MATHEMATICS

CLASS XII (Code 041) **VOLUME-1**

WITH

MCQs IN MATHEMATICS

Based on the latest revised syllabus prescribed by CBSE for Class XII under 10+2 Pattern of Senior School Certificate Examination

(Refer: https://cbseacademic.nic.in for latest information on syllabus /marking scheme)

Dr. R.D. SHARMA

B.Sc. (Hons) (Gold Medalist), M.Sc. (Gold Medalist), Ph.D.

Former Professor and Head of Department of Sciences and Humanities
Delhi Skill and Entrepreneurship University (DSEU)
Aryabhatt DSEU Ashok Vihar Campus, Delhi

DHANPAT RAI PUBLICATIONS (P) LTD.

22, ANSARI ROAD, DARYAGANJ, NEW DELHI-110002

E-Mail: ish.dhanpat@gmail.com

Combined Price : ₹ 1345.00 for Vol. 1 & 2 (with MCQs)
(Not to be sold separately)

ISBN: 978-93-94417-61-8

EVERY GENUINE COPY OF THIS BOOK HAS A HSHF

The title of the book has been Laminated by a High Security Holographic Film (HSHF) to prevent Piracy. You can see logo of Dhanpat Rai Publications at different angles with special security features.

First Edition: 1997
Reprints: 1998-2000, 02-03, 05-06, 08-10, 12-15, 17, 19, 22
Revised Editions: 2001, 04, 07, 11, 16, 18, 20, 21, 23, 24
Revised Edition: 2025

Published by *Ish Kapur*, for Dhanpat Rai Publications (P) Ltd.
For feedback and suggestions please write to rdsmath.feedback@gmail.com

PREFACE TO THE REVISED EDITION

It gives me immense pleasure in presenting this book to my esteemed readers. This edition, like the earlier editions, has been written in accordance with the latest syllabus prescribed by the CBSE. The detailed style of presentation that popularised and characterised the previous editions has been retained.

In the present edition, questions from latest CBSE Examinations have been incorporated at the appropriate places. **Illustrative Examples** and **Exercises** given at the end of each section/ sub-section of each chapter have been arranged in increasing order of difficulty level and have been categorized into the following categories:

BASIC - Based on basic concepts and formulae

LOTS - Based on lower order thinking skills

HOTS - Based on higher order thinking skills

At the end of each chapter Exercises consistsing of **Fill in the Blank Type Questions (FBQs)** and **Very Short Answer Type Questions (VSAQs)** have been given.

The quality of the book has been augmented by the Companion book "**MCQs IN MATHEMATICS**" consisting of Solved Examples and Unsolved Exercises on each of the following :

- Multiple Choice Questions (MCQs)
- Assertion Reason based MCQs
- Case Study based MCQs
- Activities

Some new and unique features of this book are:

- ❑ Detailed Theory with Illustrations
- ❑ Algorithmic approach
- ❑ Large number of graded Illustrative Examples and Exercises
- ❑ Companion book "MCQs IN MATHEMATICS"

I hope with these new features the book will be useful to students and teachers as well.

I would like to avail this opportunity to thank my publisher Sh. Ish Kapur for putting in his continuing and sincere efforts to keep me updated about the requirements and feedback of the students and teachers. Efforts have been made to incorporate suggestions and feed back received from students and teachers as well.

In spite of my best efforts to make this edition error free, some printing errors might have crept in. I shall be grateful to the teachers and students if the same are brought to my notice.

You may send your valuable suggestions, feedback or queries by post or through e-mail to rdsmath.feedback@gmail.com

Any suggestion/criticism to enhance the quality of the book will be gratefully acknowledged.

Dr. R.D. SHARMA

CONTENTS

CONTENTS IN DETAIL

CONTENTS IN DETAIL

CHAPTER 1

RELATIONS

1.1 INTRODUCTION

In Class XI, we have introduced the notion of a relation, its domain, co-domain and range. Let us recall that a relation from a set A to a set B is a subset of $A \times B$. If R is a relation from a set A to a set B and $(a, b) \in R$, then we say that a is related to b under relation R and we write as $a\ R\ b$. If $(a, b) \notin R$, then we say that a is not related to b under R and we write as $a \not{R} b$. A relation can be represented in roster form or tabular form. Sometimes, we also describe a relation by describing the common property between the elements of ordered pairs in it. For example, a relation R on the set $A = \{1, 2, 3, 4, 5\}$ defined by $R = \{(a, b) : b = a + 2\}$ can also be expressed as: $a\ R\ b$ if and only if $b = a + 2$. In this chapter, we will study different types of relations.

1.2 RECAPITULATION

In this section, we will recall some definitions learnt in the earlier class.

CARTESIAN PRODUCT OF SETS *Let A and B be two non-empty sets. The set of all ordered pairs (a, b) such that $a \in A$ and $b \in B$ is called the cartesian product of set A with set B and is denoted by $A \times B$.*

Thus, $A \times B = \{(a, b) : a \in A \text{ and } b \in B\}$. Note that $B \times A = \{(b, a) : b \in B \text{ and } a \in A\}$

Also, $A \times B = \phi$, if $A = \phi$ or $B = \phi$

If $A = \{1, 2, 3\}$ and $B = \{x, y\}$, then

$$A \times B = \{(1, x), (1, y), (2, x), (2, y), (3, x), (3, y)\},\ B \times A = \{(x,1), (x,2), (x, 3), (y,1), (y, 2), (y, 3)\}$$

$$A \times A = \{(1, 1), (1,2), (1, 3), (2, 1), (2, 2), (2, 3), (3, 1), (3, 2), (3, 3)\}$$

and, $B \times B = \{(x, x), (x, y), (y, x), (y, y)\}$

RELATION *Let A and B be two sets. Then a relation R from set A to set B is a subset of $A \times B$.*

Thus, R is a relation from A to $B \Leftrightarrow R \subseteq A \times B$.

If R is a relation from a non-void set A to a non-void set B and if $(a, b) \in R$, then we write $a\ R\ b$ which is read as "a is related to b by the relation R". If $(a, b) \notin R$, then we write $a \not{R} b$ and we say that a is not related to b by the relation R.

If A and B are finite sets consisting of m and n elements respectively, then $A \times B$ has mn ordered pairs. Therefore, total number of relations from A to B is 2^{mn}.

DOMAIN *Let R be a relation from a set A to a set B. Then the set of all first components or coordinates of the ordered pairs belonging to R is called the domain of R.*

Thus, domain of $R = \{a : (a, b) \in R\}$. Clearly, domain of $R \subseteq A$.

If $A = \{1, 3, 5, 7\}$, $B = \{2, 4, 6, 8, 10\}$ and $R = \{(1, 8), (3, 6), (5, 2), (1, 4)\}$ is a relation from A to B, then Domain $(R) = \{1, 3, 5\}$.

RANGE *Let R be a relation from a set A to a set B. Then the set of all second components or coordinates of the ordered pairs belonging to R is called the range of R.*

Thus, Range of $R = \{b : (a, b) \in R\}$. Clearly, range of $R \subseteq B$.

If $A = \{1,3,5,7\}$, $B = \{2, 4, 6, 8, 10\}$ and $R = \{(1, 8), (3, 6), (5, 2), (1, 4)\}$ is a relation from A to B, then Range $(R) = \{8, 6, 2, 4\}$.

RELATION ON A SET *Let A be a non-void set. Then a relation from A to itself i.e. a subset of $A \times A$ is called a relation on set A.*

INVERSE OF A RELATION *Let A, B be two sets and let R be a relation from a set A to a set B. Then, the inverse of R, denoted by R^{-1}, is a relation from B to A and is defined by $R^{-1} = \{(b, a) : (a, b) \in R\}$.*

Clearly, $(a,b) \in R \Leftrightarrow (b,a) \in R^{-1}$. Also, Domain (R) = Range (R^{-1}) and, Range (R) = Domain (R^{-1})

Let $A = \{1, 2, 3\}$, $B = \{a, b, c, d\}$ be two sets and $R = \{(1, a), (1, c), (2, d), (2, c)\}$ be a relation from A to B. Then, $R^{-1} = \{(a, 1), (c, 1), (d, 2), (c, 2)\}$ is a relation from B to A.

1.3 TYPES OF RELATIONS

In this section, we intend to discuss various types of relations on a set A.

1.3.1 VOID, UNIVERSAL AND IDENTITY RELATIONS

VOID RELATION *Let A be a set. Then, $\phi \subseteq A \times A$ and so it is a relation on A. This relation is called the void or empty relation on set A.*

In other words, a relation R on a set A is called void or empty relation, if no element of A is related to any element of A.

Consider the relation R on the set $A = \{1, 2, 3, 4, 5\}$ defined by $R = \{(a, b) : a - b = 12\}$.

We observe that $a - b \neq 12$ for any two elements of A.

$\therefore$ $(a, b) \notin R$ for any $a, b \in A$.

$\Rightarrow$ R does not contain any element of $A \times A \Rightarrow R$ is empty set $\Rightarrow R$ is the void relation on A.

UNIVERSAL RELATION *Let A be a set. Then, $A \times A \subseteq A \times A$ and so it is a relation on A. This relation is called the universal relation on A.*

In other words, a relation R on a set is called universal relation, if each element of A is related to every element of A.

Consider the relation R on the set $A = \{1, 2, 3, 4, 5, 6\}$ defined by $R = \{(a, b) \in R : |a - b| \geq 0\}$.

We observe that

$|a - b| \geq 0$ for all $a, b \in A$

$\Rightarrow$ $(a, b) \in R$ for all $(a, b) \in A \times A$

$\Rightarrow$ Each element of set A is related to every element of set A

$\Rightarrow$ $R = A \times A$

$\Rightarrow$ R is universal relation on set A

NOTE *It is to note here that the void relation and the universal relation on a set A are respectively the smallest and the largest relations on set A. Both the empty (or void) relation and the universal relation are sometimes called trivial relations.*

ILLUSTRATION *Let A be the set of all students of a boys school. Show that the relation R on A given by $R = \{(a, b) : a$ is sister of $b\}$ is empty relation and $R' = \{(a, b)$: the difference between the heights of a and b is less than 5 meters$\}$ is the universal relation.*

SOLUTION Since the school is boys school. Therefore, no student of the school can be sister of any student of the school. Thus, $(a, b) \notin R$ for any $a, b \in A$.

Hence, $R = \phi$ i.e. R is the empty or void relation on A.

It is obvious that the difference between the heights of any two students of the school has to be less than 5 meters.

$\therefore$ $(a, b) \in R$ for all $a, b \in A \Rightarrow R = A \times A \Rightarrow R$ is the universal relation on set A.

IDENTITY RELATION *Let A be a set. Then, the relation $I_A = \{(a, a) : a \in A\}$ on A is called the identity relation on A.*

In other words, a relation I_A on A is called the identity relation if every element of A is related to itself only.

If $A = \{1, 2, 3\}$, then the relation $I_A = \{(1, 1), (2, 2), (3, 3)\}$ is the identity relation on set A. But, relations $R_1 = \{(1, 1), (2, 2)\}$ and $R_2 = \{(1, 1), (2, 2), (3, 3), (1, 3)\}$ are not identity relations on A, because $(3, 3) \notin R_1$ and in R_2 element 1 is related to two elements 1 and 3.

1.3.2 REFLEXIVE RELATION

DEFINITION *A relation R on a set A is said to be reflexive, if every element of A is related to itself.*

Thus, R is reflexive $\Leftrightarrow (a, a) \in R$ for all $a \in A$.

A relation R on a set A is not reflexive if there exists an element $a \in A$ such that $(a, a) \notin R$.

ILLUSTRATION 1 *Let $A = \{1, 2, 3\}$ be a set. Then $R = \{(1, 1), (2, 2), (3, 3), (1, 3), (2, 1)\}$ is a reflexive relation on A. But, $R_1 = \{(1, 1), (3, 3), (2, 1), (3, 2)\}$ is not a reflexive relation on A, because $2 \in A$ but $(2, 2) \notin R_1$.*

ILLUSTRATION 2 *The identity relation on a non-void set A is always reflexive relation on A. However, a reflexive relation on A is not necessarily the identity relation on A. For example, the relation $R = \{(a, a), (b, b), (c, c), (a, b)\}$ is a reflexive relation on set $A = \{a, b, c\}$ but it is not the identity relation on A.*

ILLUSTRATION 3 *The universal relation on a non-void set A is reflexive.*

ILLUSTRATION 4 *A relation R on N defined by $(x, y) \in R \Leftrightarrow x \geq y$ is a reflexive relation on N, because every natural number is greater than or equal to itself.*

ILLUSTRATION 5 *Let X be a non-void set and P(X) be the power set of X. A relation R on P(X) defined by $(A, B) \in R \Leftrightarrow A \subseteq B$ is a reflexive relation since every set is subset of itself.*

ILLUSTRATION 6 *Let L be the set of all lines in a plane. Then relation R on L defined by $(l_1, l_2) \in R \Leftrightarrow l_1$ is parallel to l_2 is reflexive, since every line is parallel to itself.*

1.3.3 SYMMETRIC RELATION

DEFINITION *A relation R on a set A is said to be a symmetric relation iff*

$$(a, b) \in R \Rightarrow (b, a) \in R \text{ for all } a, b \in A \text{ i.e. } aRb \Rightarrow bRa \text{ for all } a, b \in A.$$

ILLUSTRATION 1 *The identity and the universal relations on a non-void set are symmetric relations.*

ILLUSTRATION 2 *Let L be the set of all lines in a plane and let R be a relation defined on L by the rule $(x, y) \in R \Leftrightarrow x$ is perpendicular to y. Then, R is a symmetric relation on L, because $L_1 \perp L_2 \Rightarrow L_2 \perp L_1$ i.e. $(L_1, L_2) \in R \Rightarrow (L_2, L_1) \in R$.*

ILLUSTRATION 3 *Let S be a non-void set and R be a relation defined on power set P(S) by*

$$(A, B) \in R \Leftrightarrow A \subseteq B \text{ for all } A, B \in P(S). \text{ Then, R is not a symmetric relation.}$$

NOTE *A relation R on a set A is not a symmetric relation if there are at least two elements $a, b \in A$ such that $(a, b) \in R$ but $(b, a) \notin R$.*

ILLUSTRATION 4 *Let $A = \{1, 2, 3, 4\}$ and let R_1 and R_2 be relations on A given by $R_1 = \{(1, 3), (1, 4), (3, 1), (2, 2) (4, 1)\}$ and $R_2 = \{(1, 1), (2, 2), (3, 3), (1, 3)\}$. Clearly, R_1 is a symmetric relation on A. However, R_2 is not so, because $(1, 3) \in R_2$ but $(3, 1) \notin R_2$.*

NOTE *A reflexive relation on a set A is not necessarily symmetric. For example, the relation $R = \{(1, 1), (2, 2), (3, 3), (1, 3)\}$ is a reflexive relation on set $A = \{1, 2, 3\}$ but it is not symmetric.*

ILLUSTRATION 5 *Prove that a relation R on a set A is symmetric iff $R = R^{-1}$.*

SOLUTION First, let R be a symmetric relation on set A. Then, we have to prove that $R = R^{-1}$. In order to prove this we have to prove that $R \subseteq R^{-1}$ and $R^{-1} \subseteq R$.

Now, $(a, b) \in R$

$\Rightarrow$ $(b, a) \in R$ [$\because$ R is symmetric]

$\Rightarrow$ $(a, b) \in R^{-1}$ [By definition of inverse relation]

Thus, $(a, b) \in R \Rightarrow (a, b) \in R^{-1}$ for all $a, b \in A$.

So, $R \subseteq R^{-1}$ ...(i)

Now, let (x, y) be an arbitrary element of R^{-1}. Then,

$(x, y) \in R^{-1}$

$\Rightarrow$ $(y, x) \in R$ [By definition of inverse relation]

$\Rightarrow$ $(x, y) \in R$ [$\because$ R is symmetric]

Thus, $(x, y) \in R^{-1} \Rightarrow (x, y) \in R$ for all $x, y \in A$.

So, $R^{-1} \subseteq R$ ...(ii)

From (i) and (ii), we obtain: $R = R^{-1}$.

Conversely, let R be a relation on set A such that $R = R^{-1}$. Then we have to prove that R is a symmetric relation on set A. Let $(a, b) \in R$. Then,

$(a, b) \in R$

$\Rightarrow$ $(b, a) \in R^{-1}$ [by definition of inverse relation]

$\Rightarrow$ $(b, a) \in R$ [$\because R = R^{-1}$]

Thus, $(a, b) \in R \Rightarrow (b, a) \in R$ for all $a, b \in A$.

So, R is a symmetric relation on A. Hence, R is symmetric iff $R = R^{-1}$.

1.3.4 TRANSITIVE RELATION

DEFINITION *Let A be any set. A relation R on A is said to be a transitive relation iff* $(a, b) \in R$ *and* $(b, c) \in R \Rightarrow (a, c) \in R$ *for all* $a, b, c \in A$. i.e., aRb *and* $bRc \Rightarrow aRc$ *for all* $a, b\, c \in A$.

ILLUSTRATION 1 *The identity and the universal relations on a non-void set are transitive.*

ILLUSTRATION 2 *The relation R on the set N of all natural numbers defined by*
$(x, y) \in R \Leftrightarrow x$ *divides* y, *for all* $x, y \in N$ *is transitive.*

SOLUTION Let $x, y, z \in N$ be such that $(x, y) \in R$ and $(y, z) \in R$. Then,

$(x, y) \in R$ and $(y, z) \in R$

$\Rightarrow$ x divides y and, y divides z

$\Rightarrow$ There exist $p, q \in N$ such that $y = xp$ and $z = yq$

$\Rightarrow$ $z = (xp)\, q$

$\Rightarrow$ $z = x\, (pq)$

$\Rightarrow$ x divides z [$\because$ $pq \in N$]

$\Rightarrow$ $(x, z) \in R$

Thus, $(x, y) \in R, (y, z) \in R \Rightarrow (x, z) \in R$ for all $x, y, z \in N$. Hence, R is a transitive relation on N.

ILLUSTRATION 3 *On the set N of natural numbers, the relation R defined by* $xRy \Rightarrow x$ *is less than* y *is transitive, because for any* $x, y, z \in N$, we find that

$x < y$ *and* $y < z \Rightarrow x < z$ *i.e.,* xRy *and* $yRz \Rightarrow xRz$

ILLUSTRATION 4 *Let S be a non-void set and R be a relation defined on power set P(S) by* $(A, B) \in R \Leftrightarrow A \subseteq B$ *for all* $A, B \in P(S)$. *Then, R is a transitive relation on P(S), because for any* $A, B, C \in P(S)$

$(A, B) \in R$ and $(B, C) \in R \Rightarrow A \subseteq B$ and $B \subseteq C \Rightarrow A \subseteq C \Rightarrow (A, C) \in R$

ILLUSTRATION 5 *Let L be the set of all straight lines in a plane. Then the relation "is parallel to" on L is a transitive relation, because for any* $l_1, l_2, l_3 \in L$, *we find that:* $l_1 \,||\, l_2$ and $l_2 \,||\, l_3 \Rightarrow l_1 \,||\, l_3$.

ILLUSTRATION 6 *The relation "is congruent to" on the set T of all triangles in a plane is a transitive relation.*

1.3.5 ANTISYMMETRIC RELATION

DEFINITION *A relation R on set A is said to be an antisymmetric relation iff*

$$(a, b) \in R \text{ and } (b, a) \in R \Rightarrow a = b \text{ for all } a, b \in A$$

NOTE *It follows from this definition that if $(a, b) \in R$ but $(b, a) \notin R$, then also R is an antisymmetric relation.*

ILLUSTRATION 1 *The identity relation on a set A is an antisymmetric relation.*

ILLUSTRATION 2 *The universal relation on a set A containing at least two elements is not antisymmetric, because if $a \neq b$ are in A, then a is related to b and b is related to a under the universal relation will imply that $a = b$ but $a \neq b$.*

ILLUSTRATION 3 *Let R be a relation on the set N of natural numbers defined by*

$$xRy \Leftrightarrow \text{'}x \text{ divides } y\text{' for all } x, y \in N$$

This relation is an antisymmetric relation on N. Since for any two numbers $a, b \in N$, we find that

$$a \mid b \text{ and } b \mid a \Rightarrow a = b \text{ i.e. } aRb \text{ and } bRa \Rightarrow a = b$$

It should be noted that this relation is not antisymmetric on the set Z of integers, because we find that for any non-zero integer a, $aR(-a)$ and $(-a)\,R\,a$ but $a \neq -a$.

ILLUSTRATION 4 *Let S be a non-void set and R be a relation on the power set P(S) defined by*

$$(A, B) \in R \Leftrightarrow A \subseteq B \text{ for all } A, B \in P(S)$$

Then, R is an antisymmetric relation on P(S), because

$$(A, B) \in R \text{ and } (B, A) \in R \Rightarrow A \subseteq B \text{ and } B \subseteq A \Rightarrow A = B$$

ILLUSTRATION 5 *The relation ≤("less than or equal to") on the set R of real numbers is antisymmetric, because $a \leq b$ and $b \leq a \Rightarrow a = b$ for all $a, b \in R$.*

ILLUSTRATIVE EXAMPLES

BASED ON BASIC CONCEPTS (BASIC)

EXAMPLE 1 *Three relations R_1, R_2 and R_3 are defined on set $A = \{a, b, c\}$ as follows:*

(i) $R_1 = \{(a, a), (a, b), (a, c), (b, b), (b, c), (c, a), (c, b), (c, c)\}$,

(ii) $R_2 = \{(a, b), (b, a), (a, c), (c, a)\}$

(iii) $R_3 = \{(a, b), (b, c), (c, a)\}$.

Find whether each of R_1, R_2 and R_3 is reflexive, symmetric and transitive.

SOLUTION (i) *Reflexive:* Clearly $(a, a), (b, b), (c, c) \in R_1$. So, R_1 is reflexive on A.

Symmetric: We observe that $(a, b) \in R_1$ but $(b, a) \notin R_1$. So, R_1 is not a symmetric relation on A.

Transitive: We find that $(b, c) \in R_1$ and $(c, a) \in R_1$ but $(b, a) \notin R_1$. So, R_1 is not a transitive relation on A.

(ii) *Reflexive:* Since $(a, a), (b, b)$ and (c, c) are not in R_2. So, it is not a reflexive relation on A.

Symmetric: We find that the ordered pairs obtained by interchanging the components of ordered pairs in R_2 are also in R_2. So, R_2 is a symmetric relation on A.

Transitive: Clearly $(a, b) \in R_2$ and $(b, a) \in R_2$ but $(a, a) \notin R_2$. So, it is not a transitive relation on A.

(iii) *Reflexive:* Since none of $(a, a), (b, b)$ and (c, c) is an element of R_3. So, R_3 is not reflexive on A.

Symmetric: Clearly, $(b, c) \in R_3$ but $(c, b) \notin R_3$. So, R_3 is not a symmetric relation on A.

Transitive: Clearly, $(a, b) \in R_3$ and $(b, c) \in R_3$ but $(a, c) \notin R_3$. So, R_3 is not a transitive relation on A.

EXAMPLE 2 *Show that the relation R on the set $A = \{1, 2, 3\}$ given by $R = \{(1, 1), (2, 2), (3, 3), (1, 2), (2, 3)\}$ is reflexive but neither symmetric nor transitive.* **[NCERT]**

SOLUTION Since $1, 2, 3 \in A$ and $(1, 1), (2, 2), (3, 3) \in R$ i.e. for each $a \in A$, $(a, a) \in R$. So, R is reflexive.

We observe that $(1, 2) \in R$ but $(2, 1) \notin R$. So, R is not symmetric.

Also, $(1, 2) \in R$ and $(2, 3) \in R$ but $(1, 3) \notin R$. So, R is not transitive.

EXAMPLE 3 *Show that the relation R on the set $A = \{1, 2, 3\}$ given by $R = \{(1, 2), (2, 1)\}$ is symmetric but neither reflexive nor transitive.* **[NCERT]**

SOLUTION We observe that $(1, 1)$, $(2, 2)$ and $(3, 3)$ do not belong to R. So, R is not reflexive.

Clearly, $(1, 2) \in R$ and $(2, 1) \in R$. So, R is symmetric.

As $(1, 2) \in R$ and $(2, 1) \in R$ but $(1, 1) \notin R$. So, R is not transitive.

EXAMPLE 4 *Check the following relations R and S for reflexivity, symmetry and transitivity:*

(i) *aRb iff b is divisible by a, where $a, b \in N$*

(ii) *$l_1 \, S \, l_2$ iff $l_1 \perp l_2$, where l_1 and l_2 are straight lines in a plane.* **[NCERT]**

SOLUTION (i) We have, $aRb \Leftrightarrow a \mid b$ for all $a, b \in N$.

Reflexivity: For any $a \in N$, we find that $a \mid a \Rightarrow aRa$. Thus, aRa for all $a \in N$.

So, R is reflexive on N.

Symmetry: R is not symmetric because if $a \mid b$, then b may not divide a. For example, $2 \mid 6$ but $6 \nmid 2$.

Transitivity: Let $a, b, c \in N$ such that aRb and bRc. Then,

$$aRb \text{ and } bRc \Rightarrow a \mid b \text{ and } b \mid c \Rightarrow a \mid c \Rightarrow aRc.$$

So, R is a transitive relation on N.

(ii) Let L be the set of all lines in a plane. We are given that $l_1 \, S \, l_2 \Leftrightarrow l_1 \perp l_2$ for all $l_1, l_2 \in L$.

Reflexivity: S is not reflexive because a line cannot be perpendicular to itself i.e. $l \perp l$ is not true.

Symmetry: Let $l_1, l_2 \in L$ such that $l_1 \, S \, l_2$. Then, $l_1 \, S \, l_2 \Rightarrow l_1 \perp l_2 \Rightarrow l_2 \perp l_1 \Rightarrow l_2 \, S \, l_1$.

So, S is symmetric on L.

Transitive: S is not transitive, because $l_1 \perp l_2$ and $l_2 \perp l_3$ does not imply that $l_1 \perp l_3$.

EXAMPLE 5 *Let a relation R_1 on the set R of real numbers be defined as $(a, b) \in R_1 \Leftrightarrow 1 + ab > 0$ for all $a, b \in R$. Show that R_1 is reflexive and symmetric but not transitive.*

SOLUTION We observe the following properties of relation R_1:

Reflexivity: Let a be an arbitrary element of R. Then,

$$a \in R$$

$$\Rightarrow \quad 1 + a.a = 1 + a^2 > 0 \qquad [\because a^2 > 0 \text{ for all } a \in R]$$

$$\Rightarrow \quad (a, a) \in R_1 \qquad [\text{By definition of } R_1]$$

Thus, $(a, a) \in R_1$ for all $a \in R$. So, R_1 is reflexive on R.

Symmetry: Let $(a, b) \in R_1$. Then,

$$(a, b) \in R_1$$

$$\Rightarrow \quad 1 + ab > 0$$

$$\Rightarrow \quad 1 + ba > 0 \qquad [\because ab = ba \text{ for all } a, b \in R]$$

$$\Rightarrow \quad (b, a) \in R_1 \qquad [\text{By definition of } R_1]$$

Thus, $(a, b) \in R_1 \Rightarrow (b, a) \in R_1$ for all $a, b \in R$. So, R_1 is symmetric on R.

Transitivity: We observe that $(1, 1/2) \in R_1$ and $(1/2, -1) \in R_1$ but $(1, -1) \notin R_1$ because $1 + 1 \times (-1) = 0 \not> 0$. So, R_1 is not transitive on R.

EXAMPLE 6 *Determine whether each of the following relations are reflexive, symmetric and transitive:*

(i) *Relation R on the set $A = \{1, 2, 3, \ldots, 13, 14\}$ defined as $R = \{(x, y) : 3x - y = 0\}$*

(ii) *Relation R on the set N of all natural numbers defined as* $R = \{(x, y) : y = x + 5 \text{ and } x < 4\}$

(iii) *Relation R on the set* $A = \{1, 2, 3, 4, 5, 6\}$ *defined as* $R = \{(x, y) : y \text{ is divisible by } x\}$

(iv) *Relation R on the set Z of all integer defined as* $R = \{(x, y) : x - y \text{ is an integer}\}$ [NCERT]

SOLUTION (i) We have, $R = \{(x, y) : 3x - y = 0\}$, where $x, y \in A = \{1, 2, 3, \ldots, 13, 14\}$

i.e., $R = \{(1, 3), (2, 6), (3, 9), (4, 12)\}$

Reflexivity: Clearly, $(1, 1) \notin R$. So, R is not a reflexive relation on A.

Symmetry: We observe that $(1, 3) \in R$ but $(3, 1) \notin R$. So, R is not a symmetric relation A.

Transitivity: We observe that $(1, 3) \in R$ and $(3, 9) \in R$ but $(1, 9) \notin R$. So, R is not a transitive relation A.

(ii) We have, $R = \{(x, y) : y = x + 5 \text{ and } x < 4, \text{ where } x, y \in N\}$ i.e. $R = \{(1, 6), (2, 7), (3, 8)\}$

Reflexivity: Clearly, $(1, 1), (2, 2)$ etc. are not in R. So, R is not reflexive.

Symmetry: We find that $(1, 6) \in R$ but $(6, 1) \notin R$. So, R is not symmetric.

Transitivity: Since $(1, 6) \in R$ and there is no order pair in R which has 6 as the first element. Same is the case for $(2, 7)$ and $(3, 8)$. So, R is transitive.

(iii) $R = \{(x, y) : y \text{ is divisible by } x\}$, where $x, y \in A = \{1, 2, 3, 4, 5, 6\}$.

Reflexivity: We know that

x is divisible by x for all $x \in A \Rightarrow (x, x) \in R$ for all $x \in A \Rightarrow R$ is reflexive on set A.

Symmetry: We observe that 6 is divisible by 2 but 2 is not divisible by 6. This means that $(2, 6) \in R$ but $(6, 2) \notin R$. So, R is not symmetric on set A.

Transitivity: Let $(x, y) \in R$ and $(y, z) \in R$. Then,

$(x, y) \in R$ and $(y, z) \in R$.

$\Rightarrow$ y is divisible by x and, z is divisible by $y \Rightarrow z$ is divisible by $x \Rightarrow (x, z) \in R$

So, R is transitive relation on A.

(iv) We have, $R = \{(x, y) : x - y \text{ is an integer, where } x, y \in Z\}$

Reflexivity: We find that

$x - x = 0$, which is an integer for all $x \in Z \Rightarrow (x, x) \in R$ for all $x \in Z \Rightarrow R$ is reflexive on Z.

Symmetry: Let $(x, y) \in R$. Then,

$(x, y) \in R$

$\Rightarrow$ $x - y$ is an integer, say, λ

$\Rightarrow$ $y - x = -\lambda$ $[\because \lambda \in Z \Rightarrow -\lambda \in Z]$

$\Rightarrow$ $y - x$ is an integer

$\Rightarrow$ $(y, x) \in R$

Thus, $(x, y) \in R \Rightarrow (y, x) \in R$ for all $x, y \in Z$. So, R is symmetric on Z.

Transivity: Let $(x, y) \in R$ and $(y, z) \in R$. Then,

$(x, y) \in R$ and $(y, z) \in R$

$\Rightarrow$ $x - y$ and $y - z$ are integers

$\Rightarrow$ $(x - y) + (y - z)$ is an integer [$\because$ Sum of two integers is an integer]

$\Rightarrow$ $x - z$ is an integer $\Rightarrow (x, z) \in R$

So, R is transitive on Z.

BASED ON LOWER ORDER THINKING SKILLS (LOTS)

EXAMPLE 7 *Show that the relation R on* $\mathbf{R}$ *defined as* $R = \{(a, b) : a \leq b\}$, *is reflexive and transitive but not symmetric.* [NCERT, CBSE 2019]

SOLUTION We have, $R = \{(a, b) : a \leq b\}$, where $a, b \in \mathbf{R}$.

Reflexivity: For any $a \in \mathbf{R}$, we find that

$a \leq a \Rightarrow (a, a) \in R$ for all $a \in \mathbf{R} \Rightarrow R$ is reflexive.

Symmetry: We observe that $(2, 3) \in R$ but $(3, 2) \notin R$. So, R is not symmetric.

Transitivity: Let $(a, b) \in R$ and $(b, c) \in R$. Then,

$$(a, b) \in R \text{ and } (b, c) \in R \Rightarrow a \leq b \text{ and } b \leq c \Rightarrow a \leq c \Rightarrow (a, c) \in R$$

So, R is transitive.

EXAMPLE 8 *Let S be the set of all points in a plane and R be a relation on S defined as* $R = \{(P, Q)$*: Distance between P and Q is less than 2 units*$\}$.

Show that R is reflexive and symmetric but not transitive.

SOLUTION We observe the following properties of relation R:

Reflexivity: For any point P in set S, we find that

Distance between P and itself is 0 which is less than 2 units $\Rightarrow (P, P) \in R$

Thus, $(P, P) \in R$ for all $P \in S$. So, R is reflexive on S.

Symmetry: Let P and Q be two points in S such that $(P, Q) \in R$. Then,

$(P, Q) \in R$

$\Rightarrow$ Distance between P and Q is less than 2 units.

$\Rightarrow$ Distance between Q and P is less than 2 units $\Rightarrow (Q, P) \in R$

So, R is symmetric on S.

Transitivity: Consider points P, Q and R having coordinates (0, 0), (1.5, 0) and (3.2, 0). We observe that the distance between P and Q is 1.5 units which is less than 2 units and the distance between Q and R is 1.7 units which is also less than 2 units. But, the distance between P and R is 3.2 which is not less than 2 units. This means that $(P, Q) \in R$ and $(Q, R) \in R$ but $(P, R) \notin R$. So, R is not transitive on S.

BASED ON HIGHER ORDER THINKING SKILLS (HOTS)

EXAMPLE 9 *Let* $X = \{1, 2, 3, 4, 5, 6, 7, 8, 9\}$. *Let* R_1 *be a relation on X given by* $R_1 = \{(x, y) : x - y$ *is divisible by* $3\}$ *and* R_2 *be another relation on X given by* $R_2 = \{(x, y) : \{x, y\} \subset \{1, 4, 7\}$ *or* $\{x, y\} \subset \{2, 5, 8\}$ *or* $\{x, y\} \subset \{3, 6, 9\}\}$. *Show that* $R_1 = R_2$. **[NCERT]**

SOLUTION Clearly, R_1 and R_2 are subsets of $X \times X$. In order to prove that $R_1 = R_2$, it is sufficient to show that $R_1 \subset R_2$ and $R_2 \subset R_1$.

We observe that the difference between any two elements of each of the sets $\{1, 4, 7\}$, $\{2, 5, 8\}$ and $\{3, 6, 9\}$ is a multiple of 3.

Let (x, y) be an arbitrary element of R_1. Then,

$(x, y) \in R_1$

$\Rightarrow$ $x - y$ is divisible by 3.

$\Rightarrow$ $x - y$ is a multiple of 3.

$\Rightarrow$ $\{x, y\} \subset \{1, 4, 7\}$ or $\{x, y\} \subset \{2, 5, 8\}$ or $\{x, y\} \subset \{3, 6, 9\} \Rightarrow (x, y) \in R_2$

Thus, $(x, y) \in R_1 \Rightarrow (x, y) \in R_2$. So, $R_1 \subset R_2$ ...(i)

Now, let (a, b) be an arbitrary element of R_2. Then,

$(a, b) \in R_2$

$\Rightarrow$ $\{a, b\} \subset \{1, 4, 7\}$ or $\{a, b\} \subset \{2, 5, 8\}$ or $\{a, b\} \subset \{3, 6, 9\}$

$\Rightarrow$ $a - b$ is divisible by 3 $\Rightarrow (a, b) \in R_1$

Thus, $(a, b) \in R_2 \Rightarrow (a, b) \in R_1$. So, $R_2 \subset R_1$ ...(ii)

From (i) and (ii), we get: $R_1 = R_2$

EXAMPLE 10 *Show that the relation R on the set* **R** *of all real numbers, defined as* $R = \{(a, b) : a \leq b^2\}$ *is neither reflexive nor symmetric nor transitive. Also, determine* $x \in \mathbf{R}$ *such that* $(x, x) \in$ R.

[NCERT, CBSE 2024]

SOLUTION We have, $R = \{(a, b) : a \le b^2\}$, where $a, b \in \mathbf{R}$.

Reflexivity: We observe that $\frac{1}{2} \le \left(\frac{1}{2}\right)^2$ is not true. Therefore, $\left(\frac{1}{2}, \frac{1}{2}\right) \notin R$. So, R is not reflexive.

Symmetry: We observe that $-1 \le 3^2$ but $3 \nleq (-1)^2$ i.e. $(-1, 3) \in R$ but $(3, -1) \notin R$. So, R is not symmetric.

Transivity: We observe that

$$2 \le (-3)^2 \text{ and } -3 \le 1^2 \text{ but } 2 \nleq 1^2 \text{ i.e. } (2, -3) \in R \text{ and } (-3, -1) \in R \text{ but } (2, 1) \notin R.$$

So, R is not transitive.

Now, $(x, x) \in R \Rightarrow x \le x^2 \Rightarrow x^2 - x \ge 0 \Rightarrow x(x-1) \ge 0 \Rightarrow x \in (-\infty, 0] \cup [1, \infty)$

EXAMPLE 11 *Check whether the relation S in the set of real numbers R defined by*

$$S = \{(a, b) : a - b + \sqrt{2} \text{ is an irrational number}\}$$

is reflexive, symmetric or transitive. **[CBSE 2024]**

SOLUTION *Reflexivity*: For any $a \in R$, we find that

$a - a + \sqrt{2} = \sqrt{2}$, which is an irrational number.

$\therefore$ $(a, a) \in S$ for all $a \in R$.

So, S is reflexive relation in R.

Symmetry: We observe that

$\sqrt{2} - 2 + \sqrt{2}$ is an irrational number $\Rightarrow (\sqrt{2}, 2) \in S$

But, $2 - \sqrt{2} + \sqrt{2} = 2$ is not an irrational number $\Rightarrow (\sqrt{2}, 2) \notin S$

Thus, $(\sqrt{2}, 2) \in S$ but $(2, \sqrt{2}) \notin S$. So, S is not symmetric in R.

Transitivity: We observe that $(2, \sqrt{3}) \in S$ and $(\sqrt{3}, \sqrt{2}) \in S$. But, $(2, \sqrt{2}) \notin S$.

So, S is not transitive in R.

EXAMPLE 12 *Let* $A = \{1, 2, 3\}$. *Then, show that the number of relations containing* $(1, 2)$ *and* $(2, 3)$ *which are reflexive and transitive but not symmetric is three.* **[NCERT]**

SOLUTION The smallest reflexive relation on set A containing $(1, 2)$ and $(2, 3)$ is

$$R = \{(1, 1), (2, 2), (3, 3), (1, 2), (2, 3)\}$$

Since $(1, 2) \in R$ and $(2, 3) \in R$ but $(1, 3) \notin R$. So, R is not transitive. To make it transitive we have to include $(1,3)$ in R. Including $(1,3)$ in R, we get: $R_1 = \{(1, 1), (2, 2), (3, 3), (1, 2), (2, 3), (1, 3)\}$.

This is reflexive and transitive but not symmetric as $(1, 3) \in R_1$ but $(3, 1) \notin R_1$.

Now, if we add the pair $(2, 1)$ to R_1 to get: $R_2 = \{(1, 1), (2, 2), (3, 3), (1, 2), (2, 3), (1, 3), (2, 1)\}$. The relation R_2 is reflexive and transitive but not symmetric. Similarly, by adding $(3, 2)$ to R_1, we get $R_3 = \{(1, 1), (2, 2), (3, 3), (1, 2), (2, 3), (1, 3), (3, 2)\}$, which is reflexive and transitive but not symmetric.

By adding $(3, 1)$ to R_1, we obtain $\{(1, 1), (2, 2), (3, 3), (1, 2), (2, 3), (1, 3), (3, 1)\}$. This relation is reflexive but not symmetric and transitive.

We observe that out of ordered pairs $(2, 1)$, $(3, 2)$ and $(3, 1)$ if we add any two ordered pairs at a time to R_1, then to maintain the transitivity we will be forced to add the remaining third pair and in this process the relation will become symmetric also which is not required. Hence, the total number of reflexive, transitive but not symmetric relations containing $(1, 2)$ and $(2, 3)$ is three.

EXERCISE 1.1

BASIC

1. Let A be the set of all human beings in a town at a particular time. Determine whether each of the following relations are reflexive, symmetric and transitive:
   (i) $R = \{(x, y) : x$ and y work at the same place$\}$
   (ii) $R = \{(x, y) : x$ and y live in the same locality$\}$
   (iii) $R = \{(x, y) : x$ is wife of $y\}$ (iv) $R = \{(x, y) : x$ is father of $y\}$ **[NCERT]**
2. Relations R_1, R_2, R_3 and R_4 are defined on a set $A = \{a, b, c\}$ as follows:
   $R_1 = \{(a, a), (a, b), (a, c), (b, b), (b, c), (c, a), (c, b), (c, c)\}$, $R_2 = \{(a, a)\}$, $R_3 = \{(b, c)\}$,
   $R_4 = \{(a, b), (b, c), (c, a)\}$.
   Find whether or not each of the relations R_1, R_2, R_3, R_4 on A is (i) reflexive (ii) symmetric (iii) transitive.
3. Test whether the following relations R_1, R_2, and R_3 are (i) reflexive (ii) symmetric and (iii) transitive:
   (i) R_1 on Q_0 defined by $(a, b) \in R_1 \Leftrightarrow a = 1/b$
   (ii) R_2 on Z defined by $(a, b) \in R_2 \Leftrightarrow |a - b| \le 5$
   (iii) R_3 on R defined by $(a, b) \in R_3 \Leftrightarrow a^2 - 4ab + 3b^2 = 0$.
4. Let $A = \{1, 2, 3\}$, and let $R_1 = \{(1, 1), (1, 3), (3, 1), (2, 2), (2, 1), (3, 3)\}$, $R_2 = \{(2,2), (3, 1), (1, 3)\}$, $R_3 = \{(1, 3), (3, 3)\}$. Find whether or not each of the relations R_1, R_2, R_3 on A is (i) reflexive (ii) symmetric (iii) transitive.

BASED ON LOTS

5. Each of the following defines a relation on N:
   (i) $x > y, x, y \in N$ (ii) $x + y = 10, x, y \in N$
   (iii) xy is square of an integer $x, y \in N$ (iv) $x + 4y = 10, x, y \in N$
   Determine which of the above relations are reflexive, symmetric and transitive. **[NCERT EXEMPLAR]**
6. The following relations are defined on the set of real numbers:
   (i) aRb iff $a - b > 0$ (ii) aRb iff $1 + ab > 0$ (iii) aRb iff $|a| \le b$.
   Find whether these relations are reflexive, symmetric or transitive.
7. Check whether the relation R defined on the set $A = \{1, 2, 3, 4, 5, 6\}$ as $R = \{(a, b) : b = a + 1\}$ is reflexive, symmetric or transitive. **[NCERT]**
8. (i) Check whether the relation R on **R** defined by $R = \{(a, b) : a \le b^3\}$ is reflexive, symmetric or transitive. **[NCERT, CBSE 2010]**
   (ii) Check if the relation R in the set of all real numbers defined as $R = \{(a, b) : a < b\}$ is
   (i) symmetric (ii) transitive **[CBSE 2020]**
9. Prove that every identity relation on a set is reflexive, but the converse is not necessarily true.
10. If $A = \{1, 2, 3, 4\}$, define relations on A which have properties of being
    (i) reflexive, transitive but not symmetric.
    (ii) symmetric but neither reflexive nor transitive.
    (iii) reflexive, symmetric and transitive. **[NCERT EXEMPLAR]**
11. Let R be a relation defined on the set of natural numbers N as
    $R = \{(x, y) : x, y \in N, 2x + y = 41\}$
    Find the domain and range of R. Also, verify whether R is (i) reflexive, (ii) symmetric (iii) transitive. **[CBSE 2014]**
12. An integer m is said to be related to another integer n if m is a multiple of n. Check if the relation is symmetric, reflexive and transitive.

13. Show that the relation "$\geq$" on the set R of all real numbers is reflexive and transitive but not symmetric.
14. Give an example of a relation which is
    (i) reflexive and symmetric but not transitive.
    (ii) reflexive and transitive but not symmetric.
    (iii) symmetric and transitive but not reflexive.
    (iv) symmetric but neither reflexive nor transitive.
    (v) transitive but neither reflexive nor symmetric. [NCERT]
15. Let W denote the set of words in the English dictionary. Define the relation R by $R = \{(x, y) \in W \times W$ such that x and y have at least one letter in common$\}$. Show that this relation R is reflexive and symmetric but not transitive. [CBSE 2020]
16. A relation R is defined on the set **R** of all real numbers as $R = \{(x,y) : x.y$ is an irrational number$\}$ check whether R is reflexive, symmetric and transitive. [CBSE 2023]
17. A relation R on set $A = \{1, 2, 3, 4, 5\}$ is defined as $R = \{(x, y) : |x^2 - y^2| < 8\}$. Check whether the relation R is reflexive, symmetric and transitive. [CBSE 2024]

BASED ON HOTS

18. Is it true that every relation which is symmetric and transitive is also reflexive? Give reasons.
19. Given the relation $R = \{(1, 2), (2, 3)\}$ on the set $A = \{1, 2, 3\}$, add a minimum number of ordered pairs so that the enlarged relation is symmetric, transitive and reflexive.
20. Let $A = \{1, 2, 3\}$ and $R = \{(1, 2), (1, 1), (2, 3)\}$ be a relation on A. What minimum number of ordered pairs may be added to R so that it may become a transitive relation on A.
21. Let $A = \{a, b, c\}$ and the relation R be defined on A as follows: $R = \{(a, a), (b, c), (a, b)\}$. Then, write minimum number of ordered pairs to be added in R to make it reflexive and transitive. [NCERT EXEMPLAR]

ANSWERS

1. (i) Reflexive, symmetric and transitive
   (ii) Reflexive, symmetric and transitive
   (iii) Neither reflexive, nor symmetric but transitive
   (iv) neither reflexive nor symmetric nor transitive
2. R_1 is reflexive but neither symmetric nor transitive.
   R_2 is symmetric and transitive but not reflexive.
   R_3 is transitive but neither reflexive nor symmetric.
   R_4 is neither reflexive nor symmetric nor transitive.
3. (i) R_1 is symmetric but it is neither reflexive nor transitive
   (ii) R_2 is reflexive and symmetric but it is not transitive
   (iii) R_3 is reflexive but it is neither symmetric nor transitive.
4. R_1 is reflexive but neither symmetric nor transitive
   R_2 is symmetric but neither reflexive nor transitive.
   R_3 is transitive but neither reflexive nor symmetric.
5. (i) transitive (ii) symmetric (iii) reflexive, symmetric and transitive (iv) transitive.
6. (i) Transitive (ii) Reflexive and symmetric but not transitive (iii) Transitive neither reflexive nor symmetric.
7. Neither reflexive nor symmetric nor transitive
8. (i) Neither reflexive nor symmetric nor transitive. (ii) Transitive but not symmetric.
10. (i) $R = \{(1, 1), (2, 2), (3, 3), (4, 4), (1, 2)\}$ (ii) $R = \{(1, 2), (2, 1)\}$
    (iii) $R = \{(1, 1), (2, 2), (3, 3), (4, 4), (1, 2), (2, 1)\}$
11. Domain $R = \{1, 2, 3, ..., 19, 20\}$, Range $R = \{39, 37, 35, ..., 7, 5, 3, 1\}$.
    R is neither reflexive nor symmetric and is not transitive.

12. Reflexive and transitive but not symmetric.

14. (i) $R = \{(1, 1), (2, 2), (3, 3), (1, 3), (3, 1) (2, 3), (3, 2)\}$ on $A = \{1, 2, 3\}$
  (ii) $R = \{(1, 1), (2, 2), (3, 3), (1, 3)\}$ on $A = \{1, 2, 3\}$
  (iii) $R = \{(1, 3), (3, 1), (1, 1), (3, 3)\}$ on $A = \{1, 2, 3\}$
  (iv) $R = \{(1, 1), (1, 3), (3, 1), (2, 3), (3, 2)\}$ on $A = \{1, 2, 3\}$ (v) $R = \{(1, 1)\}$ on $A = \{1, 2, 3\}$

16. Symmetric only 17. Reflexive and symmetric but not transitive.

18. No. Relation $R = \{(1, 1), (1, 2), (2, 1), (2, 2)\}$ on $A = \{1, 2, 3\}$ is symmetric and transitive but not reflexive.

19. (1, 1), (2, 2), (3, 3), (1, 3), (2, 1), (3, 2), (3, 1) 20. (1, 3), One 21. $(b, b), (c, c), (a, c)$

HINTS TO SELECTED PROBLEMS

1. (iv) The relation R on the set A of all human beings in a town is given by $(x, y) \in R$ iff x is father of y.

Reflexivity: Since a person x cannot be father of himself. So, $(x, x) \notin A$. Consequently, R is not reflexive.

Symmetry: Let $x, y \in A$ be such that $(x, y) \in R$. Then,

$(x, y) \in R \Rightarrow x$ is father of $y \Rightarrow y$ cannot be father of $x \Rightarrow (y, x) \notin R$

So, R is not symmetric.

Transitivity: Let $x, y, z \in A$ be such that $(x, y) \in R$ and $(y, z) \in R$. Then,

$(x, y) \in R$ and $(y, z) \in R$

$\Rightarrow$ x is father of y and y is father of $z \Rightarrow x$ is grandfather of $z \Rightarrow (x, z) \notin R$

7. The relation R on set $A = \{1, 2, 3, 4, 5, 6\}$ is defined as $(a, b) \in R$ iff $b = a + 1$. Therefore, $R = \{(1, 2), (2, 3), (3, 4), (4, 5), (5, 6)\}$. Clearly, $(a, a) \notin R$ for any $a \in A$. So, R is not reflective on A. We observe that $(1, 2) \in R$ but $(2, 1) \notin R$. So, R is not symmetric. We also observe that $(1, 2) \in R$ and $(2, 3) \in R$ but $(1, 3) \notin R$. So, R is not transitive.

8. The relation R on **R** is defined by $R = \{(a, b) : a \leq b^3\}$. We observe that $(-2) \in R$ is such that $(-2) \leq (-2)^3$ is not true. So, R is not reflexive.

Since $1 \leq (3^{1/3})^3$ but $3^{1/3} \not\leq 1$ i.e. $(1, 3^{1/3}) \in R$ but $(3^{1/3}, 1) \notin R$. So, R is not symmetric.

R is not transitive because $(5, 2) \in R$ and $(2, 2^{1/3}) \in R$ but $(5, 2^{1/3}) \notin R$.

9. Let I be the identity relation on a set A. Then, $(a, a) \in I$ for all $a \in A \Rightarrow I$ is reflexive.
Converse: The relation $\{(1, 1), (2, 2), (3, 3), (1, 3)\}$ is a reflexive relation on set $A = \{1, 2, 3\}$ but it is not the identity relation on A.

18. A relation R on the set Z of integers defined by $(a, b) \in R \Leftrightarrow a$ and b are both odd, is symmetric and transitive but it is not reflexive. Because no even integer is related to itself.

19. For reflexivity, we must add (1, 1), (2, 2) and (3, 3). For symmetry and transitivity we must add (2, 1), (3, 2), (1, 3), (3, 1) in R.

1.3.5 EQUIVALENCE RELATION AND EQUIVALENCE CLASSES

DEFINITION *A relation R on a set A is said to be an equivalence relation on A iff it is*

(i) reflexive i.e. $(a, a) \in R$ for all $a \in A$.

(ii) symmetric i.e. $(a, b) \in R \Rightarrow (b, a) \in R$ for all $a, b \in A$.

and, (iii) transitive i.e. $(a, b) \in R$ and $(b, c) \in R \Rightarrow (a, c) \in R$ for all $a, b, c \in A$.

Consider the relation R defined on the set Z of integers by the rule

$(x, y) \in R \Leftrightarrow x - y$ is divisible by 2.

This relation R has the following properties:

Reflexivity: For any $x \in Z$, we find that

$$x - x = 0 \Rightarrow x - x = 0 \times 2 \Rightarrow x - x \text{ is divisible by } 2 \Rightarrow (x, x) \in R$$

Thus, $(x, x) \in R$ for all $x \in Z$. So, R is a reflexive relation on Z.

Symmetry: For any $x, y \in Z$, we find that

$(x, y) \in R \Rightarrow x - y$ is divisible by 2

$\Rightarrow \quad x - y = 2\lambda$ for some $\lambda \in Z \Rightarrow y - x = 2(-\lambda) \Rightarrow y - x$ is divisible by $2 \Rightarrow (y, x) \in R$

Thus, $(x, y) \in R \Rightarrow (y, x) \in R$ for all $x, y \in Z$. So, R is a symmetric relation on Z.

Transitivity: For any $x, y, z \in Z$, we find that

$(x, y) \in R$ and $(y, z) \in R$

$\Rightarrow \quad x - y$ is divisible by 2 and $y - z$ is divisible by 2

$\Rightarrow \quad x - y = 2p$ and $y - z = 2q$ for some $p, q \in Z$

$\Rightarrow \quad (x - y) + (y - z) = 2p + 2q \Rightarrow x - z = 2(p + q) \Rightarrow x - z$ is divisible by $2 \Rightarrow (x, z) \in R$

Thus, $(x\ y) \in R$ and $(y, z) \in R \Rightarrow (x, z) \in R$ for all $x, y, z \in Z$.

So, R is a transitive relation on Z. Hence, R is an equivalence relation on Z.

Let us now find the sets of integers realted to various integers in Z. For any integer a, let $[a]$ denote the set of integers related to a under relation R i.e. $[a] = \{x \in Z : (x, a) \in R\}$. Then, we find that

$[0] = \{x \in Z : (x, 0) \in R\} = \{x \in Z : x - 0 \text{ is divisible } 2\} = \{x \in Z : x \text{ is divisible by } 2\}$

$= \{0, \pm 2, \pm 4, \pm 6, \ldots\}$

$[1] = \{x \in Z : (x, 1) \in R\} = \{x \in Z : x - 1 \text{ is divisible by } 2\} = \{x \in Z : x - 1 = 2\lambda, \lambda \in Z\}$

$= \{x \in Z : x = 2\lambda + 1, \lambda \in Z\} = \{\pm 1, \pm 3, \pm 5, \pm 5, \pm 7, \ldots\}$

$[2] = \{x \in Z : (x, 2) \in R\} = \{x \in Z : x - 2 \text{ is divisible by } 2\}$

$= \{x \in Z : x - 2 = 2\lambda, \lambda \in Z\} = \{x \in Z : x = 2 + 2\lambda, \lambda \in Z\}$

$= \{0, \pm 2, \pm 4, \pm 6, \ldots\}$, which is same as the set $[0]$

$[3] = \{x \in Z : (x, 3) \in R\} = \{x \in Z : x - 3 \text{ is divisible by } 2\}$

$= \{x \in Z : x - 3 = 2\lambda, \lambda \in Z\} = \{x \in Z : x = 3 + 2\lambda, \lambda \in Z\}$

$= \{\pm 1, \pm 3, \pm 5 \pm 7, \ldots\}$, which is sam as the set $[1]$

Continuing in this manner, we find that

$[0] = [2] = [4] = [6] = \ldots; \ [1] = [3] = [5] = [7] = \ldots$ and, $[0] \cap [1] = \phi$. Also, $Z = [0] \cup [1]$.

Thus, R partitions the set Z into two pairwise disjoint sets known as equivalence classes.

Similarly, the relation R on Z given by

$$(x, y) \in R \Leftrightarrow x - y \text{ is divisible by } 3$$

partitions Z into 3 pairwise disjoints sets i.e. equivalence classes given by

$[0] = \{-6, -3, 0, 3, 6, 9, \ldots\}$, $[1] = \{\ldots, -8, -5, -2, 1, 4, 7, 10, \ldots\}$, $[2] = \{\ldots, 7, -4, -1, 2, 5, 8, 11, \ldots\}$

such that $Z = [0] \cup [1] \cup [2]$.

It is evident from the above discussion that an equivalence relation R defined on a set A partitions the set A into pairwise disjoint subsets. These subsets are called equivalence classes determined by relation R. The set of all elements of A related to an element $a \in A$ is denoted by $[a]$ i.e. $[a] = \{x \in A : (x, a) \in R\}$. This is an equivalence class. Corresponding to every element in A there is an equivalence class. Any two equivalence classes are either identical or disjoint. The collection of all equivalence classes forms a partition of set A.

ILLUSTRATION *Let R be the equivalence relation in the set $A = \{0, 1, 2, 3, 4, 5\}$ given by $R = \{(a, b) : 2 \text{ divides } (a - b)\}$. Write the equivalence class $[0]$.* **[CBSE 2014]**

SOLUTION Clearly, the equivalence class $[0]$ is the set of those elements in A which are related to 0 under the relation R. i.e. $[0] = \{(a, 0) \in R : a \in A\}$.

Now, $(a, 0) \in R$

$\Rightarrow$ $a - 0$ is divisible by 2 and $a \in A \Rightarrow a \in A$ such that 2 divides a $\Rightarrow a = 0, 2, 4$

Thus, $[0] = \{0, 2, 4\}$.

ILLUSTRATIVE EXAMPLES

BASED ON BASIC CONCEPTS (BASIC)

EXAMPLE 1 *Let R be a relation on the set of all lines in a plane defined by $(l_1, l_2) \in R \Leftrightarrow$ line l_1 is parallel to line l_2. Show that R is an equivalence relation.*

SOLUTION Let L be the given set of all lines in a plane. Then, we observe the following properties.

Reflexive: For each line $l \in L$, we find that

$$l \,||\, l \Rightarrow (l, l) \in R \text{ for all } l \in L \Rightarrow R \text{ is reflexive}$$

Symmetric: Let $l_1, l_2 \in L$ such that $(l_1, l_2) \in R$. Then,

$$(l_1, l_2) \in R \Rightarrow l_1 \,||\, l_2 \Rightarrow l_2 \,||\, l_1 \Rightarrow (l_2, l_1) \in R. \text{ So, } R \text{ is symmetric on } L.$$

Transitive: Let $l_1, l_2, l_3 \in L$ such that $(l_1, l_2) \in R$ and $(l_2, l_3) \in R$. Then,

$$(l_1, l_2) \in R \text{ and } (l_2, l_3) \in R \Rightarrow l_1 \,||\, l_2 \text{ and } l_2 \,||\, l_3 \Rightarrow l_1 \,||\, l_3 \Rightarrow (l_1, l_3) \in R. \text{ So, } R \text{ is transitive on } L.$$

Hence, R being reflexive, symmetric and transitive is an equivalence relation on L.

EXAMPLE 2 *Show that the relation 'is congruent to' on the set of all triangles in a plane is an equivalence relation.*

SOLUTION Let S be the set of all triangles in a plane and let R be the relation on S defined by

$$(\Delta_1, \Delta_2) \in R \Leftrightarrow \text{triangle } \Delta_1 \text{ is congruent to triangle } \Delta_2.$$

We observe the following properties of relation R:

Reflexivity: For each triangle $\Delta \in S$, we find that

$$\Delta \cong \Delta \Rightarrow (\Delta, \Delta) \in R \text{ for all } \Delta \in S \Rightarrow R \text{ is reflexive on } S$$

Symmetry: Let $\Delta_1, \Delta_2 \in S$ such that $(\Delta_1, \Delta_2) \in R$. Then,

$$(\Delta_1, \Delta_2) \in R \Rightarrow \Delta_1 \cong \Delta_2 \Rightarrow \Delta_2 \cong \Delta_1 \Rightarrow (\Delta_2, \Delta_1) \in R. \text{ So, } R \text{ is symmetric on } S$$

Transitivity: Let $\Delta_1, \Delta_2, \Delta_3 \in S$ such that $(\Delta_1, \Delta_2) \in R$ and $(\Delta_2, \Delta_3) \in R$. Then,

$$(\Delta_1, \Delta_2) \in R \text{ and } (\Delta_2, \Delta_3) \in R \Rightarrow \Delta_1 \cong \Delta_2 \text{ and } \Delta_2 \cong \Delta_3 \Rightarrow \Delta_1 \cong \Delta_3 \Rightarrow (\Delta_1, \Delta_3) \in R$$

So, R is transitive on S.

Hence, R being reflexive, symmetric and transitive, is an equivalence relation on S.

EXAMPLE 3 *Show that the relation R defined on the set A of all triangles in a plane as $R = \{(T_1, T_2) : T_1$ is similar to $T_2\}$ is an equivalence relation.*

Consider three right angled triangles T_1 with sides 3, 4, 5; T_2 with sides 5, 12, 13 and T_3 with sides 6, 8, 10. Which triangles among T_1, T_2 and T_3 are related? [NCERT]

SOLUTION We observe the following properties of relation R.

Reflexivity: We know that every triangle is similar to itself.

$\therefore$ $(T, T) \in R$ for all $T \in A \Rightarrow R$ is reflexive.

Symmetry: Let $T_1, T_2 \in A$ such that $(T_1, T_2) \in R$. Then,

$$(T_1, T_2) \in R \Rightarrow T_1 \text{ is similar to } T_2 \Rightarrow T_2 \text{ is similar to } T_1 \Rightarrow (T_2, T_1) \in R$$

So, R is symmetric.

Transitivity: Let $T_1, T_2, T_3 \in A$ such that $(T_1, T_2) \in R$ and $(T_2, T_3) \in R$. Then,

$$(T_1, T_2) \in R \text{ and } (T_2, T_3) \in R$$

$\Rightarrow$ T_1 is similar to T_2 and T_2 is similar to $T_3 \Rightarrow T_1$ is similar to $T_3 \Rightarrow (T_1, T_3) \in R$

So, R is transitive. Hence, R is an equivalence relation on set A.

In triangles T_1 and T_3, we observe that the corresponding angles are equal and the corresponding sides are proportional i.e. $\frac{3}{6}=\frac{4}{8}=\frac{5}{10}$. Hence, T_1 and T_3 are related.

EXAMPLE 4 *Let n be a positive integer. Prove that the relation R on the set Z of all integers defined by* $(x, y) \in R \Leftrightarrow x-y$ *is divisible by n, is an equivalence relation on Z.* **[NCERT EXEMPLAR]**

SOLUTION We observe the following properties of relation R.

Reflexivity: For any $a \in Z$

$$a-a = 0 = 0 \times n \Rightarrow a-a \text{ is divisible by } n \Rightarrow (a, a) \in R$$

Thus, $(a, a) \in R$ for all $a \in Z$. So, R is reflexive on Z

Symmetry: Let $(a, b) \in R$. Then,

$(a, b) \in R$

$\Rightarrow$ $(a-b)$ is divisible by n

$\Rightarrow$ $(a-b) = np$ for some $p \in Z$

$\Rightarrow$ $b-a = n(-p)$ $[\because p \in Z \Rightarrow -p \in Z]$

$\Rightarrow$ $b-a$ is divisible by n

$\Rightarrow$ $(b, a) \in R$

Thus, $(a, b) \in R \Rightarrow (b, a) \in R$ for all $a, b \in Z$. So, R is symmetric on Z.

Transitivity: Let $a, b, c \in Z$ such that $(a, b) \in R$ and $(b, c) \in R$. Then,

$(a, b) \in R \Rightarrow (a-b)$ is divisible by $n \Rightarrow a-b = np$ for some $p \in Z$

and, $(b, c) \in R \Rightarrow (b-c)$ is divisible by $n \Rightarrow b-c = nq$ for some $q \in Z$

$\therefore$ $(a, b) \in R$ and $(b, c) \in R \Rightarrow a-b = np$ and $b-c = nq \Rightarrow (a-b)+(b-c) = np+nq$

$\Rightarrow$ $a-c = n(p+q) \Rightarrow a-c$ is divisible by n $[\because p, q \in Z \Rightarrow p+q \in Z]$

$\Rightarrow$ $(a, c) \in R$

Thus, $(a, b) \in R$ and $(b, c) \in R \Rightarrow (a, c) \in R$ for all $a, b, c \in Z$. So, R is transitive relation on Z.

Thus, R being reflexive, symmetric and transitive, is an equivalence relation on Z.

EXAMPLE 5 *Show that the relation R on the set A of all the books in a library of a college given by* $R = \{(x, y) : x$ *and* y *have the same number of pages}, is an equivalence relation.* **[NCERT]**

SOLUTION We observe the following properties of relation R.

Reflexivity: For any book x in set A, we observe that x and x have the same number of pages.

$\therefore$ $(x, x) \in R$

Thus, $(x, x) \in R$ for all $x \in A$. So, R is reflexive.

Symmetry: Let $(x, y) \in R$. Then,

$(x, y) \in R$

$\Rightarrow$ x and y have the same number of pages $\Rightarrow$ y and x have the same number of pages

$\Rightarrow$ $(y, x) \in R$

Thus, $(x, y) \in R \Rightarrow (y, x) \in R$. So, R is symmetric.

Transitivity: Let $(x, y) \in R$ and $(y, z) \in R$. Then,

$(x, y) \in R$ and $(y, z) \in R$

$\Rightarrow$ (x and y have the same number of pages) and (y and z have the same number of pages)

$\Rightarrow$ x and z have the same number of pages $\Rightarrow (x, z) \in R$

So, R is transitive.

Thus, R is reflexive, symmetric and transitive. Hence, R is an equivalence relation.

REMARK *Let m be an arbitrary but fixed integer. Two integers a and b are said to be congruence modulo m if $a-b$ is divisible by m and we write $a \equiv b \pmod m$.*

Thus, $a \equiv b \pmod m \Leftrightarrow a-b$ *is divisible by m.*

For example, $18 \equiv 3 \pmod 5$ *because* $18-3=15$ *which is divisible by 5. Similarly,* $3 \equiv 13 \pmod 2$ *because* $3-13=-10$*, which is divisible by 2. But,* $25 \not\equiv 2 \pmod 4$ *because 4 is not a divisor of* $25-2=23$.

EXAMPLE 6 *Prove that the relation 'congruence modulo m' on the set Z of all integers is an equivalence relation.*

SOLUTION We observe the following properties of the given relation.

Reflexivity: Let a be an arbitrary integer. Then,

$$a-a = 0 = 0 \times m \Rightarrow a-a \text{ is divisible by } m \Rightarrow a \equiv a \pmod m$$

Thus, $a \equiv a$ (mod m) for all $a \in Z$. So, "congruence modulo m" is reflexive.

Symmetry: Let $a, b \in Z$ such that $a \equiv b \pmod m$. Then,

$a \equiv b \pmod m$

$\Rightarrow$ $a-b$ is divisible by m

$\Rightarrow$ $a-b = \lambda m$ for $\lambda \in Z$

$\Rightarrow$ $b-a = (-\lambda)m$

$\Rightarrow$ $b-a$ is divisible by m

$\Rightarrow$ $b \equiv a \pmod m$ $[\because \lambda \in Z \Rightarrow -\lambda \in Z]$

So, "congruence modulo m" is symmetric on Z.

Transitivity: Let $a, b, c \in Z$ such that $a \equiv b$ (mod m) and $b \equiv c \pmod m$. Then,

$a \equiv b \text{ (mod m)} \Rightarrow a-b$ is divisible by $m \Rightarrow a-b = \lambda_1 m$ for some $\lambda_1 \in Z$

$b \equiv c \text{ (mod m)} \Rightarrow b-c$ is divisible by $m \Rightarrow b-c = \lambda_2$ m for some $\lambda_2 \in Z$

$\therefore$ $(a-b)+(b-c) = \lambda_1 m + \lambda_2 m = (\lambda_1 + \lambda_2) m$

$\Rightarrow$ $a-c = \lambda_3 m$, where $\lambda_3 = \lambda_1 + \lambda_2 \in Z \Rightarrow a \equiv c \pmod m$

Thus, $a \equiv b \pmod m$ and $b \equiv c$ (mod m) $\Rightarrow a \equiv c \pmod m$. So, "congruence modulo m" is transitive on Z.

Hence, "congruence modulo m" is an equivalence relation on Z.

BASED ON LOWER ORDER THINKING SKILLS (LOTS)

EXAMPLE 7 *Given a non-empty set X, consider P (X) which is the set of all subsets of X. Define a relation in P (X) as follows:*

For subsets A, B in P (X), A R B if $A \subset B$. Is R an equivalence relation on P (X)? Justify your answer. **[NCERT]**

SOLUTION It is given that for any A, B in $P(X)$: $ARB \Leftrightarrow A \subset B$

We observe the following properties of R.

Reflexivity: For any A in $P(X)$, we find that : $A \subset A \Rightarrow ARA$. So, R is reflexive on $P(X)$.

Symmetry: Let A, B in $P(X)$ be such that ARB. Then, $ARB \Rightarrow A \subset B$.

This need not imply that $B \subset A$. In fact it is possible only when $A = B$.

Also, we know that $\{1, 2\} \subset \{1, 2, 3\}$, but $\{1, 2, 3\} \not\subset \{1, 2\}$. So, R is not a symmetric relation on $P(X)$.

Transitivity: Let A, B, C be in $P(X)$ such that

$$A\,R\,B \text{ and } B\,R\,C \Rightarrow A \subset B \text{ and } B \subset C \Rightarrow A \subset C \Rightarrow A\,R\,C$$

So, R is a transitive relation on P (X).

Thus, R is reflexive and transitive relation on P (X) but it is not symmetric.

Hence, R is not an equivalence relation on P (X).

EXAMPLE 8 *Show that the relation R on the set* $A = \{1, 2, 3, 4, 5\}$, *given by* $R = \{(a, b) : |a - b| \text{ is even }\}$, is an equivalence relation.

Show that all the elements of $\{1, 3, 5\}$ *are related to each other and all the elements of* $\{2, 4\}$ *are related to each other. But, no element of* $\{1, 3, 5\}$ *is related to any element of* $\{2, 4\}$. **[NCERT, CBSE 2009]**

SOLUTION We have,

$$R = \{(a, b) : |a - b| \text{ is even}\}, \text{ where } a, b \in A = \{1, 2, 3, 4, 5\}.$$

We observe the following properties of relation R.

Reflexivity: For any $a \in A$, we find that: $|a - a| = 0$, which is even

$\therefore$ $(a, a) \in R$ for all $a \in A$. So, R is reflexive.

Symmetry: Let $(a, b) \in R$. Then,

$(a, b) \in R \Rightarrow |a - b|$ is even $\Rightarrow |b - a|$ is even $\Rightarrow (b, a) \in R$

Thus, $(a, b) \in R \Rightarrow (b, a) \in R$. So, R is symmetric.

Transitivity: Let $(a, b) \in R$ and $(b, c) \in R$. Then,

$(a, b) \in R$ and $(b, c) \in R$

$\Rightarrow$ $|a - b|$ is even and $|b - c|$ is even

$\Rightarrow$ (a and b both are even or both are odd) and (b and c both are even or both are odd)

Now two cases arise:

Case I *When b is even:* In this case,

$(a, b) \in R$ and $(b, c) \in R$

$\Rightarrow$ $|a - b|$ is even and $|b - c|$ is even [$\because$ b is even]

$\Rightarrow$ a is even and c is even

$\Rightarrow$ $|a - c|$ is even $\Rightarrow (a, c) \in R$

Case II *When b is odd*: In this case,

$(a, b) \in R$ and $(b, c) \in R$

$\Rightarrow$ $|a - b|$ is even and $|b - c|$ is even [$\because$ b is odd]

$\Rightarrow$ a is odd and c is odd

$\Rightarrow$ $|a - c|$ is even $\Rightarrow (a, c) \in R$

Thus, $(a, b) \in R$ and $(b, c) \in R \Rightarrow (a, c) \in R$. So, R is transitive.

Hence, R is an equivalence relation.

We know that the difference of any two odd (even) natural numbers is always an even natural number. Therefore, all the elements of set $\{1, 3, 5\}$ are related to each other and all the elements of $\{2, 4\}$ are related to each other.

We know that the difference of an even natural number and an odd natural number is an odd natural number. Therefore, no element of $\{1, 3, 5\}$ is related to any element of $\{2, 4\}$.

EXAMPLE 9 *Show that the relation R on the set* $A = \{x \in Z : 0 \le x \le 12\}$, *given by* $R = \{(a, b) : |a - b|$ *is a multiple of* $4\}$ *is an equivalence relation. Find the set of all elements related to 1 i.e. equivalence class* [1]. **[NCERT, CBSE 2010, 2018, 2019]**

SOLUTION We have,

$$R = \{(a, b) : |a - b| \text{ is a multiple of } 4\}, \text{ where } a, b \in A = \{x \in Z : 0 \le x \le 12\} = \{0, 1, 2, \dots, 12\}.$$

We observe the following properties of relation R.

Reflexivity: For any $a \in A$, we find that

$$|a-a|=0, \text{ which is a multiple of } 4 \Rightarrow (a, a) \in R$$

Thus, $(a, a) \in R$ for all $a \in A$. So, R is reflexive.

Symmetry: Let $(a, b) \in R$. Then,

$$(a, b) \in R \Rightarrow |a-b| \text{ is a multiple of } 4 \Rightarrow |a-b| = 4\lambda \text{ for some } \lambda \in N$$

$\Rightarrow$ $|b-a| = 4\lambda$ for some $\lambda \in N$

$\Rightarrow$ $(b, a) \in R$ $[\because |a-b| = |b-a|]$

So, R is symmetric.

Transitivity: Let $(a, b) \in R$ and $(b, c) \in R$. Then,

$(a, b) \in R$ and $(b, c) \in R$

$\Rightarrow$ $|a-b|$ is a multiple of 4 and $|b-c|$ is a multiple of 4

$\Rightarrow$ $|a-b| = 4\lambda$ and $|b-c| = 4\mu$ for some $\lambda, \mu \in N$

$\Rightarrow$ $a-b = \pm 4\lambda$ and $b-c = \pm 4\mu$

$\Rightarrow$ $a-c = \pm 4\lambda \pm 4\mu \Rightarrow a-c$ is a multiple of $4 \Rightarrow |a-c|$ is a multiple of $4 \Rightarrow (a, c) \in R$

Thus, $(a, b) \in R$ and $(b, c) \in R \Rightarrow (a, c) \in R$

So, R is transitive. Hence, R is an equivalence relation.

Let x be an element of A such that $(x, 1) \in R$. Then,

$$|x-1| \text{ is a multiple of } 4 \Rightarrow |x-1| = 0, 4, 8, 12 \Rightarrow x-1 = 0, 4, 8, 12 \Rightarrow x = 1, 5, 9 \quad [\because 13 \notin A]$$

Hence, the set of all elements of A which are related to 1 is $\{1, 5, 9\}$ i.e. $[1] = \{1, 5, 9\}$.

EXAMPLE 10 *Show that the relation R on the set A of points in a plane, given by*

$R = \{(P, Q):$ *Distance of the point P from the origin is same as the distance of the point Q from the origin*$\}$,

is an equivalence relation. Further show that the set of all points related to a point $P \neq (0, 0)$ is the circle passing through P with origin as centre. **[NCERT]**

SOLUTION Let O denote the origin in the given plane. Then, $R = \{(P, Q): OP = OQ\}$.

We observe the following properties of relation R.

Reflexivity: For any point P in set A, we find that

$$OP = OP \Rightarrow (P, P) \in R$$

Thus, $(P, P) \in R$ for all $P \in A$. So, R is reflexive.

Symmetry: Let P and Q be two points in set A such that

$$(P, Q) \in R \Rightarrow OP = OQ \Rightarrow OQ = OP \Rightarrow (Q, P) \in R$$

Thus, $(P, Q) \in R \Rightarrow (Q, P) \in R$ for all $P, Q \in A$. So, R is symmetric.

Transitivity: Let P, Q and S be three points in set A such that

$$(P, Q) \in R \text{ and } (Q, S) \in R \Rightarrow OP = OQ \text{ and } OQ = OS \Rightarrow OP = OS \Rightarrow (P, S) \in R$$

Thus, $(P, Q) \in R$ and $(Q, S) \in R \Rightarrow (P, S) \in R$ for all $P, Q, S \in A$. So, R is transitive.

Hence, R is an equivalence relation.

Let P be a fixed point in set A and Q be any point in set A such that $(P, Q) \in R$. Then,

$(P, Q) \in R$

$\Rightarrow$ $OP = OQ$

$\Rightarrow$ Q moves in the plane in such a way that its distance from the origin O $(0, 0)$ is always same and is equal to OP.

$\Rightarrow$ Locus of Q is a circle with centre at the origin and radius OP.

Hence, the set of all points related to P is the circle passing through P with origin O as centre.

EXAMPLE 11 *The Earth has 24 time zones, defined by dividing the Earth into 24 equal longitudinal segments. These are the regions on Earth that have the same standard time. For example, USA and India fall in different time zones, but Sri Lanka and India are in the same time zone. A relation R is defined on the set U = {All people on the Earth} such that R = {(x, y): the time difference between the time zones x and y reside in is 6 hours}.*

(i) *Check whether the relation R is reflexive, symmetric and transitive.*

(ii) *Is relation R an equivalence relation?*

SOLUTION (i) *Reflexivity:* For any $x \in U$, we find that the time difference between time zones where x and x reside is zero hours. Therefore, $(x, x) \notin R$ for any $x \in U$. So, R *is not reflexive.*

Symmetry: Let $x, y \in U$ be such that

$(x, y) \in R$

$\Rightarrow$ Time difference between time zones where x and y reside is 6 hours

$\Rightarrow$ Time difference between time zones where y and x reside is 6 hours

$\Rightarrow$ $(y, x) \in R$

Thus, $(x, y) \in R \Rightarrow (y, x) \in R$ for all $x, y \in R$. So, R is symmetric.

Transitivity: Let $(x, y) \in R$ and $(y, z) \in R$. Then,

$(x, y) \in R$ and $(y, z) \in R$

$\Rightarrow$ The time difference between the time zones where x and y reside is 6 hours and the time difference between the time zones where y and z reside is 6 hours

$\Rightarrow$ The time difference between the time zones where x and z reside is either 0 hours or 12 hours.

$\Rightarrow$ $(x, z) \notin R$.

So, R is not a transitive relation.

(ii) We find that the relation R is neither reflexive no transitive. Hence, it is not an equivalence relation.

BASED ON HIGHER ORDER THINKING SKILLS (HOTS)

EXAMPLE 12 *Prove that the relation R on the set N × N defined by*

$(a, b)\ R\ (c, d) \Leftrightarrow a + d = b + c$ *for all* $(a, b), (c, d) \in N \times N$ *is an equivalence relation.*

Also, find the equivalence classes $[(2, 3)]$ *and* $[(1, 3)]$. **[CBSE 2010]**

SOLUTION We observe the following properties of relation R.

Reflexivity: Let (a, b) be an arbitrary element of $N \times N$. Then,

$(a, b) \in N \times N$

$\Rightarrow$ $a, b \in N$

$\Rightarrow$ $a + b = b + a$ [By commutativity of addition on N]

$\Rightarrow$ $(a, b)\ R\ (a, b)$

Thus, $(a, b)\ R\ (a, b)$ for all $(a, b) \in N \times N$. So, R is reflexive on $N \times N$.

Symmetry: Let $(a, b), (c, d) \in N \times N$ be such that $(a, b)\ R\ (c, d)$. Then,

$(a, b)\ R\ (c, d)$

$\Rightarrow$ $a + d = b + c$

$\Rightarrow$ $c + b = d + a$ [By commutativity of addition on N]

$\Rightarrow$ $(c, d)\ R\ (a, b)$ [By definition of R]

Thus, $(a, b)\ R\ (c, d) \Rightarrow (c, d)\ R\ (a, b)$ for all $(a, b), (c, d) \in N \times N$. So, R is symmetric on $N \times N$.

Transitivity: Let $(a, b), (c, d), (e, f) \in N \times N$ such that $(a, b)\ R\ (c, d)$ and $(c, d)\ R\ (e, f)$. Then,

$$\left.\begin{array}{l}(a, b)\ R\ (c, d) \Rightarrow a+d = b+c \\ (c, d)\ R\ (e, f) \Rightarrow c+f = d+e\end{array}\right\} \Rightarrow (a+d)+(c+f) = (b+c)+(d+e)$$

$$\Rightarrow a+f = b+e \Rightarrow (a, b)\ R\ (e, f)$$

Thus, $(a, b)\ R\ (c, d)$ and $(c, d)\ R\ (e, f) \Rightarrow (a, b)\ R\ (e, f)$ for all $(a, b), (c, d), (e, f) \in N \times N$.

So, R is transitive on $N \times N$.

Hence, R being reflexive, symmetric and transitive, is an equivalence relation on $N \times N$.

$$[(2, 3)] = \{(x, y) \in N \times N : (x, y)\ R\ (2, 3)\} = \{(x, y) \in N \times N : x+3 = y+2\}$$
$$= \{(x, y) \in N \times N : x-y = 1\} = \{(x, y) \in N \times N : y = x+1\}$$
$$= \{(x, x+1) : x \in N\} = \{(1, 2), (2, 3), (3, 4), (4, 5), \ldots\}$$
$$[(7, 3)] = \{(x, y) \in N \times N : (x, y)\ R\ (7, 3)\} = \{(x, y) \in N \times N : x+3 = y+7\}$$
$$= \{(x, y) \in N \times N : y = x-4\} = \{(x, x-4) \in N \times N : x \in N\}$$
$$= \{(5, 1), (6, 2), (7, 3), (8, 4), (9, 5), \ldots\}$$

EXAMPLE 13 *Let $A = \{1, 2, 3, \ldots, 9\}$ and R be the relation on $A \times A$ defined by $(a, b)\ R\ (c, d)$ if $a+d = b+c$ for all $(a, b), (c, d) \in A \times A$. Prove that R is an equivalence relation and also obtain the equivalence class $[(2, 5)]$.*

[NCERT EXEMPLAR, CBSE 2014]

SOLUTION We observe the following properties of relation R.

Reflexivity: Let (a, b) be an arbitrary element of $A \times A$. Then,

$(a, b) \in A \times A \Rightarrow a, b \in A \Rightarrow a+b = b+a$ [By commutativity of addition on N]

$\Rightarrow$ $(a, b)\ R\ (a, b)$

Thus, $(a, b)\ R\ (a, b)$ for all $(a, b) \in A \times A$. So, R is reflexive on $A \times A$.

Symmetry: Let $(a, b), (c, d) \in A \times A$ be such that $(a, b)\ R\ (c, d)$. Then,

$(a, b)\ R\ (c, d) \Rightarrow a+d = b+c \Rightarrow c+b = d+a$ [By commutativity of addition on N]

$\Rightarrow$ $(c, d)\ R\ (a, b)$

Thus, $(a, b)\ R\ (c, d) \Rightarrow (c, d)\ R\ (a, b)$ for all $(a, b), (c, d) \in A \times A$. So, R is symmetric on $A \times A$.

Transitivity: Let $(a, b), (c, d), (e, f) \in A \times A$ such that $(a, b)\ R\ (c, d)$ and $(c, d)\ R\ (e, f)$. Then,

$$\left.\begin{array}{l}(a, b)\ R\ (c, d) \Rightarrow a+d = b+c \\ (c, d)\ R\ (e, f) \Rightarrow c+f = d+e\end{array}\right\} \Rightarrow (a+d)+(c+f) = (b+c)+(d+e) \Rightarrow a+f = b+e \Rightarrow (a,b)\,R\,(e,f)$$

Thus, $(a, b)\ R\ (c, d)$ and $(c, d)\ R\ (e, f) \Rightarrow (a, b)\ R\ (e, f)$ for all $(a, b), (c, d), (e, f) \in A \times A$.

So, R is a transitive relation on $A \times A$. Hence, R is an equivalence relation on $A \times A$.

Now,

$$[(2, 5)] = \{(x, y) \in A \times A : (x, y)\ R\ (2, 5)\} = \{(x, y) \in A \times A : x+5 = y+2\} = \{(x, y) \in A \times A : y = x+3\}$$
$$= \{(x, x+3) : x \in A \text{ and } x+3 \in A\} = \{(1, 4), (2, 5), (3, 6), (4, 7), (5, 8), (6, 9)\}$$

EXAMPLE 14 *Let N be the set of all natural numbers and let R be a relation on $N \times N$, defined by*

$$(a, b)\ R\ (c, d) \Leftrightarrow ad = bc \text{ for all } (a, b), (c, d) \in N \times N.$$

Show that R is an equivalence relation on $N \times N$. Also, find the equivalence class $[(2, 6)]$.

SOLUTION We observe the following properties of relation R.

Reflexivity: Let (a, b) be an arbitrary element of $N \times N$. Then,

$(a, b) \in N \times N \Rightarrow a, b \in N \Rightarrow ab = ba$ [By commutativity of multiplication on N]

$\Rightarrow$ $(a, b)\ R\ (a, b)$

Thus, $(a, b)\ R\ (a, b)$ for all $(a, b) \in N \times N$. So, R is reflexive on $N \times N$.

Symmetry: Let (a, b), (c, d) $\in N \times N$ be such that $(a, b)\ R\ (c, d)$. Then,

$(a, b)\ R\ (c, d) \Rightarrow ad = bc \Rightarrow cb = da$ [By commutativity of multiplication on N]

$\Rightarrow$ $(c, d)\ R\ (a, b)$

Thus, $(a, b) R (c, d) \Rightarrow (c, d) R (a, b)$ for all $(a, b), (c, d) \in N \times N$. So, R is symmetric on $N \times N$.

Transitivity: Let $(a, b), (c, d), (e, f) \in N \times N$ such that $(a, b) R (c, d)$ and $(c, d) R (e, f)$. Then,

$$\left.\begin{array}{l}(a, b) R (c, d) \Rightarrow ad = bc \\ (c, d) R (e, f) \Rightarrow cf = de\end{array}\right\} \Rightarrow (ad)(cf) = (bc)(de) \Rightarrow af = be \Rightarrow (a, b) R (e, f)$$

Thus, $(a, b) R (c, d)$ and $(c, d) R (e, f) \Rightarrow (a, b) R (e, f)$ for all $(a, b), (c, d), (e, f) \in N \times N$.

So, R is transitive on $N \times N$.

Hence, R being reflexive, symmetric and transitive, is an equivalence relation on $N \times N$.

$$[(2, 6)] = \{(x, y) \in N \times N : (x, y) R (2, 6)\} = \{(x, y) \in N \times N : 3x = y\} = \{(x, 3x) : x \in N\}$$
$$= \{(1, 3), (2, 6), (3, 9), (4, 12), \dots\}$$

EXAMPLE 15 *Let N denote the set of all natural numbers and R be the relation on $N \times N$ defined by $(a, b) R (c, d) \Leftrightarrow ad(b + c) = bc(a + d)$. Check whether R is an equivalence relation on $N \times N$.* **[CBSE 2015, 2023]**

SOLUTION We observe the following properties of relation R.

Reflexivity: Let (a, b) be an arbitrary element of $N \times N$. Then,

$(a, b) \in N \times N$

$\Rightarrow a, b \in N$

$\Rightarrow ab(b + a) = ba(a + b)$ [By commutativity of addition and multiplication on N]

$\Rightarrow (a, b) R (a, b)$

Thus, $(a, b) R (a, b)$ for all $(a, b) \in N \times N$. So, R is reflexive on $N \times N$.

Symmetry: Let $(a, b), (c, d) \in N \times N$ be such that $(a, b) R (c, d)$. Then,

$(a, b) R (c, d)$

$\Rightarrow ad(b + c) = bc(a + d)$

$\Rightarrow cb(d + a) = da(c + b)$ [By commutativity of addition and multiplication on N]

$\Rightarrow (c, d) R (a, b)$

Thus, $(a, b) R (c, d) \Rightarrow (c, d) R (a, b)$ for all $(a, b), (c, d) \in N \times N$.

So, R is symmetric on $N \times N$.

Transitivity: Let $(a, b), (c, d), (e, f) \in N \times N$ such that $(a, b) R (c, d)$ and $(c, d) R (e, f)$. Then,

$$(a, b) R (c, d) \Rightarrow ad(b + c) = bc(a + d) \Rightarrow \frac{b + c}{bc} = \frac{a + d}{ad} \Rightarrow \frac{1}{b} + \frac{1}{c} = \frac{1}{a} + \frac{1}{d} \quad \text{...(i)}$$

and, $$(c, d) R (e, f) \Rightarrow cf(d + e) = de(c + f) \Rightarrow \frac{d + e}{de} = \frac{c + f}{cf} \Rightarrow \frac{1}{d} + \frac{1}{e} = \frac{1}{c} + \frac{1}{f} \quad \text{...(ii)}$$

Adding (i) and (ii), we get

$$\left(\frac{1}{b} + \frac{1}{c}\right) + \left(\frac{1}{d} + \frac{1}{e}\right) = \left(\frac{1}{a} + \frac{1}{d}\right) + \left(\frac{1}{c} + \frac{1}{f}\right)$$

$$\Rightarrow \frac{1}{b} + \frac{1}{e} = \frac{1}{a} + \frac{1}{f} \Rightarrow \frac{b + e}{be} = \frac{a + f}{af} \Rightarrow af(b + e) = be(a + f) \Rightarrow (a, b) R (e, f)$$

Thus, $(a, b) R (c, d)$ and $(c, d) R (e, f) \Rightarrow (a, b) R (e, f)$ for all $(a, b), (c, d), (e, f) \in N \times N$.

So, R is transitive on $N \times N$.

Hence, R being reflexive, symmetric and transitive, is an equivalence relation on $N \times N$.

EXAMPLE 16 *Show that the number of equivalence relations on the set $\{1, 2, 3\}$ containing $(1, 2)$ and $(2, 1)$ is two.* **[NCERT]**

SOLUTION The smallest equivalence relation R_1 containing $(1, 2)$ and $(2, 1)$ is

$$R_1 = \{(1, 1), (2, 2), (3, 3), (1, 2), (2, 1)\}$$

Now, we are left with four ordered pairs namely (2, 3), (3, 2), (1, 3) and (3, 1). If we add any one, say (2, 3) to R_1, then for symmetry we must add (3, 2) and then for transitivity we are forced to add (1, 3) and (3, 1). Thus, the only equivalence relation other than R_1 is the universal relation. Hence, the total number of equivalence relations containing (1, 2) and (2, 1) is two.

EXAMPLE 17 *On the set N of all natural numbers, a relation R is defined as follows:*
nRm ⇔ Each of the natural numbers n and m leaves the same remainder less than 5 when divided by 5. Show that R is an equivalence relation. Also, obtain the pairwise disjoint subsets determined by R.

SOLUTION We observe the following properties of relation R.

Reflexivity: Let a be an arbitrary element of N. Then, either a is less than 5 and if $a \geq 5$, then on dividing a by 5 we obtain a remainder as one of the numbers 0, 1, 2, 3, 4.
Thus, aRa for all $a \in N$. So, R is reflexive on N.

Symmetry: Let $a, b \in N$ such that aRb. Then,

$aRb \Rightarrow$ Each of a and b leaves the same remainder less than 5 when divided by 5

$\Rightarrow$ Each of b and a leave the same remainder less than 5 when divided by 5

Thus, $aRb \Rightarrow bRa$ for all $a, b \in N$. So, R is symmetric.

Transitivity: Let $a, b, c \in N$ be such that aRb and bRc. Then,

$aRb \Rightarrow$ Each of a and b leaves the same remainder less than 5 when divided by 5

$bRc \Rightarrow$ Each of b and c leaves the same remainder less than 5 when divided by 5

$\therefore$ Each of a and c leaves the same remainder less than 5 when divided by 5

$\Rightarrow$ aRc

Thus, aRb and $bRc \Rightarrow aRc$ for all $a, b, c \in N$. So, R is a transitive relation on N.

Hence, R is an equivalence relation on N. Let us now find the equivalence classes.

$[1] = \{x \in N : x\ R\ 1\}$
$= \{x \in N : x$ and 1 leave the remainder less than 5 when divided by 5$\}$
$= \{x \in N : x$ leaves the remainder 1 when divided by 5$\} = \{1, 6, 11, 16, 21, ...\}$

$[2] = \{x \in N : x\ R\ 2\}$
$= \{x \in N :$ Each of x and 2 leave the remainder less than 5 when divided by 5$\}$
$= \{x \in N : x$ leaves the remainder 2 when divided by 5$\} = \{2, 7, 12, 17, 22, ...\}$

$[3] = \{x \in N : x\ R\ 3\}$
$= \{x \in N :$ Each of x and 3 leave the remainder less than 5 when divided by 5$\}$
$= \{x \in N : x$ leaves the remainder 3 when divided by 5$\} = \{3, 8, 13, 18, 23, ...\}$

$[4] = \{x \in N : x\ R\ 4\}$
$= \{x \in N :$ Each of x and 4 leave the remainder less than 5 when divided by 5$\}$
$= \{x \in N : x$ leaves the remainder 4 when divided by 5$\} = \{4, 9, 14, 19, ...\}$

$[5] = \{x \in N : x\ R\ 5\}$
$= \{x \in N :$ Each of x and 5 leave the remainder less than 5 when divided by 5$\}$
$= \{x \in N : x$ leaves the remainder 0 when divided by 5$\} = \{5, 10, 15, ...\}$

Proceeding in this manner we find that

$[1] = [6] = [11] ...; [2] = [7] = [12] ...; [3] = [8] = [13] ...; [4] = [9] = [14] ...$ and, $[5] = [10] = [15] = ...$

Thus, we obtain the disjoint equivalence classes: [1], [2], [3], [4], [5] such that $N = [1] \cup [2] \cup [3] \cup [4] \cup [5]$

EXERCISE 1.2

BASIC

1. Show that the relation R defined by $R = \{(a, b) : a - b$ is divisible by 3; $a, b \in Z\}$ is an equivalence relation. [CBSE 2008]

2. Show that the relation R on the set Z of integers, given by $R = \{(a, b) : 2 \text{ divides } a - b\}$, is an equivalence relation. **[NCERT]**
3. Prove that the relation R on Z defined by $(a, b) \in R \Leftrightarrow a - b$ is divisible by 5 is an equivalence relation on Z. **[CBSE 2010]**
4. Let n be a fixed positive integer. Define a relation R on Z as follows:
   $(a, b) \in R \Leftrightarrow a - b$ is divisible by n. Show that R is an equivalence relation on Z.
5. (i) Let Z be the set of integers. Show that the relation $R = \{(a, b) : a, b \in Z \text{ and } a + b \text{ is even}\}$ is an equivalence relation on Z.
   (ii) Prove that the relation R in the set of integers Z defined as $R = \{(a, b) : 2 \text{ divides } (a + b)\}$ is an equivalence relation. Also, determine the equivalence class [3]. **[CBSE 2024]**
6. m is said to be related to n if m and n are integers and $m - n$ is divisible by 13. Does this define an equivalence relation?

BASED ON LOTS

7. Let R be a relation on the set A of ordered pairs of non-zero integers defined by $(x, y)\ R\ (u, v)$ iff $xv = yu$. Show that R is an equivalence relation. **[NCERT]**
8. Show that the relation R on the set $A = \{x \in Z ; 0 \leq x \leq 12\}$, given by $R = \{(a, b) : a = b\}$, is an equivalence relation. Find the set of all elements related to 1.
9. Let L be the set of all lines in XY-plane and R be the relation in L defined as $R = \{(L_1, L_2) : L_1$ is parallel to $L_2\}$. Show that R is an equivalence relation. Find the set of all lines related to the line $y = 2x + 4$.
10. Show that the relation R, defined on the set A of all polygons as
    $R = \{(P_1, P_2) : P_1 \text{ and } P_2 \text{ have same number of sides}\}$,
    is an equivalence relation. What is the set of all elements in A related to the right angle triangle T with sides 3, 4 and 5? **[NCERT]**
11. Let R be the relation defined on the set $A = \{1, 2, 3, 4, 5, 6, 7\}$ by $R = \{(a, b) : \text{both } a \text{ and } b \text{ are either odd or even}\}$. Show that R is an equivalence relation. Further, show that all the elements of the subset $\{1, 3, 5, 7\}$ are related to each other and all the elements of the subset $\{2, 4, 6\}$ are related to each other, but no element of the subset $\{1, 3, 5, 7\}$ is related to any element of the subset $\{2, 4, 6\}$. **[NCERT]**
12. Check whether the relation R on the set N of natural numbers given by $R = \{(a, b) : a \text{ is divisor of } b\}$ is reflexive, symmetric or transitive. Also, determine whether R is an equivalence relation. **[CBSE 2020]**
13. A relation R is defined on $N \times N$ (where N is the set of natural numbers) as: $(a, b)\ R\ (c, d) \Leftrightarrow a - c = b - d$. Show that R is an equivalence relation. [CBSE 2024]
14. A relation R on set $A = \{-4, -3, -2, -1, 0, 1, 2, 3, 4\}$ be defined as $R = \{(x, y) : x + y \text{ is an integer divisible by } 2\}$. Show that R is an equivalence relation. Also, write the equivalence class [2]. [CBSE 2024]

BASED ON HOTS

15. Let S be a relation on the set R of all real numbers defined by $S = \{(a, b) \in R \times R : a^2 + b^2 = 1\}$.
    Prove that S is not an equivalence relation on R.
16. Let Z be the set of all integers and Z_0 be the set of all non-zero integers. Let a relation R on $Z \times Z_0$ be defined as : $(a, b)\ R\ (c, d) \Leftrightarrow ad = bc$ for all $(a, b), (c, d) \in Z \times Z_0$
    Prove that R is an equivalence relation on $Z \times Z_0$.
17. Let C be the set of all complex numbers and C_0 be the set of all non-zero complex numbers.
    Let a relation R on C_0 be defined as $z_1\ R\ z_2 \Leftrightarrow \dfrac{z_1 - z_2}{z_1 + z_2}$ is real for all $z_1, z_2 \in C_0$. Show that R is an equivalence relation.

ANSWERS

5. (ii) $[3] = \{..., -5, -3, -1, 1, 3, 5, ...\}$

8. $\{1\}$

9. $\{y = 2x + c : c \in R\}$

10. Set of all triangles

12. Reflexive and Transitive but not Symmetric

14. $[2] = \{-4, -2, 0, 2, 4\}$

HINTS TO SELECTED PROBLEMS

2. The relation R on Z is given by $R = \{(a, b) : 2 \text{ divides } a - b\}$. We observe the following properties of relation R.

Reflexivity: For any $a \in Z$, we find that

$$a - a = 0 = 0 \times 2 \Rightarrow 2 \text{ divides } a - a \Rightarrow (a, a) \in R$$

So, R is a reflexive relation on Z.

Symmetry: Let $a, b \in Z$ be such that

$$(a, b) \in R$$

$\Rightarrow$ 2 divides $a - b \Rightarrow a - b = 2\lambda$ for some $\lambda \in Z \Rightarrow b - a = 2(-\lambda)$, where $-\lambda \in Z$

$\Rightarrow$ 2 divides $b - a \Rightarrow (b, a) \in R$

Thus, $(a, b) \in R \Rightarrow (b, a) \in R$. So, R is a symmetric relation on Z.

Transitivity: Let $a, b, c \in Z$ be such that $(a, b) \in R$ and $(b, c) \in R$. Then,

$(a, b) \in R \Rightarrow$ 2 divides $b - a \Rightarrow b - a = 2\lambda$ for some $\lambda \in Z$

and, $(b, c) \in R \Rightarrow$ 2 divides $c - b \Rightarrow c - b = 2\mu$ for some $\mu \in Z$

$\therefore \quad b - a + c - b = 2(\lambda + \mu) \Rightarrow c - a = 2(\lambda + \mu)$, where $\lambda + \mu \in Z$

$\Rightarrow$ 2 divides $c - a \Rightarrow (a, c) \in R$

Thus, $(a, b) \in R$ and $(b, c) \in R \Rightarrow (a, c) \in R$. So, R is a transitive relation on Z.

Hence, R is an equivalence relation on Z.

7. The relation R on $Z_0 \times Z_0$ is defined by $(x, y) R (u, v) \Leftrightarrow xv = yu$ for all $(x, y), (u, v) \in Z_0 \times Z_0$

We observe the following properties of R on $Z_0 \times Z_0$.

Reflexivity: For any $(x, y) \in Z_0 \times Z_0$

$$xy = yx \Rightarrow (x, y) R (x, y) \qquad [\because \text{Multiplication is commutative on } Z_0]$$

Thus, $(x, y) R (x, y)$ for all $(x, y) \in Z_0 \times Z_0$. So, R is a reflexive relation on $Z_0 \times Z_0$.

Symmetry: Let $(x, y), (u, v) \in Z_0 \times Z_0$ such that $(x, y) R ((u, v)$. Then,

$$(x, y) R (u, v) \Rightarrow xv = yu \Rightarrow uy = vx \Rightarrow (u, v) R (x, y)$$

Thus, $(x, y) R (u, v) \Rightarrow (u, v) R (x, y)$ for all $(x, y), (u, v) \in Z_0 \times Z_0$.

So, R is a symmetric relation on Z_0.

Transitivity: Let $(x, y), (u, v), (a, b) \in Z_0 \times Z_0$ be such that $(x, y) R (u, v)$ and $(u, v) R (a, b)$. Then,

$$\left.\begin{array}{r} (x, y) R (u, v) \Rightarrow xv = yu \\ \text{and, } (u, v) R (a, b) \Rightarrow ub = va \end{array}\right\} \Rightarrow (xv)(ub) = (yv)(va) \Rightarrow xb = ya \Rightarrow (x, y) R (a, b)$$

So, R is a transitive relation on $Z_0 \times Z_0$. Hence, R is an equivalence relation on $Z_0 \times Z_0$.

10. The relation R on the set of A of all polygons is defined as $R = \{(P_1, P_2) : P_1$ and P_2 have same number of sides$\}$. We observe the following properties of R on A.

Reflexivity: Let P be any polygon in A. Then,

P and P have same number of sides $\Rightarrow (P, P) \in R$

Thus, $(P, P) \in R$ for all $P \in A$. So, R is a reflexive relation on A.

Symmetry: Let P_1, P_2 be two polygons in A such that $(P_1, P_2) \in R$. Then,

$(P_1, P_2) \in R \Rightarrow P_1$ and P_2 have same number of sides

$\Rightarrow \quad P_2$ and P_1 have same number of sides $\Rightarrow (P_2, P_1) \in R$

So, R is symmetric on A.

Transitivity: Let P_1, P_2, P_3 be three polygons in A such that $(P_1, P_2) \in R$ and $(P_2, P_3) \in R$. Then,

$(P_1, P_2) \in R \Rightarrow P_1$ and P_2 have same number of sides

and, $(P_2, P_3) \in R \Rightarrow P_2$ and P_3 have same number of sides

$\therefore$ P_1 and P_3 have same number of sides $\Rightarrow (P_1, P_3) \in R$

Thus, $(P_1, P_2) \in R$ and $(P_2, P_3) \in R \Rightarrow (P_1, P_3) \in R$. So, R is a transitive relation on A.

Hence, R is an equivalence relation on A.

Let P be a polygon in A such that $(P, T) \in R$, where T is a right angled triangle with sides 3, 4 and 5. Then,

$(P, T) \in R \Rightarrow$ Polygon P and triangle T have same number of sides $\Rightarrow P$ is any triangle in A

Hence, the set of all elements in A related to T is the set of all triangles in A.

11. The relation R on set $A = \{1, 2, 3, 4, 5, 6, 7\}$ is defined by $R = \{(a, b)$: both a and b are either odd or even$\}$. We observe the following properties of R on A:

Reflexivity: Clearly, $(1, 1), (2, 2), (3, 3), (4, 4), (5, 5), (6, 6), (7, 7) \in R$. So, R is a reflexive relation on A.

Symmetry: Let $a, b \in A$ be such that $(a, b) \in R$. Then,

$(a, b) \in R \Rightarrow$ Both a and b are either odd or even

$\Rightarrow$ Both b and a are either odd or even $\Rightarrow (b, a) \in R$

Thus, $(a, b) \in R \Rightarrow (b, a) \in R$ for all $a, b \in A$. So, R is a symmetric relation on A.

Transitivity: Let $a, b, c \in Z$ be such that $(a, b) \in R, (b, c) \in R$. Then,

$(a, b) \in R \Rightarrow$ Both a and b are either odd or even

$(b, c) \in R \Rightarrow$ Both b and c are either odd or even

If both a and b are even, then $(b, c) \in R \Rightarrow$ Both b and c are even

$\therefore$ Both a and c are even

If both a and b are odd, then $(b, c) \in R \Rightarrow$ Both b and c are odd

$\therefore$ Both a and c are odd

Thus, both a and c are even or odd. Therefore, $(a, c) \in R$.

So, $(a, b) \in R$ and $(b, c) \in R \Rightarrow (a, c) \in R$.

Consequently, R is a transitive relation on A. Hence, R is an equivalence relation on A.

We observe that two numbers in A are related if both are odd or both are even. Since $\{1, 3, 5, 7\}$ has all odd numbers of A. So, all the numbers of $\{1, 3, 5, 7\}$ are related to each other. Similarly, all the numbers of $\{2, 4, 6\}$ are related to each other as it contains all even numbers of set A. An even odd number in A is related to an even (odd) number in A. So, no number of the subset $\{1, 3, 5, 7\}$ is related to any number of the subset $\{2, 4, 6\}$.

1.4 SOME USEFUL RESULTS ON RELATIONS

In this section, we shall discuss some useful results on relations as theorems.

THEOREM 1 *If R and S are two equivalence relations on a set A, then $R \cap S$ is also an equivalence relation on A.*

OR

The intersection of two equivalence relations on a set is an equivalence relation on the set. **[NCERT]**

PROOF It is given that R and S are relations on set A.

$\therefore$ $R \subseteq A \times A$ and $S \subseteq A \times A \Rightarrow R \cap S \subseteq A \times A \Rightarrow R \cap S$ is also a relation on A.

Now, we shall show that it is an equivalence relation on A. We observe the following properties of relation $R \cap S$.

Reflexivity: Let a be an arbitrary element of A. Then,

$a \in A \Rightarrow (a, a) \in R$ and $(a, a) \in S$ [$\because$ R and S are reflexive]

$\Rightarrow$ $(a, a) \in R \cap S$

Thus, $(a, a) \in R \cap S$ for all $a \in A$. So, $R \cap S$ is a reflexive relation on A.

Symmetry: Let $a, b \in A$ such that $(a, b) \in R \cap S$. Then,

$(a, b) \in R \cap S$

$\Rightarrow$ $(a, b) \in R$ and $(a, b) \in S$

$\Rightarrow$ $(b, a) \in R$ and $(b, a) \in S$ [$\because$ R and S are symmetric]

$\Rightarrow$ $(b, a) \in R \cap S$

Thus, $(a, b) \in R \cap S \Rightarrow (b, a) \in R \cap S$ for all $(a, b) \in R \cap S$. So, $R \cap S$ is symmetric on A.

Transitivity: Let $a, b, c \in A$ such that $(a, b) \in R \cap S$ and $(b, c) \in R \cap S$. Then,

$(a, b) \in R \cap S$ and $(b, c) \in R \cap S$

$\Rightarrow$ $\{(a, b) \in R$ and $(a, b) \in S)\}$ and $\{(b, c) \in R$ and $(b, c) \in S)\}$

$\Rightarrow$ $\{(a, b) \in R, (b, c) \in R\}$ and $\{(a, b) \in S, (b, c) \in S\}$

$\Rightarrow$ $(a, c) \in R$ and $(a, c) \in S$ $\left[\begin{array}{l}\because R \text{ and } S \text{ are transitive.} \\ \therefore (a, b) \in R \text{ and } (b, c) \in R \Rightarrow (a, c) \in R \\ \quad (a, b) \in S \text{ and } (b, c) \in S \Rightarrow (a, c) \in S\end{array}\right]$

$\Rightarrow$ $(a, c) \in R \cap S$

Thus, $(a, b) \in R \cap S$ and $(b, c) \in R \cap S \Rightarrow (a, c) \in R \cap S$.

So, $R \cap S$ is transitive on A.

Hence, $R \cap S$ is an equivalence relation on A.

THEOREM 2 *The union of two equivalence relations on a set is not necessarily an equivalence relation on the set.*

PROOF Let $A = \{a, b, c\}$ and let R and S be two relations on A, given by

$R = \{(a, a), (b, b), (c, c), (a, b), (b, a)\}$ and, $S = \{(a, a), (b, b), (c, c), (b, c), (c, b)\}$

It can be easily seen that each one of R and S is an equivalence relation on A. But, $R \cup S$ is not transitive, because $(a, b) \in R \cup S$ and $(b, c) \in R \cup S$ but $(a, c) \notin R \cup S$.

Hence, $R \cup S$ is not an equivalence relation on A.

THEOREM 3 *If R is an equivalence relation on a set A, then R^{-1} is also an equivalence relation on A.*

OR

The inverse of an equivalence relation is an equivalence relation.

PROOF Since R is a relation on A.

$\therefore$ $R \subseteq A \times A \Rightarrow R^{-1} \subseteq A \times A \Rightarrow R^{-1}$ is also a relation on A.

Now, we shall show that R^{-1} is an equivalence relation on A.

We observe the following properties of relation R^{-1}.

Reflexivity: Let a be an arbitrary element of A. Then,

$a \in A$

$\Rightarrow$ $(a, a) \in R$ [$\because R$ is reflexive]

$\Rightarrow \quad (a, a) \in R^{-1}$ [By definition of R^{-1}]

Thus, $(a, a) \in R^{-1}$ for all $a \in A$. So, R^{-1} is reflexive on A.

Symmetry: Let $(a, b) \in R^{-1}$. Then,

$(a, b) \in R^{-1}$

$\Rightarrow \quad (b, a) \in R$ [By definition of R^{-1}]

$\Rightarrow \quad (a, b) \in R$ [$\because R$ is symmetric]

$\Rightarrow \quad (b, a) \in R^{-1}$ [By definition of R^{-1}]

Thus, $(a, b) \in R^{-1} \Rightarrow (b, a) \in R^{-1}$ for all $a, b \in A$. So, R^{-1} is symmetric on A.

Transitivity: Let $(a, b) \in R^{-1}$ and $(b, c) \in R^{-1}$. Then,

$(a, b) \in R^{-1}$ and $(b, c) \in R^{-1}$

$\Rightarrow \quad (b, a) \in R$ and $(c, b) \in R$ [By definition of R^{-1}]

$\Rightarrow \quad (c, b) \in R$ and $(b, a) \in R$

$\Rightarrow \quad (c, a) \in R$ [$\because R$ is transitive]

$\Rightarrow \quad (a, c) \in R^{-1}$ [By definition of R^{-1}]

Thus, $(a, b) \in R^{-1}$ and $(b, c) \in R^{-1} \Rightarrow (a, c) \in R^{-1}$ for all $a, b, c \in A$. So, R^{-1} is transitive on A.

Hence, R^{-1} is an equivalence relation on A.

EXERCISE 1.3

BASIC

1. If R and S are relations on a set A, then prove the following:
   (i) R and S are symmetric $\Rightarrow R \cap S$ and $R \cup S$ are symmetric
   (ii) R is reflexive and S is any relation $\Rightarrow R \cup S$ is reflexive.
2. If R and S are transitive relations on a set A, then prove that $R \cup S$ may not be a transitive relation on A.

FILL IN THE BLANKS TYPE QUESTIONS (FBQs)

1. If $R = \left\{(x, y) : x^2 + y^2 \leq 4, x, y \in Z\right\}$ is a relation in Z, then the domain of R is ....
2. Let R be a relation in N defined by $R = \{(x, y) : x + 2y = 8\}$, then the range of R is ....
3. The number of relations on a finite set having 5 elements is ....
4. Let $A = \{1, 2, 3, 4\}$ and R be the relation on A defined by $\{(a, b) : a, b \in A, a \times b$ is an even number$\}$, then the range of R is ....
5. Let $A = \{1, 2, 3, 4, 5\}$. The domain of the relation on A defined by $R = \{(x, y) : y = 2x - 1\}$, is ....
6. If R s a relation defined on set $A = \{1, 2, 3\}$ by the rule $(a, b) \in R \Leftrightarrow |a^2 - b^2| \leq 5$, then $R^{-1} =$ ....

7. If R is a relation from $A = \{11, 12, 13\}$ to $B = \{8, 10, 12\}$ defined by $y = x - 3$, then $R^{-1} =$ ....
8. The smallest equivalence relation on the set $A = \{a, b, c, d\}$ is ....
9. The largest equivalence relation on the set $A = \{1, 2, 3\}$ is ....
10. Let R be the equivalence relation on the set Z of integers given by $R = \{(a, b) : 3$ divides $a - b\}$. Then the equivalence class [0] is equal to ....
11. Let R be a relation on the set Z of all integers defined as $(x, y) \in R \Leftrightarrow x - y$ is divisible by 2. Then, the equivalence class [1] is ....
12. The relation $R = \{(1, 2), (1, 3)\}$ on set $A = \{1, 2, 3\}$ is .... only.
13. A relation in a set A is called ....relation, if each element of A is related to itself. [CBSE 2020]
14. A relation R on a set A is called a .... relation, if $(a_1, a_2) \in R$ implies $(a_2, a_1) \in R$ for all $a_1, a_2 \in A$. [CBSE 2020]

ANSWERS

1. $\{-2, -1, 0, 1, 2\}$ 2. $\{1, 2, 3\}$ 3. 2^{25} 4. $\{2, 4\}$ 5. $\{1, 2, 3\}$
6. $\{(1,1), (2, 1), (1, 2), (2, 2), (3, 2), (2, 3), (3, 3)\}$ 7. $\{(8, 11), (10, 13)\}$
8. $\{(a, a), (b, b), (c, c), (d, d)\}$ 9. $A \times A$ 10. $\{0, \pm 3, \pm 6, \pm 9, \ldots\ldots\}$
11. $\{\pm 1, \pm 3, \pm 5, \pm 7, \ldots\ldots\}$ 12. transitive 13. reflexive 14. symmetric

VERY SHORT ANSWER QUESTIONS (VSAQs)

Answer each of the following questions in one word or one sentence or as per exact requirement of the question:

1. Write the domain of the relation R defined on the set Z of integers as follows:
$(a, b) \in R \Leftrightarrow a^2 + b^2 = 25$
2. If $R = \{(x, y) : x^2 + y^2 \leq 4 ; x, y \in Z\}$ is a relation on Z, write the domain of R.
3. Write the identity relation on set $A = \{a, b, c\}$.
4. Write the smallest reflexive relation on set $A = \{1, 2, 3, 4\}$.
5. If $R = \{(x, y) : x + 2y = 8\}$ is a relation on N, then write the range of R. [CBSE 2014]
6. If R is a symmetric relation on a set A, then write a relation between R and R^{-1}.
7. Let $R = \{(x, y) : |x^2 - y^2| < 1\}$ be a relation on set $A = \{1, 2, 3, 4, 5\}$. Write R as a set of ordered pairs.
8. If $A = \{2, 3, 4\}, B = \{1, 3, 7\}$ and $R = \{(x, y) : x \in A, y \in B$ and $x < y\}$ is a relation from A to B, then write R^{-1}.
9. Let $A = \{3, 5, 7\}, B = \{2, 6, 10\}$ and R be a relation from A to B defined by $R = \{(x, y) : x$ and y are relatively prime$\}$. Then, write R and R^{-1}.
10. Define a reflexive relation.
11. Define a symmetric relation.

12. Define a transitive relation.
13. Define an equivalence relation.
14. If $A = \{3, 5, 7\}$ and $B = \{2, 4, 9\}$ and R is a relation given by "is less than", write R as a set ordered pairs.
15. $A = \{1, 2, 3, 4, 5, 6, 7, 8\}$ and if $R = \{(x, y) : y$ is one half of $x; x, y \in A\}$ is a relation on A, then write R as a set of ordered pairs.
16. Let $A = \{2, 3, 4, 5\}$ and $B = \{1, 3, 4\}$. If R is the relation from A to B given by $a R b$ iff "a is a divisor of b". Write R as a set of ordered pairs.
17. State the reason for the relation R on the set $\{1, 2, 3\}$ given by $R = \{(1, 2), (2, 1)\}$ not to be transitive. [CBSE 2011]
18. Let $R = \{(a, a^3) : a$ is a prime number less than $5\}$ be a relation. Find the range of R. [CBSE 2014]
19. Let R be the equivalence relation on the set Z of integers given by $R = \{(a, b) : 2$ divides $a - b\}$. Write the equivalence class [0]. [NCERT EXEMPLAR]
20. For the set $A = \{1, 2, 3\}$, define a relation R on the set A as follows:

$$R = \{(1, 1), (2, 2), (3, 3), (1, 3)\}$$

Write the ordered pairs to be added to R to make the smallest equivalence relation.
21. Let $A = \{0, 1, 2, 3\}$ and R be a relation on A defined as

$$R = \{(0, 0), (0, 1), (0, 3), (1, 0), (1, 1), (2, 2), (3, 0), (3, 3)\}$$

Is R reflexive? symmetric" transitive?
22. Let the relation R be defined on the set $A = \{1, 2, 3, 4, 5\}$ by $R = \{(a, b) : |a^2 - b^2| < 8\}$. Write R as a set of ordered pairs.
23. Let the relation R be defined on N by aRb iff $2a + 3b = 30$. Then write R as a set of ordered pairs.
24. Write the smallest equivalence relation on the set $A = \{1, 2, 3\}$.

ANSWERS

1. $\{0, \pm 3, \pm 4, \pm 5\}$
2. $\{0, \pm 1, \pm 2\}$
3. $\{(a, a), (b, b), (c, c)\}$
4. $\{(1, 1), (2, 2), (3, 3), (4, 4)\}$
5. $\{1, 2, 3\}$
6. $R = R^{-1}$
7. $\{(1, 1), (2, 2), (3, 3), (4, 4), (5, 5)\}$
8. $R^{-1} = \{(3, 2), (7, 2), (7, 3), (7, 4)\}$
9. $R = \{(3, 2), (3, 10), (5, 2), (5, 6), (7, 2), (7, 6), (7, 10)\}$
$R^{-1} = \{(2, 3), (10, 3), (2, 5), (6, 5), (2, 7), (6, 7), (10, 7)\}$

14. $R = \{(3, 4), (3, 9), (5, 9), (7, 9)\}$
15. $R = \{(2, 1), (4, 2), (6, 3), (8, 4)\}$
16. $\{(2, 4), (4, 4), (3, 3)\}$
17. $(1, 2) \in R$ and $(2, 1) \in R$ but $(1, 1) \notin R$
18. $\{8, 27\}$
19. $[0] = \{0, \pm 2, \pm 4, \pm 6, ..\}$
20. $(3, 1)$
21. Reflexive and symmetric
22. $R = \{(1, 1), (1, 2), (2, 1), (2, 2), (2, 3), (3, 2), (3, 3), (3, 4), (4, 3), (4, 4), (5, 5)\}$
23. $R = \{(3, 8), (6, 6), (9, 4), (12, 2)\}$
24. $\{(1, 1), (2, 2), (3, 3)\}$

HINTS TO SELECTED PROBLEMS

17. We observe that $(1, 2) \in R$ and $(2, 1) \in R$ but $(1, 1) \notin R$. Hence, R is not transitive.

18. We have,

$$R = \{(a, a^3) : a \text{ is prime less than } 5\} = \{(a, a^3) : a = 2, 3\} = \{(2, 8), (3, 27)\}$$

$\therefore$ Range $(R) = \{8, 27\}$

19. We have, $R = \{(a, b) : 2 \text{ divides } a - b\}$

For any $a \in Z$, $[a] = \{x : (x, a) \in R\} = \{x : 2 \text{ divides } x - a\}$

$\therefore$ $[0] = \{x \in Z : 2 \text{ divides } x - 0\} = \{x \in Z : 2 \text{ divides } x\} = \{0, \pm 2, \pm 4, \pm 6, \ldots\}$

CHAPTER 2

FUNCTIONS

2.1 INTRODUCTION

The concept of function is of paramount importance in Mathematics and among other disciplines as well. In earlier class we have introduced the notion of function and we have learnt about some special functions like identity function, constant function, polynomial function, rational function, modulus function, greatest integer function, signum function etc. along with their graphs. Addition, subtraction, multiplication and division of two real functions have also been studied in the earlier class. In this chapter, we would like to extend our study about functions from where we finished in earlier class. We will study about various kinds of functions, composition of functions and inverse of a function. Let us first recapitulate what we have learnt about functions in earlier class.

2.2 RECAPITULATION

FUNCTION AS A SET OF ORDERED PAIRS *Let A and B be two non-empty sets. A relation f from A to B i.e. a sub set of $A \times B$ is called a function (or a mapping or a map) from A to B, if*

(i) *for each $a \in A$ there exists $b \in B$ such that $(a, b) \in f$.*

(ii) $(a, b) \in f$ *and* $(a, c) \in f \Rightarrow b = c$.

Thus, a non-void subset of $A \times B$ is a function from A to B if each element of A appears in some ordered pair in f and no two ordered pairs in f have the same first element.

If $(a, b) \in f$, then b in called the image of a under f.

FUNCTION AS A CORRESPONDENCE *Let A and B be two non-empty sets. Then a function 'f' from set A to set B is a rule or method or correspondence which associates elements of set A to elements of set B such that:*

(i) *all elements of set A are associated to elements in set B.*

(ii) *an element of set A is associated to a unique element in set B.*

In other words, a function 'f' from a set A to a set B associates each element of set A to a unique element of set B.

Terms such as "map" (or "mapping"), "correspondence" are used as synonyms for "function".

If f is a function from a set A to a set B, then we write $f : A \to B$ or $A \xrightarrow{f} B$, which is read as *f is a function from A to B* or *f maps A to B.*

If an element $a \in A$ is associated to an element $b \in B$, then b is called "*the f-image of a*" or "*image of a under f*" or" *the value of the function f at a*". Also, a is called the pre-image of b under the function f. We write it as $b = f(a)$.

The set A is known as the domain of f and the set B is known as the co-domain of f. The set of all f-images of elements of A is known as the range of f or image set of A under f and is denoted by $f(A)$.

Thus, $f(A) = \{f(x) : x \in A\} =$ Range of f.

A visual representation of a function is shown in Fig. 2.1.

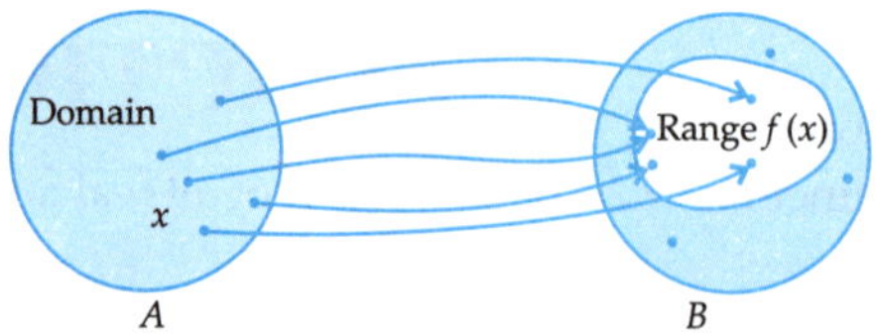

Fig. 2.1 Visual representation of a function.

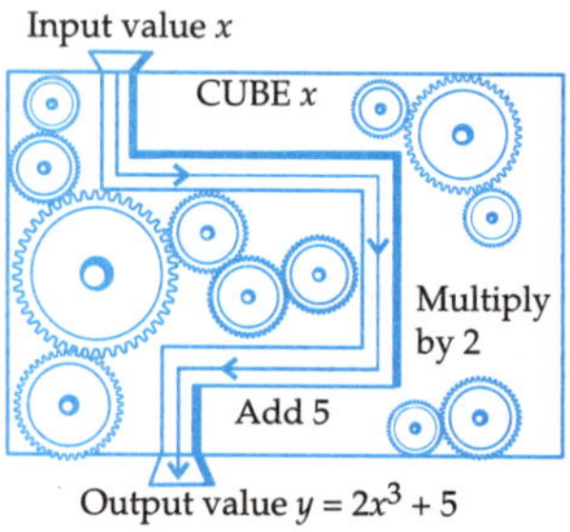

Fig. 2.2 Function as a machine.

FUNCTION AS A MACHINE *A function can also be regarded as a machine that gives unique output in set B corresponding to each input from the set A just as the function 'machine' shown in Fig. 2.2 which generate an output* $y = 2x^3 + 5$ *for each input x.*

Usually, real functions are described by using a mathematical formula. It is traditional to let x denote the input and y the corresponding output and to describe the function we write an equation relating x and y. In such an equation x and y are called variables. Because the value of the variable y is determined by that of the variable x, so we call y *the dependent variable* and x the *independent variable.*

If A and B are two sets having m and n elements respectively, then total number of functions from A to B is n^m.

A function $f : A \to B$ is called a real valued function if B is a subset of R (set of all real numbers).

If A and B both are subsets of R, then f is called a real function.

In order to represent a real function $y = f(x)$ geometrically as a graph, we use a cartesian coordinate system on which units for the independent variable x are marked on the horizontal axis i.e. x-axis and units for the dependent variable y on the vertical axis i.e. y-axis.

GRAPH OF A FUNCTION *The graph of a real function f consists of points whose coordinates* (x, y) *satisfy* $y = f(x)$, *for all* $x \in$ Domain (f).

In this section, we shall discuss graphs of some standard real functions.

By the definition of a real function f, for a given x in its domain there is only one number $y = f(x)$ in its range. Geometrically, this means that any vertical line $x = a$ crosses the graph of $f(x)$ at most once only. This observation leads to the following useful criterion for checking whether a curve in a plane is the graph of a function or not.

VERTICAL LINE TEST *A curve in a plane represents the graph of a real function if and only if no vertical line intersects it more than once.*

The curves shown in Fig. 2.3 (a) are the graphs of function whereas the curves shown in Fig. 2.3 (b) are not the graphs of functions as there exist vertical lines which intersect them more than once.

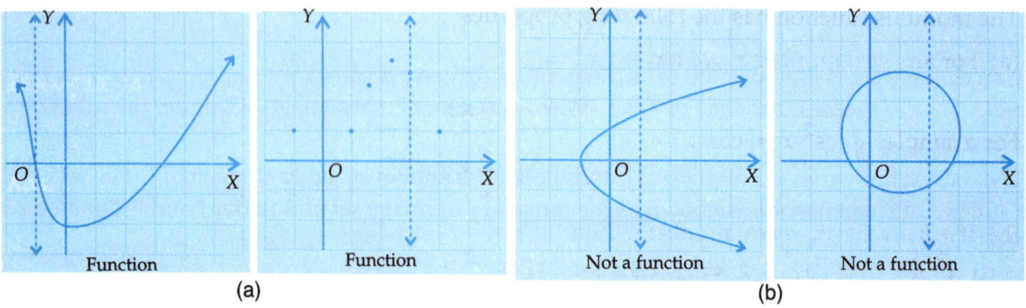

Fig. 2.3 Vertical line test

Following are some standard real functions which will occur very frequently in the study of calculus.

CONSTANT FUNCTION *If k is a fixed real number, then a function $f(x)$ given by $f(x) = k$ for all $x \in R$ is called a constant function.*

Sometimes we also call it the constant function k.

We observe that the domain of the constant function $f(x) = k$ is the set R of all real numbers and range of f is the singleton set $\{k\}$.

The graph of a constant function $f(x) = k$ is a straight line parallel to x-axis (see Fig. 2.4) which is above or below x-axis according as k is positive or negative. If $k = 0$, then the straight line is coincident to x-axis.

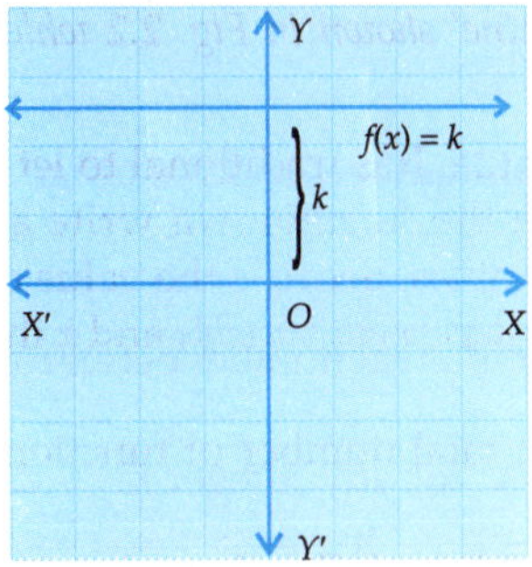

Fig. 2.4 Constant function

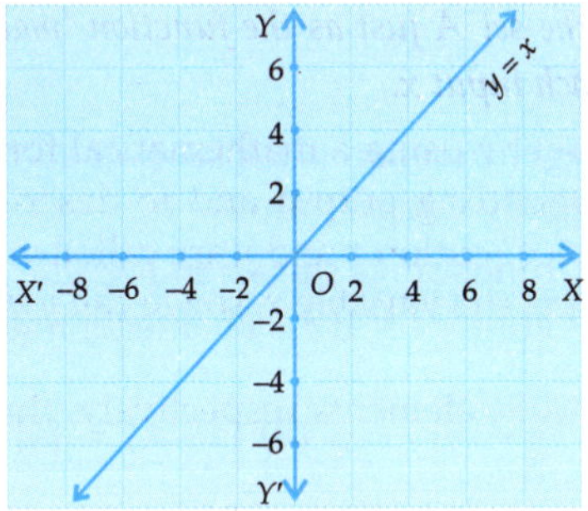

Fig. 2.5 Identity function

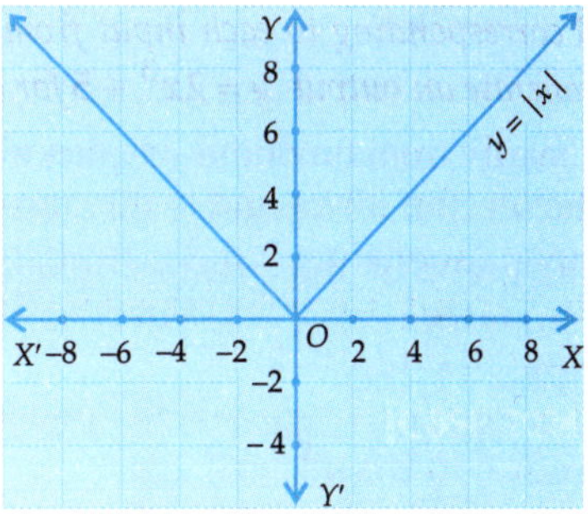

Fig. 2.6 Modulus function

IDENTITY FUNCTION *The function that associates each real number to itself is called the identity function and is usually denoted by I.*

Thus, the function $I : R \to R$ defined by $I(x) = x$ for all $x \in R$ is called the identity function.

Clearly, the domain and range of the identity function are both equal to R.

The graph of the identity function is a straight line passing through the origin and inclined at an angle of $45°$ with X-axis as shown in Fig. 2.5.

MODULUS FUNCTION *The function $f(x)$ defined by $f(x) = |x| = \begin{cases} x, & \text{when } x \geq 0 \\ -x, & \text{when } x < 0 \end{cases}$ is called the modulus function.*

It is also called the absolute value function.

We observe that the domain of the modulus function is the set R of all real numbers and the range is the set of all non-negative real numbers i.e. $R^+ = \{x \in R : x \geq 0\}$.

The graph of the modulus function is as shown in Fig. 2.6 for $x > 0$, the graph coincides with the graph of the identity function i.e. the line $y = x$ and for $x < 0$, it is coincident to the line $y = -x$.

The modulus function has the following properties:

(a) For any real number x, we have: $\sqrt{x^2} = |x|$

For example, $\sqrt{\cos^2 x} = |\cos x| = \begin{cases} \cos x, & 0 \leq x \leq \frac{\pi}{2} \\ -\cos x, & \frac{\pi}{2} < x \leq \pi \end{cases}$

(b) If a, b are positive real numbers, then

(i) $x^2 \leq a^2 \Leftrightarrow |x| \leq a \Leftrightarrow -a \leq x \leq a$ (ii) $x^2 \geq a^2 \Leftrightarrow |x| \geq a \Leftrightarrow x \leq -a$ or, $x \geq a$

(iii) $x^2 < a^2 \Leftrightarrow |x| < a \Leftrightarrow -a < x < a$ (iv) $x^2 > a^2 \Leftrightarrow |x| > a \Leftrightarrow x < -a$ or, $x > a$

(v) $a^2 \leq x^2 \leq b^2 \Leftrightarrow a \leq |x| \leq b \Leftrightarrow x \in [-b, -a] \cup [a, b]$

(vi) $a^2 < x^2 < b^2 \Leftrightarrow a < |x| < b \Leftrightarrow \in (-b, -a) \cup (a, b)$

(c) For real numbers x and y, we have

(i) $|x + y| = |x| + |y|$, if $(x \geq 0$ and $y \geq 0)$ or, $(x < 0$ and $y < 0)$

(ii) $|x - y| = |x| - |y|$, if $(x \geq 0$ and $|x| \geq |y|)$ or, $(x \leq 0, y \leq 0$ and $|x| \geq |y|)$

(iii) $|x \pm y| \leq |x| + |y|$ (iv) $|x \pm y| > ||x| - |y||$

GREATEST INTEGER FUNCTION (FLOOR FUNCTION) For any real number x, we use the symbol $[x]$ or, $\lfloor x \rfloor$ to denote the greatest integer less than or equal to x. For example,

$$[2.75] = 2, [3] = 3, [0.74] = 0, [-7.45] = -8 \text{ etc.}$$

The function $f : R \to R$ defined by $f(x) = [x]$ for all $x \in R$ is called the greatest integer function or the floor function.

It is also called a step function.

Clearly, domain of the greatest integer function is the set R of all real numbers and the range is the set Z of all integers as it attains only integer values.

The graph of the greatest integer function is shown in Fig. 2.7.

PROPERTIES OF GREATEST INTEGER FUNCTION If n is an integer and x is a real number between n and $n + 1$, then

(i) $[-n] = -[n]$

(ii) $[x + k] = [x] + k$ for any integer k.

(iii) $[-x] = -[x] - 1$

(iv) $[x] + [-x] = \begin{cases} -1, & \text{if } x \notin Z \\ 0, & \text{if } x \in Z \end{cases}$

(v) $[x] - [-x] = \begin{cases} 2[x] + 1, & \text{if } x \notin Z \\ 2[x], & \text{if } x \in Z \end{cases}$

(vi) $[x] \geq k \Rightarrow x > k$, where $k \in Z$

(vii) $[x] \leq k \Rightarrow x < k + 1$, where $k \in Z$

(viii) $[x] > k \Rightarrow x \geq k + 1$, were $k \in Z$

(ix) $[x] < k \Rightarrow x < k$, where $k \in Z$

(x) $[x + y] = [x] + [y + x - [x]]$ for all $x, y \in R$

(xi) $[x] + \left[x + \frac{1}{n}\right] + \left[x + \frac{2}{n}\right] + \ldots + \left[x + \frac{n-1}{n}\right] = [nx], n \in N.$

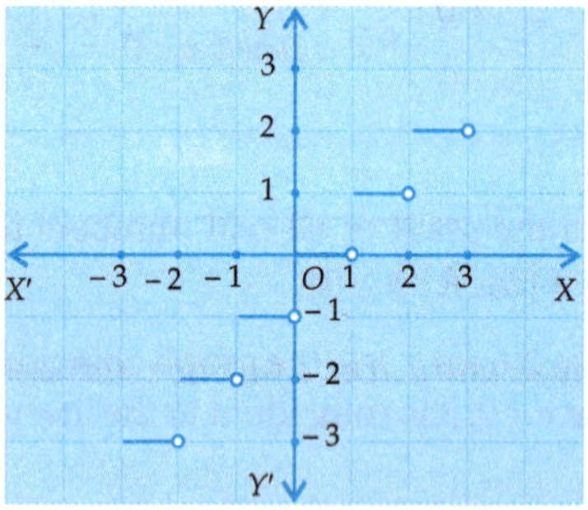

Fig. 2.7 Greatest integer function

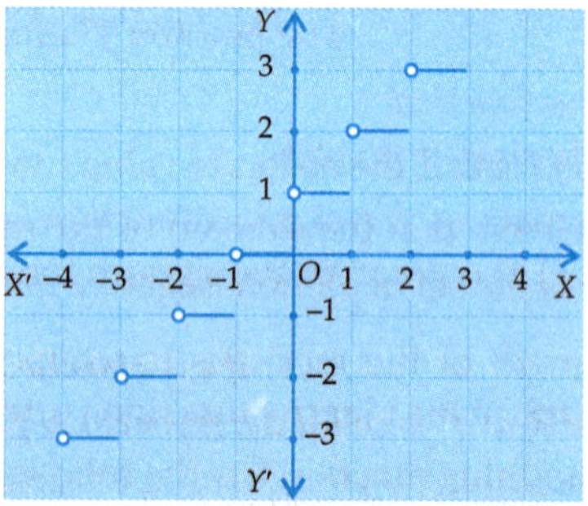

Fig. 2.8 Smallest integer function

SMALLEST INTEGER FUNCTION (CEILING FUNCTION) For any real number x, we use the symbol $\lceil x \rceil$ to denote the smallest integer greater than or equal to x.

For example, $\lceil 4.7 \rceil = 5, \lceil -7.2 \rceil = -7, \lceil 5 \rceil = 5, \lceil 0.75 \rceil = 1$ etc.

The function $f : R \to R$ defined by $f(x) = \lceil x \rceil$ for all $x \in R$ is called the smallest integer function or the ceiling function.

It is also a step function. We observe that the domain of the smallest integer function is the set R of all real numbers and its range is the set Z of all integers. The graph of the smallest integer function is as shown in Fig. 2.8.

PROPERTIES OF SMALLEST INTEGER FUNCTION Following are some properties of smallest integer function:

(i) $\lceil -n \rceil = -\lceil n \rceil$, where $n \in Z$ (ii) $\lceil -x \rceil = -\lceil x \rceil + 1$, where $x \in R - Z$

(iii) $\lceil x+n \rceil = \lceil x \rceil + n$, where $x \in R - Z$ and $n \in Z$ (iv) $\lceil x \rceil + \lceil -x \rceil = \begin{cases} 1 , & \text{if } x \notin Z \\ 0 , & \text{if } x \in Z \end{cases}$

(v) $\lceil x \rceil + \lceil -x \rceil = \begin{cases} 2\lceil x \rceil - 1, & \text{if } x \notin Z \\ 2\lceil x \rceil , & \text{if } x \in Z \end{cases}$

FRACTIONAL PART FUNCTION For any real number x, we use the symbol $\{x\}$ to denote the fractional part or decimal part of x. For example, $\{3.45\} = 0.45$, $\{-2.75\} = 0.25$, $\{-0.55\} = 0.45$, $\{3\} = 0$, $\{-7\} = 0$ etc.

The function $f : R \to R$ defined by $f(x) = \{x\}$ for all $x \in R$ is called the fractional part function.

We observe that the domain of the fractional part function is the set R of all real numbers and the range is the set $[0, 1)$. It is evident from the definition that

$$f(x) = \{x\} = x - [x] \quad \text{for all } x \in R$$

The graph of the fractional part function is as shown in Fig. 2.9.

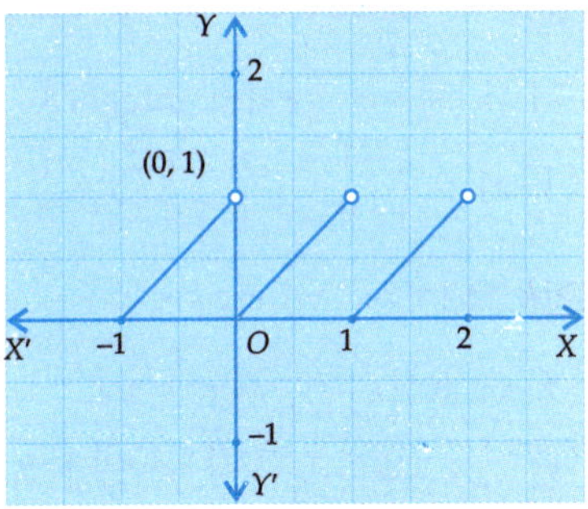

Fig. 2.9 Fractional part function

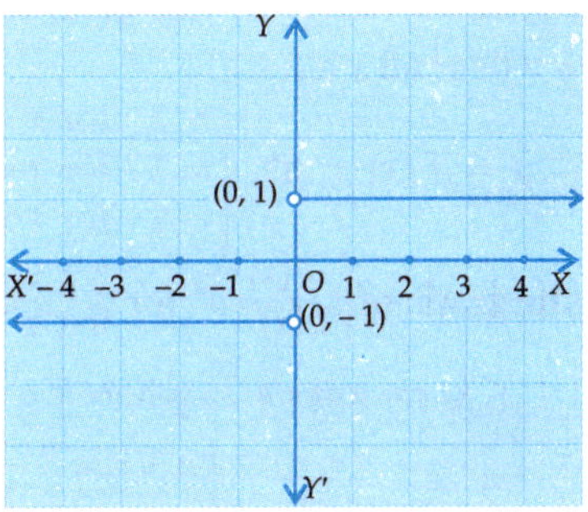

Fig. 2.10 Signum function

SIGNUM FUNCTION *The function f defined by* $f(x) = \begin{cases} \dfrac{|x|}{x} , & x \neq 0 \\ 0 , & x = 0 \end{cases}$ or, $f(x) = \begin{cases} 1 , & x > 0 \\ 0 , & x = 0 \\ -1 , & x < 0 \end{cases}$ *is called the signum function.*

The domain of the signum function is the set R of all real numbers and the range is the set $\{-1, 0, 1\}$ The graph of the signum function is as shown in Fig. 2.10.

EXPONENTIAL FUNCTION *If a is a positive real number other than unity, then a function that associates each $x \in R$ to a^x is called the exponential function.*

In other words, a function $f : R \to R$ defined by $f(x) = a^x$, where $a > 0$ and $a \neq 1$ is called the exponential function.

We observe that the domain of an exponential function is R the set of all real numbers and the range is the set $(0, \infty)$ as it attains only positive values. As $a > 0$ and $a \neq 1$. So, we have the following cases.

CASE I *When* $a > 1$: We observe that the values of $y = f(x) = a^x$ increase as the values of x increase.

Also, $f(x) = a^x \begin{cases} < 1 & \text{for } x < 0 \\ = 1 & \text{for } x = 0 \\ > 1 & \text{for } x > 0. \end{cases}$

Thus, the graph of $f(x) = a^x$ for $a > 1$ as shown in Fig. 2.11.

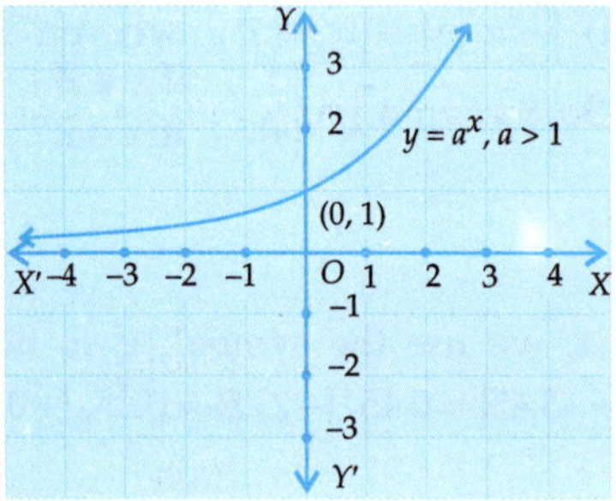

Fig. 2.11 Exponential function

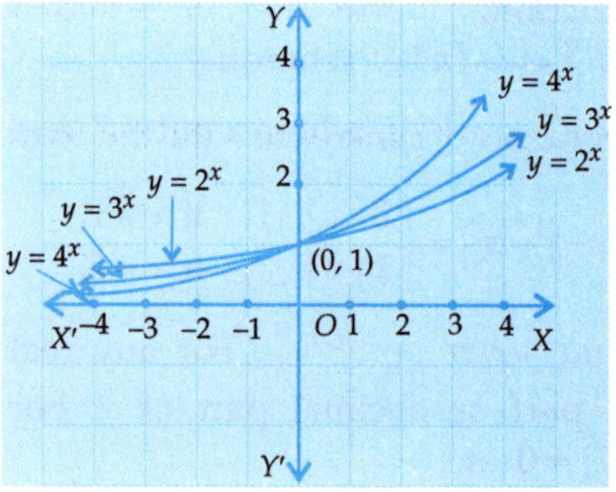

Fig. 2.12 Exponential functions on same scale

We also observe that:

$$2^x < 3^x < 4^x < \ldots \text{ for all } x > 0;\ 2^x = 3^x = 4^x = \ldots = 1 \text{ for } x = 0;\ 2^x > 3^x > 4^x > \ldots \text{ for } x < 0$$

So, the graphs of $f(x) = 2^x$, $f(x) = 3^x$, $f(x) = 4^x$ etc. are as shown in Fig. 2.12.

Case II *When* $0 < a < 1$: In this case, the values of $y = f(x) = a^x$ decrease with the increase in x and $y > 0$ for all $x \in R$.

Also, $$y = f(x) = a^x \begin{cases} > 1 & \text{for } x < 0 \\ = 1 & \text{for } x = 0 \\ < 1 & \text{for } x > 0 \end{cases}$$

Thus, the graph of $f(x) = a^x$ for $0 < a < 1$ is as shown in Fig. 2.13.

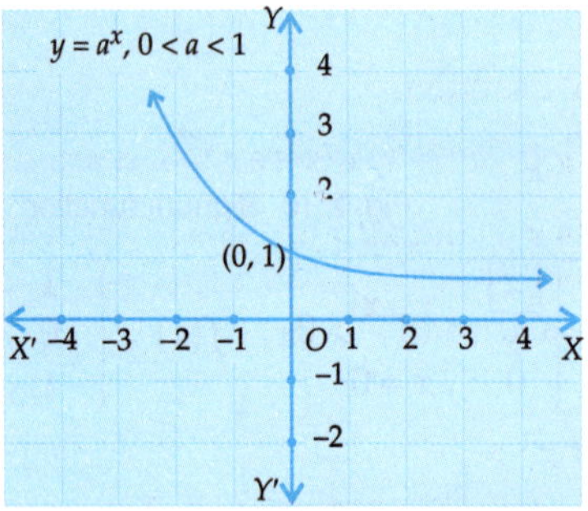

Fig. 2.13 Exponential Function

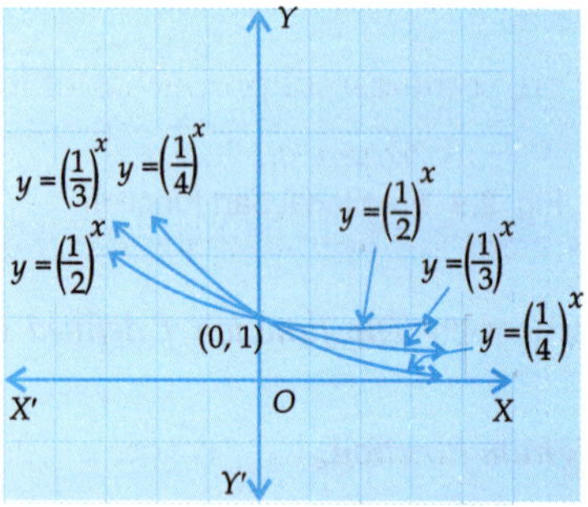

Fig. 2.14 Exponential functions on same scale

The graphs of $f(x) = a^x$, $0 < a < 1$ for different values of a are shown in Fig. 2.14.

REMARK *We have,* $2 < e < 3$. *Therefore, graph of* $f(x) = e^x$ *is identical to that of* $f(x) = a^x$ *for* $a > 1$ *and the graph of* $f(x) = e^{-x}$ *is identical to that of* $f(x) = a^x$ *for* $0 < a < 1$.

LOGARITHMIC FUNCTION *If* $a > 0$ *and* $a \neq 1$, *then the function defined by* $f(x) = \log_a x$, $x > 0$ *is called the logarithmic function.*

In earlier classes we have learnt that the logarithmic function and the exponential function are inverse functions.

i.e. $\log_a x = y \Leftrightarrow x = a^y$

We observe that the domain of the logarithmic function is the set of all positive real numbers i.e. $(0, \infty)$ and the range is the set R of all real numbers.

As $a > 0$ and $a \neq 1$. So, we have the following cases.

Case I *When* $a > 1$: In this case, we obtain: $y = \log_a x \begin{cases} < 0 & \text{for } 0 < x < 1 \\ = 0 & \text{for } x = 1 \\ > 0 & \text{for } x > 1 \end{cases}$

Also, the values of y increase with the increase in x. So, the graph of $y = \log_a x$ is as shown in Fig. 2.15.

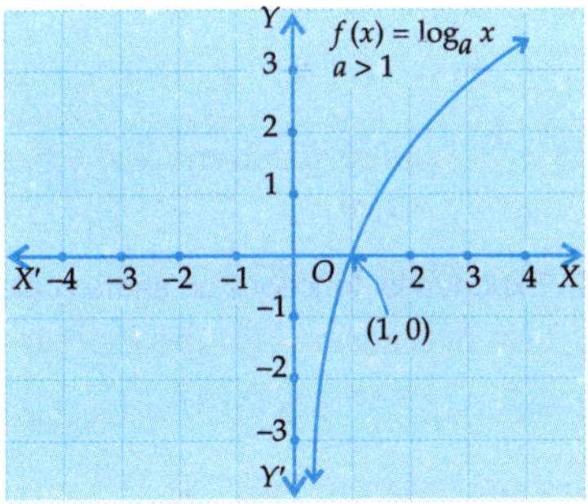

Fig. 2.15 Logarithmic function $f(x) = \log_a x, a > 1$

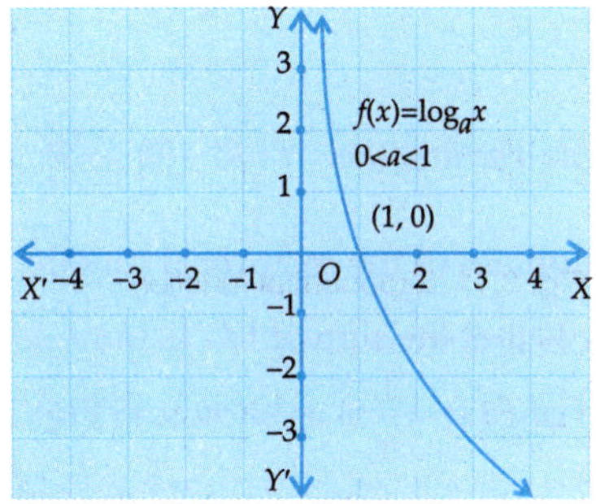

Fig. 2.16 Logarithmic function $f(x) = \log_a x, 0 < a < 1$

Case II When $0 < a < 1$: In this case, we obtain: $y = \log_a x \begin{cases} > 0 & \text{for } 0 < x < 1 \\ = 0 & \text{for } x = 1 \\ < 0 & \text{for } x > 1 \end{cases}$

Also, the values of y decrease with the increase in x. So, the graph of $y = \log_a x$ is as shown in Fig. 2.16.

Following are some useful properties of logarithmic function:

(i) $\log_a 1 = 0$, where $a > 0, a \neq 1$ (ii) $\log_a a = 1$, where $a > 0, a \neq 1$

(iii) $\log_a (xy) = \log_a |x| + \log_a |y|$, where $a > 0, a \neq 1$ and $xy > 0$

(iv) $\log_a \left(\frac{x}{y}\right) = \log_a |x| - \log_a |y|$, where $a > 0, a \neq 1$ and $\frac{x}{y} > 0$

(v) $\log_a (x^n) = n \log_a |x|$, where $a > 0, a \neq 1$ and $x^n > 0$

(vi) $\log_{a^n} x^m = \frac{m}{n} \log_{|a|} |x|$, where $a > 0, a \neq 1$ and $x^m > 0, a^n > 0$

(vii) $x^{\log_a y} = y^{\log_a x}$, where $x > 0, y > 0, a > 0, a \neq 1$

(viii) If $a > 1$, then the values of $f(x) = \log_a x$ increase with the increase in x.

i.e. $x < y \Leftrightarrow \log_a x < \log_a y$. Also, $\log_a x \begin{cases} < 0 & \text{for } 0 < x < 1 \\ = 0 & \text{for } x = 1 \\ > 0 & \text{for } x > 1. \end{cases}$

(ix) If $0 < a < 1$, then the values of $f(x) = \log_a x$ decrease with the increase in x.

i.e. $x < y \Leftrightarrow \log_a x > \log_a y$. Also, $\log_a x \begin{cases} > 0 & \text{for } 0 < x < 1 \\ = 0 & \text{for } x = 1 \\ < 0 & \text{for } x > 1 \end{cases}$

(x) $\log_a x = \frac{1}{\log_x a}$ for $a > 0, a \neq 1$ and $x > 0, x \neq 1$.

REMARK *Functions $f(x) = \log_a x$ and $g(x) = a^x$ are inverse of each other. So, their graphs are mirror images of each other in the line mirror $y = x$.*

RECIPROCAL FUNCTION The function that associates a real number x to its reciprocal $\frac{1}{x}$ is called the reciprocal function. Since $\frac{1}{x}$ is not defined for $x = 0$. So, we define the reciprocal function as follows:

DEFINITION *The function $f : R - \{0\} \to R$ defined by $f(x) = \frac{1}{x}$ is called the reciprocal function.*

Clearly, domain of the reciprocal function is $R - \{0\}$ and its range is also $R - \{0\}$.

We observe that the sign of $1/x$ is same as that of x and $1/x$ decreases with the increase in x. So, the graph of $f(x) = \frac{1}{x}$ is as shown in Fig. 2.17.

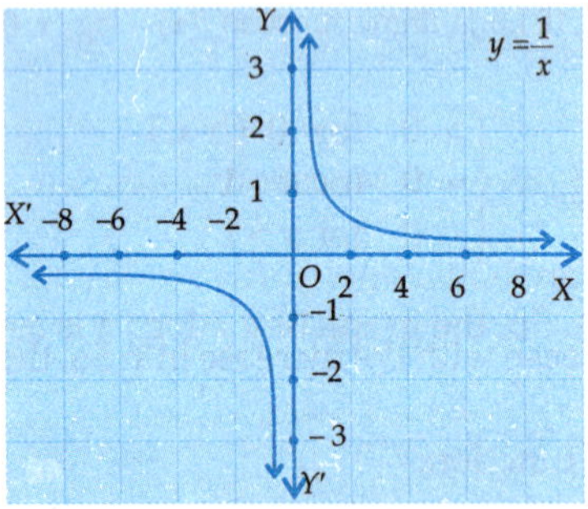

Fig. 2.17 Reciprocal function

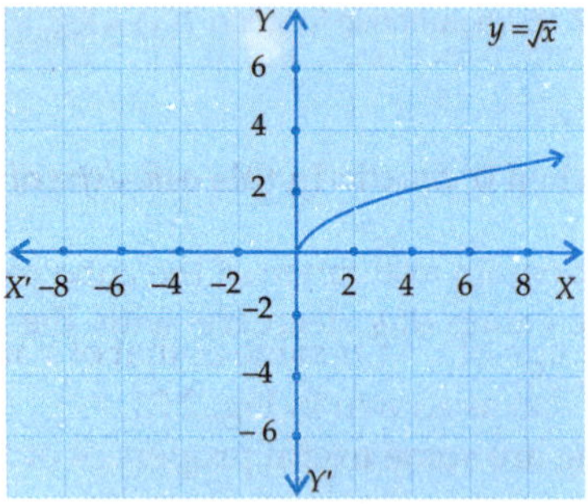

Fig. 2.18 Square root function

SQUARE ROOT FUNCTION The function that associates a real number x to $+\sqrt{x}$ is called the square root function. Since $\sqrt{x}$ is real for $x \geq 0$. So, we defined the square root function as follows:

DEFINITION *The function $f : R^+ \to R$ defined by $f(x) = +\sqrt{x}$ is called the square root function.*

Clearly, domain of the square root function is R^+ i.e. $[0, \infty)$ and its range is also $[0, \infty)$.

We observe that the values of $f(x) = +\sqrt{x}$ increase with the increase in x. So, the graph of $f(x) = +\sqrt{x}$ is as shown in Fig. 2.18.

SQUARE FUNCTION The function that associates a real number x to its square i.e. x^2 is called the square function. Since x^2 is defined for all $x \in R$. So, we define the square function as follows:

DEFINITION *The function $f : R \to R$ defined by $f(x) = x^2$ is called the square function.*

Clearly, domain of the square function is R and its range is the set of all non-negative real numbers i.e. $[0, \infty)$. The graph of $f(x) = x^2$ is parabola as shown in Fig. 2.19.

CUBE FUNCTION The function that associate a real number x to its cube is called the cube function. We observe that x^3 is meaningful for all $x \in R$. So, we define the cube function as follows:

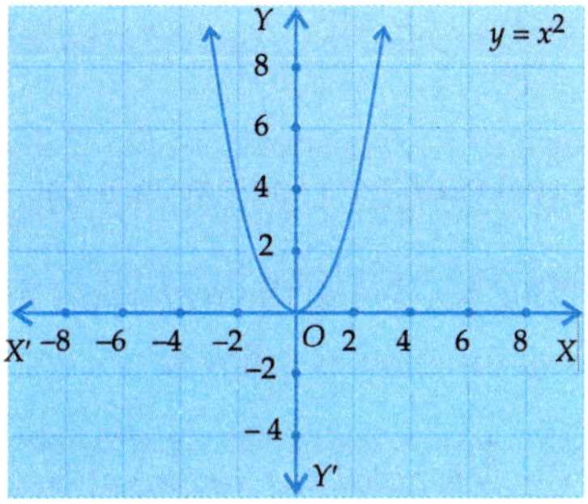

Fig. 2.19 Square function

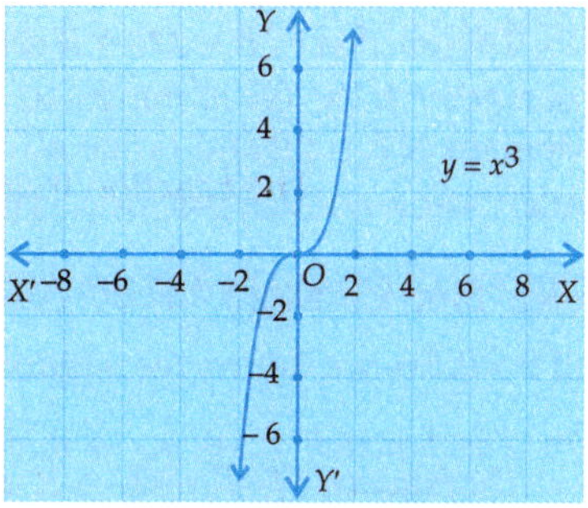

Fig. 2.20 Cube function

DEFINITION *The function $f: R \to R$ defined by $f(x) = x^3$ is called the cube function.*

We observe that the sign of x^3 is same as that of x and the values of x^3 increase with the increase in x. So, the graph of $f(x) = x^3$ is as shown in Fig. 2.20. Clearly, the graph is symmetrical in opposite quadrants.

CUBE ROOT FUNCTION The function that associates a real number x to its cube root $x^{1/3}$ is called the cube root function. Clearly, $x^{1/3}$ is defined for all $x \in R$. So, we define the cube root function as follows:

DEFINITION *The function $f: R \to R$ defined by $f(x) = x^{1/3}$ is called the cube root function.*

Clearly, domain and range of the cube root function are both equal to R.

Also, the sign of $x^{1/3}$ is same as that of x and $x^{1/3}$ increase with the increase in x. So, the graph of $f(x) = x^{1/3}$ is as shown in Fig. 2.21.

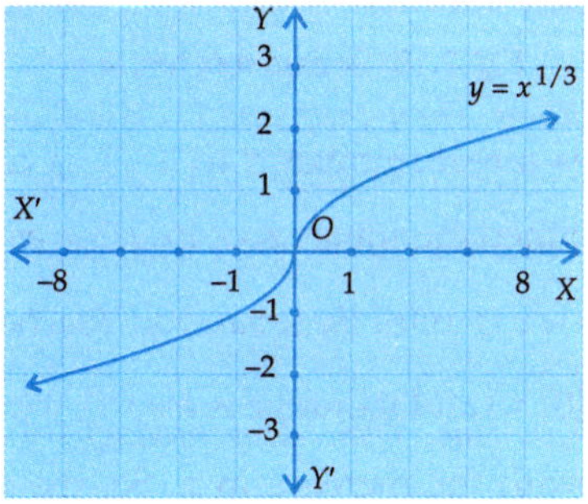

Fig. 2.21 Cube root function

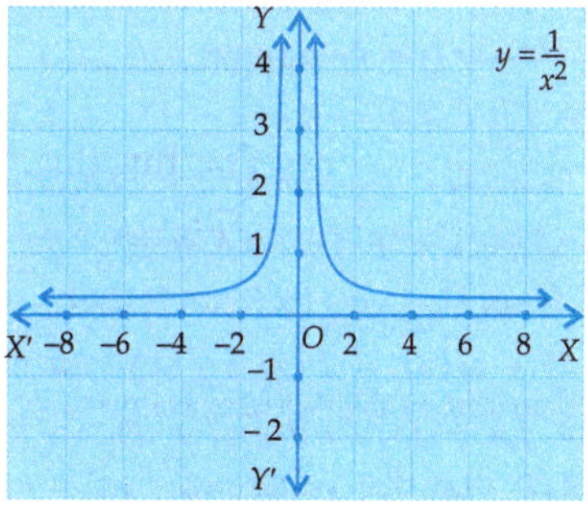

Fig. 2.22 Reciprocal squared function $f(x) = \frac{1}{x^2}$

REMARK 1 *A function $f: R \to R$ is said to be a polynomial function if $f(x)$ is a polynomial in x. For example, $f(x) = x^2 - x + 4$, $g(x) = x^3 + 3x^2 + \sqrt{2}\,x - 1$ etc are polynomial functions.*

REMARK 2 *A function of the form $f(x) = \frac{p(x)}{q(x)}$, where $p(x)$ and $q(x)$ are polynomials and $q(x) \neq 0$, is called a rational function. The domain of a rational function $f(x) = \frac{p(x)}{q(x)}$ is the set of all real numbers, except points where $q(x) = 0$.*

RECIPROCAL SQUARED FUNCTION The function that associates every non-zero real number x to the reciprocal of its square x^2 is called the reciprocal squared function. Clearly, $\frac{1}{x^2}$ is defined for non-zero x. So, we define the reciprocal squared function as follows:

DEFINITION *The function $f: R - \{0\} \rightarrow R$ defined by $f(x) = \frac{1}{x^2}$ is called the reciprocal squared function.*

Clearly, domain of $R - \{0\}$ and range is $(0, \infty)$. The graph of $f(x)$ is shown in Fig. 2.22.

SQUARE ROOT RECIPROCAL FUNCTION The function that associates every positive real number x to the reciprocal of its square root $\sqrt{x}$ is called the square root reciprocal function. Clearly, $\frac{1}{\sqrt{x}}$ is real for all $x > 0$. So, we define the square root reciprocal function as follows:

DEFINITION *The function $f: (0, \infty) \rightarrow R$ defined by $f(x) = \frac{1}{\sqrt{x}}$ is called the square root reciprocal function.*

Clearly, domain and range of f are both $(0, \infty)$. The graph of $f(x)$ is shown in Fig. 2.23.

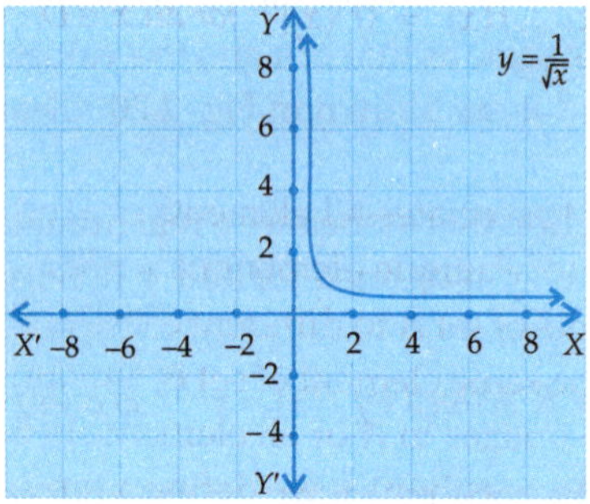

Fig. 2.23 Square root reciprocal function

2.2.1 OPERATIONS ON REAL FUNCTIONS

In this section, we shall recall various operations, namely addition, subtraction, multiplication, division etc. on real functions.

ADDITION *Let $f: D_1 \rightarrow R$ and $g: D_2 \rightarrow R$ be two real functions. Then, their sum $f + g$ is defined as that function from $D_1 \cap D_2$ to R which associates each $x \in D_1 \cap D_2$ to the number $f(x) + g(x)$.*

In other words, if $f: D_1 \rightarrow R$ and $g: D_2 \rightarrow R$ are two real functions, then their sum $f + g$ is a function from $D_1 \cap D_2$ to R such that

$$(f + g)(x) = f(x) + g(x) \quad \text{for all } x \in D_1 \cap D_2$$

PRODUCT *Let $f: D_1 \rightarrow R$ and $g: D_2 \rightarrow R$ be two real functions. Then, their product (or pointwise multiplication) $f\,g$ is a function from $D_1 \cap D_2$ to R and is defined as*

$$(f\,g)(x) = f(x)\,g(x) \quad \textit{for all } x \in D_1 \cap D_2$$

DIFFERENCE (SUBTRACTION) *Let $f: D_1 \rightarrow R$ and $g: D_2 \rightarrow R$ be two real functions. Then the difference of g from f is denoted by $f - g$ and is defined as*

$$(f - g)(x) = f(x) - g(x) \quad \textit{for all } x \in D_1 \cap D_2$$

QUOTIENT *Let $f: D_1 \rightarrow R$ and $g: D_2 \rightarrow R$ be two real functions. Then the quotient of f by g is denoted by $\frac{f}{g}$ and it is a function from $D_1 \cap D_2 - \{x : g(x) = 0\}$ to R defined by*

$$\left(\frac{f}{g}\right)(x) = \frac{f(x)}{g(x)} \quad \textit{for all } x \in D_1 \cap D_2 - \{x : g(x) = 0\}$$

MULTIPLICATION OF A FUNCTION BY A SCALAR *Let $f: D \rightarrow R$ ba a real function and α be a scalar (real number). Then the product αf is a function from D to R and is defined as*

$(\alpha f)(x) = \alpha f(x)$ *for all* $x \in D$.

RECIPROCAL OF A FUNCTION *If* $f : D \to R$ *is a real function, then its reciprocal function* $\frac{1}{f}$ *is a function from* $D - \{x : f(x) = 0\}$ *to* R *and is defined as* $\left(\frac{1}{f}\right)(x) = \frac{1}{f(x)}$.

REMARK 1 *The sum, difference product and quotient are defined for real functions only on their common domain. These operations do not make any sense for general functions even if their domains are same, because the sum, difference, product and quotient may or may not be meaningful for the elements in their common domain.*

REMARK 2 *For any real function* $f : D \to R$ *and* $n \in N$, *we define*

$$\underbrace{(ff \dots f)}_{n-\text{times}}(x) = \underbrace{f(x)f(x)\dots f(x)}_{n-\text{times}} = \{f(x)\}^n \text{ for all } x \in D$$

2.3 KINDS OF FUNCTIONS

If $f : A \to B$ is a function, then f associates all elements of set A to elements in set B such that an element of set A is associated to a unique element of set B. Following these two conditions we may associate different elements of set A to different elements of set B or more than one element of set A may be associated to the same element of set B. Similarly, there may be some elements in B which do not have their pre-images in A or all elements in B may have their pre-images in A. Corresponding to each of these possibilities we define a type of a function as given below.

2.3.1 ONE-ONE FUNCTION (INJECTION)

DEFINITION *A function* $f : A \to B$ *is said to be a one-one function or an injection if different elements of A have different images in B.*

Thus, $f : A \to B$ is one-one

$\Leftrightarrow$ $a \neq b \Rightarrow f(a) \neq f(b)$ for all $a, b \in A$ $\Leftrightarrow$ $f(a) = f(b) \Rightarrow a = b$ for all $a, b \in A$

ILLUSTRATION 1 *A function which associates to each country in the world, its capital, is one-one because different countries have their different capitals.*

ILLUSTRATION 2 *Let* $f : A \to B$ *and* $g : X \to Y$ *be two functions represented by the following diagrams:*

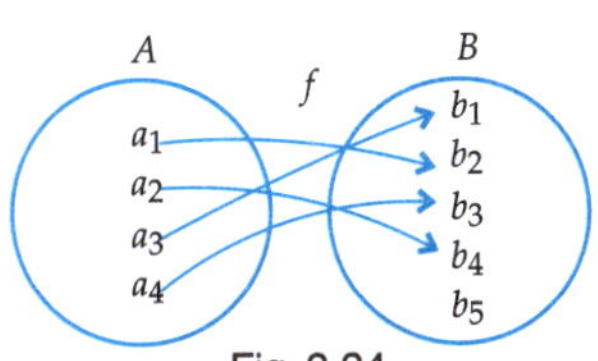

Fig. 2.24

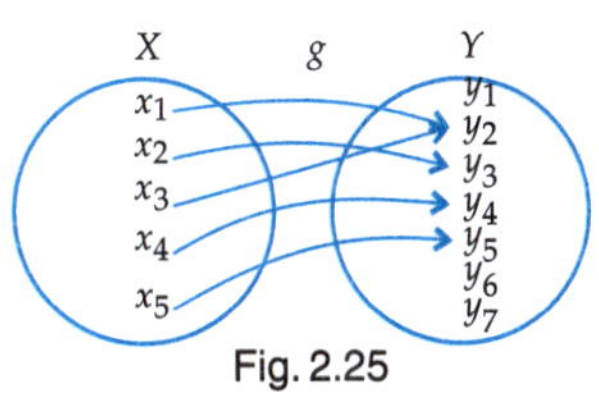

Fig. 2.25

Clearly, $f : A \to B$ is a one-one function. But, $g : X \to Y$ is not one-one because two distinct elements x_1 and x_3 have the same image under function g.

ILLUSTRATION 3 *Let* $A = \{1, 2, 3, 4\}$, $B = \{1, 2, 3, 4, 5, 6\}$ *and* $f : A \to B$ *be a function defined by* $f(x) = x + 2$ *for all* $x \in A$.

We observe that f as a set of ordered pairs can be written as $f = \{(1, 3), (2, 4), (3, 5), (4, 6)\}$

Clearly, different elements in A have different images under function f. So, $f : A \to B$ is an injection.

ILLUSTRATION 4 *Let* $A = \{1, 2, 3\}$, $B = \{4, 5, 6, 7\}$ *and let* $f = \{(1, 4), (2, 5), (3, 6)\}$ *be a function from A to B. Then,* $f(1) = 4$, $f(2) = 5$ *and* $f(3) = 6$. *Clearly, different elements of A have different images in B. So, f is a one-one function.*

Let $f : A \to B$ be a function such that A is an infinite set and we wish to check the injectivity of f. In such a case it is not possible to list the images of all elements of set A to see whether different elements of A have different images or not. The following algorithm provides a systematic procedure to check the injectivity of a function.

ALGORITHM

Step I *Take two arbitrary elements x, y (say) in the domain of f.*

Step II *Put* $f(x) = f(y)$

Step III *Solve* $f(x) = f(y)$. *If it gives* $x = y$ *only, then* $f : A \to B$ *is a one-one function (or an injection). Otherwise not.*

NOTE *Let* $f : A \to B$ *and let* $x, y \in A$. *Then,* $x = y \Rightarrow f(x) = f(y)$ *is always true from the definition. But,* $f(x) = f(y) \Rightarrow x = y$ *is true only when f is one-one.*

ILLUSTRATION 5 *Find whether the following functions are one-one or not:*

(i) $f : R \to R$ *given by* $f(x) = x^3 + 2$ *for all* $x \in R$.

(ii) $f : Z \to Z$ *given by* $f(x) = x^2 + 1$ *for all* $x \in Z$

SOLUTION (i) Let x, y be two arbitrary elements of R (domain of f) such that $f(x) = f(y)$. Then,

$$f(x) = f(y) \Rightarrow x^3 + 2 = y^3 + 2 \Rightarrow x^3 = y^3 \Rightarrow x = y$$

Hence, f is a one-one function from R to itself.

(ii) Let x, y be two arbitrary elements of Z such that $f(x) = f(y)$. Then,

$$f(x) = f(y) \Rightarrow x^2 + 1 = y^2 + 1 \Rightarrow x^2 = y^2 \Rightarrow x = \pm y$$

Here, $f(x) = f(y)$ does not provide the unique solution $x = y$ but it provides $x = \pm y$. So, f is not a one-one function. Infact, $f(2) = 2^2 + 1 = 5$ and $f(-2) = (-2)^2 + 1 = 5$. So, 2 and –2 are two distinct elements having the same image.

NOTE *If A and B are two sets having m* and *n elements respectively such that* $m \le n$, *then total numbers of one-one functions from A to B is* ${}^nC_m \times m!$.

2.3.2 MANY-ONE FUNCTION

DEFINITION *A function* $f : A \to B$ *is said to be a many-one function if two or more elements of set A have the same image in B.*

Thus, $f : A \to B$ is a many-one function if there exist $x, y \in A$ such that $x \ne y$ but $f(x) = f(y)$.

In other words, $f : A \to B$ is a many-one function if it is not a one-one function.

ILLUSTRATION 1 *Let* $f : A \to B$ *and* $g : X \to Y$ *be two functions represented by the following diagrams:*

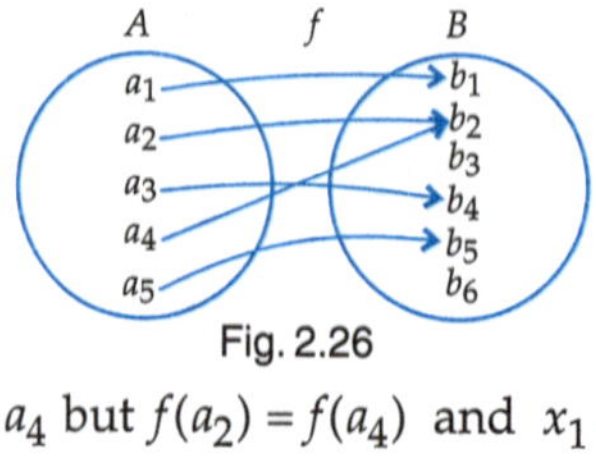

Fig. 2.26

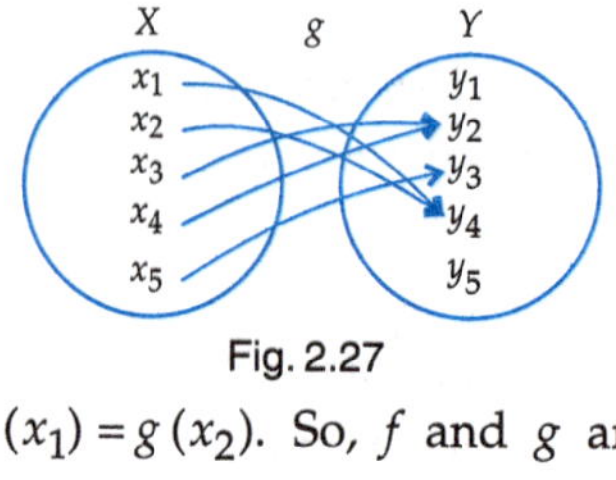

Fig. 2.27

Clearly, $a_2 \ne a_4$ but $f(a_2) = f(a_4)$ and $x_1 \ne x_2$ but $g(x_1) = g(x_2)$. So, f and g are many-one functions.

ILLUSTRATION 2 *Let* $A = \{-1, 1, -2, 2\}$ *and* $B = \{1, 4, 9, 16\}$. *Consider* $f : A \to B$ *given by* $f(x) = x^2$. *Then,* $f(-1) = 1$, $f(1) = 1$, $f(-2) = 4$ *and* $f(2) = 4$. *Thus, 1 and –1 have the same image. Similarly, 2 and –2 also have the same image. So, f is a many-one function.*

ILLUSTRATION 3 *Consider a function* $f : Z \to Z$ *given by* $f(x) = |x|$ *for all* $x \in Z$. *Then, f is a many-one function because for every* $a \in Z$, $a \ne 0$, *we find that*

$$a \ne -a, \text{ but } |a| = |-a| \Rightarrow f(a) = f(-a) \qquad [\because |a| = |-a|]$$

ILLUSTRATION 4 *Show that the function $f: Z \to Z$ defined by $f(x) = x^2 + x$ for all $x \in Z$, is a many-one function.*

SOLUTION Let $x, y \in Z$. Then,

$$f(x) = f(y) \Rightarrow x^2 + x = y^2 + y \Rightarrow (x^2 - y^2) + (x - y) = 0$$

$$\Rightarrow \quad (x - y)(x + y + 1) = 0 \Rightarrow x = y \text{ or}, y = -x - 1.$$

Since $f(x) = f(y)$ does not provide the unique solution $x = y$ but it also provides $y = -x - 1$. This means that $x \neq y$ but $f(x) = f(y)$ when $y = -x - 1$. For example, if we put $x = 1$ in $y = -x - 1$ we obtain $y = -2$. This shows that 1 and –2 have the same image under f. Hence, f is a many-one function.

2.3.3 ONTO FUNCTION (SURJECTION)

DEFINITION *A function $f: A \to B$ is said to be an onto function or a surjection if every element of B is the f-image of some element of A i.e., if $f(A) = B$ or range of f is the co-domain of f.*

Thus, $f: A \to B$ is a surjection iff for each $b \in B$, there exists $a \in A$ such that $f(a) = b$.

INTO FUNCTION *A function $f: A \to B$ is an into function if there exists an element in B having no pre-image in A.*

In other words, $f: A \to B$ is an into function if it is not an onto function.

ILLUSTRATION 1 *Let $f: A \to B$ and $g: X \to Y$ be two functions represented by the following diagrams:*

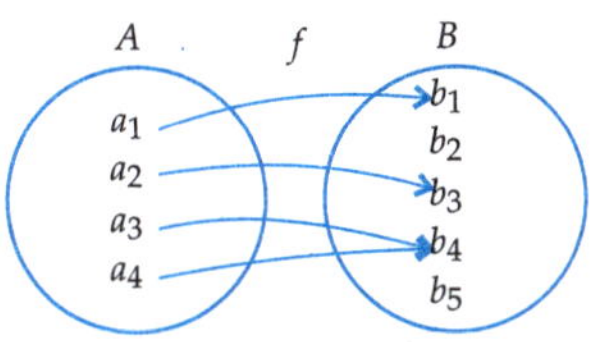

Fig. 2.28

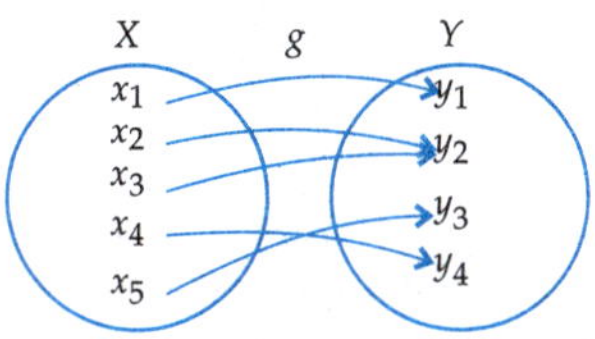

Fig. 2.29

Clearly, b_2 and b_5 are two elements in B which do not have their pre-images in A. So, $f: A \to B$ is an into function.

Under function g every element in Y has its pre-image X. So, $g: X \to Y$ is an onto function.

ILLUSTRATION 2 *Let $A = \{-1, 1, 2, -2\}$, $B = \{1, 4\}$ and $f: A \to B$ be a function defined by $f(x) = x^2$. Then, f is onto, because $f(A) = \{f(-1), f(1), f(2), f(-2)\} = \{1, 4\} = B$.*

ILLUSTRATION 3 *A function $f: N \to N$ defined by $f(x) = 2x$ is not an onto function, because $f(N) = \{2, 4, 6, \ldots\} \neq N$ (co-domain). In otherwords, range $(f) \neq$ co-domain of f.*

The following algorithm can be used to check the subjectivity of a real function.

ALGORITHM

Let $f: A \to B$ be the given function.

Step I *Choose an arbitrary element y in B.*

Step II *Put $f(x) = y$*

Step III *Solve the equation $f(x) = y$ for x and obtain x in terms of y. Let $x = g(y)$*

Step IV *If for all values of $y \in B$, the values of x obtained from $x = g(y)$ are in A, then f is onto. If there are some $y \in B$ for which x, given by $x = g(y)$, is not in A. Then, f is not onto.*

Following illustration will illustrate the above algorithm.

ILLUSTRATION 4 *Discuss the surjectivity of the following functions:*

(i) $f: R \to R$ given by $f(x) = x^3 + 2$ for all $x \in R$.

(ii) $f: R \to R$ given by $f(x) = x^2 + 2$ for all $x \in R$.

(iii) $f: Z \to Z$ given by $f(x) = 3x + 2$ for all $x \in Z$.

SOLUTION (i) Let y be an arbitrary element of R. Then, $f(x) = y \Rightarrow x^3 + 2 = y \Rightarrow x = (y-2)^{1/3}$.

Clearly, for all $y \in R, (y-2)^{1/3}$ is a real number. Thus, for all $y \in R$ (co-domain) there exists $x = (y-2)^{1/3}$ in R (domain) such that $f(x) = x^3 + 2 = y$. Hence, $f : R \to R$ is an onto function.

(ii) Clearly, $f(x) = x^2 + 2 \geq 2$ for all $x \in R$. So, negative real numbers in R(co-domain) do not have their pre-images in R(domain). Hence, f is not an onto function.

(iii) Let y be an arbitrary element of Z(co-domain). Then, $f(x) = y \Rightarrow 3x + 2 = y \Rightarrow x = \frac{y-2}{3}$.

Clearly, if $y = 0$, then $x = -2/3 \notin Z$. Thus, $y = 0 \in Z$ does not have its pre-image in Z(domain). Hence, f is not an onto function.

ILLUSTRATION 5 *Show that the function $f : N \to N$ given by $f(1) = f(2) = 1$ and $f(x) = x - 1$ for every $x \geq 2$, is onto but not one-one.* **[NCERT]**

SOLUTION It is given that $f(x) = \begin{cases} 1 & \text{, when } x = 1, 2 \\ x - 1, & \text{when } x \geq 2 \end{cases}$

Clearly, $f(1) = f(2) = 1$ i.e. 1 and 2 have the same image. So, $f : N \to N$ is a many-one function. Let y be an arbitrary element in N (Co-domain). Then, $f(x) = y \Rightarrow x - 1 = y \Rightarrow x = y + 1$. Clearly, $y + 1 \in N$ (domain) for all $y \in N$ (Co-domain). Thus, for each $y \in N$ (co-domain) there exists $y + 1 \in N$ (domain) such that $f(y+1) = y + 1 - 1 = y$. So, $f : N \to N$ is an onto function.

ILLUSTRATION 6 *Show that the Signum function $f : R \to R$, given by $f(x) = \begin{cases} 1, & \text{if } x > 0 \\ 0, & \text{if } x = 0 \\ -1, & \text{if } x < 0 \end{cases}$ is neither one-one nor onto.* **[NCERT]**

SOLUTION Clearly, all positive real numbers have the same image equal to 1. So, f is a many-one function. We observe that the range of f is $\{-1, 0, 1\}$ which is not equal to the co-domain of f. So, f is not onto. Hence, f is neither one-one nor onto.

2.3.4 BIJECTION (ONE-ONE ONTO FUNCTION)

DEFINITION *A function $f : A \to B$ is a bijection if it is one-one as well as onto.*

In other words, a function $f : A \to B$ is a bijection, if it is

(i) one-one i.e. $f(x) = f(y) \Rightarrow x = y$ for all $x, y \in A$.

(ii) onto i.e. for all $y \in B$, there exists $x \in A$ such that $f(x) = y$.

ILLUSTRATION 1 *Let $f : A \to B$ be a function represented by the diagram shown in Fig. 2.30. Clearly, f is a bijection since it is both injective as well as surjective.*

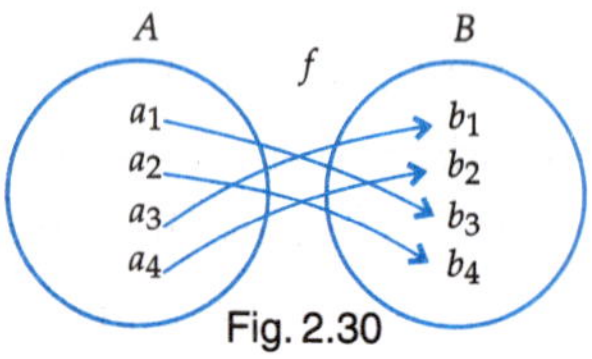

Fig. 2.30

ILLUSTRATION 2 *Prove that the function $f : Q \to Q$ given by $f(x) = 2x - 3$ for all $x \in Q$ is a bijection.*

SOLUTION We observe the following properties of f.

Injectivity: Let x, y be two arbitrary elements in Q. Then,

$$f(x) = f(y) \Rightarrow 2x - 3 = 2y - 3 \Rightarrow 2x = 2y \Rightarrow x = y$$

Thus, $f(x) = f(y) \Rightarrow x = y$ for all $x, y \in Q$. So, f is an injective map.

Surjectivity : Let y be an arbitrary element of Q. Then, $f(x) = y \Rightarrow 2x - 3 = y \Rightarrow x = \frac{y+3}{2}$.

Clearly, for all $y \in Q$ the value of x given by $x = \frac{y+3}{2} \in Q$. Thus, for all $y \in Q$ (co-domain) there exists $x \in Q$ (domain) given by $x = \frac{y+3}{2}$ such that $f(x) = f\left(\frac{y+3}{2}\right) = 2\left(\frac{y+3}{2}\right) - 3 = y$. That is every element in the co-domain has its pre-image in x. So, f is a surjection.

Hence, $f: Q \to Q$ is a bijection.

ILLUSTRATION 3 *Show that the function $f: R \to R$ defined by $f(x) = 3x^3 + 5$ for all $x \in R$ is a bijection.*

SOLUTION We observe the following properties of f.

Injectivity: Let x, y be any two elements of R(domain). Then,

$$f(x) = f(y) \Rightarrow 3x^3 + 5 = 3y^3 + 5 \Rightarrow x^3 = y^3 \Rightarrow x = y$$

Thus, $f(x) = f(y) \Rightarrow x = y$ for all $x, y \in R$. So, f is an injective map.

Surjectivity : Let y be an arbitrary element of R(co-domain). Then,

$$f(x) = y \Rightarrow 3x^3 + 5 = y \Rightarrow x^3 = \frac{y-5}{3} \Rightarrow x = \left(\frac{y-5}{3}\right)^{1/3}$$

Thus, we find that for all $y \in R$ (co-domain) there exists $x = \left(\frac{y-5}{3}\right)^{1/3} \in R$ (domain) such that

$$f(x) = f\left(\left(\frac{y-5}{3}\right)^{1/3}\right) = 3\left[\left(\frac{y-5}{3}\right)^{1/3}\right]^3 + 5 = y - 5 + 5 = y$$

This shows that every element in the co-domain has its pre-image in the domain. So, f is a surjection. Hence, f is a bijection.

ILLUSTRATION 4 *Let $A = \{x \in R : -1 \le x \le 1\} = B$. Show that $f: A \to B$ given by $f(x) = x|x|$ is a bijection.*

SOLUTION We observe the following properties of f.

Injectivity: Let x, y be any two elements in A. Then, $x \neq y \Rightarrow x|x| \neq y|y| \Rightarrow f(x) \neq f(y)$.

So, $f: A \to B$ is an injective map.

Surjectivity: We have, $f(x) = x|x| = \begin{cases} x^2, & \text{if } x \ge 0 \\ -x^2, & \text{if } x < 0 \end{cases}$

If $0 \le x \le 1$, then $f(x) = x^2$ takes all values between 0 and 1 including these two points. Also, if $-1 \le x < 0$, then $f(x) = -x^2$ takes all values between -1 and 0 including -1. Therefore, $f(x)$ takes every value between -1 and 1 including -1 and 1. So, range of f is same as its co-domain. Hence, $f: A \to B$ is an onto function. Thus, $f: A \to B$ is both one-one and onto. Hence, it is a bijection.

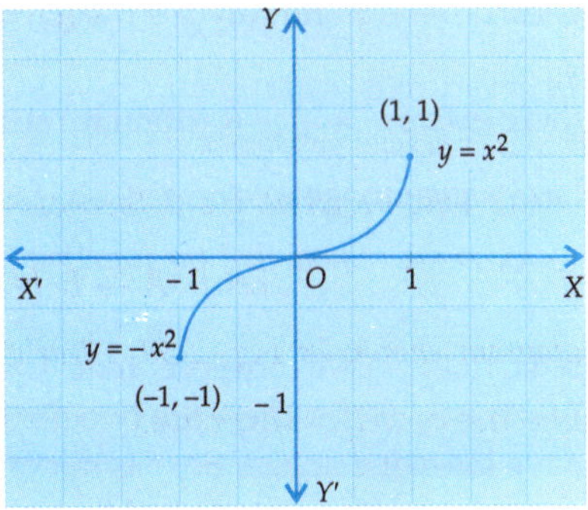

Fig. 2.31 Graph of $f(x) = x|x|$

ALITER We have, $f(x) = x|x| = \begin{cases} x^2, & \text{if } x \ge 0 \\ -x^2, & \text{if } x < 0 \end{cases}$

For $x \ge 0$, $f(x) = x^2$ represents a parabola opening upward and for $x < 0$, $f(x) = -x^2$ represents a parabola opening downward. So, the graph of $f(x)$ is as shown in Fig. 2.31.

It is evident from the graph of $f(x)$ that f is one-one and onto.

REMARK *It follows from the above discussion that if* A and B *are two finite sets and* $f: A \to B$ *is a function, then*

(i) f *is an injection* $\Rightarrow n(A) \leq n(B)$ (ii) f *is a surjection* $\Rightarrow n(B) \leq n(A)$

(iii) f *is a bijection* $\Rightarrow n(A) = n(B)$.

ILLUSTRATIVE EXAMPLES

BASED ON BASIC CONCEPTS (BASIC)

EXAMPLE 1 *Let A be the set of all* 50 *students of class XII in a central school. Let* $f: A \to N$ *be a function defined by* $f(x) =$ *Roll number of student* x*. Show that* f *is one-one but not onto.*

SOLUTION Here, f associates each students to his (her) roll number. Since no two different students of the class can have the same roll number. Therefore, f is one-one.

We observe that $f(A) =$ Range of $f = \{1, 2, 3, \dots, 50\} \neq N$ i.e. range of f is not same as its co-domain. So, f is not onto.

EXAMPLE 2 *Show that the function* $f: N \to N$*, given by* $f(x) = 2x$*, is one-one but not onto.* **[NCERT]**

SOLUTION We observe the following properties of f.

Injectivity: Let $x_1, x_2 \in N$ such that $f(x_1) = f(x_2)$. Then, $f(x_1) = f(x_2) \Rightarrow 2x_1 = 2x_2 \Rightarrow x_1 = x_2$. So, f is one-one.

Surjectivity: Clearly, f takes even values. Therefore, no odd natural number in N (co-domain) has its pre-image in domain. So, f is not onto.

EXAMPLE 3 *Prove that* $f: R \to R$*, given by* $f(x) = 2x$*, is one-one and onto.* **[NCERT]**

SOLUTION We observe the following properties of f.

Injectivity: Let $x_1, x_2 \in R$ such that $f(x_1) = f(x_2)$. Then, $f(x_1) = f(x_2) \Rightarrow 2x_1 = 2x_2 \Rightarrow x_1 = x_2$. So, $f: R \to R$ is one-one.

Surjectivity: Let y be any real number in R (co-domain). Then, $f(x) = y \Rightarrow 2x = y \Rightarrow x = \frac{y}{2}$.

Clearly, $\frac{y}{2} \in R$ for any $y \in R$ such that $f\left(\frac{y}{2}\right) = 2\left(\frac{y}{2}\right) = y$. Thus, for each $y \in R$ (co-domain) there exists $x = \frac{y}{2} \in R$ (domain) such that $f(x) = y$. This means that each element in co-domain has its pre-image in domain. So, $f: R \to R$ is onto. Hence, $f: R \to R$ is a bijection.

EXAMPLE 4 *Show that the function* $f: R \to R$*, defined as* $f(x) = x^2$*, is neither one-one nor onto.* **[NCERT]**

SOLUTION We observe that 1 and $-1 \in R$ such that $f(-1) = f(1)$ i.e. there are two distinct elements in R which have the same image. So, f is not one-one.

Since $f(x)$ assumes only non-negative values. So, no negative real number in R (co-domain) has its pre-image in domain of f i.e. R. Consequently f is not onto.

These facts are evident from the graph of $f(x)$ as shown in Fig. 2.32.

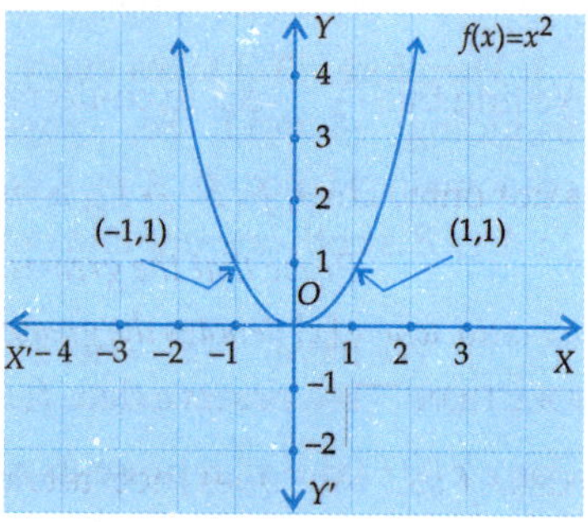

Fig. 2.32

EXAMPLE 5 *Show that $f: R \to R$, defined as $f(x) = x^3$, is a bijection.* **[NCERT]**

SOLUTION We observe the following properties of f.

Injectivity: Let $x, y \in R$ such that $f(x) = f(y)$. Then, $f(x) = f(y) \Rightarrow x^3 = y^3 \Rightarrow x = y$.

So, $f: R \to R$ is one-one.

Surjectivity: Let $y \in R$ (co-domain). Then, $f(x) = y \Rightarrow x^3 = y \Rightarrow x = y^{1/3}$.

Clearly, $y^{1/3} \in R$ (domain) for all $y \in R$ (co-domain).

Thus, for each $y \in R$ (co-domain) there exists $x = y^{1/3} \in R$ (domain) such that $f(x) = x^3 = y$.

So, $f: R \to R$ is onto. Hence, $f: R \to R$ is a bijection.

EXAMPLE 6 *Show that the function $f: R_0 \to R_0$, defined as $f(x) = \dfrac{1}{x}$, is one-one onto, where R_0 is the set of all non-zero real numbers. Is the result true, if the domain R_0 is replaced by N with co-domain being same as R_0?* **[NCERT]**

SOLUTION We observe the following properties of f.

Injectivity: Let $x, y \in R_0$ such that $f(x) = f(y)$. Then, $f(x) = f(y) \Rightarrow \dfrac{1}{x} = \dfrac{1}{y} \Rightarrow x = y$.

So, $f: R_0 \to R_0$ is one-one.

Surjectivity: Let y be an arbitrary element of R_0 (co-domain) such that $f(x) = y$. Then,

$$f(x) = y \Rightarrow \frac{1}{x} = y \Rightarrow x = \frac{1}{y}$$

Clearly, $x = \dfrac{1}{y} \in R_0$ (domain) for all $y \in R_0$ (co-domain).

Thus, for each $y \in R_0$ (co-domain) there exits $x = \dfrac{1}{y} \in R_0$ (domain) such that $f(x) = \dfrac{1}{x} = y$. So, $f: R_0 \to R_0$ is onto.

Hence, $f: R_0 \to R_0$ is one-one onto. This is also evident from the graph of $f(x)$ as shown in Fig. 2.33.

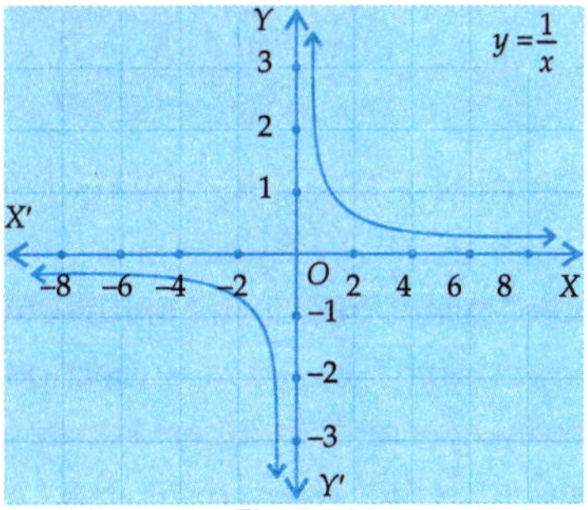

Fig. 2.33

Let us now consider $f: N \to R_0$ given by $f(x) = \dfrac{1}{x}$. For any $x, y \in N$, we find that

$$f(x) = f(y) \Rightarrow \frac{1}{x} = \frac{1}{y} \Rightarrow x = y. \text{ So, } f: N \to R_0 \text{ is one-one.}$$

We find that $\dfrac{2}{3}, \dfrac{3}{5}$ etc. in co-domain R_0 do not have their pre-image in domain N. So, $f: N \to R_0$ is not onto. Thus, $f: N \to R_0$ is one-one but not onto.

EXAMPLE 7 *Prove that the greatest integer function $f: R \to R$, given by $f(x) = [x]$, is neither one-one nor onto, where $[x]$ denotes the greatest integer less than or equal to x.* **[NCERT]**

SOLUTION We observe that $f(x) = 0$ for all $x \in [0, 1)$. So, $f: R \to R$ is not one-one.

Also, $f: R \to R$ does not attain non-integral values. Therefore, non-integer points in R (co-domain) do not have their pre-images in the domain. So, $f: R \to R$ is not onto. Hence, $f: R \to R$ is neither one-one nor onto.

This is also evident from the graph of the greatest integer function shown in Fig. 2.34.

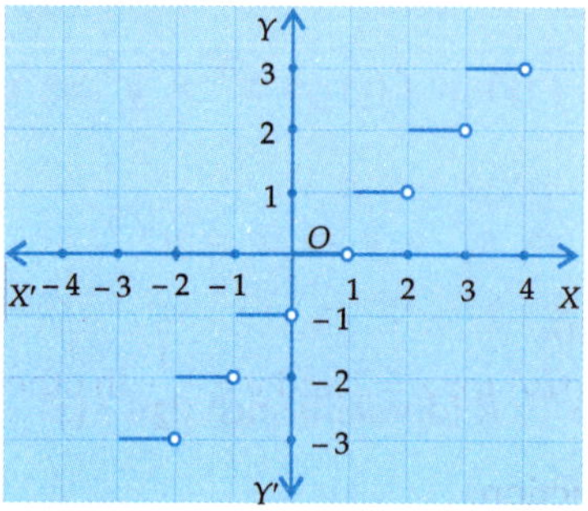

Fig. 2.34 Greatest integer function

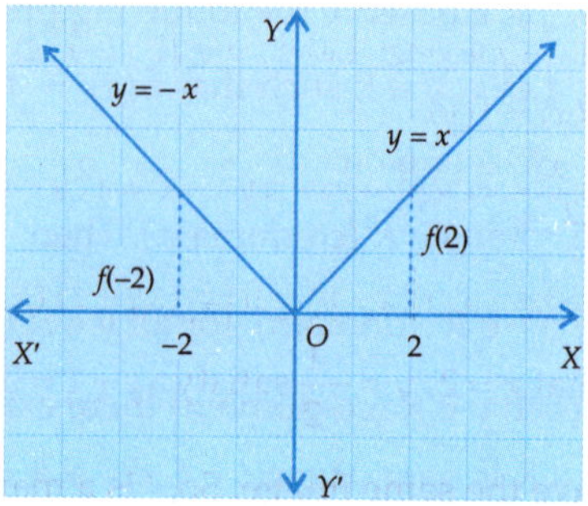

Fig. 2.35 Modulus function

EXAMPLE 8 *Show that the modulus function $f : R \to R$, given by $f(x) = |x|$ is neither one-one nor onto.* **[NCERT]**

SOLUTION We observe that $f(-2) = f(2)$. So, f is not one-one.

Also, $f(x) = |x|$ assumes only non-negative values. So, negative real numbers in R (co-domain) do not have their pre-images in R (domain). Hence, f is neither one-one nor onto.

This is also evident from the graph of $f(x) = |x|$ shown in Fig. 2.35.

BASED ON LOWER ORDER THINKING SKILLS (LOTS)

EXAMPLE 9 *Let C and R denote the set of all complex numbers and all real numbers respectively. Then show that $f : C \to R$ given by $f(z) = |z|$ for all $z \in C$ is neither one-one nor onto.*

[NCERT EXEMPLAR]

SOLUTION *Injectivity* : We find that $z_1 = 1 - i$ and $z_2 = 1 + i$ are two distinct complex numbers in C such that $|z_1| = |z_2|$ *i.e.* $z_1 \neq z_2$ but $f(z_1) = f(z_2)$. Thus, different elements in C may have the same image. So, f is not an injection.

Surjectivity: f is not a surjection, because negative real numbers in R do not have their pre-images in C. In other words, for every negative real number a there is no complex number $z \in C$ such that $f(z) = |z| = a$. So, f is not a surjection.

EXAMPLE 10 *Show that the function $f : R \to R$ given by $f(x) = ax + b$, where $a, b \in R, a \neq 0$ is a bijection.* **[CBSE 2010]**

SOLUTION *Injectivity* : Let x, y be any two real numbers. Then,

$$f(x) = f(y) \Rightarrow ax + b = ay + b \Rightarrow ax = ay \Rightarrow x = y$$

Thus, $f(x) = f(y) \Rightarrow x = y$ for all $x, y \in R$(domain). So, f is an injection.

Surjectivity: Let y be an arbitrary element of R(co-domain). Then,

$$f(x) = y \Rightarrow ax + b = y \Rightarrow x = \frac{y-b}{a}.$$

Clearly, $x = \frac{y-b}{a} \in R$ (domain) for all $y \in R$ (co-domain). Thus, for all $y \in R$ (co-domain) there exists $x = \frac{y-b}{a} \in R$ (domain) such that $f(x) = f\left(\frac{y-b}{a}\right) = a\left(\frac{y-b}{a}\right) + b = y$.

This means that every element in co-domain has its pre-image in domain. So, f is a surjection. Hence, f is a bijection.

EXAMPLE 11 *A function $f : R - \{-1, 1\} \to R$ is defined by $f(x) = \dfrac{x}{x^2 - 1}$.*

(i) Check if f is one-one *(ii) Check if f is onto.*

SOLUTION *One-one:* Let $x, y \in R - \{-1, 1\}$ be such that

$$f(x) = f(y)$$

$$\Rightarrow \quad \frac{x}{x^2-1} = \frac{y}{y^2-1} \Rightarrow xy^2 - x = x^2y - y \Rightarrow (x^2y - xy^2) + (x - y) = 0$$

$$\Rightarrow \quad xy\,(x-y) + (x-y) = 0 \Rightarrow (xy+1)\,(x-y) = 0 \Rightarrow x = y \text{ or } xy + 1 = 0$$

We find that $x = 2$, $y = -\dfrac{1}{2}$ satisfy $xy + 1 = 0$ i.e. $f(x) = f(y)$ for $x = 2$ and $y = -\dfrac{1}{2}$. In other words, 2 and $-\dfrac{1}{2}$ have the same image. So, *f* is a many-one function.

Onto: Let $f(x) = y$. Then,

$$\frac{x}{x^2-1} = y \Rightarrow x^2y - x - y = 0 \Rightarrow x = \frac{1 \pm \sqrt{1+4y^2}}{2y}$$

Clearly, $x \in R$ for all $y\,(\neq 0) \in R$ (Co-domain). So, every $y \neq 0$ in co-domain R has its pre-image in $R - \{-1, 1\}$. We observe that $y = 0$ when $x = 0$ i.e. $y = 0$ has 0 as its pre-image. Also, $x = \pm 1$, gives $y = 0$. Therefore, each $y \in R$ has its pre-image in $R - \{-1, 1\}$. Hence, *f* is onto.

EXAMPLE 12 *Let $A = R - \{2\}$* and *$B = R - \{1\}$. If $f : A \to B$ is a mapping defined by $f(x) = \dfrac{x-1}{x-2}$, show that f is bijective.*

SOLUTION *Injectivity:* Let x, y be any two elements of A. Then,

$$f(x) = f(y)$$

$$\Rightarrow \quad \frac{x-1}{x-2} = \frac{y-1}{y-2}$$

$$\Rightarrow \quad (x-1)\,(y-2) = (x-2)\,(y-1) \Rightarrow xy - y - 2x + 2 = xy - x - 2y + 2 \Rightarrow x = y$$

Thus, $f(x) = f(y) \Rightarrow x = y$ for all $x, y \in A$. So, *f* is an injective map.

Surjectivity: Let y be an arbitrary element of B. Then,

$$f(x) = y \Rightarrow \frac{x-1}{x-2} = y \Rightarrow (x-1) = y\,(x-2) \Rightarrow x = \frac{1-2y}{1-y}$$

Clearly, $x = \dfrac{1-2y}{1-y}$ is a real number for all $y \neq 1$. Also, $\dfrac{1-2y}{1-y} \neq 2$ for any y, for, if we take $\dfrac{1-2y}{1-y} = 2$, then we get $1 = 2$, which is wrong. Thus, every element y in B has its pre-image x in A given by $x = \dfrac{1-2y}{1-y}$. So, *f* is a surjective map. Hence, *f* is a bijective map.

EXAMPLE 13 *Let A and B be two sets. Show that $f : A \times B \to B \times A$ defined by $f\,(a, b) = (b, a)$ is a bijection.* **[NCERT]**

SOLUTION *Injectivity:* Let (a_1, b_1) and $(a_2, b_2) \in A \times B$ such that

$$f\,(a_1, b_1) = f\,(a_2, b_2) \Rightarrow (b_1, a_1) = (b_2, a_2) \Rightarrow b_1 = b_2 \text{ and } a_1 = a_2 \Rightarrow (a_1, b_1) = (a_2, b_2)$$

Thus, $f\,(a_1, b_1) = f\,(a_2, b_2) \Rightarrow (a_1, b_1) = (a_2, b_2)$ for all $(a_1, b_1), (a_2, b_2) \in A \times B$.

So, *f* is an injective map.

Surjectivity: Let (b, a) be an arbitrary element of $B \times A$. Then, $b \in B$ and $a \in A \Rightarrow (a, b) \in A \times B$. Thus, for all $(b, a) \in B \times A$ there exists $(a, b) \in A \times B$ such that $f(a, b) = (b, a)$. So, $f : A \times B \to B \times A$ is an onto function. Hence, f is a bijection.

EXAMPLE 14 *Let A be any non-empty set. Then, prove that the identity function on set A is a bijection.*

SOLUTION The identity function $I_A : A \to A$ is defined as $I_A(x) = x$ for all $x \in A$.

Injectivity: Let x, y be any two elements of A. Then,

$$I_A(x) = I_A(y) \Rightarrow x = y \qquad \text{[By definition of } I_A\text{]}$$

So, I_A is an injective map.

Surjectivity: Let $y \in A$. Then, there exists $x = y \in A$ such that $I_A(x) = x = y$.

So, I_A is a surjective map. Hence, $I_A : A \to A$ is a bijection.

EXAMPLE 15 *Consider the identity function $I_N : N \to N$ defined as, $I_N(x) = x$ for all $x \in N$. Show that although I_N is onto but $I_N + I_N : N \to N$ defined as $(I_N + I_N)(x) = I_N(x) + I_N(x) = x + x = 2x$ is not onto.* **[NCERT]**

SOLUTION We know that the identity function on a given set is always a bijection. Therefore, $I_N : N \to N$ is onto.

We find that, $(I_N + I_N)(x) = 2x$ for all $x \in N$. This means that under $I_N + I_N$, images of natural numbers are even natural numbers. So, odd natural numbers in N (co-domain) do not have their pre-images in domain N. For example, 1, 3, 5 etc. do not have their pre-images. So, $I_N + I_N : N \to N$ is not onto.

EXAMPLE 16 *Consider the function $f : [0, \pi/2] \to R$ given by $f(x) = \sin x$ and $g : [0, \pi/2] \to R$ given by $g(x) = \cos x$. Show that f and g are one-one, but $f + g$ is not one-one.* **[NCERT]**

SOLUTION We observe that for any two distinct elements x_1 and x_2 in $[0, \pi/2]$

$$\sin x_1 \neq \sin x_2 \text{ and } \cos x_1 \neq \cos x_2 \qquad \text{[See graphs of } f(x) = \sin x \text{ \& } f(x) = \cos x\text{]}$$

$$\Rightarrow \quad f(x_1) \neq f(x_2) \text{ and } g(x_1) \neq g(x_2) \Rightarrow f \text{ and } g \text{ are one-one.}$$

We find that

$$(f + g)(x) = f(x) + g(x) = \sin x + \cos x$$

$$\Rightarrow \quad (f + g)(0) = \sin 0 + \cos 0 = 1 \text{ and } (f + g)\left(\frac{\pi}{2}\right) = \sin\frac{\pi}{2} + \cos\frac{\pi}{2} = 1$$

Thus, $0 \neq \frac{\pi}{2}$ but, $(f + g)(0) = (f + g)\left(\frac{\pi}{2}\right)$. So, $f + g$ is not one-one.

EXAMPLE 17 *Let $f : X \to Y$ be a function. Define a relation R on X given by $R = \{(a, b) : f(a) = f(b)\}$. Show that R is an equivalence relation on X.* **[NCERT, CBSE 2010]**

SOLUTION We observe the following properties of relation R.

Reflexivity: For any $a \in X$, we find that

$$f(a) = f(a) \Rightarrow (a, a) \in R \Rightarrow R \text{ is reflexive.}$$

Symmetry: Let $a, b \in X$ be such that $(a, b) \in R$. Then,

$$(a, b) \in R \Rightarrow f(a) = f(b) \Rightarrow f(b) = f(a) \Rightarrow (b, a) \in R. \text{ So, } R \text{ is symmetric.}$$

Transitivity: Let $a, b, c \in X$ be such that $(a, b) \in R$ and $(b, c) \in R$. Then,

$$(a, b) \in R \text{ and } (b, c) \in R \Rightarrow f(a) = f(b) \text{ and } f(b) = f(c) \Rightarrow f(a) = f(c) \Rightarrow (a, c) \in R.$$

So, R is transitive. Hence, R is an equivalence relation.

BASED ON HIGHER ORDER THINKING SKILLS (HOTS)

EXAMPLE 18 *Show that the function $f: R \to R$ given by $f(x) = \cos x$ for all $x \in R$, is neither one-one nor onto.* **[NCERT EXEMPLAR]**

SOLUTION *Injectivity*: We know that $f(0) = \cos 0 = 1$ and $f(2\pi) = \cos 2\pi = 1$.

So, different elements in R may have the same image. Hence, f is not an injection.

Surjectivity: We know that $\cos x$ takes all values between -1 and 1. Therefore, its range is $[-1, 1]$. Thus, the range of $f(x)$ is not equal to its co-domain. So, f is not a surjection.

EXAMPLE 19 *Let $f: N - \{1\} \to N$ be defined by, $f(n) =$ the highest prime factor of n. Show that f is neither one-one nor onto. Find the range of f.*

SOLUTION We find that

$f(6) =$ (the highest prime factor of 6) $= 3$, $f(9) =$ (the highest prime factor of 9) $= 3$

and, $f(12) =$ (the highest prime factor of 12) $= 3$. Therefore, $f(6) = f(9) = f(12)$.

So, f is a many-one function.

Clearly, image of any $n \in N - \{1\}$ is the largest prime number that divides n. So, the range of f consists of prime numbers only. Consequently, range of $f \neq N$ (co-domain). So, f is not onto function. Hence, f is neither one-one nor onto. The range of f is the set of all prime numbers.

EXAMPLE 20 *Let $A = \{1, 2\}$. Find all one-to-one functions from A to A.*

SOLUTION Let $f: A \to A$ be a one-one function. Then, $f(1)$ has two choices, namely, 1 or 2. So, $f(1) = 1$ or, $f(1) = 2$.

Case I *When* $f(1) = 1$: As $f: A \to A$ is one-one. Therefore, $f(2) = 2$. Thus, we obtain: $f(1) = 1$ and $f(2) = 2$.

Case II *When* $f(1) = 2$: Since $f: A \to A$ is one-one. Therefore, $f(2) = 1$. Thus, in this case, we obtain: $f(1) = 2$ and $f(2) = 1$.

So, there are two one-one functions say f and g from A to A given by $f(1) = 1$, $f(2) = 2$ and, $g(1) = 2$, $g(2) = 1$.

ALITER All one-to-one functions from A to itself can be expressed in the following two row notation as follows:

$$f = \begin{pmatrix} 1 & 2 \\ 1 & 2 \end{pmatrix}, g = \begin{pmatrix} 1 & 2 \\ 2 & 1 \end{pmatrix}$$

First row contains elements of the domain and second row contains the corresponding images. Clearly, each arrangement of second row provides a one-to-one function from A to itself.

EXAMPLE 21 *Show that the function $f: R \to \{x \in R: -1 < x < 1\}$ defined by $f(x) = \frac{x}{1+|x|}$, $x \in R$ is one-one onto function.* **[NCERT]**

SOLUTION We have,
$$f(x) = \frac{x}{1+|x|} = \begin{cases} \frac{x}{1+x}, & \text{if } x \geq 0 \\ \frac{x}{1-x}, & \text{if } x < 0 \end{cases}$$

So, following cases arise:

Case I *When* $x \geq 0$: In this case, we have $f(x) = \frac{x}{1+x}$.

Injectivity: Let $x, y \in R$ such that $x \geq 0$, $y \geq 0$. Then,

$f(x) = f(y) \Rightarrow \frac{x}{1+x} = \frac{y}{1+y} \Rightarrow x + xy = y + xy \Rightarrow x = y$. So, f is an injective map.

Surjectivity: When $x \geq 0$, we find that: $f(x) = \dfrac{x}{1+x} \geq 0$ and $f(x) < 1$. Let $y \in [0, 1)$ be any real number. Then, $f(x) = y \Rightarrow \dfrac{x}{1+x} = y \Rightarrow x = \dfrac{y}{1-y}$.

Clearly, $x \geq 0$ for all $y \in [0, 1)$. Thus, for each $y \in [0, 1)$ there exists $x = \dfrac{y}{1-y} \geq 0$ such that $f(x) = y$.

So, f is an onto function from $[0, 1)$ to $[0, 1)$

Case II *When $x < 0$*: In this case, we have $f(x) = \dfrac{x}{1-x}$.

Injectivity: Let $x, y \in R$ such that $x < 0$, $y < 0$. Then,

$$f(x) = f(y) \Rightarrow \frac{x}{1-x} = \frac{y}{1-y} \Rightarrow x - xy = y - xy \Rightarrow x = y.$$ So, f is an injective map.

Surjectivity: When $x < 0$, we find that: $f(x) = \dfrac{x}{1-x} < 0$.

Also, $f(x) = \dfrac{x}{1-x} = -1 + \dfrac{1}{1-x} > -1$. Therefore, $-1 < f(x) < 0$.

Let $y \in (-1, 0)$ be an arbitrary real number such that $f(x) = y$. Then,

$$f(x) = y \Rightarrow \frac{x}{1-x} = y \Rightarrow x = \frac{y}{1+y}$$

Clearly, $x < 0$ for $y \in (-1, 0)$. Thus, for each $y \in (-1, 0)$ there exists $x = \dfrac{y}{1+y} < 0$ such that $f(x) = y$.

So, f is an onto function from $(-1, 0)$ to $(-1, 0)$.

Hence, $f : R \to \{x \in R : -1 < x < 1\}$ is a one-one onto function.

EXAMPLE 22 *Show that the function $f : R \to R$ given by $f(x) = x^3 + x$ is a bijection.*

SOLUTION *Injectivity*: Let $x, y \in R$ such that

$$
\begin{aligned}
& f(x) = f(y) \\
\Rightarrow\quad & x^3 + x = y^3 + y \\
\Rightarrow\quad & x^3 - y^3 + (x - y) = 0 \\
\Rightarrow\quad & (x-y)(x^2 + xy + y^2 + 1) = 0 \\
\Rightarrow\quad & x - y = 0 \qquad [\because x^2 + xy + y^2 \geq 0 \text{ for all } x, y \in R \therefore x^2 + xy + y^2 + 1 \geq 1 \text{ for all } x, y \in R] \\
\Rightarrow\quad & x = y
\end{aligned}
$$

Thus, $f(x) = f(y) \Rightarrow x = y$ for all $x, y \in R$. So, f is an injective map.

Surjectivity: Let y be an arbitrary element of R. Then,

$$f(x) = y \Rightarrow x^3 + x = y \Rightarrow x^3 + x - y = 0$$

We know that an odd degree equation has at least one real root. Therefore, for every real value of y, the equation $x^3 + x - y = 0$ has a real root α (say) such that

$$\alpha^3 + \alpha - y = 0 \Rightarrow \alpha^3 + \alpha = y \Rightarrow f(\alpha) = y$$

Thus, for every $y \in R$ there exists $\alpha \in R$ such that $f(\alpha) = y$. So, f is a surjective map.

Hence, $f : R \to R$ is a bijection.

EXAMPLE 23 *Show that a function $f : R \to R$ defined by $f(x) = \frac{2x}{1+x^2}$ is neither one-one nor onto. Further, find set A so that the given function $f : R \to A$ becomes an onto function.* **[CBSE 2024]**

SOLUTION We have, $f(x) = \frac{2x}{1+x^2}$. For $x, y \in R$, we find that

$$f(x) = f(y) \Rightarrow \frac{2x}{1+x^2} = \frac{2y}{1+y^2}$$

$$\Rightarrow \quad x + xy^2 = y + x^2 y \Rightarrow (x-y) = xy(x-y) \Rightarrow (xy-1)(x-y) = 0 \Rightarrow x = y \text{ or, } xy = 1.$$

Thus, $f(x) = f(y)$ for all $x, y \in R$ satisfying $xy = 1$. For example, $f(2) = f\left(\frac{1}{2}\right), f\left(\frac{2}{3}\right) = f\left(\frac{3}{2}\right)$ etc.

So, f is a many-one function.

Let us now find the range of $f(x) = \frac{2x}{1+x^2}$. Let $f(x) = y$. Then,

$$f(x) = y \Rightarrow \frac{2x}{1+x^2} = y \Rightarrow x^2 y - 2x + y = 0 \Rightarrow x = \frac{2 \pm \sqrt{4-4y^2}}{2y} = \frac{1 \pm \sqrt{1-y^2}}{y}$$

Clearly, $x \in R$, if $1 - y^2 \geq 0$ and $y \neq 0$ i.e. $y^2 - 1 \leq 0$ and $y \neq 0 \Rightarrow y \in [-1, 0) \cup (0,1]$

So, range $(f) = [-1, 0) \cup (0, 1] \neq R$ (Co-domain)

Hence, $f : R \to R$ is not onto but $f : R \to [-1, 0) \cup (0,1]$ is onto. Therefore, $A = [-1, 0) \cup (0, 1]$

EXAMPLE 24 *Show that $f : N \to N$ defined by $f(n) = \begin{cases} \frac{n+1}{2}, & \text{if } n \text{ is odd} \\ \frac{n}{2}, & \text{if } n \text{ is even} \end{cases}$ is many-one onto function.*

[NCERT, CBSE 2009]

SOLUTION We observe that $f(1) = \frac{1+1}{2} = 1$ and $f(2) = \frac{2}{2} = 1$. Thus, $1, 2 \in N$ such that $1 \neq 2$ but $f(1) = f(2)$. So, f is a many-one function.

Surjectivity Let n be an arbitrary element of N.

If n is an odd natural number, then $2n - 1$ is also an odd natural number such that

$$f(2n-1) = \frac{2n-1+1}{2} = n$$

If n is an even natural number, then $2n$ is also an even natural number such that

$$f(2n) = \frac{2n}{2} = n.$$

Thus, for every $n \in N$ (whether even or odd) there exists its pre-image in N. So, f is a surjection.

Hence, f is a many-one onto function.

EXAMPLE 25 *Show that the function $f : N \to N$ given by, $f(n) = n - (-1)^n$ for all $n \in N$ is a bijection.*

SOLUTION We have,

$$f(n) = n - (-1)^n \text{ for all } n \in N \Rightarrow f(n) = \begin{cases} n-1, & \text{if } n \text{ is even} \\ n+1, & \text{if } n \text{ is odd} \end{cases}$$

Injectivity: Let n, m be any two even natural numbers. Then, $f(n) = f(m) \Rightarrow n - 1 = m - 1 \Rightarrow n = m$.
If n, m are any two odd natural numbers. Then, $f(n) = f(m) \Rightarrow n + 1 = m + 1 \Rightarrow n = m$.

Thus in both the cases, $f(n) = f(m) \Rightarrow n = m$.

If n is even and m is odd, then $n \neq m$. Also $f(n)$ is odd and $f(m)$ is even. So, $f(n) \neq f(m)$.
Thus, $n \neq m \Rightarrow f(n) \neq f(m)$. So, f is an injective map.

Surjectivity: Let n be an arbitrary natural number. If n is an odd natural number, then there exists an even natural number $n+1$ such that $f(n+1) = n+1-1 = n$.

If n is an even natural number, then there exists an odd natural number $(n-1)$ such that $f(n-1) = n-1+1 = n$. Thus, every $n \in N$ has its pre-image in N.

So, $f: N \to N$ is a surjection. Hence, $f: N \to N$ is a bijection.

EXAMPLE 26 *Let $f: N \cup \{0\} \to N \cup \{0\}$ be defined by $f(n) = \begin{cases} n+1, & \text{if } n \text{ is even} \\ n-1, & \text{if } n \text{ is odd} \end{cases}$. Show that f is a bijection.*

SOLUTION *f is an injection :* Let $n, m \in N \cup \{0\}$.

If n and m are even, then $f(n) = f(m) \Rightarrow n+1 = m+1 \Rightarrow n = m$.

If n and m are odd, then $f(n) = f(m) \Rightarrow n-1 = m-1 \Rightarrow n = m$.

Thus, in both case, we obtain: $f(n) = f(m) \Rightarrow n = m$.

If n is odd and m is even, then $f(n) = n-1$ is even and $f(m) = m+1$ is odd. Therefore, $f(n) \neq f(m)$.
Thus, $n \neq m \Rightarrow f(n) \neq f(m)$.

Similarly, if n is even and m is odd, then $n \neq m \Rightarrow f(n) \neq f(m)$.

Hence, f is an injection.

f is a surjection : Let n be an arbitrary element of $N \cup \{0\}$.

If n is an odd natural number, there exist an even natural number $n-1 \in N \cup \{0\}$ (domain) such that $f(n-1) = n-1+1 = n$.

If n is an even natural number, then there exists an odd natural number $n+1 \in N \cup \{0\}$ (domain) such that $f(n+1) = n+1-1 = n$. Also, $f(1) = 0$.

Thus, every element of $N \cup \{0\}$ (co-domain) has its pre-image in $N \cup \{0\}$ (domain). So, f is an onto function.

EXAMPLE 27 *Let A be a finite set. If $f: A \to A$ is a one-one function, show that f is onto also.*

SOLUTION Let $A = \{a_1, a_2, a_3, ..., a_n\}$. In order to prove that f is onto function, we will have to show that every element in A (co-domain) has its pre-image in the domain A. In other words, range of $f = A$.

Since $f: A \to A$ is a one-one function. Therefore, $f(a_1), f(a_2), ..., f(a_n)$ are distinct elements of set A. But, A has only n elements. Therefore, $A = \{f(a_1), f(a_2), ..., f(a_n)\}$ i.e. Co-domain = Range.

Hence, $f: A \to A$ is onto.

EXAMPLE 28 *Let A be a finite set. If $f: A \to A$ is an onto function, show that f is one-one also.*

SOLUTION Let $A = \{a_1, a_2, \ldots, a_n\}$. In order to prove that f is a one-one function, we will have to show that $f(a_1), f(a_2), \ldots, f(a_n)$ are distinct elements of A.

Clearly, Range of $f = \{f(a_1), f(a_2), ..., f(a_n)\}$. Since $f: A \to A$ is an onto function. Therefore,

$$\text{Range of } f = A \Rightarrow \{f(a_1), f(a_2), ..., f(a_n)\} = A$$

But, A is a finite set consisting of n elements. Therefore, $f(a_1), f(a_2), f(a_3), \ldots, f(a_n)$ are distinct elements of A. Hence, $f : A \to A$ is one-one.

EXERCISE 2.1

BASIC

1. Give an example of a function
   (i) which is one-one but not onto. (ii) which is not one-one but onto.
   (iii) which is neither one-one nor onto. [NCERT EXEMPLAR]
2. Which of the following functions from A to B are one-one and onto?
   (i) $f_1 = \{(1, 3), (2, 5), (3, 7)\}$; $A = \{1, 2, 3\}$, $B = \{3, 5, 7\}$
   (ii) $f_2 = \{(2, a), (3, b), (4, c)\}$; $A = \{2, 3, 4\}$, $B = \{a, b, c\}$
   (iii) $f_3 = \{(a, x), (b, x), (c, z), (d, z)\}$; $A = \{a, b, c, d\}$, $B = \{x, y, z\}$
3. Let $A = \{-1, 0, 1\}$ and $f = \{(x, x^2) : x \in A\}$. Show that $f : A \to A$ is neither one-one nor onto.
4. Classify the following functions as injection, surjection or bijection:
   (i) $f : N \to N$ given by $f(x) = x^2$ (ii) $f : Z \to Z$ given by $f(x) = x^2$
   (iii) $f : N \to N$ given by $f(x) = x^3$ (iv) $f : Z \to Z$ given by $f(x) = x^3$
   (v) $f : R \to R$, defined by $f(x) = |x|$ (vi) $f : Z \to Z$, defined by $f(x) = x^2 + x$
   (vii) $f : Z \to Z$, defined by $f(x) = x - 5$ (viii) $f : R \to R$, defined by $f(x) = \sin x$
   (ix) $f : R \to R$, defined by $f(x) = x^3 + 1$ (x) $f : R \to R$, defined by $f(x) = x^3 - x$
   (xi) $f : R \to R$, defined by $f(x) = \sin^2 x + \cos^2 x$
   (xii) $f : Q - \{3\} \to Q$, defined by $f(x) = \dfrac{2x + 3}{x - 3}$
   (xiii) $f : Q \to Q$, defined by $f(x) = x^3 + 1$ (xiv) $f : R \to R$, defined by $f(x) = 5x^3 + 4$
   (xv) $f : R \to R$, defined by $f(x) = 3 - 4x$ (xvi) $f : R \to R$, defined by $f(x) = 1 + x^2$
   (xvii) $f : R \to R$, defined by $f(x) = \dfrac{x}{x^2 + 1}$ [NCERT EXEMPLAR, CBSE 2018]
5. Let $A = [-1, 1]$. Then, discuss whether the following functions from A to itself are one-one, onto or bijective:
   (i) $f(x) = \dfrac{x}{2}$ (ii) $g(x) = |x|$ (iii) $h(x) = x^2$ [NCERT EXEMPLAR]
6. Are the following set of ordered pairs functions? If so, examine whether the mapping is injective or surjective:
   (i) $\{(x, y) : x$ is a person, y is the mother of $x\}$ (ii) $\{(a, b) : a$ is a person, b is an ancestor of $a\}$
   [NCERT EXEMPLAR]

BASED ON LOTS

7. Prove that the function $f : N \to N$, defined by $f(x) = x^2 + x + 1$ is one-one but not onto.
8. If $f : A \to B$ is an injection such that range of $f = \{a\}$. Determine the number of elements in A.
9. (i) Show that the function $f : R - \{3\} \to R - \{1\}$ given by $f(x) = \dfrac{x - 2}{x - 3}$ is a bijection.
   [NCERT EXEMPLAR, CBSE 2012, 2024]
   (ii) Show that the function $f : R \to R$ defined as $f(x) = \dfrac{5x - 3}{4}$ is both one-one and onto.
   [CBSE 2023]
10. Let $A = \{1, 2, 3\}$. Write all one-one functions from A to itself.
11. If $f : R \to R$ be the function defined by $f(x) = 4x^3 + 7$, show that f is a bijection.
   [CBSE 2011]

12. Show that the exponential function $f : R \to R$, given by $f(x) = e^x$, is one-one but not onto. What happens if the co-domain is replaced by R_0^+ (set of all positive real numebrs).

13. Show that the logarithmic function $f : R_0^+ \to R$ given by $f(x) = \log_a x$, $a > 0$ is a bijection.

14. (i) If $A = \{1, 2, 3\}$, show that a one-one function $f : A \to A$ must be onto. [NCERT]

(ii) If $A = \{1, 2, 3\}$, show that an onto function $f : A \to A$ must be one-one. [NCERT]

15. A function $f : [-4, 4] \to [0, 4]$ is given by $f(x) = \sqrt{16 - x^2}$. Show that f is an onto function but not a one-one function. Further, find all the possible values of 'a' for which $f(a) = \sqrt{7}$. [CBSE 2023, 2024]

16. A function f is defined from R to R as $f(x) = ax + b$, such that $f(1) = 1$ and $f(2) = 3$. Find the function $f(x)$. Hence, check whether function $f(x)$ is one-one and onto or not. [CBSE 2024]

17. Let $A = R - \{3\}$ and $B = R - \{a\}$. Find the value of 'a' such that the function $f : A \to B$ defined by $f(x) = \dfrac{x-2}{x-3}$ onto. Also, check whether the given function is one-one or onto. [CBSE 2024]

BASED ON HOTS

18. Find the number of all onto functions from the set $A = \{1, 2, 3, \ldots, n\}$ to itself. [NCERT]

19. Give examples of two one-one functions f_1 and f_2 from R to R such that $f_1 + f_2 : R \to R$, defined by $(f_1 + f_2)(x) = f_1(x) + f_2(x)$ is not one-one.

20. Give examples of two surjective function f_1 and f_2 from Z to Z such that $f_1 + f_2$ is not surjective.

21. Show that if f_1 and f_2 are one-one maps from R to R, then the product $f_1 \times f_2 : R \to R$ defined by $(f_1 \times f_2)(x) = f_1(x) f_2(x)$ need not be one-one.

22. Suppose f_1 and f_2 are non-zero one-one functions from R to R. Is $\dfrac{f_1}{f_2}$ necessarily one-one? Justify your answer. Here, $\dfrac{f_1}{f_2} : R \to R$ is given by $\left(\dfrac{f_1}{f_2}\right)(x) = \dfrac{f_1(x)}{f_2(x)}$ for all $x \in R$.

23. Given $A = \{2, 3, 4\}$, $B = \{2, 5, 6, 7\}$. Construct an example of each of the following:
    (i) an injective map from A to B
    (ii) a mapping from A to B which is not injective
    (iii) a mapping from A to B.

24. Show that $f : R \to R$, given by $f(x) = x - [x]$, is neither one-one nor onto.

25. Let $f : N \to N$ be defined by $f(n) = \begin{cases} n+1, & \text{if } n \text{ is odd} \\ n-1, & \text{if } n \text{ is even} \end{cases}$. Show that f is a bijection. [CBSE 2012, NCERT]

ANSWERS

2. f_1, f_2

4. (i) one-one but not onto
(ii) Neither one-one not onto
(iii) Injective but not surjective
(iv) Injective but not surjective.
(v) Neither an injection nor a surjection
(vi) Neither Injective nor Surjective
(vii) Bijective
(viii) Neither injective nor surjective
(ix) Bijective
(x) Surjective but not injective
(xi) Neither injective nor surjective
(xii) Injective but not surjective

(xiii) Injective (xiv) Bijective (xv) Bijective
(xvi) Neither injective nor surjective. (xvii) Neither one-one nor onto

5. (i) one-one but not onto (ii) neither one-one nor onto
(iii) neither one-one nor onto

6. (i) represents a function which is surjective but not injective
(ii) does not represent a function

8. 1

10. (i) $f(1)=1, f(2)=2, f(3)=3$ (ii) $f(1)=1, f(2)=3, f(3)=2$
(iii) $f(1)=2, f(2)=3, f(3)=1$ (iv) $f(1)=2, f(2)=1, f(3)=3$
(v) $f(1)=3, f(2)=2, f(3)=1$ (vi) $f(1)=3, f(2)=1, f(3)=2$

15. ± 3 16. $f(x)=2x-1$, one-one and onto 17. $a=1$, one-one

HINTS TO SELECTED PROBLEMS

1. (i) $f: Z \to Z$ given by $f(x)=3x+2$ (ii) $f: Z \to \{0\}$ given by $f(x)=|x|$
(iii) $f: Z \to Z$ given by $f(x)=2x^2+1$

3. We have, $f(x)=x^2, x \in \{-1, 0, 1\}$. Clearly, $f(-1)=f(1)$. So, f is not one-one. Range $(f)=\{0, 1\} \neq A$. So, $f: A \to A$ is not onto.

7. We have, $f(x) = x^2+x+1$.

Injectivity: Let $x, y \in N$ be such that

$$f(x) = f(y) \Rightarrow x^2+x+1 = y^2+y+1 \Rightarrow x^2-y^2+x-y=0$$

$$\Rightarrow (x-y)(x+y+1)=0 \Rightarrow x-y = 0 \Rightarrow x = y \qquad [\because x+y+1 \neq 0 \text{ for any } x, y \in N]$$

So, f is a one-one function. Clearly, $f(x)=x^2+x+1 \geq 3$ for all $x \in N$.

So, $f(x)$ does not assume values 1 and 2. Therefore, $f: N \to N$ is not an onto function.

8. It is given that $f: A \to B$ is an injective map such that range of f is $\{a\}$. As f is an injective map, therefore different elements of A have different images in B. So, A has just one element.

9. $f: R-\{3\} \to R-\{1\}$ is given by $f(x)=\dfrac{x-2}{x-3}$

Injectivity: Let $x, y \in R-\{3\}$ be such that

$$f(x)=f(y) \Rightarrow \frac{x-2}{x-3}=\frac{y-2}{y-3} \Rightarrow 1+\frac{1}{x-3}=1+\frac{1}{y-3} \Rightarrow \frac{1}{x-3}=\frac{1}{y-3} \Rightarrow x-3=y-3 \Rightarrow x=y$$

So, f is a one-one function.

Surjectivity: Let y be an arbitrary element of $R-\{1\}$. Then,

$$f(x) = y \Rightarrow \frac{x-2}{x-3} = y \Rightarrow x=\frac{2-3y}{1-y}$$

We find that, $x = 3 \Rightarrow 1 = 0$ which is an absurd result. Therefore, $x \neq 3$. Hence, $x \in R-\{3\}$ for all $y \in R-\{1\}$. Thus, for each $y \in R-\{1\}$ there exists $x=\dfrac{2-3y}{1-y} \in R-\{3\}$ such that $f(x)=y$. So, f is an onto function.

10. All one-one functions from $A=\{1, 2, 3\}$ to itself are obtained by arranging elements of the second row in the two row notation $\begin{pmatrix} 1 & 2 & 3 \\ 1 & 2 & 3 \end{pmatrix}$.

12. For any $x, y \in R$, we find that : $f(x)=f(y) \Rightarrow e^x=e^y \Rightarrow x=y$. So, $f: R \to R$ is one-one.

Clearly, range $(f) = (0, \infty) \neq R$. So, f is not onto.

13. $f: R_0^+ \to R$ is given by $f(x) = \log_a x, a > 0$. For any $x, y \in R_0^+$, we find that

$$f(x) = f(y) \Rightarrow \log_a x = \log_a y \Rightarrow x = y.$$ So, f is one-one.

For each $y \in R$, there exists $x = a^y \in R_0^+$ such that $f(x) = \log_a a^y = y$. So, f is onto. Hence, f is a bijection.

14. (i) We have, $A = \{1, 2, 3\}$ and $f: A \to A$ is a one-one function. Therefore, $f(1), f(2), f(3)$ are distinct elements of A. But, A has three elements only. Therefore, $A = \{f(1), f(2), f(3)\}$ i.e., range $(f) = A$. So, f is onto.

(ii) We have, $A = \{1, 2, 3\}$. It is given that $f: A \to A$ is an onto function. Therefore,

$$\{f(1), f(2), f(3)\} = A$$

$\Rightarrow f(1), f(2), f(3)$ are distinct elements of $A \Rightarrow f: A \to A$ is one-one.

18. Since every onto function from A to itself is one-one (See example 22). Therefore, total number of onto functions from A to itself is same as the number of bijections from A to itself, which is equal to n!.

19. Let $f_1: R \to R$ and $f_2: R \to R$ be given by $f_1(x) = x$ and $f_2(x) = -x$.
Clearly, f_1 and f_2 are one-one. But, $(f_1 + f_2)(x) = x - x = 0$ for all $x \in R$ is not one-one.

20. Let $f_1: Z \to Z$ and $f_2: Z \to Z$ be given by $f_1(x) = x$ and $f_2(x) = -x$. Then, f_1 and f_2 are surjections, but $f_1 + f_2: Z \to Z$ is not surjection. Because, $(f_1 + f_2)(x) = x - x = 0$ for all $x \in Z$.

21. Take $f_1(x) = x$ and $f_2(x) = x$.

22. Take $f_1: R \to R$ given by $f_1(x) = x^3$ and $f_2: R \to R$ given $f_2(x) = x$.

23. We have, $f(x) = x - [x]$. Clearly, $f(x) = 0$ for all $x \in Z$. So, $f: R \to R$ is a many-one function. We find that, range $(f) = [0, 1) \neq R$. So, f is an into function.

2.4 COMPOSITION OF FUNCTIONS

Let A, B and C be three non-void sets and let $f: A \to B$, $g: B \to C$ be two functions. Since f is a function from A to B, therefore for each $x \in A$ there exists a unique element $f(x) \in B$. Again, since g is a function from B to C, therefore corresponding to $f(x) \in B$ there exists a unique element $g(f(x)) \in C$. Thus, for each $x \in A$ there exists a unique element $g(f(x)) \in C$.

It follows from the above discussion that f and g when considered together define a new function from A to C. This function is called the composition of f and g and is denoted by gof. We define it formally as follows:

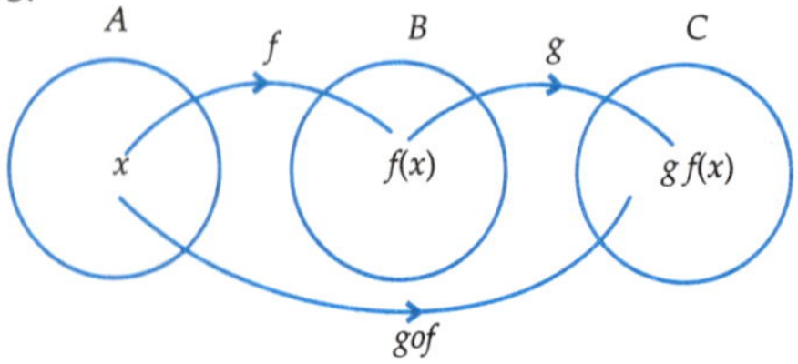

Fig. 2.36

DEFINITION *Let $f: A \to B$ and $g: B \to C$ be two functions. Then a function $gof: A \to C$ defined by*

$$(gof)(x) = g(f(x)), \text{ for all } x \in A \text{ is called the composition of } f \text{ and } g.$$

NOTE 1 *It is evident from the definition that gof is defined only if for each $x \in A$, $f(x)$ is an element of domain of g so that we can take its g-image. Hence, for the composition gof to exist, the range of f must be a subset of the domain of g as shown in Fig. 2.37.*

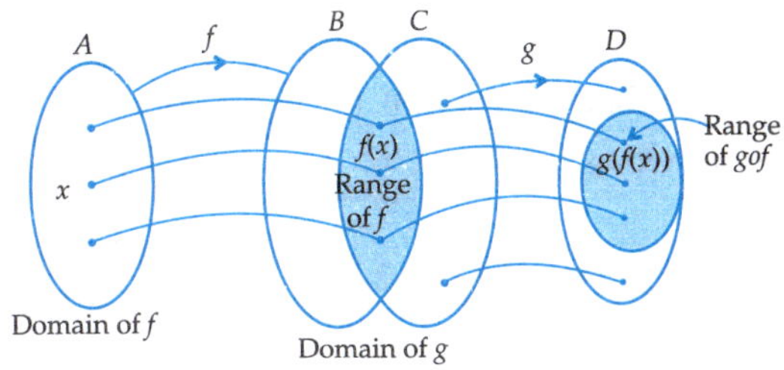

Fig. 2.37

NOTE 2 *It should be noted that gof exists iff the range of f is a subset of domain of g. Similarly, fog exists if range of g is a subset of domain of f.*

NOTE 3 *In order to visualize how functional composition works, let us think gof in terms of an "assembly line" in which f and g are arranged in series with output f (x) becoming the input of g as shown in Fig.* 2.38.

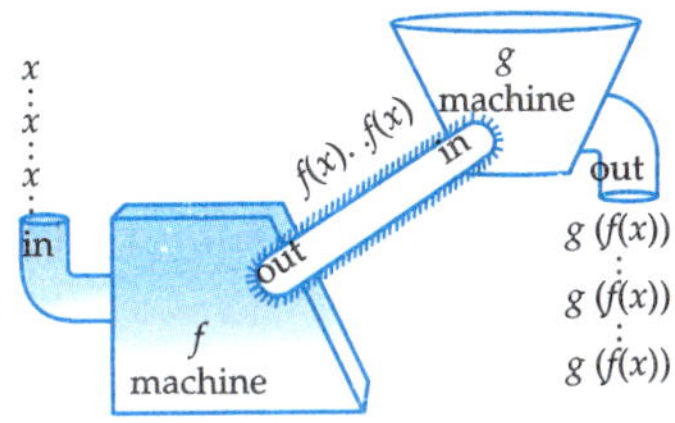

Fig. 2.38

ILLUSTRATIVE EXAMPLES

BASED ON BASIC CONCEPTS (BASIC)

EXAMPLE 1 *Let R be the set of real numbers. If* $f: R \to R$; $f(x) = x^2$ *and* $g: R \to R$; $g(x) = 2x + 1$. *Then, find fog and gof. Also, show that* $fog \neq gof$.

SOLUTION Clearly, range of f is a subset of domain of g and range of g is a subset of domain of f. So, fog and gof both exist.

Now, $(gof)(x) = g(f(x)) = g(x^2) = 2(x^2) + 1 = 2x^2 + 1$

And, $(fog)(x) = f(g(x)) = f(2x+1) = (2x+1)^2$

Clearly, $2x^2 + 1 \neq (2x+1)^2$ for all $x \in R \Rightarrow gof(x) = fog(x)$ for all $x \in R \Rightarrow gof \neq fog$.

EXAMPLE 2 *Let* $f: R \to R$; $f(x) = \sin x$ *and* $g: R \to R$; $g(x) = x^2$ *find fog and gof.*

SOLUTION Clearly, fog and gof both exist such that

$(gof)(x) = g(f(x)) = g(\sin x) = (\sin x)^2 = \sin^2 x$ and, $(fog)(x) = f(g(x)) = f(x^2) = \sin x^2$.

EXAMPLE 3 *Let* $f: \{2, 3, 4, 5\} \to \{3, 4, 5, 9\}$ *and* $g: \{3, 4, 5, 9\} \to \{7, 11, 15\}$ *be functions defined as* $f(2) = 3, f(3) = 4, f(4) = f(5) = 5$ *and,* $g(3) = g(4) = 7$ *and* $g(5) = g(9) = 11$. *Find gof.* **[NCERT]**

SOLUTION We find that Range of $f = \{3, 4, 5\}$. Clearly, it is a subset of domain of g. So, gof exists and $gof: \{2, 3, 4, 5\} \to \{7, 11, 15\}$ such that

$$gof(2) = g(f(2)) = g(3) = 7; \quad gof(3) = g(f(3)) = g(4) = 7$$

$$gof(4) = g(f(4)) = g(5) = 11 \text{ and } gof(5) = g(f(5)) = g(5) = 11$$

Hence, $gof: \{2, 3, 4, 5\} \to \{7, 11, 15\}$ such that $gof = \{(2, 7), (3, 7), (4, 11), (5, 11)\}$

EXAMPLE 4 *Let* $f: \{1, 3, 4\} \to \{1, 2, 5\}$ *and* $g: \{1, 2, 5\} \to \{1, 3\}$ *be given by* $f = \{(1, 2), (3, 5), (4, 1)\}$ *and* $g = \{(1, 3), (2, 3), (5, 1)\}$. *Write down gof.* **[NCERT]**

SOLUTION Clearly, co-domain of f is same as the domain of g. So, gof exists and $gof: \{1, 3, 4\} \to \{1, 3\}$ such that

$gof(1) = g(f(1)) = g(2) = 3$; $gof(3) = g(f(3)) = g(5) = 1$; $gof(4) = g(f(4)) = g(1) = 3$

Hence, $gof: \{1, 3, 4\} \to \{1, 3\}$ such that $gof = \{(1, 3), (3, 1), (4, 3)\}$.

EXAMPLE 5 *Find gof and fog, if $f: R \to R$ and $g: R \to R$ are given by $f(x) = |x|$ and $g(x) = |5x - 2|$.* **[NCERT]**

SOLUTION $gof(x) = g(f(x)) = g(|x|) = |5|x| - 2| = \begin{cases} |5x-2|, & \text{if } x \geq 0 \\ |-5x-2|, & \text{if } x < 0 \end{cases}$

and, $fog(x) = f(g(x)) = f(|5x-2|) = ||5x-2|| = |5x-2|$.

EXAMPLE 6 *If the functions f and g are given by $f = \{(1, 2), (3, 5), (4, 1)\}$ and $g = \{(2, 3), (5, 1), (1, 3)\}$, find range of f and g. Also, write down fog and gof as sets of ordered pairs.*

SOLUTION We find that: Range of f = Set of second components of ordered pairs in $f = \{2, 5, 1\}$
Similarly, Range of $g = \{3, 1\}$. We also find that: Domain $f = \{1, 3, 4\}$ and, Domain $g = \{2, 5, 1\}$
Clearly, Range $f \subset$ Domain g and, Range $g \subset$ Domain f. So, fog and gof both exist.

Now, $fog(2) = f(g(2)) = f(3) = 5$; $fog(5) = f(g(5)) = f(1) = 2$ and, $fog(1) = f(g(1)) = f(3) = 5$.

$\therefore$ $fog = \{(2, 5), (5, 2), (1, 5)\}$

And, $gof(1) = g(f(1)) = g(2) = 3$; $gof(3) = g(f(3)) = g(5) = 1$ and, $gof(4) = g(f(4)) = g(1) = 3$

$\therefore$ $gof = \{(1, 3), (3, 1), (4, 3)\}$

EXAMPLE 7 *If the function $f: R \to R$ be given by $f(x) = x^2 + 2$ and $g: R - \{1\} \to R$ be given by $g(x) = \frac{x}{x-1}$. Find fog and gof.* **[CBSE 2014]**

SOLUTION Clearly, range $f \subset$ domain g and, range $g \subset$ domain f. So, fog and gof both exist.

Now, $(fog)(x) = f(g(x)) = f\left(\frac{x}{x-1}\right) = \left(\frac{x}{x-1}\right)^2 + 2 = \frac{x^2}{(x-1)^2} + 2$

and, $(gof)(x) = g(f(x)) = g(x^2 + 2) = \frac{x^2 + 2}{(x^2 + 2) - 1} = \frac{x^2 + 2}{x^2 + 1}$

Hence, $gof: R \to R$ and $fog: R - \{1\} \to R$ are given by $(gof)(x) = \frac{x^2 + 2}{x^2 + 1}$ and $(fog)(x) = \frac{x^2}{(x-1)^2} + 2$.

EXAMPLE 8 *If $f, g: R \to R$ are defined respectively by $f(x) = x^2 + 3x + 1$, $g(x) = 2x - 3$, find*

(i) fog (ii) gof (iii) fof (iv) gog. **[NCERT EXEMPLAR]**

SOLUTION Clearly, Range f = Domain g and, Range g = Domain f. Therefore, fog, gof, fof and gog all exist.

(i) For any $x \in R$, we find that

$$(fog)(x) = f(g(x)) = f(2x - 3) = (2x - 3)^2 + 3(2x - 3) + 1 = 4x^2 - 6x + 1$$

So, $fog: R \to R$ is defined by $(fog)(x) = 4x^2 - 6x + 1$ for all $x \in R$.

(ii) For any $x \in R$, we find that

$$(gof)(x) = g(f(x)) = g(x^2 + 3x + 1) = 2(x^2 + 3x + 1) - 3 = 2x^2 + 6x - 1$$

So, $gof: R \to R$ is defined by $(gof)(x) = 2x^2 + 6x - 1$ for all $x \in R$

(iii) For any $x \in R$, we find that

$$(fof)(x) = f(f(x)) = f(x^2 + 3x + 1) = (x^2 + 3x + 1)^2 + 3(x^2 + 3x + 1) + 1$$

$$= x^4 + 6x^3 + 14x^2 + 15x + 5$$

So, $fof : R \to R$ is defined by $(fof)(x) = x^4 + 6x^3 + 14x^2 + 15x + 5$

(iv) For any $x \in R$, we find that

$$(gog)(x) = g(g(x)) = g(2x-3) = 2(2x-3) - 3 = 4x - 9$$

So, $gog : R \to R$ is defined by $(gog)(x) = 4x - 9$.

EXAMPLE 9 *If $f : R \to R$ is defined by $f(x) = x^2 - 3x + 2$, find $f(f(x))$.* **[NCERT]**

SOLUTION We have, $f(x) = x^2 - 3x + 2$.

$\therefore$ $f(f(x)) = f(x^2 - 3x + 2) = f(y)$, where $y = x^2 - 3x + 2$.

$$= y^2 - 3y + 2 \qquad [\because f(x) = x^2 - 3x + 2 \therefore f(y) = y^2 - 3y + 2]$$

$$= (x^2 - 3x + 2)^2 - 3(x^2 - 3x + 2) + 2 = x^4 - 6x^3 + 10x^2 - 3x.$$

BASED ON LOWER ORDER THINKING SKILLS (LOTS)

EXAMPLE 10 *If $f : R - \left\{\frac{7}{5}\right\} \to R - \left\{\frac{3}{5}\right\}$ be defined as $f(x) = \frac{3x+4}{5x-7}$ and $g : R - \left\{\frac{3}{5}\right\} \to R - \left\{\frac{7}{5}\right\}$ be defined as $g(x) = \frac{7x+4}{5x-3}$. Show that $gof = I_A$ and $fog = I_B$, where $B = R - \left\{\frac{3}{5}\right\}$ and $A = R - \left\{\frac{7}{5}\right\}$.* **[NCERT]**

SOLUTION It is given that $f : A \to B$ and $g : B \to A$. Therefore, $gof : A \to A$ and $fog : B \to B$.

$$gof(x) = g(f(x)) = g\left(\frac{3x+4}{5x-7}\right) = \frac{7\left(\frac{3x+4}{5x-7}\right)+4}{5\left(\frac{3x+4}{5x-7}\right)-3} = \frac{21x+28+20x-28}{15x+20-15x+21} = \frac{41x}{41} = x$$

Therefore, $gof : A \to A$ is such that $gof(x) = x$ for all $x \in A$. Hence, $gof = I_A$.

Now, $$fog(x) = f(g(x)) = f\left(\frac{7x+4}{5x-3}\right) = \frac{3\left(\frac{7x+4}{5x-3}\right)+4}{5\left(\frac{7x+4}{5x-3}\right)-7} = \frac{21x+12+20x-12}{35x+20-35x+21} = \frac{41x}{41} = x$$

$\therefore$ $fog : B \to B$ such that $fog(x) = x$ for all $x \in B$. Hence, $fog = I_B$.

EXAMPLE 11 *Let $f : R \to R$ be the signum function defined as $f(x) = \begin{cases} 1, & x > 0 \\ 0, & x = 0 \\ -1, & x < 0 \end{cases}$ and $g : R \to R$ be the greatest integer function given by $g(x) = [x]$. Then, prove that fog and gof coincide in $[-1, 0)$.* **[NCERT]**

SOLUTION For any $x \in [-1, 0)$, we find that

$$fog(x) = f(g(x)) = f([x]) = f(-1) = -1 \text{ and, } gof(x) = g(f(x)) = g(-1) = [-1] = -1$$

$\therefore$ $gof(x) = fog(x)$ for all $x \in [-1, 0)$

Hence, gof and fog coincide on $[-1, 0)$.

EXAMPLE 12 *Let f, g and h be functions from R to R. Show that:*

(i) $(f + g)oh = foh + goh$ (ii) $(fg)oh = (foh)(goh)$ **[NCERT]**

SOLUTION (i) Since f, g and h are functions from R to R. Therefore,

$$(f+g)\,oh : R \to R \quad \text{and} \quad foh + goh : R \to R$$

For any $x \in R$, we find that

$$((f+g)\,oh)\,(x) = (f+g)\,(h\,(x)) = f\,(h\,(x)) + g\,(h\,(x)) = foh\,(x) + goh\,(x) = (foh + goh)\,(x)$$

$\therefore \quad (f+g)\,oh = foh + goh$

(ii) Clearly, $(fg)\,oh : R \to R$ and $(foh)\,(goh) : R \to R$ such that

$$\{(fg)\,oh\}\,(x) = (fg)\,(h\,(x)) = f\,(h\,(x))\,g\,(h\,(x)) = (foh)\,(x)\,(goh)\,(x) = \{(foh).(goh)\}\,(x) \text{ for all } x \in R$$

$\therefore \quad (fg)\,oh = (foh)\,.\,(goh).$

BASED ON HIGHER ORDER THINKING SKILLS (HOTS)

EXAMPLE 13 *If $f : R \to R$ be defined by $f\,(x) = 2x$ for all $x \in R$. Find $g : R \to R$ such that $gof = I_R$.*

SOLUTION It is given that

$$gof = I_R$$

$\Rightarrow \quad gof\,(x) = I_R\,(x)$ for all $x \in R$

$\Rightarrow \quad g\,(f\,(x)) = x$ for all $x \in R$

$\Rightarrow \quad g\,(2x) = x$ for all $x \in R$

$\Rightarrow \quad g\,(y) = \dfrac{y}{2}$ for all $y \in R$, where $2x = y$

$\Rightarrow \quad g\,(x) = \dfrac{x}{2}$ for all $x \in R$.

Hence, $g : R \to R$ given by, $g\,(x) = \dfrac{x}{2}$ for all $x \in R$, is the required function.

EXAMPLE 14 *Let $A = \{x \in R : 0 \le x \le 1\}$. If $f : A \to A$ is defined by $f(x) = \begin{cases} x\,, & \text{if } x \in Q \\ 1 - x\,, & \text{if } x \notin Q \end{cases}$ then prove that $fof\,(x) = x$ for all $x \in A$.* **[NCERT EXEMPLAR]**

SOLUTION Let $x \in A$. Then, either x is rational or x is irrational. So following cases arise:

Case I *When $x \in Q$:* In this case, we have $f(x) = x$.

$\therefore \quad fof\,(x) = f\,(f\,(x)) = f\,(x) = x \qquad [\because f\,(x) = x]$

Case II *When $x \notin Q$:* In this case, we have $f\,(x) = 1 - x$.

$\therefore \quad fof\,(x) = f\,(f\,(x)) = f\,(1-x) \qquad [\because x \notin Q \;\therefore f\,(x) = 1 - x]$

$\qquad = 1 - (1 - x) = x \qquad [\because x \notin Q \Rightarrow 1 - x \notin Q \Rightarrow f\,(1-x) = 1 - (1-x)]$

Thus, $fof\,(x) = x$ whether $x \in Q$ or, $x \notin Q$. Hence, $fof\,(x) = x$ for all $x \in A$.

EXAMPLE 15 *Let $f : R \to R$ and $g : R \to R$ be two functions such that $fog\,(x) = \sin x^2$ and $gof\,(x) = \sin^2 x$. Then, find $f\,(x)$ and $g\,(x)$.*

SOLUTION We have,

$$fog\,(x) = \sin x^2 \text{ and, } gof\,(x) = \sin^2 x$$

$\Rightarrow \quad f\,(g\,(x)) = \sin\,(x^2)$ and, $g\,(f\,(x)) = (\sin x)^2 \Rightarrow f\,(x) = \sin x$ and, $g\,(x) = x^2$.

EXAMPLE 16 *If $f : R \to R$ be given by $f\,(x) = \sin^2 x + \sin^2 (x + \pi/3) + \cos x \cos\,(x + \pi/3)$ for all $x \in R$, and $g : R \to R$ be such that $g\,(5/4) = 1$, then prove that $gof : R \to R$ is a constant function.*

SOLUTION We have,

$$f\,(x) = \sin^2 x + \sin^2 (x + \pi/3) + \cos x \cos\,(x + \pi/3)$$

$$\Rightarrow \quad f\,(x) = \frac{1}{2}\left\{2\sin^2 x + 2\sin^2\left(x + \frac{\pi}{3}\right) + 2\cos x \cos\left(x + \frac{\pi}{3}\right)\right\}$$

$$\Rightarrow \quad f(x) = \frac{1}{2}\left[1 - \cos 2x + 1 - \cos\left(2x + \frac{2\pi}{3}\right) + \cos\left(2x + \frac{\pi}{3}\right) + \cos\frac{\pi}{3}\right]$$

$$\Rightarrow \quad f(x) = \frac{1}{2}\left[\frac{5}{2} - \cos 2x - \cos\left(2x + \frac{2\pi}{3}\right) + \cos\left(2x + \frac{\pi}{3}\right)\right]$$

$$\Rightarrow \quad f(x) = \frac{1}{2}\left[\frac{5}{2} - \left\{\cos(2x) + \cos\left(2x + \frac{2\pi}{3}\right)\right\} + \cos\left(2x + \frac{\pi}{3}\right)\right]$$

$$\Rightarrow \quad f(x) = \frac{1}{2}\left[\frac{5}{2} - 2\cos\left(2x + \frac{\pi}{3}\right)\cos\frac{\pi}{3} + \cos\left(2x + \frac{\pi}{3}\right)\right]$$

$$\Rightarrow \quad f(x) = \frac{1}{2}\left[\frac{5}{2} - \cos\left(2x + \frac{\pi}{3}\right) + \cos\left(2x + \frac{\pi}{3}\right)\right] = \frac{5}{4} \text{ for all } x \in R.$$

Therefore, for any $x \in R$, we obtain: $gof\,(x) = g\,(f(x)) = g\left(\frac{5}{4}\right) = 1$

Thus, $gof\,(x) = 1$ for all $x \in R$. Hence, $gof : R \to R$ is a constant function.

EXAMPLE 17 *Let $f : Z \to Z$ be defined by $f(n) = 3n$ for all $n \in Z$ and $g : Z \to Z$ be defined by*

$$g(n) = \begin{cases} \frac{n}{3}, & \text{if } n \text{ is a multiple of } 3 \\ 0, & \text{if } n \text{ is not a multiple of } 3 \end{cases}$$ *for all $n \in Z$. Show that $gof = I_Z$ and $fog \neq I_Z$.*

SOLUTION Since $f : Z \to Z$ and $g : Z \to Z$. Therefore, $gof : Z \to Z$ and $fog : Z \to Z$.

For any $n \in Z$, we obtain

$$gof\,(n) = g\,(f\,(n)) = g\,(3n) = \frac{3n}{3} = n \qquad \left[\because 3n \text{ is a multiple of } 3 \therefore f\,(3n) = \frac{3n}{3}\right]$$

$$\therefore \quad gof\,(n) = n \text{ for all } n \in Z \Rightarrow gof = I_Z.$$

For any $n \in Z$, we have

$$fog\,(n) = f\,(g\,(n)) = \begin{cases} f\left(\frac{n}{3}\right), & \text{if } n \text{ is a multiple of } 3 \\ f\,(0), & \text{if } n \text{ is not a multiple of } 3 \end{cases}$$

$$\Rightarrow \quad fog\,(n) = \begin{cases} 3\left(\frac{n}{3}\right), & \text{if } n \text{ is a multiple of } 3 \\ 3 \times 0, & \text{if } n \text{ is not a multiple of } 3 \end{cases} = \begin{cases} n, & \text{if } n \text{ is a multiple of } 3 \\ 0, & \text{if } n \text{ is not a multiple of } 3 \end{cases}$$

Clearly, $fog\,(n) \neq n$ for all $n \in Z$. In fact, $fog\,(n) = n$ only for multiple of 3. So, $fog \neq I_Z$.

EXAMPLE 18 *Let $f : R \to R$ be a function given by $f(x) = ax + b$ for all $x \in R$. Find the constants a and b such that $fof = I_R$.*

SOLUTION We have,

$$fof = I_R$$

$$\Rightarrow \quad fof\,(x) = I_R\,(x) \text{ for all } x \in R$$

$$\Rightarrow \quad f\,(f\,(x)) = x \text{ for all } x \in R \qquad [\because I_R\,(x) = x \text{ for all } x \in R]$$

$$\Rightarrow \quad f\,(ax + b) = x \text{ for all } x \in R$$

$$\Rightarrow \quad a\,(ax + b) + b = x \text{ for all } x \in R$$

$$\Rightarrow \quad (a^2 - 1)\,x + ab + b = 0 \text{ for all } x \in R$$

$$\Rightarrow \quad a^2 - 1 = 0 \text{ and } ab + b = 0 \qquad [\because (a^2 - 1)\,x + (ab + b) = 0 \text{ is an identity in } x]$$

$$\Rightarrow \quad a = \pm 1 \text{ and } b\,(a + 1) = 0$$

When $a=1$: $b(a+1) = 0 \Rightarrow 2b = 0 \Rightarrow b = 0$. Therefore, $a = 1$ and $b = 0$.

When $a=-1$: $b(a+1) = 0$ for all $b \in R$. Therefore, $a=-1$ and b can take any real value.

Hence, either $a=1$ and $b=0$, or $a=-1$ and b can take any real value.

EXAMPLE 19 *Let $f, g: R \to R$ be a two function defined as $f(x)=|x|+x$ and $g(x)=|x|-x$ for all $x \in R$. Then, find fog and gof.* **[NCERT EXEMPLAR]**

SOLUTION We have,

$$f(x)=|x|+x=\begin{cases} x+x=2x, & \text{if } x \geq 0 \\ -x+x=0, & \text{if } x<0 \end{cases} \text{ and, } g(x)=|x|-x=\begin{cases} x-x=0, & \text{if } x \geq 0 \\ -x-x=-2x, & \text{if } x<0 \end{cases}$$

The graphs of $f(x)$ and $g(x)$ are shown in Fig. 2.39 (i) and 2.39 (ii) respectively. It is event from these graphs that range $(f)=[0, \infty)$ and range $(g)=(-\infty, 0]$. Thus, range $(f) \subset$ domain (g) and range $(g) \subset$ domain (f). So, *fog* and *gof* both exist.

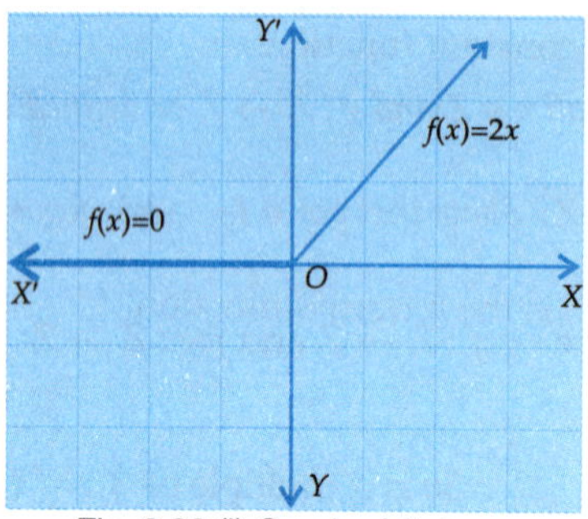

Fig. 2.39 (i) Graph of $f(x)$

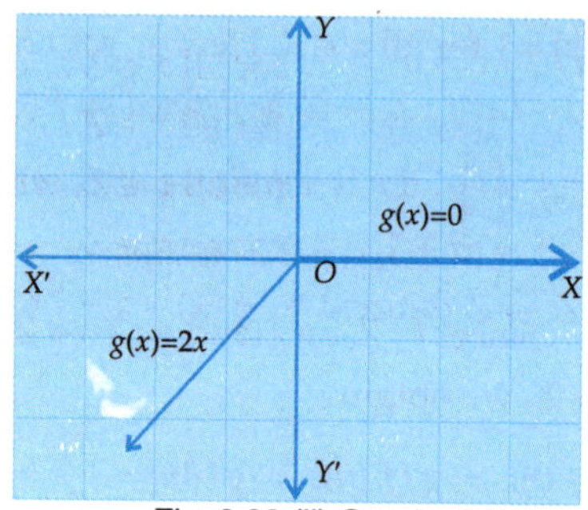

Fig. 2.39 (ii) Graph of $f(x)$

Now,

$$fog(x)=f(g(x))=\begin{cases} f(0) & , \text{if } x \geq 0 \\ f(-2x) & , \text{if } x<0 \end{cases}$$

$$\Rightarrow \quad fog(x)=\begin{cases} 2 \times 0=0, & \text{if } x \geq 0 \\ 2(-2x)=-4x, & \text{if } x<0 \end{cases} \qquad \left[\begin{array}{l} \because -2x>0 \text{ if } x<0 \\ \therefore f(-2x)=2(-2x)=-4x, \text{ if } x<0 \end{array}\right]$$

$$\text{and, } \quad gof(x)=g(f(x))=\begin{cases} g(2x), & \text{if } x \geq 0 \\ g(0), & \text{if } x<0 \end{cases}=\begin{cases} 0, & \text{if } x \geq 0 \\ 0, & \text{if } x<0 \end{cases}=0 \text{ for all } x \in R.$$

EXAMPLE 20 *Let $f: A \to A$ be a function such that $fof=f$. Show that f is onto if and only if f is one-one. Describe f in this case.*

SOLUTION We have, $fof=f$.

Let $f: A \to A$ be onto. Then, we have to prove that f is one-one.

Let $x, y, \in A$. Then, as $f: A \to A$ is onto there exist $\alpha, \beta \in A$ such that

$$f(\alpha)=x \text{ and } f(\beta)=y \qquad \text{...(i)}$$

Now, $f(x)=f(y)$

$\Rightarrow \quad f(f(\alpha))=f(f(\beta))$ [Using (i)]

$\Rightarrow \quad fof(\alpha)=fof(\beta)$

$\Rightarrow \quad f(\alpha)=f(\beta)$ $[\because fof=f]$

$\Rightarrow \quad x=y$ [Using (i)]

So, f is one-one.

Thus, $f: A \to A$ is onto $\Rightarrow f: A \to A$ is one-one.

Conversely, let $f: A \to A$ be one-one. Then, we have to prove that f is onto.

Let y be an arbitrary element in A. Then,

$$fof = f \Rightarrow fof(y) = f(y) \Rightarrow f(f(y)) = f(y) \Rightarrow f(y) = y \quad [\because f : A \to A \text{ is one-one}]$$

Thus, for all $y \in A$, there exists $y \in A$ such that $f(y) = y$. Hence, f is onto.

Now, $fof = f$

$\Rightarrow \quad fof(x) = f(x)$ for all $x \in A$

$\Rightarrow \quad f(f(x)) = f(x)$ for all $x \in A$

$\Rightarrow \quad f(\alpha) = \alpha$ for all $\alpha = f(x) \in A$

Thus, $f(x) = x$ for all $x \in A$

EXAMPLE 21 *Let $f : Z \to Z$ be defined by $f(x) = x + 2$. Find $g : Z \to Z$ such that $gof = I_Z$.*

SOLUTION It is given that

$gof = I_Z$

$\Rightarrow \quad gof(x) = I_Z(x)$ for all $x \in Z$

$\Rightarrow \quad g(f(x)) = x$ for all $x \in Z$

$\Rightarrow \quad g(x+2) = x$ for all $x \in Z$

$\Rightarrow \quad g(y) = y - 2$ for all $y \in Z$, where $x + 2 = y$

$\Rightarrow \quad g(x) = x - 2$ for all $x \in Z$.

Hence, $g : Z \to Z$ defined by $g(x) = x - 2$ for all $x \in Z$, is the required function.

EXERCISE 2.2

BASIC

1. Let $f = \{(3, 1), (9, 3), (12, 4)\}$ and $g = \{(1, 3), (3, 3), (4, 9), (5, 9)\}$. Show that gof and fog are both defined. Also, find fog and gof.
2. Let $f = \{(1, -1), (4, -2), (9, -3), (16, 4)\}$ and $g = \{(-1, -2), (-2, -4), (-3, -6), (4, 8)\}$. Show that gof is defined while fog is not defined. Also, find gof.
3. Let $A = \{a, b, c\}$, $B = \{u\, v, w\}$ and let f and g be two functions from A to B and from B to A respectively defined as: $f = \{(a, v), (b, u), (c, w)\}$, $g = \{(u, b), (v, a), (w, c)\}$.
   Show that f and g both are bijections and find fog and gof.
4. Find $fog(2)$ and $gof(1)$ when: $f : R \to R$; $f(x) = x^2 + 8$ and $g : R \to R$; $g(x) = 3x^3 + 1$.
5. Let $f : R \to R$ and $g : R \to R$ be defined by $f(x) = x^2$ and $g(x) = x + 1$. Show that $fog \neq gof$.
6. Let R^+ be the set of all non-negative real numbers. If $f : R^+ \to R^+$ and $g : R^+ \to R^+$ are defined as $f(x) = x^2$ and $g(x) = +\sqrt{x}$. Find fog and gof. Are they equal functions.

BASED ON LOTS

7. Find gof and fog when $f : R \to R$ and $g : R \to R$ are defined by
   (i) $f(x) = 2x + 3$ and $g(x) = x^2 + 5$ (ii) $f(x) = 2x + x^2$ and $g(x) = x^3$
   (iii) $f(x) = x^2 + 8$ and $g(x) = 3x^3 + 1$ (iv) $f(x) = x$ and $g(x) = |x|$
   (v) $f(x) = x^2 + 2x - 3$ and $g(x) = 3x - 4$ (vi) $f(x) = 8x^3$ and $g(x) = x^{1/3}$
8. Let $f : R \to R$ and $g : R \to R$ be defined by $f(x) = x + 1$ and $g(x) = x - 1$. Show that $fog = gof = I_R$.
9. Verify associativity for the following three mappings : $f : N \to Z_0$ (the set of non-zero integers), $g : Z_0 \to Q$ and $h : Q \to R$ given by $f(x) = 2x$, $g(x) = 1/x$ and $h(x) = e^x$.

10. If $f(x)=\frac{1-x}{1+x}$, then find $fof(x)$. [CBSE 2020]

11. Consider $f:N\to N, g:N\to N$ and $h:N\to R$ defined as $f(x)=2x$, $g(y)=3y+4$ and $h(z)=\sin z$ for all $x, y, z\in N$. Show that $ho(gof)=(hog)\,of$. [NCERT]

BASED ON HOTS

12. Give examples of two functions $f:N\to N$ and $g:N\to N$ such that gof is onto but f is not onto. [NCERT]

13. Give examples of two functions $f:N\to Z$ and $g:Z\to Z$ such that gof is injective but g is not injective. [NCERT]

14. If $f:A\to B$ and $g:B\to C$ are one-one functions, show that gof is a one-one function.

15. If $f:A\to B$ and $g:B\to C$ are onto functions show that gof is an onto function.

ANSWERS

1. $gof=\{(3,3),(9,3),(12,9)\}$ $fog=\{(1,1),(3,1),(4,3)\,(5,3)\}$
2. $gof=\{(1,-2),(4,-4),(9,-6),(16,8)\}$
3. $fog=\{(u,u),(v,v),(w,w)\}$ $gof=\{(a,a),(b,b),(c,c)\}$ 4. $fog(2)=633,\ gof(1)=2188$
6. $fog(x)=x,\ gof(x)=x$, Yes
7. (i) $gof(x)=4x^2+12x+14,\ fog(x)=2x^2+13$
   (ii) $gof(x)=(x^2+2x)^3,\ fog(x)=2x^3+x^6$
   (iii) $gof(x)=3(x^2+8)^3+1,\ fog(x)=9x^6+6x^3+9$
   (iv) $gof(x)=|x|,\ fog(x)=|x|$ (v) $gof(x)=3x^2+6x-13,\ fog(x)=9x^2-18x+5$
   (vi) $gof(x)=2x,\ fog(x)=8x$ 10. $fof(x)=x$

HINTS TO SELECTED PROBLEMS

2. We have, Range $g=\{-2,-4,-6,8\}$, Domain $f=\{1,4,9,16\}$,
Range $f=\{-1,-2,-3,4\}$, Domain $g=\{-1,-2,-3,4\}$.
Clearly, Range f = Domain g but, Range $g\not\subset$ Domain f. So, fog is not defined but gof is defined.

11. We have, $f(x)=2x$, $g(y)=3y+4$ and $h(z)=\sin z$ for all $x,y,z\in N$

$\therefore\quad gof(x)=g(f(x))=g(2x)=3(2x)+4=6x+4$

$\Rightarrow\quad \{ho(gof)\}(x)=h\{(gof)(x)\}=h(6x+4)=\sin(6x+4)$ ...(i)

$(hog)(x)=h(g(x))=h(3x+4)=\sin(3x+4)$

$\therefore\quad \{(hog)\,of\}(x)=(hog)(f(x))=(hog)(2x)=\sin 2(3x+4)=\sin(6x+4)$ ...(ii)

From (i) and (ii), we get: $ho(gof)=(hog)\,of$

12. If $f(x)=x+1$ and $g(x)=\begin{cases}x-1, & \text{if } x>1\\ 1, & \text{if } x=1\end{cases}$, then $f:N\to N$ is not onto because

Range $(f)=N-\{1\}\neq$ Co–domain of f.

Now, $gof(x)=g(f(x))=g(x+1)=x+1-1=x$ $[\because x+1>1]$

Clearly, gof, being identity function, is onto.

13. Let $f:N\to N$ and $g:Z\to Z$ be given by $f(x)=x$ and $g(x)=|x|$. Then, g is not injective as $g(-2)=g(2)=2$. We observe that $gof:N\to Z$ is given by $gof(x)=g(f(x))=g(x)=|x|=x$
Clearly, gof is injective but g is not injective.

*2.4.1 PROPERTIES OF COMPOSITION OF FUNCTIONS

THEOREM 1 *The composition of functions is not commutative i.e. $fog \neq gof$.*

PROOF Let $f : A \to B$ and $g : B \to C$ be two functions. Then, the function gof exists because the range of f is a subset of the domain of g. But, fog cannot exist unless the range of g is a subset of domain of f i.e. unless $C \subset A$. As such we find that fog does not exist if $C \not\subset A$ but fog will be a function from B to itself if $A = C$. Thus, if $A = C$.

$$f : A \to B \text{ and } g : B \to A \Rightarrow gof : A \to A \text{ and } fog : B \to B$$

Now, we find that both fog and gof exist but they cannot be equal if A and B are two distinct sets, which are their domains. However if $A = B = C$, then both gof and fog exist and both are from A to itself, even then they may not be equal as shown in Example 1 on page 2.35.

Hence, in general the composition of functions is not necessarily commutative.

THEOREM 2 *The composition of functions is associative i.e. if f, g, h are three functions such that $(fog)oh$ and $fo\,(goh)$ exist, then $(fog)\,oh = fo\,(goh)$.* [NCERT]

PROOF Let A, B, C, D be four non-void sets. Let $h : A \to B$, $g : B \to C$ and $f : C \to D$ be three functions. Then,

$$h : A \to B,\ g : B \to C,\ f : C \to D \Rightarrow fog : B \to D \text{ and } h : A \to B \Rightarrow (fog)\,oh : A \to D$$

Again, $h : A \to B,\ g : B \to C,\ f : C \to D \Rightarrow f : C \to D$ and $goh : A \to C \Rightarrow fo\,(goh) : A \to D$

Thus, $(fog)oh$ and $fo(goh)$ are functions from set A to set D.

Now, we shall show that $\{(fog)oh\}\,(x) = \{fo\,(goh)\}\,(x)$ for all $x \in A$.

Let x be an arbitrary element of A and let $y \in B, z \in C$ such that $h\,(x) = y$ and $g(y) = z$. Then,

$$\begin{aligned}
\{(fog)\,oh\}\,(x) &= (fog)\,\{h\,(x)\} \\
&= (fog)\,(y) && [\because\ h\,(x) = y] \\
&= f\,(g\,(y)) \\
&= f\,(z) && [\because\ g\,(y) = z] \quad \text{...(i)}
\end{aligned}$$

And,
$$\begin{aligned}
\{fo\,(goh)\}\,(x) &= f\,\{(goh)\,(x)\} \\
&= f\,\{g\,(h\,(x))\} \\
&= f\,\{g\,(y)\} && [\because\ h\,(x) = y] \\
&= f\,(z) && [\because\ g\,(y) = z] \quad \text{...(ii)}
\end{aligned}$$

From (i) and (ii), we obtain: $\{(fog)\,oh\}\,(x) = \{fo\,(goh)\}\,(x)$ for all $x \in A$.

Hence, $(fog)\,oh = fo\,(goh)$.

THEOREM 3 *The composition of two bijections is a bijection i.e. if f and g are two bijections, then gof is also a bijection.* [NCERT]

PROOF Let $f : A \to B$ and $g : B \to C$ be two bijections. Then, gof exists such that $gof : A \to C$.

We have to prove that gof is injective as well as surjective map.

Injectivity: Let x, y be two arbitrary elements of A. Then,

$\Rightarrow \quad (gof\,)\,(x) = (gof)\,(y)$

$\Rightarrow \quad g\,(f\,(x)) = g\,(f\,(y))$

$\Rightarrow \quad f(x) = f(y)$ [$\because$ g is an injective map]

$\Rightarrow \quad x = y$ [$\because$ f is an injective map]

Thus, $(gof\,)\,(x) = (gof\,)\,(y)$ for all $x, y \in A$. So, gof is an injective map.

Surjectivity: In order to prove the surjectivity of gof, we have to show that every element in C has its pre-image in A i.e. for all $z \in C$, there exists $x \in A$ such that $(gof)\,(x) = z$.

May be skipped. Not from examination point of view.

Let z be an arbitrary element of C. Then,

$z \in C \Rightarrow$ there exists $y \in B$ such that $g(y) = z$ [$\because$ g is a surjective map]

and, $y \in B \Rightarrow$ there exists $x \in A$ such that $f(x) = y$ [$\because$ f is a surjective map]

Thus, we find that for every $z \in C$, there exists $x \in A$ such that

$$(gof)(x) = g(f(x)) = g(y) = z.$$

i.e. every element of C is the gof-image of some element of A.

So, gof is a surjective map.

Hence, gof being both injective as well as surjective, is a bijective map.

THEOREM 4 *Let $f: A \to B$. Then, $f o I_A = I_B o f = f$ i.e. the composition of any function with the identity function is the function itself.*

PROOF Since $I_A : A \to A$ and $f : A \to B$, therefore $fo I_A : A \to B$. Now let x be an arbitrary element of A. Then,

$$(fo I_A)(x) = f(I_A(x)) = f(x) \quad [\because I_A(x) = x \text{ for all } x \in A]$$

$$\therefore \quad fo I_A = f$$

Again, $f : A \to B$ and $I_B : B \to B \Rightarrow I_B o f : A \to B$.

Now, let x be an arbitrary element of B. Let $f(x) = y$. Then, $y \in B$.

$$\therefore \quad (I_B o f)(x) = I_B(f(x))$$

$$\Rightarrow \quad (I_B o f)(x) = I_B(y) \quad [\because f(x) = y]$$

$$\Rightarrow \quad (I_B o f)(x) = y$$

$$\Rightarrow \quad (I_B o f)(x) = f(x) \quad [\because I_B(y) = y \text{ for all } y \in B]$$

$$\therefore \quad I_B o f = f$$

Hence, $f o I_A = I_B o f = f$

THEOREM 5 *Let $f : A \to B$, $g : B \to A$ be two functions such that $gof = I_A$. Then, f is an injection and g is a surjection.*

PROOF *f is an injection:* Let $x, y \in A$ be such that $f(x) = f(y)$. Then,

$$f(x) = f(y)$$

$$\Rightarrow \quad g(f(x)) = g(f(y))$$

$$\Rightarrow \quad gof(x) = gof(y)$$

$$\Rightarrow \quad I_A(x) = I_A(y) \quad [\because gof = I_A \text{ (Given)}]$$

$$\Rightarrow \quad x = y \quad [\text{By definition of } I_A]$$

Thus, $f(x) = f(y) \Rightarrow x = y$ for all $x, y \in A$.

So, f is an injective map.

g is a surjection: As $g : B \to A$ therefore to prove that g is a surjection. It is sufficient to prove that every element in A has its pre-image in B.

Let x be an arbitrary element of A. Then, as $f : A \to B$ is a function therefore $f(x) \in B$. Let $f(x) = y$. Then,

$$g(y) = g(f(x))$$

$$\Rightarrow \quad g(y) = gof(x)$$

$$\Rightarrow \quad g(y) = I_A(x) \quad [\because gof = I_A]$$

$$\Rightarrow \quad g(y) = x$$

Thus, for every $x \in A$ there exists $y = f(x) \in B$ such that $g(y) = x$. So, g is a surjection.

THEOREM 6 *Let $f : A \to B$ and $g : B \to A$ be two function such that $fog = I_B$. Then, f is a surjection and g is an injection.*

PROOF *f is a surjection* : In order to prove that $f: A \to B$ is a surjection, it is sufficient to prove that every element in B has its pre-image in A. Let b be an arbitrary element of B. Since $g: B \to A$. Therefore, $g(b) \in A$.

Let $g(b) = a$.

$\therefore \quad f(a) = f(g(b))$ $\quad [\because a = g(b)]$

$\Rightarrow \quad f(a) = fog(b)$

$\Rightarrow \quad f(a) = I_B(b)$ $\quad [\because fog = I_B]$

$\Rightarrow \quad f(a) = b$

Thus, for every $b \in B$ there exists $a \in A$ such that $f(a) = b$. So, f is a surjection.

g is an injection: Let x, y be any two elements of B such that $g(x) = g(y)$. Then,

$g(x) = g(y)$

$\Rightarrow \quad f(g(x)) = f(g(y))$

$\Rightarrow \quad fog(x) = fog(y)$

$\Rightarrow \quad I_B(x) = I_B(y)$ $\quad [\because fog = I_B]$

$\Rightarrow \quad x = y$

Thus, $g(x) = g(y) \Rightarrow x = y$ for all $x, y, \in B$.

So, g is an injection.

THEOREM 7 *Let $f: A \to B$ and $g: B \to C$ be two functions. Then,*

(i) *$gof: A \to C$ is onto $\Rightarrow$ $g: B \to C$ is onto*

(ii) *$gof: A \to C$ is one-one $\Rightarrow$ $f: A \to B$ is one-one*

(iii) *$gof: A \to C$ is onto and $g: B \to C$ is one-one $\Rightarrow$ $f: A \to B$ is onto*

(iv) *$gof: A \to C$ is one-one and $f: A \to B$ is onto $\Rightarrow$ $g: B \to C$ is one-one.*

PROOF (i) In order to prove that $g: B \to C$ is onto whenever $gof: A \to C$ is onto, it is sufficient to prove that for all $z \in C$ there exists $y \in B$ such that $g(y) = z$.

Let z be an arbitrary element of C. Since $gof: A \to C$ is onto. Therefore, there exists $x \in A$ such that

$gof(x) = z$

$\Rightarrow \quad g(f(x)) = z$

$\Rightarrow \quad g(y) = z$, where $y = f(x) \in B$.

Thus, for all $z \in C$, there exists $y = f(x) \in B$ such that $g(y) = z$.

Hence, $g: B \to C$ is onto.

(ii) In order to prove that $f: A \to B$ is one-one, it is sufficient to prove that

$f(x) = f(y) \Rightarrow x = y$ for all $x, y \in A$.

Let $x, y \in A$ such that $f(x) = f(y)$. Then,

$f(x) = f(y)$

$\Rightarrow \quad g(f(x)) = g(f(y))$ $\quad [\because g: B \to C$ is a function$]$

$\Rightarrow \quad gof(x) = gof(y)$

$\Rightarrow \quad x = y$ $\quad [\because gof: A \to C$ is one-one$]$

Hence, $f: A \to B$ is one-one.

(iii) In order to prove that $f: A \to B$ is onto, it is sufficient to prove that for all $y \in B$ there exists $x \in A$ such that $f(x) = y$. Let y be an arbitrary element of B. Then,

$g(y) \in C$ $\quad [\because g: B \to C]$

Since $gof: A \to C$ is an onto function. Therefore, for any $g(y) \in C$ there exists $x \in A$ such that

$$gof(x) = g(y)$$
$$\Rightarrow \quad g(f(x)) = g(y)$$
$$\Rightarrow \quad f(x) = y \qquad [\because g \text{ is one-one}]$$

Thus, for all $y \in B$ there exists $x \in A$ such that $f(x) = y$.

Hence, $f : A \to B$ is onto.

(iv) Let $y_1, y_2, \in B$ such that $g(y_1) = g(y_2)$. In order to prove that g is one-one, it is sufficient to prove that $y_1 = y_2$.

Since $f : A \to B$ is onto and $y_1, y_2 \in B$. So, there exist $x_1, x_2 \in A$ such that $f(x_1) = y_1$ and $f(x_2) = y_2$.

Now, $g(y_1) = g(y_2)$
$$\Rightarrow \quad g(f(x_1)) = g(f(x_2))$$
$$\Rightarrow \quad gof(x_1) = gof(x_2)$$
$$\Rightarrow \quad x_1 = x_2 \qquad [\because gof : A \to C \text{ is one-one}]$$
$$\Rightarrow \quad f(x_1) = f(x_2) \qquad [\because f : A \to B \text{ is a function}]$$
$$\Rightarrow \quad y_1 = y_2$$

Hence, $g : B \to C$ is one-one.

2.5 INVERSE OF AN ELEMENT

Let A and B be two sets and let $f : A \to B$ be a mapping. As we have discussed earlier that if $a \in A$ is associated to $b \in B$ under the function f, then 'b' is called the f image of 'a' and we write it as $b = f(a)$. We also say that 'a' is the pre-image or inverse element of 'b' under f and we write $a = f^{-1}(b)$.

It should be noted that the inverse of an element under a function may consist of a single element, two or more elements or no element depending on whether function is injective or many-one; onto or into. If $f : A \to B$ is a many-one and into function, then the inverse of some elements of B may or may not exist or the inverse of some element of B may consists of more than one element. If f is a bijection, then for each $b \in B$, $f^{-1}(b)$ exists and it consists of a single element only.

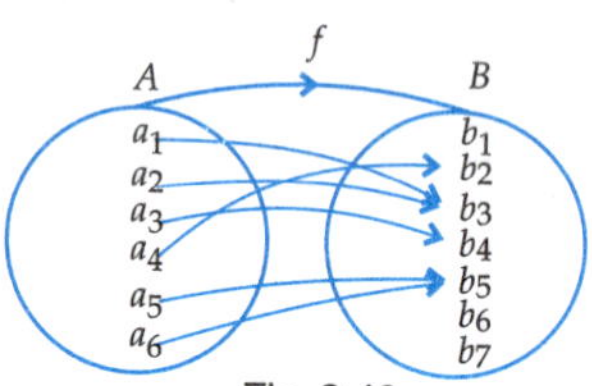

Fig. 2.40

If f is represented by Fig. 2.40 , then we find that: $f^{-1}(b_1) = \phi$, $f^{-1}(b_2) = a_4$, $f^{-1}(b_3) = \{a_1, a_2\}$, $f^{-1}(b_4) = a_3$, $f^{-1}(b_5) = \{a_5, a_6\}$, $f^{-1}(b_6) = \phi$ and, $f^{-1}(b_7) = \phi$

ILLUSTRATIVE EXAMPLES

BASED ON BASIC CONCEPTS (BASIC)

EXAMPLE 1 *If $f : Q \to Q$ is given by $f(x) = x^2$, then find:* (i) $f^{-1}(9)$ (ii) $f^{-1}(-5)$ (iii) $f^{-1}(0)$

SOLUTION (i) Let $f^{-1}(9) = x$. Then, $f(x) = 9 \Rightarrow x^2 = 9 \Rightarrow x = \pm 3$.

$\therefore \quad f^{-1}(9) = \{-3, 3\}$.

(ii) Let $f^{-1}(-5) = x$. Then, $f(x) = -5 \Rightarrow x^2 = -5$, which is not possible for any $x \in Q$.

$\therefore \quad f^{-1}(-5) = \phi$

(iii) Let $f^{-1}(0) = x$. Then, $f(x) = 0 \Rightarrow x^2 = 0 \Rightarrow x = 0$. So, $f^{-1}(0) = \{0\}$.

EXAMPLE 2 *If the function $f : R \to R$ be defined by $f(x) = x^2 + 5x + 9$, find $f^{-1}(8)$ and $f^{-1}(9)$.*

SOLUTION Let $f^{-1}(8) = x$. Then, $f(x) = 8 \Rightarrow x^2 + 5x + 9 = 8 \Rightarrow x = \frac{-5 \pm \sqrt{21}}{2}$ which are in R.

$$\therefore \quad f^{-1}(8) = \left\{\frac{-5+\sqrt{21}}{2}, \frac{-5-\sqrt{21}}{2}\right\}$$

Now, let $f^{-1}(9) = x$. Then, $f(x) = 9$.

$\Rightarrow \quad x^2 + 5x + 9 = 9 \Rightarrow x^2 + 5x = 0 \Rightarrow x(x+5) = 0 \Rightarrow x = 0, -5$, which are in R

$\therefore \quad f^{-1}(9) = \{0, -5\}$

EXAMPLE 3 *If the function $f: C \to C$ be defined by $f(x) = x^2 - 1$, find $f^{-1}(-5)$ and $f^{-1}(8)$.*

SOLUTION Let $f^{-1}(-5) = x$. Then,

$f(x) = -5 \Rightarrow x^2 - 1 = -5 \Rightarrow x^2 = -4 \Rightarrow x = \sqrt{-4} \Rightarrow x = \pm 2i$, which are in C.

$\therefore \quad f^{-1}(-5) = \{2i, -2i\}$

Again, let $f^{-1}(8) = x$. Then, $f(x) = 8 \Rightarrow x^2 - 1 = 8 \Rightarrow x^2 = 9 \Rightarrow x = \pm 3$, which are in C.

$\therefore \quad f^{-1}(8) = \{-3, 3\}$

EXAMPLE 4 *Let $f: R \to R$ be defined as $f(x) = x^2 + 1$. Find:*

(i) $f^{-1}(-5)$ (ii) $f^{-1}(26)$ (iii) $f^{-1}\{10, 37\}$

SOLUTION (i) Let $f^{-1}(-5) = x$. Then,

$f(x) = -5 \Rightarrow x^2 + 1 = -5 \Rightarrow x^2 = -6 \Rightarrow x = \pm\sqrt{-6}$, which is not in R.

So, $f^{-1}(-5) = \phi$.

(ii) Let $f^{-1}(26) = x$. Then, $f(x) = 26 \Rightarrow x^2 + 1 = 26 \Rightarrow x^2 = 25 \Rightarrow x = \pm 5$, which are real numbers

$\therefore \quad f^{-1}(26) = \{-5, 5\}$

(iii) $f^{-1}\{10, 37\} = \{x \in R : f(x) = 10 \text{ or } f(x) = 37\}, = \{x \in R : x^2 + 1 = 10 \text{ or } x^2 + 1 = 37\}$

$= \{x \in R : x^2 = 9 \text{ or } x^2 = 36\} = \{3, -3, 6, -6\}$

2.6 INVERSE OF A FUNCTION

Let A and B be two sets and let $f: A \to B$ be a function. If we follow a rule in which elements of B are associated to their pre-images, then we find that under such a rule there may be some elements in B which are not associated to elements in A. This happens when f is not an onto map. Therefore all elements in B will be associated to some elements in A if f is an onto map. Also, if it is a many-one function then under the said rule an element in B may be associated to more than one element in A. Therefore an element in B will be associated to a unique element in A if f is an injective map.

It follows from the above discussion that if $f: A \to B$ is a bijection, we can define a new function from B to A which associates each element $y \in B$ to its pre-image $f^{-1}(y) \in A$. Such a function is known as the inverse of function f and is denoted by f^{-1}.

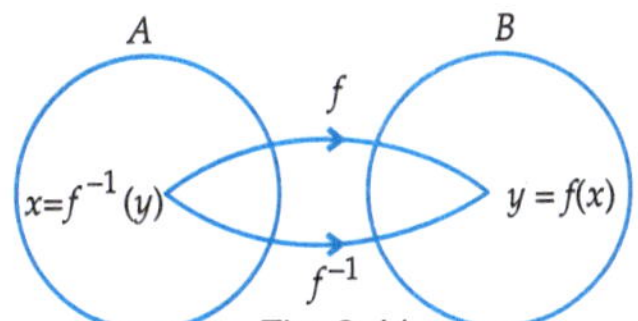

Fig. 2.41

DEFINITION *Let $f: A \to B$ be a bijection. Then a function $g: B \to A$ which associates each element $y \in B$ to a unique element $x \in A$ such that $f(x) = y$ is called the inverse of f.*

i.e., $f(x) = y \Leftrightarrow g(y) = x$

The inverse of f is generally denoted by f^{-1}.

Thus, if $f: A \to B$ is a bijection, then $f^{-1}: B \to A$ is such that $f(x) = y \Leftrightarrow f^{-1}(y) = x$.

In order to find the inverse of a bijection, we may follow the following algorithm.

ALGORITHM

Let $f: A \to B$ be a bijection. To find the inverse of f we follow the following steps:

Step I *Put $f(x) = y$, where $y \in B$ and $x \in A$.*

Step II *Solve $f(x) = y$ to obtain x in terms of y.*

Step III *In the relation obtained in step II replace x by $f^{-1}(y)$ to obtain the required inverse of f.*

Following examples will illustrate the above algorithm.

ILLUSTRATIVE EXAMPLES

BASED ON BASIC CONCEPTS (BASIC)

EXAMPLE 1 *If $A = \{1, 2, 3, 4\}$, $B = \{2, 4, 6, 8\}$ and $f: A \to B$ is given by $f(x) = 2x$, then write f and f^{-1} as a set of ordered pairs.*

SOLUTION Clearly, $f(1) = 2$, $f(2) = 4$, $f(3) = 6$ and $f(4) = 8$.

$\therefore$ $f = \{(1, 2), (2, 4), (3, 6), (4, 8)\}$ which is clearly a bijection.

On interchanging the components of ordered pairs in f, we obtain

$$f^{-1} = \{(2, 1), (4, 2), (6, 3), (8, 4)\}.$$

EXAMPLE 2 *Let $S = \{1, 2, 3\}$. Determine whether the function $f: S \to S$ defined as below have inverse. Find f^{-1}, if it exists.*

(i) $f = \{(1, 1), (2, 2), (3, 3)\}$ (ii) $f = \{(1, 2), (2, 1), (3, 1)\}$ (iii) $f = \{(1, 3), (3, 2), (2, 1)\}$ **[NCERT]**

SOLUTION (i) Clearly, $f: S \to S$ is a bijection. So, f is invertible and its inverse is given by $f^{-1} = \{(1, 1), (2, 2), (3, 3)\}$.

(ii) Clearly, $f(2) = f(3) = 1$. Therefore, f is may-one and hence it is not invertible.

(iii) Clearly, $f: S \to S$ is a bijection and hence invertible. The inverse of f is given by

$$f^{-1} = \{(3, 1), (2, 3), (1, 2)\}.$$

EXAMPLE 3 *Consider $f: \{1, 2, 3\} \to \{a, b, c\}$ given by $f(1) = a$, $f(2) = b$ and $f(3) = c$. Find the inverse $(f^{-1})^{-1}$ of f^{-1}. Show that $(f^{-1})^{-1} = f$.* **[NCERT]**

SOLUTION We have, $f = \{(1, a), (2, b), (3, c)\}$ ...(i)

Clearly, f is a bijection and hence invertible. The inverse of f is given by

$$f^{-1} = \{(a, 1), (b, 2), (c, 3)\} \Rightarrow (f^{-1})^{-1} = \{(1, a), (2, b), (3, c)\} \quad ...(ii)$$

From (i) and (ii), we find that: $(f^{-1})^{-1} = f$.

EXAMPLE 4 *If $f: R \to R$ is defined by $f(x) = 2x + 7$. Prove that f is a bijection. Also, find the inverse of f.*

SOLUTION *Injectivity* : Let x, y be any two elements of R. Then,

$$f(x) = f(y) \Rightarrow 2x + 7 = 2y + 7 \Rightarrow x = y$$

$\therefore$ f is an injective map.

Surjectivity : Let y be an arbitrary element of R(co-domain). Then,

$$y = f(x) \Rightarrow y = 2x + 7 \Rightarrow x = \frac{y - 7}{2}.$$

Clearly, $x = \frac{y-7}{2} \in R$ for all $y \in R$. Thus, for all $y \in R$ (co-domain) there exists $x = \frac{y-7}{2} \in R$ such that $f(x) = y$. In other words every element in R (co-domain) has its pre-image in R (domain). Therefore, f is a surjective map. Hence, f is a bijection. Consequently f^{-1} exists.

Inverse of f: Let $x \in R$ (domain) and $y \in R$ (co-domain) such that $f(x) = y$. Then,

$$f(x) = y \Rightarrow 2x + 7 = y \Rightarrow x = \frac{y-7}{2} \Rightarrow f^{-1}(y) = \frac{y-7}{2}.$$

Thus, $f^{-1} : R \to R$ is defined as $f^{-1}(x) = \frac{x-7}{2}$ for all $x \in R$.

EXAMPLE 5 *If $f : R \to R$ is a bijection given by $f(x) = x^3 + 3$, find $f^{-1}(x)$.*

SOLUTION Let $f(x) = y$. Then,

$$f(x) = y \Rightarrow x^3 + 3 = y \Rightarrow x = (y-3)^{1/3} \Rightarrow f^{-1}(y) = (y-3)^{1/3}$$

Thus, $f^{-1} : R \to R$ is defined as $f^{-1}(x) = (x-3)^{1/3}$ for all $x \in R$.

EXAMPLE 6 *Let $f : R \to R$ be defined by $f(x) = 3x - 7$. Show that f is invertible and hence find f^{-1}.*

SOLUTION In order to prove that f is invertible, it is sufficient to prove that f is a bijection.

Injectivity: Let $x, y \in R$. Then, $f(x) = f(y) \Rightarrow 3x - 7 = 3y - 7 \Rightarrow x = y$.

Thus, $f(x) = f(y) \Rightarrow x = y$ for all $x, y \in R$. So, f is an injection.

Surjectivity: Let y be an arbitrary element of R. Then,

$$f(x) = y \Rightarrow 3x - 7 = y \Rightarrow x = \frac{y+7}{3}$$

Clearly, $\frac{y+7}{3} \in R$ for all $y \in R$. Thus, for all $y \in R$ there exists $x = \frac{y+7}{3} \in R$ such that

$$f(x) = f\left(\frac{y+7}{3}\right) = 3\left(\frac{y+7}{3}\right) - 7 = y$$

So, f is a surjection. Hence, $f : R \to R$ is a bijection. Consequently, it is invertible.

Let $f(x) = y$. Then,

$$f(x) = y \Rightarrow 3x - 7 = y \Rightarrow x = \frac{y+7}{3} \Rightarrow f^{-1}(y) = \frac{y+7}{3}$$

Therefore, $f^{-1} : R \to R$ is given by $f^{-1}(x) = \frac{x+7}{3}$.

EXAMPLE 7 *Show that $f : R - \{0\} \to R - \{0\}$ given by $f(x) = \frac{3}{x}$ is invertible and it is inverse of itself.*

SOLUTION In order to prove that f is invertible, it is sufficient to show that it is a bijection.

f is an injection: Let $x, y \in R - \{0\}$ such that $f(x) = f(y)$. Then,

$$f(x) = f(y) \Rightarrow \frac{3}{x} = \frac{3}{y} \Rightarrow x = y$$

Thus, $f(x) = f(y) \Rightarrow x = y$ for all $x, y \in R - \{0\}$. So, f is an injection.

f is a surjection: Let y be an arbitrary element of $R - \{0\}$. Then, $f(x) = y \Rightarrow \frac{3}{x} = y \Rightarrow x = \frac{3}{y}$.

Thus, for each $y \in R - \{0\}$, there exists $x = \frac{3}{y} \in R - \{0\}$ such that $f(x) = f\left(\frac{3}{y}\right) = \frac{3}{3/y} = y$. So, f is a surjection. Hence, f is a bijection. Consequently, it is invertible.

Let $f(x) = y$. Then,

$$f(x) = y \Rightarrow \frac{3}{x} = y \Rightarrow x = \frac{3}{y} \Rightarrow f^{-1}(y) = \frac{3}{y}$$

Thus, f^{-1} is given by $f^{-1}(x) = \frac{3}{x}$ for all $x \in R - \{0\}$. Clearly, $f(x) = f^{-1}(x)$ for all $x \in R - \{0\}$. Hence, f is inverse of itself.

BASED ON HIGHER ORDER THINKING SKILLS (HOTS)

EXAMPLE 8 Let $f : N \cup \{0\} \to N \cup \{0\}$ *be defined by* $f(n) = \begin{cases} n+1, \text{ if } n \text{ is even} \\ n-1, \text{ if } n \text{ is odd} \end{cases}$. *Show that f is invertible and* $f = f^{-1}$. **[CBSE 2014, NCERT]**

SOLUTION In Example 24 on page 2.23, we have proved that f is a bijection. So, it is invertible. In order to find f^{-1}, let $n, m \in N \cup \{0\}$ such that

$$f(n) = m$$

$$\Rightarrow \quad n+1 = m, \text{ if } n \text{ is even}$$

$$n-1 = m, \text{ if } n \text{ is odd}$$

$$\Rightarrow \quad n = \begin{cases} m-1, \text{ if } m \text{ is odd} \\ m+1, \text{ if } m \text{ is even} \end{cases} \qquad \begin{bmatrix} \text{If } n \text{ is even, then } n+1 = m \text{ is odd} \\ \text{If } n \text{ is odd, then } n-1 = m \text{ is even} \end{bmatrix}$$

$$\Rightarrow \quad f^{-1}(m) = \begin{cases} m-1, \text{ if } m \text{ is odd} \\ m+1, \text{ if } m \text{ is even} \end{cases}$$

Hence, $f^{-1}(n) = \begin{cases} n+1, \text{ if } n \text{ is even} \\ n-1, \text{ if } n \text{ is odd} \end{cases}$. Clearly, $f = f^{-1}$.

*2.6.1 PROPERTIES OF INVERSE OF A FUNCTION

THEOREM 1 *The inverse of a bijection is unique.* **[NCERT]**

PROOF Let $f : A \to B$ be a bijection. If possible, let $g : B \to A$ and $h : B \to A$ be two inverses of f. We have to prove that $g = h$. In order to prove this it is sufficient to show that $g(y) = h(y)$ for all $y \in B$. Let y be an arbitrary element of B.

Let $g(y) = x_1$ and $h(y) = x_2$. Then,

$$g(y) = x_1 \Rightarrow f(x_1) = y \qquad [\because g \text{ is inverse of } f]$$

and $$h(y) = x_2 \Rightarrow f(x_2) = y \qquad [\because h \text{ is inverse of } f]$$

$$\therefore \quad f(x_1) = f(x_2)$$

$$\Rightarrow \quad x_1 = x_2 \qquad [\because f \text{ is one-one}]$$

$$\Rightarrow \quad g(y) = h(y)$$

Thus, $g(y) = h(y)$ for all $y \in B$. Hence, $g = h$

THEOREM 2 *The inverse of a bijection is also a bijection.*

PROOF Let $f : A \to B$ be a bijection and let $g : B \to A$ be its inverse. We have to show that g is a bijection.

Injectivity of g: Let $y_1, y_2, \in B$ such that $g(y_1) = x_1$ and $g(y_2) = x_2$.

Since g is the inverse of f.

$$\therefore \quad g(y_1) = x_1 \Rightarrow f(x_1) = y_1 \text{ and } g(y_2) = x_2 \Rightarrow f(x_2) = y_2.$$

May be skipped. Not from examination point of view.

Now, $g(y_1) = g(y_2) \Rightarrow x_1 = x_2 \Rightarrow f(x_1) = f(x_2) \Rightarrow y_1 = y_2$

$\therefore$ g is an injective map.

Surjectivity of g: In order to prove that $g: B \to A$ is a surjection, we have to show that every element in A has its pre-image in B under funtion g. So, let x be an arbitrary element of A. Then,

$x \in A$

$\Rightarrow$ there exists $y \in B$ such that $f(x) = y$ [$\because$ f is a function from A to B]

$\Rightarrow$ there exists $y \in B$ such that $g(y) = x$ [$\because$ g is inverse of f]

Thus, for each $x \in A$, there exists $y \in B$ such that $g(y) = x$. So, g is a surjective map.

Hence, g is a bijection.

THEOREM 3 *If $f: A \to B$ is a bijection and $g: B \to A$ is the inverse of f, then $fog = I_B$ and $gof = I_A$, where I_A and I_B are the identity functions on the sets A and B respectively.*

PROOF In order to prove that $gof = I_A$ and $fog = I_B$, we have to prove that

$(gof)(x) = x$ for all $x \in A$ and $(fog)(y) = y$ for all $y \in B$

Let x be an element of A such that $f(x) = y$. Then,

$g(y) = x$ [$\because$ g is inverse of f]

Now, $(gof)(x) = g(f(x)) = g(y) = x \Rightarrow (gof)(x) = x$ for all $x \in A \Rightarrow gof = I_A$.

We have,

$(fog)(y) = f(g(y)) = f(x) = y \Rightarrow fog(y) = y$ for all $y \in B \Rightarrow fog = I_B$.

Hence, $gof = I_A$ and $fog = I_B$.

REMARK *In the above property, if we have $B = A$. Then, we find that for every bijection $f: A \to A$ there exists a bijection $g: A \to A$ such that $fog = gof = I_A$.*

THEOREM 4 *If $f: A \to B$ and $g: B \to C$ are two bijections, then $gof: A \to C$ is a bijection and $(gof)^{-1} = f^{-1}og^{-1}$.* **[NCERT]**

PROOF It is given that

$$\left.\begin{array}{l} f: A \to B \text{ is a bijection} \\ g: B \to C \text{ is a bijection} \end{array}\right\} \Rightarrow gof: A \to C \text{ is a bijection} \Rightarrow (gof)^{-1}: C \to A \text{ exists.}$$

Now, $$\left.\begin{array}{l} f: A \to B \text{ is a bijection} \Rightarrow f^{-1}: B \to A \text{ is a bijection} \\ g: B \to C \text{ is a bijection} \Rightarrow g^{-1}: C \to B \text{ is a bijection} \end{array}\right\} \Rightarrow f^{-1}og^{-1}: C \to A$$

Let $x \in A, y \in B$ and $z \in C$ such that $f(x) = y$ and $g(y) = z$. Then,

$(gof)(x) = g(f(x)) = g(y) = z \Rightarrow (gof)^{-1}(z) = x$ ...(i)

Now, $f(x) = y$ and $g(y) = z \Rightarrow f^{-1}(y) = x$ and, $g^{-1}(z) = y$

$\therefore$ $(f^{-1}og^{-1})(z) = f^{-1}(g^{-1}(z)) = f^{-1}(y) = x$ ...(ii)

From (i) and (ii), we obtain: $(gof)^{-1}(z) = (f^{-1}og^{-1})(z)$ for all $z \in C$.

Hence, $(gof)^{-1} = f^{-1}og^{-1}$.

THEOREM 5 *Let $f: A \to B$ and $g: B \to A$ be two functions such that $gof = I_A$ and $fog = I_B$. Then, f and g are bijections and $g = f^{-1}$.*

PROOF *f is one-one :* Let $x, y \in A$ such that $f(x) = f(y)$. Then,

$f(x) = f(y)$

$\Rightarrow \quad g(f(x)) = g(f(y))$

$\Rightarrow \quad (gof)(x) = (gof)(y) \Rightarrow I_A(x) = I_A(y) \Rightarrow x = y$ $\quad [\because gof = I_A]$

$\therefore \quad f$ is a one-one map.

f is onto : Let $y \in B$ and let $g(y) = x$. Then,

$g(y) = x$

$\Rightarrow \quad f(g(y)) = f(x)$

$\Rightarrow \quad (fog)(y) = f(x)$

$\Rightarrow \quad I_B(y) = f(x)$ $\quad [\because fog = I_B]$

$\Rightarrow \quad y = f(x)$ $\quad [\because I_B(y) = y]$

Thus, for each $y \in B$, there exists $x \in A$ such that $f(x) = y$. So, f is onto. Hence, f is a bijection.

Similarly, it can be proved that g is a bijection. Now we shall show that $g = f^{-1}$.

Since $f: A \to B$ is a bijection. Therefore, f^{-1} exists.

Now, $\quad fog = I_B$

$\Rightarrow \quad f^{-1} o (fog) = f^{-1} o I_B$

$\Rightarrow \quad (f^{-1} of) og = f^{-1} o I_B$ $\quad$ [By associativity]

$\Rightarrow \quad I_A o g = f^{-1} o I_B$ $\quad [\because f^{-1} of = I_A]$

$\Rightarrow \quad g = f^{-1}$ $\quad [\because I_A og = g$ and $f^{-1} o I_B = f^{-1}]$

Hence, $g = f^{-1}$

THEOREM 6 *Let $f: A \to B$ be an invertible function. Show that the inverse of f^{-1} is f.*

i.e., $\quad (f^{-1})^{-1} = f.$ **[NCERT]**

SOLUTION Since inverse of a bijection is also a bijection. Therefore, $f^{-1}: B \to A$ is a bijection and hence invertible. As $f^{-1}: B \to A$ is a bijection. Therefore, $(f^{-1})^{-1}: A \to B$ is also a bijection.

Let x be an arbitrary element of A such that $f(x) = y$. Then,

$f^{-1}(y) = x$ $\quad [\because f^{-1}$ is the inverse of $f]$

$\Rightarrow \quad (f^{-1})^{-1}(x) = y$ $\quad [\because (f^{-1})^{-1}$ is the inverse of $f^{-1}]$

$\Rightarrow \quad (f^{-1})^{-1}(x) = f(x)$ $\quad [\because f(x) = y]$

Since x is an arbitrary element of A. Therefore, $(f^{-1})^{-1}(x) = f(x)$ for all $x \in A$.

Hence, $(f^{-1})^{-1} = f.$ **Q.E.D.**

ALITER Since $f: A \to B$ is invertible and $f^{-1}: B \to A$ is inverse of f.

$\therefore \quad f^{-1} of = I_A$ and $fof^{-1} = I_B \Rightarrow f$ is inverse of $f^{-1} \Rightarrow f = (f^{-1})^{-1}$ **Q.E.D.**

REMARK 1 *Sometimes $f: A \to B$ is one-one but not onto. In such a case f is not invertible. But, $f: A \to$ Range (f) is both one and onto. So, it is invertible and its inverse can be found.*

2.6.2 RELATION BETWEEN GRAPHS OF A FUNCTION AND ITS INVERSE

The graph of a bijection f and its inverse f^{-1} are closely related. If (a, b) is a point on the graph of f, then $b = f(a)$ and $a = f^{-1}(b)$. As $b \in$ Domain of f^{-1}, therefore $(b, f^{-1}(b))$ is a point on the graph of f^{-1}. But, $(b, f^{-1}(b)) = (b, a)$. Therefore, (b, a) is on the graph of f^{-1}. Thus, if (a, b) is a point on the graph of f, then (b, a) is a point on the graph of f^{-1}. But, (a, b) and (b, a) are reflections of one another in the line $y = x$. Thus, the graph of f^{-1} may be obtained by reflecting the graph of f in the line mirror $y = x$. That is the graphs of f and f^{-1} are mirror images of each other in the line mirror $y = x$ (see Fig. 2.42). It is also evident from the above discussion that if the graphs of $f(x)$ and $f^{-1}(x)$ intersect each other, their points of intersection lie on the line $y = x$. Consequently, solutions of the equation $f(x) = f^{-1}(x)$ are same as that of $f(x) = x$ or, $f^{-1}(x) = x$.

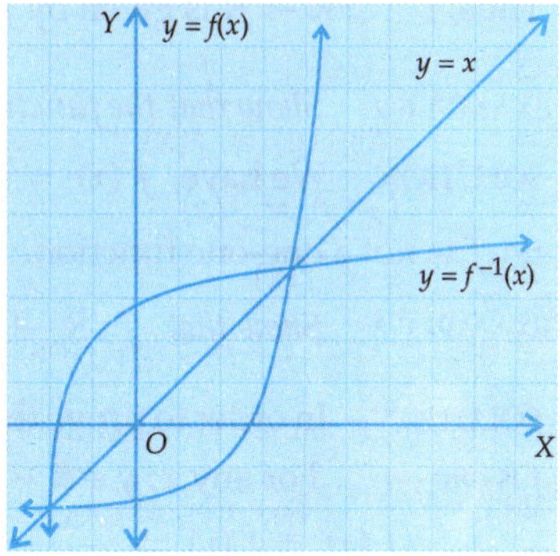

Fig. 2.42

REMARK 2 *Theorem 5 on page 2.44 suggests us an alternative method to prove the invertibility of a function. It states that if $f : A \to B$ and $g : B \to A$ are two functions such that $gof = I_A$ and $fog = I_B$, then f and g are inverse of each other.*

Theorem 5 on page 2.44 suggests the following algorithm to find the inverse of an invertible function.

ALGORITHM

Step I *Obtain the function and check its bijectivity.*

Step II *If f is a bijection, then it is invertible.*

In order to find the inverse of f, put $fof^{-1}(x) = x \Rightarrow f(f^{-1}(x)) = x$

Step III *Use the formula for $f(x)$ and replace x by $f^{-1}(x)$ in it to obtain the LHS of $f(f^{-1}(x)) = x$.*

Solve this equation for $f^{-1}(x)$ to get $f^{-1}(x)$.

Following examples will illustrate the above algorithm.

ILLUSTRATIVE EXAMPLES

BASED ON BASIC CONCEPTS (BASIC)

EXAMPLE 1 *Prove that the function $f : R \to R$ defined as $f(x) = 2x - 3$ is invertible. Also, find f^{-1}.*

SOLUTION In order to prove that f is invertible, it is sufficient to show that f is a bijection.

f is one-one : Let $x, y \in R$. Then,

$$f(x) = f(y) \Rightarrow 2x - 3 = 2y - 3 \Rightarrow x = y$$

Thus, $f(x) = f(y) \Rightarrow x = y$ for all $x, y \in R$. So, f is one-one.

f is onto : Let y be an arbitrary element in R (co-domain of f). Then,

$$f(x) = y \Rightarrow 2x - 3 = y \Rightarrow x = \frac{y+3}{2}$$

Clearly, $x = \frac{y+3}{2} \in R$ (domain) for all $y \in R$ (co-domain). Thus, for each $y \in R$ there exists $x \in R$ such that $f(x) = y$. So, f is onto.

Since $f: R \to R$ is one-one and onto both. So, it is a bijection and hence invertible.

Now,

$$fof^{-1}(x) = x \Rightarrow f(f^{-1}(x)) = x \Rightarrow 2f^{-1}(x) - 3 = x \qquad [\because f(x) = 2x - 3]$$

$$\Rightarrow \quad f^{-1}(x) = \frac{x+3}{2}$$

Thus, $f^{-1}: R \to R$ is given by $f^{-1}(x) = \frac{x+3}{2}$ for all $x \in R$.

EXAMPLE 2 *Show that the function $f: R \to R$ is given by $f(x) = x^2 + 1$ is not invertible.*

SOLUTION We have, $f(x) = x^2 + 1$. Clearly, $-2 \neq 2$ but, $f(-2) = f(2) = 5$.

So, f is not a one-one function. Hence, f is not invertible.

EXAMPLE 3 *Show that $f: R - \{-1\} \to R - \{1\}$ given by $f(x) = \frac{x}{x+1}$ is invertible. Also, find f^{-1}.*

SOLUTION In order to prove the invertibility of $f(x)$, it is sufficient to show that it is a bijection.

f is one-one : For any $x, y \in R - \{-1\}$

$$f(x) = f(y) \Rightarrow \frac{x}{x+1} = \frac{y}{y+1} \Rightarrow xy + x = xy + y \Rightarrow x = y.$$

So, f is one-one .

f is onto: Let $y \in R - \{1\}$. Then, $f(x) = y \Rightarrow \frac{x}{x+1} = y \Rightarrow x = \frac{y}{1-y}$

Clearly, $x \in R$ for all $y \in R - \{1\}$. Also, $x \neq -1$. Because,

$$x = -1 \Rightarrow \frac{y}{1-y} = -1 \Rightarrow y = -1 + y, \text{ which is not possible.}$$

Thus, for each $y \in R - \{1\}$ there exists $x = \frac{y}{1-y} \in R - \{-1\}$ such that $f(x) = \frac{x}{x+1} = \frac{\frac{y}{1-y}}{\frac{y}{1-y}+1} = y.$

So, f is onto. Thus, f is both one-one and onto. Consequently it is invertible.

Now, $fof^{-1}(x) = x$ for all $x \in R - \{1\}$

$$\Rightarrow \quad f(f^{-1}(x)) = x \Rightarrow \frac{f^{-1}(x)}{f^{-1}(x)+1} = x \Rightarrow f^{-1}(x) = \frac{x}{1-x} \text{ for all } x \in R - \{1\}.$$

EXAMPLE 4 *Show that $f: [-1, 1] \to R$, given by $f(x) = \frac{x}{x+2}$ is one-one. Find the inverse of the function $f: [-1, 1] \to$ Range (f).* **[NCERT]**

SOLUTION Let x, y be any two elements of $[-1, 1]$. Then,

$$f(x) = f(y) \Rightarrow \frac{x}{x+2} = \frac{y}{y+2} \Rightarrow xy + 2x = xy + 2y \Rightarrow x = y$$

So, $f: [-1, 1] \to$ Range (f) is one-one.

Obviously, $f: [-1, 1] \to$ Range (f) is onto and hence invertible. Let f^{-1} denote the inverse of f. Then,

$$fof^{-1}(x) = x \text{ for all } x \in \text{Range}(f)$$

$$\Rightarrow \quad f(f^{-1}(x)) = x \Rightarrow \frac{f^{-1}(x)}{f^{-1}(x)+2} = x \Rightarrow f^{-1}(x) = x f^{-1}(x) + 2x \Rightarrow f^{-1}(x) = \frac{2x}{1-x}$$

Hence, f^{-1}: Range $(f): [-1, 1]$ is given by $f^{-1}(x) = \frac{2x}{1-x}$

BASED ON LOWER ORDER THINKING SKILLS (LOTS)

EXAMPLE 5 *Let $f : R \to R$ be defined as $f(x) = 10x + 7$. Find the function $g : R \to R$ such that $gof = fog = I_R$.* [NCERT, CBSE 2011]

SOLUTION We have, $fog = I_R$

$\Rightarrow \quad fog(x) = I_R(x)$ for all $x \in R$

$\Rightarrow \quad f(g(x)) = x$ for all $x \in R \Rightarrow 10\, g(x) + 7 = x$ for all $x \in R \Rightarrow g(x) = \dfrac{x-7}{10}$ for all $x \in R$

ALITER We have, $fog = gof = I_R \Rightarrow g$ is the inverse of f. Let $f(x) = y$. Then,

$$10x + 7 = y \Rightarrow x = \frac{y-7}{10} \Rightarrow f^{-1}(y) = \frac{y-7}{10} \Rightarrow f^{-1}(x) = \frac{x-7}{10}$$

Hence, $g(x) = \dfrac{x-7}{10}$

BASED ON HIGHER ORDER THINKING SKILLS (HOTS)

EXAMPLE 6 *If the function $f : [1, \infty) \to [1, \infty)$ defined by $f(x) = 2^{x(x-1)}$ is invertible, find $f^{-1}(x)$.*

SOLUTION It is given that f is invertible with f^{-1} as its inverse.

$\therefore \quad (fof^{-1})(x) = x$ for all $x \in [1, \infty)$

$\Rightarrow f(f^{-1}(x)) = x \Rightarrow 2^{f^{-1}(x)\{f^{-1}(x) - 1\}} = x$

$\Rightarrow f^{-1}(x)\{f^{-1}(x) - 1\} = \log_2 x \Rightarrow \{f^{-1}(x)\}^2 - f^{-1}(x) - \log_2 x = 0$

$\Rightarrow f^{-1}(x) = \dfrac{1 \pm \sqrt{1 + 4\log_2 x}}{2} \Rightarrow f^{-1}(x) = \dfrac{1 + \sqrt{1 + 4\log_2 x}}{2} \quad [\because f^{-1}(x) \in [1, \infty) \therefore f^{-1}(x) \ge 1]$

EXAMPLE 7 *Find the value of parameter α for which the function $f(x) = 1 + \alpha x$, $\alpha \ne 0$ is the inverse of itself.*

SOLUTION Clearly, $f(x)$ is a bijection from R to itself.

Now, $\quad fof^{-1}(x) = x \Rightarrow f(f^{-1}(x)) = x \Rightarrow 1 + \alpha f^{-1}(x) = x \Rightarrow f^{-1}(x) = \dfrac{x-1}{\alpha}$

It is given that

$\quad f(x) = f^{-1}(x)$ for all $x \in R$

$\Rightarrow \quad 1 + \alpha x = \dfrac{x-1}{\alpha}$ for all $x \in R$

$\Rightarrow \quad \alpha x + 1 = \left(\dfrac{1}{\alpha}\right)x + \left(\dfrac{-1}{\alpha}\right)$ for all $x \in R$

$\Rightarrow \quad \alpha = \dfrac{1}{\alpha}$ and $1 = -\dfrac{1}{\alpha} \Rightarrow \alpha^2 = 1$ and $\alpha = -1 \Rightarrow \alpha = -1.$

EXAMPLE 8 *Let $f : N \to Y$ be a function defined as $f(x) = 4x + 3$, where $Y = \{y \in N : y = 4x + 3$ for some $x \in N\}$. Show that f is invertible. Find its inverse.* [NCERT]

SOLUTION In order to prove that f is invertible, it is sufficient to show that it is a bijection.

f is one-one: For any $x, y \in N$, we find that

$\quad f(x) = f(y) \Rightarrow 4x + 3 = 4y + 3 \Rightarrow x = y$

So, $f : N \to Y$ is one-one.

f is onto: Let y be an arbitrary element of Y. Then, there exists $x \in N$ such that

$\quad y = 4x + 3$ [By definition of Y]

$\Rightarrow \quad y = f(x)$

Thus, for each $y \in N$ there exists $x \in N$ such that $f(x) = y$. So, $f : N \to Y$ is onto.
Thus, $f : N \to Y$ is both one and onto. Consequently, it is invertible. Let f^{-1} be the inverse of f. Then,

$fof^{-1}(x) = x$ for all $x \in Y$

$\Rightarrow \quad f(f^{-1}(x)) = x$ for all $x \in Y$

$\Rightarrow \quad 4f^{-1}(x) + 3 = x$ for all $x \in Y$ [Using definition of f]

$\Rightarrow \quad f^{-1}(x) = \dfrac{x-3}{4}$ for all $x \in Y$

Hence, $f^{-1} : Y \to N$ is given by $f^{-1}(x) = \dfrac{x-3}{4}$ for all $x \in Y$.

EXAMPLE 9 *Let $Y = \{n^2 : n \in N\} \subset N$. Consider $f : N \to Y$ given by $f(n) = n^2$. Show that f is invertible. Find the inverse of f.* **[NCERT]**

SOLUTION In order to prove that f is invertible, it is sufficient to show that it is a bijection.
f is one-one: For any $n, m \in N$, we find that

$f(n) = f(m) \Rightarrow n^2 = m^2 \Rightarrow n = m$ [$\because n, m \in N$]

So, $f : N \to Y$ is one-one.
f is onto: Let y be an arbitrary element of Y. Then there exists $n \in N$ such that

$y = n^2$ [By definition of Y]

$\Rightarrow \quad y = f(n)$

Thus, for each $y \in Y$ there exists $n \in N$ such that $y = f(n)$. So, $f : N \to Y$ is onto.
Hence, $f : N \to Y$ is a bijection. Consequently, it is invertible.
Let f^{-1} denote the inverse of f. Then,

$fof^{-1}(x) = x$ for all $x \in Y$

$\Rightarrow \quad f(f^{-1}(x)) = x$ for all $x \in Y$

$\Rightarrow \quad \{f^{-1}(x)\}^2 = x$ for all $x \in Y$ [Using the definition of f]

$\Rightarrow \quad f^{-1}(x) = \sqrt{x}$ for all $x \in Y$

Hence, $f^{-1} : Y \to N$ is given by $f^{-1}(x) = \sqrt{x}$ for all $x \in Y$.

EXAMPLE 10 *Let $f : N \to R$ be a function defined as $f(x) = 4x^2 + 12x + 15$. Show that $f : N \to$ Range (f) is invertible. Find the inverse of f.* **[CBSE 2010]**

SOLUTION In order to prove that f is invertible, it is sufficient to show that $f : N \to$ Range (f) is a bijection.
f is one-one: For any $x, y \in N$, we find that

$f(x) = f(y)$

$\Rightarrow \quad 4x^2 + 12x + 15 = 4y^2 + 12y + 15$

$\Rightarrow \quad 4(x^2 - y^2) + 12(x - y) = 0$

$\Rightarrow \quad (x - y)(4x + 4y + 3) = 0$

$\Rightarrow \quad x - y = 0$ [$\because 4x + 4y + 3 \neq 0$ for any $x, y \in N$]

$\Rightarrow \quad x = y$

So, $f : N \to$ Range (f) is one-one.

Obviously, $f : N \to$ Range (f) is onto. Hence, $f : N \to$ Range (f) is invertible. Let f^{-1} denote the inverse of f. Then,

$$fof^{-1}(x) = x \text{ for all } x \in \text{Range}(f)$$

$\Rightarrow$ $f(f^{-1}(x)) = x$ for all $x \in$ Range(f)

$\Rightarrow$ $4\{f^{-1}(x)\}^2 + 12 f^{-1}(x) + 15 = x$ for all $x \in$ Range(f)

$\Rightarrow$ $4\{f^{-1}(x)\}^2 + 12 f^{-1}(x) + 15 - x = 0$

$\Rightarrow$ $f^{-1}(x) = \dfrac{-12 \pm \sqrt{144 - 16(15 - x)}}{8} = \dfrac{-12 \pm \sqrt{16x - 96}}{8} = \dfrac{-3 \pm \sqrt{x - 6}}{2}$

$\Rightarrow$ $f^{-1}(x) = \dfrac{-3 + \sqrt{x - 6}}{2}$ $\quad [\because f^{-1}(x) \in N \therefore f^{-1}(x) > 0]$

EXERCISE 2.3

BASIC

1. State with reasons whether following functions have inverse:
   (i) $f : \{1, 2, 3, 4\} \to \{10\}$ with $f = \{(1, 10), (2, 10), (3, 10), (4, 10)\}$
   (ii) $g : \{5, 6, 7, 8\} \to \{1, 2, 3, 4\}$ with $g = \{(5, 4), (6, 3), (7, 4), (8, 2)\}$
   (iii) $h : \{2, 3, 4, 5\} \to \{7, 9, 11, 13\}$ with $h = \{(2, 7), (3, 9), (4, 11), (5, 13)\}$
2. Find f^{-1} if it exists : $f : A \to B$ where
   (i) $A = \{0, -1, -3, 2\}$; $B = \{-9, -3, 0, 6\}$ and $f(x) = 3x$.
   (ii) $A = \{1, 3, 5, 7, 9\}$; $B = \{0, 1, 9, 25, 49, 81\}$ and $f(x) = x^2$.
3. Consider $f : \{1, 2, 3\} \to \{a, b, c\}$ and $g : \{a, b, c\} \to \{\text{apple, ball, cat}\}$ defined as $f(1) = a$, $f(2) = b$, $f(3) = c$, $g(a) = \text{apple}$, $g(b) = \text{ball}$ and $g(c) = \text{cat}$. Show that f, g and gof are invertible. Find f^{-1}, g^{-1} and $(gof)^{-1}$ and show that $(gof)^{-1} = f^{-1} o\, g^{-1}$. [NCERT]
4. Let $A = \{1, 2, 3, 4\}$; $B = \{3, 5, 7, 9\}$; $C = \{7, 23, 47, 79\}$ and $f : A \to B$, $g : B \to C$ be defined as $f(x) = 2x + 1$ and $g(x) = x^2 - 2$. Express $(gof)^{-1}$ and $f^{-1} o g^{-1}$ as the sets of ordered pairs and verify that $(gof)^{-1} = f^{-1} o g^{-1}$.
5. Show that the function $f : Q \to Q$ defined by $f(x) = 3x + 5$ is invertible. Also, find f^{-1}.
6. Consider $f : R \to R$ given by $f(x) = 4x + 3$. Show that f is invertible. Find the inverse of f. [NCERT]
7. Consider $f : R^+ \to [4, \infty)$ given by $f(x) = x^2 + 4$. Show that f is invertible with inverse f^{-1} of f given by $f^{-1}(x) = \sqrt{x - 4}$, where R^+ is the set of all non-negative real numbers. [NCERT, CBSE 2013]
8. If $f(x) = \dfrac{4x + 3}{6x - 4}$, $x \neq \dfrac{2}{3}$, show that $fof(x) = x$ for all $x \neq \dfrac{2}{3}$. What is the inverse of f? [CBSE 2012, 2013, 2020, NCERT]
9. If $f : R \to R$ be defined by $f(x) = x^3 - 3$, then prove that f^{-1} exists and find a formula for f^{-1}. Hence, find $f^{-1}(24)$ and $f^{-1}(5)$.
10. A function $f : R \to R$ is defined as $f(x) = x^3 + 4$. Is it a bijection or not? In case it is a bijection, find $f^{-1}(3)$. [CBSE 2020]
11. If $f : Q \to Q$, $g : Q \to Q$ are two functions defined by $f(x) = 2x$ and $g(x) = x + 2$, show that f and g are bijective maps. Verify that $(gof)^{-1} = f^{-1} og^{-1}$.
12. Let $A = R - \{3\}$ and $B = R - \{1\}$. Consider the function $f : A \to B$ defined by $f(x) = \dfrac{x - 2}{x - 3}$. Show that f is one-one and onto and hence find f^{-1}. [CBSE 2012, 2014]

13. Let $f : N \to N$ be a function defined as $f(x) = 9x^2 + 6x - 5$. Show that $f : N \to S$, where S is the range of f, is invertible. Find the inverse of f and hence find $f^{-1}(43)$ and $f^{-1}(163)$. **[CBSE 2016, 2017]**

14. Let $f : R - \left\{-\frac{4}{3}\right\} \to R$ be a function defined as $f(x) = \frac{4x}{3x+4}$. Show that $f : R - \left\{-\frac{4}{3}\right\} \to$ Rang (f) is one-one and onto. Hence, find f^{-1}. **[CBSE 2017, 2020, 2023]**

15. Let $A = R - \{2\}$ and $B = R - \{1\}$. If $f : A \to B$ is a function defined by $f(x) = \frac{x-1}{x-2}$, show that f is one-one and onto. Find f^{-1}. **[CBSE 2019]**

BASED ON LOTS

16. Consider $f : R^+ \to [-5, \infty)$ given by $f(x) = 9x^2 + 6x - 5$. Show that f is invertible with $f^{-1}(x) = \frac{\sqrt{x+6} - 1}{3}$. **[NCERT]**

17. Consider the function $f : R^+ \to [-9, \infty)$ given by $f(x) = 5x^2 + 6x - 9$. Prove that f is invertible with $f^{-1}(y) = \frac{\sqrt{54+5y} - 3}{5}$. **[CBSE 2015]**

18. Show that the function $f : N \to N$ defined by $f(x) = x^2 + x + 1$ is one-one but not onto. Find the inverse of $f : N \to S$, where S is range of f. **[CBSE 2019]**

19. Consider the bijective function $f : R^+ \to (7, \infty)$ given by $f(x) = 16x^2 + 24x + 7$, where R^+ is the set of positive real numbers. Find the inverse function of f. **[CBSE 2020]**

BASED ON HOTS

20. Let $f : [-1, \infty) \to [-1, \infty)$ is given by $f(x) = (x+1)^2 - 1$. Show that f is invertible. Also, find the set $S = \{x : f(x) = f^{-1}(x)\}$.

21. Let $A = \{x \in R \mid -1 \le x \le 1\}$ and let $f : A \to A, g : A \to A$ be two functions defined by $f(x) = x^2$ and $g(x) = \sin \frac{\pi x}{2}$. Show that g^{-1} exists but f^{-1} does not exist. Also, find g^{-1}.

22. Let f be a function from R to R such that $f(x) = \cos(x + 2)$. Is f invertible? Justify your answer.

23. If $A = \{1, 2, 3, 4\}$ and $B = \{a, b, c, d\}$. Define any four bijections from A to B. Also, give their inverse functions.

24. Let A and B be two sets each with finite number of elements. Assume that there is an injective map from A to B and that there is an injective map from B to A. Prove that there is a bijection from A to B.

25. If $f : A \to A, g : A \to A$ are two bijections, then prove that
    (i) fog is an injection (ii) fog is a surjection.

ANSWERS

1. (i) No, f is many-one (ii) No, g is many-one (iii) Yes, h is a bijection
2. (i) $f^{-1} = \{(-9, -3), (-3, -1), (0, 0), (6, 2)\}$ (ii) f^{-1} does not exist as f is not surjective.
3. $f^{-1} = \{(a, 1), (b, 2), (c, 3)\}$, $g^{-1} = \{(\text{apple}, a), (\text{ball}, b), (\text{cat}, c)\}$

and, $(gof)^{-1} = \{(\text{apple}, 1), (\text{ball}, 2)\ (\text{cat}, 3)\}$

4. $(gof)^{-1} = f^{-1} o g^{-1} = \{(7, 1), (23, 2), (47, 3), (79, 4)\}$ 5. $f^{-1}(x) = \frac{x-5}{3}$

6. $f^{-1}(x) = \frac{x-3}{4}$ 8. $f^{-1}(x) = \frac{4x+3}{6x-4}$ 9. $f^{-1}(x) = (3+x)^{1/3}, f^{-1}(24) = 3, f^{-1}(5) = 2$

10. Bijection, $f^{-1}(3) = -1$ 12. $f^{-1}(x) = \frac{3x-2}{x-1}$ 13. $f^{-1}(43) = 2, f^{-1}(163) = 4$

14. $f^{-1}(x) = \frac{4x}{4-3x}$ 15. $f^{-1}(x) = \frac{2x-1}{x-1}$ 18. $f^{-1}(x) = \frac{-1+\sqrt{4x-3}}{2}$

19. $f^{-1}(x) = \frac{-3+\sqrt{x+2}}{4}$ 20. $S = \{0, -1\}$ 21. $g^{-1}(x) = \left(\frac{2}{\pi}\right)\sin^{-1} x$

22. Not invertible

23. $f_1 = \{(1, a), (2, b), (3, c), (4, d)\}$, $f_1^{-1} = \{(a, 1), (b, 2), (c, 3), (d, 4)\}$

$f_2 = \{(1, a), (2, c), (3, b), (4, d)\}$, $f_2^{-1} = \{(a, 1), (c, 2), (b, 3), (d, 4)\}$

$f_3 = \{(1, d), (3, b), (2, a), (4, c)\}$, $f_3^{-1} = \{(d, 1), (b, 3), (a, 2), (c, 4)\}$ etc.

HINTS TO SELECTED PROBLEMS

3. $f : \{1, 2, 3\} \to \{a, b, c\}$ is given by $f(1) = a, f(2) = b, f(3) = c$. Clearly, it is a bijection. Similarly, $g : \{a, b, c\} \to \{\text{apple, ball, cat}\}$ given by $g(a) = \text{apple}, g(b) = \text{ball}, g(c) = \text{cat}$ is also a bijection. Since composition of two bijection is a bijection.

So, $gof : \{1, 2, 3\} \to \{\text{apple, ball, cat}\}$ is a bijection.

It is given that: $f = \{(1, a), (2, b), (3, c)\}$ and $g = \{(a, \text{apple}), (b, \text{ball}), (c, \text{cat})\}$

$\therefore$ gof $= \{(1, \text{apple}), (2, \text{ball}), (3, \text{cat})\}$

Clearly, $f^{-1} = \{(a, 1), (b, 2), (c, 3)\}$ and $g^{-1} = \{(\text{apple}, a), (\text{ball}, b), (\text{cat}, c)\}$

$\therefore$ $(gof)^{-1} = \{(\text{apple}, 1), (\text{ball}, 2), (\text{cat}, 3)\}$ ...(i)

and, $f^{-1} o g^{-1} = \{(\text{apple}, 1), (\text{ball}, 2), (\text{cat}, 3)\}$ ...(ii)

From (i) and (ii), we get $(gof)^{-1} = f^{-1} o g^{-1}$.

6. It is given that $f : R \to R$ such that $f(x) = 4x + 3$.

f is an injection: Let $x, y \in R$ be such that $f(x) = f(y) \Rightarrow 4x + 3 = 4y + 3 \Rightarrow x = y$. So, f is an injection.

f is a surjection: Let y be an arbitrary element of R (Co-domain) such that $f(x) = y$. Then,

$$f(x) = y \Rightarrow 4x + 3 = y \Rightarrow x = \frac{y-3}{4}$$

Thus, for any $y \in R$ there exists $x = \frac{y-3}{4} \in R$ such that

$$f(x) = f\left(\frac{y-3}{4}\right) = 4\left(\frac{y-3}{4}\right) + 3 = y$$

So, $f : R \to R$ is a bijection and hence invertible. Let f^{-1} denote the inverse of f. Then,

$$fof^{-1}(x) = x \text{ for all } x \in R$$

$$\Rightarrow \quad f(f^{-1}(x)) = x \text{ for all } x \in R$$

$\Rightarrow \quad 4 f^{-1}(x) + 3 = x$ for all $x \in R \Rightarrow f^{-1}(x) = \dfrac{x-3}{4}$ for all $x \in R$

7. We have, $f : R^+ \to [4, \infty)$ such that $f(x) = x^2 + 4$.

f is an injection: Let $x, y \in R^+$ such that

$$f(x) = f(y) \Rightarrow x^2 + 4 = y^2 + 4 \Rightarrow x = y \qquad [\because x, y \in R^+]$$

So, f is an injective map.

f is onto: Let $y \in [4, \infty)$. Then, $f(x) = y \Rightarrow x^2 + 4 = y \Rightarrow x = \sqrt{y-4} \qquad [\because x \in R^+]$

And, $\quad y \in [4, \infty) \Rightarrow y - 4 > 0 \Rightarrow \sqrt{y-4} > 0 \Rightarrow x = \sqrt{y-4} \in R^+$

Thus, for each $y \in [4, \infty)$ there exists $x = \sqrt{y-4} \in R^+$ such that

$$f(x) = f(\sqrt{y-4}) = (\sqrt{y-4})^2 + 4 = y.$$

So, $f : R^+ \to [4, \infty)$ is onto. Thus, $f : R^+ \to [4, \infty)$ is a bijection and hence invertible.

Let f^{-1} denote the inverse of f. Then,

$$fof^{-1}(x) = x \text{ for all } x \in [4, \infty) \Rightarrow f(f^{-1}(x)) = x \text{ for all } x \in [4, \infty)$$

$\Rightarrow \quad (f^{-1}(x))^2 + 4 = x$ for all $x \in [4, \infty) \Rightarrow f^{-1}(x) = \sqrt{x-4}$ for all $x \in [4, \infty)$

8. We have, $f(x) = \dfrac{4x+3}{6x-4}, x \neq \dfrac{2}{3}$

$$\therefore \quad fof(x) = f(f(x)) = f\left(\frac{4x+3}{67x-4}\right) = \frac{4\left(\dfrac{4x+3}{6x-4}\right)+3}{6\left(\dfrac{4x+3}{6x-4}\right)-4} = \frac{16x+12+18x-12}{24x+18-24x+16} = x$$

$\Rightarrow \quad (fof(x) = x$ for all $x \neq \dfrac{2}{3} \Rightarrow fof = I \Rightarrow f$ is inverse of itself

Hence, $f^{-1}(x) = f(x) = \dfrac{4x+3}{6x-4}$

16. We have, $f : R^+ \to [-5, \infty)$ given by $f(x) = 9x^2 + 6x - 5$.

f is an injection: For any $x, y \in R^+$

$$f(x) = f(y)$$

$\Rightarrow \quad 9x^2 + 6x - 5 = 9y^2 + 6y - 5 \Rightarrow 9(x^2 - y^2) + 6(x - y) = 0$

$\Rightarrow \quad 3(x-y)\{3(x+y)+2\} = 0$

$\Rightarrow \quad x - y = 0 \Rightarrow x = y \qquad [3(x+y) + 2 \neq 0 \text{ as } x, y \in R^+]$

So, f is an injection.

f is a surjection: Let y be an arbitrary element of $[-5, \infty)$. Then,

$$f(x) = y \Rightarrow 9x^2 + 6x - 5 = y \Rightarrow (3x+1)^2 = y + 6 \Rightarrow 3x + 1 = \sqrt{y+6} \Rightarrow x = \frac{-1+\sqrt{y+6}}{3}$$

Now, $\quad y \in [-5, \infty)$

$\Rightarrow y \geq -5 \Rightarrow y + 6 \geq 1 \Rightarrow \sqrt{y+6} \geq 1 \Rightarrow -1 + \sqrt{y+6} \geq 0 \Rightarrow \dfrac{-1+\sqrt{y+6}}{3} \geq 0$

$\Rightarrow x \geq 0 \Rightarrow x \in R^+$

Thus, for each $y \in [-5, \infty)$ there exists $x = \dfrac{-1+\sqrt{y+6}}{3} \in R^+$ such that $f(x) = y$.

So, $f : R^+ \to [-5, \infty)$ is onto.

Thus, $f : R^+ \to [-5, \infty)$ is a bijection and hence invertible. Let f^{-1} denote the inverse of f. Then,

$$(fof^{-1})(x) = x \text{ for all } x \in [-5, \infty) \Rightarrow f\left(f^{-1}(x)\right) = x \text{ for all } x \in [-5, \infty)$$

$$\Rightarrow \quad 9\left\{f^{-1}(x)\right\}^2 + 6\left\{f^{-1}(x)\right\} - 5 = x \text{ for all } x \in [-5, \infty)$$

$$\Rightarrow \quad \left\{3f^{-1}(x) + 1\right\}^2 = 6 + x \text{ for all } x \in [-5, \infty)$$

$$\Rightarrow \quad 3f^{-1}(x) + 1 = \sqrt{6+x} \text{ for all } x \in [-5, \infty) \Rightarrow f^{-1}(x) = \frac{\sqrt{x+6}-1}{3} \text{ for all } x \in [-5, \infty)$$

20. Let $f(x) = y$. Then, $f(x) = y \Rightarrow x = \sqrt{y+1} - 1 \Rightarrow f^{-1}(y) = \sqrt{y+1} - 1$.

Now, $f(x) = f^{-1}(x)$

$$\Rightarrow \quad (x+1)^2 - 1 = \sqrt{x+1} - 1$$

$$\Rightarrow \quad \sqrt{x+1}\,\{(x+1)^{3/2} - 1\} = 0 \Rightarrow x+1 = 0 \text{ or, } (x+1)^{3/2} = 1 \Rightarrow x = 0, -1$$

22. f is neither one-one nor onto. So, f is not a bijection. Hence, it is not invertible.

FILL IN THE BLANKS TYPE QUESTIONS (FBQs)

1. The total number of functions from the set $A = \{1, 2, 3, 4\}$ to the set $B = \{a, b, c\}$ is ....
2. The total number of one-one functions from the set $A = \{a, b, c\}$ to the set $B = \{x, y, z, t\}$ is ....
3. The total number of onto functions from the set $A = \{1, 2, 3, 4, 5\}$ to the set $B = \{x, y\}$ is ..... .
4. The domain of the real function $f(x) = \sqrt{16 - x^2}$ is ....
5. The domain of the real function $f(x) = \dfrac{x}{\sqrt{9 - x^2}}$ is ....
6. The range of the function $f : R \to R$ given by $f(x) = x + \sqrt{x^2}$ is ....
7. The range of the function $f : R - \{-2\} \to R$ given by $f(x) = \dfrac{x+2}{|x+2|}$ is ....
8. If $f : C \to C$ is defined by $f(x) = 8x^3$, then $f^{-1}(8) =$ ....
9. If $f : R \to R$ is defined by $f(x) = 8x^3$ then, $f^{-1}(8) =$ ....
10. If $f : R - \{0\} \to R - \{0\}$ is defined as $f(x) = \dfrac{2}{3x}$, then $f^{-1}(x) =$ ....
11. If $f : R \to R$ is defined by $f(x) = 6 - (x-9)^3$, then $f^{-1}(x) =$ ....
12. Let $A = \{1, 2, 3, 4\}$ and $f : A \to A$ be given by $f = \{(1, 4), (2, 3), (3, 2), (4, 1)\}$. Then $f^{-1} =$..........
13. If $f : R \to R$ be defined by $f(x) = (2 - x^5)^{1/5}$, then $fof(x) =$ ....

14. Let $A = \{1, 2, 3, 4, 5, ..., 10\}$ and $f : A \to A$ be an invertible function. Then, $\sum_{r=1}^{10} (f^{-1} of)(r) =$ ....

15. Let $A = \{1, 2, 3, 4, 5, 6\}$ and $B = \{2, 4, 6, 8, 10, 12\}$. If $f : A \to B$ is given by $f(x) = 2x$, then f^{-1} as set of ordered pairs, is ....

16. Let $f = \{(0, -1), (-1, 3), (2, 3), (3, 5)\}$ be a function from Z to Z defined by $f(x) = ax + b$. Then, $(a, b) =$ ....

17. Let $f : R \to R$ and $g : R \to R$ be functions defined by $f(x) = 5 - x^2$ and $g(x) = 3x - 4$. Then the value of $fog\,(-1)$ is ....

18. Let f be the greatest integer function defined as $f(x) = [x]$ and g be the modules function defined as $g(x) = |x|$, then the value of $gof\left(-\frac{5}{4}\right)$ is ....

19. If $f(x) = \cos [e]\, x + \cos [-e]\, x$, then $f(\pi) =$ ....

20. Let $A = \{1, 2, 3\}$ and $B = \{a, b\}$ be two sets. Then the number of constant functions from A to B is ....

21. If $f(x) = \cos [\pi^2]\, x + \cos [-\pi^2]\, x$, then $f\left(\frac{\pi}{2}\right) =$ ....

22. The number of onto functions from $A = \{a, b, c\}$ to $B = \{1, 2, 3, 4\}$ is.............................. .

23. If $f(0, \infty) \to R$ is given by $f(x) = \log_{10} x$, then $f^{-1}(x) =$ ....

24. If $f : R^+ \to R$ is defined as $f(x) = \log_3 x$, then $f^{-1}(x) =$ ....

25. If $f : R \to R,\ g : R \to R$ are defined by $f(x) = 5x - 3$, $g(x) = x^2 + 3$, then $(gof^{-1})(3) =$........... .

26. If $f : R \to R$ is given by $f(x) = 2x + |x|$, then $f(2x) + f(-x) + 4x =$ ....

27. If $f(x) = \frac{1-x}{1+x}$, then $fof(\cos 2\theta) =$ ....

28. Let $f(x) = \frac{x}{x-1}$ and $\frac{f(\alpha)}{f(\alpha+1)} = f(\alpha^k)$, then $k =$ ....

29. If $f(f(x)) = x + 1$ for all $x \in R$ and if $f(0) = \frac{1}{2}$, then $f(1) =$ ....

30. If $f(x) = 3x + 10$ and $g(x) = x^2 - 1$, then $(fog)^{-1}$ is equal to ....

31. Let $f = \{(1, 2), (3, 5), (4, 1)\}$ and $g = \{(2, 3), (5, 1), (1, 3)\}$. Then, $gof =$ .... and $fog =$ ....

ANSWERS

1. 81
2. 24
3. 30
4. $[-4, 4]$
5. $(-3, 3)$
6. $[0, \infty)$
7. $\{-1, 1\}$
8. $\{1, \omega, \omega^2\}$
9. $\{1\}$
10. $f^{-1}(x) = \frac{2}{3x}$
11. $f^{-1}(x) = 9 + (6 - x)^{1/3}$
12. $f^{-1} = \{(4, 1), (3, 2), (2, 3), (1, 4)\}$
13. x
14. 55
15. $f^{-1} = \{(2, 1), (4, 2), (6, 3), (8, 4), (10, 5), (12, 6)\}$
16. $(2, -1)$
17. -44
18. 2
19. 0
20. 2
21. -1
22. 0
23. 10^x
24. 3^x
25. 3
26. $2\,f(x)$

27. $\cos 2\theta$ 28. 2 29. $\frac{3}{2}$ 30. $\left(\frac{x-7}{3}\right)^{1/2}$

31. $gof = \{(1, 3), (3, 1), (4, 3)\}$ $fog = \{(2, 5), (5, 2), (1, 5)\}$

VERY SHORT ANSWER QUESTIONS (VSAQs)

Answer each of the following questions in one word or one sentence or as per exact requirement of the question:

1. Which one of the following graphs represent a function?
2. Which one of the following graphs represent a one-one function?

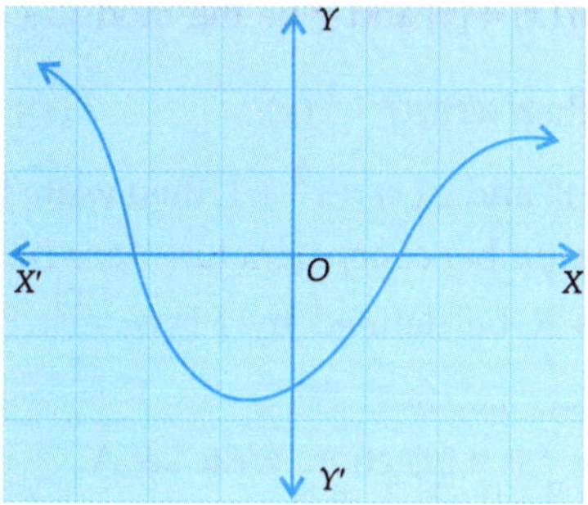

(a)

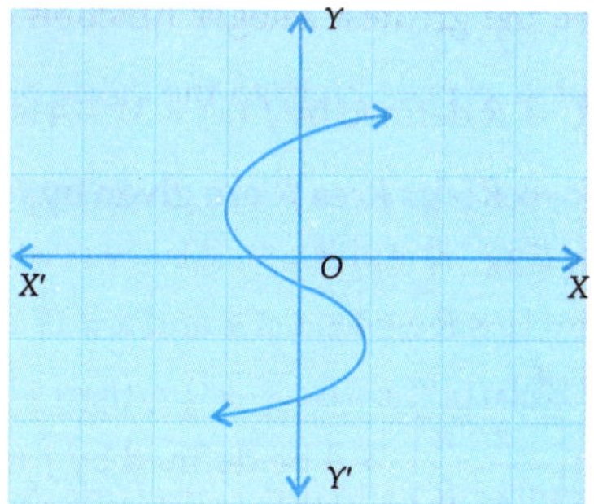

(b)

Fig. 2.43

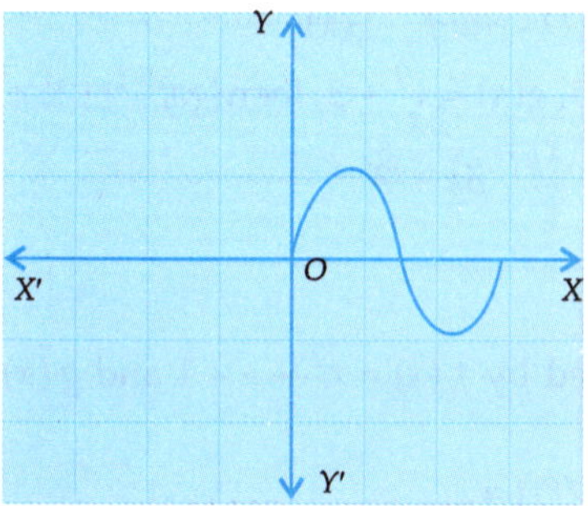

(a)

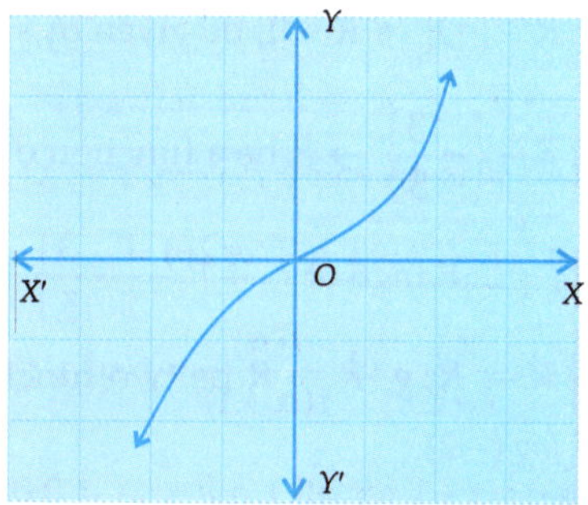

(b)

Fig. 2.44

3. If $A = \{1, 2, 3\}$ and $B = \{a, b\}$, write total number of functions from A to B.
4. If $A = \{a, b, c\}$ and $B = \{-2, -1, 0, 1, 2\}$, write total number of one-one functions from A to B.
5. Write total number of one-one functions from set $A = \{1, 2, 3, 4\}$ to set $B = \{a, b, c\}$.
6. If $f : R \to R$ is defined by $f(x) = x^2$, write $f^{-1}(25)$.
7. If $f : C \to C$ is defined by $f(x) = x^2$, write $f^{-1}(-4)$. Here, C denotes the set of all complex numbers.
8. If $f : R \to R$ is given by $f(x) = x^3$, write $f^{-1}(1)$.
9. Let C denote the set of all complex numbers. A function $f : C \to C$ is defined by $f(x) = x^3$. Write $f^{-1}(1)$.

10. Let f be a function from C (set of all complex numbers) to itself given by $f(x) = x^3$. Write $f^{-1}(-1)$.
11. Let $f : R \to R$ be defined by $f(x) = x^4$, write $f^{-1}(1)$.
12. If $f : C \to C$ is defined by $f(x) = x^4$, write $f^{-1}(1)$.
13. If $f : R \to R$ is defined by $f(x) = x^2$, find $f^{-1}(-25)$.
14. If $f : C \to C$ is defined by $f(x) = (x-2)^3$, write $f^{-1}(-1)$.
15. If $f : R \to R$ is defined by $f(x) = 10x - 7$, then write $f^{-1}(x)$.
16. Let $f : \left(-\frac{\pi}{2}, \frac{\pi}{2}\right) \to R$ be a function defined by $f(x) = \cos[x]$. Write range (f).
17. If $f : R \to R$ defined by $f(x) = 3x - 4$ is invertible then write $f^{-1}(x)$. **[CBSE 2010]**
18. If $f : R \to R$, $g : R \to R$ are given by $f(x) = (x+1)^2$ and $g(x) = x^2 + 1$, then write the value of $fog(-3)$.
19. Let $A = \{x \in R : -4 \le x \le 4 \text{ and } x \ne 0\}$ and $f : A \to R$ be defined by $f(x) = \frac{|x|}{x}$. Write the range of f.
20. Let $f : \left[-\frac{\pi}{2}, \frac{\pi}{2}\right] \to A$ be defined by $f(x) = \sin x$. If f is a bijection, write set A.
21. Let $f : R \to R^+$ be defined by $f(x) = a^x$, $a > 0$ and $a \ne 1$. Write $f^{-1}(x)$.
22. Let $f : R - \{-1\} \to R - \{1\}$ be given by $f(x) = \frac{x}{x+1}$. Write $f^{-1}(x)$.
23. Let $f : R - \left\{-\frac{3}{5}\right\} \to R$ be a function defined as $f(x) = \frac{2x}{5x+3}$.

    Write f^{-1} : Range of $f \to R - \left\{-\frac{3}{5}\right\}$.
24. Let $f : R \to R$, $g : R \to R$ be two functions defined by $f(x) = x^2 + x + 1$ and $g(x) = 1 - x^2$. Write $fog(-2)$.
25. Let $f : R \to R$ be defined as $f(x) = \frac{2x-3}{4}$. Write $fof^{-1}(1)$.
26. Let f be an invertible real function. Write $(f^{-1} of)(1) + (f^{-1} of)(2) + \ldots + (f^{-1} of)(100)$.
27. Let $A = \{1, 2, 3, 4\}$ and $B = \{a, b\}$ be two sets. Write total number of onto functions from A to B.
28. Write the domain of the real function $f(x) = \sqrt{x - [x]}$.
29. Write the domain of the real function $f(x) = \sqrt{[x] - x}$.
30. Write the domain of the real function $f(x) = \frac{1}{\sqrt{|x| - x}}$.
31. Write whether $f : R \to R$ given by $f(x) = x + \sqrt{x^2}$ is one-one, many-one, onto or into.
32. If $f(x) = x + 7$ and $g(x) = x - 7$, $x \in R$, write fog (7).
33. What is the range of the function $f(x) = \frac{|x-1|}{x-1}$? **[CBSE 2010]**

34. If $f: R \to R$ be defined by $f(x) = (3 - x^3)^{1/3}$, then find $fof(x)$. [CBSE 2010]

35. If $f: R \to R$ is defined by $f(x) = 3x + 2$, find $f(f(x))$. [CBSE 2010]

36. Let $A = \{1, 2, 3\}$, $B = \{4, 5, 6, 7\}$ and let $f = \{(1, 4), (2, 5), (3, 6)\}$ be a function from A to B. State whether f is one-one or not. [CBSE 2011]

37. If $f: \{5, 6\} \to \{2, 3\}$ and $g: \{2, 3\} \to \{5, 6\}$ are given by $f = \{(5, 2), (6, 3)\}$ and $g = \{(2, 5), (3, 6)\}$, find fog. [NCERT EXEMPLAR]

38. Let $f: R \to R$ be the function defined by $f(x) = 4x - 3$ for all $x \in R$. Then write f^{-1}.
[NCERT EXEMPLAR]

39. Which one the following relations on $A = \{1, 2, 3\}$ is a function?
$f = \{(1, 3), (2, 3), (3, 2)\}$, $g = \{(1, 2), (1, 3), (3, 1)\}$ [NCERT EXEMPLAR]

40. Write the domain of the real function f defined by $f(x) = \sqrt{25 - x^2}$. [NCERT EXEMPLAR]

41. Let $A = \{a, b, c, d\}$ and $f: A \to A$ be given by $f = \{(a, b), (b, d), (c, a), (d, c)\}$, write f^{-1}.
[NCERT EXEMPLAR]

42. Let $f, g: R \to R$ be defined by $f(x) = 2x + 1$ and $g(x) = x^2 - 2$ for all $x \in R$, respectively. Then, find gof. [NCERT EXEMPLAR]

43. If the mapping $f: \{1, 3, 4\} \to \{1, 2, 5\}$ and $g: \{1, 2, 5\} \to \{1, 3\}$, given by $f = \{(1, 2), (3, 5), (4, 1)\}$ and $g = \{(2, 3), (5, 1), (1, 3)\}$, write fog. [NCERT EXEMPLAR]

44. If a function $g = \{(1, 1), (2, 3), (3, 5), (4, 7)\}$ is described by $g(x) = \alpha x + \beta$, find the values of α and β. [NCERT EXEMPLAR]

45. If $f(x) = 4 - (x - 7)^3$, write $f^{-1}(x)$. [NCERT EXEMPLAR]

46. A function $f: A \to B$ defined as $f(x) = 2x$ is both one-one and onto. If $A = \{1, 2, 3, 4\}$, then find the set B. [CBSE 2023]

ANSWERS

1. (a) 2. (b) 3. 8 4. 60 5. 0 6. $\{-5, 5\}$
7. $\{2i, -2i\}$ 8. $\{1\}$ 9. $\{1, w, w^2\}$ 10. $\{-1, -w, -w^2\}$
11. $\{-1, 1\}$ 12. $\{-1, -i, 1, i\}$ 13. ϕ 14. $\{1, 2 - w, 2 - w^2\}$
15. $f^{-1}(x) = \dfrac{x + 7}{10}$ 16. $\{1, \cos 1, \cos 2\}$ 17. $f^{-1}(x) = \dfrac{x + 4}{3}$
18. 121 19. $\{-1, 1\}$ 20. $A = [-1, 1]$ 21. $\log_a x$
22. $f^{-1}(x) = \dfrac{x}{1 - x}$ 23. $f^{-1}(x) = \dfrac{3x}{2 - 5x}$ 24. 7 25. 1
26. 5050 27. 14 28. R 29. ϕ 30. $(-\infty, 0)$ 31. Many one-into
32. 7 33. $\{-1, 1\}$ 34. $fof(x) = x$ 35. $f(f(x)) = 9x + 9$
36. Yes 37. $fog = \{(2, 2), (3, 3)\}$ 38. $f^{-1}(x) = \dfrac{x + 3}{4}$ 39. f

40. $[-5, 5]$ **41.** $f^{-1} = \{(b, a), (d, b), (a, c), (c, d)\}$ **42.** $gof(x) = 4x^2 + 4x - 1$

43. $fog = \{(2, 5), (5, 2), (1, 5)\}$ **44.** $\alpha = 2, \beta = -1$ **45.** $f^{-1}(x) = 7 + (4 - x)^{1/3}$

46. $B = \{2, 4, 6, 8\}$.

CHAPTER 3

INVERSE TRIGONOMETRIC FUNCTIONS

3.1 INTRODUCTION

In earlier chapters, we have learnt about functions, types of functions, composition of functions and inverse of a function. In this chapter, we shall use these concepts to define the inverses of all trigonometric functions and to study their properties. Let us first recall the definition of inverse of a function.

3.2 INVERSE OF A FUNCTION

In the previous chapter, we have learnt that corresponding to every bijection (one-one onto function) $f : A \rightarrow B$ there exists a bijection $g : B \rightarrow A$ defined by

$$g(y) = x \text{ if and only } f(x) = y.$$

The function $g : B \rightarrow A$ is called the inverse of function $f : A \rightarrow B$ and is denoted by f^{-1}.

Thus, we have

$$f(x) = y \Leftrightarrow f^{-1}(y) = x$$

Also, $(f^{-1} of)(x) = f^{-1}\left(f(x)\right) = f^{-1}(y) = x, \text{ for all } x \in A.$

and, $(fo f^{-1})(y) = f\left(f^{-1}(y)\right) = f(x) = y, \text{ for all } y \in B.$

3.3 INVERSES OF TRIGONOMETRIC FUNCTIONS

We know that trigonometric functions are periodic functions, and hence, in general, all trigonometric functions are not bijections. Consequently, their inverses do not exist. However, if we restrict their domains and co-domains, they can be made bijections and we can obtain their inverses. In the following sections, we shall do all these things to obtain the inverses of trigonometric functions.

3.3.1 INVERSE OF SINE FUNCTION

Consider the function $f : R \rightarrow R$ given by $f(x) = \sin x$. The graph of this function is shown in Fig. 3.1. Clearly, it is a many-one into function as it attains same value at infinitely many points and its range $[-1, 1]$ is not same as its co-domain. We know that any function can be made an onto function, if we replace its co-domain by its range. Therefore, $f : R \rightarrow [-1, 1]$ is a many-one onto function. In order to make f a one-one function, we will have to restrict its domain in such a way that in that domain there is no turn in the graph of the function and the function takes every value between -1 and 1. It is evident from the graph of $f(x) = \sin x$ that if we take the domain as $[-\pi/2, \pi/2]$, then $f(x)$ becomes one-one. Thus, $f : [-\pi/2, \pi/2] \rightarrow [-1, 1]$ given by $f(\theta) = \sin \theta$ is a bijection and hence invertible.

The inverse of the sine function is denoted by $\sin^{-1}$. Thus, $\sin^{-1}$ is a function with domain $[-1, 1]$ and range $[-\pi/2, \pi/2]$ such that $\sin^{-1} x = \theta \Leftrightarrow \sin \theta = x$.

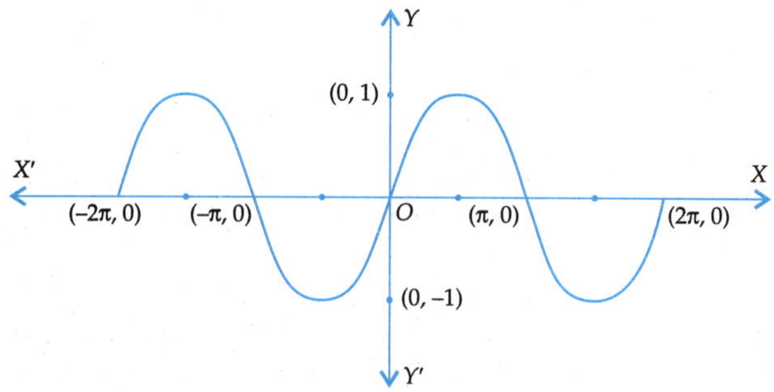

Fig. 3.1 Graph of $y = \sin x, -2\pi \le x \le 2\pi$

Also, $\sin^{-1}(\sin\theta) = \theta$ for all $\theta \in [-\pi/2, \pi/2]$ $[\because f^{-1}of(x) = f^{-1}(f(x)) = x \text{ for all } x \in D(f)]$

and, $\sin(\sin^{-1} x) = x$ for all $x \in [-1, 1]$ $[\because fof^{-1}(y) = f(f^{-1}(y)) = y \text{ for all } y \in D(f^{-1})]$

The graph of the function $f : [-\pi/2, \pi/2] \to [-1, 1]$ given by $f(x) = \sin x$ is shown in Fig. 3.2 and the graph of $\sin^{-1} : [-1, 1] \to [-\pi/2, \pi/2]$ is shown in Fig. 3.3.

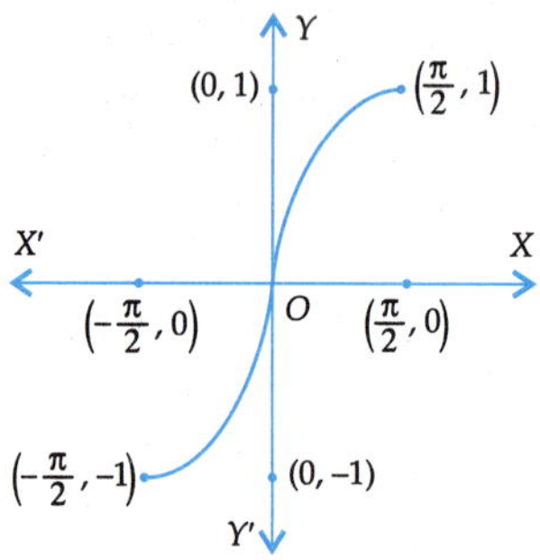

Fig. 3.2 Graph of $y = \sin x, -\frac{\pi}{2} \le x \le \frac{\pi}{2}$

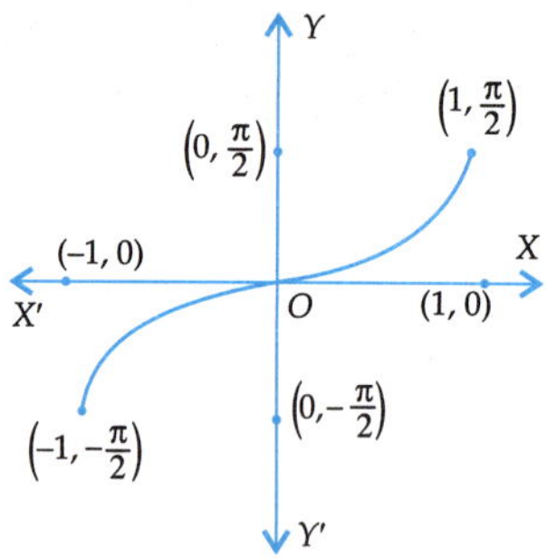

Fig. 3.3 Graph of $y = \sin^{-1} x, -1 \le x \le 1$

REMARK 1 *In the above discussion, we have restricted the domain of sine function to the interval* $[-\pi/2, \pi/2]$ *to make it a bijection. In fact, if we restrict its domain to any one of the intervals* $[-\pi/2, \pi/2]$, $[\pi/2, 3\pi/2]$, $[3\pi/2, 5\pi/2]$, $[-3\pi/2, -\pi/2]$, $[-5\pi/2, -3\pi/2]$ *or, in general* $[n\pi - \pi/2, n\pi + \pi/2]$, $n \in Z$, *then also it becomes a bijection. We can, therefore, define the inverse of the sine function in each of these intervals. Thus,* $\sin^{-1} x$ *is a function with domain* $[-1, 1]$ *and range* $[-\pi/2, \pi/2]$ *or* $[-3\pi/2, -\pi/2]$ *or* $[\pi/2, 3\pi/2]$ *and so on. Corresponding to each such interval, we get a branch of the function* $\sin^{-1} x$. *The branch of the function* $\sin^{-1} : [-1, 1] \to [-\pi/2, \pi/2]$ *called the principal value branch as shown in Fig. 3.3 and the value* $\sin^{-1} x$ *for given value of* $x \in [-1, 1]$ *is called the principal value.*

REMARK 2 *By considering* $\sin^{-1} x$ *as a function with domain* $[-1, 1]$ *and range* $[-\pi/2, \pi/2]$ *or* $[\pi/2, 3\pi/2]$ or $[3\pi/2, 5\pi/2]$ *and so on, we get different branches. If all these branches are put together and drawn on the same scale, we obtain the graph as shown in Fig. 3.4. Clearly, this graph can be obtained from the graph of sine function by interchanging the coordinate axes. The branch of* $\sin^{-1} : [-1, 1] \to [-\pi/2, \pi/2]$ *is the principal value branch and the value of* $\sin^{-1} x$ *lying in* $[-\pi/2, \pi/2]$ *for a given value of* $x \in [-1, 1]$ *is called the principal value.*

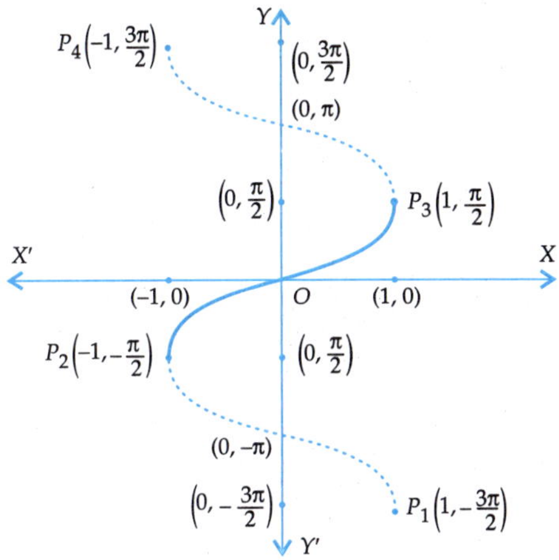

Fig. 3.4 Different branches of $y = \sin^{-1} x$ on the same scale

REMARK 3 *In chapter 2, we have learnt that the graphs of a function and its inverse (if it exists) are mirror images of each other in the line mirror $y = x$. In the above discussion, we have learnt that* $\sin^{-1}: [-1, 1] \to [-[\pi/2, \pi/2]$ *is the inverse of function* $\sin: [-\pi/2, \pi/2] \to [-1, 1]$. *Their graphs that is the curves $y = \sin x$ and $y = \sin^{-1} x$ are mirror images of each other in the line mirror $y = x$ as shown in Fig. 3.5.*

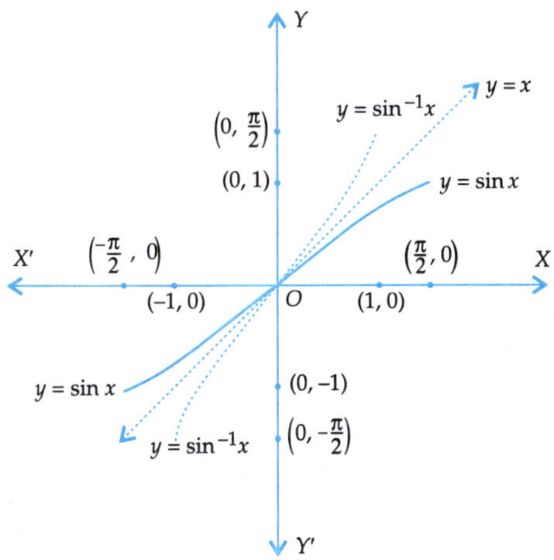

Fig. 3.5 Graphs of $y = \sin x$ and $y = \sin^{-1} x$ as mirror images of each other in line mirror $y = x$

NOTE 1 $\sin^{-1} x$ *is not equal to* $(\sin x)^{-1}$, *or* $\frac{1}{\sin x}$.

SOME OBSERVATIONS From Figures 3.2 and 3.3, we make the following observations :

(i) sin and $\sin^{-1}$ are increasing functions on $[-\pi/2, \pi/2]$ and $[-1, 1]$ respectively.

$\therefore \quad \theta_1 < \theta_2 \Rightarrow \sin\theta_1 < \sin\theta_2$ for all $\theta_1, \theta_2 \in [-\pi/2, \pi/2]$

and, $x_1 < x_2 \Rightarrow \sin^{-1} x_1 < \sin^{-1} x_2$ for all $x_1, x_2 \in [-1, 1]$

(ii) The minimum and the maximum values of $\sin^{-1} x$ are $-\frac{\pi}{2}$ and $\frac{\pi}{2}$ respectively.

(iii) $\sin^{-1} x$ attains the minimum value $-\frac{\pi}{2}$ at $x = -1$ and the maximum value $\frac{\pi}{2}$ at $x = 1$.

ILLUSTRATIVE EXAMPLES

BASED ON BASIC CONCEPTS (BASIC)

EXAMPLE 1 *Find the principal values of*

(i) $\sin^{-1}\left(\frac{\sqrt{3}}{2}\right)$ (ii) $\sin^{-1}\left(-\frac{1}{2}\right)$ [NCERT, CBSE 2011]

SOLUTION For $x \in [-1, 1]$, $\sin^{-1} x$ is an angle θ in the interval $[-\pi/2, \pi/2]$ whose sine is x i.e. $\sin\theta = x$. Therefore,

(i) $$\sin^{-1}\left(\frac{\sqrt{3}}{2}\right) = \left(\text{An angle } \theta \in \left[-\frac{\pi}{2}, \frac{\pi}{2}\right] \text{ such that } \sin\theta = \frac{\sqrt{3}}{2}\right) = \frac{\pi}{3}$$

(ii) $$\sin^{-1}\left(-\frac{1}{2}\right) = \left(\text{An angle } \theta \in \left[-\frac{\pi}{2}, \frac{\pi}{2}\right] \text{ such that } \sin\theta = -\frac{1}{2}\right) = -\frac{\pi}{6}$$

EXAMPLE 2 *Find the principal values of*

(i) $\sin^{-1}\left(\frac{1}{2}\right)$ (ii) $\sin^{-1}\left(-\frac{1}{\sqrt{2}}\right)$

SOLUTION We know that $\sin^{-1} x$ denotes an angle in the interval $[-\pi/2, \pi/2]$ whose sine is x for $x \in [-1, 1]$. Therefore,

(i) $$\sin^{-1}\left(\frac{1}{2}\right) = \left(\text{An angle } \theta \in \left[-\frac{\pi}{2}, \frac{\pi}{2}\right] \text{ such that } \sin\theta = \frac{1}{2}\right) = \frac{\pi}{6}$$

(ii) $$\sin^{-1}\left(-\frac{1}{\sqrt{2}}\right) = \left(\text{An angle } \theta \in \left[-\frac{\pi}{2}, \frac{\pi}{2}\right] \text{ such that } \sin\theta = -\frac{1}{\sqrt{2}}\right) = -\frac{\pi}{4}$$

EXAMPLE 3 *Find the value of* $\sin^{-1}\left[\cos\left\{\sin^{-1}\left(-\frac{\sqrt{3}}{2}\right)\right\}\right]$.

SOLUTION $\sin^{-1}\left[\cos\left\{\sin^{-1}\left(-\frac{\sqrt{3}}{2}\right)\right\}\right]$

$$= \sin^{-1}\left\{\cos\left(-\frac{\pi}{3}\right)\right\} = \sin^{-1}\left(\cos\frac{\pi}{3}\right) = \sin^{-1}\left(\frac{1}{2}\right) = \frac{\pi}{6} \qquad \left[\because \sin^{-1}\left(-\frac{\sqrt{3}}{2}\right) = -\frac{\pi}{3}\right]$$

BASED ON LOWER ORDER THINKING SKILLS (LOTS)

EXAMPLE 4 *Find the domain of the function* $f(x) = \sin^{-1}(2x-3)$.

SOLUTION The domain of $\sin^{-1} x$ is $[-1, 1]$. Therefore, $f(x) = \sin^{-1}(2x-3)$ is defined for all x satisfying

$$-1 \le 2x - 3 \le 1 \Rightarrow 3 - 1 \le 2x \le 3 + 1 \Rightarrow 1 \le x \le 2 \Rightarrow x \in [1, 2]$$

Hence, domain of $f(x) = \sin^{-1}(2x-3)$ is $[1, 2]$.

EXAMPLE 5 *Find the domain of* $f(x) = \sin^{-1}(-x^2)$. [NCERT EXEMPLAR]

SOLUTION The domain of $\sin^{-1} x$ is $[-1, 1]$. Therefore, $f(x) = \sin^{-1}(-x^2)$ is defined for all x satisfying

$$-1 \le -x^2 \le 1$$

$\Rightarrow \quad 1 \geq x^2 \geq -1 \Rightarrow 0 \leq x^2 \leq 1 \Rightarrow x^2 \leq 1 \Rightarrow x^2 - 1 \leq 0 \Rightarrow (x-1)(x+1) \leq 0 \Rightarrow -1 \leq x \leq 1$

Hence, the domain of $f(x) = \sin^{-1}(-x^2)$ is $[-1, 1]$.

EXAMPLE 6 *Find the domain of* $f(x) = \sin^{-1} x + \cos x$. **[NCERT EXEMPLAR]**

SOLUTION The domain of $\sin^{-1} x$ is $[-1, 1]$ and that of $\cos x$ is R. Therefore, domain of $f(x) = \sin^{-1} x + \cos x$ is $[-1, 1] \cap R = [-1, 1]$.

EXAMPLE 7 *Find the domain of the function* $f(x) = \sin^{-1} \sqrt{x-1}$. **[NCERT EXEMPLAR]**

SOLUTION The domain of $\sin^{-1} x$ is $[-1, 1]$. So, the domain of $f(x) = \sin^{-1} \sqrt{x-1}$ is the set of values of x satisfying

$$-1 \leq \sqrt{x-1} \leq 1 \Rightarrow 0 \leq \sqrt{x-1} \leq 1 \Rightarrow 0 \leq x-1 \leq 1 \Rightarrow 1 \leq x \leq 2 \Rightarrow x \in [1, 2] \quad [\because \sqrt{x-1} \geq 0]$$

Hence, the domain of $f(x) = \sin^{-1} \sqrt{x-1}$ is $[1, 2]$.

BASED ON HIGHER ORDER THINKING SKILLS (HOTS)

EXAMPLE 8 *If* $x, y, z \in [-1, 1]$ *such that* $\sin^{-1} x + \sin^{-1} y + \sin^{-1} z = -\frac{3\pi}{2}$, *find the value of* $x^2 + y^2 + z^2$.

SOLUTION We know that the minimum value of $\sin^{-1} x$ for $x \in [-1, 1]$ is $-\frac{\pi}{2}$.

$\therefore \ \sin^{-1} x \geq -\frac{\pi}{2}, \sin^{-1} y \geq -\frac{\pi}{2}$ and $\sin^{-1} z \geq -\frac{\pi}{2}$ for all $x, y, z \in [-1, 1]$

$\Rightarrow \ \sin^{-1} x + \sin^{-1} y + \sin^{-1} z \geq \left(-\frac{\pi}{2}\right) + \left(-\frac{\pi}{2}\right) + \left(-\frac{\pi}{2}\right)$

$\Rightarrow \ \sin^{-1} x + \sin^{-1} y + \sin^{-1} z \geq -\frac{3\pi}{2}$

$\therefore \ \sin^{-1} x + \sin^{-1} y + \sin^{-1} z = -\frac{3\pi}{2} \Rightarrow \sin^{-1} x = -\frac{\pi}{2}, \sin^{-1} y = -\frac{\pi}{2}, \sin^{-1} z = -\frac{\pi}{2} \Rightarrow x = y = z = -1$

Hence, $x^2 + y^2 + z^2 = (-1)^2 + (-1)^2 + (-1)^2 = 3$.

EXAMPLE 9 *Let* $x, y, z \in [-1, 1]$ *be such that* $\sin^{-1} x + \sin^{-1} y + \sin^{-1} z = \frac{3\pi}{2}$. *Find the values of*

(i) $x^{2022} + y^{2023} + z^{2024}$ (ii) $x^{2020} + y^{2022} + z^{2024} - \frac{9}{x^{2020} + y^{2022} + z^{2024}}$

SOLUTION For any $x \in [-1, 1]$, the maximum value of $\sin^{-1} x$ is $\frac{\pi}{2}$ and it attains this value at $x = 1$.

$\therefore \ \sin^{-1} x \leq \frac{\pi}{2}, \sin^{-1} y \leq \frac{\pi}{2}, \sin^{-1} z \leq \frac{\pi}{2}$ for all $x, y, z \in [-1, 1]$

$\Rightarrow \ \sin^{-1} x + \sin^{-1} y + \sin^{-1} z \leq \frac{\pi}{2} + \frac{\pi}{2} + \frac{\pi}{2}$ for all $x, y, z \in [-1, 1]$

$\Rightarrow \ \sin^{-1} x + \sin^{-1} y + \sin^{-1} z \leq \frac{3\pi}{2}$ for all $x, y, z \in [-1, 1]$

$\therefore \ \sin^{-1} x + \sin^{-1} y + \sin^{-1} z = \frac{3\pi}{2} \Rightarrow \sin^{-1} x = \frac{\pi}{2}, \sin^{-1} y = \frac{\pi}{2}, \sin^{-1} z = \frac{\pi}{2} \Rightarrow x = 1, y = 1, z = 1$

(i) $\quad x^{2022} + y^{2023} + z^{2024} = (1)^{2022} + (1)^{2023} + (1)^{2024} = 3$

(ii) $\quad x^{2020} + y^{2022} + z^{2024} - \frac{9}{x^{2020} + y^{2022} + z^{2024}} = 1 + 1 + 1 - \frac{9}{1 + 1 + 1} = 3 - 3 = 0$

EXERCISE 3.1

BASIC

1. Find the principal value of each of the following:

(i) $\sin^{-1}\left(-\frac{\sqrt{3}}{2}\right)$ (ii) $\sin^{-1}\left(\cos\frac{2\pi}{3}\right)$ (iii) $\sin^{-1}\left(\frac{\sqrt{3}-1}{2\sqrt{2}}\right)$

(iv) $\sin^{-1}\left(\frac{\sqrt{3}+1}{2\sqrt{2}}\right)$ (v) $\sin^{-1}\left(\cos\frac{3\pi}{4}\right)$ (vi) $\sin^{-1}\left(\tan\frac{5\pi}{4}\right)$

BASED ON LOTS

2. (i) $\sin^{-1}\frac{1}{2}-2\sin^{-1}\frac{1}{\sqrt{2}}$ (ii) $\sin^{-1}\left\{\cos\left(\sin^{-1}\frac{\sqrt{3}}{2}\right)\right\}$ [NCERT EXEMPLAR]

3. Find the domain of each of the following functions:

(i) $f(x)=\sin^{-1}x^2$ (ii) $f(x)=\sin^{-1}x+\sin x$ (iii) $f(x)=\sin^{-1}\sqrt{x^2-1}$

(iv) $f(x)=\sin^{-1}x+\sin^{-1}2x$ (v) $f(x)=\sin^{-1}(x^2-4)$ [CBSE 2023, 2024]

4. Draw the graph of $f(x)=\sin^{-1}x,\ x\in\left[-\frac{1}{\sqrt{2}},\frac{1}{\sqrt{2}}\right]$. Also, write range of $f(x)$. [CBSE 2023]

5. Draw the graph of $f(x)=2\sin^{-1}x,\ -1\le x\le 1$.

BASED ON HOTS

6. If $\sin^{-1}x+\sin^{-1}y+\sin^{-1}z+\sin^{-1}t=2\pi$, then find the value of $x^2+y^2+z^2+t^2$.

7. If $(\sin^{-1}x)^2+(\sin^{-1}y)^2+(\sin^{-1}z)^2=\frac{3}{4}\pi^2$, find the value of $x^2+y^2+z^2$.

ANSWERS

1. (i) $-\frac{\pi}{3}$ (ii) $-\frac{\pi}{6}$ (iii) $\frac{\pi}{12}$ (iv) $\frac{5\pi}{12}$ (v) $-\frac{\pi}{4}$

(vi) $\frac{\pi}{2}$ 2. (i) $-\frac{\pi}{3}$ (ii) $\frac{\pi}{6}$ 3. (i) $[-1,1]$ (ii) $[-1,1]$

(iii) $[-\sqrt{2},-1]\cup[1,\sqrt{2}]$ (iv) $[-1/2,1/2]$ (v) $[-\sqrt{5},-\sqrt{3}]\cup[\sqrt{3},\sqrt{5}]$

4. $\left[-\frac{\pi}{4},\frac{\pi}{4}\right]$ 6. 4 7. 3

3.3.2 INVERSE OF COSINE FUNCTION

The graph of cosine function is shown in Fig. 3.6. It is evident from the graph of $y=\cos x$ (see Fig. 3.6) that the function $f:R\to R$ given by $f(\theta)=\cos\theta$ is a many-one into function. However, $f:[0,\pi]\to[-1,1]$ is one-one onto i.e. a bijection and hence it is invertible. The inverse of cosine function is denoted by $\cos^{-1}$.

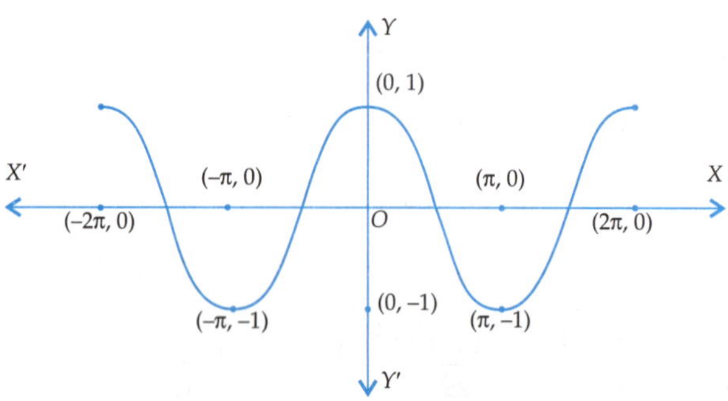

Fig. 3.6 Graph of $y=\cos x$ when $-2\pi\le x\le 2\pi$

Thus, if $\cos:[0,\pi]\to[-1,1]$ is such that $\cos\theta = x$. Then, $\cos^{-1}:[-1,1]\to[0,\pi]$ is defined as $\cos^{-1}x=\theta$. In other words: $\cos\theta = x \Leftrightarrow \cos^{-1}x=\theta$ for all $\theta\in[0,\pi]$ and $x\in[-1,1]$.

The graphs of $\cos:[0,\pi]\to[-1,1]$ and its inverse $\cos^{-1}[-1,1]\to[0,\pi]$ are shown in Figures 3.7 and 3.8 respectively. The branch of $\cos^{-1}:[-1,1]\to[0,\pi]$ is called the principal value branch and the value of $\cos^{-1}x$ lying in $[0,\pi]$ for a given value of $x\in[-1,1]$ is called the principal value.

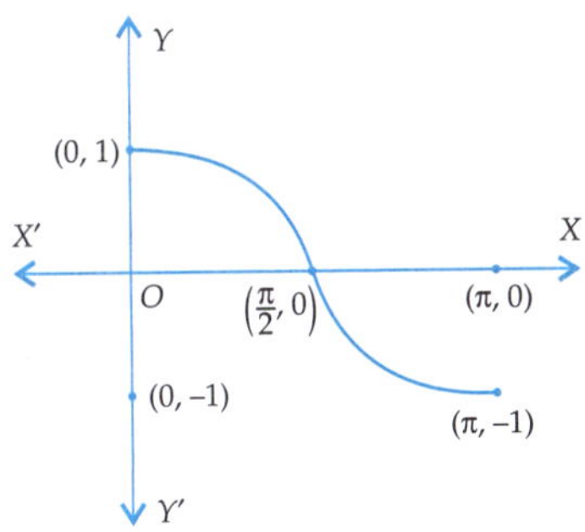

Fig. 3.7 Graph of $y=\cos x,\ 0\le x\le\pi$

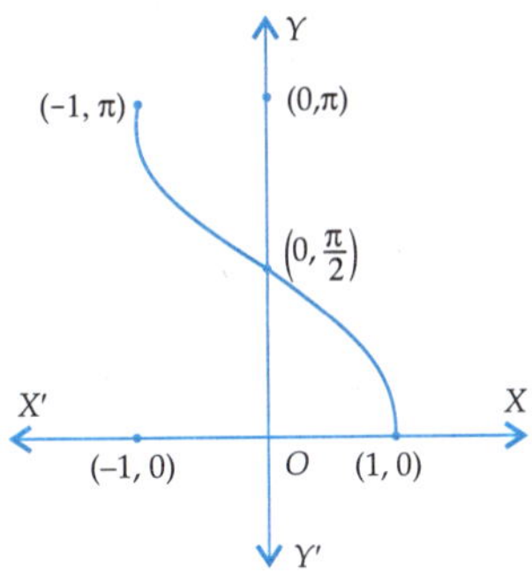

Fig. 3.8 Graph of $y=\cos^{-1}x$

SOME OBSERVATIONS It is evident from the graphs of $\cos x$ and $\cos^{-1}x$ that

(i) the domain and range of $\cos^{-1}x$ are $[-1,1]$ and $[0,\pi]$ respectively.

(ii) both cos and $\cos^{-1}$ are decreasing functions in their respective domains.

$\therefore \quad \theta_1<\theta_2 \Rightarrow \cos\theta_1>\cos\theta_2$ for all $\theta_1,\theta_2\in[0,\pi]$

and, $\quad x_1<x_2\Rightarrow \cos^{-1}x_1>\cos^{-1}x_2$ for all $x_1,x_2\in[-1,1]$

(iii) The minimum and maximum values of $\cos^{-1}x$ are 0 and π respectively which are attained at 1 and -1 respectively i.e. $\cos^{-1}(1)=0$ and $\cos^{-1}(-1)=\pi$.

ILLUSTRATIVE EXAMPLES

BASED ON BASIC CONCEPTS (BASIC)

EXAMPLE 1 *Find the domain of* $\cos^{-1}(2x-1)$.

SOLUTION The domain of $\cos^{-1}x$ is $[-1,1]$. So, the domain of $\cos^{-1}(2x-1)$ is the set of all values of x satisfying: $-1\le 2x-1\le 1 \Rightarrow 0\le 2x\le 2\Rightarrow 0\le x\le 1$.

Hence, the domain of $\cos^{-1}(2x-1)$ is $[0,1]$.

EXAMPLE 2 *Find the domain and range of the function* $f(x)=3\cos^{-1}\left(\dfrac{1}{2x-1}\right)-2$.

SOLUTION *Domain:* $f(x)$ is defined, if

$$-1\le\frac{1}{2x-1}\le 1$$

$$\Rightarrow \quad 0\le\frac{1}{2x-1}+1\le 2 \Rightarrow 0\le\frac{2x}{2x-1}\le 2\Rightarrow 0\le\frac{x}{2x-1}\le 1$$

$$\Rightarrow \quad 0\le\frac{x}{2x-1} \text{ and } \frac{x}{2x-1}\le 1\Rightarrow \frac{x}{2x-1}\ge 0 \text{ and } \frac{x}{2x-1}-1\le 0$$

$\Rightarrow \quad \frac{x}{2x-1} \geq 0$ and $\frac{1-x}{2x-1} \leq 0 \Rightarrow \frac{x}{2x-1} \geq 0$ and $\frac{x-1}{2x-1} \geq 0$

$\Rightarrow \quad x \in (-\infty, 0] \cup \left(\frac{1}{2}, \infty\right)$ and $x \in \left(-\infty, \frac{1}{2}\right) \cup [1, \infty) \Rightarrow x \in (-\infty, 0] \cup [1, \infty)$

Hence, Domain of $f(x)$ is $(-\infty, 0] \cup [1, \infty)$.

Range: For $x \in (-\infty, 0] \cup [1, \infty)$, we have

$$0 \leq \cos^{-1}\left(\frac{1}{2x-1}\right) \leq \pi$$

$\Rightarrow \quad 0 \leq 3\cos^{-1}\left(\frac{1}{2x-1}\right) \leq 3\pi \Rightarrow -2 \leq 3\cos^{-1}\left(\frac{1}{2x-1}\right) - 2 \leq 3\pi - 2$

$\Rightarrow \quad -2 \leq f(x) \leq 3\pi - 2 \Rightarrow$ Range $(f(x)) = [-2, 3\pi - 2]$

EXAMPLE 3 *Find the principal values of (i)* $\cos^{-1}\frac{\sqrt{3}}{2}$ *(ii)* $\cos^{-1}\left(-\frac{1}{2}\right)$. **[NCERT]**

SOLUTION For any $x \in [-1, 1]$, $\cos^{-1} x$ represents an angle in $[0, \pi]$ whose cosine is x. Therefore,

(i) $\cos^{-1}\left(\frac{\sqrt{3}}{2}\right) = \left(\text{An angle } \theta \in [0, \pi] \text{ such that } \cos\theta = \frac{\sqrt{3}}{2}\right) = \frac{\pi}{6}$

(ii) $\cos^{-1}\left(-\frac{1}{2}\right) = \left(\text{An angle } \theta \in [0, \pi] \text{ such that } \cos\theta = -\frac{1}{2}\right) = \frac{2\pi}{3}$

EXAMPLE 4 *Find the principal value of* $\cos^{-1}\left\{\sin\left(\cos^{-1}\frac{1}{2}\right)\right\}$.

SOLUTION We know that $\cos^{-1}\frac{1}{2} = \frac{\pi}{3}$.

$\therefore \quad \cos^{-1}\left\{\sin\left(\cos^{-1}\frac{1}{2}\right)\right\} = \cos^{-1}\left(\sin\frac{\pi}{3}\right) = \cos^{-1}\left(\frac{\sqrt{3}}{2}\right) = \frac{\pi}{6} \quad \left[\because \cos^{-1}\left(\frac{\sqrt{3}}{2}\right) = \frac{\pi}{6}\right]$

BASED ON HIGHER ORDER THINKING SKILLS (HOTS)

EXAMPLE 5 *If* $x, y, z \in [-1, 1]$ *such that* $\cos^{-1}x + \cos^{-1}y + \cos^{-1}z = 0$, *find* $x + y + z$.

SOLUTION We have,

$$x, y, z \in [-1, 1]$$

$\Rightarrow \quad -1 \leq x \leq 1, -1 \leq y \leq 1, -1, \leq z \leq 1 \Rightarrow 0 \leq \cos^{-1}x \leq \pi, 0 \leq \cos^{-1}y \leq \pi, 0 \leq \cos^{-1}z \leq \pi$

$\therefore \quad \cos^{-1}x + \cos^{-1}y + \cos^{-1}z = 0 \Rightarrow \cos^{-1}x = 0, \cos^{-1}y = 0$ and $\cos^{-1}z = 0 \Rightarrow x = y = z = 1$.

Hence, $x + y + z = 3$.

EXAMPLE 6 *If* $x, y, z \in [-1, 1]$ *such that* $\cos^{-1}x + \cos^{-1}y + \cos^{-1}z = 3\pi$, *then find the values of*

(i) $xy + yz + zx$ (ii) $x(y+z) + y(z+x) + z(x+y)$ **[NCERT EXEMPLAR]**

SOLUTION We have,

$$x, y, z \in [-1, 1]$$

$\Rightarrow \quad -1 \leq x \leq 1, -1 \leq y \leq 1, -1, \leq z \leq 1 \Rightarrow 0 \leq \cos^{-1}x \leq \pi, 0 \leq \cos^{-1}y \leq \pi, 0 \leq \cos^{-1}z \leq \pi$

$\therefore \quad \cos^{-1}x + \cos^{-1}y + \cos^{-1}z = 3\pi$

$\Rightarrow \quad \cos^{-1}x + \cos^{-1}y + \cos^{-1}z = \pi + \pi + \pi \Rightarrow \cos^{-1}x = \pi, \cos^{-1}y = \pi, \cos^{-1}z = \pi$

$\Rightarrow \quad x = -1, y = -1, z = -1.$

Therefore,

(i) $xy + yz + zx = (-1) \times (-1) + (-1) \times (-1) + (-1) \times (-1) = 1 + 1 + 1 = 3.$

(ii) $x(y+z) + y(z+x) + z(x+y) = 2(xy + yz + zx) = 2 \times 3 = 6$

EXERCISE 3.2

BASIC

1. Find the principal value of each of the following:

   (i) $\cos^{-1}\left(-\frac{\sqrt{3}}{2}\right)$ [NCERT] (ii) $\cos^{-1}\left(-\frac{1}{\sqrt{2}}\right)$ [NCERT]

   (iii) $\cos^{-1}\left(\sin\frac{4\pi}{3}\right)$ (iv) $\cos^{-1}\left(\tan\frac{3\pi}{4}\right)$

2. For the principal values, evaluate each of the following :

   (i) $\cos^{-1}\frac{1}{2} + 2\sin^{-1}\frac{1}{2}$ [NCERT, CBSE 2012] (ii) $\cos^{-1}\left(\frac{1}{2}\right) - 2\sin^{-1}\left(-\frac{1}{2}\right)$ [CBSE 2012]

   (iii) $\sin^{-1}\left(-\frac{1}{2}\right) + 2\cos^{-1}\left(-\frac{\sqrt{3}}{2}\right)$ (iv) $\sin^{-1}\left(-\frac{\sqrt{3}}{2}\right) + \cos^{-1}\left(\frac{\sqrt{3}}{2}\right)$

   (v) $3\sin^{-1}\left(\frac{1}{\sqrt{2}}\right) + 2\cos^{-1}\left(\frac{\sqrt{3}}{2}\right) + \cos^{-1}(0)$ [CBSE 2023]

BASED ON LOTS

3. Find the domain of definition of (i) $f(x) = \cos^{-1}(x^2 - 4)$ (ii) $\cos^{-1}(|x-1|)$.
4. Find the domain of $f(x) = 2\cos^{-1}2x + \sin^{-1}x$.
5. Find the domain of $f(x) = \cos^{-1}x + \cos x$.
6. Draw the graph of $\cos^{-1}x,\ x \in [-1, 0]$. Also, write its range.
7. Draw the graph of the principal branch of the function $f(x) = \cos^{-1}x$. [CBSE 2023]

ANSWERS

1. (i) $\frac{5\pi}{6}$ (ii) $\frac{3\pi}{4}$ (iii) $\frac{5\pi}{6}$ (iv) π
2. (i) $\frac{2\pi}{3}$ (ii) $\frac{2\pi}{3}$ (iii) $\frac{3\pi}{2}$ (iv) $-\frac{\pi}{6}$ (v) $\frac{19\pi}{12}$
3. (i) $[-\sqrt{5}, -\sqrt{3}] \cup [\sqrt{3}, \sqrt{5}]$ (ii) $[0, 2]$ 4. $[-1/2, 1/2]$ 5. $[-1, 1]$ 6. $\left[\frac{\pi}{2}, \pi\right]$

3.3.3 INVERSE OF TANGENT FUNCTION

Consider the function $f : R - \left\{(2n+1)\frac{\pi}{2} : n \in Z\right\} \to R$ given by $f(x) = \tan x$. The graph of this function is shown in Fig. 3.9. It is evident from the graph that $f(x) = \tan x$ is a many-one onto function and hence it is not invertible. However, the function $\tan : \left(-\frac{\pi}{2}, \frac{\pi}{2}\right) \to R$ associating each $x \in \left(-\frac{\pi}{2}, \frac{\pi}{2}\right)$ to $\tan x \in R$ is bijection and so it is invertible. The inverse of this function is denoted by $\tan^{-1}$.

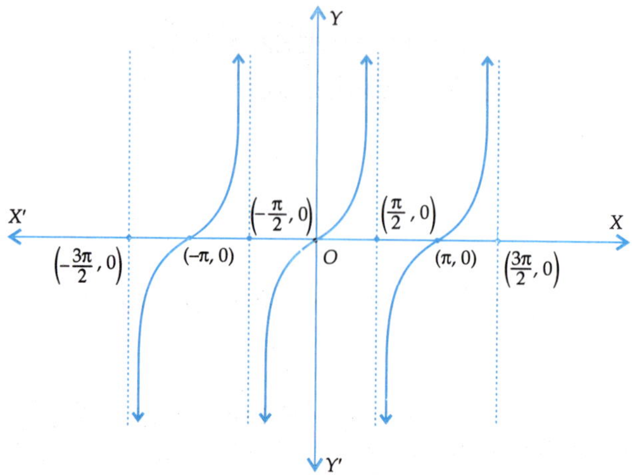

Fig. 3.9 Graph of $y = \tan x$

Clearly, $\tan^{-1}: R \to \left(-\frac{\pi}{2}, \frac{\pi}{2}\right)$ is such that $\tan^{-1} x = \theta \Leftrightarrow \tan\theta = x$.

Also, $\tan^{-1}(\tan\theta) = \theta$ for all $\theta \in \left(-\frac{\pi}{2}, \frac{\pi}{2}\right)$ and, $\tan(\tan^{-1} x) = x$ for all $x \in R$.

The graphs of the functions $\tan : \left(-\frac{\pi}{2}, \frac{\pi}{2}\right) \to R$ and $\tan^{-1} : R \to \left(-\frac{\pi}{2}, \frac{\pi}{2}\right)$ are shown in Figures 3.10 and 3.11 respectively. The branch of $\tan^{-1}: R \to (-\pi/2, \pi/2)$ is called the principal value branch and the value of $\tan^{-1} x$ lying in $(-\pi/2, \pi/2)$ for a given value of $x \in R$ is called the principal value.

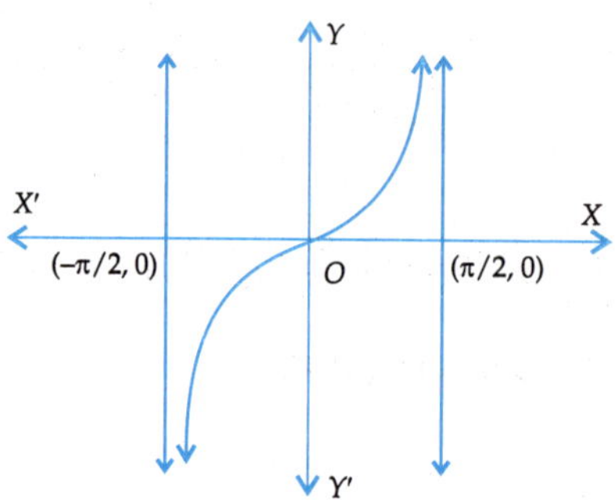

Fig. 3.10 Graph of $y = \tan x, -\frac{\pi}{2} < x < \frac{\pi}{2}$

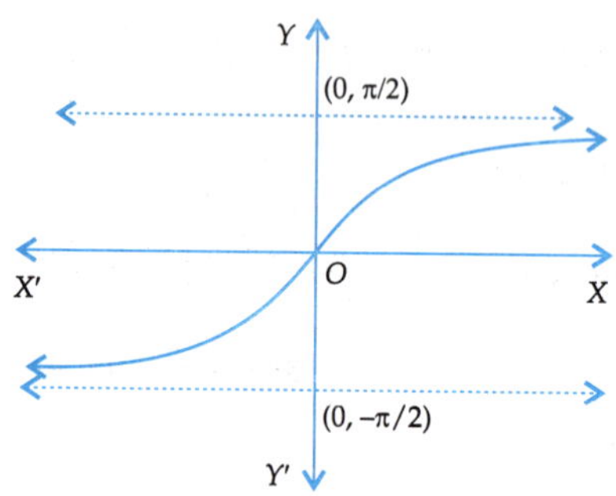

Fig. 3.11 Graph of $y = \tan^{-1} x$

SOME USEFUL OBSERVATIONS *It is evident from the graphs of* $\tan : \left(-\frac{\pi}{2}, \frac{\pi}{2}\right) \to R$ *and* $\tan^{-1} : R \to \left(-\frac{\pi}{2}, \frac{\pi}{2}\right)$ *i.e. the curves* $y = \tan x$ *and* $y = \tan^{-1} x$ *that*

(i) $-\frac{\pi}{2} < \tan^{-1} x < \frac{\pi}{2}$ for all $x \in R$ i.e. $-\frac{\pi}{2}$ and $\frac{\pi}{2}$ are minimum and maximum values of $\tan^{-1} x$ but it not does not attain these values.

(ii) both tan and $\tan^{-1}$ are increasing functions in their respective domains.

$\therefore \quad \theta_1 < \theta_2 \Rightarrow \tan\theta_1 < \tan\theta_2$ for all $\theta_1, \theta_2 \in (-\pi/2, \pi/2)$

and, $x_1 < x_2 \Rightarrow \tan^{-1} x_1 < \tan^{-1} x_2$ for all $x_1, x_2 \in R$.

ILLUSTRATIVE EXAMPLES

BASED ON BASIC CONCEPTS (BASIC)

EXAMPLE 1 *Find the principal values of each of the following :*

(i) $\tan^{-1}(-\sqrt{3})$ (ii) $\tan^{-1}(1)$ [NCERT]

(iii) $\tan^{-1}\left\{\sin\left(-\frac{\pi}{2}\right)\right\}$ [NCERT EXEMPLAR] (iv) $\tan^{-1}\left\{\cos\frac{3\pi}{2}\right\}$

SOLUTION We know that for any $x \in R$, $\tan^{-1} x$ represents an angle in $\left(-\frac{\pi}{2}, \frac{\pi}{2}\right)$ whose tangent is x. Therefore,

(i) $$\tan^{-1}(-\sqrt{3}) = \left(\text{An angle } \theta \in \left(-\frac{\pi}{2}, \frac{\pi}{2}\right) \text{such that } \tan\theta = -\sqrt{3}\right) = -\frac{\pi}{3}$$

(ii) $$\tan^{-1}(1) = \left(\text{An angle } \theta \in \left(-\frac{\pi}{2}, \frac{\pi}{2}\right) \text{such that } \tan\theta = 1\right) = \frac{\pi}{4}$$

(iii) We know that $\sin\left(-\frac{\pi}{2}\right) = -1$. Therefore, $\tan^{-1}\left\{\sin\left(-\frac{\pi}{2}\right)\right\} = \tan^{-1}(-1) = -\frac{\pi}{4}$

(iv) $$\tan^{-1}\left\{\cos\frac{3\pi}{2}\right\} = \tan^{-1}(0) = 0$$

EXAMPLE 2 *For the principal values, evaluate each of the following:*

(i) $\tan^{-1}\left\{2\cos\left(2\sin^{-1}\frac{1}{2}\right)\right\}$ [NCERT] (ii) $\cot\left[\sin^{-1}\left\{\cos\left(\tan^{-1}1\right)\right\}\right]$ [NCERT EXEMPLAR]

SOLUTION (i) We know that $\sin^{-1}\frac{1}{2} = \frac{\pi}{6}$.

$$\therefore \tan^{-1}\left\{2\cos\left(2\sin^{-1}\frac{1}{2}\right)\right\} = \tan^{-1}\left\{2\cos\left(2\times\frac{\pi}{6}\right)\right\} = \tan^{-1}\left(2\cos\frac{\pi}{3}\right) = \tan^{-1}\left(2\times\frac{1}{2}\right) = \tan^{-1}1 = \frac{\pi}{4}$$

(ii) We know that $\tan^{-1}1 = \frac{\pi}{4}$.

$$\therefore \cot\left[\sin^{-1}\left\{\cos\left(\tan^{-1}1\right)\right\}\right] = \cot\left\{\sin^{-1}\left(\cos\frac{\pi}{4}\right)\right\} = \cot\left(\sin^{-1}\frac{1}{\sqrt{2}}\right) = \cot\frac{\pi}{4} = 1$$

BASED ON HIGHER ORDER THINKING SKILLS (HOTS)

EXAMPLE 3 *Which is greater,* $\tan 1$ *or* $\tan^{-1}1$? [NCERT EXEMPLAR]

SOLUTION We know that $\tan^{-1}1 = \frac{\pi}{4}$ and $1 > \frac{\pi}{4}$. Since $\tan\theta$ is an increasing function

$$\therefore \quad 1 > \frac{\pi}{4} \Rightarrow \tan 1 > \tan\frac{\pi}{4} \Rightarrow \tan 1 > 1 \Rightarrow \tan 1 > 1 > \frac{\pi}{4} \qquad \left[\because 1 > \frac{\pi}{4}\right]$$

$$\Rightarrow \quad \tan 1 > \frac{\pi}{4} \Rightarrow \tan 1 > \tan^{-1}1 \qquad \left[\because \tan^{-1}1 = \frac{\pi}{4}\right]$$

EXAMPLE 4 *Find the minimum value of n for which* $\tan^{-1}\frac{n}{\pi} > \frac{\pi}{4}, n \in N$. [NCERT EXEMPLAR]

SOLUTION We have,

$$\tan^{-1}\frac{n}{\pi} > \frac{\pi}{4}$$

$$\Rightarrow \quad \tan^{-1}\frac{n}{\pi} > \tan^{-1}1 \qquad \left[\because \frac{\pi}{4} = \tan^{-1}1\right]$$

$\Rightarrow \quad \tan\left(\tan^{-1}\frac{n}{\pi}\right) > \tan\left(\tan^{-1}1\right)$ [$\because \tan\theta$ is an increasing function]

$\Rightarrow \quad \frac{n}{\pi} > 1$ [$\because \tan(\tan^{-1}x) = x$]

$\Rightarrow \quad n > \pi \cong 3.14 \Rightarrow n = 4, 5, 6, \ldots$

Hence, the minimum value of n is 4.

EXERCISE 3.3

BASIC

1. Find the principal value of each of the following :

(i) $\tan^{-1}\left(\frac{1}{\sqrt{3}}\right)$ (ii) $\tan^{-1}\left(-\frac{1}{\sqrt{3}}\right)$ (iii) $\tan^{-1}\left(\cos\frac{\pi}{2}\right)$ (iv) $\tan^{-1}\left(2\cos\frac{2\pi}{3}\right)$

2. For the principal values, evaluate each of the following:

(i) $\tan^{-1}(-1) + \cos^{-1}\left(-\frac{1}{\sqrt{2}}\right)$ (ii) $\tan^{-1}\left\{2\sin\left(4\cos^{-1}\frac{\sqrt{3}}{2}\right)\right\}$

3. Evaluate each of the following :

(i) $\tan^{-1}1 + \cos^{-1}\left(-\frac{1}{2}\right) + \sin^{-1}\left(-\frac{1}{2}\right)$ [NCERT]

(ii) $\tan^{-1}\left(-\frac{1}{\sqrt{3}}\right) + \tan^{-1}(-\sqrt{3}) + \tan^{-1}\left(\sin\left(-\frac{\pi}{2}\right)\right)$

(iii) $\tan^{-1}\left(\tan\frac{5\pi}{6}\right) + \cos^{-1}\left\{\cos\left(\frac{13\pi}{6}\right)\right\}$ [NCERT EXEMPLAR]

ANSWERS

1. (i) $\frac{\pi}{6}$ (ii) $-\frac{\pi}{6}$ (iii) 0 (iv) $-\frac{\pi}{4}$ 2. (i) $\frac{\pi}{2}$ (ii) $\frac{\pi}{3}$ 3. (i) $\frac{3\pi}{4}$ (ii) $-\frac{3\pi}{4}$ (iii) 0

3.3.4 INVERSE OF SECANT FUNCTION

In Class XI, we have learnt that $\sec\theta$ is not defined at odd multiples of $\pi/2$. Therefore, a rule associating $x \in R - \left\{(2n+1)\frac{\pi}{2} : n \in Z\right\}$ to $\sec x$ is a function whose graph is shown in Fig. 3.12.

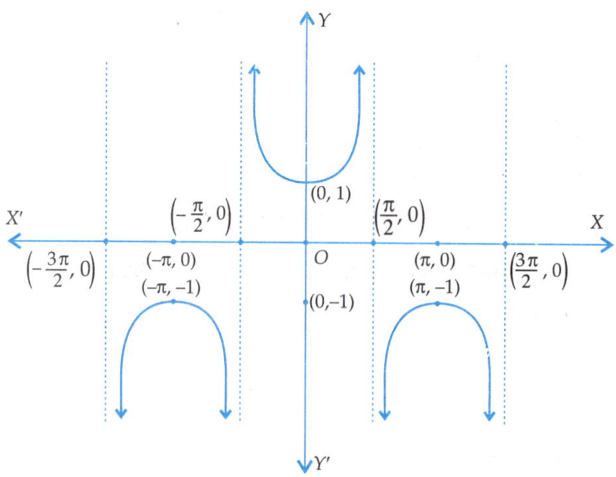

Fig. 3.12 Graph of $y = \sec x$

We observe that the function $\sec : R - \left\{(2n+1)\,\frac{\pi}{2} : n \in Z\right\} \to R$ is neither one-one nor onto but, $\sec : R - \left\{(2n+1)\,\frac{\pi}{2} : n \in Z\right\} \to (-\infty, -1] \cup [1, \infty)$ is many-one onto. If we restrict the domain to $\left[0, \frac{\pi}{2}\right) \cup \left(\frac{\pi}{2}, \pi\right]$, then the function associating each $x \in \left[0, \frac{\pi}{2}\right) \cup \left(\frac{\pi}{2}, \pi\right]$ to $\sec x \in (-\infty, -1] \cup [1, \infty)$ is a bijection as is evident from the graph of $y = \sec x$ shown in Fig. 3.13. the inverse of $\sec : \left[0, \frac{\pi}{2}\right) \cup \left(\frac{\pi}{2}, \pi\right] \to (-\infty, -1] \cup [1, \infty)$ is denoted by $\sec^{-1}$ such that $\sec^{-1}\theta = x \Leftrightarrow x = \sec\theta$.

Also, $\sec^{-1}(\sec\theta) = \theta$ for all $\theta \in [0, \pi/2) \cup (\pi/2, \pi]$ and, $\sec(\sec^{-1}x) = x$ for all $x \in (-\infty, -1] \cup [1, \infty)$ The graphs of functions $\sec : [0, \pi/2) \cup (\pi/2, \pi] \to (-\infty, -1] \cup [1, \infty)$ and $\sec^{-1} : (-\infty, -1] \cup [1, \infty) \to [0, \pi/2) \cup (\pi/2, \pi]$ are shown in Figures 3.13 and 3.14 respectively. The branch of $\sec^{-1}$ shown in Fig. 3.14 is called the principal value branch and the value of $\sec^{-1} x$ in $[0, \pi/2) \cup (\pi/2, \pi]$ for given value of $x \in (-\infty, -1] \cup [1, \infty)$ is called the principal value.

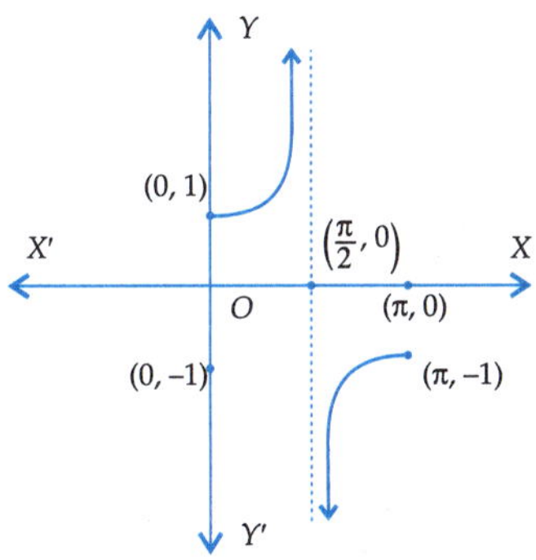

Fig. 3.13 Graph of $y = \sec x, 0 \le x \le \pi, x \ne \pi/2$

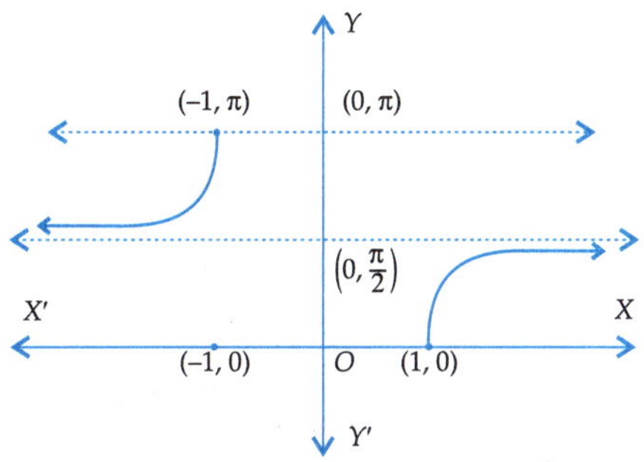

Fig. 3.14 Graph of $y = \sec^{-1} x$

SOME USEFUL OBSERVATION We make the following observations from the graphs of $\sec x$ and $\sec^{-1} x$:

(i) $\sec x$ is an increasing function on the intervals $[0, \pi/2)$ and $(\pi/2, \pi]$ but, it is neither increasing nor decreasing on $[0, \pi/2) \cup (\pi/2, \pi]$.

(ii) $\sec^{-1} x$ is an increasing function the intervals $(-\infty, -1]$ and $[1, \infty)$ but, it is neither increasing nor decreasing on $(-\infty, -1] \cup [1, \infty)$.

(iii) The maximum value of $\sec^{-1} x$ is π which it attains at $x = -1$.

(iv) The minimum value of $\sec^{-1} x$ is 0 which it attains at $x = 1$.

ILLUSTRATIVE EXAMPLES

BASED ON BASIC CONCEPTS (BASIC)

EXAMPLE 1 *Find the principal values of each of the following:*

(i) $\sec^{-1}(2)$ (ii) $\sec^{-1}\left(\frac{-2}{\sqrt{3}}\right)$.

SOLUTION For any $x \in (-\infty, -1] \cup [1, \infty)$, $\sec^{-1} x$ is an angle $\theta \in [0, \pi/2) \cup (\pi/2, \pi]$ whose secant is x i.e. $\sec\theta = x$. Therefore,

(i) $$\sec^{-1}(2) = \left(\text{An angle } \theta \in \left[0, \frac{\pi}{2}\right) \cup \left(\frac{\pi}{2}, 1\right] \text{ such that } \sec\theta = 2\right) = \frac{\pi}{3}$$

(ii) $\sec^{-1}\left(-\frac{2}{\sqrt{3}}\right)=\left(\text{An angle } \theta \in \left[0, \frac{\pi}{2}\right) \cup \left(\frac{\pi}{2}, \pi\right] \text{ such that } \sec\theta = -\frac{2}{\sqrt{3}}\right)=\frac{5\pi}{6}$

EXAMPLE 2 *Find the set of values of* $\sec^{-1}\left(\frac{\sqrt{3}}{2}\right)$.

SOLUTION We know that $\sec^{-1}x$ is defined for all $x \leq -1$ or $x \geq 1$ and $\frac{\sqrt{3}}{2} < 1$. Therefore, $\sec^{-1}\left(\frac{\sqrt{3}}{2}\right)$ is not meaningful. Hence, the set of values of $\sec^{-1}\left(\frac{\sqrt{3}}{2}\right)$ is the null set ϕ.

EXAMPLE 3 *Find the principal values of* $\sec^{-1}\frac{2}{\sqrt{3}}$ *and* $\sec^{-1}(-2)$.

SOLUTION Since $\sec^{-1}: R-(-1, 1) \to [0, \pi]-\left\{\frac{\pi}{2}\right\}$ is a bijection. Therefore, $\sec^{-1}x$ represents an angle in $[0, \pi]-\left\{\frac{\pi}{2}\right\}$ whose secant is x. Thus,

(i) $\sec^{-1}\left(\frac{2}{\sqrt{3}}\right)=\left(\text{An angle } \theta \in [0, \pi]-\left\{\frac{\pi}{2}\right\} \text{ such that } \sec\theta = \frac{2}{\sqrt{3}}\right)=\frac{\pi}{6}$

(ii) $\sec^{-1}(-2)=\left(\text{An angle } \theta \in [0, \pi]-\left\{\frac{\pi}{2}\right\} \text{ such that } \sec\theta = -2\right)=\frac{2\pi}{3}$

BASED ON HIGHER ORDER THINKING SKILLS (HOTS)

EXAMPLE 4 *Find the domain of* $\sec^{-1}(2x+1)$.

SOLUTION The domain of $\sec^{-1}x$ is $(-\infty, -1] \cup [1, \infty)$. Therefore, $\sec^{-1}(2x+1)$ is meaningful, if

$$2x+1 \geq 1 \text{ or, } 2x+1 \leq -1$$

$$\Rightarrow \quad 2x \geq 0 \text{ or, } 2x \leq -2 \Rightarrow x \geq 0 \text{ or, } x \leq -1 \Rightarrow x \in (-\infty, -1] \cup [0, \infty)$$

Hence, the domain of $\sec^{-1}(2x+1)$ is $(-\infty, -1] \cup [0, \infty)$.

EXAMPLE 5 *Find the domain of* $f(x)=\frac{1}{2}\sec^{-1}(5x-3)$.

SOLUTION $f(x)$ is defined for

$$5x-3 \leq -1 \text{ or } 5x-3 \geq 1$$

$$\Rightarrow \quad 5x \leq 2 \text{ or } 5x \geq 4 \Rightarrow x \leq \frac{2}{5} \text{ or } x \geq \frac{4}{5} \Rightarrow x \in \left(-\infty, \frac{2}{5}\right] \cup \left[\frac{4}{5}, \infty\right).$$

EXERCISE 3.4

BASIC

1. Find the principal values of each of the following:

   (i) $\sec^{-1}(-\sqrt{2})$ (ii) $\sec^{-1}(2)$ (iii) $\sec^{-1}\left(2\sin\frac{3\pi}{4}\right)$ (iv) $\sec^{-1}\left(2\tan\frac{3\pi}{4}\right)$

2. For the principal values, evaluate the following:

   (i) $\tan^{-1}\sqrt{3}-\sec^{-1}(-2)$ [CBSE 2012] (ii) $\sin^{-1}\left(-\frac{\sqrt{3}}{2}\right)-2\sec^{-1}\left(2\tan\frac{\pi}{6}\right)$

BASED ON HOTS

3. Find the domain of (i) $\sec^{-1}(3x-1)$ (ii) $\sec^{-1}x-\tan^{-1}x$

ANSWERS

1. (i) $\frac{3\pi}{4}$ (ii) $\frac{\pi}{3}$ (iii) $\frac{\pi}{4}$ (iv) $\frac{2\pi}{3}$ 2. (i) $-\frac{\pi}{3}$ (ii) $-\frac{2\pi}{3}$
3. (i) $(-\infty, 0] \cup [2/3, \infty)$ (ii) $(-\infty, -1] \cup [1, \infty)$

3.3.5 INVERSE OF COSECANT FUNCTION

In Class XI, we have learnt that the function $f(x) = \text{cosec } x$ has domain $R - \{n\pi : n \in Z\}$ and range $R - (-1, 1)$. The graph of this function is shown in Fig. 3.15. It is evident from the graph that $f : R - \{n\pi : n \in Z\} \to R$ defined as $f(x) = \text{cosec } x$ is a many-one into function and $f : R - \{n\pi : n \in Z\} \to R - (-1, 1)$ is many-one onto.

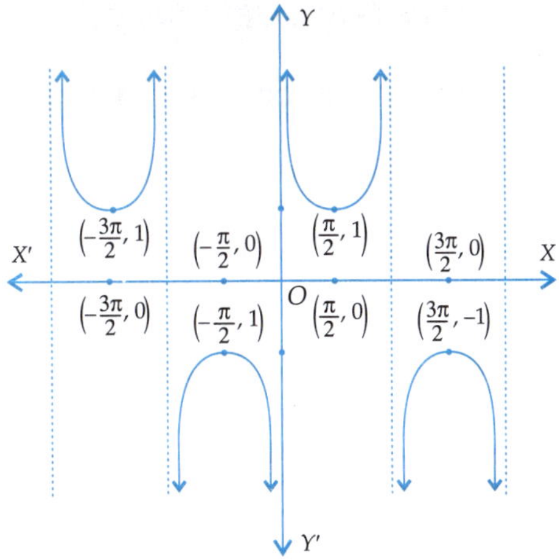

Fig. 3.15 Graph of $y = \text{cosec } x$

If we consider $f : [-\pi/2, 0) \cup (0, \pi/2] \to (-\infty, -1] \cup [1, \infty)$, then its is a bijection and hence invertible. The inverse of cosec is denoted by cosec^{-1} and is defined as

$$\text{cosec}^{-1} x = \theta \Leftrightarrow \text{cosec } \theta = x \text{ for all } \theta \in [-\pi/2, 0) \cup (0, \pi/2] \text{ and } x \in (-\infty, -1] \cup [1, \infty)$$

Also, $\text{cosec}^{-1}(\text{cosec } \theta) = \theta$ for all $\theta \in \left[-\frac{\pi}{2}, 0\right) \cup \left(0, \frac{\pi}{2}\right]$ and, $\text{cosec}(\text{cosec}^{-1} x) = x$ for all $x \in (-\infty, -1] \cup [1, \infty)$. The graphs of $\text{cosec} : [-\pi/2, 0) \cup (0, \pi/2] \to (-\infty, -1] \cup [1, \infty)$ and $\text{cosec}^{-1} : (-\infty -1] \cup [1, \infty) \to [-\pi/2, 0) \cup (0, \pi/2]$ are shown in Fig. 3.16 and 3.17 respectively.

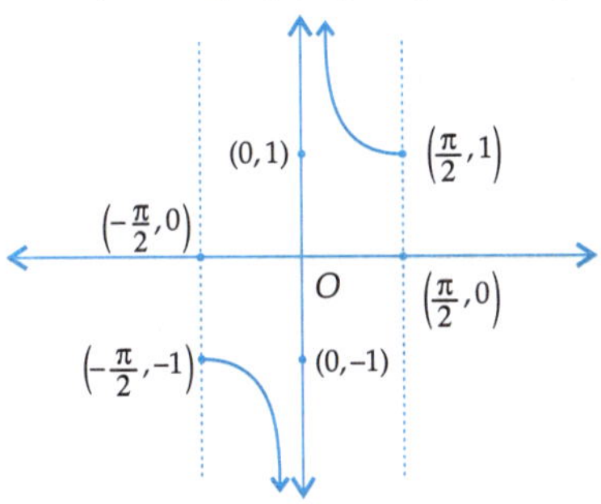

Fig. 3.16 Graph of $y = \text{cosec } x, -\frac{\pi}{2} \le x \le \frac{\pi}{2}, x \ne 0$

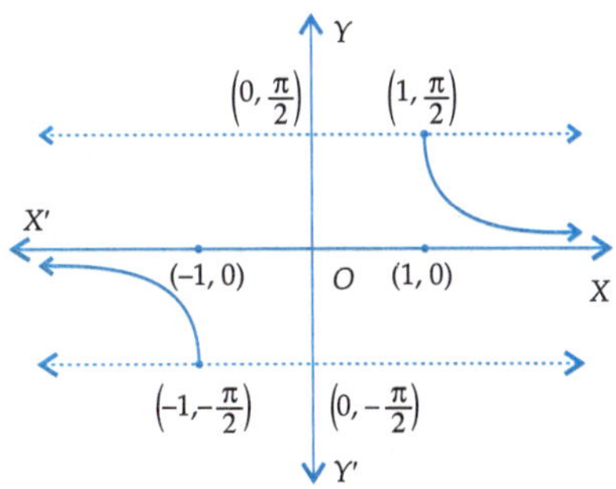

Fig. 3.17 Graph of $y = \text{cosec}^{-1} x$

The branch of $\text{cosec}^{-1} x$ shown in Fig. 3.17 is called the principal value branch and the value of $\text{cosec}^{-1} x$ lying in $[-\pi/2, 0) \cup (0, \pi/2]$ are the principal values.

SOME OBSERVATIONS It is evident from the graphs of cosec x and $\text{cosec}^{-1} x$ that

(i) cosec θ is a decreasing function on $[-\pi/2, 0)$ and $(0, \pi/2]$. But, it is neither decreasing nor increasing on $[-\pi/2, 0) \cup (0, \pi/2]$.

(ii) $\text{cosec}^{-1} x$ is decreasing on $(-\infty, -1]$ and $[1, \infty)$. But, it is neither increasing nor decreasing on $(-\infty, -1] \cup [1, \infty)$.

(iii) The maximum value of $\text{cosec}^{-1} x$ is $\pi/2$ which it attains at $x = 1$.

(iv) The minimum value is $\text{cosec}^{-1} x$ is $-\pi/2$ which it attains at $x = -1$.

ILLUSTRATIVE EXAMPLES

BASED ON BASIC CONCEPTS (BASIC)

EXAMPLE 1 *Find the principal values of* $\text{cosec}^{-1}(2)$ *and* $\text{cosec}^{-1}\left(-\frac{2}{\sqrt{3}}\right)$.

SOLUTION For $x \in (-\infty, -1] \cup [1, \infty)$, $\text{cosec}^{-1} x$ is an angle $\theta \in [-\pi/2, 0) \cup (0, \pi/2]$ such that cosec $\theta = x$.

$$\therefore \quad \text{cosec}^{-1}(2) = \left(\text{An angle } \theta \in \left[-\frac{\pi}{2}, 0\right) \cup \left(0, \frac{\pi}{2}\right] \text{ such that cosec } \theta = 2\right) = \frac{\pi}{6}$$

and,
$$\text{cosec}^{-1}\left(-\frac{2}{\sqrt{3}}\right) = \left(\text{An angle } \theta \in \left[-\frac{\pi}{2}, 0\right) \cup \left(0, \frac{\pi}{2}\right] \text{ such that cosec } \theta = -\frac{2}{\sqrt{3}}\right) = -\frac{\pi}{3}$$

EXAMPLE 2 *Find the set of values of* $\text{cosec}^{-1}\left(-\frac{1}{2}\right)$.

SOLUTION We know that $\text{cosec}^{-1} x$ is defined for all $x \leq -1$ or $x \geq 1$. So, $\text{cosec}^{-1}\left(-\frac{1}{2}\right)$ is not meaningful. Hence, the set of values of $\text{cosec}^{-1}\left(-\frac{1}{2}\right)$ is the null set ϕ.

EXAMPLE 3 *For the principal values, evaluate each of the following:*

(i) $\tan^{-1}\sqrt{3} - \sec^{-1}(-2) + \text{cosec}^{-1}\frac{2}{\sqrt{3}}$ (ii) $2\sec^{-1}(2) - 2\,\text{cosec}^{-1}(-2)$

SOLUTION (i) $\tan^{-1}\sqrt{3} - \sec^{-1}(-2) + \text{cosec}^{-1}\frac{2}{\sqrt{3}} = \frac{\pi}{3} - \frac{2\pi}{3} + \frac{\pi}{3} = 0$

(ii) $2\sec^{-1} 2 - 2\,\text{cosec}^{-1}(-2) = 2 \times \frac{\pi}{3} - 2 \times -\frac{\pi}{6} = \pi$

BASED ON HIGHER ORDER THINKING SKILLS (HOTS)

EXAMPLE 4 *If* $\text{cosec}^{-1} x + \text{cosec}^{-1} y + \text{cosec}^{-1} z = -\frac{3\pi}{2}$, *find the value of* $\frac{x}{y} + \frac{y}{z} + \frac{z}{x}$.

SOLUTION We know that the minimum value of $\text{cosec}^{-1} x$ is $-\frac{\pi}{2}$ which is attained at $x = -1$.

$$\therefore \quad \text{cosec}^{-1} x + \text{cosec}^{-1} y + \text{cosec}^{-1} z = -\frac{3\pi}{2}$$

$$\Rightarrow \quad \text{cosec}^{-1} x + \text{cosec}^{-1} y + \text{cosec}^{-1} z = \left(-\frac{\pi}{2}\right) + \left(-\frac{\pi}{2}\right) + \left(-\frac{\pi}{2}\right)$$

$\Rightarrow \quad \operatorname{cosec}^{-1} x = -\frac{\pi}{2}, \operatorname{cosec}^{-1} y = -\frac{\pi}{2}, \operatorname{cosec}^{-1} z = -\frac{\pi}{2} \Rightarrow x = -1, y = -1, z = -1$

$\therefore \quad \frac{x}{y} + \frac{y}{z} + \frac{z}{x} = \frac{(-1)}{(-1)} + \frac{(-1)}{(-1)} + \frac{(-1)}{(-1)} = 3$

EXERCISE 3.5

BASIC

1. Find the principal values of each of the following:
   (i) $\operatorname{cosec}^{-1}(-\sqrt{2})$ [NCERT]
   (ii) $\operatorname{cosec}^{-1}(-2)$
   (iii) $\operatorname{cosec}^{-1}\left(\frac{2}{\sqrt{3}}\right)$
   (iv) $\operatorname{cosec}^{-1}\left(2\cos\frac{2\pi}{3}\right)$
2. Find the set of values of $\operatorname{cosec}^{-1}\left(\frac{\sqrt{3}}{2}\right)$.
3. For the principal values, evaluate the following:
   (i) $\sin^{-1}\left(-\frac{\sqrt{3}}{2}\right) + \operatorname{cosec}^{-1}\left(-\frac{2}{\sqrt{3}}\right)$
   (ii) $\sec^{-1}(\sqrt{2}) + 2\operatorname{cosec}^{-1}(-\sqrt{2})$
   (iii) $\sin^{-1}\left[\cos\left\{2\operatorname{cosec}^{-1}(-2)\right\}\right]$
   (iv) $\operatorname{cosec}^{-1}\left(2\tan\frac{11\pi}{6}\right)$

ANSWERS

1. (i) $-\frac{\pi}{4}$ (ii) $-\frac{\pi}{6}$ (iii) $\frac{\pi}{3}$ (iv) $-\frac{\pi}{2}$ 2. ϕ 3. (i) $-\frac{2\pi}{3}$ (ii) $-\frac{\pi}{4}$ (iii) $\frac{\pi}{6}$ (iv) $-\frac{\pi}{3}$

3.3.6 INVERSE OF COTANGENT FUNCTION

We have learnt in earlier classes that the function $f(x) = \cot x$ has domain $= R - \{n\pi : n \in Z\}$ and range R. Therefore, $f : R - \{n\pi : n \in Z\} \to R$ is a many-one onto function as is evident from the curve $y = \cot x$ shown in Fig. 3.18.

If we consider $\cot : (0, \pi) \to R$, then it is a bijection and hence invertible. The inverse of this function is denoted by $\cot^{-1}$ and is defined as $\cot^{-1} x = \theta \Leftrightarrow \cot\theta = x$ for all $\theta \in (0, \pi)$ and all $x \in R$. Also, $\cot^{-1}(\cot\theta) = \theta$ for all $\theta \in (0, \pi)$ and, $\cot(\cot^{-1} x) = x$ for all $x \in R$.

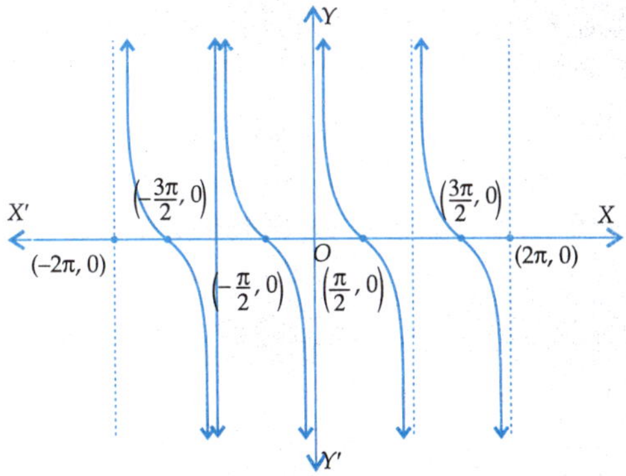

Fig. 3.18 Graph of $y = \cot x$

Graphs of $y = \cot x$ and $y = \cot^{-1} x$ are shown in Figures 3.19 and 3.20 respectively.

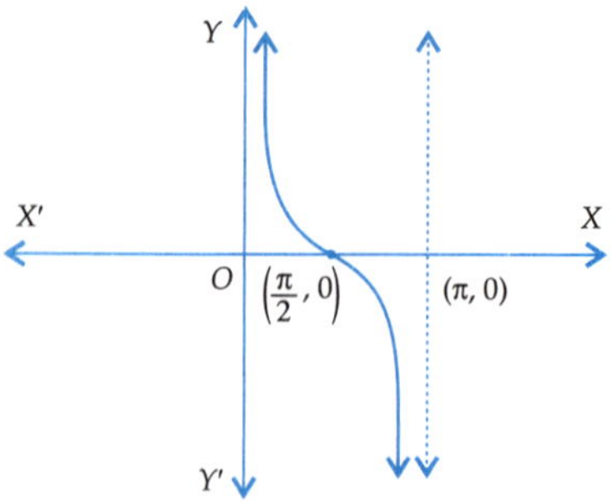

Fig. 3.19 Graph of $y = \cot x, 0 < x < \pi$

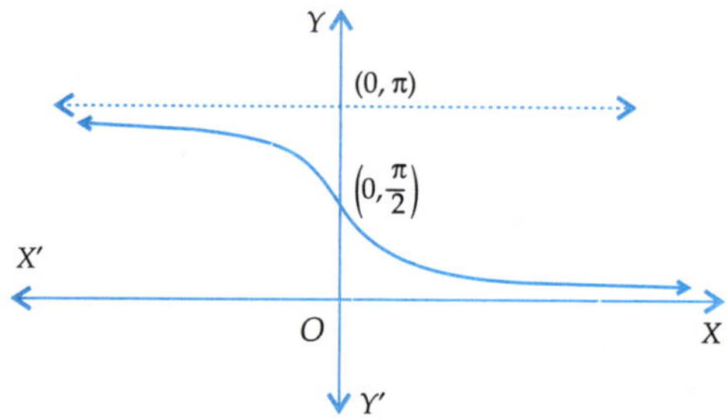

Fig. 3.20 Graph of $y = \cot^{-1} x$

The branch of $\cot^{-1} : R \to (0, \pi)$ is called the principal value branch and the value of $\cot^{-1} x$ for given x is called the principal value.

SOME USEFUL OBSERVATION It is evident from the graphs of $\cot x$ and $\cot^{-1} x$ that

(i) $\cot x$ is a decreasing function on $(0, \pi)$. i.e. $\theta_1 < \theta_2 \Rightarrow \cot \theta_1 > \cot \theta_2$ for all $\theta_1, \theta_2 \in (0, \pi)$

(ii) $\cot^{-1} x$ is a decreasing function on R. i.e. $x_1 < x_2 \Rightarrow \cot^{-1} x_1 > \cot^{-1} x_2$ for all $x_1, x_2 \in R$.

(iii) For all $x \in R$, the values of $\cot^{-1} x$ lie between 0 and π.

(iv) $\cot^{-1} x$ does not attain its minimum value zero and maximum value π at points in R.

ILLUSTRATIVE EXAMPLES

BASED ON BASIC CONCEPTS (BASIC)

EXAMPLE 1 *Find the set of values of* $\cot^{-1}(1)$ *and* $\cot^{-1}(-1)$

SOLUTION For any $x \in R$, $\cot^{-1} x$ is an angle $\theta \in (0, \pi)$ such that $\cot \theta = x$.

$$\therefore \quad \cot^{-1}(1) = \left(\text{An angle } \theta \in (0, \pi) \text{ such that } \cot \theta = 1\right) = \frac{\pi}{4}$$

$$\text{and,} \quad \cot^{-1}(-1) = \left(\text{An angle } \theta \in (0, \pi) \text{ whose cot angent is equal to } -1\right) = \frac{3\pi}{4}$$

Hence, required set is $\left\{\frac{\pi}{4}, \frac{3\pi}{3}\right\}$.

EXAMPLE 2 *Find the principal values of* $\cot^{-1}\sqrt{3}$ *and* $\cot^{-1}(-1)$.

SOLUTION We know that for any $x \in R$, $\cot^{-1} x$ denotes an angle in $(0, \pi)$ whose cotangent is x.

$$\therefore \quad \cot^{-1}\sqrt{3} = \left(\text{An angle in } (0, \pi) \text{ whose cotangent is } \sqrt{3}\right) = \frac{\pi}{6}$$

$$\text{and,} \quad \cot^{-1}(-1) = \left(\text{An angle in } (0, \pi) \text{ whose cotangent is } (-1)\right) = \frac{3\pi}{4}.$$

EXAMPLE 3 *For the principal values, evaluate the following:*

(i) $\cot^{-1}(-1) + \text{cosec}^{-1}(-\sqrt{2}) + \sec^{-1}(2)$ (ii) $\cot^{-1}(-\sqrt{3}) + \tan^{-1}(1) + \sec^{-1}\left(\frac{2}{\sqrt{3}}\right)$

SOLUTION (i) $\cot^{-1}(-1) + \text{cosec}^{-1}(-\sqrt{2}) + \text{secs}^{-1}(2) = \frac{3\pi}{4} - \frac{\pi}{4} + \frac{\pi}{3} = \frac{5\pi}{6}$

(ii) $\cot^{-1}(-\sqrt{3}) + \tan^{-1}(1) + \sec^{-1}\left(\frac{2}{\sqrt{3}}\right) = \frac{5\pi}{6} + \frac{\pi}{4} + \frac{\pi}{6} = \frac{5\pi}{4}$

EXAMPLE 4 *If* $\cot^{-1} x = \cos^{-1}(-1) - \text{cosec}^{-1}\left(\frac{2}{\sqrt{3}}\right)$, *find* $\tan^{-1}\left(\frac{1}{x}\right)$.

SOLUTION We have, $\cot^{-1} x = \cos^{-1}(-1) - \text{cosec}^{-1}\left(\frac{2}{\sqrt{3}}\right)$

$$\Rightarrow \quad \cot^{-1} x = \pi - \frac{\pi}{3} \Rightarrow \cot^{-1} x = \frac{2\pi}{3} \Rightarrow x = \cot\frac{2\pi}{3} \Rightarrow x = -\frac{1}{\sqrt{3}}$$

$$\therefore \quad \tan^{-1}\left(\frac{1}{x}\right) = \tan^{-1}(-\sqrt{3}) = -\frac{\pi}{3}$$

EXERCISE 3.6

BASIC

1. Find the principal values of each of the following:

   (i) $\cot^{-1}(-\sqrt{3})$ (ii) $\cot^{-1}(\sqrt{3})$ (iii) $\cot^{-1}\left(-\frac{1}{\sqrt{3}}\right)$ (iv) $\cot^{-1}\left(\tan\frac{3\pi}{4}\right)$

2. Find the domain of $f(x) = \cot x + \cot^{-1} x$.

3. Evaluate each of the following:

   (i) $\cot^{-1}\frac{1}{\sqrt{3}} - \text{cosec}^{-1}(-2) + \sec^{-1}\left(\frac{2}{\sqrt{3}}\right)$ (ii) $\cot^{-1}\left\{2\cos\left(\sin^{-1}\frac{\sqrt{3}}{2}\right)\right\}$

   (iii) $\text{cosec}^{-1}\left(-\frac{2}{\sqrt{3}}\right) + 2\cot^{-1}(-1)$

   (iv) $\tan^{-1}\left(-\frac{1}{\sqrt{3}}\right) + \cot^{-1}\left(\frac{1}{\sqrt{3}}\right) + \tan^{-1}\left(\sin\left(-\frac{\pi}{2}\right)\right)$ [NCERT EXEMPLAR]

ANSWERS

1. (i) $\frac{5\pi}{6}$ (ii) $\frac{\pi}{6}$ (iii) $\frac{2\pi}{3}$ (iv) $\frac{3\pi}{4}$

2. $R - \{n\pi : n \in Z\}$

3. (i) $\frac{2\pi}{3}$ (ii) $\frac{\pi}{4}$ (iii) $\frac{7\pi}{6}$ (iv) $-\frac{\pi}{12}$

As a ready reference domains, ranges and principal value branches of all inverse trigonometric functions are tabulated below.

Function	*Domain*	*Range*	*Principal value branch*
$\sin^{-1}$	$[-1, 1]$	$[-\pi/2, \pi/2]$	$y = \sin^{-1} x$ from $\left(-1, -\frac{\pi}{2}\right)$ to $\left(1, \frac{\pi}{2}\right)$
$\cos^{-1}$	$[-1, 1]$	$[0, \pi]$	$y = \cos^{-1} x$ from $(-1, \pi)$ to $(1, 0)$
$\tan^{-1}$	R	$(-\pi/2, \pi/2)$	$y = \tan^{-1} x$ from $\left(-\infty, -\frac{\pi}{2}\right)$ to $\left(\infty, \frac{\pi}{2}\right)$
cosec^{-1}	$(-\infty, -1] \cup [1, \infty)$	$[-\pi/2, \pi/2] - \{0\}$	$y = \text{cosec}^{-1} x$, from $(-\infty, 0)$ to $\left(-1, -\frac{\pi}{2}\right)$ and, from $\left(1, \frac{\pi}{2}\right)$ to $(\infty, 0)$
$\sec^{-1}$	$(-\infty, -1] \cup [1, \infty)$	$[0, \pi] - \left\{\frac{\pi}{2}\right\}$	$y = \sec^{-1} x$, from $\left(-\infty, \frac{\pi}{2}\right)$ to $(-1, \pi)$, and, from $(1, 0)$ to $\left(\infty, \frac{\pi}{2}\right)$
$\cot^{-1}$	R	$(0, \pi)$	$y = \cot^{-1} x$ from $(-\infty, \pi)$ to $(\infty, 0)$

NOTE 1 *If no branch of an inverse trigonometric function is mentioned, then it means the principal value branch of that function.*

3.4 PROPERTIES OF INVERSE TRIGONOMETRIC FUNCTIONS

In this section, we will learn about various properties of six inverse trigonometric functions defined in the previous section. These properties are very useful in simplifying expressions and solving equations involving inverse trigonometric functions.

3.4.1 PROPERTY-I

In chapter 2, we have learnt that if $f: A \to B$ is a bijection, then $f^{-1}: B \to A$ exists such that $f^{-1}of(x) = x$ or, $f^{-1}(f(x)) = x$ for all $x \in A$. In the previous section, we have learnt that $\sin: [-\pi/2, \pi/2] \to [-1, 1]$, $\cos: [0, \pi] \to [-1, 1]$, $\tan: (-\pi/2, \pi/2) \to R$, $\cot\,(0, \pi) \to R$ $\sec: [0, \pi/2) \cup (\pi/2, \pi] \to (-\infty, -1] \cup [1, \infty)$ and $\text{cosec}: [-\pi/2, 0) \cup (0, \pi/2] \to (-\infty, -1] \cup [1, \infty)$ are bijections. So, these functions and their inverses satisfy the following property.

PROPERTY-I *(i)* $\sin^{-1}(\sin\theta) = \theta$ *for all* $\theta \in [-\pi/2, \pi/2]$

(ii) $\cos^{-1}(\cos\theta) = \theta$ *for all* $\theta \in [0, \pi]$

(iii) $\tan^{-1}(\tan\theta) = \theta$ *for all* $\theta \in (-\pi/2, \pi/2)$

(iv) $\text{cosec}^{-1}(\text{cosec}\,\theta) = \theta$ *for all* $\theta \in [-\pi/2, 0) \cup (0, \pi/2]$

(v) $\sec^{-1}(\sec\theta) = \theta$ *for all* $\theta \in [0, \pi/2) \cup (\pi/2, \pi]$

(vi) $\cot^{-1}(\cot\theta) = \theta$ *for all* $\theta \in (0, \pi)$.

In the above property we observe that the relations between trigonometric functions and their inverses hold true for specific values of θ. If θ does not lie in the domain of a trigonometric function in which it is not a bijection, then the above relations do not hold good. For example, $\sin^{-1}(\sin\theta) = \theta$ holds true for $\theta \in [-\pi/2, \pi/2]$. If $\theta \notin [-\pi/2, \pi/2]$, what is the value of $\sin^{-1}(\sin\theta)$? To answer this, we partition real line into sub-intervals so that the sine function with domain any sub interval and co-domain $[-1, 1]$ is a bijection. Clearly, such sub-intervals are

$$\ldots\ldots\left[-\frac{5\pi}{2}, -\frac{3\pi}{2}\right], \left[-\frac{3\pi}{2}, -\frac{\pi}{2}\right], \left[-\frac{\pi}{2}, \frac{\pi}{2}\right], \left[\frac{\pi}{2}, \frac{3\pi}{2}\right], \left[\frac{3\pi}{2}, \frac{5\pi}{2}\right], \ldots\ldots$$

If $\theta \in \left[\frac{\pi}{2}, \frac{3\pi}{2}\right]$ i.e. $\frac{\pi}{2} \le \theta \frac{3\pi}{2}$, then $-\frac{3\pi}{2} \le -\theta \le -\frac{\pi}{2} \Rightarrow \pi - \frac{3\pi}{2} \le \pi - \theta \le \pi - \frac{\pi}{2} \Rightarrow -\frac{\pi}{2} \le \pi - \theta \le \frac{\pi}{2}$

$$\therefore \quad \sin^{-1}(\sin\theta) = \sin^{-1}\left(\sin\,(\pi - \theta)\right) = \pi - \theta$$

If $\theta \in \left[\frac{3\pi}{2}, \frac{5\pi}{2}\right]$ i.e. $\frac{3\pi}{2} \le \theta \le \frac{5\pi}{2}$, then

$$-\frac{5\pi}{2} \le -\theta \le -\frac{3\pi}{2} \Rightarrow 2\pi - \frac{5\pi}{2} \le 2\pi - \theta \le 2\pi - \frac{3\pi}{2} \Rightarrow -\frac{\pi}{2} \le 2\pi - \theta \le \frac{\pi}{2} \Rightarrow -\frac{\pi}{2} \le \theta - 2\pi \le \frac{\pi}{2}$$

$$\therefore \quad \sin^{-1}(\sin\theta) = \sin^{-1}\left(-\sin\,(2\pi - \theta)\right) = \sin^{-1}\left(\sin\,(\theta - 2\pi)\right) = \theta - 2\pi$$

If $\theta \in \left[-\frac{3\pi}{2}, -\frac{\pi}{2}\right]$ i.e. $-\frac{3\pi}{2} \le \theta \le -\frac{\pi}{2}$, then

$$-\frac{3\pi}{2} + \pi < \pi + \theta < \pi - \frac{\pi}{2} \Rightarrow -\frac{\pi}{2} \le \pi + \theta \le \frac{\pi}{2} \Rightarrow -\frac{\pi}{2} \le -\pi - \theta \le \frac{\pi}{2}$$

$\therefore \qquad \sin^{-1}(\sin\theta) = \sin^{-1}\left(-\sin(\pi+\theta)\right) = \sin^{-1}\left(\sin(-\pi-\theta)\right) = -\pi-\theta$

If $\theta \in \left[-\frac{5\pi}{2}, -\frac{3\pi}{2}\right]$ i.e. $-\frac{5\pi}{2} \le \theta \le -\frac{3\pi}{2}$, then $-\frac{5\pi}{2} + 2\pi \le 2\pi + \theta \le -\frac{3\pi}{2} + 2\pi \Rightarrow -\frac{\pi}{2} \le 2\pi + \theta \le \frac{\pi}{2}$.

$\therefore \qquad \sin^{-1}(\sin\theta) = \sin^{-1}\left(\sin(2\pi+\theta)\right) = 2\pi+\theta$

Thus, we obtain

$$\sin^{-1}(\sin\theta) = \begin{cases} 2\pi+\theta, & \text{if } -5\pi/2 \le \theta \le -3\pi/2 \\ -\pi-\theta, & \text{if } -3\pi/2 \le \theta \le -\pi/2 \\ \theta, & \text{if } -\pi/2 \le \theta \le \pi/2 \\ \pi-\theta, & \text{if } \pi/2 \le \theta \le 3\pi/2 \\ \theta-2\pi, & \text{if } 3\pi/2 \le \theta \le 5\pi/2 \\ 3\pi-\theta, & \text{if } 5\pi/2 \le \theta \le 7\pi/2 \end{cases} \quad \text{and so on.}$$

The graph of $y = \sin^{-1}(\sin x)$ is shown in Fig. 3.21. It is evident from the graph that the function $\sin^{-1}(\sin x)$ is a periodic function with period 2π.

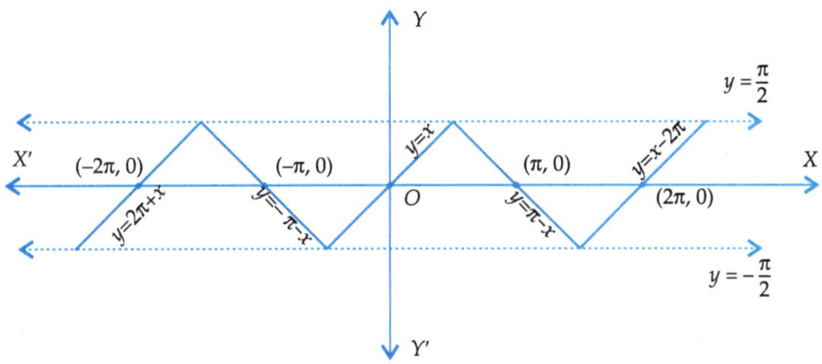

Fig. 3.21 Graph of $f(x) = \sin^{-1}(\sin x)$

Similarly, we find that

$$\cos^{-1}(\cos\theta) = \begin{cases} -2\pi-\theta, & \text{if } -3\pi \le \theta \le -2\pi \\ 2\pi+\theta, & \text{if } -2\pi \le \theta \le -\pi \\ -\theta, & \text{if } -\pi \le \theta \le 0 \\ \theta, & \text{if } 0 \le \theta \le \pi \\ 2\pi-\theta, & \text{if } \pi \le \theta \le 2\pi \\ \theta-2\pi, & \text{if } 2\pi \le \theta \le 3\pi \end{cases} \quad \text{and so on.}$$

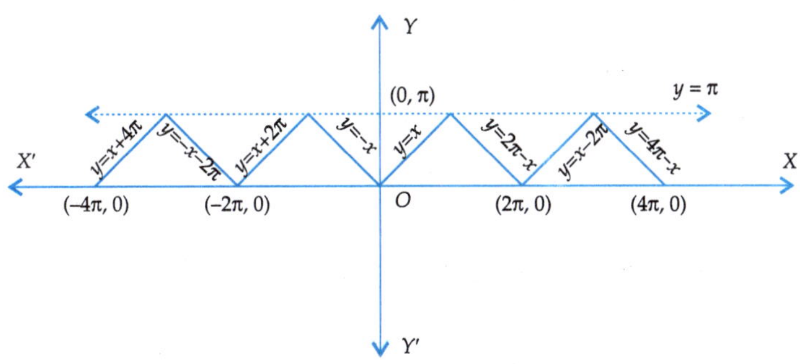

Fig. 3.22 Graph of $y = \cos^{-1}(\cos x)$

$$\tan^{-1}(\tan\theta) = \begin{cases} 2\pi+\theta, & \text{if } -5\pi/2 < \theta < -3\pi/2 \\ \pi+\theta, & \text{if } -3\pi/2 < \theta < -\pi/2 \\ \theta, & \text{if } -\pi/2 < \theta < \pi/2 \\ \theta-\pi, & \text{if } \pi/2 < \theta < 3\pi/2 \\ \theta-2\pi, & \text{if } 3\pi/2 < \theta < 5\pi/2 \end{cases} \quad \text{and so on}$$

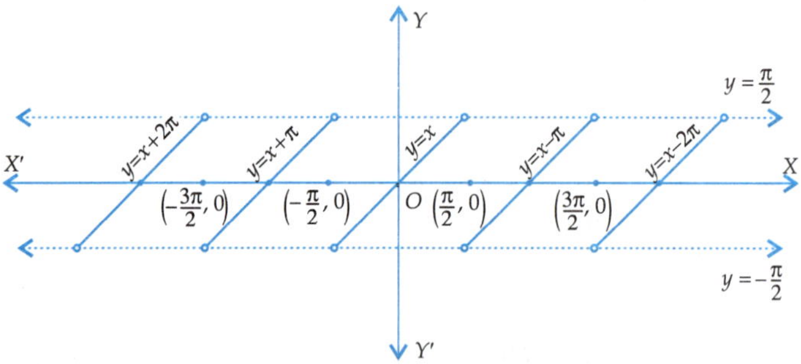

Fig. 3.23 Graph of $y = \tan^{-1}(\tan x)$

$$\sec^{-1}(\sec\theta) = \begin{cases} 2\pi+\theta, & \text{if } \theta \in \left[-2\pi, -\frac{3\pi}{2}\right) \cup \left(-\frac{3\pi}{2}, -\pi\right] \\ -\theta, & \text{if } \theta \in \left[-\pi, -\frac{\pi}{2}\right) \cup \left(-\frac{\pi}{2}, 0\right] \\ \theta, & \text{if } \theta \in \left[0, \frac{\pi}{2}\right) \cup \left(\frac{\pi}{2}, \pi\right] \\ 2\pi-\theta, & \text{if } \theta \in \left[\pi, \frac{3\pi}{2}\right) \cup \left(\frac{3\pi}{2}, 2\pi\right] \\ \theta-2\pi, & \text{if } \theta \in \left[2\pi, \frac{5\pi}{2}\right) \cup \left(\frac{5\pi}{2}, 3\pi\right] \end{cases} \quad \text{and so on}$$

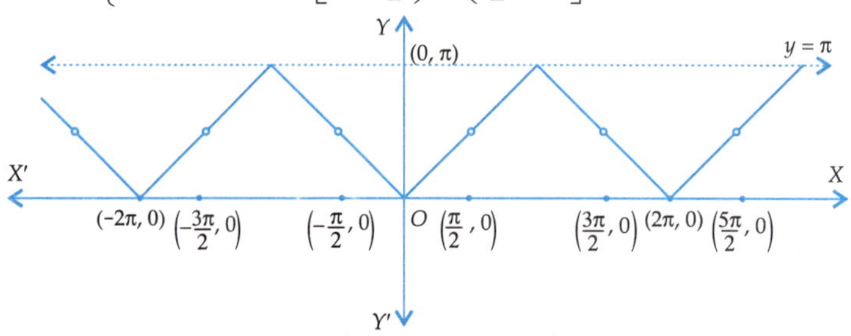

Fig. 3.24 Graph of $y = \sec^{-1}(\sec x)$

$$\operatorname{cosec}^{-1}(\operatorname{cosec}\theta) = \begin{cases} 2\pi+\theta, & \text{if } \theta \in \left[-\frac{5\pi}{2}, -2\pi\right) \cup \left(-2\pi, -\frac{3\pi}{2}\right] \\ -\pi-\theta, & \text{if } \theta \in \left[-\frac{3\pi}{2}, -\pi\right) \cup \left(-\pi, \frac{\pi}{2}\right] \\ \theta, & \text{if } \theta \in \left[-\frac{\pi}{2}, 0\right) \cup \left(0, \frac{\pi}{2}\right] \\ \pi-\theta, & \text{if } \theta \in \left[\frac{\pi}{2}, \pi\right) \cup \left(\pi, \frac{3\pi}{2}\right] \\ \theta-2\pi, & \text{if } \theta \in \left[\frac{3\pi}{2}, 2\pi\right) \cup \left(2\pi, \frac{5\pi}{2}\right] \end{cases} \quad \text{and so on}$$

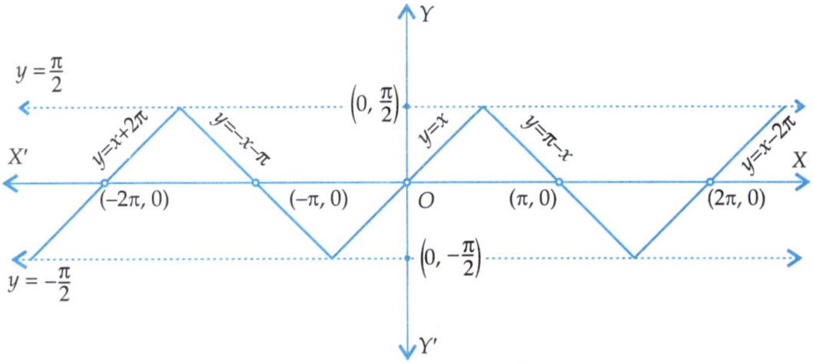

Fig. 3.25 Graph of $y = \text{cosec}^{-1}(\text{cosec } x)$

$$\cot^{-1}(\cot\theta) = \begin{cases} 2\pi+\theta, & \text{if } \theta \in (-2\pi, \pi) \\ \pi+\theta, & \text{if } \theta \in (-\pi, 0) \\ \theta, & \text{if } \theta \in (0, \pi) \\ \theta-\pi, & \text{if } \theta \in (\pi, 2\pi) \\ \theta-2\pi, & \text{if } \theta \in (2\pi, 3\pi) \quad \text{and so on} \end{cases}$$

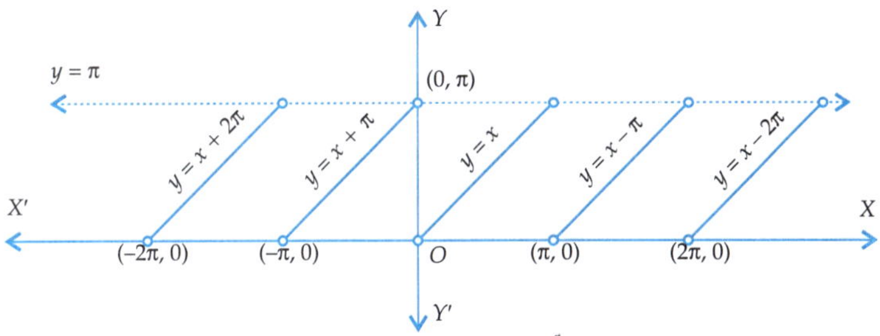

Fig. 3.26 Graph of $y = \cot^{-1}(\cot x)$

ILLUSTRATIVE EXAMPLES

BASED ON BASIC CONCEPTS (BASIC)

EXAMPLE 1 *Evaluate each of the following:*

(i) $\sin^{-1}\left(\sin\frac{\pi}{3}\right)$ (ii) $\cos^{-1}\left(\cos\frac{2\pi}{3}\right)$ (iii) $\tan^{-1}\left(\tan\frac{\pi}{4}\right)$

(iv) $\sin^{-1}\left(\sin\frac{2\pi}{3}\right)$ (v) $\cos^{-1}\left(\cos\frac{7\pi}{6}\right)$ [CBSE 2009] (vi) $\tan^{-1}\left(\tan\frac{3\pi}{4}\right)$

(vii) $\sin^{-1}\left(\sin(-600°)\right)$ [NCERT EXEMPLAR]

(viii) $\cos^{-1}\left(\cos(-680°)\right)$ [NCERT EXEMPLAR]

SOLUTION (i) We know that $\sin^{-1}(\sin\theta) = \theta$, if $-\frac{\pi}{2} \le \theta \le \frac{\pi}{2}$. Therefore, $\sin^{-1}\left(\sin\frac{\pi}{3}\right) = \frac{\pi}{3}$.

(ii) We know that $\cos^{-1}(\cos\theta) = \theta$ for $0 \le \theta \le \pi$. Therefore, $\cos^{-1}\left(\cos\frac{2\pi}{3}\right) = \frac{2\pi}{3}$.

(iii) We know that $\tan^{-1}(\tan\theta) = \theta$ for $-\frac{\pi}{2} < \theta < \frac{\pi}{2}$. Therefore, $\tan^{-1}\left(\tan\frac{\pi}{4}\right) = \frac{\pi}{4}$.

(iv) $\sin^{-1}\left(\sin\frac{2\pi}{3}\right) \neq \frac{2\pi}{3}$ as $\frac{2\pi}{3}$ does not lie between $-\frac{\pi}{2}$ and $\frac{\pi}{2}$.

Now, $\sin^{-1}\left(\sin\frac{2\pi}{3}\right) = \sin^{-1}\left\{\sin\left(\pi-\frac{\pi}{3}\right)\right\}$ $\left[\because \sin\frac{2\pi}{3} = \sin\left(\pi-\frac{\pi}{3}\right)\right]$

$= \sin^{-1}\left(\sin\frac{\pi}{3}\right) = \frac{\pi}{3}$ $[\because \sin(\pi-\theta) = \sin\theta]$

ALITER From Fig. 3.21, we find that $\sin^{-1}(\sin\theta) = \pi - \theta$ for $\frac{\pi}{2} \leq \theta \leq \frac{3\pi}{2}$.

$\therefore$ $\sin^{-1}\left(\sin\frac{2\pi}{3}\right) = \pi - \frac{2\pi}{3} = \frac{\pi}{3}$

(v) $\cos^{-1}\left(\cos\frac{7\pi}{6}\right) \neq \frac{7\pi}{6}$, because $\frac{7\pi}{6}$ does not lie between 0 and π.

$\therefore$ $\cos^{-1}\left(\cos\frac{7\pi}{6}\right) = \cos^{-1}\left\{\cos\left(2\pi-\frac{5\pi}{6}\right)\right\}$ $\left[\because \frac{7\pi}{6} = 2\pi - \frac{5\pi}{6}\right]$

$= \cos^{-1}\left(\cos\frac{5\pi}{6}\right) = \frac{5\pi}{6}$ $[\because \cos(2\pi-\theta) = \cos\theta]$

ALITER From Fig. 3.22, it is evident that $\cos^{-1}(\cos\theta) = 2\pi - \theta$ for $\pi \leq \theta \leq 2\pi$.

$\therefore$ $\cos^{-1}\left(\cos\frac{7\pi}{6}\right) = 2\pi - \frac{7\pi}{6} = \frac{5\pi}{6}$

(vi) $\tan^{-1}\left(\tan\frac{3\pi}{4}\right) \neq \frac{3\pi}{4}$, because $\frac{3\pi}{4}$ does not lie between $-\frac{\pi}{2}$ and $\frac{\pi}{2}$.

$\therefore$ $\tan^{-1}\left(\tan\frac{3\pi}{4}\right) = \tan^{-1}\left\{\tan\left(\pi-\frac{\pi}{4}\right)\right\}$ $\left[\because \frac{3\pi}{4} = \pi - \frac{\pi}{4}\right]$

$= \tan^{-1}\left(-\tan\frac{\pi}{4}\right) = \tan^{-1}\left\{\tan\left(-\frac{\pi}{4}\right)\right\} = -\frac{\pi}{4}$ $[\because \tan(\pi-\theta) = -\tan\theta]$

ALITER It is evident from Fig. 3.23 that $\tan^{-1}(\tan\theta) = \theta - \pi$ for $\frac{\pi}{2} \leq \theta \leq \frac{3\pi}{2}$.

$\therefore$ $\tan^{-1}\left(\tan\frac{3\pi}{4}\right) = \frac{3\pi}{4} - \pi = -\frac{\pi}{4}$.

(vii) $\sin^{-1}\left(\sin(-600°)\right) = \sin^{-1}\left\{\sin\left(-600\times\frac{\pi}{180}\right)\right\} = \sin^{-1}\left\{\sin\left(-\frac{10\pi}{3}\right)\right\} = \sin^{-1}\left(-\sin\frac{10\pi}{3}\right)$

$= \sin^{-1}\left\{-\sin\left(3\pi+\frac{\pi}{3}\right)\right\} = \sin^{-1}\left\{-\left(-\sin\frac{\pi}{3}\right)\right\} = \sin^{-1}\left(\sin\frac{\pi}{3}\right) = \frac{\pi}{3}$

ALITER From Fig. 3.21, we observe that $\sin^{-1}(\sin\theta) = -3\pi - \theta$ for $-\frac{7\pi}{2} \leq \theta \leq -\frac{5\pi}{2}$

$\therefore$ $\sin^{-1}\left\{\sin(-600°)\right\} = \sin^{-1}\left\{\sin\left(-\frac{10\pi}{3}\right)\right\} = -3\pi + \frac{10\pi}{3} = \frac{\pi}{3}$

(viii) $\cos^{-1}\left\{\cos(-680°)\right\} = \cos^{-1}(\cos 680°) = \cos^{-1}\left\{\cos\left(680\times\frac{\pi}{180}\right)\right\} = \cos^{-1}\left(\cos\frac{34\pi}{9}\right)$

$= \cos^{-1}\left\{\cos\left(4\pi-\frac{2\pi}{9}\right)\right\} = \cos^{-1}\left(\cos\frac{2\pi}{9}\right) = \frac{2\pi}{9}$

ALITER From Fig. 3.22, we find that $\cos^{-1}(\cos\theta) = \theta + 4\pi$, if $-4\pi \leq \theta \leq -3\pi$ and $-680° = -\frac{34\pi}{9}$

$\therefore$ $\cos^{-1}\left\{\cos(-680°)\right\} = \cos^{-1}\left\{\cos\left(-\frac{34\pi}{9}\right)\right\} = -\frac{34\pi}{9} + 4\pi = \frac{2\pi}{9}$

BASED ON LOWER ORDER THINKING SKILLS (LOTS)

EXAMPLE 2 *Express each of the following in the simplest form:*

(i) $\tan^{-1}\left\{\sqrt{\frac{1-\cos x}{1+\cos x}}\right\}, -\pi < x < \pi$ [NCERT] (ii) $\tan^{-1}\left(\frac{\cos x}{1+\sin x}\right), -\frac{\pi}{2} < x < \frac{\pi}{2}$ [CBSE 2012]

(iii) $\tan^{-1}\left(\frac{\cos x}{1-\sin x}\right), -\frac{\pi}{2} < x < \frac{\pi}{2}$ [NCERT] (iv) $\tan^{-1}\left(\frac{\cos x - \sin x}{\cos x + \sin x}\right), -\frac{\pi}{4} < x < \frac{\pi}{4}$ [NCERT]

SOLUTION (i) We have,

$$\tan^{-1}\left\{\sqrt{\frac{1-\cos x}{1+\cos x}}\right\} = \tan^{-1}\left\{\sqrt{\frac{2\sin^2\frac{x}{2}}{2\cos^2\frac{x}{2}}}\right\} = \tan^{-1}\left\{\sqrt{\tan^2\frac{x}{2}}\right\} = \tan^{-1}\left\{\left|\tan\frac{x}{2}\right|\right\}$$

$$= \begin{cases} \tan^{-1}\left(-\tan\frac{x}{2}\right) & , \text{if } -\pi < x < 0 \\ \tan^{-1}\left(\tan\frac{x}{2}\right) & , \text{if } 0 \le x < \pi \end{cases} = \begin{cases} \tan^{-1}\left\{\tan\left(-\frac{x}{2}\right)\right\} = -\frac{x}{2}, & \text{if } -\pi < x < 0 \\ \tan^{-1}\left\{\tan\frac{x}{2}\right\} = \frac{x}{2} & , \text{if } 0 < x < \pi \end{cases}$$

(ii) We have,

$$\tan^{-1}\left(\frac{\cos x}{1+\sin x}\right) = \tan^{-1}\left\{\frac{\cos^2\frac{x}{2} - \sin^2\frac{x}{2}}{\cos^2\frac{x}{2} + \sin^2\frac{x}{2} + 2\sin\frac{x}{2}\cos\frac{x}{2}}\right\}$$

$$= \tan^{-1}\left\{\frac{\left(\cos\frac{x}{2} - \sin\frac{x}{2}\right)\left(\cos\frac{x}{2} + \sin\frac{x}{2}\right)}{\left(\cos\frac{x}{2} + \sin\frac{x}{2}\right)^2}\right\}$$

$$= \tan^{-1}\left\{\frac{\cos\frac{x}{2} - \sin\frac{x}{2}}{\cos\frac{x}{2} + \sin\frac{x}{2}}\right\} = \tan^{-1}\left\{\frac{1-\tan\frac{x}{2}}{1+\tan\frac{x}{2}}\right\}$$

$$= \tan^{-1}\left\{\tan\left(\frac{\pi}{4} - \frac{x}{2}\right)\right\} = \frac{\pi}{4} - \frac{x}{2} \quad \left[\because -\frac{\pi}{2} < x < \frac{\pi}{2} \Rightarrow -\frac{\pi}{4} < -\frac{x}{2} < \frac{\pi}{4} \Rightarrow 0 < \frac{\pi}{4} - \frac{x}{2} < \frac{\pi}{2}\right]$$

ALITER We have,

$$\tan^{-1}\left(\frac{\cos x}{1+\sin x}\right) = \tan^{-1}\left\{\frac{\sin\left(\frac{\pi}{2} + x\right)}{1 - \cos\left(\frac{\pi}{2} + x\right)}\right\}$$

$$= \tan^{-1}\left\{\frac{2\sin\left(\frac{\pi}{4} + \frac{x}{2}\right)\cos\left(\frac{\pi}{4} + \frac{x}{2}\right)}{2\sin^2\left(\frac{\pi}{4} + \frac{x}{2}\right)}\right\} = \tan^{-1}\left\{\cot\left(\frac{\pi}{4} + \frac{x}{2}\right)\right\}$$

$$= \tan^{-1}\left\{\tan\left\{\frac{\pi}{2} - \left(\frac{\pi}{4} + \frac{x}{2}\right)\right\}\right\} = \tan^{-1}\left\{\tan\left(\frac{\pi}{4} - \frac{x}{2}\right)\right\} = \frac{\pi}{4} - \frac{x}{2}$$

(iii) We have,

$$\tan^{-1}\left(\frac{\cos x}{1-\sin x}\right) = \tan^{-1}\left\{\frac{\cos^2\frac{x}{2}-\sin^2\frac{x}{2}}{\cos^2\frac{x}{2}+\sin^2\frac{x}{2}-2\sin\frac{x}{2}\cos\frac{x}{2}}\right\}$$

$$= \tan^{-1}\left\{\frac{\left(\cos\frac{x}{2}+\sin\frac{x}{2}\right)\left(\cos\frac{x}{2}-\sin\frac{x}{2}\right)}{\left(\cos\frac{x}{2}-\sin\frac{x}{2}\right)^2}\right\}$$

$$= \tan^{-1}\left\{\frac{\cos\frac{x}{2}+\sin\frac{x}{2}}{\cos\frac{x}{2}-\sin\frac{x}{2}}\right\} = \tan^{-1}\left\{\frac{1+\tan\frac{x}{2}}{1-\tan\frac{x}{2}}\right\} = \tan^{-1}\left\{\tan\left(\frac{\pi}{4}+\frac{x}{2}\right)\right\}$$

$$= \frac{\pi}{4}+\frac{x}{2} \qquad \left[\because -\frac{\pi}{2}<x<\frac{\pi}{2} \Rightarrow -\frac{\pi}{4}<\frac{x}{2}<\frac{\pi}{4} \Rightarrow 0<\frac{\pi}{4}+\frac{x}{2}<\frac{\pi}{2}\right]$$

ALITER We have,

$$\tan^{-1}\left(\frac{\cos x}{1-\sin x}\right) = \tan^{-1}\left\{\frac{\sin\left(\frac{\pi}{2}-x\right)}{1-\cos\left(\frac{\pi}{2}-x\right)}\right\}$$

$$= \tan^{-1}\left\{\frac{2\sin\left(\frac{\pi}{4}-\frac{x}{2}\right)\cos\left(\frac{\pi}{4}-\frac{x}{2}\right)}{2\sin^2\left(\frac{\pi}{4}-\frac{x}{2}\right)}\right\} = \tan^{-1}\left\{\cot\left\{\frac{\pi}{4}-\frac{x}{2}\right)\right\}$$

$$= \tan^{-1}\left[\tan\left\{\frac{\pi}{2}-\left(\frac{\pi}{4}-\frac{x}{2}\right)\right\}\right] = \tan^{-1}\left\{\tan^{-1}\left(\frac{\pi}{4}+\frac{x}{2}\right)\right\} = \frac{\pi}{4}+\frac{x}{2}$$

(iv) We have,

$$\tan^{-1}\left(\frac{\cos x-\sin x}{\cos x+\sin x}\right) = \tan^{-1}\left(\frac{1-\tan x}{1+\tan x}\right) = \tan^{-1}\left\{\tan\left(\frac{\pi}{4}-x\right)\right\}$$

$$= \frac{\pi}{4}-x \qquad \left[\because -\frac{\pi}{4}<x<\frac{\pi}{4} \Rightarrow -\frac{\pi}{4}<-x<\frac{\pi}{4} \Rightarrow 0<\frac{\pi}{4}-x<\frac{\pi}{2}\right]$$

EXAMPLE 3 *Prove that:*

(i) $\tan^{-1}\left\{\frac{\sqrt{1+\cos x}+\sqrt{1-\cos x}}{\sqrt{1+\cos x}-\sqrt{1-\cos x}}\right\} = \frac{\pi}{4}+\frac{x}{2}, 0<x<\frac{\pi}{2}$

(ii) $\cot^{-1}\left\{\frac{\sqrt{1+\sin x}+\sqrt{1-\sin x}}{\sqrt{1+\sin x}-\sqrt{1-\sin x}}\right\} = \frac{x}{2}, 0<x<\frac{\pi}{2}$ **[NCERT, CBSE 2009, 2014, 2016]**

SOLUTION (i) We have,

$$\tan^{-1}\left\{\frac{\sqrt{1+\cos x}+\sqrt{1-\cos x}}{\sqrt{1+\cos x}-\sqrt{1-\cos x}}\right\} = \tan^{-1}\left\{\frac{\sqrt{2\cos^2\frac{x}{2}}+\sqrt{2\sin^2\frac{x}{2}}}{\sqrt{2\cos^2\frac{x}{2}}-\sqrt{2\sin^2\frac{x}{2}}}\right\}$$

$$= \tan^{-1}\left\{\frac{\cos\frac{x}{2}+\sin\frac{x}{2}}{\cos\frac{x}{2}-\sin\frac{x}{2}}\right\} \qquad \left[\because\ 0<\frac{x}{2}<\frac{\pi}{4}\ \therefore \cos\frac{x}{2}>0,\ \sin\frac{x}{2}>0\right]$$

$$= \tan^{-1}\left\{\frac{1+\tan\frac{x}{2}}{1-\tan\frac{x}{2}}\right\} = \tan^{-1}\left\{\tan\left(\frac{\pi}{4}+\frac{x}{2}\right)\right\} = \frac{\pi}{4}+\frac{x}{2} \quad \left[\because\ 0<x<\frac{\pi}{2}\ \therefore \frac{\pi}{4}<\frac{\pi}{4}+\frac{x}{2}<\frac{\pi}{2}\right]$$

(ii) We know that: $1 \pm \sin x = \cos^2\frac{x}{2}+\sin^2\frac{x}{2} \pm 2\sin\frac{x}{2}\cos\frac{x}{2} = \left(\cos\frac{x}{2} \pm \sin\frac{x}{2}\right)^2$

$$\therefore \quad \cot^{-1}\left\{\frac{\sqrt{1+\sin x}+\sqrt{1-\sin x}}{\sqrt{1+\sin x}-\sqrt{1-\sin x}}\right\} = \cot^{-1}\left\{\frac{\sqrt{\left(\cos\frac{x}{2}+\sin\frac{x}{2}\right)^2}+\sqrt{\left(\cos\frac{x}{2}-\sin\frac{x}{2}\right)^2}}{\sqrt{\left(\cos\frac{x}{2}+\sin\frac{x}{2}\right)^2}-\sqrt{\left(\cos\frac{x}{2}-\sin\frac{x}{2}\right)^2}}\right\}$$

$$= \cot^{-1}\left\{\frac{\left|\cos\frac{x}{2}+\sin\frac{x}{2}\right|+\left|\cos\frac{x}{2}-\sin\frac{x}{2}\right|}{\left|\cos\frac{x}{2}+\sin\frac{x}{2}\right|-\left|\cos\frac{x}{2}-\sin\frac{x}{2}\right|}\right\} \qquad \left[\because\ \sqrt{x^2}=|x|\right]$$

$$= \cot^{-1}\left\{\frac{\left(\cos\frac{x}{2}+\sin\frac{x}{2}\right)+\left(\cos\frac{x}{2}-\sin\frac{x}{2}\right)}{\left(\cos\frac{x}{2}+\sin\frac{x}{2}\right)-\left(\cos\frac{x}{2}-\sin\frac{x}{2}\right)}\right\} \qquad \left[\because\ 0<\frac{x}{2}<\frac{\pi}{4}\ \therefore \cos\frac{x}{2}>\sin\frac{x}{2}\right]$$

$$= \cot^{-1}\left(\cot\frac{x}{2}\right) = \frac{x}{2} \qquad \left[\because\ 0<\frac{x}{2}<\frac{\pi}{4}\right]$$

EXAMPLE 4 *Prove that:*

(i) $\tan^{-1}\left\{\frac{\sqrt{1+\cos x}+\sqrt{1-\cos x}}{\sqrt{1+\cos x}-\sqrt{1-\cos x}}\right\} = \frac{\pi}{4}-\frac{x}{2}$, if $\pi < x < \frac{3\pi}{2}$

(ii) $\cot^{-1}\left\{\frac{\sqrt{1+\sin x}+\sqrt{1-\sin x}}{\sqrt{1+\sin x}-\sqrt{1-\sin x}}\right\} = \frac{\pi}{2}-\frac{x}{2}$, if $\frac{\pi}{2} < x < \pi$ **[CBSE 2011]**

SOLUTION (i) We have,

$$\tan^{-1}\left\{\frac{\sqrt{1+\cos x}+\sqrt{1-\cos x}}{\sqrt{1+\cos x}-\sqrt{1-\cos x}}\right\}$$

$$= \tan^{-1}\left\{\frac{\sqrt{2\cos^2\frac{x}{2}}+\sqrt{2\sin^2\frac{x}{2}}}{\sqrt{2\cos^2\frac{x}{2}}-\sqrt{2\sin^2\frac{x}{2}}}\right\} = \tan^{-1}\left\{\frac{\sqrt{2}\left|\cos\frac{x}{2}\right|+\sqrt{2}\left|\sin\frac{x}{2}\right|}{\sqrt{2}\left|\cos\frac{x}{2}\right|-\sqrt{2}\left|\sin\frac{x}{2}\right|}\right\}$$

$$= \tan^{-1}\left\{\frac{-\cos\frac{x}{2}+\sin\frac{x}{2}}{-\cos\frac{x}{2}-\sin\frac{x}{2}}\right\} \qquad \left[\begin{array}{l}\because\ \pi<x<\frac{3\pi}{2} \Rightarrow \frac{\pi}{2}<\frac{x}{2}<\frac{3\pi}{4}\\ \therefore \left|\cos\frac{x}{2}\right| = -\cos\frac{x}{2},\ \left|\sin\frac{x}{2}\right| = \sin\frac{x}{2}\end{array}\right]$$

$$= \tan^{-1}\left\{\frac{\cos\frac{x}{2}-\sin\frac{x}{2}}{\cos\frac{x}{2}+\sin\frac{x}{2}}\right\} = \tan^{-1}\left\{\frac{1-\tan\frac{x}{2}}{1+\tan\frac{x}{2}}\right\}$$

$$= \tan^{-1}\left\{\tan\left(\frac{\pi}{4}-\frac{x}{2}\right)\right\} = \frac{\pi}{4}-\frac{x}{2} \qquad \left[\because\ \pi < x < \frac{3\pi}{2} \therefore -\frac{\pi}{2} < \frac{\pi}{4}-\frac{x}{2} < -\frac{\pi}{4}\right]$$

(ii) We have,

$$\cot^{-1}\left\{\frac{\sqrt{1+\sin x}+\sqrt{1-\sin x}}{\sqrt{1+\sin x}-\sqrt{1-\sin x}}\right\} = \cot^{-1}\left\{\frac{\sqrt{\left(\cos\frac{x}{2}+\sin\frac{x}{2}\right)^2}+\sqrt{\left(\cos\frac{x}{2}-\sin\frac{x}{2}\right)^2}}{\sqrt{\left(\cos\frac{x}{2}+\sin\frac{x}{2}\right)^2}-\sqrt{\left(\cos\frac{x}{2}-\sin\frac{x}{2}\right)^2}}\right\}$$

$$= \cot^{-1}\left\{\frac{\left|\cos\frac{x}{2}+\sin\frac{x}{2}\right|+\left|\cos\frac{x}{2}-\sin\frac{x}{2}\right|}{\left|\cos\frac{x}{2}+\sin\frac{x}{2}\right|-\left|\cos\frac{x}{2}-\sin\frac{x}{2}\right|}\right\}$$

$$= \cot^{-1}\left\{\frac{\left(\cos\frac{x}{2}+\sin\frac{x}{2}\right)-\left(\cos\frac{x}{2}-\sin\frac{x}{2}\right)}{\left(\cos\frac{x}{2}+\sin\frac{x}{2}\right)+\left(\cos\frac{x}{2}-\sin\frac{x}{2}\right)}\right\} \qquad \left[\because\ \frac{\pi}{2} < x < \pi \Rightarrow \frac{\pi}{4} < \frac{x}{2} < \frac{\pi}{2} \Rightarrow \cos\frac{x}{2} < \sin\frac{x}{2}\right]$$

$$= \cot^{-1}\left(\tan\frac{x}{2}\right) = \cot^{-1}\left\{\cot\left(\frac{\pi}{2}-\frac{x}{2}\right)\right\} = \frac{\pi}{2}-\frac{x}{2} \qquad \left[\because \frac{\pi}{2} < x < \pi \Rightarrow 0 < \frac{\pi}{2}-\frac{x}{2} < \frac{\pi}{4}\right]$$

REMARK *In order to simplify trigonometrical expressions involving inverse trigonometrical functions, following substitutions are very useful:*

Expression	*Substitution*
$a^2 + x^2$	$x = a\tan\theta$ or, $x = a\cot\theta$
$a^2 - x^2$	$x = a\sin\theta$ or, $x = a\cos\theta$
$x^2 - a^2$	$x = a\sec\theta$ or, $x = a\,\text{cosec}\,\theta$
$\sqrt{\frac{a-x}{a+x}}$ or, $\sqrt{\frac{a+x}{a-x}}$	$x = a\cos 2\theta$
$\sqrt{\frac{a^2-x^2}{a^2+x^2}}$ or, $\sqrt{\frac{a^2+x^2}{a^2-x^2}}$	$x^2 = a^2\cos 2\theta$

EXAMPLE 5 *Write the following functions in the simplest form:*

(i) $\tan^{-1}\left\{\frac{x}{\sqrt{a^2-x^2}}\right\}, -a < x < a$ [NCERT] (ii) $\tan^{-1}\left\{\sqrt{\frac{a-x}{a+x}}\right\}, -a < x < a$

(iii) $\sin^{-1}\left\{\frac{x}{\sqrt{x^2+a^2}}\right\}$ (iv) $\cos^{-1}\left\{\frac{x}{\sqrt{x^2+a^2}}\right\}$

SOLUTION (i) Putting $x = a\sin\theta$, we obtain

$$\tan^{-1}\left\{\frac{x}{\sqrt{a^2-x^2}}\right\} = \tan^{-1}\left\{\frac{a\sin\theta}{\sqrt{a^2-a^2\sin^2\theta}}\right\} = \tan^{-1}\left\{\frac{a\sin\theta}{a\cos\theta}\right\}$$

$$= \tan^{-1}(\tan\theta) = \theta = \sin^{-1}\frac{x}{a} \qquad \left[\because x = a\sin\theta \Rightarrow \sin\theta = \frac{x}{a} \Rightarrow \theta = \sin^{-1}\frac{x}{a}\right]$$

(ii) Putting $x = a\cos\theta$, we obtain

$$\tan^{-1}\sqrt{\frac{a-x}{a+x}} = \tan^{-1}\sqrt{\frac{a-a\cos\theta}{a+a\cos\theta}} = \tan^{-1}\sqrt{\frac{1-\cos\theta}{1+\cos\theta}} = \tan^{-1}\sqrt{\frac{2\sin^2\frac{\theta}{2}}{2\cos^2\frac{\theta}{2}}}$$

$$= \tan^{-1}\left(\left|\tan\frac{\theta}{2}\right|\right)$$

$$= \tan^{-1}\left(\tan\frac{\theta}{2}\right) \qquad \left[\because -a < x < a \Rightarrow 0 < \theta < \pi \Rightarrow 0 < \frac{\theta}{2} < \frac{\pi}{2} \therefore \left|\tan\frac{\theta}{2}\right| = \tan\frac{\theta}{2}\right]$$

$$= \frac{\theta}{2} = \frac{1}{2}\cos^{-1}\frac{x}{a} \qquad \left[\because x = a\cos\theta \Rightarrow \cos\theta = \frac{x}{a} \Rightarrow \theta = \cos^{-1}\frac{x}{a}\right]$$

(iii) Putting $x = a\tan\theta$, we obtain

$$\sin^{-1}\left\{\frac{x}{\sqrt{x^2+a^2}}\right\} = \sin^{-1}\left\{\frac{a\tan\theta}{\sqrt{a^2\tan^2\theta+a^2}}\right\} = \sin^{-1}\left\{\frac{a\tan\theta}{a\sec\theta}\right\} = \sin^{-1}(\sin\theta)$$

$$= \theta = \tan^{-1}\frac{x}{a} \qquad \left[\because x = a\tan\theta \Rightarrow \tan\theta = \frac{x}{a} \Rightarrow \theta = \tan^{-1}\frac{x}{a}\right]$$

(iv) Putting $x = a\cot\theta$, we obtain

$$\cos^{-1}\left\{\frac{x}{\sqrt{x^2+a^2}}\right\} = \cos^{-1}\left\{\frac{a\cot\theta}{\sqrt{a^2\cot^2\theta+a^2}}\right\} = \cos^{-1}\left\{\frac{a\cot\theta}{a\,\mathrm{cosec}\,\theta}\right\}$$

$$= \cos^{-1}(\cos\theta) = \theta = \cot^{-1}\frac{x}{a} \left[\because x = a\cot\theta \Rightarrow \cot\theta = \frac{x}{a} \Rightarrow \cot^{-1}\frac{x}{a} = \theta\right]$$

EXAMPLE 6 *Prove that:*

(i) $\tan^{-1}\left\{\frac{\sqrt{1+x}-\sqrt{1-x}}{\sqrt{1+x}+\sqrt{1-x}}\right\} = \frac{\pi}{4} - \frac{1}{2}\cos^{-1}x,\ 0 < x < 1$

[NCERT, CBSE 2010, 2011, 2014, 2017]

(ii) $\tan^{-1}\left\{\frac{\sqrt{1+x^2}+\sqrt{1-x^2}}{\sqrt{1+x^2}-\sqrt{1-x^2}}\right\} = \frac{\pi}{4} + \frac{1}{2}\cos^{-1}x^2,\ -1 < x < 1$ **[NCERT EXEMPLAR]**

SOLUTION (i) Putting $x = \cos 2\theta$, we obtain

$$\tan^{-1}\left\{\frac{\sqrt{1+\cos 2\theta}-\sqrt{1-\cos 2\theta}}{\sqrt{1+\cos 2\theta}+\sqrt{1-\cos 2\theta}}\right\} = \tan^{-1}\left\{\frac{\sqrt{2\cos^2\theta}-\sqrt{2\sin^2\theta}}{\sqrt{2\cos^2\theta}+\sqrt{2\sin^2\theta}}\right\}$$

$$= \tan^{-1}\left\{\frac{\cos\theta-\sin\theta}{\cos\theta+\sin\theta}\right\} \qquad \left[\because 0 < x < 1 \Rightarrow 0 < \cos 2\theta < 1 \Rightarrow 0 < 2\theta < \frac{\pi}{2} \Rightarrow 0 < \theta < \frac{\pi}{4}\right]$$

$$= \tan^{-1}\left\{\frac{1-\tan\theta}{1+\tan\theta}\right\} = \tan^{-1}\left\{\tan\left(\frac{\pi}{4}-\theta\right)\right\} = \frac{\pi}{4}-\theta \quad \left[\because 0<\theta<\frac{\pi}{4} \Rightarrow 0<\frac{\pi}{4}-\theta<\frac{\pi}{4}\right]$$

$$= \frac{\pi}{4}-\frac{1}{2}\cos^{-1}x \quad \left[\because \cos 2\theta = x \therefore 2\theta = \cos^{-1}x \Rightarrow \theta = \frac{1}{2}\cos^{-1}x\right]$$

(ii) Putting $x^2 = \cos 2\theta$, we obtain

$$\tan^{-1}\left\{\frac{\sqrt{1+\cos 2\theta}+\sqrt{1-\cos 2\theta}}{\sqrt{1+\cos 2\theta}-\sqrt{1-\cos 2\theta}}\right\} = \tan^{-1}\left\{\frac{\sqrt{2\cos^2\theta}+\sqrt{2\sin^2\theta}}{\sqrt{2\cos^2\theta}-\sqrt{2\sin^2\theta}}\right\}$$

$$= \tan^{-1}\left\{\frac{\cos\theta+\sin\theta}{\cos\theta-\sin\theta}\right\} = \tan^{-1}\left\{\frac{1+\tan\theta}{1-\tan\theta}\right\} = \tan^{-1}\left\{\tan\left(\frac{\pi}{4}+\theta\right)\right\}$$

$$= \frac{\pi}{4}+\theta \quad \left[\because -1<x<1 \Rightarrow 0<x^2<1 \Rightarrow 0<2\theta<\frac{\pi}{2} \Rightarrow 0<\theta<\frac{\pi}{4}\right]$$

$$= \frac{\pi}{4}+\frac{1}{2}\cos^{-1}x^2 \quad \left[\because x^2 = \cos 2\theta \Rightarrow 2\theta = \cos^{-1}x^2 \Rightarrow \theta = \frac{1}{2}\cos^{-1}x^2\right]$$

EXAMPLE 7 *Simplify each of the following:*

(i) $\cos^{-1}\left(\frac{3}{5}\cos x+\frac{4}{5}\sin x\right)$, *where* $\frac{\pi}{2} \le x \le \frac{3\pi}{4}$ **[NCERT EXEMPLAR]**

(ii) $\sin^{-1}\left(\frac{5}{13}\cos x+\frac{12}{13}\sin x\right)$

SOLUTION (i) In order to simplify $\cos^{-1}\left(\frac{3}{5}\cos x+\frac{4}{5}\sin x\right)$, we will have to express $\frac{3}{5}\cos x+\frac{4}{5}\sin x$ in the form of cosine of some expression. For this, let $\frac{3}{5} = r\cos\theta$ and $\frac{4}{5} = r\sin\theta$. Then,

$$r = \sqrt{\left(\frac{3}{5}\right)^2+\left(\frac{4}{5}\right)^2} = 1 \text{ and, } \tan\theta = \frac{r\sin\theta}{r\cos\theta} = \frac{4}{3}$$

$\Rightarrow$ $r = 1$ and, $\theta = \tan^{-1}\frac{4}{3} \Rightarrow \frac{3}{5} = \cos\theta$ and $\frac{4}{5} = \sin\theta$, where $\theta = \tan^{-1}\frac{4}{3}$

$$\therefore \cos^{-1}\left(\frac{3}{5}\cos x+\frac{4}{5}\sin x\right) = \cos^{-1}(\cos\theta\cos x+\sin\theta\sin x) = \cos^{-1}\{\cos(x-\theta)\}$$

$$= x-\theta = x-\tan^{-1}\frac{4}{3}.$$

(ii) In order to simplify $\sin^{-1}\left(\frac{5}{13}\cos x+\frac{12}{13}\sin x\right)$, we will have to express $\frac{5}{13}\cos x+\frac{12}{13}\sin x$ in the form of sine of some expression. For this, let $\frac{5}{13} = r\sin\theta$ and $\frac{12}{13} = r\cos\theta$. Then,

$$r = \sqrt{\left(\frac{5}{13}\right)^2+\left(\frac{12}{13}\right)^2} = 1 \text{ and, } \tan\theta = \frac{r\sin\theta}{r\cos\theta} = \frac{5}{12}$$

$\Rightarrow \quad r = 1$ and, $\theta = \tan^{-1}\dfrac{5}{12} \Rightarrow \dfrac{5}{13} = \sin\theta$ and $\dfrac{12}{13} = \cos\theta$, where $\theta = \tan^{-1}\dfrac{5}{12}$

$$\therefore \quad \sin^{-1}\left(\frac{5}{13}\cos x + \frac{12}{13}\sin x\right) = \sin^{-1}(\sin\theta\cos x + \cos\theta\sin x) = \sin^{-1}\{\sin(x+\theta)\}$$

$$= x + \theta = x + \tan^{-1}\frac{5}{12}$$

EXAMPLE 8 *Simplify each of the following:*

(i) $\sin^{-1}\left(\dfrac{\sin x + \cos x}{\sqrt{2}}\right), -\dfrac{\pi}{4} < x < \dfrac{\pi}{4}$ (ii) $\cos^{-1}\left(\dfrac{\sin x + \cos x}{\sqrt{2}}\right), \dfrac{\pi}{4} < x < \dfrac{5\pi}{4}$

SOLUTION (i) $\sin^{-1}\left(\dfrac{\sin x + \cos x}{\sqrt{2}}\right)$

$$= \sin^{-1}\left(\frac{1}{\sqrt{2}}\sin x + \frac{1}{\sqrt{2}}\cos x\right) = \sin^{-1}\left(\sin x\cos\frac{\pi}{4} + \cos x\sin\frac{\pi}{4}\right)$$

$$= \sin^{-1}\left\{\sin\left(x + \frac{\pi}{4}\right)\right\} = x + \frac{\pi}{4} \qquad \left[\because -\frac{\pi}{4} < x < \frac{\pi}{4} \Rightarrow 0 < x + \frac{\pi}{4} < \frac{\pi}{2}\right]$$

(ii) $\cos^{-1}\left(\dfrac{\sin x + \cos x}{\sqrt{2}}\right)$

$$= \cos^{-1}\left(\frac{1}{\sqrt{2}}\sin x + \frac{1}{\sqrt{2}}\cos x\right) = \cos^{-1}\left(\sin x\sin\frac{\pi}{4} + \cos x\cos\frac{\pi}{4}\right)$$

$$= \cos^{-1}\left\{\cos\left(x - \frac{\pi}{4}\right)\right\} = x - \frac{\pi}{4} \qquad \left[\because \frac{\pi}{4} < x < \frac{5\pi}{4} \Rightarrow 0 < x - \frac{\pi}{4} < \pi\right]$$

REMARK *This example can also be solved by using the procedure used in the earlier example.*

BASED ON HIGHER ORDER THINKING SKILLS (HOTS)

EXAMPLE 9 *Simplify each of the the following:*

(i) $\sin^{-1}\left(\dfrac{\sin x + \cos x}{\sqrt{2}}\right), \dfrac{\pi}{4} < x < \dfrac{5\pi}{4}$ (ii) $\cos^{-1}\left(\dfrac{\sin x + \cos x}{\sqrt{2}}\right), \dfrac{5\pi}{4} < x < \dfrac{9\pi}{4}$

SOLUTION (i) $\sin^{-1}\left(\dfrac{\sin x + \cos x}{\sqrt{2}}\right)$

$$= \sin^{-1}\left(\frac{1}{\sqrt{2}}\sin x + \frac{1}{\sqrt{2}}\cos x\right) = \sin^{-1}\left(\cos\frac{\pi}{4}\sin x + \sin\frac{\pi}{4}\cos x\right) = \sin^{-1}\left\{\sin\left(x + \frac{\pi}{4}\right)\right\}$$

$$= \pi - \left(x + \frac{\pi}{4}\right) = \frac{3\pi}{4} - x \qquad \left[\because \frac{\pi}{4} < x < \frac{5\pi}{4} \Rightarrow \frac{\pi}{2} < x + \frac{\pi}{4} < \frac{3\pi}{2} \Rightarrow -\frac{\pi}{2} < \pi - \left(x + \frac{\pi}{4}\right) < \frac{\pi}{2}\right]$$

(ii) $\cos^{-1}\left(\dfrac{\sin x + \cos x}{\sqrt{2}}\right)$

$$= \cos^{-1}\left(\frac{1}{\sqrt{2}}\sin x + \frac{1}{\sqrt{2}}\cos x\right) = \cos^{-1}\left(\cos x\cos\frac{\pi}{4} + \sin x\sin\frac{\pi}{4}\right) = \cos^{-1}\left\{\cos\left(x - \frac{\pi}{4}\right)\right\}$$

$$= 2\pi - \left(x - \frac{\pi}{4}\right) = \frac{9\pi}{4} - x \qquad \left[\because \frac{5\pi}{4} < x < \frac{9\pi}{4} \Rightarrow \pi < x - \frac{\pi}{4} < 2\pi \Rightarrow 0 < 2\pi - \left(x - \frac{\pi}{4}\right) < \pi\right]$$

EXAMPLE 10 *Evaluate the following:*

(i) $\sin^{-1}(\sin 10)$ (ii) $\sin^{-1}(\sin 5)$ (iii) $\cos^{-1}(\cos 10)$ (iv) $\tan^{-1}\{\tan(-6)\}$

SOLUTION (i) We know that $\sin^{-1}(\sin\theta) = \theta$, if $-\frac{\pi}{2} \le \theta \le \frac{\pi}{2}$. Here, $\theta = 10$ radians which does not lie between $-\frac{\pi}{2}$ and $\frac{\pi}{2}$. But, $3\pi - \theta$ i.e. $3\pi - 10$ lies between $-\frac{\pi}{2}$ and $\frac{\pi}{2}$. Also, $\sin(3\pi - 10) = \sin 10$.

$\therefore \quad \sin^{-1}(\sin 10) = \sin^{-1}(\sin(3\pi - 10)) = 3\pi - 10.$

ALITER We know that $3\pi < 10^c < \frac{7\pi}{2}$ and $\sin^{-1}(\sin\theta) = 3\pi - \theta$ for $\frac{5\pi}{2} \le \theta \le \frac{7\pi}{2}$.

$\therefore \quad \sin^{-1}(\sin 10) = 3\pi - 10.$

(ii) Here, $\theta = 5$ radians. Clearly, it does not lie between $-\frac{\pi}{2}$ and $\frac{\pi}{2}$. But, $2\pi - 5$ and $5 - 2\pi$ both lie between $-\frac{\pi}{2}$ and $\frac{\pi}{2}$ such that $\sin(5 - 2\pi) = \sin(-(2\pi - 5)) = -\sin(2\pi - 5) = -(-\sin 5) = \sin 5$.

$\therefore \quad \sin^{-1}(\sin 5) = \sin^{-1}(\sin(5 - 2\pi)) = 5 - 2\pi.$

ALITER We know that $\frac{3\pi}{2} < 5^c < \frac{5\pi}{2}$ and $\sin^{-1}(\sin\theta) = \theta - 2\pi$ for $\frac{3\pi}{2} \le \theta \le \frac{5\pi}{2}$ (see Fig. 3.21)

$\therefore \quad \sin^{-1}(\sin 5) = 5 - 2\pi.$

(iii) We know that $\cos^{-1}(\cos\theta) = \theta$, if $0 \le \theta \le \pi$. Here, $\theta = 10$ radians. Clearly, it does not lie between 0 and π. However, $(4\pi - 10)$ lies between 0 and π such that $\cos(4\pi - 10) = \cos 10$.

$\therefore \quad \cos^{-1}(\cos 10) = \cos^{-1}(\cos(4\pi - 10)) = 4\pi - 10$

ALITER We know that $3\pi < 10^c < 4\pi$ and $\cos^{-1}(\cos\theta) = 4\pi - \theta$ for $3\pi < \theta < 4\pi$ (see Fig. 3.22)

$\therefore \quad \cos^{-1}(\cos 10) = 4\pi - 10.$

(iv) We know that $\tan^{-1}(\tan\theta) = \theta$, if $-\frac{\pi}{2} < \theta < \frac{\pi}{2}$. Here, $\theta = -6$ radians which does not lie between $-\frac{\pi}{2}$ and $\frac{\pi}{2}$. However, $2\pi - 6$ lies between $-\frac{\pi}{2}$ and $\frac{\pi}{2}$ such that $\tan(2\pi - 6) = -\tan 6 = \tan(-6)$.

$\therefore \quad \tan^{-1}\{\tan(-6)\} = \tan^{-1}\{\tan(2\pi - 6)\} = 2\pi - 6$

ALITER We know that $-2\pi < -6^c < -\frac{3\pi}{2}$ and $\tan^{-1}(\tan\theta) = \theta + 2\pi$ for $-2\pi < \theta < -\frac{3\pi}{2}$ (see Fig. 3.23). Therefore, $\tan^{-1}(\tan(-6)) = 2\pi - 6$.

EXERCISE 3.7

BASIC

1. Evaluate each of the following:

(i) $\sin^{-1}\left(\sin\frac{\pi}{6}\right)$ (ii) $\sin^{-1}\left(\sin\frac{7\pi}{6}\right)$ (iii) $\sin^{-1}\left(\sin\frac{5\pi}{6}\right)$

(iv) $\sin^{-1}\left(\sin\frac{13\pi}{7}\right)$ (v) $\sin^{-1}\left(\sin\frac{17\pi}{8}\right)$ (vi) $\sin^{-1}\left\{\left(\sin -\frac{17\pi}{8}\right)\right\}$

(vii) $\sin^{-1}(\sin 3)$ (viii) $\sin^{-1}(\sin 4)$ (ix) $\sin^{-1}(\sin 12)$

(x) $\sin^{-1}(\sin 2)$ (xi) $\cos^{-1}\left(\cos -\frac{7\pi}{6}\right)$ [CBSE 2023]

2. Evaluate each of the following:

(i) $\cos^{-1}\left\{\cos\left(-\frac{\pi}{4}\right)\right\}$ (ii) $\cos^{-1}\left(\cos\frac{5\pi}{4}\right)$ (iii) $\cos^{-1}\left(\cos\frac{4\pi}{3}\right)$

(iv) $\cos^{-1}\left(\cos\frac{13\pi}{6}\right)$ (v) $\cos^{-1}(\cos 3)$ (vi) $\cos^{-1}(\cos 4)$

(vii) $\cos^{-1}(\cos 5)$ (viii) $\cos^{-1}(\cos 12)$

3. Evaluate each of the following:

(i) $\tan^{-1}\left(\tan\frac{\pi}{3}\right)$ (ii) $\tan^{-1}\left(\tan\frac{6\pi}{7}\right)$ (iii) $\tan^{-1}\left(\tan\frac{7\pi}{6}\right)$ [NCERT]

(iv) $\tan^{-1}\left(\tan\frac{9\pi}{4}\right)$ (v) $\tan^{-1}(\tan 1)$ (vi) $\tan^{-1}(\tan 2)$

(vii) $\tan^{-1}(\tan 4)$ (viii) $\tan^{-1}(\tan 12)$

4. Evaluate each of the following:

(i) $\sec^{-1}\left(\sec\frac{\pi}{3}\right)$ (ii) $\sec^{-1}\left(\sec\frac{2\pi}{3}\right)$ (iii) $\sec^{-1}\left(\sec\frac{5\pi}{4}\right)$

(iv) $\sec^{-1}\left(\sec\frac{7\pi}{3}\right)$ (v) $\sec^{-1}\left(\sec\frac{9\pi}{5}\right)$ (vi) $\sec^{-1}\left\{\sec\left(-\frac{7\pi}{3}\right)\right\}$

(vii) $\sec^{-1}\left(\sec\frac{13\pi}{4}\right)$ (viii) $\sec^{-1}\left(\sec\frac{25\pi}{6}\right)$

5. Evaluate each of the following:

(i) $\operatorname{cosec}^{-1}\left(\operatorname{cosec}\frac{\pi}{4}\right)$ (ii) $\operatorname{cosec}^{-1}\left(\operatorname{cosec}\frac{3\pi}{4}\right)$ (iii) $\operatorname{cosec}^{-1}\left(\operatorname{cosec}\frac{6\pi}{5}\right)$

(iv) $\operatorname{cosec}^{-1}\left(\operatorname{cosec}\frac{11\pi}{6}\right)$ (v) $\operatorname{cosec}^{-1}\left(\operatorname{cosec}\frac{13\pi}{6}\right)$ (vi) $\operatorname{cosec}^{-1}\left\{\operatorname{cosec}\left(-\frac{9\pi}{4}\right)\right\}$

6. Evaluate each of the following:

(i) $\cot^{-1}\left(\cot\frac{\pi}{3}\right)$ (ii) $\cot^{-1}\left(\cot\frac{4\pi}{3}\right)$ (iii) $\cot^{-1}\left(\cot\frac{9\pi}{4}\right)$

(iv) $\cot^{-1}\left(\cot\frac{19\pi}{6}\right)$ (v) $\cot^{-1}\left\{\cot\left(-\frac{8\pi}{3}\right)\right\}$ (vi) $\cot^{-1}\left\{\cot\left(\frac{21\pi}{4}\right)\right\}$

(vii) $\sin^{-1}\left(\sin\frac{3\pi}{4}\right)+\cos^{-1}(\cos\pi)+\tan^{-1}1$ [CBSE 2023]

(viii) $\sin^{-1}\left(\sin\frac{3\pi}{4}\right)+\cos^{-1}\left(\cos\frac{3\pi}{4}\right)+\tan^{-1}1$ [CBSE 2023]

BASED ON LOTS

7. Write each of the following in the simplest form:

(i) $\cot^{-1}\left\{\frac{a}{\sqrt{x^2-a^2}}\right\}, |x|>a$ (ii) $\tan^{-1}\left\{x+\sqrt{1+x^2}\right\}, x\in R$

(iii) $\tan^{-1}\left\{\sqrt{1+x^2}-x\right\}, x\in R$ (iv) $\tan^{-1}\left\{\frac{\sqrt{1+x^2}-1}{x}\right\}, x\neq 0$

(v) $\tan^{-1}\left\{\frac{\sqrt{1+x^2}+1}{x}\right\}, x\neq 0$ (vi) $\tan^{-1}\sqrt{\frac{a-x}{a+x}}, -a<x<a$

(vii) $\tan^{-1}\left\{\dfrac{x}{a+\sqrt{a^2-x^2}}\right\}, -a<x<a$ (viii) $\sin^{-1}\left\{\dfrac{x+\sqrt{1-x^2}}{\sqrt{2}}\right\}, -\dfrac{1}{2}<x<\dfrac{1}{\sqrt{2}}$

(ix) $\sin^{-1}\left\{\dfrac{\sqrt{1+x}+\sqrt{1-x}}{2}\right\}, 0<x<1$ (x) $\sin\left\{2\tan^{-1}\sqrt{\dfrac{1-x}{1+x}}\right\}$

ANSWERS

1. (i) $\frac{\pi}{6}$ (ii) $-\frac{\pi}{6}$ (iii) $\frac{\pi}{6}$ (iv) $-\frac{\pi}{7}$ (v) $\frac{\pi}{8}$ (vi) $-\frac{\pi}{8}$
(vii) $\pi-3$ (viii) $\pi-4$ (ix) $12-4\pi$ (x) $\pi-2$ (xi) $\frac{5\pi}{6}$
2. (i) $\frac{\pi}{4}$ (ii) $\frac{3\pi}{4}$ (iii) $\frac{2\pi}{3}$ (iv) $\frac{\pi}{6}$ (v) 3 (vi) $2\pi-4$
(vii) $2\pi-5$ (viii) $4\pi-12$
3. (i) $\frac{\pi}{3}$ (ii) $-\frac{\pi}{7}$ (iii) $\frac{\pi}{6}$ (iv) $\frac{\pi}{4}$ (v) 1 (vi) $2-\pi$
(vii) $4-\pi$ (viii) $12-4\pi$
4. (i) $\frac{\pi}{3}$ (ii) $\frac{2\pi}{3}$ (iii) $\frac{3\pi}{4}$ (iv) $\frac{\pi}{3}$ (v) $\frac{\pi}{5}$ (vi) $\frac{\pi}{3}$
(vii) $\frac{3\pi}{4}$ (viii) $\frac{\pi}{6}$
5. (i) $\frac{\pi}{4}$ (ii) $\frac{\pi}{4}$ (iii) $-\frac{\pi}{5}$ (iv) $-\frac{\pi}{6}$
(v) $\frac{\pi}{6}$ (vi) $-\frac{\pi}{4}$
6. (i) $\frac{\pi}{3}$ (ii) $\frac{\pi}{3}$ (iii) $\frac{\pi}{4}$ (iv) $\frac{\pi}{6}$
(v) $\frac{\pi}{3}$ (vi) $\frac{\pi}{4}$ (vii) $\frac{3\pi}{2}$ (viii) $\frac{5\pi}{4}$
7. (i) $\sec^{-1}\frac{x}{a}$ (ii) $\frac{\pi}{2}-\frac{1}{2}\cot^{-1}x$ (iii) $\frac{1}{2}\cot^{-1}x$ (iv) $\frac{1}{2}\tan^{-1}x$
(v) $\frac{\pi}{2}-\frac{1}{2}\tan^{-1}x$ (vi) $\frac{1}{2}\cos^{-1}\frac{x}{a}$ (vii) $\frac{1}{2}\sin^{-1}\frac{x}{a}$
(viii) $\frac{\pi}{4}+\sin^{-1}x$ (ix) $\frac{\pi}{4}+\frac{1}{2}\cos^{-1}x$ (x) $\sqrt{1-x^2}$

HINTS TO SELECTED PROBLEMS

7. (ii) Putting $x=\cot\theta$, we obtain

$$\tan^{-1}\left\{x+\sqrt{1+x^2}\right\} = \tan^{-1}(\cot\theta+\operatorname{cosec}\theta) = \tan^{-1}\left(\frac{1+\cos\theta}{\sin\theta}\right)$$

$$= \tan^{-1}\left\{\frac{2\cos^2\frac{\theta}{2}}{2\sin\frac{\theta}{2}\cos\frac{\theta}{2}}\right\} = \tan^{-1}\left(\cot\frac{\theta}{2}\right) = \tan^{-1}\left\{\tan\left(\frac{\pi}{2}-\frac{\theta}{2}\right)\right\} = \frac{\pi}{2}-\frac{\theta}{2}$$

$$= \frac{\pi}{2}-\frac{1}{2}\cot^{-1}x$$

(ix) Putting $x=\sin\theta$, we obtain

$$\sin^{-1}\left\{\frac{x+\sqrt{1-x^2}}{2}\right\} = \sin^{-1}\left\{\frac{\sin\theta+\cos\theta}{\sqrt{2}}\right\} = \sin^{-1}\left\{\sin\left(\frac{\pi}{4}+\theta\right)\right\} = \frac{\pi}{4}+\theta$$

$$= \frac{\pi}{4}+\sin^{-1}x$$

3.4.2 PROPERTY-II

Let b, p and h denote respectively the base, perpendicular and hypotenuse of a right triangle PQR and let $\angle QPR = \theta$. *Then,*

$$\sin\theta = \frac{p}{h},\ \cos\theta = \frac{b}{h},\ \tan\theta = \frac{p}{b},\ \text{cosec}\ \theta = \frac{h}{p},\ \sec\theta = \frac{h}{b} \text{ and } \cot\theta = \frac{b}{p}$$

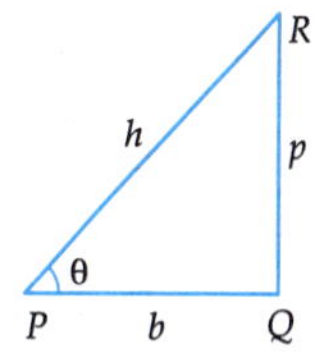

Fig. 3.27

$\therefore$ $$\theta = \sin^{-1}\left(\frac{p}{h}\right), \theta = \cos^{-1}\left(\frac{b}{h}\right), \theta = \tan^{-1}\left(\frac{p}{b}\right), \theta = \text{cosec}^{-1}\left(\frac{h}{p}\right),$$

$$\theta = \sec^{-1}\left(\frac{h}{b}\right) \text{ and, } \theta = \cot^{-1}\left(\frac{b}{p}\right)$$

$\Rightarrow$ $$\sin^{-1}\left(\frac{p}{h}\right) = \cos^{-1}\left(\frac{b}{h}\right) = \tan^{-1}\left(\frac{p}{b}\right) = \text{cosec}^{-1}\left(\frac{h}{p}\right) = \sec^{-1}\left(\frac{h}{b}\right) = \cot^{-1}\left(\frac{b}{p}\right)$$

It follows from the above result that any inverse trigonometric function can be expressed interms of the remaining five inverse trigonometric functions. For example, if $\sin^{-1}\left(\frac{5}{13}\right)$ is to be expressed interms of other five inverse trigonometric functions, then we construct a right triangle with perpendicular $p = 5$ and hypotenuse $h = 13$. The base b of this triangle is $b = 12$.

$\therefore$ $$\sin^{-1}\left(\frac{5}{13}\right) = \cos^{-1}\left(\frac{12}{13}\right) = \tan^{-1}\left(\frac{5}{12}\right) = \text{cosec}^{-1}\left(\frac{13}{5}\right) = \sec^{-1}\left(\frac{13}{12}\right) = \cot^{-1}\left(\frac{12}{5}\right)$$

In Chapter 2, we have learnt that if $f : A \to B$ is a bijection, then $f^{-1} : B \to A$ exists such that $fof^{-1}(x) = x$ or, $f(f^{-1}(x)) = x$ for all $x \in B$. Applying this property on various trigonometric functions and their inverses, we obtain the following property.

PROPERTY

(i) $\sin(\sin^{-1} x) = x$, for all $x \in [-1, 1]$ (ii) $\cos(\cos^{-1} x) = x$, for all $x \in [-1, 1]$

(iii) $\tan(\tan^{-1} x) = x$, for all $x \in R$ (iv) $\cot(\cot^{-1} x) = x$, for all $x \in R$.

(v) $\text{cosec}(\text{cosec}^{-1} x) = x$, for all $x \in (-\infty, -1] \cup [1, \infty)$

(vi) $\sec(\sec^{-1} x) = x$, for all $x \in (-\infty, -1] \cup [1, \infty)$

This property and the above discussion help us in finding the values of expression of the form $f(g^{-1}(x))$, where f and g are trigonometric functions. We may use the following algorithm for the same.

ALGORITHM

Step I *Obtain the expression and express it in the form* $f(g^{-1}(x))$, *where f and g are trigonometric functions.*

Step II *Express* $g^{-1}(x)$ *in terms of* f^{-1} *by using the following results:*

$$\sin^{-1}\left(\frac{p}{h}\right) = \cos^{-1}\left(\frac{b}{h}\right) = \tan^{-1}\left(\frac{p}{b}\right) = \text{cosec}^{-1}\left(\frac{h}{p}\right) = \sec^{-1}\left(\frac{h}{b}\right) = \cot^{-1}\left(\frac{b}{p}\right),$$

where p, b and h denote respectively the perpendicular, base and hypotenuse of a right triangle.

Step III *Let* $g^{-1}(x) = f^{-1}(y)$. *Replace* $g^{-1}(x)$ *by* $f^{-1}(y)$ *in* $f(g^{-1}(x))$ *and use property-II to get*

$$f(g^{-1}(x)) = f(f^{-1}(y)) = y.$$

Following example will illustrate the above algorithm.

ILLUSTRATIVE EXAMPLES

BASED ON BASIC CONCEPTS (BASIC)

EXAMPLE 1 *Evaluate each of the following:*

(i) $\sin\left(\sin^{-1}\frac{5}{13}\right)$ (ii) $\sin\left(\cos^{-1}\frac{4}{5}\right)$ (iii) $\sin\left(\tan^{-1}\frac{15}{8}\right)$

(iv) $\sin\left(\cot^{-1}\frac{4}{3}\right)$ (v) $\sin\left(\sec^{-1}\frac{17}{15}\right)$ (vi) $\sin\left(\text{cosec}^{-1}\frac{17}{8}\right)$

SOLUTION (i) Using $\sin(\sin^{-1}x) = x, x \in [-1, 1]$, we obtain: $\sin\left(\sin^{-1}\frac{5}{13}\right) = \frac{5}{13}$.

(ii) In order to express $\cos^{-1}\frac{4}{5}$ in terms of $\sin^{-1}$, let us construct a right triangle with base $b = 4$ and hypotenuse $h = 5$. The perpendicular of such triangle is $p = 3$.

$\therefore \quad \cos^{-1}\frac{4}{5} = \sin^{-1}\frac{3}{5}$ $\left[\because \cos^{-1}\frac{b}{h} = \sin^{-1}\frac{p}{h}\right]$

Hence, $\sin\left(\cos^{-1}\frac{4}{5}\right) = \sin\left(\sin^{-1}\frac{3}{5}\right) = \frac{3}{5}$

(iii) The right triangle with base $b = 15$ and perpendicular $p = 8$ has hypotenuse $h = 17$.

$\therefore \quad \tan^{-1}\frac{15}{8} = \sin^{-1}\frac{15}{17}$

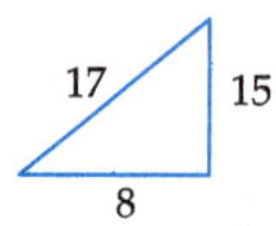

Hence, $\sin\left(\tan^{-1}\frac{15}{8}\right) = \sin\left(\sin^{-1}\frac{15}{17}\right) = \frac{15}{17}$

(iv) The hypotenuse of the right triangle with base $b = 4$, perpendicular $p = 3$ is $h = 5$.

$\therefore \quad \cot^{-1}\frac{4}{3} = \sin^{-1}\frac{3}{5}$

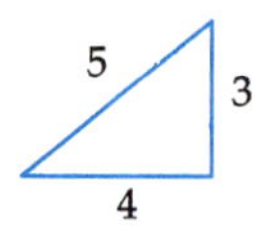

Hence, $\sin\left(\cot^{-1}\frac{4}{3}\right) = \sin\left(\sin^{-1}\frac{3}{5}\right) = \frac{3}{5}$

(v) The right triangle with base $b = 15$ and hypotenuse $h = 17$ has perpendicular $p = 8$ has hypotenuse $h = 17$.

$\therefore \quad \sec^{-1}\frac{17}{15} = \sin^{-1}\frac{8}{17}$

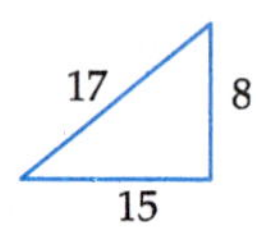

Hence, $\sin\left(\sec^{-1}\frac{17}{15}\right) = \sin\left(\sin^{-1}\frac{8}{17}\right) = \frac{8}{17}$.

(vi) The right triangle with base $b = 15$ and perpendicular $p = 8$ has hypotenuse $h = 17$.

$\therefore \quad \text{cosec}^{-1}\left(\frac{17}{8}\right) = \sin^{-1}\left(\frac{8}{17}\right)$

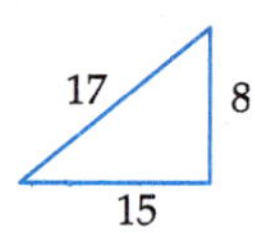

Hence, $\sin\left(\text{cosec}^{-1}\frac{17}{8}\right) = \sin\left(\sin^{-1}\frac{8}{17}\right) = \frac{8}{17}$

EXAMPLE 2 *Evaluate each of the following:*

(i) $\cos\left(\cos^{-1}\frac{5}{13}\right)$ (ii) $\cos\left(\sin^{-1}\frac{8}{17}\right)$ (iii) $\cos\left(\tan^{-1}\frac{3}{4}\right)$

(iv) $\cos\left(\cot^{-1}\frac{15}{8}\right)$ (v) $\cos\left(\sec^{-1}\frac{5}{3}\right)$ (vi) $\cos\left(\operatorname{cosec}^{-1}\frac{13}{12}\right)$

SOLUTION (i) $\cos\left(\cos^{-1}\frac{5}{13}\right)=\frac{5}{13}$

(ii) The right triangle with perpendicular $p=8$ and hypotenuse $h=17$ has base $b=15$.

$\therefore \quad \sin^{-1}\left(\frac{8}{17}\right)=\cos^{-1}\left(\frac{15}{17}\right)$

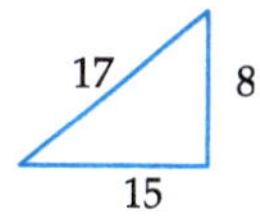

Hence, $\cos\left(\sin^{-1}\frac{8}{17}\right)=\cos\left(\cos^{-1}\frac{15}{17}\right)=\frac{15}{17}$

(iii) The right triangle with perpendicular $p=3$ and base $b=4$ has hypotenuse $h=5$.

$\therefore \quad \tan^{-1}\left(\frac{3}{4}\right)=\cos^{-1}\left(\frac{4}{5}\right)$

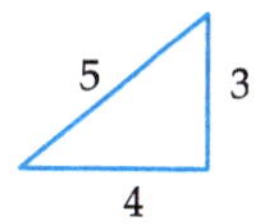

Hence, $\cos\left(\tan^{-1}\frac{3}{4}\right)=\cos\left(\cos^{-1}\frac{4}{5}\right)=\frac{4}{5}$

(iv) The right triangle with base $b=15$ and perpendicular $p=8$ has hypotenuse $h=17$.

$\therefore \quad \cot^{-1}\left(\frac{15}{8}\right)=\cos^{-1}\left(\frac{15}{17}\right)$

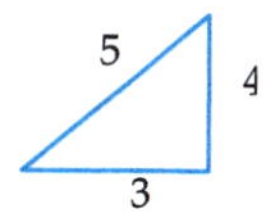

Hence, $\cos\left(\cot^{-1}\frac{15}{8}\right)=\cos\left(\cos^{-1}\frac{15}{17}\right)=\frac{15}{17}$

(v) We find that the right triangle with hypotenuse $h=5$ and base $b=3$ has perpendicular $p=4$.

$\therefore \quad \sec^{-1}\frac{5}{3}=\cos^{-1}\frac{3}{5}$

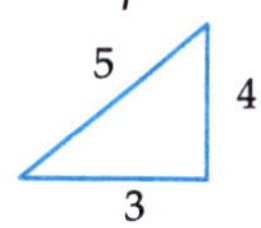

Hence, $\cos\left(\sec^{-1}\frac{5}{3}\right)=\cos\left(\cos^{-1}\frac{3}{5}\right)=\frac{3}{5}$

(vi) Clearly, the right triangle with hypotenuse $h=13$ and perpendicular $p=12$ has base $b=5$.

$\therefore \quad \operatorname{cosec}^{-1}\frac{13}{12}=\cos^{-1}\frac{5}{13}$

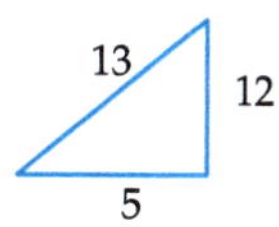

Hence, $\cos\left(\operatorname{cosec}^{-1}\frac{13}{12}\right)=\cos\left(\cos^{-1}\frac{5}{13}\right)=\frac{5}{13}$

EXAMPLE 3 *Evaluate each of the following:*

(i) $\tan\left(\tan^{-1}\frac{3}{4}\right)$ (ii) $\tan\left(\sin^{-1}\frac{5}{13}\right)$ (iii) $\tan\left(\cos^{-1}\frac{8}{17}\right)$

(iv) $\tan\left(\operatorname{cosec}^{-1}\frac{13}{5}\right)$ (v) $\tan\left(\sec^{-1}\frac{13}{12}\right)$ (vi) $\tan\left(\cot^{-1}\frac{8}{15}\right)$

SOLUTION (i) $\tan\left(\tan^{-1}\frac{3}{4}\right)=\frac{3}{4}$

(ii) The right triangle with perpendicular $p=5$ and hypotenuse $h=13$ has base $b=12$.

$\therefore \quad \sin^{-1}\frac{5}{13}=\tan^{-1}\frac{5}{12}$

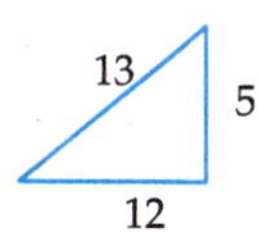

Hence, $\tan\left(\sin^{-1}\frac{5}{13}\right)=\tan\left(\tan^{-1}\frac{5}{12}\right)=\frac{5}{12}$

(iii) The right triangle with base $b=8$, hypotenuse $h=17$ has perpendicular $p=15$.

$\therefore \qquad \cos^{-1}\frac{8}{17} = \tan^{-1}\frac{15}{8}$

Hence, $\tan\left(\cos^{-1}\frac{8}{17}\right) = \tan\left(\tan^{-1}\frac{15}{8}\right) = \frac{15}{8}$

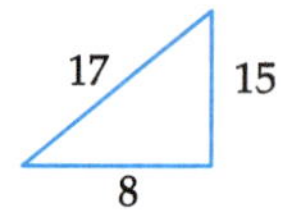

(iv) We find that the right triangle with perpendicular $p = 5$ and hypotenuse $h = 13$ has its base $b = 12$.

$\therefore \qquad \operatorname{cosec}^{-1}\left(\frac{13}{5}\right) = \tan^{-1}\left(\frac{5}{12}\right)$

Hence, $\tan\left\{\operatorname{cosec}^{-1}\frac{13}{5}\right\} = \tan\left(\tan^{-1}\frac{5}{12}\right) = \frac{5}{12}$

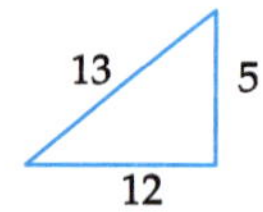

(v) The right triangle with base $b = 12$ and hypotenuse $h = 13$ has perpendicular $p = 5$.

$\therefore \qquad \sec^{-1}\frac{13}{12} = \tan^{-1}\frac{5}{12}$

Hence, $\tan\left(\sec^{-1}\frac{13}{12}\right) = \tan\left(\tan^{-1}\frac{5}{12}\right) = \frac{5}{12}$

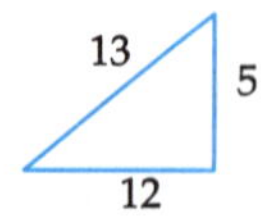

(vi) Clearly, the right triangle with base $b = 8$ and perpendicular $p = 15$ has hypotenuse $h = 17$.

$\therefore \quad \cot^{-1}\left(\frac{8}{15}\right) = \tan^{-1}\frac{15}{8}$

Hence, $\tan\left(\cot^{-1}\frac{8}{15}\right) = \tan\left(\tan^{-1}\frac{15}{8}\right) = \frac{15}{8}$

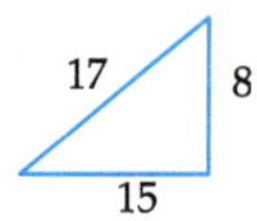

EXAMPLE 4 *Evaluate:* (i) $\sin\ (\cot^{-1} x)$ (ii) $\cos\ (\tan^{-1} x)$

SOLUTION (i) We have to find the value of $\sin\ (\cot^{-1} x) = \sin\left(\cot^{-1}\frac{x}{1}\right)$. The right triangle with base $b = x$, perpendicular $p = 1$ has hypotenuse $h = \sqrt{1+x^2}$.

$\therefore \qquad \cot^{-1} x = \sin^{-1}\frac{1}{\sqrt{1+x^2}}$

Hence, $\sin\ (\cot^{-1} x) = \sin\left(\sin^{-1}\frac{1}{\sqrt{1+x^2}}\right) = \frac{1}{\sqrt{1+x^2}}$

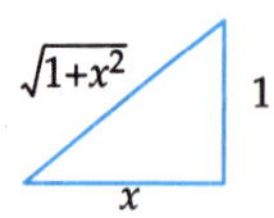

(ii) $\cos\ (\tan^{-1} x) = \cos\left(\tan^{-1}\frac{x}{1}\right)$. The right triangle with perpendicular $p = x$ and base $b = 1$ has its hypotenuse $h = \sqrt{1+x^2}$.

$\therefore \qquad \tan^{-1} x = \cos^{-1}\frac{1}{\sqrt{1+x^2}}$

Hence, $\cos\ (\tan^{-1} x) = \cos\left(\cos^{-1}\frac{1}{\sqrt{1+x^2}}\right) = \frac{1}{\sqrt{1+x^2}}$

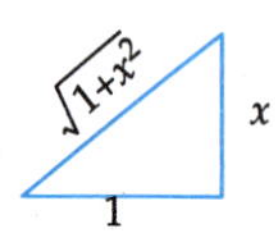

BASED ON LOWER ORDER THINKING SKILLS (LOTS)

EXAMPLE 5 *Evaluate:* $\cos\left(\sin^{-1}\frac{1}{4} + \sec^{-1}\frac{4}{3}\right)$. [NCERT EXEMPLAR]

SOLUTION $\cos\left(\sin^{-1}\frac{1}{4} + \sec^{-1}\frac{4}{3}\right) = \cos\left(\sin^{-1}\frac{1}{4} + \cos^{-1}\frac{3}{4}\right)$ $\left[\because \sec^{-1}\frac{4}{3} = \cos^{-1}\frac{3}{4}\right]$

$$= \cos\left(\sin^{-1}\frac{1}{4}\right)\cos\left(\cos^{-1}\frac{3}{4}\right) - \sin\left(\sin^{-1}\frac{1}{4}\right)\sin\left(\cos^{-1}\frac{3}{4}\right)$$

$$= \cos\left(\cos^{-1}\frac{\sqrt{15}}{4}\right)\cos\left(\cos^{-1}\frac{3}{4}\right) - \sin\left(\sin^{-1}\frac{1}{4}\right)\sin\left(\sin^{-1}\frac{\sqrt{7}}{4}\right) \quad \left[\because \sin^{-1}\frac{1}{4} = \cos^{-1}\frac{\sqrt{15}}{4} \;\&\; \cos^{-1}\frac{3}{4} = \sin^{-1}\frac{\sqrt{7}}{4}\right]$$

$$= \frac{\sqrt{15}}{4}\times\frac{3}{4} - \frac{1}{4}\times\frac{\sqrt{7}}{4} = \frac{3\sqrt{15}-\sqrt{7}}{16}$$

EXAMPLE 6 *Evaluate :* $\sin\left(\cos^{-1}\frac{3}{5} + \operatorname{cosec}^{-1}\frac{13}{5}\right)$.

SOLUTION $\sin\left(\cos^{-1}\frac{3}{5} + \operatorname{cosec}^{-1}\frac{13}{5}\right)$

$$= \sin\left(\cos^{-1}\frac{3}{5}\right)\cos\left(\operatorname{cosec}^{-1}\frac{13}{5}\right) + \cos\left(\cos^{-1}\frac{3}{5}\right)\sin\left(\operatorname{cosec}^{-1}\frac{13}{5}\right)$$

$$= \sin\left(\sin^{-1}\frac{4}{5}\right)\cos\left(\cos^{-1}\frac{12}{13}\right) + \cos\left(\cos^{-1}\frac{3}{5}\right)\sin\left(\sin^{-1}\frac{5}{13}\right) = \frac{4}{5}\times\frac{12}{13} + \frac{3}{5}\times\frac{5}{13} = \frac{63}{65}$$

EXAMPLE 7 *Find the value of the expression* $\sin\left[\cot^{-1}\left\{\cos(\tan^{-1}1)\right\}\right]$ **[NCERT EXEMPLAR]**

SOLUTION $\sin\left[\cot^{-1}\left\{\cos(\tan^{-1}1)\right\}\right] = \sin\left\{\cot^{-1}\left(\cos\frac{\pi}{4}\right)\right\}$ $\left[\because \tan^{-1}1 = \frac{\pi}{4}\right]$

$$= \sin\left(\cot^{-1}\frac{1}{\sqrt{2}}\right) = \sin\left(\sin^{-1}\frac{\sqrt{2}}{\sqrt{3}}\right) \quad \left[\because \cot^{-1}\frac{1}{\sqrt{2}} = \sin^{-1}\frac{\sqrt{2}}{\sqrt{3}}\right]$$

EXAMPLE 8 *Prove that:*

(i) $\sec^2(\tan^{-1}2) + \operatorname{cosec}^2(\cot^{-1}3) = 15$

(ii) $\tan^2(\sec^{-1}2) + \cot^2(\operatorname{cosec}^{-1}3) = 11$ **[NCERT EXEMPLAR]**

SOLUTION (i) We have,

$$\sec^2(\tan^{-1}2) + \operatorname{cosec}^2(\cot^{-1}3)$$

$$= \{\sec(\tan^{-1}2)\}^2 + \{\operatorname{cosec}(\cot^{-1}3)\}^2 = \left\{\sec\left(\tan^{-1}\frac{2}{1}\right)\right\}^2 + \left\{\operatorname{cosec}\left(\cot^{-1}\frac{3}{1}\right)\right\}^2$$

$$= \{\sec(\sec^{-1}\sqrt{5})\}^2 + \{\operatorname{cosec}(\operatorname{cosec}^{-1}\sqrt{10})\}^2 = (\sqrt{5})^2 + (\sqrt{10})^2 = 15$$

ALITER $\sec^2(\tan^{-1}2) + \operatorname{cosec}^2(\cot^{-1}3) = 1 + \tan^2(\tan^{-1}2) + 1 + \cot^2(\cot^{-1}3)$

$$= 1 + \{\tan(\tan^{-1}2)\}^2 + 1 + \{\cot(\cot^{-1}3)\}^2 = 1 + 2^2 + 1 + 3^2 = 15$$

(ii) $\tan^2(\sec^{-1}2) + \cot^2(\operatorname{cosec}^{-1}3) = \sec^2(\sec^{-1}2) - 1 + \operatorname{cosec}^2(\operatorname{cosec}^{-1}3) - 1$

$$= \{\sec(\sec^{-1}2)\}^2 - 1 + \{\operatorname{cosec}(\operatorname{cosec}^{-1}3)\}^2 - 1 = 2^2 - 1 + 3^2 - 1 = 11$$

ALITER $\tan^2(\sec^{-1}2) + \cot^2(\operatorname{cosec}^{-1}3)$

$$= \left\{\tan\left(\sec^{-1}\frac{2}{1}\right)\right\}^2 + \left\{\cot\left(\operatorname{cosec}^{-1}\frac{3}{1}\right)\right\}^2 = \left\{\tan\left(\tan^{-1}\frac{\sqrt{3}}{1}\right)\right\}^2 + \left\{\cot\left(\cot^{-1}\frac{2\sqrt{2}}{1}\right)\right\}^2$$

$$= (\sqrt{3})^2 + (2\sqrt{2})^2 = 3 + 8 = 11$$

EXAMPLE 9 *Prove that:* (i) $\sin\left[\cot^{-1}\left\{\cos(\tan^{-1}x)\right\}\right]=\sqrt{\dfrac{x^2+1}{x^2+2}}$

(ii) $\cos\left[\tan^{-1}\left\{\sin(\cot^{-1}x)\right\}\right]=\sqrt{\dfrac{x^2+1}{x^2+2}}$ **[CBSE 2010]**

SOLUTION (i) We find that

$$\cos(\tan^{-1}x)=\cos\left\{\cos^{-1}\frac{1}{\sqrt{1+x^2}}\right\}=\frac{1}{\sqrt{1+x^2}}\qquad\left[\because \tan^{-1}x=\cos^{-1}\frac{1}{\sqrt{1+x^2}}\right]$$

$\therefore$ $\sin\left[\cot^{-1}\left\{\cos(\tan^{-1}x)\right\}\right]$

$$=\sin\left\{\cot^{-1}\frac{1}{\sqrt{1+x^2}}\right\}=\sin\left\{\sin^{-1}\frac{\sqrt{1+x^2}}{\sqrt{2+x^2}}\right\}=\frac{\sqrt{1+x^2}}{\sqrt{2+x^2}}=\sqrt{\frac{x^2+1}{x^2+2}}$$

(ii) We find that $\sin(\cot^{-1}x)=\sin\left\{\sin^{-1}\dfrac{1}{\sqrt{1+x^2}}\right\}=\dfrac{1}{\sqrt{1+x^2}}$

$\therefore$ $\cos\left[\tan^{-1}\left\{\sin(\cot^{-1}x)\right\}\right]$

$$=\cos\left\{\tan^{-1}\frac{1}{\sqrt{1+x^2}}\right\}=\cos\left\{\cos^{-1}\frac{\sqrt{1+x^2}}{\sqrt{2+x^2}}\right\}=\sqrt{\frac{1+x^2}{2+x^2}}=\sqrt{\frac{x^2+1}{x^2+2}}$$

EXAMPLE 10 *If* $\sin\left\{\cot^{-1}(x+1)\right\}=\cos(\tan^{-1}x)$, *then find x.* **[CBSE 2015]**

SOLUTION We have,

$$\sin\left\{\cot^{-1}(x+1)\right\}=\cos(\tan^{-1}x)$$

$$\Rightarrow \sin\left\{\sin^{-1}\frac{1}{\sqrt{x^2+2x+2}}\right\}=\cos\left(\cos^{-1}\frac{1}{\sqrt{1+x^2}}\right)$$

$$\Rightarrow \frac{1}{\sqrt{x^2+2x+2}}=\frac{1}{\sqrt{1+x^2}}\Rightarrow\sqrt{x^2+2x+2}=\sqrt{1+x^2}\Rightarrow x^2+2x+2=x^2+1\Rightarrow 2x=-1\Rightarrow x=-\frac{1}{2}$$

Hence, $x=-\dfrac{1}{2}$ is a root of the given equation.

EXAMPLE 11 *Solve the following equation for x :*

(i) $\cos(\tan^{-1}x)=\sin\left(\cot^{-1}\dfrac{3}{4}\right)$

(ii) $\tan(\cos^{-1}x)=\sin\left(\cot^{-1}\dfrac{1}{2}\right)$ **[CBSE 2013, 2014, 2017, NCERT EXEMPLAR]**

SOLUTION (i) We have,

$$\cos(\tan^{-1}x)=\sin\left(\cot^{-1}\frac{3}{4}\right)\Rightarrow\cos\left(\cos^{-1}\frac{1}{\sqrt{1+x^2}}\right)=\sin\left(\sin^{-1}\frac{4}{5}\right)$$

$$\Rightarrow\quad \frac{1}{\sqrt{1+x^2}}=\frac{4}{5}\Rightarrow 4\sqrt{1+x^2}=5\Rightarrow 16(1+x^2)=25\Rightarrow 16x^2=9\Rightarrow x=\pm\frac{3}{4}$$

(ii) We have, $\tan(\cos^{-1}x)=\sin\left(\cot^{-1}\frac{1}{2}\right) \Rightarrow \tan\left(\tan^{-1}\frac{\sqrt{1-x^2}}{x}\right)=\sin\left(\sin^{-1}\frac{2}{\sqrt{5}}\right)$

$$\Rightarrow \quad \frac{\sqrt{1-x^2}}{x}=\frac{2}{\sqrt{5}} \Rightarrow \frac{1-x^2}{x^2}=\frac{4}{5} \Rightarrow 4x^2=5-5x^2 \Rightarrow 9x^2=5 \Rightarrow x=\pm\frac{\sqrt{5}}{3}$$

But, for $x=-\frac{\sqrt{5}}{3}$ we find that LHS is negative where as RHS is positive. Hence, $x=\frac{\sqrt{5}}{3}$.

EXERCISE 3.8

BASIC

1. Evaluate each of the following:

(i) $\sin\left(\sin^{-1}\frac{7}{25}\right)$ (ii) $\sin\left(\cos^{-1}\frac{5}{13}\right)$ (iii) $\sin\left(\tan^{-1}\frac{24}{7}\right)$

(iv) $\sin\left(\sec^{-1}\frac{17}{8}\right)$ (v) $\operatorname{cosec}\left(\cos^{-1}\frac{3}{5}\right)$ (vi) $\sec\left(\sin^{-1}\frac{12}{13}\right)$

(vii) $\tan\left(\cos^{-1}\frac{8}{17}\right)$ (viii) $\cot\left(\cos^{-1}\frac{3}{5}\right)$ (ix) $\cos\left(\tan^{-1}\frac{24}{7}\right)$

2. Prove the following results:

(i) $\tan\left(\cos^{-1}\frac{4}{5}+\tan^{-1}\frac{2}{3}\right)=\frac{17}{6}$ (ii) $\cos\left(\sin^{-1}\frac{3}{5}+\cot^{-1}\frac{3}{2}\right)=\frac{6}{5\sqrt{13}}$ [CBSE 2012]

(iii) $\tan\left(\sin^{-1}\frac{5}{13}+\cos^{-1}\frac{3}{5}\right)=\frac{63}{16}$ (iv) $\sin\left(\cos^{-1}\frac{3}{5}+\sin^{-1}\frac{5}{13}\right)=\frac{63}{65}$

BASED ON LOTS

3. Solve : $\cos\left(\sin^{-1}x\right)=\frac{1}{6}$

4. Solve : $\cos\left\{2\sin^{-1}(-x)\right\}=0$

5. Simplify : $\cos^{-1}x+\cos^{-1}\left\{\frac{x}{2}+\frac{\sqrt{3-3x^2}}{2}\right\}$; $\frac{1}{2}\le x\le 1$ [CBSE 2024]

ANSWERS

1. (i) $\frac{7}{25}$ (ii) $\frac{12}{13}$ (iii) $\frac{24}{25}$ (iv) $\frac{15}{17}$

(v) $\frac{5}{4}$ (vi) $\frac{13}{5}$ (vii) $\frac{15}{8}$ (viii) $\frac{3}{4}$

(ix) $\frac{7}{25}$

3. $\pm\frac{\sqrt{35}}{6}$

4. $\pm\frac{1}{\sqrt{2}}$

5. $\frac{\pi}{3}$

*4.3.3 PROPERTIES III & IV

PROPERTY-III *Prove that:*

(i) $\sin^{-1}(-x) = -\sin^{-1}x$, for all $x\in[-1,1]$ (ii) $\cos^{-1}(-x)=\pi-\cos^{-1}x$, for all $x\in[-1,1]$

(iii) $\tan^{-1}(-x) = -\tan^{-1}x$, for all $x\in R$ (iv) $\cot^{-1}(-x)=\pi-\cot^{-1}x$, for all $x\in R$

(v) $\operatorname{cosec}^{-1}(-x)=-\operatorname{cosec}^{-1}x$, for all $x\in(-\infty,-1]\cup[1,\infty)$

(vi) $\sec^{-1}(-x) = \pi-\sec^{-1}x$, for all $x\in(-\infty,-1]\cup[1,\infty)$

PROOF (i) Clearly, $-x\in[-1,1]$ for all $x\in[-1,1]$. Let $\sin^{-1}(-x) = \theta$ ...(i)

*May be skipped. Not from examination point of view.

Then, $-x = \sin\theta \Rightarrow x = -\sin\theta \Rightarrow x = \sin(-\theta)$

$\Rightarrow \quad -\theta = \sin^{-1} x \qquad [\because x\ [-1, 1] \text{ and } -\theta \in [-\pi/2, \pi/2] \text{ for all } \theta \in [-\pi/2, \pi/2]]$

$\Rightarrow \quad \theta = -\sin^{-1} x$ ...(ii)

From (i) and (ii), we get: $\sin^{-1}(-x) = -\sin^{-1} x$

(ii) Clearly, $-x \in [-1, 1]$ for all $x \in [-1, 1]$. Let $\cos^{-1}(-x) = \theta$. ...(i)

Then, $-x = \cos\theta \Rightarrow x = -\cos\theta \Rightarrow x = \cos(\pi - \theta)$

$\Rightarrow \quad \cos^{-1} x = \pi - \theta \qquad [\because x \in [-1, 1] \text{ and } \pi - \theta \in [0, \pi] \text{ for all } \theta \in [0, \pi]]$

$\Rightarrow \quad \theta = \pi - \cos^{-1} x$ ...(ii)

From (i) and (ii), we get: $\cos^{-1}(-x) = \pi - \cos^{-1} x$

Similarly, other results can be proved.

***PROPERTY IV** *Prove that:*

(i) $\sin^{-1}\left(\frac{1}{x}\right) = \text{cosec}^{-1} x,$ *for all* $x \in (-\infty, -1] \cup [1, \infty)$

(ii) $\cos^{-1}\left(\frac{1}{x}\right) = \sec^{-1} x,$ *for all* $x \in (-\infty, -1] \cup [1, \infty)$

(iii) $\tan^{-1}\left(\frac{1}{x}\right) = \begin{cases} \cot^{-1} x & , \textit{for } x > 0 \\ -\pi + \cot^{-1} x, & \textit{for } x < 0 \end{cases}$

ILLUSTRATIVE EXAMPLES

BASED ON BASIC CONCEPTS (BASIC)

EXAMPLE 1 *Evaluate:*

(i) $\cos\left\{\sin^{-1}\left(-\frac{5}{13}\right)\right\}$ (ii) $\cot\left\{\sin^{-1}\left(-\frac{7}{25}\right)\right\}$ (iii) $\sec\left\{\sin^{-1}\left(-\frac{8}{17}\right)\right\}$

SOLUTION We know that $\sin^{-1}(-x) = -\sin^{-1} x$ for all $x \in [-1, 1]$. Therefore,

(i) $\cos\left\{\sin^{-1}\left(-\frac{5}{13}\right)\right\} = \cos\left(-\sin^{-1}\frac{5}{13}\right) = \cos\left(\sin^{-1}\frac{5}{13}\right) = \cos\left(\cos^{-1}\frac{12}{13}\right) = \frac{12}{13}$

(ii) $\cot\left\{\sin^{-1}\left(-\frac{7}{25}\right)\right\} = \cot\left(-\sin^{-1}\frac{7}{25}\right) = -\cot\left(\sin^{-1}\frac{7}{25}\right) = -\cot\left(\cot^{-1}\frac{24}{7}\right) = -\frac{24}{7}$

(iii) $\sec\left\{\sin^{-1}\left(-\frac{8}{17}\right)\right\} = \sec\left(-\sin^{-1}\frac{8}{17}\right) = \sec\left(\sin^{-1}\frac{8}{17}\right) = \sec\left(\sec^{-1}\frac{17}{15}\right) = \frac{17}{15}$

EXAMPLE 2 *Evaluate:*

(i) $\sin\left\{\cos^{-1}\left(-\frac{3}{5}\right)\right\}$ (ii) $\tan\left\{\cos^{-1}\left(-\frac{12}{13}\right)\right\}$ (iii) $\text{cosec}\left\{\cos^{-1}\left(-\frac{12}{13}\right)\right\}$

SOLUTION We know that $\cos^{-1}(-x) = \pi - \cos^{-1} x$ for all $x \in [-1, 1]$. Therefore,

(i) $\sin\left\{\cos^{-1}\left(-\frac{3}{5}\right)\right\} = \sin\left\{\pi - \cos^{-1}\frac{3}{5}\right\} = \sin\left(\cos^{-1}\frac{3}{5}\right) = \sin\left(\sin^{-1}\frac{4}{5}\right) = \frac{4}{5}$

*May be skipped. Not from examination point of view.

(ii) $\tan\left\{\cos^{-1}\left(-\frac{12}{13}\right)\right\} = \tan\left\{\pi - \cos^{-1}\frac{12}{13}\right\} = -\tan\left(\cos^{-1}\frac{12}{13}\right) = -\tan\left(\tan^{-1}\frac{5}{12}\right) = -\frac{5}{12}$

(iii) $\operatorname{cosec}\left\{\cos^{-1}\left(-\frac{12}{13}\right)\right\} = \operatorname{cosec}\left\{\pi - \cos^{-1}\frac{12}{13}\right\} = \operatorname{cosec}\left(\cot^{-1}\frac{12}{13}\right) = \operatorname{cosec}\left(\operatorname{cosec}^{-1}\frac{13}{5}\right) = \frac{13}{5}$

EXAMPLE 3 *Evaluate:*

(i) $\sin\left\{\tan^{-1}\left(-\frac{7}{24}\right)\right\}$ (ii) $\cos\left\{\cot^{-1}\left(-\frac{5}{12}\right)\right\}$ (iii) $\operatorname{cosec}\left\{\cot^{-1}\left(-\frac{4}{3}\right)\right\}$

SOLUTION We know that $\tan^{-1}(-x) = -\tan^{-1}x$ and $\cot^{-1}(-x) = \pi - \cot^{-1}x$ for all $x \in R$. Therefore,

(i) $\sin\left\{\tan^{-1}\left(-\frac{7}{24}\right)\right\} = \sin\left(-\tan^{-1}\frac{7}{24}\right) = -\sin\left(\tan^{-1}\frac{7}{24}\right) = -\sin\left(\sin^{-1}\frac{7}{25}\right) = -\frac{7}{25}$

(ii) $\cos\left\{\cot^{-1}\left(-\frac{5}{12}\right)\right\} = \cos\left(\pi - \cot^{-1}\frac{5}{12}\right) = -\cos\left(\cot^{-1}\frac{5}{12}\right) = -\cos\left(\cos^{-1}\frac{5}{13}\right) = -\frac{5}{13}$

(iii) $\operatorname{cosec}\left\{\cot^{-1}\left(-\frac{4}{3}\right)\right\} = \operatorname{cosec}\left(\pi - \cot^{-1}\frac{4}{3}\right) = \operatorname{cosec}\left(\cot^{-1}\frac{4}{3}\right) = \operatorname{cosec}\left(\operatorname{cosec}^{-1}\frac{5}{3}\right) = \frac{5}{3}$

EXAMPLE 4 *Prove that :* $\sin^{-1}\left(-\frac{4}{5}\right) = \tan^{-1}\left(-\frac{4}{3}\right) = \cos^{-1}\left(-\frac{3}{5}\right) - \pi$

SOLUTION We find that : $\sin^{-1}\left(-\frac{4}{5}\right) = -\sin^{-1}\left(\frac{4}{5}\right) = -\tan^{-1}\left(\frac{4}{3}\right) = \tan^{-1}\left(-\frac{4}{3}\right)$

and, $\cos^{-1}\left(-\frac{3}{5}\right) - \pi = \left(\pi - \cos^{-1}\frac{3}{5}\right) - \pi = -\cos^{-1}\frac{3}{5} = -\tan^{-1}\left(\frac{4}{3}\right) = \tan^{-1}\left(-\frac{4}{3}\right)$

Hence, $\sin^{-1}\left(-\frac{4}{5}\right) = \tan^{-1}\left(-\frac{4}{3}\right) = \cos^{-1}\left(-\frac{3}{5}\right) - \pi$

BASED ON LOWER ORDER THINKING SKILLS (LOTS)

EXAMPLE 5 *Prove that* $\tan^{-1}x + \tan^{-1}\frac{1}{x} = \begin{cases} \pi/2, & \text{if } x > 0 \\ -\pi/2, & \text{if } x < 0 \end{cases}$

SOLUTION We have, $\tan^{-1}\left(\frac{1}{x}\right) = \begin{cases} \cot^{-1}x, & \text{for } x > 0 \\ -\pi + \cot^{-1}x, & \text{for } x < 0 \end{cases}$

$$\therefore \quad \tan^{-1}x + \tan^{-1}\left(\frac{1}{x}\right) = \begin{cases} \tan^{-1}x + \cot^{-1}x = \pi/2, & \text{if } x > 0 \\ \tan^{-1}x + \cot^{-1}x - \pi = \pi/2 - \pi = -\pi/2, & \text{if } x < 0 \end{cases}$$

EXERCISE 3.9

BASIC

1. Evaluate :

(i) $\cos\left\{\sin^{-1}\left(-\frac{7}{25}\right)\right\}$ (ii) $\sec\left\{\cot^{-1}\left(-\frac{5}{12}\right)\right\}$ (iii) $\cot\left\{\sec^{-1}\left(-\frac{13}{5}\right)\right\}$

2. Evaluate :

(i) $\tan\left\{\cos^{-1}\left(-\frac{7}{25}\right)\right\}$ (ii) $\operatorname{cosec}\left\{\cot^{-1}\left(-\frac{12}{5}\right)\right\}$ (iii) $\cos\left\{\tan^{-1}\left(-\frac{3}{4}\right)\right\}$

3. Evaluate : $\sin\left\{\cos^{-1}\left(-\frac{3}{5}\right)+\cot^{-1}\left(-\frac{5}{12}\right)\right\}$.

ANSWERS

1. (i) $\frac{24}{25}$ (ii) $-\frac{13}{5}$ (iii) $-\frac{5}{12}$ 2. (i) $-\frac{24}{7}$ (ii) $\frac{13}{5}$ (iii) $\frac{4}{5}$ 3. $-\frac{56}{65}$

*4.3.4 PROPERTY V

PROPERTY V *Prove that:*

(i) $\sin^{-1}x+\cos^{-1}x=\frac{\pi}{2}$, *for all* $x\in[-1, 1]$ (ii) $\tan^{-1}x+\cot^{-1}x=\frac{\pi}{2}$, *for all* $x\in R$

(iii) $\sec^{-1}x+\operatorname{cosec}^{-1}x=\frac{\pi}{2}$, *for all* $x\in(-\infty, -1]\cup[1, \infty)$.

ILLUSTRATIVE EXAMPLES

BASED ON BASIC CONCEPTS (BASIC)

EXAMPLE 1 *Find the value of* $\cot(\tan^{-1}a+\cot^{-1}a)$. [CBSE 2012, NCERT]

SOLUTION We know that $\tan^{-1}a+\cot^{-1}a=\frac{\pi}{2}$.

$$\therefore \quad \cot(\tan^{-1}a+\cot^{-1}a)=\cot\frac{\pi}{2}=0$$

EXAMPLE 2 *If* $-1\le x, y\le 1$ *such that* $\sin^{-1}x+\sin^{-1}y=\frac{\pi}{2}$, *find the value of* $\cos^{-1}x+\cos^{-1}y$. [NCERT EXEMPLAR]

SOLUTION We have,

$$\sin^{-1}x+\sin^{-1}y=\frac{\pi}{2}$$

$$\Rightarrow \quad \left(\frac{\pi}{2}-\cos^{-1}x\right)+\left(\frac{\pi}{2}-\cos^{-1}y\right)=\frac{\pi}{2} \quad \left[\because \sin^{-1}x+\cos^{-1}x=\frac{\pi}{2} \text{ and } \sin^{-1}y+\cos^{-1}y=\frac{\pi}{2}\right]$$

$$\Rightarrow \quad \pi-(\cos^{-1}x+\cos^{-1}y)=\frac{\pi}{2} \Rightarrow \cos^{-1}x+\cos^{-1}y=\frac{\pi}{2}$$

EXAMPLE 3 *If* $\tan^{-1}x+\tan^{-1}y=\frac{4\pi}{5}$, *find* $\cot^{-1}x+\cot^{-1}y$. [NCERT EXEMPLAR]

SOLUTION We have,

$$\tan^{-1}x+\tan^{-1}y=\frac{4\pi}{5}$$

$$\Rightarrow \quad \left(\frac{\pi}{2}-\cot^{-1}x\right)+\left(\frac{\pi}{2}-\cot^{-1}y\right)=\frac{4\pi}{5} \quad \left[\because \tan^{-1}x+\cot^{-1}x=\frac{\pi}{2}, \tan^{-1}y+\cot^{-1}y=\frac{\pi}{2}\right]$$

$$\Rightarrow \quad \pi-(\cot^{-1}x+\cot^{-1}y)=\frac{4\pi}{5} \Rightarrow \cot^{-1}x+\cot^{-1}y=\pi-\frac{4\pi}{5} \Rightarrow \cot^{-1}x+\cot^{-1}y=\frac{\pi}{5}$$

EXAMPLE 4 *If* $\tan^{-1}x-\cot^{-1}x=\tan^{-1}\frac{1}{\sqrt{3}}$, *find the value of* x. [NCERT EXEMPLAR]

SOLUTION We have,

$$\tan^{-1}x-\cot^{-1}x=\tan^{-1}\frac{1}{\sqrt{3}} \Rightarrow \tan^{-1}x-\cot^{-1}x=\frac{\pi}{6} \quad \text{...(i)}$$

May be skipped. Not from examination point of view.

We know that: $\tan^{-1}x+\cot^{-1}x=\frac{\pi}{2}$ ...(ii)

Adding (i) and (ii), we obtain: $2\tan^{-1}x=\frac{2\pi}{3} \Rightarrow \tan^{-1}x=\frac{\pi}{3} \Rightarrow x=\tan\frac{\pi}{3}=\sqrt{3}$

EXAMPLE 5 *If* $\sin\left(\cos^{-1}\frac{5}{13}+\sin^{-1}x\right)=1$, *find the value of x.*

SOLUTION We have, $\sin\left(\cos^{-1}\frac{5}{13}+\sin^{-1}x\right)=1$

$\Rightarrow \quad \cos^{-1}\frac{5}{13}+\sin^{-1}x=\frac{\pi}{2}$

$\Rightarrow \quad \sin^{-1}x=\frac{\pi}{2}-\cos^{-1}\frac{5}{13} \Rightarrow \sin^{-1}x=\sin^{-1}\frac{5}{13} \Rightarrow x=\frac{5}{13}$ $\quad\left[\because \sin^{-1}\frac{5}{13}+\cos^{-1}\frac{5}{13}=\frac{\pi}{2}\right]$

EXAMPLE 6 *If* $\sin\left(\sin^{-1}\frac{1}{5}+\cos^{-1}x\right)=1$, *then find the value of x.* **[NCERT, CBSE 2014]**

SOLUTION We have, $\sin\left(\sin^{-1}\frac{1}{5}+\cos^{-1}x\right)=1$

$\Rightarrow \quad \sin^{-1}\frac{1}{5}+\cos^{-1}x=\frac{\pi}{2}$

$\Rightarrow \quad \cos^{-1}x=\frac{\pi}{2}-\sin^{-1}\frac{1}{5}$

$\Rightarrow \quad \cos^{-1}x=\cos^{-1}\frac{1}{5} \Rightarrow x=\frac{1}{5}$ $\quad\left[\because \sin^{-1}\frac{1}{5}+\cos^{-1}\frac{1}{5}=\frac{\pi}{2}\right]$

EXAMPLE 7 *If* $\cos\left(\sin^{-1}\frac{2}{5}+\cos^{-1}x\right)=0$, *find the value of x.* **[NCERT EXEMPLAR]**

SOLUTION We have, $\cos\left(\sin^{-1}\frac{2}{5}+\cos^{-1}x\right)=0$

$\Rightarrow \quad \sin^{-1}\frac{2}{5}+\cos^{-1}x=\frac{\pi}{2} \Rightarrow \cos^{-1}x=\frac{\pi}{2}-\sin^{-1}\frac{2}{5}$

$\Rightarrow \quad \cos^{-1}x=\cos^{-1}\frac{2}{5} \Rightarrow x=\frac{2}{5}$ $\quad\left[\because \sin^{-1}\frac{2}{5}+\cos^{-1}\frac{2}{5}=\frac{\pi}{2}\right]$

EXAMPLE 8 *Evaluate:* $\cos(2\cos^{-1}x+\sin^{-1}x)$ *at* $x=\frac{1}{5}$.

SOLUTION We have,

$\cos(2\cos^{-1}x+\sin^{-1}x)$

$=\cos(\cos^{-1}x+\cos^{-1}x+\sin^{-1}x)=\cos\left(\cos^{-1}x+\frac{\pi}{2}\right)$ $\quad\left[\because \cos^{-1}x+\sin^{-1}x=\frac{\pi}{2}\right]$

$=-\sin(\cos^{-1}x)=-\sin\left(\sin^{-1}\sqrt{1-x^2}\right)=-\sqrt{1-x^2}$

Putting $x=\frac{1}{5}$, we obtain: $\cos\left(2\cos^{-1}x+\sin^{-1}x\right)=-\sqrt{1-\frac{1}{25}}=-\sqrt{\frac{24}{25}}$

EXERCISE 3.10

BASIC

1. Evaluate:

(i) $\cot\left(\sin^{-1}\frac{3}{4}+\sec^{-1}\frac{4}{3}\right)$ (ii) $\sin\left(\tan^{-1}x+\tan^{-1}\frac{1}{x}\right)$ for $x<0$

(iii) $\sin\left(\tan^{-1}x+\tan^{-1}\frac{1}{x}\right)$ for $x>0$ (iv) $\cot\left(\tan^{-1}a+\cot^{-1}a\right)$ **[CBSE 2012]**

(v) $\cos\left(\sec^{-1}x+\operatorname{cosec}^{-1}x\right), |x|\geq 1$

2. If $\cos^{-1}x+\cos^{-1}y=\frac{\pi}{4}$, find the value of $\sin^{-1}x+\sin^{-1}y$.

BASED ON LOTS

3. If $\sin^{-1}x+\sin^{-1}y=\frac{\pi}{3}$ and $\cos^{-1}x-\cos^{-1}y=\frac{\pi}{6}$, find the values of x and y.

4. If $\cot\left(\cos^{-1}\frac{3}{5}+\sin^{-1}x\right)=0$, find the values of x.

5. If $(\sin^{-1}x)^2+(\cos^{-1}x)^2=\frac{17\pi^2}{36}$, find x.

6. Solve : $\sin\left\{\sin^{-1}\frac{1}{5}+\cos^{-1}x\right\}=1$ [CBSE 2014, NCERT]

7. Solve the following equations:

(i) $\sin^{-1}x=\frac{\pi}{6}+\cos^{-1}x$ (ii) $4\sin^{-1}x=\pi-\cos^{-1}x$

(iii) $\tan^{-1}x+2\cot^{-1}x=\frac{2\pi}{3}$ (iv) $5\tan^{-1}x+3\cot^{-1}x=2\pi$

ANSWERS

1. (i) 0 (ii) −1 (iii) 1 (iv) 0 (v) 0

2. $\frac{3\pi}{4}$ 3. $x=\frac{\sqrt{3}-1}{2\sqrt{2}}, y=\frac{1}{\sqrt{2}}$ 4. $x=\frac{3}{5}$ 5. $x=-\frac{1}{2}$

6. $x=\frac{1}{5}$ 7. (i) $x=\frac{\sqrt{3}}{2}$ (ii) $x=\frac{1}{2}$ (iii) $x=\sqrt{3}$ (iv) 1

HINTS TO SELECTED PROBLEMS

6. We have, $\sin\left(\sin^{-1}\frac{1}{5}+\cos^{-1}x\right)=1$

$\Rightarrow \quad \sin^{-1}\frac{1}{5}+\cos^{-1}x=\frac{\pi}{2} \Rightarrow \cos^{-1}x=\frac{\pi}{2}-\sin^{-1}\frac{1}{5} \Rightarrow \cos^{-1}x=\cos^{-1}\frac{1}{5} \Rightarrow x=\frac{1}{5}$

7. (i) We have, $\sin^{-1}x=\frac{\pi}{6}+\cos^{-1}x$

$\Rightarrow \quad \sin^{-1}x-\cos^{-1}x=\frac{\pi}{6} \Rightarrow \sin^{-1}x-\left(\frac{\pi}{2}-\sin^{-1}x\right)=\frac{\pi}{6}$ $\left[\because \sin^{-1}x+\cos^{-1}x=\frac{\pi}{2}\right]$

$\Rightarrow \quad 2\sin^{-1}x=\frac{2\pi}{3} \Rightarrow \sin^{-1}x=\frac{\pi}{3} \Rightarrow x=\frac{\sqrt{3}}{2}$

*4.3.6 PROPERTY-VI

PROPERTY VI *Prove that:*

(i) $$\tan^{-1}x+\tan^{-1}y=\begin{cases}\tan^{-1}\left(\dfrac{x+y}{1-xy}\right), & \text{if } xy<1\\ \pi+\tan^{-1}\left(\dfrac{x+y}{1-xy}\right), & \text{if } x>0, y>0 \text{ and } xy>1\\ -\pi+\tan^{-1}\left(\dfrac{x+y}{1-xy}\right), & \text{if } x<0, y<0 \text{ and } xy>1\end{cases}$$

**May be skipped. Not from examination point of view.*

(ii) $$\tan^{-1}x-\tan^{-1}y=\begin{cases}\tan^{-1}\left(\dfrac{x-y}{1+xy}\right) & \text{, if } xy>-1\\ \pi+\tan^{-1}\left(\dfrac{x-y}{1+xy}\right) & \text{, if } x>0,\ y<0 \text{ and } xy<-1\\ -\pi+\tan^{-1}\left(\dfrac{x-y}{1+xy}\right) & \text{, if } x<0,\ y>0 \text{ and } xy<-1\end{cases}$$

ILLUSTRATIVE EXAMPLES

BASED ON BASIC CONCEPTS (BASIC)

EXAMPLE 1 *Prove that :* $\tan^{-1}\dfrac{2}{11}+\tan^{-1}\dfrac{7}{24}=\tan^{-1}\dfrac{1}{2}$

SOLUTION $\tan^{-1}\dfrac{2}{11}+\tan^{-1}\dfrac{7}{24}$

$$=\tan^{-1}\left\{\frac{\frac{2}{11}+\frac{7}{24}}{1-\frac{2}{11}\times\frac{7}{24}}\right\} \qquad \left[\because \tan^{-1}x+\tan^{-1}y=\tan^{-1}\left(\frac{x+y}{1-xy}\right), \text{If } xy<1\right]$$

$$=\tan^{-1}\left\{\frac{48+77}{264-14}\right\}=\tan^{-1}\left(\frac{125}{250}\right)=\tan^{-1}\left(\frac{1}{2}\right)$$

EXAMPLE 2 *Prove that:* $\tan^{-1}2+\tan^{-1}3=\dfrac{3\pi}{4}$

SOLUTION $\tan^{-1}2+\tan^{-1}3$

$$=\pi+\tan^{-1}\left\{\frac{2+3}{1-2\times 3}\right\} \qquad \left[\because \tan^{-1}x+\tan^{-1}y=\pi+\tan^{-1}\left(\frac{x+y}{1-xy}\right), \text{if } xy>1\right]$$

$$=\pi+\tan^{-1}(-1)=\pi-\frac{\pi}{4}=\frac{3\pi}{4}$$

EXAMPLE 3 *Prove that:* $\tan^{-1}1+\tan^{-1}2+\tan^{-1}3=\pi$ **[CBSE 2010]**

SOLUTION $\tan^{-1}1+\tan^{-1}2+\tan^{-1}3=\tan^{-1}1+(\tan^{-1}2+\tan^{-1}3)$

$$=\frac{\pi}{4}+\frac{3\pi}{4}=\pi$$ [See Example 2]

EXAMPLE 4 *Prove that:* $\sin^{-1}\dfrac{12}{13}+\cos^{-1}\dfrac{4}{5}+\tan^{-1}\dfrac{63}{16}=\pi$

SOLUTION We have,

$$\sin^{-1}\frac{12}{13}+\cos^{-1}\frac{4}{5}+\tan^{-1}\frac{63}{16}$$

$$=\tan^{-1}\frac{12}{5}+\tan^{-1}\frac{3}{4}+\tan^{-1}\frac{63}{16} \qquad \left[\because \sin^{-1}\frac{12}{13}=\tan^{-1}\frac{12}{5}\ \&\ \cos^{-1}\frac{4}{5}=\tan^{-1}\frac{3}{4}\right]$$

$$=\pi+\tan^{-1}\left\{\frac{\frac{12}{5}+\frac{3}{4}}{1-\frac{12}{5}\times\frac{3}{4}}\right\}+\tan^{-1}\frac{63}{16} \qquad \left[\begin{array}{l}\because \tan^{-1}x+\tan^{-1}y\\ =\pi+\tan^{-1}\left(\frac{x+y}{1-xy}\right), \text{if } xy>1\end{array}\right]$$

$$= \pi + \tan^{-1}\left(\frac{63}{-16}\right) + \tan^{-1}\left(\frac{63}{16}\right)$$

$$= \pi - \tan^{-1}\frac{63}{16} + \tan^{-1}\frac{63}{16} = \pi \qquad [\because \tan^{-1}(-x) = -\tan^{-1}x]$$

BASED ON LOWER ORDER THINKING SKILLS (LOTS)

EXAMPLE 5 *If* $\tan^{-1}2 + \tan^{-1}3 + \theta = \pi$, *find the value of* θ.

SOLUTION We have, $\tan^{-1}2 + \tan^{-1}3 + \theta = \pi \Rightarrow \tan^{-1}2 + \tan^{-1}3 = \pi - \theta$

$$\Rightarrow \quad \pi + \tan^{-1}\left(\frac{2+3}{1-2\times 3}\right) = \pi - \theta \Rightarrow \pi + \tan^{-1}(-1) = \pi - \theta \Rightarrow \pi - \frac{\pi}{4} = \pi - \theta \Rightarrow \theta = \frac{\pi}{4}$$

EXAMPLE 6 *Prove that:*

(i) $\tan^{-1}\frac{1}{7} + \tan^{-1}\frac{1}{13} = \tan^{-1}\frac{2}{9}$ (ii) $\tan^{-1}\frac{1}{2} + \tan^{-1}\frac{1}{5} + \tan^{-1}\frac{1}{8} = \frac{\pi}{4}$

[CBSE 2011, 2013]

(iii) $\tan^{-1}\frac{3}{4} + \tan^{-1}\frac{3}{5} - \tan^{-1}\frac{8}{19} = \frac{\pi}{4}$ (iv) $\tan^{-1}\frac{1}{5} + \tan^{-1}\frac{1}{7} + \tan^{-1}\frac{1}{3} + \tan^{-1}\frac{1}{8} = \frac{\pi}{4}$

[NCERT, CBSE 2008, 2010, 2016]

(v) $\cot^{-1}7 + \cot^{-1}8 + \cot^{-1}18 = \cot^{-1}3$ **[NCERT EXEMPLAR, CBSE 2014]**

SOLUTION (i) LHS $= \tan^{-1}\frac{1}{7} + \tan^{-1}\frac{1}{13}$

$$= \tan^{-1}\left\{\frac{\frac{1}{7}+\frac{1}{13}}{1-\frac{1}{7}\times\frac{1}{13}}\right\} \qquad \left[\because \tan^{-1}x + \tan^{-1}y = \tan^{-1}\frac{x+y}{1-xy}, \text{ if } xy < 1\right]$$

$$= \tan^{-1}\frac{20}{90} = \tan^{-1}\frac{2}{9} = \text{R.H.S.}$$

(ii) $$\text{LHS} = \tan^{-1}\frac{1}{2} + \tan^{-1}\frac{1}{5} + \tan^{-1}\frac{1}{8} = \left\{\tan^{-1}\frac{1}{2} + \tan^{-1}\frac{1}{5}\right\} + \tan^{-1}\frac{1}{8}$$

$$= \tan^{-1}\left\{\frac{\frac{1}{2}+\frac{1}{5}}{1-\frac{1}{2}\times\frac{1}{5}}\right\} + \tan^{-1}\frac{1}{8}\left[\because \tan^{-1}x + \tan^{-1}y = \tan^{-1}\left(\frac{x+y}{1-xy}\right), \text{ if } xy < 1\right]$$

$$= \tan^{-1}\frac{7}{9} + \tan^{-1}\frac{1}{8} = \tan^{-1}\left\{\frac{\frac{7}{9}+\frac{1}{8}}{1-\frac{7}{9}\times\frac{1}{8}}\right\} = \tan^{-1}\left(\frac{65}{65}\right) = \tan^{-1}1 = \frac{\pi}{4} = \text{R.H.S.}$$

(iii) $$\text{LHS} = \tan^{-1}\frac{3}{4} + \tan^{-1}\frac{3}{5} - \tan^{-1}\frac{8}{19} = \left\{\tan^{-1}\frac{3}{4} + \tan^{-1}\frac{3}{5}\right\} - \tan^{-1}\frac{8}{19}$$

$$= \tan^{-1}\left\{\frac{\frac{3}{4}+\frac{3}{5}}{1-\frac{3}{4}\times\frac{3}{5}}\right\} - \tan^{-1}\frac{8}{19} = \tan^{-1}\frac{27}{11} - \tan^{-1}\frac{8}{19} = \tan^{-1}\left\{\frac{\frac{27}{11}-\frac{8}{19}}{1+\frac{27}{11}\times\frac{8}{19}}\right\}$$

$$= \tan^{-1}\frac{425}{425} = \tan^{-1}1 = \frac{\pi}{4} = \text{R.H.S.}$$

(iv) $\text{LHS} = \tan^{-1}\frac{1}{5} + \tan^{-1}\frac{1}{7} + \tan^{-1}\frac{1}{3} + \tan^{-1}\frac{1}{8}$

$$= \left(\tan^{-1}\frac{1}{5} + \tan^{-1}\frac{1}{7}\right) + \left(\tan^{-1}\frac{1}{3} + \tan^{-1}\frac{1}{8}\right)$$

$$= \tan^{-1}\left(\frac{\frac{1}{5}+\frac{1}{7}}{1-\frac{1}{5}\times\frac{1}{7}}\right) + \tan^{-1}\left(\frac{\frac{1}{3}+\frac{1}{8}}{1-\frac{1}{3}\times\frac{1}{8}}\right) = \tan^{-1}\frac{6}{17} + \tan^{-1}\frac{11}{23}$$

$$= \tan^{-1}\left(\frac{\frac{6}{17}+\frac{11}{23}}{1-\frac{6}{17}\times\frac{11}{23}}\right) = \tan^{-1}\left(\frac{325}{325}\right) = \tan^{-1}1 = \frac{\pi}{4} = \text{R.H.S.}$$

(v) $\text{LHS} = \cos^{-1}7 + \cot^{-1}8 + \cot^{-1}18$

$$= \tan^{-1}\frac{1}{7} + \tan^{-1}\frac{1}{8} + \tan^{-1}\frac{1}{18} \qquad \left[\because\ \cot^{-1}(x) = \tan^{-1}\frac{1}{x},\ \text{if } x > 0\right]$$

$$= \left\{\tan^{-1}\frac{1}{7} + \tan^{-1}\frac{1}{8}\right\} + \tan^{-1}\frac{1}{18} = \tan^{-1}\left\{\frac{\frac{1}{7}+\frac{1}{8}}{1-\frac{1}{7}\times\frac{1}{8}}\right\} + \tan^{-1}\frac{1}{18} \left[\because\ xy = \frac{1}{7}\times\frac{1}{8} < 1\right]$$

$$= \tan^{-1}\frac{3}{11} + \tan^{-1}\frac{1}{18} = \tan^{-1}\left\{\frac{\frac{3}{11}+\frac{1}{18}}{1-\frac{3}{11}\times\frac{1}{18}}\right\} \qquad \left[\because\ xy = \frac{3}{11}\times\frac{1}{18} < 1\right]$$

$$= \tan^{-1}\frac{65}{195} = \tan^{-1}\frac{1}{3} = \cot^{-1}3.$$

EXAMPLE 7 *Simplify each of the following:*

(i) $\tan^{-1}\left(\frac{a+bx}{b-ax}\right), x < \frac{b}{a}$

(ii) $\tan^{-1}\left(\frac{a\cos x - b\sin x}{b\cos x + a\sin x}\right), -\frac{\pi}{2} < x < \frac{\pi}{2}, \frac{a}{b}\tan x > -1$ **[NCERT]**

(iii) $\tan^{-1}\left(\frac{3a^2x - x^3}{a^3 - 3ax^2}\right), -\frac{1}{\sqrt{3}} < \frac{x}{a} < \frac{1}{\sqrt{3}}$ **[NCERT]**

SOLUTION (i) $\tan^{-1}\left(\frac{a+bx}{b-ax}\right) = \tan^{-1}\left(\frac{\frac{a}{b}+x}{1-\frac{a}{b}x}\right) = \tan^{-1}\frac{a}{b} + \tan^{-1}x$

(ii) $\tan^{-1}\left(\frac{a\cos x - b\sin x}{b\cos x + a\sin x}\right) = \tan^{-1}\left(\frac{\frac{a}{b} - \tan x}{1+\frac{a}{b}\tan x}\right) = \tan^{-1}\frac{a}{b} - \tan^{-1}(\tan x) = \tan^{-1}\frac{a}{b} - x$

(iii) $\tan^{-1}\left(\dfrac{3a^2x-x^3}{a^3-3ax^2}\right)=\tan^{-1}\left\{\dfrac{3\left(\dfrac{x}{a}\right)-\left(\dfrac{x}{a}\right)^3}{1-3\left(\dfrac{x}{a}\right)^2}\right\}=3\tan^{-1}\dfrac{x}{a}$ $\left[\because \tan^{-1}\left(\dfrac{3x-x^3}{1-3x^2}\right)=3\tan^{-1}x\right]$

EXAMPLE 8 *Prove that:* $\tan^{-1}\dfrac{1-x}{1+x}-\tan^{-1}\dfrac{1-y}{1+y}=\sin^{-1}\dfrac{y-x}{\sqrt{1+x^2}\sqrt{1+y^2}}$.

SOLUTION We have,

$$\text{LHS}=\tan^{-1}\frac{1-x}{1+x}-\tan^{-1}\frac{1-y}{1+y}=(\tan^{-1}1-\tan^{-1}x)-(\tan^{-1}1-\tan^{-1}y)$$

$$=\tan^{-1}y-\tan^{-1}x=\tan^{-1}\left(\frac{y-x}{1+yx}\right)$$

$$=\sin^{-1}\frac{y-x}{\sqrt{(1+yx)^2+(y-x)^2}}=\sin^{-1}\left\{\frac{y-x}{\sqrt{(1+x^2)(1+y^2)}}\right\}=\text{RHS}.$$

EXAMPLE 9 *If* $a>b>c>0$, *prove that:* $\cot^{-1}\left(\dfrac{ab+1}{a-b}\right)+\cot^{-1}\left(\dfrac{bc+1}{b-c}\right)+\cot^{-1}\left(\dfrac{ca+1}{c-a}\right)=\pi$

SOLUTION We know that

$$\tan^{-1}\left(\frac{1}{x}\right)=\begin{cases}\cot^{-1}x & \text{, for } x>0\\ -\pi+\cot^{-1}x & \text{, for } x<0\end{cases}\Rightarrow \cot^{-1}x=\begin{cases}\tan^{-1}\dfrac{1}{x} & \text{, for } x>0\\ \pi+\tan^{-1}\dfrac{1}{x} & \text{, for } x<0\end{cases}$$

It is given that $a>b>c>0$. Therefore, $a-b>0$, $b-c>0$ and $c-a<0$.

$$\Rightarrow \quad \cot^{-1}\left(\frac{ab+1}{a-b}\right)=\tan^{-1}\left(\frac{a-b}{1+ab}\right),\ \cot^{-1}\left(\frac{bc+1}{b-c}\right)=\tan^{-1}\left(\frac{b-c}{1+bc}\right)$$

and, $$\cot^{-1}\left(\frac{ca+1}{c-a}\right)=\pi+\tan^{-1}\left(\frac{c-a}{1+ac}\right)$$

$$\therefore \quad \cot^{-1}\left(\frac{ab+1}{a-b}\right)+\cot^{-1}\left(\frac{bc+1}{b-c}\right)+\cot^{-1}\left(\frac{ca+1}{c-a}\right)$$

$$=\tan^{-1}\left(\frac{a-b}{1+ab}\right)+\tan^{-1}\left(\frac{b-c}{1+bc}\right)+\pi+\tan^{-1}\left(\frac{c-a}{1+ca}\right)$$

$$=\tan^{-1}a-\tan^{-1}b+\tan^{-1}b-\tan^{-1}c+\pi+\tan^{-1}c-\tan^{-1}a=\pi.$$

EXAMPLE 10 *Solve the following equations:*

(i) $\tan^{-1}\dfrac{x-1}{x-2}+\tan^{-1}\dfrac{x+1}{x+2}=\dfrac{\pi}{4}$ [NCERT, CBSE 2010]

(ii) $\tan^{-1}2x+\tan^{-1}3x=\dfrac{\pi}{4}$ [NCERT, CBSE 2009, 2012]

(iii) $\tan^{-1}\dfrac{x-1}{x+1}+\tan^{-1}\dfrac{2x-1}{2x+1}=\tan^{-1}\dfrac{23}{36}$

SOLUTION (i) We have,

$$\tan^{-1}\frac{x-1}{x-2}+\tan^{-1}\frac{x+1}{x+2}=\frac{\pi}{4}\Rightarrow \tan^{-1}\frac{x-1}{x-2}+\tan^{-1}\frac{x+1}{x+2}=\tan^{-1}1$$

$$\Rightarrow \quad \tan^{-1}\frac{x-1}{x-2}=\tan^{-1}1-\tan^{-1}\frac{x+1}{x+2}\Rightarrow \tan^{-1}\frac{x-1}{x-2}=\tan^{-1}\left(\frac{1-\frac{x+1}{x+2}}{1+\frac{x+1}{x+2}}\right)$$

$$\Rightarrow \quad \tan^{-1}\frac{x-1}{x-2}=\tan^{-1}\frac{x+2-x-1}{x+2+x+1}\Rightarrow \tan^{-1}\frac{x-1}{x-2}=\tan^{-1}\frac{1}{2x+3}$$

$$\Rightarrow \quad \frac{x-1}{x-2}=\frac{1}{2x+3}$$

$$\Rightarrow \quad (2x+3)(x-1)=x-2\Rightarrow 2x^2+x-3=x-2\Rightarrow 2x^2-1=0\Rightarrow x=\pm\frac{1}{\sqrt{2}}$$

(ii) We have,

$$\tan^{-1}2x+\tan^{-1}3x=\frac{\pi}{4}\Rightarrow \tan^{-1}\left\{\frac{2x+3x}{1-2x\times 3x}\right\}=\tan^{-1}1,\ \text{if } 6x^2<1$$

$$\Rightarrow \quad \frac{5x}{1-6x^2}=1,\ \text{if } 6x^2<1\Rightarrow 6x^2+5x-1=0 \text{ and } x^2<\frac{1}{6}$$

$$\Rightarrow \quad (6x-1)(x+1)=0 \text{ and } -\frac{1}{\sqrt{6}}<x<\frac{1}{\sqrt{6}}\Rightarrow x=-1,\frac{1}{6} \text{ and } -\frac{1}{\sqrt{6}}<x<\frac{1}{\sqrt{6}}\Rightarrow x=\frac{1}{6}$$

(iii) We have,

$$\tan^{-1}\frac{x-1}{x+1}+\tan^{-1}\frac{2x-1}{2x+1}=\tan^{-1}\frac{23}{36}$$

$$\Rightarrow \quad \tan^{-1}\left\{\frac{\frac{x-1}{x+1}+\frac{2x-1}{2x+1}}{1-\frac{x-1}{x+1}\cdot\frac{2x-1}{2x+1}}\right\}=\tan^{-1}\frac{23}{36},\ \text{if } \frac{(x-1)(2x-1)}{(x+1)(2x+1)}<1$$

$$\Rightarrow \quad \tan^{-1}\left(\frac{2x^2-1}{3x}\right)=\tan^{-1}\frac{23}{36} \text{ and } \frac{(x-1)(2x-1)}{(x+1)(2x+1)}-1<0$$

$$\Rightarrow \quad \frac{2x^2-1}{3x}=\frac{23}{36} \quad \text{and } \frac{-6x}{(x+1)(2x+1)}<0$$

$$\Rightarrow \quad 24x^2-23x-12=0 \text{ and } \frac{x}{(x+1)(2x+1)}>0$$

$$\Rightarrow \quad (3x-4)(8x+3)=0 \text{ and } x\in(-1,-1/2)\cup(0,\infty)\Rightarrow x=\frac{4}{3}$$

EXERCISE 3.11

BASIC

1. Prove the following results:

(i) $\tan^{-1}\frac{1}{7}+\tan^{-1}\frac{1}{13}=\tan^{-1}\frac{2}{9}$

(ii) $\sin^{-1}\frac{12}{13}+\cos^{-1}\frac{4}{5}+\tan^{-1}\frac{63}{16}=\pi$

(iii) $\tan^{-1}\frac{1}{4}+\tan^{-1}\frac{2}{9}=\sin^{-1}\frac{1}{\sqrt{5}}$ [NCERT EXEMPLAR, CBSE 2020]

2. Find the value of $\tan^{-1}\left(\frac{x}{y}\right)-\tan^{-1}\left(\frac{x-y}{x+y}\right)$ [CBSE 2011]

BASED ON LOTS

3. Solve the following equations for x :

(i) $\tan^{-1}2x+\tan^{-1}3x=n\pi+\frac{3\pi}{4}$

(ii) $\tan^{-1}(x+1)+\tan^{-1}(x-1)=\tan^{-1}\frac{8}{31}$

(iii) $\tan^{-1}(x-1)+\tan^{-1}x+\tan^{-1}(x+1)=\tan^{-1}3x$

(iv) $\tan^{-1}\left(\frac{1-x}{1+x}\right)-\frac{1}{2}\tan^{-1}x=0$, where $x>0$ [NCERT, CBSE 2008, 2010, 2011]

(v) $\cot^{-1}x-\cot^{-1}(x+2)=\frac{\pi}{12}$, where $x>0$

(vi) $\tan^{-1}(x+2)+\tan^{-1}(x-2)=\tan^{-1}\left(\frac{8}{79}\right)$, $x>0$ [CBSE 2010]

(vii) $\tan^{-1}\frac{x}{2}+\tan^{-1}\frac{x}{3}=\frac{\pi}{4}$, $0<x<\sqrt{6}$ [CBSE 2010C]

(viii) $\tan^{-1}\left(\frac{x-2}{x-4}\right)+\tan^{-1}\left(\frac{x+2}{x+4}\right)=\frac{\pi}{4}$ [CBSE 2014]

(ix) $\tan^{-1}(2+x)+\tan^{-1}(2-x)=\tan^{-1}\frac{2}{3}$, where $x<-\sqrt{3}$ or, $x>\sqrt{3}$

(x) $\tan^{-1}\frac{x-2}{x-1}+\tan^{-1}\frac{x+2}{x+1}=\frac{\pi}{4}$ [CBSE 2016]

(xi) $\tan^{-1}4x+\tan^{-1}6x=\frac{\pi}{4}$ [CBSE 2019]

BASED ON HOTS

4. Sum the series : $\tan^{-1}\frac{1}{3}+\tan^{-1}\frac{2}{9}+\tan^{-1}\frac{4}{33}+\ldots+\tan^{-1}\frac{2^{n-1}}{1+2^{2n-1}}$

ANSWERS

3. (i) $-\frac{1}{6}$ (ii) $\frac{1}{4}$ (iii) $0, \pm\frac{1}{2}$ (iv) $\frac{1}{\sqrt{3}}$ (v) $\sqrt{3}$ (vi) $\frac{1}{4}$

(vii) 1 (viii) $\pm\sqrt{2}$ (ix) ± 3 (x) $\pm\sqrt{\frac{7}{2}}$ (xi) $\frac{1}{12}$ 4. $\tan^{-1}2^n-\frac{\pi}{4}$

HINTS TO SELECTED PROBLEMS

2. $\tan^{-1}\frac{x}{y}-\tan^{-1}\left(\frac{x-y}{x+y}\right)=\tan^{-1}\frac{x}{y}+\tan^{-1}\left(\frac{y-x}{y+x}\right)=\tan^{-1}\frac{x}{y}+\tan^{-1}\left(\frac{1-x/y}{1+x/y}\right)$

$$=\tan^{-1}\frac{x}{y}+\tan^{-1}1-\tan^{-1}\frac{x}{y}=\tan^{-1}1=\frac{\pi}{4}$$

3. (iv) We have, $\tan^{-1}\left(\frac{1-x}{1+x}\right)-\frac{1}{2}\tan^{-1}x=0,\ x>0$

$$\Rightarrow \tan^{-1} 1 - \tan^{-1} x - \frac{1}{2}\tan^{-1} x = 0 \Rightarrow \frac{\pi}{4} - \frac{3}{2}\tan^{-1} x = 0 \Rightarrow \tan^{-1} x = \frac{\pi}{6} \Rightarrow x = \tan\frac{\pi}{6} = \frac{1}{\sqrt{3}}$$

(v) $$\tan^{-1}\frac{1}{x} - \tan^{-1}\frac{1}{x+2} = \frac{\pi}{12} \Rightarrow \tan^{-1}\left\{\frac{\frac{1}{x} - \frac{1}{x+2}}{1 + \frac{1}{x(x+2)}}\right\} = \frac{\pi}{12}$$

$$\Rightarrow \quad \tan^{-1}\left(\frac{2}{x^2+2x+1}\right) = \frac{\pi}{12} \Rightarrow \frac{2}{x^2+2x+1} = \tan\frac{\pi}{12}$$

$$\Rightarrow \quad \frac{2}{x^2+2x+1} = \frac{\sqrt{3}-1}{\sqrt{3}+1} \Rightarrow \frac{2}{x^2+2x+1} = \frac{2}{(\sqrt{3}+1)^2} \Rightarrow (x+1)^2 = (\sqrt{3}+1)^2 \Rightarrow x = \sqrt{3}$$

*4.3.7 PROPERTY VII

PROPERTY VII *Prove that:*

(i) $$\sin^{-1} x + \sin^{-1} y = \begin{cases} \sin^{-1}\left\{x\sqrt{1-y^2} + y\sqrt{1-x^2}\right\} & \text{, if } -1 \le x, y \le 1 \text{ and } x^2+y^2 \le 1 \\ & \text{or} \\ & \text{if } xy < 0 \text{ and } x^2+y^2 > 1 \\ \pi - \sin^{-1}\left\{x\sqrt{1-y^2} + y\sqrt{1-x^2}\right\} & \text{, if } 0 < x, y \le 1 \text{ and } x^2+y^2 > 1 \\ -\pi - \sin^{-1}\left\{x\sqrt{1-y^2} + y\sqrt{1-x^2}\right\} & \text{, if } -1 \le x, y < 0 \text{ and } x^2+y^2 > 1 \end{cases}$$

(ii) $$\sin^{-1} x - \sin^{-1} y = \begin{cases} \sin^{-1}\left\{x\sqrt{1-y^2} - y\sqrt{1-x^2}\right\} & \text{, if } -1 \le x, y \le 1 \text{ and } x^2+y^2 \le 1 \\ & \text{or} \\ & \text{if } xy > 0 \text{ and } x^2+y^2 > 1 \\ \pi - \sin^{-1}\left\{x\sqrt{1-y^2} - y\sqrt{1-x^2}\right\} & \text{, if } 0 < x \le 1, -1 \le y \le 0 \text{ and } x^2+y^2 > 1 \\ -\pi - \sin^{-1}\left\{x\sqrt{1-y^2} - y\sqrt{1-x^2}\right\} & \text{, if } -1 \le x < 0, 0 < y \le 1 \text{ and } x^2+y^2 > 1 \end{cases}$$

ILLUSTRATIVE EXAMPLES

BASED ON BASIC CONCEPTS (BASIC)

EXAMPLE 1 *Prove that:* $\sin^{-1}\frac{8}{17} + \sin^{-1}\frac{3}{5} = \sin^{-1}\frac{77}{85} = \tan^{-1}\left(\frac{77}{36}\right)$

[CBSE 2012, NCERT]

SOLUTION $$\sin^{-1}\frac{8}{17} + \sin^{-1}\frac{3}{5} = \sin^{-1}\left\{\frac{8}{17}\sqrt{1-\left(\frac{3}{5}\right)^2} + \frac{3}{5}\sqrt{1-\left(\frac{8}{17}\right)^2}\right\}$$

$$= \sin^{-1}\left\{\frac{8}{17}\times\frac{4}{5} + \frac{3}{5}\times\frac{15}{17}\right\} = \sin^{-1}\left(\frac{77}{85}\right) = \tan^{-1}\left(\frac{77}{36}\right)$$

**May be skipped. Not from examination point of view.*

EXAMPLE 2 *Prove that:* $\cos^{-1}\frac{12}{13}+\sin^{-1}\frac{3}{5}=\sin^{-1}\frac{56}{65}$ [NCERT, CBSE 2010, 2012]

SOLUTION We have,

$$\cos^{-1}\frac{12}{13}+\sin^{-1}\frac{3}{5}=\sin^{-1}\frac{5}{13}+\sin^{-1}\frac{3}{5} \qquad \left[\because \cos^{-1}\frac{12}{13}=\sin^{-1}\frac{5}{13}\right]$$

$$=\sin^{-1}\left\{\frac{5}{13}\times\sqrt{1-\left(\frac{3}{5}\right)^2}+\frac{3}{5}\times\sqrt{1-\left(\frac{5}{13}\right)^2}\right\}=\sin^{-1}\left\{\frac{5}{13}\times\frac{4}{5}+\frac{3}{5}\times\frac{12}{13}\right\}=\sin^{-1}\frac{56}{65}$$

EXAMPLE 3 *Prove that:*

(i) $\sin^{-1}\frac{3}{5}+\sin^{-1}\frac{8}{17}=\sin^{-1}\frac{77}{85}$ [NCERT EXEMPLAR]

(ii) $\sin^{-1}\frac{4}{5}+\sin^{-1}\frac{5}{13}+\sin^{-1}\frac{16}{65}=\frac{\pi}{2}$ [CBSE 2009]

(iii) $\sin^{-1}\frac{3}{5}+\sin^{-1}\frac{8}{17}=\cos^{-1}\frac{36}{85}$ [CBSE 2010]

(iv) $\sin^{-1}\frac{3}{5}+\cos^{-1}\frac{12}{13}=\cos^{-1}\frac{33}{65}=\sin^{-1}\frac{56}{65}$ [CBSE 2010]

SOLUTION Using $\sin^{-1}x\pm\sin^{-1}y=\sin^{-1}\left\{x\sqrt{1-y^2}\pm y\sqrt{1-x^2}\right\}$, we obtain

(i) $\sin^{-1}\frac{3}{5}+\sin^{-1}\frac{8}{17}$

$$=\sin^{-1}\left\{\frac{3}{5}\sqrt{1-\left(\frac{8}{17}\right)^2}+\frac{8}{17}\sqrt{1-\left(\frac{3}{5}\right)^2}\right\}=\sin^{-1}\left\{\frac{3}{5}\times\frac{15}{17}+\frac{8}{17}\times\frac{4}{5}\right\}=\sin^{-1}\frac{77}{85}$$

(ii) $\sin^{-1}\frac{4}{5}+\sin^{-1}\frac{5}{13}+\sin^{-1}\frac{16}{65}$

$$=\left\{\sin^{-1}\frac{4}{5}+\sin^{-1}\frac{5}{13}\right\}+\sin^{-1}\frac{16}{65}=\sin^{-1}\left\{\frac{4}{5}\sqrt{1-\left(\frac{5}{13}\right)^2}+\frac{5}{13}\sqrt{1-\left(\frac{4}{5}\right)^2}\right\}+\sin^{-1}\frac{16}{65}$$

$$=\sin^{-1}\left\{\frac{4}{5}\times\frac{12}{13}+\frac{5}{13}\times\frac{3}{5}\right\}+\sin^{-1}\frac{16}{65}=\sin^{-1}\frac{63}{65}+\sin^{-1}\frac{16}{65}$$

$$=\cos^{-1}\frac{16}{65}+\sin^{-1}\frac{16}{65} \qquad \left[\because \sin^{-1}\frac{63}{65}=\cos^{-1}\sqrt{1-\left(\frac{63}{65}\right)^2}=\cos^{-1}\frac{16}{65}\right]$$

$$=\frac{\pi}{2} \qquad \left[\because \sin^{-1}x+\cos^{-1}x=\frac{\pi}{2}\right]$$

(iii) $\sin^{-1}\frac{3}{5}+\sin^{-1}\frac{8}{17}$

$$=\sin^{-1}\left\{\frac{3}{5}\sqrt{1-\left(\frac{8}{17}\right)^2}+\frac{8}{17}\sqrt{1-\left(\frac{3}{5}\right)^2}\right\}=\sin^{-1}\left\{\frac{3}{5}\times\frac{15}{17}+\frac{8}{17}\times\frac{4}{5}\right\}$$

$$=\sin^{-1}\frac{77}{85}=\cos^{-1}\sqrt{1-\left(\frac{77}{85}\right)^2}=\cos^{-1}\frac{36}{85} \qquad \left[\because \sin^{-1}x=\cos^{-1}\sqrt{1-x^2}\right]$$

(iv) $\sin^{-1}\frac{3}{5}+\cos^{-1}\frac{12}{13}$

$= \sin^{-1}\frac{3}{5}+\sin^{-1}\frac{5}{13}$ $\quad [\because \cos^{-1}x=\sin^{-1}\sqrt{1-x^2}]$

$= \sin^{-1}\left\{\frac{3}{5}\times\sqrt{1-\left(\frac{5}{13}\right)^2}+\frac{5}{13}\times\sqrt{1-\left(\frac{3}{5}\right)^2}\right\}$

$= \sin^{-1}\left\{\frac{3}{5}\times\frac{12}{13}+\frac{5}{13}\times\frac{4}{5}\right\} = \sin^{-1}\frac{56}{65} = \cos^{-1}\sqrt{1-\left(\frac{56}{65}\right)^2} = \cos^{-1}\frac{33}{65}$

EXERCISE 3.12

BASIC

1. Evaluate : $\cos\left(\sin^{-1}\frac{3}{5}+\sin^{-1}\frac{5}{13}\right)$

2. Prove the following results :

(i) $\sin^{-1}\left(\frac{63}{65}\right)=\sin^{-1}\left(\frac{5}{13}\right)+\cos^{-1}\left(\frac{3}{5}\right)$ [CBSE 2012]

(ii) $\sin^{-1}\left(\frac{5}{13}\right)+\cos^{-1}\frac{3}{5}=\tan^{-1}\frac{63}{16}$ [NCERT EXEMPLAR]

(iii) $\frac{9\pi}{8}-\frac{9}{4}\sin^{-1}\left(\frac{1}{3}\right)=\frac{9}{4}\sin^{-1}\left(\frac{2\sqrt{2}}{3}\right)$ [NCERT]

BASED ON LOTS

3. Solve the following :

(i) $\sin^{-1}x+\sin^{-1}2x=\frac{\pi}{3}$

(ii) $\cos^{-1}x+\sin^{-1}\frac{x}{2}-\frac{\pi}{6}=0$ [CBSE 2010]

(iii) $\sin^{-1}\frac{5}{x}+\sin^{-1}\frac{12}{x}=\frac{\pi}{2}, x>0$ [CBSE 2020]

ANSWERS

1. $\frac{33}{65}$ 3. (i) $\frac{1}{2}\sqrt{\frac{3}{7}}$ (ii) 1 (iii) 13

*4.3.8 PROPERTY-VIII

PROPERTY VIII *Prove that:*

(i) $\cos^{-1}x+\cos^{-1}y=\begin{cases}\cos^{-1}\left\{xy-\sqrt{1-x^2}\sqrt{1-y^2}\right\}, & \text{if } -1\le x, y\le 1 \text{ and } x+y\ge 0\\ 2\pi-\cos^{-1}\left\{xy-\sqrt{1-x^2}\sqrt{1-y^2}\right\}, & \text{if } -1\le x, y\le 1 \text{ and } x+y\le 0\end{cases}$

(ii) $\cos^{-1}x-\cos^{-1}y=\begin{cases}\cos^{-1}\left\{xy+\sqrt{1-x^2}\sqrt{1-y^2}\right\}, & \text{if } -1\le x, y\le 1 \text{ and } x\le y\\ -\cos^{-1}\left\{xy+\sqrt{1-x^2}\sqrt{1-y^2}\right\}, & \text{if } -1\le y\le 0, 0<x\le 1 \text{ and } x\ge y\end{cases}$

*May be skipped. Not from examination point of view.

ILLUSTRATIVE EXAMPLES

BASED ON BASIC CONCEPTS (BASIC)

EXAMPLE 1 *Prove that:* $\cos^{-1}\frac{4}{5}+\cos^{-1}\frac{12}{13}=\cos^{-1}\frac{33}{65}$ [NCERT, CBSE 2010, 2012]

SOLUTION $\cos^{-1}\frac{4}{5}+\cos^{-1}\frac{12}{13}$

$$=\cos^{-1}\left\{\frac{4}{5}\times\frac{12}{13}-\sqrt{1-\left(\frac{4}{5}\right)^2}\sqrt{1-\left(\frac{12}{13}\right)^2}\right\}$$

$$=\cos^{-1}\left\{\frac{4}{5}\times\frac{12}{13}-\frac{3}{5}\times\frac{5}{13}\right\}=\cos^{-1}\left\{\frac{48}{65}-\frac{15}{65}\right\}=\cos^{-1}\frac{33}{65}$$

EXAMPLE 2 *Prove that:* $\sin^{-1}\frac{3}{5}-\sin^{-1}\frac{8}{17}=\cos^{-1}\frac{84}{85}$ [NCERT]

SOLUTION $\sin^{-1}\frac{3}{5}-\sin^{-1}\frac{8}{17}$

$$=\cos^{-1}\frac{4}{5}-\cos^{-1}\frac{15}{17}\qquad\left[\because\ \sin^{-1}\frac{3}{5}=\cos^{-1}\frac{4}{5},\ \sin^{-1}\frac{8}{17}=\cos^{-1}\frac{15}{17}\right]$$

$$=\cos^{-1}\left\{\frac{4}{5}\times\frac{15}{17}+\sqrt{1-\left(\frac{4}{5}\right)^2}\times\sqrt{1-\left(\frac{15}{17}\right)^2}\right\}$$

$$=\cos^{-1}\left\{\frac{4}{5}\times\frac{15}{17}+\frac{3}{5}\times\frac{8}{17}\right\}=\cos^{-1}\left\{\frac{60}{85}+\frac{24}{85}\right\}=\cos^{-1}\frac{84}{85}$$

BASED ON LOWER ORDER THINKING SKILLS (LOTS)

EXAMPLE 3 *If* $\cos^{-1}\frac{x}{a}+\cos^{-1}\frac{y}{b}=\alpha$, *prove that* $\frac{x^2}{a^2}-\frac{2xy}{ab}\cos\alpha+\frac{y^2}{b^2}=\sin^2\alpha.$

SOLUTION We have, [CBSE 2016]

$$\cos^{-1}\frac{x}{a}+\cos^{-1}\frac{y}{b}=\alpha$$

$$\Rightarrow\quad \cos^{-1}\left\{\frac{xy}{ab}-\sqrt{1-\frac{x^2}{a^2}}\sqrt{1-\frac{y^2}{b^2}}\right\}=\alpha\Rightarrow\frac{xy}{ab}-\sqrt{1-\frac{x^2}{a^2}}\sqrt{1-\frac{y^2}{b^2}}=\cos\alpha$$

$$\Rightarrow\quad \frac{xy}{ab}-\cos\alpha=\sqrt{1-\frac{x^2}{a^2}}\sqrt{1-\frac{y^2}{b^2}}\quad\Rightarrow\left(\frac{xy}{ab}-\cos\alpha\right)^2=\left(1-\frac{x^2}{a^2}\right)\left(1-\frac{y^2}{b^2}\right)$$

$$\Rightarrow\quad \frac{x^2y^2}{a^2b^2}-\frac{2xy}{ab}\cos\alpha+\cos^2\alpha=1-\frac{x^2}{a^2}-\frac{y^2}{b^2}+\frac{x^2y^2}{a^2b^2}$$

$$\Rightarrow\quad \frac{x^2}{a^2}+\frac{y^2}{b^2}-\frac{2xy}{ab}\cos\alpha=1-\cos^2\alpha\Rightarrow\frac{x^2}{a^2}+\frac{y^2}{b^2}-\frac{2xy}{ab}\cos\alpha=\sin^2\alpha$$

BASED ON HIGHER ORDER THINKING SKILLS (HOTS)

EXAMPLE 4 *If* $\cos^{-1}x+\cos^{-1}y+\cos^{-1}z=\pi$, *prove that* $x^2+y^2+z^2+2xyz=1.$

SOLUTION We have,

$$\cos^{-1} x + \cos^{-1} y + \cos^{-1} z = \pi$$

$$\Rightarrow \quad \cos^{-1} x + \cos^{-1} y = \pi - \cos^{-1} z$$

$$\Rightarrow \quad \cos^{-1} x + \cos^{-1} y = \cos^{-1}(-z) \qquad [\because \cos^{-1}(-z) = \pi - \cos^{-1} z]$$

$$\Rightarrow \quad \cos^{-1}\left\{xy - \sqrt{1-x^2}\,\sqrt{1-y^2}\right\} = \cos^{-1}(-z)$$

$$\Rightarrow \quad xy - \sqrt{1-x^2}\,\sqrt{1-y^2} = -z$$

$$\Rightarrow \quad (xy+z)^2 = (1-x^2)(1-y^2)$$

$$\Rightarrow \quad x^2 y^2 + z^2 + 2xyz = 1 - x^2 - y^2 + x^2 y^2 \Rightarrow x^2 + y^2 + z^2 + 2xyz = 1$$

EXERCISE 3.13

BASED ON LOTS

1. If $\cos^{-1}\frac{x}{2} + \cos^{-1}\frac{y}{3} = \alpha$, then prove that $9x^2 - 12xy\cos\alpha + 4y^2 = 36\sin^2\alpha$.
2. Solve the equation: $\cos^{-1}\frac{a}{x} - \cos^{-1}\frac{b}{x} = \cos^{-1}\frac{1}{b} - \cos^{-1}\frac{1}{a}$
3. Solve : $\cos^{-1}\sqrt{3}x + \cos^{-1}x = \frac{\pi}{2}$
4. Prove that:

   (i) $\cos^{-1}\frac{4}{5} + \cos^{-1}\frac{12}{13} = \cos^{-1}\frac{33}{65}$ [CBSE 2012]

   (ii) $\cos^{-1}\frac{12}{13} + \sin^{-1}\frac{3}{5} = \sin^{-1}\frac{56}{65}$ [CBSE 2019]

ANSWERS

2. $x = ab$ 3. $x = \frac{1}{2}$

*4.3.9 PROPERTY-IX

PROPERTY IX *Prove that:*

(i) $$2\sin^{-1} x = \begin{cases} \sin^{-1}(2x\sqrt{1-x^2}) & , \text{if } -\frac{1}{\sqrt{2}} \le x \le \frac{1}{\sqrt{2}} \\ \pi - \sin^{-1}(2x\sqrt{1-x^2}) & , \text{if } \frac{1}{\sqrt{2}} \le x \le 1 \\ -\pi - \sin^{-1}(2x\sqrt{1-x^2}) & , \text{if } -1 \le x \le -\frac{1}{\sqrt{2}} \end{cases}$$ [NCERT]

(ii) $$3\sin^{-1} x = \begin{cases} \sin^{-1}(3x - 4x^3) & , \text{if } -\frac{1}{2} \le x \le \frac{1}{2} \\ \pi - \sin^{-1}(3x - 4x^3) & , \text{if } \frac{1}{2} < x \le 1 \\ -\pi - \sin^{-1}(3x - 4x^3) & , \text{if } -1 \le x < -\frac{1}{2} \end{cases}$$ [CBSE 2018]

May be skipped. Not from examination point of view.

ILLUSTRATIVE EXAMPLES

BASED ON BASIC CONCEPTS (BASIC)

EXAMPLE 1 *Evaluate:* (i) $\sin(2\sin^{-1} 0.6)$ (ii) $\sin(2\sin^{-1} 0.8)$

SOLUTION (i) $\sin(2\sin^{-1} 0.6)$

$$= \sin\left[\sin^{-1}\left\{2 \times 0.6 \times \sqrt{1-(0.6)^2}\right\}\right] \quad \left[\because 2\sin^{-1} x = \sin^{-1}\left(2x\sqrt{1-x^2}\right), \text{ if } -\frac{1}{\sqrt{2}} \le x \le \frac{1}{\sqrt{2}}\right]$$

$$= \sin(\sin^{-1} 0.96) = 0.96$$

(ii) $\sin(2\sin^{-1} 0.8)$

$$= \sin\left[\pi - \sin^{-1}\left\{2 \times 0.8 \times \sqrt{1-(0.8)^2}\right\}\right] \left[\because 2\sin^{-1} x = \pi - \sin^{-1}\left(2x\sqrt{1-x^2}\right), \text{ if, } \frac{1}{\sqrt{2}} \le x < 1\right]$$

$$= \sin(\pi - \sin^{-1} 0.96) = \sin\left\{\sin^{-1}(0.96)\right\} = 0.96 \quad [\because \sin(\pi-\theta) = \sin\theta]$$

EXAMPLE 2 *Evaluate:* $\sin(3\sin^{-1} 0.4)$

SOLUTION Using $3\sin^{-1} x = \sin^{-1}(3x - 4x^3)$, we obtain

$$\sin(3\sin^{-1} 0.4) = \sin\left[\sin^{-1}\left\{3 \times 0.4 - 4 \times (0.4)^3\right\}\right]$$

$$= \sin\left\{\sin^{-1}(1.2 - 0.256)\right\} = \sin\left\{\sin^{-1}(0.944)\right\} = 0.944$$

*3.3.10 PROPERTIES X-XII

PROPERTY X *Prove that*

(i) $$2\cos^{-1} x = \begin{cases} \cos^{-1}(2x^2-1) & \text{, if } 0 \le x \le 1 \\ 2\pi - \cos^{-1}(2x^2-1) & \text{, if } -1 \le x \le 0 \end{cases}$$

(ii) $$3\cos^{-1} x = \begin{cases} \cos^{-1}(4x^3-3x) & \text{, if } \frac{1}{2} \le x \le 1 \\ 2\pi - \cos^{-1}(4x^3-3x) & \text{, if } -\frac{1}{2} \le x \le \frac{1}{2} \\ 2\pi + \cos^{-1}(4x^3-3x) & \text{, if } -1 \le x \le -\frac{1}{2} \end{cases}$$

***PROPERTY XI** *Prove that:*

(i) $$2\tan^{-1} x = \begin{cases} \tan^{-1}\left(\frac{2x}{1-x^2}\right) & \text{, if } -1 < x < 1 \\ \pi + \tan^{-1}\left(\frac{2x}{1-x^2}\right) & \text{, if } x > 1 \\ -\pi + \tan^{-1}\left(\frac{2x}{1-x^2}\right) & \text{, if } x < -1 \end{cases}$$

**May be skipped. Not from examination point of view.*

$$\text{(ii)}\ 3\tan^{-1}x = \begin{cases} \tan^{-1}\left(\dfrac{3x-x^3}{1-3x^2}\right), & \text{if } -\dfrac{1}{\sqrt{3}} < x < \dfrac{1}{\sqrt{3}} \\ \pi + \tan^{-1}\left(\dfrac{3x-x^3}{1-3x^2}\right), & \text{if } x > \dfrac{1}{\sqrt{3}} \\ -\pi + \tan^{-1}\left(\dfrac{3x-x^3}{1-3x^2}\right), & \text{if } x < -\dfrac{1}{\sqrt{3}} \end{cases}$$

***PROPERTY XII** *Prove that:*

$$\text{(i)}\ 2\tan^{-1}x = \begin{cases} \sin^{-1}\left(\dfrac{2x}{1+x^2}\right), & \text{if } -1 \le x \le 1 \\ \pi - \sin^{-1}\left(\dfrac{2x}{1+x^2}\right), & \text{if } x > 1 \\ -\pi - \sin^{-1}\left(\dfrac{2x}{1+x^2}\right), & \text{if } x < -1 \end{cases}$$

$$\text{(ii)}\ 2\tan^{-1}x = \begin{cases} \cos^{-1}\left(\dfrac{1-x^2}{1+x^2}\right), & \text{if } 0 \le x < \infty \\ -\cos^{-1}\left(\dfrac{1-x^2}{1+x^2}\right), & \text{if } -\infty < x \le 0 \end{cases}$$

ILLUSTRATIVE EXAMPLES

BASED ON BASIC CONCEPTS (BASIC)

EXAMPLE 1 *Prove that:*

$$\tan^{-1}x + \tan^{-1}\left(\frac{2x}{1-x^2}\right) = \tan^{-1}\left(\frac{3x-x^3}{1-3x^2}\right), |x| < \frac{1}{\sqrt{3}}$$ [NCERT, CBSE 2010]

SOLUTION $\tan^{-1}x + \tan^{-1}\left(\dfrac{2x}{1-x^2}\right)$

$$= \tan^{-1}\left\{\frac{x + \dfrac{2x}{1-x^2}}{1 - \dfrac{2x^2}{1-x^2}}\right\} \qquad \left[\because \tan^{-1}x + \tan^{-1}y = \tan^{-1}\left(\frac{x+y}{1-xy}\right), \text{if } xy < 1\right]$$

$$= \tan^{-1}\left(\frac{x-x^3+2x}{1-x^2-2x^2}\right) = \tan^{-1}\left(\frac{3x-x^3}{1-3x^2}\right)$$

ALITER $\text{LHS} = \tan^{-1}x + \tan^{-1}\left(\dfrac{2x}{1-x^2}\right) = \tan^{-1}x + 2\tan^{-1}x \qquad \left[\because -\dfrac{1}{\sqrt{3}} < x < \dfrac{1}{\sqrt{3}}\right]$

$$= 3\tan^{-1}x = \tan^{-1}\left(\frac{3x-x^3}{1-3x^2}\right) = \text{RHS}$$

**May be skipped. Not from examination point of view.*

EXAMPLE 2 *Simplify:* $\tan^{-1}\left(\dfrac{3a^2x-x^3}{a^3-3ax^2}\right), -\dfrac{1}{\sqrt{3}}<\dfrac{x}{a}<\dfrac{1}{\sqrt{3}}$ **[NCERT]**

SOLUTION $\tan^{-1}\left(\dfrac{3a^2x-x^3}{a^3-3ax^2}\right)$

$$= \tan^{-1}\left\{\frac{3\left(\frac{x}{a}\right)-\left(\frac{x}{a}\right)^3}{1-3\left(\frac{x}{a}\right)^2}\right\} = 3\tan^{-1}\frac{x}{a} \qquad \left[\because \tan^{-1}\left(\frac{3x-x^3}{1-3x^2}\right)=3\tan^{-1}x\right]$$

EXAMPLE 3 *Prove that:* $2\tan^{-1}\dfrac{1}{2}+\tan^{-1}\dfrac{1}{7}=\tan^{-1}\dfrac{31}{17}$

SOLUTION $2\tan^{-1}\dfrac{1}{2}+\tan^{-1}\dfrac{1}{7}$

$$= \tan^{-1}\left\{\frac{2\times\frac{1}{2}}{1-\left(\frac{1}{2}\right)^2}\right\}+\tan^{-1}\frac{1}{7} \qquad \left[\because 2\tan^{-1}x=\tan^{-1}\left(\frac{2x}{1-x^2}\right), \text{ if } -1<x<1\right]$$

$$= \tan^{-1}\frac{4}{3}+\tan^{-1}\frac{1}{7} = \tan^{-1}\left\{\frac{\frac{4}{3}+\frac{1}{7}}{1-\frac{4}{3}\times\frac{1}{7}}\right\} = \tan^{-1}\frac{31}{17}$$

EXAMPLE 4 *Evaluate:* $\tan\left(2\tan^{-1}\dfrac{1}{5}\right)$ **[CBSE 2013]**

SOLUTION $\tan\left(2\tan^{-1}\dfrac{1}{5}\right) = \tan\left\{\tan^{-1}\left(\dfrac{2\times\frac{1}{5}}{1-\frac{1}{25}}\right)\right\} = \tan\left(\tan^{-1}\dfrac{5}{12}\right)=\dfrac{5}{12}$

EXAMPLE 5 *Prove that:* $2\sin^{-1}\dfrac{3}{5}-\tan^{-1}\dfrac{17}{31}=\dfrac{\pi}{4}$ **[NCERT EXEMPLAR]**

SOLUTION $2\sin^{-1}\dfrac{3}{5}-\tan^{-1}\dfrac{17}{31}$

$$= 2\tan^{-1}\frac{3}{4}-\tan^{-1}\frac{17}{31} \qquad \left[\because \sin^{-1}\frac{3}{5}=\tan^{-1}\frac{3}{4}\right]$$

$$= \tan^{-1}\left\{\frac{2\times\frac{3}{4}}{1-\left(\frac{3}{4}\right)^2}\right\}-\tan^{-1}\frac{17}{31} \qquad \left[\because 2\tan^{-1}x=\tan^{-1}\frac{2x}{1-x^2} \text{ for } |x|<1\right]$$

$$= \tan^{-1}\frac{24}{7}-\tan^{-1}\frac{17}{13} = \tan^{-1}\left(\frac{\frac{24}{7}-\frac{17}{31}}{1+\frac{24}{7}\times\frac{17}{31}}\right) = \tan^{-1}1=\frac{\pi}{4}$$

BASED ON LOWER ORDER THINKING SKILLS (LOTS)

EXAMPLE 6 *Prove that:* $\tan \frac{1}{2}\left\{\sin^{-1}\frac{2x}{1+x^2}+\cos^{-1}\frac{1-y^2}{1+y^2}\right\}=\frac{x+y}{1-xy}$, *if* $|x|<1, y>0$ *and* $xy<1$. **[NCERT, CBSE 2013]**

SOLUTION We know that

$$\cos^{-1}\frac{1-y^2}{1+y^2}=2\tan^{-1}y \text{ for all } y\geq 0 \text{ and, } \sin^{-1}\frac{2x}{1+x^2}=2\tan^{-1}x \text{ for all } x\in[-1,1]$$

$$\therefore \quad \text{LHS}=\tan\frac{1}{2}\left\{\sin^{-1}\frac{2x}{1+x^2}+\cos^{-1}\frac{1-y^2}{1+y^2}\right\}=\tan\frac{1}{2}\left\{2\tan^{-1}x+2\tan^{-1}y\right\}$$

$$=\tan\left(\tan^{-1}x+\tan^{-1}y\right)=\tan\left\{\tan^{-1}\left(\frac{x+y}{1-xy}\right)\right\}=\frac{x+y}{1-xy}=\text{RHS} \quad [\because\ xy<1]$$

EXAMPLE 7 *Find the value of:* $\sin\left\{2\cot^{-1}\left(-\frac{5}{12}\right)\right\}$. **[NCERT EXEMPLAR]**

SOLUTION $\sin\left\{2\cot^{-1}\left(-\frac{5}{12}\right)\right\}=\sin\left\{2\left(\pi-\cot^{-1}\frac{5}{12}\right)\right\}$ $\quad [\because\ \cot^{-1}(-x)=\pi-\cot^{-1}x]$

$$=\sin\left(2\pi-2\cot^{-1}\frac{5}{12}\right)=-\sin\left(2\cot^{-1}\frac{5}{12}\right) \quad [\because \sin(2\pi-\theta)=-\sin\theta]$$

$$=-\sin\left(2\tan^{-1}\frac{12}{5}\right) \quad \left[\because\ \cot^{-1}x=\tan^{-1}\frac{1}{x} \text{ for } x>0\right]$$

$$=-\sin\left\{\pi-\sin^{-1}\left(\frac{2\times\frac{12}{5}}{1+\left(\frac{12}{5}\right)^2}\right)\right\} \quad \left[\because\ 2\tan^{-1}x=\pi-\sin^{-1}\left(\frac{2x}{1+x^2}\right) \text{ for } x>1\right]$$

$$=-\sin\left(\pi-\sin^{-1}\frac{120}{169}\right)=-\sin\left(\sin^{-1}\frac{120}{169}\right)=-\frac{120}{169}$$

EXAMPLE 8 *Show that:* $2\tan^{-1}(-3)=-\frac{\pi}{2}+\tan^{-1}\left(-\frac{4}{3}\right)$. **[NCERT EXEMPLAR]**

SOLUTION $\text{LHS}=2\tan^{-1}(-3)=-2\tan^{-1}3$ $\quad [\because\ \tan^{-1}(-x)=-\tan^{-1}x]$

$$=-\left\{\pi+\tan^{-1}\left(\frac{2\times 3}{1-3^2}\right)\right\} \quad \left[\because\ 2\tan^{-1}x=\pi+\tan^{-1}\left(\frac{2x}{1-x^2}\right), \text{ if } x>1\right]$$

$$=-\pi-\tan^{-1}\left(-\frac{3}{4}\right)=-\pi+\tan^{-1}\frac{3}{4} \quad \left[\because\ \tan^{-1}(-x)=-\tan^{-1}x\right]$$

$$=-\pi+\left(\frac{\pi}{2}-\cot^{-1}\frac{3}{4}\right) \quad \left[\because\ \tan^{-1}x=\frac{\pi}{2}-\cot^{-1}x\right]$$

$$=-\frac{\pi}{2}-\cot^{-1}\frac{3}{4}=-\frac{\pi}{2}-\tan^{-1}\frac{4}{3} \quad \left[\because \cot^{-1}x=\tan^{-1}\left(\frac{1}{x}\right) \text{ for } x>0\right]$$

$$=-\frac{\pi}{2}+\tan^{-1}\left(-\frac{4}{3}\right)=\text{RHS}$$

EXAMPLE 9 *Show that:* $\cos\left(2\tan^{-1}\frac{1}{7}\right)=\sin\left(4\tan^{-1}\frac{1}{3}\right)$ **[NCERT EXEMPLAR]**

SOLUTION We have,

$$\text{LHS}=\cos\left(2\tan^{-1}\frac{1}{7}\right)=\cos\left\{\cos^{-1}\left(\frac{1-\frac{1}{49}}{1+\frac{1}{49}}\right)\right\}\qquad\left[\because 2\tan^{-1}x=\cos^{-1}\left(\frac{1-x^2}{1+x^2}\right)\text{ for } 0\le x<\infty\right]$$

$$=\cos\left\{\cos^{-1}\left(\frac{24}{25}\right)\right\}=\frac{24}{25}\qquad\ldots\text{(i)}$$

and,

$$\text{RHS}=\sin\left(4\tan^{-1}\frac{1}{3}\right)=\sin\left\{2\left(2\tan^{-1}\frac{1}{3}\right)\right\}$$

$$=\sin\left\{2\tan^{-1}\left(\frac{2\times\frac{1}{3}}{1-\frac{1}{9}}\right)\right\}\qquad\left[\because 2\tan^{-1}x=\tan^{-1}\left(\frac{2x}{1-x^2}\right)\text{ for } -1<x<1\right]$$

$$=\sin\left(2\tan^{-1}\frac{3}{4}\right)=\sin\left\{\sin^{-1}\left(\frac{2\times\frac{3}{4}}{1+\frac{9}{16}}\right)\right\}\qquad\left[\because 2\tan^{-1}x=\sin^{-1}\left(\frac{2x}{1+x^2}\right),\text{ if } -1<x<1\right]$$

$$=\sin\left(\sin^{-1}\frac{24}{25}\right)=\frac{24}{25}\qquad\ldots\text{(ii)}$$

From (i) and (ii), we obtain

$$\cos\left(2\tan^{-1}\frac{1}{7}\right)=\sin\left(4\tan^{-1}\frac{1}{3}\right)$$

EXAMPLE 10 *Prove that:* $\tan^{-1}\sqrt{x}=\frac{1}{2}\cos^{-1}\left(\frac{1-x}{1+x}\right)$, $x\in[0,1]$ **[NCERT, CBSE 2010]**

SOLUTION We have,

$$\frac{1}{2}\cos^{-1}\left(\frac{1-x}{1+x}\right)=\frac{1}{2}\cos^{-1}\left\{\frac{1-(\sqrt{x})^2}{1+(\sqrt{x})^2}\right\}=\frac{1}{2}\times 2\tan^{-1}\sqrt{x}=\tan^{-1}\sqrt{x}.$$

ALITER Putting $x=\tan^2\theta$, we obtain

$$\text{RHS}=\frac{1}{2}\cos^{-1}\left(\frac{1-x}{1+x}\right)=\frac{1}{2}\cos^{-1}\left(\frac{1-\tan^2\theta}{1+\tan^2\theta}\right)=\frac{1}{2}\cos^{-1}(\cos 2\theta)=\theta=\tan^{-1}\sqrt{x}=\text{LHS}$$

EXAMPLE 11 *Find the value of the expression:* $\sin\left(2\tan^{-1}\frac{1}{3}\right)+\cos\left(\tan^{-1}2\sqrt{2}\right)$.

[NCERT EXEMPLAR]

SOLUTION $\sin\left(2\tan^{-1}\frac{1}{3}\right)+\cos\left(\tan^{-1}2\sqrt{2}\right)$

$$=\sin\left\{\sin^{-1}\left(\frac{2\times\frac{1}{3}}{1+\frac{1}{9}}\right)\right\}+\cos\left(\cos^{-1}\frac{1}{3}\right)\qquad\left[\because 2\tan^{-1}x=\sin^{-1}\left(\frac{2x}{1+x^2}\right),\text{ if } -1<x<1\right]$$

$$= \sin\left(\sin^{-1}\frac{3}{5}\right) + \cos\left(\cos^{-1}\frac{1}{3}\right) = \frac{3}{5} + \frac{1}{3} = \frac{14}{15}$$

EXAMPLE 12 *Prove the following:*

(i) $4\tan^{-1}\frac{1}{5} - \tan^{-1}\frac{1}{70} + \tan^{-1}\frac{1}{99} = \frac{\pi}{4}$ (ii) $2\tan^{-1}\frac{1}{5} + \sec^{-1}\frac{5\sqrt{2}}{7} + 2\tan^{-1}\frac{1}{8} = \frac{\pi}{4}$

[CBSE 2014]

SOLUTION (i) We have,

$$4\tan^{-1}\frac{1}{5} - \tan^{-1}\frac{1}{70} + \tan^{-1}\frac{1}{99}$$

$$= 2\left\{2\tan^{-1}\frac{1}{5}\right\} - \tan^{-1}\frac{1}{70} + \tan^{-1}\frac{1}{99}$$

$$= 2\tan^{-1}\left\{\frac{2\times 1/5}{1-(1/5)^2}\right\} - \tan^{-1}\frac{1}{70} + \tan^{-1}\frac{1}{99} \qquad \left[\because\ 2\tan^{-1}x = \tan^{-1}\frac{2x}{1-x^2},\ \text{if } |x|<1\right]$$

$$= 2\tan^{-1}\frac{5}{12} - \left\{\tan^{-1}\frac{1}{70} - \tan^{-1}\frac{1}{99}\right\}$$

$$= \tan^{-1}\left\{\frac{2\times 5/12}{1-(5/12)^2}\right\} - \tan^{-1}\left\{\frac{\frac{1}{70}-\frac{1}{99}}{1+\frac{1}{70}\times\frac{1}{99}}\right\} = \tan^{-1}\frac{120}{119} - \tan^{-1}\frac{29}{6931}$$

$$= \tan^{-1}\frac{120}{119} - \tan^{-1}\frac{1}{239} = \tan^{-1}\left\{\frac{\frac{120}{119}-\frac{1}{239}}{1+\frac{120}{119}\times\frac{1}{239}}\right\} = \tan^{-1}1 = \frac{\pi}{4}$$

(ii) $2\tan^{-1}\frac{1}{5} + \sec^{-1}\frac{5\sqrt{2}}{7} + 2\tan^{-1}\frac{1}{8}$

$$= 2\left\{\tan^{-1}\frac{1}{5} + \tan^{-1}\frac{1}{8}\right\} + \sec^{-1}\frac{5\sqrt{2}}{7}$$

$$= 2\tan^{-1}\left\{\frac{\frac{1}{5}+\frac{1}{8}}{1-\frac{1}{5}\times\frac{1}{8}}\right\} + \tan^{-1}\sqrt{\left(\frac{5\sqrt{2}}{7}\right)^2 - 1} \qquad \left[\because\ \sec^{-1}x = \tan^{-1}\sqrt{x^2-1}\right]$$

$$= 2\tan^{-1}\frac{13}{39} + \tan^{-1}\frac{1}{7} = 2\tan^{-1}\frac{1}{3} + \tan^{-1}\frac{1}{7}$$

$$= \tan^{-1}\left\{\frac{2\times 1/3}{1-(1/3)^2}\right\} + \tan^{-1}\frac{1}{7} \qquad \left[\because\ 2\tan^{-1}x = \tan^{-1}\frac{2x}{1-x^2},\ \text{if } |x|<1\right]$$

$$= \tan^{-1}\frac{3}{4} + \tan^{-1}\frac{1}{7} = \tan^{-1}\left\{\frac{\frac{3}{4}+\frac{1}{7}}{1-\frac{3}{4}\times\frac{1}{7}}\right\} = \tan^{-1}1 = \frac{\pi}{4}$$

EXAMPLE 13 *Evaluate:*

(i) $\tan\left\{2\tan^{-1}\frac{1}{5} - \frac{\pi}{4}\right\}$ (ii) $\tan\left\{\frac{1}{2}\cos^{-1}\frac{\sqrt{5}}{3}\right\}$

SOLUTION (i) $\tan\left\{2\tan^{-1}\frac{1}{5}-\frac{\pi}{4}\right\}$

$$= \tan\left\{\tan^{-1}\left(\frac{2\times\frac{1}{5}}{1-\frac{1}{25}}\right)-\tan^{-1}1\right\} \qquad \left[\because 2\tan^{-1}x=\tan^{-1}\left(\frac{2x}{1-x^2}\right), \text{ if } |x|<1\right]$$

$$= \tan\left\{\tan^{-1}\frac{5}{12}-\tan^{-1}1\right\} = \tan\left\{\tan^{-1}\left(\frac{\frac{5}{12}-1}{1+\frac{5}{12}}\right)\right\} = \tan\left\{\tan^{-1}\left(\frac{-7}{17}\right)\right\} = \frac{-7}{17}$$

(ii) Let $\cos^{-1}\frac{\sqrt{5}}{3}=\theta$. Then, $\cos\theta=\frac{\sqrt{5}}{3}$.

$$\therefore \quad \tan\left(\frac{1}{2}\cos^{-1}\frac{\sqrt{5}}{3}\right) = \tan\frac{\theta}{2} = \sqrt{\frac{1-\cos\theta}{1+\cos\theta}} = \sqrt{\frac{1-\frac{\sqrt{5}}{3}}{1+\frac{\sqrt{5}}{3}}} = \sqrt{\frac{3-\sqrt{5}}{3+\sqrt{5}}}$$

$$= \sqrt{\frac{(3-\sqrt{5})^2}{(3+\sqrt{5})(3-\sqrt{5})}} = \sqrt{\frac{(3-\sqrt{5})^2}{9-5}} = \frac{3-\sqrt{5}}{2}$$

EXAMPLE 14 *Solve for x*: $2\tan^{-1}(\cos x)=\tan^{-1}(2\operatorname{cosec} x)$.

[NCERT EXEMPLAR, CBSE 2009, 2010 C, 2014, 2016]

SOLUTION We have,

$$2\tan^{-1}(\cos x) = \tan^{-1}(2\operatorname{cosec} x)$$

$$\Rightarrow \quad \tan^{-1}\left(\frac{2\cos x}{1-\cos^2 x}\right) = \tan^{-1}(2\operatorname{cosec} x)$$

$$\Rightarrow \quad \frac{2\cos x}{\sin^2 x} = 2\operatorname{cosec} x \Rightarrow \cos x=\sin x \Rightarrow \tan x=1 \Rightarrow \tan x=\tan\frac{\pi}{4} \Rightarrow x=n\pi+\frac{\pi}{4}, n\in Z$$

EXAMPLE 15 *Solve the following equations:*

(i) $\sin^{-1}(1-x)-2\sin^{-1}x=\frac{\pi}{2}$ **[CBSE 2020]** (ii) $\sin\left[2\cos^{-1}\left\{\cot(2\tan^{-1}x)\right\}\right]=0$

(iii) $\sin^{-1}x+\sin^{-1}(1-x)=\cos^{-1}x$ **[NCERT EXEMPLAR, CBSE 2016]**

SOLUTION (i) We have,

$$\sin^{-1}(1-x)-2\sin^{-1}x = \frac{\pi}{2}$$

$$\Rightarrow \quad \sin^{-1}(1-x) = \frac{\pi}{2}+2\sin^{-1}x$$

$$\Rightarrow \quad \sin\left\{\sin^{-1}(1-x)\right\} = \sin\left(\frac{\pi}{2}+2\sin^{-1}x\right)$$

$$\Rightarrow \quad 1-x = \cos(2\sin^{-1}x)$$

$$\Rightarrow \quad 1-x = \cos\left\{\cos^{-1}(1-2x^2)\right\} \qquad [\because 2\sin^{-1}x=\cos^{-1}(1-2x^2)]$$

$$\Rightarrow \quad 1-x = (1-2x^2) \Rightarrow x = 2x^2 \Rightarrow x(2x-1) = 0 \Rightarrow x = 0, \frac{1}{2}$$

For, $x=\frac{1}{2}$, we obtain

$$\text{LHS} = \sin^{-1}(1-x) - 2\sin^{-1}x = \sin^{-1}\frac{1}{2} - 2\sin^{-1}\frac{1}{2} = -\sin^{-1}\frac{1}{2} = -\frac{\pi}{6} \neq \text{R.H.S.}$$

So, $x = 1/2$ is not a root of the given equation.

Clearly, $x = 0$ satisfies the given equation. Hence, $x = 0$ is a root of the given equation.

(ii) We have,

$$\sin\left[2\cos^{-1}\left\{\cot(2\tan^{-1}x)\right\}\right] = 0$$

$$\Rightarrow \sin\left[2\cos^{-1}\left\{\cot\left(\tan^{-1}\left(\frac{2x}{1-x^2}\right)\right)\right\}\right] = 0 \qquad \left[\because 2\tan^{-1}x = \tan^{-1}\frac{2x}{1-x^2}\right]$$

$$\Rightarrow \sin\left[2\cos^{-1}\left\{\cot\left(\cot^{-1}\left(\frac{1-x^2}{2x}\right)\right)\right\}\right] = 0 \qquad \left[\because \cot^{-1}x = \tan^{-1}\frac{1}{x}\right]$$

$$\Rightarrow \sin\left[2\cos^{-1}\left(\frac{1-x^2}{2x}\right)\right] = 0$$

$$\Rightarrow \sin\left[\sin^{-1}\left\{2\left(\frac{1-x^2}{2x}\right)\sqrt{1-\left(\frac{1-x^2}{2x}\right)^2}\right\}\right] = 0 \qquad \left[\because 2\cos^{-1}x = \sin^{-1}(2x\sqrt{1-x^2})\right]$$

$$\Rightarrow \left(\frac{1-x^2}{x}\right)\sqrt{1-\left(\frac{1-x^2}{2x}\right)^2} = 0 \Rightarrow \frac{1-x^2}{x} = 0 \text{ or, } \sqrt{1-\left(\frac{1-x^2}{2x}\right)^2} = 0$$

$$\Rightarrow 1-x^2 = 0 \text{ or, } \left(\frac{1-x^2}{2x}\right)^2 = 1 \Rightarrow x = \pm 1 \text{ or, } (1-x^2)^2 = 4x^2$$

Now, $(1-x^2)^2 = 4x^2 \Rightarrow (1-x^2)^2 - (2x)^2 = 0 \Rightarrow (1-x^2-2x)(1-x^2+2x) = 0$

$\Rightarrow \quad 1-x^2-2x = 0 \text{ or, } 1-x^2+2x = 0 \Rightarrow x^2+2x-1 = 0 \text{ or, } x^2-2x-1 = 0$

$\Rightarrow \quad x = -1 \pm \sqrt{2} \text{ or, } x = 1 \pm \sqrt{2}$

Hence, $x = \pm 1, -1 \pm \sqrt{2}, 1 \pm \sqrt{2}$ are the roots of the given equation.

(iii) We have,

$$\sin^{-1}x + \sin^{-1}(1-x) = \cos^{-1}x$$

$$\Rightarrow \sin^{-1}x + \sin^{-1}(1-x) = \frac{\pi}{2} - \sin^{-1}x \qquad \left[\because \cos^{-1}x = \frac{\pi}{2} - \sin^{-1}x\right]$$

$$\Rightarrow \sin^{-1}(1-x) = \frac{\pi}{2} - 2\sin^{-1}x$$

$$\Rightarrow \sin\left\{\sin^{-1}(1-x)\right\} = \sin\left(\frac{\pi}{2} - 2\sin^{-1}x\right)$$

$$\Rightarrow 1-x = \cos(2\sin^{-1}x)$$

$$\Rightarrow 1-x = \cos\left\{\cos^{-1}(1-2x^2)\right\} \qquad \left[\because 2\sin^{-1}x = \cos^{-1}(1-2x^2)\right]$$

$$\Rightarrow 1-x = 1-2x^2 \Rightarrow 2x^2 - x = 0 \Rightarrow x(2x-1) = 0 \Rightarrow x = 0 \text{ or, } x = \frac{1}{2}$$

Clearly, these values satisfy the given equation. Hence, $x = 0, \frac{1}{2}$ are the roots of the given equation.

EXAMPLE 16 *Solve for* x: $\tan^{-1}\left(\frac{2x}{1-x^2}\right) + \cot^{-1}\left(\frac{1-x^2}{2x}\right) = \frac{\pi}{3}, -1 < x < 1$ [CBSE 2011]

SOLUTION We know that

$$\tan^{-1}\left(\frac{1}{x}\right) = \begin{cases} \cot^{-1} x & , \text{ if } x > 0 \\ -\pi + \cot^{-1} x, & \text{if } x < 0 \end{cases} \quad \text{i.e. } \cot^{-1} x = \begin{cases} \tan^{-1}\left(\frac{1}{x}\right) & , \text{ if } x > 0 \\ \pi + \tan^{-1}\left(\frac{1}{x}\right), & \text{if } x < 0 \end{cases}$$

So, following cases arise:

Case I *When* $0 < x < 1$: In this case, we have

$$\cot^{-1}\left(\frac{1-x^2}{2x}\right) = \tan^{-1}\left(\frac{2x}{1-x^2}\right) \qquad \ldots(i)$$

Given equation is

$$\tan^{-1}\left(\frac{2x}{1-x^2}\right) + \cot^{-1}\left(\frac{1-x^2}{2x}\right) = \frac{\pi}{3}$$

$$\Rightarrow \quad 2\tan^{-1}\left(\frac{2x}{1-x^2}\right) = \frac{\pi}{3} \qquad \text{[Using (i)]}$$

$$\Rightarrow \quad 4\tan^{-1} x = \frac{\pi}{3} \Rightarrow \tan^{-1} x = \frac{\pi}{12} \Rightarrow x = \tan\frac{\pi}{12} = \tan 15° = \frac{\sqrt{3}-1}{\sqrt{3}+1}$$

Case II *When* $-1 < x < 0$: In this case, we have

$$\cot^{-1}\left(\frac{1-x^2}{2x}\right) = \pi + \tan^{-1}\left(\frac{2x}{1-x^2}\right) \qquad \ldots(ii)$$

Given equation is

$$\tan^{-1}\left(\frac{2x}{1-x^2}\right) + \cot^{-1}\left(\frac{1-x^2}{2x}\right) = \frac{\pi}{3} \Rightarrow \tan^{-1}\left(\frac{2x}{1-x^2}\right) + \pi + \tan^{-1}\left(\frac{2x}{1-x^2}\right) = \frac{\pi}{3} \quad \text{[Using (i)]}$$

$$\Rightarrow 2\tan^{-1}\left(\frac{2x}{1-x^2}\right) = -\frac{2\pi}{3} \Rightarrow 4\tan^{-1} x = -\frac{2\pi}{3} \Rightarrow \tan^{-1} x = -\frac{\pi}{6} \Rightarrow x = \tan\left(-\frac{\pi}{6}\right) = -\frac{1}{\sqrt{3}}$$

Case III *When* $x = 0$: In this case, we have

$$\text{LHS} = \tan^{-1}\left(\frac{2x}{1-x^2}\right) + \cot^{-1}\left(\frac{1-x^2}{2x}\right) = \tan^{-1}(0) + \cot^{-1}(\infty) = \frac{\pi}{2} \text{ and, RHS } = \frac{\pi}{3}$$

So, $x = 0$ is not a solution of the given equation.

Hence, $x = \frac{\sqrt{3}-1}{\sqrt{3}+1}$ and $x = \frac{1}{\sqrt{3}}$ are solutions of the given equation.

EXERCISE 3.14

BASIC

1. Evaluate the following:

(i) $\tan\left\{2\tan^{-1}\frac{1}{5}-\frac{\pi}{4}\right\}$ (ii) $\tan\left(\frac{1}{2}\sin^{-1}\frac{3}{4}\right)$ [CBSE 2013, NCERT EXEMPLAR]

(iii) $\sin\left(\frac{1}{2}\cos^{-1}\frac{4}{5}\right)$ (iv) $\sin\left(2\tan^{-1}\frac{2}{3}\right)+\cos\left(\tan^{-1}\sqrt{3}\right)$ [NCERT EXEMPLAR]

2. Prove the following results:

(i) $2\sin^{-1}\frac{3}{5}=\tan^{-1}\frac{24}{7}$ (ii) $4\tan^{-1}\frac{1}{5}-\tan^{-1}\frac{1}{239}=\frac{\pi}{4}$ [NCERT EXEMPLAR]

(iii) $\tan^{-1}\frac{2}{3}=\frac{1}{2}\tan^{-1}\frac{12}{5}$ (iv) $\tan^{-1}\frac{1}{7}+2\tan^{-1}\frac{1}{3}=\frac{\pi}{4}$ [CBSE 2010]

(v) $\sin^{-1}\frac{4}{5}+2\tan^{-1}\frac{1}{3}=\frac{\pi}{2}$ (vi) $2\sin^{-1}\frac{3}{5}-\tan^{-1}\frac{17}{31}=\frac{\pi}{4}$

(vii) $2\tan^{-1}\frac{1}{5}+\tan^{-1}\frac{1}{8}=\tan^{-1}\frac{4}{7}$ [NCERT]

(viii) $2\tan^{-1}\frac{3}{4}-\tan^{-1}\frac{17}{31}=\frac{\pi}{4}$ [CBSE 2011]

(ix) $2\tan^{-1}\frac{1}{2}+\tan^{-1}\frac{1}{7}=\tan^{-1}\frac{31}{17}$ [CBSE 2011, 2020]

(x) $\tan^{-1}\frac{1}{4}+\tan^{-1}\frac{2}{9}=\frac{1}{2}\cos^{-1}\frac{3}{5}=\frac{1}{2}\sin^{-1}\frac{4}{5}$ [CBSE 2010 C]

3. Find the values of each of the following:

(i) $\tan^{-1}\left\{2\cos\left(2\sin^{-1}\frac{1}{2}\right)\right\}$ (ii) $\cos\left(\sec^{-1}x+\operatorname{cosec}^{-1}x\right), |x|\geq 1$

4. If $\sin^{-1}\frac{2a}{1+a^2}-\cos^{-1}\frac{1-b^2}{1+b^2}=\tan^{-1}\frac{2x}{1-x^2}$, then prove that $x=\frac{a-b}{1+ab}$.

BASED ON LOTS

5. Prove that:

(i) $\tan^{-1}\left(\frac{1-x^2}{2x}\right)+\cot^{-1}\left(\frac{1-x^2}{2x}\right)=\frac{\pi}{2}$ (ii) $\sin\left\{\tan^{-1}\frac{1-x^2}{2x}+\cos^{-1}\frac{1-x^2}{1+x^2}\right\}=1$

(iii) $\sin^{-1}\left(2x\sqrt{1-x^2}\right)=2\cos^{-1}x, \frac{1}{\sqrt{2}}\leq x\leq 1$ [CBSE 2020]

6. If $\sin^{-1}\frac{2a}{1+a^2}+\sin^{-1}\frac{2b}{1+b^2}=2\tan^{-1}x$, prove that $x=\frac{a+b}{1-ab}$.

7. Show that $2\tan^{-1}x+\sin^{-1}\frac{2x}{1+x^2}$ is constant for $x\geq 1$, find that constant.

8. Solve the following equations for x :

(i) $\tan^{-1}\frac{1}{4}+2\tan^{-1}\frac{1}{5}+\tan^{-1}\frac{1}{6}+\tan^{-1}\frac{1}{x}=\frac{\pi}{4}$

(ii) $3\sin^{-1}\frac{2x}{1+x^2} - 4\cos^{-1}\frac{1-x^2}{1+x^2} + 2\tan^{-1}\frac{2x}{1-x^2} = \frac{\pi}{3}$

(iii) $\tan^{-1}\left(\frac{2x}{1-x^2}\right) + \cot^{-1}\left(\frac{1-x^2}{2x}\right) = \frac{2\pi}{3}, x > 0$ [CBSE 2010]

(iv) $2\tan^{-1}(\sin x) = \tan^{-1}(2\sec x), x \neq \frac{\pi}{2}$ [CBSE 2012]

(v) $\cos^{-1}\left(\frac{x^2-1}{x^2+1}\right) + \frac{1}{2}\tan^{-1}\left(\frac{2x}{1-x^2}\right) = \frac{2\pi}{3}$

(vi) $\tan^{-1}\left(\frac{x-2}{x-1}\right) + \tan^{-1}\left(\frac{x+2}{x+1}\right) = \frac{\pi}{4}$ [CBSE 2016]

ANSWERS

1. (i) $-\frac{7}{17}$ (ii) $\frac{4-\sqrt{7}}{3}$ (iii) $\frac{1}{\sqrt{10}}$ (iv) $\frac{37}{26}$ 3. (i) $\frac{\pi}{4}$ (ii) 0 7. π

8. (i) $-\frac{461}{9}$ (ii) $\frac{1}{\sqrt{3}}$ (iii) $\frac{1}{\sqrt{3}}$ (iv) $x = n\pi + \frac{\pi}{4}, n \in Z$ (v) $x = \sqrt{3}$ (vi) $\pm\sqrt{\frac{7}{2}}$

FILL IN THE BLANKS TYPE QUESTIONS (FBQs)

1. The value of $\sec^2(\tan^{-1}2) + \text{cosec}^2(\cot^{-1}3)$ is ....
2. If $\sin^{-1}x - \cos^{-1}x = \frac{\pi}{6}$, then $x =$ ....
3. The range of $\sin^{-1}x + \cos^{-1}x + \tan^{-1}x$ is ....
4. If $\sin^{-1}x = \frac{\pi}{5}$ for some $x \in (-1, 1)$, then the value of $\cos^{-1}x$ is ....
5. If $x < 0$, then $\tan^{-1}x + \tan^{-1}\frac{1}{x}$ is equal to ....
6. The value of $\tan^{-1}2 + \tan^{-1}3$ is ....
7. If $\tan^{-1}\frac{1}{\sqrt{3}} + \cot^{-1}x = \frac{\pi}{2}$, then $x =$ ....
8. If $\tan^{-1}x - \tan^{-1}y = \frac{\pi}{4}$, then $x - y - xy =$ ....
9. The value of $\cot(\tan^{-1}x + \cot^{-1}x)$ for all $x \in R$, is.............................. .
10. If $\cos^{-1}x + \cos^{-1}y = \frac{\pi}{3}$, then $\sin^{-1}x + \sin^{-1}y =$ ....
11. If $x > 0, y > 0, xy > 1$, then $\tan^{-1}x + \tan^{-1}y =$ ....
12. If $3\sin^{-1}x = \pi - \cos^{-1}x$, then $x =$ ....
13. If $\tan^{-1}x + \tan^{-1}y = \frac{5\pi}{6}$, then $\cot^{-1}x + \cot^{-1}y =$ ....
14. If $\tan^{-1}x - \cot^{-1}x = \tan^{-1}\sqrt{3}$, then $x =$ ....

15. If $\sin^{-1}x+\sin^{-1}y+\sin^{-1}z=-\frac{3\pi}{2}$, then $xyz=$ ....

16. The value of $\cos^{-1}\left\{\sin\left(\cos^{-1}\frac{1}{2}\right)\right\}$ is ....

17. The value of $\tan\left[\cos^{-1}\left\{\sin\left(\cot^{-1}1\right)\right\}\right]$ is ....

18. The value of $\tan^2(\sec^{-1}3)+\cot^2(\text{cosec}^{-1}4)$ is ....

19. If $\tan^{-1}(\cot\theta)=2\theta$, then $\theta=$ ....

20. The value of $\sin^{-1}\left(\cos\frac{33\pi}{5}\right)$ is ....

21. If $\tan^{-1}x+\tan^{-1}y=\frac{4\pi}{5}$, then $\cot^{-1}x+\cot^{-1}y=$ ....

22. If $3\tan^{-1}x+\cot^{-1}x=\pi$, then $x=$ ....

23. If $\tan^{-1}2$, $\tan^{-1}3$ are measures of two angles of a triangle, then the measure of its third angle is ....

24. If $\tan^{-1}\frac{a}{x}+\tan^{-1}\frac{b}{x}=\frac{\pi}{2}$, then $x=$ ....

25. If $\cos(2\sin^{-1}x)=\frac{1}{9}$, then the value of x is ....

26. If $0<x<\frac{\pi}{2}$, then $\sin^{-1}(\cos x)+\cos^{-1}(\sin x)=$ ....

27. If $\tan^{-1}x=\frac{\pi}{4}-\tan^{-1}\frac{1}{3}$, then $x=$ ....

28. If $\tan^{-1}x+\tan^{-1}\frac{1}{2}=\frac{\pi}{4}$, then $x=$ ....

29. $\cot\left(\frac{\pi}{4}-2\cot^{-1}3\right)$ is equal to ....

30. $\tan^{-1}\left(\tan\frac{2\pi}{3}\right)$ is equal to ....

31. If $y=2\tan^{-1}x+\sin^{-1}\left(\frac{2x}{1+x^2}\right)$ for all x, then y lies in the interval....... [NCERT EXEMPLAR]

32. The result $\tan^{-1}x-\tan^{-1}y=\tan^{-1}\left(\frac{x-y}{1+xy}\right)$ is true when value of xy is...........

[NCERT EXENMPLAR]

33. The value of $\cot^{-1}(-x)$ for all $x\in R$ in terms of $\cot^{-1}x$ is.......... [NCERT EXEMPLAR]

34. The principal value of $\cos^{-1}\left(-\frac{1}{2}\right)$ is .... [CBSE 2020]

35. The range of the principal value branch of $y=\sec^{-1}x$ is .... [CBSE 2020]

ANSWERS

1. 15	2. $\frac{\sqrt{3}}{2}$	3. $\left[\frac{\pi}{4}, \frac{3\pi}{4}\right]$	4. $\frac{3\pi}{10}$	5. $-\frac{\pi}{2}$
6. $\frac{3\pi}{4}$	7. $\frac{1}{\sqrt{3}}$	8. 1	9. 0	10. $\frac{2\pi}{3}$
11. $\pi + \tan^{-1}\left(\frac{x+y}{1-xy}\right)$		12. $\frac{1}{\sqrt{2}}$	13. $\frac{\pi}{6}$	14. $\tan\frac{5\pi}{12}$
15. -1	16. $\frac{\pi}{6}$	17. 1	18. 23	19. $\frac{\pi}{6}$
20. $-\frac{\pi}{10}$	21. $\frac{\pi}{5}$	22. 1	23. $\frac{\pi}{4}$	24. $\sqrt{ab}$
25. $\pm\frac{2}{3}$	26. $\pi - 2x$	27. $\frac{1}{2}$	28. $\frac{1}{3}$	29. 7
30. $-\frac{\pi}{3}$	31. $(-2\pi, 2\pi)$	32. $xy > -1$	33. $\pi - \cot^{-1} x$	34. $\frac{2\pi}{3}$
35. $(-\infty, -1] \cup [1, \infty)$				

VERY SHORT ANSWER QUESTIONS (VSAQs)

Answer each of the following questions in one word or one sentence or as per exact requirement of the question:

1. Write the value of $\sin^{-1}\left(-\frac{\sqrt{3}}{2}\right) + \cos^{-1}\left(-\frac{1}{2}\right)$.
2. Write the difference between maximum and minimum values of $\sin^{-1} x$ for $x \in [-1, 1]$.
3. If $\sin^{-1} x + \sin^{-1} y + \sin^{-1} z = \frac{3\pi}{2}$, then write the value of $x + y + z$.
4. If $x > 1$, then write the value of $\sin^{-1}\left(\frac{2x}{1+x^2}\right)$ in terms of $\tan^{-1} x$.
5. If $x < 0$, then write the value of $\cos^{-1}\left(\frac{1-x^2}{1+x^2}\right)$ in terms of $\tan^{-1} x$.
6. Write the value of $\tan^{-1} x + \tan^{-1}\left(\frac{1}{x}\right)$ for $x > 0$.
7. Write the value of $\tan^{-1} x + \tan^{-1}\left(\frac{1}{x}\right)$ for $x < 0$.
8. What is the value of $\cos^{-1}\left(\cos\frac{2\pi}{3}\right) + \sin^{-1}\left(\sin\frac{2\pi}{3}\right)$?
9. If $-1 < x < 0$, then write the value of $\sin^{-1}\left(\frac{2x}{1+x^2}\right) + \cos^{-1}\left(\frac{1-x^2}{1+x^2}\right)$.
10. Write the value of $\sin(\cot^{-1} x)$.
11. Write the value of $\cos^{-1}\left(\frac{1}{2}\right) + 2\sin^{-1}\left(\frac{1}{2}\right)$.

12. Write the range of $\tan^{-1} x$.

13. Write the value of $\cos^{-1}(\cos 1540°)$.

14. Write the value of $\sin^{-1}(\sin(-600°))$.

15. Write the value of $\cos\left(2\sin^{-1}\frac{1}{3}\right)$.

16. Write the value of $\sin^{-1}(\sin 1550°)$.

17. Evaluate: $\sin\left(\frac{1}{2}\cos^{-1}\frac{4}{5}\right)$.

18. Evaluate: $\sin\left(\tan^{-1}\frac{3}{4}\right)$.

19. Write the value of $\cos^{-1}\left(\tan\frac{3\pi}{4}\right)$.

20. Write the value of $\cos\left(2\sin^{-1}\frac{1}{2}\right)$.

21. Write the value of $\cos^{-1}(\cos 350°) - \sin^{-1}(\sin 350°)$

22. Write the value of $\cos^2\left(\frac{1}{2}\cos^{-1}\frac{3}{5}\right)$.

23. If $\tan^{-1} x + \tan^{-1} y = \frac{\pi}{4}$, then write the value of $x + y + xy$. [CBSE 2014]

24. Write the value of $\cos^{-1}(\cos 6)$.

25. Write the value of $\sin^{-1}\left(\cos\frac{\pi}{9}\right)$.

26. Write the value of $\sin\left\{\frac{\pi}{3} - \sin^{-1}\left(-\frac{1}{2}\right)\right\}$. [CBSE 2011]

27. Write the value of $\tan^{-1}\left\{\tan\left(\frac{15\pi}{4}\right)\right\}$.

28. Write the value of $2\sin^{-1}\frac{1}{2} + \cos^{-1}\left(-\frac{1}{2}\right)$. [CBSE 2014]

29. Write the value of $\tan^{-1}\frac{a}{b} - \tan^{-1}\left(\frac{a-b}{a+b}\right)$.

30. Write the value of $\cos^{-1}\left(\cos\frac{5\pi}{4}\right)$.

31. Show that $\sin^{-1}(2x\sqrt{1-x^2}) = 2\sin^{-1} x$

32. Evaluate: $\sin^{-1}\left(\sin\frac{3\pi}{5}\right)$. [CBSE 2009]

33. If $\tan^{-1}(\sqrt{3}) + \cot^{-1} x = \frac{\pi}{2}$, find x. [CBSE 2010]

34. If $\sin^{-1}\left(\frac{1}{3}\right) + \cos^{-1} x = \frac{\pi}{2}$, then find x. [CBSE 2010]

35. Write the value of $\sin^{-1}\left(\frac{1}{3}\right)-\cos^{-1}\left(-\frac{1}{3}\right)$.

36. If $4\sin^{-1}x+\cos^{-1}x=\pi$, then what is the value of x?

37. If $x<0, y<0$ such that $xy=1$, then write the value of $\tan^{-1}x+\tan^{-1}y$.

38. What is the principal value of $\sin^{-1}\left(-\frac{\sqrt{3}}{2}\right)$? [CBSE 2010]

39. Write the principal value of $\sin^{-1}\left(-\frac{1}{2}\right)$. [CBSE 2011]

40. Write the principal value of $\cos^{-1}\left(\cos\frac{2\pi}{3}\right)+\sin^{-1}\left(\sin\frac{2\pi}{3}\right)$.

41. Write the value of $\tan\left(2\tan^{-1}\frac{1}{5}\right)$. [CBSE 2013]

42. Write the principal value of $\tan^{-1}(1)+\cos^{-1}\left(-\frac{1}{2}\right)$. [CBSE 2013]

43. Write the value of $\tan^{-1}\left\{2\sin\left(2\cos^{-1}\frac{\sqrt{3}}{2}\right)\right\}$. [CBSE 2013]

44. Write the principal value of $\tan^{-1}\sqrt{3}+\cot^{-1}\sqrt{3}$. [CBSE 21013]

45. Write the principal value of $\cos^{-1}(\cos 680°)$. [CBSE 2014]

46. Write the value of $\sin^{-1}\left(\sin\frac{3\pi}{5}\right)$. [NCERT EXEMPLAR]

47. Write the value of $\sec^{-1}\left(\frac{1}{2}\right)$. [NCERT EXEMPLAR]

48. Write the value of $\cos^{-1}\left(\cos\frac{14\pi}{3}\right)$. [NCERT EXEMPLAR]

49. Write the value of $\cos\left(\sin^{-1}x+\cos^{-1}x\right), |x|\le 1$. [NCERT EXEMPLAR]

50. Write the value of the expression $\tan\left(\frac{\sin^{-1}x+\cos^{-1}x}{2}\right)$, when $x=\frac{\sqrt{3}}{2}$.

[NCERT EXEMPLAR]

51. Write the principal value of $\sin^{-1}\left\{\cos\left(\sin^{-1}\frac{1}{2}\right)\right\}$. [NCERT EXEMPLAR]

52. The set of values of $\operatorname{cosec}^{-1}\left(\frac{\sqrt{3}}{2}\right)$.

53. Write the value of $\tan^{-1}\left(\frac{1}{x}\right)$ for $x<0$ in terms of $\cot^{-1}(x)$.

54. Write the value of $\cot^{-1}(-x)$ for all $x \in R$ in terms of $\cot^{-1} x$.

55. Write the value of $\cos\left(\frac{\tan^{-1} x + \cot^{-1} x}{3}\right)$, when $x = -\frac{1}{\sqrt{3}}$.

56. If $\cos(\tan^{-1} x + \cot^{-1}\sqrt{3}) = 0$, find the value of x. [NCERT EXEMPLAR]

57. Find the value of $2\sec^{-1} 2 + \sin^{-1}\left(\frac{1}{2}\right)$.

58. If $\cos\left(\sin^{-1}\frac{2}{5} + \cos^{-1} x\right) = 0$, find the value of x.

59. Find the value of $\cos^{-1}\left(\cos\frac{13\pi}{6}\right)$.

60. Find the value of $\tan^{-1}\left(\tan\frac{9\pi}{8}\right)$.

61. Find the value of $\tan^{-1}\sqrt{3} - \cot^{-1}(-\sqrt{3})$. [CBSE 2018]

62. Find the value of $\sin^{-1}\left\{\sin\left(\frac{-17\pi}{8}\right)\right\}$. [CBSE 2020]

63. Two angles of a triangle are $\cot^{-1} 2$ and $\cot^{-1} 3$. The third angle of the triangle is...... [CBSE 2020]

64. Find the value of $\tan^{-1}\left\{2\cos\left(2\sin^{-1}\frac{1}{2}\right)\right\} + \tan^{-1} 1$. [CBSE 2023]

65. Write the domain and range (principal value branch) of $f(x) = \tan^{-1} x$. [CBSE 2023]

66. Find the value of k, if $\sin^{-1}\left\{k\tan\left(2\cos^{-1}\frac{\sqrt{3}}{2}\right)\right\} = \frac{\pi}{3}$. [CBSE 2024]

67. If $a = \sin^{-1}\left(\frac{\sqrt{2}}{2}\right) + \cos^{-1}\left(-\frac{1}{2}\right)$ and $b = \tan^{-1}\sqrt{3} - \cot^{-1}\left(-\frac{1}{\sqrt{3}}\right)$, then find the value of $a + b$. [CBSE 2024]

68. Find the value of $\tan^{-1}\left(-\frac{1}{\sqrt{3}}\right) + \cot^{-1}\left(\frac{1}{\sqrt{3}}\right) + \tan^{-1}\left\{\sin\left(-\frac{\pi}{2}\right)\right\}$. [CBSE 2024]

69. Evaluate: $\sec^2\left(\tan^{-1}\frac{1}{2}\right) + \operatorname{cosec}^2\left(\cot^{-1}\frac{1}{3}\right)$. [CBSE 2024]

70. Find the value of $\sin^2\left\{\cos^{-1}\left(\frac{3}{5}\right)\right\} + \tan^2\left\{\sec^{-1}(3)\right\}$. [CBSE 2024]

71. Evaluate : $\cot^2\left\{\operatorname{cosec}^{-1}(3)\right\} + \sin^2\left\{\cos^{-1}\left(\frac{1}{3}\right)\right\}$. [CBSE 2024]

72. Find the principal value of $\tan^{-1}(1) + \cos^{-1}\left(-\frac{1}{2}\right) + \sin^{-1}\left(-\frac{1}{\sqrt{2}}\right)$. [CBSE 2024]

73. Find the value of $\cos^{-1}\left(\frac{1}{2}\right) - \tan^{-1}\left(-\frac{1}{\sqrt{3}}\right) + \operatorname{cosec}^{-1}(-2)$. [CBSE 2024]

ANSWERS

1. $\frac{\pi}{3}$ 2. π 3. 3 4. $\pi - 2\tan^{-1} x$ 5. $-2\tan^{-1} x$
6. $\frac{\pi}{2}$ 7. $-\frac{\pi}{2}$ 8. π 9. 0 10. $\frac{1}{\sqrt{1+x^2}}$ 11. $\frac{2\pi}{3}$
12. $\left(-\frac{\pi}{2}, \frac{\pi}{2}\right)$ 13. 100° 14. 60° 15. $\frac{7}{9}$ 16. 70 17. $\frac{1}{\sqrt{10}}$
18. $\frac{3}{5}$ 19. π 20. $\frac{1}{2}$ 21. 20° 22. $\frac{4}{5}$ 23. 1
24. $2\pi - 6$ 25. $\frac{7\pi}{18}$ 26. 1 27. $-\frac{\pi}{4}$ 28. π 29. $\frac{\pi}{4}$
30. $\frac{3\pi}{4}$ 32. $\frac{2\pi}{5}$ 33. $\sqrt{3}$ 34. $\frac{1}{3}$ 35. $-\frac{\pi}{2}$ 36. $\frac{1}{2}$
37. $-\frac{\pi}{2}$ 38. $-\frac{\pi}{3}$ 39. $\frac{-\pi}{6}$ 40. π 41. $\frac{5}{12}$ 42. $\frac{11\pi}{12}$
43. $\frac{\pi}{3}$ 44. $\frac{\pi}{2}$ 45. 40° 46. $\frac{2\pi}{5}$ 47. ϕ 48. $\frac{2\pi}{3}$
49. 0 50. 1 51. $\frac{\pi}{3}$ 52. ϕ 53. $-\pi + \cot^{-1} x$ 54. $\pi - \cot^{-1} x$
55. $\frac{\sqrt{3}}{2}$ 56. $\sqrt{3}$ 57. $\frac{5\pi}{6}$ 58. $\frac{2}{5}$ 59. $\frac{\pi}{6}$ 60. $\frac{\pi}{8}$
61. $-\frac{\pi}{2}$ 62. $-\frac{\pi}{8}$ 63. $\frac{3\pi}{4}$ 64. $\frac{\pi}{2}$ 65. $R, \left(-\frac{\pi}{2}, \frac{\pi}{2}\right)$ 66. $\frac{1}{2}$
67. $-\frac{3\pi}{4}$ 68. $-\frac{\pi}{12}$ 69. $\frac{13}{36}$ 70. $\frac{216}{25}$ 71. $\frac{80}{9}$ 72. $\frac{2\pi}{3}$
73. $\frac{\pi}{3}$

CHAPTER 4

ALGEBRA OF MATRICES

4.1 MATRIX

DEFINITION *A set of mn numbers (real or imaginary) arranged in the form of a rectangular array of m rows and n columns is called an $m \times n$ matrix (to be read as 'm by n' matrix).*

An $m \times n$ matrix is usually written as

$$A = \begin{bmatrix} a_{11} & a_{12} & a_{13} & \dots & a_{1j} & \dots & a_{1n} \\ a_{21} & a_{22} & a_{23} & \dots & a_{2j} & \dots & a_{2n} \\ \vdots & \vdots & \vdots & & \vdots & & \vdots \\ a_{i1} & a_{i2} & a_{i3} & \dots & a_{ij} & \dots & a_{in} \\ \vdots & \vdots & \vdots & & \vdots & & \vdots \\ a_{m1} & a_{m2} & a_{m3} & \dots & a_{mj} & \dots & a_{mn} \end{bmatrix}$$

In compact form the above matrix is represented by $A = [a_{ij}]_{m \times n}$ or, $A = [a_{ij}]$.

The numbers $a_{11}, a_{12}, \dots$ etc. are known as the elements of the matrix A. The element a_{ij} belongs to i^{th} row and j^{th} column and is called the $(i, j)^{th}$ element of the matrix $A = [a_{ij}]$. Thus, in the element a_{ij} the first subscript i always denotes the number of row and the second subscript j, number of column in which the element occurs.

Following are some examples of matrices:

(i) $A = \begin{bmatrix} 2 & 1 & -1 \\ 1 & 3 & 2 \end{bmatrix}$ is a matrix having 2 rows and 3 columns and so it is a matrix of order 2×3 such that $a_{11} = 2, a_{12} = 1, a_{13} = -1, a_{21} = 1, a_{22} = 3, a_{23} = 2$.

(ii) $B = \begin{bmatrix} \sin x & \cos x \\ \cos x & -\sin x \end{bmatrix}$ is a matrix having 2 rows and 2 columns and so it is a matrix of order 2×2 such that $b_{11} = \sin x, b_{12} = \cos x, b_{21} = \cos x, b_{22} = -\sin x$.

NOTE *It is to note here that to define a matrix we must define its order and its elements either by a general formula (See illustration given below) or separately.*

ILLUSTRATION *Construct a 3×4 matrix $A = [a_{ij}]$ whose elements are given by*

(i) $a_{ij} = i + j$ (ii) $a_{ij} = i - j$

SOLUTION (i) We have,

$$A = \begin{bmatrix} a_{11} & a_{12} & a_{13} & a_{14} \\ a_{21} & a_{22} & a_{23} & a_{24} \\ a_{31} & a_{32} & a_{33} & a_{34} \end{bmatrix}, \text{ where } a_{ij} = i + j.$$

$\therefore \quad a_{11} = 1 + 1 = 2, \quad a_{12} = 1 + 2 = 3, \quad a_{13} = 1 + 3 = 4, \quad a_{14} = 1 + 4 = 5.$

Similarly, $a_{21} = 3, \ a_{22} = 4, \ a_{23} = 5, \ a_{24} = 6$ and $a_{31} = 4, \ a_{32} = 5, \ a_{33} = 6, \ a_{34} = 7$.

Hence, $A = \begin{bmatrix} 2 & 3 & 4 & 5 \\ 3 & 4 & 5 & 6 \\ 4 & 5 & 6 & 7 \end{bmatrix}$

(ii) Proceeding as above, we obtain

$$A = \begin{bmatrix} 0 & -1 & -2 & -3 \\ 1 & 0 & -1 & -2 \\ 2 & 1 & 0 & -1 \end{bmatrix}.$$

4.2 TYPES OF MATRICES

ROW MATRIX *A matrix having only one row is called a row-matrix or a row-vector.*

For example, $A = [1 \;\; 2 \; -1 \; -2]$ is a row matrix of order 1×4.

COLUMN MATRIX *A matrix having only one column is called a column matrix or a column-vector.*

For example, $A = \begin{bmatrix} 1 \\ 2 \\ -1 \end{bmatrix}$ and $B = \begin{bmatrix} 3 \\ 2 \\ 5 \\ 4 \end{bmatrix}$ are column-matrices of orders 3×1 and 4×1 respectively.

SQUARE MATRIX *A matrix in which the number of rows is equal to the number of columns, say n, is called a square matrix of order n.*

A square matrix of order n is also called a n-rowed square matrix. The elements a_{ij} of a square matrix $A = [a_{ij}]_{n \times n}$ for which $i = j$ i.e. the elements $a_{11}, a_{22}, \ldots, a_{nn}$ are called the diagonal elements and the line along which they lie is called the *principal diagonal* or leading diagonal of the matrix.

For example, the matrix $\begin{bmatrix} 2 & 1 & -1 \\ 3 & -2 & 5 \\ 1 & 5 & -3 \end{bmatrix}$ is square matrix of order 3 in which the diagonal elements are 2, – 2 and – 3.

DIAGONAL MATRIX *A square matrix $A = [a_{ij}]_{n \times n}$ is called a diagonal matrix if all the elements, except those in the leading diagonal, are zero i.e. $a_{ij} = 0$ for all $i \neq j$.*

A diagonal matrix of order $n \times n$ having $d_1, d_2, \ldots, d_n$ as diagonal elements is denoted by diag $[d_1, d_2, \ldots, d_n]$.

For example, the matrix $A = \begin{bmatrix} 1 & 0 & 0 \\ 0 & 2 & 0 \\ 0 & 0 & 3 \end{bmatrix}$ is a diagonal matrix, to be denoted by $A = \text{diag}\,[1, 2, 3]$.

SCALAR MATRIX *A square matrix $A = [a_{ij}]_{n \times n}$ is called a scalar matrix if*

(i) $a_{ij} = 0$ *for all* $i \neq j$ *and,* (ii) $a_{ii} = c$ *for all* i, *where* $c \neq 0$.

In other words, a diagonal matrix in which all the diagonal elements are equal is called the scalar matrix.

For example, the matrices $A = \begin{bmatrix} 2 & 0 \\ 0 & 2 \end{bmatrix}$, $B = \begin{bmatrix} 1-2i & 0 & 0 \\ 0 & 1-2i & 0 \\ 0 & 0 & 1-2i \end{bmatrix}$ are scalar matrices of orders 2 and 3 respectively.

IDENTITY OR UNIT MATRIX *A square matrix $A = [a_{ij}]_{n \times n}$ is called an identity or unit matrix if*

(i) $a_{ij} = 0$ *for all* $i \neq j$ *and,* (ii) $a_{ii} = 1$ *for all* i

In other words, a square matrix each of whose diagonal element is unity and each of whose non-diagonal elements is equal to zero is called an identity or unit matrix.

The identity matrix of order n is denoted by I_n.

For example, the matrices $I_2 = \begin{bmatrix} 1 & 0 \\ 0 & 1 \end{bmatrix}$, $I_3 = \begin{bmatrix} 1 & 0 & 0 \\ 0 & 1 & 0 \\ 0 & 0 & 1 \end{bmatrix}$ are identity matrices of orders 2 and 3 respectively.

NULL MATRIX *A matrix whose all elements are zero is called a null matrix or a zero matrix.*

For example, $\begin{bmatrix} 0 & 0 \\ 0 & 0 \end{bmatrix}$ *and* $\begin{bmatrix} 0 & 0 & 0 \\ 0 & 0 & 0 \end{bmatrix}$ *are null matrices of orders* 2×2 *and* 2×3 *respectively.*

UPPER TRIANGULAR MATRIX *A square matrix* $A = [a_{ij}]$ *is called an upper triangular matrix if* $a_{ij} = 0$ *for all* $i > j$.

Thus, in an upper triangular matrix, all elements below the main diagonal are zero.

For example, $A = \begin{bmatrix} 1 & 2 & 4 & 3 \\ 0 & 5 & 1 & 3 \\ 0 & 0 & 2 & 9 \\ 0 & 0 & 0 & 5 \end{bmatrix}$ is an upper triangular matrix.

LOWER TRIANGULAR MATRIX *A square matrix* $A = [a_{ij}]$ *is called a lower triangular matrix if* $a_{ij} = 0$ *for all* $i < j$.

Thus, in a lower triangular matrix, all elements above the main diagonal are zero.

For example, $A = \begin{bmatrix} 2 & 0 & 0 \\ 3 & 2 & 0 \\ 4 & 5 & 3 \end{bmatrix}$ is a lower triangular matrix of order 3.

A triangular matrix $A = [a_{ij}]$ of order $n \times n$ is called a strictly triangular iff $a_{ii} = 0$ for all $i = 1, 2, ..., n$.

4.3 EQUALITY OF MATRICES

DEFINITION *Two matrices* $A = [a_{ij}]_{m \times n}$ *and* $B = [b_{ij}]_{r \times s}$ *are equal if*

(i) $m = r$ *i.e. the number of rows in A equals the number of rows in B*

(ii) $n = s$ *i.e. the number of columns in A equals the number of columns in B*

(iii) $a_{ij} = b_{ij}$ *for* $i = 1, 2, \dots, m$ *and* $j = 1, 2, \dots, n$.

If two matrices A and B are equal, we write $A = B$, otherwise we write $A \neq B$.

The matrices $A = \begin{bmatrix} 3 & 2 & 1 \\ x & y & 5 \\ 1 & -1 & 4 \end{bmatrix}$ and $B = \begin{bmatrix} 3 & 2 & 1 \\ -1 & 0 & 5 \\ 1 & -1 & z \end{bmatrix}$ are equal if $x = -1$, $y = 0$ and $z = 4$.

Matrices $\begin{bmatrix} 0 & 0 \\ 0 & 0 \end{bmatrix}$ and $\begin{bmatrix} 0 & 0 & 0 \\ 0 & 0 & 0 \end{bmatrix}$ are not equal, because their orders are not same.

ILLUSTRATION 1 *If* $\begin{bmatrix} x - y & 2x + z \\ 2x - y & 3z + w \end{bmatrix} = \begin{bmatrix} -1 & 5 \\ 0 & 13 \end{bmatrix}$, *find* x, y, z, w. **[CBSE 2002 C, 2013]**

SOLUTION Since the corresponding elements of two equal matrices are equal. Therefore,

$$\begin{bmatrix} x - y & 2x + z \\ 2x - y & 3z + w \end{bmatrix} = \begin{bmatrix} -1 & 5 \\ 0 & 13 \end{bmatrix} \Rightarrow x - y = -1,\ 2x + z = 5,\ 2x - y = 0,\ 3z + w = 13.$$

Solving the equations $x - y = -1$ and $2x - y = 0$ as simultaneous linear equations, we get $x = 1$, $y = 2$.

Now putting $x = 1$ in $2x + z = 5$, we obtain $z = 3$. Substituting $z = 3$ in $3z + w = 13$, we obtain $w = 4$.

Thus, $x = 1$, $y = 2$, $z = 3$ and $w = 4$.

ILLUSTRATION 2 *Find the values of x, y, z and a which satisfy the matrix equation*

$$\begin{bmatrix} x+3 & 2y+x \\ z-1 & 4a-6 \end{bmatrix} = \begin{bmatrix} 0 & -7 \\ 3 & 2a \end{bmatrix}$$

SOLUTION The corresponding elements of two equal matrices are equal.

$$\therefore \quad \begin{bmatrix} x+3 & 2y+x \\ z-1 & 4a-6 \end{bmatrix} = \begin{bmatrix} 0 & -7 \\ 3 & 2a \end{bmatrix} \Rightarrow x+3=0,\ 2y+x=-7,\ z-1=3 \text{ and } 4a-6=2a.$$

Solving these equations, we obtain : $a = 3,\ x = -3,\ y = -2,\ z = 4.$

ILLUSTRATIVE EXAMPLES

BASED ON BASIC CONCEPTS (BASIC)

EXAMPLE 1 *A matrix has 12 elements. What are the possible orders it can have?*

SOLUTION We know that if a matrix is of order $m \times n$, then it has mn elements. Therefore, to find all possible orders of a matrix with 12 elements, we will have to find all ordered pairs (a, b) such that a and b are factors of 12. Clearly, all possible ordered pairs of this type are :

$$(1, 12), (12, 1), (3, 4), (4, 3), (2, 6), (6, 2)$$

Hence, possible orders of the matrix are: 1×12, 12×1, 3×4, 4×3, 2×6 and 6×2.

EXAMPLE 2 *If* $A = [a_{ij}]$ *is a matrix given by* $A = [a_{ij}] = \begin{bmatrix} 4 & -2 & 1 & 3 \\ 5 & 7 & 9 & 6 \\ 21 & 15 & 18 & -25 \end{bmatrix}$, *write the order of A and find the elements* a_{24}, a_{34}. *Also, show that* $a_{32} = a_{23} + a_{24}$.

SOLUTION We observe that there are 3 rows and 4 columns in matrix A. Therefore, it is of order 3×4. The element lying at the intersection of 2nd row and fourth column is 6. Therefore, $a_{24} = 6$. Similarly, the element lying at the intersection of third row and fourth column is – 25. Therefore, $a_{34} = -25$. Similarly, $a_{32} = 15$, $a_{23} = 9$ and $a_{24} = 6$.

Clearly, $a_{32} = 15 = 9 + 6 = a_{23} + a_{24}$.

EXAMPLE 3 *Construct a* 2×2 *matrix* $A = [a_{ij}]$ *whose elements are given by* $a_{ij} = \dfrac{(i+2j)^2}{2}$.

SOLUTION Here $a_{ij} = \dfrac{(i+2j)^2}{2}$, $1 \le i \le 2$ and $1 \le j \le 2$. [NCERT]

$$\therefore \quad a_{11} = \frac{(1+2\times 1)^2}{2} = \frac{(1+2)^2}{2} = \frac{9}{2},\quad a_{12} = \frac{(1+2\times 2)^2}{2} = \frac{25}{2}$$

$$a_{21} = \frac{(2+2\times 1)^2}{2} = 8 \text{ and } a_{22} = \frac{(2+2\times 2)^2}{2} = 18$$

$$\text{Hence, } A = \begin{bmatrix} a_{11} & a_{12} \\ a_{21} & a_{22} \end{bmatrix} = \begin{bmatrix} \frac{9}{2} & \frac{25}{2} \\ 8 & 18 \end{bmatrix}$$

EXAMPLE 4 *Construct a* 2×3 *matrix* $A = [a_{ij}]$ *whose elements are given by* $a_{ij} = \dfrac{i-j}{i+j}$.

SOLUTION We have, $a_{ij} = \dfrac{i-j}{i+j}$, $1 \le i \le 2$ and $1 \le j \le 3$. Therefore,

$$a_{11} = 0,\ a_{12} = -\frac{1}{3},\ a_{13} = -\frac{1}{2},\ a_{21} = \frac{1}{3},\ a_{22} = 0 \text{ and } a_{23} = -\frac{1}{5}.$$

$$\therefore \quad A = \begin{bmatrix} 0 & -\frac{1}{3} & -\frac{1}{2} \\ \frac{1}{3} & 0 & -\frac{1}{5} \end{bmatrix}$$

EXAMPLE 5 *Construct a* 3×2 *matrix* $A = [a_{ij}]$ *whose elements are given by*

(i) $a_{ij} = e^{ix} \sin jx$ (ii) $a_{ij} = e^{-ix} \cos\left(\frac{\pi}{2}i + jx\right)$

SOLUTION (i) It is given that $A = [a_{ij}]$ is a 3×2 matrix such that $a_{ij} = e^{ix} \sin jx, 1 \le i \le 3$ and $1 \le j \le 2$. Therefore, $a_{11} = e^x \sin x$, $a_{12} = e^x \sin 2x$, $a_{21} = e^{2x} \sin x$, $a_{22} = e^{2x} \sin 2x, a_{31} = e^{3x} \sin x$ and $a_{32} = e^{3x} \sin 2x$.

$$\text{Hence,} \quad A = \begin{bmatrix} a_{11} & a_{12} \\ a_{21} & a_{22} \\ a_{31} & a_{32} \end{bmatrix} = \begin{bmatrix} e^x \sin x & e^x \sin 2x \\ e^{2x} \sin x & e^{2x} \sin 2x \\ e^{3x} \sin x & e^{3x} \sin 2x \end{bmatrix}$$

(ii) It is given that $A = [a_{ij}]$ is a 3×2 matrix such that $a_{ij} = e^{-ix} \cos\left(\frac{\pi}{2}i + jx\right), 1 \le i \le 3$ and $1 \le j \le 2$.

$$\therefore \quad a_{11} = e^{-x} \cos\left(\frac{\pi}{2} + x\right) = -e^{-x} \sin x, a_{12} = e^{-x} \cos\left(\frac{\pi}{2} + 2x\right) = -e^{-x} \sin 2x$$

$$a_{21} = e^{-2x} \cos(\pi + x) = -e^{-2x} \cos x, a_{22} = e^{-2x} \cos(\pi + 2x) = -e^{-2x} \cos 2x$$

$$a_{31} = e^{-3x} \cos\left(\frac{3\pi}{2} + x\right) = e^{-3x} \sin x, a_{32} = e^{-3x} \cos\left(\frac{3\pi}{2} + 2x\right) = e^{-3x} \sin 2x$$

$$\text{Hence,} \quad A = \begin{bmatrix} a_{11} & a_{12} \\ a_{21} & a_{22} \\ a_{31} & a_{32} \end{bmatrix} = \begin{bmatrix} -e^{-x} \sin x & -e^{-x} \sin 2x \\ -e^{-2x} \cos x & -e^{-2x} \cos 2x \\ e^{-3x} \sin x & e^{-3x} \sin 2x \end{bmatrix}$$

EXAMPLE 6 *Find x, y, z and w such that* $\begin{bmatrix} x - y & 2z + w \\ 2x - y & 2x + w \end{bmatrix} = \begin{bmatrix} 5 & 3 \\ 12 & 15 \end{bmatrix}$.

SOLUTION We know that the corresponding elements of two equal matrices are equal.

$$\therefore \quad \begin{bmatrix} x - y & 2z + w \\ 2x - y & 2x + w \end{bmatrix} = \begin{bmatrix} 5 & 3 \\ 12 & 15 \end{bmatrix} \Rightarrow x - y = 5, 2z + w = 3, \ 2x - y = 12 \text{ and } 2x + w = 15$$

Solving $x - y = 5$ and $2x - y = 12$ as simultaneous linear equations, we get $x = 7$, $y = 2$. Putting $x = 7$ in equation $2x + w = 15$, we get $w = 1$. Putting $w = 1$ in $2z + w = 3$, we get $z = 1$. Hence, $x = 7, y = 2, z = 1$ and $w = 1$.

EXAMPLE 7 *Consider the following information regarding the number of men and women workers in three factories I, II and III.*

	Men workers	*Women workers*
I	30	25
II	25	31
III	27	26

Represent the above information in the form of 3×2 *matrix. What does the entry in the third row and second column represent?*

SOLUTION The given information can be represented in the form of a 3×2 matrix as follows:

$$\begin{matrix} & \text{Men workers} & \text{Women workers} \\ \text{I} \\ \text{II} \\ \text{III} \end{matrix} \begin{bmatrix} 30 & 25 \\ 25 & 31 \\ 27 & 26 \end{bmatrix}$$

The entry in third row and second column represents the number of women workers in factory III.

BASED ON LOWER ORDER THINKING SKILLS (LOTS)

EXAMPLE 8 *If* $\begin{bmatrix} a+b & 2 \\ 5 & ab \end{bmatrix} = \begin{bmatrix} 6 & 2 \\ 5 & 8 \end{bmatrix}$, *find the values of a and b.*

SOLUTION The corresponding elements of two equal matrices are equal.

$\therefore \quad \begin{bmatrix} a+b & 2 \\ 5 & ab \end{bmatrix} = \begin{bmatrix} 6 & 2 \\ 5 & 8 \end{bmatrix} \Rightarrow a+b=6$ and $ab=8 \Rightarrow a+\dfrac{8}{a}=6 \qquad [\because ab=8 \Rightarrow b=8/a]$

$\Rightarrow \quad a^2+8=6a \Rightarrow a^2-6a+8=0 \Rightarrow (a-4)(a-2)=0 \Rightarrow a=2, 4.$

Now, $a=2$ and $ab=8 \Rightarrow b=4$ and, $a=4$ and $ab=8 \Rightarrow b=2$.

Hence, $a=2$ and $b=4$, or $a=4$ and $b=2$.

EXAMPLE 9 *For what values of x and y are the following matrices equal?*

$$A = \begin{bmatrix} 2x+1 & 3y \\ 0 & y^2-5y \end{bmatrix}, B = \begin{bmatrix} x+3 & y^2+2 \\ 0 & -6 \end{bmatrix}$$

SOLUTION The corresponding elements of two equal matrices are equal. Therefore,

$$\begin{bmatrix} 2x+1 & 3y \\ 0 & y^2-5y \end{bmatrix} = \begin{bmatrix} x+3 & y^2+2 \\ 0 & -6 \end{bmatrix}$$

$\Rightarrow \quad 2x+1=x+3, \quad 3y=y^2+2$ and $y^2-5y=-6$

$\Rightarrow \quad x=2, y^2-3y+2=0$ and $y^2-5y+6=0$

$\Rightarrow \quad x=2, (y-1)(y-2)=0$ and $(y-2)(y=3)=0 \Rightarrow x=2, y=1, 2$ and $y=2, 3$

$\Rightarrow \quad x=2, y=2 \qquad [\because y=1, 2$ and $y=2, 3 \Rightarrow y=2]$

EXERCISE 4.1

BASIC

1. If a matrix has 8 elements, what are the possible orders it can have? What if it has 5 elements? **[NCERT]**
2. If $A=[a_{ij}]=\begin{bmatrix} 2 & 3 & -5 \\ 1 & 4 & 9 \\ 0 & 7 & -2 \end{bmatrix}$ and $B=[b_{ij}]=\begin{bmatrix} 2 & -1 \\ -3 & 4 \\ 1 & 2 \end{bmatrix}$ then find: (i) $a_{22}+b_{21}$ (i) $a_{11}b_{11}+a_{22}b_{22}$
3. Let A be a matrix of order 3×4. If R_1 denotes the first row of A and C_2 denotes its second column, then determine the orders of matrices R_1 and C_2.
4. Construct a 2×3 matrix $A=[a_{ij}]$ whose elements a_{ij} are given by:

   (i) $a_{ij}=i\times j$ (ii) $a_{ij}=2i-j$ (iii) $a_{ij}=i+j$ (iv) $a_{ij}=\dfrac{(i+j)^2}{2}$
5. Construct a 2×2 matrix $A=[a_{ij}]$ whose elements a_{ij} are given by:

   (i) $\dfrac{(i+j)^2}{2}$ **[NCERT]** (ii) $a_{ij}=\dfrac{(i-j)^2}{2}$

   (iii) $a_{ij}=\dfrac{(i-2j)^2}{2}$ **[CBSE 2002, NCERT EXEMPLAR]** (iv) $a_{ij}=\dfrac{(2i+j)^2}{2}$ **[CBSE 2002]**

(v) $a_{ij} = \frac{|2i-3j|}{2}$ [NCERT EXEMPLAR] (vi) $a_{ij} = \frac{|-3i+j|}{2}$ [NCERT]

(vii) $a_{ij} = e^{2ix} \sin xj$ [NCERT EXEMPLAR]

6. Construct a 3×4 matrix $A = [a_{ij}]$ whose elements a_{ij} are given by:

(i) $a_{ij} = i + j$ (ii) $a_{ij} = i - j$ (iii) $a_{ij} = 2i$

(iv) $a_{ij} = j$ (v) $a_{ij} = \frac{1}{2} |-3i + j|$ [NCERT]

7. Construct a 4×3 matrix $A = [a_{ij}]$ whose elements a_{ij} are given by:

(i) $a_{ij} = 2i + \frac{i}{j}$ (ii) $a_{ij} = \frac{i-j}{i+j}$ (iii) $a_{ij} = i$

8. Find x, y, a and b, if $\begin{bmatrix} 3x+4y & 2 & x-2y \\ a+b & 2a-b & -1 \end{bmatrix} = \begin{bmatrix} 2 & 2 & 4 \\ 5 & -5 & -1 \end{bmatrix}$.

9. Find x, y, a and b, if $\begin{bmatrix} 2x-3y & a-b & 3 \\ 1 & x+4y & 3a+4b \end{bmatrix} = \begin{bmatrix} 1 & -2 & 3 \\ 1 & 6 & 29 \end{bmatrix}$.

10. Find the values of a, b, c and d, if $\begin{bmatrix} 2a+b & a-2b \\ 5c-d & 4c+3d \end{bmatrix} = \begin{bmatrix} 4 & -3 \\ 11 & 24 \end{bmatrix}$. [NCERT]

11. Find x, y and z so that $A = B$, where $A = \begin{bmatrix} x-2 & 3 & 2z \\ 18z & y+2 & 6z \end{bmatrix}$, $B = \begin{bmatrix} y & z & 6 \\ 6y & x & 2y \end{bmatrix}$.

12. If $\begin{bmatrix} x & 3x-y \\ 2x+z & 3y-\omega \end{bmatrix} = \begin{bmatrix} 3 & 2 \\ 4 & 7 \end{bmatrix}$, find x, y, z, ω.

13. If $\begin{bmatrix} x-y & z \\ 2x-y & \omega \end{bmatrix} = \begin{bmatrix} -1 & 4 \\ 0 & 5 \end{bmatrix}$, find x, y, z, ω. [CBSE 2014]

14. If $\begin{bmatrix} x+3 & z+4 & 2y-7 \\ 4x+6 & a-1 & 0 \\ b-3 & 3b & z+2c \end{bmatrix} = \begin{bmatrix} 0 & 6 & 3y-2 \\ 2x & -3 & 2c+2 \\ 2b+4 & -21 & 0 \end{bmatrix}$ [NCERT]

Obtain the values of a, b, c, x, y and z.

15. If $\begin{bmatrix} 2x+1 & 5x \\ 0 & y^2+1 \end{bmatrix} = \begin{bmatrix} x+3 & 10 \\ 0 & 26 \end{bmatrix}$, find the value of $(x+y)$. [CBSE 2012]

16. If $\begin{bmatrix} xy & 4 \\ z+6 & x+y \end{bmatrix} = \begin{bmatrix} 8 & w \\ 0 & 6 \end{bmatrix}$, then find the values of x, y, z and w. [NCERT EXEMPLAR]

17. Give an example of: (i) a row matrix which is also a column matrix
(ii) a diagonal matrix which is not scalar (iii) a triangular matrix.

BASED ON LOTS

18. The sales figure of two car dealers during January 2013 showed that dealer A sold 5 deluxe, 3 premium and 4 standard cars, while dealer B sold 7 deluxe, 2 premium and 3 standard cars. Total sales over the 2 month period of January-February revealed that dealer A sold 8 deluxe 7 premium and 6 standard cars. In the same 2 month period, dealer B sold 10 deluxe, 5 premium and 7 standard cars. Write 2×3 matrices summarizing sales data for January and 2-month period for each dealer.

19. For what values of x and y are the following matrices equal?

$$A = \begin{bmatrix} 2x+1 & 2y \\ 0 & y^2-5y \end{bmatrix},\ B = \begin{bmatrix} x+3 & y^2+2 \\ 0 & -6 \end{bmatrix}$$

20. Find the values of x and y if $\begin{bmatrix} x+10 & y^2+2y \\ 0 & -4 \end{bmatrix} = \begin{bmatrix} 3x+4 & 3 \\ 0 & y^2-5y \end{bmatrix}$

21. Find the values of a and b if $A = B$, where $A = \begin{bmatrix} a+4 & 3b \\ 8 & -6 \end{bmatrix}$, $B = \begin{bmatrix} 2a+2 & b^2+2 \\ 8 & b^2-10 \end{bmatrix}$

[NCERT EXEMPLAR]

ANSWERS

1. (i) $1\times 8, 8\times 1, 2\times 4, 4\times 2$ (ii) $1\times 5, 5\times 1$

2. (i) 1 (ii) 20

3. $1\times 4,\ 3\times 1$

4. (i) $\begin{bmatrix} 1 & 2 & 3 \\ 2 & 4 & 6 \end{bmatrix}$ (ii) $\begin{bmatrix} 1 & 0 & -1 \\ 3 & 2 & 1 \end{bmatrix}$ (iii) $\begin{bmatrix} 2 & 3 & 4 \\ 3 & 4 & 5 \end{bmatrix}$ (iv) $\begin{bmatrix} 2 & 9/2 & 8 \\ 9/2 & 8 & 25/2 \end{bmatrix}$

5. (i) $\begin{bmatrix} 2 & 9/2 \\ 9/2 & 8 \end{bmatrix}$ (ii) $\begin{bmatrix} 0 & 1/2 \\ 1/2 & 0 \end{bmatrix}$ (iii) $\begin{bmatrix} 1/2 & 9/2 \\ 0 & 2 \end{bmatrix}$ (iv) $\begin{bmatrix} 9/2 & 8 \\ 25/2 & 18 \end{bmatrix}$

(v) $\begin{bmatrix} 1/2 & 2 \\ 1/2 & 1 \end{bmatrix}$ (vi) $\begin{bmatrix} 1 & 1/2 \\ 5/2 & 2 \end{bmatrix}$

6. (i) $\begin{bmatrix} 2 & 3 & 4 & 5 \\ 3 & 4 & 5 & 6 \\ 4 & 5 & 6 & 7 \end{bmatrix}$ (ii) $\begin{bmatrix} 0 & -1 & -2 & -3 \\ 1 & 0 & -1 & -2 \\ 2 & 1 & 0 & -1 \end{bmatrix}$ (iii) $\begin{bmatrix} 2 & 2 & 2 & 2 \\ 4 & 4 & 4 & 4 \\ 6 & 6 & 6 & 6 \end{bmatrix}$ (iv) $\begin{bmatrix} 1 & 2 & 3 & 4 \\ 1 & 2 & 3 & 4 \\ 1 & 2 & 3 & 4 \end{bmatrix}$

(v) $\begin{bmatrix} 1 & 1/2 & 0 & 1/2 \\ 5/2 & 2 & 3/2 & 1 \\ 4 & 7/2 & 3 & 5/2 \end{bmatrix}$

7. (i) $\begin{bmatrix} 3 & 5/2 & 7/3 \\ 6 & 5 & 14/3 \\ 9 & 15/2 & 7 \\ 12 & 10 & 28/3 \end{bmatrix}$ (ii) $\begin{bmatrix} 0 & -1/3 & -1/2 \\ 1/3 & 0 & -1/5 \\ 1/2 & 1/5 & 0 \\ 3/5 & 1/3 & 1/7 \end{bmatrix}$ (iii) $\begin{bmatrix} 1 & 1 & 1 \\ 2 & 2 & 2 \\ 3 & 3 & 3 \\ 4 & 4 & 4 \end{bmatrix}$

8. $x=2, y=-1, a=0, b=5$

9. $x=2, y=1, a=3, b=5$

10. $a=1, b=2, c=3, d=4$

11. $x=11, y=9, z=3$

12. $x = 3, y = 7, z = -2, \omega = 14$

13. $x = 1, y = 2, z = 4, \omega = 5$

14. $a=-2, b=-7, c=-1, x=-3, y=-5, z=2$

15. $7, -3$

16. $x=2, y=4, z=-6, w=4$ or $x=4, y=2, z=-6, w=4$

17. (i) [5] (ii) $\begin{bmatrix} 2 & 0 & 0 \\ 0 & 3 & 0 \\ 0 & 0 & -1 \end{bmatrix}$ (iii) $\begin{bmatrix} 4 & 3 & 5 \\ 0 & 7 & 1 \\ 0 & 0 & 2 \end{bmatrix}$

18.

	Deluxe	Premium	Standard
Dealer A	5	3	4
Dealer B	7	2	3

,

	Deluxe	Premium	Standard
Dealer A	8	7	6
Dealer B	10	5	7

19. A and B cannot be equal for any value of y.

20. $x = 3, y = 1$

21. $a=2, b=2$

4.4 ADDITION OF MATRICES

DEFINITION *Let A, B be two matrices, each of order $m \times n$. Then their sum $A + B$ is a matrix of order $m \times n$ and is obtained by adding the corresponding elements of A and B.*

Thus, if $A = [a_{ij}]_{m \times n}$ and $B = [b_{ij}]_{m \times n}$ are two matrices of the same order, their sum $A + B$ is defined to be the matrix of order $m \times n$ such that

$$(A + B)_{ij} = a_{ij} + b_{ij} \quad \text{for } i = 1, 2, ..., m \quad \text{and} \quad j = 1, 2, ..., n$$

NOTE *The sum of two matrices is defined only when they are of the same order.*

If $A = \begin{bmatrix} 1 & 2 & 3 \\ 4 & 5 & 6 \end{bmatrix}$, $B = \begin{bmatrix} 6 & 5 & 4 \\ 3 & 2 & 1 \end{bmatrix}$, then $A + B = \begin{bmatrix} 1+6 & 2+5 & 3+4 \\ 4+3 & 5+2 & 6+1 \end{bmatrix} = \begin{bmatrix} 7 & 7 & 7 \\ 7 & 7 & 7 \end{bmatrix}$

If $A = \begin{bmatrix} 1 & 2 & 3 \\ 4 & 5 & 6 \end{bmatrix}$, $B = \begin{bmatrix} -1 & 2 & 1 \\ 3 & 2 & 1 \\ 2 & 5 & -2 \end{bmatrix}$, then $A + B$ is not defined, because A and B are not of the same order.

For the following pairs of matrices $A + B$ is not defined because they are of different orders:

(i) $A = \begin{bmatrix} 1 & -1 \\ 2 & 0 \end{bmatrix}$, $B = \begin{bmatrix} 2 \\ 3 \end{bmatrix}$ (ii) $A = \begin{bmatrix} 0 & 0 & 5 \\ 1 & -1 & 0 \end{bmatrix}$, $B = \begin{bmatrix} 1 & 2 \\ 3 & -1 \\ 4 & 5 \end{bmatrix}$

4.4.1 PROPERTIES OF MATRIX ADDITION

THEOREM 1 *(Commutativity) If A and B are two $m \times n$ matrices, then $A + B = B + A$. i.e. matrix addition is commutative.*

PROOF Let $A = [a_{ij}]$, $B = [b_{ij}]$ be two $m \times n$ matrices. Then, $A + B$ and $B + A$ both are $m \times n$ matrices such that

$$\begin{aligned} (A + B)_{ij} &= a_{ij} + b_{ij} && \text{[By definition of addition]} \\ &= b_{ij} + a_{ij} && \text{[By commutativity of addition of numbers]} \\ &= (B + A)_{ij} && \text{[By definition of addition]} \\ &= (B + A)_{ij} && \text{for } i = 1, 2, ..., m \text{ and } j = 1, 2, ..., n \end{aligned}$$

Thus, $A + B$ and $B + A$ are two matrices such that their orders are same and the corresponding elements are equal. Hence, $A + B = B + A$.

Q.E.D.

NOTE *To prove that two matrices are equal it is required to prove that their orders are same and the corresponding elements are equal.*

THEOREM 2 *(Associativity) If A, B, C are three matrices of the same order, then*

$(A + B) + C = A + (B + C)$ i.e. matrix addition is associative.

PROOF Let $A = [a_{ij}]$, $B = [b_{ij}]$ and $C = [c_{ij}]$ be three $m \times n$ matrices. Then, $(A + B) + C$ and $A + (B + C)$ are $m \times n$ matrices such that

$$\begin{aligned} ((A + B) + C)_{ij} &= (A + B)_{ij} + (C)_{ij} && \text{[By definition of addition]} \\ &= (a_{ij} + b_{ij}) + c_{ij} && \text{[By definition of addition]} \\ &= a_{ij} + (b_{ij} + c_{ij}) && \text{[By associativity of addition of numbers]} \\ &= (A)_{ij} + (B + C)_{ij} && \text{[By definition of addition]} \\ &= (A + (B + C))_{ij} && \text{[By definition of addition]} \\ &= (A + (B + C))_{ij} && \text{for } i = 1, 2, ..., m \text{ and } j = 1, 2, ..., n \end{aligned}$$

Thus, $(A + B) + C$ and $A + (B + C)$ are two matrices such that their orders are same and the corresponding elements are equal. Hence, $(A + B) + C = A + (B + C)$.

Q.E.D.

THEOREM 3 *(Existence of Identity) The null matrix is the identity element for matrix addition,*
i.e. $A + O = A = O + A$.

PROOF Let $A = [a_{ij}]$ be any matrix of order $m \times n$ and O be a null matrix of order $m \times n$. Then, $A + O$ and $O + A$ are $m \times n$ matrices such that

$$(A + O)_{ij} = a_{ij} + 0 = a_{ij} = (A)_{ij} \text{ and, } (O + A)_{ij} = 0 + a_{ij} = a_{ij} = (A)_{ij} \text{ for all } i, j$$

Hence, $A + O = A = O + A$. **Q.E.D.**

THEOREM 4 *(Existence of Inverse) For every matrix* $A = [a_{ij}]_{m \times n}$ *there exists a matrix* $[-a_{ij}]_{m \times n}$, *denoted by* $-A$, *such that* $A + (-A) = O = (-A) + A$.

PROOF We have,

$$(A + (-A))_{ij} = a_{ij} + (-a_{ij}) = a_{ij} - a_{ij} = 0 \text{ and, } ((-A) + A)_{ij} = (-a_{ij}) + a_{ij} = -a_{ij} + a_{ij} = 0 \text{ for all } i, j.$$

Hence, $A + (-A) = O = (-A) + A$.

Q.E.D.

The matrix $-A = [-a_{ij}]_{m \times n}$ is called the additive inverse of the matrix $A = [a_{ij}]_{m \times n}$.

If $A = \begin{bmatrix} 1 & -2 & 4 & 3 \\ 2 & 5 & 7 & -4 \end{bmatrix}$, then $(-A) = \begin{bmatrix} -1 & 2 & -4 & -3 \\ -2 & -5 & -7 & 4 \end{bmatrix}$.

THEOREM 5 *(Cancellation laws) If A, B, C are matrices of the same order, then*

$A + B = A + C \Rightarrow B = C$ *[Left cancellation law]*

and, $B + A = C + A \Rightarrow B = C$ *[Right cancellation law]*

PROOF We have,

$A + B = A + C$

$\Rightarrow (-A) + (A + B) = (-A) + (A + C)$ [Adding $(-A)$ on both sides]

$\Rightarrow (-A + A) + B = (-A + A) + C$ [By associativity of addition]

$\Rightarrow O + B = O + C$ [$\because -A + A = O$]

$\Rightarrow B = C$ [$\because$ O is the additive identity]

Similarly, we can prove that : $B + A = C + A \Rightarrow B = C$.

Q.E.D.

4.5 MULTIPLICATION OF A MATRIX BY A SCALAR (SCALAR MULTIPLICATION)

DEFINITION *Let* $A = [a_{ij}]$ *be an* $m \times n$ *matrix and k be any number called a scalar. Then the matrix obtained by multiplying every element of A by k is called the scalar multiple of A by k and is denoted by kA.*

Thus, $kA = [k\, a_{ij}]_{m \times n}$

For example, if $A = \begin{bmatrix} 1 & 2 & 5 \\ -2 & 3 & 4 \\ 1 & 2 & -1 \end{bmatrix}$, then $3A = \begin{bmatrix} 3 & 6 & 15 \\ -6 & 9 & 12 \\ 3 & 6 & -3 \end{bmatrix}$ and $\frac{1}{2}A = \begin{bmatrix} \frac{1}{2} & 1 & \frac{5}{2} \\ -1 & \frac{3}{2} & 2 \\ \frac{1}{2} & 1 & \frac{-1}{2} \end{bmatrix}$.

4.5.1 PROPERTIES OF SCALAR MULTIPLICATION

Various properties of scalar multiplication are stated and proved in the following theorem.

THEOREM *If* $A = [a_{ij}]_{m \times n}$, $B = [b_{ij}]_{m \times n}$ *are two matrices and k, l are scalars, then*

(i) $k(A + B) = kA + kB$ (ii) $(k + l)A = kA + lA$

(iii) $(kl)A = k(lA) = l(kA)$ (iv) $(-k)A = -(kA) = k(-A)$

(v) $1A = A$ (vi) $(-1)A = -A$

PROOF (i) Since A and B are matrices of the same order $m \times n$, $A + B$ is also a matrix of order $m \times n$. Therefore, $k(A + B)$ is also of order $m \times n$. Further, kA and kB are of order $m \times n$. Therefore, $kA + kB$ is also of order $m \times n$. Thus, $k(A + B)$ and $kA + kB$ are matrices of the same order such that

$$
\begin{aligned}
(k(A+B))_{ij} &= k(A+B)_{ij} && \text{[By definition of scalar multiplication]}\\
&= k(a_{ij}+b_{ij}) && \text{[By definition of addition of matrices]}\\
&= k\,a_{ij}+k\,b_{ij} && \text{[By distributivity of multiplication over addition]}\\
&= (kA)_{ij}+(kB)_{ij} && \text{[By definition of scalar multiplication]}\\
&= (kA+kB)_{ij} && \text{[By definition of matrix addition]}\\
&= (kA+kB)_{ij} && \text{for } i=1,2,\dots,m \text{ and } j=1,2,\dots,n
\end{aligned}
$$

Hence, $k(A + B) = kA + kB$ [By definition of equality of two matrices]

(ii) Since k and l are scalars, $k + l$ is also a scalar. Therefore, $(k + l)A$ is a matrix of order $m \times n$. Also, kA and lA are $m \times n$ matrices. Therefore, $kA + lA$ is also an $m \times n$ matrix.

Thus, $(k + l)A$ and $kA + lA$ are two matrices of the same order $m \times n$ such that

$$
\begin{aligned}
((k+l)A)_{ij} &= (k+l)\,a_{ij} && \text{[By definition of scalar multiplication]}\\
&= ka_{ij}+la_{ij} && \text{[By distributivity of multiplication over addition]}\\
&= (kA)_{ij}+(lA)_{ij} && \text{[By definition of scalar multiplication]}\\
&= (kA+lA)_{ij} && \text{[By definition of addition of matrices]}\\
&= (kA+lA)_{ij} && \text{for } i=1,2,\dots,m \text{ and } j=1,2,\dots,n
\end{aligned}
$$

Hence, $(k + l)A = kA + lA$. [By definition of equality of two matrices]

(iii) Since k and l are scalars, kl is also a scalar. Therefore, $(kl)A$ is an $m \times n$ matrix. Also, note that lA and kA are matrices of order $m \times n$. Therefore, $k(lA)$ and $l(kA)$ are matrices of order $m \times n$.

Thus, $(kl)A$ and $k(lA)$ are two matrices of the same order $m \times n$ such that

$$
\begin{aligned}
((kl)A)_{ij} &= (kl)\,a_{ij} && \text{[By definition of scalar multiplication]}\\
&= k(la_{ij}) && \text{[By association of multiplication]}\\
&= k(lA)_{ij} && \text{[By definition of scalar multiplication]}\\
&= (k(lA))_{ij} && \text{[By definition of scalar multiplication]}\\
&= (k(lA))_{ij} && \text{for } i=1,2,\dots,m \text{ and } j=1,2,\dots,n
\end{aligned}
$$

Hence, $(kl)A = k(lA)$. [By definition of equality of two matrices]

Similarly, it can be proved that $(kl)A = l(kA)$. Hence, $(kl)A = k(lA) = l(kA)$.

(iv) Putting $l = -1$ in (iii), we obtain: $(-k)A = k(-A) = -(kA)$

(v) Putting $k = -1$ in (iv), we obtain: $1A = A$.

(vi) Putting $k = 1$ in (iv), we obtain: $(-1)A = -A$. Q.E.D.

4.6 SUBTRACTION OF MATRICES

DEFINITION *For two matrices A and B of the same order, the subtraction of matrix B from matrix A is denoted by $A - B$ and is defined as $A - B = A + (-B)$.*

For example, if $A = \begin{bmatrix} -3 & 2 & 1 \\ 1 & -4 & 7 \end{bmatrix}$ and $B = \begin{bmatrix} 3 & 5 & -2 \\ -1 & 4 & -2 \end{bmatrix}$, then

$$A - B = A + (-B) = \begin{bmatrix} -3 & 2 & 1 \\ 1 & -4 & 7 \end{bmatrix} + \begin{bmatrix} -3 & -5 & 2 \\ 1 & -4 & 2 \end{bmatrix} = \begin{bmatrix} -6 & -3 & 3 \\ 2 & -8 & 9 \end{bmatrix}$$

ILLUSTRATION *If* $A = \begin{bmatrix} 2 & 3 & 4 \\ 0 & 4 & 6 \\ 5 & 8 & 9 \end{bmatrix}$, $B = \begin{bmatrix} 3 & 0 & 5 \\ 5 & 3 & 2 \\ 0 & 4 & 7 \end{bmatrix}$, *find* $3A - 2B$.

SOLUTION We find that $3A - 2B = 3A + (-2)B$

$$\therefore \quad 3A - 2B = \begin{bmatrix} 6 & 9 & 12 \\ 0 & 12 & 18 \\ 15 & 24 & 27 \end{bmatrix} + \begin{bmatrix} -6 & 0 & -10 \\ -10 & -6 & -4 \\ 0 & -8 & -14 \end{bmatrix} = \begin{bmatrix} 0 & 9 & 2 \\ -10 & 6 & 14 \\ 15 & 16 & 13 \end{bmatrix}$$

ILLUSTRATIVE EXAMPLES

BASED ON BASIC CONCEPTS (BASIC)

EXAMPLE 1 *If* $A = \begin{bmatrix} 2 & 3 & -5 \\ 1 & 2 & -1 \end{bmatrix}$ *and* $B = \begin{bmatrix} 0 & 5 & 1 \\ -2 & 7 & 3 \end{bmatrix}$, *find* $A + B$ *and* $A - B$.

SOLUTION Clearly, A and B both are matrices of the same order 2×3. So, $A + B$ and $A - B$ both are defined.

Now,

$$A + B = \begin{bmatrix} 2 & 3 & -5 \\ 1 & 2 & -1 \end{bmatrix} + \begin{bmatrix} 0 & 5 & 1 \\ -2 & 7 & 3 \end{bmatrix} = \begin{bmatrix} 2+0 & 3+5 & -5+1 \\ 1-2 & 2+7 & -1+3 \end{bmatrix} = \begin{bmatrix} 2 & 8 & -4 \\ -1 & 9 & 2 \end{bmatrix}$$

and, $$A - B = A + (-B) = \begin{bmatrix} 2 & 3 & -5 \\ 1 & 2 & -1 \end{bmatrix} + (-1)\begin{bmatrix} 0 & 5 & 1 \\ -2 & 7 & 3 \end{bmatrix} = \begin{bmatrix} 2 & 3 & -5 \\ 1 & 2 & -1 \end{bmatrix} + \begin{bmatrix} 0 & -5 & -1 \\ 2 & -7 & -3 \end{bmatrix}$$

$$= \begin{bmatrix} 2+0 & 3-5 & -5-1 \\ 1+2 & 2-7 & -1-3 \end{bmatrix} = \begin{bmatrix} 2 & -2 & -6 \\ 3 & -5 & -4 \end{bmatrix}$$

EXAMPLE 2 *If* $A = \begin{bmatrix} 2 & -1 \\ 3 & 1 \end{bmatrix}$ *and* $B = \begin{bmatrix} 1 & 4 \\ 7 & 2 \end{bmatrix}$, *find* $3A - 2B$.

SOLUTION Clearly,

$$3A = \begin{bmatrix} 6 & -3 \\ 9 & 3 \end{bmatrix} \text{ and, } (-2)B = \begin{bmatrix} -2 & -8 \\ -14 & -4 \end{bmatrix}$$

$$\therefore \quad 3A - 2B = 3A + (-2)B = \begin{bmatrix} 6 & -3 \\ 9 & 3 \end{bmatrix} + \begin{bmatrix} -2 & -8 \\ -14 & -4 \end{bmatrix} = \begin{bmatrix} 6+(-2) & -3+(-8) \\ 9+(-14) & 3+(-4) \end{bmatrix} = \begin{bmatrix} 4 & -11 \\ -5 & -1 \end{bmatrix}$$

EXAMPLE 3 *If* $A = diag(1 \ \ -1 \ \ 2)$ *and* $B = diag(2 \ \ 3 \ \ -1)$, *find* $A + B$, $3A + 4B$.

SOLUTION We have,

$$A = \begin{bmatrix} 1 & 0 & 0 \\ 0 & -1 & 0 \\ 0 & 0 & 2 \end{bmatrix} \text{ and, } B = \begin{bmatrix} 2 & 0 & 0 \\ 0 & 3 & 0 \\ 0 & 0 & -1 \end{bmatrix}$$

$$\therefore \quad A + B = \begin{bmatrix} 1 & 0 & 0 \\ 0 & -1 & 0 \\ 0 & 0 & 2 \end{bmatrix} + \begin{bmatrix} 2 & 0 & 0 \\ 0 & 3 & 0 \\ 0 & 0 & -1 \end{bmatrix} = \begin{bmatrix} 3 & 0 & 0 \\ 0 & 2 & 0 \\ 0 & 0 & 1 \end{bmatrix} = \text{diag}(3 \ \ 2 \ \ 1)$$

and, $$3A + 4B = \begin{bmatrix} 3 & 0 & 0 \\ 0 & -3 & 0 \\ 0 & 0 & 6 \end{bmatrix} + \begin{bmatrix} 8 & 0 & 0 \\ 0 & 12 & 0 \\ 0 & 0 & -4 \end{bmatrix} = \begin{bmatrix} 11 & 0 & 0 \\ 0 & 9 & 0 \\ 0 & 0 & 2 \end{bmatrix} = \text{diag}(11 \ \ 9 \ \ 2)$$

REMARK *It is evident from the above example that if* $A = \text{diag}(a_1 \;\; a_2 \;\; a_3 \; \dots \; a_n)$ *and* $B = \text{diag}(b_1 \;\; b_2 \;\; b_3 \; \dots \; b_n)$ *Then,* $A + B = \text{diag}(a_1 + b_1 \;\; a_2 + b_2 \;\; a_3 + b_3 \dots a_n + b_n)$.

EXAMPLE 4 *Simplify:* $\cos\theta \begin{bmatrix} \cos\theta & \sin\theta \\ -\sin\theta & \cos\theta \end{bmatrix} + \sin\theta \begin{bmatrix} \sin\theta & -\cos\theta \\ \cos\theta & \sin\theta \end{bmatrix}$ [CBSE 2012, NCERT]

SOLUTION We have,

$$\cos\theta \begin{bmatrix} \cos\theta & \sin\theta \\ -\sin\theta & \cos\theta \end{bmatrix} + \sin\theta \begin{bmatrix} \sin\theta & -\cos\theta \\ \cos\theta & \sin\theta \end{bmatrix}$$

$$= \begin{bmatrix} \cos^2\theta & \sin\theta\cos\theta \\ -\sin\theta\cos\theta & \cos^2\theta \end{bmatrix} + \begin{bmatrix} \sin^2\theta & -\sin\theta\cos\theta \\ \sin\theta\cos\theta & \sin^2\theta \end{bmatrix}$$

$$= \begin{bmatrix} \cos^2\theta + \sin^2\theta & \sin\theta\cos\theta - \sin\theta\cos\theta \\ -\sin\theta\cos\theta + \sin\theta\cos\theta & \cos^2\theta + \sin^2\theta \end{bmatrix} = \begin{bmatrix} 1 & 0 \\ 0 & 1 \end{bmatrix}.$$

EXAMPLE 5 *Find a matrix X such that* $2A + B + X = O$*, where* $A = \begin{bmatrix} -1 & 2 \\ 3 & 4 \end{bmatrix}$ *and,* $B = \begin{bmatrix} 3 & -2 \\ 1 & 5 \end{bmatrix}$.

[CBSE 2000]

SOLUTION We have,

$$2A + B + X = O$$

$$\Rightarrow \quad X = -2A - B$$

$$\Rightarrow \quad X = -2\begin{bmatrix} -1 & 2 \\ 3 & 4 \end{bmatrix} - \begin{bmatrix} 3 & -2 \\ 1 & 5 \end{bmatrix} = \begin{bmatrix} 2 & -4 \\ -6 & -8 \end{bmatrix} + \begin{bmatrix} -3 & 2 \\ -1 & -5 \end{bmatrix} = \begin{bmatrix} 2-3 & -4+2 \\ -6-1 & -8-5 \end{bmatrix} = \begin{bmatrix} -1 & -2 \\ -7 & -13 \end{bmatrix}$$

EXAMPLE 6 *Find a matrix A such that* $2A - 3B + 5C = O$*, where* $B = \begin{bmatrix} -2 & 2 & 0 \\ 3 & 1 & 4 \end{bmatrix}$ *and* $C = \begin{bmatrix} 2 & 0 & -2 \\ 7 & 1 & 6 \end{bmatrix}$. [CBSE 2019]

SOLUTION We have,

$$2A - 3B + 5C = O$$

$$\Rightarrow \quad 2A = 3B - 5C$$

$$\Rightarrow \quad 2A = 3\begin{bmatrix} -2 & 2 & 0 \\ 3 & 1 & 4 \end{bmatrix} - 5\begin{bmatrix} 2 & 0 & -2 \\ 7 & 1 & 6 \end{bmatrix} = \begin{bmatrix} -6 & 6 & 0 \\ 9 & 3 & 12 \end{bmatrix} + \begin{bmatrix} -10 & 0 & 10 \\ -35 & -5 & -30 \end{bmatrix}$$

$$\Rightarrow \quad 2A = \begin{bmatrix} -6-10 & 6+0 & 0+10 \\ 9-35 & 3-5 & 12-30 \end{bmatrix} = \begin{bmatrix} -16 & 6 & 10 \\ -26 & -2 & -18 \end{bmatrix}$$

$$\Rightarrow \quad A = \frac{1}{2}\begin{bmatrix} -16 & 6 & 10 \\ -26 & -2 & -18 \end{bmatrix} = \begin{bmatrix} -8 & 3 & 5 \\ -13 & -1 & -9 \end{bmatrix}.$$

BASED ON LOWER ORDER THINKING SKILLS (LOTS)

EXAMPLE 7 *Find X and Y, if* $X + Y = \begin{bmatrix} 7 & 0 \\ 2 & 5 \end{bmatrix}$ *and* $X - Y = \begin{bmatrix} 3 & 0 \\ 0 & 3 \end{bmatrix}$.

SOLUTION We have, [NCERT]

$$X + Y = \begin{bmatrix} 7 & 0 \\ 2 & 5 \end{bmatrix} \text{ and, } X - Y = \begin{bmatrix} 3 & 0 \\ 0 & 3 \end{bmatrix}$$

$$\therefore \quad (X + Y) + (X - Y) = \begin{bmatrix} 7 & 0 \\ 2 & 5 \end{bmatrix} + \begin{bmatrix} 3 & 0 \\ 0 & 3 \end{bmatrix} = \begin{bmatrix} 7+3 & 0+0 \\ 2+0 & 5+3 \end{bmatrix}$$

$$\Rightarrow \quad 2X = \begin{bmatrix} 10 & 0 \\ 2 & 8 \end{bmatrix} \Rightarrow X = \frac{1}{2}\begin{bmatrix} 10 & 0 \\ 2 & 8 \end{bmatrix} = \begin{bmatrix} 5 & 0 \\ 1 & 4 \end{bmatrix}$$

and, $(X+Y)-(X-Y) = \begin{bmatrix} 7 & 0 \\ 2 & 5 \end{bmatrix} - \begin{bmatrix} 3 & 0 \\ 0 & 3 \end{bmatrix} = \begin{bmatrix} 7 & 0 \\ 2 & 5 \end{bmatrix} + \begin{bmatrix} -3 & 0 \\ 0 & -3 \end{bmatrix} = \begin{bmatrix} 7-3 & 0+0 \\ 2+0 & 5-3 \end{bmatrix}$

$\Rightarrow \quad 2Y = \begin{bmatrix} 4 & 0 \\ 2 & 2 \end{bmatrix} \Rightarrow Y = \frac{1}{2}\begin{bmatrix} 4 & 0 \\ 2 & 2 \end{bmatrix} = \begin{bmatrix} 2 & 0 \\ 1 & 1 \end{bmatrix}$

Hence, $X = \begin{bmatrix} 5 & 0 \\ 1 & 4 \end{bmatrix}$ and $Y = \begin{bmatrix} 2 & 0 \\ 1 & 1 \end{bmatrix}$

EXAMPLE 8 *Find a matrix A, if* $A + \begin{bmatrix} 2 & 3 \\ -1 & 4 \end{bmatrix} = \begin{bmatrix} 3 & -6 \\ -3 & 8 \end{bmatrix}$.

SOLUTION Let $B = \begin{bmatrix} 2 & 3 \\ -1 & 4 \end{bmatrix}$ and $C = \begin{bmatrix} 3 & -6 \\ -3 & 8 \end{bmatrix}$. Then, the given matrix equation is $A+B=C$.

Now, $A + B = C$

$\Rightarrow \quad (A+B)+(-B) = C+(-B)$ [Adding $-B$ on both sides]

$\Rightarrow \quad A+(B+(-B)) = C+(-B)$ [Using associativity of matrix addition on LHS]

$\Rightarrow \quad A+O = C-B$

$\Rightarrow \quad A = C-B.$

$\therefore \quad A = \begin{bmatrix} 3 & -6 \\ -3 & 8 \end{bmatrix} + \begin{bmatrix} -2 & -3 \\ 1 & -4 \end{bmatrix} = \begin{bmatrix} 3-2 & -6-3 \\ -3+1 & 8-4 \end{bmatrix} = \begin{bmatrix} 1 & -9 \\ -2 & 4 \end{bmatrix}$

EXAMPLE 9 *Find* x, y, z, t *if* $2\begin{bmatrix} x & z \\ y & t \end{bmatrix} + 3\begin{bmatrix} 1 & -1 \\ 0 & 2 \end{bmatrix} = 3\begin{bmatrix} 3 & 5 \\ 4 & 6 \end{bmatrix}$.

SOLUTION The given matrix equation can be written as [NCERT]

$$\begin{bmatrix} 2x & 2z \\ 2y & 2t \end{bmatrix} + \begin{bmatrix} 3 & -3 \\ 0 & 6 \end{bmatrix} = \begin{bmatrix} 9 & 15 \\ 12 & 18 \end{bmatrix}$$

$$\Rightarrow \quad \begin{bmatrix} 2x+3 & 2z-3 \\ 2y & 2t+6 \end{bmatrix} = \begin{bmatrix} 9 & 15 \\ 12 & 18 \end{bmatrix}$$

$\Rightarrow \quad 2x+3=9,\ 2z-3=15,\ 2y=12$ and $2t+6=18$ [By definition of equality of addition]

$\Rightarrow \quad x=3, z=9, y=6$ and $t=6$.

EXAMPLE 10 *Find non-zero values of x satisfying the matrix equation:*

$$x\begin{bmatrix} 2x & 2 \\ 3 & x \end{bmatrix} + 2\begin{bmatrix} 8 & 5x \\ 4 & 4x \end{bmatrix} = 2\begin{bmatrix} x^2+8 & 24 \\ 10 & 6x \end{bmatrix}$$

SOLUTION We have, [NCERT EXEMPLAR]

$$x\begin{bmatrix} 2x & 2 \\ 3 & x \end{bmatrix} + 2\begin{bmatrix} 8 & 5x \\ 4 & 4x \end{bmatrix} = 2\begin{bmatrix} x^2+8 & 24 \\ 10 & 6x \end{bmatrix}$$

$$\Rightarrow \quad \begin{bmatrix} 2x^2 & 2x \\ 3x & x^2 \end{bmatrix} + \begin{bmatrix} 16 & 10x \\ 8 & 8x \end{bmatrix} = \begin{bmatrix} 2x^2+16 & 48 \\ 20 & 12x \end{bmatrix}$$

$$\Rightarrow \quad \begin{bmatrix} 2x^2+16 & 2x+10x \\ 3x+8 & x^2+8x \end{bmatrix} = \begin{bmatrix} 2x^2+16 & 48 \\ 20 & 12x \end{bmatrix}$$

$\Rightarrow \quad 2x^2+16=2x^2+16,\ 2x+10x=48,\ 3x+8=20$ and $x^2+8x=12x$

$\Rightarrow \quad 12x=48,\ 3x=12$ and $x^2-4x=0 \Rightarrow x=4$ and, $x(x-4)=0 \Rightarrow x=4$ and $x=0, 4 \Rightarrow x=4$

EXAMPLE 11 *Solve the matrix equation* $\begin{bmatrix} x^2 \\ y^2 \end{bmatrix} - 3\begin{bmatrix} x \\ 2y \end{bmatrix} = \begin{bmatrix} -2 \\ 9 \end{bmatrix}$.

SOLUTION We have,

$$\begin{bmatrix} x^2 \\ y^2 \end{bmatrix} - 3\begin{bmatrix} x \\ 2y \end{bmatrix} = \begin{bmatrix} -2 \\ 9 \end{bmatrix} \Rightarrow \begin{bmatrix} x^2 \\ y^2 \end{bmatrix} - \begin{bmatrix} 3x \\ 6y \end{bmatrix} = \begin{bmatrix} -2 \\ 9 \end{bmatrix} \Rightarrow \begin{bmatrix} x^2 - 3x \\ y^2 - 6y \end{bmatrix} = \begin{bmatrix} -2 \\ 9 \end{bmatrix}$$

$$\Rightarrow \quad x^2 - 3x = -2 \text{ and } y^2 - 6y = 9 \Rightarrow x^2 - 3x + 2 = 0 \text{ and } y^2 - 6y - 9 = 0$$

$$\Rightarrow \quad (x-1)(x-2) = 0 \text{ and } y = \frac{6 \pm \sqrt{36+36}}{2} \Rightarrow x = 1, 2 \text{ and } y = 3 \pm 3\sqrt{2}$$

EXAMPLE 12 *If A, B and C are three matrices of the same order, then prove that*

$$A = B \Rightarrow A + C = B + C.$$

SOLUTION Let $A = [a_{ij}]_{m \times n}$, $B = [b_{ij}]_{m \times n}$ and $C = [c_{ij}]_{m \times n}$ be three matrices of the same order $m \times n$. Then, $A + C$ and $B + C$ are also of the same order $m \times n$.

Now, $A = B$

$\Rightarrow \quad a_{ij} = b_{ij}$ for all $i = 1, 2, ..., m;\ j = 1, 2, ..., n$

$\Rightarrow \quad a_{ij} + c_{ij} = b_{ij} + c_{ij}$ for all $i = 1, 2, ..., m;\ j = 1, 2, ..., n$ [Adding c_{ij} on both sides]

$\Rightarrow \quad (A + C)_{ij} = (B + C)_{ij}$ for all $i = 1, 2, ..., m;\ j = 1, 2, ..., n$

$\Rightarrow \quad A + C = B + C.$

EXAMPLE 13 *Two farmers Ram Kishan and Gurcharan Singh cultivate only three varities of rice namely Basmati, Permal and Naura. The sale (in ₹) of these varities of rice by both the farmers in the month of September and October are given by the following matrices A and B*

September sales (in ₹)

$$A = \begin{array}{c} \textit{Basmati} \quad \textit{Permal} \quad \textit{Naura} \\ \begin{bmatrix} 10{,}000 & 20{,}000 & 30{,}000 \\ 50{,}000 & 30{,}000 & 10{,}000 \end{bmatrix} \end{array} \begin{array}{l} \textit{Ram Kishan} \\ \textit{Gurcharan Singh} \end{array}$$

October sales (in ₹)

$$B = \begin{array}{c} \textit{Basmati} \quad \textit{Permal} \quad \textit{Naura} \\ \begin{bmatrix} 5{,}000 & 10{,}000 & 6{,}000 \\ 20{,}000 & 10{,}000 & 10{,}000 \end{bmatrix} \end{array} \begin{array}{l} \textit{Ram Kishan} \\ \textit{Gurcharan Singh} \end{array}$$

Find:

(i) *What were the combined sales in September and October for each farmer in each variety.*

(ii) *What was the change in sales from September to October?*

(iii) *If both farmers receive 2% profit on gross rupees sales, compute the profit for each farmer and for each variety sold in October.*

SOLUTION (i) The combined sales in September and October is given by $A + B$.

Clearly,

$$A + B = \begin{array}{c} \text{Basmati} \qquad \text{Permal} \qquad \text{Naura} \\ \begin{bmatrix} 10{,}000 + 5000 & 20{,}000 + 10{,}000 & 30{,}000 + 6000 \\ 50{,}000 + 20{,}000 & 30{,}000 + 10{,}000 & 10{,}000 + 10{,}000 \end{bmatrix} \end{array} \begin{array}{l} \text{Ram Kishan} \\ \text{Gurcharan Singh} \end{array}$$

$$\Rightarrow \quad A + B = \begin{array}{c} \text{Basmati} \quad \text{Permal} \quad \text{Naura} \\ \begin{bmatrix} 15{,}000 & 30{,}000 & 36{,}000 \\ 70{,}000 & 40{,}000 & 20{,}000 \end{bmatrix} \end{array} \begin{array}{l} \text{Ram Kishan} \\ \text{Gurcharan Singh} \end{array}$$

(ii) The change in sales from September to October is given by $A - B$.

Clearly,

$$A-B=\begin{bmatrix} 10{,}000-5{,}000 & 20{,}000-10{,}000 & 30{,}000-6000 \\ 50{,}000-20{,}000 & 30{,}000-10{,}000 & 10{,}000-10{,}000 \end{bmatrix}\begin{matrix}\text{Ram Kishan}\\ \text{Gurcharan Singh}\end{matrix}$$

(columns: Basmati, Permal, Naura)

$$A-B=\begin{bmatrix} 5{,}000 & 10{,}000 & 24{,}000 \\ 30{,}000 & 20{,}000 & 0 \end{bmatrix}\begin{matrix}\text{Ram Kishan}\\ \text{Gurcharan Singh}\end{matrix}$$

(columns: Basmati, Permal, Naura)

(iii) The profit for each farmer and for each variety sold in October at the rate of 2% of gross sale is given by

$$2\% \text{ of } B=\frac{2}{100}\times B=0.02\,B=0.02\begin{bmatrix} 5{,}000 & 10{,}000 & 6{,}000 \\ 20{,}000 & 10{,}000 & 10{,}000 \end{bmatrix}\begin{matrix}\text{Ram Kishan}\\ \text{Gurcharan Singh}\end{matrix}$$

(columns: Basmati, Permal, Naura)

$$=\begin{bmatrix} 100 & 200 & 120 \\ 400 & 200 & 200 \end{bmatrix}\begin{matrix}\text{Ram Kishan}\\ \text{Gurcharan Singh}\end{matrix}$$

(columns: Basmati, Permal, Naura)

Thus, in October Ram Kishan receives ₹ 100, ₹ 200 and ₹ 120 as profit in the sale of each variety of rice respectively, and Gurcharan Singh receives profit of ₹ 400, ₹ 200 and ₹ 200 in each variety of rice respectively.

EXERCISE 4.2

BASIC

1. Compute the following sums:

(i) $\begin{bmatrix} 3 & -2 \\ 1 & 4 \end{bmatrix}+\begin{bmatrix} -2 & 4 \\ 1 & 3 \end{bmatrix}$ (ii) $\begin{bmatrix} 2 & 1 & 3 \\ 0 & 3 & 5 \\ -1 & 2 & 5 \end{bmatrix}+\begin{bmatrix} 1 & -2 & 3 \\ 2 & 6 & 1 \\ 0 & -3 & 1 \end{bmatrix}$

2. Let $A=\begin{bmatrix} 2 & 4 \\ 3 & 2 \end{bmatrix}$, $B=\begin{bmatrix} 1 & 3 \\ -2 & 5 \end{bmatrix}$ and $C=\begin{bmatrix} -2 & 5 \\ 3 & 4 \end{bmatrix}$. Find each of the following:

(i) $2A-3B$ (ii) $B-4C$ (iii) $3A-C$ (iv) $3A-2B+3C$

3. If $A=\begin{bmatrix} 2 & 3 \\ 5 & 7 \end{bmatrix}$, $B=\begin{bmatrix} -1 & 0 & 2 \\ 3 & 4 & 1 \end{bmatrix}$, $C=\begin{bmatrix} -1 & 2 & 3 \\ 2 & 1 & 0 \end{bmatrix}$, find

(i) $A+B$ and $B+C$ (ii) $2B+3A$ and $3C-4B$.

4. Let $A=\begin{bmatrix} -1 & 0 & 2 \\ 3 & 1 & 4 \end{bmatrix}$, $B=\begin{bmatrix} 0 & -2 & 5 \\ 1 & -3 & 1 \end{bmatrix}$ and $C=\begin{bmatrix} 1 & -5 & 2 \\ 6 & 0 & -4 \end{bmatrix}$. Compute $2A-3B+4C$.

5. If $A=\text{diag}\,(2\quad -5\quad 9)$, $B=\text{diag}\,(1\quad 1\quad -4)$ and $C=\text{diag}\,(-6\quad 3\quad 4)$, find

(i) $A-2B$ (ii) $B+C-2A$ (iii) $2A+3B-5C$

6. Given the matrices

$$A=\begin{bmatrix} 2 & 1 & 1 \\ 3 & -1 & 0 \\ 0 & 2 & 4 \end{bmatrix},\quad B=\begin{bmatrix} 9 & 7 & -1 \\ 3 & 5 & 4 \\ 2 & 1 & 6 \end{bmatrix}\quad \text{and}\quad C=\begin{bmatrix} 2 & -4 & 3 \\ 1 & -1 & 0 \\ 9 & 4 & 5 \end{bmatrix}$$

Verify that $(A+B)+C=A+(B+C)$.

BASED ON LOTS

7. Find matrices X and Y, if $X+Y=\begin{bmatrix} 5 & 2 \\ 0 & 9 \end{bmatrix}$ and $X-Y=\begin{bmatrix} 3 & 6 \\ 0 & -1 \end{bmatrix}$. [NCERT]

8. Find X, if $Y = \begin{bmatrix} 3 & 2 \\ 1 & 4 \end{bmatrix}$ and $2X + Y = \begin{bmatrix} 1 & 0 \\ -3 & 2 \end{bmatrix}$. **[NCERT]**

9. Find matrices X and Y, if $2X - Y = \begin{bmatrix} 6 & -6 & 0 \\ -4 & 2 & 1 \end{bmatrix}$ and $X + 2Y = \begin{bmatrix} 3 & 2 & 5 \\ -2 & 1 & -7 \end{bmatrix}$.

10. If $X - Y = \begin{bmatrix} 1 & 1 & 1 \\ 1 & 1 & 0 \\ 1 & 0 & 0 \end{bmatrix}$ and $X + Y = \begin{bmatrix} 3 & 5 & 1 \\ -1 & 1 & 4 \\ 11 & 8 & 0 \end{bmatrix}$, find X and Y.

11. Find matrix A, if $\begin{bmatrix} 1 & 2 & -1 \\ 0 & 4 & 9 \end{bmatrix} + A = \begin{bmatrix} 9 & -1 & 4 \\ -2 & 1 & 3 \end{bmatrix}$.

12. If $A = \begin{bmatrix} 9 & 1 \\ 7 & 8 \end{bmatrix}$, $B = \begin{bmatrix} 1 & 5 \\ 7 & 12 \end{bmatrix}$, find matrix C such that $5A + 3B + 2C$ is a null matrix.

13. If $A = \begin{bmatrix} 2 & -2 \\ 4 & 2 \\ -5 & 1 \end{bmatrix}$, $B = \begin{bmatrix} 8 & 0 \\ 4 & -2 \\ 3 & 6 \end{bmatrix}$, find matrix X such that $2A + 3X = 5B$.

14. If $A = \begin{bmatrix} 1 & -3 & 2 \\ 2 & 0 & 2 \end{bmatrix}$ and, $B = \begin{bmatrix} 2 & -1 & -1 \\ 1 & 0 & -1 \end{bmatrix}$, find the matrix C such that $A + B + C$ is zero matrix.

15. Find x, y satisfying the matrix equations

(i) $\begin{bmatrix} x-y & 2 & -2 \\ 4 & x & 6 \end{bmatrix} + \begin{bmatrix} 3 & -2 & 2 \\ 1 & 0 & -1 \end{bmatrix} = \begin{bmatrix} 6 & 0 & 0 \\ 5 & 2x+y & 5 \end{bmatrix}$

(ii) $[x \;\; y+2 \;\; z-3] + [y \;\; 4 \;\; 5] = [4 \;\; 9 \;\; 12]$

(iii) $x\begin{bmatrix} 2 \\ 1 \end{bmatrix} + y\begin{bmatrix} 3 \\ 5 \end{bmatrix} + \begin{bmatrix} -8 \\ -11 \end{bmatrix} = O$ **[NCERT EXEMPLAR]**

16. If $2\begin{bmatrix} 3 & 4 \\ 5 & x \end{bmatrix} + \begin{bmatrix} 1 & y \\ 0 & 1 \end{bmatrix} = \begin{bmatrix} 7 & 0 \\ 10 & 5 \end{bmatrix}$, find x and y.

17. Find the value of λ, a non-zero scalar, if $\lambda\begin{bmatrix} 1 & 0 & 2 \\ 3 & 4 & 5 \end{bmatrix} + 2\begin{bmatrix} 1 & 2 & 3 \\ -1 & -3 & 2 \end{bmatrix} = \begin{bmatrix} 4 & 4 & 10 \\ 4 & 2 & 14 \end{bmatrix}$.

18. (i) Find a matrix X such that $2A + B + X = O$, where $A = \begin{bmatrix} -1 & 2 \\ 3 & 4 \end{bmatrix}$, $B = \begin{bmatrix} 3 & -2 \\ 1 & 5 \end{bmatrix}$ **[CBSE 2000]**

(ii) If $A = \begin{bmatrix} 8 & 0 \\ 4 & -2 \\ 3 & 6 \end{bmatrix}$ and $B = \begin{bmatrix} 2 & -2 \\ 4 & 2 \\ -5 & 1 \end{bmatrix}$, then find the matrix X of order 3×2 such that $2A + 3X = 5B$. **[NCERT]**

19. Find x, y, z and t, if

(i) $3\begin{bmatrix} x & y \\ z & t \end{bmatrix} = \begin{bmatrix} x & 6 \\ -1 & 2t \end{bmatrix} + \begin{bmatrix} 4 & x+y \\ z+t & 3 \end{bmatrix}$ **[NCERT]**

(ii) $2\begin{bmatrix} x & 5 \\ 7 & y-3 \end{bmatrix} + \begin{bmatrix} 3 & 4 \\ 1 & 2 \end{bmatrix} = \begin{bmatrix} 7 & 14 \\ 15 & 14 \end{bmatrix}$ **[NCERT EXEMPLAR, CBSE 2002, 2012]**

20. If X and Y are 2×2 matrices, then solve the following matrix equations for X and Y.

$2X + 3Y = \begin{bmatrix} 2 & 3 \\ 4 & 0 \end{bmatrix}$, $3X + 2Y = \begin{bmatrix} -2 & 2 \\ 1 & -5 \end{bmatrix}$ **[NCERT EXEMPLAR]**

21. In a certain city there are 30 colleges. Each college has 15 peons, 6 clerks, 1 typist and 1 section officer. Express the given information as a column matrix. Using scalar multiplication, find the total number of posts of each kind in all the colleges.

22. The monthly incomes of Aryan and Babban are in the ratio 3 : 4 and their monthly expenditures are in the ratio 5 : 7. If each saves ₹ 15000 per month, find their monthly incomes using matrix method. This problem reflects which value? [CBSE 2016]

ANSWERS

1. (i) $\begin{bmatrix} 1 & 2 \\ 2 & 7 \end{bmatrix}$ (ii) $\begin{bmatrix} 3 & -1 & 6 \\ 2 & 9 & 6 \\ -1 & -1 & 6 \end{bmatrix}$

2. (i) $\begin{bmatrix} 1 & -1 \\ 12 & -11 \end{bmatrix}$ (ii) $\begin{bmatrix} 9 & -17 \\ -14 & -11 \end{bmatrix}$ (iii) $\begin{bmatrix} 8 & 7 \\ 6 & 2 \end{bmatrix}$ (iv) $\begin{bmatrix} -2 & 21 \\ 22 & 8 \end{bmatrix}$

3. (i) $A + B$ does not exist, $B + C = \begin{bmatrix} -2 & 2 & 5 \\ 5 & 5 & 1 \end{bmatrix}$.

(ii) $2B + 3A$ does not exit, $3C - 4B = \begin{bmatrix} 1 & 6 & 1 \\ -6 & -13 & -4 \end{bmatrix}$ 4. $\begin{bmatrix} 2 & -14 & -3 \\ 27 & 11 & -11 \end{bmatrix}$

5. (i) diag $(0 \quad -7 \quad 17)$ (ii) diag $(-9 \quad 14 \quad -18)$ (iii) diag $(37 \quad -22 \quad -14)$

7. $X = \begin{bmatrix} 4 & 4 \\ 0 & 4 \end{bmatrix}, Y = \begin{bmatrix} 1 & -2 \\ 0 & 5 \end{bmatrix}$ 8. $\begin{bmatrix} -1 & -1 \\ -2 & -1 \end{bmatrix}$

9. $X = \begin{bmatrix} 3 & -2 & 1 \\ -2 & 1 & -1 \end{bmatrix}, Y = \begin{bmatrix} 0 & 2 & 2 \\ 0 & 0 & -3 \end{bmatrix}$ 10. $X = \begin{bmatrix} 2 & 3 & 1 \\ 0 & 1 & 2 \\ 6 & 4 & 0 \end{bmatrix}, Y = \begin{bmatrix} 1 & 2 & 0 \\ -1 & 0 & 2 \\ 5 & 4 & 0 \end{bmatrix}$

11. $\begin{bmatrix} 8 & -3 & 5 \\ -2 & -3 & -6 \end{bmatrix}$ 12. $\begin{bmatrix} -24 & -10 \\ -28 & -38 \end{bmatrix}$ 13. $\begin{bmatrix} 12 & 4/3 \\ 4 & -14/3 \\ 25/3 & 28/3 \end{bmatrix}$

14. $\begin{bmatrix} -3 & 4 & -1 \\ -3 & 0 & -1 \end{bmatrix}$ 15. (i) $x = \frac{3}{2}, y = -\frac{3}{2}$ (ii) $x = 1, y = 3, z = 10$ (iii) $x = 1, y = 2$

16. $x = 2, y = -8$ 17. $\lambda = 2$ 18. (i) $\begin{bmatrix} -1 & -2 \\ -7 & -13 \end{bmatrix}$ (ii) $\begin{bmatrix} -2 & -10/3 \\ 4 & 14/3 \\ -31/3 & -7/3 \end{bmatrix}$

19. (i) $x = 2, y = 4, t = 3, z = 1$ (ii) $x = 2, y = 9$ 20. $X = \begin{bmatrix} -2 & 0 \\ -1 & -3 \end{bmatrix}, Y = \begin{bmatrix} 2 & 1 \\ 2 & 2 \end{bmatrix}$

21. $A = \begin{bmatrix} 15 \\ 6 \\ 1 \\ 1 \end{bmatrix}, 30A = \begin{bmatrix} 450 \\ 180 \\ 30 \\ 30 \end{bmatrix}$ 22. ₹ 90,000, ₹ 120,000

4.7 MULTIPLICATION OF MATRICES

Let us first define the product of a row matrix and a column matrix.

Let $A = [a_1 \; a_2 \ldots a_n]$ be a row matrix and $B = \begin{bmatrix} b_1 \\ b_2 \\ \vdots \\ b_n \end{bmatrix}$ be a column matrix. Then, we define

$$AB = a_1 b_1 + a_2 b_2 + \ldots + a_n b_n .$$

For example, if $A = [1 \ \ -2 \ \ 3 \ \ 4]$ and $B = \begin{bmatrix} 5 \\ -4 \\ 1 \\ -2 \end{bmatrix}$. Then,

$$AB = [1 \ \ -2 \ \ 3 \ \ 4] \begin{bmatrix} 5 \\ -4 \\ 1 \\ -2 \end{bmatrix} = 1 \times 5 + (-2)(-4) + 3 \times 1 + 4 \times (-2) = 5 + 8 + 3 - 8 = 8$$

Using the product of a row matrix and a column matrix, let us now define the multiplication of any two matrices.

DEFINITION *Two matrices A and B are conformable for the product AB if the number of columns in A (pre-multiplier) is same as the number of rows in B (post-multiplier).*

Thus, if $A = [a_{ij}]_{m \times n}$ and $B = [b_{ij}]_{n \times p}$ are two matrices of orders $m \times n$ and $n \times p$ respectively, then their product AB is of orders $m \times p$ and is defined as

$$(AB)_{ij} = (i^{th} \text{ row of } A)(j^{th} \text{ column of } B) \quad \text{for all } i = 1, 2, \ldots, m \text{ and } j = 1, 2, \ldots, p.$$

$$\Rightarrow \quad (AB)_{ij} = [a_{i1} \ a_{i2} \ \ldots \ a_{in}] \begin{bmatrix} b_{1j} \\ b_{2j} \\ \vdots \\ b_{nj} \end{bmatrix}$$

$$\Rightarrow \quad (AB)_{ij} = a_{i1} b_{1j} + a_{i2} b_{2j} + \ldots + a_{ir} b_{rj} + \ldots + a_{in} b_{nj} = \sum_{r=1}^{n} a_{ir} b_{rj}$$

NOTE *If A and B are two matrices such that AB exists, then BA may or may not exist.*

ILLUSTRATION 1 *If* $A = \begin{bmatrix} 2 & 1 & 3 \\ 3 & -2 & 1 \\ -1 & 0 & 1 \end{bmatrix}$ *and* $B = \begin{bmatrix} 1 & -2 \\ 2 & 1 \\ 4 & -3 \end{bmatrix}$, *then A is a 3×3 matrix and B is a 3×2 matrix. Therefore, A and B are conformable for the product AB and it is of order 3×2 such that*

$$(AB)_{11} = (\text{First row of } A)(\text{First column of } B) = [2 \ 1 \ 3] \begin{bmatrix} 1 \\ 2 \\ 4 \end{bmatrix} = 2 \times 1 + 1 \times 2 + 3 \times 4 = 16$$

$$(AB)_{12} = (\text{First row of } A)(\text{Second column of } B) = [2 \ 1 \ 3] \begin{bmatrix} -2 \\ 1 \\ -3 \end{bmatrix} = 2 \times -2 + 1 \times 1 + 3 \times -3 = -12$$

$$(AB)_{21} = (\text{Second row of } A)(\text{First column of } B) = [3 \ -2 \ 1] \begin{bmatrix} 1 \\ 2 \\ 4 \end{bmatrix} = 3 \times 1 + (-2) \times 2 + 1 \times 4 = 3$$

Similarly, we obtain: $(AB)_{22} = -11$, $(AB)_{31} = 3$ and $(AB)_{32} = -1$.

$$\therefore \quad AB = \begin{bmatrix} 16 & -12 \\ 3 & -11 \\ 3 & -1 \end{bmatrix}$$

NOTE *In this case BA does not exist, because the number of columns in B is not same as the number of rows in A.*

ILLUSTRATION 2 *Let* $A = \begin{bmatrix} 1 & -2 & 3 \\ 3 & 2 & -1 \end{bmatrix}$ *and* $B = \begin{bmatrix} 2 & 3 \\ -1 & 2 \\ 4 & -5 \end{bmatrix}$. *Find AB and BA and show that* $AB \neq BA$.

SOLUTION Here, A is a 2×3 matrix and B is a 3×2 matrix. So, AB exists and it is of order 2×2.

$$\therefore \quad AB = \begin{bmatrix} 1 & -2 & 3 \\ 3 & 2 & -1 \end{bmatrix} \begin{bmatrix} 2 & 3 \\ -1 & 2 \\ 4 & -5 \end{bmatrix} = \begin{bmatrix} 2+2+12 & 3-4-15 \\ 6-2-4 & 9+4+5 \end{bmatrix} = \begin{bmatrix} 16 & -16 \\ 0 & 18 \end{bmatrix}$$

Again, B is a 3×2 matrix and A is a 2×3 matrix. So, BA exists and it is or order 3×3.

$$\therefore \quad BA = \begin{bmatrix} 2 & 3 \\ -1 & 2 \\ 4 & -5 \end{bmatrix} \begin{bmatrix} 1 & -2 & 3 \\ 3 & 2 & -1 \end{bmatrix} = \begin{bmatrix} 2+9 & -4+6 & 6-3 \\ -1+6 & 2+4 & -3-2 \\ 4-15 & -8-10 & 12+5 \end{bmatrix} = \begin{bmatrix} 11 & 2 & 3 \\ 5 & 6 & -5 \\ -11 & -18 & 17 \end{bmatrix}$$

Clearly, $AB \neq BA$.

4.7.1 PROPERTIES OF MATRIX MULTIPLICATION

THEOREM 1 *Matrix multiplication is not commutative in general.*

PROOF Let A and B be two matrices such that AB exists. Then it is quite possible that BA may not exist. For example, if A is a 3×3 matrix and B is a 3×2 matrix, then AB exists but BA does not exist. Similarly, if BA exists, then AB may not exist. Further, if AB and BA both exist, then they may not be equal as shown in illustration 2 (given above). Hence, in general, $AB \neq BA$.

Q.E.D.

THEOREM 2 *Matrix multiplication is associative i.e.* $(AB)C = A(BC)$, *whenever both sides are defined.*

PROOF Let $A = [a_{ij}]_{m \times n}$, $B = [b_{ij}]_{n \times p}$ and $C = [c_{ij}]_{p \times q}$. Then AB is an $m \times p$ matrix and so $(AB)C$ is a $m \times q$ matrix. Clearly, BC is of order $n \times q$ and so $A(BC)$ is of order $m \times q$. Thus, $(AB)C$ and $A(BC)$ are of the same order.

$$\text{Now,} \quad ((AB)C)_{ij} = \sum_{r=1}^{p} (AB)_{ir} (C)_{rj}$$

$$= \sum_{r=1}^{p} \left(\sum_{s=1}^{n} a_{is} b_{sr} \right) c_{rj} = \sum_{r=1}^{p} \sum_{s=1}^{n} (a_{is} b_{sr}) c_{rj}$$

$$= \sum_{r=1}^{p} \sum_{s=1}^{n} a_{is} (b_{sr} c_{rj}) \qquad \text{[By associativity of multiplication of numbers]}$$

$$= \sum_{s=1}^{n} a_{is} \left(\sum_{r=1}^{p} (b_{sr} c_{rj}) \right) = \sum_{s=1}^{n} a_{is} (BC)_{sj} = (A(BC))_{ij} \quad \text{for all } i, j$$

Thus, $(AB)C$ and $A(BC)$ are matrices of the same order such that their corresponding elements are equal. Hence, $(AB)C = A(BC)$.

Q.E.D.

THEOREM 3 *Matrix multiplication is distributive over matrix addition.*
i.e. (i) $A(B+C) = AB + AC$ (ii) $(A+B)C = AC + BC$
whenever both sides of equality are defined.

PROOF Let $A = [a_{ij}]_{m \times n}$, $B = [b_{ij}]_{n \times p}$ and $C = [c_{ij}]_{n \times p}$ be three matrices. Then, $B + C$ is of order $n \times p$ and so $A(B+C)$ is of order $m \times p$. Since AB and AC both are of the same order $m \times p$. Therefore, $AB + AC$ is of order $m \times p$. Thus, $A(B+C)$ and $AB + AC$ are of the same order $m \times p$ such that

$$(A(B+C))_{ij} = \sum_{r=1}^{n} a_{ir}(B+C)_{rj} = \sum_{r=1}^{n} a_{ir}(b_{rj}+c_{rj}) = \sum_{r=1}^{n} a_{ir} b_{rj} + \sum_{r=1}^{n} a_{ir} c_{rj}$$

$$= (AB)_{ij} + (AC)_{ij} = (AB+AC)_{ij} \quad \text{for all } i, j$$

Thus, $A(B+C)$ and $AB+AC$ are two matrices of the same order such that their corresponding elements are equal. Hence, $A(B+C) = AB+AC$.

Similarly, $(A+B)C = AC+BC$.

Q.E.D.

THEOREM 4 *If A is an $m \times n$ matrix, then $I_m A = A = A I_n$.*

PROOF Let $A = [a_{ij}]_{m \times n}$. Then, $I_m A$ and AI_n are of the same order $m \times n$ such that

$$(I_m A)_{ij} = \sum_{r=1}^{m} (I_m)_{ir} (A)_{rj} = \sum_{r=1}^{m} (I_m)_{ir} a_{rj} = (I_m)_{i1} a_{1j} + (I_m)_{i2} a_{2j} + \ldots + (I_m)_{ii} a_{ij} + \ldots + (I_m)_{im} a_{mj}$$

$$= a_{ij} \text{ for all } i, j \qquad \left[\because (I_m)_{ir} = \begin{cases} 0 & \text{for } r \neq i \\ 1 & \text{for } r = i \end{cases}\right]$$

$\therefore \quad I_m A = A.$

Now, $$(A I_n)_{ij} = \sum_{r=1}^{n} (A)_{ir} (I_n)_{rj} = \sum_{r=1}^{n} a_{ir} (I_n)_{rj} = a_{i1}(I_n)_{1j} + a_{i2}(I_n)_{2j} + \ldots + a_{ij}(I_n)_{jj} + \ldots + a_{in}(I_n)_{nj}$$

$$= a_{ij} \text{ for all } i, j \qquad [\because (I_n)_{jj} = 1 \text{ and } (I_n)_{rj} = 0 \text{ for } r \neq j]$$

Thus, AI_n and A are matrices of the same order such that their corresponding elements are equal. So, $AI_n = A$. Hence, $I_m A = A = AI_n$. Q.E.D.

REMARK 1 *The product of two matrices can be the null matrix while neither of them is the null matrix.*

For example, if $A = \begin{bmatrix} 0 & 2 \\ 0 & 0 \end{bmatrix}$ *and* $B = \begin{bmatrix} 1 & 0 \\ 0 & 0 \end{bmatrix}$, *then* $AB = \begin{bmatrix} 0 & 0 \\ 0 & 0 \end{bmatrix}$ *while neither A nor B is the null matrix.*

THEOREM 5 *If A is $m \times n$ matrix and O is a null matrix, then*

(i) $A_{m \times n} O_{n \times p} = O_{m \times p}$ (ii) $O_{p \times m} A_{m \times n} = O_{p \times n}$

i.e. the product of the matrix with a null matrix is always a null matrix.

PROOF (i) Let $A = [a_{ij}]_{m \times n}$ and $O_{n \times p} = [b_{ij}]_{n \times p}$, where $b_{ij} = 0$ for all i, j. Then, $A_{m \times n} O_{n \times p}$ is an $m \times p$ matrix such that

$$(A_{m \times n} O_{n \times p})_{ij} = \sum_{r=1}^{n} a_{ir} b_{rj} = 0 \quad \text{for all } i, j \qquad [b_{ij} = 0 \text{ for all } i, j]$$

Thus, $A_{m \times n} O_{n \times p}$ and $O_{m \times p}$ are two matrices of the same order such that their corresponding elements are equal. Hence, $A_{m \times n} \cdot O_{n \times p} = O_{n \times p}$.

(ii) Proceed as in (i). Q.E.D.

REMARK 2 *In the case of matrix multiplication if $AB = O$, then it does not necessarily imply that $BA = O$.*

For example, if $A = \begin{bmatrix} 0 & 1 \\ 0 & 0 \end{bmatrix}$ *and* $B = \begin{bmatrix} 1 & 0 \\ 0 & 0 \end{bmatrix}$. *Then,* $AB = O$. *But,* $BA = \begin{bmatrix} 1 & 0 \\ 0 & 0 \end{bmatrix}\begin{bmatrix} 0 & 1 \\ 0 & 0 \end{bmatrix} = \begin{bmatrix} 0 & 1 \\ 0 & 0 \end{bmatrix} \neq O.$

Thus, $AB = O$ *while* $BA \neq O$.

4.7.2 POSITIVE INTEGRAL POWERS OF A SQUARE MATRIX

For any square matrix, we define

(i) $A^1 = A$ *and,* (ii) $A^{n+1} = A^n \cdot A$, where $n \in N$.

It is evident from this definition that $A^2 = AA$, $A^3 = A^2 A = (AA)A$. etc.

It can be easily shown that

(i) $A^m A^n = A^{m+n}$ and, (ii) $(A^m)^n = A^{mn}$ for all $m, n \in N$.

MATRIX POLYNOMIAL *Let $f(x) = a_0 x^n + a_1 x^{n-1} + a_2 x^{n-2} + \ldots + a_{n-1} x + a_n$ be a polynomial and let A be a square matrix of order n. Then,*

$$f(A) = a_0 A^n + a_1 A^{n-1} + a_2 A^{n-2} + .. + a_{n-1} A + a_n I_n$$

is called a matrix polynomial.

For example, if $f(x) = x^2 - 3x + 2$ is a polynomial and A is a square matrix, then $f(A) = A^2 - 3A + 2I$ is a matrix polynomial.

ILLUSTRATIVE EXAMPLES

BASED ON BASIC CONCEPTS (BASIC)

Type I ON MULTIPLICATION OF MATRICES

EXAMPLE 1 *If A, B, C are three matrices such that* $A = [x\ y\ z]$, $B = \begin{bmatrix} a & h & g \\ h & b & f \\ g & f & c \end{bmatrix}$, $C = \begin{bmatrix} x \\ y \\ z \end{bmatrix}$, *find ABC.*

SOLUTION Since the product of matrices is associative. Therefore, we can find ABC either by computing $(AB)C$ or by computing $A(BC)$. Let us compute $A(BC)$.

Since B is a 3×3 matrix and C is 3×1 matrix. Therefore, BC is of order 3×1 and is given by

$$BC = \begin{bmatrix} a & h & g \\ h & b & f \\ g & f & c \end{bmatrix} \begin{bmatrix} x \\ y \\ z \end{bmatrix} = \begin{bmatrix} ax + hy + gz \\ hx + by + fz \\ gx + fy + cz \end{bmatrix}$$

Clearly, A is of order 1×3 and BC is of order 3×1. Therefore, $A(BC)$ is of order 1×1 and is given by

$$A(BC) = [x\ y\ z] \begin{bmatrix} ax + hy + gz \\ hx + by + fz \\ gx + fy + cz \end{bmatrix} = x(ax + hy + gz) + y(hx + by + fz) + z(gx + fy + cz)$$

$$= ax^2 + 2hxy + by^2 + cz^2 + 2fyz + 2gzx$$

EXAMPLE 2 *If* $A = \begin{bmatrix} 1 & -1 \\ 2 & 3 \end{bmatrix}$, $B = \begin{bmatrix} 2 & 1 \\ 1 & 0 \end{bmatrix}$, *prove that* $(A + B)^2 \neq A^2 + 2AB + B^2$.

SOLUTION We have,

$$A = \begin{bmatrix} 1 & -1 \\ 2 & 3 \end{bmatrix} \text{ and } B = \begin{bmatrix} 2 & 1 \\ 1 & 0 \end{bmatrix}$$

$$\therefore \quad A^2 = AA = \begin{bmatrix} 1 & -1 \\ 2 & 3 \end{bmatrix} \begin{bmatrix} 1 & -1 \\ 2 & 3 \end{bmatrix} = \begin{bmatrix} -1 & -4 \\ 8 & 7 \end{bmatrix},$$

$$AB = \begin{bmatrix} 1 & -1 \\ 2 & 3 \end{bmatrix} \begin{bmatrix} 2 & 1 \\ 1 & 0 \end{bmatrix} = \begin{bmatrix} 1 & 1 \\ 7 & 2 \end{bmatrix} \Rightarrow 2AB = \begin{bmatrix} 2 & 2 \\ 14 & 4 \end{bmatrix}$$

$$\text{and,} \quad B^2 = BB = \begin{bmatrix} 2 & 1 \\ 1 & 0 \end{bmatrix} \begin{bmatrix} 2 & 1 \\ 1 & 0 \end{bmatrix} = \begin{bmatrix} 5 & 2 \\ 2 & 1 \end{bmatrix}$$

$$\therefore \quad A^2 + 2AB + B^2 = \begin{bmatrix} -1 & -4 \\ 8 & 7 \end{bmatrix} + \begin{bmatrix} 2 & 2 \\ 14 & 4 \end{bmatrix} + \begin{bmatrix} 5 & 2 \\ 2 & 1 \end{bmatrix} = \begin{bmatrix} 6 & 0 \\ 24 & 12 \end{bmatrix} \quad \text{...(i)}$$

$$\text{Now,} \quad A + B = \begin{bmatrix} 1 & -1 \\ 2 & 3 \end{bmatrix} + \begin{bmatrix} 2 & 1 \\ 1 & 0 \end{bmatrix} = \begin{bmatrix} 3 & 0 \\ 3 & 3 \end{bmatrix}$$

$$\Rightarrow \quad (A+B)^2 = (A+B)(A+B) = \begin{bmatrix} 3 & 0 \\ 3 & 3 \end{bmatrix}\begin{bmatrix} 3 & 0 \\ 3 & 3 \end{bmatrix} = \begin{bmatrix} 9 & 0 \\ 18 & 9 \end{bmatrix} \qquad ...(ii)$$

From (i) and (ii), we obtain that $(A+B)^2 \neq A^2 + 2AB + B^2$.

EXAMPLE 3 *If* $A = \begin{bmatrix} 1 & -1 \\ 2 & -1 \end{bmatrix}$, $B = \begin{bmatrix} a & 1 \\ b & -1 \end{bmatrix}$ *and* $(A+B)^2 = A^2 + B^2$, *find a and b.*

SOLUTION We have, [CBSE 2015]

$$(A+B)^2 = A^2 + B^2$$

$$\Rightarrow \quad (A+B)(A+B) = A^2 + B^2$$

$$\Rightarrow \quad (A+B)A + (A+B)B = A^2 + B^2 \qquad \text{[By distributive law]}$$

$$\Rightarrow \quad A^2 + BA + AB + B^2 = A^2 + B^2 \qquad \text{[By distributive law]}$$

$$\Rightarrow \quad BA + AB = O$$

$$\Rightarrow \quad \begin{bmatrix} a & 1 \\ b & -1 \end{bmatrix}\begin{bmatrix} 1 & -1 \\ 2 & -1 \end{bmatrix} + \begin{bmatrix} 1 & -1 \\ 2 & -1 \end{bmatrix}\begin{bmatrix} a & 1 \\ b & -1 \end{bmatrix} = \begin{bmatrix} 0 & 0 \\ 0 & 0 \end{bmatrix}$$

$$\Rightarrow \quad \begin{bmatrix} a+2 & -a-1 \\ b-2 & -b+1 \end{bmatrix} + \begin{bmatrix} a-b & 2 \\ 2a-b & 3 \end{bmatrix} = \begin{bmatrix} 0 & 0 \\ 0 & 0 \end{bmatrix}$$

$$\Rightarrow \quad \begin{bmatrix} 2a-b+2 & -a+1 \\ 2a-2 & -b+4 \end{bmatrix} = \begin{bmatrix} 0 & 0 \\ 0 & 0 \end{bmatrix}$$

$$\Rightarrow \quad 2a-b+2=0,\ -a+1=0,\ 2a-2=0 \text{ and } -b+4=0 \Rightarrow a=1, b=4$$

EXAMPLE 4 *If* $A = \begin{bmatrix} 0 & 1 \\ -1 & 0 \end{bmatrix}$, *find x and y such that* $(xI + yA)^2 = A$.

SOLUTION We have, $A = \begin{bmatrix} 0 & 1 \\ -1 & 0 \end{bmatrix}$

$$\therefore \quad xI + yA = x\begin{bmatrix} 1 & 0 \\ 0 & 1 \end{bmatrix} + y\begin{bmatrix} 0 & 1 \\ -1 & 0 \end{bmatrix} = \begin{bmatrix} x & 0 \\ 0 & x \end{bmatrix} + \begin{bmatrix} 0 & y \\ -y & 0 \end{bmatrix} = \begin{bmatrix} x & y \\ -y & x \end{bmatrix}$$

Given that $(xI + yA)^2 = A$

$$\Rightarrow \quad \begin{bmatrix} x & y \\ -y & x \end{bmatrix}\begin{bmatrix} x & y \\ -y & x \end{bmatrix} = \begin{bmatrix} 0 & 1 \\ -1 & 0 \end{bmatrix}$$

$$\Rightarrow \quad \begin{bmatrix} x^2-y^2 & 2xy \\ -2xy & x^2-y^2 \end{bmatrix} = \begin{bmatrix} 0 & 1 \\ -1 & 0 \end{bmatrix}$$

$$\Rightarrow \quad x^2-y^2 = 0,\ 2xy = 1,\ -2xy = -1 \text{ and } x^2-y^2 = 0$$

$$\Rightarrow \quad x^2-y^2 = 0 \text{ and } 2xy = 1 \Rightarrow x = \pm y \text{ and } 2xy = 1$$

Now two cases arise.

Case I *When* $x = y$ *and* $2xy = 1$: In this case, we have $x = y$ and $2xy = 1 \Rightarrow 2x^2 = 1 \Rightarrow x = \pm\frac{1}{\sqrt{2}}$.

$$\therefore \quad \left(x = \frac{1}{\sqrt{2}} \text{ and } y = \frac{1}{\sqrt{2}}\right) \text{ or, } \left(x = -\frac{1}{\sqrt{2}} \text{ and } y = -\frac{1}{\sqrt{2}}\right)$$

Case II *When* $x = -y$ *and* $2xy = 1$: In this case, we have $x = -y$ and $2xy = 1 \Rightarrow -2x^2 = 1 \Rightarrow x = \pm\frac{i}{\sqrt{2}}$.

$$\therefore \quad \left(x = \frac{i}{\sqrt{2}} \text{ and } y = -\frac{i}{\sqrt{2}}\right) \text{ or, } \left(x = -\frac{i}{\sqrt{2}} \text{ and } y = \frac{i}{\sqrt{2}}\right)$$

EXAMPLE 5 *If* $A = \begin{bmatrix} \alpha & 0 \\ 1 & 1 \end{bmatrix}$ *and* $B = \begin{bmatrix} 1 & 0 \\ 5 & 1 \end{bmatrix}$, *find the values of* α *for which* $A^2 = B$.

SOLUTION Given that

$$A^2 = B$$

$$\Rightarrow \begin{bmatrix} \alpha & 0 \\ 1 & 1 \end{bmatrix}\begin{bmatrix} \alpha & 0 \\ 1 & 1 \end{bmatrix} = \begin{bmatrix} 1 & 0 \\ 5 & 1 \end{bmatrix} \Rightarrow \begin{bmatrix} \alpha^2 + 0 & 0 + 0 \\ \alpha + 1 & 0 + 1 \end{bmatrix} = \begin{bmatrix} 1 & 0 \\ 5 & 1 \end{bmatrix} \Rightarrow \begin{bmatrix} \alpha^2 & 0 \\ \alpha + 1 & 1 \end{bmatrix} = \begin{bmatrix} 1 & 0 \\ 5 & 1 \end{bmatrix}$$

$\Rightarrow \quad \alpha^2 = 1$ and $\alpha + 1 = 5 \Rightarrow \alpha = \pm 1$ and $\alpha = 4$, which is not possible.

Hence, there is no value of α for which $A^2 = B$ is true.

EXAMPLE 6 *Let* $A = \begin{bmatrix} 2 & -1 \\ 3 & 4 \end{bmatrix}$, $B = \begin{bmatrix} 5 & 2 \\ 7 & 4 \end{bmatrix}$, $C = \begin{bmatrix} 2 & 5 \\ 3 & 8 \end{bmatrix}$. *Find a matrix D such that* $CD - AB = O$.

[NCERT, CBSE 201?]

SOLUTION Let $D = \begin{bmatrix} a & b \\ x & y \end{bmatrix}$. Then,

$$CD - AB = O$$

$$\Rightarrow \quad CD = AB$$

$$\Rightarrow \begin{bmatrix} 2 & 5 \\ 3 & 8 \end{bmatrix}\begin{bmatrix} a & b \\ x & y \end{bmatrix} = \begin{bmatrix} 2 & -1 \\ 3 & 4 \end{bmatrix}\begin{bmatrix} 5 & 2 \\ 7 & 4 \end{bmatrix}$$

$$\Rightarrow \begin{bmatrix} 2a + 5x & 2b + 5y \\ 3a + 8x & 3b + 8y \end{bmatrix} = \begin{bmatrix} 10 - 7 & 4 - 4 \\ 15 + 28 & 6 + 16 \end{bmatrix} \Rightarrow \begin{bmatrix} 2a + 5x & 2b + 5y \\ 3a + 8x & 3b + 8y \end{bmatrix} = \begin{bmatrix} 3 & 0 \\ 43 & 22 \end{bmatrix}$$

$\Rightarrow \quad 2a + 5x = 3,\ 3a + 8x = 43,\ 2b + 5y = 0$ and $3b + 8y = 22$

Solving $2a + 5x = 3$ and $3a + 8x = 43$, we get: $a = -191$ and $x = 77$.

Solving $2b + 5y = 0$ and $3b + 8y = 22$, we get: $b = -110$ and $y = 44$.

$$\therefore \quad D = \begin{bmatrix} a & b \\ x & y \end{bmatrix} = \begin{bmatrix} -191 & -110 \\ 77 & 44 \end{bmatrix}$$

EXAMPLE 7 *Find the value of x such that* $[1\ \ x\ \ 1]\begin{bmatrix} 1 & 3 & 2 \\ 2 & 5 & 1 \\ 15 & 3 & 2 \end{bmatrix}\begin{bmatrix} 1 \\ 2 \\ x \end{bmatrix} = 0$.

SOLUTION We have, **[CBSE 2006, NCERT EXEMPLAR]**

$$[1\ \ x\ \ 1]\begin{bmatrix} 1 & 3 & 2 \\ 2 & 5 & 1 \\ 15 & 3 & 2 \end{bmatrix}\begin{bmatrix} 1 \\ 2 \\ x \end{bmatrix} = 0 \Rightarrow [1\ \ x\ \ 1]\begin{bmatrix} 7 + 2x \\ 12 + x \\ 21 + 2x \end{bmatrix} = 0$$

$\Rightarrow 7 + 2x + 12x + x^2 + 21 + 2x = 0 \Rightarrow x^2 + 16x + 28 = 0 \Rightarrow (x + 14)(x + 2) = 0 \Rightarrow x = -2$ or -14.

EXAMPLE 8 *If* $A = \begin{bmatrix} 1 & 0 \\ -1 & 7 \end{bmatrix}$ *and* $I = \begin{bmatrix} 1 & 0 \\ 0 & 1 \end{bmatrix}$, *then find k so that* $A^2 = 8A + kI$.

SOLUTION We have, $A = \begin{bmatrix} 1 & 0 \\ -1 & 7 \end{bmatrix}$ **[CBSE 2005]**

$$\therefore \quad A^2 = AA = \begin{bmatrix} 1 & 0 \\ -1 & 7 \end{bmatrix}\begin{bmatrix} 1 & 0 \\ -1 & 7 \end{bmatrix} = \begin{bmatrix} 1 & 0 \\ -8 & 49 \end{bmatrix}$$

and, $\quad 8A + kI = 8\begin{bmatrix} 1 & 0 \\ -1 & 7 \end{bmatrix} + k\begin{bmatrix} 1 & 0 \\ 0 & 1 \end{bmatrix} = \begin{bmatrix} 8 & 0 \\ -8 & 56 \end{bmatrix} + \begin{bmatrix} k & 0 \\ 0 & k \end{bmatrix} = \begin{bmatrix} 8 + k & 0 \\ -8 & 56 + k \end{bmatrix}$

$$\therefore \quad A^2 = 8A + kI \begin{bmatrix} 1 & 0 \\ -8 & 49 \end{bmatrix} = \begin{bmatrix} 8 + k & 0 \\ -8 & 56 + k \end{bmatrix} \Rightarrow 1 = 8 + k \text{ and } 56 + k = 49 \Rightarrow k = -7.$$

EXAMPLE 9 *If* $\begin{bmatrix} 2 & -1 \\ 1 & 0 \\ -3 & 4 \end{bmatrix} A = \begin{bmatrix} -1 & -8 & -10 \\ 1 & -2 & -5 \\ 9 & 22 & 15 \end{bmatrix}$, *find A.* [NCERT EXEMPLAR]

SOLUTION Since the product matrix is a 3×3 matrix and the premultiplier of A is a 3×2 matrix. Therefore, A is 2×3 matrix. Let $A = \begin{bmatrix} x & y & z \\ a & b & c \end{bmatrix}$. Then, the given equation becomes

$$\begin{bmatrix} 2 & -1 \\ 1 & 0 \\ -3 & 4 \end{bmatrix} \begin{bmatrix} x & y & z \\ a & b & c \end{bmatrix} = \begin{bmatrix} -1 & -8 & -10 \\ 1 & -2 & -5 \\ 9 & 22 & 15 \end{bmatrix}$$

$$\Rightarrow \quad \begin{bmatrix} 2x-a & 2y-b & 2z-c \\ x & y & z \\ -3x+4a & -3y+4b & -3z+4c \end{bmatrix} = \begin{bmatrix} -1 & -8 & -10 \\ 1 & -2 & -5 \\ 9 & 22 & 15 \end{bmatrix}$$

$\Rightarrow \quad 2x - a = -1,\ x = 1,\ -3x + 4a = 9,\ 2y - b = -8,\ y = -2, -3y + 4b = 22,\ 2z - c = -0,$
$z = -5,\ -3z + 4c = 15$

$\Rightarrow \quad x = 1, a = 3, y = -2, b = 4, z = -5$ and $c = 0$

Hence, $A = \begin{bmatrix} 1 & -2 & -5 \\ 3 & 4 & 0 \end{bmatrix}$

Type II ON MATRIX POLYNOMIALS AND MATRIX POLYNOMIAL EQUATIONS

EXAMPLE 10 *Let* $f(x) = x^2 - 5x + 6$. *Find* $f(A)$, *if* $A = \begin{bmatrix} 2 & 0 & 1 \\ 2 & 1 & 3 \\ 1 & -1 & 0 \end{bmatrix}$.

SOLUTION First, we note that by $f(A)$ we mean the matrix polynomial $A^2 - 5A + 6I_3$. That is, to obtain $f(A)$, x is replaced by A and the constant term is multiplied by the identity matrix of order same as that of A.

Now, $A^2 = AA = \begin{bmatrix} 2 & 0 & 1 \\ 2 & 1 & 3 \\ 1 & -1 & 0 \end{bmatrix} \begin{bmatrix} 2 & 0 & 1 \\ 2 & 1 & 3 \\ 1 & -1 & 0 \end{bmatrix} = \begin{bmatrix} 4+0+1 & 0+0-1 & 2+0+0 \\ 4+2+3 & 0+1-3 & 2+3+0 \\ 2-2+0 & 0-1+0 & 1-3+0 \end{bmatrix} = \begin{bmatrix} 5 & -1 & 2 \\ 9 & -2 & 5 \\ 0 & -1 & -2 \end{bmatrix}$

$-5A = \begin{bmatrix} (-5)\times 2 & (-5)\times 0 & (-5)\times 1 \\ (-5)\times 2 & (-5)\times 1 & (-5)\times 3 \\ (-5)\times 1 & (-5)\times(-1) & (-5)\times 0 \end{bmatrix} = \begin{bmatrix} -10 & 0 & -5 \\ -10 & -5 & -15 \\ -5 & 5 & 0 \end{bmatrix}$ and, $6I_3 = 6\begin{bmatrix} 1 & 0 & 0 \\ 0 & 1 & 0 \\ 0 & 0 & 1 \end{bmatrix} = \begin{bmatrix} 6 & 0 & 0 \\ 0 & 6 & 0 \\ 0 & 0 & 6 \end{bmatrix}$

$$\therefore \quad f(A) = A^2 - 5A + 6I_3 = \begin{bmatrix} 5 & -1 & 2 \\ 9 & -2 & 5 \\ 0 & -1 & -2 \end{bmatrix} + \begin{bmatrix} -10 & 0 & -5 \\ -10 & -5 & -15 \\ -5 & 5 & 0 \end{bmatrix} + \begin{bmatrix} 6 & 0 & 0 \\ 0 & 6 & 0 \\ 0 & 0 & 6 \end{bmatrix} = \begin{bmatrix} 1 & -1 & -3 \\ -1 & -1 & -10 \\ -5 & 4 & 4 \end{bmatrix}.$$

EXAMPLE 11 *If* $A = \begin{bmatrix} 3 & 1 \\ -1 & 2 \end{bmatrix}$, *show that* $A^2 - 5A + 7I_2 = O$.

SOLUTION We have, $A = \begin{bmatrix} 3 & 1 \\ -1 & 2 \end{bmatrix}$

$$\therefore \quad A^2 = \begin{bmatrix} 3 & 1 \\ -1 & 2 \end{bmatrix} \begin{bmatrix} 3 & 1 \\ -1 & 2 \end{bmatrix} = \begin{bmatrix} 9-1 & 3+2 \\ -3-2 & -1+4 \end{bmatrix} = \begin{bmatrix} 8 & 5 \\ -5 & 3 \end{bmatrix}$$

$$-5A = \begin{bmatrix} (-5)\times 3 & (-5)\times 1 \\ (-5)\times(-1) & (-5)\times 2 \end{bmatrix} = \begin{bmatrix} -15 & -5 \\ 5 & -10 \end{bmatrix} \text{ and, } 7I_2 = 7\begin{bmatrix} 1 & 0 \\ 0 & 1 \end{bmatrix} = \begin{bmatrix} 7 & 0 \\ 0 & 7 \end{bmatrix}$$

$$\therefore \quad A^2 - 5A + 7I_2 = \begin{bmatrix} 8 & 5 \\ -5 & 3 \end{bmatrix} + \begin{bmatrix} -15 & -5 \\ 5 & -10 \end{bmatrix} + \begin{bmatrix} 7 & 0 \\ 0 & 7 \end{bmatrix} = \begin{bmatrix} 8-15+7 & 5-5+0 \\ -5+5+0 & 3-10+7 \end{bmatrix} = \begin{bmatrix} 0 & 0 \\ 0 & 0 \end{bmatrix}$$

Type III ON PRINCIPLE OF MATHEMATICAL INDUCTION

The Principle of Mathematical Induction:

Let $P(n)$ be a statement involving positive integer n such that

(i) $P(1)$ is true i.e. the statement is true for $n = 1$, and

(ii) $P(m+1)$ is true whenever $P(m)$ is true i.e. the truth of $P(m)$ implies the truth of $P(m+1)$.

Then, $P(n)$ is true for all positive integer n.

EXAMPLE 12 *Prove the following by the principle of mathematical induction:*

If $A = \begin{bmatrix} 3 & -4 \\ 1 & -1 \end{bmatrix}$, *then* $A^n = \begin{bmatrix} 1+2n & -4n \\ n & 1-2n \end{bmatrix}$ *for every positive integer n.* **[NCERT]**

SOLUTION We shall prove the result by mathematical induction on n.

Step 1 When $n = 1$, by the definition of integral powers of a matrix, we have

$$A^1 = A = \begin{bmatrix} 3 & -4 \\ 1 & -1 \end{bmatrix} = \begin{bmatrix} 1+2(1) & -4(1) \\ 1 & 1-2(1) \end{bmatrix}$$

So, the result is true for n = 1.

Step 2 Let the result be true for n = m. Then,

$$A^m = \begin{bmatrix} 1+2m & -4m \\ m & 1-2m \end{bmatrix} \quad \text{...(i)}$$

Now, we will show that the result is true for $n = m+1$ i.e. $A^{m+1} = \begin{bmatrix} 1+2(m+1) & -4(m+1) \\ m+1 & 1-2(m+1) \end{bmatrix}$

By the definition of integral powers of a square matrix, we obtain

$$A^{m+1} = A^m A$$

$$\Rightarrow A^{m+1} = \begin{bmatrix} 1+2m & -4m \\ m & 1-2m \end{bmatrix}\begin{bmatrix} 3 & -4 \\ 1 & -1 \end{bmatrix} \quad \text{[By supposition (i)]}$$

$$\Rightarrow A^{m+1} = \begin{bmatrix} 3+6m-4m & -4-8m+4m \\ 3m+1-2m & -4m-1+2m \end{bmatrix} = \begin{bmatrix} 3+2m & -4-4m \\ m+1 & -1-2m \end{bmatrix} = \begin{bmatrix} 1+2(m+1) & -4(m+1) \\ m+1 & 1-2(m+1) \end{bmatrix}$$

This shows that the result is true for $n = m+1$, whenever it is true for $n = m$.

Hence, by the principle of mathematical induction, the result is valid for any positive integer n.

EXAMPLE 13 *If* $A_\alpha = \begin{bmatrix} \cos\alpha & \sin\alpha \\ -\sin\alpha & \cos\alpha \end{bmatrix}$, *then prove that*

(i) $A_\alpha A_\beta = A_{\alpha+\beta}$ (ii) $(A_\alpha)^n = \begin{bmatrix} \cos n\alpha & \sin n\alpha \\ -\sin n\alpha & \cos n\alpha \end{bmatrix}$ *for every positive integer n.*

[NCERT, CBSE 2004]

SOLUTION (i) We find that

$$A_\alpha A_\beta = \begin{bmatrix} \cos\alpha & \sin\alpha \\ -\sin\alpha & \cos\alpha \end{bmatrix}\begin{bmatrix} \cos\beta & \sin\beta \\ -\sin\beta & \cos\beta \end{bmatrix}$$

$$= \begin{bmatrix} \cos\alpha\cos\beta - \sin\alpha\sin\beta & \sin\alpha\cos\beta + \cos\alpha\sin\beta \\ -\sin\alpha\cos\beta - \cos\alpha\sin\beta & \cos\alpha\cos\beta - \sin\alpha\sin\beta \end{bmatrix} = \begin{bmatrix} \cos(\alpha+\beta) & \sin(\alpha+\beta) \\ -\sin(\alpha+\beta) & \cos(\alpha+\beta) \end{bmatrix}$$

$$= A_{\alpha+\beta}.$$

(ii) We shall prove the result by mathematical induction on n.

Step 1 When $n = 1$, by the definition of integral powers of a matrix, we obtain

$$(A_\alpha)^1 = A_\alpha = \begin{bmatrix} \cos\alpha & \sin\alpha \\ -\sin\alpha & \cos\alpha \end{bmatrix} = \begin{bmatrix} \cos(1.\alpha) & \sin(1.\alpha) \\ -\sin(1.\alpha) & \cos(1.\alpha) \end{bmatrix}$$

So, the result is true for $n = 1$.

Step 2 Let the result be true for $n = m$. Then,

$$(A_\alpha)^m = \begin{bmatrix} \cos m\alpha & \sin m\alpha \\ -\sin m\alpha & \cos m\alpha \end{bmatrix} \quad \text{...(i)}$$

Now, we will show that the result is true for $n = m + 1$ i.e. $(A_\alpha)^{m+1} = \begin{bmatrix} \cos(m+1)\alpha & \sin(m+1)\alpha \\ -\sin(m+1)\alpha & \cos(m+1)\alpha \end{bmatrix}$

By the definition of integral powers of a square matrix, we have

$$(A_\alpha)^{m+1} = (A_\alpha)^m A_\alpha$$

$$\Rightarrow \quad (A_\alpha)^{m+1} = \begin{bmatrix} \cos m\alpha & \sin m\alpha \\ -\sin m\alpha & \cos m\alpha \end{bmatrix}\begin{bmatrix} \cos\alpha & \sin\alpha \\ -\sin\alpha & \cos\alpha \end{bmatrix} \quad \text{[By assumption (i)]}$$

$$\Rightarrow \quad (A_\alpha)^{m+1} = \begin{bmatrix} \cos m\alpha\cos\alpha - \sin m\alpha\sin\alpha & \cos m\alpha\sin\alpha + \sin m\alpha\cos\alpha \\ -\sin m\alpha\cos\alpha - \cos m\alpha\sin\alpha & -\sin m\alpha\sin\alpha + \cos m\alpha\cos\alpha \end{bmatrix}$$

$$\Rightarrow \quad (A_\alpha)^{m+1} = \begin{bmatrix} \cos(m\alpha+\alpha) & \sin(m\alpha+\alpha) \\ -\sin(m\alpha+\alpha) & \cos(m\alpha+\alpha) \end{bmatrix} = \begin{bmatrix} \cos(m+1)\alpha & \sin(m+1)\alpha \\ -\sin(m+1)\alpha & \cos(m+1)\alpha \end{bmatrix}$$

This shows that the result is true for $n = m + 1$, whenever it is true for $n = m$.

Hence, by the principle of mathematical induction, the result is valid for any positive integer n.

EXAMPLE 14 *If a is a non-zero real or complex number. Use the principle of mathematical induction to prove that:*

If $A = \begin{bmatrix} a & 1 \\ 0 & a \end{bmatrix}$, *then* $A^n = \begin{bmatrix} a^n & na^{n-1} \\ 0 & a^n \end{bmatrix}$ *for every positive integer n.*

SOLUTION We have, $A = \begin{bmatrix} a & 1 \\ 0 & a \end{bmatrix}$

Step 1 When $n = 1$, by the definition of integral powers of a matrix, we have

$A^1 = A = \begin{bmatrix} a & 1 \\ 0 & a \end{bmatrix} = \begin{bmatrix} a^1 & 1\,(a^{1-1}) \\ 0 & a^1 \end{bmatrix}$. So, the result is true for $n = 1$.

Step 2 Let the result be true for $n = m$. Then, $A^m = \begin{bmatrix} a^m & ma^{m-1} \\ 0 & a^m \end{bmatrix}$. ...(i)

Now we will show that the result is true for $n = m + 1$. i.e. $A^{m+1} = \begin{bmatrix} a^{m+1} & (m+1)\,a^m \\ 0 & a^{m+1} \end{bmatrix}$.

By using the definition of integral powers of a square matrix, we obtain

$$A^{m+1} = A^m A = \begin{bmatrix} a^m & ma^{m-1} \\ 0 & a^m \end{bmatrix}\begin{bmatrix} a & 1 \\ 0 & a \end{bmatrix} = \begin{bmatrix} a^m \times a + 0 \times ma^{m-1} & a^m \times 1 + ma^{m-1} \times a^1 \\ a \times 0 + 0 \times a^m & 0 \times 1 + a^m \times a \end{bmatrix}$$

$$\Rightarrow \quad A^{m+1} = \begin{bmatrix} a^{m+1} & a^m + ma^m \\ 0 & a^{m+1} \end{bmatrix} = \begin{bmatrix} a^{m+1} & (m+1)\,a^m \\ 0 & a^{m+1} \end{bmatrix}$$

This shows that the result is true for $n = m + 1$, whenever it is true for $n = m$.

Hence, by the principle of mathematical induction, the result is true for any positive integer n.

EXAMPLE 15 *If* $A = \begin{bmatrix} 1 & 1 & 1 \\ 1 & 1 & 1 \\ 1 & 1 & 1 \end{bmatrix}$, *then prove that* $A^n = \begin{bmatrix} 3^{n-1} & 3^{n-1} & 3^{n-1} \\ 3^{n-1} & 3^{n-1} & 3^{n-1} \\ 3^{n-1} & 3^{n-1} & 3^{n-1} \end{bmatrix}$ *for every positive integer n.* **[NCERT]**

SOLUTION We shall prove the result by the principle of mathematical induction on n.

Step 1 When $n = 1$, by the definition of integral powers of a matrix, we obtain

$$A^1 = A = \begin{bmatrix} 1 & 1 & 1 \\ 1 & 1 & 1 \\ 1 & 1 & 1 \end{bmatrix} = \begin{bmatrix} 3^{1-1} & 3^{1-1} & 3^{1-1} \\ 3^{1-1} & 3^{1-1} & 3^{1-1} \\ 3^{1-1} & 3^{1-1} & 3^{1-1} \end{bmatrix}.$$ So, the result is true for $n = 1$.

Step 2 Let the result be true for $n = m$. Then, $A^m = \begin{bmatrix} 3^{m-1} & 3^{m-1} & 3^{m-1} \\ 3^{m-1} & 3^{m-1} & 3^{m-1} \\ 3^{m-1} & 3^{m-1} & 3^{m-1} \end{bmatrix}$ ...(i)

Now we shall show that the result is true for $n = m + 1$ i.e. $A^{m+1} = \begin{bmatrix} 3^m & 3^m & 3^m \\ 3^m & 3^m & 3^m \\ 3^m & 3^m & 3^m \end{bmatrix}$.

By using the definition of integral powers of a matrix, we obtain

$$A^{m+1} = A^m A$$

$$\Rightarrow \quad A^{m+1} = \begin{bmatrix} 3^{m-1} & 3^{m-1} & 3^{m-1} \\ 3^{m-1} & 3^{m-1} & 3^{m-1} \\ 3^{m-1} & 3^{m-1} & 3^{m-1} \end{bmatrix} \begin{bmatrix} 1 & 1 & 1 \\ 1 & 1 & 1 \\ 1 & 1 & 1 \end{bmatrix} \quad \text{[Using (i)]}$$

$$\Rightarrow \quad A^{m+1} = \begin{bmatrix} 3^{m-1} + 3^{m-1} + 3^{m-1} & 3^{m-1} + 3^{m-1} + 3^{m-1} & 3^{m-1} + 3^{m-1} + 3^{m-1} \\ 3^{m-1} + 3^{m-1} + 3^{m-1} & 3^{m-1} + 3^{m-1} + 3^{m-1} & 3^{m-1} + 3^{m-1} + 3^{m-1} \\ 3^{m-1} + 3^{m-1} + 3^{m-1} & 3^{m-1} + 3^{m-1} + 3^{m-1} & 3^{m-1} + 3^{m-1} + 3^{m-1} \end{bmatrix}$$

$$\Rightarrow \quad A^{m+1} = \begin{bmatrix} 3 \times 3^{m-1} & 3 \times 3^{m-1} & 3 \times 3^{m-1} \\ 3 \times 3^{m-1} & 3 \times 3^{m-1} & 3 \times 3^{m-1} \\ 3 \times 3^{m-1} & 3 \times 3^{m-1} & 3 \times 3^{m-1} \end{bmatrix} = \begin{bmatrix} 3^m & 3^m & 3^m \\ 3^m & 3^m & 3^m \\ 3^m & 3^m & 3^m \end{bmatrix}$$

This shows that the result is true for $n = m + 1$, whenever it is true for $n = m$.

Hence, by the principle of mathematical induction, the result is valid for any positive integer n.

Type IV MISCELLANEOUS PROBLEMS

EXAMPLE 16 *Under what conditions is the matrix equation* $A^2 - B^2 = (A - B)(A + B)$ *is true?*

SOLUTION We have,

$$A^2 - B^2 = (A - B)(A + B)$$

$$\Leftrightarrow \quad A^2 - B^2 = (A - B) A + (A - B) B \quad \left[\begin{array}{l}\text{By disributivity of matrix muliplication} \\ \text{over matrix addition}\end{array}\right]$$

$\Leftrightarrow \quad A^2 - B^2 = A^2 - BA + AB - B^2$ [By disributivity of matrix muliplication over matrix addition]

$\Leftrightarrow \quad O = A^2 - BA + AB - B^2 - A^2 + B^2 \Leftrightarrow O = -\ BA + AB \Leftrightarrow AB = BA$

Thus the given matrix equation is true if the matrices A and B commute with each other.

EXAMPLE 17 *If A is any $m \times n$ matrix such that AB and BA are both defined show that B is an $n \times m$ matrix.*

SOLUTION Since A is an $m \times n$ matrix such that AB exists. Therefore, the number of rows in B should be equal to the number of columns in A. Thus, B has n rows. Further, BA exists, therefore the number of columns in B should be equal to the number of rows in A. So B has m columns.Hence, B is an $n \times m$ matrix.

EXAMPLE 18 *A, B are two matrices such that AB and $A + B$ are both defined; show that A, B are square matrices of the same order.*

SOLUTION Let A be an $m \times n$ matrix. Since $A + B$ is defined, therefore B is also an $m \times n$ matrix. Further since AB exists, therefore the number of columns in A is same as the number of rows in B i.e. $n = m$. Hence, A and B are square matrices of the same order.

EXAMPLE 19 *If A and B are square matrices of order n, then prove that A and B will commute iff $A - \lambda I$ and $B - \lambda I$ commute for every scalar λ.*

SOLUTION $A - \lambda I$ and $B - \lambda I$ commute

$\Leftrightarrow \quad (A - \lambda I)(B - \lambda I) = (B - \lambda I)(A - \lambda I)$

$\Leftrightarrow \quad AB - \lambda IA - \lambda IB + \lambda^2 I^2 = BA - \lambda BI - \lambda IA + \lambda^2 I^2$

$\Leftrightarrow \quad AB - \lambda A - \lambda B + \lambda^2 I = BA - \lambda B - \lambda A + \lambda^2 I \Leftrightarrow AB = BA \Leftrightarrow$ A and B commute.

EXAMPLE 20 *If $AB = A$ and $BA = B$, then show that $A^2 = A$, $B^2 = B$.*

SOLUTION We have, $AB = A$ and $BA = B$

Now, $AB = A$

$(AB)A = AA$ [Multiplying both sides on right by A]

$\Rightarrow \quad A(BA) = A^2$ [By associativity of matrix multiplication]

$\Rightarrow \quad AB = A^2$ [$\because BA = B$]

$\Rightarrow \quad A = A^2$ [$\because AB = A$]

Similarly, it can be proved that $B^2 = B$.

EXAMPLE 21 *Give an example of two matrices A and B such that* **[NCERT EXEMPLAR]**

(i) $A \neq O,\ B \neq O,\ AB = O$ and $BA \neq O$

(ii) $A \neq O,\ B \neq O,\ AB = BA = O$.

SOLUTION (i) If $A = \begin{bmatrix} 1 & 0 \\ 0 & 0 \end{bmatrix}$ and $B = \begin{bmatrix} 0 & 0 \\ 3 & 0 \end{bmatrix}$, then $A \neq O,\ B \neq O$.

But, $AB = \begin{bmatrix} 1 & 0 \\ 0 & 0 \end{bmatrix}\begin{bmatrix} 0 & 0 \\ 3 & 0 \end{bmatrix} = \begin{bmatrix} 0 & 0 \\ 0 & 0 \end{bmatrix} = O$ and, $BA = \begin{bmatrix} 0 & 0 \\ 3 & 0 \end{bmatrix}\begin{bmatrix} 1 & 0 \\ 0 & 0 \end{bmatrix} = \begin{bmatrix} 0 & 0 \\ 3 & 0 \end{bmatrix} \neq O$

(ii) If $A = \begin{bmatrix} 1 & 1 \\ 1 & 1 \end{bmatrix}$ and $B = \begin{bmatrix} 1 & -1 \\ -1 & 1 \end{bmatrix}$, then $A \neq O,\ B \neq O$.

But, $AB = \begin{bmatrix} 1 & 1 \\ 1 & 1 \end{bmatrix}\begin{bmatrix} 1 & -1 \\ -1 & 1 \end{bmatrix} = \begin{bmatrix} 1-1 & -1+1 \\ 1-1 & -1+1 \end{bmatrix} = \begin{bmatrix} 0 & 0 \\ 0 & 0 \end{bmatrix} = O$

and, $BA = \begin{bmatrix} 1 & -1 \\ -1 & 1 \end{bmatrix}\begin{bmatrix} 1 & 1 \\ 1 & 1 \end{bmatrix} = \begin{bmatrix} 1-1 & 1-1 \\ -1+1 & -1+1 \end{bmatrix} = \begin{bmatrix} 0 & 0 \\ 0 & 0 \end{bmatrix} = O$

EXAMPLE 22 *Give an example of three matrices A, B, C such that $AB = AC$ but $B \neq C$.*

[NCERT EXEMPLAR]

SOLUTION Let $A = \begin{bmatrix} 1 & 0 \\ 0 & 0 \end{bmatrix}$, $B = \begin{bmatrix} 0 & 0 \\ -1 & 0 \end{bmatrix}$ and $C = \begin{bmatrix} 0 & 0 \\ 0 & 1 \end{bmatrix}$. Then, it can be easily verified that $AB = AC = O$. But $B \neq C$.

Type V ON APPLICATIONS OF MATRICES

EXAMPLE 23 *There are two families A and B. There are 4 men, 6 women and 2 children in family A and 2 men, 2 women and 4 children in family B. The recommended daily allowance for calories is : Man : 2400, woman : 1900, child : 1800 and for proteins is : Man : 55 gm, woman : 45 gm and child : 33 gm.*

Represent the above information by matrices. Using matrix multiplication, calculate the total requirement of calories and proteins for each of the two families.

SOLUTION The members of the two families can be represented by a 2×3 matrix F given below.

$$F = \begin{array}{c} \\ A \\ B \end{array} \begin{array}{c} \begin{matrix} M & W & C \end{matrix} \\ \begin{bmatrix} 4 & 6 & 2 \\ 2 & 2 & 4 \end{bmatrix} \end{array}$$

and the recommended daily allowance of calories and proteins for each member can be represented by 3×2 matrix R as given below.

$$R = \begin{array}{c} \\ M \\ W \\ C \end{array} \begin{array}{c} \begin{matrix} \text{Calories} & \text{Proteins} \end{matrix} \\ \begin{bmatrix} 2400 & 55 \\ 1900 & 45 \\ 1800 & 33 \end{bmatrix} \end{array}$$

The total requirement of calories and proteins for each of the two families is given by the matrix multiplication FR as given below.

$$FR = \begin{bmatrix} 4 & 6 & 2 \\ 2 & 2 & 4 \end{bmatrix} \begin{bmatrix} 2400 & 55 \\ 1900 & 45 \\ 1800 & 33 \end{bmatrix} = \begin{array}{c} A \\ B \end{array} \begin{bmatrix} 24600 & 556 \\ 15800 & 332 \end{bmatrix}$$

Hence, family A requires 24600 calories and 556 gm proteins and family B requires 15,800 calories and 332 gm proteins.

EXAMPLE 24 *Use matrix multiplication to divide ₹ 30,000 in two parts such that the total annual interest at 9% on the first part and 11% on the second part amounts ₹ 3060.*

SOLUTION Let the two parts be ₹ x and ₹ $(30000 - x)$ respectively. Let A be the 1×2 matrix representing these two parts

i.e. $$A = \begin{array}{c} \begin{matrix} \text{Part I} & \text{Part II} \end{matrix} \\ [x \quad 30000 - x] \end{array}$$

Let R denote the 2×1 matrix representing the annual interest rates of interest on two parts i.e.

$$R = \begin{array}{c} \text{Part I} \\ \text{Part II} \end{array} \begin{bmatrix} 0.09 \\ 0.11 \end{bmatrix}$$

The total annual interest on the two parts is given by the matrix multiplication AR.

$\therefore \quad AR = 3060$

$\Rightarrow \quad [x \quad 30000 - x] \begin{bmatrix} 0.09 \\ 0.11 \end{bmatrix} = 3060$

$\Rightarrow \quad 0.09\,x + 0.11\,(30000 - x) = 3060$

$\Rightarrow \quad \frac{9}{100} x + \frac{11}{100} (30000 - x) = 3060 \Rightarrow 9x + 330000 - 11\,x = 306000 \Rightarrow x = 12{,}000$

Hence two parts of ₹ 30,000 are ₹ 12,000 and ₹ 18,000 respectively.

EXAMPLE 25 *Three schools A, B and C organised a mela for collecting funds for helping the rehabilitation of flood victims. They sold hand made fans, mats and plates from recyled material at a cost of ₹ 25, ₹ 100 and ₹ 50 each. The number of articles sold are given below:*

Article \ School	A	B	C
Hand-fans	40	25	35
Mats	50	40	50
Plates	20	30	40

Find the funds collected by each school separately by sailing the above articles. Also, find the total funds collected for the purpose. **[CBSE 2015]**

SOLUTION Three items sold by three schools are represented by the following 3×3 matrix Q as given below.

$$Q = \begin{matrix} & \text{Hand-fans} & \text{Mats} & \text{Plates} \\ A \\ B \\ C \end{matrix} \begin{bmatrix} 40 & 50 & 20 \\ 25 & 40 & 30 \\ 35 & 50 & 40 \end{bmatrix}$$

The price matrix representing price of of three articles in ₹ is a 3×1 matrix given by

$$P = \begin{matrix} \text{Hand-fan} \\ \text{Mat} \\ \text{Plate} \end{matrix} \begin{bmatrix} 25 \\ 100 \\ 50 \end{bmatrix}$$

The funds collected by schools A, B and C separately by selling three articles are given by the product matrix QP.

$\therefore$

$$QP = \begin{matrix} A \\ B \\ C \end{matrix} \begin{bmatrix} 40 & 50 & 20 \\ 25 & 40 & 30 \\ 35 & 50 & 40 \end{bmatrix} \begin{bmatrix} 25 \\ 100 \\ 50 \end{bmatrix} \quad (\text{columns: Hand-fans, Mats, Plates})$$

$$\Rightarrow \quad QP = \begin{matrix} A \\ B \\ C \end{matrix} \begin{bmatrix} 40 \times 25 + 50 \times 100 + 20 \times 50 \\ 25 \times 25 + 40 \times 100 + 30 \times 50 \\ 35 \times 25 + 50 \times 100 + 40 \times 50 \end{bmatrix} = \begin{matrix} A \\ B \\ C \end{matrix} \begin{bmatrix} ₹7000 \\ ₹6125 \\ ₹7875 \end{bmatrix}$$

Hence, the funds collected by schools A, B and C are ₹ 7000, ₹ 6125 and ₹ 7875 respectively.
The total funds collected = ₹ (7000 + 6125 + 7875) = ₹21000.

BASED ON LOWER ORDER THINKING SKILLS (LOTS)

Type I ON MULTIPLICATION OF MATRICES

EXAMPLE 26 *Prove that the product of matrices*

$$\begin{bmatrix} \cos^2\theta & \cos\theta\sin\theta \\ \cos\theta\sin\theta & \sin^2\theta \end{bmatrix} \text{ and } \begin{bmatrix} \cos^2\phi & \cos\phi\sin\phi \\ \cos\phi\sin\phi & \sin^2\phi \end{bmatrix}$$

is the null matrix, when θ and ϕ differ by an odd multiple of $\frac{\pi}{2}$.

SOLUTION We have,

$$\begin{bmatrix} \cos^2\theta & \cos\theta\sin\theta \\ \cos\theta\sin\theta & \sin^2\theta \end{bmatrix} \begin{bmatrix} \cos^2\phi & \cos\phi\sin\phi \\ \cos\phi\sin\phi & \sin^2\phi \end{bmatrix}$$

$$= \begin{bmatrix} \cos^2\theta\cos^2\phi + \cos\theta\cos\phi\sin\theta\sin\phi & \cos^2\theta\cos\phi\sin\phi + \cos\theta\sin\theta\sin^2\phi \\ \cos^2\phi\cos\theta\sin\theta + \sin^2\theta\cos\phi\sin\phi & \cos\theta\sin\theta\cos\phi\sin\phi + \sin^2\theta\sin^2\phi \end{bmatrix}$$

$$= \begin{bmatrix} \cos\theta\cos\phi\cos(\theta-\phi) & \cos\theta\sin\phi\cos(\theta-\phi) \\ \sin\theta\cos\phi\cos(\theta-\phi) & \sin\theta\sin\phi\cos(\theta-\phi) \end{bmatrix}$$

$$= \begin{bmatrix} 0 & 0 \\ 0 & 0 \end{bmatrix} \qquad \left[\because \theta - \phi = (2n+1)\frac{\pi}{2}, n \in Z \therefore \cos(\theta-\phi) = \cos(2n+1)\frac{\pi}{2} = 0\right]$$

EXAMPLE 27 *Let* $A = \begin{bmatrix} 0 & -\tan(\alpha/2) \\ \tan(\alpha/2) & 0 \end{bmatrix}$ *and I be the identity matrix of order 2. Show that* $I + A = (I - A)\begin{bmatrix} \cos\alpha & -\sin\alpha \\ \sin\alpha & \cos\alpha \end{bmatrix}$. **[NCERT]**

SOLUTION We have,

$$I + A = \begin{bmatrix} 1 & 0 \\ 0 & 1 \end{bmatrix} + \begin{bmatrix} 0 & -\tan\frac{\alpha}{2} \\ \tan\frac{\alpha}{2} & 0 \end{bmatrix} = \begin{bmatrix} 1 & -\tan\frac{\alpha}{2} \\ \tan\frac{\alpha}{2} & 1 \end{bmatrix}$$

and, $$I - A = \begin{bmatrix} 1 & 0 \\ 0 & 1 \end{bmatrix} + \begin{bmatrix} 0 & \tan\frac{\alpha}{2} \\ -\tan\frac{\alpha}{2} & 0 \end{bmatrix} = \begin{bmatrix} 1 & \tan\frac{\alpha}{2} \\ -\tan\frac{\alpha}{2} & 1 \end{bmatrix}.$$

$$\therefore \quad (I-A)\begin{bmatrix} \cos\alpha & -\sin\alpha \\ \sin\alpha & \cos\alpha \end{bmatrix} = \begin{bmatrix} 1 & \tan\frac{\alpha}{2} \\ -\tan\frac{\alpha}{2} & 1 \end{bmatrix}\begin{bmatrix} \cos\alpha & -\sin\alpha \\ \sin\alpha & \cos\alpha \end{bmatrix}$$

$$\Rightarrow \quad (I-A)\begin{bmatrix} \cos\alpha & -\sin\alpha \\ \sin\alpha & \cos\alpha \end{bmatrix} = \begin{bmatrix} 1 & \tan\frac{\alpha}{2} \\ -\tan\frac{\alpha}{2} & 1 \end{bmatrix}\begin{bmatrix} \dfrac{1-\tan^2\frac{\alpha}{2}}{1+\tan^2\frac{\alpha}{2}} & -\dfrac{2\tan\frac{\alpha}{2}}{1+\tan^2\frac{\alpha}{2}} \\ \dfrac{2\tan\frac{\alpha}{2}}{1+\tan^2\frac{\alpha}{2}} & \dfrac{1-\tan^2\frac{\alpha}{2}}{1+\tan^2\frac{\alpha}{2}} \end{bmatrix}$$

$$\Rightarrow \quad (I-A)\begin{bmatrix} \cos\alpha & -\sin\alpha \\ \sin\alpha & \cos\alpha \end{bmatrix} = \begin{bmatrix} 1 & t \\ -t & 1 \end{bmatrix}\begin{bmatrix} \dfrac{1-t^2}{1+t^2} & -\dfrac{2t}{1+t^2} \\ \dfrac{2t}{1+t^2} & \dfrac{1-t^2}{1+t^2} \end{bmatrix}, \text{ where } t = \tan\frac{\alpha}{2}.$$

$$\Rightarrow \quad (I-A)\begin{bmatrix} \cos\alpha & -\sin\alpha \\ \sin\alpha & \cos\alpha \end{bmatrix} = \begin{bmatrix} \dfrac{1-t^2+2t^2}{1+t^2} & \dfrac{-2t+t-t^3}{1+t^2} \\ \dfrac{-t+t^3+2t}{1+t^2} & \dfrac{2t^2+1-t^2}{1+t^2} \end{bmatrix}$$

$$\Rightarrow \quad (I-A)\begin{bmatrix} \cos\alpha & -\sin\alpha \\ \sin\alpha & \cos\alpha \end{bmatrix} = \begin{bmatrix} \dfrac{1+t^2}{1+t^2} & \dfrac{-t(1+t^2)}{1+t^2} \\ \dfrac{t(1+t^2)}{1+t^2} & \dfrac{1+t^2}{1+t^2} \end{bmatrix} = \begin{bmatrix} 1 & -t \\ t & 1 \end{bmatrix}$$

$$\Rightarrow \quad (I-A)\begin{bmatrix} \cos\alpha & -\sin\alpha \\ \sin\alpha & \cos\alpha \end{bmatrix} = \begin{bmatrix} 1 & -\tan\frac{\alpha}{2} \\ \tan\frac{\alpha}{2} & 1 \end{bmatrix} = I + A$$

EXAMPLE 28 *Let* $F(x)=\begin{bmatrix}\cos x & -\sin x & 0\\ \sin x & \cos x & 0\\ 0 & 0 & 1\end{bmatrix}$. *Show that*

(i) $F(x)\,F(y)=F(x+y)$ [NCERT] *(ii)* $F(x)\,F(-y)=F(x-y)$ [CBSE 2023]

SOLUTION (i) We have,

$$F(x)\cdot F(y)=\begin{bmatrix}\cos x & -\sin x & 0\\ \sin x & \cos x & 0\\ 0 & 0 & 1\end{bmatrix}\begin{bmatrix}\cos y & -\sin y & 0\\ \sin y & \cos y & 0\\ 0 & 0 & 1\end{bmatrix}$$

$$\Rightarrow \quad F(x)\cdot F(y)=\begin{bmatrix}\cos x\cos y-\sin x\sin y & -\sin y\cos x-\sin x\cos y & 0\\ \sin x\cos y+\cos x\sin y & -\sin x\sin y+\cos x\cos y & 0\\ 0 & 0 & 1\end{bmatrix}$$

$$\Rightarrow \quad F(x)\cdot F(y)=\begin{bmatrix}\cos(x+y) & -\sin(x+y) & 0\\ \sin(x+y) & \cos(x+y) & 0\\ 0 & 0 & 1\end{bmatrix}=F(x+y)$$

(ii)
$$F(x)\,F(-y)=\begin{bmatrix}\cos x & -\sin x & 0\\ \sin x & \cos x & 0\\ 0 & 0 & 1\end{bmatrix}\begin{bmatrix}\cos(-y) & -\sin(-y) & 0\\ \sin(-y) & \cos(-y) & 0\\ 0 & 0 & 1\end{bmatrix}$$

$$\Rightarrow \quad F(x)\,F(-y)=\begin{bmatrix}\cos x & -\sin x & 0\\ \sin x & \cos x & 0\\ 0 & 0 & 1\end{bmatrix}\begin{bmatrix}\cos y & \sin y & 0\\ -\sin y & \cos y & 0\\ 0 & 0 & 1\end{bmatrix}$$

$$\Rightarrow \quad F(x)\,F(-y)=\begin{bmatrix}\cos x\cos y+\sin x\sin y & \cos x\sin y-\sin x\cos y & 0\\ \sin x\cos y-\cos x\sin y & \sin x\sin y+\cos x\cos y & 0\\ 0 & 0 & 1\end{bmatrix}$$

$$\Rightarrow \quad F(x)\,F(-y)=\begin{bmatrix}\cos(x-y) & -\sin(x-y) & 0\\ \sin(x-y) & \cos(x-y) & 0\\ 0 & 0 & 1\end{bmatrix}=F(x-y)$$

Type II ON MATRIX POLYNOMIALS AND MATRIX POLYNOMIAL EQUATIONS

EXAMPLE 29 *Let* $A=\begin{bmatrix}2 & 3\\ -1 & 2\end{bmatrix}$ *and* $f(x)=x^2-4x+7$. *Show that* $f(A)=O$. *Use this result to find* A^5.

[NCERT EXEMPLAR]

SOLUTION We have, $f(x)=x^2-4x+7$. Therefore, $f(A)=A^2-4A+7I_2$.

Now, $A^2=\begin{bmatrix}2 & 3\\ -1 & 2\end{bmatrix}\begin{bmatrix}2 & 3\\ -1 & 2\end{bmatrix}=\begin{bmatrix}4-3 & 6+6\\ -2-2 & -3+4\end{bmatrix}=\begin{bmatrix}1 & 12\\ -4 & 1\end{bmatrix}$,

$-4A=\begin{bmatrix}-8 & -12\\ 4 & -8\end{bmatrix}$ and, $7I_2=\begin{bmatrix}7 & 0\\ 0 & 7\end{bmatrix}$

$\therefore \quad f(A)=A^2-4A+7I_2$

$\Rightarrow \quad f(A)=\begin{bmatrix}1 & 12\\ -4 & 1\end{bmatrix}+\begin{bmatrix}-8 & -12\\ 4 & -8\end{bmatrix}+\begin{bmatrix}7 & 0\\ 0 & 7\end{bmatrix}=\begin{bmatrix}1-8+7 & 12-12+0\\ -4+4+0 & 1-8+7\end{bmatrix}=\begin{bmatrix}0 & 0\\ 0 & 0\end{bmatrix}=O$

Now, $f(A)=O$

$\Rightarrow \quad A^2-4A+7I_2=O$

$\Rightarrow \quad A^2=4A-7I_2$

$\Rightarrow \quad A^3=A^2A=(4A-7I_2)A=4A^2-7I_2A$

$\Rightarrow \quad A^3 = 4(4A - 7I_2) - 7A$ [Using : $A^2 = 4A - 7I_2$]

$\Rightarrow \quad A^3 = 9A - 28I_2$

$\Rightarrow \quad A^4 = A^3 A = (9A - 28I_2)\,A$

$\Rightarrow \quad A^4 = 9A^2 - 28A = 9(4A - 7I_2) - 28A$ [Using : $A^2 = 4A - 7I_2$]

$\Rightarrow \quad A^4 = 36A - 63I_2 - 28A = 8A - 63I_2$

$\Rightarrow \quad A^5 = A^4\,A = (8A - 63I_2)\,A = 8A^2 - 63I_2\,A$

$\Rightarrow \quad A^5 = 8(4A - 7I_2) - 63A = -31A - 56I_2$ [Using : $A^2 = 4A - 7I_2$]

$$\Rightarrow \quad A^5 = -31\begin{bmatrix} 2 & 3 \\ -1 & 2 \end{bmatrix} - 56\begin{bmatrix} 1 & 0 \\ 0 & 1 \end{bmatrix} = \begin{bmatrix} -62 & -93 \\ 31 & -62 \end{bmatrix} + \begin{bmatrix} -56 & 0 \\ 0 & -56 \end{bmatrix} = \begin{bmatrix} -118 & -93 \\ 31 & -118 \end{bmatrix}.$$

Type III ON PRINCIPLE OF MATHEMATICAL INDUCTION

EXAMPLE 30 *If* $A = \begin{bmatrix} 0 & 1 \\ 0 & 0 \end{bmatrix}$, *prove that* $(aI + bA)^n = a^n I + na^{n-1} bA$ *where I is a unit matrix of order 2 and n is a positive integer.* [NCERT]

SOLUTION We shall prove the result by mathematical induction on n.

Step 1 When $n = 1$, by the definition of integral powers of a matrix, we have

$$(aI + bA)^1 = aI + bA = a^1 I + 1\,a^0\,bA = a^1 I + 1a^{1-1}\,bA$$

So, the result is true for $n = 1$.

Step 2 Let the result be true for $n = m$. Then, $(aI + bA)^m = a^m I + ma^{m-1}\,bA$ ...(i)

Now we shall show that the result is true for $n = m + 1$.

i.e. $\quad (aI + bA)^{m+1} = a^{m+1} I + (m+1)\,a^m\,bA$

By using the definition of integral powers of a matrix, we obtain

$$\begin{aligned}
(aI + bA)^{m+1} &= (aI + bA)^m\,(aI + bA) \\
&= (a^m I + ma^{m-1} bA)\,(aI + bA) && \text{[Using (i)]} \\
&= (a^m I)(aI) + (a^m I)(bA) + (ma^{m-1} bA)(aI) + (ma^{m-1} bA)(bA) \\
&= (a^m a)(I\,.\,I) + a^m b\,(IA) + ma^m b\,(AI) + ma^{m-1} b^2\,(AA) \\
&= a^{m+1} I + a^m bA + ma^m bA + ma^{m-1} b^2 A^2 && [\because IA = AI = A,\ I\,.\,I = I] \\
&= a^{m+1} I + (ma^m b + a^m b)\,A + ma^{m-1} b^2 A^2 \\
&= a^{m+1} I + (m+1)\,a^m\,bA + ma^{m-1} b^2\,O && [\because A^2 = O] \\
&= a^{m+1} I + (m+1)\,a^m\,bA
\end{aligned}$$

This shows that the result is true for $n = m + 1$, whenever it is true for $n = m$.

Hence, by the principle of mathematical induction, the result is valid for any positive integer n.

EXAMPLE 31 *Let A, B be two matrices such that they commute. Show that for any positive integer n*

(i) $AB^n = B^n A$ (ii) $(AB)^n = A^n B^n$ [NCERT EXEMPLAR]

SOLUTION (i) We shall prove the result by the principle of mathematical induction on n.

Step 1 When $n = 1$, by the definition of integral powers of a matrix, we have

$$\begin{aligned}
AB^1 &= AB = BA && [\because AB = BA \text{ (given)}] \\
&= B^1 A && [\because B^1 = B]
\end{aligned}$$

So, that result is true for $n = 1$.

Step 2 Let the result be true for $n = m$. Then, $AB^m = B^m A$. ...(i)

We shall now show that the result is true for $n = m + 1$ i.e. $AB^{m+1} = B^{m+1}A$.

By the definition of integral powers of a matrix, we obtain

$$\begin{aligned}
AB^{m+1} &= A(B^m B) = A(BB^m) \\
&= (AB)B^m && \text{[By associativity of matrix multiplication]} \\
&= (BA)B^m && [\because AB = BA \text{ (given)}] \\
&= B(AB^m) && \text{[By associativity of matrix multiplication]} \\
&= B(B^m A) && \text{[Using induction assumption (i)]} \\
&= (BB^m)A && \text{[By associativity of matrix multiplication]} \\
&= B^{m+1}A && \text{[By definition of integral powers]}
\end{aligned}$$

This shows that the result is true for $n = m + 1$, whenever it is true for $n = m$.

Hence, by the principle of mathematical induction, the result is true for any positive integer n.

(ii) We shall prove this result also by the principle of mathematical induction on n.

Step 1 When $n = 1$, by the definition of integral powers of a matrix, we have

$$(AB)^1 = AB = A^1 B^1 \qquad [\because A^1 = A, B^1 = B]$$

So, the result is true for $n = 1$.

Step 2 Let the result be true for $n = m$. Then, $(AB)^m = A^m B^m$ ...(i)

Now we shall show that the result is true for $n = m + 1$ i.e. $(AB)^{m+1} = A^{m+1}B^{m+1}$.

By using the definition of integral powers of a matrix, we obtain

$$\begin{aligned}
(AB)^{m+1} &= (AB)^m (AB) \\
&= (A^m B^m)(AB) && \text{[By induction assumption (i)]} \\
&= A^m (B^m (AB)) && \text{[By associativity of matrix multiplication]} \\
&= A^m (B^m (BA)) && [\because AB = BA \text{ (given)}] \\
&= A^m ((B^m B)A) && \text{[By associativity of matrix multiplication]} \\
&= A^m (B^{m+1}A) && \text{[By definition of integral powers]} \\
&= A^m (AB^{m+1}) && [\because AB^n = B^n A \text{ for all } n \in N \text{ (proved in (i))}] \\
&= (A^m A)B^{m+1} && \text{[By associativity of matrix multiplication]} \\
&= A^{m+1}B^{m+1}
\end{aligned}$$

This shows that the result is true for $n = m + 1$, whenever it is true for $n = m$.

Hence, by the principle of mathematical induction, the result is true for every positive integer n.

EXAMPLE 32 *If A is a square matrix such that $A^2 = A$, show that $(I + A)^3 = 7A + I$.*

[NCERT EXEMPLAR]

SOLUTION Using matrix multiplication, we obtain

$$\begin{aligned}
(I + A)^2 &= (I + A)(I + A) \\
&= I(I + A) + A(I + A) && \text{[By distributivity of multiplication over addition]} \\
&= I^2 + IA + AI + A^2 \\
&= I + A + A + A^2 && [\because IA = AI = A] \\
&= I + 2A + A^2 = I + 2A + A = I + 3A && [\because A^2 = A]
\end{aligned}$$

$\therefore \quad (I+A)^3 = (I+A)^2 (I+A)$

$= (I+3A)(I+A)$

$= I(I+A) + 3A(I+A) = I^2 + IA + 3(AI) + 3(AA)$

$= I + A + 3A + 3A^2$ $\quad [\because IA = AI = A]$

$= I + A + 3A + 3A = I + 7A$ $\quad [\because A^2 = A]$

EXAMPLE 33 *If A is a square matrix such that* $A^2 = I$*, then find the simplified value of* $(A-I)^3 + (A+I)^3 - 7A$. **[CBSE 2016]**

SOLUTION We have, $A^2 = I$

$\therefore \quad A^3 = A^2 A = IA = A$ ...(i)

We know that

$$(A+B)^3 = A^3 + 3A^2B + 3AB^2 + B^3 \text{ and, } (A-B)^3 = A^3 - 3A^2B + 3AB^2 - B^3$$

provided that $AB = BA$.

Since $AI = IA = A$.

$\therefore \quad (A+I)^3 = A^3 + 3A^2I + 3AI^2 + I^3$ and $(A-I)^3 = A^3 - 3A^2I + 3AI^2 - I^3$

$\Rightarrow \quad (A+I)^3 = A^3 + 3A^2 + 3A + I$ and $(A-I)^3 = A^3 - 3A^2 + 3A - I$

$\therefore \quad (A+I)^3 + (A-I)^3 = 2(A^3 + 3A) = 2(A + 3A) = 8A$ [Using (i)]

Hence, $(A-I)^3 + (A+I)^3 - 7A = 8A - 7A = A$.

EXAMPLE 34 *If* $A = [3 \quad 5]$, $B = [7 \quad 3]$*, then find a non-zero matrix C such that* $AC = BC$.

[NCERT EXEMPLAR]

SOLUTION Clearly, A and B are 1×2 matrix. Therefore, products AC and BC exist if C is of order $2 \times n$, where $n \in N$.

Now, following cases arise.

Case I *When* $n = 1$: In this case, matrix C is a 2×1 matrix. So, let $C = \begin{bmatrix} a \\ b \end{bmatrix}$. Then,

$AC = BC$

$\Rightarrow \quad [3 \quad 5]\begin{bmatrix} a \\ b \end{bmatrix} = [7 \quad 3]\begin{bmatrix} a \\ b \end{bmatrix} \Rightarrow 3a + 5b = 7a + 3b \Rightarrow 4a = 2b \Rightarrow 2a = b$

$\therefore \quad C = \begin{bmatrix} a \\ 2a \end{bmatrix}$, where $a \in R$.

Case II *When* $n = 2$: In this case, matrix C is a 2×2 matrix. So, let $C = \begin{bmatrix} a & x \\ b & y \end{bmatrix}$. Then,

$AC = BC$

$\Rightarrow \quad [3 \quad 5]\begin{bmatrix} a & x \\ b & y \end{bmatrix} = [7 \quad 3]\begin{bmatrix} a & x \\ b & y \end{bmatrix}$

$\Rightarrow \quad [3a + 5b \quad 3x + 5y] = [7a + 3b \quad 7x + 3y] \Rightarrow 3a + 5b = 7a + 3b$ and $3x + 5y = 7x + 3y$

$\Rightarrow \quad b = 2a$ and $y = 2x$.

$\therefore \quad C = \begin{bmatrix} a & x \\ 2a & 2x \end{bmatrix}$, where $a, x \in R$.

Similarly, if $n = 3$

$$C = \begin{bmatrix} a & x & y \\ 2a & 2x & 2y \end{bmatrix}, \text{ where } a, x, y \in R \text{ and so on.}$$

EXERCISE 4.3

BASIC

1. Compute the indicated products:

(i) $\begin{bmatrix} a & b \\ -b & a \end{bmatrix}\begin{bmatrix} a & -b \\ b & a \end{bmatrix}$ (ii) $\begin{bmatrix} 1 & -2 \\ 2 & 3 \end{bmatrix}\begin{bmatrix} 1 & 2 & 3 \\ -3 & 2 & -1 \end{bmatrix}$ (iii) $\begin{bmatrix} 2 & 3 & 4 \\ 3 & 4 & 5 \\ 4 & 5 & 6 \end{bmatrix}\begin{bmatrix} 1 & -3 & 5 \\ 0 & 2 & 4 \\ 3 & 0 & 5 \end{bmatrix}$

2. Show that $AB \neq BA$ in each of the following cases:

(i) $A = \begin{bmatrix} 5 & -1 \\ 6 & 7 \end{bmatrix}$ and $B = \begin{bmatrix} 2 & 1 \\ 3 & 4 \end{bmatrix}$ (ii) $A = \begin{bmatrix} -1 & 1 & 0 \\ 0 & -1 & 1 \\ 2 & 3 & 4 \end{bmatrix}$ and $B = \begin{bmatrix} 1 & 2 & 3 \\ 0 & 1 & 0 \\ 1 & 1 & 0 \end{bmatrix}$

(iii) $A = \begin{bmatrix} 1 & 3 & 0 \\ 1 & 1 & 0 \\ 4 & 1 & 0 \end{bmatrix}$ and $B = \begin{bmatrix} 0 & 1 & 0 \\ 1 & 0 & 0 \\ 0 & 5 & 1 \end{bmatrix}$

3. Compute the products AB and BA whichever exists in each of the following cases:

(i) $A = \begin{bmatrix} 1 & -2 \\ 2 & 3 \end{bmatrix}$ and $B = \begin{bmatrix} 1 & 2 & 3 \\ 2 & 3 & 1 \end{bmatrix}$ (ii) $A = \begin{bmatrix} 3 & 2 \\ -1 & 0 \\ -1 & 1 \end{bmatrix}$ and $B = \begin{bmatrix} 4 & 5 & 6 \\ 0 & 1 & 2 \end{bmatrix}$

(iii) $A = [1 \ -1 \ 2 \ 3]$ and $B = \begin{bmatrix} 0 \\ 1 \\ 3 \\ 2 \end{bmatrix}$ (iv) $[a \ b]\begin{bmatrix} c \\ d \end{bmatrix} + [a \ b \ c \ d]\begin{bmatrix} a \\ b \\ c \\ d \end{bmatrix}$

4. Show that $AB \neq BA$ in each of the following cases:

(i) $A = \begin{bmatrix} 1 & 3 & -1 \\ 2 & -1 & -1 \\ 3 & 0 & -1 \end{bmatrix}$ and $B = \begin{bmatrix} -2 & 3 & -1 \\ -1 & 2 & -1 \\ -6 & 9 & -4 \end{bmatrix}$ (ii) $A = \begin{bmatrix} 10 & -4 & -1 \\ 11 & 5 & 0 \\ 9 & -5 & 1 \end{bmatrix}$ and $B = \begin{bmatrix} 1 & 2 & 2 \\ 3 & 4 & 1 \\ 1 & 3 & 2 \end{bmatrix}$

5. Evaluate the following:

(i) $\left(\begin{bmatrix} 1 & 3 \\ -1 & -4 \end{bmatrix} + \begin{bmatrix} 3 & -2 \\ -1 & 1 \end{bmatrix}\right)\begin{bmatrix} 1 & 3 & 5 \\ 2 & 4 & 6 \end{bmatrix}$ (ii) $[1 \ 2 \ 3]\begin{bmatrix} 1 & 0 & 2 \\ 2 & 0 & 1 \\ 0 & 1 & 2 \end{bmatrix}\begin{bmatrix} 2 \\ 4 \\ 6 \end{bmatrix}$

(iii) $\begin{bmatrix} 1 & -1 \\ 0 & 2 \\ 2 & 3 \end{bmatrix}\left(\begin{bmatrix} 1 & 0 & 2 \\ 2 & 0 & 1 \end{bmatrix} - \begin{bmatrix} 0 & 1 & 2 \\ 1 & 0 & 2 \end{bmatrix}\right)$

6. If $A = \begin{bmatrix} 1 & 0 \\ 0 & 1 \end{bmatrix}, B = \begin{bmatrix} 1 & 0 \\ 0 & -1 \end{bmatrix}$ and $C = \begin{bmatrix} 0 & 1 \\ 1 & 0 \end{bmatrix}$, then show that $A^2 = B^2 = C^2 = I_2$.

7. If $A = \begin{bmatrix} 2 & -1 \\ 3 & 2 \end{bmatrix}$ and $B = \begin{bmatrix} 0 & 4 \\ -1 & 7 \end{bmatrix}$, find $3A^2 - 2B + I$. [CBSE 2005]

8. If $A = \begin{bmatrix} 4 & 2 \\ -1 & 1 \end{bmatrix}$, prove that $(A - 2I)(A - 3I) = O$.

9. If $A = \begin{bmatrix} 1 & 1 \\ 0 & 1 \end{bmatrix}$, show that $A^2 = \begin{bmatrix} 1 & 2 \\ 0 & 1 \end{bmatrix}$ and $A^3 = \begin{bmatrix} 1 & 3 \\ 0 & 1 \end{bmatrix}$.

10. If $A=\begin{bmatrix} ab & b^2 \\ -a^2 & -ab \end{bmatrix}$, show that $A^2=O$.

11. If $A=\begin{bmatrix} \cos 2\theta & \sin 2\theta \\ -\sin 2\theta & \cos 2\theta \end{bmatrix}$, find A^2. **[CBSE 2000C]**

12. If $A=\begin{bmatrix} 2 & -3 & -5 \\ -1 & 4 & 5 \\ 1 & -3 & -4 \end{bmatrix}$ and $B=\begin{bmatrix} -1 & 3 & 5 \\ 1 & -3 & -5 \\ -1 & 3 & 5 \end{bmatrix}$, show that $AB=BA=O_{3\times 3}$.

13. If $A=\begin{bmatrix} 0 & c & -b \\ -c & 0 & a \\ b & -a & 0 \end{bmatrix}$ and $B=\begin{bmatrix} a^2 & ab & ac \\ ab & b^2 & bc \\ ac & bc & c^2 \end{bmatrix}$, show that $AB=BA=O_{3\times 3}$.

14. If $A=\begin{bmatrix} 2 & -3 & -5 \\ -1 & 4 & 5 \\ 1 & -3 & -4 \end{bmatrix}$ and $B=\begin{bmatrix} 2 & -2 & -4 \\ -1 & 3 & 4 \\ 1 & -2 & -3 \end{bmatrix}$, show that $AB=A$ and $BA=B$.

15. Let $A=\begin{bmatrix} -1 & 1 & -1 \\ 3 & -3 & 3 \\ 5 & 5 & 5 \end{bmatrix}$ and $B=\begin{bmatrix} 0 & 4 & 3 \\ 1 & -3 & -3 \\ -1 & 4 & 4 \end{bmatrix}$, compute A^2-B^2.

16. For the following matrices verify the associativity of matrix multiplication i.e. $(AB)C=A(BC)$.

(i) $A=\begin{bmatrix} 1 & 2 & 0 \\ -1 & 0 & 1 \end{bmatrix}$, $B=\begin{bmatrix} 1 & 0 \\ -1 & 2 \\ 0 & 3 \end{bmatrix}$ and $C=\begin{bmatrix} 1 \\ -1 \end{bmatrix}$

(ii) $A=\begin{bmatrix} 4 & 2 & 3 \\ 1 & 1 & 2 \\ 3 & 0 & 1 \end{bmatrix}$, $B=\begin{bmatrix} 1 & -1 & 1 \\ 0 & 1 & 2 \\ 2 & -1 & 1 \end{bmatrix}$ and $C=\begin{bmatrix} 1 & 2 & -1 \\ 3 & 0 & 1 \\ 0 & 0 & 1 \end{bmatrix}$.

17. For the following matrices verify the distributivity of matrix multiplication over matrix addition i.e. $A(B+C)=AB+AC$.

(i) $A=\begin{bmatrix} 1 & -1 \\ 0 & 2 \end{bmatrix}$, $B=\begin{bmatrix} -1 & 0 \\ 2 & 1 \end{bmatrix}$ and $C=\begin{bmatrix} 0 & 1 \\ 1 & -1 \end{bmatrix}$

(ii) $A=\begin{bmatrix} 2 & -1 \\ 1 & 1 \\ -1 & 2 \end{bmatrix}$, $B=\begin{bmatrix} 0 & 1 \\ 1 & 1 \end{bmatrix}$ and $C=\begin{bmatrix} 1 & -1 \\ 0 & 1 \end{bmatrix}$.

18. If $A=\begin{bmatrix} 1 & 0 & -2 \\ 3 & -1 & 0 \\ -2 & 1 & 1 \end{bmatrix}$, $B=\begin{bmatrix} 0 & 5 & -4 \\ -2 & 1 & 3 \\ -1 & 0 & 2 \end{bmatrix}$ and $C=\begin{bmatrix} 1 & 5 & 2 \\ -1 & 1 & 0 \\ 0 & -1 & 1 \end{bmatrix}$, verify that $A(B-C)=AB-AC$.

19. Compute the elements a_{43} and a_{22} of the matrix:

$$A=\begin{bmatrix} 0 & 1 & 0 \\ 2 & 0 & 2 \\ 0 & 3 & 2 \\ 4 & 0 & 4 \end{bmatrix}\begin{bmatrix} 2 & -1 \\ -3 & 2 \\ 4 & 3 \end{bmatrix}\begin{bmatrix} 0 & 1 & -1 & 2 & -2 \\ 3 & -3 & 4 & -4 & 0 \end{bmatrix}$$

20. If $A=\begin{bmatrix} 0 & 1 & 0 \\ 0 & 0 & 1 \\ p & q & r \end{bmatrix}$ and I is the identity matrix of order 3, show that $A^3=pI+qA+rA^2$.

21. If w is a complex cube root of unity, show that
$$\left(\begin{bmatrix} 1 & w & w^2 \\ w & w^2 & 1 \\ w^2 & 1 & w \end{bmatrix} + \begin{bmatrix} w & w^2 & 1 \\ w^2 & 1 & w \\ w & w^2 & 1 \end{bmatrix}\right)\begin{bmatrix} 1 \\ w \\ w^2 \end{bmatrix} = \begin{bmatrix} 0 \\ 0 \\ 0 \end{bmatrix}$$

22. If $A = \begin{bmatrix} 2 & -3 & -5 \\ -1 & 4 & 5 \\ 1 & -3 & -4 \end{bmatrix}$, show that $A^2 = A$.

23. If $A = \begin{bmatrix} 4 & -1 & -4 \\ 3 & 0 & -4 \\ 3 & -1 & -3 \end{bmatrix}$, show that $A^2 = I_3$.

24. (i) If $[1 \quad 1 \quad x]\begin{bmatrix} 1 & 0 & 2 \\ 0 & 2 & 1 \\ 2 & 1 & 0 \end{bmatrix}\begin{bmatrix} 1 \\ 1 \\ 1 \end{bmatrix} = 0$, find x.

(ii) If $\begin{bmatrix} 2 & 3 \\ 5 & 7 \end{bmatrix}\begin{bmatrix} 1 & -3 \\ -2 & 4 \end{bmatrix} = \begin{bmatrix} -4 & 6 \\ -9 & x \end{bmatrix}$, find x. **[CBSE 2012]**

25. If $[x \quad 4 \quad 1]\begin{bmatrix} 2 & 1 & 2 \\ 1 & 0 & 2 \\ 0 & 2 & -4 \end{bmatrix}\begin{bmatrix} x \\ 4 \\ -1 \end{bmatrix} = 0$, find x.

26. If $[1 \quad -1 \quad x]\begin{bmatrix} 0 & 1 & -1 \\ 2 & 1 & 3 \\ 1 & 1 & 1 \end{bmatrix}\begin{bmatrix} 0 \\ 1 \\ 1 \end{bmatrix} = 0$, find x.

27. If $A = \begin{bmatrix} 3 & -2 \\ 4 & -2 \end{bmatrix}$ and $I = \begin{bmatrix} 1 & 0 \\ 0 & 1 \end{bmatrix}$, then prove that $A^2 - A + 2I = O$.

28. If $A = \begin{bmatrix} 3 & 1 \\ -1 & 2 \end{bmatrix}$ and $I = \begin{bmatrix} 1 & 0 \\ 0 & 1 \end{bmatrix}$, then find λ so that $A^2 = 5A + \lambda I$.

29. If $A = \begin{bmatrix} 3 & 1 \\ -1 & 2 \end{bmatrix}$, show that $A^2 - 5A + 7I_2 = O$. **[CBSE 2003, 2007]**

30. If A is a square matrix such that $A^2 = A$, then find $(2I + A)^3 - 19A$. **[CBSE 2020]**

31. Show that the matrix $A = \begin{bmatrix} 2 & 3 \\ 1 & 2 \end{bmatrix}$ satisfies the equation $A^3 - 4A^2 + A = O$. **[CBSE 2005]**

32. Show that the matrix $A = \begin{bmatrix} 5 & 3 \\ 12 & 7 \end{bmatrix}$ is a root of the equation $A^2 - 12A - I = O$.

33. If $A = \begin{bmatrix} 3 & -5 \\ -4 & 2 \end{bmatrix}$, find $A^2 - 5A - 14I$. **[CBSE 2004]**

BASED ON LOTS

34. If $A = \begin{bmatrix} 3 & 1 \\ -1 & 2 \end{bmatrix}$, show that $A^2 - 5A + 7I = O$. Use this to find A^4. **[NCERT]**

35. If $A = \begin{bmatrix} 3 & -2 \\ 4 & -2 \end{bmatrix}$, find k such that $A^2 = kA - 2I_2$. **[NCERT, CBSE 2003]**

36. If $A = \begin{bmatrix} 1 & 0 \\ -1 & 7 \end{bmatrix}$, find k such that $A^2 - 8A + kI = O$. [CBSE 2005]

37. If $A = \begin{bmatrix} 1 & 2 \\ 2 & 1 \end{bmatrix}$ and $f(x) = x^2 - 2x - 3$, show that $f(A) = O$. [CBSE 2005]

38. If $A = \begin{bmatrix} 2 & 3 \\ 1 & 2 \end{bmatrix}$ and $I = \begin{bmatrix} 1 & 0 \\ 0 & 1 \end{bmatrix}$, then find λ, μ so that $A^2 = \lambda A + \mu I$

39. Find the value of x for which the matrix product $\begin{bmatrix} 2 & 0 & 7 \\ 0 & 1 & 0 \\ 1 & -2 & 1 \end{bmatrix} \begin{bmatrix} -x & 14x & 7x \\ 0 & 1 & 0 \\ x & -4x & -2x \end{bmatrix}$ equal to an identity matrix.

40. Solve the matrix equations:

(i) $[x \quad 1] \begin{bmatrix} 1 & 0 \\ -2 & -3 \end{bmatrix} \begin{bmatrix} x \\ 5 \end{bmatrix} = 0$

(ii) $[1 \quad 2 \quad 1] \begin{bmatrix} 1 & 2 & 0 \\ 2 & 0 & 1 \\ 1 & 0 & 2 \end{bmatrix} \begin{bmatrix} 0 \\ 2 \\ x \end{bmatrix} = 0$ [NCERT]

(iii) $[x \; -5 \; -1] \begin{bmatrix} 1 & 0 & 2 \\ 0 & 2 & 1 \\ 2 & 0 & 3 \end{bmatrix} \begin{bmatrix} x \\ 4 \\ 1 \end{bmatrix} = 0$ [NCERT]

(iv) $[2x \quad 3] \begin{bmatrix} 1 & 2 \\ -3 & 0 \end{bmatrix} \begin{bmatrix} x \\ 8 \end{bmatrix} = 0$

41. If $A = \begin{bmatrix} 1 & 2 & 3 \\ 3 & -2 & 1 \\ 4 & 2 & 1 \end{bmatrix}$, then show that $A^3 - 23A - 40I = O$. [CBSE 2023]

42. If $f(x) = x^2 - 2x$, find $f(A)$, where $A = \begin{bmatrix} 0 & 1 & 2 \\ 4 & 5 & 0 \\ 0 & 2 & 3 \end{bmatrix}$.

43. If $f(x) = x^3 + 4x^2 - x$, find $f(A)$, where $A = \begin{bmatrix} 0 & 1 & 2 \\ 2 & -3 & 0 \\ 1 & -1 & 0 \end{bmatrix}$.

44. If $A = \begin{bmatrix} 1 & 0 & 2 \\ 0 & 2 & 1 \\ 2 & 0 & 3 \end{bmatrix}$, then show that A is a root of the polynomial $f(x) = x^3 - 6x^2 + 7x + 2$.

[NCERT, CBSE 2023]

45. If $A = \begin{bmatrix} 1 & 2 & 2 \\ 2 & 1 & 2 \\ 2 & 2 & 1 \end{bmatrix}$, then prove that $A^2 - 4A - 5I = O$. [CBSE 2008]

46. If $A = \begin{bmatrix} 3 & 2 & 0 \\ 1 & 4 & 0 \\ 0 & 0 & 5 \end{bmatrix}$, show that $A^2 - 7A + 10I_3 = O$.

47. Without using the concept of inverse of a matrix, find the matrix $\begin{bmatrix} x & y \\ z & u \end{bmatrix}$ such that

$$\begin{bmatrix} 5 & -7 \\ -2 & 3 \end{bmatrix} \begin{bmatrix} x & y \\ z & u \end{bmatrix} = \begin{bmatrix} -16 & -6 \\ 7 & 2 \end{bmatrix}.$$

48. Find the matrix A such that

(i) $\begin{bmatrix} 1 & 1 \\ 0 & 1 \end{bmatrix} A = \begin{bmatrix} 3 & 3 & 5 \\ 1 & 0 & 1 \end{bmatrix}$

(ii) $A \begin{bmatrix} 1 & 2 & 3 \\ 4 & 5 & 6 \end{bmatrix} = \begin{bmatrix} -7 & -8 & -9 \\ 2 & 4 & 6 \end{bmatrix}$ [NCERT]

(iii) $\begin{bmatrix} 4 \\ 1 \\ 3 \end{bmatrix} A = \begin{bmatrix} -4 & 8 & 4 \\ -1 & 2 & 1 \\ -3 & 6 & 3 \end{bmatrix}$ [NCERT EXEMPLAR]

(iv) $[2\ 1\ 3] \begin{bmatrix} -1 & 0 & -1 \\ -1 & 1 & 0 \\ 0 & 1 & 1 \end{bmatrix} \begin{bmatrix} 1 \\ 0 \\ -1 \end{bmatrix} = A$ [NCERT EXEMPLAR]

(v) $\begin{bmatrix} 2 & -1 \\ 1 & 0 \\ -3 & 4 \end{bmatrix} A = \begin{bmatrix} -1 & -8 & -10 \\ 1 & -2 & -5 \\ 9 & 22 & 15 \end{bmatrix}$ [CBSE 2017]

(vi) $A \begin{bmatrix} 1 & 2 & 3 \\ 4 & 5 & 6 \end{bmatrix} = \begin{bmatrix} -7 & -8 & -9 \\ 2 & 4 & 6 \\ 11 & 10 & 9 \end{bmatrix}$ [CBSE 2017]

49. Find a 2×2 matrix A such that $A \begin{bmatrix} 1 & -2 \\ 1 & 4 \end{bmatrix} = 6I_2$.

50. If $A = \begin{bmatrix} -3 & 2 \\ 1 & -1 \end{bmatrix}$ and $I = \begin{bmatrix} 1 & 0 \\ 0 & 1 \end{bmatrix}$, find scalar k so that $A^2 + I = kA$. [CBSE 2020]

51. If $A = \begin{bmatrix} 0 & -x \\ x & 0 \end{bmatrix}$, $B = \begin{bmatrix} 0 & 1 \\ 1 & 0 \end{bmatrix}$ and $x^2 = -1$, then show that $(A+B)^2 = A^2 + B^2$.

[NCERT EXEMPLAR]

52. If $A = \begin{bmatrix} 1 & 0 & -3 \\ 2 & 1 & 3 \\ 0 & 1 & 1 \end{bmatrix}$, then verify that $A^2 + A = A(A+I)$, where I is the identity matrix.

[NCERT EXEMPLAR]

53. If $A = \begin{bmatrix} 3 & -5 \\ -4 & 2 \end{bmatrix}$, then find $A^2 - 5A - 14I$. Hence, obtain A^3. [NCERT EXEMPLAR]

54. (i) If $P(x) = \begin{bmatrix} \cos x & \sin x \\ -\sin x & \cos x \end{bmatrix}$, then show that $P(x)\, P(y) = P(x+y) = P(y)\, P(x)$.

(ii) If $P = \begin{bmatrix} x & 0 & 0 \\ 0 & y & 0 \\ 0 & 0 & z \end{bmatrix}$ and $Q = \begin{bmatrix} a & 0 & 0 \\ 0 & b & 0 \\ 0 & 0 & c \end{bmatrix}$, prove that $PQ = \begin{bmatrix} xa & 0 & 0 \\ 0 & yb & 0 \\ 0 & 0 & zc \end{bmatrix} = QP$

[NCERT EXEMPLAR]

55. If $A = \begin{bmatrix} 2 & 0 & 1 \\ 2 & 1 & 3 \\ 1 & -1 & 0 \end{bmatrix}$, find $A^2 - 5A + 4I$ and hence find a matrix X such that $A^2 - 5A + 4I + X = O$. [CBSE 2015]

56. If $A = \begin{bmatrix} 1 & 1 \\ 0 & 1 \end{bmatrix}$, prove that $A^n = \begin{bmatrix} 1 & n \\ 0 & 1 \end{bmatrix}$ for all positive integers n.

57. If $A = \begin{bmatrix} a & b \\ 0 & 1 \end{bmatrix}$, prove that $A^n = \begin{bmatrix} a^n & b\left(\dfrac{a^n - 1}{a - 1}\right) \\ 0 & 1 \end{bmatrix}$ for every positive integer n.

58. If $A = \begin{bmatrix} \cos\theta & i\sin\theta \\ i\sin\theta & \cos\theta \end{bmatrix}$, then prove by principle of mathematical induction that

$A^n = \begin{bmatrix} \cos n\theta & i\sin n\theta \\ i\sin n\theta & \cos n\theta \end{bmatrix}$ for all $n \in N$. [CBSE 2005]

59. If $A = \begin{bmatrix} \cos\alpha + \sin\alpha & \sqrt{2}\sin\alpha \\ -\sqrt{2}\sin\alpha & \cos\alpha - \sin\alpha \end{bmatrix}$, prove that $A^n = \begin{bmatrix} \cos n\alpha + \sin n\alpha & \sqrt{2}\sin n\alpha \\ -\sqrt{2}\sin n\alpha & \cos n\alpha - \sin n\alpha \end{bmatrix}$ for all $n \in N$.

60. If $A = \begin{bmatrix} 1 & 1 & 1 \\ 0 & 1 & 1 \\ 0 & 0 & 1 \end{bmatrix}$, then use the principle of mathematical induction to show that

$$A^n = \begin{bmatrix} 1 & n & n(n+1)/2 \\ 0 & 1 & n \\ 0 & 0 & 1 \end{bmatrix} \text{ for every positive integer } n.$$

61. If B, C are n rowed square matrices and if $A = B + C,\ BC = CB,\ C^2 = O$, then show that for every $n \in N,\ A^{n+1} = B^n (B + (n+1)C)$.

62. If $A = \text{diag}(a\ \ b\ \ c)$, show that $A^n = \text{diag}(a^n\ \ b^n\ \ c^n)$ for all positive integer n.

63. If A is a square matrix, using mathematical induction prove that $(A^T)^n = (A^n)^T$ for all $n \in N$.

[NCERT EXEMPLAR]

64. A matrix X has $a + b$ rows and $a + 2$ columns while the matrix Y has $b + 1$ rows and $a + 3$ columns. Both matrices XY and YX exist. Find a and b. Can you say XY and YX are of the same type? Are they equal.

65. Give examples of matrices
    (i) A and B such that $AB \neq BA$.
    (ii) A and B such that $AB = O$ but $A \neq O, B \neq O$.
    (iii) A and B such that $AB = O$ but $BA \neq O$.
    (iv) A, B and C such that $AB = AC$ but $B \neq C, A \neq O$.

66. Let A and B be square matrices of the same order. Does $(A + B)^2 = A^2 + 2AB + B^2$ hold? If not, why?

67. If A and B are square matrices of the same order, explain, why in general
    (i) $(A + B)^2 \neq A^2 + 2\,AB + B^2$ (ii) $(A - B)^2 \neq A^2 - 2\,AB + B^2$
    (iii) $(A + B)(A - B) \neq A^2 - B^2$.

68. Let A and B be square matrices of the same order 3×3. Is $(AB)^2 = A^2 B^2$? Give reasons.

[NCERT EXEMPLAR]

69. If A and B are square matrices of the same order such that $AB = BA$, then show that $(A + B)^2 = A^2 + 2AB + B^2$. **[NCERT EXEMPLAR]**

70. Let $A = \begin{bmatrix} 1 & 1 & 1 \\ 3 & 3 & 3 \end{bmatrix}$, $B = \begin{bmatrix} 3 & 1 \\ 5 & 2 \\ -2 & 4 \end{bmatrix}$ and $C = \begin{bmatrix} 4 & 2 \\ -3 & 5 \\ 5 & 0 \end{bmatrix}$.

    Verify that $AB = AC$ though $B \neq C, A \neq O$.

71. Three shopkeepers A, B and C go to a store to buy stationary. A purchases 12 dozen notebooks, 5 dozen pens and 6 dozen pencils. B purchases 10 dozen notebooks, 6 dozen pens and 7 dozen pencils. C purchases 11 dozen notebooks, 13 dozen pens and 8 dozen pencils. A notebook costs 40 paise, a pen costs ₹ 1.25 and a pencil costs 35 paise. Use matrix multiplication to calculate each individual's bill.

72. The cooperative stores of a particular school has 10 dozen physics books, 8 dozen chemistry books and 5 dozen mathematics books. Their selling prices are ₹ 8.30, ₹ 3.45 and ₹ 4.50 each respectively. Find the total amount the store will receive from selling all the items.

73. In a legislative assembly election, a political group hired a public relations firm to promote its candidates in three ways: telephone, house calls and letters. The cost per contact (in paise) is given matrix A as

$$\begin{array}{c} \text{Cost per contact} \\ A = \begin{bmatrix} 40 \\ 100 \\ 50 \end{bmatrix} \begin{array}{l} \text{Telephone} \\ \text{House call} \\ \text{Letter} \end{array} \end{array}$$

The number of contacts of each type made in two cities X and Y is given in matrix B as

$$\begin{array}{cccc} & \text{Telephone} & \text{House call} & \text{Letter} \end{array}$$
$$B = \begin{bmatrix} 1000 & 500 & 5000 \\ 3000 & 1000 & 10000 \end{bmatrix} \begin{array}{l} \to X \\ \to Y \end{array}$$

Find the total amount spent by the group in the two cities X and Y.

74. A trust fund has ₹ 30000 that must be invested in two different types of bonds. The first bond pays 5% interest per year, and the second bond pays 7% interest per year. Using matrix multiplication, determine how to divide ₹ 30000 among the two types of bonds. If the trust fund must obtain an annual total interest of (i) ₹ 1800 (ii) ₹ 2000. **[NCERT]**

75. To promote making of toilets for women, an organisation tried to generate awareness through (i) house calls (ii) letters, and (iii) announcements. The cost for each mode per attempt is given below:

(i) ₹ 50 (ii) ₹ 20 (iii) ₹ 40

The number of attempts made in three villages X, Y and Z are given below:

	(i)	(ii)	(iii)
X	400	300	100
Y	300	250	75
Z	500	400	150

Find the total cost incurred by the organisation for three villages separately, using matrices. **[CBSE 2015]**

76. There are 2 families A and B. There are 4 men, 6 women and 2 children in family A, and 2 men, 2 women and 4 children in family B. The recommend daily amount of calories is 2400 for men, 1900 for women, 1800 for children and 45 grams of proteins for men, 55 grams for women and 33 grams for children. Represent the above information using matrix. Using matrix multiplication, calculate the total requirement of calories and proteins for each of the two families. What awareness can you create among people about the planned diet from this question? **[CBSE 2015]**

77. In a parliament election, a political party hired a public relations firm to promote its candidates in three ways — telephone, house calls and letters. The cost per contact (in paisa) is given in matrix A as

$$A = \begin{bmatrix} 140 \\ 200 \\ 150 \end{bmatrix} \begin{array}{l} \text{Telephone} \\ \text{House calls} \\ \text{Letters} \end{array}$$

The number of contacts of each type made in two cities X and Y is given in the matrix B as

$$\begin{array}{cccc} & \text{Telephone} & \text{House call} & \text{Letters} \end{array}$$
$$B = \begin{bmatrix} 1000 & 500 & 5000 \\ 3000 & 1000 & 10000 \end{bmatrix} \begin{array}{l} \text{City } X \\ \text{City } Y \end{array}$$

Find the total amount spent by the party in the two cities.

What should one consider before casting his/her vote — party's promotional activity or their social activities? [CBSE 2015]

78. The monthly incomes of Aryan and Babbar are in the ratio 3 : 4 and their monthly expenditures are in the ratio 5 : 7. If each saves ₹ 15000 per month, find their monthly incomes using matrix method. This problem reflects which value? [CBSE 2016]

79. A trust invested some money in two type of bonds. The first bond pays 10% interest and second bond pays 12% interest. The trust received ₹ 2800 as interest. However, if trust had interchanged money in bonds, they would have got ₹ 100 less as interest. Using matrix method, find the amount invested by the trust. [CBSE 2016]

ANSWERS

1. (i) $\begin{bmatrix} a^2+b^2 & 0 \\ 0 & a^2+b^2 \end{bmatrix}$ (ii) $\begin{bmatrix} 7 & -2 & 5 \\ -7 & 10 & 3 \end{bmatrix}$ (iii) $\begin{bmatrix} 14 & 0 & 42 \\ 18 & -1 & 56 \\ 22 & -2 & 70 \end{bmatrix}$

3. (i) $AB = \begin{bmatrix} -3 & -4 & 1 \\ 8 & 13 & 9 \end{bmatrix}$, BA does not exist (ii) $AB = \begin{bmatrix} 12 & 17 & 22 \\ -4 & -5 & -6 \\ -4 & -4 & -4 \end{bmatrix}$, $BA = \begin{bmatrix} 1 & 14 \\ -3 & 2 \end{bmatrix}$

(iii) $AB = [11]$, $BA = \begin{bmatrix} 0 & 0 & 0 & 0 \\ 1 & -1 & 2 & 3 \\ 3 & -3 & 6 & 9 \\ 2 & -2 & 4 & 6 \end{bmatrix}$ (iv) $[a^2+b^2+c^2+d^2+ac+bd]$

5. (i) $\begin{bmatrix} 6 & 16 & 26 \\ -8 & -18 & -28 \end{bmatrix}$ (ii) [82] (iii) $\begin{bmatrix} 0 & -1 & 1 \\ 2 & 0 & -2 \\ 5 & -2 & -3 \end{bmatrix}$ 7. $\begin{bmatrix} 4 & -20 \\ 38 & -10 \end{bmatrix}$

11. $\begin{bmatrix} \cos 4\theta & \sin 4\theta \\ -\sin 4\theta & \cos 4\theta \end{bmatrix}$ 15. $\begin{bmatrix} -2 & -9 & -1 \\ 3 & 26 & 3 \\ 35 & 15 & 34 \end{bmatrix}$ 19. $a_{43} = 8, a_{22} = 0$

24. (i) $x = -2$ (ii) $x = 13$ 25. $x = -2, -1$ 26. 2

28. -7 30. $8I$ 33. $\begin{bmatrix} 0 & 0 \\ 0 & 0 \end{bmatrix}$ 34. (ii) $\begin{bmatrix} 39 & 55 \\ -55 & -16 \end{bmatrix}$ 35. $k = 1$

36. $k = 7$ 38. $\lambda = 4, \mu = -1$ 39. $\frac{1}{5}$

40. (i) $x = -3, 5$ (ii) $x = -1$ (iii) $x = 4\sqrt{3}$ (iv) $x = 0, -\frac{23}{2}$

41. $\begin{bmatrix} 6 & -14 & 10 \\ -21 & 36 & -25 \\ -3 & 5 & -5 \end{bmatrix}$ 42. $\begin{bmatrix} 4 & 7 & 2 \\ 12 & 19 & 8 \\ 8 & 12 & 3 \end{bmatrix}$ 43. $\begin{bmatrix} 6 & -2 & 6 \\ 0 & 4 & 4 \\ 1 & 1 & 4 \end{bmatrix}$

47. $\begin{bmatrix} 1 & -4 \\ 3 & -2 \end{bmatrix}$ 48. (i) $\begin{bmatrix} 2 & 3 & 4 \\ 1 & 0 & 1 \end{bmatrix}$ (ii) $\begin{bmatrix} 1 & -2 \\ 2 & 0 \end{bmatrix}$ (iii) $[-1 \ \ 2 \ \ 1]$ (iv) $[-4]$ (v) $\begin{bmatrix} 1 & -2 & -5 \\ 3 & 4 & 0 \end{bmatrix}$

(vi) $\begin{bmatrix} 1 & -2 \\ 2 & 0 \\ -5 & 4 \end{bmatrix}$ 49. $\begin{bmatrix} 4 & 2 \\ -1 & 1 \end{bmatrix}$ 50. -4 53. $\begin{bmatrix} 187 & -195 \\ -156 & 148 \end{bmatrix}$

55. $\begin{bmatrix} -1 & -1 & -3 \\ -1 & -3 & -10 \\ -5 & 4 & 2 \end{bmatrix}$, $\begin{bmatrix} 1 & 1 & 3 \\ 1 & 3 & 10 \\ 5 & -4 & -2 \end{bmatrix}$ 64. $a = 2, b = 3$, No 68. True when $AB = BA$

71. ₹ 157.80, ₹ 167.40, ₹ 281.40 72. ₹1597.20 73. ₹ 3400, ₹ 7200

74. (i) ₹ 15000 each (ii) ₹ 5000, ₹ 25000

75. X: ₹ 30,000
Y: ₹ 23,000
Z: ₹ 39,000

76.

	Calories	Proteins
Family A:	24600	576
Family B:	15800	332

77. X: ₹ 9900
Y: ₹ 21200

78. ₹ 90,000, ₹ 120,000

79. ₹ 10,000, ₹ 15,000

HINTS TO SELECTED PROBLEMS

34. We have,

$$A = \begin{bmatrix} 3 & 1 \\ -1 & 2 \end{bmatrix}$$

$$\Rightarrow \quad A^2 = AA = \begin{bmatrix} 3 & 1 \\ -1 & 2 \end{bmatrix}\begin{bmatrix} 3 & 1 \\ -1 & 2 \end{bmatrix} = \begin{bmatrix} 9-1 & 3+2 \\ -3-2 & -1+4 \end{bmatrix} = \begin{bmatrix} 8 & 5 \\ -5 & 3 \end{bmatrix}$$

$$\therefore \quad A^2 - 5A + 7I = \begin{bmatrix} 8 & 5 \\ -5 & 3 \end{bmatrix} + \begin{bmatrix} -15 & -5 \\ 5 & -10 \end{bmatrix} + \begin{bmatrix} 7 & 0 \\ 0 & 7 \end{bmatrix} = \begin{bmatrix} 8-15+7 & 5-5+0 \\ -5+5+0 & 3-10+7 \end{bmatrix} = \begin{bmatrix} 0 & 0 \\ 0 & 0 \end{bmatrix} = O$$

$$\Rightarrow \quad A^2 = 5A - 7I$$

$$\therefore \quad A^4 = A^2 A^2 = (5A - 7I)(5A - 7I) = 5A(5A - 7I) - 7I(5A - 7I)$$

$$= 25A^2 - 35AI - 35IA + 49II = 25A^2 - 35A - 35A + 49I$$

$$= 25A^2 - 70A + 49I = 25(5A - 7I) - 70A + 49I$$

$$= 125A - 175I - 70A + 49I = 55A - 126I$$

$$= 55\begin{bmatrix} 3 & 1 \\ -1 & 2 \end{bmatrix} - 126\begin{bmatrix} 1 & 0 \\ 0 & 1 \end{bmatrix} = \begin{bmatrix} 165 & 55 \\ -55 & 110 \end{bmatrix} + \begin{bmatrix} -126 & 0 \\ 0 & -126 \end{bmatrix} = \begin{bmatrix} 39 & 55 \\ -55 & -16 \end{bmatrix}$$

35. We have, $A = \begin{bmatrix} 3 & -2 \\ 4 & -2 \end{bmatrix}$

$$\therefore \quad A^2 = \begin{bmatrix} 3 & -2 \\ 4 & -2 \end{bmatrix}\begin{bmatrix} 3 & -2 \\ 4 & -2 \end{bmatrix} = \begin{bmatrix} 9-8 & -6+4 \\ 12-8 & -8+4 \end{bmatrix} = \begin{bmatrix} 1 & -2 \\ 4 & -4 \end{bmatrix}$$

It is given that $A^2 = kA - 2I_2$

$$\therefore \quad \begin{bmatrix} 1 & -2 \\ 4 & -4 \end{bmatrix} = k\begin{bmatrix} 3 & -2 \\ 4 & -2 \end{bmatrix} - 2\begin{bmatrix} 1 & 0 \\ 0 & 1 \end{bmatrix} \Rightarrow \begin{bmatrix} 1 & -2 \\ 4 & -4 \end{bmatrix} = \begin{bmatrix} 3k-2 & -2k \\ 4k & -2k-2 \end{bmatrix}$$

$$\Rightarrow \quad 3k - 2 = 1,\ 4k = 4,\ -2k = -2 \text{ and } -2k - 2 = -4 \Rightarrow k = 1$$

40. (ii) $[1 \quad 2 \quad 1]\begin{bmatrix} 1 & 2 & 0 \\ 2 & 0 & 1 \\ 1 & 0 & 2 \end{bmatrix}\begin{bmatrix} 0 \\ 2 \\ x \end{bmatrix} = 0 \Rightarrow [1 \quad 2 \quad 1]\begin{bmatrix} 4 \\ x \\ 2x \end{bmatrix} = 0 \Rightarrow 4 + 2x + 2x = 0 \Rightarrow x = -1$

44. We have, $A = \begin{bmatrix} 1 & 0 & 2 \\ 0 & 2 & 1 \\ 2 & 0 & 3 \end{bmatrix}$ and $f(x) = x^3 - 6x^2 + 7x + 2$. Therefore, $f(A) = A^3 - 6A^2 + 7A + 2I_3$.

Now, $A^2 = AA = \begin{bmatrix} 1 & 0 & 2 \\ 0 & 2 & 1 \\ 2 & 0 & 3 \end{bmatrix}\begin{bmatrix} 1 & 0 & 2 \\ 0 & 2 & 1 \\ 2 & 0 & 3 \end{bmatrix} = \begin{bmatrix} 5 & 0 & 8 \\ 2 & 4 & 5 \\ 8 & 0 & 13 \end{bmatrix}$

$$\Rightarrow \quad A^3 = A^2 A = \begin{bmatrix} 5 & 0 & 8 \\ 2 & 4 & 5 \\ 8 & 0 & 13 \end{bmatrix}\begin{bmatrix} 1 & 0 & 2 \\ 0 & 2 & 1 \\ 2 & 0 & 3 \end{bmatrix} = \begin{bmatrix} 21 & 0 & 34 \\ 12 & 8 & 23 \\ 34 & 0 & 55 \end{bmatrix}$$

$$\therefore \quad f(A) = A^3 - 6A^2 + 7A + 2I_3$$

$$\Rightarrow \quad f(A) = \begin{bmatrix} 21 & 0 & 34 \\ 12 & 8 & 23 \\ 34 & 0 & 55 \end{bmatrix} - 6\begin{bmatrix} 5 & 0 & 8 \\ 2 & 4 & 5 \\ 8 & 0 & 13 \end{bmatrix} + \begin{bmatrix} 7 & 0 & 14 \\ 0 & 14 & 7 \\ 14 & 0 & 21 \end{bmatrix} + \begin{bmatrix} 2 & 0 & 0 \\ 0 & 2 & 0 \\ 0 & 0 & 2 \end{bmatrix} = \begin{bmatrix} 0 & 0 & 0 \\ 0 & 0 & 0 \\ 0 & 0 & 0 \end{bmatrix} = O$$

Hence, A is a root of the polynomial $f(x) = x^3 - 6x^2 + 7x + 2$.

48. (ii) We have to find a matrix A satisfying the equation $A\begin{bmatrix} 1 & 2 & 3 \\ 4 & 5 & 6 \end{bmatrix} = \begin{bmatrix} -7 & -8 & -9 \\ 2 & 4 & 6 \end{bmatrix}$.

Clearly, the product of A with a 2×3 matrix is a 2×3 matrix. Therefore, A is a 2×2 matrix.

Let $A = \begin{bmatrix} a & b \\ c & d \end{bmatrix}$. Then,

$$A\begin{bmatrix} 1 & 2 & 3 \\ 4 & 5 & 6 \end{bmatrix} = \begin{bmatrix} -7 & -8 & -9 \\ 2 & 4 & 6 \end{bmatrix} \Rightarrow \begin{bmatrix} a & b \\ c & d \end{bmatrix}\begin{bmatrix} 1 & 2 & 3 \\ 4 & 5 & 6 \end{bmatrix} = \begin{bmatrix} -7 & -8 & -9 \\ 2 & 4 & 6 \end{bmatrix}$$

$$\Rightarrow \quad \begin{bmatrix} a+4b & 2a+5b & 3a+6b \\ c+4d & 2c+5d & 3c+6d \end{bmatrix} = \begin{bmatrix} -7 & -8 & -9 \\ 2 & 4 & 6 \end{bmatrix}$$

$$\Rightarrow \quad a+4b = -7,\ 2a+5b = -8,\ 3a+6b = -9,\ c+4d = 2,\ 2c+5d = 4,\ 3c+6d = 6$$

$$\Rightarrow \quad a = 1,\ b = -2,\ c = 2,\ d = 0$$

$$\therefore \quad A = \begin{bmatrix} 1 & -2 \\ 2 & 0 \end{bmatrix}$$

65. (ii) $A = \begin{bmatrix} 5 & 0 \\ 0 & 0 \end{bmatrix}, B = \begin{bmatrix} 0 & 0 \\ -1 & 0 \end{bmatrix}$ (iii) $A = \begin{bmatrix} 1 & 0 \\ 0 & 0 \end{bmatrix}, B = \begin{bmatrix} 0 & 0 \\ 2 & 1 \end{bmatrix}$

(iv) $A = \begin{bmatrix} 2 & 0 \\ 0 & 0 \end{bmatrix}, B = \begin{bmatrix} 3 & 0 \\ 0 & 0 \end{bmatrix}, C = \begin{bmatrix} 3 & 0 \\ 0 & 1 \end{bmatrix}$

74. Let ₹ x be invested in first bond and ₹ y be invested in second bond. Let A be the investment matrix and B be the interest per rupee matrix. Then,

$$A = [x \quad y] \text{ and } B = \begin{bmatrix} \frac{5}{100} \\ \frac{7}{100} \end{bmatrix}. \text{ Total annual interest } = AB = [x \quad y]\begin{bmatrix} \frac{5}{100} \\ \frac{7}{100} \end{bmatrix} = \frac{5x}{100} + \frac{7y}{100}$$

Also, $x + y = 30000$ ...(i)

(i) If total interest is ₹ 1800. Then, $\frac{5x}{100} + \frac{7y}{100} = 1800 \Rightarrow 5x + 7y = 180000$ ...(ii)

Solving (i) and (ii), we get : $x = y = 15000$.

(ii) If total interest is ₹ 2000. Then, $\frac{5x}{100} + \frac{7y}{100} = 2000 \Rightarrow 5x + 7y = 200000$ ...(iii)

Solving (i) and (iii), we get : $x = 5000$ and $y = 25000$

76. Let F be the family matrix and R be the requirement matrix. Then,

$$F = \begin{array}{c} \\ \text{Family } A \\ \text{Family } B \end{array}\begin{array}{c} \begin{array}{ccc} \text{Men} & \text{Women} & \text{Children} \end{array} \\ \begin{bmatrix} 4 & 6 & 2 \\ 2 & 2 & 4 \end{bmatrix} \end{array} \text{ and, } R = \begin{array}{c} \\ \text{Men} \\ \text{Women} \\ \text{Children} \end{array}\begin{array}{c} \begin{array}{cc} \text{Calories} & \text{Proteins} \end{array} \\ \begin{bmatrix} 2400 & 45 \\ 1900 & 55 \\ 1800 & 33 \end{bmatrix} \end{array}$$

Total requirement of calories and proteins of each of the two families is given by the matrix product

$$FR = \begin{matrix} \\ \text{Family } A \\ \text{Family } B \end{matrix}\begin{matrix} \text{Men} & \text{Women} & \text{Children} \\ \left[\begin{matrix} 4 \\ 2 \end{matrix}\right. & \begin{matrix} 6 \\ 2 \end{matrix} & \left.\begin{matrix} 2 \\ 4 \end{matrix}\right] \end{matrix} \quad \begin{matrix} \\ \text{Men} \\ \text{Women} \\ \text{Children} \end{matrix}\begin{matrix} \text{Calories} & \text{Proteins} \\ \left[\begin{matrix} 2400 \\ 1900 \\ 1800 \end{matrix}\right. & \left.\begin{matrix} 45 \\ 55 \\ 33 \end{matrix}\right] \end{matrix}$$

$$\Rightarrow \quad FR = \begin{matrix} \\ \text{Family } A \\ \text{Family } B \end{matrix}\begin{matrix} \text{Calories} & \text{Proteins} \\ \left[\begin{matrix} 24600 \\ 15800 \end{matrix}\right. & \left.\begin{matrix} 576 \\ 332 \end{matrix}\right] \end{matrix}$$

4.8 TRANSPOSE OF A MATRIX

DEFINITION *Let $A = [a_{ij}]$ be an $m \times n$ matrix. Then, the transpose of A, denoted by A^T or A', is an $n \times m$ matrix such that*

$$(A^T)_{ij} = a_{ji} \text{ for all } i = 1, 2, \ldots, n; j = 1, 2, \ldots, m.$$

Thus, A^T is obtained from A by changing its rows into columns and columns into rows.

For example, if $A = \begin{bmatrix} 1 & 2 & 3 & 4 \\ 2 & 3 & 4 & 1 \\ 3 & 2 & 1 & 4 \end{bmatrix}$, then $A^T = \begin{bmatrix} 1 & 2 & 3 \\ 2 & 3 & 2 \\ 3 & 4 & 1 \\ 4 & 1 & 4 \end{bmatrix}$.

The first row of A^T is the first column of A. The second row of A^T is the second column of A and so on.

4.8.1 PROPERTIES OF TRANSPOSE

We shall now state and prove some properties of transpose of a matrix as theorems given below.

THEOREM 1 *For any matrix A, $(A^T)^T = A$.*

PROOF Let $A = [a_{ij}]$ be an $m \times n$ matrix. Then, A^T is an $n \times m$ matrix and so $(A^T)^T$ is an $m \times n$ matrix. Thus, the matrices A and $(A^T)^T$ are of the same order such that

$$\left((A^T)^T\right)_{ij} = (A^T)_{ji} \qquad \text{[By the definition of transpose]}$$

$$\Rightarrow \quad \left((A^T)^T\right)_{ij} = (A)_{ij} \text{ for all } i = 1, 2, \ldots, m \text{ and } j = 1, 2, \ldots, n$$

Hence, by the definition of equality of two matrices, we obtain

$$(A^T)^T = A.$$

Q.E.D.

THEOREM 2 *For any two matrices A and B of the same order, $(A + B)^T = A^T + B^T$.*

PROOF Let $A = [a_{ij}]_{m \times n}$ and $B = [b_{ij}]_{m \times n}$. Then, $A + B$ will be a matrix of the order $m \times n$ and so $(A + B)^T$ will be a matrix of order $n \times m$. Since A^T and B^T are both $n \times m$ matrices. Therefore, $A^T + B^T$ will be a matrix of the order $n \times m$. Thus, the matrices $(A + B)^T$ and $A^T + B^T$ are of the same order such that

$$\begin{aligned} ((A + B)^T))_{ij} &= (A + B)_{ji} && \text{[By the definition of transpose]} \\ &= a_{ji} + b_{ji} && \text{[By the definition of addition]} \\ &= (A^T)_{ij} + (B^T)_{ij} \\ &= (A^T + B^T)_{ij} \quad \text{for all } i, j && \text{[By the definition of addition]} \end{aligned}$$

Hence, by the definition of equality of two matrices, we obtain : $(A + B)^T = A^T + B^T$. Q.E.D.

THEOREM 3 *If A is a matrix and k is a scalar, then $(kA)^T = k(A^T)$.*

PROOF Let $A = [a_{ij}]$ be an $m \times n$ matrix. Then, for any scalar k, kA is also an $m \times n$ matrix and so $(kA)^T$ is an $n \times m$ matrix. Again A^T is an $n \times m$ matrix and so kA^T is an $n \times m$ matrix. Thus, the two matrices $(kA)^T$ and kA^T are of the same order such that

$$((kA)^T)_{ij} = (kA)_{ji} \quad \text{[By the definition of transpose]}$$

$$= k\, a_{ji} \quad \text{[By the definition of scalar multiplication]}$$

$$= k\,(A^T)_{ij} \quad \text{[By the definition of transpose]}$$

$$= (kA^T)_{ij} \quad \text{[By the definition of scalar multiplication]}$$

Hence, by the definition of equality of two matrices, we obtain : $(kA)^T = k\,A^T$. **Q.E.D.**

THEOREM 4 *If A and B are two matrices such that AB is defined, then $(AB)^T = B^T A^T$.*

PROOF Let $A = [a_{ij}]_{m \times n}$ and $B = [b_{ij}]_{n \times p}$ be two matrices. Then AB is an $m \times p$ matrix and therefore $(AB)^T$ is a $p \times m$ matrix. Since A^T and B^T are $n \times m$ and $p \times n$ matrices, therefore $B^T A^T$ is a $p \times m$ matrix. Thus, the two matrices $(AB)^T$ and $B^T A^T$ are of the same order such that

$$((AB)^T)_{ij} = (AB)_{ji} \quad \text{[By the definition of transpose]}$$

$$= \sum_{r=1}^{n} a_{jr}\, b_{ri} \quad \text{[By the definition of matrix multiplication]}$$

$$= \sum_{r=1}^{n} b_{ri}\, a_{jr} \quad \text{[By commutativity of multiplication of numbers]}$$

$$= \sum_{r=1}^{n} (B^T)_{ir}\, (A^T)_{rj} \quad \text{[By definition of transpose]}$$

$$= (B^T A^T)_{ij} \quad \text{[By definition of multiplication of matrices]}$$

Hence, by the definition of equality of two matrices, we obtain $(AB)^T = B^T A^T$.

Q.E.D.

GENERALISATION *If A, B, C are three matrices confirmable for the products $(AB)\,C$ and $A\,(BC)$, then $(ABC)^T = C^T B^T A^T$.*

REMARK *The above law is called the reversal law for transposes i.e. the transpose of the product is the product of the transposes taken in the reverse order.*

ILLUSTRATIVE EXAMPLES

BASED ON BASIC CONCEPTS (BASIC)

EXAMPLE 1 *If $A = \begin{bmatrix} -1 \\ 2 \\ 3 \end{bmatrix}$ and $B = [-2 \;\; -1 \;\; -4]$, verify that $(AB)^T = B^T A^T$.*

SOLUTION We have, **[CBSE 2002, 2005]**

$$A = \begin{bmatrix} -1 \\ 2 \\ 3 \end{bmatrix} \text{ and } B = [-2 \;\; -1 \;\; -4]$$

$$\therefore \quad AB = \begin{bmatrix} -1 \\ 2 \\ 3 \end{bmatrix} [-2 \quad -1 \quad -4] = \begin{bmatrix} 2 & 1 & 4 \\ -4 & -2 & -8 \\ -6 & -3 & -12 \end{bmatrix} \Rightarrow (AB)^T = \begin{bmatrix} 2 & -4 & -6 \\ 1 & -2 & -3 \\ 4 & -8 & -12 \end{bmatrix} \quad ...(i)$$

Also, $$B^T A^T = [-2 \quad -1 \quad -4]^T \begin{bmatrix} -1 \\ 2 \\ 3 \end{bmatrix}^T = \begin{bmatrix} -2 \\ -1 \\ -4 \end{bmatrix} [-1 \quad 2 \quad 3] = \begin{bmatrix} 2 & -4 & -6 \\ 1 & -2 & -3 \\ 4 & -8 & -12 \end{bmatrix} \quad ...(ii)$$

From (i) and (ii), we observe that $(AB)^T = B^T A^T$.

BASED ON LOWER ORDER THINKING SKILLS (LOTS)

EXAMPLE 2 *If* $A = \begin{bmatrix} \cos\theta & -\sin\theta \\ \sin\theta & \cos\theta \end{bmatrix}$, *then find the values of* θ *satisfying the equation* $A^T + A = I_2$.

SOLUTION We have,

$$A = \begin{bmatrix} \cos\theta & -\sin\theta \\ \sin\theta & \cos\theta \end{bmatrix} \Rightarrow A^T = \begin{bmatrix} \cos\theta & \sin\theta \\ -\sin\theta & \cos\theta \end{bmatrix}$$

Now, $A^T + A = I_2$

$$\Rightarrow \quad \begin{bmatrix} \cos\theta & \sin\theta \\ -\sin\theta & \cos\theta \end{bmatrix} + \begin{bmatrix} \cos\theta & -\sin\theta \\ \sin\theta & \cos\theta \end{bmatrix} = \begin{bmatrix} 1 & 0 \\ 0 & 1 \end{bmatrix} \Rightarrow \begin{bmatrix} 2\cos\theta & 0 \\ 0 & 2\cos\theta \end{bmatrix} = \begin{bmatrix} 1 & 0 \\ 0 & 1 \end{bmatrix}$$

$$\Rightarrow \quad 2\cos\theta = 1 \Rightarrow \cos\theta = \frac{1}{2} \Rightarrow \cos\theta = \cos\frac{\pi}{3} \Rightarrow \theta = 2n\pi \pm \frac{\pi}{3}, \quad n \in Z$$

EXAMPLE 3 *If* $A = \begin{bmatrix} 1 & 2 & 2 \\ 2 & 1 & -2 \\ a & 2 & b \end{bmatrix}$ *is a matrix satisfying* $AA^T = 9I_3$, *then find the values of a and b.*

SOLUTION We have,

$$A = \begin{bmatrix} 1 & 2 & 2 \\ 2 & 1 & -2 \\ a & 2 & b \end{bmatrix} \Rightarrow A^T = \begin{bmatrix} 1 & 2 & a \\ 2 & 1 & 2 \\ 2 & -2 & b \end{bmatrix}$$

$$\therefore \quad AA^T = 9I_3$$

$$\Rightarrow \quad \begin{bmatrix} 1 & 2 & 2 \\ 2 & 1 & -2 \\ a & 2 & b \end{bmatrix} \begin{bmatrix} 1 & 2 & a \\ 2 & 1 & 2 \\ 2 & -2 & b \end{bmatrix} = 9 \begin{bmatrix} 1 & 0 & 0 \\ 0 & 1 & 0 \\ 0 & 0 & 1 \end{bmatrix}$$

$$\Rightarrow \quad \begin{bmatrix} 9 & 0 & a+2b+4 \\ 0 & 9 & 2a+2-2b \\ a+2b+4 & 2a+2-2b & a^2+4+b^2 \end{bmatrix} = \begin{bmatrix} 9 & 0 & 0 \\ 0 & 9 & 0 \\ 0 & 0 & 9 \end{bmatrix}$$

$$\Rightarrow \quad a+2b+4 = 0, \; 2a+2-2b = 0 \text{ and } a^2+4+b^2 = 9$$

$$\Rightarrow \quad a+2b+4 = 0, \; a-b+1 = 0 \text{ and } a^2+b^2 = 5$$

Solving $a+2b+4 = 0$ and $a-b+1 = 0$, we get: $a = -2$ and $b = -1$.

EXAMPLE 4 *Find the values of* x, y, z *if the matrix* $A = \begin{bmatrix} 0 & 2y & z \\ x & y & -z \\ x & -y & z \end{bmatrix}$ *satisfy the equation* $A^T A = I_3$. [NCERT]

SOLUTION We have,

$$A = \begin{bmatrix} 0 & 2y & z \\ x & y & -z \\ x & -y & z \end{bmatrix} \Rightarrow A^T = \begin{bmatrix} 0 & x & x \\ 2y & y & -y \\ z & -z & z \end{bmatrix}$$

It is given that

$$A^T A = I_3$$

$$\Rightarrow \begin{bmatrix} 0 & x & x \\ 2y & y & -y \\ z & -z & z \end{bmatrix} \begin{bmatrix} 0 & 2y & z \\ x & y & -z \\ x & -y & z \end{bmatrix} = \begin{bmatrix} 1 & 0 & 0 \\ 0 & 1 & 0 \\ 0 & 0 & 1 \end{bmatrix}$$

$$\Rightarrow \begin{bmatrix} 2x^2 & 0 & 0 \\ 0 & 6y^2 & 0 \\ 0 & 0 & 3z^2 \end{bmatrix} = \begin{bmatrix} 1 & 0 & 0 \\ 0 & 1 & 0 \\ 0 & 0 & 1 \end{bmatrix}$$

$$\Rightarrow 2x^2 = 1,\ 6y^2 = 1,\ 3z^2 = 1 \Rightarrow x = \pm \frac{1}{\sqrt{2}}, y = \pm \frac{1}{\sqrt{6}}, z = \pm \frac{1}{\sqrt{3}}$$

EXERCISE 4.4

BASIC

1. Let $A = \begin{bmatrix} 2 & -3 \\ -7 & 5 \end{bmatrix}$ and $B = \begin{bmatrix} 1 & 0 \\ 2 & -4 \end{bmatrix}$, verify that

   (i) $(2A)^T = 2A^T$ (ii) $(A+B)^T = A^T + B^T$ (iii) $(A-B)^T = A^T - B^T$ (iv) $(AB)^T = B^T A^T$

2. If $A = \begin{bmatrix} 3 \\ 5 \\ 2 \end{bmatrix}$ and $B = [1 \quad 0 \quad 4]$, verify that $(AB)^T = B^T A^T$. [CBSE 2002]

3. Let $A = \begin{bmatrix} 1 & -1 & 0 \\ 2 & 1 & 3 \\ 1 & 2 & 1 \end{bmatrix}$ and $B = \begin{bmatrix} 1 & 2 & 3 \\ 2 & 1 & 3 \\ 0 & 1 & 1 \end{bmatrix}$. Find A^T, B^T and verify that

   (i) $(A+B)^T = A^T + B^T$ (ii) $(AB)^T = B^T A^T$ (iii) $(2A)^T = 2A^T$

4. If $A = \begin{bmatrix} -2 \\ 4 \\ 5 \end{bmatrix}$, $B = [1\,3 \quad -6]$, verify that $(AB)^T = B^T A^T$.

5. If $A = \begin{bmatrix} 2 & 4 & -1 \\ -1 & 0 & 2 \end{bmatrix}$, $B = \begin{bmatrix} 3 & 4 \\ -1 & 2 \\ 2 & 1 \end{bmatrix}$, find $(AB)^T$.

6. (i) For two matrices A and B, $A = \begin{bmatrix} 2 & 1 & 3 \\ 4 & 1 & 0 \end{bmatrix}$, $B = \begin{bmatrix} 1 & -1 \\ 0 & 2 \\ 5 & 0 \end{bmatrix}$ verify that $(AB)^T = B^T A^T$.

   (ii) For the matrices A and B, verify that $(AB)^T = B^T A^T$, where $A = \begin{bmatrix} 1 & 3 \\ 2 & 4 \end{bmatrix}$, $B = \begin{bmatrix} 1 & 4 \\ 2 & 5 \end{bmatrix}$

7. If $A^T = \begin{bmatrix} 3 & 4 \\ -1 & 2 \\ 0 & 1 \end{bmatrix}$ and $B = \begin{bmatrix} -1 & 2 & 1 \\ 1 & 2 & 3 \end{bmatrix}$, find $A^T - B^T$. [CBSE 2012]

BASED ON LOTS

8. If $A = \begin{bmatrix} \cos\alpha & \sin\alpha \\ -\sin\alpha & \cos\alpha \end{bmatrix}$, then verify that $A^T A = I_2$. [NCERT]

9. If $A = \begin{bmatrix} \sin\alpha & \cos\alpha \\ -\cos\alpha & \sin\alpha \end{bmatrix}$, verify that $A^T A = I_2$. [NCERT]

BASED ON HOTS

10. If l_i, m_i, n_i ; $i = 1, 2, 3$ denote the direction cosines of three mutually perpendicular vectors in space, prove that $AA^T = I$, where $A = \begin{bmatrix} l_1 & m_1 & n_1 \\ l_2 & m_2 & n_2 \\ l_3 & m_3 & n_3 \end{bmatrix}$.

ANSWERS

5. $\begin{bmatrix} 0 & 1 \\ 15 & -2 \end{bmatrix}$ 7. $\begin{bmatrix} 4 & 3 \\ -3 & 0 \\ -1 & -2 \end{bmatrix}$

4.9 SYMMETRIC AND SKEW-SYMMETRIC MATRICES

SYMMETRIC MATRIX *A square matrix $A = [a_{ij}]$ is called a symmetric matrix, if $a_{ij} = a_{ji}$ for all i, j.*

For example, the matrix $A = \begin{bmatrix} 3 & -1 & 1 \\ -1 & 2 & 5 \\ 1 & 5 & -2 \end{bmatrix}$ is symmetric, because $a_{12} = -1 = a_{21}, a_{13} = 1 = a_{31}$, $a_{23} = 5 = a_{32}$ i.e. $a_{ij} = a_{ji}$ for all i, j.

It follows from the definition of a symmetric matrix that A is symmetric, iff

$$a_{ij} = a_{ji} \text{ for all } i, j \Leftrightarrow (A)_{ij} = (A^T)_{ij} \text{ for all } i, j \Leftrightarrow A = A^T.$$

Thus, a square matrix A is a symmetric matrix iff $A^T = A$.

Matrices $A = \begin{bmatrix} a & h & g \\ h & b & f \\ g & f & c \end{bmatrix}$, $B = \begin{bmatrix} 2+i & 1 & 3 \\ 1 & 2 & 3+2i \\ 3 & 3+2i & 4 \end{bmatrix}$ are symmetric matrices, because $A^T = A$ and $B^T = B$.

SKEW-SYMMETRIC MATRIX *A square matrix $A = [a_{ij}]$ is a skew-symmetric matrix if $a_{ij} = -a_{ji}$ for all i, j.*

For example, the matrix $A = \begin{bmatrix} 0 & 2 & -3 \\ -2 & 0 & 5 \\ 3 & -5 & 0 \end{bmatrix}$ is skew-symmetric, because

$$a_{12} = 2,\ a_{21} = -2 \Rightarrow a_{12} = -a_{21};\ a_{13} = -3,\ a_{31} = 3 \Rightarrow a_{13} = -a_{31};$$

and, $\quad a_{23} = 5,\ a_{32} = -5 \Rightarrow a_{23} = -a_{32}$

It follows from the definition of a skew-symmetric matrix that A is skew-symmetric iff

$$\Leftrightarrow a_{ij} = -a_{ji} \text{ for all } i, j \Leftrightarrow (A)_{ij} = -(A^T)_{ij} \text{ for all } i, j \Leftrightarrow A = -A^T \Leftrightarrow A^T = -A.$$

Thus, a square matrix A is a skew-symmetric matrix iff $A^T = -A$.

Matrices $A = \begin{bmatrix} 0 & 2i & 3 \\ -2i & 0 & 4 \\ -3 & -4 & 0 \end{bmatrix}, B = \begin{bmatrix} 0 & -3 & 5 \\ 3 & 0 & 2 \\ -5 & -2 & 0 \end{bmatrix}$ are skew-symmetric matrices because $A^T = -A$ and $B^T = -B$.

ILLUSTRATIVE EXAMPLES

BASED ON BASIC CONCEPTS (BASIC)

EXAMPLE 1 *Show that the elements on the main diagonal of a skew-symmetric matrix are all zero.* **[CBSE 2017]**

SOLUTION Let $A = [a_{ij}]$ be a skew-symmetric matrix. Then,

$a_{ij} = -a_{ji}$ for all i, j [By definition]

$\Rightarrow$ $a_{ii} = -a_{ii}$ for all values of i

$\Rightarrow$ $2a_{ii} = 0 \Rightarrow a_{ii} = 0$ for all values of $i \Rightarrow a_{11} = a_{22} = a_{33} = \dots = a_{nn} = 0.$

EXAMPLE 2 *If the matrix* $A = \begin{bmatrix} 0 & a & 3 \\ 2 & b & -1 \\ c & 1 & 0 \end{bmatrix}$ *is skew-symmetric, find the values of a, b and c.* **[NCERT EXEMPLAR]**

SOLUTION For a skew-symmetric $A = [a_{ij}]$, we have $a_{ij} = -a_{ji}$ for all $i \neq j$ and $a_{ii} = 0$ for all i.

Thus, if $A = \begin{bmatrix} 0 & a & 3 \\ 2 & b & -1 \\ c & 1 & 0 \end{bmatrix}$ is skew-symmetric, then

$a_{22} = 0, a_{12} = -a_{21}$ and $a_{31} = -a_{13} \Rightarrow b = 0, \ a = -2$ and $c = -3$

ALITER *If* $A = \begin{bmatrix} 0 & a & 3 \\ 2 & b & -1 \\ c & 1 & 0 \end{bmatrix}$ *is skew-symmetric, then*

$A^T = -A$

$$\Rightarrow \begin{bmatrix} 0 & a & 3 \\ 2 & b & -1 \\ c & 1 & 0 \end{bmatrix}^T = -\begin{bmatrix} 0 & a & 3 \\ 2 & b & -1 \\ c & 1 & 0 \end{bmatrix} \Rightarrow \begin{bmatrix} 0 & 2 & c \\ a & b & 1 \\ 3 & -1 & 0 \end{bmatrix} = \begin{bmatrix} 0 & -a & -3 \\ -2 & -b & 1 \\ -c & -1 & 0 \end{bmatrix}$$

$\Rightarrow$ $2 = -a, c = -3$ and $b = -b \Rightarrow a = -2, c = -3$ and $2b = 0 \Rightarrow a = -2, b = 0$ and $c = -3$

EXAMPLE 3 *Let A be a square matrix. Then,*

(i) $A + A^T$ *is a symmetric matrix* **[NCERT]** (ii) $A - A^T$ *is a skew-symmetric matrix.* **[NCERT]**

(iii) AA^T *and* $A^T A$ *are symmetric matrices.*

SOLUTION (i) Let $P = A + A^T$. Then,

$P^T = (A + A^T)^T = A^T + (A^T)^T$ [$\because (A+B)^T = A^T + B^T$]

$\Rightarrow$ $P^T = A^T + A$ [$\because (A^T)^T = A$]

$\Rightarrow$ $P^T = A + A^T = P$ [By commutativity of matrix addition]

$\therefore$ P is a symmetric matrix.

(ii) Let $Q = A - A^T$. Then,

$$Q^T = (A - A^T)^T = A^T - (A^T)^T \qquad [\because (A+B)^T = A^T + B^T]$$

$\Rightarrow \quad Q^T = A^T - A = -(A - A^T) = -Q \qquad [\because (A^T)^T = A]$

$\Rightarrow \quad Q$ is skew-symmetric

(iii) We find that

$$(AA^T)^T = (A^T)^T A^T \qquad \text{[By reversal law]}$$

$\Rightarrow \quad (AA^T)^T = AA^T \qquad [\because (A^T)^T = A]$

$\Rightarrow \quad AA^T$ is symmetric

Similarly, *it can be proved that* $A^T A$ is symmetric.

BASED ON LOWER ORDER THINKING SKILLS (LOTS)

EXAMPLE 4 *Prove that every square matrix can be uniquely expressed as the sum of a symmetric matrix and a skew-symmetric matrix.* [NCERT]

SOLUTION Let A be a square matrix. Then,

$$A = \frac{1}{2}(A + A^T) + \frac{1}{2}(A - A^T) = P + Q \text{ (say), where } P = \frac{1}{2}(A + A^T) \text{ and } Q = \frac{1}{2}(A - A^T).$$

Now, $P^T = \left(\frac{1}{2}(A + A^T)\right)^T = \frac{1}{2}(A + A^T)^T \qquad [\because (kA)^T = k A^T]$

$\Rightarrow \quad P^T = \frac{1}{2}(A^T + (A^T)^T) \qquad [\because (A+B)^T = A^T + B^T]$

$\Rightarrow \quad P^T = \frac{1}{2}(A^T + A) \qquad [\because (A^T)^T = A]$

$\Rightarrow \quad P^T = \frac{1}{2}(A + A^T) = P \qquad$ [By commutativity of matrix addition]

$\therefore \quad P$ is a symmetric matrix.

And, $Q^T = \left(\frac{1}{2}(A - A^T)\right)^T = \frac{1}{2}(A - A^T)^T = \frac{1}{2}(A^T - (A^T)^T) = \frac{1}{2}(A^T - A) = -\frac{1}{2}(A - A^T) = -Q$

$\therefore \quad Q$ is a skew-symmetric matrix.

Thus, $A = P + Q$, where P is a symmetric matrix and Q is a skew-symmetric matrix.

Hence, A is expressible as the sum of a symmetric and a skew-symmetric matrix.

Uniqueness: If possible, let $A = R + S$, where R is symmetric and S is skew-symmetric. Then,

$$A^T = (R + S)^T = R^T + S^T = R - S \qquad [\because R^T = R \text{ and } S^T = -S]$$

Now, $A = R + S$ and $A^T = R - S \Rightarrow R = \frac{1}{2}(A + A^T) = P, S = \frac{1}{2}(A - A^T) = Q.$

Hence, A is uniquely expressible as the sum of a symmetric and a skew-symmetric matrix.

EXAMPLE 5 *If A and B are symmetric matrices, then show that AB is symmetric iff AB = BA i.e. A and B commute.* [NCERT]

SOLUTION AB is symmetric

$\Leftrightarrow \quad (AB)^T = AB$

$\Leftrightarrow \quad B^T A^T = AB \qquad [\because (AB)^T = B^T A^T]$

$\Leftrightarrow \quad BA = AB \qquad [\because A \text{ and } B \text{ are symmetric matrices } \therefore A^T = A, B^T = B]$

EXAMPLE 6 *Show that the matrix $B^T AB$ is symmetric or skew-symmetric according as A is symmetric or skew-symmetric.* [NCERT EXEMPLAR]

SOLUTION Case I Let A be a symmetric matrix. Then, $A^T = A$.

Now, $(B^T AB)^T = B^T A^T (B^T)^T$ [By reversal law]

$= B^T A^T B$ [$\because (B^T)^T = B$]

$= B^T AB$ [$\because A^T = A$]

$\therefore$ $B^T AB$ is a symmetric matrix.

Case II Let A be a skew-symmetric matrix. Then, $A^T = -A$.

Now,

$(B^T AB)^T = B^T A^T (B^T)^T$ [By reversal law]

$= B^T A^T B$ [$\because (B^T)^T = B$]

$= B^T (-A) B = -B^T AB$ [$\because A^T = -A$]

$\therefore$ $B^T AB$ is a skew-symmetric matrix.

EXAMPLE 7 *Let A and B be symmetric matrices of the same order. Then, show that*

(i) *$A + B$ is a symmetric matrix.* (ii) *$AB - BA$ is a skew-symmetric matrix.* [NCERT]

(iii) *$AB + BA$ is a symmetric matrix.*

SOLUTION Since A and B are symmetric matrices. Therefore, $A^T = A$ and $B^T = B$.

(i) We find that: $(A + B)^T = A^T + B^T = A + B$ [$\because A^T = A, B^T = B$]

$\therefore$ $A + B$ is symmetric

(ii) We find that

$(AB - BA)^T = (AB)^T - (BA)^T = B^T A^T - A^T B^T$ [By reversal law]

$= BA - AB = -(AB - BA)$ [$\because B^T = B, A^T = A$]

$\therefore$ $AB - BA$ is skew-symmetric.

(iii) We find that

$(AB + BA)^T = (AB)^T + (BA)^T$

$= B^T A^T + A^T B^T$ [By reversal law]

$= BA + AB = AB + BA$ [$\because A^T = A, B^T = B$]

$\therefore$ $AB + BA$ is symmetric matrix.

EXAMPLE 8 *Express the matrix $A = \begin{bmatrix} 3 & 2 & 3 \\ 4 & 5 & 3 \\ 2 & 4 & 5 \end{bmatrix}$ as the sum of a symmetric and a skew-symmetric matrix.*

SOLUTION We have,

$$A = \begin{bmatrix} 3 & 2 & 3 \\ 4 & 5 & 3 \\ 2 & 4 & 5 \end{bmatrix} \Rightarrow A^T = \begin{bmatrix} 3 & 4 & 2 \\ 2 & 5 & 4 \\ 3 & 3 & 5 \end{bmatrix}$$

$\therefore \quad A + A^T = \begin{bmatrix} 3 & 2 & 3 \\ 4 & 5 & 3 \\ 2 & 4 & 5 \end{bmatrix} + \begin{bmatrix} 3 & 4 & 2 \\ 2 & 5 & 4 \\ 3 & 3 & 5 \end{bmatrix} = \begin{bmatrix} 6 & 6 & 5 \\ 6 & 10 & 7 \\ 5 & 7 & 10 \end{bmatrix}$

and, $A - A^T = \begin{bmatrix} 3 & 2 & 3 \\ 4 & 5 & 3 \\ 2 & 4 & 5 \end{bmatrix} - \begin{bmatrix} 3 & 4 & 2 \\ 2 & 5 & 4 \\ 3 & 3 & 5 \end{bmatrix} = \begin{bmatrix} 0 & -2 & 1 \\ 2 & 0 & -1 \\ -1 & 1 & 0 \end{bmatrix}$

Let $P = \frac{1}{2}(A + A^T) = \begin{bmatrix} 3 & 3 & 5/2 \\ 3 & 5 & 7/2 \\ 5/2 & 7/2 & 5 \end{bmatrix}$ and, $Q = \frac{1}{2}(A - A^T) = \begin{bmatrix} 0 & -1 & 1/2 \\ 1 & 0 & -1/2 \\ -1/2 & 1/2 & 0 \end{bmatrix}$.

Then, $P^T = \begin{bmatrix} 3 & 3 & 5/2 \\ 3 & 5 & 7/2 \\ 5/2 & 7/2 & 5 \end{bmatrix}^T = \begin{bmatrix} 3 & 3 & 5/2 \\ 3 & 5 & 7/2 \\ 5/2 & 7/2 & 5 \end{bmatrix} = P$

and, $Q^T = \begin{bmatrix} 0 & -1 & 1/2 \\ 1 & 0 & -1/2 \\ -1/2 & 1/2 & 0 \end{bmatrix}^T = \begin{bmatrix} 0 & 1 & -1/2 \\ -1 & 0 & 1/2 \\ 1/2 & -1/2 & 0 \end{bmatrix} = -\begin{bmatrix} 0 & -1 & 1/2 \\ 1 & 0 & -1/2 \\ -1/2 & 1/2 & 0 \end{bmatrix} = -Q$

Thus, P is symmetric and Q is skew-symmetric.

Also, $P + Q = \begin{bmatrix} 3 & 3 & 5/2 \\ 3 & 5 & 5/2 \\ 5/2 & 7/2 & 5 \end{bmatrix} + \begin{bmatrix} 0 & -1 & 5/2 \\ 1 & 0 & 5/2 \\ -1/2 & 5/2 & 0 \end{bmatrix} = \begin{bmatrix} 3 & 2 & 3 \\ 4 & 5 & 3 \\ 2 & 4 & 5 \end{bmatrix} = A$

Thus, A is expressible as the sum of a symmetric matrix P and a skew-symmetric matrix Q.

EXAMPLE 9 *If A is a symmetric matrix and B is skew-symmetric matrix such that $A + B = \begin{bmatrix} 2 & 3 \\ 5 & -1 \end{bmatrix}$, then find AB.*

SOLUTION It is given that A is a symmetric matrix and B is a skew-symmetric matrix. Therefore, $A^T = A$ and $B^T = -B$.

Now $A + B = \begin{bmatrix} 2 & 3 \\ 5 & -1 \end{bmatrix}$ ...(i)

$\Rightarrow \quad (A + B)^T = \begin{bmatrix} 2 & 3 \\ 5 & -1 \end{bmatrix}^T \Rightarrow A^T + B^T = \begin{bmatrix} 2 & 5 \\ 3 & -1 \end{bmatrix} \Rightarrow A - B = \begin{bmatrix} 2 & 5 \\ 3 & -1 \end{bmatrix}$ ...(ii)

Adding (i) and (ii), we obtain

$$2A = \begin{bmatrix} 2 & 3 \\ 5 & -1 \end{bmatrix} + \begin{bmatrix} 2 & 5 \\ 3 & -1 \end{bmatrix} = \begin{bmatrix} 2+2 & 3+5 \\ 5+3 & -1-1 \end{bmatrix} = \begin{bmatrix} 4 & 8 \\ 8 & -2 \end{bmatrix} \Rightarrow A = \frac{1}{2}\begin{bmatrix} 4 & 8 \\ 8 & -2 \end{bmatrix} = \begin{bmatrix} 2 & 4 \\ 4 & -1 \end{bmatrix} \quad \text{...(iii)}$$

From (i) and (iii), we obtain

$$\begin{bmatrix} 2 & 4 \\ 4 & -1 \end{bmatrix} + B \begin{bmatrix} 2 & 3 \\ 5 & -1 \end{bmatrix} \Rightarrow B = \begin{bmatrix} 2 & 3 \\ 5 & -1 \end{bmatrix} - \begin{bmatrix} 2 & 4 \\ 4 & -1 \end{bmatrix} = \begin{bmatrix} 0 & -1 \\ 1 & 0 \end{bmatrix}$$

$\therefore \quad AB = \begin{bmatrix} 2 & 4 \\ 4 & -1 \end{bmatrix}\begin{bmatrix} 0 & -1 \\ 1 & 0 \end{bmatrix} = \begin{bmatrix} 0+4 & -2+0 \\ 0-1 & -4+0 \end{bmatrix} = \begin{bmatrix} 4 & -2 \\ -1 & -4 \end{bmatrix}$

EXAMPLE 10 *The sum of a matrix and its transpose is* $\begin{bmatrix} 6 & -1 \\ -1 & 4 \end{bmatrix}$. *Find one such matrix for which this holds true.*

SOLUTION Let $A = \begin{bmatrix} a & b \\ c & d \end{bmatrix}$ be the given matrix. It is given that

$$A + A^T = \begin{bmatrix} 6 & -1 \\ -1 & 4 \end{bmatrix}$$

$$\Rightarrow \quad \begin{bmatrix} a & b \\ c & d \end{bmatrix} + \begin{bmatrix} a & c \\ b & d \end{bmatrix} = \begin{bmatrix} 6 & -1 \\ -1 & 4 \end{bmatrix}$$

$$\Rightarrow \quad \begin{bmatrix} 2a & b+c \\ c+b & 2d \end{bmatrix} = \begin{bmatrix} 6 & -1 \\ -1 & 4 \end{bmatrix} \Rightarrow 2a = 6, 2d = 4 \text{ and } b + c = -1 \Rightarrow a = 3, d = 2 \text{ and } c = -1 - b$$

$$\therefore \quad A = \begin{bmatrix} 3 & b \\ -1-b & 2 \end{bmatrix}, \text{ where } b \text{ is any real number.}$$

This, gives a family of matrices satisfying the given condition. Putting $b = 0$ (say), we obtain a particular matrix $A = \begin{bmatrix} 3 & 0 \\ -1 & 2 \end{bmatrix}$.

BASED ON HIGHER ORDER THINKING SKILLS (HOTS)

EXAMPLE 11 *Show that all positive integral powers of a symmetric matrix are symmetric.*

SOLUTION Let A be a symmetric matrix and $n \in N$. Then,

$$(A^n)^T = (AAA \ldots A \text{ upto } n\text{-times})^T$$

$$= (A^T A^T A^T \ldots A^T \text{ upto } n\text{-times}) \qquad \text{[By reversal law]}$$

$$= (A^T)^n = A^n \qquad [\because A^T = A]$$

Hence, A^n is also a symmetric matrix.

EXAMPLE 12 *Show that positive odd integral powers of a skew-symmetric matrix are skew-symmetric and positive even integral powers of a skew-symmetric matrix are symmetric.*

SOLUTION Let A be a skew-symmetric matrix. Then, $A^T = -A$.

We have, $(A^n)^T = (A^T)^n$ for all $n \in N$. [See Example 9]

$$\therefore \quad (A^n)^T = (-A)^n \qquad [\because A^T = -A]$$

$$= (-1)^n A^n = \begin{cases} A^n, & \text{if } n \text{ is even} \\ -A^n, & \text{if } n \text{ is odd} \end{cases}$$

Hence, A^n is symmetric if n is even and skew-symmetric if n is odd.

EXAMPLE 13 *A matrix which is both symmetric as well as skew-symmetric is a null matrix.*

[NCERT EXEMPLAR, CBSE 2020]

SOLUTION Let $A = [a_{ij}]$ a matrix which is both symmetric and skew-symmetric.

Now, $A = [a_{ij}]$ is a symmetric matrix $\Rightarrow a_{ij} = a_{ji}$ for all i, j ...(i)

Also, $A = [a_{ij}]$ is a skew-symmetric matrix.

$\therefore \quad a_{ij} = -a_{ji}$ for all $i, j \Rightarrow a_{ji} = -a_{ij}$ for all i, j ...(ii)

From (i) and (ii), we obtain

$a_{ij} = -a_{ij}$ for all $i, j \Rightarrow 2a_{ij} = 0$ for all $i, j \Rightarrow a_{ij} = 0$ for all $i, j \Rightarrow A = [a_{ij}]$ is a null matrix.

EXERCISE 4.5

BASIC

1. If $A = \begin{bmatrix} 2 & 3 \\ 4 & 5 \end{bmatrix}$, prove that $A - A^T$ is a skew-symmetric matrix. [CBSE 2001]

2. For the matrix $A = \begin{bmatrix} 2 & 3 \\ 5 & 7 \end{bmatrix}$, find $A + A^T$ and verify that it is a symmetric matrix. [CBSE 2019]

3. If $\begin{bmatrix} 4 & x+2 \\ 2x-3 & x+1 \end{bmatrix}$ is a symmetric matrix, then find the value of x. [CBSE 2020]

4. If the matrix $A = \begin{bmatrix} 5 & 2 & x \\ y & z & -3 \\ 4 & t & -7 \end{bmatrix}$ is a symmetric matrix, find x, y, z and t.

BASED ON LOTS

5. Express the matrix $A = \begin{bmatrix} 3 & -4 \\ 1 & -1 \end{bmatrix}$ as the sum of a symmetric and a skew-symmetric matrix.

6. Let $A = \begin{bmatrix} 3 & 2 & 7 \\ 1 & 4 & 3 \\ -2 & 5 & 8 \end{bmatrix}$. Find matrices X and Y such that $X + Y = A$, where X is a symmetric and Y is a skew-symmetric matrix.

7. Express the matrix $\begin{bmatrix} 3 & -2 & -4 \\ 3 & -2 & -5 \\ -1 & 1 & 2 \end{bmatrix}$ as the sum of a symmetric and skew-symmetric matrix and verify your result. [CBSE 2010]

ANSWERS

2. $A = \begin{bmatrix} 4 & 8 \\ 8 & 14 \end{bmatrix}$ 3. 5 4. $x = 4, y = 2, z \in C, t = -3$

5. Symmetric matrix $= \begin{bmatrix} 3 & -3/2 \\ -3/2 & -1 \end{bmatrix}$, Skew-symmetric matrix $= \begin{bmatrix} 0 & -5/2 \\ 5/2 & 0 \end{bmatrix}$

6. $X = \begin{bmatrix} 3 & 3/2 & 5/2 \\ 3/2 & 4 & 4 \\ 5/2 & 4 & 8 \end{bmatrix}$, $Y = \begin{bmatrix} 0 & 1/2 & 9/2 \\ -1/2 & 0 & -1 \\ -9/2 & 1 & 0 \end{bmatrix}$

7. Symmetric matrix $= \begin{bmatrix} 3 & 1/2 & -5/2 \\ 1/2 & -2 & -2 \\ -5/2 & -2 & 2 \end{bmatrix}$, Skew-symmetric matrix $= \begin{bmatrix} 0 & -5/2 & -3/2 \\ 5/2 & 0 & -3 \\ 3/2 & 3 & 0 \end{bmatrix}$

FILL IN THE BLANKS TYPE QUESTIONS (FBQs)

1. If A and B are two matrices of orders $a \times 3$ and $3 \times b$ respectively such that AB exists and is of order 2×4. Then, $(a, b) =$ ....

2. If P and Q are two matrices of orders $3 \times n$ and $n \times p$ respectively then the order of the matrix PQ is ....

3. If $A=\begin{bmatrix}-1 & 2 & 3x\\ 2y & 4 & -1\\ 6 & 5 & 0\end{bmatrix}$ is a symmetric matrix, then the value of $2x+y$ is ....

4. If a, b are positive integers such that $a<b$ and $[a \quad b]\begin{bmatrix}a\\ b\end{bmatrix}=25$, then $(a, b)=$ ....

5. If $A=\begin{bmatrix}\frac{1}{3} & 2\\ 0 & 2x-3\end{bmatrix}$, $B=\begin{bmatrix}3 & 6\\ 0 & -1\end{bmatrix}$ and $AB=I$, then $x=$ ....

6. If $A=\begin{bmatrix}x & 1\\ -1 & -x\end{bmatrix}$ satisfies the equation $A^2=O$, then $x=$ ....

7. If A is an $m\times n$ matrix and B is a matrix such that both AB and BA are defined, then the order of B is ....

8. If $A=\begin{bmatrix}0 & 2 & 0\\ 0 & 0 & 3\\ -2 & 2 & 0\end{bmatrix}$ and $B=\begin{bmatrix}1 & 2 & 3\\ 3 & 4 & 5\\ 5 & -4 & 0\end{bmatrix}$, then $(AB)_{33}=$ ....

9. If $A=\begin{bmatrix}3 & 0 & 0\\ 0 & 3 & 0\\ 0 & 0 & 3\end{bmatrix}$, then $A^4=$ ....

10. If $A=\text{diag}\,(2, -1, 3)$, $B=\text{diag}\,(-1, 3, 2)$, then $A^2B=$ ....

11. $\begin{bmatrix}1\\ -1\\ 2\end{bmatrix}[2 \quad 1 \quad -1]=$ ....

12. If $A=\begin{bmatrix}x & 1\\ 1 & 0\end{bmatrix}$ and A^2 is the identity matrix, then $x=$ ....

13. If $e\begin{bmatrix}e^x & e^y\\ e^y & e^x\end{bmatrix}=\begin{bmatrix}1 & 1\\ 1 & 1\end{bmatrix}$, then $x=$ ...., $y=$ ....

14. If $A=\begin{bmatrix}0 & 2\\ 3 & -4\end{bmatrix}$ and $kA=\begin{bmatrix}0 & 3a\\ 2b & 24\end{bmatrix}$, then $(k, a, b)=$ ....

15. If $A=\begin{bmatrix}\cos\theta & \sin\theta\\ -\sin\theta & \cos\theta\end{bmatrix}$, then $AA^T=$ ....

16. If A is 3×4 matrix and B is a matrix such that A^TB and BA^T are both defined. Then the order of B is ....

17. If $A=\begin{bmatrix}1\\ 2\\ 3\end{bmatrix}$, then $AA^T=$ ....

18. If $f(x)=\begin{bmatrix}\cos x & \sin x\\ -\sin x & \cos x\end{bmatrix}$ and $f(x)\,f(y)=f(z)$, then $z=$ ....

19. If A, B and C are $m \times n, n \times p$ and $p \times q$ matrices respectively such that $(BC)\, A$ is defined, then $m =$ ....

20. If $A = \begin{bmatrix} 2 & 0 & 0 \\ 0 & 2 & 0 \\ 0 & 0 & 2 \end{bmatrix}$ such that $A^5 = \lambda A$, then $\lambda =$ ....

21. If the matrices $A = \begin{bmatrix} a & b \\ c & d \end{bmatrix}$ and $B = \begin{bmatrix} 1 & 1 \\ 0 & 1 \end{bmatrix}$ commute with each other, then $C =$ ....

22. If $A = \begin{bmatrix} 4 & x+2 \\ 2x-3 & x+1 \end{bmatrix}$ is a symmetric matrix, then $x =$ ....

23. If A and B are two skew-symmetric matrices of same order, then AB is symmetric if......................... . **[NCERT EXEMPLAR]**

24. If A and B are matrices of the same order, then $(3A - 2B)^T$ is equal to ....

25. Addition of matrices is defined if order of the matrices is ....

26. If A and B are symmetric matrices of the same order, then AB is symmetric iff........................ . **[NCERT EXEMPLAR]**

27. If A is symmetric matrix, then $B^T AB$ is .... **[NCERT EXEMPLAR]**

28. If A is a skew-symmetric matrix, then A^2 is a .... matrix. **[NCERT EXEMPLAR]**

29. If A is a symmetric matrix, then A^3 is a .... matrix. **[NCERT EXEMPLAR]**

30. If A is a skew-symmetric matrix, then kA is a ....(k is any scalar). **[NCERT EXEMPLAR]**

31. If A and B are symmetric matrices of the same order, then
    (i) $AB - BA$ is a ....
    (ii) $BA - 2AB$ is a .... **[NCERT EXEMPLAR]**

32. In applying one or more row operations while finding A^{-1} by elementary row operations, we obtain all zeroes in one or more row, then A^{-1} ....

33. The product of any matrix by the scalar .... is the null matrix.

34. A matrix which is not a square matrix is called .... matrix.

35. The sum of two skew-symmetric matrices is always .... matrix.

36. A and B are square matrices of the same order, then ....
    (i) $(AB)^T =$......... (ii) $(kA)^T =$.......... (iii) $(k\,(A - B))^T =$....... where k is any scalar.

37. .... matrix is both symmetric and skew-symmetric matrix. **[CBSE 2020]**

38. Matrix multiplication is .... over matrix addition.

39. The negative of a matrix is obtained by multiplying it by ....

40. If A is a non-singular matrix, then $(A^T)^{-1} =$ ....

41. If $A + B = \begin{bmatrix} 1 & 0 \\ 1 & 1 \end{bmatrix}$ and $A - 2B = \begin{bmatrix} -1 & 1 \\ 0 & -1 \end{bmatrix}$, then $A =$......................... . **[CBSE 2020]**

42. Given a skew-symmetric matrix $A=\begin{bmatrix}0 & a & 1\\ -1 & b & 1\\ -1 & c & 0\end{bmatrix}$ the value of $(a+b+c)^2$ is .... [CBSE 2020]

43. If $[3 \quad -2 \quad 0]\begin{bmatrix}2\\ k\\ -5\end{bmatrix}=0$, then the value of k is .... [CBSE 2020]

ANSWERS

1. (2, 4) 2. $3\times p$ 3. 5 4. (3, 4) 5. 1
6. ± 1 7. $n\times m$ 8. 4 9. $3^4 I_3$
10. diag (−4, 3, 18) 11. $\begin{bmatrix}2 & 1 & -1\\ -2 & -1 & 1\\ 4 & 2 & -2\end{bmatrix}$ 12. 0 13. $x=-1, y=-1$
14. (−6, −4, −9) 15. I 16. 3×4 17. $\begin{bmatrix}1 & 2 & 3\\ 2 & 4 & 6\\ 3 & 6 & 9\end{bmatrix}$
18. $x+y$ 19. q 20. 16 21. 0 22. 5
23. $AB=BA$ 24. $3A^T-2B^T$ 25. same 26. $AB=BA$
27. symmetric 28. symmetric 29. symmetric 30. skew-symmetric
31. (i) skew-symmetric (ii) neither symmetric nor skew-symmetric
32. does not exist 33. zero 34. rectangular 35. skew-symmetric
36. (i) $B^T A^T$ (ii) $k\,A^T$ (iii) $k\,(A^T-B^T)$ 37. null matrix
38. distributive 39. −1 40. $(A^{-1})^T$ 41. $A=\begin{bmatrix}1/3 & 1/3\\ 2/3 & 1/3\end{bmatrix}$
42. 0 43. 3

VERY SHORT ANSWER QUESTIONS (VSAQs)

Answer each of the following questions in one word or one sentence or as per exact requirement of the question:

1. If A is an $m\times n$ matrix and B is $n\times p$ matrix does AB exist? If yes, write its order.
2. If $A=\begin{bmatrix}2 & 1 & 4\\ 4 & 1 & 5\end{bmatrix}$ and $B=\begin{bmatrix}3 & -1\\ 2 & 2\\ 1 & 3\end{bmatrix}$. Write the orders of AB and BA.
3. If $A=\begin{bmatrix}4 & 3\\ 1 & 2\end{bmatrix}$ and $B=\begin{bmatrix}-4\\ 3\end{bmatrix}$, write AB.
4. If $A=\begin{bmatrix}1\\ 2\\ 3\end{bmatrix}$, write AA^T. [CBSE 2009]
5. Give an example of two non-zero 2×2 matrices A and B such that $AB=O$.
6. If $A=\begin{bmatrix}2 & 3\\ 5 & 7\end{bmatrix}$, find $A+A^T$.

7. If $A = \begin{bmatrix} i & 0 \\ 0 & i \end{bmatrix}$, write A^2.

8. If $A = \begin{bmatrix} \cos x & \sin x \\ -\sin x & \cos x \end{bmatrix}$, find x satisfying $0 < x < \frac{\pi}{2}$ when $A + A^T = I$

9. If $A = \begin{bmatrix} \cos x & -\sin x \\ \sin x & \cos x \end{bmatrix}$, find AA^T

10. If $\begin{bmatrix} 1 & 0 \\ y & 5 \end{bmatrix} + 2\begin{bmatrix} x & 0 \\ 1 & -2 \end{bmatrix} = I$, where I is 2×2 unit matrix. Find x and y.

11. If $A = \begin{bmatrix} 1 & -1 \\ -1 & 1 \end{bmatrix}$, satisfies the matrix equation $A^2 = kA$, write the value of k.

12. If $A = \begin{bmatrix} 1 & 1 \\ 1 & 1 \end{bmatrix}$ satisfies $A^4 = \lambda A$, then write the value of λ.

13. If $A = \begin{bmatrix} -1 & 0 & 0 \\ 0 & -1 & 0 \\ 0 & 0 & -1 \end{bmatrix}$, find A^2.

14. If $A = \begin{bmatrix} -1 & 0 & 0 \\ 0 & -1 & 0 \\ 0 & 0 & -1 \end{bmatrix}$, find A^3.

15. If $A = \begin{bmatrix} -3 & 0 \\ 0 & -3 \end{bmatrix}$, find A^4.

16. If $[x \quad 2] \begin{bmatrix} 3 \\ 4 \end{bmatrix} = 2$, find x

17. If $A = [a_{ij}]$ is a 2×2 matrix such that $a_{ij} = i + 2j$, write A. **[CBSE 2008]**

18. Write matrix A satisfying $A + \begin{bmatrix} 2 & 3 \\ -1 & 4 \end{bmatrix} = \begin{bmatrix} 3 & -6 \\ -3 & 8 \end{bmatrix}$.

19. If $A = [a_{ij}]$ is a square matrix such that $a_{ij} = i^2 - j^2$, then write whether A is symmetric or skew-symmetric.

20. For any square matrix write whether AA^T is symmetric or skew-symmetric.

21. If $A = [a_{ij}]$ is a skew-symmetric matrix, then write the value of $\sum_i a_{ii}$.

22. If $A = [a_{ij}]$ is a skew-symmetric matrix, then write the value of $\sum_i \sum_j a_{ij}$.

23. If A and B are symmetric matrices, then write the condition for which AB is also symmetric.

24. If B is a skew-symmetric matrix, write whether the matrix $AB\,A^T$ is symmetric or skew-symmetric.

25. If B is a symmetric matrix, write whether the matrix $AB\,A^T$ is symmetric or skew-symmetric.

26. If A is a skew-symmetric and $n \in N$ such that $(A^n)^T = \lambda A^n$, write the value of λ.

27. If A is a symmetric matrix and $n \in N$, write whether A^n is symmetric or skew-symmetric or neither of these two.

28. If A is a skew-symmetric matrix and n is an even natural number, write whether A^n is symmetric or skew-symmetric or neither of these two.

29. If A is a skew-symmetric matrix and n is an odd natural number, write whether A^n is symmetric or skew-symmetric or neither of the two.

30. If A and B are symmetric matrices of the same order, write whether $AB - BA$ is symmetric or skew-symmetric or neither of the two.

31. Write a square matrix which is both symmetric as well as skew-symmetric.

32. Find the values of x and y, if $2\begin{bmatrix} 1 & 3 \\ 0 & x \end{bmatrix} + \begin{bmatrix} y & 0 \\ 1 & 2 \end{bmatrix} = \begin{bmatrix} 5 & 6 \\ 1 & 8 \end{bmatrix}$. [CBSE 2008, 2019]

33. If $\begin{bmatrix} x+3 & 4 \\ y-4 & x+y \end{bmatrix} = \begin{bmatrix} 5 & 4 \\ 3 & 9 \end{bmatrix}$, find x and y. [CBSE 2008]

34. Find the value of x from the following: $\begin{bmatrix} 2x-y & 5 \\ 3 & y \end{bmatrix} = \begin{bmatrix} 6 & 5 \\ 3 & -2 \end{bmatrix}$. [CBSE 2009]

35. Find the value of y, if $\begin{bmatrix} x-y & 2 \\ x & 5 \end{bmatrix} = \begin{bmatrix} 2 & 2 \\ 3 & 5 \end{bmatrix}$. [CBSE 2009]

36. Find the value of x, if $\begin{bmatrix} 3x+y & -y \\ 2y-x & 3 \end{bmatrix} = \begin{bmatrix} 1 & 2 \\ -5 & 3 \end{bmatrix}$. [CBSE 2009]

37. If matrix $A = [1 \ \ 2 \ \ 3]$, write AA^T. [CBSE 2009]

38. If $\begin{bmatrix} 2x+y & 3y \\ 0 & 4 \end{bmatrix} = \begin{bmatrix} 6 & 0 \\ 6 & 4 \end{bmatrix}$, then find x. [CBSE 2010]

39. If $A = \begin{bmatrix} 1 & 2 \\ 3 & 4 \end{bmatrix}$, find $A + A^T$. [CBSE 2010]

40. If $\begin{bmatrix} a+b & 2 \\ 5 & b \end{bmatrix} = \begin{bmatrix} 6 & 2 \\ 5 & 2 \end{bmatrix}$, then find a.

41. If A is a matrix of order 3×4 and B is a matrix of order 4×3, find the order of the matrix of AB. [CBSE 2010]

42. If $A = \begin{bmatrix} \cos\alpha & -\sin\alpha \\ \sin\alpha & \cos\alpha \end{bmatrix}$ is identity matrix, then write the value of α. [CBSE 2010]

43. If $\begin{bmatrix} 1 & 2 \\ 3 & 4 \end{bmatrix}\begin{bmatrix} 3 & 1 \\ 2 & 5 \end{bmatrix} = \begin{bmatrix} 7 & 11 \\ k & 23 \end{bmatrix}$, then write the value of k. [CBSE 2010]

44. If I is the identity matrix and A is a square matrix such that $A^2 = A$, then what is the value of $(I + A)^2 - 3A$?

45. If $A = \begin{bmatrix} 1 & 2 \\ 0 & 3 \end{bmatrix}$ is written as $B + C$, where B is a symmetric matrix and C is a skew-symmetric matrix, then find B.

46. If A is 2×3 matrix and B is a matrix such that $A^T B$ and BA^T both are defined, then what is the order of B?

47. What is the total number of 2×2 matrices with each entry 0 or 1?

48. If $\begin{bmatrix} x & x-y \\ 2x+y & 7 \end{bmatrix} = \begin{bmatrix} 3 & 1 \\ 8 & 7 \end{bmatrix}$, then find the value of y. [CBSE 2011]

49. If a matrix has 5 elements, write all possible orders it can have. [CBSE 2011]

50. For a 2×2 matrix $A = [a_{ij}]$ whose elements are given by $a_{ij} = \frac{i}{j}$, write the value of a_{12}. [CBSE 2011]

51. If $x\begin{bmatrix} 2 \\ 3 \end{bmatrix} + y\begin{bmatrix} -1 \\ 1 \end{bmatrix} = \begin{bmatrix} 10 \\ 5 \end{bmatrix}$, find the value of x. [CBSE 2012]

52. If $\begin{bmatrix} 9 & -1 & 4 \\ -2 & 1 & 3 \end{bmatrix} = A + \begin{bmatrix} 1 & 2 & -1 \\ 0 & 4 & 9 \end{bmatrix}$, then find matrix A. [CBSE 2013]

53. If $\begin{bmatrix} a-b & 2a+c \\ 2a-b & 3c+d \end{bmatrix} = \begin{bmatrix} -1 & 5 \\ 0 & 13 \end{bmatrix}$, find the value of b. [CBSE 2013]

54. For what value of x, is the matrix $A = \begin{bmatrix} 0 & 1 & -2 \\ -1 & 0 & 3 \\ x & -3 & 0 \end{bmatrix}$ a skew-symmetric matrix? [CBSE 2013]

55. If matrix $A = \begin{bmatrix} 2 & -2 \\ -2 & 2 \end{bmatrix}$ and $A^2 = pA$, then write the value of p. [CBSE 2013]

56. If A is a square matrix such that $A^2 = A$, then write the value of $7A - (I + A)^3$, where I is the identity matrix. [CBSE 2014]

57. If $2\begin{bmatrix} 3 & 4 \\ 5 & x \end{bmatrix} + \begin{bmatrix} 1 & y \\ 0 & 1 \end{bmatrix} = \begin{bmatrix} 7 & 0 \\ 10 & 5 \end{bmatrix}$, find $x - y$. [CBSE 2014]

58. If $[x \ \ 1]\begin{bmatrix} 1 & 0 \\ -2 & 0 \end{bmatrix} = O$, find x. [CBSE 2014]

59. If $\begin{bmatrix} a+4 & 3b \\ 8 & -6 \end{bmatrix} = \begin{bmatrix} 2a+2 & b+2 \\ 8 & a-8b \end{bmatrix}$, write the value of $a - 2b$. [CBSE 2014]

60. Write a 2×2 matrix which is both symmetric and skew-symmetric. [CBSE 2014]

61. If $\begin{bmatrix} xy & 4 \\ z+6 & x+y \end{bmatrix} = \begin{bmatrix} 8 & w \\ 0 & 6 \end{bmatrix}$, write the value of $(x + y + z)$. [CBSE 2014]

62. Construct a 2×2 matrix $A = [a_{ij}]$ whose elements a_{ij} are given by $a_{ij} = \begin{cases} \frac{|-3i+j|}{2}, & \text{if } i \neq j \\ (I+j)^2, & \text{if } i = j \end{cases}$

63. If $\begin{bmatrix} x+y \\ x-y \end{bmatrix} = \begin{bmatrix} 2 & 1 \\ 4 & 3 \end{bmatrix}\begin{bmatrix} 1 \\ -2 \end{bmatrix}$, then write the value of (x, y).

64. Matrix $A = \begin{bmatrix} 0 & 2b & -2 \\ 3 & 1 & 3 \\ 3a & 3 & -1 \end{bmatrix}$ is given to be symmetric, find the values of a and b. [CBSE 2016]

65. Write the number of all possible matrices of order 2×2 with each entry 1, 2 or 3. [CBSE 2016]

66. If $[2 \;\; 1 \;\; 3]\begin{bmatrix}-1 & 0 & -1\\ -1 & 1 & 0\\ 0 & 1 & 1\end{bmatrix}\begin{bmatrix}1\\ 0\\ -1\end{bmatrix} = A$, then write the order of matrix A. [CBSE 2016]

67. If $A = \begin{bmatrix}3 & 5\\ 7 & 9\end{bmatrix}$ is written as $A = P + Q$, where as $A = P + Q$, where P is symmetric and Q is skew-symmetric matrix, then write the matrix P. [CBSE 2016]

68. Let A and B be matrices of orders 3×2 and 2×4 respectively. Write the order of matrix AB. [CBSE 2017]

69. If the matrix $A = \begin{bmatrix}0 & a & -3\\ 2 & 0 & -1\\ b & 1 & 0\end{bmatrix}$ is skew-symmetric, find the values of 'a' and 'b'. [CBSE 2018]

ANSWERS

1. Yes, $m \times p$
2. 2×2 and 3×3
3. $\begin{bmatrix}-7\\ 2\end{bmatrix}$
4. $\begin{bmatrix}1 & 2 & 3\\ 2 & 4 & 6\\ 3 & 6 & 9\end{bmatrix}$
5. $A = \begin{bmatrix}2 & 0\\ 3 & 0\end{bmatrix}, B = \begin{bmatrix}0 & 0\\ 2 & -1\end{bmatrix}$
6. $\begin{bmatrix}4 & 8\\ 8 & 14\end{bmatrix}$
7. $\begin{bmatrix}-1 & 0\\ 0 & -1\end{bmatrix}$
8. $\frac{\pi}{3}$
9. $\begin{bmatrix}1 & 0\\ 0 & 1\end{bmatrix}$
10. $x = 0, y = -2$
11. 2
12. 8
13. $-A$ or, I_3
14. A
15. $\begin{bmatrix}81 & 0\\ 0 & 81\end{bmatrix}$
16. -2
17. $\begin{bmatrix}3 & 5\\ 4 & 6\end{bmatrix}$
18. $\begin{bmatrix}1 & -9\\ -2 & 4\end{bmatrix}$
19. skew-symmetric
20. symmetric
21. 0
22. 0
23. $AB = BA$
24. skew-symmetric
25. symmetric
26. $(-1)^n$
27. symmetric
28. symmetric
29. skew-symmetric
30. skew-symmetric
31. null matrix
32. $x = 3, y = 3$
33. $x = 2, y = 7$
34. $x = 2$
35. $y = 1$
36. $x = 1$
37. 14
38. $x = 3, y = 0$
39. $\begin{bmatrix}2 & 5\\ 5 & 8\end{bmatrix}$
40. 4
41. 3×3
42. $\alpha = 0$
43. 17
44. I
45. $\begin{bmatrix}1 & 1\\ 1 & 3\end{bmatrix}$
46. 2×3
47. 16
48. 2
49. $1 \times 5, 5 \times 1$
50. 1/2
51. $x = 3$
52. $\begin{bmatrix}8 & -3 & 5\\ -2 & -3 & -6\end{bmatrix}$
53. $b = 2$
54. $x = 2$
55. 4
56. $-I$
57. $x = 2, y = -8$
58. $x = 2$
59. 0
60. $\begin{bmatrix}0 & 0\\ 0 & 0\end{bmatrix}$
61. 0

62. $\begin{bmatrix} 4 & 1/2 \\ 5/2 & 16 \end{bmatrix}$ 63. $(-1, 1)$ 64. $a = -\frac{2}{3}, b = \frac{3}{2}$ 65. $3^4 = 81$ 66. 1×1

67. $\begin{bmatrix} 3 & 6 \\ 6 & 9 \end{bmatrix}$ 68. 3×4 69. $a = -2, b = 3$

CHAPTER 5

DETERMINANTS

5.1 DETERMINANTS

DEFINITION *Every square matrix can be associated to an expression or a number which is known as its determinant. If $A = [a_{ij}]$ is a square matrix of order n, then the determinant of A is denoted by det A or, $|A|$ or,*

$$\begin{vmatrix} a_{11} & a_{12} & \cdots & a_{1j} & \cdots & a_{1n} \\ a_{21} & a_{22} & \cdots & a_{2j} & \cdots & a_{2n} \\ \vdots & \vdots & & & & \\ a_{i1} & a_{i2} & \cdots & a_{ij} & \cdots & a_{in} \\ \vdots & \vdots & & \vdots & & \vdots \\ a_{n1} & a_{n2} & \cdots & a_{nj} & \cdots & a_{nn} \end{vmatrix}$$

5.1.1 DETERMINANT OF A SQUARE MATRIX OF ORDER 1

If $A = [a_{11}]$ is a square matrix of order 1, then the determinant of A is defined as

$$|A| = a_{11} \quad or, \quad |a_{11}| = a_{11}$$

5.1.2 DETERMINANT OF A SQUARE MATRIX OF ORDER 2

If $A = \begin{bmatrix} a_{11} & a_{12} \\ a_{21} & a_{22} \end{bmatrix}$ is a square matrix of order 2, then the expression $a_{11}\, a_{22} - a_{12}\, a_{21}$ is defined as the determinant of A.

i.e. $$|A| = \begin{vmatrix} a_{11} & a_{12} \\ a_{21} & a_{22} \end{vmatrix} = a_{11}\, a_{22} - a_{12}\, a_{21} \qquad \text{...(i)}$$

Thus, the determinant of a square matrix of order 2 is equal to the product of the diagonal elements minus the product of off-diagonal elements.

ILLUSTRATION *Evaluate:*

(i) $\begin{vmatrix} 5 & 4 \\ -2 & 3 \end{vmatrix}$ (ii) $\begin{vmatrix} \sin\theta & \cos\theta \\ -\cos\theta & \sin\theta \end{vmatrix}$ (iii) $\begin{vmatrix} x-1 & 1 \\ x^3 & x^2+x+1 \end{vmatrix}$

(iv) $\begin{vmatrix} x^2+xy+y^2 & x+y \\ x^2-xy+y^2 & x-y \end{vmatrix}$ (v) $\begin{vmatrix} 1 & \log_b a \\ \log_a b & 1 \end{vmatrix}$

SOLUTION By definition, we obtain

(i) $$\begin{vmatrix} 5 & 4 \\ -2 & 3 \end{vmatrix} = 5 \times 3 - 4 \times -2 = 15 + 8 = 23$$

(ii) $$\begin{vmatrix} \sin\theta & \cos\theta \\ -\cos\theta & \sin\theta \end{vmatrix} = \sin^2\theta - (-\cos^2\theta) = \sin^2\theta + \cos^2\theta = 1.$$

(iii) $$\begin{vmatrix} x-1 & 1 \\ x^3 & x^2+x+1 \end{vmatrix} = (x-1)(x^2+x+1) - x^3 = (x^3-1) - x^3 = -1.$$

(iv) $$\begin{vmatrix} x^2+xy+y^2 & x+y \\ x^2-xy+y^2 & x-y \end{vmatrix} = (x^2+xy+y^2)(x-y) - (x^2-xy+y^2)(x+y)$$

$$= (x^3 - y^3) - (x^3 + y^3) = -2y^3$$

(v) $\begin{vmatrix} 1 & \log_a b \\ \log_a b & 1 \end{vmatrix} = 1 - \log_b a \times \log_a b = 1 - 1 = 0$ $\left[\because \log_b a = \dfrac{1}{\log_a b}\right]$

5.1.3 DETERMINANT OF A SQUARE MATRIX OF ORDER 3

If $A = \begin{bmatrix} a_{11} & a_{12} & a_{13} \\ a_{21} & a_{22} & a_{23} \\ a_{31} & a_{32} & a_{33} \end{bmatrix}$ is a square matrix of order 3, then the expression

$$a_{11}\, a_{22}\, a_{33} + a_{12}\, a_{23}\, a_{31} + a_{13}\, a_{32}\, a_{21} - a_{11}\, a_{23}\, a_{32} - a_{22}\, a_{13}\, a_{31} - a_{12}\, a_{21}\, a_{33}$$

is defined as the determinant of A

i.e. $|A| = \begin{vmatrix} a_{11} & a_{12} & a_{13} \\ a_{21} & a_{22} & a_{23} \\ a_{31} & a_{32} & a_{33} \end{vmatrix}$

$$= a_{11}\, a_{22}\, a_{33} + a_{12}\, a_{23}\, a_{31} + a_{13}\, a_{32}\, a_{21} - a_{11}\, a_{23}\, a_{32} - a_{22}\, a_{31}\, a_{13} - a_{33}\, a_{12}\, a_{21} \quad ...(ii)$$

or, $|A| = \begin{vmatrix} a_{11} & a_{12} & a_{13} \\ a_{21} & a_{22} & a_{23} \\ a_{31} & a_{32} & a_{33} \end{vmatrix}$

$\Rightarrow \quad |A| = a_{11}(a_{22}\, a_{33} - a_{23}\, a_{32}) - a_{12}(a_{33}\, a_{21} - a_{23}\, a_{31}) + a_{13}(a_{32}\, a_{21} - a_{22}\, a_{31})$

$\Rightarrow \quad |A| = a_{11}\begin{vmatrix} a_{22} & a_{23} \\ a_{32} & a_{33} \end{vmatrix} - a_{12}\begin{vmatrix} a_{21} & a_{23} \\ a_{31} & a_{33} \end{vmatrix} + a_{13}\begin{vmatrix} a_{21} & a_{22} \\ a_{31} & a_{32} \end{vmatrix}$ [Using notation given in 5.1.2]

$\Rightarrow \quad |A| = (-1)^{1+1} a_{11}\begin{vmatrix} a_{22} & a_{23} \\ a_{32} & a_{33} \end{vmatrix} + (-1)^{1+2} a_{12}\begin{vmatrix} a_{21} & a_{23} \\ a_{31} & a_{33} \end{vmatrix} + (-1)^{1+3} a_{13}\begin{vmatrix} a_{21} & a_{22} \\ a_{31} & a_{32} \end{vmatrix}$

Thus the determinant of a square matrix of order 3 is the sum of the product of elements a_{1j} in first row with $(-1)^{1+j}$ times the determinant of a 2×2 sub-matrix obtained by leaving the first row and column passing through the element.

The above expansion of $|A|$ is known as the expansion along first row. For example, if $A = \begin{bmatrix} 3 & -2 & 4 \\ 1 & 2 & 1 \\ 0 & 1 & -1 \end{bmatrix}$ is a square matrix of order 3, then

$$|A| = \begin{vmatrix} 3 & -2 & 4 \\ 1 & 2 & 1 \\ 0 & 1 & -1 \end{vmatrix} = (-1)^{1+1} \times 3\begin{vmatrix} 2 & 1 \\ 1 & -1 \end{vmatrix} + (-1)^{1+2}(-2)\begin{vmatrix} 1 & 1 \\ 0 & -1 \end{vmatrix} + (-1)^{1+3}\, 4\begin{vmatrix} 1 & 2 \\ 0 & 1 \end{vmatrix}$$

$$= 3(-2-1) + 2(-1-0) + 4(1-0) = -9 - 2 + 4 = -7$$

There are three rows and three columns in a square matrix of order 3. The expression (ii) for the determinant of a square matrix of order 3 can be arranged in various forms to obtain the expansion of $|A|$ along any of its rows or columns. Infact, to expand $|A|$ about a row or a column we multiply each element a_{ij} in i^{th} row with $(-1)^{i+j}$ times the determinant of the sub-matrix obtained by leaving the row and column passing through the element.

For example,

$$|A| = \begin{vmatrix} a_{11} & a_{12} & a_{13} \\ a_{21} & a_{22} & a_{23} \\ a_{31} & a_{32} & a_{33} \end{vmatrix} = (-1)^{2+1} a_{21}\begin{vmatrix} a_{12} & a_{13} \\ a_{32} & a_{33} \end{vmatrix} + (-1)^{2+2} a_{22}\begin{vmatrix} a_{11} & a_{13} \\ a_{31} & a_{33} \end{vmatrix} + (-1)^{2+3} a_{23}\begin{vmatrix} a_{11} & a_{12} \\ a_{31} & a_{32} \end{vmatrix}$$

is the expansion of $|A|$ about second row.

The expansion of $|A|$ about 2nd column is given as

$$|A| = (-1)^{1+2} a_{12}\begin{vmatrix} a_{21} & a_{23} \\ a_{31} & a_{33} \end{vmatrix} + (-1)^{2+2} a_{22}\begin{vmatrix} a_{11} & a_{13} \\ a_{31} & a_{33} \end{vmatrix} + (-1)^{3+2} a_{32}\begin{vmatrix} a_{11} & a_{13} \\ a_{21} & a_{23} \end{vmatrix}$$

ILLUSTRATION 1 *Evaluate* $\Delta = \begin{vmatrix} 2 & 3 & -2 \\ 1 & 2 & 3 \\ -2 & 1 & -3 \end{vmatrix}$ *by expanding it along the second row.*

SOLUTION By using the definition, of expansion along second row, we obtain

$$\Delta = \begin{vmatrix} 2 & 3 & -2 \\ 1 & 2 & 3 \\ -2 & 1 & -3 \end{vmatrix} = (-1)^{2+1}(1)\begin{vmatrix} 3 & -2 \\ 1 & -3 \end{vmatrix} + (-1)^{2+2}(2)\begin{vmatrix} 2 & -2 \\ -2 & -3 \end{vmatrix} + (-1)^{2+3}(3)\begin{vmatrix} 2 & 3 \\ -2 & 1 \end{vmatrix}$$

$$= -\begin{vmatrix} 3 & -2 \\ 1 & -3 \end{vmatrix} + 2\begin{vmatrix} 2 & -2 \\ -2 & -3 \end{vmatrix} - 3\begin{vmatrix} 3 & 3 \\ -2 & 1 \end{vmatrix} = -(-9+2) + 2(-6-4) - 3(2+6) = -37.$$

ILLUSTRATION 2 *Evaluate the determinant* $D = \begin{vmatrix} 2 & 3 & -2 \\ 1 & 2 & 3 \\ -2 & 1 & -3 \end{vmatrix}$ *by expanding it along first column.*

SOLUTION By using the definition, of expansion along first column, we obtain

$$D = \begin{vmatrix} 2 & 3 & -2 \\ 1 & 2 & 3 \\ -2 & 1 & -3 \end{vmatrix} = (-1)^{1+1}(2)\begin{vmatrix} 2 & 3 \\ 1 & -3 \end{vmatrix} + (-1)^{2+1}(1)\begin{vmatrix} 3 & -2 \\ 1 & -3 \end{vmatrix} + (-1)^{3+1}(-2)\begin{vmatrix} 3 & -2 \\ 2 & 3 \end{vmatrix}$$

$$= 2\begin{vmatrix} 2 & 3 \\ 1 & -3 \end{vmatrix} - \begin{vmatrix} 3 & -2 \\ 1 & -3 \end{vmatrix} - 2\begin{vmatrix} 3 & -2 \\ 2 & 3 \end{vmatrix} = 2(-6-3) - (-9+2) - 2(9+4) = -37.$$

NOTE 1 *Only square matrices have their determinants. The matrices which are not square do not have determinants.*

NOTE 2 *The determinant of a square matrix of order 3 can be expanded along any row or column.*

NOTE 3 *If a row or a column of a determinant consists of all zeros, then the value of the determinant is zero.*

5.1.4 DETERMINANT OF A SQUARE MATRIX OF ORDER 4 OR MORE

To evaluate the determinant of a square matrix of order 4 or more we follow the same procedure as discussed in evaluating the determinant of a square matrix of order 3.

For example,

$$\Delta = \begin{vmatrix} 1 & 2 & -1 & 3 \\ 2 & 1 & -2 & 3 \\ 3 & 1 & 2 & 1 \\ 1 & -1 & 0 & 2 \end{vmatrix}$$

$$\Rightarrow \quad \Delta = (-1)^{1+1}(1)\begin{vmatrix} 1 & -2 & 3 \\ 1 & 2 & 1 \\ -1 & 0 & 2 \end{vmatrix} + (-1)^{1+2}(2)\begin{vmatrix} 2 & -2 & 3 \\ 3 & 2 & 1 \\ 1 & 0 & 2 \end{vmatrix} + (-1)^{1+3}(-1)\begin{vmatrix} 2 & 1 & 3 \\ 3 & 1 & 1 \\ 1 & -1 & 2 \end{vmatrix} + (-1)^{1+4}(3)\begin{vmatrix} 2 & 1 & -2 \\ 3 & 1 & 2 \\ 1 & -1 & 0 \end{vmatrix}$$

$$\Rightarrow \quad \Delta = 1(16) - 2(12) + (-1)(-11) - 3(14) = -39.$$

REMARK *It is evident from the above discussion that every square matrix* $A = [a_{ij}]$ *of order n can be associated to a number (real or complex) or an expression which is called determinant of the square matrix A. Thus, determinant may be thought as a function from the set M of all square matrices to the set of all numbers (real or complex).*

5.2 SINGULAR MATRIX

DEFINITION *A square matrix is a singular matrix if its determinant is zero. Otherwise, it is a non-singular matrix.*

ILLUSTRATION 1 *For what value of x the matrix* $A = \begin{bmatrix} 1 & -2 & 3 \\ 1 & 2 & 1 \\ x & 2 & -3 \end{bmatrix}$ *is singular?*

SOLUTION The matrix A is singular, if

$$|A| = 0$$

$$\Rightarrow \quad \begin{vmatrix} 1 & -2 & 3 \\ 1 & 2 & 1 \\ x & 2 & -3 \end{vmatrix} = 0$$

$$\Rightarrow \quad 1\begin{vmatrix} 2 & 1 \\ 2 & -3 \end{vmatrix} + 2\begin{vmatrix} 1 & 1 \\ x & -3 \end{vmatrix} + 3\begin{vmatrix} 1 & 2 \\ x & 2 \end{vmatrix} = 0$$

$$\Rightarrow \quad (-6-2) + 2(-3-x) + 3(2-2x) = 0 \Rightarrow -8-6-2x+6-6x = 0 \Rightarrow -8x-8 = 0 \Rightarrow x = -1.$$

ILLUSTRATION 2 *Determine the values of x for which the matrix* $A = \begin{bmatrix} x+1 & -3 & 4 \\ -5 & x+2 & 2 \\ 4 & 1 & x-6 \end{bmatrix}$ *is singular.*

SOLUTION Given matrix A is a singular matrix, if

$$|A| = 0$$

$$\Rightarrow \quad \begin{vmatrix} x+1 & -3 & 4 \\ -5 & x+2 & 2 \\ 4 & 1 & x-6 \end{vmatrix} = 0$$

$$\Rightarrow \quad (x+1)\begin{vmatrix} x+2 & 2 \\ 1 & x-6 \end{vmatrix} - (-3)\begin{vmatrix} -5 & 2 \\ 4 & x-6 \end{vmatrix} + 4\begin{vmatrix} -5 & x+2 \\ 4 & 1 \end{vmatrix} = 0$$

$$\Rightarrow \quad (x+1)\{(x+2)(x-6)-2\} + 3\{-5x+30-8\} + 4\{-5-4x-8\} = 0$$

$$\Rightarrow \quad (x+1)(x^2-4x-14) + 3(-5x+22) + 4(-4x-13) = 0$$

$$\Rightarrow \quad x(x^2-3x-49) = 0 \Rightarrow x = 0,\ x = \frac{1}{2}(3 \pm \sqrt{205})$$

5.3 MINORS AND COFACTOR

MINOR *Let* $A = [a_{ij}]$ *be a square matrix of order n. The minor* M_{ij} *of* a_{ij} *in A is the determinant of the square sub-matrix of order (n – 1) obtained by leaving* i^{th} *row and* j^{th} *column of A.*

For example, if $A = \begin{bmatrix} 4 & -7 \\ -3 & 2 \end{bmatrix}$, then

$M_{11} =$ Minor of $a_{11} = 2$, $M_{12} =$ Minor of $a_{12} = -3$, $M_{21} =$ Minor of $a_{21} = -7$, $M_{22} =$ Minor of $a_{22} = 4$

If $A = \begin{bmatrix} 1 & 2 & 3 \\ -3 & 2 & -1 \\ 2 & -4 & 3 \end{bmatrix}$, then

M_{11} = Minor of a_{11}

= Determinant of the 2×2 square sub-matrix obtained by leaving first row and first column of A

$$= \begin{vmatrix} 2 & -1 \\ -4 & 3 \end{vmatrix} = 2.$$

Similarly, we obtain

$$M_{12} = \text{Minor of } a_{12} = \begin{vmatrix} -3 & -1 \\ 2 & 3 \end{vmatrix} = -7, \quad M_{13} = \text{Minor of } a_{13} = \begin{vmatrix} -3 & 2 \\ 2 & -4 \end{vmatrix} = 8$$

$$M_{21} = \text{Minor of } a_{21} = \begin{vmatrix} 2 & 3 \\ -4 & 3 \end{vmatrix} = 18, \quad M_{22} = \text{Minor of } a_{22} = \begin{vmatrix} 1 & 3 \\ 2 & 3 \end{vmatrix} = -3 \text{ etc.}$$

COFACTOR *Let $A = [a_{ij}]$ be a square matrix of order n. The cofactor C_{ij} of a_{ij} in A is equal to $(-1)^{i+j}$ times the determinant of the sub-matrix of order $(n-1)$ obtained by leaving i^{th} row and j^{th} column of A.*

It follows from this definition that

$$C_{ij} = \text{Cofactor of } a_{ij} \text{ in } A = (-1)^{i+j} M_{ij}, \quad \text{where } M_{ij} \text{ is minor of } a_{ij} \text{ in } A.$$

Thus, we have $C_{ij} = \begin{cases} M_{ij}, & \text{if } i+j \text{ is even} \\ -M_{ij}, & \text{if } i+j \text{ is odd} \end{cases}$

For example, if $A = \begin{bmatrix} 4 & -7 \\ -3 & 2 \end{bmatrix}$, then

$$C_{11} = (-1)^{1+1} M_{11} = M_{11} = 2, \quad C_{12} = (-1)^{1+2} M_{12} = -M_{12} = -(-3) = 3,$$

$$C_{21} = (-1)^{2+1} M_{21} = -M_{21} = -(-7) = 7, \quad \text{and} \quad C_{22} = (-1)^{2+2} M_{22} = 4$$

If $A = \begin{bmatrix} 1 & 2 & 3 \\ -3 & 2 & -1 \\ 2 & -4 & 3 \end{bmatrix}$, then

$$C_{11} = (-1)^{1+1} M_{11} = M_{11} = \begin{vmatrix} 2 & -1 \\ -4 & 3 \end{vmatrix} = 2,$$

$$C_{12} = (-1)^{1+2} M_{12} = -M_{12} = -\begin{vmatrix} -3 & -1 \\ 2 & 3 \end{vmatrix} = -(-9+2) = 7$$

$$C_{13} = (-1)^{1+3} M_{13} = M_{13} = \begin{vmatrix} -3 & 2 \\ 2 & -4 \end{vmatrix} = 8, C_{23} = (-1)^{2+3} M_{23} = -M_{23} = -\begin{vmatrix} 1 & 2 \\ 2 & -4 \end{vmatrix} = 8 \text{ etc.}$$

REMARK *In some books the minors and cofactors are defined for the elements of a determinant. Infact, minors and cofactors are defined for the elements of a square matrix.*

ILLUSTRATIVE EXAMPLES

BASED ON BASIC CONCEPTS (BASIC)

EXAMPLE 1 *If $A = \begin{bmatrix} 1 & 3 \\ 2 & 1 \end{bmatrix}$, find the determinant of the matrix $A^2 - 2A$.*

SOLUTION We have, $A = \begin{bmatrix} 1 & 3 \\ 2 & 1 \end{bmatrix}$

$$\therefore \quad A^2 - 2A = \begin{bmatrix} 1 & 3 \\ 2 & 1 \end{bmatrix} \begin{bmatrix} 1 & 3 \\ 2 & 1 \end{bmatrix} - 2\begin{bmatrix} 1 & 3 \\ 2 & 1 \end{bmatrix}$$

$$\Rightarrow \quad A^2 - 2A = \begin{bmatrix} 1+6 & 3+3 \\ 2+2 & 6+1 \end{bmatrix} - \begin{bmatrix} 2 & 6 \\ 4 & 2 \end{bmatrix} = \begin{bmatrix} 7 & 6 \\ 4 & 7 \end{bmatrix} - \begin{bmatrix} 2 & 6 \\ 4 & 2 \end{bmatrix} = \begin{bmatrix} 7-2 & 6-6 \\ 4-4 & 7-2 \end{bmatrix} = \begin{bmatrix} 5 & 0 \\ 0 & 5 \end{bmatrix}$$

$$\therefore \quad |A^2 - 2A| = \begin{vmatrix} 5 & 0 \\ 0 & 5 \end{vmatrix} = 25 - 0 = 25.$$

EXAMPLE 2 *If $A = \begin{bmatrix} 1 & 2 \\ 4 & 2 \end{bmatrix}$, then show that $|2A| = 4|A|$.*

SOLUTION We have, **[NCERT]**

$$A = \begin{bmatrix} 1 & 2 \\ 4 & 2 \end{bmatrix} \Rightarrow 2A = \begin{bmatrix} 2 & 4 \\ 8 & 4 \end{bmatrix}$$

$$\therefore \quad |A| = \begin{vmatrix} 1 & 2 \\ 4 & 2 \end{vmatrix} = 2 - 8 = -6 \text{ and } |2A| = \begin{vmatrix} 2 & 4 \\ 8 & 4 \end{vmatrix} = 8 - 32 = -24 = 4 \times (-6)$$

Clearly, $|2A| = 4|A|$.

EXAMPLE 3 *If* $\begin{vmatrix} x-2 & -3 \\ 3x & 2x \end{vmatrix} = 3$, *find the values of* x.

SOLUTION We have,

$$\begin{vmatrix} x-2 & -3 \\ 3x & 2x \end{vmatrix} = 3$$

$$\Rightarrow \quad (x-2) \times 2x - (-3) \times 3x = 3 \Rightarrow 2x(x-2) + 9x = 3 \Rightarrow 2x^2 - 4x + 9x = 3$$

$$\Rightarrow \quad 2x^2 + 5x - 3 = 0 \Rightarrow (2x-1)(x+3) = 0 \Rightarrow 2x - 1 = 0 \text{ or, } x + 3 = 0 \Rightarrow x = \frac{1}{2}, -3.$$

BASED ON LOWER ORDER THINKING SKILLS (LOTS)

EXAMPLE 4 *Let* $\begin{vmatrix} 3 & y \\ x & 1 \end{vmatrix} = \begin{vmatrix} 3 & 2 \\ 4 & 1 \end{vmatrix}$. *Find possible values of x and y if x, y are natural numbers.*

SOLUTION We have,

$$\begin{vmatrix} 3 & y \\ x & 1 \end{vmatrix} = \begin{vmatrix} 3 & 2 \\ 4 & 1 \end{vmatrix}$$

$$\Rightarrow \quad 3 - xy = 3 - 8 \Rightarrow xy = 8 \Rightarrow x = 1, y = 8; x = 2, y = 4; x = 4, y = 2; x = 8, y = 1$$

EXAMPLE 5 *Evaluate the determinant* $\Delta = \begin{vmatrix} \log_3 512 & \log_4 3 \\ \log_3 8 & \log_4 9 \end{vmatrix}$.

SOLUTION We have,

$$\Delta = \begin{vmatrix} \log_3 512 & \log_4 3 \\ \log_3 8 & \log_4 9 \end{vmatrix} = \begin{vmatrix} \log_3 2^9 & \log_{2^2} 3 \\ \log_3 2^3 & \log_{2^2} 3^2 \end{vmatrix}$$

$$\Rightarrow \quad \Delta = \begin{vmatrix} 9 \log_3 2 & \frac{1}{2} \log_2 3 \\ 3 \log_3 2 & \frac{2}{2} \log_2 3 \end{vmatrix} \qquad \left[\because \log_{a^p} m^n = \frac{n}{p} \log_a m\right]$$

$$\Rightarrow \quad \Delta = \begin{vmatrix} 9 \log_3 2 & \frac{1}{2} \log_2 3 \\ 3 \log_3 2 & \log_2 3 \end{vmatrix} = (9 \log_3 2) \times (\log_2 3) - \left(\frac{1}{2} \log_2 3\right)(3 \log_3 2)$$

$$\Rightarrow \quad \Delta = 9(\log_3 2 \times \log_2 3) - \frac{3}{2}(\log_2 3 \times \log_3 2) = 9 - \frac{3}{2} = \frac{15}{2} \qquad [\because \log_b a \times \log_a b = 1]$$

EXAMPLE 6 *Find the minors and cofactors of elements of the matrix* $A = [a_{ij}] = \begin{bmatrix} 1 & 3 & -2 \\ 4 & -5 & 6 \\ 3 & 5 & 2 \end{bmatrix}$.

SOLUTION Let M_{ij} and C_{ij} denote respectively the minor and cofactor of element a_{ij} in A. Then,

$$M_{11} = \begin{vmatrix} -5 & 6 \\ 5 & 2 \end{vmatrix} = -10 - 30 = -40 \Rightarrow C_{11} = M_{11} = -40$$

$$M_{12} = \begin{vmatrix} 4 & 6 \\ 3 & 2 \end{vmatrix} = 8 - 18 = -10 \qquad \Rightarrow C_{12} = -M_{12} = 10$$

$$M_{13} = \begin{vmatrix} 4 & -5 \\ 3 & 5 \end{vmatrix} = 20 + 15 = 35 \Rightarrow C_{13} = M_{13} = 35$$

$$M_{21} = \begin{vmatrix} 3 & -2 \\ 5 & 2 \end{vmatrix} = 6 + 10 = 16 \Rightarrow C_{21} = -M_{21} = -16$$

$$M_{22} = \begin{vmatrix} 1 & -2 \\ 3 & 2 \end{vmatrix} = 2 + 6 = 8 \Rightarrow C_{22} = M_{22} = 8$$

$$M_{23} = \begin{vmatrix} 1 & 3 \\ 3 & 5 \end{vmatrix} = 5 - 9 = -4 \Rightarrow C_{23} = -M_{23} = 4$$

$$M_{31} = \begin{vmatrix} 3 & -2 \\ -5 & 6 \end{vmatrix} = 18 - 10 = 8 \Rightarrow C_{31} = M_{31} = 8$$

$$M_{32} = \begin{vmatrix} 1 & -2 \\ 4 & 6 \end{vmatrix} = 6 + 8 = 14 \Rightarrow C_{32} = -M_{32} = -14$$

$$M_{33} = \begin{vmatrix} 1 & 3 \\ 4 & -5 \end{vmatrix} = -5 - 12 = -17 \Rightarrow C_{33} = M_{33} = -17$$

BASED ON HIGHER ORDER THINKING SKILLS (HOTS)

EXAMPLE 7 *Evaluate the determinant* $\Delta = \begin{vmatrix} 1 & \sin\theta & 1 \\ -\sin\theta & 1 & \sin\theta \\ -1 & -\sin\theta & 1 \end{vmatrix}$. *Also, prove that* $2 \le \Delta \le 4$

SOLUTION We have,

$$\Delta = \begin{vmatrix} 1 & \sin\theta & 1 \\ -\sin\theta & 1 & \sin\theta \\ -1 & -\sin\theta & 1 \end{vmatrix}$$

On expanding along first row, we obtain

$$\Delta = 1 \times \begin{vmatrix} 1 & \sin\theta \\ -\sin\theta & 1 \end{vmatrix} - \sin\theta \begin{vmatrix} -\sin\theta & \sin\theta \\ -1 & 1 \end{vmatrix} + 1 \times \begin{vmatrix} -\sin\theta & 1 \\ -1 & -\sin\theta \end{vmatrix}$$

$$= 1 \times (1 + \sin^2\theta) - \sin\theta(-\sin\theta + \sin\theta) + 1 \times (\sin^2\theta + 1)$$

$$= (1 + \sin^2\theta) - 0 + (\sin^2\theta + 1) = 2 + 2\sin^2\theta = 2(1 + \sin^2\theta)$$

We know that

$$-1 \le \sin\theta \le 1 \quad \text{for all } \theta$$

$$\Rightarrow \quad 0 \le \sin^2\theta \le 1 \quad \text{for all } \theta$$

$$\Rightarrow \quad 1 + 0 \le 1 + \sin^2\theta \le 1 + 1 \quad \text{for all } \theta$$

$$\Rightarrow \quad 1 \le 1 + \sin^2\theta \le 2 \text{ for all } \theta \Rightarrow 2 \le 2(1 + \sin^2\theta) \le 4 \text{ for all } \theta \Rightarrow 2 \le \Delta \le 4. \text{ for all } \theta$$

EXAMPLE 8 *If* $[\cdot]$ *denotes the greatest integer less than or equal to the real number under consideration, and* $-1 \le x < 0$, $0 \le y < 1$, $1 \le z < 2$, *then find the value of the following determinant:*

$$\Delta = \begin{vmatrix} [x]+1 & [y] & [z] \\ [x] & [y]+1 & [z] \\ [x] & [y] & [z]+1 \end{vmatrix}$$

SOLUTION We have, $-1 \le x < 0$, $0 \le y < 1$ and $1 \le z < 2 \Rightarrow [x] = -1$, $[y] = 0$ and $[z] = 1$.

$$\therefore \quad \Delta = \begin{vmatrix} [x]+1 & [y] & [z] \\ [x] & [y]+1 & [z] \\ [x] & [y] & [z]+1 \end{vmatrix} = \begin{vmatrix} 0 & 0 & 1 \\ -1 & 1 & 1 \\ -1 & 0 & 2 \end{vmatrix}$$

$$\Rightarrow \quad \Delta = 0 \times \begin{vmatrix} 1 & 1 \\ 0 & 2 \end{vmatrix} - 0 \times \begin{vmatrix} -1 & 1 \\ -1 & 2 \end{vmatrix} + 1 \times \begin{vmatrix} -1 & 1 \\ -1 & 0 \end{vmatrix} \quad \text{[Expanding along first row]}$$

$$\Rightarrow \quad \Delta = 0(2-0) - 0(-2+1) + 1 \times (0+1) = 1.$$

EXAMPLE 9 *Prove that the determinant* $\begin{vmatrix} x & \sin\theta & \cos\theta \\ -\sin\theta & -x & 1 \\ \cos\theta & 1 & x \end{vmatrix}$ *is independent of* θ.

[NCERT, CBSE 2023]

SOLUTION We have,

$$\Delta = \begin{vmatrix} x & \sin\theta & \cos\theta \\ -\sin\theta & -x & 1 \\ \cos\theta & 1 & x \end{vmatrix}$$

$$\Rightarrow \quad \Delta = x \begin{vmatrix} -x & 1 \\ 1 & x \end{vmatrix} - \sin\theta \begin{vmatrix} -\sin\theta & 1 \\ \cos\theta & x \end{vmatrix} + \cos\theta \begin{vmatrix} -\sin\theta & -x \\ \cos\theta & 1 \end{vmatrix} \quad \text{[Expanding along first row]}$$

$$\Rightarrow \quad \Delta = x(-x^2-1) - \sin\theta(-x\sin\theta - \cos\theta) + \cos\theta(-\sin\theta + x\cos\theta)$$

$$\Rightarrow \quad \Delta = -x^3 - x + x\sin^2\theta + \sin\theta\cos\theta - \sin\theta\cos\theta + x\cos^2\theta$$

$$\Rightarrow \quad \Delta = -x^3 - x + x(\sin^2\theta + \cos^2\theta) = -x^3 - x + x = -x^3,$$ which is independent of θ.

EXERCISE 5.1

BASIC

1. Write the minors and cofactors of each element of the first column of the following matrices and hence evaluate the determinant in each case:

(i) $A = \begin{bmatrix} 5 & 20 \\ 0 & -1 \end{bmatrix}$ (ii) $A = \begin{bmatrix} 1 & -3 & 2 \\ 4 & -1 & 2 \\ 3 & 5 & 2 \end{bmatrix}$ (iii) $A = \begin{bmatrix} 1 & a & bc \\ 1 & b & ca \\ 1 & c & ab \end{bmatrix}$

(iv) $A = \begin{bmatrix} a & h & g \\ h & b & f \\ g & f & c \end{bmatrix}$ (v) $A = \begin{bmatrix} 2 & -1 & 0 & 1 \\ -3 & 0 & 1 & -2 \\ 1 & 1 & -1 & 1 \\ 2 & -1 & 5 & 0 \end{bmatrix}$

2. Evaluate the following determinants:

(i) $\begin{vmatrix} x & -7 \\ x & 5x+1 \end{vmatrix}$ (ii) $\begin{vmatrix} \cos\theta & -\sin\theta \\ \sin\theta & \cos\theta \end{vmatrix}$ (iii) $\begin{vmatrix} \cos 15^\circ & \sin 15^\circ \\ \sin 75^\circ & \cos 75^\circ \end{vmatrix}$ (iv) $\begin{vmatrix} a+ib & c+id \\ -c+id & a-ib \end{vmatrix}$

[CBSE 2008]

3. Evaluate: $\begin{vmatrix} 2 & 3 & 7 \\ 13 & 17 & 5 \\ 15 & 20 & 12 \end{vmatrix}^2$.

4. Show that $\begin{vmatrix} \sin 10^\circ & -\cos 10^\circ \\ \sin 80^\circ & \cos 80^\circ \end{vmatrix} = 1$

5. Evaluate $\begin{vmatrix} 2 & 3 & -5 \\ 7 & 1 & -2 \\ -3 & 4 & 1 \end{vmatrix}$ by two methods.

BASED ON LOTS

6. Evaluate: $\Delta = \begin{vmatrix} 0 & \sin\alpha & -\cos\alpha \\ -\sin\alpha & 0 & \sin\beta \\ \cos\alpha & -\sin\beta & 0 \end{vmatrix}$ [NCERT]

7. Evaluate: $\Delta = \begin{vmatrix} \cos\alpha\cos\beta & \cos\alpha\sin\beta & -\sin\alpha \\ -\sin\beta & \cos\beta & 0 \\ \sin\alpha\cos\beta & \sin\alpha\sin\beta & \cos\alpha \end{vmatrix}$ [NCERT]

8. If $A = \begin{bmatrix} 2 & 5 \\ 2 & 1 \end{bmatrix}$ and $B = \begin{bmatrix} 4 & -3 \\ 2 & 5 \end{bmatrix}$, verify that $|AB| = |A||B|$.

9. If $A = \begin{bmatrix} 1 & 0 & 1 \\ 0 & 1 & 2 \\ 0 & 0 & 4 \end{bmatrix}$, then show that $|3A| = 27|A|$.

10. Find the values of x, if

(i) $\begin{vmatrix} 2 & 4 \\ 5 & 1 \end{vmatrix} = \begin{vmatrix} 2x & 4 \\ 6 & x \end{vmatrix}$ [NCERT]

(ii) $\begin{vmatrix} 3 & x \\ x & 1 \end{vmatrix} = \begin{vmatrix} 3 & 2 \\ 4 & 1 \end{vmatrix}$ [NCERT]

(iii) $\begin{vmatrix} x+1 & x-1 \\ x-3 & x+2 \end{vmatrix} = \begin{vmatrix} 4 & -1 \\ 1 & 3 \end{vmatrix}$ [CBSE 2013]

(iv) $\begin{vmatrix} 2x & 5 \\ 8 & x \end{vmatrix} = \begin{vmatrix} 6 & 5 \\ 8 & 3 \end{vmatrix}$ [NCERT EXEMPLAR]

11. Find the integral value of x, if $\begin{vmatrix} x^2 & x & 1 \\ 0 & 2 & 1 \\ 3 & 1 & 4 \end{vmatrix} = 28$.

12. For what value of x the matrix A is singular?

(i) $A = \begin{bmatrix} 1+x & 7 \\ 3-x & 8 \end{bmatrix}$ [CBSE 2012]

(ii) $A = \begin{bmatrix} x-1 & 1 & 1 \\ 1 & x-1 & 1 \\ 1 & 1 & x-1 \end{bmatrix}$

ANSWERS

1. *Minors* / *Cofactors*

(i) $M_{11} = -1, M_{21} = 20$; $C_{11} = -1, C_{21} = -20$

(ii) $M_{11} = -12, M_{21} = -16, M_{31} = -4$; $C_{11} = -12, C_{21} = 16, C_{31} = -4$

(iii) $M_{11} = a(b^2 - c^2), M_{21} = b(a^2 - c^2), M_{31} = c(a^2 - b^2)$; $C_{11} = a(b^2 - c^2), C_{21} = -b(a^2 - c^2), C_{31} = c(a^2 - b^2)$

(iv) $M_{11} = bc - f^2, M_{21} = hc - fg, M_{31} = hf - bg$; $C_{11} = bc - f^2, C_{21} = fg - ch, C_{31} = hf - bg$

(v) $M_{11} = -9, M_{21} = 9, M_{31} = -9, M_{41} = 0$; $C_{11} = -9, C_{21} = -9, C_{31} = -9, C_{41} = 0$

2. (i) $5x^2 + 8x$ (ii) 1 (iii) 0 (iv) $a^2 + b^2 + c^2 + d^2$ 3. 0 5. -140

6. 0 7. 1 10. (i) $\pm\sqrt{3}$ (ii) $\pm 2\sqrt{2}$ (iii) 2 (iv) ± 3 11. 2 12. (i) $\frac{13}{15}$ (ii) $-1, 2$

HINTS TO SELECTED PROBLEMS

6. We have, $\Delta = \begin{vmatrix} 0 & \sin\alpha & -\cos\alpha \\ -\sin\alpha & 0 & \sin\beta \\ \cos\alpha & -\sin\beta & 0 \end{vmatrix}$

On expanding along first row, we get

$$\Delta = 0\begin{vmatrix} 0 & \sin\beta \\ -\sin\beta & 0 \end{vmatrix} - \sin\alpha\begin{vmatrix} -\sin\alpha & \sin\beta \\ \cos\alpha & 0 \end{vmatrix} - \cos\alpha\begin{vmatrix} -\sin\alpha & 0 \\ \cos\alpha & -\sin\beta \end{vmatrix}$$

$\Rightarrow \Delta = -\sin\alpha(0 - \sin\beta\cos\alpha) - \cos\alpha(\sin\alpha\sin\beta) = \sin\alpha\cos\alpha\sin\beta - \sin\alpha\cos\alpha\sin\beta = 0$

On expanding along first row, we get

$$\Delta = 0\begin{vmatrix} 0 & \sin\beta \\ -\sin\beta & 0 \end{vmatrix} - \sin\alpha\begin{vmatrix} -\sin\alpha & \sin\beta \\ \cos\alpha & 0 \end{vmatrix} - \cos\alpha\begin{vmatrix} -\sin\alpha & 0 \\ \cos\alpha & -\sin\beta \end{vmatrix}$$

$\Rightarrow \Delta = -\sin\alpha\,(0 - \sin\beta\cos\alpha) - \cos\alpha\,(\sin\alpha\sin\beta) = \sin\alpha\cos\alpha\sin\beta - \sin\alpha\cos\alpha\sin\beta = 0$

7. We have, $\Delta = \begin{vmatrix} \cos\alpha\cos\beta & \cos\alpha\sin\beta & -\sin\alpha \\ -\sin\beta & \cos\beta & 0 \\ \sin\alpha\cos\beta & \sin\alpha\sin\beta & \cos\alpha \end{vmatrix}$

On expanding along first row, we get

$$\Delta = \cos\alpha\cos\beta \begin{vmatrix} \cos\beta & 0 \\ \sin\alpha\sin\beta & \cos\alpha \end{vmatrix} - \cos\alpha\sin\beta \begin{vmatrix} -\sin\beta & 0 \\ \sin\alpha\cos\beta & \cos\alpha \end{vmatrix} - \sin\alpha \begin{vmatrix} -\sin\beta & \cos\beta \\ \sin\alpha\cos\beta & \sin\alpha\sin\beta \end{vmatrix}$$

$$\Rightarrow \Delta = \cos\alpha\cos\beta\,(\cos\alpha\cos\beta - 0) - \cos\alpha\sin\beta\,(-\cos\alpha\sin\beta - 0) - \sin\alpha\,(-\sin\alpha\sin^2\beta - \sin\alpha\cos^2\beta)$$

$$\Rightarrow \Delta = \cos^2\alpha\cos^2\beta + \cos^2\alpha\sin^2\beta + \sin^2\alpha$$

$$\Rightarrow \Delta = \cos^2\alpha\,(\cos^2\beta + \sin^2\beta) + \sin^2\alpha = \cos^2\alpha + \sin^2\alpha = 1$$

10. (i) $\begin{vmatrix} 2 & 4 \\ 5 & 1 \end{vmatrix} = \begin{vmatrix} 2x & 4 \\ 6 & x \end{vmatrix} \Rightarrow 2 - 20 = 2x^2 - 24 \Rightarrow 2x^2 = 6 \Rightarrow x = \pm\sqrt{3}$

(ii) $\begin{vmatrix} 3 & x \\ x & 1 \end{vmatrix} = \begin{vmatrix} 3 & 2 \\ 4 & 1 \end{vmatrix} \Rightarrow 3 - x^2 = 3 - 8 \Rightarrow x^2 = 8 \Rightarrow x = \pm 2\sqrt{2}$

*5.4 PROPERTIES OF DETERMINANTS

In section 5.1, we have defined the determinant of a square matrix of order 4 or less. Infact, these definitions are consequences of the general definition of the determinant of a square matrix of any order which needs so many advanced concepts. These concepts are beyond the scope of this book. Using the said definition and some other advanced concepts we can prove the following properties. But, the concepts used in the definition itself are very advanced. Therefore we mention these properties and verify them for a determinant of a square matrix of order 3.

PROPERTY 1 *Let $A = [a_{ij}]$ be a square matrix of order n, then the sum of the product of elements of any row (column) with their cofactors is always equal to $|A|$ or, det (A).*

i.e. $\sum_{j=1}^{n} a_{ij} C_{ij} = |A|$ and, $\sum_{i=1}^{n} a_{ij} C_{ij} = |A|$.

VERIFICATION Let $A = \begin{bmatrix} a_{11} & a_{12} & a_{13} \\ a_{21} & a_{22} & a_{23} \\ a_{31} & a_{32} & a_{33} \end{bmatrix}$ be a square matrix of order 3. Then, by definition, we obtain

$$|A| = \begin{vmatrix} a_{11} & a_{12} & a_{13} \\ a_{21} & a_{22} & a_{23} \\ a_{31} & a_{32} & a_{33} \end{vmatrix}$$

$$\Rightarrow |A| = (-1)^{1+1} a_{11} \begin{vmatrix} a_{22} & a_{23} \\ a_{32} & a_{33} \end{vmatrix} + (-1)^{1+2} a_{12} \begin{vmatrix} a_{21} & a_{23} \\ a_{31} & a_{33} \end{vmatrix} + (-1)^{1+3} a_{13} \begin{vmatrix} a_{21} & a_{22} \\ a_{31} & a_{32} \end{vmatrix}$$

[Expanding along first row]

$\Rightarrow |A| = a_{11} C_{11} + a_{12} C_{12} + a_{13} C_{13}$ [By using the definition of cofactors]

**May be skipped. Not from examination point of view.*

Similarly, we obtain

$$|A| = a_{21} C_{21} + a_{22} C_{22} + a_{23} C_{23}, \; |A| = a_{31} C_{31} + a_{32} C_{32} + a_{33} C_{33},$$
$$|A| = a_{11} C_{11} + a_{21} C_{21} + a_{31} C_{31} \quad \text{etc.}$$

PROPERTY 2 *Let $A = [a_{ij}]$ be a square matrix of order n, then the sum of the product of elements of any row (column) with the cofactors of the corresponding elements of some other row (column) is zero.*

i.e. $$\sum_{j=1}^{n} a_{ij} C_{kj} = 0 \quad \textit{and,} \quad \sum_{i=1}^{n} a_{ij} C_{ik} = 0.$$

VERIFICATION Let $A = \begin{bmatrix} a_{11} & a_{12} & a_{13} \\ a_{21} & a_{22} & a_{23} \\ a_{31} & a_{32} & a_{33} \end{bmatrix}$ be a square matrix of order 3. Then, the sum of the product of elements of first row with the cofactors of elements in second row is given by

$$a_{11} C_{21} + a_{12} C_{22} + a_{13} C_{23}$$
$$= a_{11} (-1)^{2+1} \begin{vmatrix} a_{12} & a_{13} \\ a_{32} & a_{33} \end{vmatrix} + a_{12} (-1)^{2+2} \begin{vmatrix} a_{11} & a_{13} \\ a_{31} & a_{33} \end{vmatrix} + a_{13} (-1)^{2+3} \begin{vmatrix} a_{11} & a_{12} \\ a_{31} & a_{32} \end{vmatrix}$$
$$= - a_{11} (a_{12} a_{33} - a_{13} a_{32}) + a_{12} (a_{11} a_{33} - a_{13} a_{31}) - a_{13} (a_{11} a_{32} - a_{12} a_{31})$$
$$= 0$$

Similarly, we obtain

$$a_{11} C_{31} + a_{12} C_{32} + a_{13} C_{33} = 0, \quad a_{21} C_{11} + a_{22} C_{12} + a_{23} C_{13} = 0 \quad \text{etc.}$$

PROPERTY 3 *Let $A = [a_{ij}]$ be a square matrix of order n, then $|A| = |A^T|$.*

By the abuse of language this property is also stated as follows:

The value of a determinant remains unchanged if its rows and columns are interchanged.

VERIFICATION Let $A = \begin{bmatrix} a_1 & b_1 & c_1 \\ a_2 & b_2 & c_2 \\ a_3 & b_3 & c_3 \end{bmatrix}$ be a square matrix of order 3. Then, $A^T = \begin{bmatrix} a_1 & a_2 & a_3 \\ b_1 & b_2 & b_3 \\ c_1 & c_2 & c_3 \end{bmatrix}$.

Now, $$|A| = \begin{vmatrix} a_1 & b_1 & c_1 \\ a_2 & b_2 & c_2 \\ a_3 & b_3 & c_3 \end{vmatrix}$$

$$\Rightarrow \quad |A| = (-1)^{1+1} a_1 \begin{vmatrix} b_2 & c_2 \\ b_3 & c_3 \end{vmatrix} + (-1)^{1+2} b_1 \begin{vmatrix} a_2 & c_2 \\ a_3 & c_3 \end{vmatrix} + (-1)^{1+3} c_1 \begin{vmatrix} a_2 & b_2 \\ a_3 & b_3 \end{vmatrix}$$

[Expanding along first row]

$$\Rightarrow \quad |A| = a_1 (b_2 c_3 - b_3 c_2) - b_1 (a_2 c_3 - a_3 c_2) + c_1 (a_2 b_3 - a_3 b_2) \quad \text{...(i)}$$

and, $$|A^T| = \begin{vmatrix} a_1 & a_2 & a_3 \\ b_1 & b_2 & b_3 \\ c_1 & c_2 & c_3 \end{vmatrix}$$

$$\Rightarrow \quad |A^T| = (-1)^{1+1} a_1 \begin{vmatrix} b_2 & b_3 \\ c_2 & c_3 \end{vmatrix} + (-1)^{1+2} b_1 \begin{vmatrix} a_2 & a_3 \\ c_2 & c_3 \end{vmatrix} + (-1)^{1+3} c_1 \begin{vmatrix} a_2 & a_3 \\ b_2 & b_3 \end{vmatrix}$$

[Expanding along first column]

$$\Rightarrow \quad |A^T| = a_1 (b_2 c_3 - b_3 c_2) - b_1 \cdot (a_2 c_3 - a_3 c_2) + c_1 (a_2 b_3 - a_3 b_2) \quad \text{...(ii)}$$

From (i) and (ii), we obtain $|A| = |A^T|$.

PROPERTY 4 *Let $A = [a_{ij}]$ be a square matrix of order $n (\geq 2)$ and let B be a matrix obtained from A by interchanging any two rows (columns) of A, then $|B| = -|A|$.*

Conventionally this property is also stated as:

If any two rows (columns) of a determinant are interchanged, then the value of the determinant changes by minus sign only.

VERIFICATION Let $A = \begin{bmatrix} a_1 & b_1 & c_1 \\ a_2 & b_2 & c_2 \\ a_3 & b_3 & c_3 \end{bmatrix}$ be a square matrix of order 3 and let B be the matrix obtained from A by interchanging first and third row i.e. $B = \begin{bmatrix} a_3 & b_3 & c_3 \\ a_2 & b_2 & c_2 \\ a_1 & b_1 & c_1 \end{bmatrix}$.

Then, $|A| = \begin{vmatrix} a_1 & b_1 & c_1 \\ a_2 & b_2 & c_2 \\ a_3 & b_3 & c_3 \end{vmatrix} = (-1)^{1+1} a_1 \begin{vmatrix} b_2 & c_2 \\ b_3 & c_3 \end{vmatrix} + (-1)^{1+2} b_1 \begin{vmatrix} a_2 & c_2 \\ a_3 & c_3 \end{vmatrix} + (-1)^{1+3} c_1 \begin{vmatrix} a_2 & b_2 \\ a_3 & b_3 \end{vmatrix}$

[Expanding along first row]

$\Rightarrow \quad |A| = a_1 (b_2 c_3 - b_3 c_2) - b_1 (a_2 c_3 - a_3 c_2) + c_1 (a_2 b_3 - a_3 b_2)$ ...(i)

and, $|B| = \begin{vmatrix} a_3 & b_3 & c_3 \\ a_2 & b_2 & c_2 \\ a_1 & b_1 & c_1 \end{vmatrix} = (-1)^{3+1} a_1 \begin{vmatrix} b_3 & c_3 \\ b_2 & c_2 \end{vmatrix} + (-1)^{3+2} b_1 \begin{vmatrix} a_3 & c_3 \\ a_2 & c_2 \end{vmatrix} + (-1)^{3+3} c_1 \begin{vmatrix} a_3 & b_3 \\ a_2 & b_2 \end{vmatrix}$

[Expanding along first row]

$\Rightarrow \quad |B| = -[a_1 (b_2 c_3 - b_3 c_2) - b_1 (a_2 c_3 - a_3 c_2) + c_1 (a_2 b_3 - a_3 b_2)]$ ...(ii)

From (i) and (ii), we obtain : $|B| = -|A|$.

PROPERTY 5 *If any two rows (columns) of a square matrix $A = [a_{ij}]$ of order $n (> 2)$ are identical, then its determinant is zero i.e. $|A| = 0$.*

Conventionally this property is stated as:

If any two rows or columns of a determinant are identical, then its value is zero.

VERIFICATION Let $A = \begin{bmatrix} a_1 & b_1 & c_1 \\ a_2 & b_2 & c_2 \\ a_1 & b_1 & c_1 \end{bmatrix}$ be a matrix having first and third rows identical and let B be the matrix obtained from A by interchanging the first and third rows. Then, by property 4, we obtain

$$|B| = -|A| \quad \text{...(i)}$$

But, $B = \begin{bmatrix} a_1 & b_1 & c_1 \\ a_2 & b_2 & c_2 \\ a_1 & b_1 & c_1 \end{bmatrix} = A$. Therefore, $|B| = |A|$ ...(ii)

From (i) and (ii), we obtain

$$|A| = -|A| \Rightarrow 2|A| = 0 \Rightarrow |A| = 0.$$

PROPERTY 6 *Let $A = [a_{ij}]$ be a square matrix of order n, and let B be the matrix obtained from A by multiplying each element of a row (column) of A by a scalar k, then $|B| = k|A|$.*

Conventionally this property is also stated as:

If each element of a row (column) of a determinant is multiplied by a constant k, then the value of the new determinant is k times the value of the original determinant.

VERIFICATION Let $A = \begin{bmatrix} a_1 & b_1 & c_1 \\ a_2 & b_2 & c_2 \\ a_3 & b_3 & c_3 \end{bmatrix}$ be a square matrix order 3, and let B be a matrix obtained from A by multiplying each element of second row by the same constant k, then

$$B = \begin{bmatrix} a_1 & b_1 & c_1 \\ ka_2 & kb_2 & kc_2 \\ a_3 & b_3 & c_3 \end{bmatrix}.$$

Now,

$$|A| = \begin{vmatrix} a_1 & b_1 & c_1 \\ a_2 & b_2 & c_2 \\ a_3 & b_3 & c_3 \end{vmatrix} = a_1 (b_2 c_3 - b_3 c_2) - b_1 (a_2 c_3 - a_3 c_2) + c_1 (a_2 b_3 - a_3 b_2) \quad \text{...(i)}$$

and, $$|B| = \begin{vmatrix} a_1 & b_1 & c_1 \\ ka_2 & kb_2 & kc_2 \\ a_3 & b_3 & c_3 \end{vmatrix}$$

$$\Rightarrow \quad |B| = a_1 (kb_2 c_3 - kb_3 c_2) - b_1 (ka_2 c_3 - ka_3 c_2) + c_1 (ka_2 b_3 - kb_2 a_3)$$

[On expanding along first row]

$$\Rightarrow \quad |B| = k [a_1 (b_2 c_3 - b_3 c_2) - b_1 (a_2 c_3 - a_3 c_2) + c_1 (a_2 b_3 - a_3 b_2)] \quad \text{...(ii)}$$

From (i) and (ii), we obtain $|B| = k|A|$.

REMARK 1 *It follows from the above property that we can take out any common factor from any one row or any one column of a given determinant.*

REMARK 2 *Let $A = [a_{ij}]$ be a square matrix of order n, then $|kA| = k^n |A|$, because k is common from each row of kA.*

PROPERTY 7 *Let A be a square matrix such that each element of a row (column) of A is expressed as the sum of two or more terms. Then, the determinant of A can be expressed as the sum of the determinants of two or more matrices of the same order.*

Conventionally this property is also stated as:

If each element of a row (column) of a determinant is expressed as a sum of two or more terms, then the determinant can be expressed as the sum of two or more determinants.

VERIFICATION Let $A = \begin{bmatrix} a_1 + \alpha_1 & b_1 + \beta_1 & c_1 + \gamma_1 \\ a_2 & b_2 & c_2 \\ a_3 & b_3 & c_3 \end{bmatrix}$ be a square matrix such that each element in first row of A is the sum of two elements. Then,

$$|A| = \begin{vmatrix} a_1 + \alpha_1 & b_1 + \beta_1 & c_1 + \gamma_1 \\ a_2 & b_2 & c_2 \\ a_3 & b_3 & c_3 \end{vmatrix}$$

$$\Rightarrow \quad |A| = (a_1 + \alpha_1) \begin{vmatrix} b_2 & c_2 \\ b_3 & c_3 \end{vmatrix} - (b_1 + \beta_1) \begin{vmatrix} a_2 & c_2 \\ a_3 & c_3 \end{vmatrix} + (c_1 + \gamma_1) \begin{vmatrix} a_2 & b_2 \\ a_3 & b_3 \end{vmatrix} \quad \begin{bmatrix} \text{Expanding along} \\ \text{first row} \end{bmatrix}$$

$$\Rightarrow \quad |A| = \left\{ a_1 \begin{vmatrix} b_2 & c_2 \\ b_3 & c_3 \end{vmatrix} - b_1 \begin{vmatrix} a_2 & c_2 \\ a_3 & c_3 \end{vmatrix} + c_1 \begin{vmatrix} a_2 & b_2 \\ a_3 & b_3 \end{vmatrix} \right\} + \left\{ \alpha_1 \begin{vmatrix} b_2 & c_2 \\ b_3 & c_3 \end{vmatrix} - \beta_1 \begin{vmatrix} a_2 & c_2 \\ a_3 & c_3 \end{vmatrix} + \gamma_1 \begin{vmatrix} a_2 & b_2 \\ a_3 & b_3 \end{vmatrix} \right\}$$

$$\Rightarrow \quad |A| = \begin{vmatrix} a_1 & b_1 & c_1 \\ a_2 & b_2 & c_2 \\ a_3 & b_3 & c_3 \end{vmatrix} + \begin{vmatrix} \alpha_1 & \beta_1 & \gamma_1 \\ a_2 & b_2 & c_2 \\ a_3 & b_3 & c_3 \end{vmatrix}$$

$$\Rightarrow \quad |A| = |B| + |C|, \text{ where } B = \begin{bmatrix} a_1 & b_1 & c_1 \\ a_2 & b_2 & c_2 \\ a_3 & b_3 & c_3 \end{bmatrix} \text{ and } C = \begin{bmatrix} \alpha_1 & \beta_1 & \gamma_1 \\ a_2 & b_2 & c_2 \\ a_3 & b_3 & c_3 \end{bmatrix}.$$

PROPERTY 8 *Let A be a square matrix and B be a matrix obtained from A by adding to a row (column) of A a scalar multiple of another row (column) of A, then* $|B| = |A|$.

This property is conventionally stated as:

If each element of a row (column) of a determinant is multiplied by the same constant and then added to the corresponding elements of some other row (column), then the value of the determinant remains same.

VERIFICATION Let $A = \begin{bmatrix} a_1 & b_1 & c_1 \\ a_2 & b_2 & c_2 \\ a_3 & b_3 & c_3 \end{bmatrix}$ be a matrix and let $B = \begin{bmatrix} a_1 + kb_1 & b_1 & c_1 \\ a_2 + kb_2 & b_2 & c_2 \\ a_3 + kb_3 & b_3 & c_3 \end{bmatrix}$ be the matrix obtained from A by multiplying the elements of second column by k and then adding them to the corresponding elements of first column. Then,

$$|B| = \begin{vmatrix} a_1 + kb_1 & b_1 & c_1 \\ a_2 + kb_2 & b_2 & c_2 \\ a_3 + kb_3 & b_3 & c_3 \end{vmatrix}$$

$$\Rightarrow \quad |B| = \begin{vmatrix} a_1 & b_1 & c_1 \\ a_2 & b_2 & c_2 \\ a_3 & b_3 & c_3 \end{vmatrix} + \begin{vmatrix} kb_1 & b_1 & c_1 \\ kb_2 & b_2 & c_2 \\ kb_3 & b_3 & c_3 \end{vmatrix} \qquad \text{[Using property 7]}$$

$$\Rightarrow \quad |B| = \begin{vmatrix} a_1 & b_1 & c_1 \\ a_2 & b_2 & c_2 \\ a_3 & b_3 & c_3 \end{vmatrix} + k \begin{vmatrix} b_1 & b_1 & c_1 \\ b_2 & b_2 & c_2 \\ b_3 & b_3 & c_3 \end{vmatrix} \qquad \text{[Using property 6]}$$

$$\Rightarrow \quad |B| = |A| + k\,0 = |A| \qquad \text{[Using property 5]}$$

PROPERTY 9 *Let A be a square matrix order* $n\ (\geq 2)$ *such that each element in a row (column) of A is zero, then* $|A| = 0$.

Conventionally this property is also stated as:

If each element of a row (column) of a determinant is zero, then its value is zero.

VERIFICATION Let $A = \begin{bmatrix} 0 & 0 & 0 \\ a_2 & b_2 & c_2 \\ a_3 & b_3 & c_3 \end{bmatrix}$ be a square matrix. Then,

$$|A| = \begin{vmatrix} 0 & 0 & 0 \\ a_2 & b_2 & c_2 \\ a_3 & b_3 & c_3 \end{vmatrix} = 0 \begin{vmatrix} b_2 & c_2 \\ b_3 & c_3 \end{vmatrix} - 0 \begin{vmatrix} a_2 & c_2 \\ a_3 & c_3 \end{vmatrix} + 0 \begin{vmatrix} a_2 & b_2 \\ a_3 & b_3 \end{vmatrix} = 0. \qquad \begin{bmatrix}\text{Expanding along} \\ \text{first row}\end{bmatrix}$$

PROPERTY 10 *If* $A = [a_{ij}]$ *is a diagonal matrix of order* $n\ (\geq 2)$, *then* $|A| = a_{11} \times a_{22} \times a_{33} \times \ldots \times a_{nn}$.

PROPERTY 11 *If A and B are square matrices of the same order, then* $|AB| = |A|\ |B|$.

PROPERTY 12 *Let* $A = [a_{ij}]$ *be a square matrix of order n and let* c_{ij} = *cofactor of* a_{ij} *in A for* $i, j = 1, 2, \ldots, n$. *If* $C = [c_{ij}]$ *is the matrix of cofactors of elements in A, then* $|C| = |A|^{n-1}$.

VERIFICATION Let $A = \begin{bmatrix} a_{11} & a_{12} & a_{13} \\ a_{21} & a_{22} & a_{23} \\ a_{31} & a_{32} & a_{33} \end{bmatrix}$ and $C = \begin{bmatrix} c_{11} & c_{12} & c_{13} \\ c_{21} & c_{22} & c_{23} \\ c_{31} & c_{32} & c_{33} \end{bmatrix}$, where C_{ij} = cofactor of a_{ij} in A. Then,

$$CA^T = \begin{bmatrix} c_{11} & c_{12} & c_{13} \\ c_{21} & c_{22} & c_{23} \\ c_{31} & c_{32} & c_{33} \end{bmatrix} \begin{bmatrix} a_{11} & a_{21} & a_{31} \\ a_{12} & a_{22} & a_{32} \\ a_{13} & a_{23} & a_{33} \end{bmatrix}$$

$$\Rightarrow \quad CA^T = \begin{bmatrix} a_{11} c_{11} + a_{12} c_{12} + a_{13} c_{13} & a_{21} c_{11} + a_{22} c_{12} + a_{23} c_{13} & a_{31} c_{11} + a_{32} c_{12} + a_{13} c_{33} \\ a_{11} c_{21} + a_{12} c_{22} + a_{13} c_{23} & a_{21} c_{21} + a_{22} c_{22} + a_{23} c_{23} & a_{31} c_{21} + a_{32} c_{22} + a_{33} c_{23} \\ a_{11} c_{31} + a_{12} c_{32} + a_{13} c_{33} & a_{21} c_{31} + a_{22} c_{32} + a_{23} c_{33} & a_{31} c_{31} + a_{32} c_{32} + a_{33} c_{33} \end{bmatrix}$$

$$\Rightarrow \quad CA^T = \begin{bmatrix} |A| & 0 & 0 \\ 0 & |A| & 0 \\ 0 & 0 & |A| \end{bmatrix} \qquad \text{[Using Properties 1 and 2]}$$

$$\Rightarrow \quad |CA^T| = \begin{vmatrix} |A| & 0 & 0 \\ 0 & |A| & 0 \\ 0 & 0 & |A| \end{vmatrix} = |A|^3$$

$$\Rightarrow \quad |C|\,|A^T| = |A|^3 \Rightarrow |C|\,|A| = |A|^3 \Rightarrow |C| = |A|^2 \qquad [\because |A^T| = |A|]$$

*5.5 EVALUATION OF DETERMINANTS

If A is a square matrix of order 2, then its determinant can be easily found. But, to evaluate determinants of square matrices of higher orders, we should always try to introduce zeros at maximum number of places in a particular row (column) by using the properties given in section 5.4 and then we should expand the determinant along that row (column).

We shall be using the following notations to evaluate a determinant:

(i) R_i to denote i^{th} row.

(ii) $R_i \leftrightarrow R_j$ to denote the interchange of ith and j^{th} rows.

(iii) $R_i \to R_i + \lambda R_j$ to denote the addition of λ times the elements of jth row to the corresponding elements of ith row.

(iv) $R_i(\lambda)$ to denote the multiplication of all elements of ith row by λ.

Similar notations are used to denote column operations if R is replaced by C.

ILLUSTRATIVE EXAMPLES

BASED ON BASIC CONCEPTS (BASIC)

Type I DETERMINANTS IN WHICH TWO ROWS (COLUMNS) BECOME IDENTICAL BY APPLYING THE PROPERTIES OF DETERMINANTS

EXAMPLE 1 *Without expanding evaluate the determinant* $\begin{vmatrix} 41 & 1 & 5 \\ 79 & 7 & 9 \\ 29 & 5 & 3 \end{vmatrix}$.

SOLUTION Let $\Delta = \begin{vmatrix} 41 & 1 & 5 \\ 79 & 7 & 9 \\ 29 & 5 & 3 \end{vmatrix}$. Applying $C_1 \to C_1 + (-8)\,C_3$, we get

$$\Delta = \begin{vmatrix} 1 & 1 & 5 \\ 7 & 7 & 9 \\ 5 & 5 & 3 \end{vmatrix} = 0 \qquad [\because C_1 \text{ and } C_2 \text{ are identical}]$$

May be skipped. Not from examination point of view.

EXAMPLE 2 *If w is a complex cube root of unity. Show that* $\begin{vmatrix} 1 & w & w^2 \\ w & w^2 & 1 \\ w^2 & 1 & w \end{vmatrix} = 0$.

SOLUTION Let $\Delta = \begin{vmatrix} 1 & w & w^2 \\ w & w^2 & 1 \\ w^2 & 1 & w \end{vmatrix}$. Applying $C_1 \to C_1 + C_2 + C_3$, we get

$$\Delta = \begin{vmatrix} 1+w+w^2 & w & w^2 \\ w+w^2+1 & w^2 & 1 \\ w^2+1+w & 1 & w \end{vmatrix} = \begin{vmatrix} 0 & w & w^2 \\ 0 & w^2 & 1 \\ 0 & 1 & w \end{vmatrix} \qquad [\because\ 1+w+w^2=0]$$

$\Rightarrow \quad \Delta = 0$ $\qquad$ [$\because$ C_1 consists of all zeros]

EXAMPLE 3 *Show that* $\begin{vmatrix} 1 & a & b+c \\ 1 & b & c+a \\ 1 & c & a+b \end{vmatrix} = 0$.

SOLUTION Let $\Delta = \begin{vmatrix} 1 & a & b+c \\ 1 & b & c+a \\ 1 & c & a+b \end{vmatrix}$. Applying $C_2 \to C_2 + C_3$, we get

$$\Delta = \begin{vmatrix} 1 & a+b+c & b+c \\ 1 & b+c+a & c+a \\ 1 & c+a+b & a+b \end{vmatrix}$$

$$\Rightarrow \quad \Delta = (a+b+c)\begin{vmatrix} 1 & 1 & b+c \\ 1 & 1 & c+a \\ 1 & 1 & a+b \end{vmatrix} \qquad [\text{Taking out } a+b+c \text{ common from } C_2]$$

$\Rightarrow \quad \Delta = (a+b+c) \times 0 = 0$ $\qquad$ [$\because$ C_1 and C_2 are identical]

EXAMPLE 4 *Show that* $\begin{vmatrix} b-c & c-a & a-b \\ c-a & a-b & b-c \\ a-b & b-c & c-a \end{vmatrix}$. **[NCERT, CBSE 2009]**

SOLUTION Let $\Delta = \begin{vmatrix} b-c & c-a & a-b \\ c-a & a-b & b-c \\ a-b & b-c & c-a \end{vmatrix}$. Applying $C_1 \to C_1 + C_2 + C_3$, we get

$$\Delta = \begin{vmatrix} 0 & c-a & a-b \\ 0 & a-b & b-c \\ 0 & b-c & c-a \end{vmatrix} = 0 \qquad [\because\ C_1 \text{ consists of all zeros}]$$

EXAMPLE 5 *Show that* $\begin{vmatrix} 1 & bc & a(b+c) \\ 1 & ca & b(c+a) \\ 1 & ab & c(a+b) \end{vmatrix} = 0$. **[NCERT]**

SOLUTION Let $\Delta = \begin{vmatrix} 1 & bc & a(b+c) \\ 1 & ca & b(c+a) \\ 1 & ab & c(a+b) \end{vmatrix}$. Applying $C_3 \to C_2 + C_3$, we get

$$\Delta = \begin{vmatrix} 1 & bc & ab+bc+ca \\ 1 & ca & ab+bc+ca \\ 1 & ab & ab+bc+ca \end{vmatrix}$$

$\Rightarrow \quad \Delta = (ab+bc+ca)\begin{vmatrix} 1 & bc & 1 \\ 1 & ca & 1 \\ 1 & ab & 1 \end{vmatrix}$ [Taking out $ab+bc+ca$ common from C_3]

$\Rightarrow \quad \Delta = (ab+bc+ca) \times 0 = 0.$ [$\because$ C_1 and C_3 are identical]

EXAMPLE 6 *Without expanding prove that :* $\begin{vmatrix} x+y & y+z & z+x \\ z & x & y \\ 1 & 1 & 1 \end{vmatrix} = 0.$ **[NCERT]**

SOLUTION Let $\Delta = \begin{vmatrix} x+y & y+z & z+x \\ z & x & y \\ 1 & 1 & 1 \end{vmatrix}$. Applying $R_1 \to R_1 + R_2$, we get

$$\Delta = \begin{vmatrix} x+y+z & x+y+z & x+y+z \\ z & x & y \\ 1 & 1 & 1 \end{vmatrix}$$

$\Rightarrow \quad \Delta = (x+y+z)\begin{vmatrix} 1 & 1 & 1 \\ z & x & y \\ 1 & 1 & 1 \end{vmatrix}$ [Taking out $(x+y+z)$ common from R_1]

$\Rightarrow \quad \Delta = (x+y+z) \times 0 = 0$ [$\because$ R_1 and R_3 are identical]

EXAMPLE 7 *Without expanding show that:* $\Delta = \begin{vmatrix} \operatorname{cosec}^2\theta & \cot^2\theta & 1 \\ \cot^2\theta & \operatorname{cosec}^2\theta & -1 \\ 42 & 40 & 2 \end{vmatrix} = 0.$

[NCERT EXEMPLAR]

SOLUTION Applying $C_1 \to C_1 - C_2$, we obtain

$\Delta = \begin{vmatrix} \operatorname{cosec}^2\theta - \cot^2\theta & \cot^2\theta & 1 \\ \cot^2\theta - \operatorname{cosec}^2\theta & \operatorname{cosec}^2\theta & -1 \\ 42-40 & 40 & 2 \end{vmatrix} = \begin{vmatrix} 1 & \cot^2\theta & 1 \\ -1 & \operatorname{cosec}^2\theta & -1 \\ 2 & 40 & 2 \end{vmatrix} = 0$ [$\because$ C_1 and C_3 are identical]

EXAMPLE 8 *Find the value of the determinant* $\Delta = \begin{vmatrix} 2 & 3 & 4 \\ 5 & 6 & 8 \\ 6x & 9x & 12x \end{vmatrix}$. **[CBSE 2009]**

SOLUTION Taking $3x$ common from R_3, we get

$\Delta = 3x\begin{vmatrix} 2 & 3 & 4 \\ 5 & 6 & 8 \\ 2 & 3 & 4 \end{vmatrix} = 3x \times 0 = 0$ [$\because$ R_1 and R_3 are identical]

EXAMPLE 9 *Without expanding show that* $\begin{vmatrix} b^2c^2 & bc & b+c \\ c^2a^2 & ca & c+a \\ a^2b^2 & ab & a+b \end{vmatrix} = 0.$

[NCERT EXEMPLAR, CBSE 2001 C]

SOLUTION Let $\Delta = \begin{vmatrix} b^2c^2 & bc & b+c \\ c^2a^2 & ca & c+a \\ a^2b^2 & ab & a+b \end{vmatrix}$. Applying $R_1 \to R_1(a)$, $R_2 \to R_2(b)$ and $R_3 \to R_3(c)$,

we get

$$\Delta = \frac{1}{abc}\begin{vmatrix} ab^2 c^2 & abc & ab+ac \\ bc^2 a^2 & abc & bc+ba \\ ca^2 b^2 & abc & ac+bc \end{vmatrix}$$ $\left[\because R_1, R_2\ R_3 \text{ are multiplied by } a, b \text{ and } c \text{ respectively, therefore we divide by } abc\right]$

$\Rightarrow$ $$\Delta = \frac{1}{abc}(abc)^2\begin{vmatrix} bc & 1 & ab+ac \\ ca & 1 & bc+ba \\ ab & 1 & ac+bc \end{vmatrix}$$ [Taking out abc common from C_1 and C_2]

$\Rightarrow$ $$\Delta = abc\begin{vmatrix} bc & 1 & ab+bc+ca \\ ca & 1 & ab+bc+ca \\ ab & 1 & ab+bc+ca \end{vmatrix}$$ [Applying $C_3 \to C_3 + C_1$]

$\Rightarrow$ $$\Delta = abc\,(ab+bc+ca)\begin{vmatrix} bc & 1 & 1 \\ ca & 1 & 1 \\ ab & 1 & 1 \end{vmatrix}$$ [Taking out $ab+bc+ca$ common from C_3]

$\Rightarrow$ $\Delta = abc\,(ab+bc+ca) \times 0 = 0$ [$\because$ C_2 and C_3 are identical]

EXAMPLE 10 *Without expanding evaluate the determinant* $\begin{vmatrix} \sin\alpha & \cos\alpha & \sin(\alpha+\delta) \\ \sin\beta & \cos\beta & \sin(\beta+\delta) \\ \sin\gamma & \cos\gamma & \sin(\gamma+\delta) \end{vmatrix}$.

SOLUTION Let $\Delta = \begin{vmatrix} \sin\alpha & \cos\alpha & \sin(\alpha+\delta) \\ \sin\beta & \cos\beta & \sin(\beta+\delta) \\ \sin\gamma & \cos\gamma & \sin(\gamma+\delta) \end{vmatrix}$.

$\Rightarrow$ $$\Delta = \begin{vmatrix} \sin\alpha & \cos\alpha & \sin\alpha\cos\delta + \cos\alpha\sin\delta \\ \sin\beta & \cos\beta & \sin\beta\cos\delta + \cos\beta\sin\delta \\ \sin\gamma & \cos\gamma & \sin\gamma\cos\delta + \cos\gamma\sin\delta \end{vmatrix}$$ [$\because$ $\sin(A+B) = \sin A\cos B + \cos A \sin B$]

$\Rightarrow$ $$\Delta = \begin{vmatrix} \sin\alpha & \cos\alpha & 0 \\ \sin\beta & \cos\beta & 0 \\ \sin\gamma & \cos\gamma & 0 \end{vmatrix}$$ [Applying $C_3 \to C_3 - (\cos\delta)\,C_1 - (\sin\delta)\,C_2$]

$\Rightarrow$ $\Delta = 0$ [$\because$ C_3 consists of all zeros]

EXAMPLE 11 *Without expanding evaluate the determinant* $\begin{vmatrix} (a^x+a^{-x})^2 & (a^x-a^{-x})^2 & 1 \\ (a^y+a^{-y})^2 & (a^y-a^{-y})^2 & 1 \\ (a^z+a^{-z})^2 & (a^z-a^{-z})^2 & 1 \end{vmatrix}$, *where* $a, > 0$ *and* $x, y, z \in R$.

SOLUTION Let Δ be the given determinant. Applying $C_1 \to C_1 - C_2$, we get

$$\Delta = \begin{vmatrix} (a^x+a^{-x})^2-(a^x-a^{-x})^2 & (a^x-a^{-x})^2 & 1 \\ (a^y+a^{-y})^2-(a^y-a^{-y})^2 & (a^y-a^{-y})^2 & 1 \\ (a^z+a^{-z})^2-(a^z-a^{-z})^2 & (a^z-a^{-z})^2 & 1 \end{vmatrix}$$

$\Rightarrow$ $$\Delta = \begin{vmatrix} 4 & (a^x-a^{-x})^2 & 1 \\ 4 & (a^y-a^{-y})^2 & 1 \\ 4 & (a^z-a^{-z})^2 & 1 \end{vmatrix}$$ [Using : $(a+b)^2 - (a-b)^2 = 4ab$]

$$\Rightarrow \quad \Delta = 4\begin{vmatrix} 1 & (a^x - a^{-x})^2 & 1 \\ 1 & (a^y - a^{-y})^2 & 1 \\ 1 & (a^z - a^{-z})^2 & 1 \end{vmatrix} \qquad \text{[Taking out 4 common from } C_1]$$

$$\Rightarrow \quad \Delta = 4 \times 0 = 0 \qquad [\because C_1 \text{ and } C_3 \text{ are identical}]$$

EXAMPLE 12 *If a, b, c are in A.P., find the value of* $\begin{vmatrix} 2y+4 & 5y+7 & 8y+a \\ 3y+5 & 6y+8 & 9y+b \\ 4y+6 & 7y+9 & 10y+c \end{vmatrix}$. **[NCERT]**

SOLUTION Applying $R_2 \to R_2\,(2)$, we get

$$\Delta = \frac{1}{2}\begin{vmatrix} 2y+4 & 5y+7 & 8y+a \\ 6y+10 & 12y+16 & 18y+2b \\ 4y+6 & 7y+9 & 10y+c \end{vmatrix}$$

$$\Rightarrow \quad \Delta = \frac{1}{2}\begin{vmatrix} 2y+4 & 5y+7 & 8y+a \\ 0 & 0 & 2b-(a+c) \\ 4y+6 & 7y+9 & 10y+c \end{vmatrix} \qquad \text{Applying } R_2 \to R_2 - (R_1 + R_3)$$

$$\Rightarrow \quad \Delta = \frac{1}{2}\begin{vmatrix} 2y+4 & 5y+7 & 8y+a \\ 0 & 0 & 0 \\ 4y+6 & 7y+9 & 10y+c \end{vmatrix} \qquad [\because a, b, c \text{ are in A.P.} \therefore 2b = a + c]$$

$$\Rightarrow \quad \Delta = 0 \qquad [\because R_2 \text{ consists of zeros only}]$$

REMARK *The transformation* $R_1 \to R_1 + R_3 - 2R_2$ *can also be used to get the value of* Δ.

EXAMPLE 13 *Without expanding evaluate the determinant* $\Delta = \begin{vmatrix} 265 & 240 & 219 \\ 240 & 225 & 198 \\ 219 & 198 & 181 \end{vmatrix}$.

SOLUTION Applying $C_1 \to C_1 - C_3$ and $C_2 \to C_2 - C_3$, we get

$$\Delta = \begin{vmatrix} 46 & 21 & 219 \\ 42 & 27 & 198 \\ 38 & 17 & 181 \end{vmatrix}$$

$$\Rightarrow \quad \Delta = \begin{vmatrix} 4 & 21 & 9 \\ -12 & 27 & -72 \\ 4 & 17 & 11 \end{vmatrix} \qquad [\text{Applying } C_1 \to C_1 - 2C_2 \text{ and } C_3 \to C_3 - 10C_2]$$

$$\Rightarrow \quad \Delta = \begin{vmatrix} 0 & 4 & -2 \\ 0 & 78 & -39 \\ 4 & 17 & 11 \end{vmatrix} \qquad [\text{Applying } R_1 \to R_1 - R_3 \text{ and } R_2 \to R_2 + 3R_3]$$

$$\Rightarrow \quad \Delta = 2\,(39)\begin{vmatrix} 0 & 2 & -1 \\ 0 & 2 & -1 \\ 4 & 17 & 11 \end{vmatrix} \qquad [\text{Taking 2 common from } R_1 \text{ and 39 common from } R_2]$$

$$\Rightarrow \quad \Delta = 78 \times 0 \qquad [\because R_1 \text{ and } R_2 \text{ are identical}]$$

Type II EVALUATING DETERMINANTS BY USING THE PROPERTIES OF DETERMINANTS AND PROVING IDENTITIES

EXAMPLE 14 *If* $\Delta_1 = \begin{vmatrix} 1 & 1 & 1 \\ x^2 & y^2 & z^2 \\ x & y & z \end{vmatrix}$ *and* $\Delta_2 = \begin{vmatrix} 1 & 1 & 1 \\ yz & zx & xy \\ x & y & z \end{vmatrix}$, *without expanding prove that* $\Delta_1 = \Delta_2$.

SOLUTION Applying $C_1 \to C_1 (x), C_2 \to C_2 (y)$ and $C_3 \to C_3 (z)$, we get

$$\Delta_2 = \frac{1}{xyz}\begin{vmatrix} x & y & z \\ xyz & xyz & xyz \\ x^2 & y^2 & z^2 \end{vmatrix} = \frac{xyz}{xyz}\begin{vmatrix} x & y & z \\ 1 & 1 & 1 \\ x^2 & y^2 & z^2 \end{vmatrix} \quad \text{[Taking } xyz \text{ common from } R_2]$$

$$\Rightarrow \quad \Delta_2 = -\begin{vmatrix} 1 & 1 & 1 \\ x & y & z \\ x^2 & y^2 & z^2 \end{vmatrix} \quad [\text{Applying } R_2 \leftrightarrow R_1]$$

$$\Rightarrow \quad \Delta_2 = \begin{vmatrix} 1 & 1 & 1 \\ x^2 & y^2 & z^2 \\ x & y & z \end{vmatrix} = \Delta_1 \quad [\text{Applying } R_2 \leftrightarrow R_3]$$

EXAMPLE 15 *Let* $\Delta = \begin{vmatrix} Ax & x^2 & 1 \\ By & y^2 & 1 \\ Cz & z^2 & 1 \end{vmatrix}$ *and* $\Delta_1 = \begin{vmatrix} A & B & C \\ x & y & z \\ yz & zx & xy \end{vmatrix}$, *then show that* $\Delta_1 = \Delta$.

SOLUTION We have,

$$\Delta_1 = \begin{vmatrix} A & B & C \\ x & y & z \\ yz & zx & xy \end{vmatrix}$$

$$\Rightarrow \quad \Delta_1 = \frac{1}{xyz}\begin{vmatrix} Ax & By & Cz \\ x^2 & y^2 & z^2 \\ xyz & xyz & xyz \end{vmatrix} \quad [\text{Applying } C_1 \to C_1 x, C_2 \to C_2 y, C_3 \to C_3 z]$$

$$\Rightarrow \quad \Delta_1 = \frac{xyz}{xyz}\begin{vmatrix} Ax & By & Cz \\ x^2 & y^2 & z^2 \\ 1 & 1 & 1 \end{vmatrix} \quad [\text{Taking } xyz \text{ common from } R_3]$$

$$\Rightarrow \quad \Delta_1 = \begin{vmatrix} Ax & By & Cz \\ x^2 & y^2 & z^2 \\ 1 & 1 & 1 \end{vmatrix}$$

$$\Rightarrow \quad \Delta_1 = \begin{vmatrix} Ax & x^2 & 1 \\ By & y^2 & 1 \\ Cz & z^2 & 1 \end{vmatrix} = \Delta. \quad [\text{Interchanging rows and columns}]$$

EXAMPLE 16 *If* $\Delta_1 = \begin{vmatrix} a & b & c \\ x & y & z \\ p & q & r \end{vmatrix}$ *and* $\Delta_2 = \begin{vmatrix} q & -b & y \\ -p & a & -x \\ r & -c & z \end{vmatrix}$, *without expanding or evaluating* Δ_1 *and* Δ_2, *show that* $\Delta_1 + \Delta_2 = 0$.

SOLUTION Taking -1 common from second row, we obtain

$$\Delta_2 = -\begin{vmatrix} q & -b & y \\ p & -a & x \\ r & -c & z \end{vmatrix}$$

$$\Rightarrow \quad \Delta_2 = \begin{vmatrix} q & b & y \\ p & a & x \\ r & c & z \end{vmatrix} \quad [\text{Taking } (-1) \text{ common from } C_2]$$

$$\Rightarrow \quad \Delta_2 = \begin{vmatrix} q & p & r \\ b & a & c \\ y & x & z \end{vmatrix} \quad \text{[Interchanging row and columns]}$$

$$\Rightarrow \quad \Delta_2 = -\begin{vmatrix} p & q & r \\ a & b & c \\ x & y & z \end{vmatrix} \quad \text{[Applying } C_2 \leftrightarrow C_1\text{]}$$

$$\Rightarrow \quad \Delta_2 = \begin{vmatrix} a & b & c \\ p & q & r \\ x & y & z \end{vmatrix} \quad \text{[Applying } R_1 \leftrightarrow R_2\text{]}$$

$$\Rightarrow \quad \Delta_2 = -\begin{vmatrix} a & b & c \\ x & y & z \\ p & q & r \end{vmatrix} \quad \text{[Applying } R_2 \leftrightarrow R_3\text{]}$$

$$\Rightarrow \quad \Delta_2 = -\Delta_1 \Rightarrow \Delta_1 + \Delta_2 = 0$$

EXAMPLE 17 *If A is a skew-symmetric matrix of odd order n, then $|A| = O$.*

SOLUTION Since A is a skew-symmetric matrix. Therefore,

$$A^T = -A$$

$$\Rightarrow \quad |A^T| = |-A|$$

$$\Rightarrow \quad |A^T| = (-1)^n |A| \quad [\because |kA| = k^n |A|]$$

$$\Rightarrow \quad |A| = (-1)^n |A| \quad [\because |A^T| = |A|]$$

$$\Rightarrow \quad |A| = -|A| \Rightarrow 2|A| = 0 \Rightarrow |A| = 0 \quad [\because n \text{ is odd}]$$

Hence, the determinant of a skew-symmetric matrix of odd order is zero.

EXAMPLE 18 *Prove that:* $\begin{vmatrix} 0 & a & -b \\ -a & 0 & -c \\ b & c & 0 \end{vmatrix} = 0.$

SOLUTION Let $\Delta = \begin{vmatrix} 0 & a & -b \\ -a & 0 & -c \\ b & c & 0 \end{vmatrix}$. Then,

$$\Delta = (-1)^3 \begin{vmatrix} 0 & -a & b \\ a & 0 & c \\ -b & -c & 0 \end{vmatrix} \quad \text{[Taking } (-1) \text{ common from each row]}$$

$$\Rightarrow \quad \Delta = -\begin{vmatrix} 0 & a & -b \\ -a & 0 & -c \\ b & c & 0 \end{vmatrix} \quad \text{[Interchanging rows and columns]}$$

$$\Rightarrow \quad \Delta = -\Delta \Rightarrow 2\Delta = 0 \Rightarrow \Delta = 0.$$

ALITER Clearly, $A = \begin{bmatrix} 0 & a & -b \\ -a & 0 & -c \\ b & c & 0 \end{bmatrix}$ is a skew-symmetric matrix of odd order. Therefore, $|A| = 0$.

EXAMPLE 19 *Without expanding or evaluating show that* $\begin{vmatrix} 0 & b-a & c-a \\ a-b & 0 & c-b \\ a-c & b-c & 0 \end{vmatrix} = 0.$

[NCERT EXEMPLAR]

SOLUTION Let $\Delta = \begin{vmatrix} 0 & b-a & c-a \\ a-b & 0 & c-b \\ a-c & b-c & 0 \end{vmatrix}$. Then,

$$\Delta = \begin{vmatrix} 0 & -(a-b) & -(a-c) \\ (a-b) & 0 & -(b-c) \\ (a-c) & (b-c) & 0 \end{vmatrix} = \begin{vmatrix} 0 & -(a-b) & -(a-c) \\ (a-b) & 0 & -(b-c) \\ (a-c) & (b-c) & 0 \end{vmatrix}$$

$\Rightarrow \quad \Delta = (-1)^3 \begin{vmatrix} 0 & (a-b) & (a-c) \\ -(a-b) & 0 & (b-c) \\ -(a-c) & -(b-c) & 0 \end{vmatrix}$ [Taking –1 common from each row]

$\Rightarrow \quad \Delta = -\begin{vmatrix} 0 & -(a-b) & -(a-c) \\ (a-b) & 0 & -(b-c) \\ (a-c) & (b-c) & 0 \end{vmatrix}$ [Interchanging rows and columns]

$\Rightarrow \quad \Delta = -\Delta \Rightarrow 2\Delta = 0 \Rightarrow \Delta = 0$

ALITER Clearly, given determinant is the determinant of a skew-symmetric matrix of odd order. So, its value is zero.

EXAMPLE 20 *Without expanding, prove that* $\begin{vmatrix} a+bx & c+dx & p+qx \\ ax+b & cx+d & px+q \\ u & v & w \end{vmatrix} = (1-x^2) \begin{vmatrix} a & c & p \\ b & d & q \\ u & v & w \end{vmatrix}$.

[NCERT]

SOLUTION Applying $R_1 \to R_1 - x R_2$ to Δ, we get

$$\Delta = \begin{vmatrix} a(1-x^2) & c(1-x^2) & p(1-x^2) \\ ax+b & cx+d & px+q \\ u & v & w \end{vmatrix} = (1-x^2) \begin{vmatrix} a & c & p \\ ax+b & cx+d & px+q \\ u & v & w \end{vmatrix}$$

$\Rightarrow \quad \Delta = (1-x^2) \begin{vmatrix} a & c & p \\ b & d & q \\ u & v & w \end{vmatrix}$ [Applying $R_2 \to R_2 - xR_1$]

EXAMPLE 21 *Prove that:* $\begin{vmatrix} -a^2 & ab & ac \\ ba & -b^2 & bc \\ ac & bc & -c^2 \end{vmatrix} = 4a^2 b^2 c^2$. [NCERT, CBSE 2011]

SOLUTION Let $\Delta = \begin{vmatrix} -a^2 & ab & ac \\ ba & -b^2 & bc \\ ac & bc & -c^2 \end{vmatrix}$. Then,

$\Delta = abc \begin{vmatrix} -a & b & c \\ a & -b & c \\ a & b & -c \end{vmatrix}$ [Taking a, b and c common from R_1, R_2 and R_3 respectively]

$\Rightarrow \quad \Delta = a^2 b^2 c^2 \begin{vmatrix} -1 & 1 & 1 \\ 1 & -1 & 1 \\ 1 & 1 & -1 \end{vmatrix}$ [Taking a, b and c common from C_1, C_2 and C_3 respectively]

$$\Rightarrow \quad \Delta = a^2 b^2 c^2 \begin{vmatrix} -1 & 0 & 0 \\ 1 & 0 & 2 \\ 1 & 2 & 0 \end{vmatrix} \quad [\text{Applying } C_2 \to C_2 + C_1, C_3 \to C_3 + C_1]$$

$$\Rightarrow \quad \Delta = a^2 b^2 c^2 \times (-1) \times \begin{vmatrix} 0 & 2 \\ 2 & 0 \end{vmatrix} \quad [\text{Expanding along } R_1]$$

$$\Rightarrow \quad \Delta = a^2 b^2 c^2 (-1)(0-4) = 4a^2 b^2 c^2$$

EXAMPLE 22 *Prove that:* $\begin{vmatrix} 1 & 1 & 1 \\ 1 & 1+x & 1 \\ 1 & 1 & 1+y \end{vmatrix} = xy.$ **[NCERT]**

SOLUTION Let $\Delta = \begin{vmatrix} 1 & 1 & 1 \\ 1 & 1+x & 1 \\ 1 & 1 & 1+y \end{vmatrix}$. Applying $C_2 \to C_2 - C_1$ and $C_3 \to C_3 - C_1$, we get

$$\Delta = \begin{vmatrix} 1 & 0 & 0 \\ 1 & x & 0 \\ 1 & 0 & y \end{vmatrix} = 1 \times \begin{vmatrix} x & 0 \\ 0 & y \end{vmatrix} - 0 \times \begin{vmatrix} 1 & 0 \\ 1 & y \end{vmatrix} + 0 \times \begin{vmatrix} 1 & x \\ 1 & 0 \end{vmatrix} = xy \quad [\text{On expanding along } R_1]$$

EXAMPLE 23 *Evaluate:* $\begin{vmatrix} 1 & a & a^2 \\ 1 & b & b^2 \\ 1 & c & c^2 \end{vmatrix}$. **[NCERT]**

SOLUTION Let Δ be the given determinant. Applying $R_2 \to R_2 - R_1$ and $R_3 \to R_3 - R_1$, we get

$$\Delta = \begin{vmatrix} 1 & a & a^2 \\ 0 & b-a & b^2-a^2 \\ 0 & c-a & c^2-a^2 \end{vmatrix}$$

$$\Rightarrow \quad \Delta = (b-a)(c-a) \begin{vmatrix} 1 & a & a^2 \\ 0 & 1 & b+a \\ 0 & 1 & c+a \end{vmatrix} \quad [\text{Taking out } (b-a) \text{ common from } R_2 \text{ \& } (c-a) \text{ from } R_3]$$

$$\Rightarrow \quad \Delta = (b-a)(c-a) \begin{vmatrix} 1 & a & a^2 \\ 0 & 1 & b+a \\ 0 & 0 & c-b \end{vmatrix} \quad [\text{Applying } R_3 \to R_3 - R_2]$$

$$\Rightarrow \quad \Delta = (b-a)(c-a)(c-b) \begin{vmatrix} 1 & a & a^2 \\ 0 & 1 & b+a \\ 0 & 0 & 1 \end{vmatrix} \quad [\text{Taking out } (c-b) \text{ common from } R_3]$$

$$\Rightarrow \quad \Delta = (b-a)(c-a)(c-b) \times 1 \times \begin{vmatrix} 1 & b+a \\ 0 & 1 \end{vmatrix} \quad [\text{Expanding along } C_1]$$

$$\Rightarrow \quad \Delta = (b-a)(c-a)(c-b) \times 1 = (a-b)(b-c)(c-a)$$

REMARK *The reader is advised to remember the value of this determinant as a standard result.*

EXAMPLE 24 *Show that:* $\begin{vmatrix} x & y & z \\ x^2 & y^2 & z^2 \\ x^3 & y^3 & z^3 \end{vmatrix} = xyz(x-y)(y-z)(z-x).$ **[CBSE 2000, 2010 C, 2011]**

SOLUTION Let $\Delta = \begin{vmatrix} x & y & z \\ x^2 & y^2 & z^2 \\ x^3 & y^3 & z^3 \end{vmatrix}$. Taking x, y and z common from C_1, C_2 and C_3 respectively, we get

$$\Delta = xyz \begin{vmatrix} 1 & 1 & 1 \\ x & y & z \\ x^2 & y^2 & z^2 \end{vmatrix}$$

$$\Rightarrow \quad \Delta = xyz \begin{vmatrix} 1 & 0 & 0 \\ x & y-x & z-x \\ x^2 & y^2-x^2 & z^2-x^2 \end{vmatrix} \quad [\text{Applying } C_2 \to C_2 - C_1 \text{ and } C_3 \to C_3 - C_1]$$

$$\Rightarrow \quad \Delta = xyz\,(y-x)\,(z-x) \begin{vmatrix} 1 & 0 & 0 \\ x & 1 & 1 \\ x^2 & y+x & z+x \end{vmatrix} \quad \begin{bmatrix} \text{Taking } (y-x) \text{ and } (z-x) \text{ common from} \\ C_2 \text{ from } C_3 \text{ respectively.} \end{bmatrix}$$

$$\Rightarrow \quad \Delta = xyz\,(y-x)\,(z-x) \times 1 \times \begin{vmatrix} 1 & 1 \\ y+x & z+x \end{vmatrix} \quad [\text{Expanding along } R_1]$$

$$\Rightarrow \quad \Delta = xyz\,(y-x)\,(z-x)\,(z+x-y-x) = xyz\,(x-y)\,(y-z)\,(z-x)$$

EXAMPLE 25 *Prove that:* $\begin{vmatrix} \alpha & \beta & \gamma \\ \alpha^2 & \beta^2 & \gamma^2 \\ \beta+\gamma & \gamma+\alpha & \alpha+\beta \end{vmatrix} = (\alpha-\beta)\,(\beta-\gamma)\,(\gamma-\alpha)\,(\alpha+\beta+\gamma).$

[NCERT, CBSE 2007C, 2008, 2010 C]

SOLUTION Let $\Delta = \begin{vmatrix} \alpha & \beta & \gamma \\ \alpha^2 & \beta^2 & \gamma^2 \\ \beta+\gamma & \gamma+\alpha & \alpha+\beta \end{vmatrix}$. Applying $R_3 \to R_1 + R_3$, we get

$$\Delta = \begin{vmatrix} \alpha & \beta & \gamma \\ \alpha^2 & \beta^2 & \gamma^2 \\ \alpha+\beta+\gamma & \alpha+\beta+\gamma & \alpha+\beta+\gamma \end{vmatrix}$$

$$\Rightarrow \quad \Delta = (\alpha+\beta+\gamma) \begin{vmatrix} \alpha & \beta & \gamma \\ \alpha^2 & \beta^2 & \gamma^2 \\ 1 & 1 & 1 \end{vmatrix} \quad [\text{Taking out } (\alpha+\beta+\gamma) \text{ common from } R_3]$$

$$\Rightarrow \quad \Delta = (\alpha+\beta+\gamma) \begin{vmatrix} \alpha & \beta-\alpha & \gamma-\alpha \\ \alpha^2 & \beta^2-\alpha^2 & \gamma^2-\alpha^2 \\ 1 & 0 & 0 \end{vmatrix} \quad [\text{Applying } C_1 \to C_2 - C_1 \text{ and } C_3 \to C_3 - C_1]$$

$$\Rightarrow \quad \Delta = (\alpha+\beta+\gamma)\,(\beta-\alpha)\,(\gamma-\alpha) \begin{vmatrix} \alpha & 1 & 1 \\ \alpha^2 & \beta+\alpha & \gamma+\alpha \\ 1 & 0 & 0 \end{vmatrix} \quad \begin{bmatrix} \text{Taking } (\beta-\alpha) \text{ common from} \\ C_2 \text{ and } (\gamma-\alpha) \text{ from } C_3 \end{bmatrix}$$

$$\Rightarrow \quad \Delta = (\alpha+\beta+\gamma)\,(\beta-\alpha)\,(\gamma-\alpha) \times 1 \times \begin{vmatrix} 1 & 1 \\ \beta+\alpha & \gamma+\alpha \end{vmatrix} \quad [\text{Expanding along } R_3]$$

$$\Rightarrow \quad \Delta = (\alpha+\beta+\gamma)\,(\beta-\alpha)\,(\gamma-\alpha)\,(\gamma+\alpha-\beta-\alpha) = (\alpha-\beta)\,(\beta-\gamma)\,(\gamma-\alpha)\,(\alpha+\beta+\gamma).$$

EXAMPLE 26 *Prove that:* $\begin{vmatrix} 1 & a & a^3 \\ 1 & b & b^3 \\ 1 & c & c^3 \end{vmatrix} = (a-b)(b-c)(c-a)(a+b+c)$

[NCERT, CBSE 2011, 2012, 2013]

SOLUTION Let $\Delta = \begin{vmatrix} 1 & a & a^3 \\ 1 & b & b^3 \\ 1 & c & c^3 \end{vmatrix}$. Applying $R_2 \to R_2 - R_1$ and $R_3 \to R_3 - R_1$, we obtain

$$\Delta = \begin{vmatrix} 1 & a & a^3 \\ 0 & b-a & b^3-a^3 \\ 0 & c-a & c^3-a^3 \end{vmatrix}$$

$\Rightarrow \quad \Delta = (b-a)(c-a)\begin{vmatrix} 1 & a & a^3 \\ 0 & 1 & b^2+a^2+ab \\ 0 & 1 & c^2+a^2+ac \end{vmatrix}$ [Taking out $(b-a)$ from R_2 and $(c-a)$ from R_3]

$\Rightarrow \quad \Delta = (b-a)(c-a)\begin{vmatrix} 1 & a & a^3 \\ 0 & 0 & (b^2-c^2)+(ab-ac) \\ 0 & 1 & c^2+a^2+ac \end{vmatrix}$ [Applying $R_2 \to R_2 - R_3$]

$\Rightarrow \quad \Delta = (b-a)(c-a)\begin{vmatrix} 1 & a & a^3 \\ 0 & 0 & (b-c)(b+c+a) \\ 0 & 1 & c^2+a^2+ac \end{vmatrix}$

$\Rightarrow \quad \Delta = (b-a)(c-a)(b-c)\begin{vmatrix} 1 & a & a^3 \\ 0 & 0 & a+b+c \\ 0 & 1 & c^2+a^2+ac \end{vmatrix}$ [Taking out $(b-c)$ common from R_2]

$\Rightarrow \quad \Delta = (b-a)(c-a)(b-c) \times 1 \times \begin{vmatrix} 0 & a+b+c \\ 1 & c^2+a^2+ac \end{vmatrix}$ [Expanding along C_1]

$\Rightarrow \quad \Delta = (b-a)(c-a)(b-c)\{0-(a+b+c)\} = (a-b)(b-c)(c-a)(a+b+c).$

EXAMPLE 27 *Show that* $\begin{vmatrix} a & b & c \\ a^2 & b^2 & c^2 \\ bc & ca & ab \end{vmatrix} = \begin{vmatrix} 1 & 1 & 1 \\ a^2 & b^2 & c^2 \\ a^3 & b^3 & c^3 \end{vmatrix} = (a-b)(b-c)(c-a)(ab+bc+ca).$

[NCERT, CBSE 2007, 2011, 2013, 2014]

SOLUTION Let $\Delta = \begin{vmatrix} a & b & c \\ a^2 & b^2 & c^2 \\ bc & ca & ab \end{vmatrix}$. Multiplying C_1, C_2 and C_3 by a, b and c respectively, we get

$\Delta = \dfrac{1}{abc}\begin{vmatrix} a^2 & b^2 & c^2 \\ a^3 & b^3 & c^3 \\ abc & abc & abc \end{vmatrix} = \dfrac{abc}{abc}\begin{vmatrix} a^2 & b^2 & c^2 \\ a^3 & b^3 & c^3 \\ 1 & 1 & 1 \end{vmatrix}$ [Taking abc common from R_3]

$$\Rightarrow \quad \Delta = -\begin{vmatrix} a^2 & b^2 & c^2 \\ 1 & 1 & 1 \\ a^3 & b^3 & c^3 \end{vmatrix} \qquad [\text{Applying } R_2 \leftrightarrow R_3]$$

$$\Rightarrow \quad \Delta = \begin{vmatrix} 1 & 1 & 1 \\ a^2 & b^2 & c^2 \\ a^3 & b^3 & c^3 \end{vmatrix} \qquad [\text{Applying } R_1 \leftrightarrow R_2]$$

$$\Rightarrow \quad \Delta = \begin{vmatrix} 1 & 0 & 0 \\ a^2 & b^2 - a^2 & c^2 - a^2 \\ a^3 & b^3 - a^3 & c^3 - a^3 \end{vmatrix} \qquad [\text{Applying } C_2 \to C_2 - C_1 \text{ and } C_3 \to C_3 - C_1]$$

$$\Rightarrow \quad \Delta = \begin{vmatrix} 1 & 0 & 0 \\ a^2 & (b-a)(b+a) & (c-a)(c+a) \\ a^3 & (b-a)(b^2 + ba + a^2) & (c-a)(c^2 + ca + a^2) \end{vmatrix}$$

$$\Rightarrow \quad \Delta = (b-a)(c-a)\begin{vmatrix} 1 & 0 & 0 \\ a^2 & b+a & c+a \\ a^3 & b^2 + a^2 + ab & c^2 + ac + a^2 \end{vmatrix} \qquad \begin{bmatrix}\text{Taking } (b-a) \text{ and } (c-a) \text{ common} \\ \text{from } C_2 \text{ and } C_3 \text{ respectively}\end{bmatrix}$$

$$\Rightarrow \quad \Delta = (b-a)(c-a) \times 1 \times \begin{vmatrix} b+a & c+a \\ b^2 + a^2 + ab & c^2 + a^2 + ac \end{vmatrix} \qquad [\text{Expanding along } R_1]$$

$$\Rightarrow \quad \Delta = (b-a)(c-a)\begin{vmatrix} b-c & c+a \\ b^2 - c^2 + ab - ac & c^2 + a^2 + ac \end{vmatrix} \qquad [\text{Applying } C_1 \to C_1 - C_2]$$

$$\Rightarrow \quad \Delta = (b-a)(c-a)\begin{vmatrix} b-c & c+a \\ (b^2 - c^2) + a(b-c) & c^2 + a^2 + ac \end{vmatrix}$$

$$\Rightarrow \quad \Delta = (b-a)(c-a)(b-c)\begin{vmatrix} 1 & c+a \\ b+c+a & c^2 + a^2 + ac \end{vmatrix} \qquad [\text{Taking } (b-c) \text{ common from } C_1]$$

$$\Rightarrow \quad \Delta = (b-a)(c-a)(b-c)(c^2 + a^2 + ac - bc - c^2 - ac - ab - ac - a^2)$$

$$\Rightarrow \quad \Delta = (b-a)(c-a)(b-c)(-bc - ab - ac) = (a-b)(b-c)(c-a)(ab + bc + ca).$$

EXAMPLE 28 *If* $x \neq y \neq z$ *and* $\begin{vmatrix} x & x^2 & 1+x^3 \\ y & y^2 & 1+y^3 \\ z & z^2 & 1+z^3 \end{vmatrix} = 0$, *then prove that* $xyz = -1$.

[NCERT, CBSE 2011, 2020]

SOLUTION We have,

$$\Delta = \begin{vmatrix} x & x^2 & 1+x^3 \\ y & y^2 & 1+y^3 \\ z & z^2 & 1+z^3 \end{vmatrix}$$

$$\Rightarrow \quad \Delta = \begin{vmatrix} x & x^2 & 1 \\ y & y^2 & 1 \\ z & z^2 & 1 \end{vmatrix} + \begin{vmatrix} x & x^2 & x^3 \\ y & y^2 & y^3 \\ z & z^2 & z^3 \end{vmatrix} \qquad \begin{bmatrix}\text{Since each element of third} \\ \text{column is sum of two elements}\end{bmatrix}$$

$$\Rightarrow \quad \Delta = \begin{vmatrix} x & x^2 & 1 \\ y & y^2 & 1 \\ z & z^2 & 1 \end{vmatrix} + xyz \begin{vmatrix} 1 & x & x^2 \\ 1 & y & y^2 \\ 1 & z & z^2 \end{vmatrix} \qquad \left[\begin{array}{l}\text{Taking } x, y \text{ and } z \text{ common from } C_1, \\ C_2, \text{ and } C_3 \text{ in second determinant}\end{array}\right]$$

$$\Rightarrow \quad \Delta = -\begin{vmatrix} x & 1 & x^2 \\ y & 1 & y^2 \\ z & 1 & z^2 \end{vmatrix} + xyz \begin{vmatrix} 1 & x & x^2 \\ 1 & y & y^2 \\ 1 & z & z^2 \end{vmatrix} \qquad [\text{Interchanging } C_2 \text{ and } C_3 \text{ in first determinant}]$$

$$\Rightarrow \quad \Delta = \begin{vmatrix} 1 & x & x^2 \\ 1 & y & y^2 \\ 1 & z & z^2 \end{vmatrix} + xyz \begin{vmatrix} 1 & x & x^2 \\ 1 & y & y^2 \\ 1 & z & z^2 \end{vmatrix} \qquad [\text{Interchanging } C_1 \text{ and } C_2 \text{ in first determinant}]$$

$$\Rightarrow \quad \Delta = \begin{vmatrix} 1 & x & x^2 \\ 1 & y & y^2 \\ 1 & z & z^2 \end{vmatrix} (1 + xyz)$$

$$\Rightarrow \quad \Delta = \begin{vmatrix} 1 & x & x^2 \\ 0 & y-x & y^2-x^2 \\ 0 & z-x & z^2-x^2 \end{vmatrix} (1 + xyz) \qquad [\text{Applying } R_2 \to R_2 - R_1 \text{ and } R_3 \to R_3 - R_1]$$

$$\Rightarrow \quad \Delta = (y-x)(z-x) \begin{vmatrix} 1 & x & x^2 \\ 0 & 1 & y+x \\ 0 & 1 & z+x \end{vmatrix} (1 + xyz) \qquad \left[\begin{array}{l}\text{Taking } (y-x) \text{ and } (z-x) \\ \text{common } R_2 \text{ and } R_3 \text{ resp.}\end{array}\right]$$

$$\Rightarrow \quad \Delta = (y-x)(z-x) \times 1 \times \begin{vmatrix} 1 & y+x \\ 1 & z+x \end{vmatrix} (1 + xyz) \qquad [\text{Expanding along } C_1]$$

$$\Rightarrow \quad \Delta = (y-x)(z-x)(z+x-y-x)(1+xyz)$$

$$\Rightarrow \quad \Delta = (y-x)(z-x)(z-y)(1+xyz) = (x-y)(y-z)(z-x)(1+xyz)$$

$$\therefore \quad \Delta = 0$$

$$\Rightarrow \quad (x-y)(y-z)(z-x)(1+xyz) = 0$$

$$\Rightarrow \quad 1 + xyz = 0 \qquad [\because\ x \neq y \neq z \Rightarrow x-y \neq 0,\ y-z \neq 0 \text{ and } z-x \neq 0]$$

$$\Rightarrow \quad xyz = -1.$$

EXAMPLE 29 *For any scalar p prove that* $\Delta = \begin{vmatrix} x & x^2 & 1+px^3 \\ y & y^2 & 1+py^3 \\ z & z^2 & 1+pz^3 \end{vmatrix} = (1+pxyz)(x-y)(y-z)(z-x).$

[NCERT, CBSE 2010]

SOLUTION We have,

$$\Delta = \begin{vmatrix} x & x^2 & 1+px^3 \\ y & y^2 & 1+py^3 \\ z & z^2 & 1+pz^3 \end{vmatrix}$$

$$\Rightarrow \quad \Delta = \begin{vmatrix} x & x^2 & 1 \\ y & y^2 & 1 \\ z & z^2 & 1 \end{vmatrix} + \begin{vmatrix} x & x^2 & px^3 \\ y & y^2 & py^3 \\ z & z^2 & pz^3 \end{vmatrix}$$ [$\because$ Each element in III column is sum of two elements]

$$\Rightarrow \quad \Delta = -\begin{vmatrix} 1 & x^2 & x \\ 1 & y^2 & y \\ 1 & z^2 & z \end{vmatrix} + pxyz \begin{vmatrix} 1 & x & x^2 \\ 1 & y & y^2 \\ 1 & z & z^2 \end{vmatrix}$$ [Interchanging C_1 and C_3 in first det. Taking x, y, z common from R_1, R_2, R_3 respectively and p from C_3 in 2nd det.]

$$\Rightarrow \quad \Delta = \begin{vmatrix} 1 & x & x^2 \\ 1 & y & y^2 \\ 1 & z & z^2 \end{vmatrix} + pxyz \begin{vmatrix} 1 & x & x^2 \\ 1 & y & y^2 \\ 1 & z & z^2 \end{vmatrix}$$ [Interchanging C_2 and C_3 in first determinant]

$$\Rightarrow \quad \Delta = (1 + pxyz) \begin{vmatrix} 1 & x & x^2 \\ 1 & y & y^2 \\ 1 & z & z^2 \end{vmatrix}$$

$$\Rightarrow \quad \Delta = (1 + pxyz) \begin{vmatrix} 1 & x & x^2 \\ 0 & y-x & y^2-x^2 \\ 0 & z-x & z^2-x^2 \end{vmatrix}$$ [Applying $R_2 \to R_2 - R_1$ and $R_3 \to R_3 - R_1$]

$$\Rightarrow \quad \Delta = (1 + pxyz)(y-x)(z-x) \begin{vmatrix} 1 & x & x^2 \\ 0 & 1 & y+x \\ 0 & 1 & z+x \end{vmatrix}$$ [Taking $(y-x)$ and $(z-x)$ common from R_2 and R_3 respectively]

$$\Rightarrow \quad \Delta = (1 + pxyz)(y-x)(z-x) \begin{vmatrix} 1 & y+x \\ 1 & z+x \end{vmatrix}$$ [Expanding along C_1]

$$\Rightarrow \quad \Delta = (1 + pxyz)(y-x)(z-x)(z+x-y-x) = (1 + pxyz)(x-y)(y-z)(z-x)$$

EXAMPLE 30 *Evaluate:* $\Delta = \begin{vmatrix} 10! & 11! & 12! \\ 11! & 12! & 13! \\ 12! & 13! & 14! \end{vmatrix}$.

SOLUTION We have,

$$\Delta = \begin{vmatrix} 10! & 11! & 12! \\ 11! & 12! & 13! \\ 12! & 13! & 14! \end{vmatrix} = \begin{vmatrix} 10! & 11 \times 10! & 12 \times 11 \times 10! \\ 11! & 12 \times 11! & 13 \times 12 \times 11! \\ 12! & 13 \times 12! & 14 \times 13 \times 12! \end{vmatrix}$$

$$\Rightarrow \quad \Delta = 10! \times 11! \times 12! \begin{vmatrix} 1 & 11 & 132 \\ 1 & 12 & 156 \\ 1 & 13 & 182 \end{vmatrix}$$ [Taking 10!, 11! and 12! common from R_1, R_2 and R_3 respectively]

$$\Rightarrow \quad \Delta = 10! \times 11! \times 12! \begin{vmatrix} 1 & 11 & 132 \\ 0 & 1 & 24 \\ 0 & 2 & 50 \end{vmatrix}$$ [Applying $R_2 \to R_2 - R_1$, $R_3 \to R_3 - R_1$]

$$\Rightarrow \quad \Delta = 10! \times 11! \times 12! \times \begin{vmatrix} 1 & 24 \\ 2 & 50 \end{vmatrix} = (10! \times 11! \times 12!) \times 2$$ [Expanding along C_1]

EXAMPLE 31 *Prove that:* $\begin{vmatrix} x+y & x & x \\ 5x+4y & 4x & 2x \\ 10x+8y & 8x & 3x \end{vmatrix} = x^3$. [CBSE 2002 C, 2009, 2014]

SOLUTION Let $\Delta = \begin{vmatrix} x+y & x & x \\ 5x+4y & 4x & 2x \\ 10x+8y & 8x & 3x \end{vmatrix}$.

Since each element in the first column of Δ is the sum of two elements. Therefore, Δ can be expressed as the sum of two determinants given by

$$\Delta = \begin{vmatrix} x & x & x \\ 5x & 4x & 2x \\ 10x & 8x & 3x \end{vmatrix} + \begin{vmatrix} y & x & x \\ 4y & 4x & 2x \\ 8y & 8x & 3x \end{vmatrix} = x^3 \begin{vmatrix} 1 & 1 & 1 \\ 5 & 4 & 2 \\ 10 & 8 & 3 \end{vmatrix} + yx^2 \begin{vmatrix} 1 & 1 & 1 \\ 4 & 4 & 2 \\ 8 & 8 & 3 \end{vmatrix}$$

$\Rightarrow \quad \Delta = x^3 \begin{vmatrix} 1 & 1 & 1 \\ 5 & 4 & 2 \\ 10 & 8 & 3 \end{vmatrix} + yx^2 \times 0$ [$\because$ C_1 and C_2 are identical in the second determinant]

$\Rightarrow \quad \Delta = x^3 \begin{vmatrix} 0 & 0 & 1 \\ 3 & 2 & 2 \\ 7 & 5 & 3 \end{vmatrix}$ [Applying $C_1 \to C_1 - C_3, C_2 \to C_2 - C_3$]

$\Rightarrow \quad \Delta = x^3 \times 1 \times \begin{vmatrix} 3 & 2 \\ 7 & 5 \end{vmatrix} = x^3 (15 - 14) = x^3$ [Expanding along R_1]

EXAMPLE 32 *Show that:* $\begin{vmatrix} 1 & 1+p & 1+p+q \\ 2 & 3+2p & 1+3p+2q \\ 3 & 6+3p & 1+6p+3q \end{vmatrix} = 1.$ **[CBSE 2009]**

SOLUTION Let $\Delta = \begin{vmatrix} 1 & 1+p & 1+p+q \\ 2 & 3+2p & 1+3p+2q \\ 3 & 6+3p & 1+6p+3q \end{vmatrix}$. Applying $C_2 \to C_2 - pC_1$ and $C_3 \to C_3 - qC_1$,

we get

$$\Delta = \begin{vmatrix} 1 & 1 & 1+p \\ 2 & 3 & 1+3p \\ 3 & 6 & 1+6p \end{vmatrix} = \begin{vmatrix} 1 & 1 & 1 \\ 2 & 3 & 1 \\ 3 & 6 & 1 \end{vmatrix} \quad \text{[Applying } C_3 \to C_3 - pC_2\text{]}$$

$\Rightarrow \quad \Delta = \begin{vmatrix} 0 & 0 & 1 \\ 1 & 2 & 1 \\ 2 & 5 & 1 \end{vmatrix}$ [Applying $C_1 \to C_1 - C_3, C_2 \to C_2 - C_3$]

$\Rightarrow \quad \Delta = 5 - 4 = 1$ [Expanding along R_1]

EXAMPLE 33 *Show that:* $\begin{vmatrix} a & a+b & a+b+c \\ 2a & 3a+2b & 4a+3b+2c \\ 3a & 6a+3b & 10a+6b+3c \end{vmatrix} = a^3.$ **[NCERT, CBSE 2012]**

SOLUTION Let $\Delta = \begin{vmatrix} a & a+b & a+b+c \\ 2a & 3a+2b & 4a+3b+2c \\ 3a & 6a+3b & 10a+6b+3c \end{vmatrix}$.

Since each element of the second column is sum of two elements. Therefore, Δ can be written as the sum of two determinants as follows:

$$\Delta = \begin{vmatrix} a & a & a+b+c \\ 2a & 3a & 4a+3b+2c \\ 3a & 6a & 10a+6b+3c \end{vmatrix} + \begin{vmatrix} a & b & a+b+c \\ 2a & 2b & 4a+3b+2c \\ 3a & 3b & 10a+6b+3c \end{vmatrix}$$

$\Rightarrow \quad \Delta = \begin{vmatrix} a & a & a+b+c \\ 2a & 3a & 4a+3b+2c \\ 3a & 6a & 10a+6b+3c \end{vmatrix} + ab \begin{vmatrix} 1 & 1 & a+b+c \\ 2 & 2 & 4a+3b+2c \\ 3 & 3 & 10a+6b+3c \end{vmatrix}$ [Taking a and b common from C_1 and C_2 of second determinant]

$\Rightarrow \quad \Delta = \begin{vmatrix} a & a & a+b+c \\ 2a & 3a & 4a+3b+2c \\ 3a & 6a & 10a+6b+3c \end{vmatrix} + ab \times 0$ [$\because C_2$ & C_3 are identical in second determinant]

$\Rightarrow \quad \Delta = \begin{vmatrix} a & a & a \\ 2a & 3a & 4a \\ 3a & 6a & 10a \end{vmatrix} + \begin{vmatrix} a & a & b \\ 2a & 3a & 3b \\ 3a & 6a & 6b \end{vmatrix} + \begin{vmatrix} a & a & c \\ 2a & 3a & 2c \\ 3a & 6a & 3c \end{vmatrix}$

$\Rightarrow \quad \Delta = a^3 \begin{vmatrix} 1 & 1 & 1 \\ 2 & 3 & 4 \\ 3 & 6 & 10 \end{vmatrix} + a^2b \begin{vmatrix} 1 & 1 & 1 \\ 2 & 3 & 3 \\ 3 & 6 & 6 \end{vmatrix} + a^2c \begin{vmatrix} 1 & 1 & 1 \\ 2 & 3 & 2 \\ 3 & 6 & 3 \end{vmatrix}$

$\Rightarrow \quad \Delta = a^3 \begin{vmatrix} 1 & 1 & 1 \\ 2 & 3 & 4 \\ 3 & 6 & 10 \end{vmatrix} + a^2 b \times 0 + a^2 c \times 0$ [$\because C_2$ and C_3 are identical in second det. and C_1 and C_3 are identical in third det.]

$\Rightarrow \quad \Delta = a^3 \begin{vmatrix} 1 & 0 & 0 \\ 2 & 1 & 2 \\ 3 & 3 & 7 \end{vmatrix}$ [Applying $C_2 \to C_2 - C_1, C_3 \to C_3 - C_1$]

$\Rightarrow \quad \Delta = a^3 \times 1 \times \begin{vmatrix} 1 & 2 \\ 3 & 7 \end{vmatrix} = a^3 (7-6) = a^3$ [Expanding along R_1]

ALITER Let $\Delta = \begin{vmatrix} a & a+b & a+b+c \\ 2a & 3a+2b & 4a+3b+2c \\ 3a & 6a+3b & 10a+6b+3c \end{vmatrix}$. Taking '$a$' common from C_1, we obtain

$\Delta = a \begin{vmatrix} 1 & a+b & a+b+c \\ 2 & 3a+2b & 4a+3b+2c \\ 3 & 6a+3b & 10a+6b+3c \end{vmatrix}$

$\Rightarrow \quad \Delta = a \begin{vmatrix} 1 & a & a+b \\ 2 & 3a & 4a+3b \\ 3 & 6a & 10a+6b \end{vmatrix}$ [Applying $C_2 \to C_2 - bC_1, C_3 \to C_3 - cC_1$]

$\Rightarrow \quad \Delta = a^2 \begin{vmatrix} 1 & 1 & a+b \\ 2 & 3 & 4a+3b \\ 3 & 6 & 10a+6b \end{vmatrix}$ [Taking a common from C_2]

$\Rightarrow \quad \Delta = a^2 \begin{vmatrix} 1 & 1 & a \\ 2 & 3 & 4a \\ 3 & 6 & 10a \end{vmatrix}$ [Applying $C_3 \to C_3 - b\,C_2$]

$\Rightarrow \quad \Delta = a^3 \begin{vmatrix} 1 & 1 & 1 \\ 2 & 3 & 4 \\ 3 & 6 & 10 \end{vmatrix}$ [Taking a common from C_3]

$\Rightarrow \quad \Delta = a^3 \begin{vmatrix} 1 & 0 & 0 \\ 2 & 1 & 2 \\ 3 & 3 & 7 \end{vmatrix}$ [Applying $C_2 \to C_2 - C_1, C_3 \to C_3 - C_1$]

$\Rightarrow \quad \Delta = a^3 \times 1 = a^3$ [Expanding along R_1]

EXAMPLE 34 *Show that:* $\begin{vmatrix} b+c & c+a & a+b \\ q+r & r+p & p+q \\ y+z & z+x & x+y \end{vmatrix} = 2\begin{vmatrix} a & b & c \\ p & q & r \\ x & y & z \end{vmatrix}$. **[CBSE 2004, 2006, 2010, 2012, 2014]**

SOLUTION Let $\Delta = \begin{vmatrix} b+c & c+a & a+b \\ q+r & r+p & p+q \\ y+z & z+x & x+y \end{vmatrix}$. Applying $C_1 \to C_1 + C_2 + C_3$, we get

$$\Delta = \begin{vmatrix} 2(a+b+c) & c+a & a+b \\ 2(p+q+r) & r+p & p+q \\ 2(x+y+z) & z+x & x+y \end{vmatrix} = 2\begin{vmatrix} a+b+c & c+a & a+b \\ p+q+r & r+p & p+q \\ x+y+z & z+x & x+y \end{vmatrix} \quad \text{[Taking 2 common from } C_1]$$

$$\Rightarrow \quad \Delta = 2\begin{vmatrix} a+b+c & -b & -c \\ p+q+r & -q & -r \\ x+y+z & -y & -z \end{vmatrix} \quad [\text{Applying } C_2 \to C_2 - C_1, C_3 \to C_3 - C_1]$$

$$\Rightarrow \quad \Delta = 2\begin{vmatrix} a & -b & -c \\ p & -q & -r \\ x & -y & -z \end{vmatrix} \quad [\text{Applying } C_1 \to C_1 + C_2 + C_3]$$

$$\Rightarrow \quad \Delta = 2(-1)^2\begin{vmatrix} a & b & c \\ p & q & r \\ x & y & z \end{vmatrix} = 2\begin{vmatrix} a & b & c \\ p & q & r \\ x & y & z \end{vmatrix} \quad [\text{Taking } (-1) \text{ common from both } C_2 \text{ and } C_3]$$

EXAMPLE 35 *Prove that* $\begin{vmatrix} 1+a & 1 & 1 \\ 1 & 1+b & 1 \\ 1 & 1 & 1+c \end{vmatrix} = abc\left(1 + \frac{1}{a} + \frac{1}{b} + \frac{1}{c}\right) = abc + bc + ca + ab.$

[NCERT, CBSE 2004, 2009, 2012, 2014]

SOLUTION Let $\Delta = \begin{vmatrix} 1+a & 1 & 1 \\ 1 & 1+b & 1 \\ 1 & 1 & 1+c \end{vmatrix}$. Taking a, b and c common from C_1, C_2 and C_3 respectively, we obtain

$$\Delta = abc\begin{vmatrix} 1/a + 1 & 1/b & 1/c \\ 1/a & 1 + 1/b & 1/c \\ 1/a & 1/b & 1 + 1/c \end{vmatrix}$$

$$\Delta = abc\begin{vmatrix} 1 + 1/a + 1/b + 1/c & 1/b & 1/c \\ 1 + 1/a + 1/b + 1/c & 1 + 1/b & 1/c \\ 1 + 1/a + 1/b + 1/c & 1/b & 1 + 1/c \end{vmatrix} \quad [\text{Applying } C_1 \to C_1 + C_2 + C_3]$$

$$\Rightarrow \quad \Delta = abc\left(1 + \frac{1}{a} + \frac{1}{b} + \frac{1}{c}\right)\begin{vmatrix} 1 & 1/b & 1/c \\ 1 & 1 + 1/b & 1/c \\ 1 & 1/b & 1 + 1/c \end{vmatrix} \quad \left[\text{Taking} \left(1 + \frac{1}{a} + \frac{1}{b} + \frac{1}{c}\right) \text{common from } C_1\right]$$

$$\Rightarrow \quad \Delta = abc\left(1 + \frac{1}{a} + \frac{1}{b} + \frac{1}{c}\right)\begin{vmatrix} 1 & 1/b & 1/c \\ 0 & 1 & 0 \\ 0 & 0 & 1 \end{vmatrix} \quad [\text{Applying } R_2 \to R_2 - R_1, R_3 \to R_3 - R_1]$$

$$\Rightarrow \quad \Delta = abc\left(1 + \frac{1}{a} + \frac{1}{b} + \frac{1}{c}\right) \times 1 \times \begin{vmatrix} 1 & 0 \\ 0 & 1 \end{vmatrix} \quad [\text{Expanding along } C_1]$$

$$\Rightarrow \quad \Delta = abc\left(1 + \frac{1}{a} + \frac{1}{b} + \frac{1}{c}\right).$$

EXERCISE 5.2

BASIC

1. *Evaluate the following determinant:*

(i) $\begin{vmatrix} 1 & 3 & 5 \\ 2 & 6 & 10 \\ 31 & 11 & 38 \end{vmatrix}$ (ii) $\begin{vmatrix} 67 & 19 & 21 \\ 39 & 13 & 14 \\ 81 & 24 & 26 \end{vmatrix}$ (iii) $\begin{vmatrix} a & h & g \\ h & b & f \\ g & f & c \end{vmatrix}$

(iv) $\begin{vmatrix} 1 & -3 & 2 \\ 4 & -1 & 2 \\ 3 & 5 & 2 \end{vmatrix}$ (v) $\begin{vmatrix} 1 & 4 & 9 \\ 4 & 9 & 16 \\ 9 & 16 & 25 \end{vmatrix}$ (vi) $\begin{vmatrix} 6 & -3 & 2 \\ 2 & -1 & 2 \\ -10 & 5 & 2 \end{vmatrix}$

(vii) $\begin{vmatrix} 1 & 3 & 9 & 27 \\ 3 & 9 & 27 & 1 \\ 9 & 27 & 1 & 3 \\ 27 & 1 & 3 & 9 \end{vmatrix}$ (viii) $\begin{vmatrix} 102 & 18 & 36 \\ 1 & 3 & 4 \\ 17 & 3 & 6 \end{vmatrix}$ [CBSE 2012]

2. Without expanding, show that the value of each of the following determinants is zero:

(i) $\begin{vmatrix} 8 & 2 & 7 \\ 12 & 3 & 5 \\ 16 & 4 & 3 \end{vmatrix}$ (ii) $\begin{vmatrix} 6 & -3 & 2 \\ 2 & -1 & 2 \\ -10 & 5 & 2 \end{vmatrix}$ (iii) $\begin{vmatrix} 2 & 3 & 7 \\ 13 & 17 & 5 \\ 15 & 20 & 12 \end{vmatrix}$

(iv) $\begin{vmatrix} 1/a & a^2 & bc \\ 1/b & b^2 & ac \\ 1/c & c^2 & ab \end{vmatrix}$ (v) $\begin{vmatrix} a+b & 2a+b & 3a+b \\ 2a+b & 3a+b & 4a+b \\ 4a+b & 5a+b & 6a+b \end{vmatrix}$ (vi) $\begin{vmatrix} 1 & a & a^2-bc \\ 1 & b & b^2-ac \\ 1 & c & c^2-ab \end{vmatrix}$

(vii) $\begin{vmatrix} 49 & 1 & 6 \\ 39 & 7 & 4 \\ 26 & 2 & 3 \end{vmatrix}$ (viii) $\begin{vmatrix} 0 & x & y \\ -x & 0 & z \\ -y & -z & 0 \end{vmatrix}$ (ix) $\begin{vmatrix} 1 & 43 & 6 \\ 7 & 35 & 4 \\ 3 & 17 & 2 \end{vmatrix}$

(x) $\begin{vmatrix} 1^2 & 2^2 & 3^2 & 4^2 \\ 2^2 & 3^2 & 4^2 & 5^2 \\ 3^2 & 4^2 & 5^2 & 6^2 \\ 4^2 & 5^2 & 6^2 & 7^2 \end{vmatrix}$ (xi) $\begin{vmatrix} a & b & c \\ a+2x & b+2y & c+2z \\ x & y & z \end{vmatrix}$ (xii) $\begin{vmatrix} (2^x+2^{-x})^2 & (2^x-2^{-x})^2 & 1 \\ (3^x+3^{-x})^2 & (3^x-3^{-x})^2 & 1 \\ (4^x+4^{-x})^2 & (4^x-4^{-x}) & 1 \end{vmatrix}$

(xiii) $\begin{vmatrix} \sin\alpha & \cos\alpha & \cos(\alpha+\delta) \\ \sin\beta & \cos\beta & \cos(\beta+\delta) \\ \sin\gamma & \cos\gamma & \cos(\gamma+\delta) \end{vmatrix}$ (xiv) $\begin{vmatrix} \sin^2 23^\circ & \sin^2 67^\circ & \cos 180^\circ \\ -\sin^2 67^\circ & -\sin^2 23^\circ & \cos^2 180^\circ \\ \cos 180^\circ & \sin^2 23^\circ & \sin^2 67^\circ \end{vmatrix}$

(xv) $\begin{vmatrix} \cos(x+y) & -\sin(x+y) & \cos 2y \\ \sin x & \cos x & \sin y \\ -\cos x & \sin x & -\cos y \end{vmatrix}$ (xvi) $\begin{vmatrix} \sqrt{23}+\sqrt{3} & \sqrt{5} & \sqrt{5} \\ \sqrt{15}+\sqrt{46} & 5 & \sqrt{10} \\ 3+\sqrt{115} & \sqrt{15} & 5 \end{vmatrix}$

(xvii) $\begin{vmatrix} \sin^2 A & \cot A & 1 \\ \sin^2 B & \cot B & 1 \\ \sin^2 C & \cot C & 1 \end{vmatrix}$, where A, B, C are the angles of ΔABC.

Evaluate the following (3 – 9):

3. $\begin{vmatrix} a & b+c & a^2 \\ b & c+a & b^2 \\ c & a+b & c^2 \end{vmatrix}$ [CBSE 2006]

4. $\begin{vmatrix} 1 & a & bc \\ 1 & b & ca \\ 1 & c & ab \end{vmatrix}$ [NCERT, CBSE 2006]

5. $\begin{vmatrix} x+\lambda & x & x \\ x & x+\lambda & x \\ x & x & x+\lambda \end{vmatrix}$ [NCERT]

6. $\begin{vmatrix} a & b & c \\ c & a & b \\ b & c & a \end{vmatrix}$ [CBSE 2004]

7. $\begin{vmatrix} x & 1 & 1 \\ 1 & x & 1 \\ 1 & 1 & x \end{vmatrix}$

8. $\begin{vmatrix} 0 & xy^2 & xz^2 \\ x^2y & 0 & yz^2 \\ x^2z & zy^2 & 0 \end{vmatrix}$ [NCERT EXEMPLAR]

9. $\begin{vmatrix} a+x & y & z \\ x & a+y & z \\ x & y & a+z \end{vmatrix}$ [NCERT EXEMPLAR]

10. If $\Delta = \begin{vmatrix} 1 & x & x^2 \\ 1 & y & y^2 \\ 1 & z & z^2 \end{vmatrix}$, $\Delta_1 = \begin{vmatrix} 1 & 1 & 1 \\ yz & zx & xy \\ x & y & z \end{vmatrix}$, then prove that $\Delta + \Delta_1 = 0$. [NCERT EXEMPLAR]

BASED ON LOTS

Prove the following identities (11 –45):

11. $\begin{vmatrix} a & b & c \\ a-b & b-c & c-a \\ b+c & c+a & a+b \end{vmatrix} = a^3 + b^3 + c^3 - 3abc$ [CBSE 2009. 2019]

12. $\begin{vmatrix} b+c & a-b & a \\ c+a & b-c & b \\ a+b & c-a & c \end{vmatrix} = 3abc - a^3 - b^3 - c^3$

13. $\begin{vmatrix} a+b & b+c & c+a \\ b+c & c+a & a+b \\ c+a & a+b & b+c \end{vmatrix} = 2\begin{vmatrix} a & b & c \\ b & c & a \\ c & a & b \end{vmatrix}$ [CBSE 2001, 2004, 2006 C, 2007]

14. $\begin{vmatrix} a+b+2c & a & b \\ c & b+c+2a & b \\ c & a & c+a+2b \end{vmatrix} = 2\,(a+b+c)^3$ [NCERT, CBSE 2006C, 2008, 2014]

15. $\begin{vmatrix} a-b-c & 2a & 2a \\ 2b & b-c-a & 2b \\ 2c & 2c & c-a-b \end{vmatrix} = (a+b+c)^3$ [CBSE 2000C, 04, 07, NCERT EXEMPLAR]

16. $\begin{vmatrix} 1 & b+c & b^2+c^2 \\ 1 & c+a & c^2+a^2 \\ 1 & a+b & a^2+b^2 \end{vmatrix} = (a-b)\,(b-c)\,(c-a)$ [CBSE 2002]

17. $\begin{vmatrix} a & a+b & a+2b \\ a+2b & a & a+b \\ a+b & a+2b & a \end{vmatrix} = 9(a+b)b^2$ [CBSE 2002, 2013, 2017]

18. $\begin{vmatrix} 1 & a & bc \\ 1 & b & ca \\ 1 & c & ab \end{vmatrix} = \begin{vmatrix} 1 & a & a^2 \\ 1 & b & b^2 \\ 1 & c & c^2 \end{vmatrix}$

19. $\begin{vmatrix} z & x & y \\ z^2 & x^2 & y^2 \\ z^4 & x^4 & y^4 \end{vmatrix} = \begin{vmatrix} x & y & z \\ x^2 & y^2 & z^2 \\ x^4 & y^4 & z^4 \end{vmatrix} = \begin{vmatrix} x^2 & y^2 & z^2 \\ x^4 & y^4 & z^4 \\ x & y & z \end{vmatrix} = xyz(x-y)(y-z)(z-x)\ (x+y+z).$

ANSWERS

1. (i) 0 (ii) -43 (iii) $abc + 2fgh - af^2 - bg^2 - ch^2$
(iv) 40 (v) -8 (vi) 0 (vii) 512000 (viii) 0

3. $-(a+b+c)(a-b)(b-c)(c-a)$
4. $(a-b)(b-c)(c-a)$
5. $\lambda^2(3x+\lambda)$
6. $(a+b+c)(a^2+b^2+c^2-ab-bc-ca)$
7. $(x-1)^2(x+2)$
8. $2x^3y^3z^3$
9. $a^2(a+x+y+z)$

5.6 APPLICATIONS OF DETERMINANTS TO COORDINATE GEOMETRY

5.6.1 AREA OF A TRIANGLE

We know that the area of triangle whose vertices are $(x_1, y_1), (x_2, y_2)$ and (x_3, y_3) is given by the expression:

$$\Delta = \frac{1}{2}\left\{x_1(y_2-y_3) + x_2(y_3-y_1) + x_3(y_1-y_2)\right\} \quad ...(i)$$

Also, $\begin{vmatrix} x_1 & y_1 & 1 \\ x_2 & y_2 & 1 \\ x_3 & y_3 & 1 \end{vmatrix} = x_1\begin{vmatrix} y_2 & 1 \\ y_3 & 1 \end{vmatrix} - x_2\begin{vmatrix} y_1 & 1 \\ y_3 & 1 \end{vmatrix} + x_3\begin{vmatrix} y_1 & 1 \\ y_2 & 1 \end{vmatrix}$ [Expanding along C_1]

$$= x_1(y_2-y_3) - x_2(y_1-y_3) + x_3(y_1-y_2)$$

$$= x_1(y_2-y_3) + x_2(y_3-y_1) + x_3(y_1-y_2) \quad ...(ii)$$

From (i) and (ii), we obtain : $\Delta = \frac{1}{2}\begin{vmatrix} x_1 & y_1 & 1 \\ x_2 & y_2 & 1 \\ x_3 & y_3 & 1 \end{vmatrix}$

Thus, the area of a triangle having vertices at $(x_1, y_1), (x_2, y_2)$ and (x_3, y_3) is the absolute value of Δ given by

$$\Delta = \frac{1}{2}\begin{vmatrix} x_1 & y_1 & 1 \\ x_2 & y_2 & 1 \\ x_3 & y_3 & 1 \end{vmatrix}$$

NOTE *Since area is always a positive quantity, therefore we always take the absolute value of the determinant for the area.*

5.6.2 CONDITION OF COLLINEARITY OF THREE POINTS

Let $A(x_1, y_1)$, $B(x_2, y_2)$ and $C(x_3, y_3)$ be three points. Then,

$$A, B, C \text{ are collinear} \Leftrightarrow \text{Area of triangle } ABC = 0 \Leftrightarrow \frac{1}{2}\begin{vmatrix} x_1 & y_1 & 1 \\ x_2 & y_2 & 1 \\ x_3 & y_3 & 1 \end{vmatrix} = 0 \Leftrightarrow \begin{vmatrix} x_1 & y_1 & 1 \\ x_2 & y_2 & 1 \\ x_3 & y_3 & 1 \end{vmatrix} = 0$$

5.6.3 EQUATION OF A LINE PASSING THROUGH TWO GIVEN POINTS

Let the two point be $A(x_1, y_1)$ and $B(x_2, y_2)$. Let $P(x, y)$ be any point on the line joining A and B. Then, points P, A and B are collinear.

$$\therefore \quad \begin{vmatrix} x & y & 1 \\ x_1 & y_1 & 1 \\ x_2 & y_2 & 1 \end{vmatrix} = 0$$

Thus, the equation of the line joining points (x_1, y_1) and (x_2, y_2) is given by $\begin{vmatrix} x & y & 1 \\ x_1 & y_1 & 1 \\ x_2 & y_2 & 1 \end{vmatrix} = 0$

ILLUSTRATIVE EXAMPLES

BASED ON BASIC CONCEPTS (BASIC)

EXAMPLE 1 *Find the area of the triangle with vertices $A(5, 4)$, $B(-2, 4)$ and $C(2, -6)$.*

SOLUTION The area Δ of triangle ABC is given by

$$\Delta = \frac{1}{2}\begin{vmatrix} 5 & 4 & 1 \\ -2 & 4 & 1 \\ 2 & -6 & 1 \end{vmatrix} = \frac{1}{2}\begin{vmatrix} 5 & 4 & 1 \\ -7 & 0 & 0 \\ -3 & -10 & 0 \end{vmatrix} \quad [\text{Applying } R_2 \to R_2 - R_1 \text{ and } R_3 \to R_3 - R_1]$$

$$\Rightarrow \quad \Delta = \frac{1}{2} \times 1 \times \begin{vmatrix} -7 & 0 \\ -3 & -10 \end{vmatrix} = \frac{1}{2}(70 - 0) = 35 \text{ sq. units.} \quad [\text{Expanding along } C_3]$$

EXAMPLE 2 *Show that the points $(a, b + c)$, $(b, c + a)$ and $(c, a + b)$ are collinear.*

SOLUTION We have,

$$\Delta = \begin{vmatrix} a & b+c & 1 \\ b & c+a & 1 \\ c & a+b & 1 \end{vmatrix} = \begin{vmatrix} a & a+b+c & 1 \\ b & b+c+a & 1 \\ c & c+a+b & 1 \end{vmatrix} \quad [\text{Applying } C_2 \to C_2 + C_1]$$

$$\Rightarrow \quad \Delta = (a+b+c)\begin{vmatrix} a & 1 & 1 \\ b & 1 & 1 \\ c & 1 & 1 \end{vmatrix} \quad [\text{Taking } (a+b+c) \text{ common from } C_2]$$

$$\Rightarrow \quad \Delta = (a+b+c) \times 0 = 0. \quad [\because C_2 \text{ and } C_3 \text{ are identical}]$$

Hence, the given points are collinear.

EXAMPLE 3 *If the points (a_1, b_1), (a_2, b_2) and $(a_1 + a_2, b_1 + b_2)$ are collinear, show that $a_1 b_2 = a_2 b_1$.*

SOLUTION If given points are collinear, then

$$\begin{vmatrix} a_1 & b_1 & 1 \\ a_2 & b_2 & 1 \\ a_1 + a_2 & b_1 + b_2 & 1 \end{vmatrix} = 0$$

$$\Rightarrow \quad \begin{vmatrix} a_1 & b_1 & 1 \\ a_2 - a_1 & b_2 - b_1 & 0 \\ a_2 & b_2 & 0 \end{vmatrix} = 0 \qquad \text{[Applying } R_2 \to R_2 - R_1, R_3 \to R_3 - R_1\text{]}$$

$$\Rightarrow \quad \begin{vmatrix} a_2 - a_1 & b_2 - b_1 \\ a_2 & b_2 \end{vmatrix} = 0 \qquad \text{[Expanding along } C_3\text{]}$$

$$\Rightarrow \quad \begin{vmatrix} -a_1 & -b_1 \\ a_2 & b_2 \end{vmatrix} = 0 \qquad \text{[Applying } R_1 \to R_1 - R_2\text{]}$$

$$\Rightarrow \quad -a_1 b_2 + a_2 b_1 = 0 \Rightarrow a_1 b_2 = a_2 b_1$$

EXAMPLE 4 *If the points* $(2, -3), (\lambda, -1)$ *and* $(0, 4)$ *are collinear, find the value of* λ.

SOLUTION If given points are collinear, then

$$\begin{vmatrix} 2 & -3 & 1 \\ \lambda & -1 & 1 \\ 0 & 4 & 1 \end{vmatrix} = 0 \Rightarrow \begin{vmatrix} 2 & -3 & 1 \\ \lambda - 2 & 2 & 0 \\ -2 & 7 & 0 \end{vmatrix} = 0 \quad \text{[Applying } R_2 \to R_2 - R_1 \text{ and } R_3 \to R_3 - R_1\text{]}$$

$$\Rightarrow \quad \begin{vmatrix} \lambda - 2 & 2 \\ -2 & 7 \end{vmatrix} = 0 \qquad \text{[Expanding along } C_3\text{]}$$

$$\Rightarrow \quad 7\lambda - 14 + 4 = 0 \Rightarrow \lambda = 10/7.$$

EXAMPLE 5 *Using determinants, find the area of the triangle whose vertices are* $(-2, 4), (2, -6)$ *and* $(5, 4)$*. Are the given points collinear?*

SOLUTION Let Δ be the area of the triangle. Then,

$$\Delta = \frac{1}{2}\begin{vmatrix} -2 & 4 & 1 \\ 2 & -6 & 1 \\ 5 & 4 & 1 \end{vmatrix} = \frac{1}{2}\begin{vmatrix} -2 & 4 & 1 \\ 4 & -10 & 0 \\ 7 & 0 & 0 \end{vmatrix} \quad \text{[Applying } R_2 \to R_2 - R_1 \text{ and } R_3 \to R_3 - R_1\text{]}$$

$$\Rightarrow \quad \Delta = \frac{1}{2}\begin{vmatrix} 4 & -10 \\ 7 & 0 \end{vmatrix} \qquad \text{[By expanding along } C_1\text{]}$$

$$\Rightarrow \quad \Delta = \frac{1}{2}(70) = 35 \text{ sq. units.}$$

Clearly, $\Delta \neq 0$, therefore given points are not collinear.

EXAMPLE 6 *Find the equation of the line joining* $A(1, 3)$ *and* $B(0, 0)$ *using determinants and find* k *if* $D(k, 0)$ *is a point such that area of* $\Delta\, ABD$ *is 3 sq. units.* **[CBSE 2013, 2020]**

SOLUTION Let $P(x, y)$ be any point on line AB. Then,

Area of $\Delta\, ABP = 0$

$$\Rightarrow \quad \frac{1}{2}\begin{vmatrix} 1 & 3 & 1 \\ 0 & 0 & 1 \\ x & y & 1 \end{vmatrix} = 0 \Rightarrow \frac{1}{2}\{1(0 - y) - 3(0 - x) + 1(0 - 0)\} = 0$$

$\Rightarrow \quad 3x - y = 0$, which is the required equation of AB.

Now, Area of $\Delta\, ABD = 3$ sq. units

$$\Rightarrow \quad \frac{1}{2}\begin{vmatrix} 1 & 3 & 1 \\ 0 & 0 & 1 \\ k & 0 & 1 \end{vmatrix} = \pm 3$$

$$\Rightarrow \quad \begin{vmatrix} 1 & 3 & 1 \\ 0 & 0 & 1 \\ k & 0 & 1 \end{vmatrix} = \pm 6 \Rightarrow 1(0-0) - 3(0-k) + 1(0-0) = \pm 6 \Rightarrow 3k = \pm 6 \Rightarrow k = \pm 2$$

BASED ON HIGHER ORDER THINKING SKILLS (HOTS)

EXAMPLE 7 *If $A(x_1, y_1)$, $B(x_2, y_2)$ and $C(x_3, y_3)$ are vertices of an equilateral triangle whose each side is equal to a, then prove that* $\begin{vmatrix} x_1 & y_1 & 2 \\ x_2 & y_2 & 2 \\ x_3 & y_3 & 2 \end{vmatrix}^2 = 3a^4$. **[NCERT EXEMPLAR]**

SOLUTION Let Δ be the area of triangle ABC. Then,

$$\Delta = \frac{1}{2}\begin{vmatrix} x_1 & y_1 & 1 \\ x_2 & y_2 & 1 \\ x_3 & y_3 & 1 \end{vmatrix}$$

$$\Rightarrow \quad 2\Delta = \begin{vmatrix} x_1 & y_1 & 1 \\ x_2 & y_2 & 1 \\ x_3 & y_3 & 1 \end{vmatrix}$$

$$\Rightarrow \quad 4\Delta = 2\begin{vmatrix} x_1 & y_1 & 1 \\ x_2 & y_2 & 1 \\ x_3 & y_3 & 1 \end{vmatrix} = \begin{vmatrix} x_1 & y_1 & 2 \\ x_2 & y_2 & 2 \\ x_3 & y_3 & 2 \end{vmatrix}$$

$$\Rightarrow \quad 16\Delta^2 = \begin{vmatrix} x_1 & y_1 & 2 \\ x_2 & y_2 & 2 \\ x_3 & y_3 & 2 \end{vmatrix}^2 \qquad ...(i)$$

But, the area of an equilateral triangle with each side equal to a is $\frac{\sqrt{3}}{4}a^2$.

$$\therefore \quad \Delta = \frac{\sqrt{3}}{4}a^2 \Rightarrow 16\Delta^2 = 3a^4 \qquad ...(ii)$$

From (i) and (ii), we obtain $\begin{vmatrix} x_1 & y_1 & 2 \\ x_2 & y_2 & 2 \\ x_3 & y_3 & 2 \end{vmatrix}^2 = 3a^4$.

EXAMPLE 8 *A triangle has its three sides equal to a, b and c. If the coordinates of its vertices are $A(x_1, y_1)$, $B(x_2, y_2)$ and $C(x_3, y_3)$, show that*

$$\begin{vmatrix} x_1 & y_1 & 2 \\ x_2 & y_2 & 2 \\ x_3 & y_3 & 2 \end{vmatrix}^2 = (a+b+c)(b+c-a)(c+a-b)(a+b-c).$$

SOLUTION Let Δ be the area of triangle ABC. Then,

$$\Delta = \frac{1}{2}\begin{vmatrix} x_1 & y_1 & 1 \\ x_2 & y_2 & 1 \\ x_3 & y_3 & 1 \end{vmatrix} \Rightarrow 2\Delta = \begin{vmatrix} x_1 & y_1 & 1 \\ x_2 & y_2 & 1 \\ x_3 & y_3 & 1 \end{vmatrix}$$

$$\Rightarrow \quad 4\Delta = 2\begin{vmatrix} x_1 & y_1 & 1 \\ x_2 & y_2 & 1 \\ x_3 & y_3 & 1 \end{vmatrix} = \begin{vmatrix} x_1 & y_1 & 2 \\ x_2 & y_2 & 2 \\ x_3 & y_3 & 2 \end{vmatrix} \Rightarrow 16\Delta^2 = \begin{vmatrix} x_1 & y_1 & 2 \\ x_2 & y_2 & 2 \\ x_3 & y_3 & 2 \end{vmatrix}^2 \qquad ...(i)$$

We also know that the area of triangle ABC is given by

$$\Delta = \sqrt{s(s-a)(s-b)(s-c)}, \text{ where } s = \frac{1}{2}(a+b+c)$$

But, $s = \frac{1}{2}(a+b+c) \Rightarrow s-a = \frac{1}{2}(a+b+c) - a = \frac{1}{2}(b+c-a)$.

Similarly, $s-b = \frac{1}{2}(c+a-b)$ and $s-c = \frac{1}{2}(a+b-c)$.

$$\therefore \quad \Delta^2 = \frac{1}{2}(a+b+c) \times \frac{1}{2}(b+c-a) \times \frac{1}{2}(c+a-b) \times \frac{1}{2}(a+b-c)$$

$$\Rightarrow \quad 16\,\Delta^2 = (a+b+c)(b+c-a)(c+a-b)(a+b+c) \qquad \text{...(ii)}$$

From (i) and (ii), we get : $\begin{vmatrix} x_1 & y_1 & 2 \\ x_2 & y_2 & 2 \\ x_3 & y_3 & 2 \end{vmatrix}^2 = (a+b+c)(b+c-a)(c+a-b)(a+b-c)$

EXERCISE 5.3

BASIC

1. Find the area of the triangle with vertices at the points:
   (i) $(3, 8), (-4, 2)$ and $(5, -1)$ (ii) $(2, 7), (1, 1)$ and $(10, 8)$
   (iii) $(-1, -8), (-2, -3)$ and $(3, 2)$ (iv) $(0, 0), (6, 0)$ and $(4, 3)$.
2. Using determinants show that the following points are collinear:
   (i) $(5, 5), (-5, 1)$ and $(10, 7)$ (ii) $(1, -1), (2, 1)$ and $(4, 5)$
   (iii) $(3, -2), (8, 8)$ and $(5, 2)$ (iv) $(2, 3), (-1, -2)$ and $(5, 8)$
3. If the points $(a, 0)$, $(0, b)$ and $(1, 1)$ are collinear, prove that $a + b = ab$.
4. Using determinants prove that the points (a, b), (a', b') and $(a - a', b - b')$ are collinear if $ab' = a'b$.
5. Find the value of λ so that the points $(1, -5), (-4, 5)$ and $(\lambda, 7)$ are collinear.
6. Find the value of x if the area of Δ is 35 square cms with vertices $(x, 4), (2, -6)$ and $(5, 4)$.
7. Using determinants, find the area of the triangle whose vertices are $(1, 4), (2, 3)$ and $(-5, -3)$. Are the given points collinear?
8. Using determinants, find the area of the triangle with vertices $(-3, 5), (3, -6)$ and $(7, 2)$.
9. Using determinants, find the value of k so that the points $(k, 2-2k)$, $(-k+1, 2k)$ and $(-4-k, 6-2k)$ may be collinear.
10. If the points $(x, -2), (5, 2)$ and $(8, 8)$ are collinear, find x using determinants.
11. If the points $(3, -2), (x, 2)$ and $(8, 8)$ are collinear, find x using determinant.
12. Using determinants, find the equation of the line joining the points
    (i) $(1, 2)$ and $(3, 6)$ (ii) $(3, 1)$ and $(9, 3)$
13. Find values of k, if area of triangle is 4 square units whose vertices are
    (i) $(k, 0), (4, 0)$ and $(0, 2)$ (ii) $(-2, 0), (0, 4)$ and $(0, k)$
14. Using determinants, find the area of ΔPQR with vertices $P(3, 1)$, $Q(9, 3)$ and $R(5, 7)$. Also, find the equation of line PQ using determinants. [CBSE 2023]

ANSWERS

1. (i) $\frac{75}{2}$ sq. units (ii) $\frac{47}{2}$ sq. units (iii) 15 sq. units (iv) 9 sq. units
5. $\lambda = -5$
6. $x = -2, 12$
7. $\frac{13}{2}$ sq. units, No
8. 46 sq. units
9. $k = -1,\ 1/2$
10. $x = 3$
11. $x = 5$
12. (i) $y = 2x$ (ii) $x = 3y$
13. (i) $k = 0, 8$ (ii) $0, 8$
14. 16 sq. units, $x = 3y$

FILL IN THE BLANKS TYPE QUESTIONS (FBQs)

1. If $A = \text{diag}\,(1, 2, 3)$, then $|A| =$ ....
2. If A is a skew-symmetric matrix of order 3×3, then $|A| =$ .... [CBSE 2020]
3. If the matrix $A = \begin{bmatrix} 1 & 3 & x+2 \\ 2 & 4 & 8 \\ 3 & 5 & 10 \end{bmatrix}$ is singular, then $x =$ ....
4. If A and B are non-singular square matrices of order n such that $A = kB$, then $\frac{|A|}{|B|} =$ ....
5. The set of real values of a for which the matrix $A = \begin{bmatrix} a & 2 \\ 2 & 4 \end{bmatrix}$ is non-singular is ....
6. If A is a 2×2 matrix such that $|A| = 5$, then $|5A| =$ ....
7. If A and B are square matrices of order 3 such that $|A| = -1, |B| = 3$, then $|3AB| =$ .... [CBSE 2020]
8. If $A = \begin{bmatrix} \alpha & 2 \\ 2 & \alpha \end{bmatrix}$ and $|A^3| = 125$, then $\alpha =$ ....
9. If $A = \begin{bmatrix} \ln x & -1 \\ -\ln x & 2 \end{bmatrix}$ and if $\det(A) = 2$, then $x =$ ....
10. If I is the identity matrix of order 10, then determinant of I is ....
11. If $|A|$ denotes the value of the determinant of a square matrix of order 3, then $|-2A| =$ ....
12. Let $A = [a_{ij}]$ be a 3×3 matrix such that $|A| = 5$. If C_{ij} = Cofactor of a_{ij} in A. Then $a_{11} C_{11} + a_{12} C_{12} + a_{13} C_{13} =$ ....
13. In the above question, $a_{11} C_{21} + a_{12} C_{22} + a_{13} C_{23} =$ ....
14. If $A =$ diag (2, 3, 4), then $|A^2| =$ ....
15. Let $A = [a_{ij}]$ be a square matrix of order 3 with $|A| = 2$ and let $C = [c_{ij}]$, where c_{ij} = cofactor of a_{ij} in A. Then, $|C| =$ ....
16. The value of the determinant $\Delta = \begin{vmatrix} 1 & 2 & 3 \\ 4 & 5 & 6 \\ 3x & 6x & 9x \end{vmatrix}$ is ....

17. The value of the determinant $\Delta = \begin{vmatrix} \sec^2\theta & \tan^2\theta & 1 \\ \tan^2\theta & \sec^2\theta & -1 \\ 22 & 20 & 2 \end{vmatrix}$ is ....

18. The value of the determinant $\Delta = \begin{vmatrix} 0 & x-y & y-z \\ y-x & 0 & z-x \\ z-y & x-z & 0 \end{vmatrix}$ is ....

19. Let $A = [a_{ij}]$ and $B = [b_{ij}]$ be a square matrices of order 3 such that

$b_{i1} = 2\,a_{i1},\quad b_{i2} = 3\,a_{i2}$ and $b_{i3} = 4\,a_{i3}, i = 1, 2, 3$

If $|A| = 5$, then $|B| =$ ....

20. If A and B are square matrices of order 3 such that $|A| = -2, |B| = 4$, then $|2AB| =$ ....

21. The value of determinant $\begin{vmatrix} \cos(x+y) & -\sin(x+y) & \cos 2y \\ \sin x & \cos x & \sin y \\ -\cos x & \sin x & \sin y \end{vmatrix}$ depends on.................... only.

[NCERT EXEMPLAR]

22. If $x, y, z \in R$, then the value of the determinant $\begin{vmatrix} (2^x + 2^{-x})^2 & (2^x - 2^{-x})^2 & 1 \\ (3^x + 3^{-x})^2 & (3^x - 3^{-x})^2 & 1 \\ (4^x + 4^{-x})^2 & (4^x - 4^{-x})^2 & 1 \end{vmatrix}$ is equal to............................ . [NCERT EXEMPLAR]

23. If $f(x) = \begin{vmatrix} (1+x)^{17} & (1+x)^{19} & (1+x)^{23} \\ (1+x)^{23} & (1+x)^{29} & (1+x)^{34} \\ (1+x)^{41} & (1+x)^{43} & (1+x)^{47} \end{vmatrix} = A + Bx + Cx^2 +$ ...., then $A =$............ .

[NCERT EXEMPLAR)

24. If $\cos 2\theta = 0$, then $\begin{vmatrix} 0 & \cos\theta & \sin\theta \\ \cos\theta & \sin\theta & 0 \\ \sin\theta & 0 & \cos\theta \end{vmatrix}^2 =$ .... [NCERT EXEMPLAR)

25. If A is a matrix of order 3×3, then the number of minors in A is ....[NCERT EXEMPLAR)

26. If $x = -9$ is a root of $\begin{vmatrix} x & 3 & 7 \\ 2 & x & 2 \\ 7 & 6 & x \end{vmatrix} = 0$, then other two roots are ....[NCERT EXEMPLAR)

27. $\begin{vmatrix} 0 & xyz & x-z \\ y-x & 0 & y-z \\ z-x & z-y & 0 \end{vmatrix} =$............................ . [NCERT EXEMPLAR]

28. If A and B are square matrices of order 3 and $|A| = 5, |B| = 5$, then $|3AB| =$ ....

29. If $\begin{vmatrix} x+1 & x+2 & x+a \\ x+2 & x+3 & x+b \\ x+3 & x+4 & x+c \end{vmatrix} = 0$, then a, b, c are in............................ .

30. The value of the determinant $\begin{vmatrix} \sin A & \cos A & \sin A+\cos B \\ \sin B & \cos A & \sin B+\cos B \\ \sin C & \cos A & \sin C+\cos B \end{vmatrix}$ is.............................. .

31. If the determinant $\begin{vmatrix} x+a & p+u & l+f \\ y+b & q+v & m+g \\ z+c & r+w & n+h \end{vmatrix}$ splits into exactly k determinants of order 3, each element of which contains only one term, then $k=$ ....

32. The maximum value of $\begin{vmatrix} 1 & 1 & 1 \\ 1 & 1+\sin\theta & 1 \\ 1 & 1 & 1+\cos\theta \end{vmatrix}$ is ....

33. If A, B, C are the angles of a triangle, then $\begin{vmatrix} \sin^2 A & \cot A & 1 \\ \sin^2 B & \cot B & 1 \\ \sin^2 C & \cot C & 1 \end{vmatrix} =$ ....[NCERT EXEMPLAR]

34. The determinant $A=\begin{vmatrix} \sqrt{23}+\sqrt{3} & \sqrt{5} & \sqrt{5} \\ \sqrt{15}+\sqrt{46} & 5 & \sqrt{10} \\ 3+\sqrt{115} & \sqrt{15} & 5 \end{vmatrix}$ is equal to is equal to.............

[NCERT EXEMPLAR]

35. The value of the determinant $\Delta=\begin{vmatrix} \sin^2 33° & \sin^2 57° & \cos 180° \\ -\sin^2 57° & -\sin^2 33° & \cos^2 180° \\ \cos 180° & \sin^2 33° & \sin^2 57° \end{vmatrix}$ is equal to ....

[NCERT EXEMPLAR]

36. If $\begin{vmatrix} 2-x & 2+x & 2+x \\ 2+x & 2-x & 2+x \\ 2+x & 2+x & 2-x \end{vmatrix}=0$, then $x=$ .... [NCERT EXEMPLAR]

37. If A is a square matrix of order 3 and $|A|=2$, then $|-AA^T|=$ .... [CBSE 2020]

38. If $A=\begin{bmatrix} 3 & -5 \\ 2 & 0 \end{bmatrix}$ and $B=\begin{bmatrix} 1 & 17 \\ 0 & -10 \end{bmatrix}$, then $|AB|=$.................... [CBSE 2020]

ANSWERS

1. 6
2. 0
3. 4
4. k^n
5. $R-\{1\}$
6. 125
7. −81
8. ± 3
9. e^2
10. 1
11. $-8|A|$
12. 5
13. 0
14. 576
15. 4
16. 0
17. 0
18. 0
19. 120
20. − 64
21. y
22. zero
23. zero
24. $\frac{1}{2}$
25. 9
26. 2, 7
27. $(y-z)(z-x)(y-x+xyz)$
28. 405
29. AP
30. zero
31. 8
32. $\frac{1}{2}$
33. zero
34. zero
35. zero
36. 0, − 6
37. − 4
38. − 100

VERY SHORT ANSWER QUESTIONS (VSAQs)

Answer each of the following questions in one word or one sentence or as per exact requirement of the question:

1. If A is a singular matrix, then write the value of $|A|$.
2. For what value of x, the matrix $\begin{bmatrix} 5-x & x+1 \\ 2 & 4 \end{bmatrix}$ is singular? [CBSE 2011]
3. Write the value of the determinant $\begin{vmatrix} 2 & 3 & 4 \\ 2x & 3x & 4x \\ 5 & 6 & 8 \end{vmatrix}$.
4. State whether the matrix $\begin{bmatrix} 2 & 3 \\ 6 & 4 \end{bmatrix}$ is singular or nonsingular.
5. Find the value of the determinant $\begin{vmatrix} 4200 & 4201 \\ 4202 & 4203 \end{vmatrix}$.
6. Find the value of the determinant $\begin{vmatrix} 101 & 102 & 103 \\ 104 & 105 & 106 \\ 107 & 108 & 109 \end{vmatrix}$
7. Write the value of the determinant $\begin{vmatrix} a & 1 & b+c \\ b & 1 & c+a \\ c & 1 & a+b \end{vmatrix}$.
8. If $A = \begin{bmatrix} 0 & i \\ i & 1 \end{bmatrix}$ and $B = \begin{bmatrix} 0 & 1 \\ 1 & 0 \end{bmatrix}$, find the value of $|A| + |B|$.
9. If $A = \begin{bmatrix} 1 & 2 \\ 3 & -1 \end{bmatrix}$ and $B = \begin{bmatrix} 1 & 0 \\ -1 & 0 \end{bmatrix}$, find $|AB|$.
10. Evaluate: $\begin{vmatrix} 4785 & 4787 \\ 4789 & 4791 \end{vmatrix}$.
11. If w is an imaginary cube root of unity, find the value of $\begin{vmatrix} 1 & w & w^2 \\ w & w^2 & 1 \\ w^2 & 1 & w \end{vmatrix}$.
12. If $A = \begin{bmatrix} 1 & 2 \\ 3 & -1 \end{bmatrix}$ and $B = \begin{bmatrix} 1 & -4 \\ 3 & -2 \end{bmatrix}$, find $|AB|$.
13. If $A = [a_{ij}]$ is a 3×3 diagonal matrix such that $a_{11} = 1$, $a_{22} = 2$ and $a_{33} = 3$, then find $|A|$.
14. If $A = [a_{ij}]$ is a 3×3 scalar matrix such that $a_{11} = 2$, then write the value of $|A|$.
15. If I_3 denotes identity matrix of order 3×3, write the value of its determinant.
16. A matrix A of order 3×3 has determinant 5. What is the value of $|3A|$? [CBSE 2012]
17. On expanding by first row, the value of the determinant of 3×3 square matrix $A = [a_{ij}]$ is $a_{11}C_{11} + a_{12}C_{12} + a_{13}C_{13}$, where C_{ij} is the cofactor of a_{ij} in A. Write the expression for its value on expanding by second column.
18. Let $A = [a_{ij}]$ be a square matrix of order 3×3 and C_{ij} denote cofactor of a_{ij} in A. If $|A| = 5$, write the value of $a_{31}C_{31} + a_{32}C_{32} + a_{33}C_{33}$.
19. In question 18, write the value of $a_{11}C_{21} + a_{12}C_{22} + a_{13}C_{23}$. [CBSE 2020]

20. Write the value of $\begin{vmatrix} \sin 20^\circ & -\cos 20^\circ \\ \sin 70^\circ & \cos 70^\circ \end{vmatrix}$.

21. If A is a square matrix satisfying $A^T A = I$, write the value of $|A|$.

22. If A and B are square matrices of the same order such that $|A| = 3$ and $AB = I$, then write the value of $|B|$.

23. A is a skew-symmetric of order 3, write the value of $|A|$.

24. If A is a square matrix of order 3 with determinant 4, then write the value of $|-A|$.

25. If A is a square matrix such that $|A| = 2$, write the value of $|AA^T|$.

26. Find the value of the determinant $\begin{vmatrix} 243 & 156 & 300 \\ 81 & 52 & 100 \\ -3 & 0 & 4 \end{vmatrix}$.

27. Write the value of the determinant $\begin{vmatrix} 2 & -3 & 5 \\ 4 & -6 & 10 \\ 6 & -9 & 15 \end{vmatrix}$.

28. If the matrix $\begin{bmatrix} 5x & 2 \\ -10 & 1 \end{bmatrix}$ is singular, find the value of x.

29. If A is a square matrix of order $n \times n$ such that $|A| = \lambda$, then write the value of $|-A|$.

30. Find the value of the determinant $\begin{vmatrix} 2^2 & 2^3 & 2^4 \\ 2^3 & 2^4 & 2^5 \\ 2^4 & 2^5 & 2^6 \end{vmatrix}$.

31. If A and B are non-singular matrices of the same order, write whether AB is singular or non-singular.

32. A matrix of order 3×3 has determinant 2. What is the value of $|A(3I)|$, where I is the identy matrix of order 3×3.

33. If A and B are square matrices of order 3 such that $|A| = -1$, $|B| = 3$, then find the value of $|3AB|$.

34. Write the value of $\begin{vmatrix} a+ib & c+id \\ -c+id & a-ib \end{vmatrix}$. [CBSE 2008]

35. Write the cofactor of a_{12} in the matrix $\begin{bmatrix} 2 & -3 & 5 \\ 6 & 0 & 4 \\ 1 & 5 & -7 \end{bmatrix}$. [CBSE 2008]

36. If $\begin{vmatrix} 2x+5 & 3 \\ 5x+2 & 9 \end{vmatrix} = 0$, find x. [CBSE 2008]

37. Find the value of x from the following: $\begin{vmatrix} x & 4 \\ 2 & 2x \end{vmatrix} = 0$ [CBSE 2009]

38. Write the value of the determinant $\begin{vmatrix} 2 & 3 & 4 \\ 5 & 6 & 8 \\ 6x & 9x & 12x \end{vmatrix}$ [CBSE 2009]

39. If $|A| = 2$, where A is 2×2 matrix, find $|\text{adj } A|$. [CBSE 2010]

40. What is the value of the determinant $\begin{vmatrix} 0 & 2 & 0 \\ 2 & 3 & 4 \\ 4 & 5 & 6 \end{vmatrix}$? [CBSE 2010]

41. For what value of x is the matrix $\begin{bmatrix} 6-x & 4 \\ 3-x & 1 \end{bmatrix}$ singular? [CBSE 2011]

42. A matrix A of order 3×3 is such that $|A| = 4$. Find the value of $|2A|$. [CBSE 2011]

43. Evaluate: $\begin{vmatrix} \cos 15° & \sin 15° \\ \sin 75° & \cos 75° \end{vmatrix}$. [CBSE 2011]

44. If $A = \begin{bmatrix} 5 & 3 & 8 \\ 2 & 0 & 1 \\ 1 & 2 & 3 \end{bmatrix}$. Write the cofactor of the element a_{32}. [CBSE 2012]

45. If $\begin{vmatrix} x+1 & x-1 \\ x-3 & x+2 \end{vmatrix} = \begin{vmatrix} 4 & -1 \\ 1 & 3 \end{vmatrix}$, then write the value of x. [CBSE 2013]

46. If $\begin{vmatrix} 2x & x+3 \\ 2(x+1) & x+1 \end{vmatrix} = \begin{vmatrix} 1 & 5 \\ 3 & 3 \end{vmatrix}$, then write the value of x. [CBSE 2013]

47. If $\begin{vmatrix} 3x & 7 \\ -2 & 4 \end{vmatrix} = \begin{vmatrix} 8 & 7 \\ 6 & 4 \end{vmatrix}$, find the value of x. [CBSE 2014]

48. If $\begin{vmatrix} 2x & 5 \\ 8 & x \end{vmatrix} = \begin{vmatrix} 6 & -2 \\ 7 & 3 \end{vmatrix}$, write the value of x. [CBSE 2014]

49. If A is a 3×3 matrix, $|A| \neq 0$ and $|3A| = k|A|$ then write the value of k. [CBSE 2014]

50. Write the value of the determinant $\begin{vmatrix} p & p+1 \\ p-1 & p \end{vmatrix}$. [CBSE 2014]

51. Write the value of the determinant $\begin{vmatrix} x+y & y+z & z+x \\ z & x & y \\ -3 & -3 & -3 \end{vmatrix}$. [CBSE 2015]

52. If $A = \begin{bmatrix} \cos\theta & \sin\theta \\ -\sin\theta & \cos\theta \end{bmatrix}$, then for any natural number, find the value of Det (A^n). [CBSE 2015]

53. Find the maximum value of $\begin{vmatrix} 1 & 1 & 1 \\ 1 & 1+\sin\theta & 1 \\ 1 & 1 & 1+\cos\theta \end{vmatrix}$ [CBSE 2016]

54. If $x \in N$ and $\begin{vmatrix} x+3 & -2 \\ -3x & 2x \end{vmatrix} = 8$, then find the value of x. [CBSE 2016]

55. If $\begin{vmatrix} x & \sin\theta & \cos\theta \\ -\sin\theta & -x & 1 \\ \cos\theta & 1 & x \end{vmatrix} = 8$, write the value of x. [CBSE 2016]

56. If A is a 3×3 matrix, then what will be the value of k if Det $(A^{-1}) = (\text{Det } A)^k$? [CBSE 2017]

57. A and B are square matrices of the same order 3, such that $AB = 2I$ and $|A| = 2$, write the value of $|B|$. [CBSE 2019]

58. A square matrix A is said to be singular, if .... [CBSE 2020]

ANSWERS

1. 0	2. 3	3. 0	4. Non-singular	5. -2	6. 0	7. 0
8. 0	9. 0	10. -8	11. 0	12. -70	13. 6	14. 8
15. 1	16. 135	17. $a_{12}C_{12} + a_{22}C_{22} + a_{32}C_{32}$	18. 5	19. 0	20. 1	21. ± 1
22. 1/3	23. 0	24. -4	25. 4	26. 0	27. 0	28. -4
29. $(-1)^n \lambda$	30. 0	31. Non-singular	32. 54	33. -81	34. $a^2 + b^2 + c^2 + d^2$	35. 46
36. -13	37. ± 2	38. 0	39. 8	40. 8	41. 2	42. 32
43. 0	44. 11	45. 2	46. 1	47. -2	48. ± 6	49. 27
50. 1	51. 0	52. 1	53. $\frac{1}{2}$	54. ± 2	55. $-2, -2w, -2w^2$	56. $k = -1$
57. 4	58. 0					

CHAPTER 6

ADJOINT AND INVERSE OF A MATRIX

6.1 ADJOINT OF A SQUARE MATRIX

ADJOINT *Let $A = [a_{ij}]$ be a square matrix of order n and let C_{ij} be cofactor of a_{ij} in A. Then the transpose of the matrix of cofactors of elements of A is called the adjoint of A and is denoted by adj A.*

Thus, $\text{adj } A = [C_{ij}]^T \Rightarrow (\text{adj } A)_{ij} = C_{ji}$ = Cofactor of a_{ji} in A.

If $$A = \begin{bmatrix} a_{11} & a_{12} & a_{13} \\ a_{21} & a_{22} & a_{23} \\ a_{31} & a_{32} & a_{33} \end{bmatrix}, \text{ then, adj } A = \begin{bmatrix} C_{11} & C_{12} & C_{13} \\ C_{21} & C_{22} & C_{23} \\ C_{31} & C_{32} & C_{33} \end{bmatrix}^T = \begin{bmatrix} C_{11} & C_{21} & C_{31} \\ C_{12} & C_{22} & C_{32} \\ C_{13} & C_{23} & C_{33} \end{bmatrix},$$

where C_{ij} denotes the cofactor of a_{ij} in A.

ILLUSTRATION 1 *Find the adjoint of matrix* $A = [a_{ij}] = \begin{bmatrix} p & q \\ r & s \end{bmatrix}$.

SOLUTION We have,

Cofactor of $a_{11} = s$, Cofactor of $a_{12} = -r$, Cofactor of $a_{21} = -q$ and, Cofactor of $a_{22} = p$.

$$\therefore \quad \text{adj } A = \begin{bmatrix} s & -r \\ -q & p \end{bmatrix}^T = \begin{bmatrix} s & -q \\ -r & p \end{bmatrix}$$

RULE *It is evident from this example that the adjoint of a square matrix of order 2 can be easily obtained by interchanging the diagonal elements and changing signs of off-diagonal elements.*

If $A = \begin{bmatrix} -2 & 3 \\ -5 & 4 \end{bmatrix}$, *then by the above rule, we obtain* adj $A = \begin{bmatrix} 4 & -3 \\ 5 & -2 \end{bmatrix}$.

ILLUSTRATION 2 *Find the adjoint of matrix* $A = [a_{ij}] = \begin{bmatrix} 1 & 1 & 1 \\ 2 & 1 & -3 \\ -1 & 2 & 3 \end{bmatrix}$.

SOLUTION Let C_{ij} be cofactor of a_{ij} in A. Then, the cofactors of elements of A are given by

$$C_{11} = \begin{vmatrix} 1 & -3 \\ 2 & 3 \end{vmatrix} = 9, \quad C_{12} = -\begin{vmatrix} 2 & -3 \\ -1 & 3 \end{vmatrix} = -3, \quad C_{13} = \begin{vmatrix} 2 & 1 \\ -1 & 2 \end{vmatrix} = 5$$

$$C_{21} = -\begin{vmatrix} 1 & 1 \\ 2 & 3 \end{vmatrix} = -1, \quad C_{22} = \begin{vmatrix} 1 & 1 \\ -1 & 3 \end{vmatrix} = 4, \quad C_{23} = -\begin{vmatrix} 1 & 1 \\ -1 & 2 \end{vmatrix} = -3$$

$$C_{31} = \begin{vmatrix} 1 & 1 \\ 1 & -3 \end{vmatrix} = -4, \quad C_{32} = -\begin{vmatrix} 1 & 1 \\ 2 & -3 \end{vmatrix} = 5, \quad C_{33} = \begin{vmatrix} 1 & 1 \\ 2 & 1 \end{vmatrix} = -1$$

$$\therefore \quad \text{adj } A = \begin{bmatrix} 9 & -3 & 5 \\ -1 & 4 & -3 \\ -4 & 5 & -1 \end{bmatrix}^T = \begin{bmatrix} 9 & -1 & -4 \\ -3 & 4 & 5 \\ 5 & -3 & -1 \end{bmatrix}$$

THEOREM 1 *Let A be a square matrix of order n. Then,* $A\,(\text{adj } A) = |A|\, I_n = (\text{adj } A)\, A$.

PROOF Let $A = [a_{ij}]$, and let C_{ij} be cofactor of a_{ij} in A. Then,

$$(\text{adj } A)_{ij} = C_{ji} \quad \text{for all } i, j = 1, 2, \ldots, n$$

Since A and adj A are both square matrices of the same order $n \times n$. Therefore, both A (adj A) and (adj A) A exist and are of the same order $n \times n$.

Now,

$$(A\,(\text{adj } A))_{ij} = \sum_{r=1}^{n} (A)_{ir}\,(\text{adj } A)_{rj} \quad \text{[By definition of multiplication of two matrices]}$$

$$= \sum_{r=1}^{n} a_{ir}\,C_{rj} = \begin{cases} |A| & , \text{ if } i = j \\ 0 & , \text{ if } i \neq j \end{cases} \quad \text{[By property 1 and 2 of section 5.4]}$$

Thus, each diagonal element of A (adj A) is equal to $|A|$ and all non-diagonal elements are equal to zero.

$$\therefore \quad A\,(\text{adj } A) = \begin{bmatrix} |A| & 0 & 0 & \ldots & 0 \\ 0 & |A| & 0 & \ldots & 0 \\ 0 & 0 & |A| & \ldots & 0 \\ \vdots & \vdots & \vdots & & \\ 0 & 0 & 0 & \ldots & |A| \end{bmatrix} = |A|\,I_n$$

Similarly, we obtain

$$((\text{adj } A)\,A)_{ij} = \sum_{r=1}^{n} (\text{adj } A)_{ir}\,(A)_{rj}$$

$$\Rightarrow \quad ((\text{adj } A)\,A)_{ij} = \sum_{r=1}^{n} C_{ri}\,a_{rj}$$

$$\Rightarrow \quad ((\text{adj } A)\,A)_{ij} = \begin{cases} |A| & , \text{ if } i = j \\ 0 & , \text{ if } i \neq j \end{cases} \quad \text{[By property 1 and 2 of section 5.4]}$$

Hence, $A\,(\text{adj } A) = |A|\,I_n = (\text{adj } A)\,A$.

Q.E.D.

ILLUSTRATION 3 *Compute the adjoint of the matrix A given by* $A = \begin{bmatrix} 1 & 4 & 5 \\ 3 & 2 & 6 \\ 0 & 1 & 0 \end{bmatrix}$ *and verify that* $A\,(\text{adj } A) = |A|\,I = (\text{adj } A)\,A$.

SOLUTION We have,

$$|A| = \begin{vmatrix} 1 & 4 & 5 \\ 3 & 2 & 6 \\ 0 & 1 & 0 \end{vmatrix} = 1\,(0-6) - 4\,(0-0) + 5\,(3-0) = 9$$

Let C_{ij} be cofactor of a_{ij} in A. Then, the cofactors of elements of A are given by

$$C_{11} = \begin{vmatrix} 2 & 6 \\ 1 & 0 \end{vmatrix} = -6, \quad C_{12} = -\begin{vmatrix} 3 & 6 \\ 0 & 0 \end{vmatrix} = 0, \quad C_{13} = \begin{vmatrix} 3 & 2 \\ 0 & 1 \end{vmatrix} = 3$$

$$C_{21} = -\begin{vmatrix} 4 & 5 \\ 1 & 0 \end{vmatrix} = 5, \quad C_{22} = \begin{vmatrix} 1 & 5 \\ 0 & 0 \end{vmatrix} = 0, \quad C_{23} = -\begin{vmatrix} 1 & 4 \\ 0 & 1 \end{vmatrix} = -1$$

$$C_{31} = \begin{vmatrix} 4 & 5 \\ 2 & 6 \end{vmatrix} = 14, \quad C_{32} = -\begin{vmatrix} 1 & 5 \\ 3 & 6 \end{vmatrix} = 9, \quad C_{33} = \begin{vmatrix} 1 & 4 \\ 3 & 2 \end{vmatrix} = -10$$

$$\therefore \quad \text{adj } A = \begin{bmatrix} -6 & 0 & 3 \\ 5 & 0 & -1 \\ 14 & 9 & -10 \end{bmatrix}^T = \begin{bmatrix} -6 & 5 & 14 \\ 0 & 0 & 9 \\ 3 & -1 & -10 \end{bmatrix}$$

Now, $A(\text{adj } A) = \begin{bmatrix} 1 & 4 & 5 \\ 3 & 2 & 6 \\ 0 & 1 & 0 \end{bmatrix} \begin{bmatrix} -6 & 5 & 14 \\ 0 & 0 & 9 \\ 3 & -1 & -10 \end{bmatrix} = \begin{bmatrix} 9 & 0 & 0 \\ 0 & 9 & 0 \\ 0 & 0 & 9 \end{bmatrix} = 9 \begin{bmatrix} 1 & 0 & 0 \\ 0 & 1 & 0 \\ 0 & 0 & 1 \end{bmatrix} = |A| I$

and, $(\text{adj } A) A = \begin{bmatrix} -6 & 5 & 14 \\ 0 & 0 & 9 \\ 3 & -1 & -10 \end{bmatrix} \begin{bmatrix} 1 & 4 & 5 \\ 3 & 2 & 6 \\ 0 & 1 & 0 \end{bmatrix} = \begin{bmatrix} 9 & 0 & 0 \\ 0 & 9 & 0 \\ 0 & 0 & 9 \end{bmatrix} = 9 \begin{bmatrix} 1 & 0 & 0 \\ 0 & 1 & 0 \\ 0 & 0 & 1 \end{bmatrix} = |A| I$

Hence, $A(\text{adj } A) = |A| I = (\text{adj } A) A$.

6.2 INVERSE OF A MATRIX

INVERSE *A square matrix of order n is invertible if there exists a square matrix B of the same order such that* $AB = I_n = BA$.

In such a case, we say that the inverse of A is B and we write, $A^{-1} = B$.

THEOREM 1 *Every invertible matrix possesses a unique inverse.*

PROOF Let A be an invertible matrix of order $n \times n$. Let B and C be two inverses of A. Then,

$AB = BA = I_n$ ...(i) and $AC = CA = I_n$ ...(ii)

Now, $AB = I_n$

$\Rightarrow C(AB) = C I_n$ [Pre-multiplying both sides by C)

$\Rightarrow (CA) B = C I_n$ [By associativity of multiplication]

$\Rightarrow I_n B = C I_n$ [$\because CA = I_n$ from (ii)]

$\Rightarrow B = C$ [$\because I_n B = B$ and $C I_n = C$]

Hence, an invertible matrix possesses a unique inverse.

Q.E.D.

COROLLARY *If A is an invertible matrix, then* $(A^{-1})^{-1} = A$.

PROOF Since A^{-1} is inverse of A. Therefore,

$AA^{-1} = I = A^{-1} A \Rightarrow A$ is the inverse of A^{-1} i.e. $A = (A^{-1})^{-1}$.

THEOREM 2 *A square matrix is invertible iff it is non-singular.*

PROOF Let A be an invertible matrix. Then, there exists a matrix B such that

$AB = I_n = BA$

$\Rightarrow |AB| = |I_n|$

$\Rightarrow |A|\,|B| = 1$ [$\because |AB| = |A||B|$]

$\Rightarrow |A| \neq 0 \Rightarrow A$ is a non-singular matrix.

Conversely, let A be a non-singular square matrix of order n. Then,

$A(\text{adj } A) = |A| I_n = (\text{adj } A) A$ [See Theorem 1 on page 6.1]

$\Rightarrow A\left(\frac{1}{|A|} \text{adj } A\right) = I_n = \left(\frac{1}{|A|} \text{adj } A\right) A$ $\left[\because |A| \neq 0 \;\therefore\; \frac{1}{|A|} \text{ exists}\right]$

$\Rightarrow A^{-1} = \frac{1}{|A|} \text{adj } A$ [By definition of inverse]

Hence, A is an invertible matrix such that $A^{-1} = \frac{1}{|A|} \text{adj } A$.

Q.E.D.

REMARK *This theorem provides us a formula for finding the inverse of a non-singular square matrix. The inverse of A is given by*

$$A^{-1} = \frac{1}{|A|} \cdot \text{adj } A$$

In order to find the inverse of a square matrix, we may use the following algorithm.

ALGORITHM

Step I *Find* $|A|$

Step II *If* $|A| = 0$, *then write "A is a singular matrix and hence not invertible".*
Else write "A is a non-singular and hence invertible".

Step III *Calculate the cofactors of elements of A.*

Step IV *Write the matrix of cofactors of elements of A and then obtain its transpose to obtain adj A.*

Step V *Find the inverse of A by using the formula:* $A^{-1} = \frac{1}{|A|}\text{ adj } A$.

ILLUSTRATION 1 *Find the inverse of the matrix* $\begin{bmatrix} 2 & -1 \\ 3 & 4 \end{bmatrix}$.

SOLUTION Let $A = \begin{bmatrix} 2 & -1 \\ 3 & 4 \end{bmatrix}$. Then, $|A| = \begin{vmatrix} 2 & -1 \\ 3 & 4 \end{vmatrix} = 8 + 3 = 11 \neq 0$.

So, A is a non-singular matrix and therefore it is invertible. Let C_{ij} be cofactor of a_{ij} in A. Then, the cofactors of elements of A are given by

$$C_{11} = 4,\ C_{12} = -3,\ C_{21} = -(-1) = 1 \text{ and } C_{22} = 2.$$

$$\therefore \quad adj\ A = \begin{bmatrix} 4 & -3 \\ 1 & 2 \end{bmatrix}^T = \begin{bmatrix} 4 & 1 \\ -3 & 2 \end{bmatrix}$$

Hence, $A^{-1} = \frac{1}{|A|}\, adj\ A = \frac{1}{11}\begin{bmatrix} 4 & 1 \\ -3 & 2 \end{bmatrix} = \begin{bmatrix} 4/11 & 1/11 \\ -3/11 & 2/11 \end{bmatrix}$

ILLUSTRATION 2 *Find the inverse of the matrix* $A = \begin{bmatrix} 8 & 4 & 2 \\ 2 & 9 & 4 \\ 1 & 2 & 8 \end{bmatrix}$.

SOLUTION We find that

$$|A| = \begin{vmatrix} 8 & 4 & 2 \\ 2 & 9 & 4 \\ 1 & 2 & 8 \end{vmatrix} = 8\,(72-8) - 4\,(16-4) + 2\,(4-9) = 454 \neq 0$$

Thus, A is a non-singular matrix and hence it is invertible. Let C_{ij} be cofactor of a_{ij} in A. Then,

$$C_{11} = \begin{vmatrix} 9 & 4 \\ 2 & 8 \end{vmatrix} = 64, \quad C_{12} = -\begin{vmatrix} 2 & 4 \\ 1 & 8 \end{vmatrix} = -12, \quad C_{13} = \begin{vmatrix} 2 & 9 \\ 1 & 2 \end{vmatrix} = -5$$

$$C_{21} = -\begin{vmatrix} 4 & 2 \\ 2 & 8 \end{vmatrix} = -28, \quad C_{22} = \begin{vmatrix} 8 & 2 \\ 1 & 8 \end{vmatrix} = 62, \quad C_{23} = -\begin{vmatrix} 8 & 4 \\ 1 & 2 \end{vmatrix} = -12$$

$$C_{31} = \begin{vmatrix} 4 & 2 \\ 9 & 4 \end{vmatrix} = -2, \quad C_{32} = -\begin{vmatrix} 8 & 2 \\ 2 & 4 \end{vmatrix} = -28, \quad C_{33} = \begin{vmatrix} 8 & 4 \\ 2 & 9 \end{vmatrix} = 64$$

$$\therefore \quad \text{adj } A = \begin{bmatrix} 64 & -12 & -5 \\ -28 & 62 & -12 \\ -2 & -28 & 64 \end{bmatrix}^T = \begin{bmatrix} 64 & -28 & -2 \\ -12 & 62 & -28 \\ -5 & -12 & 64 \end{bmatrix}$$

Hence, $A^{-1} = \frac{1}{|A|}\text{ adj } A = \frac{1}{454}\begin{bmatrix} 64 & -28 & -2 \\ -12 & 62 & -28 \\ -5 & -12 & 64 \end{bmatrix}$

6.3 SOME USEFUL RESULTS ON INVERTIBLE MATRICES

In this section, we shall discuss some useful results on inverse of a matrix. We shall state and prove these results as theorems given below.

THEOREM 1 *(Cancellation Laws) Let A, B, C be square matrices of the same order n. If A is a non-singular matrix, then*

(i) $AB = AC \Rightarrow B = C$ [*Left cancellation law*] (ii) $BA = CA \Rightarrow B = C$ [*Right Cancellation law*]

PROOF (i) Since A is a non-singular matrix i.e. $|A| \neq 0$. So, A^{-1} exists.

Now, $AB = AC$

$\Rightarrow A^{-1}(AB) = A^{-1}(AC)$ [Pre-multiplying both sides by A^{-1}]

$\Rightarrow (A^{-1}A)B = (A^{-1}A)C$ [By associativity of multiplication]

$\Rightarrow I_n B = I_n C$ [$\because A^{-1}A = I_n$]

$\Rightarrow B = C$ [$\because I_n B = B$ and $I_n C = C$]

Similarly, we can prove that $BA = CA \Rightarrow B = C$.

Q.E.D.

REMARK *The result $AB = AC \Rightarrow B = C$ is true only when $|A| \neq 0$. Otherwise we can find matrices such that $AB = AC$ but $B \neq C$ as given below.*

Let $A = \begin{bmatrix} 1 & 2 \\ 3 & 6 \end{bmatrix}, B = \begin{bmatrix} -2 & 0 \\ 0 & 0 \end{bmatrix}, C = \begin{bmatrix} 0 & 0 \\ -1 & 0 \end{bmatrix}$. *Then*

$AB = \begin{bmatrix} 1 & 2 \\ 3 & 6 \end{bmatrix}\begin{bmatrix} -2 & 0 \\ 0 & 0 \end{bmatrix} = \begin{bmatrix} -2 & 0 \\ -6 & 0 \end{bmatrix}$ *and* $AC = \begin{bmatrix} 1 & 2 \\ 3 & 6 \end{bmatrix}\begin{bmatrix} 0 & 0 \\ -1 & 0 \end{bmatrix} = \begin{bmatrix} -2 & 0 \\ -6 & 0 \end{bmatrix}$.

Clearly, $AB = AC$ but $B \neq C$.

THEOREM 2 *(Reversal Law) If A and B are invertible matrices of the same order, then show that AB is invertible and $(AB)^{-1} = B^{-1}A^{-1}$.*

PROOF It is given that A and B are invertible matrices.

$\therefore |A| \neq 0$ and $|B| \neq 0 \Rightarrow |A|\,|B| \neq 0 \Rightarrow |AB| \neq 0$ [$\because |AB| = |A|\,|B|$]

$\Rightarrow AB$ is a invertible matrix.

Now,

$(AB)(B^{-1}A^{-1}) = A(BB^{-1})A^{-1}$ [By associativity of multiplication]

$\Rightarrow (AB)(B^{-1}A^{-1}) = (AI_n)A^{-1}$ [$\because BB^{-1} = I_n$]

$\Rightarrow (AB)(B^{-1}A^{-1}) = AA^{-1}$ [$\because AI_n = A$]

$\Rightarrow (AB)(B^{-1}A^{-1}) = I_n$ [$\because AA^{-1} = I_n$]

and, $(B^{-1}A^{-1})(AB) = B^{-1}(A^{-1}A)B$ [By associativity of multiplication]

$\Rightarrow (B^{-1}A^{-1})(AB) = B^{-1}(I_n B)$ [$\because A^{-1}A = I_n$]

$\Rightarrow (B^{-1}A^{-1})(AB) = B^{-1}B$ [$\because I_n B = B$]

$\Rightarrow (B^{-1}A^{-1})(AB) = I_n$ [$\because B^{-1}B = I_n$]

Thus, $(AB)(B^{-1}A^{-1}) = I_n = (B^{-1}A^{-1})(AB)$.

Hence, $(AB)^{-1} = B^{-1}A^{-1}$. Q.E.D

REMARK *If A, B, C are invertible matrices, of the same order then $(ABC)^{-1} = C^{-1}B^{-1}A^{-1}$.*

THEOREM 3 *If A is an invertible square matrix, then A^T is also invertible and $(A^T)^{-1} = (A^{-1})^T$.*

PROOF Since A is invertible matrix.

$\therefore |A| \neq 0 \Rightarrow |A^T| \neq 0 \Rightarrow A^T$ is also invertible [$\because |A^T| = |A|$]

Now,

$$AA^{-1} = I_n = A^{-1}A$$

$\Rightarrow \quad (AA^{-1})^T = (I_n)^T = (A^{-1}A)^T$

$\Rightarrow \quad (A^{-1})^T (A^T) = I_n = A^T (A^{-1})^T$ [By reversal law for transpose]

$\Rightarrow \quad (A^T)^{-1} = (A^{-1})^T$ [By definition of inverse]

Q.E.D

THEOREM 4 *The inverse of an invertible symmetric matrix is a symmetric matrix.*

PROOF Let A be an invertible symmetric matrix. Then, $|A| \neq 0$ and $A^T = A$.

Now, $(A^{-1})^T = (A^T)^{-1} = A^{-1}$ [$\because A^T = A$]

$\therefore \quad A^{-1}$ is a symmetric matrix.

ALITER Let A be a non-singular symmetric matrix. Then, A^{-1} exists.

Now, $AA^{-1} = I = A^{-1}A$

$\Rightarrow \quad (AA^{-1})^T = (I)^T = (A^{-1}A)^T$

$\Rightarrow \quad (A^{-1})^T A^T = I = A^T (A^{-1})^T$

$\Rightarrow \quad (A^{-1})^T A = I = A(A^{-1})^T$ [$\because A^T = A$]

$\Rightarrow \quad A^{-1} = (A^{-1})^T$ [By definition of inverse]

$\Rightarrow \quad A^{-1}$ is symmetric.

Q.E.D

THEOREM 5 *Let A be a non-singular square matrix of order n. Then, $|\text{adj } A| = |A|^{n-1}$.*

PROOF We have,

$$A(\text{adj } A) = |A| I_n$$

$$\Rightarrow \quad A(\text{adj } A) = \begin{bmatrix} |A| & 0 & 0 & \dots & 0 \\ 0 & |A| & 0 & \dots & 0 \\ 0 & 0 & |A| & \dots & 0 \\ \vdots & \vdots & \vdots & & \\ 0 & 0 & 0 & \dots & |A| \end{bmatrix}_{n \times n}$$

$$\Rightarrow \quad |A(\text{adj } A)| = \begin{vmatrix} |A| & 0 & 0 & \dots & 0 \\ 0 & |A| & 0 & \dots & 0 \\ 0 & 0 & |A| & \dots & 0 \\ \vdots & \vdots & \vdots & & \\ 0 & 0 & 0 & \dots & |A| \end{vmatrix} = |A|^n$$

$\Rightarrow \quad |A| |\text{adj } A| = |A|^n$ [$\because |AB| = |A| |B|$]

$\Rightarrow \quad |\text{adj } A| = |A|^{n-1}$.

Q.E.D

ILLUSTRATION 1 *If A is an invertible matrix of order 3 and $|A| = 5$, then find $|\text{adj } A|$.* **[CBSE 2009]**

SOLUTION Here A is an invertible matrix of order 3.

$\therefore \quad |\text{adj } A| = |A|^2$ [Using: $|\text{adj } A| = |A|^{n-1}$]

$\Rightarrow \quad |\text{adj } A| = 5^2 = 25$ [$\because |A| = 5$ (given)]

THEOREM 6 *If A and B are non-singular square matrices of the same order, then*

$$\text{adj } AB = (\text{adj } B)(\text{adj } A)$$

PROOF Since A and B are non-singular square matrices of the same order. Therefore, AB exists such that $|AB| = |A||B| \neq 0$ [$\because |A| \neq 0, |B| \neq 0$]

We know that $(AB)\,(\text{adj } AB) = |AB|\, I_n$ ...(i)

Also, $(AB)\,(\text{adj } B \text{ adj } A) = (A\,(B \cdot \text{adj } B)\text{ adj } A)$ [By associativity of multiplication]

$= (A\,|B|\,I_n)\text{ adj } A$ [$\because$ $B \text{ adj } B = |B|\, I_n$]

$= |B|\,(A \text{ adj } A)$ [$\because$ $A\, I_n = A$]

$= |B|(\,|A|\, I_n)$ [$\because$ $A \text{ adj } A = |A|\, I_n$]

$= |A|\;|B|\, I_n$

$= |AB|\, I_n$ [$\because$ $|AB| = |A|\;|B|$]

Thus, $(AB)\,(\text{adj } B \text{ adj } A) = |AB|\, I_n$ ...(ii)

From (i) and (ii), we get

$$(AB)\,(\text{adj } AB) = (AB)\,(\text{adj } B \cdot \text{adj } A)$$

$$\Rightarrow \quad (AB)^{-1}\,((AB)\,(\text{adj } AB)) = (AB)^{-1}\,((AB)\,(\text{adj } B\,.\,\text{adj } A))$$

$$\Rightarrow \quad ((AB)^{-1}\,(AB))\,(\text{adj } AB) = ((AB)^{-1}\,(AB))\;(\text{adj } B\,.\,\text{adj } A)$$

$$\Rightarrow \quad I\,(\text{adj } AB) = I\,(\text{adj } B\,.\,\text{adj } A)$$

$$\Rightarrow \quad \text{adj } AB = \text{adj } B\,.\,\text{adj } A$$

Q.E.D

THEOREM 7 *If A is an invertible square matrix, then adj $A^T = (\text{adj } A)^T$.*

PROOF Since A is an invertible matrix.

$$\therefore \quad |A| \neq 0$$

$$\Rightarrow \quad |A^T| \neq 0 \qquad [\because\ |A^T| = |A|]$$

$\Rightarrow$ A^T is invertible.

We know that

$$A \text{ adj } A = |A|\, I_n \Rightarrow (A \text{ adj } A)^T = (\,|A|\, I_n)^T \Rightarrow (\text{adj } A)^T\,(A^T) = |A|\, I_n \qquad \text{...(i)}$$

Also,

$$(\text{adj } A^T)\,(A^T) = |A^T|\, I_n \Rightarrow (\text{adj } A^T)\,(A^T) = |A|\, I_n \qquad \text{...(ii)}$$

From (i) and (ii), we get

$$(\text{adj } A^T)\,(A^T) = (\text{adj } A)^T\,(A^T) \Rightarrow \text{adj } A^T = (\text{adj } A)^T \qquad \text{[By right cancellation law]}$$

Q.E.D

THEOREM 8 *Prove that adjoint of a symmetric matrix is also a symmetric matrix.*

PROOF Let A be a symmetric matrix. Then, $A^T = A$

We know that

$$(\text{adj } A)^T = (\text{adj } A^T)$$

$$\Rightarrow \quad (\text{adj } A)^T = \text{adj } A \qquad [\because\ A^T = A]$$

$\Rightarrow$ adj A is a symmetric matrix.

Q.E.D.

THEOREM 9 *If A is a non-singular square matrix, then* $\text{adj}\,(\text{adj } A) = |A|^{n-2}\, A$.

PROOF We know that $B\,(\text{adj } B) = |B|\, I_n$ for every square matrix of order n.

Replacing B by adj A, we get

$$(\text{adj } A)\,[\text{adj}\,(\text{adj } A)] = |\text{adj } A|\, I_n$$

$$\Rightarrow \quad (\text{adj } A)\,[\text{adj}\,(\text{adj } A)] = |A|^{n-1}\, I_n \qquad [\because\ |\text{adj } A| = |A|^{n-1}]$$

$$\Rightarrow \quad A\,\{(\text{adj } A)\,(\text{adj adj } A)\} = A\,\{|A|^{n-1}\, I_n\} \qquad \text{[Pre-multiplying both sides by } A]$$

$$\Rightarrow \quad (A \text{ adj } A)\,(\text{adj adj } A) = |A|^{n-1}\,(A I_n) \qquad \text{[By associativity of multiplication]}$$

$$\Rightarrow \quad |A|\, I_n\, (\text{adj adj } A) = |A|^{n-1} A \qquad [\because AI_n = A \text{ and } A \text{ adj } A = |A|\, I_n]$$

$$\Rightarrow \quad |A|\, (I_n\, (\text{adj adj } A)) = |A|^{n-1} A$$

$$\Rightarrow \quad |A|\, (\text{adj adj } A) = |A|^{n-1} A$$

$$\Rightarrow \quad \text{adj adj } A = |A|^{n-2} A. \qquad \left[\text{Multiplying both sides by } \frac{1}{|A|}\right]$$

Q.E.D

COROLLARY *If A is a non-singular matrix of order n, then $|\text{adj}\,(\text{adj}\,A)| = |A|^{(n-1)^2}$*

PROOF We know that

$$\text{adj}\,(\text{adj}\,A) = |A|^{n-2} A$$

$$\Rightarrow \quad |\text{adj}\,(\text{adj}\,A)| = ||A|^{n-2} A|$$

$$\Rightarrow \quad |\text{adj}\,(\text{adj}\,A)| = |A|^{n(n-2)} |A| \qquad [\because |kA| = k^n |A|]$$

$$\Rightarrow \quad |\text{adj}\,(\text{adj}\,A)| = |A|^{n^2-2n+1} = |A|^{(n-1)^2}$$

ILLUSTRATION 2 *If A is an invertible matrix of order 3×3 such that $|A| = 2$. Then, find* adj (adj A).

SOLUTION Replacing n by 3 in the above theorem, we get

$$\text{adj}\,(\text{adj}\,A) = |A|^{3-2} A = |A|\, A = 2A$$

ILLUSTRATION 3 *If A is a square matrix of order 3 such that $|A| = 2$, then write the value of $|\text{adj}\,(\text{adj}\,A)|$.*

SOLUTION If A is a square matrix of order n, then $|\text{adj}\,(\text{adj}\,A)| = |A|^{(n-1)^2}$.

Here A is a square matrix of order 3 such that $|A| = 2$.

$$\therefore \quad |\text{adj}\,(\text{adj}\,A)| = 2^{(3-1)^2} = 2^4 = 16$$

ILLUSTRATION 4 *If $A = \begin{bmatrix} 3 & 0 & -1 \\ 2 & 3 & 0 \\ 0 & 4 & 1 \end{bmatrix}$, then find $|\text{adj}\,(\text{adj}\,A)|$.*

SOLUTION Here, $|A| = \begin{vmatrix} 3 & 0 & -1 \\ 2 & 3 & 0 \\ 0 & 4 & 1 \end{vmatrix} = 3(3-0) - 0(2-0) - 1(8-0) = 1$

If A is a square matrix of order n, then $|\text{adj}\,(\text{adj}\,A)| = |A|^{(n-1)^2}$

So, for the given matrix, we obtain : $|\text{adj}\,(\text{adj}\,A)| = |A|^4 = 1$

THEOREM 10 *If the product of two non-null square matrices is a null matrix, show that both of them must be singular matrices.*

PROOF Let A and B be two non-null square matrices of the same order $n \times n$. It is given that $AB = O$ (null matrix). If possible, let B be *a* non-singular matrix. Then, B^{-1} exists.

$$\therefore \quad AB = O$$

$$\Rightarrow \quad (AB)\, B^{-1} = OB^{-1} \qquad [\text{Post-multiplying both sides by } B^{-1}]$$

$$\Rightarrow \quad A\,(BB^{-1}) = O \qquad [\text{By associativity of multiplication}]$$

$$\Rightarrow \quad AI_n = O \qquad [\because BB^{-1} = I_n]$$

$$\Rightarrow \quad A = O.$$

But, A is a non-null matrix. Therefore, our supposition is wrong. Hence, B is a singular matrix. Similarly it can be shown that A is a singular matrix.

Q.E.D.

THEOREM 11 *If A is a non-singular matrix, then prove that* $|A^{-1}| = |A|^{-1}$ i.e. $|A^{-1}| = \frac{1}{|A|}$.

PROOF Since $|A| \neq 0$, therefore A^{-1} exists such that

$$AA^{-1} = I = A^{-1}A$$

$\Rightarrow \quad |AA^{-1}| = |I|$ [Taking determinant of both sides]

$\Rightarrow \quad |A|\,|A^{-1}| = 1$ [$\because$ $|AB| = |A|\,|B|$ and $|I| = 1$]

$\Rightarrow \quad |A^{-1}| = \frac{1}{|A|}$. [$\because$ $|A| \neq 0$]

Q.E.D.

ILLUSTRATIVE EXAMPLES

BASED ON BASIC CONCEPTS (BASIC)

Type I **FINDING THE ADJOINT AND INVERSE OF A MATRIX**

EXAMPLE 1 *If* $A = \begin{bmatrix} a & b \\ c & d \end{bmatrix}$, *find adj A.*

SOLUTION Let C_{ij} be the cofactor of a_{ij} in $A = [a_{ij}]$. Then,

C_{11} = Cofactor of $a_{11} = (-1)^{1+1} d = d$, C_{12} = Cofactor of $a_{12} = -(-1)^{1+2} c = -c$

C_{21} = Cofactor of $a_{21} = (-1)^{2+1} b = -b$ and, C_{22} = Cofactor of $a_{22} = (-1)^{2+2} a = a$

$$\therefore \quad \text{adj } A = \begin{bmatrix} C_{11} & C_{12} \\ C_{21} & C_{22} \end{bmatrix}^T = \begin{bmatrix} d & -c \\ -b & a \end{bmatrix}^T = \begin{bmatrix} d & -b \\ -c & a \end{bmatrix}.$$

EXAMPLE 2 *If* $A = \begin{bmatrix} \cos\alpha & -\sin\alpha & 0 \\ \sin\alpha & \cos\alpha & 0 \\ 0 & 0 & 1 \end{bmatrix}$, *find adj A and verify that* $A\,(\text{adj } A) = (\text{adj } A)\,A = |A|\,I_3$.

[CBSE 2016]

SOLUTION Let C_{ij} be the cofactor of a_{ij} in $A = [a_{ij}]$. Then,

$$C_{11} = (-1)^{1+1}\begin{vmatrix} \cos\alpha & 0 \\ 0 & 1 \end{vmatrix} = \cos\alpha, \quad C_{12} = (-1)^{1+2}\begin{vmatrix} \sin\alpha & 0 \\ 0 & 1 \end{vmatrix} = -\sin\alpha,$$

$$C_{13} = (-1)^{1+3}\begin{vmatrix} \sin\alpha & \cos\alpha \\ 0 & 0 \end{vmatrix} = 0, \quad C_{21} = (-1)^{2+1}\begin{vmatrix} -\sin\alpha & 0 \\ 0 & 1 \end{vmatrix} = \sin\alpha,$$

$$C_{22} = (-1)^{2+2}\begin{vmatrix} \cos\alpha & 0 \\ 0 & 1 \end{vmatrix} = \cos\alpha, \quad C_{23} = (-1)^{2+3}\begin{vmatrix} \cos\alpha & -\sin\alpha \\ 0 & 0 \end{vmatrix} = 0,$$

$$C_{31} = (-1)^{3+1}\begin{vmatrix} -\sin\alpha & 0 \\ \cos\alpha & 0 \end{vmatrix} = 0, \quad C_{32} = (-1)^{3+2}\begin{vmatrix} \cos\alpha & 0 \\ \sin\alpha & 0 \end{vmatrix} = 0,$$

and, $$C_{33} = (-1)^{3+3}\begin{vmatrix} \cos\alpha & -\sin\alpha \\ \sin\alpha & \cos\alpha \end{vmatrix} = \cos^2\alpha + \sin^2\alpha = 1$$

$$\therefore \quad \text{adj } A = \begin{bmatrix} \cos\alpha & -\sin\alpha & 0 \\ \sin\alpha & \cos\alpha & 0 \\ 0 & 0 & 1 \end{bmatrix}^T = \begin{bmatrix} \cos\alpha & \sin\alpha & 0 \\ -\sin\alpha & \cos\alpha & 0 \\ 0 & 0 & 1 \end{bmatrix}$$

and, $\quad |A| = a_{11}C_{11} + a_{12}C_{12} + a_{13}C_{13}$

$\Rightarrow \quad |A| = (\cos\alpha)(\cos\alpha) + (-\sin\alpha)(-\sin\alpha) + 0 \times 0 = \cos^2\alpha + \sin^2\alpha = 1.$

Now,

$$A\,(\text{adj } A)=\begin{bmatrix}\cos\alpha & -\sin\alpha & 0\\ \sin\alpha & \cos\alpha & 0\\ 0 & 0 & 1\end{bmatrix}\begin{bmatrix}\cos\alpha & \sin\alpha & 0\\ -\sin\alpha & \cos\alpha & 0\\ 0 & 0 & 1\end{bmatrix}$$

$$\Rightarrow \quad A\,(\text{adj } A)=\begin{bmatrix}\cos^2\alpha+\sin^2\alpha & \sin\alpha\cos\alpha-\cos\alpha\sin\alpha & 0\\ \cos\alpha\sin\alpha-\sin\alpha\cos\alpha & \sin^2+\cos^2\alpha & 0\\ 0 & 0 & 1\end{bmatrix}$$

$$\Rightarrow \quad A\,(\text{adj } A)=\begin{bmatrix}1 & 0 & 0\\ 0 & 1 & 0\\ 0 & 0 & 1\end{bmatrix}=|A|\,I \qquad [\because |A|=1]$$

and,

$$(\text{adj } A)\,A=\begin{bmatrix}\cos\alpha & \sin\alpha & 0\\ -\sin\alpha & \cos\alpha & 0\\ 0 & 0 & 1\end{bmatrix}\begin{bmatrix}\cos\alpha & -\sin\alpha & 0\\ \sin\alpha & \cos\alpha & 0\\ 0 & 0 & 1\end{bmatrix}$$

$$\Rightarrow \quad (\text{adj } A)\,A=\begin{bmatrix}\cos^2\alpha+\sin^2\alpha & -\sin\alpha\cos\alpha+\cos\alpha\sin\alpha & 0\\ -\sin\alpha\cos\alpha+\cos\alpha\sin\alpha & \sin^2\alpha+\cos^2\alpha & 0\\ 0 & 0 & 1\end{bmatrix}$$

$$\Rightarrow \quad (\text{adj } A)\,A=\begin{bmatrix}1 & 0 & 0\\ 0 & 1 & 0\\ 0 & 0 & 1\end{bmatrix}=|A|\,I \qquad [\because |A|=1]$$

Hence, $A\,(\text{adj } A)=|A|\,I=(\text{adj } A)\,A$ is verified.

EXAMPLE 3 *If* $A=\begin{bmatrix}2 & 3\\ 5 & -2\end{bmatrix}$, *show that* $A^{-1}=\frac{1}{19}A$.

SOLUTION We have, $|A|=\begin{vmatrix}2 & 3\\ 5 & -2\end{vmatrix}=-4-15=-19\neq 0$. Therefore, A is invertible.

Let C_{ij} be the cofactor of a_{ij} in $A=[a_{ij}]$. Then,

$$C_{11}=-2,\ C_{12}=-5,\ C_{21}=-3 \text{ and } C_{22}=2.$$

$$\therefore \quad \text{adj } A=\begin{bmatrix}-2 & -5\\ -3 & 2\end{bmatrix}^T=\begin{bmatrix}-2 & -3\\ -5 & 2\end{bmatrix}$$

Now, $A^{-1}=\frac{1}{|A|}\text{adj } A \Rightarrow A^{-1}=\frac{1}{-19}\begin{bmatrix}-2 & -3\\ -5 & 2\end{bmatrix}=\frac{1}{19}\begin{bmatrix}2 & 3\\ 5 & -2\end{bmatrix}=\frac{1}{19}A.$

EXAMPLE 4 *Find the inverse of* $A=\begin{bmatrix}1 & 3 & 3\\ 1 & 4 & 3\\ 1 & 3 & 4\end{bmatrix}$ *and verify that* $A^{-1}A=I_3$.

SOLUTION We have, $A=\begin{bmatrix}1 & 3 & 3\\ 1 & 4 & 3\\ 1 & 3 & 4\end{bmatrix}$.

$$\therefore \quad |A|=\begin{vmatrix}1 & 3 & 3\\ 1 & 4 & 3\\ 1 & 3 & 4\end{vmatrix}=(16-9)-3(4-3)+3(3-4)=7-3-3=1\neq 0.$$ So, A is invertible.

Let C_{ij} be the cofactor of a_{ij} in $A=[a_{ij}]$. Then,

$$C_{11}=(-1)^{1+1}\begin{vmatrix}4 & 3\\ 3 & 4\end{vmatrix}=7,\quad C_{12}=(-1)^{1+2}\begin{vmatrix}1 & 3\\ 1 & 4\end{vmatrix}=-1,\quad C_{13}=(-1)^{1+3}\begin{vmatrix}1 & 4\\ 1 & 3\end{vmatrix}=-1$$

$$C_{21}=(-1)^{2+1}\begin{vmatrix}3&3\\3&4\end{vmatrix}=-3,\quad C_{22}=(-1)^{2+2}\begin{vmatrix}1&3\\1&4\end{vmatrix}=1,\quad C_{23}=(-1)^{2+3}\begin{vmatrix}1&3\\1&3\end{vmatrix}=0$$

$$C_{31}=(-1)^{3+1}\begin{vmatrix}3&3\\4&3\end{vmatrix}=-3,\quad C_{32}=(-1)^{3+2}\begin{vmatrix}1&3\\1&3\end{vmatrix}=0,\quad C_{33}=(-1)^{3+3}\begin{vmatrix}1&3\\1&4\end{vmatrix}=1$$

$$\therefore\quad \text{adj } A=\begin{bmatrix}C_{11}&C_{12}&C_{13}\\C_{21}&C_{22}&C_{23}\\C_{31}&C_{32}&C_{33}\end{bmatrix}^T=\begin{bmatrix}7&-1&-1\\-3&1&0\\-3&0&1\end{bmatrix}^T=\begin{bmatrix}7&-3&-3\\-1&1&0\\-1&0&1\end{bmatrix}$$

Now, $A^{-1}=\dfrac{1}{|A|}\text{adj } A$

$$\Rightarrow A^{-1}=\frac{1}{1}\begin{bmatrix}7&-3&-3\\-1&1&0\\-1&0&1\end{bmatrix}=\begin{bmatrix}7&-3&-3\\-1&1&0\\-1&0&1\end{bmatrix}$$

$$\therefore\quad A^{-1}A=\begin{bmatrix}7&-3&-3\\-1&1&0\\-1&0&1\end{bmatrix}\begin{bmatrix}1&3&3\\1&4&3\\1&3&4\end{bmatrix}=\begin{bmatrix}7-3-3&21-12-9&21-9-12\\-1+1+0&-3+4+0&-3+3+0\\-1+0+1&-3+0+3&-3+0+4\end{bmatrix}=\begin{bmatrix}1&0&0\\0&1&0\\0&0&1\end{bmatrix}$$

EXAMPLE 5 *If* $A=\begin{bmatrix}1&\tan x\\-\tan x&1\end{bmatrix}$, *show that* $A^T A^{-1}=\begin{bmatrix}\cos 2x&-\sin 2x\\\sin 2x&\cos 2x\end{bmatrix}$.

SOLUTION Clearly, $|A|=\begin{vmatrix}1&\tan x\\-\tan x&1\end{vmatrix}=1+\tan^2 x\neq 0$

So, A is invertible. Let C_{ij} be the cofactor of a_{ij} in $A=[a_{ij}]$. Then,

$$C_{11}=(-1)^{1+1}1=1,\quad C_{12}=(-1)^{1+2}(-\tan x)=\tan x$$

$$C_{21}=(-1)^{2+1}\tan x=-\tan x\quad\text{and}\quad C_{22}=(-1)^{2+2}1=1$$

$$\therefore\quad \text{adj } A=\begin{bmatrix}C_{11}&C_{12}\\C_{21}&C_{22}\end{bmatrix}^T\begin{bmatrix}1&\tan x\\-\tan x&1\end{bmatrix}^T=\begin{bmatrix}1&-\tan x\\\tan x&1\end{bmatrix}.$$

Now,

$$A^{-1}=\frac{1}{|A|}\text{adj } A=\frac{1}{1+\tan^2 x}\begin{bmatrix}1&-\tan x\\\tan x&1\end{bmatrix}=\begin{bmatrix}\dfrac{1}{1+\tan^2 x}&-\dfrac{\tan x}{1+\tan^2 x}\\\dfrac{\tan x}{1+\tan^2 x}&\dfrac{1}{1+\tan^2 x}\end{bmatrix}$$

$$\therefore\quad A^T A^{-1}=\begin{bmatrix}1&-\tan x\\\tan x&1\end{bmatrix}\begin{bmatrix}\dfrac{1}{1+\tan^2 x}&\dfrac{-\tan x}{1+\tan^2 x}\\\dfrac{\tan x}{1+\tan^2 x}&\dfrac{1}{1+\tan^2 x}\end{bmatrix}$$

$$\Rightarrow\quad A^T A^{-1}=\begin{bmatrix}\dfrac{1}{1+\tan^2 x}-\dfrac{\tan^2 x}{1+\tan^2 x}&-\dfrac{\tan x}{1+\tan^2 x}-\dfrac{\tan x}{1+\tan^2 x}\\\dfrac{\tan x}{1+\tan^2 x}+\dfrac{\tan x}{1+\tan^2 x}&-\dfrac{\tan^2 x}{1+\tan^2 x}+\dfrac{1}{1+\tan^2 x}\end{bmatrix}$$

$$\Rightarrow\quad A^T A^{-1}=\begin{bmatrix}\dfrac{1-\tan^2 x}{1+\tan^2 x}&-\dfrac{2\tan x}{1+\tan^2 x}\\\dfrac{2\tan x}{1+\tan^2 x}&\dfrac{1-\tan^2 x}{1+\tan^2 x}\end{bmatrix}=\begin{bmatrix}\cos 2x&-\sin 2x\\\sin 2x&\cos 2x\end{bmatrix}$$

EXAMPLE 6 *If* $A=\begin{bmatrix}3 & 2\\ 7 & 5\end{bmatrix}$ *and* $B=\begin{bmatrix}6 & 7\\ 8 & 9\end{bmatrix}$, *verify that* $(AB)^{-1}=B^{-1}A^{-1}$. [NCERT]

SOLUTION Clearly, $|A|=\begin{vmatrix}3 & 2\\ 7 & 5\end{vmatrix}=15-14=1\neq 0$. So, A is invertible.

Let A_{ij} be the cofactor of elements a_{ij} in $A=[a_{ij}]$. Then,

$A_{11}=(-1)^{1+1}5=5,\quad A_{12}=(-1)^{1+2}7=-7, A_{21}=(-1)^{2+1}2=-2$ and $A_{22}=(-1)^{2+2}3=3.$

$$\therefore \quad \text{adj } A=\begin{bmatrix}A_{11} & A_{12}\\ A_{21} & A_{22}\end{bmatrix}^T=\begin{bmatrix}5 & -7\\ -2 & 3\end{bmatrix}^T=\begin{bmatrix}5 & -2\\ -7 & 3\end{bmatrix}$$

Hence, $A^{-1}=\frac{1}{|A|}\text{adj } A=\begin{bmatrix}5 & -2\\ -7 & 3\end{bmatrix}$

Now, $B=\begin{bmatrix}6 & 7\\ 8 & 9\end{bmatrix}\Rightarrow |B|=\begin{vmatrix}6 & 7\\ 8 & 9\end{vmatrix}=54-56=-2\neq 0$. So, B is invertible.

Let B_{ij} be the cofactors of b_{ij} in $B=[b_{ij}]$. Then,

$B_{11}=(-1)^{1+1}9=9,\quad B_{12}=(-1)^{1+2}8=-8, B_{21}=(-1)^{2+1}7=-7$ and $B_{22}=(-1)^{2+2}6=6.$

$$\therefore \quad \text{adj } B=\begin{bmatrix}B_{11} & B_{12}\\ B_{21} & B_{22}\end{bmatrix}^T=\begin{bmatrix}9 & -8\\ -7 & 6\end{bmatrix}^T=\begin{bmatrix}9 & -7\\ -8 & 6\end{bmatrix}$$

Hence, $B^{-1}=\frac{1}{|B|}\text{adj } B=-\frac{1}{2}\begin{bmatrix}9 & -7\\ -8 & 6\end{bmatrix}$

We know that adj AB = adj B . adj A.

$$\therefore \quad \text{adj } AB=\begin{bmatrix}9 & -7\\ -8 & 6\end{bmatrix}\begin{bmatrix}5 & -2\\ -7 & 3\end{bmatrix}=\begin{bmatrix}94 & -39\\ -82 & 34\end{bmatrix}$$

We also know that $|AB|=|A|\,|B|$. Therefore, $|AB|=1\times -2=-2\neq 0$. So, AB is invertible.

Hence, $(AB)^{-1}=\frac{1}{|AB|}\text{adj }(AB)=\frac{1}{-2}\begin{bmatrix}94 & -39\\ -82 & 34\end{bmatrix}=-\frac{1}{2}\begin{bmatrix}94 & -39\\ -82 & 34\end{bmatrix}$ ...(i)

Also, $B^{-1}A^{-1}=-\frac{1}{2}\begin{bmatrix}9 & -7\\ -8 & 6\end{bmatrix}\begin{bmatrix}5 & -2\\ -7 & 3\end{bmatrix}=-\frac{1}{2}\begin{bmatrix}94 & -39\\ -82 & 34\end{bmatrix}$ ...(ii)

From (i) and (ii), we get : $(AB)^{-1}=B^{-1}A^{-1}$.

NOTE *Students are advised not to find the product AB and* $(AB)^{-1}$ *by the usual technique.*

Type II FINDING THE INVERSE OF A MATRIX *A* WHEN IT SATISFIES SOME MATRIX EQUATION *f(A)* = *O*.

EXAMPLE 7 *Show that* $A=\begin{bmatrix}2 & -3\\ 3 & 4\end{bmatrix}$ *satisfies the equation* $x^2-6x+17=0$. *Hence, find* A^{-1}.

[CBSE 2007]

SOLUTION We have, $A=\begin{bmatrix}2 & -3\\ 3 & 4\end{bmatrix}$.

$$\therefore \quad A^2=AA=\begin{bmatrix}2 & -3\\ 3 & 4\end{bmatrix}\begin{bmatrix}2 & -3\\ 3 & 4\end{bmatrix}=\begin{bmatrix}4-9 & -6-12\\ 6+12 & -9+16\end{bmatrix}=\begin{bmatrix}-5 & -18\\ 18 & 7\end{bmatrix}$$

$$-6A=(-6)\begin{bmatrix}2 & -3\\ 3 & 4\end{bmatrix}=\begin{bmatrix}-12 & 18\\ -18 & -24\end{bmatrix} \text{ and, } 17I=17\begin{bmatrix}1 & 0\\ 0 & 1\end{bmatrix}=\begin{bmatrix}17 & 0\\ 0 & 17\end{bmatrix}.$$

$$\therefore \quad A^2 - 6A + 17I_2 = \begin{bmatrix} -5 & -18 \\ 18 & 7 \end{bmatrix} + \begin{bmatrix} -12 & 18 \\ -18 & -24 \end{bmatrix} + \begin{bmatrix} 17 & 0 \\ 0 & 17 \end{bmatrix}$$

$$\Rightarrow \quad A^2 - 6A + 17I_2 = \begin{bmatrix} -5-12+17 & -18+18+0 \\ 18-18+0 & 7-24+17 \end{bmatrix} = \begin{bmatrix} 0 & 0 \\ 0 & 0 \end{bmatrix} = O.$$

Hence, the matrix A satisfies the equation $x^2 - 6x + 17 = 0$.

Now,

$$A^2 - 6A + 17I_2 = O$$

$$\Rightarrow \quad A^2 - 6A = -17I_2$$

$$\Rightarrow \quad A^{-1}(A^2 - 6A) = A^{-1}(-17I_2) \qquad \text{[Pre-multiplying both sides by } A^{-1}]$$

$$\Rightarrow \quad A^{-1}A^2 - 6A^{-1}A = -17(A^{-1}I_2)$$

$$\Rightarrow \quad A - 6I_2 = -17A^{-1}$$

$$\Rightarrow \quad A^{-1} = -\frac{1}{17}(A - 6I_2) = \frac{1}{17}(6I_2 - A) = \frac{1}{17}\left\{\begin{bmatrix} 6 & 0 \\ 0 & 6 \end{bmatrix} - \begin{bmatrix} 2 & -3 \\ 3 & 4 \end{bmatrix}\right\} = \frac{1}{17}\begin{bmatrix} 4 & 3 \\ -3 & 2 \end{bmatrix}$$

EXAMPLE 8 *For the matrix* $A = \begin{bmatrix} 3 & 1 \\ 7 & 5 \end{bmatrix}$, *find* x and y *so that* $A^2 + xI = yA$.

Hence, find A^{-1}.

SOLUTION We have, $A = \begin{bmatrix} 3 & 1 \\ 7 & 5 \end{bmatrix}$.

$$\therefore \quad A^2 = AA = \begin{bmatrix} 3 & 1 \\ 7 & 5 \end{bmatrix}\begin{bmatrix} 3 & 1 \\ 7 & 5 \end{bmatrix} = \begin{bmatrix} 9+7 & 3+5 \\ 21+35 & 7+25 \end{bmatrix} = \begin{bmatrix} 16 & 8 \\ 56 & 32 \end{bmatrix}$$

Now, $A^2 + xI = yA$

$$\Rightarrow \quad \begin{bmatrix} 16 & 8 \\ 56 & 32 \end{bmatrix} + x\begin{bmatrix} 1 & 0 \\ 0 & 1 \end{bmatrix} = y\begin{bmatrix} 3 & 1 \\ 7 & 5 \end{bmatrix} \Rightarrow \begin{bmatrix} 16+x & 8+0 \\ 56+0 & 32+x \end{bmatrix} = \begin{bmatrix} 3y & y \\ 7y & 5y \end{bmatrix}$$

$$\Rightarrow \quad 16 + x = 3y,\ y = 8,\ 7y = 56,\ 5y = 32 + x$$

Putting $y = 8$ in $16 + x = 3y$, we get: $x = 24 - 16 = 8$.

Clearly $x = 8$ and $y = 8$ also satisfy equations $7y = 56$ and $5y = 32 + x$. Hence, $x = 8$ and $y = 8$.

Now, $|A| = \begin{vmatrix} 3 & 1 \\ 7 & 5 \end{vmatrix} = 8 \neq 0$. So, A is invertible.

Putting $x = 8$, $y = 8$ in $A^2 + xI = yA$, we get

$$A^2 + 8I = 8A$$

$$\Rightarrow \quad A^{-1}(A^2 + 8I) = A^{-1}(8A) \qquad \text{[Pre-multiplying throughout by } A^{-1}]$$

$$\Rightarrow \quad A^{-1}A^2 + 8A^{-1}I = 8(A^{-1}A)$$

$$\Rightarrow \quad A + 8A^{-1} = 8I \qquad [\because A^{-1}A^2 = (A^{-1}A)A = IA = A,\ A^{-1}I = A^{-1} \text{ and, } A^{-1}A = I]$$

$$\Rightarrow \quad 8A^{-1} = 8I - A$$

$$\Rightarrow \quad A^{-1} = \frac{1}{8}(8I - A) = \frac{1}{8}\left\{\begin{bmatrix} 8 & 0 \\ 0 & 8 \end{bmatrix} - \begin{bmatrix} 3 & 1 \\ 7 & 5 \end{bmatrix}\right\} = \frac{1}{8}\begin{bmatrix} 8-3 & 0-1 \\ 0-7 & 8-5 \end{bmatrix} = \frac{1}{8}\begin{bmatrix} 5 & -1 \\ -7 & 3 \end{bmatrix} = \begin{bmatrix} 5/8 & -1/8 \\ -7/8 & 3/8 \end{bmatrix}$$

EXAMPLE 9 *For the matrix* $A = \begin{bmatrix} 3 & 2 \\ 1 & 1 \end{bmatrix}$, *find the numbers a and b such that* $A^2 + aA + bI = O$.

Hence, find A^{-1}. [NCERT]

SOLUTION We have, $A = \begin{bmatrix} 3 & 2 \\ 1 & 1 \end{bmatrix}$. Therefore, $A^2 = AA = \begin{bmatrix} 3 & 2 \\ 1 & 1 \end{bmatrix}\begin{bmatrix} 3 & 2 \\ 1 & 1 \end{bmatrix} = \begin{bmatrix} 11 & 8 \\ 4 & 3 \end{bmatrix}$.

Now, $A^2 + aA + bI = O$ ...(i)

$\Rightarrow \begin{bmatrix} 11 & 8 \\ 4 & 3 \end{bmatrix} + a\begin{bmatrix} 3 & 2 \\ 1 & 1 \end{bmatrix} + b\begin{bmatrix} 1 & 0 \\ 0 & 1 \end{bmatrix} = \begin{bmatrix} 0 & 0 \\ 0 & 0 \end{bmatrix} \Rightarrow \begin{bmatrix} 11+3a+b & 8+2a \\ 4+a & 3+a+b \end{bmatrix} = \begin{bmatrix} 0 & 0 \\ 0 & 0 \end{bmatrix}$

$\Rightarrow 11 + 3a + b = 0, 8 + 2a = 0, 4 + a = 0$ and $3 + a + b = 0 \Rightarrow a = -4$ and $b = 1$

Putting $a = -4$ and $b = 1$ in (i), we get

$$A^2 - 4A + I = O \Rightarrow 4A - A^2 = I \Rightarrow A(4I - A) = I$$

$$\Rightarrow A^{-1} = 4I - A = \begin{bmatrix} 4 & 0 \\ 0 & 4 \end{bmatrix} - \begin{bmatrix} 3 & 2 \\ 1 & 1 \end{bmatrix} = \begin{bmatrix} 1 & -2 \\ -1 & 3 \end{bmatrix}$$

EXAMPLE 10 *Show that the matrix* $A = \begin{bmatrix} 1 & 2 & 2 \\ 2 & 1 & 2 \\ 2 & 2 & 1 \end{bmatrix}$ *satisfies the equation* $A^2 - 4A - 5I_3 = O$ *and hence find* A^{-1}. [CBSE 2004]

SOLUTION We have, $A = \begin{bmatrix} 1 & 2 & 2 \\ 2 & 1 & 2 \\ 2 & 2 & 1 \end{bmatrix}$

$\therefore A^2 = AA = \begin{bmatrix} 1 & 2 & 2 \\ 2 & 1 & 2 \\ 2 & 2 & 1 \end{bmatrix}\begin{bmatrix} 1 & 2 & 2 \\ 2 & 1 & 2 \\ 2 & 2 & 1 \end{bmatrix} = \begin{bmatrix} 9 & 8 & 8 \\ 8 & 9 & 8 \\ 8 & 8 & 9 \end{bmatrix}$, $4A = \begin{bmatrix} 4 & 8 & 8 \\ 8 & 4 & 8 \\ 8 & 8 & 4 \end{bmatrix}$ and, $5I_3 = \begin{bmatrix} 5 & 0 & 0 \\ 0 & 5 & 0 \\ 0 & 0 & 5 \end{bmatrix}$.

$$\therefore A^2 - 4A - 5I_3 = \begin{bmatrix} 9 & 8 & 8 \\ 8 & 9 & 8 \\ 8 & 8 & 9 \end{bmatrix} - \begin{bmatrix} 4 & 8 & 8 \\ 8 & 4 & 8 \\ 8 & 8 & 4 \end{bmatrix} - \begin{bmatrix} 5 & 0 & 0 \\ 0 & 5 & 0 \\ 0 & 0 & 5 \end{bmatrix}$$

$$\Rightarrow A^2 - 4A - 5I_3 = \begin{bmatrix} 9-4-5 & 8-8-0 & 8-8-0 \\ 8-8-0 & 9-4-5 & 8-8-0 \\ 8-8-0 & 8-8-0 & 9-4-5 \end{bmatrix} = \begin{bmatrix} 0 & 0 & 0 \\ 0 & 0 & 0 \\ 0 & 0 & 0 \end{bmatrix} = O$$

Now, $A^2 - 4A - 5I_3 = O$

$\Rightarrow A^2 - 4A = 5I_3$

$\Rightarrow A^{-1}A^2 - 4A^{-1}A = 5A^{-1}I_3$ [Pre-multiplying throughout by A^{-1}]

$\Rightarrow A - 4I = 5A^{-1}$ [$\because A^{-1}A^2 = (A^{-1}A)A = IA = A$]

$\Rightarrow A^{-1} = \frac{1}{5}(A - 4I)$

$$\Rightarrow A^{-1} = \frac{1}{5}\left\{\begin{bmatrix} 1 & 2 & 2 \\ 2 & 1 & 2 \\ 2 & 2 & 1 \end{bmatrix} - \begin{bmatrix} 4 & 0 & 0 \\ 0 & 4 & 0 \\ 0 & 0 & 4 \end{bmatrix}\right\} = \frac{1}{5}\begin{bmatrix} -3 & 2 & 2 \\ 2 & -3 & 2 \\ 2 & 2 & -3 \end{bmatrix} = \frac{1}{5}\begin{bmatrix} -3/5 & 2/5 & 2/5 \\ 2/5 & -2/5 & 2/5 \\ 2/5 & 2/5 & -3/5 \end{bmatrix}$$

Type III FINDING THE INVERSE OF A MATRIX BY USING THE DEFINITION OF INVERSE

EXAMPLE 11 *If* $A = \begin{bmatrix} 1 & -1 & 1 \\ 2 & -1 & 0 \\ 1 & 0 & 0 \end{bmatrix}$, *show that* $A^{-1} = A^2$.

SOLUTION We know that a matrix B is the inverse of a matrix A if $AB = I = BA$. Here, we have to show that A^2 is the inverse of A. Therefore, it is sufficient to prove that $A^2 A = I$ or, $A^3 = I$.

Now, $A^2 = AA$

$$\Rightarrow \quad A^2 = \begin{bmatrix} 1 & -1 & 1 \\ 2 & -1 & 0 \\ 1 & 0 & 0 \end{bmatrix}\begin{bmatrix} 1 & -1 & 1 \\ 2 & -1 & 0 \\ 1 & 0 & 0 \end{bmatrix} = \begin{bmatrix} 1-2+1 & -1+1+0 & 1+0+0 \\ 2-2+0 & -2+1+0 & 2+0+0 \\ 1+0+0 & -1+0+0 & 1+0+0 \end{bmatrix} = \begin{bmatrix} 0 & 0 & 1 \\ 0 & -1 & 2 \\ 1 & -1 & 1 \end{bmatrix}$$

and, $A^3 = A^2 A$

$$\Rightarrow \quad A^3 = \begin{bmatrix} 0 & 0 & 1 \\ 0 & -1 & 2 \\ 1 & -1 & 1 \end{bmatrix}\begin{bmatrix} 1 & -1 & 1 \\ 2 & -1 & 0 \\ 1 & 0 & 0 \end{bmatrix} = \begin{bmatrix} 0+0+1 & 0+0+0 & 0+0+0 \\ 0-2+2 & 0+1+0 & 0+0+0 \\ 1-2+1 & -1+1+0 & 1+0+0 \end{bmatrix} = \begin{bmatrix} 1 & 0 & 0 \\ 0 & 1 & 0 \\ 0 & 0 & 1 \end{bmatrix} = I$$

Hence, $A^2 = A^{-1}$.

Type IV ON SOLVING MATRIX EQUATIONS

EXAMPLE 12 *Find a 2×2 matrix B such that* $B\begin{bmatrix} 1 & -2 \\ 1 & 4 \end{bmatrix} = \begin{bmatrix} 6 & 0 \\ 0 & 6 \end{bmatrix}$.

SOLUTION Let $A = \begin{bmatrix} 1 & -2 \\ 1 & 4 \end{bmatrix}$ and $C = \begin{bmatrix} 6 & 0 \\ 0 & 6 \end{bmatrix}$. Then, $|A| = \begin{vmatrix} 1 & -2 \\ 1 & 4 \end{vmatrix} = 6 \neq 0$. So, A is invertible.

The given matrix equation is

$$B\begin{bmatrix} 1 & -2 \\ 1 & 4 \end{bmatrix} = \begin{bmatrix} 6 & 0 \\ 0 & 6 \end{bmatrix}$$

$\Rightarrow \quad BA = C$

$\Rightarrow \quad (BA)\, A^{-1} = CA^{-1}$ [Post-multiplying throughout by A^{-1}]

$\Rightarrow \quad B\,(AA)^{-1} = CA^{-1} \Rightarrow BI = CA^{-1} \Rightarrow B = CA^{-1}$.

Let C_{ij} be the cofactor of a_{ij} in $A = [a_{ij}]$. Then,

$$C_{11} = (-1)^{1+1} 4 = 4,\ C_{12} = (-1)^{1+2} 1 = -1,\ C_{21} = (-1)^{2+1}(-2) = 2 \text{ and, } C_{22} = (-1)^{2+2}\, 1 = 1.$$

$$\therefore \quad \text{adj } A = \begin{bmatrix} C_{11} & C_{12} \\ C_{21} & C_{22} \end{bmatrix}^T = \begin{bmatrix} 4 & -1 \\ 2 & 1 \end{bmatrix}^T = \begin{bmatrix} 4 & 2 \\ -1 & 1 \end{bmatrix}$$

Hence, $A^{-1} = \dfrac{1}{|A|} \text{adj } A = \dfrac{1}{6}\begin{bmatrix} 4 & 2 \\ -1 & 1 \end{bmatrix}$

Now,

$$B = CA^{-1}$$

$$\Rightarrow \quad B = \begin{bmatrix} 6 & 0 \\ 0 & 6 \end{bmatrix} \frac{1}{6}\begin{bmatrix} 4 & 2 \\ -1 & 1 \end{bmatrix} = \frac{1}{6}\begin{bmatrix} 6 & 0 \\ 0 & 6 \end{bmatrix}\begin{bmatrix} 4 & 2 \\ -1 & 1 \end{bmatrix} = \frac{1}{6}\begin{bmatrix} 24+0 & 12+0 \\ 0-6 & 0+6 \end{bmatrix} = \begin{bmatrix} 4 & 2 \\ -1 & 1 \end{bmatrix}$$

EXAMPLE 13 *Find the matrix A satisfying the matrix equation* $\begin{bmatrix} 2 & 1 \\ 3 & 2 \end{bmatrix} A \begin{bmatrix} -3 & 2 \\ 5 & -3 \end{bmatrix} = \begin{bmatrix} 1 & 0 \\ 0 & 1 \end{bmatrix}$.

SOLUTION Let $B = \begin{bmatrix} 2 & 1 \\ 3 & 2 \end{bmatrix}$ and $C = \begin{bmatrix} -3 & 2 \\ 5 & -3 \end{bmatrix}$. Then,

$$|B| = \begin{vmatrix} 2 & 1 \\ 3 & 2 \end{vmatrix} = 4 - 3 = 1 \neq 0 \text{ and, } |C| = \begin{vmatrix} -3 & 2 \\ 5 & -3 \end{vmatrix} = 9 - 10 = -1 \neq 0.$$

So, B and C are invertible matrices. The given matrix equation is $BAC = I$.

Now, $\quad BAC = I$

$\Rightarrow \quad B^{-1}(BAC)\, C^{-1} = B^{-1}\, IC^{-1}$

$\Rightarrow \quad (B^{-1} B)\, A\, (CC^{-1}) = B^{-1} C^{-1} \Rightarrow IAI = B^{-1} C^{-1} \Rightarrow A = B^{-1} C^{-1}$ ...(i)

Let B_{ij} be the cofactor of elements b_{ij} in $B = [b_{ij}]$. Then,

$B_{11} = (-1)^{1+1}\, 2 = 2,\ B_{12} = (-1)^{1+2}\, 3 = -3,\quad B_{21} = (-1)^{2+1}\, 1 = -1$ and, $B_{22} = (-1)^{2+2}\, 2 = 2.$

$\therefore \quad \text{adj } B = \begin{bmatrix} B_{11} & B_{12} \\ B_{21} & B_{22} \end{bmatrix}^T = \begin{bmatrix} 2 & -3 \\ -1 & 2 \end{bmatrix}^T = \begin{bmatrix} 2 & -1 \\ -3 & 2 \end{bmatrix}$

So, $\quad B^{-1} = \dfrac{1}{|B|} \text{adj } B = \begin{bmatrix} 2 & -1 \\ -3 & 2 \end{bmatrix}.$ $\qquad [\because |B| = 1]$

Let C_{ij} be the cofactors of elements c_{ij} in $C = [c_{ij}]$. Then,

$C_{11} = (-1)^{1+1}(-3) = -3,\ C_{12} = (-1)^{1+2}\, 5 = -5,\quad C_{21} = (-1)^{2+1}\, 2 = -2$

and, $\quad C_{22} = (-1)^{2+2}(-3) = -3.$

$\therefore \quad \text{adj } C = \begin{bmatrix} C_{11} & C_{12} \\ C_{21} & C_{22} \end{bmatrix}^T = \begin{bmatrix} -3 & -5 \\ -2 & -3 \end{bmatrix}^T = \begin{bmatrix} -3 & -2 \\ -5 & -3 \end{bmatrix}$

So, $\quad C^{-1} = \dfrac{1}{|C|} \text{adj } C = -\begin{bmatrix} -3 & -2 \\ -5 & -3 \end{bmatrix} = \begin{bmatrix} 3 & 2 \\ 5 & 3 \end{bmatrix}$ $\qquad [\because |C| = -1]$

Substituting the values of B^{-1} and C^{-1} in (i), we get

$$A = B^{-1} C^{-1} = \begin{bmatrix} 2 & -1 \\ -3 & 2 \end{bmatrix} \begin{bmatrix} 3 & 2 \\ 5 & 3 \end{bmatrix} = \begin{bmatrix} 6-5 & 4-3 \\ -9+10 & -6+6 \end{bmatrix} = \begin{bmatrix} 1 & 1 \\ 1 & 0 \end{bmatrix}$$

EXAMPLE 14 *Find the matrix X for which* $\begin{bmatrix} 1 & -4 \\ 3 & -2 \end{bmatrix} X = \begin{bmatrix} -16 & -6 \\ 7 & 2 \end{bmatrix}.$

SOLUTION Let $A = \begin{bmatrix} 1 & -4 \\ 3 & -2 \end{bmatrix}$ and $B = \begin{bmatrix} -16 & -6 \\ 7 & 2 \end{bmatrix}$. Then the given matrix equation is $AX = B$.

$\therefore \quad |A| = \begin{vmatrix} 1 & -4 \\ 3 & -2 \end{vmatrix} = -2 + 12 = 10 \neq 0.$

So, A is an invertible matrix. Let C_{ij} be the cofactors of elements a_{ij} in $A = [a_{ij}]$. Then,

$C_{11} = (-1)^{1+1}(-2) = -2,\ C_{12} = (-1)^{1+2}\, 3 = -3,\ C_{21} = (-1)^{2+1}(-4) = 4$

and, $\quad C_{22} = (-1)^{2+2}\, 1 = 1.$

$\therefore \quad \text{adj } A = \begin{bmatrix} -2 & -3 \\ 4 & 1 \end{bmatrix}^T = \begin{bmatrix} -2 & 4 \\ -3 & 1 \end{bmatrix}$ and, $A^{-1} = \dfrac{1}{|A|} \text{adj } A = \dfrac{1}{10}\begin{bmatrix} -2 & 4 \\ -3 & 1 \end{bmatrix}.$

Now, $\quad AX = B$

$\Rightarrow \quad A^{-1}(AX) = A^{-1}B \Rightarrow (A^{-1}A)X = A^{-1}B \Rightarrow IX = A^{-1}B \Rightarrow X = A^{-1}B.$

$\Rightarrow \quad X = \dfrac{1}{10}\begin{bmatrix} -2 & 4 \\ -3 & 1 \end{bmatrix}\begin{bmatrix} -16 & -6 \\ 7 & 2 \end{bmatrix} = \dfrac{1}{10}\begin{bmatrix} 32+28 & 12+8 \\ 48+7 & 18+2 \end{bmatrix} = \begin{bmatrix} 6 & 2 \\ 11/2 & 2 \end{bmatrix}.$

BASED ON LOWER ORDER THINKING SKILLS (LOTS)

EXAMPLE 15 *If* $A = \begin{bmatrix} 0 & 1 & 3 \\ 1 & 2 & x \\ 2 & 3 & 1 \end{bmatrix}$ *and* $A^{-1} = \begin{bmatrix} 1/2 & -4 & 5/2 \\ -1/2 & 3 & -3/2 \\ 1/2 & y & 1/2 \end{bmatrix}$, *find x, y.*

SOLUTION We know that

$AA^{-1} = I_3$

$$\Rightarrow \quad \begin{bmatrix} 0 & 1 & 3 \\ 1 & 2 & x \\ 2 & 3 & 1 \end{bmatrix} \begin{bmatrix} 1/2 & -4 & 5/2 \\ -1/2 & 3 & -3/2 \\ 1/2 & y & 1/2 \end{bmatrix} = \begin{bmatrix} 1 & 0 & 0 \\ 0 & 1 & 0 \\ 0 & 0 & 1 \end{bmatrix}$$

$$\Rightarrow \quad \begin{bmatrix} 1 & 3+3y & 0 \\ -\frac{1}{2}+\frac{x}{2} & 2+xy & -\frac{1}{2}+\frac{x}{2} \\ 0 & 1+y & 1 \end{bmatrix} = \begin{bmatrix} 1 & 0 & 0 \\ 0 & 1 & 0 \\ 0 & 0 & 1 \end{bmatrix}$$

$$\Rightarrow \quad 3+3y=0 \; -\frac{1}{2}+\frac{x}{2}=0, \;\; 2+xy=1, \;\; 1+y=0 \Rightarrow x=1, y=-1$$

EXAMPLE 16 *If* $A = \begin{bmatrix} \cos\alpha & \sin\alpha \\ -\sin\alpha & \cos\alpha \end{bmatrix}$ *is such that* $A^T = A^{-1}$, *find* α.

SOLUTION It is given that

$$A^T = A^{-1}$$

$$\Rightarrow \quad AA^T = AA^{-1} \qquad \text{[Premultiplying by } A]$$

$$\Rightarrow \quad AA^T = I \qquad [\because AA^{-1} = 1]$$

Now,

$$AA^T = \begin{bmatrix} \cos\alpha & \sin\alpha \\ -\sin\alpha & \cos\alpha \end{bmatrix} \begin{bmatrix} \cos\alpha & -\sin\alpha \\ \sin\alpha & \cos\alpha \end{bmatrix}$$

$$\Rightarrow \quad AA^T = \begin{bmatrix} \cos^2\alpha + \sin^2\alpha & -\sin\alpha\cos\alpha + \sin\alpha\cos\alpha \\ -\cos\alpha\sin\alpha + \sin\alpha\cos\alpha & \sin^2\alpha + \cos^2\alpha \end{bmatrix} = \begin{bmatrix} 1 & 0 \\ 0 & 1 \end{bmatrix}$$

Thus, $AA^T = I$ is true for all α. Hence, α can take any real value.

EXAMPLE 17 *If matrix* $A = \begin{bmatrix} 0 & 2y & z \\ x & y & -z \\ x & -y & z \end{bmatrix}$ *satisfies* $A^T = A^{-1}$, *find* x, y, z. **[NCERT EXEMPLAR]**

SOLUTION It is given that the matrix A satisfies the relation

$$A^T = A^{-1}$$

$$\Rightarrow \quad AA^T = I \qquad [\text{Putting } A^{-1} = A^T \text{ in } AA^{-1} = I]$$

$$\Rightarrow \quad \begin{bmatrix} 0 & 2y & z \\ x & y & -z \\ x & -y & z \end{bmatrix} \begin{bmatrix} 0 & x & x \\ 2y & y & -y \\ z & -z & z \end{bmatrix} = \begin{bmatrix} 1 & 0 & 0 \\ 0 & 1 & 0 \\ 0 & 0 & 1 \end{bmatrix}$$

$$\Rightarrow \quad \begin{bmatrix} 4y^2+z^2 & 2y^2-z^2 & -2y^2+z^2 \\ 2y^2-z^2 & x^2+y^2+z^2 & x^2-y^2-z^2 \\ -2y^2+z^2 & x^2-y^2-z^2 & x^2+y^2+z^2 \end{bmatrix} = \begin{bmatrix} 1 & 0 & 0 \\ 0 & 1 & 0 \\ 0 & 0 & 1 \end{bmatrix}$$

$$\Rightarrow \quad 4y^2+z^2=1, \;\; 2y^2-z^2=0, \;\; x^2+y^2+z^2=1, \;\; x^2-y^2-z^2=0$$

Now, $4y^2+z^2=1$ and $2y^2-z^2=0 \Rightarrow (4y^2+z^2)+(2y^2-z^2)=1 \Rightarrow 6y^2=1 \Rightarrow y=\pm\frac{1}{\sqrt{6}}$

Putting $y=\pm\frac{1}{\sqrt{6}}$ in $2y^2-z^2=0$, we obtain $z=\pm\frac{1}{\sqrt{3}}$.

Substituting $y=\pm\frac{1}{\sqrt{6}}, z=\pm\frac{1}{\sqrt{3}}$ in $x^2-y^2-z^2=0$, we obtain:

$$x^2 - \frac{1}{6} - \frac{1}{3} = 0 \Rightarrow x^2 = \frac{1}{2} \Rightarrow x = \pm \frac{1}{\sqrt{2}}$$

Hence, $x = \pm \frac{1}{\sqrt{2}}, y = \pm \frac{1}{\sqrt{6}}, z = \pm \frac{1}{\sqrt{3}}$.

BASED ON HIGHER ORDER THINKING SKILLS (HOTS)

Type V ON FINDING A NON-SINGULAR MATRIX A WHEN | A | AND adj A ARE GIVEN

EXAMPLE 18 *Find the matrix A such that* $|A| = 2$ *and* $adj\ A = \begin{bmatrix} 2 & 2 & 0 \\ 2 & 5 & 1 \\ 0 & 1 & 1 \end{bmatrix}$.

SOLUTION We know that

$$A\,(\text{adj } A) = |A|\, I$$

$\Rightarrow \quad A = |A|\, I\, (\text{adj } A)^{-1}$

$\Rightarrow \quad A = |A|\, (\text{adj } A)^{-1}$

$\Rightarrow \quad A = 2\,(\text{adj } A)^{-1}$ $\quad [\because |A| = 2]$

$\Rightarrow \quad A = 2B^{-1}$, where $B = \text{adj } A$

Now, $B = \text{adj } A = \begin{bmatrix} 2 & 2 & 0 \\ 2 & 5 & 1 \\ 0 & 1 & 1 \end{bmatrix}$

$\therefore \quad |B| = |\text{adj } A| = |A|^{3-1} = |A|^2 = 4$ $\quad [\because |\text{adj } A| = |A|^{n-1}]$

Let C_{ij} be the cofactor of $(B)_{ij}$ in matrix B. Then,

$$C_{11} = 4, C_{12} = -2, C_{13} = 2, C_{21} = -2, C_{22} = 2, C_{23} = -2, C_{31} = 2, C_{32} = -2 \text{ and } C_{33} = 6$$

$\therefore \quad \text{adj } B = \begin{bmatrix} 4 & -2 & 2 \\ -2 & 2 & -2 \\ 2 & -2 & 6 \end{bmatrix}^T = \begin{bmatrix} 4 & -2 & 2 \\ -2 & 2 & -2 \\ 2 & -2 & 6 \end{bmatrix}$ and, $B^{-1} = \frac{1}{|B|} \text{adj } B = \frac{1}{4}\begin{bmatrix} 4 & -2 & 2 \\ -2 & 2 & -2 \\ 2 & -2 & 6 \end{bmatrix}$

$\Rightarrow \quad (\text{adj } A)^{-1} = \frac{1}{4}\begin{bmatrix} 4 & -2 & 2 \\ -2 & 2 & -2 \\ 2 & -2 & 6 \end{bmatrix}$

Hence, $A = 2\,(\text{adj } A)^{-1} = \frac{1}{2}\begin{bmatrix} 4 & -2 & 2 \\ -2 & 2 & -2 \\ 2 & -2 & 6 \end{bmatrix} = \begin{bmatrix} 2 & -1 & 1 \\ -1 & 1 & -1 \\ 1 & -1 & 3 \end{bmatrix}$

ALITER We have,

$$A^{-1} = \frac{1}{|A|} \text{adj } A = \frac{1}{2}\begin{bmatrix} 2 & 2 & 0 \\ 2 & 5 & 1 \\ 0 & 1 & 1 \end{bmatrix} = \begin{bmatrix} 1 & 1 & 0 \\ 1 & 5/2 & 1/2 \\ 0 & 1/2 & 1/2 \end{bmatrix}$$

Since $A = (A^{-1})^{-1}$. So, let us find the inverse of A^{-1}.

$$|A^{-1}| = \frac{1}{|A|} \Rightarrow |A|^{-1} = \frac{1}{2}$$

Let C_{ij} be the cofact of $(i, j)^{\text{th}}$ element of A^{-1}. Then,

$$C_{11} = 1, C_{12} = -\frac{1}{2}, C_{13} = \frac{1}{2}, C_{21} = -\frac{1}{2}, C_{22} = \frac{1}{2}, C_{23} = -\frac{1}{2} C_{31} = \frac{1}{2}, C_{32} = -\frac{1}{2} \text{ and } C_{33} = \frac{3}{2}$$

$$\therefore \quad \text{adj}(A^{-1}) = \begin{bmatrix} 1 & -1/2 & 1/2 \\ -1/2 & 1/2 & -1/2 \\ 1/2 & -1/2 & 3/2 \end{bmatrix} \begin{bmatrix} 1 & -1/2 & 1/2 \\ -1/2 & 1/2 & -1/2 \\ 1/2 & -1/2 & 3/2 \end{bmatrix}$$

Hence, $A = (A^{-1})^{-1} = \dfrac{1}{|A^{-1}|} \text{adj}(A^{-1}) = 2\begin{bmatrix} 1 & -1/2 & 1/2 \\ -1/2 & 1/2 & -1/2 \\ 1/2 & -1/2 & 3/2 \end{bmatrix} = \begin{bmatrix} 2 & -1 & 1 \\ -1 & 1 & -1 \\ 1 & -1 & 3 \end{bmatrix}$

Type VI ON FINDING $(\text{adj}\, A)^{-1}$ WHEN MATRIX A IS GIVEN

EXAMPLE 19 *If A is a non-singular matrix, prove that :*

(i) *adj (A) is also non-singular.* (ii) $(\text{adj}\, A)^{-1} = \dfrac{1}{|A|} A.$

SOLUTION (i) We know that

$$A\,(\text{adj}\, A) = |A|\, I_n = (\text{adj}\, A)\, A$$

$\Rightarrow \quad |A\,(\text{adj}\, A)| = ||A|\, I_n|$

$\Rightarrow \quad |A||\text{adj}\, A| = |A|^n\, |I_n|$

$\Rightarrow \quad |\text{adj}\, A| = |A|^{n-1}$ $\quad [\because |A| \neq 0]$

$\Rightarrow \quad |\text{adj}\, A| \neq 0 \Rightarrow$ adj A is non-singular. $\quad [\because |A| \neq 0]$

(ii) We know that

$$A\,(\text{adj}\, A) = |A|\, I_n = (\text{adj}\, A)\, A$$

$\Rightarrow \quad \left(\dfrac{1}{|A|} A\right)(\text{adj}\, A) = I_n = (\text{adj}\, A)\left(\dfrac{1}{|A|} A\right)$ $\quad [\because |A| \neq 0]$

$\Rightarrow \quad (\text{adj}\, A)^{-1} = \dfrac{1}{|A|} A.$

EXAMPLE 20 *If A is a non-singular matrix, prove that* $(\text{adj}\, A)^{-1} = (\text{adj}\, A^{-1})$.

SOLUTION We have,

$$AA^{-1} = I$$

$\Rightarrow \quad \text{adj}(AA^{-1}) = \text{adj}(I)$

$\Rightarrow \quad (\text{adj}\, A^{-1})(\text{adj}\, A) = I$ $\quad [\because \text{adj}(AB) = (\text{adj}\, B)(\text{adj}\, A) \text{ and } \text{adj}(I) = I]$

$\Rightarrow \quad (\text{adj}\, A)^{-1} = \text{adj}\, A^{-1}$

EXAMPLE 21 *Find the non-singular matrices A, if its is given that* $\text{adj}(A) = \begin{bmatrix} -1 & -2 & 1 \\ 3 & 0 & -3 \\ 1 & -4 & 1 \end{bmatrix}$.

SOLUTION We know that $(\text{adj}\, A)^{-1} = \dfrac{A}{|A|}$. Therefore,

$$A = |A|\,(\text{adj}\, A)^{-1} = |A| \frac{1}{|\text{adj}\, A|} \text{adj}(\text{adj}\, A) \quad \ldots\text{(i)}$$

Now, $\text{adj}(A) = \begin{bmatrix} -1 & -2 & 1 \\ 3 & 0 & -3 \\ 1 & -4 & 1 \end{bmatrix}$

$$\Rightarrow \quad |\text{adj } A| = \begin{vmatrix} -1 & -2 & 1 \\ 3 & 0 & -3 \\ 1 & -4 & 1 \end{vmatrix} = -1(0-12) + 2(3+3) + 1(-12-0) = 12$$

$$\Rightarrow \quad |A|^2 = 12 \Rightarrow |A| = \pm 2\sqrt{3} \qquad [\because |\text{adj } A| = |A|^{n-1}]$$

Let C_{ij} be the cofactor of $(\text{adj } A)_{ij}$ in (adj A). Then,

$$C_{11} = -12, C_{12} = -6, C_{13} = -12, C_{21} = -2, C_{22} = -2, C_{23} = -6, C_{31} = 6, C_{32} = 0, C_{33} = 6$$

$$\therefore \quad \text{adj}(\text{adj } A) = \begin{bmatrix} -12 & -6 & -12 \\ -2 & -2 & -6 \\ 6 & 0 & 6 \end{bmatrix}^T = \begin{bmatrix} -12 & -2 & 6 \\ -6 & -2 & 0 \\ -12 & -6 & 6 \end{bmatrix}$$

Substituting the values of $|A|$, $|\text{adj } A|$ and adj (adj A) in (i), we get

$$A = \pm \frac{2\sqrt{3}}{12} \begin{bmatrix} -12 & -2 & 6 \\ -6 & -2 & 0 \\ -12 & -6 & 6 \end{bmatrix} = \pm \frac{1}{\sqrt{3}} \begin{bmatrix} -6 & -1 & 3 \\ -3 & -1 & 0 \\ -6 & -3 & 3 \end{bmatrix}$$

EXAMPLE 22 *If* $A = \begin{bmatrix} 2 & -1 & 1 \\ -1 & 2 & -1 \\ 1 & -1 & 2 \end{bmatrix}$, *find* $(\text{adj } A)^{-1}$ *and* $(\text{adj } A^{-1})$.

SOLUTION We have, $A = \begin{bmatrix} 2 & -1 & 1 \\ -1 & 2 & -1 \\ 1 & -1 & 2 \end{bmatrix}$

$$\therefore \quad |A| = 2(4-1) + 1(-2+1) + 1(1-2) = 4$$

We know that $(\text{adj } A)^{-1} = \frac{1}{|A|} A$.

$$\therefore \quad (\text{adj } A)^{-1} = \frac{1}{4} \begin{bmatrix} 2 & -1 & 1 \\ -1 & 2 & -1 \\ 1 & -1 & 2 \end{bmatrix}$$

We also know that $(\text{adj } A^{-1}) = (\text{adj } A)^{-1}$.

$$\therefore \quad \text{adj } A^{-1} = \frac{1}{4} \begin{bmatrix} 2 & -1 & 1 \\ -1 & 2 & -1 \\ 1 & -1 & 2 \end{bmatrix}$$

Type VII MISCELLANEOUS PROBLEMS

EXAMPLE 23 *Let A be a non-singular matrix. Show that $A^T A^{-1}$ is symmetric iff $A^2 = (A^T)^2$.*

SOLUTION First, let $A^T A^{-1}$ be symmetric. Then,

$$(A^T A^{-1})^T = A^T A^{-1}$$

$$\Rightarrow \quad (A^{-1})^T (A^T)^T = A^T A^{-1}$$

$$\Rightarrow \quad (A^T)^{-1} A = A^T A^{-1} \qquad \left[\because (A^{-1})^T = (A^T)^{-1}\right]$$

$$\Rightarrow \quad A^T\left((A^T)^{-1} A\right) A = A^T (A^T A^{-1}) A \Rightarrow \left(A^T (A^T)^{-1}\right) AA = (A^T A^T)(A^{-1} A)$$

$$\Rightarrow \quad I A^2 = (A^T)^2 I \Rightarrow A^2 = (A^T)^2 \text{ or, } (A^T)^2 = A^2$$

Conversely, let A be a non-singular matrix such that $A^2 = (A^T)^2$. Then,

$$A^2 = (A^T)^2$$

$\Rightarrow \quad AA = A^T A^T$

$\Rightarrow \quad (A^T)^{-1}(AA)\, A^{-1} = (A^T)^{-1}(A^T A^T)\, A^{-1}$ $\left[\begin{array}{l}\text{Pre and post multiplying by } (A^T)^{-1} \\ \text{and } A^{-1} \text{ respectively}\end{array}\right]$

$\Rightarrow \quad \left((A^{-1})^T A\right)(AA^{-1}) = \left((A^T)^{-1} A^T\right)(A^T A^{-1}) \Rightarrow \left((A^{-1})^T A\right) I = I\,(A^T A^{-1})$

$\Rightarrow \quad (A^{-1})^T A = A^T A^{-1} \Rightarrow (A^{-1})^T (A^T)^T = A^T A^{-1} \Rightarrow (A^T A^{-1})^T = A^T A^{-1}$

$\Rightarrow \quad A^T A^{-1}$ is a symmetric matrix.

EXERCISE 6.1

BASIC

1. Find the adjoint of each of the following matrices:

(i) $\begin{bmatrix} -3 & 5 \\ 2 & 4 \end{bmatrix}$ [CBSE 2020] (ii) $\begin{bmatrix} a & b \\ c & d \end{bmatrix}$ (iii) $\begin{bmatrix} \cos\alpha & \sin\alpha \\ \sin\alpha & \cos\alpha \end{bmatrix}$ (iv) $\begin{bmatrix} 1 & \tan\alpha/2 \\ -\tan\alpha/2 & 1 \end{bmatrix}$

Verify that $(\text{adj } A)\, A = |A|\, I = A\,(\text{adj } A)$ for the above matrices.

2. Compute the adjoint of each of the following matrices:

(i) $\begin{bmatrix} 1 & 2 & 2 \\ 2 & 1 & 2 \\ 2 & 2 & 1 \end{bmatrix}$ (ii) $\begin{bmatrix} 1 & 2 & 5 \\ 2 & 3 & 1 \\ -1 & 1 & 1 \end{bmatrix}$ (iii) $\begin{bmatrix} 2 & -1 & 3 \\ 4 & 2 & 5 \\ 0 & 4 & -1 \end{bmatrix}$ (iv) $\begin{bmatrix} 2 & 0 & -1 \\ 5 & 1 & 0 \\ 1 & 1 & 3 \end{bmatrix}$

Verify that $(\text{adj } A)\, A = |A|\, I = A\,(\text{adj } A)$ for the above matrices.

3. For the matrix $A = \begin{bmatrix} 1 & -1 & 1 \\ 2 & 3 & 0 \\ 18 & 2 & 10 \end{bmatrix}$, show that $A\,(\text{adj } A) = O$.

4. If $A = \begin{bmatrix} -4 & -3 & -3 \\ 1 & 0 & 1 \\ 4 & 4 & 3 \end{bmatrix}$, show that $\text{adj } A = A$.

5. If $A = \begin{bmatrix} -1 & -2 & -2 \\ 2 & 1 & -2 \\ 2 & -2 & 1 \end{bmatrix}$, show that $\text{adj } A = 3A^T$.

6. Find $A\,(\text{adj } A)$ for the matrix $A = \begin{bmatrix} 1 & -2 & 3 \\ 0 & 2 & -1 \\ -4 & 5 & 2 \end{bmatrix}$.

7. Find the inverse of each of the following matrices:

(i) $\begin{bmatrix} \cos\theta & \sin\theta \\ -\sin\theta & \cos\theta \end{bmatrix}$ (ii) $\begin{bmatrix} 0 & 1 \\ 1 & 0 \end{bmatrix}$ (iii) $\begin{bmatrix} a & b \\ c & \dfrac{1+bc}{a} \end{bmatrix}$ (iv) $\begin{bmatrix} 2 & 5 \\ -3 & 1 \end{bmatrix}$

8. Find the inverse of each of the following matrices.

(i) $\begin{bmatrix} 1 & 2 & 3 \\ 2 & 3 & 1 \\ 3 & 1 & 2 \end{bmatrix}$ (ii) $\begin{bmatrix} 1 & 2 & 5 \\ 1 & -1 & -1 \\ 2 & 3 & -1 \end{bmatrix}$ (iii) $\begin{bmatrix} 2 & -1 & 1 \\ -1 & 2 & -1 \\ 1 & -1 & 2 \end{bmatrix}$ (iv) $\begin{bmatrix} 2 & 0 & -1 \\ 5 & 1 & 0 \\ 0 & 1 & 3 \end{bmatrix}$

(v) $\begin{bmatrix} 0 & 1 & -1 \\ 4 & -3 & 4 \\ 3 & -3 & 4 \end{bmatrix}$ (vi) $\begin{bmatrix} 0 & 0 & -1 \\ 3 & 4 & 5 \\ -2 & -4 & -7 \end{bmatrix}$ (vii) $\begin{bmatrix} 1 & 0 & 0 \\ 0 & \cos\alpha & \sin\alpha \\ 0 & \sin\alpha & -\cos\alpha \end{bmatrix}$

9. Find the inverse of each of the following matrices and verify that $A^{-1}A = I_3$.

(i) $\begin{bmatrix} 1 & 3 & 3 \\ 1 & 4 & 3 \\ 1 & 3 & 4 \end{bmatrix}$ (ii) $\begin{bmatrix} 2 & 3 & 1 \\ 3 & 4 & 1 \\ 3 & 7 & 2 \end{bmatrix}$

10. For the following pairs of matrices verify that $(AB)^{-1} = B^{-1}A^{-1}$:

(i) $A = \begin{bmatrix} 3 & 2 \\ 7 & 5 \end{bmatrix}$ and $B = \begin{bmatrix} 4 & 6 \\ 3 & 2 \end{bmatrix}$ (ii) $A = \begin{bmatrix} 2 & 1 \\ 5 & 3 \end{bmatrix}$ and $B = \begin{bmatrix} 4 & 5 \\ 3 & 4 \end{bmatrix}$

11. Let $A = \begin{bmatrix} 3 & 2 \\ 7 & 5 \end{bmatrix}$ and $B = \begin{bmatrix} 6 & 7 \\ 8 & 9 \end{bmatrix}$. Find $(AB)^{-1}$

12. Given $A = \begin{bmatrix} 2 & -3 \\ -4 & 7 \end{bmatrix}$, compute A^{-1} and show that $2A^{-1} = 9I - A$. **[CBSE 2018]**

13. If $A = \begin{bmatrix} 4 & 5 \\ 2 & 1 \end{bmatrix}$, then show that $A - 3I = 2(I + 3A^{-1})$.

14. Find the inverse of the matrix $A = \begin{bmatrix} a & b \\ c & \dfrac{1+bc}{a} \end{bmatrix}$ and show that $aA^{-1} = (a^2 + bc + 1)I - aA$.

15. Given $A = \begin{bmatrix} 5 & 0 & 4 \\ 2 & 3 & 2 \\ 1 & 2 & 1 \end{bmatrix}$, $B^{-1} = \begin{bmatrix} 1 & 3 & 3 \\ 1 & 4 & 3 \\ 1 & 3 & 4 \end{bmatrix}$. Compute $(AB)^{-1}$. **[NCERT]**

16. If $A = \begin{bmatrix} 1 & \cot x \\ -\cot x & 1 \end{bmatrix}$, show that $A^T A^{-1} = \begin{bmatrix} -\cos 2x & -\sin 2x \\ \sin 2x & -\cos 2x \end{bmatrix}$. **[CBSE 2024]**

17. Let $F(\alpha) = \begin{bmatrix} \cos\alpha & -\sin\alpha & 0 \\ \sin\alpha & \cos\alpha & 0 \\ 0 & 0 & 1 \end{bmatrix}$ and $G(\beta) = \begin{bmatrix} \cos\beta & 0 & \sin\beta \\ 0 & 1 & 0 \\ -\sin\beta & 0 & \cos\beta \end{bmatrix}$. Show that

(i) $[F(\alpha)]^{-1} = F(-\alpha)$ (ii) $[G(\beta)]^{-1} = G(-\beta)$ (iii) $[F(\alpha)\,G(\beta)]^{-1} = G(-\beta)\,F(-\alpha)$.

18. If $A = \begin{bmatrix} 2 & 3 \\ 1 & 2 \end{bmatrix}$, verify that $A^2 - 4A + I = O$, where $I = \begin{bmatrix} 1 & 0 \\ 0 & 1 \end{bmatrix}$ and $O = \begin{bmatrix} 0 & 0 \\ 0 & 0 \end{bmatrix}$. Hence, find A^{-1}. **[NCERT]**

19. Show that $A = \begin{bmatrix} -8 & 5 \\ 2 & 4 \end{bmatrix}$ satisfies the equation $A^2 + 4A - 42I = O$. Hence, find A^{-1}.

20. If $A = \begin{bmatrix} 3 & 1 \\ -1 & 2 \end{bmatrix}$, show that $A^2 - 5A + 7I = O$. Hence, find A^{-1}. **[NCERT, CBSE 2007]**

21. If $A = \begin{bmatrix} 4 & 3 \\ 2 & 5 \end{bmatrix}$, find x and y such that $A^2 - xA + yI = O$. Hence, evaluate A^{-1}.

22. If $A = \begin{bmatrix} 3 & -2 \\ 4 & -2 \end{bmatrix}$, find the value of λ so that $A^2 = \lambda A - 2I$. Hence, find A^{-1}. **[CBSE 2007]**

23. Show that $A = \begin{bmatrix} 5 & 3 \\ -1 & -2 \end{bmatrix}$ satisfies the equation $x^2 - 3x - 7 = 0$. Thus, find A^{-1}.

24. For the matrix $A = \begin{bmatrix} 1 & 1 & 1 \\ 1 & 2 & -3 \\ 2 & -1 & 3 \end{bmatrix}$. Show that $A^3 - 6A^2 + 5A + 11 I_3 = O$. Hence, find A^{-1}.

[NCERT]

25. Show that the matrix, $A = \begin{bmatrix} 1 & 0 & -2 \\ -2 & -1 & 2 \\ 3 & 4 & 1 \end{bmatrix}$ satisfies the equation, $A^3 - A^2 - 3A - I_3 = O$.

Hence, find A^{-1}.

26. If $A = \begin{bmatrix} 2 & -1 & 1 \\ -1 & 2 & -1 \\ 1 & -1 & 2 \end{bmatrix}$. Verify that $A^3 - 6A^2 + 9A - 4I = O$ and hence find A^{-1}. [NCERT]

27. (i) If $A = \frac{1}{9}\begin{bmatrix} -8 & 1 & 4 \\ 4 & 4 & 7 \\ 1 & -8 & 4 \end{bmatrix}$, prove that $A^{-1} = A^T$.

(ii) Given a square matrix A of order 3 such that $A^2 = \begin{bmatrix} 3 & -4 & 4 \\ 0 & -1 & 0 \\ -2 & 2 & -3 \end{bmatrix}$ show that $A^3 = A^{-1}$.

[CBSE 2024]

28. If $A = \begin{bmatrix} 3 & -3 & 4 \\ 2 & -3 & 4 \\ 0 & -1 & 1 \end{bmatrix}$, show that $A^{-1} = A^3$.

29. If $A = \begin{bmatrix} -1 & 2 & 0 \\ -1 & 1 & 1 \\ 0 & 1 & 0 \end{bmatrix}$, show that $A^2 = A^{-1}$.

30. Solve the matrix equation $\begin{bmatrix} 5 & 4 \\ 1 & 1 \end{bmatrix} X = \begin{bmatrix} 1 & -2 \\ 1 & 3 \end{bmatrix}$, where X is a 2×2 matrix.

31. (i) Find the matrix X satisfying the matrix equation: $X \begin{bmatrix} 5 & 3 \\ -1 & -2 \end{bmatrix} = \begin{bmatrix} 14 & 7 \\ 7 & 7 \end{bmatrix}$.

(ii) Find a matrix A such that $A \begin{bmatrix} 4 & 0 \\ -1 & -2 \end{bmatrix} = \begin{bmatrix} 17 & 10 \\ 0 & -16 \end{bmatrix}$. Also, find A^{-1}. [CBSE 2024]

32. Find the matrix X for which: $\begin{bmatrix} 3 & 2 \\ 7 & 5 \end{bmatrix} X \begin{bmatrix} -1 & 1 \\ -2 & 1 \end{bmatrix} = \begin{bmatrix} 2 & -1 \\ 0 & 4 \end{bmatrix}$.

33. Find the matrix X satisfying the equation: $\begin{bmatrix} 2 & 1 \\ 5 & 3 \end{bmatrix} X \begin{bmatrix} 5 & 3 \\ 3 & 2 \end{bmatrix} = \begin{bmatrix} 1 & 0 \\ 0 & 1 \end{bmatrix}$.

34. If $A = \begin{bmatrix} 1 & 2 & 2 \\ 2 & 1 & 2 \\ 2 & 2 & 1 \end{bmatrix}$, find A^{-1} and prove that $A^2 - 4A - 5I = O$.

BASED ON LOTS

35. If A is a square matrix of order n, prove that $|A \text{ adj } A| = |A|^n$.

36. If $A^{-1} = \begin{bmatrix} 3 & -1 & 1 \\ -15 & 6 & -5 \\ 5 & -2 & 2 \end{bmatrix}$ and $B = \begin{bmatrix} 1 & 2 & -2 \\ -1 & 3 & 0 \\ 0 & -2 & 1 \end{bmatrix}$, find $(AB)^{-1}$. [CBSE 2012]

37. If $A=\begin{bmatrix}1 & -2 & 3\\ 0 & -1 & 4\\ -2 & 2 & 1\end{bmatrix}$, find $(A^T)^{-1}$. [CBSE 2015]

38. Find the adjoint of the matrix $A=\begin{bmatrix}-1 & -2 & -2\\ 2 & 1 & -2\\ 2 & -2 & 1\end{bmatrix}$ and hence show that $A\,(\text{adj}\,A)=|A|\,I_3$. [CBSE 2015]

39. If $A=\begin{bmatrix}0 & 1 & 1\\ 1 & 0 & 1\\ 1 & 1 & 0\end{bmatrix}$, find A^{-1} and show that $A^{-1}=\frac{1}{2}(A^2-3I)$. [NCERT EXEMPLAR]

40. If $A=\begin{bmatrix}1 & 2 & -2\\ -1 & 3 & 0\\ 0 & -2 & 1\end{bmatrix}$ and $B^{-1}=\begin{bmatrix}3 & -1 & 1\\ -15 & 6 & -5\\ 5 & -2 & 2\end{bmatrix}$, find $(AB)^{-1}$. [CBSE 2023]

41. If $A=\begin{bmatrix}-1 & a & 2\\ 1 & 2 & x\\ 3 & 1 & 1\end{bmatrix}$ and $A^{-1}=\begin{bmatrix}1 & -1 & 1\\ -8 & 7 & -5\\ b & y & 3\end{bmatrix}$, find the value of $(a+x)-(b+y)$. [CBSE 2024]

ANSWERS

1. (i) $\begin{bmatrix}4 & -5\\ -2 & -3\end{bmatrix}$ (ii) $\begin{bmatrix}d & -b\\ -c & a\end{bmatrix}$ (iii) $\begin{bmatrix}\cos\alpha & -\sin\alpha\\ -\sin\alpha & \cos\alpha\end{bmatrix}$ (iv) $\begin{bmatrix}1 & -\tan\alpha/2\\ \tan\alpha/2 & 1\end{bmatrix}$

2. (i) $\begin{bmatrix}-3 & 2 & 2\\ 2 & -3 & 2\\ 2 & 2 & -3\end{bmatrix}$ (ii) $\begin{bmatrix}2 & 3 & -13\\ -3 & 6 & 9\\ 5 & -3 & -1\end{bmatrix}$ (iii) $\begin{bmatrix}-22 & 11 & -11\\ 4 & -2 & 2\\ 16 & -8 & 8\end{bmatrix}$

(iv) $\begin{bmatrix}3 & -1 & 1\\ -15 & 7 & -5\\ 4 & -2 & 2\end{bmatrix}$

6. $\begin{bmatrix}25 & 0 & 0\\ 0 & 25 & 0\\ 0 & 0 & 25\end{bmatrix}$

7. (i) $\begin{bmatrix}\cos\theta & -\sin\theta\\ \sin\theta & \cos\theta\end{bmatrix}$ (ii) $\begin{bmatrix}0 & 1\\ 1 & 0\end{bmatrix}$ (iii) $\begin{bmatrix}\frac{1+bc}{a} & -b\\ -c & a\end{bmatrix}$ (iv) $\frac{1}{17}\begin{bmatrix}1 & -5\\ 3 & 2\end{bmatrix}$

8. (i) $\frac{1}{18}\begin{bmatrix}-5 & 1 & 7\\ 1 & 7 & -5\\ 7 & -5 & 1\end{bmatrix}$ (ii) $\frac{1}{27}\begin{bmatrix}4 & 17 & 3\\ -1 & -11 & 6\\ 5 & 1 & -3\end{bmatrix}$ (iii) $\frac{1}{4}\begin{bmatrix}3 & 1 & -1\\ 1 & 3 & 1\\ -1 & 1 & 3\end{bmatrix}$

(iv) $\begin{bmatrix}3 & -1 & 1\\ -15 & 6 & -5\\ 5 & -2 & 2\end{bmatrix}$ (v) $\begin{bmatrix}0 & 1 & -1\\ 4 & -3 & 4\\ 3 & -3 & 4\end{bmatrix}$ (vi) $\frac{1}{4}\begin{bmatrix}-8 & 4 & 4\\ 11 & -2 & -3\\ -4 & 0 & 0\end{bmatrix}$

(vii) $\begin{bmatrix}1 & 0 & 0\\ 0 & \cos\alpha & \sin\alpha\\ 0 & \sin\alpha & -\cos\alpha\end{bmatrix}$

9. (i) $\begin{bmatrix}7 & -3 & -3\\ -1 & 1 & 0\\ -1 & 0 & 1\end{bmatrix}$ (ii) $\frac{1}{2}\begin{bmatrix}1 & 1 & -1\\ -3 & 1 & 1\\ 9 & -5 & -1\end{bmatrix}$

11. $\begin{bmatrix}-47 & \frac{39}{2}\\ 41 & -17\end{bmatrix}$

14. $\begin{bmatrix}\frac{1+bc}{a} & -b\\ -c & a\end{bmatrix}$

15. $\begin{bmatrix}-2 & 19 & -27\\ -2 & 18 & -25\\ -3 & 29 & -42\end{bmatrix}$

18. $\begin{bmatrix} 2 & -3 \\ -1 & 2 \end{bmatrix}$ 19. $\frac{1}{42}\begin{bmatrix} -4 & 5 \\ 2 & 8 \end{bmatrix}$ 20. $\frac{1}{7}\begin{bmatrix} 2 & -1 \\ 1 & 3 \end{bmatrix}$

21. $x = 9,\ y = 14,\ \frac{1}{14}\begin{bmatrix} 5 & -3 \\ -2 & 4 \end{bmatrix}$ 22. $\lambda = 1, A^{-1} = \frac{1}{2}\begin{bmatrix} -2 & 2 \\ -4 & 3 \end{bmatrix}$

23. $\frac{1}{7}\begin{bmatrix} 2 & 3 \\ -1 & -5 \end{bmatrix}$ 24. $\frac{1}{11}\begin{bmatrix} -3 & 4 & 5 \\ 9 & -1 & -4 \\ 5 & -3 & -1 \end{bmatrix}$ 25. $\begin{bmatrix} -9 & -8 & -2 \\ 8 & 7 & 2 \\ -5 & -4 & -1 \end{bmatrix}$ 26. $\frac{1}{4}\begin{bmatrix} 3 & 1 & -1 \\ 1 & 3 & 1 \\ -1 & 1 & 3 \end{bmatrix}$

30. $\begin{bmatrix} -3 & -14 \\ 4 & 17 \end{bmatrix}$ 31. (i) $\begin{bmatrix} 3 & 1 \\ 1 & -2 \end{bmatrix}$ (ii) $A = \begin{bmatrix} 3 & -5 \\ 2 & 8 \end{bmatrix}, A^{-1} = \frac{1}{34}\begin{bmatrix} 8 & 5 \\ -2 & 3 \end{bmatrix}$

32. $\begin{bmatrix} -16 & 3 \\ 24 & -5 \end{bmatrix}$ 33. $\begin{bmatrix} 9 & -14 \\ -16 & 25 \end{bmatrix}$ 34. $\frac{1}{5}\begin{bmatrix} -3 & 2 & 2 \\ 2 & -3 & 2 \\ 2 & 2 & -3 \end{bmatrix}$

36. $\begin{bmatrix} 9 & -3 & 5 \\ -2 & 1 & 0 \\ 1 & 0 & 2 \end{bmatrix}$ 37. $\begin{bmatrix} -9 & -8 & -2 \\ 8 & 7 & 2 \\ -5 & -4 & -1 \end{bmatrix}$ 40. $\begin{bmatrix} 10 & 7 & 21 \\ -49 & -34 & -103 \\ 17 & 12 & 36 \end{bmatrix}$ 41. 3

HINTS TO SELECTED PROBLEMS

15. We have to find $(AB)^{-1}$ and we are given the values of A and B^{-1}. But, $(AB)^{-1} = B^{-1}A^{-1}$.

So, we need to find A^{-1}.

Now, $A = \begin{bmatrix} 5 & 0 & 4 \\ 2 & 3 & 2 \\ 1 & 2 & 1 \end{bmatrix} \Rightarrow |A| = 5(3-4) - 0(2-2) + 4(4-3) = -5+4 = -1 \neq 0$

So, A^{-1} exists.

Let C_{ij} be cofactor of a_{ij} in $A = [a_{ij}]$. Then,

$C_{11} = 3-4 = -1, C_{12} = -(2-2) = 0, \quad C_{13} = 4-3 = 1, C_{21} = -(0-8) = 8$

$C_{22} = 5-4 = 1, \quad C_{23} = -(10-0) = -10, C_{31} = (0-12) = -12,$

$C_{32} = -(10-8) = -2, C_{33} = 15$

$$\therefore \quad \text{adj } A = \begin{bmatrix} C_{11} & C_{12} & C_{13} \\ C_{21} & C_{22} & C_{23} \\ C_{31} & C_{32} & C_{33} \end{bmatrix}^T = \begin{bmatrix} -1 & 0 & 1 \\ 8 & 1 & -10 \\ -12 & -2 & 15 \end{bmatrix}^T = \begin{bmatrix} -1 & 8 & -12 \\ 0 & 1 & -2 \\ 1 & -10 & 15 \end{bmatrix}$$

$$\text{So,} \quad A^{-1} = \frac{1}{|A|}\text{adj } A = \begin{bmatrix} 1 & -8 & 12 \\ 0 & -1 & 2 \\ -1 & 10 & -15 \end{bmatrix}$$

$$\text{Hence,} \quad (AB)^{-1} = B^{-1}A^{-1} = \begin{bmatrix} 1 & 3 & 3 \\ 1 & 4 & 3 \\ 1 & 3 & 4 \end{bmatrix}\begin{bmatrix} 1 & -8 & 12 \\ 0 & -1 & 2 \\ -1 & 10 & -15 \end{bmatrix} = \begin{bmatrix} -2 & 19 & -27 \\ -2 & 18 & -25 \\ -3 & 29 & -42 \end{bmatrix}$$

18. We have, $A = \begin{bmatrix} 2 & 3 \\ 1 & 2 \end{bmatrix}$

$$\therefore \quad A^2 = AA = \begin{bmatrix} 2 & 3 \\ 1 & 2 \end{bmatrix}\begin{bmatrix} 2 & 3 \\ 1 & 2 \end{bmatrix} = \begin{bmatrix} 7 & 12 \\ 4 & 7 \end{bmatrix}$$

$$\therefore \quad A^2 - 4A + I = \begin{bmatrix} 7 & 12 \\ 4 & 7 \end{bmatrix} - 4\begin{bmatrix} 2 & 3 \\ 1 & 2 \end{bmatrix} + \begin{bmatrix} 1 & 0 \\ 0 & 1 \end{bmatrix} = \begin{bmatrix} 0 & 0 \\ 0 & 0 \end{bmatrix} = O$$

$\Rightarrow \quad A^{-1}(A^2 - 4A + I) = A^{-1}O$ [Multiplying both sides by A^{-1}]

$\Rightarrow \quad A^{-1}A^2 - 4A^{-1}A + A^{-1}I = O \Rightarrow A - 4I + A^{-1} = O$

$\Rightarrow \quad A^{-1} = 4I - A = \begin{bmatrix} 4 & 0 \\ 0 & 4 \end{bmatrix} - \begin{bmatrix} 2 & 3 \\ 1 & 2 \end{bmatrix} = \begin{bmatrix} 2 & -3 \\ -1 & 2 \end{bmatrix}$

20. We have, $A = \begin{bmatrix} 3 & 1 \\ -1 & 2 \end{bmatrix}$

$\therefore \quad A^2 = AA = \begin{bmatrix} 3 & 1 \\ -1 & 2 \end{bmatrix}\begin{bmatrix} 3 & 1 \\ -1 & 2 \end{bmatrix} = \begin{bmatrix} 8 & 5 \\ -5 & 3 \end{bmatrix}$

So, $A^2 - 5A + 7I = \begin{bmatrix} 8 & 5 \\ -5 & 3 \end{bmatrix} - 5\begin{bmatrix} 3 & 1 \\ -1 & 2 \end{bmatrix} + 7\begin{bmatrix} 1 & 0 \\ 0 & 1 \end{bmatrix} = \begin{bmatrix} 8-15+7 & 5-5+0 \\ -5+5+0 & 3-10+7 \end{bmatrix} = \begin{bmatrix} 0 & 0 \\ 0 & 0 \end{bmatrix} = O$

Now, $A^2 - 5A + 7I = O$

$\Rightarrow \quad A^{-1}(A^2 - 5A + 7I) = A^{-1}O$ [Multiplying throughout by A^{-1}]

$\Rightarrow \quad A^{-1}A^2 - 5A^{-1}A + 7A^{-1}I = O$

$\Rightarrow \quad A - 5I + 7A^{-1} = O \Rightarrow 7A^{-1} = 5I - A$

$\Rightarrow \quad 7A^{-1} = \begin{bmatrix} 5 & 0 \\ 0 & 5 \end{bmatrix} - \begin{bmatrix} 3 & 1 \\ -1 & 2 \end{bmatrix} = \begin{bmatrix} 2 & -1 \\ 1 & 3 \end{bmatrix} \Rightarrow A^{-1} = \frac{1}{7}\begin{bmatrix} 2 & -1 \\ 1 & 3 \end{bmatrix}$

24. We have, $A = \begin{bmatrix} 1 & 1 & 1 \\ 1 & 2 & -3 \\ 2 & -1 & 3 \end{bmatrix}$

$\therefore \quad A^2 = AA = \begin{bmatrix} 1 & 1 & 1 \\ 1 & 2 & -3 \\ 2 & -1 & 3 \end{bmatrix}\begin{bmatrix} 1 & 1 & 1 \\ 1 & 2 & -3 \\ 2 & -1 & 3 \end{bmatrix} = \begin{bmatrix} 4 & 2 & 1 \\ -3 & 8 & -14 \\ 7 & -3 & 14 \end{bmatrix}$

and, $A^3 = A^2A = \begin{bmatrix} 4 & 2 & 1 \\ -3 & 8 & -14 \\ 7 & -3 & 14 \end{bmatrix}\begin{bmatrix} 1 & 1 & 1 \\ 1 & 2 & -3 \\ 2 & -1 & 3 \end{bmatrix} = \begin{bmatrix} 8 & 7 & 1 \\ -23 & 27 & -69 \\ 32 & -13 & 58 \end{bmatrix}$

$\therefore \quad A^3 - 6A^2 + 5A + 11I_3$

$= \begin{bmatrix} 8 & 7 & 1 \\ -23 & 27 & -69 \\ 32 & -13 & 58 \end{bmatrix} - 6\begin{bmatrix} 4 & 2 & 1 \\ -3 & 8 & -14 \\ 7 & -3 & 14 \end{bmatrix} + 5\begin{bmatrix} 1 & 1 & 1 \\ 1 & 2 & -3 \\ 2 & -1 & 3 \end{bmatrix} + 11\begin{bmatrix} 1 & 0 & 0 \\ 0 & 1 & 0 \\ 0 & 0 & 1 \end{bmatrix}$

$= \begin{bmatrix} 8-24+5+11 & 7-12+5+0 & 1-6+5+0 \\ -23+18+5+0 & 27-48+10+11 & -69+84-15+0 \\ 32-42+10+0 & -13+18-5+0 & 58-84+15+1 \end{bmatrix} = \begin{bmatrix} 0 & 0 & 0 \\ 0 & 0 & 0 \\ 0 & 0 & 0 \end{bmatrix} = O$

Now, $A^3 - 6A^2 + 5A + 11I_3 = O$

$\Rightarrow \quad A^{-1}(A^3 - 6A^2 + 5A + 11I_3) = A^{-1}O$ [Multiplying both sides by A^{-1}]

$\Rightarrow \quad A^2 - 6A + 5I + 11A^{-1} = O$

$\Rightarrow \quad 11A^{-1} = -A^2 + 6A - 5I$

$\Rightarrow \quad 11A^{-1} = -\begin{bmatrix} 4 & 2 & 1 \\ -3 & 8 & -14 \\ 7 & -3 & 14 \end{bmatrix} + 6\begin{bmatrix} 1 & 1 & 1 \\ 1 & 2 & -3 \\ 2 & -1 & 3 \end{bmatrix} - 5\begin{bmatrix} 1 & 0 & 0 \\ 0 & 1 & 0 \\ 0 & 0 & 1 \end{bmatrix}$

$$\Rightarrow \quad 11A^{-1} = \begin{bmatrix} -4+6-5 & -2+6+0 & -1+6+0 \\ 3+6+0 & -8+12-5 & 14-18+0 \\ -7+12+0 & 3-6+0 & -14+18-5 \end{bmatrix} = \begin{bmatrix} -3 & 4 & 5 \\ 9 & -1 & -4 \\ 5 & -3 & -1 \end{bmatrix}$$

$$\Rightarrow \quad A^{-1} = \frac{1}{11}\begin{bmatrix} -3 & 4 & 5 \\ 9 & -1 & -4 \\ 5 & -3 & -1 \end{bmatrix}$$

26. We have, $A = \begin{bmatrix} 2 & -1 & 1 \\ -1 & 2 & -1 \\ 1 & -1 & 2 \end{bmatrix}$

$$\therefore \quad A^2 = AA = \begin{bmatrix} 2 & -1 & 1 \\ -1 & 2 & -1 \\ 1 & -1 & 2 \end{bmatrix}\begin{bmatrix} 2 & -1 & 1 \\ -1 & 2 & -1 \\ 1 & -1 & 2 \end{bmatrix} = \begin{bmatrix} 6 & -5 & 5 \\ -5 & 6 & -5 \\ 5 & -5 & 6 \end{bmatrix}$$

$$\text{and,} \quad A^3 = A^2 A = \begin{bmatrix} 6 & -5 & 5 \\ -5 & 6 & -5 \\ 5 & -5 & 6 \end{bmatrix}\begin{bmatrix} 2 & -1 & 1 \\ -1 & 2 & -1 \\ 1 & -1 & 2 \end{bmatrix} = \begin{bmatrix} 22 & -21 & 21 \\ -21 & 22 & -21 \\ 21 & -21 & 22 \end{bmatrix}$$

$$\therefore \quad A^3 - 6A^2 + 9A - 4I$$

$$= \begin{bmatrix} 22 & -21 & 21 \\ -21 & 22 & -21 \\ 21 & -21 & 22 \end{bmatrix} + \begin{bmatrix} -36 & 30 & -30 \\ 30 & -36 & 30 \\ -30 & 30 & -36 \end{bmatrix} + \begin{bmatrix} 18 & -9 & 9 \\ -9 & 18 & -9 \\ 9 & -9 & 18 \end{bmatrix} + \begin{bmatrix} -4 & 0 & 0 \\ 0 & -4 & 0 \\ 0 & 0 & -4 \end{bmatrix}$$

$$= \begin{bmatrix} 22-36+18-4 & -21+30-9+0 & 21-30+9+0 \\ -21+30-9+0 & 22-36+18-4 & -21+30-9+0 \\ 21-30+9+0 & -21+30-9+0 & 22-36+18-4 \end{bmatrix} = \begin{bmatrix} 0 & 0 & 0 \\ 0 & 0 & 0 \\ 0 & 0 & 0 \end{bmatrix} = O$$

Now, $A^3 - 6A^2 + 9A - 4I = O$

$\Rightarrow \quad A^{-1}(A^3 - 6A^2 + 9A - 4I) = A^{-1}O$ [Multiplying both sides by A^{-1}]

$\Rightarrow \quad A^2 - 6A + 9I - 4A^{-1} = O$

$\Rightarrow \quad 4A^{-1} = A^2 - 6A + 9I$

$$\Rightarrow \quad 4A^{-1} = \begin{bmatrix} 6 & -5 & 5 \\ -5 & 6 & -5 \\ 5 & -5 & 6 \end{bmatrix} + \begin{bmatrix} -12 & 6 & -6 \\ 6 & -12 & 6 \\ -6 & 6 & -12 \end{bmatrix} + \begin{bmatrix} 9 & 0 & 0 \\ 0 & 9 & 0 \\ 0 & 0 & 9 \end{bmatrix}$$

$$\Rightarrow \quad 4A^{-1} = \begin{bmatrix} 6-12+9 & -5+6+0 & 5-6+0 \\ -5+6+0 & 6-12+9 & -5+6+0 \\ 5-6+0 & -5+6+0 & 6-12+9 \end{bmatrix} = \begin{bmatrix} 3 & 1 & -1 \\ 1 & 3 & 1 \\ -1 & 1 & 3 \end{bmatrix}$$

$$\therefore \quad A^{-1} = \frac{1}{4}\begin{bmatrix} 3 & 1 & -1 \\ 1 & 3 & 1 \\ -1 & 1 & 3 \end{bmatrix}$$

FILL IN THE BLANKS TYPE QUESTIONS (FBQs)

1. If A is a unit matrix of order n, then A (adj A) = ...
2. If A is a non-singular square matrix such that $A^3 = I$, then A^{-1} =......................... .
3. If A and B are square matrices of the same order and $AB = 3I$, then A^{-1} = ...

4. If the matrix $A=\begin{bmatrix}1 & a & 2\\ 1 & 2 & 5\\ 2 & 1 & 1\end{bmatrix}$ is not invertible, then $a=$ ....

5. If A is a singular matrix, then A (adj A) = ...

6. Let A be a square matrix of order 3 such that $|A|=11$ and B be the matrix of cofactors of elements of A. Then, $|B|^2=$ ....

7. If A is a square matrix of order 2 such that $A(\text{adj}A)=\begin{bmatrix}10 & 0\\ 0 & 10\end{bmatrix}$, then $|A|=$ ....

8. If A is an invertible matrix of order 3 and $|A|=3$, then $|\text{adj } A|=$ ....

9. If A is an invertible matrix of order 3 and $|A|=5$, then adj (adj A) = ...

10. If A is an invertible matrix of order 3 and $|A|=4$, then $|\text{adj (adj } A)|=$ ....

11. If $A=$ diag (1, 2, 3), then $|\text{adj (adj } A)|=$ ....

12. If A is a square matrix of order 3 such that $|A|=\frac{5}{2}$, then $|A^{-1}|=$ ....

13. If A is a square matrix such that A (adj A) $=10I$, then $|A|=$ ....

14. Let A be a square matrix of order 3 and $B=|A|A^{-1}$. If $|A|=-5$, then $|B|=$ ....

15. If k is a scalar and I is a unit matrix of order 3, then adj (kI) = ...

16. If $A=\begin{bmatrix}\cos x & \sin x\\ -\sin x & \cos x\end{bmatrix}$ and A (adj A) $=\begin{bmatrix}k & 0\\ 0 & k\end{bmatrix}$, then $k=$ ....

17. If A is a non-singular matrix of order 3, then adj (adj A) is equal to ....

18. If $A=[a_{ij}]_{2\times 2}$, where $a_{ij}=\begin{cases} i+j, \text{ if } i\neq j\\ i^2-2j, \text{ if } i=j\end{cases}$, then $A^{-1}=$ ....

19. If $A=\begin{bmatrix}0 & 3\\ 2 & 0\end{bmatrix}$ and $A^{-1}=\lambda$ (adj A), then $\lambda=$ ....

20. If A is a 3×3 non-singular matrix such that $AA^T=A^TA$ and $B=A^{-1}A^T$, then $BB^T=$ ....

21. If A and B are two square matrices of the same order such that $B=-A^{-1}BA$, then $(A+B)^2=$ ....

22. If A is a non-singular matrix of order 3×3, then $(A^3)^{-1}=$ ....

23. If A be a square matrix such that $|\text{adj } A|=|A|^2$, then the order of A is ....

24. If $A=\begin{bmatrix}x & 5 & 2\\ 2 & y & 3\\ 1 & 1 & z\end{bmatrix}$, $xyz=80$, $3x+2y+10z=20$ and A adj $A=kI$, then $k=$...... .

[NCERT EXEMPLAR]

25. For $A=\begin{bmatrix}3 & -4\\ 1 & -1\end{bmatrix}$, write A^{-1}. [CBSE 2020]

ANSWERS

1. A 2. A^2 3. $\frac{1}{3}B$ 4. 1 5. Null matrix 6. 11^4 7. 10
8. 9 9. $5A$ 10. 4^4 11. 6^4 12. $\frac{2}{5}$ 13. 10 14. 25 15. k^2I

16. 1 17. $|A|A$ 18. $\frac{1}{9}\begin{bmatrix} 0 & 3 \\ 3 & 1 \end{bmatrix}$ 19. $-\frac{1}{6}$ 20. I 21. $A^2 + B^2$

22. $(A^{-1})^3$ 23. 3×3 24. 79 25. $\begin{bmatrix} -1 & 4 \\ -1 & 3 \end{bmatrix}$

VERY SHORT ANSWER QUESTIONS (VSAQs)

Answer each of the following questions in one word or one sentence or as per exact requirement of the question:

1. Write the adjoint of the matrix $A = \begin{bmatrix} -3 & 4 \\ 7 & -2 \end{bmatrix}$.
2. If A is a square matrix such that $A\,(\text{adj}\,A) = 5I$, where I denotes the identity matrix of the same order. Then, find the value of $|A|$.
3. If A is a square matrix of order 3 such that $|A| = 5$, write the value of $|\text{adj}\,A|$. **[CBSE 2009]**
4. If A is a square matrix of order 3 such that $|\text{adj}\,A| = 64$, find $|A|$.
5. If A is a non-singular square matrix such that $|A| = 10$, find $|A^{-1}|$.
6. If A, B, C are three non-null square matrices of the same order, write the condition on A such that $AB = AC \Rightarrow B = C$.
7. If A is a non-singular square matrix such that $A^{-1} = \begin{bmatrix} 5 & 3 \\ -2 & -1 \end{bmatrix}$, then find $(A^T)^{-1}$.
8. If $\text{adj}\,A = \begin{bmatrix} 2 & 3 \\ 4 & -1 \end{bmatrix}$ and $\text{adj}\,B = \begin{bmatrix} 1 & -2 \\ -3 & 1 \end{bmatrix}$, find $\text{adj}\,AB$.
9. If A is a symmetric matrix, write whether A^T is symmetric or skew-symmetric.
10. If A is a square matrix of order 3 such that $|A| = 2$, then write the value of $\text{adj}\,(\text{adj}\,A)$.
11. If A is a square matrix of order 3 such that $|A| = 3$, then find the value of $|\text{adj}\,(\text{adj}\,A)|$.
12. If A is a square matrix of order 3 such that $\text{adj}\,(2A) = k\,\text{adj}\,(A)$, then write the value of k.
13. If A is a square matrix, then write the matrix $\text{adj}\,(A^T) - (\text{adj}\,A)^T$.
14. Let A be a 3×3 square matrix such that $A\,(\text{adj}\,A) = 2\,I$, where I is the identity matrix. Write the value of $|\text{adj}\,A|$.
15. If A is a non-singular symmetric matrix, write whether A^{-1} is symmetric or skew-symmetric.
16. If $A = \begin{bmatrix} \cos\theta & \sin\theta \\ -\sin\theta & \cos\theta \end{bmatrix}$ and $A\,(\text{adj}\,A) = \begin{bmatrix} k & 0 \\ 0 & k \end{bmatrix}$, then find the value of k.
17. If A is an invertible matrix such that $|A^{-1}| = 2$, find the value of $|A|$.
18. If A is a square matrix such that $A\,(\text{adj}\,A) = \begin{bmatrix} 5 & 0 & 0 \\ 0 & 5 & 0 \\ 0 & 0 & 5 \end{bmatrix}$, then write the value of $|\text{adj}\,A|$.
19. If $A = \begin{bmatrix} 2 & 3 \\ 5 & -2 \end{bmatrix}$ be such that $A^{-1} = k\,A$, then find the value of k.
20. Let A be a square matrix such that $A^2 - A + I = O$, then write A^{-1} in terms of A.

21. If C_{ij} is the cofactor of the element a_{ij} of the matrix $A = \begin{bmatrix} 2 & -3 & 5 \\ 6 & 0 & 4 \\ 1 & 5 & -7 \end{bmatrix}$, then write the value of $a_{32}\, C_{32}$. [CBSE 2013]

22. Find the inverse of the matrix $\begin{bmatrix} 3 & -2 \\ -7 & 5 \end{bmatrix}$

23. Find the inverse of the matrix $\begin{bmatrix} \cos\theta & \sin\theta \\ -\sin\theta & \cos\theta \end{bmatrix}$.

24. If $A = \begin{bmatrix} 1 & -3 \\ 2 & 0 \end{bmatrix}$, write adj A.

25. If $A = \begin{bmatrix} a & b \\ c & d \end{bmatrix}$, $B = \begin{bmatrix} 1 & 0 \\ 0 & 1 \end{bmatrix}$, find adj (AB).

26. If $A = \begin{bmatrix} 3 & 1 \\ 2 & -3 \end{bmatrix}$, then find $|\text{adj } A|$. [CBSE 2010]

27. If $A = \begin{bmatrix} 2 & 3 \\ 5 & -2 \end{bmatrix}$, write A^{-1} in terms of A. [CBSE 2011]

28. Write A^{-1} for $A = \begin{bmatrix} 2 & 5 \\ 1 & 3 \end{bmatrix}$

29. Use elementary column operation $C_2 \to C_2 + 2C_1$ in the following matrix equation :

$$\begin{bmatrix} 2 & 1 \\ 2 & 0 \end{bmatrix} = \begin{bmatrix} 3 & 1 \\ 2 & 0 \end{bmatrix} \begin{bmatrix} 1 & 0 \\ -1 & 1 \end{bmatrix}$$ [CBSE 2016]

30. In the following matrix equation use elementary operation $R_2 \to R_2 + R_1$ and the equation thus obtained:

$$\begin{bmatrix} 2 & 3 \\ 1 & 4 \end{bmatrix} \begin{bmatrix} 1 & 0 \\ 2 & -1 \end{bmatrix} = \begin{bmatrix} 8 & -3 \\ 9 & -4 \end{bmatrix}$$ [CBSE 2017]

31. If A is a square matrix with $|A| = 4$ then find the value of $|A.(\text{adj } A)|$. [CBSE 2019]

ANSWERS

1. $\begin{bmatrix} -2 & -4 \\ -7 & -3 \end{bmatrix}$ 2. 5 3. 25 4. ± 8 5. $\frac{1}{10}$

6. A must be invertible or $|A| \neq 0$ 7. $\begin{bmatrix} 5 & -2 \\ 3 & -1 \end{bmatrix}$ 8. $\begin{bmatrix} -6 & 5 \\ -2 & -10 \end{bmatrix}$ 9. symmetric

10. $2A$ 11. 81 12. 4 13. Null matrix 14. 4

15. symmetric 16. 1 17. $\frac{1}{2}$ 18. 25 19. $\frac{1}{19}$

20. $A^{-1} = (I - A)$ 21. 110 22. $\begin{bmatrix} 5 & 2 \\ 7 & 3 \end{bmatrix}$ 23. $\begin{bmatrix} \cos\theta & -\sin\theta \\ \sin\theta & \cos\theta \end{bmatrix}$

24. $\begin{bmatrix} 0 & 3 \\ -2 & 1 \end{bmatrix}$ 25. $\begin{bmatrix} d & -b \\ -c & a \end{bmatrix}$ 26. -11 27. $A^{-1} = \frac{1}{19} A$

28. $A^{-1} = \begin{bmatrix} 3 & -5 \\ -1 & 2 \end{bmatrix}$ 29. $\begin{bmatrix} 2 & 5 \\ 2 & 4 \end{bmatrix} = \begin{bmatrix} 3 & 1 \\ 2 & 0 \end{bmatrix} \begin{bmatrix} 1 & 2 \\ -1 & -1 \end{bmatrix}$ 30. $\begin{bmatrix} 2 & 3 \\ 3 & 7 \end{bmatrix} \begin{bmatrix} 1 & 0 \\ 2 & -1 \end{bmatrix} = \begin{bmatrix} 8 & -3 \\ 17 & -7 \end{bmatrix}$

31. $4^{O(A)}$

CHAPTER 7

SOLUTION OF SIMULTANEOUS LINEAR EQUATIONS

7.1 INTRODUCTION

Consider the following system of m linear equations in n unknowns:

$$\begin{array}{l} a_{11}\, x_1 + a_{12}\, x_2 + \dots + a_{1n}\, x_n = b_1 \\ a_{21}\, x_1 + a_{22}\, x_2 + \dots + a_{2n}\, x_n = b_2 \\ \dots \quad \dots \quad \dots \quad \dots \quad \dots \\ \dots \quad \dots \quad \dots \quad \dots \quad \dots \\ a_{m1}\, x_1 + a_{m2}\, x_2 + \dots + a_{mn}\, x_n = b_m \end{array} \qquad \text{...(i)}$$

This system of equations can be written in matrix form as

$$\begin{bmatrix} a_{11} & a_{12} & \cdots & a_{1n} \\ a_{21} & a_{22} & \cdots & a_{2n} \\ \vdots & \vdots & & \\ a_{m1} & a_{m2} & \cdots & a_{mn} \end{bmatrix} \begin{bmatrix} x_1 \\ x_2 \\ \vdots \\ x_n \end{bmatrix} = \begin{bmatrix} b_1 \\ b_2 \\ \vdots \\ b_n \end{bmatrix}$$

or $\quad AX = B$, where $A = \begin{bmatrix} a_{11} & a_{12} & \cdots & a_{1n} \\ a_{21} & a_{22} & \cdots & a_{2n} \\ \vdots & \vdots & & \\ a_{m1} & a_{m2} & \cdots & a_{mn} \end{bmatrix}_{m \times n}$, $X = \begin{bmatrix} x_1 \\ x_2 \\ \vdots \\ x_n \end{bmatrix}_{n \times 1}$ and $B = \begin{bmatrix} b_1 \\ b_2 \\ \vdots \\ b_n \end{bmatrix}_{n \times 1}$

The $m \times n$ matrix A is called the *coefficient matrix* of the system of linear equations.

ILLUSTRATION *Express the following system of simultaneous linear equation as a matrix equation:*

$$\begin{aligned} 2x + 3y - z &= 1 \\ x + y + 2z &= 2 \\ 2x - y + z &= 3 \end{aligned}$$

SOLUTION The given system of equations can be written in matrix form as

$$\begin{bmatrix} 2 & 3 & -1 \\ 1 & 1 & 2 \\ 2 & -1 & 1 \end{bmatrix} \begin{bmatrix} x \\ y \\ z \end{bmatrix} = \begin{bmatrix} 1 \\ 2 \\ 3 \end{bmatrix} \text{ or, } AX = B, \text{ where } A = \begin{bmatrix} 2 & 3 & -1 \\ 1 & 1 & 2 \\ 2 & -1 & 1 \end{bmatrix}, X = \begin{bmatrix} x \\ y \\ z \end{bmatrix} \text{ and } B = \begin{bmatrix} 1 \\ 2 \\ 3 \end{bmatrix}$$

SOLUTION *A set of values of the variables $x_1, x_2, \dots x_n$ which simultaneously satisfy all the equations is called a solution of the system of equations.*

For example, $x = 2, y = -3$ is a solution of the system of linear equations

$$\begin{aligned} 3x + y &= 3 \\ 2x + y &= 1 \end{aligned}$$

because $3(2) + (-3) = 3$ and, $2(2) + (-3) = 1$.

CONSISTENT SYSTEM *If the system of equations has one or more solutions, then it is said to be a consistent system of equations, otherwise it is an inconsistent system of equations.*

For example, the system of linear equations

$$2x + 3y = 5$$
$$4x + 6y = 10$$

is consistent, because $x = 1, y = 1$ and $x = 2, y = 1/3$ are solutions of it.

However, the system of linear equations

$$2x + 3y = 5$$
$$4x + 6y = 9$$

is inconsistent, because there is no set of values of x, y which satisfy the two equations simultaneously.

HOMOGENEOUS AND NON-HOMOGENEOUS SYSTEMS *A system of equations $AX = B$ is called a homogeneous system if $B = O$. Otherwise, it is called a non-homogeneous system of equations.*

For example, the system of equations

$$2x + 3y = 0$$
$$3x - y = 0$$

is a homogeneous system of linear equations whereas the system of equations given by

$$2x + 3y = 1$$
$$3x - y = 5$$

is a non-homogeneous system of linear equations.

7.2 MATRIX METHOD FOR THE SOLUTION OF A NON-HOMOGENEOUS SYSTEM

In the previous section, we have seen that a system of simultaneous linear equations can be expressed as a matrix equation. In this section, we shall discuss about a method for solving a system of non-homogenous simultaneous linear equations in which the number of unknowns is same as the number of equations. In this method, we will use the inverse of the coefficient matrix. So, it is also known as matrix method.

THEOREM 1 *If A is a non-singular matrix, then the system of equations given by $AX = B$ has the unique solution given by $X = A^{-1}B$.*

PROOF We have, $AX = B$, where $|A| \neq 0$. Since $|A| \neq 0$, therefore A^{-1} exists.

Pre-multiplying both sides of $AX = B$ by A^{-1}, we get

$$A^{-1}(AX) = A^{-1}B \Rightarrow (A^{-1}A)X = A^{-1}B \Rightarrow IX = A^{-1}B \Rightarrow X = A^{-1}B$$

Thus, the system of equations $AX = B$ has a solution given by $X = A^{-1}B$.

Uniqueness: If possible, let X_1 and X_2 be two solutions of $AX = B$. Then,

$$AX_1 = B \text{ and } AX_2 = B$$

$$\Rightarrow \quad AX_1 = AX_2$$

$$\Rightarrow \quad A^{-1}(AX_1) = A^{-1}(AX_2) \Rightarrow (A^{-1}A)X_1 = (A^{-1}A)X_2 \Rightarrow IX_1 = IX_2 \Rightarrow X_1 = X_2.$$

Hence, the given system of equations has the unique solution given by $X = A^{-1}B$.

Q.E.D.

In the above theorem, we have proved that a non-homogenous system $AX = B$ of n simultaneous linear equations with n-unknowns has the unique solution given by $X = A^{-1}B$, if A is a non-singular matrix. Now, a natural question arises, what happens when A is a singular matrix? In order to answer this, let us consider the following system of equations:

$$2x + y = 3$$
$$4x + 2y = 6$$

This system of equations can be written in matrix form as

$$\begin{bmatrix} 2 & 1 \\ 4 & 2 \end{bmatrix} \begin{bmatrix} x \\ y \end{bmatrix} = \begin{bmatrix} 3 \\ 6 \end{bmatrix}, \text{ or } AX = B \text{ where } A = \begin{bmatrix} 2 & 1 \\ 4 & 2 \end{bmatrix}, X = \begin{bmatrix} x \\ y \end{bmatrix} \text{ and } B = \begin{bmatrix} 3 \\ 6 \end{bmatrix}$$

Clearly, $|A| = 0$. Also, the system of equations has infinitely many solutions as the two equations represent coincident lines in xy-plane.

Now, consider the following system of equations:

$$2x + y = 3$$
$$4x + 2y = 5$$

For this system of equations also the determinant of the coefficient matrix A is zero i.e. A is a singular matrix. But, the system has no solution i.e. it is an inconsistent system of equations, as the lines represented by the two equations are non-coincident parallel lines.

It follows from the above discussion that the system of equations $AX = B$ may be inconsistent or it may be consistent with infinitely many solutions when the coefficient matrix A is singular.

We now state and prove the following criterion for the consistency or inconsistency of a non-homogenous system of linear equations.

THEOREM 2 *(Criterion of consistency) Let $AX = B$ be a system of n-linear equations in n unknowns.*

(i) *If $|A| \neq 0$, then the system is consistent and has the unique solution given by $X = A^{-1}B$.*

(ii) *If $|A| = 0$ and $(adj\ A)\ B = O$, then the system is consistent and has infinitely many solutions.*

(iii) *If $|A| = 0$ and $(adj\ A)\ B \neq O$, then the system is inconsistent.*

PROOF (i) See Theorem 1

(ii) We have,

$$AX = B, \text{ where } |A| = 0.$$

$\Rightarrow \quad (adj\ A)\ (AX) = (adj\ A)\ B$

$\Rightarrow \quad ((adj\ A)\ A)X = (adj\ A)\ B$

$\Rightarrow \quad (|A|\ I_n)X = (adj\ A)\ B \qquad [\because (adj\ A)\ A = |A|\ I_n]$

$\Rightarrow \quad |A|\ X = (adj\ A)\ B$

If $|A| = 0$ and $(adj\ A)\ B = O$, then $|A|\ X = (adj\ A)\ B$ is true for every value of X.

So, the system of equations $AX = B$ is consistent and it has infinitely many solutions.

(iii) If $|A| = 0$ and $(adj\ A)B \neq O$, then the equation $|A|\ X = (adj\ A)\ B$ is not true because its LHS is always a null matrix whereas the RHS is non-null matrix. So, the system is inconsistent.

Q.E.D.

The above discussion suggests the following algorithm to solve a system of simultaneous linear equations.

ALGORITHM

Step I *Obtain the system of equations and express it in the matrix equation from $AX = B$.*

Step II *Find $|A|$.*

Step III *If $|A| \neq 0$, then the given system of equations is consistent with unique solution. To obtain the solution compute A^{-1} by using $A^{-1} = \frac{1}{|A|}$ adj A and use the formula $X = A^{-1}\ B$.*

Step IV *If $|A| = 0$, then the given system of equations is either inconsistent or it has infinitely many solutions. To distinguish these two proceed as follows:*

Compute $(adj\ A)\ B$.

If $(adj\ A)\ B \neq O$, then the given system of equations is inconsistent i.e. it has no solution.

If $(adj\ A)\ B = O$, then the given system of equations is consistent with infinitely many solutions.

In order to find these infinitely many solutions, replace one of the variables by some real number. This will reduce the number of variables by one. Now, take any two out of the three equations and solve them by matrix method.

Following examples will illustrate the above algorithm.

ILLUSTRATIVE EXAMPLES

BASED ON BASIC CONCEPTS (BASIC)

Type I **SOLVING THE GIVEN SYSTEM OF LINEAR EQUATIONS WHEN THE COEFFICIENT MATRIX IS NON-SINGULAR**

EXAMPLE 1 *Use matrix method to solve the following system of equations :*

$$5x - 7y = 2, 7x - 5y = 3$$

SOLUTION The given system of equations can be written as

$$5x - 7y = 2$$
$$7x - 5y = 3$$

or, $\begin{bmatrix} 5 & -7 \\ 7 & -5 \end{bmatrix}\begin{bmatrix} x \\ y \end{bmatrix} = \begin{bmatrix} 2 \\ 3 \end{bmatrix}$ or, $AX = B$ where $A = \begin{bmatrix} 5 & -7 \\ 7 & -5 \end{bmatrix}$, $X = \begin{bmatrix} x \\ y \end{bmatrix}$ and $B = \begin{bmatrix} 2 \\ 3 \end{bmatrix}$

Now, $|A| = \begin{vmatrix} 5 & -7 \\ 7 & -5 \end{vmatrix} = -25 + 49 = 24 \neq 0$. So, the given system has a unique solution given by $X = A^{-1}B$.

Let C_{ij} be the cofactors of elements a_{ij} in $A = [a_{ij}]$. Then,

$C_{11} = (-1)^{1+1}(-5) = -5$, $C_{12} = (-1)^{1+2}7 = -7$, $C_{21} = (-1)^{2+1}(-7) = 7$, $C_{22} = (-1)^{2+2}5 = 5$.

$$\therefore \quad \text{adj}\, A = \begin{bmatrix} -5 & -7 \\ 7 & 5 \end{bmatrix}^T = \begin{bmatrix} -5 & 7 \\ -7 & 5 \end{bmatrix} \text{ and, } A^{-1} = \frac{1}{|A|}\text{adj}\, A = \frac{1}{24}\begin{bmatrix} -5 & 7 \\ -7 & 5 \end{bmatrix}$$

$$\therefore \quad X = A^{-1}B = \frac{1}{24}\begin{bmatrix} -5 & 7 \\ -7 & 5 \end{bmatrix}\begin{bmatrix} 2 \\ 3 \end{bmatrix} = \frac{1}{24}\begin{bmatrix} -10+21 \\ -14+15 \end{bmatrix} = \begin{bmatrix} 11/24 \\ 1/24 \end{bmatrix}$$

$$\Rightarrow \quad \begin{bmatrix} x \\ y \end{bmatrix} = \begin{bmatrix} 11/24 \\ 1/24 \end{bmatrix} \Rightarrow x = \frac{11}{24} \text{ and } y = \frac{1}{24}$$

Hence, $x = 11/24$ and $y = 1/24$ is the required solution.

EXAMPLE 2 *Use matrix method to solve the following system of equations:*

$$x - 2y - 4 = 0, -3x + 5y + 7 = 0$$

SOLUTION The given system of equations can be written as

$$x - 2y = 4$$
$$-3x + 5y = -7$$

or, $\begin{bmatrix} 1 & -2 \\ -3 & 5 \end{bmatrix}\begin{bmatrix} x \\ y \end{bmatrix} = \begin{bmatrix} 4 \\ -7 \end{bmatrix}$ or, $AX = B$ where $A = \begin{bmatrix} 1 & -2 \\ -3 & 5 \end{bmatrix}$, $X = \begin{bmatrix} x \\ y \end{bmatrix}$ and $B = \begin{bmatrix} 4 \\ -7 \end{bmatrix}$

Now, $|A| = \begin{vmatrix} 1 & -2 \\ -3 & 5 \end{vmatrix} = 5 - 6 = -1 \neq 0$

So, the given system has a unique solution given by $X = A^{-1}B$. Let C_{ij} be the co-factors of elements a_{ij} in $A = [a_{ij}]$. Then,

$$C_{11} = (-1)^{1+1}5 = 5, C_{12} = (-1)^{1+2}(-3) = 3, C_{21} = (-1)^{2+1}(-2) = 2$$

and $C_{22} = (-1)^{2+2}1 = 1.$

$\therefore \quad \text{adj}\, A = \begin{bmatrix} 5 & 3 \\ 2 & 1 \end{bmatrix}^T = \begin{bmatrix} 5 & 2 \\ 3 & 1 \end{bmatrix}$ and, $A^{-1} = \frac{1}{|A|}\, \text{adj}\, A = \frac{1}{(-1)} \begin{bmatrix} 5 & 2 \\ 3 & 1 \end{bmatrix} = \begin{bmatrix} -5 & -2 \\ -3 & -1 \end{bmatrix}$

$\therefore \quad X = A^{-1} B = \begin{bmatrix} -5 & -2 \\ -3 & -1 \end{bmatrix} \begin{bmatrix} 4 \\ -7 \end{bmatrix} = \begin{bmatrix} -20 & +14 \\ -12 & +7 \end{bmatrix} = \begin{bmatrix} -6 \\ -5 \end{bmatrix} \Rightarrow \begin{bmatrix} x \\ y \end{bmatrix} = \begin{bmatrix} -6 \\ -5 \end{bmatrix}$

$\Rightarrow \quad x = -6$ and $y = -5$

Hence, $x = -6$ and $y = -5$ is the required solution.

EXAMPLE 3 *Solve the following system of equations, using matrix method:*

$x + 2y + z = 7, \; x + 3z = 11, \; 2x - 3y = 1$ **[CBSE 2002, 2003, 2005]**

SOLUTION The given system of equations is

$$\begin{aligned} x + 2y + z &= 7 \\ x + 0y + 3z &= 11 \\ 2x - 3y + 0z &= 1 \end{aligned} \quad \text{or,} \quad \begin{bmatrix} 1 & 2 & 1 \\ 1 & 0 & 3 \\ 2 & -3 & 0 \end{bmatrix} \begin{bmatrix} x \\ y \\ z \end{bmatrix} = \begin{bmatrix} 7 \\ 11 \\ 1 \end{bmatrix}$$

or, $AX = B$, where $A = \begin{bmatrix} 1 & 2 & 1 \\ 1 & 0 & 3 \\ 2 & -3 & 0 \end{bmatrix}$, $X = \begin{bmatrix} x \\ y \\ z \end{bmatrix}$ and $B = \begin{bmatrix} 7 \\ 11 \\ 1 \end{bmatrix}$

Now, $|A| = \begin{vmatrix} 1 & 2 & 1 \\ 1 & 0 & 3 \\ 2 & -3 & 0 \end{vmatrix} = 1(0+9) - 2(0-6) + 1(-3-0) = 9 + 12 - 3 = 18 \neq 0$

So, the given system of equations has a unique solution given by $X = A^{-1} B$. Let C_{ij} be the co-factors of elements a_{ij} in $A = [a_{ij}]$. Then,

$C_{11} = (-1)^{1+1} \begin{vmatrix} 0 & 3 \\ -3 & 0 \end{vmatrix} = 9, \qquad C_{12} = (-1)^{1+2} \begin{vmatrix} 1 & 3 \\ 2 & 0 \end{vmatrix} = 6,$

$C_{13} = (-1)^{1+3} \begin{vmatrix} 1 & 0 \\ 2 & -3 \end{vmatrix} = -3, \qquad C_{21} = (-1)^{2+1} \begin{vmatrix} 2 & 1 \\ -3 & 0 \end{vmatrix} = -3,$

$C_{22} = (-1)^{2+2} \begin{vmatrix} 1 & 1 \\ 2 & 0 \end{vmatrix} = -2, \qquad C_{23} = (-1)^{2+3} \begin{vmatrix} 1 & 2 \\ 2 & -3 \end{vmatrix} = 7,$

$C_{31} = (-1)^{3+1} \begin{vmatrix} 2 & 1 \\ 0 & 3 \end{vmatrix} = 6, \qquad C_{32} = (-1)^{3+2} \begin{vmatrix} 1 & 1 \\ 1 & 3 \end{vmatrix} = -2,$

and, $C_{33} = (-1)^{3+3} \begin{vmatrix} 1 & 2 \\ 1 & 0 \end{vmatrix} = -2$

$\therefore \quad \text{adj}\, A = \begin{bmatrix} 9 & 6 & -3 \\ -3 & -2 & 7 \\ 6 & -2 & -2 \end{bmatrix}^T = \begin{bmatrix} 9 & -3 & 6 \\ 6 & -2 & -2 \\ -3 & 7 & -2 \end{bmatrix}$ and, $A^{-1} = \frac{1}{|A|}\, \text{adj}\, A = \frac{1}{18} \begin{bmatrix} 9 & -3 & 6 \\ 6 & -2 & -2 \\ -3 & 7 & -2 \end{bmatrix}$

Now, $X = A^{-1} B$

$$\Rightarrow \quad X = \frac{1}{18} \begin{bmatrix} 9 & -3 & 6 \\ 6 & -2 & -2 \\ -3 & 7 & -2 \end{bmatrix} \begin{bmatrix} 7 \\ 11 \\ 1 \end{bmatrix} = \frac{1}{18} \begin{bmatrix} 63 & -33 & +6 \\ 42 & -22 & -2 \\ -21 & +77 & -2 \end{bmatrix} = \frac{1}{18} \begin{bmatrix} 36 \\ 18 \\ 54 \end{bmatrix} = \begin{bmatrix} 2 \\ 1 \\ 3 \end{bmatrix}$$

$$\Rightarrow \quad \begin{bmatrix} x \\ y \\ z \end{bmatrix} = \begin{bmatrix} 2 \\ 1 \\ 3 \end{bmatrix} \Rightarrow x = 2, \; y = 1 \text{ and } z = 3$$

Hence, $x = 2$, $y = 1$ and $z = 3$ is the required solution.

Type II SOLVING THE GIVEN SYSTEM OF EQUATIONS WHEN THE COEFFICIENT MATRIX IS SINGULAR

EXAMPLE 4 *Use matrix method to examine the following system of equations for consistency or inconsistency:*

$$4x - 2y = 3, \qquad 6x - 3y = 5$$

SOLUTION The given system of equations can be written as

$$AX = B, \text{ where } A = \begin{bmatrix} 4 & -2 \\ 6 & -3 \end{bmatrix}, X = \begin{bmatrix} x \\ y \end{bmatrix} \text{ and } B = \begin{bmatrix} 3 \\ 5 \end{bmatrix}.$$

Now, $|A| = \begin{vmatrix} 4 & -2 \\ 6 & -3 \end{vmatrix} = -12 + 12 = 0$

So, the given system of equations is inconsistent or it has infinitely many solutions according as (adj A) $B \neq O$ or, (adj A) $B = O$ respectively. Let C_{ij} be the co-factors of elements a_{ij} in $A = [a_{ij}]$. Then,

$$C_{11} = (-1)^{1+1}(-3) = -3, C_{12} = (-1)^{1+2}\, 6 = -6, C_{21} = (-1)^{2+1}(-2) = 2, C_{22} = (-1)^{2+2}(4) = 4$$

$$\therefore \qquad \text{adj } A = \begin{bmatrix} -3 & -6 \\ 2 & 4 \end{bmatrix}^T = \begin{bmatrix} -3 & 2 \\ -6 & 4 \end{bmatrix}$$

So, $$(\text{adj } A)\, B = \begin{bmatrix} -3 & 2 \\ -6 & 4 \end{bmatrix} \begin{bmatrix} 3 \\ 5 \end{bmatrix} = \begin{bmatrix} -9 & +10 \\ -18 & +20 \end{bmatrix} = \begin{bmatrix} 1 \\ 2 \end{bmatrix} \neq O$$

Hence, the given system of equations is inconsistent.

EXAMPLE 5 *Show that the following system of equations is consistent.*

$$2x - y + 3z = 5, \; 3x + 2y - z = 7, \; 4x + 5y - 5z = 9$$

Also, find the solution.

SOLUTION The given system of equation can be written in matrix form as

$$\begin{bmatrix} 2 & -1 & 3 \\ 3 & 2 & -1 \\ 4 & 5 & -5 \end{bmatrix} \begin{bmatrix} x \\ y \\ z \end{bmatrix} = \begin{bmatrix} 5 \\ 7 \\ 9 \end{bmatrix}$$

or, $$AX = B, \text{ where } A = \begin{bmatrix} 2 & -1 & 3 \\ 3 & 2 & -1 \\ 4 & 5 & -5 \end{bmatrix}, X = \begin{bmatrix} x \\ y \\ z \end{bmatrix} \text{ and } B = \begin{bmatrix} 5 \\ 7 \\ 9 \end{bmatrix}$$

Now, $$|A| = \begin{vmatrix} 2 & -1 & 3 \\ 3 & 2 & -1 \\ 4 & 5 & -5 \end{vmatrix} = 2(-10+5) + 1(-15+4) + 3(15-8) = 0$$

So, A is singular. Thus, the given system of equations is either inconsistent or it is consistent wit h infinitely many solutions according as (adj A) $B \neq O$ or, (adj A) $B = O$ respectively.

Let C_{ij} be the co-factors of elements a_{ij} in $A = [a_{ij}]$. Then,

$$C_{11} = (-1)^{1+1}\begin{vmatrix} 2 & -1 \\ 5 & -5 \end{vmatrix} = -5, \qquad C_{12} = (-1)^{1+2}\begin{vmatrix} 3 & -1 \\ 4 & -5 \end{vmatrix} = 11,$$

$$C_{13} = (-1)^{1+3}\begin{vmatrix} 3 & 2 \\ 4 & 5 \end{vmatrix} = 7, \qquad C_{21} = (-1)^{2+1}\begin{vmatrix} -1 & 3 \\ 5 & -5 \end{vmatrix} = 10,$$

$$C_{22} = (-1)^{2+2}\begin{vmatrix} 2 & 3 \\ 4 & -5 \end{vmatrix} = -22, \qquad C_{23} = (-1)^{2+3}\begin{vmatrix} 2 & -1 \\ 4 & 5 \end{vmatrix} = -14,$$

$$C_{31} = (-1)^{3+1}\begin{vmatrix} -1 & 3 \\ 2 & -1 \end{vmatrix} = -5, \qquad C_{32} = (-1)^{3+2}\begin{vmatrix} 2 & 3 \\ 3 & -1 \end{vmatrix} = 11$$

and, $$C_{33} = (-1)^{3+3}\begin{vmatrix} 2 & -1 \\ 3 & 2 \end{vmatrix} = 7,$$

$$\therefore \quad (\text{adj } A) = \begin{bmatrix} -5 & 11 & 7 \\ 10 & -22 & -14 \\ -5 & 11 & 7 \end{bmatrix}^T = \begin{bmatrix} -5 & 10 & -5 \\ 11 & -22 & 11 \\ 7 & -14 & 7 \end{bmatrix}$$

$$\Rightarrow \quad (\text{adj } A)\, B = \begin{bmatrix} -5 & 10 & -5 \\ 11 & -22 & 11 \\ 7 & -14 & 7 \end{bmatrix} \begin{bmatrix} 5 \\ 7 \\ 9 \end{bmatrix} = \begin{bmatrix} -25 & +70 & -45 \\ 55 & -154 & +99 \\ 35 & -98 & +63 \end{bmatrix} = \begin{bmatrix} 0 \\ 0 \\ 0 \end{bmatrix} = O$$

Thus, $AX = B$ has infinitely many solutions. To find these solutions, we put $z = k$ in the first two equations and write them as follows:

$$2x - y = 5 - 3k \quad \text{and} \quad 3x + 2y = 7 + k$$

$$\text{or,} \quad \begin{bmatrix} 2 & -1 \\ 3 & 2 \end{bmatrix} \begin{bmatrix} x \\ y \end{bmatrix} = \begin{bmatrix} 5 - 3k \\ 7 + k \end{bmatrix}$$

$$\text{or,} \quad AX = B, \text{ where } A = \begin{bmatrix} 2 & -1 \\ 3 & 2 \end{bmatrix}, X = \begin{bmatrix} x \\ y \end{bmatrix} \text{ and } B = \begin{bmatrix} 5 - 3k \\ 7 + k \end{bmatrix}$$

$$\text{Now,} \quad |A| = \begin{vmatrix} 2 & -1 \\ 3 & 2 \end{vmatrix} = 4 + 3 = 7 \neq 0 \quad \text{and} \quad \text{adj } A = \begin{bmatrix} 2 & 1 \\ -3 & 2 \end{bmatrix}$$

$$\therefore \quad A^{-1} = \frac{1}{|A|}(\text{adj } A) = \frac{1}{7}\begin{bmatrix} 2 & 1 \\ -3 & 2 \end{bmatrix}$$

$$\text{Now,} \quad X = A^{-1} B$$

$$\Rightarrow \quad \begin{bmatrix} x \\ y \end{bmatrix} = \frac{1}{7}\begin{bmatrix} 2 & 1 \\ -3 & 2 \end{bmatrix} \begin{bmatrix} 5 & -3k \\ 7 & +k \end{bmatrix} = \frac{1}{7}\begin{bmatrix} 10 - 6k + 7 + k \\ -15 + 9k + 2k + 14 \end{bmatrix} = \begin{bmatrix} \dfrac{17 - 5k}{7} \\ \dfrac{11k - 1}{7} \end{bmatrix}$$

$$\Rightarrow \quad x = \frac{17 - 5k}{7}, y = \frac{11k - 1}{7}$$

These values of x, y and $z = k$ also satisfy the third equation. Hence, $x = \dfrac{17 - 5k}{7}, y = \dfrac{11k - 1}{7}$ and $z = k$, where k is any real number satisfy the given system of equations.

BASED ON LOWER ORDER THINKING SKILLS (LOTS)

Type III SOLVING A SYSTEM OF LINEAR EQUATIONS WHEN THE INVERSE OF THE COEFFICIENT MATRIX IS OBTAINED FROM SOME GIVEN RELATION

EXAMPLE 6 *If* $A = \begin{bmatrix} 1 & -1 & 1 \\ 2 & 1 & -3 \\ 1 & 1 & 1 \end{bmatrix}$, *find* A^{-1} *and hence solve the system of linear equations*

$$x + 2y + z = 4, \quad -x + y + z = 0, \quad x - 3y + z = 2.$$

SOLUTION We have, $A = \begin{bmatrix} 1 & -1 & 1 \\ 2 & 1 & -3 \\ 1 & 1 & 1 \end{bmatrix}$

$$\therefore \quad |A| = \begin{vmatrix} 1 & -1 & 1 \\ 2 & 1 & -3 \\ 1 & 1 & 1 \end{vmatrix} = 1(1 + 3) + 1(2 + 3) + 1(2 - 1) = 10 \neq 0$$

So, A is invertible.

Let C_{ij} be the co-factors of elements a_{ij} in $A\,[a_{ij}]$. Then,

$$C_{11} = (-1)^{1+1}\begin{vmatrix} 1 & -3 \\ 1 & 1 \end{vmatrix} = 4, \qquad C_{12} = (-1)^{1+2}\begin{vmatrix} 2 & -3 \\ 1 & 1 \end{vmatrix} = -5,$$

$$C_{13} = (-1)^{1+3}\begin{vmatrix} 2 & 1 \\ 1 & 1 \end{vmatrix} = 1, \qquad C_{21} = (-1)^{2+1}\begin{vmatrix} -1 & 1 \\ 1 & 1 \end{vmatrix} = 2,$$

$$C_{22} = (-1)^{2+2}\begin{vmatrix} 1 & 1 \\ 1 & 1 \end{vmatrix} = 0, \qquad C_{23} = (-1)^{2+3}\begin{vmatrix} 1 & -1 \\ 1 & 1 \end{vmatrix} = -2$$

$$C_{31} = (-1)^{3+1}\begin{vmatrix} -1 & 1 \\ 1 & -3 \end{vmatrix} = 2, \qquad C_{32} = (-1)^{3+2}\begin{vmatrix} 1 & 1 \\ 2 & -3 \end{vmatrix} = 5,$$

and, $C_{33} = (-1)^{3+3}\begin{vmatrix} 1 & -1 \\ 2 & 1 \end{vmatrix} = 3$

$$\therefore \quad \text{adj } A = \begin{bmatrix} 4 & -5 & 1 \\ 2 & 0 & -2 \\ 2 & 5 & 3 \end{bmatrix}^T = \begin{bmatrix} 4 & 2 & 2 \\ -5 & 0 & 5 \\ 1 & -2 & 3 \end{bmatrix} \text{ and, } A^{-1} = \frac{1}{|A|}\text{adj } A = \frac{1}{10}\begin{bmatrix} 4 & 2 & 2 \\ -5 & 0 & 5 \\ 1 & -2 & 3 \end{bmatrix} \quad \ldots\text{(i)}$$

The given system of equations is expressible as

$$\begin{bmatrix} 1 & 2 & 1 \\ -1 & 1 & 1 \\ 1 & -3 & 1 \end{bmatrix}\begin{bmatrix} x \\ y \\ z \end{bmatrix} = \begin{bmatrix} 4 \\ 0 \\ 2 \end{bmatrix} \text{ or, } A^T X = B \text{ where } X = \begin{bmatrix} x \\ y \\ z \end{bmatrix} \text{ and } B = \begin{bmatrix} 4 \\ 0 \\ 2 \end{bmatrix}$$

Now, $|A^T| = |A| = 10 \neq 0$. So, the given system of equations is consistent with a unique solution given by

$$X = (A^T)^{-1} B = (A^{-1})^T B \qquad [\because (A^T)^{-1} = (A^{-1})^T]$$

$$\Rightarrow \quad \begin{bmatrix} x \\ y \\ z \end{bmatrix} = \frac{1}{10}\begin{bmatrix} 4 & 2 & 2 \\ -5 & 0 & 5 \\ 1 & -2 & 3 \end{bmatrix}^T \begin{bmatrix} 4 \\ 0 \\ 2 \end{bmatrix} \qquad \text{[Using } (i)]$$

$$\Rightarrow \quad \begin{bmatrix} x \\ y \\ z \end{bmatrix} = \frac{1}{10}\begin{bmatrix} 4 & -5 & 1 \\ 2 & 0 & -2 \\ 2 & 5 & 3 \end{bmatrix}\begin{bmatrix} 4 \\ 0 \\ 2 \end{bmatrix} = \frac{1}{10}\begin{bmatrix} 16+0+2 \\ 8+0-4 \\ 8+0+6 \end{bmatrix} = \begin{bmatrix} 9/5 \\ 2/5 \\ 7/5 \end{bmatrix}$$

$$\Rightarrow \quad x = 9/5, \; y = 2/5 \text{ and } z = 7/5$$

Hence, $x = 9/5, y = 2/5, z = 7/5$ is the required solution.

EXAMPLE 7 *Determine the product* $\begin{bmatrix} -4 & 4 & 4 \\ -7 & 1 & 3 \\ 5 & -3 & -1 \end{bmatrix}\begin{bmatrix} 1 & -1 & 1 \\ 1 & -2 & -2 \\ 2 & 1 & 3 \end{bmatrix}$ *and use it to solve the system of equations:*

$$x - y + z = 4, x - 2y - 2z = 9, \; 2x + y + 3z = 1. \qquad \textbf{[CBSE 2024]}$$

SOLUTION Let $A = \begin{bmatrix} 1 & -1 & 1 \\ 1 & -2 & -2 \\ 2 & 1 & 3 \end{bmatrix}$ and $C = \begin{bmatrix} -4 & 4 & 4 \\ -7 & 1 & 3 \\ 5 & -3 & -1 \end{bmatrix}$. Then the given product is

$$CA = \begin{bmatrix} -4 & 4 & 4 \\ -7 & 1 & 3 \\ 5 & -3 & -1 \end{bmatrix}\begin{bmatrix} 1 & -1 & 1 \\ 1 & -2 & -2 \\ 2 & 1 & 3 \end{bmatrix}$$

$$\Rightarrow \quad CA = \begin{bmatrix} -4+4+8 & 4-8+4 & -4-8+12 \\ -7+1+6 & 7-2+3 & -7-2+9 \\ 5-3-2 & -5+6-1 & 5+6-3 \end{bmatrix} = \begin{bmatrix} 8 & 0 & 0 \\ 0 & 8 & 0 \\ 0 & 0 & 8 \end{bmatrix} = 8\begin{bmatrix} 1 & 0 & 0 \\ 0 & 1 & 0 \\ 0 & 0 & 1 \end{bmatrix} = 8I_3$$

$$\Rightarrow \quad \frac{1}{8}CA = I_3 \Rightarrow \left(\frac{1}{8}C\right)A = I_3 \Rightarrow A^{-1} = \frac{1}{8}C \qquad \text{[By definition of inverse]}$$

$$\Rightarrow \quad A^{-1} = \frac{1}{8}\begin{bmatrix} -4 & 4 & 4 \\ -7 & 1 & 3 \\ 5 & -3 & -1 \end{bmatrix} \quad \text{...(i)}$$

The given system of equations can be written in matrix form as

$$\begin{bmatrix} 1 & -1 & 1 \\ 1 & -2 & -2 \\ 2 & 1 & 3 \end{bmatrix}\begin{bmatrix} x \\ y \\ z \end{bmatrix} = \begin{bmatrix} 4 \\ 9 \\ 1 \end{bmatrix}$$

or, $\quad AX = B$, where $A = \begin{bmatrix} 1 & -1 & 1 \\ 1 & -2 & -2 \\ 2 & 1 & 3 \end{bmatrix}$, $X = \begin{bmatrix} x \\ y \\ z \end{bmatrix}$ and $B = \begin{bmatrix} 4 \\ 9 \\ 1 \end{bmatrix}$

The solution of this system of equations is given by

$$X = A^{-1}B = \frac{1}{8}\begin{bmatrix} -4 & 4 & 4 \\ -7 & 1 & 3 \\ 5 & -3 & -1 \end{bmatrix}\begin{bmatrix} 4 \\ 9 \\ 1 \end{bmatrix} \quad \text{[Using (i)]}$$

$$\Rightarrow \quad \begin{bmatrix} x \\ y \\ z \end{bmatrix} = \frac{1}{8}\begin{bmatrix} -16+36+4 \\ -28+9+3 \\ 20-27-1 \end{bmatrix} = \frac{1}{8}\begin{bmatrix} 24 \\ -16 \\ -8 \end{bmatrix} = \begin{bmatrix} 3 \\ -2 \\ -1 \end{bmatrix} \Rightarrow x = 3,\ y = -2 \text{ and } z = -1$$

EXAMPLE 8 *Find* A^{-1}, *where* $A = \begin{bmatrix} 1 & 2 & -3 \\ 2 & 3 & 2 \\ 3 & -3 & -4 \end{bmatrix}$. *Hence solve the system of equations*

$x + 2y - 3z = -4,\ 2x + 3y + 2z = 2,\ 3x - 3y - 4z = 11.$ **[CBSE 2019, 2020, 2024]**

SOLUTION We have,

$$A = \begin{bmatrix} 1 & 2 & -3 \\ 2 & 3 & 2 \\ 3 & -3 & -4 \end{bmatrix} \Rightarrow |A| = \begin{vmatrix} 1 & 2 & -3 \\ 2 & 3 & 2 \\ 3 & -3 & -4 \end{vmatrix} = -6 + 28 + 45 = 67 \neq 0$$

So, A is invertible. Let C_{ij} be the co-factors of a_{ij} in $A = [a_{ij}]$. Then,

$$C_{11} = (-1)^{1+1}\begin{vmatrix} 3 & 2 \\ -3 & -4 \end{vmatrix} = -6, \qquad C_{12} = (-1)^{1+2}\begin{vmatrix} 2 & 2 \\ 3 & -4 \end{vmatrix} = 14,$$

$$C_{13} = (-1)^{1+3}\begin{vmatrix} 2 & 3 \\ 3 & -3 \end{vmatrix} = -15, \qquad C_{21} = (-1)^{2+1}\begin{vmatrix} 2 & -3 \\ -3 & -4 \end{vmatrix} = 17,$$

$$C_{22} = (-1)^{2+2}\begin{vmatrix} 1 & -3 \\ 3 & -4 \end{vmatrix} = 5, \qquad C_{23} = (-1)^{2+3}\begin{vmatrix} 1 & 2 \\ 3 & -3 \end{vmatrix} = 9$$

$$C_{31} = (-1)^{3+1}\begin{vmatrix} 2 & -3 \\ 3 & 2 \end{vmatrix} = 13, \qquad C_{32} = (-1)^{3+2}\begin{vmatrix} 1 & -3 \\ 2 & 2 \end{vmatrix} = -8,$$

and, $\quad C_{33} = (-1)^{3+3}\begin{vmatrix} 1 & 2 \\ 2 & 3 \end{vmatrix} = -1$

$$\therefore \quad \text{adj } A = \begin{bmatrix} -6 & 14 & -15 \\ 17 & 5 & 9 \\ 13 & -8 & -1 \end{bmatrix}^T = \begin{bmatrix} -6 & 17 & 13 \\ 14 & 5 & -8 \\ -15 & 9 & -1 \end{bmatrix}$$

$$\text{So,} \quad A^{-1} = \frac{1}{|A|}\text{adj } A = \frac{1}{67}\begin{bmatrix} -6 & 17 & 13 \\ 14 & 5 & -8 \\ -15 & 9 & -1 \end{bmatrix} \quad \text{...(i)}$$

The given system of equations is

$$x + 2y - 3z = -4$$
$$2x + 3y + 2z = -2$$
$$3x - 3y - 4z = 11$$

or, $AX = B$, where $A = \begin{bmatrix} 1 & 1 & -3 \\ 2 & 3 & 2 \\ 3 & -3 & -4 \end{bmatrix}$, $X = \begin{bmatrix} x \\ y \\ z \end{bmatrix}$ and $B = \begin{bmatrix} -4 \\ 2 \\ 11 \end{bmatrix}$

As discussed above A is non-singular and so invertible. The inverse of A is given by (i).

The solution of the given system of equations is given by

$$X = A^{-1} B$$

$$\Rightarrow \begin{bmatrix} x \\ y \\ z \end{bmatrix} = \frac{1}{67}\begin{bmatrix} -6 & 17 & 13 \\ 14 & 5 & -8 \\ -15 & 9 & -1 \end{bmatrix}\begin{bmatrix} -4 \\ 2 \\ 11 \end{bmatrix} = \frac{1}{67}\begin{bmatrix} 24 & +34 & +143 \\ -56 & +10 & -88 \\ 60 & +18 & -11 \end{bmatrix} = \begin{bmatrix} 3 \\ -2 \\ 1 \end{bmatrix}$$

$\Rightarrow$ $x = 3,\ y = -2$ and $z = 1$ is the required solution.

Type IV ON APPLICATIONS OF SIMULTANEOUS LINEAR EQUATIONS

EXAMPLE 9 *The sum of three numbers is 6. If we multiply the third number by 2 and add the first number to the result, we get 7. By adding second and third numbers to three times the first number, we get 12. Using matrices find the numbers.* [CBSE 2019]

SOLUTION Let the three numbers be x, y and z respectively. Then,

$x + y + z = 6$ [Given]

Also, $x + 2z = 7$

and, $3x + y + z = 12$

Thus, we obtain the following system of simultaneous linear equations:

$$x + y + z = 6$$
$$x + 0y + 2z = 7$$
$$3x + y + z = 12$$

The above system of equations can be written in matrix form as

$$\begin{bmatrix} 1 & 1 & 1 \\ 1 & 0 & 2 \\ 3 & 1 & 1 \end{bmatrix}\begin{bmatrix} x \\ y \\ z \end{bmatrix} = \begin{bmatrix} 6 \\ 7 \\ 12 \end{bmatrix}$$

or, $AX = B$, where $A = \begin{bmatrix} 1 & 1 & 1 \\ 1 & 0 & 2 \\ 3 & 1 & 1 \end{bmatrix}$, $X = \begin{bmatrix} x \\ y \\ z \end{bmatrix}$ and $B = \begin{bmatrix} 6 \\ 7 \\ 12 \end{bmatrix}$

Now, $|A| = \begin{vmatrix} 1 & 1 & 1 \\ 1 & 0 & 2 \\ 3 & 1 & 1 \end{vmatrix} = 1(0-2) - (1-6) + 1(1-0) = -2 + 5 + 1 = 4 \neq 0$

So, the above system of equations has a unique solution given by $X = A^{-1} B$.

Let C_{ij} be the cofactor of a_{ij} in $A = [a_{ij}]$. Then,

$C_{11} = -2, C_{12} = 5, C_{13} = 1, C_{21} = 0, C_{22} = -2, C_{23} = 2, C_{31} = 2, C_{32} = -1$ and $C_{33} = -1$

$\therefore$ $\text{adj}\, A = \begin{bmatrix} -2 & 5 & 1 \\ 0 & -2 & 2 \\ 2 & -1 & -1 \end{bmatrix}^T = \begin{bmatrix} -2 & 0 & 2 \\ 5 & -2 & -1 \\ 1 & 2 & -1 \end{bmatrix}$ and, $A^{-1} = \frac{1}{|A|}\text{adj}\, A = \frac{1}{4}\begin{bmatrix} -2 & 0 & 2 \\ 5 & -2 & -1 \\ 1 & 2 & -1 \end{bmatrix}$

Now, $X = A^{-1} B$

$$\Rightarrow \quad X = \frac{1}{4}\begin{bmatrix} -2 & 0 & 2 \\ 5 & -2 & -1 \\ 1 & 2 & -1 \end{bmatrix}\begin{bmatrix} 6 \\ 7 \\ 12 \end{bmatrix} = \frac{1}{4}\begin{bmatrix} -12 & +0 & +24 \\ 30 & -14 & -12 \\ 6 & +14 & -12 \end{bmatrix} = \begin{bmatrix} 3 \\ 1 \\ 2 \end{bmatrix}$$

$$\Rightarrow \quad \begin{bmatrix} x \\ y \\ z \end{bmatrix} = \begin{bmatrix} 3 \\ 1 \\ 2 \end{bmatrix} \Rightarrow x = 3, y = 1 \text{ and } z = 2.$$

Hence, the three numbers are 3, 1 and 2 respectively.

EXAMPLE 10 *An amount of ₹ 5000 is put into three investments at the rate of interest of 6%, 7% and 8% per annum respectively. The total annual income is ₹ 358. If the combined income from the first two investments is ₹ 70 more than the income from the third, find the amount of each investment by matrix method.*

SOLUTION Let x, y and z ₹ be the investments at the rates of interest of 6%, 7% and 8% per annum respectively. Then,

Total investment = ₹ 5000

$$\Rightarrow \quad x + y + z = 5000.$$

Now, Income from first investment of ₹ x = ₹ $\frac{6x}{100}$

Income from second investment of ₹ y = ₹ $\frac{7y}{100}$

Income from third investment of ₹ z = ₹ $\frac{8z}{100}$.

$$\therefore \quad \text{Total annual income} = ₹\left(\frac{6x}{100} + \frac{7y}{100} + \frac{8z}{100}\right)$$

$$\Rightarrow \quad \frac{6x}{100} + \frac{7y}{100} + \frac{8z}{100} = 358 \qquad [\because \text{Total annual income} = ₹\ 358]$$

$$\Rightarrow \quad 6x + 7y + 8z = 35800.$$

It is given that the combined income from the first two investments is ₹ 70 more than the income from the third.

$$\therefore \quad \frac{6x}{100} + \frac{7y}{100} = 70 + \frac{8z}{100} \Rightarrow 6x + 7y - 8z = 7000.$$

Thus, we obtain the following system of simultaneous linear equations:

$$x + y + z = 5000$$
$$6x + 7y + 8z = 35800$$
$$6x + 7y - 8z = 7000$$

This system of equations can be written in matrix form as follows:

$$\begin{bmatrix} 1 & 1 & 1 \\ 6 & 7 & 8 \\ 6 & 7 & -8 \end{bmatrix}\begin{bmatrix} x \\ y \\ z \end{bmatrix} = \begin{bmatrix} 5000 \\ 35800 \\ 7000 \end{bmatrix}$$

or, $AX = B$, where $A = \begin{bmatrix} 1 & 1 & 1 \\ 6 & 7 & 8 \\ 6 & 7 & -8 \end{bmatrix}, X = \begin{bmatrix} x \\ y \\ z \end{bmatrix}$ and $B = \begin{bmatrix} 5000 \\ 35800 \\ 7000 \end{bmatrix}$

Now, $|A| = \begin{vmatrix} 1 & 1 & 1 \\ 6 & 7 & 8 \\ 6 & 7 & -8 \end{vmatrix} = 1(-56-56) - (-48-48) + (42-42) = -16 \neq 0.$

So, A^{-1} exists and the solution of the given system of equations is given by $X = A^{-1} B$.

Let C_{ij} be the cofactor of a_{ij} in $A = [a_{ij}]$. Then,

$C_{11} = -112, C_{12} = 96, C_{13} = 0, C_{21} = 15, C_{22} = -14,$
$C_{23} = -1, C_{31} = 1, C_{32} = -2$ and $C_{33} = 1.$

$$\therefore \quad \text{adj } A = \begin{bmatrix} -112 & 96 & 0 \\ 15 & -14 & -1 \\ 1 & -2 & 1 \end{bmatrix}^T = \begin{bmatrix} -112 & 15 & 1 \\ 96 & -14 & -2 \\ 0 & -1 & 1 \end{bmatrix}$$

So, $$A^{-1} = \frac{1}{|A|}(\text{adj } A) = -\frac{1}{16}\begin{bmatrix} -112 & 15 & 1 \\ 96 & -14 & -2 \\ 0 & -1 & 1 \end{bmatrix}$$

Hence, the solution is given by

$$X = A^{-1}B = -\frac{1}{16}\begin{bmatrix} -112 & 15 & 1 \\ 96 & -14 & -2 \\ 0 & -1 & 1 \end{bmatrix}\begin{bmatrix} 5000 \\ 35800 \\ 7000 \end{bmatrix} = -\frac{1}{16}\begin{bmatrix} -560000 & +537000 & +7000 \\ 480000 & -501200 & -14000 \\ 0 & -35800 & +7000 \end{bmatrix}$$

$$\Rightarrow \quad \begin{bmatrix} x \\ y \\ z \end{bmatrix} = \begin{bmatrix} 1000 \\ 2200 \\ 1800 \end{bmatrix} \Rightarrow x = 1000, y = 2200 \text{ and } z = 1800$$

Hence, three investments are of ₹ 1000, ₹ 2200 and ₹ 1800 respectively.

EXAMPLE 11 *A mixture is to be made of three foods A, B, C. The three foods A, B, C contain nutrients P, Q, R as shown below:*

Food	*Ounces per pound of Nutrient*		
	P	*Q*	*R*
A	1	2	5
B	3	1	1
C	4	2	1

How to form a mixture which will have 8 ounces of P, 5 ounces of Q and 7 ounces of R?

SOLUTION Let x pounds of food A, y pounds of food B and z pounds of food C be needed to form the mixture.

Since one pound of food A contains 1 ounce of nutrient P. So, x pounds of food A will contain x ounces of nutrient P. Similarly, the amount of nutrient P in y pounds of food B and z pounds of food C are $3y$ and $4z$ ounces respectively. Therefore,

Total quantity of nutrient P in x pounds of food A, y pounds of food B and z pounds of food C is $x + 3y + 4z$ ounces.

$\therefore \quad x + 3y + 4z = 8$

Similarly, $2x + y + 2z = 5$ [For nutrient Q]

and $5x + y + z = 7$ [For nutrient R]

The above system of simultaneous linear equations can be written in matrix form as

$$\begin{bmatrix} 1 & 3 & 4 \\ 2 & 1 & 2 \\ 5 & 1 & 1 \end{bmatrix}\begin{bmatrix} x \\ y \\ z \end{bmatrix} = \begin{bmatrix} 8 \\ 5 \\ 7 \end{bmatrix}$$

or, $AX = B$, where $A = \begin{bmatrix} 1 & 3 & 4 \\ 2 & 1 & 2 \\ 5 & 1 & 1 \end{bmatrix}$, $x = \begin{bmatrix} x \\ y \\ z \end{bmatrix}$ and $B = \begin{bmatrix} 8 \\ 5 \\ 7 \end{bmatrix}$

Now, $$|A| = \begin{vmatrix} 1 & 3 & 4 \\ 2 & 1 & 2 \\ 5 & 1 & 1 \end{vmatrix} = 1(1-2) - 3(2-10) + 4(2-5) = -1 + 24 - 12 = 11 \neq 0$$

So, A^{-1} exists.

Let C_{ij} be the cofactor of a_{ij} in $A = [a_{ij}]$. Then,

$$C_{11} = -1, C_{12} = 8, C_{13} = -3, C_{21} = 1, C_{22} = -19,$$
$$C_{23} = 14,\ C_{31} = 22, C_{32} = 6 \text{ and } C_{33} = -5$$

$$\therefore \quad \text{adj}\, A = \begin{bmatrix} -1 & 8 & -3 \\ 1 & -19 & 14 \\ 2 & 6 & -5 \end{bmatrix}^T = \begin{bmatrix} -1 & 1 & 2 \\ 8 & -19 & 6 \\ -3 & 14 & -5 \end{bmatrix}$$

$$\Rightarrow \quad A^{-1} = \frac{1}{|A|}\text{adj}\, A = \frac{1}{11}\begin{bmatrix} -1 & 1 & 2 \\ 8 & -19 & 6 \\ -3 & 14 & -5 \end{bmatrix}$$

Thus, the solution of the system of equations is given by

$$X = A^{-1}B = \frac{1}{11}\begin{bmatrix} -1 & 1 & 2 \\ 8 & -19 & 6 \\ -3 & 14 & -5 \end{bmatrix}\begin{bmatrix} 8 \\ 5 \\ 7 \end{bmatrix} = \frac{1}{11}\begin{bmatrix} -8 & +5 & +14 \\ 64 & -95 & +42 \\ -24 & +70 & -35 \end{bmatrix} = \frac{1}{11}\begin{bmatrix} 11 \\ 11 \\ 11 \end{bmatrix} = \begin{bmatrix} 1 \\ 1 \\ 1 \end{bmatrix}$$

$$\Rightarrow \quad \begin{bmatrix} x \\ y \\ z \end{bmatrix} = \begin{bmatrix} 1 \\ 1 \\ 1 \end{bmatrix} \Rightarrow x = 1, y = 1 \text{ and } z = 1.$$

Hence, the mixture is formed by mixing one pound of each of the foods *A*, *B* and *C*.

EXAMPLE 12 *Abdul threw a basketball in the direction of the basketball hoop which traversed a parabolic path in a vertical plane as shown below.*

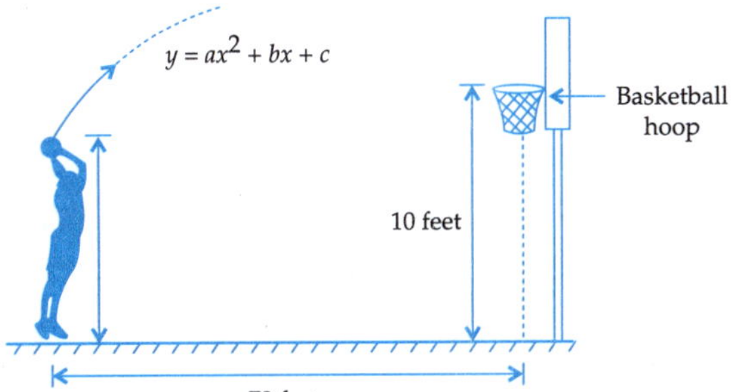

Fig. 7.1

The equation of the path traversed by the ball is $y = ax^2 + bx + c$ with respect to a xy-coordinate system in the vertical plane. The ball traversed through the points (10, 16), (20, 22) and (30, 25). The basketball hoop is at a horizontal distance of 70 feet from Abdul. The height of the basketball hoop is 10 feet from the floor to the top edge of the rim. Did the ball successfully go through the hoop?

SOLUTION Given that the equation of the path traversed by the ball is $y = ax^2 + bx + c$ and the ball traversed through the points (10, 16), (20, 22) and (30, 25). Therefore, these points satisfy the equation of the path i.e. $y = ax^2 + bx + c$.

$$\therefore \quad 100a + 10b + c = 16$$
$$400a + 20b + c = 22$$
$$900a + 30b + c = 25$$

This system of equations can be written in matrix form as

$$\begin{bmatrix} 100 & 10 & 1 \\ 400 & 20 & 1 \\ 900 & 30 & 1 \end{bmatrix}\begin{bmatrix} a \\ b \\ c \end{bmatrix} = \begin{bmatrix} 16 \\ 22 \\ 25 \end{bmatrix} \text{ or, } AX = B, \text{ where } A = \begin{bmatrix} 100 & 10 & 1 \\ 400 & 20 & 1 \\ 900 & 30 & 1 \end{bmatrix}, X = \begin{bmatrix} a \\ b \\ c \end{bmatrix} \text{ and } B = \begin{bmatrix} 16 \\ 22 \\ 25 \end{bmatrix}$$

$$\therefore \quad |A| = (12000 - 18000) - (3000 - 9000) + (2000 - 4000) = -2000 \neq 0$$

So, *A* is invertible matrix.

$\therefore \qquad AX = B \Rightarrow X = A^{-1} B$ ...(i)

Let C_{ij} be the cofactor of a_{ij} in $A = [a_{ij}]$. Then,

$$C_{11} = \begin{vmatrix} 20 & 1 \\ 30 & 1 \end{vmatrix} = -10, \quad C_{12} = -\begin{vmatrix} 400 & 1 \\ 900 & 1 \end{vmatrix} = 500, \quad C_{13} = \begin{vmatrix} 400 & 20 \\ 900 & 30 \end{vmatrix} = -6000$$

$$C_{21} = -\begin{vmatrix} 10 & 1 \\ 30 & 1 \end{vmatrix} = 20, \quad C_{22} = \begin{vmatrix} 100 & 1 \\ 900 & 1 \end{vmatrix} = -800, \quad C_{23} = -\begin{vmatrix} 100 & 10 \\ 900 & 30 \end{vmatrix} = 6000$$

$$C_{31} = \begin{vmatrix} 10 & 1 \\ 20 & 1 \end{vmatrix} = -10, \quad C_{32} = -\begin{vmatrix} 100 & 1 \\ 400 & 1 \end{vmatrix} = 300, \quad C_{33} = \begin{vmatrix} 100 & 10 \\ 400 & 20 \end{vmatrix} = -2000$$

$$\therefore \qquad \text{adj } A = \begin{bmatrix} -10 & 500 & -6000 \\ 20 & -800 & 6000 \\ -10 & 300 & -2000 \end{bmatrix}^T = \begin{bmatrix} -10 & 20 & -10 \\ 500 & -800 & 300 \\ -6000 & 6000 & -2000 \end{bmatrix}^T$$

So, $$A^{-1} = \frac{1}{|A|} \text{adj } A = -\frac{1}{2000} \begin{bmatrix} -10 & 20 & -10 \\ 500 & -800 & 300 \\ -6000 & 6000 & -2000 \end{bmatrix} = \begin{bmatrix} \frac{1}{200} & -\frac{1}{100} & \frac{1}{200} \\ -\frac{1}{4} & \frac{2}{5} & -\frac{3}{20} \\ 3 & -3 & 1 \end{bmatrix}$$

Substituting the value of A^{-1} in (i), we obtain

$$\begin{bmatrix} a \\ b \\ c \end{bmatrix} = \begin{bmatrix} \frac{1}{200} & -\frac{1}{100} & \frac{1}{200} \\ -\frac{1}{4} & \frac{2}{5} & -\frac{3}{20} \\ 3 & -3 & 1 \end{bmatrix} \begin{bmatrix} 16 \\ 22 \\ 25 \end{bmatrix} = \begin{bmatrix} -\frac{3}{2000} \\ \frac{21}{20} \\ 7 \end{bmatrix} \Rightarrow a = -\frac{3}{200}, b = \frac{21}{20} \text{ and } c = 7.$$

Substituting the values of a, b and c in $y = ax^2 + bx + c$, we obtain

$$y = -\frac{3}{200} x^2 + \frac{21}{20} x + 7 \qquad ...(ii)$$

This is the equation of the path traversed by the ball. The coordinates of the centre of the hoop are (70, 10), if the ball goes through the hoop, this point must satisfy the equation (ii). For $x = 70$, we obtain

$$y = -\frac{3}{200} \times 4900 + \frac{21}{20} \times 70 + 7 = 7$$

Thus, (70, 10) does not satisfy equation of the path. Hence, the ball did not go through the hoop.

EXERCISE 7.1

BASIC

1. Solve the following system of equations by matrix method:

(i) $5x + 7y + 2 = 0$, $4x + 6y + 3 = 0$

(ii) $5x + 2y = 3$, $3x + 2y = 5$

(iii) $3x + 4y - 5 = 0$, $x - y + 3 = 0$

(iv) $3x + y = 19$, $3x - y = 23$

(v) $3x + 7y = 4$, $x + 2y = -1$

(vi) $3x + y = 7$, $5x + 3y = 12$

2. Solve the following system of equations by matrix method:

(i) $x + y - z = 3$, $2x + 3y + z = 10$, $3x - y - 7z = 1$

(ii) $x + y + z = 3$, $2x - y + z = -1$, $2x + y - 3z = -9$ [CBSE 2004, 2005]

(iii) $x + 2y + 3z = 6$, $2x - y + z = 2$, $3x + 2y - 2z = 3$ [CBSE 2023]

(iv) $3x + 4y + 7z = 14$, $2x - y + 3z = 4$, $x + 2y - 3z = 0$

(v) $\frac{2}{x} - \frac{3}{y} + \frac{3}{z} = 10$, $\frac{1}{x} + \frac{1}{y} + \frac{1}{z} = 10$, $\frac{3}{x} - \frac{1}{y} + \frac{2}{z} = 13$ [CBSE 2005, 07]

(vi) $5x + 3y + z = 16$, $2x + y + 3z = 19$, $x + 2y + 4z = 25$

(vii) $3x + 4y + 2z = 8$, $2y - 3z = 3$, $x - 2y + 6z = -2$

(viii) $2x + y + z = 2$, $x + 3y - z = 5$, $3x + y - 2z = 6$ [CBSE 2008]

(ix) $2x + 6y = 2$, $3x - z = -8$, $2x - y + z = -3$ [CBSE 2003]

(x) $x - y + z = 2$, $2x - y = 0$, $2y - z = 1$ [CBSE 2003]

(xi) $8x + 4y + 3z = 18$, $2x + y + z = 5$, $x + 2y + z = 5$ [CBSE 2008]

(xii) $x + y + z = 6$, $x + 2z = 7$, $3x + y + z = 12$ [CBSE 2009]

(xiii) $\frac{2}{x} + \frac{3}{y} + \frac{10}{z} = 4$, $\frac{4}{x} - \frac{6}{y} + \frac{5}{z} = 1$, $\frac{6}{x} + \frac{9}{y} - \frac{20}{z} = 2$; $x, y, z \neq 0$ [CBSE 2011, 2024]

(xiv) $x - y + 2z = 7$, $3x + 4y - 5z = -5$, $2x - y + 3z = 12$ [CBSE 2012]

3. Show that each of the following systems of linear equations is consistent and also find their solutions:

(i) $6x + 4y = 2$, $9x + 6y = 3$

(ii) $2x + 3y = 5$, $6x + 9y = 15$

(iii) $5x + 3y + 7z = 4$, $3x + 26y + 2z = 9$, $7x + 2y + 10z = 5$

(iv) $x - y + z = 3$, $2x + y - z = 2$, $-x - 2y + 2z = 1$

(v) $x + y + z = 6$, $x + 2y + 3z = 14$, $x + 4y + 7z = 30$

(vi) $2x + 2y - 2z = 1$, $4x + 4y - z = 2$, $6x + 6y + 2z = 3$

4. Show that each one of the following systems of linear equations is inconsistent:

(i) $2x + 5y = 7$, $6x + 15y = 13$

(ii) $2x + 3y = 5$, $6x + 9y = 10$

(iii) $4x - 2y = 3$, $6x - 3y = 5$

(iv) $4x - 5y - 2z = 2$, $5x - 4y + 2z = -2$, $2x + 2y + 8z = -1$

(v) $3x - y - 2z = 2$, $2y - z = -1$, $3x - 5y = 3$

(vi) $x + y - 2z = 5$, $x - 2y + z = -2$, $-2x + y + z = 4$

BASED ON LOTS

5. If $A = \begin{bmatrix} 1 & -1 & 0 \\ 2 & 3 & 4 \\ 0 & 1 & 2 \end{bmatrix}$ and $B = \begin{bmatrix} 2 & 2 & -4 \\ -4 & 2 & -4 \\ 2 & -1 & 5 \end{bmatrix}$ are two square matrices, find AB and hence solve the system of linear equations:

$x - y = 3,\ 2x + 3y + 4z = 17,\ y + 2z = 7$ **[CBSE 2010, 2012]**

6. If $A = \begin{bmatrix} 2 & -3 & 5 \\ 3 & 2 & -4 \\ 1 & 1 & -2 \end{bmatrix}$, find A^{-1} and hence solve the system of linear equations:

$2x - 3y + 5z = 11,\ 3x + 2y - 4z = -5,\ x + y - 2z = -3$ **[CBSE 2007, 2009, 2012, 2018, 2020]**

7. Find A^{-1}, if $A = \begin{bmatrix} 1 & 2 & 5 \\ 1 & -1 & -1 \\ 2 & 3 & -1 \end{bmatrix}$. Hence, solve the following system of linear equations:

$x + 2y + 5z = 10,\ x - y - z = -2,\ 2x + 3y - z = -11$ **[CBSE 2010, 2012]**

8. (i) If $A = \begin{bmatrix} 1 & -2 & 0 \\ 2 & 1 & 3 \\ 0 & -2 & 1 \end{bmatrix}$, find A^{-1}. Using A^{-1}, solve the system of linear equations:

$x - 2y = 10,\ 2x + y + 3z = 8,\ -2y + z = 7$ **[CBSE 2024]**

(ii) $A = \begin{bmatrix} 3 & -4 & 2 \\ 2 & 3 & 5 \\ 1 & 0 & 1 \end{bmatrix}$, find A^{-1} and hence solve the following system of equations:

$3x - 4y + 2z = -1,\ 2x + 3y + 5z = 7,\ x + z = 2$ **[CBSE 2011]**

(iii) $A = \begin{bmatrix} 1 & -2 & 0 \\ 2 & 1 & 3 \\ 0 & -2 & 1 \end{bmatrix}$ and $B = \begin{bmatrix} 7 & 2 & -6 \\ -2 & 1 & -3 \\ -4 & 2 & 5 \end{bmatrix}$, find AB. Hence, solve the system of equations:

$x - 2y = 10,\ 2x + y + 3z = 8$ and $-2y + z = 7$ **[CBSE 2011]**

(iv) If $A = \begin{bmatrix} 1 & 2 & 0 \\ -2 & -1 & -2 \\ 0 & -1 & 1 \end{bmatrix}$, find A^{-1}. Using A^{-1}, solve the system of linear equations

$x - 2y = 10,\ 2x - y - z = 8,\ -2y + z = 7$ **[NCERT EXEMPLAR]**

(v) Given $A = \begin{bmatrix} 2 & 2 & -4 \\ -4 & 2 & -4 \\ 2 & -1 & 5 \end{bmatrix}$, $B = \begin{bmatrix} 1 & -1 & 0 \\ 2 & 3 & 4 \\ 0 & 1 & 2 \end{bmatrix}$, find BA and use this to solve the system of equations $y + 2z = 7,\ x - y = 3,\ 2x + 3y + 4z = 17$ **[NCERT EXEMPLAR]**

(vi) If $A = \begin{bmatrix} 2 & 3 & 1 \\ 1 & 2 & 2 \\ -3 & 1 & -1 \end{bmatrix}$, find A^{-1} and hence solve the system of equations

$2x + y - 3z = 13,\ 3x + 2y + z = 4,\ x + 2y - z = 8.$ **[CBSE 2017]**

(vii) Use the product $\begin{bmatrix} 1 & -1 & 2 \\ 0 & 2 & -3 \\ 3 & -2 & 4 \end{bmatrix} \begin{bmatrix} -2 & 0 & 1 \\ 9 & 2 & -3 \\ 6 & 1 & -2 \end{bmatrix}$ to solve the system of equations

$x + 3z = -9,\ -x + 2y - 2z = 4,\ 2x - 3y + 4z = -3.$ **[CBSE 2017]**

(viii) If $A = \begin{bmatrix} 3 & 2 \\ 5 & -7 \end{bmatrix}$, then find A^{-1} and use it to solve the following system of the equations: $3x+5y=11,\ 2x-7y=-3.$ **[CBSE 2023]**

(ix) If $A = \begin{bmatrix} -3 & -2 & -4 \\ 2 & 1 & 2 \\ 2 & 1 & 3 \end{bmatrix}$, $B = \begin{bmatrix} 1 & 2 & 0 \\ -2 & -1 & -2 \\ 0 & -1 & 1 \end{bmatrix}$, then find AB and use it to solve the following system of equations: $x-2y=3,\ 2x-y-z=2, -2y+z=3.$ **[CBSE 2023]**

(x) Find the product of the matrices $\begin{bmatrix} 1 & 2 & -3 \\ 2 & 3 & 2 \\ 3 & -3 & -4 \end{bmatrix}\begin{bmatrix} -6 & 17 & 13 \\ 14 & 5 & -8 \\ -15 & 9 & -1 \end{bmatrix}$ and hence solve the system of linear equations: $x+2y-3z=-4, 2x+3y+2z=2,\ 3x-3y-4z=11.$ **[CBSE 2024]**

9. The sum of three numbers is 2. If twice the second number is added to the sum of first and third, the sum is 1. By adding second and third number to five times the first number, we get 6. Find the three numbers by using matrices.

10. An amount of ₹ 10,000 is put into three investments at the rate of 10, 12 and 15% per annum. The combined income is ₹ 1310 and the combined income of first and second investment is ₹ 190 short of the income from the third. Find the investment in each using matrix method.

11. A company produces three products every day. Their production on a certain day is 45 tons. It is found that the production of third product exceeds the production of first product by 8 tons while the total production of first and third product is twice the production of second product. Determine the production level of each product using matrix method.

12. The prices of three commodities P, Q and R are ₹ x, y and z per unit respectively. A purchases 4 units of R and sells 3 units of P and 5 units of Q. B purchases 3 units of Q and sells 2 units of P and 1 unit of R. C purchases 1 unit of P and sells 4 units of Q and 6 units of R. In the process A, B and C earn ₹ 6000, ₹ 5000 and ₹ 13000 respectively. If selling the units is positive earning and buying the units is negative earnings, find the price per unit of three commodities by using matrix method.

13. The management committee of a residential colony decided to award some of its members (say x) for honesty, some (say y) for helping others (say z) for supervising the workers to keep the colony neat and clean. The sum of all the awardees is 12. Three times the sum of awardees for cooperation and supervision added to two times the number of awardees for honesty is 33. If the sum of the number of awardees for honesty and supervision is twice the number of awardees for helping others, using matrix method, find the number of awardees of each category. Apart from these values, namely, honesty, cooperation and supervision, suggest one more value which the management must include for awards. **[CBSE 2013]**

14. A school wants to award its students for the values of Honesty, Regularity and Hardwork with a total cash award of ₹ 6000. Three times the award money for Hardwork added to that given for honesty amounts to ₹ 11000. The award money given for Honesty and Hardwork together is double the one given for Regularity. Represent the above situation algebraically and find the award for each value, using matrix method. Apart from these values, namely, Honesty, Regularity and Hardwork, suggest one more value which the school must include for awards. **[CBSE 2013]**

15. Two institutions decided to award their employees for the three values of resourcefulness, competence and determination in the form of prizes at the rate of ₹ x, ₹ y and ₹ z respectively per person. The first institution decided to award respectively 4, 3 and 2 employees with a

total prize money of ₹ 37000 and the second institution decided to award respectively 5, 3 and 4 employees with a total prize money of ₹ 47000. If all the three prizes per person together amount to ₹ 12000, then using matrix method find the value of x, y and z. What values are described in this equations? [CBSE 2013]

16. Two factories decided to award their employees for three values of (a) adaptable to new techniques, (b) careful and alert in difficult situations and (c) keeping calm in tense situations, at the rate of ₹ x, ₹ y and ₹ z per person respectively. The first factory decided to honour respectively 2, 4 and 3 employees with a total prize money of ₹ 29000. The second factory decided to honour respectively 5, 2 and 3 employees with the prize money of ₹ 30500. If the three prizes per person together cost ₹ 9500, then
   (i) represent the above situation by a matrix equation and form linear equations using matrix multiplication.
   (ii) Solve these equations using matrices.
   (iii) Which values are reflected in the questions? [CBSE 2013]

17. Two schools A and B want to award their selected students on the values of sincerity, truthfulness and helpfulness. The school A wants to award ₹ x each ₹ y each and ₹ z each for the three respective values to 3, 2 and 1 students respectively with a total award money of ₹ 16,00. School B wants to spend ₹ 2,300 to award its 4, 1 and 3 students on the respective values (by giving the same award money to the three values as before). If the total amount of award for one prize on each value is ₹ 900, using matrices, find the award money for each value. Apart from these three values, suggest one more value which should be considered for award. [CBSE 2014]

18. Two schools P and Q want to award their selected students on the values of Discipline, Politeness and Punctuality. The school P wants to award ₹ x each , ₹ y each and ₹ z each for the three respectively values to its 3, 2 and 1 students with a total award money of ₹ 1,000. School Q wants to spend ₹ 1,500 to award its 4, 1 and 3 students on the respective values (by giving the same award money for three values as before). If the total amount of awards for one prize on each value is ₹ 600, using matrices, find the award money for each value. Apart from the above three values, suggest one more value for awards. [CBSE 2014]

19. Two schools P and Q want to award their selected students on the values of Tolerance, Kindness and Leadership. The school P wants to award ₹ x each, ₹ y each and ₹ z each for the three respective values to 3, 2 and 1 students respectively with a total award money of ₹ 2,200. School Q wants to spend ₹ 3,100 to award its 4, 1 and 3 students on the respective values (by giving the same award money to the three values as school P). If the total amount of award for one prize on each values is ₹ 1,200, using matrices, find the award money for each value.

    Apart from these three values, suggest one more value which should be considered for award. [CBSE 2014]

20. A total amount of ₹ 7000 is deposited in three different saving bank accounts with annual interest rates 5%, 8% and $8\frac{1}{2}\%$ respectively. The total annual interest from these three accounts is ₹ 550. Equal amounts have been deposited in the 5% and 8% savings accounts. Find the amount deposited in each of the three accounts, with the help of matrices. [CBSE 2014]

21. A shopkeeper has 3 varieties of pens 'A', 'B' and 'C'. Meenu purchased 1 pen of each variety for a total of ₹ 21. Jeen purchased 4 pens of 'A' variety, 3 pens of 'B' variety and 2 pens of 'C' variety for ₹ 60. While Shikha purchased 6 pens of 'A' variety, 2 pens of 'B' variety and 3 pens of 'C' variety for ₹ 70. Using matrix method find the cost of each pen. [CBSE 2016]

ANSWERS

1. (i) $x=\frac{9}{2},\ y=-\frac{7}{2}$ (ii) $x=-1,\ y=4$ (iii) $x=-1,\ y=2$
   (iv) $x=7,\ y=-2$ (v) $x=-15,\ y=7$ (vi) $x=\frac{9}{4},\ y=\frac{1}{4}$
2. (i) $x=3,\ y=1,\ z=1$ (ii) $x=-\frac{8}{7}, y=\frac{10}{7}, z=\frac{19}{7}$ (iii) $x=1,\ y=1,\ z=1$
   (iv) $x=1,\ y=1,\ z=1$ (v) $x=\frac{1}{2}, y=\frac{1}{3}, z=\frac{1}{5}$ (vi) $x=1,\ y=2,\ z=5$
   (vii) $x=-2,\ y=3,\ z=1$ (viii) $x=1,\ y=1,\ z=-1$ (ix) $x=-2, y=1, z=2$
   (x) $x=1, y=2, z=3$ (xi) $x=1,\ y=1,\ z=2$ (xii) $x=3, y=2, z=1$
   (xiii) $x=2, y=3, z=5$ (xiv) $x=2, y=1, z=3$ (xii) $x=3,\ y=1,\ z=2$
3. (i) $x=\frac{1-2k}{3},\ y=k$ (ii) $x=\frac{5-3k}{2},\ y=k$
   (iii) $x=\frac{7-16k}{11},\ y=\frac{k+3}{11},\ z=k$ (iv) $x=\frac{5}{3},\ y=\frac{-4}{3}+k,\ z=k$
   (v) $x=k-2,\ y=8-2k,\ z=k$ (vi) $x=\frac{1}{2}-k,\ y=k,\ z=0$
5. $x=2,\ y=-1,\ z=4$ 6. $x=1,\ y=2,\ z=3$ 7. $x=-1,\ y=-2,\ z=3$
8. (i) $x=4,\ y=-3,\ z=1$ (ii) $x=3, y=2, z=-1$ (iii) $x=4, y=-3, z=1$
   (iv) $x=0, y=-5, z=-3$ (v) $x=2, y=-1, z=4$ (vi) $z=1\ y=2, z=-3$
   (vii) $x=36, y=5, z=-15$ (viii) $x=2, y=1$ (ix) $x=1, y=-1, z=1$
   (x) Product $=67I_3$; $x=3, y=-2, z=1$
9. $1, -1, 2$ 10. ₹ 2000, ₹ 3000, ₹ 5000 11. $11, 15, 19$
12. $x=3000, y=1000, z=2000$ 13. $x=3, y=4, z=5$
14. $x=500, y=2000, z=3500$ 15. $x=4000, y=5000, z=3000$
16. $x=2500,\ y=3000,\ z=4000$ 17. $x=200, y=300, z=400$ 18. $x=100, y=200, z=300$
19. $x=300, y=400, z=500$ 20. ₹ 1125, ₹ 1125, ₹ 4750
21. Variety A : ₹ 5, Variety B: ₹ 8, Variety C : ₹ 8

HINTS TO SELECTED PROBLEMS

13. The given data suggests the following equations:
    $$x+y+z=12,\ x-2y+z=0,\ 2x+3y+3z=33$$
14. Let the award money for Honesty, Regularity and Hardwork be ₹ x, y and z respectively. Then, $x+y+z=6000,\ x+3z=11000$ and $x-2y+z=0$.
15. $4x+3y+2z=37000,\quad 5x+3y+4z=47000,\quad x+y+z=12000$
16. $2x+4y+3z=29000,\quad 5x+2y+3z=30500,\quad x+y+z=9500$

7.3 SOLUTION OF HOMOGENEOUS SYSTEM OF LINEAR EQUATIONS

In chapter 6, we have learnt about determinant method to solve a homogeneous system of linear equations. In this section, we shall discuss matrix method to solve the same.

Let $AX=O$ be a homogeneous system of n linear equations with n unknowns.

Let us now discuss two cases:

Case I *When* $|A|\neq 0$ *i.e. matrix A is non-singular.*

If $|A|\neq 0$, then A^{-1} exists.

$\therefore\quad AX=O$

$\Rightarrow\quad A^{-1}(AX)=A^{-1}O$

$\Rightarrow \quad (A^{-1}A)X = O \Rightarrow I_n X = O \Rightarrow X = O$

$\Rightarrow \quad x_1 = x_2 = \ldots = x_n = 0$

Thus, if the coefficient matrix A is a non-singular, then the homogeneous system of equations has the unique solution $X = O$ i.e. $x_1 = x_2 = \ldots = x_n = 0$.

This solution is known as the trivial solution.

Case II *When* $|A| = 0$ *i.e. matrix A singular.*

If $|A| = 0$, then $(adj\ A)\ B = (adj\ A)\ O = O$

i.e. the condition of consistency is always satisfied. So, the given system of equations is consistent and it has infinitely many solutions which can be obtained by giving any real value to one of the variables and then solving the remaining equations by matrix method.

In order to solve a homogeneous system of the three linear equations with 3 unknowns x, y, z, we may use the following algorithm.

ALGORITHM

Step I *Obtain the system of equations and express it in the matrix equation of the form* $AX = O$.

Step II *Find* $|A|$.

Step III *If* $|A| \neq 0$, *then* $x = y = z = 0$ *is the only solution of the homogeneous system. So, write* $x = 0$, $y = 0, z = 0$ *as the solution.*

Step IV *If* $|A| = 0$, *then the system has infinitely many solutions. In order to find these solutions put* $z = k$ *(any real number) and solve any two equations for x and y by the matrix method. The values of x and y so obtained with* $z = k$ *give a solution of the system.*

Following examples will illustrate the above procedure.

ILLUSTRATIVE EXAMPLES

BASED ON BASIC CONCEPTS (BASIC)

Type I WHEN THE DETERMINANT OF THE COEFFICIENT MATRIX IS NON-SINGULAR

EXAMPLE 1 *Solve the following system of homogeneous equations:*

$$2x + 3y - z = 0$$
$$x - y - 2z = 0$$
$$3x + y + 3z = 0$$

SOLUTION The given system of homogeneous equations can be written as

$$\begin{bmatrix} 2 & 3 & -1 \\ 1 & -1 & -2 \\ 3 & 1 & 3 \end{bmatrix} \begin{bmatrix} x \\ y \\ z \end{bmatrix} = \begin{bmatrix} 0 \\ 0 \\ 0 \end{bmatrix}$$

or, $\quad AX = O$, where $A = \begin{bmatrix} 2 & 3 & -1 \\ 1 & -1 & -2 \\ 3 & 1 & 3 \end{bmatrix}$, $X = \begin{bmatrix} x \\ y \\ z \end{bmatrix}$ and $O = \begin{bmatrix} 0 \\ 0 \\ 0 \end{bmatrix}$

Now, $\quad |A| = \begin{vmatrix} 2 & 3 & -1 \\ 1 & -1 & -2 \\ 3 & 1 & 3 \end{vmatrix} = -2 - 27 - 4 = -33 \neq 0.$

Thus $|A| \neq 0$. So, the given system has only the trivial solution given by $x = y = z = 0$.

Type II WHEN THE DETERMINANT OF THE COEFFICIENT MATRIX IS SINGULAR

EXAMPLE 2 *Show that the homogeneous system of equations*

$$x-2y+z=0,\ x+y-z=0,\ 3x+6y-5z=0$$

has a non-trivial solution. Also, find the solution.

SOLUTION The given system of homogeneous equations can be written in matrix form as

$$\begin{bmatrix} 1 & -2 & 1 \\ 1 & 1 & -1 \\ 3 & 6 & -5 \end{bmatrix}\begin{bmatrix} x \\ y \\ z \end{bmatrix}=\begin{bmatrix} 0 \\ 0 \\ 0 \end{bmatrix}$$

or, $AX = O$, where $A=\begin{bmatrix} 1 & -2 & 1 \\ 1 & 1 & -1 \\ 3 & 6 & -5 \end{bmatrix}$, $X=\begin{bmatrix} x \\ y \\ z \end{bmatrix}$ and $O=\begin{bmatrix} 0 \\ 0 \\ 0 \end{bmatrix}$.

Now, $|A|=\begin{vmatrix} 1 & -2 & 1 \\ 1 & 1 & -1 \\ 3 & 6 & -5 \end{vmatrix}=1(-5+6)+2(-5+3)+1(6-3)=0.$

So, the given system of equations has a non-trivial solution. To find these solutions, we put $z=k$ in the first two equations and write them as follows:

$$x-2y=-k \text{ and } x+y=k.$$

or, $\begin{bmatrix} 1 & -2 \\ 1 & 1 \end{bmatrix}\begin{bmatrix} x \\ y \end{bmatrix}=\begin{bmatrix} -k \\ k \end{bmatrix}$ or, $AX=B$ where $A=\begin{bmatrix} 1 & -2 \\ 1 & 1 \end{bmatrix}$, $X=\begin{bmatrix} x \\ y \end{bmatrix}$ and $B=\begin{bmatrix} -k \\ k \end{bmatrix}$.

Now, $|A|=\begin{vmatrix} 1 & -2 \\ 1 & 1 \end{vmatrix}=3\neq 0$. So, A^{-1} exists.

Clearly, $\text{adj } A=\begin{bmatrix} 1 & 2 \\ -1 & 1 \end{bmatrix}$ and $A^{-1}=\frac{1}{|A|}\text{adj } A=\frac{1}{3}\begin{bmatrix} 1 & 2 \\ -1 & 1 \end{bmatrix}$

$\therefore\quad X=A^{-1}B \Rightarrow \begin{bmatrix} x \\ y \end{bmatrix}=\frac{1}{3}\begin{bmatrix} 1 & 2 \\ -1 & 1 \end{bmatrix}\begin{bmatrix} -k \\ k \end{bmatrix}=\begin{bmatrix} k/3 \\ 2k/3 \end{bmatrix}\Rightarrow x=k/3,\ y=2k/3.$

These values of x, y and z also satisfy the third equation.

Hence $x=k/3$, $y=2k/3$ and $z=k$, where k is any real number satisfy the given system of equations.

EXERCISE 7.2

BASIC

Solve the following systems of homogeneous linear equations by matrix method:

1. $2x-y+z=0$, $3x+2y-z=0$, $x+4y+3z=0$
2. $2x-y+2z=0$, $5x+3y-z=0$, $x+5y-5z=0$
3. $3x-y+2z=0$, $4x+3y+3z=0$, $5x+7y+4z=0$
4. $x+y-6z=0$, $x-y+2z=0$, $-3x+y+2z=0$
5. $x+y+z=0$, $x-y-5z=0$, $x+2y+4z=0$
6. $x+y-z=0$, $x-2y+z=0$, $3x+6y-5z=0$
7. $3x+y-2z=0$, $x+y+z=0$, $x-2y+z=0$
8. $2x+3y-z=0$, $x-y-2z=0$, $3x+y+3z=0$

ANSWERS

1. $x = y = z = 0$
2. $x = \frac{-5k}{11},\ y = \frac{12k}{11},\ z = k$
3. $x = \frac{-9k}{13},\ y = \frac{-k}{13},\ z = k$
4. $x = 2k,\ y = 4k,\ z = k$
5. $x = 2k,\ y = -3k,\ z = k$
6. $x = k,\ y = 2k,\ z = 3k$
7. $x = y = z = 0$
8. $x = y = z = 0$
5. $x = 2, y = 3, z = -1$
6. 2

FILL IN THE BLANKS TYPE QUESTIONS (FBQs)

1. If the system of equations $x + ay = 0$, $az + y = 0$, $ax + z = 0$ has infinitely many solutions, then $a =$ ....
2. If the system of equations $x + y + z = 6$, $x + 2y + 3z = 10$, $x + 2y + \lambda z = 12$ is inconsistent, then $\lambda =$ ....
3. The number of solutions of the system of equations $x + 2y + z = 3$, $2x + 3y + z = 3$, $3x + 5y + 2z = 1$ is ....
4. If the system of equations $2x - y - z = 12$, $x - 2y + z = -4$, $x + y + \lambda z = 4$ has no solution, then $\lambda =$ ....
5. If the system of equations $x - ky - z = 0$, $kx - y - z = 0$, $x + y - z = 0$ has a non-zero solution, then the values of k are ....
6. The real value of λ for which the system of equations $\lambda x + y + z = 0$, $-x + \lambda y + z = 0$, $-x - y + \lambda z = 0$ has a non-zero solution, is ....
7. The set of values of k for which the system of equations $x + y + z = 2$, $2x + y - z = 3$, $3x + 2y + kz = 4$ has a unique solution, is ....

ANSWERS

1. –1 2. 3 3. 0 4. $\lambda = -2$ 5. 1, –1 6. 0 7. $R - \{0\}$

VERY SHORT ANSWER QUESTIONS (VSAQs)

Answer each of the following questions in one word or one sentence or as per exact requirement of the question:

1. If $\begin{bmatrix} 1 & 0 & 0 \\ 0 & 1 & 0 \\ 0 & 0 & 1 \end{bmatrix} \begin{bmatrix} x \\ y \\ z \end{bmatrix} = \begin{bmatrix} 1 \\ -1 \\ 0 \end{bmatrix}$, find x, y and z.
2. If $\begin{bmatrix} 1 & 0 & 0 \\ 0 & -1 & 0 \\ 0 & 0 & -1 \end{bmatrix} \begin{bmatrix} x \\ y \\ z \end{bmatrix} = \begin{bmatrix} 1 \\ 0 \\ 1 \end{bmatrix}$, find x, y and z.
3. If $\begin{bmatrix} 1 & 0 & 0 \\ 0 & y & 0 \\ 0 & 0 & 1 \end{bmatrix} \begin{bmatrix} x \\ -1 \\ z \end{bmatrix} = \begin{bmatrix} 1 \\ 0 \\ 1 \end{bmatrix}$, find x, y and z.
4. Solve $\begin{bmatrix} 3 & -4 \\ 9 & 2 \end{bmatrix} \begin{bmatrix} x \\ y \end{bmatrix} = \begin{bmatrix} 10 \\ 2 \end{bmatrix}$ for x and y.

5. If $\begin{bmatrix} 1 & 0 & 0 \\ 0 & 0 & 1 \\ 0 & 1 & 0 \end{bmatrix} \begin{bmatrix} x \\ y \\ z \end{bmatrix} = \begin{bmatrix} 2 \\ -1 \\ 3 \end{bmatrix}$, find x, y, z.

6. If $A = \begin{bmatrix} 2 & 4 \\ 4 & 3 \end{bmatrix}$, $X = \begin{bmatrix} n \\ 1 \end{bmatrix}$, $B = \begin{bmatrix} 8 \\ 11 \end{bmatrix}$ and $AX = B$, then find n.

ANSWERS

1. $x = 1, y = -1, z = 0$
2. $x = 1, y = 0, z = -1$
3. $x = 1, y = 0, z = 1$
4. $x = \frac{2}{3}, y = -2$
5. $x = 2, y = 3, z = -1$
6. 2

CHAPTER 8

CONTINUITY

8.1 INTUTIVE NOTION OF CONTINUITY

Intutively a function is continuous in its domain if its graph is a curve without breaks or jumps throughout its domain and a function is continuous at a point in its domain if its graph does not have breaks or jumps in the immediate neighbourhood of the point. Consider the graph of a function $f(x)$ shown in Fig. 8.1. It is evident from the graph that $f(x)$ is not defined at $x = a$. Consequently, there is hole in the curve $y = f(x)$ and so $f(x)$ is not continuous at $x = a$. We also observe that $L = R$ i.e. $\lim\limits_{x \to a^-} f(x) = \lim\limits_{x \to a^+} f(x)$ and so $\lim\limits_{x \to a} f(x)$ exists. Thus, the continuity of $f(x)$ at $x = a$ is destroyed, if $\lim\limits_{x \to a} f(x)$ exists but $f(x)$ is not defined at $x = a$.

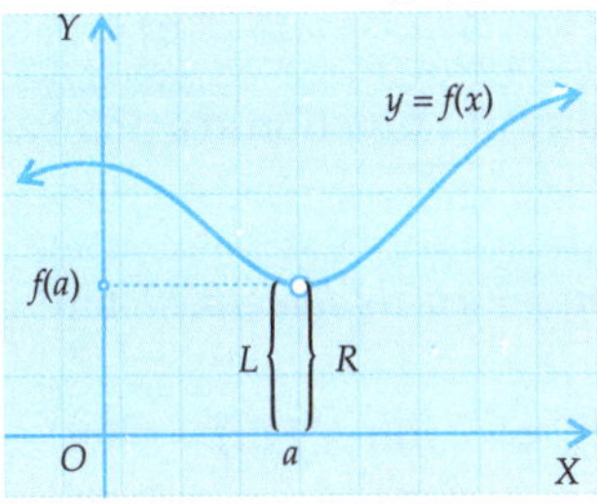

$f(a)$ is not defined, $\lim\limits_{x \to a} f(x)$ exists

Fig. 8.1

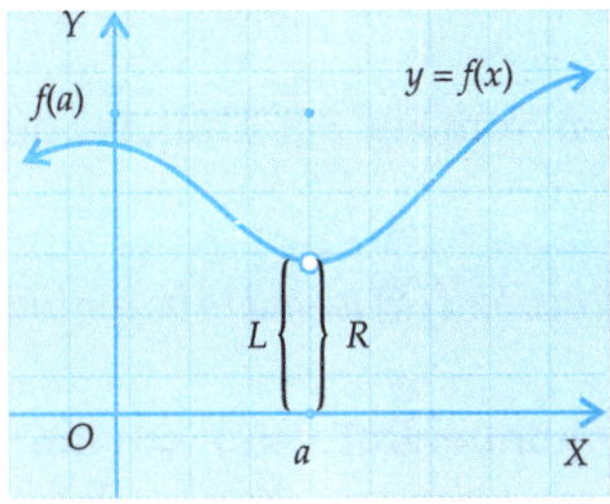

$f(a)$ is defined, $\lim\limits_{x \to a} f(x)$ exists and not equal to $f(a)$

Fig. 8.2

Let us now consider the function f whose graph is shown in Fig. 8.2. Clearly, $L = R$ i.e. $\lim\limits_{x \to a^-} f(x) = \lim\limits_{x \to a^+} f(x)$. Consequently $\lim\limits_{x \to a} f(x)$ exists. But, there is hole in the curve because $\lim\limits_{x \to a} f(x)$ is not equal to $f(a)$. So, $f(x)$ becomes discontinuous at $x = a$ if, $\lim\limits_{x \to a} f(x)$ exists but it is not equal to the value of f at $x = a$.

In Fig. 8.3, we observe that $L \neq R$ i.e. $\lim\limits_{x \to a^-} f(x) \neq \lim\limits_{x \to a^+} f(x)$. So, $\lim\limits_{x \to a} f(x)$ does not exist. Also, $f(x)$ is not continuous at $x = a$. Thus, the continuity of f at $x = a$ is also destroyed, if $\lim\limits_{x \to a} f(x)$ does not exist. This happens due to the jump in the values of $f(x)$ as x crosses 'a'.

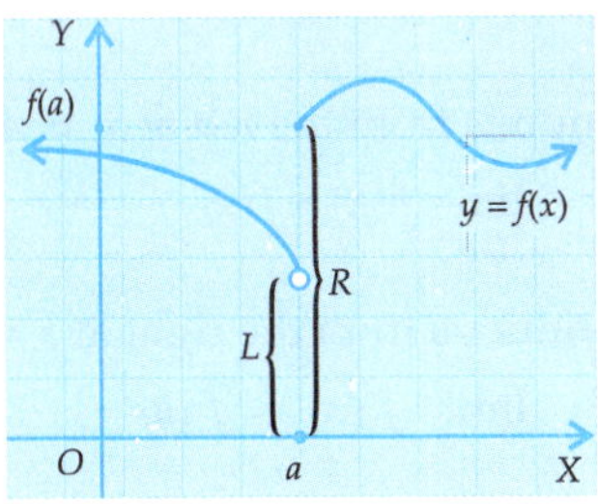

$\lim\limits_{x \to a^-} f(x)$ is not same as $\lim\limits_{x \to a^+} f(x)$

Fig. 8.3

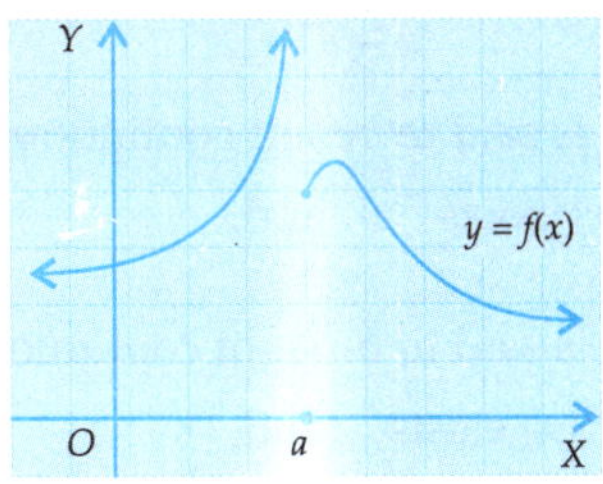

$f(x)$ is defined at $x = a$, $\lim\limits_{x \to a^-} f(x) = +\infty$

Fig. 8.4 (i)

The continuity of a function f is also destroyed if either of the two limits $\lim_{x \to a^-} f(x)$ and $\lim_{x \to a^+} f(x)$ or both tend to $+\infty$ or $-\infty$ and $f(a)$ is finite as is evident from Fig. 8.4 (i), (ii).

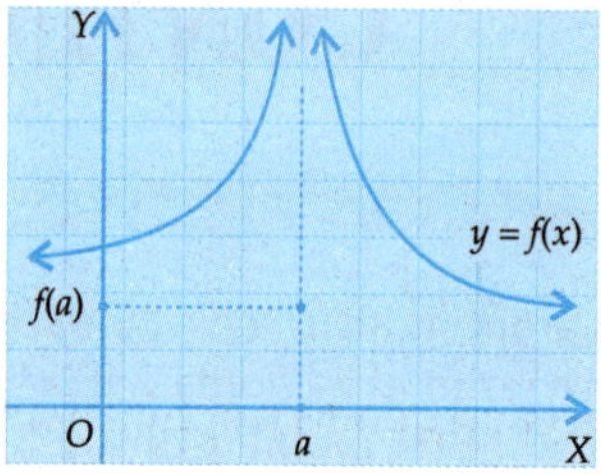

$f(x)$ is defined at $x = a$, $\lim_{x \to a^-} f(x) = +\infty$ and $\lim_{x \to a^+} f(x) = +\infty$

Fig. 8.4 (ii)

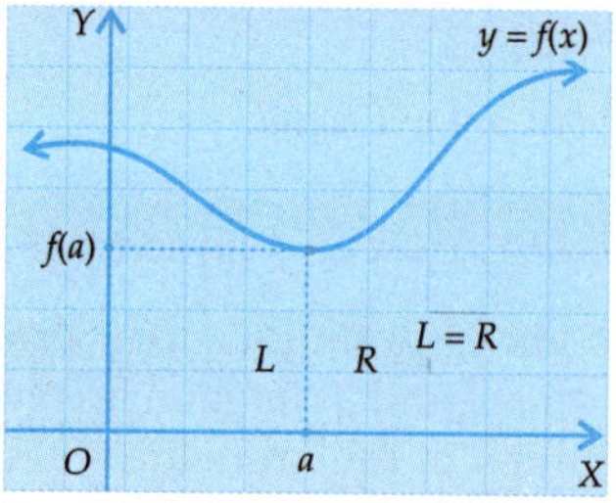

$\lim_{x \to a} f(a)$ exists and is equal to $f(a)$.
Function $f(x)$ is continuous at point $x = a$

Fig. 8.5

It follows from the above discussion that a function $f(x)$ can be continuous at a point $x = a$ iff

(i) $f(a)$ is defined, (ii) $\lim_{x \to a} f(x)$ exists and, (iii) $\lim_{x \to a} f(x) = f(a)$.

This is also evident from Fig. 8.5. Thus, we define continuity of a function at a point as follows.

8.2 CONTINUITY AT A POINT

DEFINITION *A function $f(x)$ is said to be continuous at a point $x = a$ of its domain, iff* $\lim_{x \to a} f(x) = f(a)$.

Thus,

$$(f(x) \text{ is continuous at } x = a) \Leftrightarrow \lim_{x \to a} f(x) = f(a) \Leftrightarrow \lim_{x \to a^-} f(x) = \lim_{x \to a^+} f(x) = f(a)$$

If $f(x)$ is not continuous at a point $x = a$, then it is said to be discontinuous at $x = a$.

If $\lim_{x \to a^-} f(x) = \lim_{x \to a^+} f(x) \neq f(a)$, then the discontinuity is known as the *removable discontinuity*, because $f(x)$ can be made continuous by redefining it at point $x = a$ in such a way that $f(a) = \lim_{x \to a} f(x)$.

If $\lim_{x \to a^-} f(x) \neq \lim_{x \to a^+} f(x)$, then $f(x)$ is said to have a *discontinuity of first kind.*

A function $f(x)$ is said to have a discontinuity of *the second kind* at $x = a$ iff

$\lim_{x \to a^-} f(x)$ or, $\lim_{x \to a^+} f(x)$ or, both do not exist.

A function $f(x)$ is said to be left continuous or continuous from the left at $x = a$, iff

(i) $\lim_{x \to a^-} f(x)$ exists and, (ii) $\lim_{x \to a^-} f(x) = f(a)$

A function $f(x)$ is said to be right continuous or continuous from the right at $x = a$, iff

(i) $\lim_{x \to a^+} f(x)$ exists and, (ii) $\lim_{x \to a^+} f(x) = f(a)$

It follows from the above definitions that

$f(x)$ is continuous at $x = a$ iff it is both left as well as right continuous at $x = a$.

REMARK *A function $f(x)$ fails to be continuous at $x = a$ for any of the following reasons.*

(i) $\lim_{x \to a} f(x)$ *exists but it is not equal to* $f(a)$. (ii) $\lim_{x \to a} f(x)$ *does not exist.*

This happens if either $\lim_{x \to a^-} f(x)$ *does not exist or,* $\lim_{x \to a^+} f(x)$ *does not exist or both* $\lim_{x \to a^-} f(x)$ *and* $\lim_{x \to a^+} f(x)$ *exist but are not equal.*

(iii) *f is not defined at $x = a$ i.e. $f(a)$ does not exist.*

8.3 ALGEBRA OF CONTINUOUS FUNCTIONS

Regarding the continuity of the sum, difference, product and quotient of functions, we have the following theorems.

THEOREM 1 *Let f and g be two real functions, continuous at $x = a$. Let α be a real number. Then,*

(i) *$f + g$ is continuous at $x = a$.* (ii) *$f - g$ is continuous at $x = a$.*

(iii) *αf is continuous at $x = a$.* (iv) *fg is continuous at $x = a$.*

(v) *$\frac{1}{f}$ is continuous at $x = a$, provided that $f(a) \neq 0$.*

(vi) *$\frac{f}{g}$ is continuous at $x = a$, provided that $g(a) \neq 0$.*

PROOF Since f and g are continuous at $x = a$. Therefore, $\lim_{x \to a} f(x) = f(a)$ and $\lim_{x \to a} g(x) = g(a)$.

(i) We find that

$$\lim_{x \to a} (f+g)(x) = \lim_{x \to a} (f(x) + g(x)) = \lim_{x \to a} f(x) + \lim_{x \to a} g(x)$$

$$= f(a) + g(a) \qquad \left[\because \lim_{x \to a} f(x) = f(a) \text{ and, } \lim_{x \to a} g(x) = g(a)\right]$$

$$= (f+g)(a)$$

$\therefore$ $f + g$ is continuous at $x = a$.

(ii) We find that

$$\lim_{x \to a} (f-g)(x) = \lim_{x \to a} (f(x) - g(x)) = \lim_{x \to a} f(x) - \lim_{x \to a} g(x)$$

$$= f(a) - g(a) \qquad \left[\because \lim_{x \to a} f(x) = f(a) \text{ and, } \lim_{x \to a} g(x) = g(a)\right]$$

$$= (f-g)(a)$$

$\therefore$ $f - g$ is continuous at $x = a$.

(iii) We find that

$$\lim_{x \to a} (\alpha f)(x) = \lim_{x \to a} \alpha f(x) = \alpha \lim_{x \to a} f(x) = \alpha f(a) \qquad \left[\because \lim_{x \to a} f(x) = f(a)\right]$$

$\therefore$ αf is continuous at $x = a$.

(iv) We find that

$$\lim_{x \to a} (fg)(x) = \lim_{x \to a} \{f(x)\, g(x)\} = \lim_{x \to a} f(x) \lim_{x \to a} g(x) = f(a)\, g(a) = (fg)(a)$$

So, fg is continuous at $x = a$.

(v) We find that

$$\lim_{x \to a} \left(\frac{1}{f}\right)(x) = \lim_{x \to a} \left(\frac{1}{f(x)}\right) = \frac{1}{\lim\limits_{x \to a} f(x)} = \frac{1}{f(a)} = \left(\frac{1}{f}\right)(a)$$

So, $\frac{1}{f}$ is continuous at $x = a$

(vi) We find that

$$\lim_{x \to a} \left(\frac{f}{g}\right)(x) = \lim_{x \to a} \left\{\frac{f(x)}{g(x)}\right\} = \frac{\lim\limits_{x \to a} f(x)}{\lim\limits_{x \to a} g(x)} = \frac{f(a)}{g(a)} = \left(\frac{f}{g}\right)(a)$$

So, $\frac{f}{g}$ is continuous at $x = a$.

THEOREM 2 *Let f and g be real functions such that fog is defined. If g is continuous at $x = a$ and f is continuous at $g(a)$, show that fog is continuous at $x = a$.*

PROOF Since fog is defined. Therefore, Range (g) $\subset$ Domain $(f) \Rightarrow g(x) \in$ Domain (f) for all $x \in$ Domain (g)

Now, $g(x)$ is continuous at $x = a \Rightarrow \lim\limits_{x \to a} g(x) = g(a)$ ...(i)

f is continuous at $g(a)$

$$\Rightarrow \lim_{g(x) \to g(a)} f(g(x)) = f(g(a))$$

$$\Rightarrow \lim_{x \to a} f(g(x)) = f(g(a)) \qquad [\text{From (i)}, x \to a \Rightarrow g(x) \to g(a)]$$

$$\Rightarrow \lim_{x \to a} (fog)(x) = (fog)(a) \Rightarrow fog \text{ is continuous at } x = a.$$

ILLUSTRATIVE EXAMPLES

BASED ON BASIC CONCEPTS (BASIC)

Type I **ON TESTING CONTINUITY OF A FUNCTION AT A POINT WHEN THE FUNCTION HAS SAME DEFINITION ON BOTH SIDES OF THE GIVEN POINT**

EXAMPLE 1 *Test the continuity of the following function at the origin:* $f(x) = \begin{cases} \frac{|x|}{x} & ; \ x \neq 0 \\ 1 & ; \ x = 0 \end{cases}$

SOLUTION We observe that:

$$(\text{LHL at } x = 0) = \lim_{x \to 0^-} f(x) = \lim_{h \to 0} f(0 - h) = \lim_{h \to 0} f(-h)$$

$$= \lim_{h \to 0} \frac{|-h|}{-h} = \lim_{h \to 0} \frac{h}{-h} = \lim_{h \to 0} -1 = -1$$

and, $$(\text{RHL at } x = 0) = \lim_{x \to 0^+} f(x) = \lim_{h \to 0} f(0 + h) = \lim_{h \to 0} f(h)$$

$$= \lim_{h \to 0} \frac{|h|}{h} = \lim_{h \to 0} \frac{h}{h} = \lim_{h \to 0} 1 = 1$$

Thus, we obtain : $\lim\limits_{x \to 0^-} f(x) \neq \lim\limits_{x \to 0^+} f(x)$. Hence, $f(x)$ is not continuous at the origin.

ALITER We have,

$$f(x) = \begin{cases} \frac{|x|}{x} & ; \; x \neq 0 \\ 1 & ; \; x = 0 \end{cases} \text{ or, } f(x) = \begin{cases} \frac{x}{x} = 1 & ; x > 0 \\ \frac{-x}{x} = -1 & ; x < 0 \\ 1 & ; x = 0 \end{cases} \qquad \left[\because |x| = \begin{cases} x, & x \geq 0 \\ -x, & x < 0 \end{cases} \right]$$

$\therefore$ $$(\text{LHL at } x = 0) = \lim_{x \to 0^-} f(x) = \lim_{x \to 0} -1 = -1 \qquad \left[\begin{array}{l} \because f(x) = -1 \text{ for } x < 0 \text{ and } x \to 0^- \\ \text{means that } x < 0 \text{ such that } x \to 0 \end{array} \right]$$

$$(\text{RHL at } x = 0) = \lim_{x \to 0^+} f(x) = \lim_{x \to 0} 1 = 1 \qquad \left[\begin{array}{l} \because f(x) = 1 \text{ for } x > 0 \text{ and } x \to 0^+ \\ \text{means that } x > 0 \text{ such that } x \to 0 \end{array} \right]$$

$\therefore$ $$\lim_{x \to 0^-} f(x) \neq \lim_{x \to 0^+} f(x).$$

Hence, $f(x)$ is not continuous at the origin.

EXAMPLE 2 *Show that the function $f(x)$ given by* $f(x) = \begin{cases} \frac{\sin x}{x} + \cos x, & x \neq 0 \\ 2 & , x = 0 \end{cases}$ *is continuous at $x = 0$.*

SOLUTION We observe that

$$(\text{LHL at } x = 0) = \lim_{x \to 0^-} f(x) = \lim_{h \to 0} f(0 - h) = \lim_{h \to 0} f(-h)$$

$$= \lim_{h \to 0} \frac{\sin(-h)}{-h} + \cos(-h) = \lim_{h \to 0} \frac{\sin h}{h} + \lim_{h \to 0} \cos h = 1 + 1 = 2$$

$$(\text{RHL at } x = 0) = \lim_{x \to 0^+} f(x) = \lim_{h \to 0} f(0 + h) = \lim_{h \to 0} f(h)$$

$$= \lim_{h \to 0} \frac{\sin h}{h} + \cos h = \lim_{h \to 0} \frac{\sin h}{h} + \lim_{h \to 0} \cos h = 1 + 1 = 2$$

and, $f(0) = 2$

$\therefore$ $\lim\limits_{x \to 0^-} f(x) = \lim\limits_{x \to 0^+} f(x) = f(0)$. Hence, $f(x)$ is continuous at $x = 0$.

EXAMPLE 3 *Examine the function $f(t)$ given by* $f(t) = \begin{cases} \frac{\cos t}{\pi/2 - t} & ; \; t \neq \pi/2 \\ 1 & ; \; t = \pi/2 \end{cases}$ *for continuity at $t = \pi/2$.*

SOLUTION We observe that:

$$(\text{LHL at } t = \pi/2) = \lim_{t \to \pi/2^-} f(t)$$

$$= \lim_{h \to 0} f\left(\frac{\pi}{2} - h\right) = \lim_{h \to 0} \frac{\cos(\pi/2 - h)}{\pi/2 - (\pi/2 - h)} = \lim_{h \to 0} \frac{\sin h}{h} = 1$$

and, $$(\text{RHL at } t = \pi/2) = \lim_{t \to \pi/2^+} f(t)$$

$$= \lim_{h \to 0} f\left(\frac{\pi}{2} + h\right) = \lim_{h \to 0} \frac{\cos(\pi/2 + h)}{\pi/2 - (\pi/2 + h)} = \lim_{h \to 0} \frac{-\sin h}{-h} = \lim_{h \to 0} \frac{\sin h}{h} = 1$$

and, $f(\pi/2) = 1$.

$\therefore$ $\lim\limits_{t \to \pi/2^-} f(t) = \lim\limits_{t \to \pi/2^+} f(t) = f(\pi/2)$. So, $f(t)$ is continuous at $t = \pi/2$.

Type II **ON TESTING CONTINUITY OF A FUNCTION AT A POINT WHEN THE FUNCTION HAS DIFFERENT DEFINITIONS ON BOTH SIDES OF THE GIVEN POINT**

Let a function $f(x)$ be defined as

$$f(x)=\begin{cases}\phi(x) & ; \text{ if } x<a\\ \psi(x) & ; \text{ if } x\geq a\end{cases} \text{ or, } f(x)=\begin{cases}\phi(x) & ; \text{ if } x\leq a\\ \psi(x) & ; \text{ if } x>a\end{cases} \text{ or, } f(x)=\begin{cases}\phi(x) & ; \text{ if } x<a\\ k & ; \text{ if } x=a\\ \psi(x) & ; \text{ if } x>a\end{cases}$$

To test the continuity of such functions at $x = a$, we have to find left hand and right hand limits of $f(x)$ at $x=a$. For finding these two limits one can use the method which we have used in previous examples or we can use the following method:

$$(\text{LHL at } x=a) = \lim_{x\to a^-} f(x) = \lim_{x\to a} \phi(x) \quad \left[\begin{array}{l} \because x\to a^- \Leftrightarrow x< \text{ and } x\to a \\ \therefore \lim\limits_{x\to a^-} f(x) = \lim\limits_{x\to a} \phi(x)\ [\because f(x)=\phi(x) \text{ for } x<a] \end{array}\right]$$

Now, $\lim\limits_{x\to a} \phi(x)$ can be calculated by various methods of evaluating limits as discussed in the chapter on limits.

Similarly, we have

$$(\text{RHL at } x=a) = \lim_{x\to a^+} f(x) = \lim_{x\to a} \psi(x) \quad \left[\begin{array}{l} \because x\to a^+ \Leftrightarrow x>a\ \&\ x\to a \\ \therefore \lim\limits_{x\to a^+} f(x) = \lim\limits_{x\to a} \psi(x)\ [\because f(x)=\psi(x) \text{ for } x>a] \end{array}\right]$$

Now, $\lim\limits_{x\to a} \psi(x)$ can be calculated by various methods of evaluating limits.

EXAMPLE 4 *Discuss the continuity of the function $f(x)$ at $x=1/2$, where*

$$f(x) = \begin{cases} 1/2-x & ; \ 0\leq x<1/2 \\ 1 & ; \ x=1/2 \\ 3/2-x & ; \ 1/2<x\leq 1 \end{cases}$$ **[CBSE 2011]**

SOLUTION We observe that:

$$(\text{LHL at } x=1/2) = \lim_{x\to 1/2^-} f(x) = \lim_{x\to 1/2} (1/2-x) \quad \left[\because f(x)=\frac{1}{2}-x \text{ for } 0\leq x<\frac{1}{2}\right]$$

$$= 1/2-1/2 = 0 \quad \text{[Using direct substitution method]}$$

and, $$(\text{RHL at } x=1/2) = \lim_{x\to 1/2^+} f(x) = \lim_{x\to 1/2} (3/2-x) \quad \left[\because f(x)=\frac{3}{2}-x \text{ for } \frac{1}{2}<x\leq 1\right]$$

$$= 3/2-1/2 = 1 \quad \text{[Using direct substitution method]}$$

Clearly, $\lim\limits_{x\to 1/2^-} f(x) \neq \lim\limits_{x\to 1/2^+} f(x)$.

Hence, $f(x)$ is not continuous at $x=1/2$. Clearly, $f(x)$ has discontinuity of first kind at $x=1/2$.

EXAMPLE 5 *Discuss the continuity of the function f(x) given by* $f(x) = \begin{cases} 2-x, & x<2 \\ 2+x, & x\geq 2 \end{cases}$ *at $x=2$.*

SOLUTION We observe that:

$$(\text{LHL at } x=2) = \lim_{x\to 2^-} f(x) = \lim_{x\to 2} (2-x) = 2-2=0 \quad [\because f(x)=2-x \text{ for } x<2]$$

and, $$(\text{RHL at } x=2) = \lim_{x\to 2^+} f(x) = \lim_{x\to 2} (2+x) = 2+2=4 \quad [\because f(x)=2+x= \text{ for } x\geq 2]$$

$\because \quad \lim_{x \to 2^-} f(x) \neq \lim_{x \to 2^+} f(x)$. Hence, $f(x)$ is not continuous at $x = 2$.

EXAMPLE 6 *Show that* $f(x) = \begin{cases} 5x-4, & \text{when } 0 < x \le 1 \\ 4x^3 - 3x, & \text{when } 1 < x < 2 \end{cases}$ *is continuous at* $x = 1$.

SOLUTION We have,

$$(\text{LHL at } x=1) = \lim_{x \to 1^-} f(x) = \lim_{x \to 1} 5x - 4 = 5 \times 1 - 4 = 1 \quad [\because f(x) = 5x - 4, \text{ when } x \le 1]$$

$$(\text{RHL at } x=1) = \lim_{x \to 1^+} f(x) = \lim_{x \to 1} 4x^3 - 3x = 4(1)^3 - 3(1) = 1 \; [\because f(x) = 4x^3 - 3x, x > 1]$$

and, $f(1) = 5 \times 1 - 4 = 1 \quad [\because f(x) = 5x - 4, \text{ where } x \le 1]$

$\therefore \quad \lim_{x \to 1^-} f(x) = f(1) = \lim_{x \to 1^+} f(x)$. So, $f(x)$ is continuous at $x = 1$.

EXAMPLE 7 *Show that the function* $f(x) = 2x - |x|$ *is continuous at* $x = 0$. **[CBSE 2002]**

SOLUTION We have,

$$f(x) = 2x - |x| = \begin{cases} 2x - x, & \text{if } x \ge 0 \\ 2x - (-x), & \text{if } x < 0 \end{cases} = \begin{cases} x, & \text{if } x \ge 0 \\ 3x, & \text{if } x < 0 \end{cases}$$

Now,

$$(\text{LHL at } x=0) = \lim_{x \to 0^-} f(x) = \lim_{x \to 0^-} 3x = 3 \times 0 = 0$$

$$(\text{RHL at } x=0) = \lim_{x \to 0^+} f(x) = \lim_{x \to 0^+} x = 0 \text{ and, } f(0) = 0$$

$\therefore \quad \lim_{x \to 0^-} f(x) = \lim_{x \to 0^+} f(x) = f(0)$. So, $f(x)$ is continuous at $x = 0$.

Type III ON FINDING THE VALUE(S) OF A CONSTANT GIVEN IN THE DEFINITION OF A FUNCTION WHEN IT IS CONTINUOUS AT AN INDICATED POINT

A function $f(x)$ is continuous at a point $x = a$ iff $\lim_{x \to a^-} f(x) = \lim_{x \to a^+} f(x) = f(a)$.

But, $\lim_{x \to a^-} f(x) = \lim_{x \to a^+} f(x) \Rightarrow \lim_{x \to a} f(x)$ exists.

Thus, $f(x)$ is continuous at $x = a$ iff $\lim_{x \to a} f(x) = f(a)$.

We will use this result in finding unknown quantity in the definition of a function when it is given to be continuous at a given point.

EXAMPLE 8 *Determine the value of k for which the function* $f(x) = \begin{cases} \dfrac{x^2 - 9}{x - 3}, & x \ne 3 \\ k, & x = 3 \end{cases}$ *is continuous at* $x = 3$.

SOLUTION It is given that $f(x)$ is continuous at $x = 3$.

$$\therefore \quad \lim_{x \to 3} f(x) = f(3)$$

$$\Rightarrow \quad \lim_{x \to 3} f(x) = k \quad [\because f(3) = k]$$

$$\Rightarrow \quad \lim_{x \to 3} \frac{x^2 - 9}{x - 3} = k \Rightarrow \lim_{x \to 3} \frac{(x-3)(x+3)}{x - 3} = k \Rightarrow \lim_{x \to 3} (x + 3) = k \Rightarrow 6 = k$$

Thus, $f(x)$ is continuous at $x = 3$, if $k = 6$.

EXAMPLE 9 *Find the value of the constant λ so that the function given below is continuous at x = – 1.*

$$f(x) = \begin{cases} \dfrac{x^2 - 2x - 3}{x+1}, & x \neq -1 \\ \lambda, & x = -1 \end{cases}$$

SOLUTION Given that $f(x)$ is continuous at $x = -1$.

$\therefore \quad \lim_{x \to -1} f(x) = f(-1)$

$\Rightarrow \quad \lim_{x \to -1} \dfrac{x^2 - 2x - 3}{x+1} = \lambda \qquad [\because f(-1) = \lambda]$

$\Rightarrow \quad \lim_{x \to -1} \dfrac{(x-3)(x+1)}{x+1} = \lambda \Rightarrow \lim_{x \to -1} (x-3) = \lambda \Rightarrow -4 = \lambda$

So, $f(x)$ is continuous at $x = -1$, if $\lambda = -4$.

EXAMPLE 10 *Find the value of 'a' if the function f(x) defined by* $f(x) = \begin{cases} 2x-1, & x<2 \\ a, & x=2 \\ x+1, & x>2 \end{cases}$ *is continuous at x = 2.*

SOLUTION We find that:

$$(\text{LHL at } x = 2) = \lim_{x \to 2^-} f(x) = \lim_{x \to 2} (2x-1) = 2 \times 2 - 1 = 3,$$

$$(\text{RHL at } x = 2) = \lim_{x \to 2^+} f(x) = \lim_{x \to 2} (x+1) = 2+1 = 3, \text{ and, } f(2) = a$$

Since $f(x)$ is continuous at $x = 2$. Therefore,

$$\lim_{x \to 2^-} f(x) = \lim_{x \to 2^+} f(x) = f(2) \Rightarrow 3 = 3 = a \Rightarrow a = 3$$

Thus, $f(x)$is continuous at $x = 2$, if $a = 3$.

BASED ON LOWER ORDER THINKING SKILLS (LOTS)

Type I ON TESTING CONTINUITY OF A FUNCTION AT A POINT WHEN THE FUNCTION HAS SAME DEFINITION ON BOTH SIDES OF THE GIVEN POINT

EXAMPLE 11 *Show that the function f(x) given by* $f(x) = \begin{cases} x \sin \dfrac{1}{x}, & x \neq 0 \\ 0, & x = 0 \end{cases}$ *is continuous at x = 0.*

[NCERT EXEMPLAR, CBSE 2024]

SOLUTION We observe that:

$$(\text{LHL at } x = 0) = \lim_{x \to 0^-} f(x) = \lim_{h \to 0} f(0-h) = \lim_{h \to 0} f(-h) = \lim_{h \to 0} -h \sin\left(\frac{1}{-h}\right)$$

$$= \lim_{h \to 0} h \sin\left(\frac{1}{h}\right) = 0 \times (\text{an oscillating number between} -1 \text{ and } 1) = 0$$

$$(\text{RHL at } x = 0) = \lim_{x \to 0^+} f(x) = \lim_{h \to 0} f(0+h) = \lim_{h \to 0} f(h) = \lim_{h \to 0} h \sin\left(\frac{1}{h}\right)$$

$$= 0 \times (\text{an oscillating number between } -1 \text{ and } 1) = 0$$

and, $f(0) = 0$.

Thus, we find that : $\lim_{x \to 0^-} f(x) = \lim_{x \to 0^+} f(x) = f(0)$. Hence, $f(x)$ is continuous at $x = 0$.

EXAMPLE 12 *Show that the function $f(x)$ given by* $f(x)=\begin{cases}\dfrac{e^{1/x}-1}{e^{1/x}+1}, & when\ x\neq 0\\ 0, & when\ x=0\end{cases}$ *is discontinuous at $x=0$.* [NCERT EXEMPLAR]

SOLUTION We observe that:

$$(\text{LHL at } x=0)=\lim_{x\to 0^-} f(x)=\lim_{h\to 0} f(0-h)=\lim_{h\to 0} f(-h)$$

$$=\lim_{h\to 0}\frac{e^{-1/h}-1}{e^{-1/h}+1}=\lim_{h\to 0}\frac{\frac{1}{e^{1/h}}-1}{\frac{1}{e^{1/h}}+1}=\frac{0-1}{0+1}=-1 \qquad \left[\because \lim_{h\to 0}\frac{1}{e^{1/h}}=0\right]$$

and, $$(\text{RHL at } x=0)=\lim_{x\to 0^+} f(x)=\lim_{h\to 0} f(0+h)=\lim_{h\to 0} f(h)$$

$$=\lim_{h\to 0}\frac{e^{1/h}-1}{e^{1/h}+1}=\lim_{h\to 0}\frac{1-1/e^{1/h}}{1+1/e^{1/h}}=\frac{1-0}{1+0}=1$$

$\therefore$ (LHL at $x=0$) $\neq$ (RHL at $x=0$)

So, $f(x)$ is not continuous at $x=0$ and has a discontinuity of first kind at $x=0$.

Type II ON TESTING CONTINUITY OF A FUNCTION AT A POINT WHEN THE FUNCTION HAS DIFFERENT DEFINITIONS ON BOTH SIDES OF THE GIVEN POINT

EXAMPLE 13 *Discuss the continuity of the function of given by $f(x)=|x-1|+|x-2|$ at $x=1$ and $x=2$.*

SOLUTION We have,

$$f(x)=|x-1|+|x-2|$$

$$\Rightarrow \quad f(x)=\begin{cases}-(x-1)-(x-2), & \text{if } x<1\\ (x-1)-(x-2), & \text{if } 1\leq x<2\\ (x-1)+(x-2), & \text{if } x\geq 2\end{cases} \Rightarrow f(x)=\begin{cases}-2x+3, & \text{if } x<1\\ 1, & \text{if } 1\leq x<2\\ 2x-3, & x\geq 2\end{cases}$$

Continuity at $x=1$:

$$\lim_{x\to 1^-} f(x)=\lim_{x\to 1^-}(-2x+3)=-2\times 1+3=1,\ \lim_{x\to 1^+} f(x)=\lim_{x\to 1^+} 1=1 \text{ and, } f(1)=1.$$

$\therefore$ $\displaystyle\lim_{x\to 1^-} f(x)=f(1)=\lim_{x\to 1^+} f(x)$. So, $f(x)$ is continuous at $x=1$.

Continuity at $x=2$:

$$\lim_{x\to 2^-} f(x)=\lim_{x\to 2^-} 1=1,\ \lim_{x\to 2^+} f(x)=\lim_{x\to 2}(2x-3)=2\times 2-3=1$$

and, $f(2)=2\times 2-3=1$.

$\therefore$ $\displaystyle\lim_{x\to 2^-} f(x)=\lim_{x\to 2^+} f(x)=f(2)$. So, $f(x)$ is continuous at $x=2$.

Type III ON FINDING THE VALUE(S) OF A CONSTANT GIVEN IN THE DEFINITION OF A FUNCTION WHEN IT IS CONTINUOUS AT AN INDICATED POINT

EXAMPLE 14 *Find the value of the constant k so that the function given below is continuous at $x=0$.*

$$f(x)=\begin{cases}\dfrac{1-\cos 2x}{2x^2}, & x\neq 0\\ k, & x=0\end{cases}$$ [CBSE 2023]

SOLUTION It is given that the function $f(x)$ is continuous at $x = 0$.

$$\therefore \quad \lim_{x \to 0} f(x) = f(0)$$

$$\Rightarrow \quad \lim_{x \to 0} \frac{1 - \cos 2x}{2x^2} = k \qquad [\because f(0) = k]$$

$$\Rightarrow \quad \lim_{x \to 0} \frac{2 \sin^2 x}{2x^2} = k \Rightarrow \lim_{x \to 0} \left(\frac{\sin x}{x}\right)^2 = k \Rightarrow 1^2 = k \Rightarrow k = 1$$

Thus, $f(x)$ is continuous at $x = 0$, if $k = 1$.

EXAMPLE 15 *If the function $f(x)$ defined by* $f(x) = \begin{cases} \dfrac{\log(1 + ax) - \log(1 - bx)}{x} & , \text{ if } x \neq 0 \\ k & , \text{ if } x = 0 \end{cases}$ *is continuous at $x = 0$, find k.*

SOLUTION Since $f(x)$ is continuous at $x = 0$.

$$\therefore \quad \lim_{x \to 0} f(x) = f(0)$$

$$\Rightarrow \quad \lim_{x \to 0} \frac{\log(1 + ax) - \log(1 - bx)}{x} = k \qquad [\because f(0) = k]$$

$$\Rightarrow \quad \lim_{x \to 0} \left\{\frac{\log(1 + ax)}{x} - \frac{\log(1 - bx)}{x}\right\} = k$$

$$\Rightarrow \quad \lim_{x \to 0} \frac{\log(1 + ax)}{x} - \lim_{x \to 0} \frac{\log(1 - bx)}{x} = k$$

$$\Rightarrow \quad a \lim_{x \to 0} \frac{\log(1 + ax)}{ax} - (-b) \lim_{x \to 0} \frac{\log(1 - bx)}{(-b)\,x} = k$$

$$\Rightarrow \quad a(1) - (-b)(1) = k \Rightarrow a + b = k \qquad \left[\text{Using: } \lim_{x \to 0} \frac{\log(1 + x)}{x} = 1\right]$$

Thus, $f(x)$ is continuous at $x = 0$, if $k = a + b$.

EXAMPLE 16 *Find the values of 'a' so that the function f(x) defined by* $f(x) = \begin{cases} \dfrac{\sin^2 ax}{x^2} & , x \neq 0 \\ 1 & , x = 0 \end{cases}$ *may be continuous at $x = 0$.* **[CBSE 2023]**

SOLUTION The function $f(x)$ will be continuous at $x = 0$, iff

$$\lim_{x \to 0} f(x) = f(0)$$

$$\Rightarrow \quad \lim_{x \to 0} \frac{\sin^2 ax}{x^2} = 1 \qquad [\because f(0) = 1]$$

$$\Rightarrow \quad a^2 \lim_{x \to 0} \left(\frac{\sin ax}{ax}\right)^2 = 1 \Rightarrow a^2 (1)^2 = 1 \Rightarrow a = \pm 1$$

Thus, $f(x)$ will be continuous at $x = 0$, if $a = \pm 1$.

EXAMPLE 17 *If the function f (x) given by* $f(x) = \begin{cases} 3ax + b & , \text{ if } x > 1 \\ 11 & , \text{ if } x = 1 \\ 5ax - 2b & , \text{ if } x < 1 \end{cases}$ *is continuous at $x = 1$, find the values of a and b.* **[CBSE 2002, 2010, 2011, 2012]**

SOLUTION We find that:

$$(\text{LHL at } x=1) = \lim_{x \to 1^-} f(x) = \lim_{x \to 1^-} (5ax - 2b) = 5a - 2b$$

$$(\text{RHL at } x=1) = \lim_{x \to 1^+} f(x) = \lim_{x \to 1^+} (3ax + b) = 3a + b \text{ and, } f(1) = 11.$$

Since $f(x)$ is continuous at $x = 1$.

$$\therefore \quad \lim_{x \to 1^-} f(x) = \lim_{x \to 1^+} f(x) = f(1)$$

$$\lim_{x \to 1^-} f(x) = f(1) \text{ and, } \lim_{x \to 1^+} f(x) = f(1)$$

$$\Rightarrow \quad 5a - 2b = 3a + b = 11 \Rightarrow 5a - 2b = 11 \text{ and } 3a + b = 11 \Rightarrow a = 3 \text{ and } b = 2$$

EXAMPLE 18 *Let* $f(x) = \begin{cases} \dfrac{1 - \cos 4x}{x^2}, & \text{if } x < 0 \\ a, & \text{if } x = 0 \\ \dfrac{\sqrt{x}}{\sqrt{16 + \sqrt{x}} - 4}, & \text{if } x > 0 \end{cases}$. *Determine the value of a so that* $f(x)$ *is continuous at* $x = 0$. [CBSE 2010, 2012, 2013, NCERT EXEMPLAR]

SOLUTION For $f(x)$ to be continuous at $x = 0$, we must have

$$\lim_{x \to 0^-} f(x) = \lim_{x \to 0^+} f(x) = f(0)$$

$$\Rightarrow \quad \lim_{x \to 0^-} f(x) = \lim_{x \to 0^+} f(x) = a \qquad \text{...(i)}$$

$$\text{Now,} \quad \lim_{x \to 0^-} f(x) = \lim_{x \to 0} \frac{1 - \cos 4x}{x^2} \qquad \left[\because f(x) = \frac{1 - \cos 4x}{x^2} \text{ for } x < 0\right]$$

$$\Rightarrow \quad \lim_{x \to 0^-} f(x) = \lim_{x \to 0} \frac{2\sin^2 2x}{x^2}$$

$$\Rightarrow \quad \lim_{x \to 0^-} f(x) = 2 \lim_{x \to 0} \left(\frac{\sin 2x}{x}\right)^2 = 2 \times 4 \times \lim_{x \to 0} \left(\frac{\sin 2x}{2x}\right)^2 = 8(1)^2 = 8 \qquad \text{...(ii)}$$

$$\text{and,} \quad \lim_{x \to 0^+} f(x) = \lim_{x \to 0} \frac{\sqrt{x}}{\sqrt{16 + \sqrt{x}} - 4} \qquad \left[\because f(x) = \frac{\sqrt{x}}{\sqrt{16 + \sqrt{x}} - 4} \text{ for } x > 0\right]$$

$$\Rightarrow \quad \lim_{x \to 0^+} f(x) = \lim_{x \to 0} \frac{\sqrt{x}}{16 + \sqrt{x} - 16} \left(\sqrt{16 + \sqrt{x}} + 4\right)$$

$$\Rightarrow \quad \lim_{x \to 0^+} f(x) = \lim_{x \to 0} \left(\sqrt{16 + \sqrt{x}} + 4\right) = 4 + 4 = 8 \qquad \text{...(iii)}$$

From (i), (ii) and (iii), we get $a = 8$.

BASED ON HIGHER ORDER THINKING SKILLS (HOTS)

EXAMPLE 19 *Determine* $f(0)$ *so that the function* $f(x)$ *defined by* $f(x) = \dfrac{(4^x - 1)^3}{\sin \dfrac{x}{4} \log\left(1 + \dfrac{x^2}{3}\right)}$ *becomes continuous at* $x = 0$.

SOLUTION For $f(x)$ to be continuous at $x = 0$, we must have

$$\lim_{x \to 0} f(x) = f(0)$$

$$\Rightarrow \quad f(0) = \lim_{x \to 0} f(x) = \lim_{x \to 0} \frac{(4^x - 1)^3}{\sin \frac{x}{4} \log\left(1 + \frac{x^2}{3}\right)} = \lim_{x \to 0} \frac{\left(\frac{4^x - 1}{x}\right)^3}{\left(\frac{\sin \frac{x}{4}}{4 \times \frac{x}{4}}\right)\left(\frac{\log\left(1 + \frac{x^2}{3}\right)}{\frac{x^2}{3} \times 3}\right)}$$

$$\Rightarrow \quad f(0) = \frac{(\log_e 4)^3}{\frac{1}{4} \times \frac{1}{3}} = 12 (\log_e 4)^3.$$

EXAMPLE 20 *If* $f(x) = \frac{\sqrt{2} \cos x - 1}{\cot x - 1}$, $x \neq \frac{\pi}{4}$. *Find the value of* $f\left(\frac{\pi}{4}\right)$ *so that* $f(x)$ *becomes continuous at* $x = \pi/4$. [NCERT EXEMPLAR]

SOLUTION For $f(x)$ to be continuous at $x = \frac{\pi}{4}$, we must have

$$\lim_{x \to \pi/4} f(x) = f\left(\frac{\pi}{4}\right)$$

$$\Rightarrow \quad f\left(\frac{\pi}{4}\right) = \lim_{x \to \pi/4} \frac{\sqrt{2} \cos x - 1}{\cot x - 1}$$

$$\Rightarrow \quad f\left(\frac{\pi}{4}\right) = \lim_{x \to \pi/4} \frac{\sqrt{2}\left(\cos x - \cos \frac{\pi}{4}\right)}{\cot x - \cot \frac{\pi}{4}} = -\sqrt{2} \lim_{x \to \pi/4} \frac{2 \sin\left(\frac{x}{2} - \frac{\pi}{8}\right) \sin\left(\frac{x}{2} + \frac{\pi}{8}\right)}{\left(\cos x \sin \frac{\pi}{4} - \sin x \cos \frac{\pi}{4}\right)} \times \sin x \sin \frac{\pi}{4}$$

$$\Rightarrow \quad f\left(\frac{\pi}{4}\right) = -2\sqrt{2} \lim_{x \to \pi/4} \frac{\sin\left(\frac{x}{2} - \frac{\pi}{8}\right) \sin\left(\frac{x}{2} + \frac{\pi}{8}\right)}{-\sin\left(x - \frac{\pi}{4}\right)} \times \sin x \sin \frac{\pi}{4}$$

$$\Rightarrow \quad f\left(\frac{\pi}{4}\right) = -2\sqrt{2} \lim_{x \to \pi/4} \frac{\sin\left(\frac{x}{2} - \frac{\pi}{8}\right) \sin\left(\frac{x}{2} + \frac{\pi}{8}\right)}{-2 \sin\left(\frac{x}{2} - \frac{\pi}{8}\right) \cos\left(\frac{x}{2} - \frac{\pi}{8}\right)} \times \sin x \sin \frac{\pi}{4}$$

$$\Rightarrow \quad f\left(\frac{\pi}{4}\right) = \sqrt{2} \lim_{x \to \pi/4} \frac{\sin\left(\frac{x}{2} + \frac{\pi}{8}\right)}{\cos\left(\frac{x}{2} - \frac{\pi}{8}\right)} \times \sin x \sin \frac{\pi}{4} = \sqrt{2} \frac{\sin\left(\frac{\pi}{8} + \frac{\pi}{8}\right)}{\cos\left(\frac{\pi}{8} - \frac{\pi}{8}\right)} \times \sin \frac{\pi}{4} \sin \frac{\pi}{4} = \left(\sin \frac{\pi}{4}\right)^2 = \frac{1}{2}$$

EXAMPLE 21 *Prove that the greatest integer function* $[x]$ *is continuous at all points except at integer points.* [NCERT]

SOLUTION Let $f(x) = [x]$ be the greatest integer function and let k be any integer. Then,

$$f(x) = [x] = \begin{cases} k - 1, & \text{if } k - 1 \leq x < k \\ k, & \text{if } k \leq x < k + 1 \end{cases} \qquad \text{[By definition of } [x]]$$

Now,

$$(\text{LHL at } x = k) = \lim_{x \to k^-} f(x) = \lim_{h \to 0} f(k-h) = \lim_{h \to 0} [k-h]$$

$$= \lim_{h \to 0} (k-1) = k-1 \qquad [\because k-1 \le k-h < k \;\therefore [k-h] = k-1]$$

and,

$$(\text{RHL at } x = k) = \lim_{x \to k^+} f(x) = \lim_{h \to 0} f(k+h) = \lim_{h \to 0} [k+h]$$

$$= \lim_{h \to 0} k = k \qquad [\because k \le k+h < k+1 \;\therefore [k+h] = k]$$

$$\therefore \quad \lim_{x \to k^-} f(x) \ne \lim_{x \to k^+} f(x).$$

So, $f(x)$ is not continuous at $x = k$.

Since k is an arbitrary integer. Therefore, $f(x)$ is not continuous at integer points.

Let a be any real number other than an integer. Then, there exists an integer k such that $k-1 < a < k$.

Now,

$$(\text{LHL at } x = a) = \lim_{x \to a^-} f(x) = \lim_{h \to 0} f(a-h) = \lim_{h \to 0} [a-h]$$

$$= \lim_{h \to 0} k-1 = k-1 \qquad [\because k-1 < a-h < k \;\therefore [a-h] = k-1]$$

$$(\text{RHL at } x = a) = \lim_{x \to a^+} f(x) = \lim_{h \to 0} f(a+h)$$

$$= \lim_{h \to 0} [a+h] = \lim_{h \to 0} (k-1) = k-1 \qquad \left[\begin{array}{l}\because k-1 < a+h < k \\ \therefore [a+h] = k-1\end{array}\right]$$

and, $\quad f(a) = [a] = k-1 \qquad [\because k-1 < a < k \;\therefore [a] = k-1]$

Thus, $\displaystyle \lim_{x - a^-} f(x) = \lim_{x \to a^+} f(x) = f(a)$

So, $f(x)$ is continuous at $x = a$. Since a is an arbitrary real number, other than an integer. Therefore, $f(x)$ is continuous at all real points except integer points.

EXAMPLE 22 *Let $f(x+y) = f(x) + f(y)$ for all $x, y \in R$. If $f(x)$ is continuous at $x = 0$, show that $f(x)$ is continuous at all x.*

SOLUTION Since $f(x)$ is continuous at $x = 0$. Therefore,

$$\lim_{x \to 0^-} f(x) = \lim_{x \to 0^+} f(x) = f(0)$$

$$\Rightarrow \quad \lim_{h \to 0} f(0-h) = \lim_{h \to 0} f(0+h) = f(0)$$

$$\Rightarrow \quad \lim_{h \to 0} f(0+(-h)) = \lim_{h \to 0} f(0+h) = f(0)$$

$$\Rightarrow \quad \lim_{h \to 0} [f(0) + f(-h)] = \lim_{h \to 0} [f(0) + f(h)] = f(0) \qquad [\text{Using}: f(x+y) = f(x) + f(y)]$$

$$\Rightarrow \quad f(0) + \lim_{h \to 0} f(-h) = f(0) + \lim_{h \to 0} f(h) = f(0)$$

$$\Rightarrow \quad \lim_{h \to 0} f(-h) = \lim_{h \to 0} f(h) = 0 \qquad \text{...(i)}$$

Let a be any real number. Then,

$$\lim_{x \to a^-} f(x) = \lim_{h \to 0} f(a-h) = \lim_{h \to 0} f(a+(-h))$$

$\Rightarrow \quad \lim_{x \to a^-} f(x) = \lim_{h \to 0} [f(a) + f(-h)]$ $\quad [\because f(x+y) = f(x) + f(y)]$

$\Rightarrow \quad \lim_{x \to a^-} f(x) = f(a) + \lim_{h \to 0} f(-h)$

$\Rightarrow \quad \lim_{x \to a^-} f(x) = f(a) + 0$ $\quad$ [Using (i)]

$\Rightarrow \quad \lim_{x \to a^-} f(x) = f(a).$

and, $\quad \lim_{x \to a^+} f(x) = \lim_{h \to 0} f(a+h)$

$\Rightarrow \quad \lim_{x \to a^+} f(x) = \lim_{h \to 0} [f(a) + f(h)]$ $\quad [\because f(x+y) = f(x) + f(y)]$

$\Rightarrow \quad \lim_{x \to a^+} f(x) = f(a) + \lim_{h \to 0} f(h)$

$\Rightarrow \quad \lim_{x \to a^+} f(x) = f(a) + 0 = f(a)$ $\quad$ [Using (i)]

Thus, we have

$$\lim_{x \to a^-} f(x) = \lim_{x \to a^+} f(x) = f(a)$$

$\therefore \quad f(x)$ is continuous at $x = a$.

Since a is an arbitrary real number. So, $f(x)$ is continuous at all $x \in R$.

Type IV ON CONTINUITY OF COMPOSITE FUNCTION

EXAMPLE 23 *Show that the function* $f(x) = |\sin x + \cos x|$ *is continuous at* $x = \pi$.

SOLUTION Let $g(x) = \sin x + \cos x$ and $h(x) = |x|$. Then,

$$(hog)(x) = h(g(x)) = h(\sin x + \cos x) = |\sin x + \cos x| = f(x)$$

In order to prove that $f(x)$ is continuous at $x = \pi$. It is sufficient to prove that $g(x)$ is continuous at $x = \pi$ and $h(x)$ is continuous at $g(\pi) = \sin \pi + \cos \pi = -1$.

Now, $\quad \lim_{x \to \pi} g(x) = \lim_{x \to \pi} (\sin x + \cos x) = \sin \pi + \cos \pi = -1$ and, $g(\pi) = -1$

$\therefore \quad \lim_{x \to \pi} g(x) = g(\pi)$. So, $g(x)$ is continuous at $x = \pi$.

Let $y = g(\pi) = -1$. Then,

$$\lim_{y \to -1} h(y) = \lim_{y \to -1} |y| = \lim_{y \to -1} -y = -(-1) = 1 \text{ and, } h(g(\pi)) = h(-1) = |-1| = 1.$$

$\therefore \quad \lim_{y \to -1} h(y) = h(g(\pi))$

$\Rightarrow \quad \lim_{g(x) \to -1} h(g(x)) = h(g(\pi)) \Rightarrow \lim_{g(x) \to g(\pi)} h(g(x)) = h(g(\pi)) \Rightarrow h(x)$ is continuous at $g(\pi)$

Hence, $f(x) = hog(x)$ is continuous at $x = \pi$.

EXERCISE 8.1

BASIC

1. A function $f(x)$ is defined as $f(x) = \begin{cases} \dfrac{x^2 - x - 6}{x - 3} & ; \text{ if } x \neq 3 \\ 5 & ; \text{ if } x = 3 \end{cases}$. Show that $f(x)$ is continuous at $x = 3$.

2. A function $f(x)$ is defined as $f(x) = \begin{cases} \dfrac{x^2 - 9}{x - 3} & ; \text{ if } x \neq 3 \\ 6 & ; \text{ if } x = 3 \end{cases}$. Show that $f(x)$ is continuous at $x = 3$.

3. If $f(x) = \begin{cases} \dfrac{x^2 - 1}{x - 1} & ; \text{ for } x \neq 1 \\ 2 & ; \text{ for } x = 1 \end{cases}$. Find whether $f(x)$ is continuous at $x = 1$.

4. If $f(x) = \begin{cases} \dfrac{\sin 3x}{x} & , \text{ when } x \neq 0 \\ 1 & , \text{ when } x = 0 \end{cases}$. Find whether $f(x)$ is continuous at $x = 0$.

5. If $f(x) = \begin{cases} e^{1/x} & , \text{ if } x \neq 0 \\ 1 & , \text{ if } x = 0 \end{cases}$. Find whether f is continuous at $x = 0$.

6. Let $f(x) = \begin{cases} \dfrac{1 - \cos x}{x^2} & , \text{ when } x \neq 0 \\ 1 & , \text{ when } x = 0 \end{cases}$. Show that $f(x)$ is discontinuous at $x = 0$.

7. Show that $f(x) = \begin{cases} \dfrac{x - |x|}{2} & , \text{ when } x \neq 0 \\ 2 & , \text{ when } x = 0 \end{cases}$ is discontinuous at $x = 0$.

8. Show that $f(x) = \begin{cases} \dfrac{|x - a|}{x - a} & , \text{ when } x \neq a \\ 1 & , \text{ when } x = a \end{cases}$ is discontinuous at $x = a$.

9. Show that $f(x) = \begin{cases} 1 + x^2 & , \text{ if } 0 \leq x \leq 1 \\ 2 - x & , \text{ if } x > 1 \end{cases}$ is discontinuous at $x = 1$.

10. Examine the continuity of the function $f(x) = \begin{cases} 3x - 2 & , x \leq 0 \\ x + 1 & , x > 0 \end{cases}$ at $x = 0$.

    Also sketch the graph of this function.

11. Discuss the continuity of the function $f(x) = \begin{cases} x & , x > 0 \\ 1 & , x = 0 \\ -x & , x < 0 \end{cases}$ at the point $x = 0$.

12. Discuss the continuity of the function $f(x) = \begin{cases} x & , 0 \leq x < 1/2 \\ 1/2 & , x = 1/2 \\ 1 - x & , 1/2 < x \leq 1 \end{cases}$ at the point $x = 1/2$.

13. Discuss the continuity of $f(x) = \begin{cases} 2x - 1 , & x < 0 \\ 2x + 1 , & x \geq 0 \end{cases}$ at $x = 0$. [CBSE 2002]

14. For what value of k is the function $f(x) = \begin{cases} \dfrac{x^2-1}{x-1}, & x \neq 1 \\ k, & x = 1 \end{cases}$ continuous at $x = 1$?

15. Determine the value of the constant k so that the function $f(x) = \begin{cases} \dfrac{x^2-3x+2}{x-1}, & \text{if } x \neq 1 \\ k, & \text{if } x = 1 \end{cases}$ is continuous at $x = 1$

16. If $f(x) = \begin{cases} \dfrac{x^2}{2}, & \text{if } 0 \leq x \leq 1 \\ 2x^2 - 3x + \dfrac{3}{2}, & \text{if } 1 < x \leq 2 \end{cases}$. Show that f is continuous at $x = 1$.

17. Prove that $f(x) = \begin{cases} \dfrac{x - |x|}{x}, & x \neq 0 \\ 2, & x = 0 \end{cases}$ is discontinuous at $x = 0$.

18. If $f(x) = \begin{cases} 2x^2 + k, & \text{if } x \geq 0 \\ -2x^2 + k, & \text{if } x < 0 \end{cases}$, then what should be the value of k so that $f(x)$ is continuous at $x = 0$.

19. For what value of λ is the function $f(x) = \begin{cases} \lambda(x^2 - 2x), & \text{if } x \leq 0 \\ 4x + 1, & \text{if } x > 0 \end{cases}$ continuous at $x = 0$? What about continuity at $x = \pm 1$? **[NCERT]**

20. For what value of k is the function $f(x) = \begin{cases} 2x + 1; & \text{if } x < 2 \\ k; & x = 2 \\ 3x - 1; & x > 2 \end{cases}$ continuous at $x = 2$? **[CBSE 2008]**

21. For what value of k is the function $f(x) = \begin{cases} \dfrac{\sin 5x}{3x}, & \text{if } x \neq 0 \\ k, & \text{if } x = 0 \end{cases}$ continuous at $x = 0$?

22. Determine the value of the constant k so that the function $f(x) = \begin{cases} kx^2, & \text{if } x \leq 2 \\ 3, & \text{if } x > 2 \end{cases}$ is continuous at $x = 2$. **[NCERT]**

23. Determine the value of the constant k so that the function $f(x) = \begin{cases} \dfrac{\sin 2x}{5x}, & \text{if } x \neq 0 \\ k, & \text{if } x = 0 \end{cases}$ is continuous at $x = 0$. **[CBSE 2007]**

24. Find the values of a so that the function $f(x) = \begin{cases} ax + 5, & \text{if } x \leq 2 \\ x - 1, & \text{if } x > 2 \end{cases}$ is continuous at $x = 2$. **[CBSE 2002]**

BASED ON LOTS

25. Discuss the continuity of the following functions at the indicated point(s):

(i) $f(x) = \begin{cases} |x| \cos\left(\dfrac{1}{x}\right), & x \neq 0 \\ 0, & x = 0 \end{cases}$ at $x = 0$ **[NCERT EXEMPLAR]**

(ii) $f(x) = \begin{cases} x^2 \sin\left(\dfrac{1}{x}\right), & x \neq 0 \\ 0, & x = 0 \end{cases}$ at $x = 0$

(iii) $f(x) = \begin{cases} (x-a) \sin\left(\dfrac{1}{x-a}\right), & x \neq a \\ 0, & x = a \end{cases}$ at $x = a$

(iv) $f(x) = \begin{cases} \dfrac{e^x - 1}{\log(1+2x)}, & \text{if } x \neq 0 \\ 7, & \text{if } x = 0 \end{cases}$ at $x = 0$

(v) $f(x) = \begin{cases} \dfrac{1-x^n}{1-x}, & x \neq 1 \\ n-1, & x = 1 \end{cases}$ $n \in N$ at $x = 1$

(vi) $f(x) = \begin{cases} \dfrac{|x^2-1|}{x-1}, & \text{for } x \neq 1 \\ 2, & \text{for } x = 1 \end{cases}$ at $x = 1$

(vii) $f(x) = \begin{cases} \dfrac{2|x| + x^2}{x}, & x \neq 0 \\ 0, & x = 0 \end{cases}$ at $x = 0$

(viii) $f(x) = \begin{cases} |x-a| \sin\left(\dfrac{1}{x-a}\right), & \text{for } x \neq a \\ 0, & \text{for } x = a \end{cases}$ at $x = a$ **[NCERT EXEMPLAR]**

26. Prove that the function $f(x) = \begin{cases} \dfrac{x}{|x| + 2x^2}, & x \neq 0 \\ k, & x = 0 \end{cases}$ remains discontinuous at $x = 0$, regardless the choice of k. **[NCERT EXEMPLAR]**

27. Find the value of k if $f(x)$ is continuous at $x = \pi/2$, where $f(x) = \begin{cases} \dfrac{k \cos x}{\pi - 2x}, & x \neq \pi/2 \\ 3, & x = \pi/2 \end{cases}$ **[NCERT]**

28. For what value of k is the function $f(x) = \begin{cases} \dfrac{\sin 2x}{x}, & x \neq 0 \\ k, & x = 0 \end{cases}$ continuous at $x = 0$?

29. If $f(x) = \dfrac{2x + 3 \sin x}{3x + 2 \sin x}$, $x \neq 0$ is continuous at $x = 0$, then find $f(0)$.

30. Find the value of k for which $f(x) = \begin{cases} \dfrac{1 - \cos 4x}{8x^2}, & \text{when } x \neq 0 \\ k, & \text{when } x = 0 \end{cases}$ is continuous at $x = 0$. **[CBSE 2000 C, 2017, NCERT EXEMPLAR]**

31. In each of the following, find the value of the constant k so that the given function is continuous at the indicated point:

(i) $f(x) = \begin{cases} \dfrac{1 - \cos 2kx}{x^2}, & \text{if } x \neq 0 \\ 8, & \text{if } x = 0 \end{cases}$ at $x = 0$

(ii) $f(x) = \begin{cases} (x-1) \tan \dfrac{\pi x}{2}, & \text{if } x \neq 1 \\ k, & \text{if } x = 1 \end{cases}$ at $x = 1$

(iii) $f(x) = \begin{cases} k(x^2 - 2x), & \text{if } x < 0 \\ \cos x, & \text{if } x \geq 0 \end{cases}$ at $x = 0$ **[NCERT]**

(iv) $f(x) = \begin{cases} kx + 1, & \text{if } x \leq \pi \\ \cos x, & \text{if } x > \pi \end{cases}$ at $x = \pi$ **[NCERT]**

(v) $f(x) = \begin{cases} kx+1, & \text{if } x \le 5 \\ 3x-5, & \text{if } x > 5 \end{cases}$ at $x = 5$

(vi) $f(x) = \begin{cases} \dfrac{x^2-25}{x-5}, & x \ne 5 \\ k, & x = 5 \end{cases}$ at $x = 5$ [CBSE 2007]

(vii) $f(x) = \begin{cases} kx^2, & x \ge 1 \\ 4, & x < 1 \end{cases}$ at $x = 1$ [CBSE 2007]

(viii) $f(x) = \begin{cases} k(x^2+2), & \text{if } x \le 0 \\ 3x+1, & \text{if } x > 0 \end{cases}$ at $x = 0$. [CBSE 2010]

(ix) $f(x) = \begin{cases} \dfrac{x^3+x^2-16x+20}{(x-2)^2}, & x \ne 2 \\ k, & x = 2 \end{cases}$ at $x = 2$. [NCERT EXEMP

32. Find the values of a and b so that the function f given by

$f(x) = \begin{cases} 1, & \text{if } x \le 3 \\ ax+b, & \text{if } 3 < x < 5 \\ 7, & \text{if } x \ge 5 \end{cases}$ is continuous at $x = 3$ and $x = 5$. [CBSE 2013]

33. Find the relationship between 'a' and 'b' so that the function 'f' defined by

$f(x) = \begin{cases} ax+1, & \text{if } x \le 3 \\ bx+3, & \text{if } x > 3 \end{cases}$ is continuous at $x = 3$. [CBSE 2011]

34. If the functions $f(x)$, defined below is continuous at $x = 0$, find the value of k:

$$f(x) = \begin{cases} \dfrac{1-\cos 2x}{2x^2}, & x < 0 \\ k, & x = 0 \\ \dfrac{x}{|x|}, & x > 0 \end{cases}$$ [CBSE 2010]

BASED ON HOTS

35. Show that $f(x) = \begin{cases} \dfrac{\sin 3x}{\tan 2x}, & \text{if } x < 0 \\ \dfrac{3}{2}, & \text{if } x = 0 \\ \dfrac{\log(1+3x)}{e^{2x}-1}, & \text{if } x > 0 \end{cases}$ is continuous at $x = 0$

36. Find the value of 'a' for which the function f defined by

$f(x) = \begin{cases} a \sin \dfrac{\pi}{2}(x+1), & x \le 0 \\ \dfrac{\tan x - \sin x}{x^3}, & x > 0 \end{cases}$ is continuous at $x = 0$. [CBSE 2011]

37. Determine the values of a, b, c for which the function

$f(x) = \begin{cases} \dfrac{\sin(a+1)x + \sin x}{x}, & \text{for } x < 0 \\ c, & \text{for } x = 0 \\ \dfrac{\sqrt{x+bx^2} - \sqrt{x}}{bx^{3/2}}, & \text{for } x > 0 \end{cases}$ is continuous at $x = 0$.

38. If $f(x) = \begin{cases} \dfrac{1-\cos kx}{x\sin x}, & x \neq 0 \\ \dfrac{1}{2}, & x = 0 \end{cases}$ is continuous at $x = 0$, find k. [NCERT EXEMPLAR]

39. If $f(x) = \begin{cases} \dfrac{x-4}{|x-4|} + a, & \text{if } x < 4 \\ a+b, & \text{if } x = 4 \\ \dfrac{x-4}{|x-4|} + b, & \text{if } x > 4 \end{cases}$ is continuous at $x = 4$, find a, b.

[NCERT EXEMPLAR, CBSE 2024]

40. Let $f(x) = \dfrac{\log\left(1+\dfrac{x}{a}\right) - \log\left(1-\dfrac{x}{b}\right)}{x}$, $x \neq 0$. Find the value of f at $x = 0$ so that f becomes continuous at $x = 0$.

41. If $f(x) = \begin{cases} \dfrac{2^{x+2}-16}{4^x-16}, & \text{if } x \neq 2 \\ k, & \text{if } x = 2 \end{cases}$ is continuous at $x = 2$, find k. [NCERT EXEMPLAR]

42. If $f(x) = \begin{cases} \dfrac{\cos^2 x - \sin^2 x - 1}{\sqrt{x^2+1}-1}, & x \neq 0 \\ k, & x = 0 \end{cases}$ is continuous at $x = 0$, find k.

43. Extend the definition of the following by continuity $f(x) = \dfrac{1-\cos 7(x-\pi)}{5(x-\pi)^2}$ at the point $x = \pi$.

44. Discuss the continuity of the $f(x)$ at the indicated points:

(i) $f(x) = |x| + |x-1|$ at $x = 0, 1$.

(ii) $f(x) = |x-1| + |x+1|$ at $x = -1, 1$. [NCERT EXEMPLAR]

45. Let $f(x) = \begin{cases} \dfrac{1-\sin^3 x}{3\cos^2 x}, & \text{if } x < \dfrac{\pi}{2} \\ a, & \text{if } x = \dfrac{\pi}{2} \\ \dfrac{b(1-\sin x)}{(\pi-2x)^2}, & \text{if } x > \dfrac{\pi}{2} \end{cases}$. If $f(x)$ is continuous at $x = \dfrac{\pi}{2}$, find a and b.

[CBSE 2008, 2016]

ANSWERS

3. Continuous 4. Discontinuous 5. Discontinuous 10. Discontinuous
11. Discontinuous 12. Continuous 13. Discontinuous 14. 2
15. -1 18. k is any real number.
19. There is no value of λ for which it is continuous at $x = 0$. At $x = \pm 1$, $f(x)$ is continuous
20. $k = 5$ 21. 5/3 22. 3/4 23. 2/5
24. -2 25. (i) Continuous (ii) Continuous (iii) Continuous
(iv) Discontinuous (v) Discontinuous (vi) Discontinuous (vii) Discontinuous
(viii) Continuous 27. 6 28. 2 29. 1 30. 1

31. (i) $k = \pm 2$ (ii) $k = \frac{-2}{\pi}$ (iii) No value of k (iv) $k = \frac{-2}{\pi}$

(v) $k = \frac{9}{5}$ (vi) $k = 10$ (vii) $k = 4$ (viii) $k = 1/2$ (ix) $k = 7$

32. $a = 3, b = -8$ 33. $3a - 3b = 2$ 34. $k = 1$ 36. $a = \frac{1}{2}$

37. $a = -\frac{3}{2}, b \in R - \{0\}, c = \frac{1}{2}$ 38. ± 1 39. $a = 1, b = -1$

40. $\frac{a+b}{ab}$ 41. $1/2$ 42. -4 43. $49/10$

44. (i) Continuous, (ii) Continuous 45. $a = \frac{1}{2}, b = 4$

HINTS TO SELECTED PROBLEMS

22. If $f(x) = \begin{cases} kx^2 & , x \leq 2 \\ 3 & , x > 2 \end{cases}$ is continuous at $x = 2$, then

$$\lim_{x \to 2^-} f(x) = \lim_{x \to 2^+} f(x) = f(2) \Rightarrow \lim_{x \to 2^-} kx^2 = \lim_{x \to 2^+} 3 = k(2)^2 \Rightarrow 4k = 3 \Rightarrow k = \frac{3}{4}$$

27. It is given that $f(x) = \begin{cases} \frac{k \cos x}{\pi - 2x} & , x \neq \frac{\pi}{2} \\ 3 & , x = \frac{\pi}{2} \end{cases}$ is continuous at $x = \frac{\pi}{2}$.

$$\therefore \quad \lim_{x \to \pi/2} f(x) = f\left(\frac{\pi}{2}\right)$$

$$\Rightarrow \quad \lim_{x \to \pi/2} \frac{k \cos x}{\pi - 2x} = 3 \Rightarrow k \lim_{x \to \pi 2} \frac{\sin(\pi/2 - x)}{2(\pi/2 - x)} = 3 \Rightarrow \frac{k}{2} \times 1 = 3 \Rightarrow k = 6$$

31. (iii) It is given that $f(x) = \begin{cases} k(x^2 - 2x), & x < 0 \\ \cos x & , x \geq 0 \end{cases}$

$$\therefore \quad \lim_{x \to 0^-} f(x) = \lim_{x \to 0^-} k(x^2 - 2x) = 0 \text{ for all } k$$

$$\lim_{x \to 0^+} f(x) = \lim_{x \to 0^+} \cos x = 1 \text{ and, } f(0) = \cos 0 = 1$$

Clearly, there is no value of k for which $\lim_{x \to 0^-} f(x) = \lim_{x \to 0^+} f(x) = f(0)$ may hold good.

Hence, there is no value of k for which $f(x)$ is continuous at $x = 0$.

(iv) It is given that $f(x) = \begin{cases} kx + 1 & , x \leq \pi \\ \cos x & , x > \pi \end{cases}$ is continuous at $x = \pi$.

$$\therefore \quad \lim_{x \to \pi^-} f(x) = \lim_{x \to \pi^+} f(x) = f(\pi)$$

$$\Rightarrow \quad \lim_{x \to \pi^-} kx + 1 = \lim_{x \to \pi^+} \cos x = k\pi + 1 \Rightarrow k\pi + 1 = \cos \pi \Rightarrow k\pi + 1 = -1 \Rightarrow k = -\frac{2}{\pi}$$

8.4 CONTINUITY ON AN INTERVAL

CONTINUITY ON AN OPEN INTERVAL *A function $f(x)$ is said to be continuous on an open interval (a, b) iff it is continuous at every point on the interval (a, b).*

CONTINUITY ON A CLOSED INTERVAL *A function $f(x)$ is said to be continuous on a closed interval $[a, b]$ iff*

(i) f is continuous on the open interval (a, b) (ii) $\lim_{x \to a^+} f(x) = f(a)$ *and, (iii)* $\lim_{x \to b^-} f(x) = f(b)$.

In other words, f(x) is continuous on [a, b] iff it is continuous on (a, b) and it is continuous at a from the right and at b from the left.

CONTINUOUS FUNCTION *A function f(x) is said to be continuous, if it is continuous at each point of its domain.*

EVERYWHERE CONTINUOUS FUNCTION *A function f(x) is said to be everywhere continuous if it is continuous on the entire real line* $(-\infty, \infty)$.

8.5 PROPERTIES OF CONTINUOUS FUNCTIONS

In this section, we shall learn some properties of continuous functions and prove the continuity of some standard real functions in their domains.

THEOREM 1 *If f and g are two continuous functions on their common domain D, then*

(i) $f + g$ *is continuous on D* (ii) $f - g$ *is continuous on D*

(iii) fg *is continuous on D* (iv) αf *is continuous on D, where* α *is any real number.*

(v) $\frac{f}{g}$ *is continuous on* $D - \{x : g(x) \neq 0\}$ (vi) $\frac{1}{f}$ *is continuous on* $D - \{x : f(x) \neq 0\}$

PROOF Let a be an arbitrary point in common domain D. Since f and g are continuous on D. So, they are also continuous at 'a'.

$$\therefore \quad \lim_{x \to a} f(x) = f(a) \text{ and } \lim_{x \to a} g(x) = g(a) \qquad \text{...(i)}$$

(i) We find that

$$\lim_{x \to a} (f + g)(x) = \lim_{x \to a} (f(x) + g(x)) = \lim_{x \to a} f(x) + \lim_{x \to a} g(x)$$

$$= f(a) + g(a) = (f + g)(a) \qquad \text{[Using (i)]}$$

$\therefore$ $f + g$ is continuous at $x = a$.

Since a is an arbitrary point in D. Hence, $f + g$ is continuous on D.

(ii) We find that

$$\lim_{x \to a} (f - g)(x) = \lim_{x \to a} (f(x) - g(x)) = \lim_{x \to a} f(x) - \lim_{x \to a} g(x)$$

$$= f(a) - g(a) = (f - g)(a) \qquad \text{[Using (i)]}$$

$\therefore$ $f - g$ is continuous at $x = a$.

Since a is an arbitrary point in D. Hence, $f - g$ is continuous in D.

(iii) We find that

$$\lim_{x \to a} (fg)(x) = \lim_{x \to a} (f(x)\ g(x)) = \lim_{x \to a} f(x) \times \lim_{x \to a} g(x)$$

$$= f(a)\, g(a) = (fg)(a) \qquad \text{[Using (i)]}$$

$\therefore$ fg is continuous at $x = a$.

Since a is an arbitrary point in D. Hence, fg is continuous in D.

(iv) We find that

$$\lim_{x \to a} (\alpha f)(x) = \lim_{x \to a} (\alpha f(x)) = \alpha \lim_{x \to a} f(x) = \alpha f(a) = (\alpha f)(a) \qquad \text{[Using (i)]}$$

$\therefore$ αf is continuous at $x = a$.

Since a is an arbitrary point in D. Hence, αf is continuous in D.

(v) Let $a \in D$ such that $g(a) \neq 0$. Then,

$$\lim_{x \to a} \left(\frac{f}{g}\right)(x) = \lim_{x \to a} \frac{f(x)}{g(x)} = \frac{\lim_{x \to a} f(x)}{\lim_{x \to a} g(x)} = \frac{f(a)}{g(a)} = \left(\frac{f}{g}\right)(a)$$

$\therefore$ $\frac{f}{g}$ is continuous at $x = a$.

Since a is an arbitrary point in D such that $g(a) \neq 0$. Hence, $\frac{f}{g}$ is continuous on $D - \{x : g(x) \neq 0\}$.

(vi) Let $a \in D$ such that $f(a) \neq 0$. Then,

$$\lim_{x \to a} \left(\frac{1}{f}\right)(x) = \lim_{x \to a} \frac{1}{f(x)} = \frac{1}{\lim_{x \to a} f(x)} = \frac{1}{f(a)} = \left(\frac{1}{f}\right)(a) \qquad \text{[Using (i)]}$$

$\therefore$ $\frac{1}{f}$ is continuous at $x = a$.

Since a is arbitrary point in D such that $f(a) \neq 0$. Hence, $1/f$ is continuous on $D - \{x : f(x) \neq 0\}$.

Q.E.D.

THEOREM 2 *The composition of two continuous functions is a continuous function.*

PROOF Let f and g be two real functions such that gof exists. Then, Range $(f) \subseteq$ Domain (g).
Let a be an arbitrary point in the domain of f. Then,

$a \in$ Domain $(f) \Rightarrow f(a) \in$ Range $(f) \Rightarrow f(a) \in$ Domain(g) [$\because$ Range $(f) \subseteq$ Domain (g)]

Since f and g are continuous on their domains. Therefore,

$a \in$ Domain (f) and $f(a) \in$ Domain (g)

$\Rightarrow$ f is continuous at $x = a$ and g is continuous at $f(a)$

$$\Rightarrow \lim_{x \to a} f(x) = f(a) \text{ and } \lim_{y \to f(a)} g(y) = g(f(a))$$

$$\Rightarrow \lim_{x \to a} f(x) = f(a) \text{ and } \lim_{f(x) \to f(a)} g(f(x)) = g(f(a)), \text{ where } y = f(x)$$

$$\Rightarrow \lim_{x \to a} g(f(x)) = g(f(a)) \qquad [\because x \to a \Rightarrow f(x) \to f(a)]$$

$$\Rightarrow \lim_{x \to a} gof(x) = gof(a) \Rightarrow gof \text{ is continuous at } x = a.$$

Since a is an arbitrary point in its domain. Hence, gof is continuous. Q.E.D.

THEOREM 3 *If f is continuous on its domain D, then $|f|$ is also continuous on D.*

PROOF Recall that $|f|$ (known as absolute function) is defined as $|f|(x) = |f(x)|$.
Let a be an arbitrary real number in D. Then, f is continuous at a.

$\therefore$ $\lim_{x \to a} f(x) = f(a)$

Now,

$$\lim_{x \to a} |f|(x) = \lim_{x \to a} |f(x)| \qquad \text{[By definition of } |f|\text{]}$$

$$\Rightarrow \lim_{x \to a} |f|(x) = \left|\lim_{x \to a} f(x)\right| = |f(a)| = |f|(a)$$

$\therefore$ $|f|$ is continuous at $x = a$.

Since a is an arbitrary point in D. Therefore, $|f|$ is continuous in D. Q.E.D.

REMARK *The converse of the above theorem may not be true. For example, consider the function*

$$f(x) = \begin{cases} 1, & \text{if } x \in Z \\ -1, & \text{if } x \in R - Z \end{cases}$$

Let a be an arbitrary integer. Then,

$$\lim_{x \to a^-} f(x) = \lim_{h \to 0} f(a-h) = \lim_{h \to 0} -1 = -1 \qquad [\because h > 0, a - h \notin Z \text{ as } h \text{ is very small}]$$

$$\lim_{x \to a^+} f(x) = \lim_{h \to 0} f(a+h) = \lim_{h \to 0} -1 = -1 \text{ and, } f(a) = 1.$$

$$\therefore \quad \lim_{x \to a^-} f(x) = \lim_{x \to a^+} f(x) \neq f(a)$$

So, f is discontinuous at $x = a$.

Now, $|f|(x) = |f(x)| = 1$ *for all* $x \in R$. *So,* $|f|$ *is a constant function and hence , it is everywhere continuous.*

THEOREM 4 *A constant function is everywhere continuous.*

PROOF Let $f(x) = c$, where c is a constant. Clearly, the domain of a constant function is R. Let a be any real number. Then,

$$\lim_{x \to a} f(x) = \lim_{x \to a} c = c \text{ and, } f(a) = c.$$

$$\therefore \quad \lim_{x \to a} f(x) = f(a) \Rightarrow f(x) \text{ is continuous at } x = a.$$

But, a is an arbitrary real number. Hence, $f(x)$ is continuous on R. **Q.E.D.**

REMARK 1 *It is evident from the graph of a constant function that is everywhere continuous.*

THEOREM 5 *The identity function is everywhere continuous.*

PROOF Let $f(x) = x$ for all $x \in R$ be the identity function. Let a be any real number. Then,

$$\lim_{x \to a} f(x) = \lim_{x \to a} x = a \text{ and, } f(a) = a.$$

$$\therefore \quad \lim_{x \to a} f(x) = f(a). \text{ So, } f(x) \text{ is continuous at } x = a.$$

Since a is an arbitrary real number. Hence, $f(x)$ is continuous on R i.e. it is everywhere continuous.

REMARK 2 *The above fact can be easily observed from the graph of the identity function.* **Q.E.D.**

THEOREM 6 *A polynomial function is everywhere continuous.*

PROOF Let $f(x) = a_0 + a_1 x + a_2 x^2 + \ldots + a_n x^n, n \in Z, n \geq 0, x \in R$ be a polynomial function.

We shall prove the theorem by induction on n.

Step I *When* $n = 0$, *we have*

$$f(x) = a_0$$

Clearly, $f(x)$ is a constant function which is everywhere continuous

When $n = 1$, we have

$$f(x) = a_0 + a_1 x.$$

Clearly, $f(x)$ is the sum of a constant function and a multiple of the identity function. So, being the sum of two everywhere continuous functions, $f(x)$ is everywhere continuous.

Step II *Let every polynomial function of degree at most n be everywhere continuous.*

Consider a general polynomial function of degree $(n + 1)$.

$$g(x) = a_0 + a_1 x + a_2 x^2 + \ldots + a_n x^n + a_{n+1} x^{n+1}, \text{ where } a_{n+1} \neq 0.$$

$$\Rightarrow \quad g(x) = a_0 + x(a_1 + a_2 x + \ldots + a_n x^{n-1} + a_{n+1} x^n)$$

Clearly, it is the sum of a constant function a_0 (which is everywhere continuous) and the product of the identity function x (which is everywhere continuous) and the polynomial function $a_1 + a_2 x + \ldots + a_{n+1} x^n$ of degree at most n (which is everywhere continuous by induction assumption). Therefore, $g(x)$ is everywhere continuous.

Hence, by the principle of mathematical induction, a polynomial function is everywhere continuous.

A simple consequence of the above theorem is the following: **Q.E.D.**

COROLLARY *Every rational function is continuous at every point in its domain.*

PROOF Let $f(x) = \dfrac{g(x)}{h(x)}$, $h(x) \neq 0$ be a rational function. Then, $g(x)$ and $h(x)$ are polynomial functions.

The domain of $f(x)$ is the set $D = R - \{x : g(x) = 0\}$.

Since polynomial functions are everywhere continuous. Therefore, $g(x)$ and $h(x)$ are continuous on D.

Hence, by theorem 1, $f(x) = \dfrac{g(x)}{h(x)}$ is continuous on D.

THEOREM 7 *The modulus function is everywhere continuous.*

PROOF We know that the identify function is everywhere continuous.

Also, if f is continuous, then $|f|$ is also continuous. Therefore, $|x|$ is everywhere continuous.

Q.E.D.

THEOREM 8 *The exponential function a^x, $a > 0$ is everywhere continuous.*

PROOF *Let* $f(x) = a^x$. Then,

$$\lim_{x \to 0} a^x = \lim_{x \to 0} \left\{\left(\frac{a^x - 1}{x}\right) x + 1\right\} = \lim_{x \to 0} \left(\frac{a^x - 1}{x}\right) \times \lim_{x \to 0} x + \lim_{x \to 0} 1 = (\log_e a \times 0) + 1 = 1.$$

Let c be an arbitrary real number. Then,

$$\lim_{x \to c^-} f(x) = \lim_{h \to 0} f(c - h) = \lim_{h \to 0} a^{c-h} = a^c \lim_{h \to 0} a^{-h} = a^c \lim_{h \to 0} \frac{1}{a^h} = a^c \times \frac{1}{1} = a^c = f(c)$$

and, $$\lim_{x \to c^+} f(x) = \lim_{h \to 0} f(c + h) = \lim_{h \to 0} a^{c+h} = a^c \lim_{h \to 0} a^h = a^c \times 1 = a^c = f(c)$$

$$\therefore \quad \lim_{x \to c^-} f(x) = \lim_{x \to c^+} f(x) = f(c)$$

So, $f(x)$ is continuous at $x = c$.

Since c is an arbitrary real number. Hence, $f(x) = a^x$ is everywhere continuous.

Q.E.D.

COROLLARY *e^x is everywhere continuous.*

THEOREM 9 *The logarithmic function is continuous in its domain.*

PROOF Let $f(x) = \log_c x$, where $c > 0$ be the logarithmic function. Clearly, domain $(f) = (0, \infty)$.

Let a be an arbitrary point in $(0, \infty)$. Then,

$$\lim_{x \to a^+} f(x) = \lim_{h \to 0} f(a + h)$$

$$\Rightarrow \quad \lim_{x \to a^+} f(x) = \lim_{h \to 0} \log_c (a+h)$$

$$\Rightarrow \quad \lim_{x \to a^+} f(x) = \lim_{h \to 0} \log_c a\left(1+\frac{h}{a}\right)$$

$$\Rightarrow \quad \lim_{x \to a^+} f(x) = \lim_{h \to 0} \left\{\log_c a + \log_c\left(1+\frac{h}{a}\right)\right\}$$

$$\Rightarrow \quad \lim_{x \to a^+} f(x) = \log_c a + \lim_{h \to 0} \log_c\left(1+\frac{h}{a}\right)$$

$$\Rightarrow \quad \lim_{x \to a^+} f(x) = \log_c a + \lim_{h \to 0} \left\{\frac{\log_c\left(1+\frac{h}{a}\right)}{\frac{h}{a}}\right\} \times \frac{h}{a}$$

$$\Rightarrow \quad \lim_{x \to a^+} f(x) = \log_c a + \lim_{h \to 0} \frac{\log_c\left(1+\frac{h}{a}\right)}{\frac{h}{a}} \times \lim_{h \to 0} \frac{h}{a}$$

$$\Rightarrow \quad \lim_{x \to a^+} f(x) = \log_c a + \log_e c \times 0 = \log_c a = f(a)$$

Similarly, we obtain : $\lim_{x \to a^-} f(x) = f(a)$

$\therefore \quad \lim_{x \to a^-} f(x) = f(a) = \lim_{h \to a^+} f(x)$. So, $f(x)$ is continuous at $x = a$.

Since a is an arbitrary point in $(0, \infty)$. Hence, $f(x)$ is continuous on $(0, \infty)$. Q.E.D.

THEOREM 10 *The sine function is everywhere continuous.*

PROOF Let $f(x) = \sin x$ and let a be an arbitrary real number. Then,

$$\lim_{x \to a^+} f(x) = \lim_{h \to 0} f(a+h)$$

$$\Rightarrow \quad \lim_{x \to a^+} f(x) = \lim_{h \to 0} \sin(a+h)$$

$$\Rightarrow \quad \lim_{x \to a^+} f(x) = \lim_{h \to 0} \{\sin a \cos h + \cos a \sin h\}$$

$$\Rightarrow \quad \lim_{x \to a^+} f(x) = \sin a\left(\lim_{h \to 0} \cos h\right) + \cos a\left(\lim_{h \to 0} \sin h\right)$$

$$\Rightarrow \quad \lim_{x \to a^+} f(x) = \sin a \times 1 + \cos a \times 0 \qquad \left[\because \lim_{h \to 0} \sin h = 0 \text{ and } \lim_{h \to 0} \cos h = 1\right]$$

$$\Rightarrow \quad \lim_{x \to a^+} f(x) = \sin a = f(a)$$

Similarly, we obtain

$$\lim_{x \to a^-} f(x) = f(a)$$

$\therefore \quad \lim_{x \to a^-} f(x) = f(a) = \lim_{x \to a^+} f(x)$. $\Rightarrow f(x)$ is continuous at $x = a$.

Since a is an arbitrary real number. Hence, $f(x) = \sin x$ is everywhere continuous. **Q.E.D.**

THEOREM 11 *The cosine function is everywhere continuous.*

PROOF Let $f(x) = \cos x$ and let a be any real number. Then,

$$\lim_{x \to a^+} f(x) = \lim_{h \to 0} f(a+h)$$

$$\Rightarrow \lim_{x \to a^+} f(x) = \lim_{h \to 0} \cos(a+h)$$

$$\Rightarrow \lim_{x \to a^+} f(x) = \lim_{h \to 0} \{\cos a \cos h - \sin a \sin h\}$$

$$\Rightarrow \lim_{x \to a^+} f(x) = \cos a \left(\lim_{h \to 0} \cos h\right) - \sin a \left(\lim_{h \to 0} \sin h\right)$$

$$\Rightarrow \lim_{x \to a^+} f(x) = (\cos a) \times 1 - \sin a \times 0 \qquad \left[\because \lim_{h \to 0} \cos h = 1 \text{ and } \lim_{h \to 0} \sin h = 0\right]$$

$$\Rightarrow \lim_{x \to a^+} f(x) = \cos a = f(a)$$

Similarly, we obtain

$$\lim_{x \to a^-} f(x) = f(a)$$

$$\therefore \lim_{x \to a^-} f(x) = \lim_{x \to a^+} f(x) = f(a). \text{ So, } f(x) \text{ is continuous at } x = a$$

Since a is an arbitrary real number. Hence, $f(x)$ is everywhere continuous. **Q.E.D.**

THEOREM 12 *The tangent function is continuous in its domain.*

PROOF Let $f(x) = \tan x$. Clearly, domain $(f) = R - \left\{(2n+1)\frac{\pi}{2} : n \in Z\right\}$

We have, $f(x) = \tan x = \dfrac{\sin x}{\cos x}$. Since $\sin x$ and $\cos x$ are everywhere continuous. Therefore, $f(x) = \tan x$ is continuous for all $x \in R$ except when $\cos x \neq 0$. But, $\cos x = 0$ at $x = (2n+1)\pi/2, n \in Z$.

Hence, $f(x) = \tan x$ is continuous for all $x \in R - \{(2n+1)\pi/2 : n \in Z\}$. **Q.E.D.**

THEOREM 13 (i) *The cosecant function is continuous in its domain.*

(ii) *The secant function is continuous in its domain.*

(iii) *The cotangent function is continuous in its domain.*

PROOF It is the direct consequence of the above Theorems and Theorem 1.

THEOREM 14 $f(x) = \sin^{-1} x$ *is continuous on* $[-1, 1]$.

PROOF Let a be an arbitrary point in $[-1, -1]$. Let $y = \sin^{-1} x$. Then, $x = \sin y$.

$$\therefore \quad x \to a \Rightarrow \sin y \to a \Rightarrow y \to \sin^{-1} a.$$

Thus, $\lim_{x \to a} f(x) = \lim_{x \to a} \sin^{-1} x = \lim_{y \to \sin^{-1} a} y = \sin^{-1} a = f(a)$

So, $f(x)$ is continuous at $x = a$.

Since a is an arbitrary point of $[-1, 1]$. Hence, $f(x) = \sin^{-1} x$ is continuous on $[-1, 1]$.

Q.E.D.

REMARK *Proceeding as above, it can be shown that all inverse trigonometric functions are continuous in their respective domains.*

ILLUSTRATIVE EXAMPLES

BASED ON BASIC CONCEPTS (BASIC)

Type I ON TESTING THE CONTINUITY OF A FUNCTION IN ITS DOMAIN

EXAMPLE 1 *If a function f is defined as* $f(x)=\begin{cases}\dfrac{|x-4|}{x-4}, & x\neq 4\\ 0, & x=4\end{cases}$*. Show that f is everywhere continuous except at* $x=4$.

SOLUTION We have,

$$f(x)=\begin{cases}\dfrac{|x-4|}{x-4}, & x\neq 4\\ 0, & x=4\end{cases}$$

$$\Rightarrow \quad f(x)=\begin{cases}\dfrac{-(x-4)}{x-4}=-1 \; ; & x<4\\ \dfrac{x-4}{x-4}=1 \; ; & x>4\\ 0 \; ; & x=4\end{cases} \qquad \left[\because |x-4|=\begin{cases}-(x-4), & x<4\\ x-4, & x\geq 4\end{cases}\right]$$

When $x<4$, we have $f(x)=-1$, which, being a constant function, is continuous at each point $x<4$.

Also, when $x>4$, we have $f(x)=1$, which, being a constant function, is continuous at each point $x>4$.

Let us consider the point $x=4$. We find that

$$\lim_{x\to 4^-} f(x)=\lim_{x\to 4} -1=-1, \quad \lim_{x\to 4^+} f(x)=\lim_{x\to 4} 1=1 \text{ and, } f(4)=0.$$

$\therefore \quad \lim_{x\to 4^-} f(x)\neq \lim_{x\to 4^+} f(x)$. So, $f(x)$ is not continuous at $x=4$.

Hence, $f(x)$ is everywhere continuous, except at $x=4$.

EXAMPLE 2 *Discuss the continuity of the function* $f(x)=\begin{cases}\dfrac{\sin 2x}{x}, & \text{if } x<0\\ x+2, & \text{if } x\geq 0\end{cases}$.

SOLUTION When $x<0$, we have $f(x)=\dfrac{\sin 2x}{x}$. We know that $\sin 2x$ as well as the identity function x both are everywhere continuous. So, the quotient function $\dfrac{\sin 2x}{x}=f(x)$ is continuous at each $x<0$.

When, $x>0$, we have $f(x)=x+2$, which being a polynomial function, is continuous at each $x>0$. Let us now consider the point $x=0$. We find that

$$\lim_{x\to 0^-} f(x)=\lim_{x\to 0}\frac{\sin 2x}{x}=2\lim_{x\to 0}\frac{\sin 2x}{2x}=2(1)=2, \quad \lim_{x\to 0^+} f(x)=\lim_{x\to 0} x+2=2$$

and, $\quad f(0)=0+2=2$

$\therefore \quad \lim_{x \to 0^-} f(x) = \lim_{x \to 0^+} f(x) = f(0)$. So, $f(x)$ is also continuous at $x = 0$.

Hence, $f(x)$ is everywhere continuous.

EXAMPLE 3 *Discuss the continuity of the function* $f(x) = \begin{cases} \frac{|x|}{x} & , \text{ if } x \neq 0 \\ 0 & , \text{ if } x = 0 \end{cases}$.

SOLUTION We have,

$$f(x) = \begin{cases} \frac{|x|}{x} & , \text{ if } x \neq 0 \\ 0 & , \text{ if } x = 0 \end{cases} \Rightarrow f(x) = \begin{cases} \frac{-x}{x} = -1 & , \text{ if } x < 0 \\ \frac{x}{x} = 1 & , \text{ if } x > 0 \\ 0 & , \text{ if } x = 0 \end{cases} \quad \left[\because |x| = \begin{cases} x, & \text{if } x > 0 \\ -x, & \text{if } x < 0 \end{cases}\right]$$

We observe that $f(x)$ is a constant function for all $x < 0$ as well as for $x > 0$. So, it is continuous for all $x > 0$ and for all $x < 0$. Consider the point $x = 0$. At $x = 0$, we find that

(LHL at $x = 0$) $= \lim_{x \to 0^-} f(x) = \lim_{x \to 0} -1 = -1$ and, (RHL at $x = 0$) $= \lim_{x \to 0^+} f(x) = \lim_{x \to 0} 1 = 1$

$\therefore \quad$ (LHL at $x = 0$) $\neq$ (RHL at $x = 0$)

So, $f(x)$ is not continuous at $x = 0$. Hence, $f(x)$ is continuous at each point, except at $x = 0$.

EXAMPLE 4 *Discuss the continuity of the function $f(x)$ given by* $f(x) = \begin{cases} 2x - 1 & , \text{ if } x < 0 \\ 2x + 1 & , \text{ if } x \geq 0 \end{cases}$

[CBSE 2002]

SOLUTION When $x < 0$, we have $f(x) = 2x - 1$. Clearly, $f(x)$ is a polynomial function for $x < 0$. So, $f(x)$ is continuous for all $x < 0$.

When $x > 0$, we have $f(x) = 2x + 1$. Clearly, $f(x)$ is a polynomial function for $x > 0$. So, it is continuous for all $x > 0$.

Let us now consider the point $x = 0$. At $x = 0$, we find that

$$\lim_{x \to 0^-} f(x) = \lim_{x \to 0} (2x - 1) = -1 \text{ and, } \lim_{x \to 0^+} f(x) = \lim_{x \to 0} (2x + 1) = 1.$$

$$\therefore \quad \lim_{x \to 0^-} f(x) \neq \lim_{x \to 0^+} f(x)$$

So, $f(x)$ is not continuous at $x = 0$. Hence, $f(x)$ is everywhere continuous except at $x = 0$.

Type II ON FINDING THE VALUE(S) OF A CONSTANT GIVEN IN THE DEFINITION OF A FUNCTION WHEN IT IS CONTINUOUS ON ITS DOMAIN

EXAMPLE 5 *Determine the value of the constant k so that the function* $f(x) = \begin{cases} k x^2 & , \text{ if } x \leq 2 \\ 3 & , \text{ if } x > 2 \end{cases}$ *is continuous.* **[NCERT]**

SOLUTION When $x \leq 2$, we have $f(x) = k x^2$, which being a polynomial function is continuous at each $x < 2$.

When $x > 2$, we have $f(x) = 3$, which being a constant function is continuous at each $x > 2$.

Let us now consider the point $x = 2$. At $x = 2$, we have

$$(\text{LHL at } x = 2) = \lim_{x \to 2^-} f(x) = \lim_{x \to 2} kx^2 = 4k \qquad [\because f(x) = kx^2 \text{ for } x \le 2]$$

$$(\text{RHL at } x = 2) = \lim_{x \to 2^+} f(x) = \lim_{x \to 2} 3 = 3 \qquad [\because f(x) = 3 \text{ for } x > 2]$$

and, $\quad f(2) = k(2)^2 = 4k.$

As $f(x)$ is continuous in its domain. Therefore, it is also continuous at $x = 2$. Consequently, we have

$$\lim_{x \to 2^-} f(x) = f(2) = \lim_{x \to 2^+} f(x) \Rightarrow 4k = 3 \Rightarrow k = \frac{3}{4}$$

EXAMPLE 6 *If* $f(x) = \begin{cases} 1 & , \text{ if } x \le 3 \\ ax + b & , \text{ if } 3 < x < 5 \\ 7 & , \text{ if } 5 \le x \end{cases}$. *Determine the values of a and b so that f(x) is continuous.*

SOLUTION The given function is a constant function for all $x < 3$ as well as for all $x > 5$. So, it is continuous for all $x < 3$ as well as for all $x > 5$. We know that a polynomial function is continuous. So, the given function is continuous for all $x \in (3, 5)$. Thus, $f(x)$ is continuous at each $x \in R$ except possibly at $x = 3$ and $x = 5$.

At $x = 3$, we have

$$\lim_{x \to 3^-} f(x) = \lim_{x \to 3} 1 = 1, \quad \lim_{x \to 3^+} f(x) = \lim_{x \to 3} ax + b = 3a + b \quad \text{and, } f(3) = 1$$

For $f(x)$ be continuous at $x = 3$, we must have

$$\lim_{x \to 3^-} f(x) = \lim_{x \to 3^+} f(x) = f(3) \Rightarrow 1 = 3a + b \qquad \text{...(i)}$$

At $x = 5$, we have

$$\lim_{x \to 5^-} f(x) = \lim_{x \to 5} ax + b = 5a + b, \quad \lim_{x \to 5^+} f(x) = \lim_{x \to 5} 7 = 7 \quad \text{and, } f(5) = 7$$

For $f(x)$ to be continuous at $x = 5$, we must have

$$\lim_{x \to 5^-} f(x) = \lim_{x \to 5^+} f(x) = f(5) \Rightarrow 5a + b = 7 \qquad \text{...(ii)}$$

Solving (i) and (ii), we get: $a = 3, b = -8$.

BASED ON LOWER ORDER THINKING SKILLS (LOTS)

EXAMPLE 7 *Show that the function f defined by* $f(x) = |1 - x + |x||$ *is everywhere continuous.* **[NCERT]**

SOLUTION Let $g(x) = 1 - x + |x|$ and $h(x) = |x|$ be two functions defined on R. Then,

$$(hog)(x) = h(g(x)) = h(1 - x + |x|) = |1 - x + |x|| = f(x) \text{ for all } x \in R.$$

Since $(1 - x)$, being a polynomial function and $|x|$ being a modulus function are continuous on R. Therefore, $g(x) = 1 - x + |x|$ is everywhere continuous. Also, $h(x) = |x|$ is everywhere continuous. Hence, $f = hog$ is everywhere continuous.

ALITER We have, $f(x) = |1 - x + |x|| = \begin{cases} |1 - x - x|, & \text{if } x < 0 \\ |1 - x + x|, & \text{if } x \ge 0 \end{cases} = \begin{cases} (1 - 2x), & \text{if } x < 0 \\ 1 & , \text{if } x \ge 0 \end{cases}$

For $x < 0$, we have $f(x) = 1 - 2x$. Clearly, $f(x)$ is a polynomial function. So, $f(x)$ is continuous for all $x < 0$.

For $x > 0$, $f(x) = 1$, being a constant function, is continuous. So, $x = 0$ is the only point of possible discontinuity.

Now, $\lim\limits_{x \to 0^-} f(x) = \lim\limits_{x \to 0} (1 - 2x) = 1$ and $\lim\limits_{x \to 0^+} f(x) = \lim\limits_{x \to 0} 1 = 1$

Thus, $\lim\limits_{x \to 0^-} f(x) = f(0) = \lim\limits_{x \to 0^+} f(x)$. So, $f(x)$ is continuous at $x = 0$. Hence, $f(x)$ is everywhere continuous.

EXAMPLE 8 *Prove that* $f(x) = \sqrt{|x| - x}$ *is continuous for all* $x \geq 0$.

SOLUTION Let $g(x) = |x| - x$ and $h(x) = \sqrt{x}$. Clearly, domain $(g) = R$ and domain $(h) = [0, \infty)$. Also, $g(x))$ and $h(x)$ are continuous in their domains.

We observe that

$$\begin{aligned} \text{Domain } (hog) &= \{x \in \text{Domain } (g) : g(x) \in \text{Domain } (h)\} \\ &= \{x \in R : |x| - x \in [0, \infty)\} = \{x \in R : x \geq 0\} = [0, \infty) \end{aligned}$$

Since $g(x)$ and $h(x)$ are continuous on their respective domains. Therefore, $hog : [0, \infty) \to R$ is also continuous.

ALITER We have, $f(x) = \sqrt{|x| - x} \Rightarrow f(x) = \begin{cases} \sqrt{x - x} = 0 & \text{, if } x \geq 0 \\ \sqrt{-x - x} = \sqrt{-2x}, & \text{if } x < 0 \end{cases}$

For $x \geq 0$, we have $f(x) = 0$, which being a constant function, is continuous.
For $x < 0$, we have $f(x) = \sqrt{-2x}$

We know that the square root function is continuous in its domain. So, $f(x) = \sqrt{-2x}$ is continuous for all $x < 0$.

Now,

$$\lim_{x \to 0^-} f(x) = \lim_{x \to 0} \sqrt{-2x} = 0 \text{ and, } \lim_{x \to 0^+} f(x) = \lim_{x \to 0} 0 = 0$$

$\therefore$ $\lim\limits_{x \to 0^-} f(x) = f(0) = \lim\limits_{x \to 0^+} f(x)$. So, $f(x)$ is continuous at $x = 0$.

Hence, $f(x)$ is everywhere continuous.

EXAMPLE 9 *Determine the value of the constant m so that the function* $f(x) = \begin{cases} m(x^2 - 2x) & , \text{ if } x < 0 \\ \cos x & , \text{ if } x \geq 0 \end{cases}$ *is continuous.*

SOLUTION When $x < 0$, we have $f(x) = m(x^2 - 2x)$, which being a polynomial is continuous at each $x < 0$.

When $x > 0$, we have $f(x) = \cos x$, which being a cosine function is continuous at each $x > 0$.
Let us now consider the point $x = 0$. At $x = 0$, we have

$$(\text{LHL at } x = 0) = \lim_{x \to 0^-} f(x) = \lim_{x \to 0} m(x^2 - 2x) = 0 \text{ for all values of } m.$$

and, $$(\text{RHL at } x = 0) = \lim_{x \to 0^+} f(x) = \lim_{x \to 0} \cos x = 1$$

Clearly, $\lim\limits_{x \to 0^-} f(x) \neq \lim\limits_{x \to 0^+} f(x)$ for any value of m. So, $f(x)$ cannot be made continuous for any value of m. In other words, the value of m does not exist for which $f(x)$ can be made continuous.

BASED ON HIGHER ORDER THINKING SKILLS (HOTS)

EXAMPLE 10 *Given* $f(x) = \frac{1}{x-1}$. *Find the points of discontinuity of the composite function* $f(f(x))$.

[NCERT EXEMPLAR]

SOLUTION We find that

$$\lim_{x \to 1^-} f(x) = \lim_{h \to 0} f(1-h) = \lim_{h \to 0} \frac{1}{-h} \to -\infty \text{ and, } \lim_{x \to 1^+} f(x) = \lim_{h \to 0} f(1+h) = \lim_{h \to 0} \frac{1}{h} \to \infty$$

$$\therefore \quad \lim_{x \to 1^-} f(x) \neq \lim_{x \to 1^+} f(x)$$

So, $f(x)$ is discontinuous at $x = 1$. Also, $f(x)$ is not defined at $x = 1$. So, for $x \neq 1$, we obtain

$$f(f(x)) = f\left(\frac{1}{x-1}\right) = \frac{1}{\frac{1}{x-1} - 1} = \frac{x-1}{2-x}$$

Let $g(x) = f(f(x)) = \frac{x-1}{2-x}$. Then,

$$\lim_{x \to 2^-} g(x) = \lim_{h \to 0} g(2-h) = \lim_{h \to 0} \frac{2-h-1}{2-(2-h)} = \lim_{h \to 0}\left(\frac{1}{h} - 1\right) \to \infty$$

and, $$\lim_{x \to 2^+} g(x) = \lim_{h \to 0} g(2+h) = \lim_{h \to 0} \frac{2+h-1}{2-(2+h)} = \lim_{h \to 0}\left(-1 - \frac{1}{h}\right) \to -\infty$$

$$\therefore \quad \lim_{x \to 2^-} g(x) \neq \lim_{x \to 2^+} g(x) \text{ or, } \lim_{x \to 2^-} f\left(f(x)\right) \neq \lim_{x \to 2^+} f\left(f(x)\right)$$

So, $f(f(x))$ is discontinuous at $x = 2$. Hence, $f(f(x))$ is discontinuous at $x = 1$ and $x = 2$.

EXERCISE 8.2

BASIC

1. Prove that the function $f(x) = \begin{cases} \frac{\sin x}{x}, & x < 0 \\ x + 1, & x \geq 0 \end{cases}$ is everywhere continuous.

2. Discuss the continuity of the function $f(x) = \begin{cases} \frac{x}{|x|}, & x \neq 0 \\ 0, & x = 0 \end{cases}$.

3. Find the points of discontinuity, if any, of the following functions:

(i) $f(x) = \begin{cases} x^3 - x^2 + 2x - 2, & \text{if } x \neq 1 \\ 4, & \text{if } x = 1 \end{cases}$ (ii) $f(x) = \begin{cases} \frac{x^4 - 16}{x - 2}, & \text{if } x \neq 2 \\ 16, & \text{if } x = 2 \end{cases}$

(iii) $f(x) = \begin{cases} \frac{\sin x}{x}, & \text{if } x < 0 \\ 2x + 3, & x \geq 0 \end{cases}$ (iv) $f(x) = \begin{cases} \frac{\sin 3x}{x}, & \text{if } x \neq 0 \\ 4, & \text{if } x = 0 \end{cases}$

(v) $f(x) = \begin{cases} \frac{\sin x}{x} + \cos x, & \text{if } x \neq 0 \\ 5, & \text{if } x = 0 \end{cases}$ (vi) $f(x) = \begin{cases} \frac{x^4 + x^3 + 2x^2}{\tan^{-1} x}, & \text{if } x \neq 0 \\ 10, & \text{if } x = 0 \end{cases}$

(vii) $f(x) = \begin{cases} \dfrac{e^x - 1}{\log_e (1+2x)}, & \text{if } x \neq 0 \\ 7, & \text{if } x = 0 \end{cases}$

(viii) $f(x) = \begin{cases} |x-3|, & \text{if } x \geq 1 \\ \dfrac{x^2}{4} - \dfrac{3x}{2} + \dfrac{13}{4}, & \text{if } x < 1 \end{cases}$

(ix) $f(x) = \begin{cases} |x| + 3, & \text{if } x \leq -3 \\ -2x, & \text{if } -3 < x < 3 \\ 6x + 2, & \text{if } x \geq 3 \end{cases}$ [CBSE 2010]

(x) $f(x) = \begin{cases} x^{10} - 1, & \text{if } x \leq 1 \\ x^2, & \text{if } x > 1 \end{cases}$ [NCERT]

(xi) $f(x) = \begin{cases} 2x, & \text{if } x < 0 \\ 0, & \text{if } 0 \leq x \leq 1 \\ 4x, & \text{if } x > 1 \end{cases}$ [NCERT]

(xii) $f(x) = \begin{cases} \sin x - \cos x, & \text{if } x \neq 0 \\ -1, & \text{if } x = 0 \end{cases}$ [NCERT]

(xiii) $f(x) = \begin{cases} -2, & \text{if } x \leq -1 \\ 2x, & \text{if } -1 < x < 1 \\ 2, & \text{if } x \geq 1 \end{cases}$ [NCERT]

4. In the following, determine the value(s) of constant(s) involved in the definition so that the given function is continuous:

(i) $f(x) = \begin{cases} \dfrac{\sin 2x}{5x}, & \text{if } x \neq 0 \\ 3k, & \text{if } x = 0 \end{cases}$

(ii) $f(x) = \begin{cases} kx + 5, & \text{if } x \leq 2 \\ x - 1, & \text{if } x > 2 \end{cases}$

(iii) $f(x) = \begin{cases} k(x^2 + 3x), & \text{if } x < 0 \\ \cos 2x, & \text{if } x \geq 0 \end{cases}$

(iv) $f(x) = \begin{cases} 2, & \text{if } x \leq 3 \\ ax + b, & \text{if } 3 < x < 5 \\ 9, & \text{if } x \geq 5 \end{cases}$

(v) $f(x) = \begin{cases} 4, & \text{if } x \leq -1 \\ ax^2 + b, & \text{if } -1 < x < 0 \\ \cos x, & \text{if } x \geq 0 \end{cases}$

(vi) $f(x) = \begin{cases} \dfrac{\sqrt{1+px} - \sqrt{1-px}}{x}, & \text{if } -1 \leq x < 0 \\ \dfrac{2x+1}{x-2}, & \text{if } 0 \leq x \leq 1 \end{cases}$ [CBSE 2013, NCERT EXEMPLAR]

(vii) $f(x) = \begin{cases} 5, & \text{if } x \leq 2 \\ ax + b, & \text{if } 2 < x < 10 \\ 21, & \text{if } x \geq 10 \end{cases}$ [NCERT]

(viii) $f(x) = \begin{cases} \dfrac{k \cos x}{\pi - 2x}, & x < \dfrac{\pi}{2} \\ 3, & x = \dfrac{\pi}{2} \\ \dfrac{3 \tan 2x}{2x - \pi}, & x > \dfrac{\pi}{2} \end{cases}$ [CBSE 2010]

BASED ON LOTS

5. The function $f(x) = \begin{cases} \dfrac{x^2}{a} & , \text{ if } 0 \le x < 1 \\ a & , \text{ if } 1 \le x < \sqrt{2} \\ \dfrac{2b^2 - 4b}{x^2} & , \text{ if } \sqrt{2} \le x < \infty \end{cases}$ is continuous on $[0, \infty)$. Find the most suitable values of a and b.

6. Find the values of a and b so that the function $f(x)$ defined by

$f(x) = \begin{cases} x + a\sqrt{2} \sin x & , \text{if } 0 \le x < \pi/4 \\ 2x \cot x + b & , \text{ if } \pi/4 \le x < \pi/2 \\ a \cos 2x - b \sin x & , \text{ if } \pi/2 \le x \le \pi \end{cases}$ becomes continuous on $[0, \pi]$.

7. The function $f(x)$ is defined by $f(x) = \begin{cases} x^2 + ax + b & , 0 \le x < 2 \\ 3x + 2 & , 2 \le x \le 4 \\ 2ax + 5b & , 4 < x \le 8 \end{cases}$. If f is continuous on $[0, 8]$, find the values of a and b.

8. Discuss the continuity of the function $f(x) = \begin{cases} 2x - 1 & , \text{ if } x < 2 \\ \dfrac{3x}{2} & , \text{ if } x \ge 2 \end{cases}$.

9. Prove that $f(x) = \begin{cases} \dfrac{\sin 3x}{x}, & x < 0 \\ x + 3 & , x \ge 0 \end{cases}$ is everywhere continuous.

10. Is $f(x) = \begin{cases} x^2 \sin \dfrac{1}{x} & , x \ne 0 \\ 0 & , x = 0 \end{cases}$ a continuous function? [NCERT]

BASED ON HOTS

11. If $f(x) = \dfrac{\tan\left(\dfrac{\pi}{4} - x\right)}{\cot 2x}$ for $x \ne \dfrac{\pi}{4}$, find the value which can be assigned to $f(x)$ at $x = \pi/4$ so that the function $f(x)$ becomes continuous every where in $[0, \pi/2]$.

12. Discuss the continuity of $f(x) = \sin |x|$. [NCERT]

13. Show that the function $g(x) = x - [x]$ is discontinuous at all integral points. Here $[x]$ denotes the greatest integer function. [NCERT]

14. Discuss the continuity of the following functions:
(i) $f(x) = \sin x + \cos x$ (ii) $f(x) = \sin x - \cos x$ (iii) $f(x) = \sin x \cos x$ [NCERT]

15. Show that $f(x) = \cos x^2$ is a continuous function. [NCERT]

16. Show that $f(x) = |\cos x|$ is a continuous function. [NCERT]

17. Find all the points of discontinuity of f defined by $f(x) = |x| - |x + 1|$. [NCERT]

18. Given the function $f(x) = \dfrac{1}{x+2}$. Find the points of discontinuity of the function $f(f(x))$.

[NCERT EXEMPLAR]

19. Find all points of discontinuity of the function $f(t) = \frac{1}{t^2 + t - 2}$, where $t = \frac{1}{x-1}$.

[NCERT EXEMPLAR]

ANSWERS

2. Discontinuous at $x = 0$
3. (i) $x = 1$ (ii) $x = 2$ (iii) $x = 0$ (iv) $x = 0$ (v) $x = 0$
(vi) $x = 0$ (vii) $x = 0$ (viii) Nowhere discontinuous
(ix) Discontinuous at $x = 3$ (x) Discontinuous at $x = 1$
(xi) Discontinuous at $x = 1$ (xii) Everywhere continuous
(xiii) Everywhere continuous
4. (i) $k = \frac{2}{15}$ (ii) $k = -2$
(iii) No value of k can make f (iv) $a = 7/2, b = -17/2$ (v) $a = 3, b = 1$
(vi) $p = -1/2$ (vii) $a = 2, b = 1$ (viii) 6
5. $a = -1, b = 1$ or $a = 1, b = 1 \pm \sqrt{2}$
6. $a = \pi/6, b = -\pi/12$
7. $a = 3, b = -2$
8. Everywhere continuous.
10. Continuous
11. $f\left(\frac{\pi}{4}\right) = \frac{1}{2}$
12. Everywhere continuous
14. (i) Everywhere continuous (ii) Everywhere continuous
(iii) Everywhere continuous
17. No point of discontinuity
18. Discontinuous at $x = -2$ and $x = -5/2$
19. Discontinuous $x = 1/2, 1, 2$.

HINTS TO SELECTED PROBLEMS

3. (x) We have,

$$f(x) = \begin{cases} x^{10} - 1, & x \le 1 \\ x^2, & x > 1 \end{cases}$$

Clearly, $f(x)$ is a polynomial function for all $x \le 1$ as well as for all $x > 1$. So, $f(x)$ is everywhere continuous except possibly at $x = 1$.

Now, $\lim_{x \to 1^-} f(x) = \lim_{x \to 1^-} x^{10} - 1 = 1 - 1 = 0$ and, $\lim_{x \to 1^+} f(x) = \lim_{x \to 1^+} x^2 = 1^2 = 1$

Clearly, $\lim_{x \to 1^-} f(x) \ne \lim_{x \to 1^+} f(x)$. So, $f(x)$ is not continuous at $x = 1$.

Hence, $f(x)$ is everywhere continuous except at $x = 1$.

(xi) We have, $f(x) = \begin{cases} 2x, & x < 0 \\ 0, & 0 \le x \le 1 \\ 4x, & x > 1 \end{cases}$

At $x = 0$, we have

$$\lim_{x \to 0^-} f(x) = \lim_{x \to 0^-} 2x = 2 \times 0 = 0, \quad \lim_{x \to 0^+} f(x) = \lim_{x \to 0^+} 0 = 0 \text{ and, } f(0) = 0$$

Thus, $\lim_{x \to 0^-} f(x) = \lim_{x \to 0^+} f(x) = f(0)$. So, $f(x)$ is continuous at $x = 0$.

At $x = 1$, we have

$$\lim_{x \to 1^-} f(x) = \lim_{x \to 1^-} 0 = 0, \quad \lim_{x \to 1^+} f(x) = \lim_{x \to 1^+} 4x = 4$$

$\therefore \quad \lim_{x \to 1^-} f(x) \neq \lim_{x \to 1^+} f(x)$. So, $f(x)$ is not continuous at $x = 1$.

For $x < 0$, $f(x)$ is a polynomial function which is everywhere continuous. For $x \in [0, 1]$, $f(x)$ is a constant function which is also continuous. For $x > 1$, $f(x)$ is a polynomial function which is everywhere continuous. Hence, $f(x)$ is everywhere continuous except at $x = 1$.

(xii) We have, $f(x) = \begin{cases} \sin x - \cos x, & x \neq 0 \\ -1, & x = 0 \end{cases}$. Clearly, $f(x)$ is continuous for all $x \neq 0$.

Now, $\lim_{x \to 0} f(x) = \lim_{x \to 0} (\sin x - \cos x) = \sin 0 - \cos 0 = -1 = f(0)$

So, $f(x)$ is continuous at $x = 0$. Hence, $f(x)$ is everywhere continuous.

(xiii) We have, $f(x) = \begin{cases} -2, & x \leq -1 \\ 2x, & -1 < x < 1 \\ 2, & x \geq 1 \end{cases}$

As $f(x)$ is a constant function for all $x < -1$ and all $x > 1$. So, $f(x)$ is continuos for all $x < -1$ and all $x > 1$. For $x \in (-1, 1)$, $f(x)$ is a polynomial function which is always continuous. Thus, $f(x)$ is continuous for all x except possible at $x = -1, 1$.

Continuity at $x = -1$: We observe that

$$\lim_{x \to -1^-} f(x) = \lim_{x \to -1^-} -2 = -2, \quad \lim_{x \to -1^+} f(x) = \lim_{x \to -1^+} 2x = -2 \text{ and, } f(-1) = -2$$

$\therefore \quad \lim_{x \to -1^-} f(x) = \lim_{x \to -1^+} f(x) = f(-1)$. So, $f(x)$ is continuous at $x = -1$.

Continuity at $x = 1$: Clearly,

$$\lim_{x \to 1^+} f(x) = \lim_{x \to 1^+} 2 = 2, \quad \lim_{x \to 1^-} f(x) = \lim_{x \to 1^-} 2x = 2 \times 1 = 2 \text{ and, } f(1) = 2$$

$$\therefore \quad \lim_{x \to 1^-} f(x) = \lim_{x \to 1^+} f(x) = f(1)$$

So, $f(x)$ is continuous at $x = 1$. Hence, $f(x)$ is everywhere continuous.

4. (vii) It is given that $f(x) = \begin{cases} 5, & x \leq 2 \\ ax + b, & 2 < x < 10 \\ 21, & x \geq 10 \end{cases}$ is everywhere continuous.

So, it is continuous at $x = 2$ and $x = 10$.

$$\therefore \quad \lim_{x \to 2^-} f(x) = \lim_{x \to 2^+} f(x) = f(2) \text{ and, } \lim_{x \to 10^-} f(x) = \lim_{x \to 10^+} f(x) = f(10)$$

$$\Rightarrow \quad \lim_{x \to 2^-} 5 = \lim_{x \to 2^+} ax + b = 5 \text{ and, } \lim_{x \to 10^-} ax + b = \lim_{x \to 10^+} 21 = 21$$

$$\Rightarrow \quad 5 = 2a + b \text{ and } 10a + b = 21 \Rightarrow a = 2, \ b = 1$$

10. We have, $f(x) = \begin{cases} x^2 \sin \dfrac{1}{x}, & x \neq 0 \\ 0, & x = 0 \end{cases}$. Clearly, $f(x)$ is continuous for all $x \neq 0$.

Now,

$$\lim_{x \to 0} f(x) = \lim_{x \to 0} x^2 \sin \frac{1}{x} = 0 \times (\text{An oscillating number between } -1 \text{ and } 1) = 0 = f(0)$$

So, $f(x)$ is continuous at $x = 0$. Hence, $f(x)$ is everywhere continuous.

12. Let a be any real number. Then,

$$\lim_{x \to a^-} f(x) = \lim_{x \to a^-} \sin|x| = \lim_{h \to 0} \sin|a-h| = \sin|a|$$

$$\lim_{x \to a^+} f(x) = \lim_{x \to a^+} \sin|x| = \lim_{h \to 0} \sin|a+h| = \sin|a| \text{ and, } f(a) = \sin|a|$$

$$\therefore \lim_{x \to a^-} f(x) = \lim_{x \to a^+} f(x) = f(a)$$

So, $f(x)$ is continuous at $x = a$. Since a is an arbitrary real number. Hence, $f(x)$ is everywhere continuous.

13. Let a be any integer. Then,

$$\lim_{x \to a^+} g(x) = \lim_{h \to 0} = g(a-h) = \lim_{h \to 0} (a-h) - [a-h] = \lim_{h \to 0} (a-h) - (a-1) = a - (a-1) = 1$$

$$\lim_{x \to a^+} g(x) = \lim_{h \to 0} g(a+h) = \lim_{h \to 0} (a+h) - [a+h] = \lim_{h \to 0} (a+h) - a = a - a = 0$$

$$\therefore \lim_{x \to a^-} g(x) \neq \lim_{x \to a^+} g(x).$$ So, $g(x)$ is discontinuous at $x = a$.

Since a is an arbitrary integer. Hence, $g(x)$ is discontinuous at all integral points.

14. We know that $\sin x$ and $\cos x$ are everywhere continuous. Therefore, $\sin x + \cos x$, $\sin x - \cos x$ and $\sin x \cos x$ are everywhere continuous.

15. Let $f(x) = \cos x^2$ and a be any real number. Then,

$$\lim_{x \to a^-} f(x) = \lim_{h \to 0} f(a-h) = \lim_{h \to 0} \cos(a-h)^2 = \cos a^2$$

$$\lim_{x \to a^+} f(x) = \lim_{h \to 0} f(a+h) = \lim_{h \to 0} \cos(a+h)^2 = \cos a^2 \text{ and, } f(a) = \cos a^2$$

$$\therefore \lim_{x \to a^-} f(x) = \lim_{x \to a^+} f(x) = f(a).$$ So, $f(x)$ is continuous at $x = a$.

Since 'a' is an arbitrary real number. Hence, $f(x)$ is everywhere continuous.

16. Let $f(x) = |\cos x|$ and a be any real number. Then,

$$\lim_{x \to a^-} f(x) = \lim_{h \to 0} f(a-h) = \lim_{h \to 0} |\cos(a-h)| = |\cos a|$$

$$\lim_{x \to a^+} f(x) = \lim_{h \to 0} f(a+h) = \lim_{h \to 0} |\cos(a+h)| = |\cos a| \text{ and, } f(a) = |\cos a|$$

$$\therefore \lim_{x \to a^-} f(x) = \lim_{x \to a^+} f(x) = f(a).$$ So, $f(x)$ is continuous at $x = a$.

Since 'a' is an arbitrary real number. Therefore, $f(x)$ is everywhere continuous.

17. We have,

$$f(x) = |x| - |x+1| = \begin{cases} -x + x + 1 & , x < -1 \\ -x - (x+1) & , -1 \le x < 0 \\ x - (x+1) & , x \ge 0 \end{cases} \Rightarrow f(x) = \begin{cases} 1 & , x < -1 \\ -2x - 1 & , -1 \le x < 0 \\ -1 & , x \ge 0 \end{cases}$$

Clearly, $f(x)$ is continuous for all x satisfying $x < -1$, $-1 < x < 0$ and $x > 0$. So, possibly points of discontinuity are $x = -1$ and $x = 0$.

Continuity at $x = -1$: Clearly,

$$\lim_{x \to -1^-} f(x) = \lim_{x \to -1^-} 1 = 1, \quad \lim_{x \to -1^+} f(x) = \lim_{x \to -1^+} (-2x - 1) = -2 \times -1 - 1 = 1$$

and, $f(-1) = -2 \times -1 - 1 = 1$

$$\therefore \quad \lim_{x \to -1^-} f(x) = \lim_{x \to -1^+} f(x) = f(-1).$$

So, $f(x)$ is continuous at $x = 1$.

Continuity at $x = 0$: Clearly,

$$\lim_{x \to 0^-} f(x) = \lim_{x \to 0^-} (-2x - 1) = -2 \times 0 - 1 = -1,$$

$$\lim_{x \to 0^+} f(x) = \lim_{x \to 0^+} -1 = -1 \text{ and, } f(0) = -2 \times 0 - 1 = -1$$

$$\therefore \quad \lim_{x \to 0^-} f(x) = \lim_{x \to 0^+} f(x) = f(0)$$

So, $f(x)$ is continuous at $x = 0$. Hence, $f(x)$ is everywhere continuous.

18. Clearly, $f(x) = \dfrac{1}{x+2}$ is discontinuous at $x = -2$. Also, it is not defined at $x = -2$.

For $x \neq -2$, we have $f(x) = f\left(\dfrac{1}{x+2}\right) = \dfrac{1}{\dfrac{1}{x+2} + 2} = \dfrac{x+2}{2x+5}$

We observe that $f(f(x))$ is discontinuous and undefined at $x = -5/2$.
Hence, $f(f(x))$ is discontinuous at $x = -2$ and $x = -5/2$.

19. We have, $f(x) = \dfrac{1}{t^2 + t - 2}$ and $t = \dfrac{1}{x-1}$. Clearly, $t = \dfrac{1}{x-1}$ is discontinuous and undefined at $x = 1$.

For $x \neq 1$, we have $f(t) = \dfrac{1}{t^2 + t - 2} = \dfrac{1}{(t+2)(t-1)}$. This is discontinuous at $t = 2$ and $t = 1$.

For $t = -2$, $t = \dfrac{1}{x-1} \Rightarrow x = \dfrac{1}{2}$ and, For $t = 1$, $t = \dfrac{1}{x-1} \Rightarrow x = 2$

Hence, f is discontinuous at $x = 1/2$, $x = 1$ and $x = 2$.

FILL IN THE BLANKS TYPE QUESTIONS (FBQs)

1. If $f(x) = \begin{cases} \dfrac{x^3 - a^3}{x - a}, & x \neq a \\ b, & x = a \end{cases}$ is continuous at $x = a$, then $b =$ ....

2. If the function $f(x) = \begin{cases} \dfrac{\sin^2 ax}{x^2}, & x \neq 0 \\ 1, & x = 0 \end{cases}$ is continuous at $x = 0$, then $a =$ ....

3. If the function $f(x) = \begin{cases} ax^2 - b, & 0 \leq x < 1 \\ 2, & x = 1 \\ x + 1, & 1 < x \leq 2 \end{cases}$ is continuous at $x = 1$, then $a - b =$ ....

4. If $f(x)=\begin{cases} x+k & , x<3 \\ 4 & , x=3 \\ 3x-5, & x>3 \end{cases}$ is continuous at $x = 3$, then $k =$ ....

5. Let $f(x)=\begin{cases} \frac{x-4}{|x-4|}+a, & x<4 \\ a+b & , x=4 \\ \frac{x-4}{|x-4|}+b & , x>4 \end{cases}$. Then $f(x)$ is continuous at $x=4$ when $a+b=$ ....

6. If $f: R \to R$ defined by $f(x)=\begin{cases} \frac{\cos 3x-\cos x}{x^2} & , x\neq 0 \\ \lambda & , x=0 \end{cases}$ is continuous at $x=0$, then $\lambda=$ ....

7. If $f(x)=\begin{cases} \frac{1-\sin x}{\pi-2x}, & x\neq \frac{\pi}{2} \\ k & , x=\frac{\pi}{2} \end{cases}$ is continuous at $x=\frac{\pi}{2}$, then $k=$ ....

8. If $f(x)=\frac{2-\sqrt{x+4}}{\sin 2x}$, $x\neq 0$, is continuous at $x=0$, then $f(0)=$ ....

9. If $f(x)=\begin{cases} \frac{x^2-9}{x-3}, & x\neq 3 \\ 2x+k & , x=3 \end{cases}$ is continuous at $x = 3$, then $k=$ ....

10. If the function $f(x)=\begin{cases} \frac{x^2-1}{x-1}, & x\neq 1 \\ k & , x=1 \end{cases}$ is given to be continuous at $x=1$, then the value of k is ....

11. The set of points where $f(x)=x-[x]$ is discontinuous is ....

12. Let $f(x)=\frac{1-\tan x}{4x-\pi}$, $x\neq\frac{\pi}{4}$, $x\in\left[0,\frac{\pi}{2}\right]$. If $f(x)$ is continuous in $\left[0,\frac{\pi}{2}\right]$, then $f\left(\frac{\pi}{4}\right)=$ ....

13. If $f(x)=x\sin\left(\frac{\pi}{x}\right)$ is everywhere continuous, then $f(0)=$ ....

14. The set of points at which the function $f(x)=\frac{1}{\log|x|}$ is not continuous, is ....

15. If $f(x)=\begin{cases} ax+1, & \text{if } x\geq 1 \\ x+2, & \text{if } x<1 \end{cases}$ is continuous, then 'a' should be equal to ....

16. If $f(x)$ is continuous at $x=a$ and $\lim_{x\to a^-} f(x)=\lim_{x\to a^+} f(x)=k$, then k is equal to ....

17. If $f(x)=\begin{cases} \frac{\sin 3x}{x}, & \text{if } x\neq 0 \\ \frac{k}{2} & , \text{if } x=0 \end{cases}$ is continuous at $x=0$, then k is equal to ....

18. The set of points of discontinuity of $f(x)=\tan x$ is ....

19. The set of points of discontinuity of $f(x)=[x]$ is ....

20. The set of points of discontinuity of $f(x) = \frac{1}{x-[x]}$ is ....

ANSWERS

1. $3a^2$	2. ± 1	3. 2	4. 1	5. 0	6. -4	7. 0
8. $-\frac{1}{8}$	9. 0	10. 2	11. Z	12. $-\frac{1}{2}$	13. 0	14. $\{-1, 0, 1\}$
15. 2	16. $f(a)$	17. 6	18. $\left\{(2n+1)\frac{\pi}{2} : n \in Z\right\}$	19. Z	20. Z	

VERY SHORT ANSWER QUESTIONS (VSAQs)

Answer each of the following questions in one word or one sentence or as per exact requirement of the questions.

1. Define continuity of a function at a point.
2. What happens to a function $f(x)$ at $x = a$, if $\lim_{x \to a} f(x) = f(a)$?
3. Find $f(0)$, so that $f(x) = \frac{x}{1 - \sqrt{1-x}}$ becomes continuous at $x = 0$.
4. If $f(x) = \begin{cases} \frac{x}{\sin 3x}, & x \neq 0 \\ k, & x = 0 \end{cases}$ is continuous at $x = 0$, then write the value of k.
5. If the function $f(x) = \frac{\sin 10x}{x}$, $x \neq 0$ is continuous at $x = 0$, find $f(0)$.
6. If $f(x) = \begin{cases} \frac{x^2 - 16}{x - 4}, & \text{if } x \neq 4 \\ k, & \text{if } x = 4 \end{cases}$ is continuous at $x = 4$, find k.
7. Determine whether $f(x) = \begin{cases} \frac{\sin x^2}{x}, & x \neq 0 \\ 0, & x = 0 \end{cases}$ is continuous at $x = 0$ or not.
8. If $f(x) = \begin{cases} \frac{1 - \cos x}{x^2}, & x \neq 0 \\ k, & x = 0 \end{cases}$ is continuous at $x = 0$, find k.
9. If $f(x) = \begin{cases} \frac{\sin^{-1} x}{x}, & x \neq 0 \\ k, & x = 0 \end{cases}$ is continuous at $x = 0$, write the value of k.
10. Write the value of b for which $f(x) = \begin{cases} 5x - 4 & 0 < x \leq 1 \\ 4x^2 + 3bx & 1 < x < 2 \end{cases}$ is continuous at $x = 1$.
11. Determine the value of constant 'k' so that the function $f(x) = \begin{cases} \frac{kx}{|x|}, & x < 0 \\ 3, & x \geq 0 \end{cases}$ is continuous at $x = 0$. [CBSE 2017]

12. Find the value of k for which the function $f(x) = \begin{cases} \dfrac{x^2 + 3x - 10}{x - 2}, & x \neq 2 \\ k, & x^2 \end{cases}$ is continuous at $x = 2$.

[C [illegible] 2017]

ANSWERS

2. $f(x)$ becomes continuous at $x = a$ 3. 2 4. $\dfrac{1}{3}$ 5. 10 6. 8

7. continuous 8. $\dfrac{1}{2}$ 9. 1 10. -1 11. -3 12. 7

CHAPTER 9

DIFFERENTIABILITY

9.1 DIFFERENTIABILITY AT A POINT

DEFINITION *Let $f(x)$ be a real valued function defined on an open interval (a, b) and let $c \in (a, b)$. Then, $f(x)$ is said to be differentiable or derivable at $x = c$, iff $\lim_{x \to c} \frac{f(x) - f(c)}{x - c}$ exists finitely.*

This limit is called the derivative or differential coefficient of the function $f(x)$ at $x = c$, and is denoted by $f'(c)$ or, $Df(c)$ or, $\left(\frac{df(x)}{dx}\right)_{x=c}$.

Thus, $f'(c) = \lim_{x \to c} \frac{f(x) - f(c)}{x - c}$.

Now,

$f(x)$ is differentiable at $x = c$

$$\Leftrightarrow \quad \lim_{x \to c} \frac{f(x) - f(c)}{x - c} \text{ exists finitely}$$

$$\Leftrightarrow \quad \lim_{x \to c^-} \frac{f(x) - f(c)}{x - c} = \lim_{x \to c^+} \frac{f(x) - f(c)}{x - c}$$

$$\Leftrightarrow \quad \lim_{h \to 0} \frac{f(c - h) - f(c)}{-h} = \lim_{h \to 0} \frac{f(c + h) - f(c)}{h}$$

$\lim_{x \to c^-} \frac{f(x) - f(c)}{x - c}$ or, $\lim_{h \to 0} \frac{f(c - h) - f(c)}{-h}$ is called the left hand derivative of $f(x)$ at $x = c$ and is denoted by $f'(c^-)$ or, $Lf'(c)$.

$\lim_{x \to c^+} \frac{f(x) - f(c)}{x - c}$ or, $\lim_{h \to 0} \frac{f(c + h) - f(c)}{h}$ is called the right hand derivative of $f(x)$ at $x = c$ and is denoted by $f'(c^+)$ or, $Rf'(c)$.

Thus, (f is differentiable at $x = c$) $\Leftrightarrow$ $Lf'(c) = Rf'(c)$.

If $Lf'(c) \neq Rf'(c)$, we say that $f(x)$ is not differentiable at $x = c$.

MEANING OF DIFFERENTIABILITY AT A POINT As we have seen in the chapter on continuity of a function that if a function $f(x)$ is continuous at a point $x = a$ (say), then its graph is an unbroken curve at $(a, f(a))$ and there are no holes and jumps in the graph of the function in the neighbourhood of point $x = a$. Now, a natural question arises: What do we mean when we say that a function $f(x)$ is differentiable at a point $x = c$? In the following discussion we shall try to answer this question.

Consider the function $f(x)$ defined on an open interval (a, b). Let $P(c, f(c))$ be a point on the curve $y = f(x)$, and let $Q(c-h, f(c-h))$, and $R(c+h, f(c+h))$ be two neighbouring points on the left and right hand side respectively of point P as shown in Fig. 9.1. Then,

$$\text{Slope of chord } PQ = \frac{f(c-h)-f(c)}{-h}$$

and, $$\text{Slope of chord } PR = \frac{f(c+h)-f(c)}{h}$$

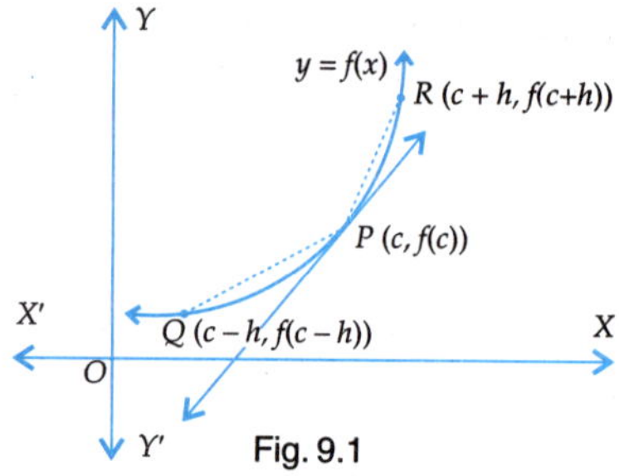

Fig. 9.1

We know that tangent to a curve at a point P (say) is the limiting position of chord PQ when Q tends to P. Therefore, as $h \to 0$ points Q and R both tend to P from left hand and right hand sides respectively. Consequently, chords PQ and PR become tangent(s) at point P.

Thus, $$\lim_{h \to 0} \frac{f(c-h)-f(c)}{-h} = \lim_{h \to 0} (\text{Slope of chord } PQ)$$

$$= \lim_{Q \to P} (\text{Slope of chord } PQ)$$

= Slope of the tangent at point P, which is the limiting position of the chords drawn on the left hand side of point P. ...(i)

and, $$\lim_{h \to 0} \frac{f(c+h)-f(c)}{h} = \lim_{h \to 0} (\text{Slope of chord } PR)$$

$$= \lim_{R \to P} (\text{Slope of chord } PR)$$

= Slope of the tangent at point P, which is the limiting position of the chords drawn on the right hand side of point P ...(ii)

Now,

$f(x)$ is differentiable at $x = c$.

$$\Leftrightarrow \quad \lim_{h \to 0} \frac{f(c-h)-f(c)}{-h} = \lim_{h \to 0} \frac{f(c+h)-f(c)}{h}$$

$\Leftrightarrow$ Slope of the tangent at point P, which is limiting position of the chords drawn on the left hand side of P is same as the slope of the tangent at point P, which is the limiting position of the chords drawn on the right hand side of P

$\Leftrightarrow$ There is a unique tangent at point P.

Thus, $f(x)$ is differentiable at point P, iff there exists a unique tangent at point P. In other words, $f(x)$ is differentiable at a point P iff the curve does not have P as a corner point.

Consider the function $f(x) = |x|$. This function is not differentiable at $x = 0$, because if we draw tangent at the origin as the limiting position of the chords on the left hand side of the origin, it is the line $y = -x$ whereas the tangent at the origin as the limiting position of the chords on the right hand side of the origin is the line $y = x$. Mathematically, left hand derivative at the origin is -1 (slope of the line $y = -x$) and the right hand derivative at the origin is 1 (slope of the line $y = x$).

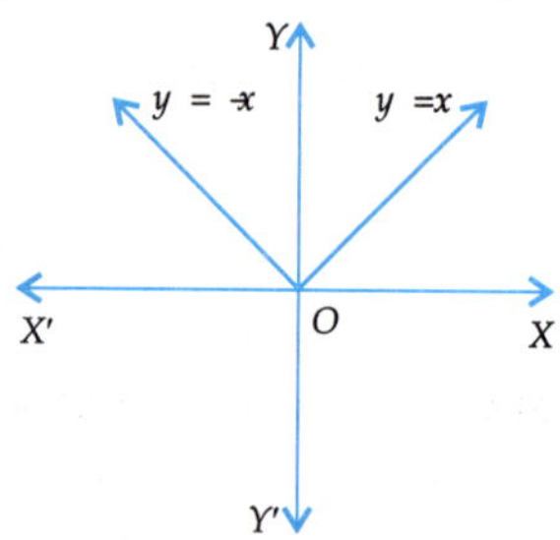

Fig. 9.2

Let $f(x)$ be a differentiable function at a point P. Then the curve $y = f(x)$ has a unique tangent at P. Since tangent at P is the limiting position of the chord PQ when $Q \to P$. So, if $f(x)$ is differentiable at a point P, then chords exist on both sides of point P. This means that the curve exists on both sides of P. Consequently $f(x)$ is continuous at P.

It follows from the above discussion that, if a function is not differentiable at $x = c$, then either it has $(c, f(c))$ as a corner point or it is discontinuous at $x = c$.

Also, every differentiable function is continuous as proved below.

THEOREM *If a function is differentiable at a point, it is necessarily continuous at that point. But, the converse is not necessarily true.*

OR

$f(x)$ is differentiable at $x = c \Rightarrow f(x)$ is continuous at $x = c$

PROOF Let a function $f(x)$ be differentiable at $x = c$. Then, $\lim_{x \to c} \frac{f(x) - f(c)}{x - c}$ exists finitely.

Let $$\lim_{x \to c} \frac{f(x) - f(c)}{x - c} = f'(c) \quad \text{...(i)}$$

In order to prove that $f(x)$ is continuous at $x = c$, it is sufficient to show that $\lim_{x \to c} f(x) = f(c)$.

Now,

$$\lim_{x \to c} f(x) = \lim_{x \to c} \left\{ \left(\frac{f(x) - f(c)}{x - c} \right)(x - c) + f(c) \right\}$$

$$\Rightarrow \quad \lim_{x \to c} f(x) = \lim_{x \to c} \left\{ \left(\frac{f(x) - f(c)}{x - c} \right)(x - c) \right\} + f(c)$$

$$\Rightarrow \quad \lim_{x \to c} f(x) = \lim_{x \to c} \left(\frac{f(x) - f(c)}{x - c} \right) \times \lim_{x \to c} (x - c) + f(c) = f'(c) \times 0 + f(c) \quad \text{[Using (i)]}$$

$$\Rightarrow \quad \lim_{x \to c} f(x) = f(c)$$

Hence, $f(x)$ is continuous at $x = c$. **Q.E.D.**

REMARK *The converse of the above theorem is not necessarily true i.e., a function may be continuous at a point but may not be differentiable at that point. For example, the function $f(x) = |x|$ is continuous at $x = 0$ but it is not differentiable at $x = 0$ (See Example 1 below.)*

ILLUSTRATIVE EXAMPLES

BASED ON BASIC CONCEPTS (BASIC)

EXAMPLE 1 *Show that $f(x) = |x|$ is not differentiable at $x = 0$.*

SOLUTION We observe that:

$$(\text{LHD at } x = 0) = \lim_{x \to 0^-} \frac{f(x) - f(0)}{x - 0} = \lim_{h \to 0} \frac{f(0 - h) - f(0)}{0 - h - 0} = \lim_{h \to 0} \frac{f(-h) - f(0)}{-h}$$

$$= \lim_{h \to 0} \frac{|-h| - |0|}{-h} = \lim_{h \to 0} \frac{|-h|}{-h} = \lim_{h \to 0} \frac{h}{-h} = \lim_{h \to 0} -1 = -1$$

and, $$(\text{RHD at } x = 0) = \lim_{x \to 0^+} \frac{f(x) - f(0)}{x - 0} = \lim_{h \to 0} \frac{f(0 + h) - f(0)}{h}$$

$$= \lim_{h \to 0} \frac{f(h) - f(0)}{h} = \lim_{h \to 0} \frac{|h| - |0|}{h} = \lim_{h \to 0} \frac{h}{h} = \lim_{h \to 0} 1 = 1$$

$\therefore$ (LHD at $x = 0$) $\neq$ (RHD at $x = 0$). So, $f(x)$ is not differentiable at $x = 0$.

EXAMPLE 2 *Show that the function* $f(x) = \begin{cases} x-1, & \text{if } x < 2 \\ 2x-3, & \text{if } x \geq 2 \end{cases}$ *is not differentiable at* $x = 2$.

SOLUTION We observe that:

$$(\text{LHD at } x = 2) = \lim_{x \to 2^-} \frac{f(x) - f(2)}{x - 2} = \lim_{x \to 2} \frac{(x-1)-(4-3)}{x-2} \quad [\because f(x) = x - 1 \text{ for } x < 2]$$

$$= \lim_{x \to 2} \frac{x-2}{x-2} = \lim_{x \to 2} 1 = 1$$

and, $$(\text{RHD at } x = 2) = \lim_{x \to 2^+} \frac{f(x) - f(2)}{x - 2} = \lim_{x \to 2} \frac{(2x-3)-(4-3)}{x-2} \quad [\because f(x) = 2x - 3 \text{ for } x \geq 2]$$

$$= \lim_{x \to 2} \frac{2x-4}{x-2} = \lim_{x \to 2} 2 = 2$$

$\therefore$ (LHD at $x = 2$) $\neq$ (RHD at $x = 2$). So, $f(x)$ is not differentiable at $x = 2$.

EXAMPLE 3 *Show that* $f(x) = x^2$ *is differentiable at* $x = 1$ *and find* $f'(1)$.

SOLUTION We observe that:

$$(\text{LHD at } x = 1) = \lim_{x \to 1^-} \frac{f(x) - f(1)}{x - 1} = \lim_{h \to 0} \frac{f(1-h) - f(1)}{1 - h - 1}$$

$$= \lim_{h \to 0} \frac{(1-h)^2 - 1^2}{-h} = \lim_{h \to 0} \frac{-2h + h^2}{-h} = \lim_{h \to 0} (2 - h) = 2.$$

and, $$(\text{RHD at } x = 1) = \lim_{x \to 1^+} \frac{f(x) - f(1)}{x - 1} = \lim_{h \to 0} \frac{f(1+h) - f(1)}{1 + h - 1}$$

$$= \lim_{h \to 0} \frac{(1+h)^2 - 1}{h} = \lim_{h \to 0} \frac{2h + h^2}{h} = \lim_{h \to 0} (2 + h) = 2$$

$\therefore$ (LHD at $x = 1$) = (RHD at $x = 1$) = 2. So, $f(x)$ is differentiable at $x = 1$ and $f'(1) = 2$.

EXAMPLE 4 *Discuss the differentiability of* $f(x) = x|x|$ *at* $x = 0$.

SOLUTION We have, $f(x) = x|x| = \begin{cases} x^2, & x \geq 0 \\ -x^2, & x < 0 \end{cases}$ **[CBSE 2020, NCERT EXEMPLAR]**

Now, $$(\text{LHD at } x = 0) = \lim_{x \to 0^-} \frac{f(x) - f(0)}{x - 0} = \lim_{x \to 0} \frac{-x^2 - 0}{x - 0} \quad [\text{Using definition of } f(x)]$$

$$= \lim_{x \to 0} -x = 0$$

and, $$(\text{RHD at } x = 0) = \lim_{x \to 0^+} \frac{f(x) - f(0)}{x - 0} = \lim_{x \to 0} \frac{x^2 - 0}{x - 0} \quad [\text{Using definition of } f(x)]$$

$$= \lim_{x \to 0} x = 0.$$

$\therefore$ (LHD at $x = 0$) = (RHD at $x = 0$). So, $f(x)$ is differentiable at $x = 0$.

BASED ON LOWER ORDER THINKING SKILLS (LOTS)

EXAMPLE 5 *If* $f(x)=\begin{cases} x^2, & \text{if } x\geq 1 \\ x, & \text{if } x<1 \end{cases}$*, then show that f is not differentiable at* $x=1$. **[CBSE 2023]**

SOLUTION We find that

$$(\text{LHD at } x=1) = \lim_{x\to 1^-} \frac{f(x)-f(1)}{x-1} = \lim_{x\to 1^-} \frac{x-1}{x-1} = \lim_{x\to 1^-} 1 = 1$$

and, $$(\text{RHD at } x=1) = \lim_{x\to 1^+} \frac{f(x)-f(1)}{x-1} = \lim_{x\to 1^+} \frac{x^2-1}{x-1} = \lim_{x\to 1^+} (x+1) = 1+1 = 2$$

Clearly, (LHD at $x=1$) $\neq$ (RHD at $x=1$). Hence, $f(x)$ is not differentiable at $x=1$.

EXAMPLE 6 *Show that the function* $f(x)=\begin{cases} x^2 \sin\left(\frac{1}{x}\right) & , \text{ if } x\neq 0 \\ 0 & , \text{ if } x=0 \end{cases}$ *is differentiable at* $x=0$ *and* $f'(0)=0$. **[NCERT EXEMPLAR]**

SOLUTION We observe that:

$$(\text{LHD at } x=0) = \lim_{x\to 0^-} \frac{f(x)-f(0)}{x-0} = \lim_{h\to 0} \frac{f(0-h)-f(0)}{0-h-0} = \lim_{h\to 0} \frac{f(-h)-f(0)}{-h}$$

$$= \lim_{h\to 0} \frac{(-h)^2 \sin\left(\frac{1}{-h}\right)-0}{-h} = \lim_{h\to 0} h \sin\left(\frac{1}{h}\right)$$

$$= 0\times(\text{an oscillating number between } -1 \text{ and } 1) = 0$$

and, $$(\text{RHD at } x=0) = \lim_{x\to 0^+} \frac{f(x)-f(0)}{x-0} = \lim_{h\to 0} \frac{f(0+h)-f(0)}{0+h-0}$$

$$= \lim_{h\to 0} \frac{f(h)-f(0)}{h} = \lim_{h\to 0} \frac{h^2 \sin\left(\frac{1}{h}\right)-0}{h} = \lim_{h\to 0} h \sin\left(\frac{1}{h}\right)$$

$$= 0\times(\text{an oscillating number between } -1 \text{ and } 1) = 0$$

$\therefore$ (LHD at $x=0$) = (RHD at $x=0$) = 0.

So, $f(x)$ is differentiable at $x=0$ and $f'(0)=0$.

EXAMPLE 7 *Show that the function* $f(x) = \begin{cases} x\sin\frac{1}{x} & , \text{ when } x\neq 0 \\ 0 & , \text{ when } x=0 \end{cases}$ *is continuous but not differentiable at* $x=0$.

SOLUTION For the continuity of the function refer Example 11 on page 9.8 of Chapter 9.

Now,

$$(\text{LHD at } x=0) = \lim_{x\to 0^-} \frac{f(x)-f(0)}{x-0} = \lim_{h\to 0} \frac{f(0-h)-f(0)}{0-h-0}$$

$$= \lim_{h\to 0} \frac{f(-h)-0}{-h} = \lim_{h\to 0} \frac{-h\sin\left(\frac{1}{-h}\right)}{-h} = -\lim_{h\to 0} \sin\left(\frac{1}{h}\right)$$

$= \text{A number which oscillates between } -1 \text{ and } 1$

$\therefore$ (LHD at $x = 0$) does not exist.

Similarly, it can be shown that RHD at $x = 0$ does not exist. Hence, $f(x)$ is not differentiable at $x = 0$.

EXAMPLE 8 *Show that the function $f(x) = |x+1| + |x-1|$ for all $x \in R$, is not differentiable at $x = -1$ and $x = 1$.* **[CBSE 2015]**

SOLUTION We have,

$$f(x) = |x-1| + |x+1| = \begin{cases} -(x+1)-(x-1) = -2x, & \text{if } x < -1 \\ x+1-(x-1) = 2, & \text{if } -1 \le x < 1 \\ x+1+x-1 = 2x, & \text{if } x \ge 1 \end{cases}$$

Differentiability at $x = -1$: We find that

$$(\text{LHD at } x = -1) = \lim_{x \to -1^-} \frac{f(x) - f(-1)}{x - (-1)}$$

$$= \lim_{x \to -1^-} \frac{-2x-2}{x+1} = \lim_{x \to -1^-} \frac{-2(x+1)}{x+1} = \lim_{x \to -1^-} (-2) = -2$$

$$(\text{RHD at } x = -1) = \lim_{x \to -1^+} \frac{f(x) - f(-1)}{x - (-1)} = \lim_{x \to -1^+} \frac{2-2}{x+1} = \lim_{x \to -1^+} \frac{0}{x+1} = \lim_{x \to -1^+} 0 = 0$$

$\therefore$ (LHD at $x = -1$) $\neq$ (RHD at $x = -1$). So, $f(x)$ is not differentiable at $x = -1$.

Differentiability at $x = 1$: We find that

$$(\text{LHD at } x = 1) = \lim_{x \to 1^-} \frac{f(x) - f(1)}{x - 1} = \lim_{x \to 1^-} \frac{2-2}{x-1} = \lim_{x \to 1^-} \frac{0}{x-1} = \lim_{x \to 1^-} 0 = 0$$

$$(\text{RHD at } x = 1) = \lim_{x \to 1^+} \frac{f(x) - f(1)}{x - 1} = \lim_{x \to 1^+} \frac{2x-2}{x-1} = \lim_{x \to 1^+} 2\left(\frac{x-1}{x-1}\right) = \lim_{x \to 1^+} 2 = 2$$

$\therefore$ (LHD at $x = 1$) $\neq$ (RHD at $x = 1$)

So, $f(x)$ is not differentiable at $x = 1$. Hence, $f(x)$ is not differentiable at $x = -1$ and $x = 1$.

EXAMPLE 9 *If $f(x)$ is differentiale at $x = a$, find* $\lim\limits_{x \to a} \frac{x f(a) - a f(x)}{x - a}$.

SOLUTION It given that $f(x)$ is differentiable at $x = a$. Therefore, $\lim\limits_{x \to a} \frac{f(x) - f(a)}{x - a}$ exists finitely.

Let $\lim\limits_{x \to a} \frac{f(x) - f(a)}{x - a} = f'(a)$

Now, $$\lim_{x \to a} \frac{x f(a) - a f(x)}{x - a} = \lim_{x \to a} \frac{x f(a) - a f(a) + a f(a) - a f(x)}{x - a}$$

$$= \lim_{x \to a} \frac{(x-a) f(a) - a\{f(x) - f(a)\}}{x - a} = \lim_{x \to a} \frac{(x-a) f(a)}{x - a} - a \lim_{x \to a} \frac{f(x) - f(a)}{x - a}$$

$$= \lim_{x \to a} f(a) - a \lim_{x \to a} \frac{f(x) - f(a)}{x - a} = f(a) - a f'(a)$$

EXAMPLE 10 *If $f(2) = 4$ and $f'(2) = 1$, then find* $\lim\limits_{x \to 2} \frac{x f(2) - 2f(x)}{x - 2}$.

SOLUTION Using definition of derivative, we obtain

$$\lim_{x \to 2} \frac{f(x) - f(2)}{x - 2} = f'(2) \Rightarrow \lim_{x \to 2} \frac{f(x) - f(2)}{x - 2} = 1 \qquad [\because f'(2) = 1] \qquad \ldots(i)$$

Now,

$$\lim_{x \to 2} \frac{x f(2) - 2f(x)}{x - 2} = \lim_{x \to 2} \frac{x f(2) - 2 f(2) + 2f(2) - 2 f(x)}{x - 2}$$

$$= \lim_{x \to 2} \frac{(x - 2) f(2) - 2 (f(x) - f(2))}{x - 2} = \lim_{x \to 2} \frac{(x - 2) f(2)}{x - 2} - 2 \lim_{x \to 2} \frac{f(x) - f(2)}{x - 2}$$

$$= f(2) - 2 f'(2) = 4 - 2 \times 1 = 2 \qquad [\text{Using (i) and } f(2) = 4]$$

EXAMPLE 11 *If $f(x)$ is differentiable at $x = a$, find* $\lim_{x \to a} \frac{x^2 f(a) - a^2 f(x)}{x - a}$.

SOLUTION It is given that $f(x)$ is differentiable at $x = a$. Therefore, $\lim_{x \to a} \frac{f(x) - f(a)}{x - a}$ exists finitely.

Let $\lim_{x \to a} \frac{f(x) - f(a)}{x - a} = f'(a)$ ...(i)

Now, $$\lim_{x \to a} \frac{x^2 f(a) - a^2 f(x)}{x - a} = \lim_{x \to a} \frac{x^2 f(a) - a^2 f(a) + a^2 f(a) - a^2 f(x)}{x - a}$$

$$= \lim_{x \to a} \frac{(x^2 - a^2) f(a) - a^2 \{f(x) - f(a)\}}{x - a} = \lim_{x \to a} \left\{ \frac{(x^2 - a^2) f(a)}{x - a} - a^2 \left(\frac{f(x) - f(a)}{x - a} \right) \right\}$$

$$= \lim_{x \to a} (x + a) f(a) - a^2 \lim_{x \to a} \frac{f(x) - f(a)}{x - a} = 2a f(a) - a^2 f'(a) \qquad [\text{Using (i)}]$$

BASED ON HIGHER ORDER THINKING SKILLS (HOTS)

EXAMPLE 12 *Discuss the differentiability of* $f(x) = \begin{cases} x e^{-\left(\frac{1}{|x|} + \frac{1}{x}\right)} & , x \neq 0 \\ 0 & , x = 0 \end{cases}$ *at $x = 0$.*

SOLUTION We observe that:

$$f(x) = \begin{cases} x e^{-\left(\frac{1}{x} + \frac{1}{x}\right)} = x e^{-2/x}, & x > 0 \\ 0 & , x = 0 \\ x e^{-\left(\frac{-1}{x} + \frac{1}{x}\right)} = x & , x < 0 \end{cases}$$

Now, $$(\text{LHD at } x = 0) = \lim_{x \to 0^-} \frac{f(x) - f(0)}{x - 0} = \lim_{x \to 0} \frac{x - 0}{x - 0} = 1 \qquad [\because f(x) = x \text{ for } x < 0 \text{ and } f(0) = 0]$$

and, $$(\text{RHD at } x = 0) = \lim_{x \to 0^+} \frac{f(x) - f(0)}{x - 0}$$

$$= \lim_{x \to 0} \frac{x e^{-2/x} - 0}{x} \qquad [\because f(x) = x e^{-2x} \text{ for } x > 0 \text{ and } f(0) = 0]$$

$$= \lim_{x \to 0} e^{-2/x} = 0.$$

$\therefore$ (LHD at $x = 0$) $\neq$ (RHD at $x = 0$). So, $f(x)$ is not differentiable at $x = 0$.

EXAMPLE 13 *For what choice of a and b is the function* $f(x)=\begin{cases} x^2 & , x \le c \\ ax+b, & x>c \end{cases}$ *is differentiable at* $x = c$.

SOLUTION It is given that $f(x)$ is differentiable at $x=c$ and every differentiable function is continuous. So, $f(x)$ is continuous at $x = c$.

$$\therefore \quad \lim_{x \to c^-} f(x) = \lim_{x \to c^+} f(x) = f(c)$$

$$\Rightarrow \quad \lim_{x \to c} x^2 = \lim_{x \to c} (ax+b) = c^2 \qquad \text{[Using definition of } f(x)]$$

$$\Rightarrow \quad c^2 = ac+b \qquad \text{...(i)}$$

Now, $f(x)$ is differentiable at $x = c$

$\Rightarrow$ (LHD at $x = c$) = (RHD at $x = c$)

$$\Rightarrow \quad \lim_{x \to c^-} \frac{f(x)-f(c)}{x-c} = \lim_{x \to c^+} \frac{f(x)-f(c)}{x-c}$$

$$\Rightarrow \quad \lim_{x \to c} \frac{x^2-c^2}{x-c} = \lim_{x \to c} \frac{(ax+b)-c^2}{x-c} \qquad \text{[Using definition of } f(x)]$$

$$\Rightarrow \quad \lim_{x \to c} \frac{x^2-c^2}{x-c} = \lim_{x \to c} \frac{ax+b-(ac+b)}{x-c} \qquad \text{[Using (i)]}$$

$$\Rightarrow \quad \lim_{x \to c} (x+c) = \lim_{x \to c} \frac{a(x-c)}{x-c} \Rightarrow \lim_{x \to c} (x+c) = \lim_{x \to c} a \Rightarrow 2c = a \qquad \text{...(ii)}$$

From (i) and (ii), we get : $c^2 = 2c^2 + b \Rightarrow b = -c^2$. Hence, $a = 2c$ and $b = -c^2$.

EXAMPLE 14 *A function* $f: R \to R$ *satisfies that equation* $f(x+y) = f(x)\, f(y)$ *for all* $x, y \in R$, $f(x) \ne 0$. *Suppose that the function* $f(x)$ *is differentiable at* $x = 0$ *and* $f'(0) = 2$. *Prove that* $f'(x) = 2f(x)$.

[NCERT EXEMPLAR]

SOLUTION We have, $f(x+y) = f(x)\, f(y)$ for all $x, y \in R$

$$\therefore \quad f(0+0) = f(0)\, f(0) \qquad \text{[Putting } x=0, y=0]$$

$$\Rightarrow \quad f(0) = f(0)\, f(0)$$

$$\Rightarrow \quad f(0)\{1-f(0)\} = 0 \qquad [\because f(x) \ne 0 \text{ for any } x \therefore f(0) \ne 0]$$

$$\Rightarrow \quad 1 - f(0) = 0 \Rightarrow f(0) = 1$$

It is given that $f(x)$ is differentiable at $x = 0$ and $f'(0) = 2$.

$$\therefore \quad f'(0) = \lim_{h \to 0} \frac{f(0+h)-f(0)}{h} \qquad \left[\text{Putting } c = 0 \text{ in } f'(c) = \lim_{h \to 0} \frac{f(c+h)-f(c)}{h}\right]$$

$$\Rightarrow \quad 2 = \lim_{h \to 0} \frac{f(h)-f(0)}{h} \Rightarrow 2 = \lim_{h \to 0} \frac{f(h)-1}{h} \qquad \text{...(i)}$$

Now,

$$f'(x) = \lim_{h \to 0} \frac{f(x+h)-f(x)}{h}$$

$$\Rightarrow \quad f'(x) = \lim_{h \to 0} \frac{f(x)f(h)-f(x)}{h} \qquad [\because f(x+y) = f(x)\, f(y) \text{ for all } x, y \in R \;\therefore\; f(x+h) = f(x)\, f(h)]$$

$$\Rightarrow \quad f'(x) = f(x) \lim_{h \to 0} \frac{f(h)-1}{h} \Rightarrow f'(x) = 2f(x) \qquad \text{[Using (i)]}$$

Hence, $f'(x) = 2f(x)$.

EXERCISE 9.1

BASIC

1. Show that $f(x) = |x - 3|$ is continuous but not differentiable at $x = 3$. [CBSE 2012, 2013]

2. Show that $f(x) = \begin{cases} 12x - 13, & \text{if } x \le 3 \\ 2x^2 + 5, & \text{if } x > 3 \end{cases}$ is differentiable at $x = 3$. Also, find $f'(3)$.

3. Show that the function f defined by $f(x) = \begin{cases} 3x - 2, & 0 < x \le 1 \\ 2x^2 - x, & 1 < x \le 2 \\ 5x - 4, & x > 2 \end{cases}$ is continuous at $x = 2$, but not differentiable thereat. [CBSE 2010]

4. Find whether the following function is differentiable at $x = 1$ and $x = 2$ or not:

$$f(x) = \begin{cases} x, & x < 1 \\ 2 - x, & 1 \le x \le 2 \\ -2 + 3x - x^2, & x > 2 \end{cases}$$ [CBSE 2015]

5. Check whether the function $f(x) = x^2|x|$ is differentiable at $x = 0$ or not. [CBSE 2024]

BASED ON LOTS

6. Show that $f(x) = x^{1/3}$ is not differentiable at $x = 0$.

7. Discuss the continuity and differentiability of the function $f(x) = |x| + |x - 1|$ in the interval $(-1, 2)$. [CBSE 2015]

8. Find the values of a and b so that the function $f(x) = \begin{cases} x^2 + 3x + a, & \text{if } x \le 1 \\ bx + 2, & \text{if } x > 1 \end{cases}$ is differentiable at each $x \in R$. [NCERT EXEMPLAR, CBSE 2016]

9. If $f(x) = \begin{cases} ax^2 - b, & \text{if } |x| < 1 \\ \dfrac{1}{|x|}, & \text{if } |x| \ge 1 \end{cases}$ is differentiable at $x = 1$, find a, b.

BASED ON HOTS

10. Show that the function $f(x) = \begin{cases} x^m \sin\left(\dfrac{1}{x}\right), & x \ne 0 \\ 0, & x = 0 \end{cases}$ is

(i) differentiable at $x = 0$, if $m > 1$

(ii) continuous but not differentiable at $x = 0$, if $0 < m < 1$

(iii) neither continuous nor differentiable, if $m \le 0$

11. Show that the function $f(x) = \begin{cases} |2x - 3|\,[x], & x \ge 1 \\ \sin\left(\dfrac{\pi x}{2}\right), & x < 1 \end{cases}$ is continuous but not differentiable at $x = 1$.

ANSWERS

3. 12
4. Not differentiable at $x = 1$, but differentiable at $x = 2$.
5. Differentiable
7. Continuous on $(-1, 2)$ but not differentiable at $x = 0, 1$.
8. $a = 3, b = 5$
9. $a = -1/2, b = -3/2$

HINTS TO SELECTED PROBLEMS

7. Use (LHD at $x = 1$) = (RHD at $x = 1$) and, $\lim_{x \to 1^-} f(x) = \lim_{x \to 1^+} f(x) = f(1)$

8. $f(x)$ can be re-written as : $f(x) = \begin{cases} -\dfrac{1}{x} & , \text{ if } x \le -1 \\ (ax^2 - b) & , \text{ if } -1 < x < 1 \\ \dfrac{1}{x} & , \text{ if } x \ge 1 \end{cases}$

Now, check continuity and differentiability of $f(x)$.

10. $f(x)$ can be re-written as : $f(x) = \begin{cases} (2x-3)[x] & , x \ge \dfrac{3}{2} \\ -(2x-3) & , 1 \le x < \dfrac{3}{2} \\ \sin\left(\dfrac{\pi x}{2}\right) & , x < 1 \end{cases}$

Now, check continuity and differentiablility of $f(x)$.

9.2 DIFFERENTIABILITY IN A SET

A function $f(x)$ defined on an open interval (a, b) is said to be differentiable or derivable in open interval (a, b) if it is differentiable at each point of (a, b).

A function $f(x)$ defined on $[a, b]$ is said to be differentiable or derivable at the end points a and b if it is differentiable from the right at a and from the left at b.

In other words, $\lim_{x \to a^+} \dfrac{f(x) - f(a)}{x - a}$ and $\lim_{x \to b^-} \dfrac{f(x) - f(b)}{x - b}$ both exist.

If f is derivable in the open interval (a, b) and also at the end points a and b, then f is said to be derivable in the closed interval $[a, b]$.

A function f is said to be a differentiable function if it is differentiable at every point of its domain.

If a function is differentiable at each $x \in R$, then it is said to be every where differentiable.

For example, a constant function, a polynomial function, $\sin x$, $\cos x$ etc. are everywhere differentiable.

SOME USEFUL RESULTS ON DIFFERENTIABILITY

(i) Every polynomial function is differentiable at each $x \in R$.

(ii) The exponential function a^x, $a > 0$ is differentiable at each $x \in R$.

(iii) Every constant function is differentiable at each $x \in R$.

(iv) The logarithmic function is differentiable at each point in its domian.

(v) Trigonometric and inverse-trigonometric functions are differentiable in their respective domains.

(vi) The sum, difference, product and quotient of two differentiable functions is differentiable.

(vii) The composition of differentiable function is a differentiable function.

(viii) If a function $f(x)$ is differentiable at every point in its domain, then

$$\lim_{h \to 0} \frac{f(x+h) - f(x)}{h} \text{ or, } \lim_{h \to 0} \frac{f(x-h) - f(x)}{-h}$$

is called the derivative or differentiation of f at x and is denoted by $f'(x)$ or, $\frac{d}{dx}(f(x))$.

ILLUSTRATIVE EXAMPLES

BASED ON BASIC CONCEPTS (BASIC)

EXAMPLE 1 *If $f(x) = x^2 + 2x + 7$, find $f'(3)$.*

SOLUTION We know that a polynomial function is everywhere differentiable. Therefore, $f(x)$ is differentiable at $x = 3$.

$$\therefore \quad f'(3) = \lim_{h \to 0} \frac{f(3+h) - f(3)}{h}$$

$$\Rightarrow \quad f'(3) = \lim_{h \to 0} \frac{\{(3+h)^2 + 2(3+h) + 7\} - \{9 + 6 + 7\}}{h} = \lim_{h \to 0} \frac{8h + h^2}{h} = \lim_{h \to 0} (8 + h) = 8.$$

EXAMPLE 2 *Find $f'(2)$ and $f'(5)$ when $f(x) = x^2 + 7x + 4$.*

SOLUTION We know that a polynomial function is everywhere differentiable. Therefore, $f(x)$ is everywhere differentiable. The derivative of f at x is given by

$$f'(x) = \lim_{h \to 0} \frac{f(x+h) - f(x)}{h} = \lim_{h \to 0} \frac{\{(x+h)^2 + 7(x+h) + 4\} - \{x^2 + 7x + 4\}}{h}$$

$$= \lim_{h \to 0} \frac{2hx + 7h + h^2}{h} = \lim_{h \to 0} (2x + 7 + h) = 2x + 7$$

Putting $x = 2$ and $x = 5$ respectively in $f'(x) = 2x + 7$, we get

$$\therefore \quad f'(2) = 2 \times 2 + 7 = 11 \text{ and } f'(5) = 2 \times 5 + 7 = 17.$$

EXAMPLE 3 *For the function f given by $f(x) = x^2 - 6x + 8$, prove that $f'(5) - 3f'(2) = f'(8)$.*

SOLUTION Clearly, $f(x)$ being a polynomial function, is everywhere differentiable. The derivative of f at x is given by

$$f'(x) = \lim_{h \to 0} \frac{f(x+h) - f(x)}{h} = \lim_{h \to 0} \frac{\{(x+h)^2 - 6(x+h) + 8\} - \{x^2 - 6x + 8\}}{h}$$

$$= \lim_{h \to 0} \frac{2hx - 6h + h^2}{h} = \lim_{h \to 0} (2x - 6 + h) = 2x - 6$$

$$\therefore \quad f'(5) - 3f'(2) = (2 \times 5 - 6) - 3(2 \times 2 - 6) = 4 + 6 = 10 \text{ and, } f'(8) = 2 \times 8 - 6 = 10.$$

Hence, $f'(5) - 3f'(2) = f'(8)$.

BASED ON LOWER ORDER THINKING SKILLS (LOTS)

EXAMPLE 4 *Discuss the continuity and differentiability of* $f(x) = \begin{cases} 1 - x & , \ x < 1 \\ (1-x)(2-x), & 1 \le x \le 2 \\ 3 - x & , \ x > 2 \end{cases}$

SOLUTION When $x < 1$, we have $f(x) = 1 - x$. We know that a polynomial function is everywhere continuous and differentiable. So, $f(x)$ is continuous and differentiable for all $x < 1$.

Similarly, $f(x)$ is continuous and differentiable for all $x \in (1, 2)$ and $x > 2$.

Thus, the possible points where we have to check the continuity and differentiability of $f(x)$ are $x = 1$ and $x = 2$.

Continuity at $x = 1$: We find that:

$$\lim_{x \to 1^-} f(x) = \lim_{x \to 1} (1 - x) = 1 - 1 = 0 \qquad [\because f(x) = 1 - x \text{ for } x < 1]$$

$$\lim_{x \to 1^+} f(x) = \lim_{x \to 1} (1 - x)(2 - x) = 0 \qquad [\because f(x) = (1 - x)(2 - x), \text{ for } 1 \le x \le 2]$$

and, $f(1) = (1 - 1)(2 - 1) = 0.$

$\therefore \quad \lim_{x \to 1^-} f(x) = \lim_{x \to 1^+} f(x) = f(1)$. So, $f(x)$ is continuous at $x = 1$.

Continuity at $x = 2$: We find that:

$$\lim_{x \to 2^-} f(x) = \lim_{x \to 2} (1 - x)(2 - x) = (2 - 1)(2 - 2) = 0 \qquad [\because f(x) = (1 - x)(2 - x) \text{ for } 1 \le x \le 2]$$

and, $\lim_{x \to 2^+} f(x) = \lim_{x \to 2} (3 - x) = 3 - 2 = 1 \qquad [\because f(x) = 3 - x \text{ for } x > 2]$

$\therefore \quad \lim_{x \to 2^-} f(x) \ne \lim_{x \to 2} f(x)$. So, $f(x)$ is not continuous at $x = 2$.

Differentiability at $x = 1$: We observe that:

$$(\text{LHD at } x = 1) = \lim_{x \to 1^-} \frac{f(x) - f(1)}{x - 1} = \lim_{x \to 1} \frac{(1 - x) - 0}{x - 1} \qquad [\text{Using definition of } f(x)]$$

$$= - \lim_{x \to 1} \frac{x - 1}{x - 1} = -1$$

and, $(\text{RHD at } x = 1) = \lim_{x \to 1^+} \frac{f(x) - f(1)}{x - 1} = \lim_{x \to 1} \frac{(1 - x)(2 - x) - 0}{x - 1} \qquad [\text{Using definition of } f(x)]$

$$= \lim_{x \to 1} \frac{(x - 1)(x - 2)}{x - 1} = \lim_{x \to 1} x - 2 = 1 - 2 = -1$$

Clearly, (LHD at $x = 1$) = (RHD at $x = 1$). So, $f(x)$ is differentiable at $x = 1$.

Differentiability at $x = 2$: Since $f(x)$ is not continuous at $x = 2$. So, it is not differentiable at $x = 2$.

EXAMPLE 5 *Discuss the differentiability of $f(x) = |x - 1| + |x - 2|$.*

SOLUTION We have,

$$f(x) = |x - 1| + |x - 2|$$

$$\Rightarrow \quad f(x) = \begin{cases} -(x - 1) - (x - 2) & \text{for } x < 1 \\ x - 1 - (x - 2) & \text{for } 1 \le x < 2 \\ (x - 1) + (x - 2) & \text{for } x \ge 2 \end{cases} \Rightarrow f(x) = \begin{cases} -2x + 3 & , x < 1 \\ 1 & , 1 \le x < 2 \\ 2x - 3 & , x \ge 2 \end{cases}$$

When $x < 1$, we have $f(x) = -2x + 3$ which, being a polynomial function is continuous and differentiable.

When $1 \le x < 2$, we have $f(x) = 1$ which, being a constant function, is differentiable on $(1, 2)$.

When $x \ge 2$, we have $f(x) = 2x - 3$ which, being a polynomial function, is differentiable for all $x > 2$.

Thus, the possible points of non-differentiability of $f(x)$ are $x = 1$ and $x = 2$. So, let us check the differentiability of $f(x)$ at these points.

Differentiability at $x = 1$:

$$(\text{LHD at } x = 1) = \lim_{x \to 1^-} \frac{f(x) - f(1)}{x - 1} = \lim_{x \to 1} \frac{(-2x + 3) - 1}{x - 1} \qquad [\because f(x) = -2x + 3 \text{ for } x < 1]$$

$$= \lim_{x \to 1} \frac{-2(x-1)}{x-1} = \lim_{x \to 1} = -2 = -2$$

and, $\quad$ (RHD at $x = 1$) $= \lim_{x \to 1^+} \frac{f(x) - f(1)}{x-1} = \lim_{x \to 1} \frac{1-1}{x-1} = 0. \quad [\because f(x) = 1 \text{ for } 1 \le x < 2]$

$\therefore$ $\quad$ (LHD at $x = 1$) $\neq$ (RHD at $x = 1$). So, $f(x)$ is not differentiable at $x = 1$.

Differentiability at $x = 2$:

(LHD at $x = 2$) $= \lim_{x \to 2^-} \frac{f(x) - f(2)}{x-2}$

$= \lim_{x \to 2} \frac{1-(2 \times 2 - 3)}{x-2} \quad [\because f(x) = 1 \text{ for } 1 \le x < 2 \;\&\; f(2) = 2 \times 2 - 3]$

$= \lim_{x \to 2} \frac{1-1}{x-2} = 0.$

and, $\quad$ (RHD at $x = 2$) $= \lim_{x \to 2^+} \frac{f(x) - f(2)}{x-2}$

$= \lim_{x \to 2} \frac{(2x-3)-(2 \times 2 - 3)}{x-2} \quad [\because f(x) = 2x - 3 \text{ for } x \ge 2]$

$= \lim_{x \to 2} \frac{2x-4}{x-2} = \lim_{x \to 2} \frac{2(x-2)}{x-2} = 2$

$\therefore$ $\quad$ (LHD at $x = 2$) $\neq$ (RHD at $= 2$). So, $f(x)$ is not differentiable at $x = 2$.

REMARK *The function f(x) given by $f(x) = |x - a_1| + |x - a_2| + |x - a_3| + \ldots + |x - a_n|$ is not differentiable at $x = a_1, a_2, a_3, \ldots, a_n$. However, it is continuous at these points.*

BASED ON HIGHER ORDER THINKING SKILLS (HOTS)

EXAMPLE 6 *If* $f(x) = \begin{cases} ax + b\,; & 0 < x \le 1 \\ 2x^2 - x\,; & 1 < x < 2 \end{cases}$ *is a differentiable function in* $(0, 2)$, *then find the values of a and b.* **[CBSE 2023]**

SOLUTION $\;$ For $0 < x \le 1$, we have $f(x) = ax + b$ which is a polynomial function. Also, $f(x) = 2x^2 - x$ is a polynomial function for $1 < x < 2$. We know that a polynomial function is everywhere differentiable. So, we shall use the diffferentiability of $f(x)$ at $x = 1$ to find the values of a and b.

Now, $\quad f(x)$ is differentiable at $x = 1$

$\Rightarrow \quad f(x)$ is continuous at $x = 1$

$\Rightarrow \quad \lim_{x \to 1^-} f(x) = \lim_{x \to 1^+} f(x) = f(1)$

$\Rightarrow \quad \lim_{x \to 1} ax + b = \lim_{x \to 1} 2x^2 - x = a \times 1 + b \Rightarrow a + b = 1 \quad$ ...(i)

Again, $f(x)$ is differentiable at $x = 1$.

$\Rightarrow \quad$ (LHD at $x = 1$) $=$ (RHD at $x = 1$)

$\Rightarrow \quad \lim_{x \to 1^-} \frac{f(x) - f(1)}{x-1} = \lim_{x \to 1^+} \frac{f(x) - f(1)}{x-1}$

$\Rightarrow \quad \lim_{x \to 1} \frac{(ax+b)-(a+b)}{x-1} = \lim_{x \to 1} \frac{(2x^2 - x)-(a+b)}{x-1}$

$\Rightarrow \quad \lim_{x \to 1} \frac{a(x-1)}{x-1} = \lim_{x \to 1} \frac{2x^2 - x - 1}{x-1}$ [Using (i)]

$\Rightarrow \quad a \lim_{x \to 1} \frac{x-1}{x-1} = \lim_{x \to 1} \frac{(2x+1)(x-1)}{x-1} \Rightarrow a \times 1 = \lim_{x \to 1} (2x+1) \Rightarrow a = 3$ ...(ii)

From (i) and (ii), we obtain: $a = 3$ and $b = -2$.

EXAMPLE 7 *If* $f(x) = \begin{cases} x^2 + 3x + a, & \text{for } x \le 1 \\ bx + 2, & \text{for } x > 1 \end{cases}$ *is everywhere differentiable, find the values of a and b.*

SOLUTION For $x \le 1$, we have $f(x) = x^2 + 3x + a$ which is a polynomial. For $x > 1$, we have $f(x) = bx + 2$ which is also a polynomial. Since a polynomial function is everywhere differentiable. Therefore, $f(x)$ is differentiable for all $x > 1$ and also for all $x < 1$. Thus, we have to use the differentiability of $f(x)$ at $x = 1$ to find the values of a and b.

Now,

$f(x)$ is differentiable at $x = 1$

$\Rightarrow \quad f(x)$ is continuous at $x = 1$

$\Rightarrow \quad \lim_{x \to 1^-} f(x) = \lim_{x \to 1^+} f(x) = f(1)$

$\Rightarrow \quad \lim_{x \to 1} x^2 + 3x + a = \lim_{x \to 1} bx + 2 = 1 + 3 + a \Rightarrow 1 + 3 + a = b + 2 \Rightarrow a - b + 2 = 0$ ...(i)

Again, $f(x)$ is differentiable at $x = 1$.

$\Rightarrow \quad$ (LHD at $x = 1$) = (RHD at $x = 1$)

$\Rightarrow \quad \lim_{x \to 1^-} \frac{f(x) - f(1)}{x - 1} = \lim_{x \to 1^+} \frac{f(x) - f(1)}{x - 1}$

$\Rightarrow \quad \lim_{x \to 1} \frac{x^2 + 3x + a - (4 + a)}{x - 1} = \lim_{x \ 1} \frac{(bx + 2) - (4 + a)}{x - 1}$

$\Rightarrow \quad \lim_{x \to 1} \frac{x^2 + 3x - 4}{x - 1} = \lim_{x \to 1} \frac{bx - (2 + a)}{x - 1}$

$\Rightarrow \quad \lim_{x \to 1} \frac{(x + 4)(x - 1)}{x - 1} = \lim_{x \to 1} \frac{bx - b}{x - 1}$ [From (i), $2 + a = b$]

$\Rightarrow \quad \lim_{x \to 1} (x + 4) = \lim_{x \to 1} b \Rightarrow 5 = b.$

Putting $b = 5$ in (i), we get $a = 3$. Hence, $a = 3$ and $b = 5$.

EXAMPLE 8 *Discuss the differentiability of* $f(x) = |\log_e x|$ *for* $x > 0$.

SOLUTION We have,

$$f(x) = |\log_e x| = \begin{cases} -\log_e x, & \text{for } 0 < x < 1 \\ \log_e x, & \text{for } x \ge 1 \end{cases}$$

Clearly, $f(x)$ is differentiable for all $x > 1$ as well as for all $x < 1$. So, we have to check its differentiability at $x = 1$.

We have,

$$(\text{LHD at } x = 1) = \lim_{x \to 1^-} \frac{f(x) - f(1)}{x - 1}$$

$$= \lim_{x \to 1^-} \frac{-\log x - \log 1}{x - 1} \qquad [\because f(x) = -\log_e x \text{ for } 0 < x < 1]$$

$$= -\lim_{x \to 1^-} \frac{\log x}{x-1} = -\lim_{h \to 0} \frac{\log(1-h)}{1-h-1} = -\lim_{h \to 0} \frac{\log(1-h)}{-h} = -1$$

and, $$(\text{RHD at } x = 1) = \lim_{x \to 1^+} \frac{f(x) - f(1)}{x - 1}$$

$$= \lim_{x \to 1^+} \frac{\log x - \log 1}{x - 1} = \lim_{h \to 0} \frac{\log(1+h)}{1+h-1} = \lim_{h \to 0} \frac{\log(1+h)}{h} = 1$$

Clearly, (LHD at $x = 1$) $\neq$ (RHD at $x = 1$). So, $f(x)$ is not differentiable at $x = 1$.

EXERCISE 9.2

BASIC

1. If f is defined by $f(x) = x^2$, find $f'(2)$.
2. If f is defined by $f(x) = x^2 - 4x + 7$, show that $f'(5) = 2f'\left(\frac{7}{2}\right)$
3. Show that the derivative of the function f given by $f(x) = 2x^3 - 9x^2 + 12x + 9$, at $x = 1$ and $x = 2$ are equal.
4. If for the function $\Phi(x) = \lambda x^2 + 7x - 4$, $\Phi'(5) = 97$, find λ.
5. If $f(x) = x^3 + 7x^2 + 8x - 9$, find $f'(4)$.
6. Find the derivative of the function f defined by $f(x) = mx + c$ at $x = 0$.

BASED ON LOTS

7. Examine the differentiability of the function f defined by

$$f(x) = \begin{cases} 2x + 3, & \text{if } -3 \le x < -2 \\ x + 1, & \text{if } -2 \le x < 0 \\ x + 2, & \text{if } \quad 0 \le x \le 1 \end{cases}$$ [NCERT EXEMPLAR]

8. Write an example of a function which is everywhere continuous but fails to be differentiable exactly at five points.

BASED ON HOTS

9. Discuss the continuity and differentiability of $f(x) = |\log|x||$.
10. Discuss the continuity and differentiability of $f(x) = e^{|x|}$.
11. Discuss the continuity and differentiability of $f(x) = \begin{cases} (x-c)\cos\left(\frac{1}{x-c}\right), & x \neq c \\ 0, & x = c \end{cases}$
12. Is $|\sin x|$ differentiable? What about $\cos|x|$?
13. Find the values of a and b so that the following function is differentiable for all values of x:

$$f(x) = \begin{cases} ax + b, & x > -1 \\ bx^2 - 3, & x \le -1 \end{cases}$$ [CBSE 2024]

ANSWERS

1. 4 4. 9 5. 112 6. m
7. Not differentiable at $x = 0$ and $x = -2$. 8. $f(x) = |x| + |x-1| + |x-2| + |x-3| + |x-4|$
9. Not differentiable at $x = \pm 1$ 10. Not differentiable at $x = 0$
11. Not differentiable at $x = c$
12. $|\sin x|$ is not differentiable at $x = n\pi, n \in Z$, $\cos|x|$ is everywhere differentiable.
13. $a = 3,\ b = -\frac{3}{2}$

FILL IN THE BLANKS TYPE QUESTIONS (FBQs)

1. The function $f(x) = |x+1|$ is not differentiable at $x =$ ....
2. The function $g(x) = |x-1| + |x+1|$ is not differentiable at $x =$ ....
3. The set of points where $f(x) = x - [x]$ not differentiable is ....
4. The number of points in $[-\pi, \pi]$ where $f(x) = \sin^{-1}(\sin x)$ is not differentiable is ....
5. The function $f(x) = \cos^{-1}(\cos x),\ x \in (-2\pi, 2\pi)$ is not differentiable at $x =$ ....
6. The function $f(x) = |\sin x|, \left[-\frac{\pi}{2}, \frac{\pi}{2}\right]$ is not differentiable at $x =$ ....
7. Let $f(x) = \begin{cases} ax^2 + 3, & x > 1 \\ x + \frac{5}{2}, & x \le 1 \end{cases}$. If $f(x)$ is differentiable at $x = 1$, then $a =$ ....
8. If $f(x) = x|x|$, then $f'(-1) =$ ....
9. If $f(x) = x|x|$, then $f'(2) =$ ....
10. The set of point where the function $f(x) = |2x-1|$ is differentiable, is ....
11. The set of points where the function $f(x) = \begin{cases} x+1, & x < 2 \\ 2x-1, & x \ge 2 \end{cases}$ is not differentiable, is ....
12. An example of a function which is everywhere continuous but fails to be differentiable exactly at two points is ....
13. The set of points where $f(x) = \cos|x|$ is differentiable, is ....
14. The set of points where $f(x) = |\sin x|$ is not differentiable, is ....
15. The set of points at which the function $f(x) = \frac{1}{\log|x|}$ is not differentiable, is ....
16. The greatest integer function $f(x) = [x],\ 0 < x < 2$ is not differentiable at $x =$......

[CBSE 2020]

ANSWERS

1. -1 2. ± 1 3. Z 4. 2 5. $\pm \pi$ 6. 0 7. $a = \frac{1}{2}$ 8. 2
9. 4 10. $R - \left\{\frac{1}{2}\right\}$ 11. $\{2\}$ 12. $f(x) = |x-1| + |x-2|$ 13. R
14. $\{0\}$ 15. $\{-1, 0, 1\}$ 16. $x = 1$

VERY SHORT ANSWERS QUESTIONS (VSAQs)

Answer each of the following questions in one word or one sentence or as per exact requirement of the question:

1. Define differentiability of a function at a point.
2. Is every differentiable function continuous?
3. Is every continuous function differentiable?
4. Give an example of a function which is continuous but not differentiable at a point.
5. If $f(x)$ is differentiable at $x = c$, then write the value of $\lim_{x \to c} f(x)$.
6. If $f(x) = |x - 2|$ write whether $f'(2)$ exists or not.
7. Write the points where $f(x) = |\log_e x|$ is not differentiable.
8. Write the points of non-differentiability of $f(x) = |\log |x||$.
9. Write the derivative of $f(x) = |x|^3$ at $x = 0$.
10. Write the number of points where $f(x) = |x| + |x - 1|$ is continuous but not differentiable.
11. If $\lim_{x \to c} \frac{f(x) - f(c)}{x - c}$ exists finitely, write the value of $\lim_{x \to c} f(x)$.
12. Write the value of the derivative of $f(x) = |x - 1| + |x - 3|$ at $x = 2$.
13. If $f(x) = \sqrt{x^2 + 9}$, write the value of $\lim_{x \to 4} \frac{f(x) - f(4)}{x - 4}$.
14. Check the differentiability of $f(x) = [x]$ at $x = -3$, where $[\cdot]$ denotes the greatest integer function. [CBSE 2024]
15. Show that the function $f(x) = |x|^3$ is differentiable at all points of its domain. [CBSE 2024]
16. Check the differentiability of $f(x) = |x - 5|$ at $x = 5$. [CBSE 2024]
17. Check the differentiablility of $f(x) = \begin{cases} x^2 + 1, 0 \le x < 1 \\ 3 - x, 1 \le x \le 2 \end{cases}$ [CBSE 2024]

ANSWERS

2. Yes 3. No 4. $f(x) = |x|$ at $x = 0$ 5. $f(c)$ 6. Does not exist 7. 1
8. ± 1 9. 0 10. $x = 0, 1$ 11. $f(c)$ 12. 0 13. $\frac{4}{5}$
14. Not differentiable 16. Not differentiable 17. Not differentiable

CHAPTER 10

DIFFERENTIATION

10.1 INTRODUCTION

In the previous chapter, we have learnt about differentiability of a function at a point. The same was extended to the domain of a function. In case, a function is differentiable at every point of its domain, then each point in its domain can be associated to the derivative of the function at that point. Such a correspondence between points in the domain and the set of values of derivatives at those points defines a new function which is known as the derivative or differentiation of the given function. In the previous class, we have studied that the derivative of a function $f(x)$ is given by

$$\frac{d}{dx}\left(f\ (x)\right) = \lim_{h \to 0} \frac{f\ (x+h) - f\ (x)}{h} \quad \text{or,} \quad \frac{d}{dx}\left(f\ (x)\right) = \lim_{h \to 0} \frac{f\ (x-h) - f\ (x)}{-h}$$

This is also called the derivative or differentiation with respect to x and is also denoted by $f'(x)$ or, $D\ f\ (x)$. Sometime the derivative or differentiation of a function $f\ (x)$ is also called the differential coefficient of $f\ (x)$. The process of finding the derivative of a function by using the above definition is called the differentiation from first principles or by *ab*-initio method or by delta method.

Following are derivatives of some standard functions which have been derived in Class XI from first principles.

(i) $\frac{d}{dx}(x^n) = n\,x^{n-1}$ (ii) $\frac{d}{dx}(e^x) = e^x$ (iii) $\frac{d}{dx}(a^x) = a^x \log_e a\,,\ a > 0$

(iv) $\frac{d}{dx}(\log_e x) = \frac{1}{x}$ (v) $\frac{d}{dx}(\log_a x) = \frac{1}{x \log_e a}\,,\ a > 0,\ a \neq 1$

(vi) $\frac{d}{dx}(\sin x) = \cos x$ (vii) $\frac{d}{dx}(\cos x) = -\sin x$ (viii) $\frac{d}{dx}(\tan x) = \sec^2 x$

(ix) $\frac{d}{dx}(\cot x) = -\operatorname{cosec}^2 x$ (x) $\frac{d}{dx}(\sec x) = \sec x \tan x$ (xi) $\frac{d}{dx}(\operatorname{cosec} x) = -\operatorname{cosec} x \cot x$

Let us now have a brief recall of what else we have studied in Class XI.

10.2 RECAPITULATION

In the previous class, we have learnt about the following fundamental rules for differentiation.

(i) Differentiation of a constant functions zero i.e., $\frac{d}{dx}(c) = 0$

(ii) Let $f\ (x)$ be a differentiable function and let c be a constant. Then, $c\,f\ (x)$ is also differentiable such that

$$\frac{d}{dx}\left(c\ f(x)\right) = c\,\frac{d}{dx}\left(f\ (x)\right)$$

i.e. the derivative of a constant times a function is the constant times the derivative of the function.

(iii) *Product rule*: If $f(x)$ and $g(x)$ are differentiable functions, then $f(x)\, g(x)$ is also differentiable function such that

$$\frac{d}{dx}\{f(x)\, g(x)\} = \frac{d}{dx}\Big(f(x)\Big) g(x) + f(x) \cdot \frac{d}{dx}\Big(g(x)\Big)$$

If $f(x)$, $g(x)$ and $h(x)$ are differentiable functions, then

$$\frac{d}{dx}\Big(f(x)\, g(x)\, h(x)\Big) = \frac{d}{dx}\Big(f(x)\Big) g(x)\, h(x) + f(x)\frac{d}{dx}\Big(g(x)\Big) h(x) + f(x)\, g(x)\frac{d}{dx}\Big(h(x)\Big)$$

(iv) *Quotient rule:* If $f(x)$ and $g(x)$ are two differentiable functions and $g(x) \neq 0$, then

$$\frac{d}{dx}\left\{\frac{f(x)}{g(x)}\right\} = \frac{g(x)\frac{d}{dx}\Big(f(x)\Big) - f(x)\frac{d}{dx}\Big(g(x)\Big)}{\{g(x)\}^2}$$

BASED ON BASIC CONCEPTS (BASIC)

ILLUSTRATION 1 *Differentiate the following functions with respect to x:*

(i) $\dfrac{2^x \cot x}{\sqrt{x}}$ (ii) $e^x \log \sqrt{x} \tan x$

SOLUTION (i) We have,

$$\frac{d}{dx}\left\{\frac{2^x \cot x}{\sqrt{x}}\right\}$$

$$= \frac{d}{dx}\left\{2^x \cot x\; x^{-1/2}\right\}$$

$$= \left\{\frac{d}{dx}(2^x)\right\}(\cot x)\; x^{-1/2} + 2^x\left\{\frac{d}{dx}(\cot x)\right\} x^{-1/2} + 2^x \cot x\left\{\frac{d}{dx}(x^{-1/2})\right\}$$

$$= 2^x \log_e 2 \cot x\, x^{-1/2} + 2^x(-\operatorname{cosec}^2 x)\, x^{-1/2} + 2^x \cot x \times -\frac{1}{2} x^{-3/2}$$

$$= \frac{2^x \log_e 2 \cot x}{\sqrt{x}} - \frac{2^x \operatorname{cosec}^2 x}{\sqrt{x}} - \frac{2^{x-1} \cot x}{x\sqrt{x}}$$

(ii) $$\frac{d}{dx}\{e^x \log \sqrt{x} \tan x\}$$

$$= \frac{d}{dx}\left\{e^x \times \frac{1}{2}\log x \times \tan x\right\}$$

$$= \frac{1}{2}\frac{d}{dx}\left\{e^x \log x \tan x\right\}$$

$$= \frac{1}{2}\left[\left\{\frac{d}{dx}(e^x)\right\}\log x \tan x + e^x\left\{\frac{d}{dx}(\log x)\right\}\tan x + e^x \log x\left\{\frac{d}{dx}(\tan x)\right\}\right]$$

$$= \frac{1}{2}\left\{e^x \log x \tan x + \frac{e^x \tan x}{x} + e^x \log x \sec^2 x\right\}$$

$$= \frac{1}{2}e^x\left\{\log x \tan x + \frac{\tan x}{x} + \log x \sec^2 x\right\}$$

ILLUSTRATION 2 *Differentiate the following functions with respect to x:*

(i) $\dfrac{e^x + \sin x}{1 + \log x}$ (ii) $\dfrac{\sin x - x \cos x}{x \sin x + \cos x}$

SOLUTION (i) We have,

$$\frac{d}{dx}\left\{\frac{e^x + \sin x}{1 + \log x}\right\}$$

$$= \frac{(1 + \log x)\dfrac{d}{dx}(e^x + \sin x) - (e^x + \sin x)\dfrac{d}{dx}(1 + \log x)}{(1 + \log x)^2}$$

$$= \frac{(1 + \log x)(e^x + \cos x) - (e^x + \sin x)\left(0 + \dfrac{1}{x}\right)}{(1 + \log x)^2} = \frac{(1 + \log x)(e^x + \cos x) - \dfrac{e^x + \sin x}{x}}{(1 + \log x)^2}$$

(ii) $$\frac{d}{dx}\left\{\frac{\sin x - x \cos x}{x \sin x + \cos x}\right\}$$

$$= \frac{(x \sin x + \cos x)\dfrac{d}{dx}(\sin x - x \cos x) - (\sin x - x \cos x)\dfrac{d}{dx}(x \sin x + \cos x)}{(x \sin x + \cos x)^2}$$

$$= \frac{(x \sin x + \cos x)(\cos x - \cos x + x \sin x) - (\sin x - x \cos x)(\sin x + x \cos x - \sin x)}{(x \sin x + \cos x)^2}$$

$$= \frac{(x \sin x + \cos x)(x \sin x) - (\sin x - x \cos x)(x \cos x)}{(x \sin x + \cos x)^2}$$

$$= \frac{(x^2 \sin^2 x + x \sin x \cos x) - (x \sin x \cos x - x^2 \cos^2 x)}{(x \sin x + \cos x)^2}$$

$$= \frac{x^2 (\sin^2 x + \cos^2 x)}{(x \sin x + \cos x)^2} = \frac{x^2}{(x \sin x + \cos x)^2}$$

BASED ON LOWER ORDER THINKING SKILLS (LOTS)

ILLUSTRATION 3 *If* $y = (1 + x)(1 + x^2)(1 + x^4)(1 + x^8) \dots (1 + x^{2^n})$, *find* $\dfrac{dy}{dx}$.

SOLUTION We have,

$$y = (1 + x)(1 + x^2)(1 + x^4)(1 + x^8) \dots (1 + x^{2^n})$$

$$\Rightarrow \quad y = \frac{(1 - x)(1 + x)(1 + x^2)(1 + x^4)(1 + x^8) \dots (1 + x^{2^n})}{1 - x}$$

$$\Rightarrow \quad y = \frac{(1 - x^2)(1 + x^2)(1 + x^4)(1 + x^8) \dots (1 + x^{2^n})}{1 - x}$$

$$\Rightarrow \quad y = \frac{1 - x^{2^{n+1}}}{1 - x}$$

$$\Rightarrow \quad \frac{dy}{dx} = \frac{(1 - x)\dfrac{d}{dx}(1 - x^{2^{n+1}}) - (1 - x^{2^{n+1}})\dfrac{d}{dx}(1 - x)}{(1 - x)^2}$$

$$\Rightarrow \quad \frac{dy}{dx} = \frac{(1-x)(-2^{n+1} x^{2^{n+1}-1}) + (1 - x^{2^{n+1}})}{(1-x)^2}$$

$$\Rightarrow \quad \frac{dy}{dx} = \frac{-2^{n+1} x^{2^{n+1}-1} + 2^{n+1} x^{2^{n+1}} + 1 - x^{2^{n+1}}}{(1-x)^2}$$

$$\Rightarrow \quad \frac{dy}{dx} = \frac{-2^{n+1} x^{2^{n+1}-1} + 1 + x^{2^{n+1}} (2^{n+1}-1)}{(1-x)^2}$$

BASED ON HIGHER ORDER THINKING SKILLS (HOTS)

ILLUSTRATION 4 *If $f(x) = |\cos x|$, find $f'\left(\frac{\pi}{4}\right)$ and $f'\left(\frac{3\pi}{4}\right)$.* [NCERT EXEMPLAR]

SOLUTION We have,

$$f(x) = |\cos x| = \begin{cases} \cos x, \text{ if } 0 < x \le \frac{\pi}{2} \\ -\cos x, \text{ if } \frac{\pi}{2} < x < \pi \end{cases} \Rightarrow f'(x) = \begin{cases} -\sin x, \text{ if } 0 < x < \frac{\pi}{2} \\ \sin x, \text{ if } \frac{\pi}{2} < x < \pi \end{cases}$$

Note that $f(x)$ is not differentiable at $x = \frac{\pi}{2}$.

$$\therefore \quad f'\left(\frac{\pi}{4}\right) = -\sin\frac{\pi}{4} = -\frac{1}{\sqrt{2}} \text{ and, } f'\left(\frac{3\pi}{4}\right) = \sin\frac{3\pi}{4} = \frac{1}{\sqrt{2}}$$

ILLUSTRATION 5 *If $f(x) = |\cos x - \sin x|$, find $f'\left(\frac{\pi}{6}\right)$ and $f'\left(\frac{\pi}{3}\right)$.* [NCERT EXEMPLAR]

SOLUTION We have,

$$f(x) = |\cos x - \sin x| = \begin{cases} \cos x - \sin x, \text{ if } 0 < x < \frac{\pi}{4} \\ -(\cos x - \sin x), \text{ if } \frac{\pi}{4} < x < \frac{\pi}{2} \end{cases}$$

$$\Rightarrow \quad f(x) = \begin{cases} \cos x - \sin x, \text{ if } 0 < x < \frac{\pi}{4} \\ \sin x - \cos x, \text{ if } \frac{\pi}{4} < x < \frac{\pi}{2} \end{cases} \Rightarrow f'(x) = \begin{cases} -\sin x - \cos x, \text{ if } 0 < x < \frac{\pi}{4} \\ \cos x + \sin x, \text{ if } \frac{\pi}{4} < x < \frac{\pi}{2} \end{cases}$$

$$\Rightarrow \quad f'\left(\frac{\pi}{6}\right) = -\sin\frac{\pi}{6} - \cos\frac{\pi}{6} = -\frac{\sqrt{3}+1}{2} \text{ and } f'\left(\frac{\pi}{3}\right) = \cos\frac{\pi}{3} + \sin\frac{\pi}{3} = \frac{\sqrt{3}+1}{2}$$

ILLUSTRATION 6 *If $f(x) = |\log x|, x > 0$, find $f'(1/e)$ and $f'(e)$.* [NCERT EXEMPLAR]

SOLUTION We have,

$$f(x) = |\log x| = \begin{cases} -\log x, \text{ if } 0 < x < 1 \\ \log x, \text{ if } x \ge 1 \end{cases} \Rightarrow f'(x) = \begin{cases} -1/x, \text{ if } 0 < x < 1 \\ 1/x, \text{ if } x > 1 \end{cases} \Rightarrow f'(e) = 1/e \text{ and } f'(1/e) = -e$$

ILLUSTRATION 7 *Show that: $\frac{d}{dx}(|x|) = \frac{x}{|x|}, x \ne 0$.* [CBSE 2024]

SOLUTION We find that $|x| = \begin{cases} x, x \ge 0 \\ -x, x < 0 \end{cases}$

$$\therefore \quad \frac{x}{|x|} = \begin{cases} \dfrac{x}{x} = 1, & x > 0 \\ \dfrac{x}{-x} = -1, & x < 0 \end{cases} \quad \ldots(i)$$

$$\Rightarrow \quad \frac{d}{dx}(|x|) = \begin{cases} \dfrac{d}{dx}(x) = 1, & x > 0 \\ \dfrac{d}{dx}(-x) = -1, & x < 0 \end{cases} \quad \ldots(ii)$$

From (i) and (ii), we obtain

$$\frac{d}{dx}(|x|) = \frac{x}{|x|}\ x \neq 0.$$

10.3 DIFFERENTIATION OF INVERSE TRIGONOMETRIC FUNCTIONS FROM FIRST PRINCIPLES

In the previous class, we have learnt that the derivative of a function $f(x)$ is given by

$$\frac{d}{dx}\left\{f(x)\right\} = \lim_{h \to 0} \frac{f(x+h) - f(x)}{h} \text{ or, } \frac{d}{dx}\left\{f(x)\right\} = \lim_{h \to 0} \frac{f(x-h) - f(x)}{-h}$$

The process of finding the derivative of a function by using the above definition is called the differentiation from first principles or, by *ab*-initio method or, by delta method.

In this section, we will find the derivatives or differentiations or differential coefficients of $\sin^{-1} x$, $\cos^{-1} x$, $\tan^{-1} x$, $\sec^{-1} x$, $\text{cosec}^{-1} x$ and $\cot^{-1} x$ from first principles.

Following results will be very useful to find the same:

(i) $\sin^{-1} x \pm \sin^{-1} y = \sin^{-1}\left\{x\sqrt{1-y^2} \pm y\sqrt{1-x^2}\right\}$

(ii) $\cos^{-1} x \pm \cos^{-1} y = \cos^{-1}\left\{xy \mp \sqrt{1-x^2}\sqrt{1-y^2}\right\}$

(iii) $\tan^{-1} x \pm \tan^{-1} y = \tan^{-1}\left\{\dfrac{x \pm y}{1 \mp xy}\right\}$

(iv) $\displaystyle\lim_{x \to a} \frac{x^n - a^n}{x - a} = n\,a^{n-1}$

(v) $\displaystyle\lim_{x \to 0} \frac{\sin x}{x} = 1,\ \lim_{x \to a} \frac{\sin(x-a)}{x-a} = 1$

(vi) $\displaystyle\lim_{x \to 0} \frac{\tan x}{x} = 1,\ \lim_{x \to a} \frac{\tan(x-a)}{x-a} = 1$

(vii) $\displaystyle\lim_{x \to 0} \frac{\sin^{-1} x}{x} = 1,\ \lim_{x \to 0} \frac{\tan^{-1} x}{x} = 1$

(viii) $\displaystyle\lim_{x \to 0} \frac{a^x - 1}{x} = \log_e a,\ a > 0, a \neq 1$

(ix) $\displaystyle\lim_{x \to 0} \frac{\log_e(1+x)}{x} = 1$

(x) $\displaystyle\lim_{x \to 0} \frac{\log_a(1+x)}{x} = \log_a e.$

THEOREM 1 *If $x \in (-1, 1)$, then the differentiation of $\sin^{-1} x$ with respect to x is* $\dfrac{1}{\sqrt{1-x^2}}$.

i.e., $$\frac{d}{dx}(\sin^{-1} x) = \frac{1}{\sqrt{1-x^2}},\ \text{for } x \in (-1, 1)$$

PROOF Let $f(x) = \sin^{-1} x$. Then, $f(x+h) = \sin^{-1}(x+h)$

$$\therefore \quad \frac{d}{dx}(f(x)) = \lim_{h \to 0} \frac{f(x+h) - f(x)}{h}$$

$$\Rightarrow \frac{d}{dx}(f(x)) = \lim_{h\to 0} \frac{\sin^{-1}(x+h) - \sin^{-1} x}{h}$$

$$\Rightarrow \frac{d}{dx}(f(x)) = \lim_{h\to 0} \frac{\sin^{-1}\left\{(x+h)\sqrt{1-x^2} - x\sqrt{1-(x+h)^2}\right\}}{h}$$

$$\Rightarrow \frac{d}{dx}(f(x)) = \lim_{h\to 0} \frac{\sin^{-1}\left\{(x+h)\sqrt{1-x^2} - x\sqrt{1-(x+h)^2}\right\}}{\left\{(x+h)\sqrt{1-x^2} - x\sqrt{1-(x+h)^2}\right\}} \times \frac{\left\{(x+h)\sqrt{1-x^2} - x\sqrt{1-(x+h)^2}\right\}}{h}$$

$$\Rightarrow \frac{d}{dx}(f(x)) = \lim_{h\to 0} \frac{\left\{(x+h)\sqrt{1-x^2} - x\sqrt{1-(x+h)^2}\right\}}{h}$$

$$\Rightarrow \frac{d}{dx}(f(x)) = \lim_{h\to 0} \frac{(x+h)^2(1-x^2) - x^2\{1-(x+h)^2\}}{h} \times \frac{1}{\left\{(x+h)\sqrt{1-x^2} + x\sqrt{1-(x+h)^2}\right\}}$$

$$\Rightarrow \frac{d}{dx}(f(x)) = \lim_{h\to 0} \frac{(x+h)^2 - x^2}{h} \times \frac{1}{\left\{(x+h)\sqrt{1-x^2} + x\sqrt{1-(x+h)^2}\right\}}$$

$$\Rightarrow \quad \frac{d}{dx}(f(x)) = \lim_{h\to 0} (2x+h) \times \frac{1}{\left\{(x+h)\sqrt{1-x^2} + x\sqrt{1-(x+h)^2}\right\}}$$

$$\Rightarrow \quad \frac{d}{dx}(f(x)) = \frac{2x}{2x\sqrt{1-x^2}} = \frac{1}{\sqrt{1-x^2}}$$

Hence, $\frac{d}{dx}(\sin^{-1} x) = \frac{1}{\sqrt{1-x^2}}$, where $-1 < x < 1$. **Q.E.D.**

THEOREM 2 *If $x \in (-1, 1)$, then the differentiation of $\cos^{-1} x$ with respect to x is $-\frac{1}{\sqrt{1-x^2}}$.*

i.e., $\frac{d}{dx}(\cos^{-1} x) = -\frac{1}{\sqrt{1-x^2}}$

PROOF Let $f(x) = \cos^{-1} x$. Then, $f(x+h) = \cos^{-1}(x+h)$

$$\therefore \quad \frac{d}{dx}(f(x)) = \lim_{h\to 0} \frac{f(x+h) - f(x)}{h}$$

$$\Rightarrow \quad \frac{d}{dx}(f(x)) = \lim_{h\to 0} \frac{\cos^{-1}(x+h) - \cos^{-1} x}{h}$$

$$\Rightarrow \quad \frac{d}{dx}(f(x)) = \lim_{h\to 0} \frac{\left\{\frac{\pi}{2} - \sin^{-1}(x+h)\right\} - \left\{\frac{\pi}{2} - \sin^{-1} x\right\}}{h} \quad \left[\because \cos^{-1} x = \frac{\pi}{2} - \sin^{-1} x\right]$$

$$\Rightarrow \quad \frac{d}{dx}(f(x)) = -\lim_{h\to 0} \frac{\sin^{-1}(x+h) - \sin^{-1} x}{h}$$

$$\Rightarrow \quad \frac{d}{dx}(f(x)) = -\frac{1}{\sqrt{1-x^2}}$$ [See Theorem 1]

Hence, $\frac{d}{dx}(\cos^{-1} x) = -\frac{1}{\sqrt{1-x^2}}$ **Q.E.D.**

THEOREM 3 *The differentiation of* $\tan^{-1} x$ *with respect to x is* $\frac{1}{1+x^2}$ i.e., $\frac{d}{dx}(\tan^{-1} x) = \frac{1}{1+x^2}$

PROOF Let $f(x) = \tan^{-1} x$. Then, $f(x+h) = \tan^{-1}(x+h)$

Now, $\frac{d}{dx}(f(x)) = \lim_{h \to 0} \frac{f(x+h) - f(x)}{h}$

$$\Rightarrow \frac{d}{dx}(f(x)) = \lim_{h \to 0} \frac{\tan^{-1}(x+h) - \tan^{-1} x}{h} = \lim_{h \to 0} \frac{\tan^{-1}\left\{\frac{x+h-x}{1+x(x+h)}\right\}}{h}$$

$$\Rightarrow \frac{d}{dx}(f(x)) = \lim_{h \to 0} \left\{\frac{\tan^{-1}\left(\frac{h}{1+x^2+hx}\right)}{\left(\frac{h}{1+x^2+hx}\right)}\right\} \times \frac{1}{(1+x^2+hx)} = 1 \times \frac{1}{1+x^2} = \frac{1}{1+x^2}$$

Hence, $\frac{d}{dx}(\tan^{-1} x) = \frac{1}{1+x^2}$ for all $x \in R$. **Q.E.D.**

THEOREM 4 *The differentiation of* $\cot^{-1} x$ *with respect to x is* $-\frac{1}{1+x^2}$ i.e., $\frac{d}{dx}(\cot^{-1} x) = -\frac{1}{1+x^2}$

PROOF Let $f(x) = \cot^{-1} x$. Then, $f(x) = \frac{\pi}{2} - \tan^{-1} x$ and so $f(x+h) = \frac{\pi}{2} - \tan^{-1}(x+h)$

$$\therefore \frac{d}{dx}(f(x)) = \lim_{h \to 0} \frac{f(x+h) - f(x)}{h}$$

$$\Rightarrow \frac{d}{dx}(f(x)) = \lim_{h \to 0} \frac{\left\{\frac{\pi}{2} - \tan^{-1}(x+h)\right\} - \left\{\frac{\pi}{2} - \tan^{-1} x\right\}}{h} = \lim_{h \to 0} \frac{\tan^{-1} x - \tan^{-1}(x+h)}{h}$$

$$\Rightarrow \frac{d}{dx}(f(x)) = \lim_{h \to 0} \frac{\tan^{-1}\left\{\frac{x-(x+h)}{1+x(x+h)}\right\}}{h} = \lim_{h \to 0} \frac{\tan^{-1}\left\{\frac{-h}{1+x^2+xh}\right\}}{h}$$

$$\Rightarrow \frac{d}{dx}(f(x)) = \lim_{h \to 0} \left\{\frac{\tan^{-1}\left(\frac{-h}{1+x^2+hx}\right)}{\left(\frac{-h}{1+x^2+hx}\right)}\right\} \times \frac{1}{1+x^2+hx} = 1 \times \frac{-1}{1+x^2} = \frac{-1}{1+x^2}$$

Hence, $\frac{d}{dx}(\cot^{-1} x) = -\frac{1}{1+x^2}$ **Q.E.D.**

THEOREM 5 *If* $x \in R - [-1, 1]$*, then the differentiation of* $\sec^{-1} x$ *with respect to x is* $\frac{1}{|x|\sqrt{x^2-1}}$.

i.e., $\frac{d}{dx}(\sec^{-1} x) = \frac{1}{|x|\sqrt{x^2-1}}$

PROOF Let $f(x) = \sec^{-1} x$. Then, $f(x) = \begin{cases} \tan^{-1}\sqrt{x^2-1}, & \text{if } x \geq 1 \\ \pi - \tan^{-1}\sqrt{x^2-1}, & \text{if } x \leq -1 \end{cases}$

Case I *When* $x > 1$.

We have, $f(x) = \tan^{-1}\sqrt{x^2-1}$ and $f(x+h) = \tan^{-1}\sqrt{(x+h)^2-1}$

$$\therefore \frac{d}{dx}(f(x)) = \lim_{h \to 0} \frac{f(x+h) - f(x)}{h}$$

$$\Rightarrow \frac{d}{dx}(f(x)) = \lim_{h \to 0} \frac{\tan^{-1}\sqrt{(x+h)^2-1} - \tan^{-1}\sqrt{x^2-1}}{h}$$

$$\Rightarrow \frac{d}{dx}(f(x)) = \lim_{h \to 0} \frac{1}{h}\tan^{-1}\left\{\frac{\sqrt{(x+h)^2-1} - \sqrt{x^2-1}}{1 + \sqrt{(x+h)^2-1} \times \sqrt{x^2-1}}\right\}$$

$$\Rightarrow \frac{d}{dx}(f(x)) = \lim_{h \to 0} \left\{\frac{\tan^{-1}\left\{\dfrac{\sqrt{(x+h)^2-1} - \sqrt{x^2-1}}{1 + \sqrt{(x+h)^2-1} \times \sqrt{x^2-1}}\right\}}{\dfrac{\sqrt{(x+h)^2-1} - \sqrt{x^2-1}}{1 + \sqrt{(x+h)^2-1} \times \sqrt{x^2-1}}}\right\} \times \frac{\sqrt{(x+h)^2-1} - \sqrt{x^2-1}}{h\left\{1 + \sqrt{(x+h)^2-1} \times \sqrt{x^2-1}\right\}}$$

$$\Rightarrow \frac{d}{dx}(f(x)) = \lim_{h \to 0} \frac{1}{h}\left\{\frac{(x+h)^2 - 1 - (x^2-1)}{1 + \sqrt{(x+h)^2-1} \times \sqrt{x^2-1}}\right\} \times \frac{1}{\sqrt{(x+h)^2-1} + \sqrt{x^2-1}}$$

$$\Rightarrow \frac{d}{dx}(f(x)) = \lim_{h \to 0} \frac{1}{h}\left\{\frac{2hx + h^2}{1 + \sqrt{(x+h)^2-1} \times \sqrt{x^2-1}}\right\} \times \frac{1}{\sqrt{(x+h)^2-1} + \sqrt{x^2-1}}$$

$$\Rightarrow \frac{d}{dx}(f(x)) = \lim_{h \to 0} \left\{\frac{2x + h}{1 + \sqrt{(x+h)^2-1} \times \sqrt{x^2-1}}\right\} \times \frac{1}{\sqrt{(x+h)^2-1} + \sqrt{x^2-1}}$$

$$\Rightarrow \frac{d}{dx}(f(x)) = \frac{2x}{1 + x^2 - 1} \times \frac{1}{\sqrt{x^2-1} + \sqrt{x^2-1}} = \frac{1}{x\sqrt{x^2-1}}$$

Case II *When* $x < -1$: Proceeding as in Case I, we obtain: $\frac{d}{dx}(\sec^{-1} x) = -\frac{1}{x\sqrt{x^2-1}}$

Thus, we obtain : $\frac{d}{dx}(\sec^{-1} x) = \begin{cases} \dfrac{1}{x\sqrt{x^2-1}} & \text{for } x > 1 \\ -\dfrac{1}{x\sqrt{x^2-1}} & \text{for } x < -1 \end{cases}$

Hence, $\frac{d}{dx}(\sec^{-1} x) = \frac{1}{|x|\sqrt{x^2-1}}$ for all $x \neq \pm 1$. **Q.E.D.**

THEOREM 6 *If $x \in R - [-1, 1]$, then the differentiation of* $\text{cosec}^{-1} x$ *with respect to x is* $\dfrac{-1}{|x|\sqrt{x^2-1}}$.

i.e., $$\frac{d}{dx}(\text{cosec}^{-1} x) = \frac{-1}{|x|\sqrt{x^2-1}} \text{ for all } x \neq \pm 1.$$

PROOF Let $f(x) = \text{cosec}^{-1} x$. Then, $f(x+h) = \text{cosec}^{-1}(x+h)$

$$\therefore \quad \frac{d}{dx}(f(x)) = \lim_{h \to 0} \frac{f(x+h) - f(x)}{h}$$

$$\Rightarrow \quad \frac{d}{dx}(f(x)) = \lim_{h \to 0} \frac{\text{cosec}^{-1}(x+h) - \text{cosec}^{-1} x}{h}$$

$$\Rightarrow \quad \frac{d}{dx}(f(x)) = \lim_{h \to 0} \frac{\left\{\frac{\pi}{2} - \sec^{-1}(x+h)\right\} - \left\{\frac{\pi}{2} - \sec^{-1} x\right\}}{h}$$

$$\Rightarrow \quad \frac{d}{dx}(f(x)) = -\lim_{h \to 0} \frac{\sec^{-1}(x+h) - \sec^{-1} x}{h}$$

$$\Rightarrow \quad \frac{d}{dx}(f(x)) = -\frac{1}{|x|\sqrt{x^2-1}}$$ [See Theorem 5]

Hence, $$\frac{d}{dx}(\text{cosec}^{-1} x) = -\frac{1}{|x|\sqrt{x^2-1}} \text{ for all } x \neq \pm 1.$$

Q.E.D.

The above results and derivatives of other standard functions are listed below for ready reference.

(i) $\dfrac{d}{dx}(x^n) = nx^{n-1}$ (ii) $\dfrac{d}{dx}(e^x) = e^x$ (iii) $\dfrac{d}{dx}(a^x) = a^x \log_e a$

(iv) $\dfrac{d}{dx}(\log_e x) = \dfrac{1}{x}$ (v) $\dfrac{d}{dx}(\log_a x) = \dfrac{1}{x \log_e a}$ (vi) $\dfrac{d}{dx}(\sin x) = \cos x$

(vii) $\dfrac{d}{dx}(\cos x) = -\sin x$ (viii) $\dfrac{d}{dx}(\tan x) = \sec^2 x$ (ix) $\dfrac{d}{dx}(\cot x) = -\text{cosec}^2 x$

(x) $\dfrac{d}{dx}(\sec x) = \sec x \tan x$ (xi) $\dfrac{d}{dx}(\text{cosec } x) = -\text{cosec } x \cot x$

(xii) $\dfrac{d}{dx}(\sin^{-1} x) = \dfrac{1}{\sqrt{1-x^2}}$ (xiii) $\dfrac{d}{dx}(\cos^{-1} x) = -\dfrac{1}{\sqrt{1-x^2}}$

(xiv) $\dfrac{d}{dx}(\tan^{-1} x) = \dfrac{1}{1+x^2}$ (xv) $\dfrac{d}{dx}(\cot^{-1} x) = -\dfrac{1}{1+x^2}$

(xvi) $\dfrac{d}{dx}(\sec^{-1} x) = \dfrac{1}{|x|\sqrt{x^2-1}}$ (xvii) $\dfrac{d}{dx}(\text{cosec}^{-1} x) = \dfrac{-1}{|x|\sqrt{x^2-1}}$

Following examples will illustrate some more applications of differentiation by first principles.

ILLUSTRATIVE EXAMPLES

BASED ON LOWER ORDER THINKING SKILLS (LOTS)

EXAMPLE 1 *Differentiate the following functions with respect to x from first-principles:*

(i) e^{x^2} (ii) e^{2x} (iii) $e^{\sqrt{x}}$ [CBSE 2003] (iv) $e^{\sin x}$

SOLUTION (i) Let $f(x) = e^{x^2}$. Then, $f(x+h) = e^{(x+h)^2}$

$$\therefore \quad \frac{d}{dx}(f(x)) = \lim_{h \to 0} \frac{f(x+h) - f(x)}{h}$$

$$\Rightarrow \quad \frac{d}{dx}(f(x)) = \lim_{h \to 0} \frac{e^{(x+h)^2} - e^{x^2}}{h} = \lim_{h \to 0} \frac{e^{x^2} e^{2hx + h^2} - e^{x^2}}{h}$$

$$\Rightarrow \quad \frac{d}{dx}(f(x)) = \lim_{h \to 0} e^{x^2} \left\{ \frac{e^{2hx + h^2} - 1}{2hx + h^2} \right\} \times \left(\frac{2hx + h^2}{h} \right)$$

$$\Rightarrow \quad \frac{d}{dx}(f(x)) = e^{x^2} \lim_{h \to 0} \left\{ \frac{e^{2hx + h^2} - 1}{2hx + h^2} \right\} \times \lim_{h \to 0} (2x + h)$$

$$\Rightarrow \quad \frac{d}{dx}(f(x)) = e^{x^2} \lim_{\theta \to 0} \left(\frac{e^{\theta} - 1}{\theta} \right) \times \lim_{h \to 0} (2x + h), \text{ where } \theta = 2hx + h^2$$

$$\Rightarrow \quad \frac{d}{dx}(f(x)) = e^{x^2} \times 1 \times 2x = 2x\, e^{x^2}$$

$$\therefore \quad \frac{d}{dx}(e^{x^2}) = 2x\, e^{x^2}$$

(ii) Let $f(x) = e^{2x}$. Then, $f(x+h) = e^{2(x+h)}$

$$\therefore \quad \frac{d}{dx}(f(x)) = \lim_{h \to 0} \frac{f(x+h) - f(x)}{h}$$

$$\Rightarrow \quad \frac{d}{dx}(f(x)) = \lim_{h \to 0} \frac{e^{2(x+h)} - e^{2x}}{h} = \lim_{h \to 0} \frac{e^{2x} . e^{2h} - e^{2x}}{h}$$

$$\Rightarrow \quad \frac{d}{dx}(f(x)) = 2e^{2x} \lim_{h \to 0} \left(\frac{e^{2h} - 1}{2h} \right) = 2e^{2x} \lim_{y \to 0} \left(\frac{e^{y} - 1}{y} \right), \text{ where } y = 2h$$

$$\Rightarrow \quad \frac{d}{dx}(f(x)) = 2e^{2x} \times 1 = 2e^{2x} \qquad \left[\because \lim_{y \to 0} \frac{e^y - 1}{y} = 1 \right]$$

$$\therefore \quad \frac{d}{dx}(e^{2x}) = 2e^{2x}$$

(iii) Let $f(x) = e^{\sqrt{x}}$. Then, $f(x+h) = e^{\sqrt{x+h}}$

$$\therefore \quad \frac{d}{dx}(f(x)) = \lim_{h \to 0} \frac{f(x+h) - f(x)}{h}$$

$$\Rightarrow \quad \frac{d}{dx}(f(x)) = \lim_{h \to 0} \frac{e^{\sqrt{x+h}} - e^{\sqrt{x}}}{h} = e^{\sqrt{x}} \lim_{h \to 0} \left(\frac{e^{\sqrt{x+h} - \sqrt{x}} - 1}{h} \right)$$

$$\Rightarrow \quad \frac{d}{dx}(f(x)) = e^{\sqrt{x}} \lim_{h \to 0} \left(\frac{e^{\sqrt{x+h} - \sqrt{x}} - 1}{\sqrt{x+h} - \sqrt{x}} \right) \times \left(\frac{\sqrt{x+h} - \sqrt{x}}{h} \right)$$

$$\Rightarrow \quad \frac{d}{dx}(f(x)) = e^{\sqrt{x}} \lim_{h \to 0} \left(\frac{e^{\sqrt{x+h} - \sqrt{x}} - 1}{\sqrt{x+h} - \sqrt{x}} \right) \times \frac{(\sqrt{x+h} - \sqrt{x})(\sqrt{x+h} + \sqrt{x})}{h(\sqrt{x+h} + \sqrt{x})}$$

$$\Rightarrow \quad \frac{d}{dx}(f(x)) = e^{\sqrt{x}} \lim_{y \to 0} \left(\frac{e^y - 1}{y} \right) \times \lim_{h \to 0} \frac{x + h - x}{h\left(\sqrt{x+h} + \sqrt{x}\right)}, \text{ where } y = \sqrt{x+h} - \sqrt{x}$$

$[\because \text{ when } h \to 0, y \to 0]$

$$\Rightarrow \quad \frac{d}{dx}(f(x)) = e^{\sqrt{x}} \times 1 \times \left(\frac{1}{\sqrt{x} + \sqrt{x}} \right) = \frac{e^{\sqrt{x}}}{2\sqrt{x}} \qquad \left[\because \lim_{y \to 0} \frac{e^y - 1}{y} = 1\right]$$

(iv) Let $f(x) = e^{\sin x}$. Then, $f(x + h) = e^{\sin(x + h)}$

$$\therefore \quad \frac{d}{dx}(f(x)) = \lim_{h \to 0} \frac{f(x+h) - f(x)}{h}$$

$$\Rightarrow \quad \frac{d}{dx}(f(x)) = \lim_{h \to 0} \frac{e^{\sin(x+h)} - e^{\sin x}}{h} = e^{\sin x} \lim_{h \to 0} \frac{e^{\sin(x+h) - \sin x} - 1}{h}$$

$$\Rightarrow \frac{d}{dx}(f(x)) = e^{\sin x} \lim_{h \to 0} \left\{ \frac{e^{\sin(x+h) - \sin x} - 1}{\sin(x+h) - \sin x} \right\} \times \left\{ \frac{\sin(x+h) - \sin x}{h} \right\}$$

$$\Rightarrow \frac{d}{dx}(f(x)) = e^{\sin x} \lim_{h \to 0} \left\{ \frac{e^{\sin(x+h) - \sin x} - 1}{\sin(x+h) - \sin x} \right\} \times \lim_{h \to 0} \frac{\sin(x+h) - \sin x}{h}$$

$$\Rightarrow \frac{d}{dx}(f(x)) = e^{\sin x} \lim_{y \to 0} \left(\frac{e^y - 1}{y} \right) \times \lim_{h \to 0} \frac{2\sin(h/2)\cos(x + h/2)}{2(h/2)}, \quad \text{where } y = \sin(x+h) - \sin x$$

$[\because \text{ when } h \to 0, y \to 0]$

$$\Rightarrow \frac{d}{dx}(f(x)) = e^{\sin x} \lim_{y \to 0} \left(\frac{e^y - 1}{y} \right) \times \lim_{h \to 0} \frac{\sin(h/2)}{h/2} \times \lim_{h \to 0} \cos(x + h/2)$$

$$\Rightarrow \frac{d}{dx}(f(x)) = e^{\sin x}(1) \times (1) \times (\cos x) = e^{\sin x} \times \cos x$$

EXAMPLE 2 *Differentiate xe^x from first principles.*

SOLUTION Let $f(x) = xe^x$. Then, $f(x + h) = (x + h)\, e^{(x + h)}$

$$\frac{d}{dx}(f(x)) = \lim_{h \to 0} \frac{f(x+h) - f(x)}{h}$$

$$\Rightarrow \quad \frac{d}{dx}(f(x)) = \lim_{h \to 0} \frac{(x+h)\, e^{x+h} - xe^x}{h} = \lim_{h \to 0} \frac{(xe^{x+h} - xe^x) + he^{x+h}}{h}$$

$$\Rightarrow \quad \frac{d}{dx}(f(x)) = \lim_{h \to 0} \left\{ xe^x \left(\frac{e^h - 1}{h} \right) + e^{x+h} \right\} = xe^x \lim_{h \to 0} \left(\frac{e^h - 1}{h} \right) + \lim_{h \to 0} e^{x+h}$$

$$\Rightarrow \quad \frac{d}{dx}(f(x)) = xe^x + e^x = (x+1)\, e^x.$$

BASED ON HIGHER ORDER THINKING SKILLS (HOTS)

EXAMPLE 3 *Differentiate* $\log \sin x$ *by first principles.*

SOLUTION Let $f(x) = \log \sin x$. Then, $f(x+h) = \log \sin (x+h)$.

$$\therefore \quad \frac{d}{dx}(f(x)) = \lim_{h \to 0} \frac{f(x+h) - f(x)}{h}$$

$$\Rightarrow \quad \frac{d}{dx}(f(x)) = \lim_{h \to 0} \frac{\log \sin (x+h) - \log \sin x}{h} = \lim_{h \to 0} \frac{\log \left\{ \frac{\sin (x+h)}{\sin x} \right\}}{h}$$

$$\Rightarrow \quad \frac{d}{dx}(f(x)) = \lim_{h \to 0} \frac{\log \left\{ 1 + \frac{\sin (x+h)}{\sin x} - 1 \right\}}{h} = \lim_{h \to 0} \frac{\log \left\{ 1 + \frac{\sin (x+h) - \sin x}{\sin x} \right\}}{h}$$

$$\Rightarrow \quad \frac{d}{dx}(f(x)) = \lim_{h \to 0} \frac{\log \left\{ 1 + \frac{\sin (x+h) - \sin x}{\sin x} \right\}}{h \left\{ \frac{\sin (x+h) - \sin x}{\sin x} \right\}} \times \left\{ \frac{\sin (x+h) - \sin x}{\sin x} \right\}$$

$$\Rightarrow \quad \frac{d}{dx}(f(x)) = \lim_{h \to 0} \frac{\log \left\{ 1 + \frac{\sin (x+h) - \sin x}{\sin x} \right\}}{\left\{ \frac{\sin (x+h) - \sin x}{\sin x} \right\}} \times \frac{\sin (x+h) - \sin x}{h} \times \frac{1}{\sin x}$$

$$\Rightarrow \quad \frac{d}{dx}(f(x)) = \lim_{h \to 0} \frac{\log \left\{ 1 + \frac{\sin (x+h) - \sin x}{\sin x} \right\}}{\left\{ \frac{\sin (x+h) - \sin x}{\sin x} \right\}} \times \lim_{h \to 0} \frac{2 \sin \frac{h}{2} \cos \left(x + \frac{h}{2} \right)}{h} \times \frac{1}{\sin x}$$

$$\Rightarrow \quad \frac{d}{dx}(f(x)) = \lim_{h \to 0} \frac{\log \left\{ 1 + \frac{\sin (x+h) - \sin x}{\sin x} \right\}}{\left\{ \frac{\sin (x+h) - \sin x}{\sin x} \right\}} \times \lim_{h \to 0} \frac{\sin \left(\frac{h}{2} \right) \cos \left(x + \frac{h}{2} \right)}{\left(\frac{h}{2} \right)} \times \frac{1}{\sin x}$$

$$\Rightarrow \quad \frac{d}{dx}(f(x)) = 1 \times \cos x \times \frac{1}{\sin x} = \cot x.$$

EXAMPLE 4 *Differentiate* $\log \sec x$ *from first principles.*

SOLUTION Let $f(x) = \log \sec x$. Then, $f(x+h) = \log \sec (x+h)$

$$\frac{d}{dx}(f(x)) = \lim_{h \to 0} \frac{f(x+h) - f(x)}{h}$$

$$\Rightarrow \quad \frac{d}{dx}(f(x)) = \lim_{h \to 0} \frac{\log \sec(x+h) - \log \sec x}{h}$$

$$\Rightarrow \quad \frac{d}{dx}(f(x)) = \lim_{h \to 0} \frac{\log\left\{\frac{\sec(x+h)}{\sec x}\right\}}{h} = \lim_{h \to 0} \frac{\log\left\{1 + \left(\frac{\cos x}{\cos(x+h)} - 1\right)\right\}}{h}$$

$$\Rightarrow \quad \frac{d}{dx}(f(x)) = \lim_{h \to 0} \frac{\log\left\{1 + \frac{\cos x - \cos(x+h)}{\cos(x+h)}\right\}}{h\left\{\frac{\cos x - \cos(x+h)}{\cos(x+h)}\right\}} \times \frac{\cos x - \cos(x+h)}{\cos(x+h)}$$

$$\Rightarrow \quad \frac{d}{dx}(f(x)) = \lim_{h \to 0} \frac{\log\left\{1 + \frac{\cos x - \cos(x+h)}{\cos(x+h)}\right\}}{\left\{\frac{\cos x - \cos(x+h)}{\cos(x+h)}\right\}} \times \lim_{h \to 0} \frac{2\sin\left(x + \frac{h}{2}\right)\sin\frac{h}{2}}{h\cos(x+h)}$$

$$\Rightarrow \quad \frac{d}{dx}(f(x)) = 1 \times \lim_{h \to 0} \frac{\sin\left(x + \frac{h}{2}\right)}{\cos(x+h)} \times \left(\frac{\sin\frac{h}{2}}{\frac{h}{2}}\right) = 1 \times \frac{\sin x}{\cos x} \times 1 = \tan x.$$

EXAMPLE 5 *If $f(x) = x\tan^{-1} x$, find $f'(\sqrt{3})$ by first principles.*

SOLUTION We have,

$$f'(x) = \lim_{h \to 0} \frac{f(x+h) - f(x)}{h}$$

$$\therefore \quad f'(\sqrt{3}) = \lim_{h \to 0} \frac{f(\sqrt{3}+h) - f(\sqrt{3})}{h} = \lim_{h \to 0} \frac{(\sqrt{3}+h)\tan^{-1}(\sqrt{3}+h) - \sqrt{3}\tan^{-1}\sqrt{3}}{h}$$

$$\Rightarrow \quad f'(\sqrt{3}) = \lim_{h \to 0} \frac{\sqrt{3}\left\{\tan^{-1}(\sqrt{3}+h) - \tan^{-1}\sqrt{3}\right\} + h\tan^{-1}(\sqrt{3}+h)}{h}$$

$$\Rightarrow \quad f'(\sqrt{3}) = \lim_{h \to 0} \frac{\sqrt{3}}{h}\tan^{-1}\left(\frac{\sqrt{3}+h-\sqrt{3}}{1+\sqrt{3}(\sqrt{3}+h)}\right) + \lim_{h \to 0} \tan^{-1}(\sqrt{3}+h)$$

$$\Rightarrow \quad f'(\sqrt{3}) = \sqrt{3}\lim_{h \to 0}\left\{\frac{\tan^{-1}\left(\frac{h}{4+\sqrt{3}h}\right)}{\frac{h}{4+\sqrt{3}h}}\right\} \times \frac{1}{4+\sqrt{3}h} + \lim_{h \to 0} \tan^{-1}(\sqrt{3}+h)$$

$$\Rightarrow \quad f'(\sqrt{3}) = \sqrt{3} \times 1 \times \frac{1}{4} + \tan^{-1}\sqrt{3} = \frac{\sqrt{3}}{4} + \tan^{-1}\sqrt{3}.$$

EXAMPLE 6 *Differentiate $\cos^{-1}(2x+3)$ from first principles.*

SOLUTION Let $f(x) = \cos^{-1}(2x+3)$. Then, $f(x+h) = \cos^{-1}(2x+3+2h)$.

$$\therefore \quad \frac{d}{dx}(f(x)) = \lim_{h \to 0} \frac{f(x+h) - f(x)}{h}$$

$$\Rightarrow \quad \frac{d}{dx}(f(x)) = \lim_{h \to 0} \frac{\cos^{-1}(2x+3+2h) - \cos^{-1}(2x+3)}{h}$$

$$\Rightarrow \quad \frac{d}{dx}(f(x)) = \lim_{h \to 0} \frac{\left\{\frac{\pi}{2} - \sin^{-1}(2x+3+2h)\right\} - \left\{\frac{\pi}{2} - \sin^{-1}(2x+3)\right\}}{h}$$

$$\Rightarrow \quad \frac{d}{dx}(f(x)) = \lim_{h \to 0} \frac{\sin^{-1}(2x+3) - \sin^{-1}(2x+3+2h)}{h}$$

$$\Rightarrow \quad \frac{d}{dx}(f(x)) = \lim_{h \to 0} \frac{\sin^{-1}\left\{(2x+3)\sqrt{1-(2x+3+2h)^2} - (2x+3+2h)\sqrt{1-(2x+3)^2}\right\}}{h}$$

$$\Rightarrow \quad \frac{d}{dx}(f(x)) = \lim_{h \to 0} \frac{\sin^{-1} Z}{Z} \times \frac{Z}{h},$$

where $Z = (2x+3)\sqrt{1-(2x+3+2h)^2} - (2x+3+2h)\sqrt{1-(2x+3)^2}$

$$\Rightarrow \quad \frac{d}{dx}(f(x)) = \lim_{h \to 0} \frac{Z}{h} \qquad \left[\because \lim_{h \to 0} \frac{\sin^{-1} Z}{Z} = 1\right]$$

$$\Rightarrow \quad \frac{d}{dx}(f(x)) = \lim_{h \to 0} \frac{(2x+3)\sqrt{1-(2x+3+2h)^2} - (2x+3+2h)\sqrt{1-(2x+3)^2}}{h}$$

$$\Rightarrow \quad \frac{d}{dx}(f(x)) = \lim_{h \to 0} \frac{(2x+3)^2\{1-(2x+3+2h)^2\} - (2x+3+2h)^2\{1-(2x+3)^2\}}{h\left\{(2x+3)\sqrt{1-(2x+3+2h)^2} + (2x+3+2h)\sqrt{1-(2x+3)^2}\right\}}$$

$$\Rightarrow \quad \frac{d}{dx}(f(x)) = \lim_{h \to 0} \frac{(2x+3)^2 - (2x+3+2h)^2}{h\left\{(2x+3)\sqrt{1-(2x+3+2h)^2} + (2x+3+2h)\sqrt{1-(2x+3)^2}\right\}}$$

$$\Rightarrow \quad \frac{d}{dx}(f(x)) = \lim_{h \to 0} \frac{-4h(2x+3) - 4h^2}{h\left\{(2x+3)\sqrt{1-(2x+3+2h)^2} + (2x+3+2h)\sqrt{1-(2x+3)^2}\right\}}$$

$$\Rightarrow \quad \frac{d}{dx}(f(x)) = \lim_{h \to 0} \frac{-4(2x+3) - 4h}{(2x+3)\sqrt{1-(2x+3+2h)^2} + (2x+3+2h)\sqrt{1-(2x+3)^2}}$$

$$\Rightarrow \quad \frac{d}{dx}(f(x)) = -\frac{4(2x+3)}{2(2x+3)\sqrt{1-(2x+3)^2}} = \frac{-2}{\sqrt{1-(2x+3)^2}}.$$

EXAMPLE 7 *Differentiate $e^{\sqrt{\tan x}}$ from first principle.*

SOLUTION Let $f(x) = e^{\sqrt{\tan x}}$. Then, $f(x+h) = e^{\sqrt{\tan(x+h)}}$

$$\Rightarrow \quad \frac{d}{dx}(f(x)) = \lim_{h \to 0} \frac{f(x+h) - f(x)}{h}$$

$$\Rightarrow \quad \frac{d}{dx}(f(x)) = \lim_{h \to 0} \frac{e^{\sqrt{\tan(x+h)}} - e^{\sqrt{\tan x}}}{h} = \lim_{h \to 0} e^{\sqrt{\tan x}} \left\{ \frac{e^{\sqrt{\tan(x+h)} - \sqrt{\tan x}} - 1}{h} \right\}$$

$$\Rightarrow \quad \frac{d}{dx}(f(x)) = e^{\sqrt{\tan x}} \lim_{h \to 0} \left\{ \frac{e^{\sqrt{\tan(x+h)} - \sqrt{\tan x}} - 1}{\sqrt{\tan(x+h)} - \sqrt{\tan x}} \times \frac{\sqrt{\tan(x+h)} - \sqrt{\tan x}}{h} \right\}$$

$$\Rightarrow \quad \frac{d}{dx}(f(x)) = e^{\sqrt{\tan x}} \times \lim_{h \to 0} \left\{ \frac{e^{\sqrt{\tan(x+h)} - \sqrt{\tan x}} - 1}{\sqrt{\tan(x+h)} - \sqrt{\tan x}} \right\} \times \lim_{h \to 0} \frac{\sqrt{\tan(x+h)} - \sqrt{\tan x}}{h}$$

$$\Rightarrow \quad \frac{d}{dx}(f(x)) = e^{\sqrt{\tan x}} \times 1 \times \lim_{h \to 0} \frac{\tan(x+h) - \tan x}{h} \times \frac{1}{\sqrt{\tan(x+h)} + \sqrt{\tan x}}$$

$$\Rightarrow \quad \frac{d}{dx}(f(x)) = e^{\sqrt{\tan x}} \times \lim_{h \to 0} \frac{\sin h}{h \cos(x+h) \cos x} \times \frac{1}{\sqrt{\tan(x+h)} + \sqrt{\tan x}}$$

$$\Rightarrow \quad \frac{d}{dx}(f(x)) = e^{\sqrt{\tan x}} \times \frac{1}{\cos^2 x} \times \frac{1}{2\sqrt{\tan x}} = \frac{e^{\sqrt{\tan x}}}{2\sqrt{\tan x}} \sec^2 x.$$

EXAMPLE 8 *Differentiate $x \tan^{-1} x$ from first principles.*

SOLUTION Let $f(x) = x \tan^{-1} x$. Then, $f(x+h) = (x+h) \tan^{-1}(x+h)$

$$\therefore \quad \frac{d}{dx}(f(x)) = \lim_{h \to 0} \frac{f(x+h) - f(x)}{h} = \lim_{h \to 0} \frac{(x+h) \tan^{-1}(x+h) - x \tan^{-1} x}{h}$$

$$\Rightarrow \quad \frac{d}{dx}(f(x)) = \lim_{h \to 0} \left[x \left\{ \frac{\tan^{-1}(x+h) - \tan^{-1} x}{h} \right\} + \frac{h \tan^{-1}(x+h)}{h} \right]$$

$$\Rightarrow \quad \frac{d}{dx}(f(x)) = \lim_{h \to 0} \left\{ \frac{x \tan^{-1}\left(\frac{x+h-x}{1+x(x+h)}\right)}{h} \right\} + \lim_{h \to 0} \tan^{-1}(x+h)$$

$$\Rightarrow \quad \frac{d}{dx}(f(x)) = x \lim_{h \to 0} \left\{ \frac{\tan^{-1}\left(\frac{h}{1+x(x+h)}\right)}{\frac{h}{1+x(x+h)}} \times \frac{1}{\{1+x(x+h)\}} \right\} + \tan^{-1} x = \frac{x}{1+x^2} + \tan^{-1} x$$

EXAMPLE 9 *Differentiate $\sin^{-1} \sqrt{x}$ $(0 < x < 1)$ from first principles.*

SOLUTION Let $f(x) = \sin^{-1} \sqrt{x}$. Then, $f(x+h) = \sin^{-1} \sqrt{x+h}$

$$\therefore \quad \frac{d}{dx}(f(x)) = \lim_{h \to 0} \frac{f(x+h) - f(x)}{h}$$

$$\Rightarrow \quad \frac{d}{dx}(f(x)) = \lim_{h \to 0} \frac{\sin^{-1}\sqrt{x+h} - \sin^{-1}\sqrt{x}}{h}$$

$$\Rightarrow \quad \frac{d}{dx}(f(x)) = \lim_{h \to 0} \frac{\sin^{-1}\left\{\sqrt{x+h}\sqrt{1-x} - \sqrt{x}\sqrt{1-x-h}\right\}}{h}$$

$$\Rightarrow \quad \frac{d}{dx}(f(x)) = \lim_{h \to 0} \frac{\sin^{-1} Z}{Z} \times \frac{Z}{h}, \text{ where } Z = \sqrt{x+h}\sqrt{1-x} - \sqrt{x}\sqrt{1-x-h}$$

$$\Rightarrow \quad \frac{d}{dx}(f(x)) = \lim_{h \to 0} \frac{Z}{h} \qquad \left[\because \lim_{h \to 0} \frac{\sin^{-1} Z}{Z} = \lim_{Z \to 0} \frac{\sin^{-1} Z}{Z} = 1\right]$$

$$\Rightarrow \quad \frac{d}{dx}(f(x)) = \lim_{h \to 0} \frac{(x+h)(1-x) - x(1-x-h)}{h} \times \frac{1}{\sqrt{x+h}\sqrt{1-x} + \sqrt{x}\sqrt{1-x-h}}$$

$$\Rightarrow \quad \frac{d}{dx}(f(x)) = \lim_{h \to 0} \frac{h(1-x+x)}{h} \times \frac{1}{\sqrt{x+h}\sqrt{1-x} + \sqrt{x}\sqrt{1-x-h}}$$

$$\Rightarrow \quad \frac{d}{dx}(f(x)) = \lim_{h \to 0} \frac{1}{\sqrt{x+h}\sqrt{1-x} + \sqrt{x}\sqrt{1-x-h}} = \frac{1}{2\sqrt{x}\sqrt{1-x}}.$$

REMARK *It should be noted that* $\frac{d}{dx}$ *is an operator such that when it is applied on* $y = f(x)$ *gives us* $\frac{d}{dx}(f(x)) = \frac{dy}{dx}$. *Also,* $\frac{dy}{dx}$ *is not simply a fraction obtained by dividing dy by dx. For example, if* $\frac{d}{dx}$ *is applied on* $\sin x$ *it gives us* $\cos x$ *i.e.,* $\frac{d}{dx}(\sin x) = \cos x$. *The operator* $\frac{d}{dx}$ *is called the differential operator.*

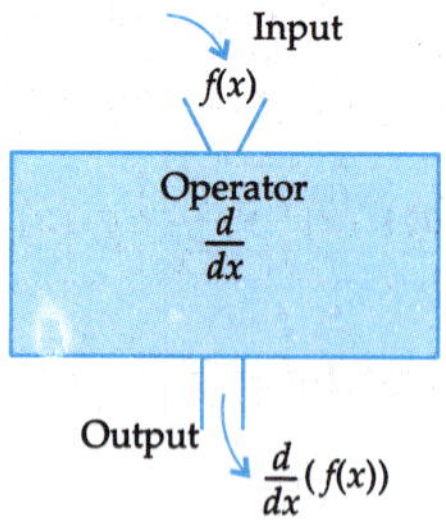

Fig. 10.1

EXERCISE 10.1

BASIC

Differentiate the following functions from first principles:

1. e^{-x} 2. e^{3x} 3. e^{ax+b} 4. $e^{\cos x}$ 5. $e^{\sqrt{2x}}$

BASED ON HOTS

Differentiate each of the following functions from first principal:

6. $\log \cos x$ 7. $e^{\sqrt{\cot x}}$ 8. $x^2 e^x$ 9. $\log \operatorname{cosec} x$ 10. $\sin^{-1}(2x+3)$

ANSWERS

1. $-e^{-x}$ 2. $3e^{3x}$ 3. ae^{ax+b} 4. $-e^{\cos x}\sin x$ 5. $\dfrac{e^{\sqrt{2x}}}{\sqrt{2x}}$ 6. $-\tan x$

7. $-\dfrac{e^{\sqrt{\cot x}}}{2\sqrt{\cot x}}\operatorname{cosec}^2 x$ 8. $(x^2+2x)\,e^x$ 9. $-\cot x$ 10. $\dfrac{2}{\sqrt{1-(2x+3)^2}}$

10.4 DIFFERENTIATION OF A FUNCTION OF A FUNCTION

In this section, we will study about the differentiation of composition of two or more functions.

THEOREM *(Chain Rule) If $f(x)$ and $g(x)$ are differentiable functions, then fog is also differentiable and*

$$(fog)'(x) = f'(g(x))\; g'(x)$$

or,
$$\frac{d}{dx}\left\{(fog)\,(x)\right\} = \frac{d}{d\,g(x)}\{f(g(x))\}\frac{d}{dx}\left(g\,(x)\right).$$

PROOF Since $f(x)$ and $g(x)$ are differentiable functions. Therefore,

$$\frac{d}{dx}(f(x)) = \lim_{h\to 0}\frac{f(x+h)-f(x)}{h} \text{ and, } \frac{d}{dx}(g(x)) = \lim_{h\to 0}\frac{g(x+h)-g(x)}{h} \qquad \text{...(i)}$$

Now,
$$\frac{d}{dx}\left\{(fog)\,(x)\right\} = \lim_{h\to 0}\frac{fog(x+h)-fog(x)}{h} = \lim_{h\to 0}\frac{f\{g(x+h)\}-f\{g(x)\}}{h}$$

$$\Rightarrow \quad \frac{d}{dx}\left\{(fog)\,(x)\right\} = \lim_{h\to 0}\frac{f\{g(x+h)\}-f\{g(x)\}}{g(x+h)-g(x)}\times\frac{g(x+h)-g(x)}{h}$$

$$\Rightarrow \quad \frac{d}{dx}\left\{(fog)\,(x)\right\} = \lim_{h\to 0}\frac{f\{g(x+h)\}-f\{g(x)\}}{g(x+h)-g(x)}\times\lim_{h\to 0}\frac{g(x+h)-g(x)}{h}$$

Given that $g(x)$ is differentiable and therefore it is continuous and hence $\lim\limits_{h\to 0} g(x+h)=g(x)$.

$$\therefore \quad \frac{d}{dx}\left\{(fog)\,(x)\right\} = \lim_{g(x+h)\to g(x)}\frac{f\{g(x+h)\}-f\{g(x)\}}{g(x+h)-g(x)}\times\lim_{h\to 0}\frac{g(x+h)-g(x)}{h}$$

$$\Rightarrow \quad \frac{d}{dx}\left\{(fog)\,(x)\right\} = \frac{d}{dg(x)}\left\{(fog)\,(x)\right\}\times\frac{d}{dx}\left\{g\,(x)\right\}.$$

REMARK 1 *The above rule can also be restated as if* $z=f(y)$ and $y=g(x)$, *then* $\dfrac{dz}{dx}=\dfrac{dz}{dy}\cdot\dfrac{dy}{dx}$

OR

Derivative of z with respect to x = (Derivative of z with respect to y) × (Derivative of y with respect to x)

REMARK 2 *This chain rule can be extended further.*

Derivative of z with respect to x = (Derivative of z with respect to u) × (Derivative of u with respect to v) × (Derivative of v with respect to x)

ILLUSTRATIVE EXAMPLES

BASED ON BASIC CONCEPTS (BASIC)

EXAMPLE 1 *Differentiate the following functions with respect to x:*

(i) $\sin(x^2+1)$ (ii) $e^{\sin x}$ (iii) $\log\sin x$

SOLUTION (i) Let $y = \sin(x^2+1)$. Putting $u = x^2+1$, we get

$$y = \sin u \text{ and } u = x^2+1 \Rightarrow \frac{dy}{du} = \cos u \text{ and } \frac{du}{dx} = 2x$$

$$\therefore \quad \frac{dy}{dx} = \frac{dy}{du} \times \frac{du}{dx} = (\cos u)\, 2x = 2x \cos(x^2+1) \qquad [\because u = x^2+1]$$

Hence, $\frac{d}{dx}\{\sin(x^2+1)\} = 2x\cos(x^2+1)$

ALITER We have,

$$\frac{d}{dx}\{\sin(x^2+1)\} = \frac{d}{d(x^2+1)}\{\sin(x^2+1)\} \times \frac{d}{dx}(x^2+1)$$

$$\Rightarrow \quad \frac{d}{dx}\{\sin(x^2+1)\} = \{\cos(x^2+1)\} \times 2x \qquad \left[\because \frac{d}{d(x^2+1)}\{\sin(x^2+1)\} = \cos(x^2+1)\right]$$

$$\Rightarrow \quad \frac{d}{dx}\{\sin(x^2+1)\} = 2x\cos(x^2+1).$$

(ii) Let $y = e^{\sin x}$. Putting $u = \sin x$, we get

$$y = e^u \text{ and } u = \sin x \Rightarrow \frac{dy}{du} = e^u \text{ and } \frac{du}{dx} = \cos x.$$

$$\therefore \quad \frac{dy}{dx} = \frac{dy}{du} \times \frac{du}{dx} = e^u \cos x = \cos x\, e^{\sin x} \qquad [\because u = \sin x]$$

Hence, $\frac{d}{dx}\{e^{\sin x}\} = e^{\sin x} \cos x.$

ALITER $\frac{d}{dx}\{e^{\sin x}\} = \frac{d}{d(\sin x)}\{e^{\sin x}\} \times \frac{d}{dx}\{\sin x\} = e^{\sin x} \times \cos x.$

(iii) Let $y = \log \sin x$. Putting $u = \sin x$, we get

$$y = \log u \text{ and } u = \sin x \Rightarrow \frac{dy}{du} = \frac{1}{u} \text{ and } \frac{du}{dx} = \cos x.$$

$$\therefore \quad \frac{dy}{dx} = \frac{dy}{du} \times \frac{du}{dx} = \frac{1}{u} \times \cos x = \frac{1}{\sin x} \times \cos x = \cot x.$$

Hence, $\frac{d}{dx}\{\log \sin x\} = \cot x.$

ALITER $\frac{d}{dx}\{\log \sin x\} = \frac{d}{d(\sin x)}\{\log \sin x\} \times \frac{d}{dx}(\sin x) = \frac{1}{\sin x} \times \cos x = \cot x$

EXAMPLE 2 *If $f(x) = |\tan 2x|$, then find the value of $f'(x)$ at $x = \frac{\pi}{3}$.* **[CBSE 2024]**

SOLUTION We have, $f(x) = |\tan 2x| = -\tan 2x$ for all x in the neighborhood of $x = \frac{\pi}{3}$.

$$\therefore \quad f'(x) = -\sec^2 2x \frac{d}{dx}(2x) = -2\sec^2 2x$$

$$\Rightarrow \quad f'\left(\frac{\pi}{3}\right) = -2\sec^2\frac{2\pi}{3} = -2 \times (-2)^2 = 8$$

EXAMPLE 3 *Differentiate the following functions with respect to x:*

(i) $\log \sin x^2$ (ii) $e^{\sin x^2}$ (iii) $\sin (e^{x^2})$

SOLUTION (i) Let $y = \log \sin x^2$. Putting $v = x^2$ and $u = \sin x^2 = \sin v$, we get

$$y = \log u,\ u = \sin v \text{ and } v = x^2 \Rightarrow \frac{dy}{du} = \frac{1}{u},\ \frac{du}{dv} = \cos v \text{ and } \frac{dv}{dx} = 2x.$$

$$\therefore \quad \frac{dy}{dx} = \frac{dy}{du} \times \frac{du}{dv} \times \frac{dv}{dx} = \frac{1}{u} \times \cos v \times 2x = \frac{1}{\sin v} \cos v \times 2x \qquad [\because u = \sin v]$$

$$\Rightarrow \quad \frac{dy}{dx} = (\cot v)\, 2x = 2x \cot x^2 \qquad [\because v = x^2]$$

Hence, $\frac{d}{dx}(\log \sin x^2) = 2x \cot x^2$

ALITER $$\frac{d}{dx}\{\log \sin x^2\} = \frac{d}{d(\sin x^2)}\{\log \sin x^2\} \times \frac{d}{d(x^2)}(\sin x^2) \times \frac{d}{dx}(x^2)$$

$$= \frac{1}{\sin x^2} \times \cos x^2 \times 2x = 2x \cot x^2.$$

(ii) Let $y = e^{\sin x^2}$. Putting $x^2 = v$ and $u = \sin x^2 = \sin v$, we get

$$y = e^u,\ u = \sin v \text{ and } v = x^2 \Rightarrow \frac{dy}{du} = e^u,\ \frac{du}{dv} = \cos v \text{ and } \frac{dv}{dx} = 2x.$$

$$\therefore \quad \frac{dy}{dx} = \frac{dy}{du} \times \frac{du}{dv} \times \frac{dv}{dx} = e^u \times \cos v \times 2x = e^{\sin v} \times \cos v \times 2x \qquad [\because u = \sin v]$$

$$\Rightarrow \quad \frac{dy}{dx} = e^{\sin x^2} \times \cos x^2 \times 2x \qquad [\because v = x^2]$$

ALITER $$\frac{d}{dx}\left(e^{\sin x^2}\right) = \frac{d}{d(\sin x^2)}\left(e^{\sin x^2}\right) \times \frac{d}{dx}\left(\sin x^2\right) \times \frac{d}{dx}(x^2) = e^{\sin x^2} \times \cos x^2 \times 2x$$

(iii) Let $y = \sin (e^{x^2})$. Putting $x^2 = v$ and $u = e^{x^2} = e^v$, we get

$$y = \sin u, \text{ where } u = e^v \text{ and } v = x^2 \Rightarrow \frac{dy}{du} = \cos u,\ \frac{du}{dv} = e^v \text{ and } \frac{dv}{dx} = 2x.$$

$$\therefore \quad \frac{dy}{dx} = \frac{dy}{du} \times \frac{du}{dv} \times \frac{dv}{dx} = \cos u \times e^v \times 2x = \cos (e^v) \times e^v \times 2x \qquad [\because u = e^v]$$

$$\Rightarrow \quad \frac{dy}{dx} = \cos (e^{x^2}) \times e^{x^2} \times 2x \qquad [\because v = x^2]$$

ALITER $$\frac{d}{dx}\{\sin e^{x^2}\} = \frac{d}{d(e^{x^2})}(\sin e^{x^2}) \times \frac{d}{d(x^2)}(e^{x^2}) \times \frac{d}{dx}(x^2) = \cos (e^{x^2}) \times e^{x^2} \times 2x$$

EXAMPLE 4 *Differentiate the following functions with respect to x:*

(i) $(x^2 + x + 1)^4$ (ii) $\sqrt{x^2 + x + 1}$ (iii) $\sin^3 x$ (iv) $\frac{1}{\sqrt{a^2 - x^2}}$

SOLUTION (i) Let $y = (x^2 + x + 1)^4$. Putting $x^2 + x + 1 = u$, we get

$$y = u^4 \text{ and } u = x^2 + x + 1 \Rightarrow \frac{dy}{du} = 4u^3 \text{ and } \frac{du}{dx} = 2x + 1$$

$\therefore \quad \dfrac{dy}{dx} = \dfrac{dy}{du} \times \dfrac{du}{dx} = 4u^3(2x+1) = 4(x^2+x+1)^3(2x+1).$

ALITER We have,

$$\frac{d}{dx}\{(x^2+x+1)^4\} = \frac{d}{d(x^2+x+1)}\{(x^2+x+1)^4\} \times \frac{d}{dx}(x^2+x+1) = 4(x^2+x+1)^3(2x+1)$$

(ii) Let $y = \sqrt{x^2+x+1}$. Putting $x^2+x+1 = u$, we get

$$y = \sqrt{u} \text{ and } u = x^2+x+1 \Rightarrow \frac{dy}{du} = \frac{1}{2}u^{\frac{1}{2}-1} = \frac{1}{2\sqrt{u}} \text{ and } \frac{du}{dx} = 2x+1$$

$$\therefore \quad \frac{dy}{dx} = \frac{dy}{du} \times \frac{du}{dx} = \frac{1}{2\sqrt{u}} \times (2x+1) = \frac{1}{2\sqrt{x^2+x+1}} \times (2x+1) \qquad [\because u = x^2+x+1]$$

ALITER We have,

$$\frac{d}{dx}\left\{\sqrt{x^2+x+1}\right\} = \frac{d}{d(x^2+x+1)}\left\{(x^2+x+1)^{1/2}\right\} \times \frac{d}{dx}(x^2+x+1)$$

$$= \frac{1}{2}(x^2+x+1)^{-1/2}(2x+1)$$

(iii) Let $y = \sin^3 x$. Putting $u = \sin x$, we get

$$y = u^3 \text{ and } u = \sin x \Rightarrow \frac{dy}{du} = 3u^2 \text{ and } \frac{du}{dx} = \cos x.$$

$$\therefore \quad \frac{dy}{dx} = \frac{dy}{du} \times \frac{du}{dx} = 3u^2 \times \cos x = 3(\sin x)^2 \times \cos x = 3\sin^2 x \cos x. \qquad [\because u = \sin x]$$

ALITER $\dfrac{d}{dx}(\sin^3 x) = \dfrac{d}{dx}\{(\sin x)^3\} = \dfrac{d}{d(\sin x)}\{(\sin x)^3\} \times \dfrac{d}{dx}(\sin x)$

$$= 3(\sin x)^{3-1} \times \cos x = 3\sin^2 x \cos x.$$

(iv) Let $y = \dfrac{1}{\sqrt{a^2-x^2}}$. Putting $u = a^2-x^2$, we get

$$y = \frac{1}{\sqrt{u}} = u^{-1/2} \text{ and } u = a^2-x^2 \Rightarrow \frac{dy}{du} = -\frac{1}{2}u^{-3/2} \text{ and } \frac{du}{dx} = -2x.$$

$$\therefore \quad \frac{dy}{dx} = \frac{dy}{du} \times \frac{du}{dx} = -\frac{1}{2}u^{-3/2} \times (-2x) = -\frac{1}{2u^{3/2}} \times (-2x) = \frac{x}{(a^2-x^2)^{3/2}} \quad [\because u = a^2-x^2]$$

ALITER $\dfrac{d}{dx}\left\{(a^2-x^2)^{-1/2}\right\} = \dfrac{d}{d(a^2-x^2)}\left\{(a^2-x^2)^{-1/2}\right\} \times \dfrac{d}{dx}\left(a^2-x^2\right)$

$$= -\frac{1}{2}\left(a^2-x^2\right)^{-3/2}(0-2x) = \frac{x}{(a^2-x^2)^{3/2}}$$

EXAMPLE 5 *If* $y = \text{cosec}(\cot^{-1} x)$, *then prove that* $\sqrt{1+x^2}\dfrac{dy}{dx} - x = 0.$ **[CBSE 2024]**

SOLUTION We have,

$$y = \text{cosec}(\cot^{-1} x) \Rightarrow y = \text{cosec}(\text{cosec}^{-1}\sqrt{1+x^2}) = \sqrt{1+x^2}$$

Now, $y = \sqrt{1+x^2}$

$$\Rightarrow \quad \frac{dy}{dx} = \frac{1}{2}(1+x^2)^{-1/2} \frac{d}{dx}(1+x^2)$$

$$\Rightarrow \quad \frac{dy}{dx} = \frac{1}{2\sqrt{1+x^2}} \times 2x = \frac{x}{\sqrt{1+x^2}} \Rightarrow \sqrt{1+x^2}\frac{dy}{dx} = x \Rightarrow \sqrt{1+x^2}\frac{dy}{dx} - x = 0$$

EXAMPLE 6 *Differentiate the following functions with respect to x:*

(i) $\log(\sec x + \tan x)$ (ii) $e^{x \sin x}$ (iii) $\sin^{-1}(x^3)$ (iv) $\sin^{-1}\left(\frac{a+b\cos x}{b+a\cos x}\right), b > a$

SOLUTION (i) Let $y = \log(\sec x + \tan x)$. Putting $u = \sec x + \tan x$, we get

$$y = \log u \text{ and } u = \sec x + \tan x \Rightarrow \frac{dy}{du} = \frac{1}{u} \text{ and } \frac{du}{dx} = \sec x \tan x + \sec^2 x.$$

$$\therefore \quad \frac{dy}{dx} = \frac{dy}{du} \times \frac{du}{dx} = \frac{1}{u} \times (\sec x \tan x + \sec^2 x) = \frac{1}{\sec x + \tan x} \sec x (\tan x + \sec x) = \sec x.$$

(ii) Let $y = e^{x \sin x}$. Putting $u = x \sin x$, we get

$$y = e^u \text{ and } u = x \sin x \Rightarrow \frac{dy}{du} = e^u \text{ and } \frac{du}{dx} = x \cos x + \sin x.$$

$$\therefore \quad \frac{dy}{dx} = \frac{dy}{du} \times \frac{du}{dx} = e^u (x \cos x + \sin x) = e^{x \sin x}(x \cos x + \sin x)$$

ALITER $\frac{d}{dx}(e^{x \sin x}) = \frac{d}{d(x \sin x)}\{e^{x \sin x}\} \times \frac{d}{dx}(x \sin x) = e^{x \sin x} \times (x \cos x + \sin x).$

(iii) Let $y = \sin^{-1} x^3$. Putting $u = x^3$, we get

$$y = \sin^{-1} u \text{ and } u = x^3 \Rightarrow \frac{dy}{du} = \frac{1}{\sqrt{1-u^2}} \text{ and } \frac{du}{dx} = 3x^2$$

$$\therefore \quad \frac{dy}{dx} = \frac{dy}{du} \times \frac{du}{dx} = \frac{1}{\sqrt{1-u^2}} \times 3x^2 = \frac{1}{\sqrt{1-x^6}} \times 3x^2$$

ALITER $\frac{d}{dx}(\sin^{-1} x^3) = \frac{d}{d(x^3)}(\sin^{-1} x^3) \times \frac{d}{dx}(x^3) = \frac{1}{\sqrt{1-x^6}} \times 3x^2$

(iv) Let $y = \sin^{-1}\left(\frac{a+b\cos x}{b+a\cos x}\right)$. Putting $u = \frac{a+b\cos x}{b+a\cos x}$, we get

$$y = \sin^{-1} u \text{ and } u = \frac{a+b\cos x}{b+a\cos x}$$

$$\Rightarrow \quad \frac{dy}{du} = \frac{1}{\sqrt{1-u^2}} \text{ and, } \frac{du}{dx} = \frac{(b+a\cos x)(0-b\sin x)-(a+b\cos x)(0-a\sin x)}{(b+a\cos x)^2}$$

$$\Rightarrow \quad \frac{dy}{du} = \frac{1}{\sqrt{1-u^2}} \text{ and, } \frac{du}{dx} = \frac{(a^2-b^2)\sin x}{(b+a\cos x)^2}$$

$$\therefore \quad \frac{dy}{dx} = \frac{dy}{du} \times \frac{du}{dx}$$

$$\Rightarrow \quad \frac{dy}{dx} = \frac{1}{\sqrt{1-u^2}} \times \frac{(a^2-b^2)\sin x}{(b+a\cos x)^2} = \frac{1}{\sqrt{1-\left(\frac{a+b\cos x}{b+a\cos x}\right)^2}} \times \frac{(a^2-b^2)\sin x}{(b+a\cos x)^2}$$

$$\Rightarrow \quad \frac{dy}{dx} = \frac{(b+a\cos x)}{\sqrt{(b+a\cos x)^2-(a+b\cos x)^2}} \times \frac{(a^2-b^2)\sin x}{(b+a\cos x)^2}$$

$$\Rightarrow \quad \frac{dy}{dx} = \frac{(a^2-b^2)\sin x}{\sqrt{b^2(1-\cos^2 x)-a^2(1-\cos^2 x)}} \times \frac{1}{(b+a\cos x)}$$

$$\Rightarrow \quad \frac{dy}{dx} = \frac{(a^2-b^2)\sin x}{\sqrt{(b^2-a^2)\sin^2 x}} \times \frac{1}{b+a\cos x} = -\frac{(b^2-a^2)\sin x}{\sqrt{b^2-a^2}\,\sin x} \times \frac{1}{b+a\cos x} = \frac{-\sqrt{b^2-a^2}}{b+a\cos x}.$$

EXAMPLE 7 *Differentiate the following functions with respect to x:*

(i) e^{e^x} (ii) $\log_7(\log_7 x)$ (iii) $\log_x 2$

SOLUTION (i) Let $y = e^{e^x}$. Putting $e^x = u$, we get

$$y = e^u \text{ and } u = e^x \Rightarrow \frac{dy}{du} = e^u \text{ and } \frac{du}{dx} = e^x$$

$$\therefore \quad \frac{dy}{dx} = \frac{dy}{du} \times \frac{du}{dx} = e^u \times e^x = e^{e^x} \times e^x \qquad [\because u = e^x]$$

ALITER $\frac{d}{dx}\left(e^{e^x}\right) = \frac{d}{d(e^x)}\left(e^{e^x}\right) \times \frac{d}{dx}(e^x) = e^{e^x} \times e^x$

(ii) Let $y = \log_7(\log_7 x)$. Putting $u = \log_7 x$, we get

$$y = \log_7 u \text{ and } u = \log_7 x \Rightarrow \frac{dy}{du} = \frac{1}{u\log_e 7} \text{ and } \frac{du}{dx} = \frac{1}{x\log_e 7}$$

$$\therefore \quad \frac{dy}{dx} = \frac{dy}{du} \times \frac{du}{dx} = \frac{1}{u\log_e 7} \times \frac{1}{x\log_e 7}$$

$$\Rightarrow \quad \frac{dy}{dx} = \frac{1}{\log_7 x \times \log_e 7 \times x\log_e 7} = \frac{1}{x(\log_7 x)(\log_e 7)^2} \qquad [\because u = \log_7 x]$$

ALITER $\frac{d}{dx}\{\log_7(\log_7 x)\} = \frac{d}{d(\log_7 x)}\left(\log_7(\log_7 x)\right) \times \frac{d}{dx}(\log_7 x) = \frac{1}{(\log_7 x)\log_e 7} \times \frac{1}{x\log_e 7}$

$$= \frac{1}{x(\log_7 x)(\log_e 7)^2}$$

(iii) Let $y = \log_x 2$. Then, $y = \frac{1}{\log_2 x}$. Putting $u = \log_2 x$, we get $\left[\because \log_b a = \frac{1}{\log_a b}\right]$

$$y = \frac{1}{u} \text{ and } u = \log_2 x \Rightarrow \frac{dy}{du} = -\frac{1}{u^2} \text{ and } \frac{du}{dx} = \frac{1}{x\log_e 2}$$

$$\therefore \quad \frac{dy}{dx} = \frac{dy}{du} \times \frac{du}{dx} = -\frac{1}{u^2} \times \frac{1}{x\log_e 2} = -\frac{1}{(\log_2 x)^2} \times \frac{1}{x\log_e 2} \qquad [\because u = \log_2 x]$$

ALITER Using chain rule, we obtain

$$\frac{d}{dx}(\log_x 2) = \frac{d}{dx}\left(\frac{1}{\log_2 x}\right) = \frac{d}{d(\log_2 x)}\left(\frac{1}{\log_2 x}\right) \times \frac{d}{dx}(\log_2 x) = -\frac{1}{(\log_2 x)^2} \times \frac{1}{x \log_e 2}$$

EXAMPLE 8 *Differentiate the following functions with respect to x:*

(i) $\sec(\log x^n)$ (ii) $\log \tan\left(\frac{\pi}{4} + \frac{x}{2}\right)$ **[CBSE 2002]** (iii) $\sqrt{\log\left\{\sin\left(\frac{x^2}{3} - 1\right)\right\}}$.

SOLUTION (i) Let $y = \sec(\log x^n)$. Putting $x^n = v$, $u = \log x^n = \log v$, we get

$$y = \sec u,\ u = \log v \text{ and } v = x^n \Rightarrow \frac{dy}{du} = \sec u \tan u,\ \frac{du}{dv} = \frac{1}{v} \text{ and } \frac{dv}{dx} = nx^{n-1}$$

$$\therefore \quad \frac{dy}{dx} = \frac{dy}{du} \times \frac{du}{dv} \times \frac{dv}{dx} = \sec u \tan u \times \frac{1}{v} \times nx^{n-1}$$

$$\Rightarrow \quad \frac{dy}{dx} = \sec(\log x^n)\tan(\log x^n) \times \frac{1}{x^n} \times nx^{n-1} = \frac{n}{x} \times \sec(\log x^n)\tan(\log x^n)$$

(ii) Let $y = \log \tan\left(\frac{\pi}{4} + \frac{x}{2}\right)$. Putting $\frac{\pi}{4} + \frac{x}{2} = v$, $\tan\left(\frac{\pi}{4} + \frac{x}{2}\right) = \tan v = u$, we get

$$y = \log u,\ u = \tan v \text{ and } v = \frac{\pi}{4} + \frac{x}{2} \Rightarrow \frac{dy}{du} = \frac{1}{u},\ \frac{du}{dv} = \sec^2 v \text{ and } \frac{du}{dx} = \frac{1}{2}.$$

$$\therefore \quad \frac{dy}{dx} = \frac{dy}{du} \times \frac{du}{dv} \times \frac{dv}{dx} = \frac{1}{u} \times \sec^2 v \times \frac{1}{2} = \frac{1}{\tan v}\sec^2 v \times \frac{1}{2} \qquad [\because u = \tan v]$$

$$\Rightarrow \quad \frac{dy}{dx} = \frac{1}{2\sin v \cos v} = \frac{1}{\sin 2v} = \frac{1}{\sin\left(\frac{\pi}{2} + x\right)} = \frac{1}{\cos x} = \sec x. \qquad \left[\because v = \frac{\pi}{4} + \frac{x}{2}\right]$$

(iii) Let $y = \sqrt{\log\left\{\sin\left(\frac{x^2}{3} - 1\right)\right\}}$

Putting $\frac{x^2}{3} - 1 = v$, $\sin\left(\frac{x^2}{3} - 1\right) = \sin v = u$ and $\log\left\{\sin\left(\frac{x^2}{3} - 1\right)\right\} = \log u = z$, we get

$$y = \sqrt{z},\ z = \log u, u = \sin v \text{ and } v = \frac{x^2}{3} - 1 \Rightarrow \frac{dy}{dz} = \frac{1}{2\sqrt{z}},\ \frac{dz}{du} = \frac{1}{u},\ \frac{du}{dv} = \cos v \text{ and } \frac{dv}{dx} = \frac{2x}{3}$$

$$\therefore \quad \frac{dy}{dx} = \frac{dy}{dz} \times \frac{dz}{du} \times \frac{du}{dv} \times \frac{dv}{dx}$$

$$\Rightarrow \frac{dy}{dx} = \left(\frac{1}{2\sqrt{z}}\right)\left(\frac{1}{u}\right)(\cos v)\left(\frac{2x}{3}\right) = \frac{x}{3} \times \frac{\cos v}{u\sqrt{\log u}} \qquad [\because z = \log u]$$

$$\Rightarrow \frac{dy}{dx} = \frac{x}{3} \times \frac{\cos\left(\frac{x^2}{3} - 1\right)}{\sin\left(\frac{x^2}{3} - 1\right)\sqrt{\log\left\{\sin\left(\frac{x^2}{3} - 1\right)\right\}}} = \frac{x \cot\left(\frac{x^2}{3} - 1\right)}{3\sqrt{\log\left\{\sin\left(\frac{x^2}{3} - 1\right)\right\}}}.$$

EXAMPLE 9 *Differentiate the following functions with respect to x:*

(i) $\log\left(x+\sqrt{a^2+x^2}\right)$ **[CBSE 2003, NCERT EXEMPLAR]** (ii) $\log\left\{\dfrac{a+b\sin x}{a-b\sin x}\right\}$

(iii) $\dfrac{e^x+e^{-x}}{e^x-e^{-x}}$ (iv) $\log\sqrt{\dfrac{1+\sin x}{1-\sin x}}$

SOLUTION (i) Let $y=\log\left(x+\sqrt{a^2+x^2}\right)$. Then,

$$\frac{dy}{dx}=\frac{d}{dx}\left\{\log\left(x+\sqrt{a^x+x^2}\right)\right\}=\frac{1}{x+\sqrt{a^2+x^2}}\times\frac{d}{dx}\left\{x+\sqrt{a^2+x^2}\right\}$$

$$\Rightarrow\quad \frac{dy}{dx}=\frac{1}{x+\sqrt{a^2+x^2}}\left\{1+\frac{1}{2}(a^2+x^2)^{-1/2}\times\frac{d}{dx}(a^2+x^2)\right\}$$

$$\Rightarrow\quad \frac{dy}{dx}=\frac{1}{x+\sqrt{a^2+x^2}}\left\{1+\frac{1}{2\sqrt{a^2+x^2}}\times 2x\right\}=\frac{1}{x+\sqrt{a^2+x^2}}\times\frac{\sqrt{a^2+x^2}+x}{\sqrt{a^2+x^2}}=\frac{1}{\sqrt{a^2+x^2}}$$

(ii) Let $y=\log\left\{\dfrac{a+b\sin x}{a-b\sin x}\right\}$. Then,

$$y=\log(a+b\sin x)-\log(a-b\sin x)$$

$$\Rightarrow\quad \frac{dy}{dx}=\frac{d}{dx}\{\log(a+b\sin x)\}-\frac{d}{dx}\{\log(a-b\sin x)\}$$

$$\Rightarrow\quad \frac{dy}{dx}=\frac{1}{a+b\sin x}\times\frac{d}{dx}(a+b\sin x)-\frac{1}{a-b\sin x}\times\frac{d}{dx}(a-b\sin x)$$

$$\Rightarrow\quad \frac{dy}{dx}=\frac{1}{a+b\sin x}\times\frac{d}{dx}(a+b\sin x)-\frac{1}{a-b\sin x}\times\frac{d}{dx}(a-b\sin x)$$

$$\Rightarrow\quad \frac{dy}{dx}=\frac{1}{a+b\sin x}(0+b\cos x)-\frac{1}{a-b\sin x}(0-b\cos x)$$

$$\Rightarrow\quad \frac{dy}{dx}=\frac{b\cos x}{a+b\sin x}+\frac{b\cos x}{a-b\sin x}=b\cos x\left\{\frac{1}{a+b\sin x}+\frac{1}{a-b\sin x}\right\}$$

$$\Rightarrow\quad \frac{dy}{dx}=b\cos x\left\{\frac{a-b\sin x+a+b\sin x}{(a+b\sin x)(a-b\sin x)}\right\}=\frac{2ab\cos x}{a^2-b^2\sin^2 x}$$

(iii) Let $y=\dfrac{e^x+e^{-x}}{e^x-e^{-x}}$. Then,

$$\frac{dy}{dx}=\frac{d}{dx}\left\{\frac{e^x+e^{-x}}{e^x-e^{-x}}\right\}$$

$$\Rightarrow\quad \frac{dy}{dx}=\frac{(e^x-e^{-x})\frac{d}{dx}(e^x+e^{-x})-(e^x+e^{-x})\frac{d}{dx}(e^x-e^{-x})}{(e^x-e^{-x})^2}$$

$$\Rightarrow\quad \frac{dy}{dx}=\frac{(e^x-e^{-x})(e^x-e^{-x})-(e^x+e^{-x})(e^x+e^{-x})}{(e^x-e^{-x})^2}\qquad\left[\because \frac{d}{dx}(e^{-x})=e^{-x}\frac{d}{dx}(-x)=-e^{-x}\right]$$

$$\Rightarrow \quad \frac{dy}{dx} = \frac{(e^x - e^{-x})^2 - (e^x + e^{-x})^2}{(e^x - e^{-x})^2} = -\frac{4}{(e^x - e^{-x})^2}$$

(iv) Let $y = \log\sqrt{\frac{1+\sin x}{1-\sin x}}$. Then,

$$y = \log\left\{\frac{1+\sin x}{1-\sin x}\right\}^{1/2} = \frac{1}{2}\log\left\{\frac{1+\sin x}{1-\sin x}\right\} = \frac{1}{2}\{\log(1+\sin x) - \log(1-\sin x)\}$$

$$\therefore \quad \frac{dy}{dx} = \frac{1}{2}\left\{\frac{d}{dx}\{\log(1+\sin x)\} - \frac{d}{dx}\{\log(1-\sin x)\}\right\}$$

$$\Rightarrow \quad \frac{dy}{dx} = \frac{1}{2}\left\{\frac{1}{1+\sin x}\times\frac{d}{dx}(1+\sin x) - \frac{1}{1-\sin x}\times\frac{d}{dx}(1-\sin x)\right\}$$

$$\Rightarrow \quad \frac{dy}{dx} = \frac{1}{2}\left\{\frac{1}{1+\sin x}(0+\cos x) - \frac{1}{1-\sin x}(0-\cos x)\right\} = \frac{1}{2}\left\{\frac{\cos x}{1+\sin x} + \frac{\cos x}{1-\sin x}\right\}$$

$$\Rightarrow \quad \frac{dy}{dx} = \frac{1}{2}\cos x\left\{\frac{1-\sin x+1+\sin x}{1-\sin^2 x}\right\} = \frac{1}{2}\cos x\left(\frac{2}{1-\sin^2 x}\right) = \frac{\cos x}{\cos^2 x} = \sec x.$$

EXAMPLE 10 *Find* $\frac{dy}{dx}$, *when*

(i) $y = e^{ax}\cos(bx+c)$ (ii) $y = \frac{e^x + \log x}{\sin 3x}$ (iii) $y = e^x \log(1+x^2)$ (iv) $y = \frac{\sin x + x^2}{\cot 2x}$

SOLUTION (i) Using product rule, we get

$$\frac{dy}{dx} = e^{ax}\times\frac{d}{dx}\{\cos(bx+c)\} + \cos(bx+c)\times\frac{d}{dx}(e^{ax})$$

$$\Rightarrow \quad \frac{dy}{dx} = e^{ax}\times -\sin(bx+c)\times\frac{d}{dx}(bx+c) + \cos(bx+c)\times e^{ax}\times\frac{d}{dx}(ax)\}$$

$$\Rightarrow \quad \frac{dy}{dx} = e^{ax}\times\{-\sin(bx+c)\}\times b + \cos(bx+c)\times e^{ax}\times a$$

$$\Rightarrow \quad \frac{dy}{dx} = e^{ax}\{-b\sin(bx+c) + a\cos(bx+c)\}.$$

(ii) Using quotient rule, we get

$$\frac{dy}{dx} = \frac{\sin 3x \times \frac{d}{dx}(e^x + \log x) - (e^x + \log x)\times\frac{d}{dx}(\sin 3x)}{(\sin 3x)^2}$$

$$\Rightarrow \quad \frac{dy}{dx} = \frac{\sin 3x\left(e^x + \frac{1}{x}\right) - (e^x + \log x)(\cos 3x)\frac{d}{dx}(3x)}{\sin^2 3x}$$

$$\Rightarrow \quad \frac{dy}{dx} = \frac{\sin 3x\left(e^x + \frac{1}{x}\right) - (e^x + \log x)(\cos 3x)\times 3}{\sin^2 3x}$$

$$\Rightarrow \quad \frac{dy}{dx} = \frac{(e^x + 1/x)\sin 3x - 3(e^x + \log x)\cos 3x}{\sin^2 3x}$$

(iii) Using product rule, we get

$$\frac{dy}{dx} = e^x \times \frac{d}{dx}\{\log(1+x^2)\} + \log(1+x^2) \times \frac{d}{dx}(e^x)$$

$$\Rightarrow \quad \frac{dy}{dx} = e^x \times \frac{1}{1+x^2} \times \frac{d}{dx}(1+x^2) + \log(1+x^2) \times e^x$$

$$\Rightarrow \quad \frac{dy}{dx} = \frac{e^x}{1+x^2} \times 2x + e^x \times \log(1+x^2) = e^x\left\{\frac{2x}{1+x^2} + \log(1+x^2)\right\}$$

(iv) We have, $y = \dfrac{\sin x + x^2}{\cot 2x} = (\sin x + x^2)\tan 2x$

Using product rule, we get

$$\frac{dy}{dx} = (\sin x + x^2)\frac{d}{dx}(\tan 2x) + \tan 2x \frac{d}{dx}(\sin x + x^2)$$

$$\Rightarrow \quad \frac{dy}{dx} = (\sin x + x^2)(\sec^2 2x)\frac{d}{dx}(2x) + (\tan 2x)\ (\cos x + 2x)$$

$$\Rightarrow \quad \frac{dy}{dx} = (\sin x + x^2)(\sec^2 2x) \times 2 + (\tan 2x)(\cos x + 2x)$$

$$\Rightarrow \quad \frac{dy}{dx} = 2(\sin x + x^2)\sec^2 2x + (\cos x + 2x)\tan 2x.$$

BASED ON LOWER ORDER THINKING SKILLS (LOTS)

EXAMPLE 11 *If* $y = \left\{x + \sqrt{x^2 + a^2}\right\}^n$, *then prove that* $\dfrac{dy}{dx} = \dfrac{ny}{\sqrt{x^2+a^2}}$.

SOLUTION We have, $y = \left\{x + \sqrt{x^2 + a^2}\right\}^n$ [CBSE 2005]

$$\therefore \quad \frac{dy}{dx} = \frac{d}{dx}\left\{x + \sqrt{x^2+a^2}\right\}^n = n\left\{x + \sqrt{x^2+a^2}\right\}^{n-1} \times \frac{d}{dx}\left\{x + \sqrt{x^2+a^2}\right\}$$

$$\Rightarrow \quad \frac{dy}{dx} = n\left\{x + \sqrt{x^2+a^2}\right\}^{n-1} \times \left\{\frac{d}{dx}(x) + \frac{d}{dx}\sqrt{x^2+a^2}\right\}$$

$$\Rightarrow \quad \frac{dy}{dx} = n\left\{x + \sqrt{x^2+a^2}\right\}^{n-1} \times \left\{1 + \frac{1}{2}(x^2+a^2)^{-1/2} \times \frac{d}{dx}(x^2+a^2)\right\}$$

$$\Rightarrow \quad \frac{dy}{dx} = n\left\{x + \sqrt{x^2+a^2}\right\}^{n-1} \times \left\{1 + \frac{1}{2\sqrt{x^2+a^2}} \times 2x\right\}$$

$$\Rightarrow \quad \frac{dy}{dx} = n\left\{x + \sqrt{x^2+a^2}\right\}^{n-1}\left\{1 + \frac{x}{\sqrt{x^2+a^2}}\right\}$$

$$\Rightarrow \quad \frac{dy}{dx} = n\left\{x + \sqrt{x^2+a^2}\right\}^{n-1}\left\{\frac{\sqrt{x^2+a^2}+x}{\sqrt{x^2+a^2}}\right\} = \frac{n\left\{x + \sqrt{x^2+a^2}\right\}^n}{\sqrt{x^2+a^2}} = \frac{ny}{\sqrt{x^2+a^2}}.$$

EXAMPLE 12 *If* $y=\dfrac{x\sin^{-1}x}{\sqrt{1-x^2}}+\log\sqrt{1-x^2}$*, then prove that* $\dfrac{dy}{dx}=\dfrac{\sin^{-1}x}{(1-x^2)^{3/2}}$.

SOLUTION We have, $y=x\sin^{-1}x\,(1-x^2)^{-1/2}+\dfrac{1}{2}\log(1-x^2)$

Differentiating with respect to x, we get

$$\frac{dy}{dx}=\frac{d}{dx}\left\{x\sin^{-1}x\,(1-x^2)^{-1/2}\right\}+\frac{1}{2}\frac{d}{dx}\left\{\log(1-x^2)\right\}$$

$$\Rightarrow\quad \frac{dy}{dx}=\sin^{-1}x\,(1-x^2)^{-1/2}\frac{d}{dx}(x)+x\frac{d}{dx}(\sin^{-1}x)\,(1-x^2)^{-1/2}+x\sin^{-1}x\frac{d}{dx}(1-x^2)^{-1/2}+\frac{1}{2}\times\frac{1}{1-x^2}\times\frac{d}{dx}(1-x^2)$$

$$\Rightarrow\quad \frac{dy}{dx}=\frac{\sin^{-1}x}{\sqrt{1-x^2}}\times 1+x\times\frac{1}{\sqrt{1-x^2}}\times\frac{1}{\sqrt{1-x^2}}+x\sin^{-1}x\times\left(-\frac{1}{2}\right)(1-x^2)^{-3/2}\frac{d}{dx}(1-x^2)+\frac{1}{2(1-x^2)}(0-2x)$$

$$\Rightarrow\quad \frac{dy}{dx}=\frac{\sin^{-1}x}{\sqrt{1-x^2}}+\frac{x}{1-x^2}-\frac{x}{2}\frac{(\sin^{-1}x)}{(1-x^2)^{3/2}}(0-2x)-\frac{x}{1-x^2}$$

$$\Rightarrow\quad \frac{dy}{dx}=\frac{\sin^{-1}x}{\sqrt{1-x^2}}+\frac{x^2\sin^{-1}x}{(1-x^2)^{3/2}}=\frac{\sin^{-1}x}{\sqrt{1-x^2}}\left\{1+\frac{x^2}{1-x^2}\right\}=\frac{\sin^{-1}x}{\sqrt{1-x^2}}\times\frac{1}{1-x^2}=\frac{\sin^{-1}x}{(1-x^2)^{3/2}}.$$

EXAMPLE 13 *Differentiate the following functions with respect to x:*

(i) $\sin(m\sin^{-1}x)$ (ii) $a^{(\sin^{-1}x)^2}$ (iii) $e^{\cos^{-1}\left(\sqrt{1-x^2}\right)}$

SOLUTION (i) We have, $y=\sin(m\sin^{-1}x)$

$$\therefore\quad \frac{dy}{dx}=\frac{d}{dx}\left\{\sin(m\sin^{-1}x)\right\}=\cos(m\sin^{-1}x)\times\frac{d}{dx}(m\sin^{-1}x)=\cos(m\sin^{-1}x)\times m\frac{d}{dx}(\sin^{-1}x)$$

$$\Rightarrow\quad \frac{dy}{dx}=\cos(m\sin^{-1}x)\times m\times\frac{1}{\sqrt{1-x^2}}=\frac{m}{\sqrt{1-x^2}}\cos(m\sin^{-1}x)$$

(ii) We have, $y=a^{(\sin^{-1}x)^2}$

$$\therefore\quad \frac{dy}{dx}=\frac{d}{dx}\left\{a^{(\sin^{-1}x)^2}\right\}=a^{(\sin^{-1}x)^2}\log a\times\frac{d}{dx}\left\{(\sin^{-1}x)^2\right\}$$

$$\Rightarrow\quad \frac{dy}{dx}=a^{(\sin^{-1}x)^2}\log a\times 2(\sin^{-1}x)^{2-1}\times\frac{d}{dx}(\sin^{-1}x)$$

$$\Rightarrow\quad \frac{dy}{dx}=a^{(\sin^{-1}x)^2}\log a\times 2\sin^{-1}x\times\frac{1}{\sqrt{1-x^2}}=\frac{2\log a\cdot\sin^{-1}x}{\sqrt{1-x^2}}\times a^{(\sin^{-1}x)^2}$$

(iii) We have, $y=e^{\cos^{-1}\sqrt{1-x^2}}$

$$\therefore \quad \frac{dy}{dx} = \frac{d}{dx}\left\{e^{\cos^{-1}\sqrt{1-x^2}}\right\} = e^{\cos^{-1}\sqrt{1-x^2}} \times \frac{d}{dx}\left\{\cos^{-1}\sqrt{1-x^2}\right\}$$

$$\Rightarrow \quad \frac{dy}{dx} = e^{\cos^{-1}\sqrt{1-x^2}} \times \frac{-1}{\sqrt{1-\left(\sqrt{1-x^2}\right)^2}} \times \frac{d}{dx}\left(\sqrt{1-x^2}\right)$$

$$\Rightarrow \quad \frac{dy}{dx} = e^{\cos^{-1}\sqrt{1-x^2}} \times \frac{-1}{\sqrt{1-(1-x^2)}} \times \frac{1}{2}(1-x^2)^{\frac{1}{2}-1} \times \frac{d}{dx}(1-x^2)$$

$$\Rightarrow \quad \frac{dy}{dx} = e^{\cos^{-1}\sqrt{1-x^2}} \times \left(-\frac{1}{x}\right) \times \frac{1}{2\sqrt{1-x^2}}(-2x) = e^{\cos^{-1}\sqrt{1-x^2}} \times \frac{1}{\sqrt{1-x^2}}.$$

EXAMPLE 14 *Differentiate the following functions with respect to x:*

(i) $\log_{10} x + \log_x 10 + \log_x x + \log_{10} 10$ (ii) $5^{3-x^2} + (3-x^2)^5$

SOLUTION (i) Let $y = \log_{10} x + \log_x 10 + \log_x x + \log_{10} 10$. Then,

$$y = \log_{10} x + \frac{1}{\log_{10} x} + 1 + 1 = \log_{10} x + (\log_{10} x)^{-1} + 2.$$

Differentiating with respect to x, we get

$$\frac{dy}{dx} = \frac{1}{x \log_e 10} + (-1)(\log_{10} x)^{-2} \times \frac{d}{dx}(\log_{10} x) + 0$$

$$\Rightarrow \quad \frac{dy}{dx} = \frac{1}{x \log_e 10} - (\log_{10} x)^{-2} \times \frac{1}{x \log_e 10}$$

$$\Rightarrow \quad \frac{dy}{dx} = \frac{1}{x \log_e 10} - \frac{1}{x(\log_{10} x)^2} \times \frac{1}{\log_e 10}$$

$$\Rightarrow \quad \frac{dy}{dx} = \frac{1}{x \log_e 10} - \frac{1}{x(\log_{10} x \cdot \log_e 10)^2}\log_e 10 = \frac{1}{x \log_e 10} - \frac{1}{x(\log_e x)^2}\log_e 10.$$

(ii) Let $y = 5^{3-x^2} + (3-x^2)^5$. Differentiating with respect to x, we get

$$\frac{dy}{dx} = \frac{d}{dx}(5^{3-x^2}) + \frac{d}{dx}\left\{(3-x^2)^5\right\}$$

$$\Rightarrow \quad \frac{dy}{dx} = 5^{3-x^2}\log_e 5 \times \frac{d}{dx}(3-x^2) + 5(3-x^2)^{5-1} \times \frac{d}{dx}(3-x^2)$$

$$\Rightarrow \quad \frac{dy}{dx} = 5^{3-x^2}\log_e 5 \times (0-2x) + 5(3-x^2)^4 \times (0-2x) = -2x\left\{5^{3-x^2}\log_e 5 + 5(3-x^2)^4\right\}.$$

EXAMPLE 15 *If* $y = \dfrac{\sqrt{a^2+x^2}+\sqrt{a^2-x^2}}{\sqrt{a^2+x^2}-\sqrt{a^2-x^2}}$, *show that* $\dfrac{dy}{dx} = -\dfrac{2a^2}{x^3}\left\{1+\dfrac{a^2}{\sqrt{a^4-x^4}}\right\}$.

SOLUTION We have,

$$y = \frac{\sqrt{a^2+x^2}+\sqrt{a^2-x^2}}{\sqrt{a^2+x^2}-\sqrt{a^2-x^2}} = \frac{\sqrt{a^2+x^2}+\sqrt{a^2-x^2}}{\sqrt{a^2+x^2}-\sqrt{a^2-x^2}} \times \frac{\sqrt{a^2+x^2}+\sqrt{a^2-x^2}}{\sqrt{a^2+x^2}+\sqrt{a^2-x^2}}$$

$$\Rightarrow \quad y = \frac{\left\{\sqrt{a^2+x^2}+\sqrt{a^2-x^2}\right\}^2}{(a^2+x^2)-(a^2-x^2)} = \frac{a^2+x^2+a^2-x^2+2\sqrt{a^2+x^2}\sqrt{a^2-x^2}}{2x^2}$$

$$\Rightarrow \quad y = \frac{2a^2+2\sqrt{a^4-x^4}}{2x^2} = \frac{a^2}{x^2}+\frac{\sqrt{a^4-x^4}}{x^2} = a^2x^{-2}+\sqrt{a^4-x^4}\,x^{-2}$$

$$\therefore \quad \frac{dy}{dx} = a^2\frac{d}{dx}(x^{-2})+\frac{d}{dx}\left\{\sqrt{a^4-x^4}\,x^{-2}\right\}$$

$$\Rightarrow \quad \frac{dy}{dx} = -2a^2x^{-3}+(-2)\,x^{-3}\sqrt{a^4-x^4}+(x^{-2})\frac{1}{2}(a^4-x^4)^{-1/2}\times\frac{d}{dx}(a^4-x^4)$$

$$\Rightarrow \quad \frac{dy}{dx} = -\frac{2a^2}{x^3}-\frac{2}{x^3}\sqrt{a^4-x^4}+\frac{1}{2x^2\sqrt{a^4-x^4}}(-4x^3)$$

$$\Rightarrow \quad \frac{dy}{dx} = -\frac{2a^2}{x^3}-\frac{2}{x^3}\sqrt{a^4-x^4}-\frac{2x}{\sqrt{a^4-x^4}} = -\frac{2a^2}{x^3}-2\left\{\frac{\sqrt{a^4-x^4}}{x^3}+\frac{x}{\sqrt{a^4-x^4}}\right\}$$

$$\Rightarrow \quad \frac{dy}{dx} = -\frac{2a^2}{x^3}-2\left\{\frac{a^4-x^4+x^4}{x^3\sqrt{a^4-x^4}}\right\} = -\frac{2a^2}{x^3}-\frac{2a^4}{x^3\sqrt{a^4-x^4}} = -\frac{2a^2}{x^3}\left\{1+\frac{a^2}{\sqrt{a^4-x^4}}\right\}$$

EXAMPLE 16 *If* $y=\sqrt{\frac{1-x}{1+x}}$, *prove that* $(1-x^2)\frac{dy}{dx}+y=0$. **[CBSE 2004]**

SOLUTION We have, $y=\sqrt{\frac{1-x}{1+x}}$. Differentiating with respect to x, we get

$$\frac{dy}{dx} = \frac{1}{2}\left(\frac{1-x}{1+x}\right)^{1/2-1}\times\frac{d}{dx}\left(\frac{1-x}{1+x}\right)$$

$$\Rightarrow \quad \frac{dy}{dx} = \frac{1}{2}\sqrt{\frac{1+x}{1-x}}\times\frac{(1+x)\frac{d}{dx}(1-x)-(1-x)\frac{d}{dx}(1+x)}{(1+x)^2}$$

$$\Rightarrow \quad \frac{dy}{dx} = \frac{1}{2}\sqrt{\frac{1+x}{1-x}}\times\frac{(1+x)(-1)-(1-x)(1)}{(1+x)^2} = \frac{1}{2}\sqrt{\frac{1+x}{1-x}}\times\frac{-1-x-1+x}{(1+x)^2}$$

$$\Rightarrow \quad \frac{dy}{dx} = -\sqrt{\frac{1+x}{1-x}}\times\frac{1}{(1+x)^2}$$

$$\Rightarrow \quad (1-x^2)\frac{dy}{dx} = -\sqrt{\frac{1+x}{1-x}}\,\frac{1}{(1+x)^2}(1-x^2) \qquad \text{[Multiplying both sides by } (1-x^2)\text{]}$$

$$\Rightarrow \quad (1-x^2)\frac{dy}{dx} = -\sqrt{\frac{1-x}{1+x}} \Rightarrow (1-x^2)\frac{dy}{dx} = -y \Rightarrow (1-x^2)\frac{dy}{dx} + y = 0$$

EXAMPLE 17 *If* $y = \sqrt{\frac{1+e^x}{1-e^x}}$, *show that* $\frac{dy}{dx} = \frac{e^x}{(1-e^x)\sqrt{1-e^{2x}}}$.

SOLUTION We have, $y = \sqrt{\frac{1+e^x}{1-e^x}}$. Differentiating both sides with respect to x, we obtain.

$$\frac{dy}{dx} = \frac{1}{2}\left(\frac{1+e^x}{1-e^x}\right)^{1/2-1} \times \frac{d}{dx}\left(\frac{1+e^x}{1-e^x}\right)$$

$$\Rightarrow \quad \frac{dy}{dx} = \frac{1}{2}\sqrt{\frac{1-e^x}{1+e^x}} \times \frac{(1-e^x)\frac{d}{dx}(1+e^x) - (1+e^x)\frac{d}{dx}(1-e^x)}{(1-e^x)^2}$$

$$\Rightarrow \quad \frac{dy}{dx} = \frac{1}{2}\sqrt{\frac{1-e^x}{1+e^x}} \times \frac{(1-e^x)\,e^x + (1+e^x)\,e^x}{(1-e^x)^2} = \frac{1}{2}\sqrt{\frac{1-e^x}{1+e^x}} \times \frac{2e^x}{(1-e^x)^2}$$

$$\Rightarrow \quad \frac{dy}{dx} = e^x\sqrt{\frac{1-e^x}{1+e^x}} \times \frac{1}{(1-e^x)^2} = \frac{e^x}{\sqrt{1+e^x}\,(1-e^x)^{3/2}}$$

$$\Rightarrow \quad \frac{dy}{dx} = \frac{e^x}{\sqrt{1+e^x}\,\sqrt{1-e^x}\,(1-e^x)} = \frac{e^x}{(1-e^x)\sqrt{1-e^{2x}}}$$

EXAMPLE 18 *If* $(1+x)^n = C_0 + C_1 x + C_2 x^2 + \ldots + C_n x^n$, *using derivatives prove that*

(i) $C_1 + 2C_2 + \ldots + nC_n = n.2^{n-1}$ (ii) $C_1 - 2C_2 + 3C_3 + \ldots + (-1)^{n-1} nC_n = 0$

SOLUTION We have, $(1+x)^n = C_0 + C_1 x + C_2 x^2 + \ldots + C_n x^n$

Differentiating both sides with respect to x, we get

$$n(1+x)^{n-1} = C_1 + 2C_2 x + 3C_3 x^2 + \ldots + nC_n x^{n-1}$$

Putting $x = 1$ and -1 successively, we get

$$C_1 + 2C_2 + 3C_3 + \ldots + nC_n = n.2^{n-1} \text{ and, } C_1 - 2C_2 + 3C_3 + \ldots + (-1)^{n-1} nC_n = 0$$

EXAMPLE 19 *Using the fact:* $\sin(A+B) = \sin A \cos B + \cos A \sin B$ *and the technique of differentiation, obtain the sum formula for* cosines.

SOLUTION We have,

$$\sin(A+B) = \sin A \cos B + \cos A \sin B$$

Taking B as a constant, A as a variable and differentiating both sides with respect to A, we get

$$\frac{d}{dA}(\sin(A+B)) = \cos B \frac{d}{dA}(\sin A) + \sin B \frac{d}{dA}(\cos A)$$

$$\Rightarrow \quad \cos(A+B) = \cos B \cos A - \sin B \sin A \text{ or, } \cos(A+B) = \cos A \cos B - \sin A \sin B.$$

BASED ON HIGHER ORDER THINKING SKILLS (HOTS)

EXAMPLE 20 *If* $f(x) = \sqrt{x^2+1}$, $g(x) = \frac{x+1}{x^2+1}$ *and* $h(x) = 2x-3$, *then find* $f'(h'(g'(x)))$. **[CBSE 2015]**

SOLUTION We have, $f(x) = \sqrt{x^2+1}$, $g(x) = \frac{x+1}{x^2+1}$ and $h(x) = 2x - 3$

$$\therefore \quad f'(x) = \frac{x}{\sqrt{x^2+1}}, g'(x) = \frac{1-2x-x^2}{(x^2+1)^2} \text{ and } h'(x) = 2 \text{ for all } x \in R$$

Now,

$$h'(x) = 2 \text{ for all } x \in R$$

$$\Rightarrow \quad h'\left(g'(x)\right) = 2 \text{ for all } x \in R$$

$$\Rightarrow \quad f'\left(h'\left(g'(x)\right)\right) = f'(2) \text{ for all } x \in R$$

$$\Rightarrow \quad f'\left(h'\left(g'(x)\right)\right) = \frac{2}{\sqrt{2^2+1}} = \frac{2}{\sqrt{5}} \text{ for all } x \in R \qquad \left[\because f'(x) = \frac{x}{\sqrt{x^2+1}} \therefore f'(2) = \frac{2}{\sqrt{5}}\right]$$

EXAMPLE 21 *If $y = f(x^2)$ and $f'(x) = e^{\sqrt{x}}$, find $\frac{dy}{dx}$.* [CBSE 2020]

SOLUTION We have, $y = f(x^2)$ and $f'(x) = e^{\sqrt{x}}$

$$\therefore \quad \frac{dy}{dx} = \frac{d}{dx}(f(x^2)) = f'(x^2)\frac{d}{dx}(x^2) = f'(x^2)\, 2x = e^{|x|}\, 2x = 2x e^{|x|} \qquad [\because f'(x) = e^{\sqrt{x}} \therefore f'(x^2) = e^{|x|}]$$

10.4.1 DIFFERENTIATION OF INVERSE TRIGONOMETRIC FUNCTIONS BY CHAIN RULE

In section 10.3, we have obtained the derivative of inverse trigonometric functions from first principles. In this section, we will obtain the same by using chain rule.

THEOREM 1 *If $x \in (-1, 1)$, then the differentiation of $\sin^{-1} x$ with respect to x is $\frac{1}{\sqrt{1-x^2}}$.*

i.e., $$\frac{d}{dx}(\sin^{-1} x) = \frac{1}{\sqrt{1-x^2}}, \text{ for } x \in (-1, 1).$$

PROOF Let $y = \sin^{-1} x$. Then, $\sin(\sin^{-1} x) = x \Rightarrow \sin y = x$

Differentiating both sides with respect to x, we get

$$1 = \frac{d}{dx}(\sin y)$$

$$\Rightarrow \quad 1 = \frac{d}{dy}(\sin y) \times \frac{dy}{dx} \qquad \text{[By chain rule]}$$

$$\Rightarrow \quad 1 = \cos y \frac{dy}{dx} \Rightarrow \frac{dy}{dx} = \frac{1}{\cos y} = \frac{1}{\sqrt{1-\sin^2 y}} = \frac{1}{\sqrt{1-x^2}}, -1 < x < 1$$

or, $$\frac{d}{dx}(\sin^{-1} x) = \frac{1}{\sqrt{1-x^2}}$$

THEOREM 2 *If $x \in (-1, 1)$, then the differentiation of $\cos^{-1} x$ with respect to x is $\frac{-1}{\sqrt{1-x^2}}$.*

i.e., $$\frac{d}{dx}(\cos^{-1} x) = \frac{-1}{\sqrt{1-x^2}}, \text{ for } x \in (-1, 1).$$

PROOF Let $y = \cos^{-1} x$. Then,

$$\cos(\cos^{-1} x) = x$$

$$\Rightarrow \quad \cos y = x$$

$$\Rightarrow \quad \frac{d}{dx}(\cos y) = \frac{d}{dx}(x) \qquad \text{[Differentiating both sides with respect to } x\text{]}$$

$\Rightarrow \quad \frac{d}{dy}(\cos y) \times \frac{dy}{dx} = 1$ [By chain rule]

$\Rightarrow \quad -\sin y \frac{dy}{dx} = 1$

$\Rightarrow \quad \frac{dy}{dx} = \frac{-1}{\sin y} = \frac{-1}{\sqrt{1-\cos^2 y}} = \frac{-1}{\sqrt{1-x^2}}, -1 < x < 1$ $[\because x = \cos y]$

or, $\quad \frac{d}{dx}(\cos^{-1} x) = \frac{1}{\sqrt{1-x^2}}, -1 < x < 1$

THEOREM 3 *The differentiation of* $\tan^{-1} x$ *with respect to x is* $\frac{1}{1+x^2}$.

i.e., $\quad \frac{d}{dx}(\tan^{-1} x) = \frac{1}{1+x^2}$

PROOF Let $y = \tan^{-1} x$. Then,

$\tan(\tan^{-1} x) = x$

$\Rightarrow \quad \tan y = x$

$\Rightarrow \quad \frac{d}{dx}(\tan y) = \frac{d}{dx}(x)$ [Differentiating both sides with respect to x]

$\Rightarrow \quad \frac{d}{dy}(\tan y) \times \frac{dy}{dx} = 1$ [By chain rule]

$\Rightarrow \quad \sec^2 y \frac{dy}{dx} = 1$

$\Rightarrow \quad \frac{dy}{dx} = \frac{1}{\sec^2 y} = \frac{1}{1+\tan^2 y} = \frac{1}{1+x^2}$

or, $\quad \frac{d}{dx}(\tan^{-1} x) = \frac{1}{1+x^2}$ $[\because y = \tan^{-1} x \text{ and } \tan y = x]$

THEOREM 4 *The differentiation of* $\cot^{-1} x$ *with respect to x is* $\frac{-1}{1+x^2}$.

i.e., $\quad \frac{d}{dx}(\cot^{-1} x) = \frac{-1}{1+x^2}$

PROOF Let $y = \cot^{-1} x$. Then,

$\cot(\cot^{-1} x) = x$

$\Rightarrow \quad \cot y = x$

$\Rightarrow \quad \frac{d}{dx}(\cot y) = \frac{d}{dx}(x)$ [Differentiating both sides with respect to x]

$\Rightarrow \quad \frac{d}{dy}(\cot y) \times \frac{dy}{dx} = 1$ [Using chain rule]

$\Rightarrow \quad -\text{cosec}^2 y \times \frac{dy}{dx} = 1$

$\Rightarrow \quad \frac{dy}{dx} = \frac{-1}{\text{cosec}^2 y} = \frac{-1}{1+\cot^2 y} = \frac{-1}{1+x^2}$

or, $\quad \frac{d}{dx}(\cot^{-1} x) = \frac{-1}{1+x^2}$ $[\because y = \cot^{-1} x \text{ and } x = \cot y]$

THEOREM 5 *If* $x \in R - [-1, 1]$, *then the differentiation of* $\sec^{-1} x$ *with respect to x is* $\frac{1}{|x|\sqrt{x^2-1}}$.

i.e., $$\frac{d}{dx}(\sec^{-1} x) = \frac{1}{|x|\sqrt{x^2-1}}, x \in R - [-1, 1].$$

PROOF Let $y = \sec^{-1} x$. Then,

$$\sec(\sec^{-1} x) = x$$

$\Rightarrow$ $\sec y = x$

$\Rightarrow$ $\frac{d}{dx}(\sec y) = \frac{d}{dx}(x)$ [Differentiating both sides with respect to x]

$\Rightarrow$ $\frac{d}{dy}(\sec y) \times \frac{dy}{dx} = 1$ [Using chain rule]

$\Rightarrow$ $\sec y \tan y \frac{dy}{dx} = 1 \Rightarrow \frac{dy}{dx} = \frac{1}{\sec y \tan y}$

If $x > 1$, then

$y \in (0, \pi/2) \Rightarrow \sec y > 0, \tan y > 0 \Rightarrow |\sec y|\,|\tan y| = \sec y \tan y$.

If $x < -1$, then

$y \in (\pi/2, \pi) \Rightarrow \sec y < 0, \tan y < 0 \Rightarrow |\sec y|\,|\tan y| = (-\sec y)(-\tan y) = \sec y \tan y$

$\therefore$ $\frac{dy}{dx} = \frac{1}{\sec y \tan y} \Rightarrow \frac{dy}{dx} = \frac{1}{|\sec y|\,|\tan y|}$

$\Rightarrow$ $\frac{dy}{dx} = \frac{1}{|\sec y|\sqrt{\tan^2 y}} = \frac{1}{|\sec y|\sqrt{\sec^2 y - 1}} = \frac{1}{|x|\sqrt{x^2-1}}$

or, $$\frac{d}{dx}(\sec^{-1} x) = \frac{1}{|x|\sqrt{x^2-1}}$$

THEOREM 6 *If $x \in R - [-1, 1]$, then the differentiation of $\text{cosec}^{-1} x$ with respect to x is* $\frac{-1}{|x|\sqrt{x^2-1}}$.

i.e., $$\frac{d}{dx}(\text{cosec}^{-1} x) = \frac{1}{|x|\sqrt{x^2-1}}$$

PROOF Let $y = \text{cosec}^{-1} x$. Then,

$$\text{cosec}(\text{cosec}^{-1} x) = x$$

$\Rightarrow$ $\text{cosec}\, y = x$

$\Rightarrow$ $\frac{d}{dx}(\text{cosec}\, y) = \frac{d}{dx}(x)$ [Differentiating both sides with respect to x]

$\Rightarrow$ $\frac{d}{dy}(\text{cosec}\, y) \times \frac{dy}{dx} = 1$ [Using chain rule]

$\Rightarrow$ $-\text{cosec}\, y \cot y \times \frac{dy}{dx} = 1 \Rightarrow \frac{dy}{dx} = \frac{-1}{\text{cosec}\, y \cot y}$

If $x > 1$, then $y\ (0, \pi/2) \Rightarrow \text{cosec}\, y > 0, \cot y > 0 \Rightarrow |\text{cosec}\, y||\cot y| = \text{cosec}\, y \cot y$

If $x < -1$, then

$y \in (-\pi/2, 0) \Rightarrow \text{cosec}\, y < 0$ and $\cot y < 0 \Rightarrow |\text{cosec}\, y||\cot y| = (-\text{cosec}\, y)(-\cot y)$

$\therefore$ $\frac{dy}{dx} = \frac{-1}{\text{cosec}\, y \cot y} \Rightarrow \frac{dy}{dx} = \frac{-1}{|\text{cosec}\, y||\cot y|} = \frac{-1}{|\text{cosec}\, y|\sqrt{\text{cosec}^2 y - 1}} = \frac{-1}{|x|\sqrt{x^2-1}}$

or, $$\frac{d}{dx}(\text{cosec}^{-1} x) = \frac{-1}{|x|\sqrt{x^2-1}}$$

EXERCISE 10.2

BASIC

Differentiate the following functions with respect to x (1-57) :

1. $\sin(3x+5)$
2. $\tan^2 x$
3. $\tan(x^\circ + 45^\circ)$
4. $\sin(\log x)$
5. $e^{\sin\sqrt{x}}$
6. $e^{\tan x}$
7. $\sin^2(2x+1)$
8. $\log_7(2x-3)$
9. $\tan 5x^\circ$
10. 2^{x^3}
11. 3^{e^x}
12. $\log_x 3$
13. 3^{x^2+2x}
14. $\sqrt{\dfrac{a^2-x^2}{a^2+x^2}}$
15. $3^{x\log x}$
16. $\sqrt{\dfrac{1+\sin x}{1-\sin x}}$
17. $\sqrt{\dfrac{1-x^2}{1+x^2}}$
18. $(\log\sin x)^2$
19. $\sqrt{\dfrac{1+x}{1-x}}$
20. $\sin\left(\dfrac{1+x^2}{1-x^2}\right)$
21. $e^{3x}\cos 2x$
22. $\sin(\log\sin x)$
23. $e^{\tan 3x}$
24. $e^{\sqrt{\cot x}}$
25. $\log\left(\dfrac{\sin x}{1+\cos x}\right)$
26. $\log\sqrt{\dfrac{1-\cos x}{1+\cos x}}$ [CBSE 2003]
27. $\tan(e^{\sin x})$
28. $\log(x+\sqrt{x^2+1})$
29. $\dfrac{e^x\log x}{x^2}$
30. $\dfrac{3x^2\sin x}{\sqrt{7-x^2}}$
31. $\dfrac{e^{2x}+e^{-2x}}{e^{2x}-e^{-2x}}$
32. $\log\left(\dfrac{x^2+x+1}{x^2-x+1}\right)$
33. $\tan^{-1}(e^x)$
34. $e^{\sin^{-1}2x}$
35. $\sin(2\sin^{-1}x)$
36. $e^{\tan^{-1}\sqrt{x}}$
37. $\sqrt{\tan^{-1}\left(\dfrac{x}{2}\right)}$
38. $\log(\tan^{-1}x)$
39. $\dfrac{2^x\cos x}{(x^2+3)^2}$
40. $\sin^2\{\log(2x+3)\}$
41. $e^x\log\sin 2x$
42. $(\sin^{-1}x^4)^4$
43. $\sin^{-1}\left(\dfrac{x}{\sqrt{x^2+a^2}}\right)$
44. $\dfrac{e^x\sin x}{(x^2+2)^3}$
45. $3e^{-3x}\log(1+x)$
46. $\dfrac{x^2+2}{\sqrt{\cos x}}$
47. $\dfrac{x^2(1-x^2)^3}{\cos 2x}$
48. $\log\left\{\cot\left(\dfrac{\pi}{4}+\dfrac{x}{2}\right)\right\}$
49. $e^{ax}\sec x\tan 2x$
50. $\log(\cos x^2)$
51. $\cos(\log x)^2$
52. $\log\sqrt{\dfrac{x-1}{x+1}}$
53. $\log(\text{cosec}\,x-\cot x)$
54. $x\sin 2x+5^x+k^k+(\tan^2 x)^3$
55. $\log(3x+2)-x^2\log(2x-1)$
56. $\dfrac{\sqrt{x^2+1}+\sqrt{x^2-1}}{\sqrt{x^2+1}-\sqrt{x^2-1}}$
57. $\log\left\{x+2+\sqrt{x^2+4x+1}\right\}$
58. If $y=\dfrac{e^x-e^{-x}}{e^x+e^{-x}}$, prove that $\dfrac{dy}{dx}=1-y^2$
59. If $y=\sqrt{x^2+a^2}$, prove that $y\dfrac{dy}{dx}-x=0$
60. If $y=e^x+e^{-x}$, prove that $\dfrac{dy}{dx}=\sqrt{y^2-4}$ [CBSE 2020]

61. If $y=\sqrt{a^2-x^2}$, prove that $y\frac{dy}{dx}+x=0$

62. If $xy=4$, prove that $x\left(\frac{dy}{dx}+y^2\right)=3y$

63. If $f(x)=\sqrt{\frac{\sec x-1}{\sec x+1}}$, find $f'\left(\frac{\pi}{3}\right)$. [CBSE 2020]

64. If $f(x)=\sqrt{\tan\sqrt{x}}$, then (i) find $f'\left(\frac{\pi^2}{16}\right)$ (ii) prove that $\sqrt{x}\frac{dy}{dx}=\frac{1+y^4}{4y}$. [CBSE 2020, 2024]

65. If $y=\frac{x}{x+2}$, prove that $x\frac{dy}{dx}=(1-y)y$

66. If $y=\sqrt{x}+\frac{1}{\sqrt{x}}$, prove that $2x\frac{dy}{dx}=\sqrt{x}-\frac{1}{\sqrt{x}}$

67. If $y=\log\sqrt{\frac{1+\tan x}{1-\tan x}}$, prove that $\frac{dy}{dx}=\sec 2x$. [CBSE 2011]

68. If $y=\frac{x\sin^{-1}x}{\sqrt{1-x^2}}$, prove that $(1-x^2)\frac{dy}{dx}=x+\frac{y}{x}$.

69. If $y=x\sin^{-1}x+\sqrt{1-x^2}$, prove that $\frac{dy}{dx}=\sin^{-1}x$.

70. If $y=(1-x)\log(x-1)-(x+1)\log(x+1)$, prove that $\frac{dy}{dx}-\log\left(\frac{x-1}{1+x}\right)$

71. If $y=\log\left(\sqrt{x}+\frac{1}{\sqrt{x}}\right)$, prove that $\frac{dy}{dx}=\frac{x-1}{2x(x+1)}$

72. If $y=\sqrt{x+1}+\sqrt{x-1}$, prove that $\sqrt{x^2-1}\frac{dy}{dx}=\frac{1}{2}y$

73. If $y=\frac{1}{2}\log\left(\frac{1-\cos 2x}{1+\cos 2x}\right)$, prove that $\frac{dy}{dx}=2\operatorname{cosec}2x$

74. Prove that $\frac{d}{dx}\left\{\frac{x}{2}\sqrt{a^2-x^2}+\frac{a^2}{2}\sin^{-1}\frac{x}{a}\right\}=\sqrt{a^2-x^2}$ [CBSE 2004]

75. If $y=\log\left\{\sqrt{x-1}-\sqrt{x+1}\right\}$, show that $\frac{dy}{dx}=\frac{-1}{2\sqrt{x^2-1}}$

76. If $y=\left(x+\sqrt{x^2-1}\right)^2$, then show that $(x^2-1)\left(\frac{dy}{dx}\right)^2=4y^2$. [CBSE 2023]

77. If $y=\cos^3(\sec^2 2t)$, find $\frac{dy}{dt}$. [CBSE 2024]

ANSWERS

1. $3\cos(3x+5)$

2. $2\tan x\sec^2 x$

3. $\frac{\pi}{180}\sec^2(x^\circ+45^\circ)$

4. $\frac{1}{x}\cos(\log x)$

5. $\frac{\cos\sqrt{x}\,e^{\sin\sqrt{x}}}{2\sqrt{x}}$

6. $e^{\tan x}\sec^2 x$

7. $2\sin(4x+2)$

8. $\frac{2}{(2x-3)\log_e 7}$

9. $\frac{5\pi}{180}\sec^2(5x^\circ)$

10. $3x^2 \cdot 2^{x^3} \log 2$

11. $3^{e^x} \log 3 \cdot e^x$

12. $-\dfrac{1}{x \log_e 3 (\log_3 x)^2}$

13. $(3^{x^2+2x} \log 3)(2x+2)$

14. $\dfrac{-2a^2 x}{\sqrt{a^2-x^2}\,(a^2+x^2)^{3/2}}$

15. $3^{x \log x} (\log 3)(1+\log x)$

16. $\sec x(\tan x + \sec x)$

17. $\dfrac{-2x}{\sqrt{1-x^2}\,(1+x^2)^{3/2}}$

18. $2(\log \sin x)\cot x$

19. $\dfrac{1}{\sqrt{1+x}\,(1-x)^{3/2}}$

20. $\dfrac{4x}{(1-x^2)^2} \cos\left(\dfrac{1+x^2}{1-x^2}\right)$

21. $e^{3x}(3\cos 2x - 2\sin 2x)$

22. $\cos(\log \sin x) \cdot \cot x$

23. $3\, e^{\tan 3x} \cdot \sec^2 3x$

24. $-\dfrac{1}{2} \dfrac{e^{\sqrt{\cot x}}}{\sqrt{\cot x}} \times \operatorname{cosec}^2 x$

25. $\operatorname{cosec} x$

26. $\operatorname{cosec} x$

27. $\sec^2(e^{\sin x})\, e^{\sin x} \cos x$

28. $\dfrac{1}{\sqrt{x^2+1}}$

29. $e^x x^{-2}\left(\log x + \dfrac{1}{x} - \dfrac{2}{x} \log x\right)$

30. $\dfrac{6x \sin x + 3x^2 \cos x}{\sqrt{7-x^2}} + \dfrac{3x^3 \sin x}{(7-x^2)^{3/2}}$

31. $\dfrac{-8}{(e^{2x}-e^{-2x})^2}$

32. $-\dfrac{2(x^2-1)}{x^4+x^2+1}$

33. $\dfrac{e^x}{1+e^{2x}}$

34. $\dfrac{2}{\sqrt{1-4x^2}}\, e^{\sin^{-1} 2x}$

35. $\cos(2\sin^{-1} x) \cdot \dfrac{2}{\sqrt{1-x^2}}$

36. $\dfrac{e^{\tan^{-1}\sqrt{x}}}{2\sqrt{x}\,(1+x)}$

37. $\dfrac{1}{(4+x^2)\sqrt{\tan^{-1}\left(\dfrac{x}{2}\right)}}$

38. $\dfrac{1}{(1+x^2)\tan^{-1} x}$

39. $\dfrac{2^x}{(x^2+3)^2}\left\{\cos x \cdot \log_e 2 - \sin x - \dfrac{4x \cos x}{x^2+3}\right\}$

40. $\sin\{2\log(2x+3)\} \cdot \left(\dfrac{2}{2x+3}\right)$

41. $2\, e^x \cot 2x + e^x \log \sin 2x$

42. $\dfrac{16x^3(\sin^{-1} x^4)^3}{\sqrt{1-x^8}}$

43. $\dfrac{a}{a^2+x^2}$

44. $\dfrac{e^x \sin x + e^x \cos x}{(x^2+2)^3} - \dfrac{6x\, e^x \sin x}{(x^2+2)^4}$

45. $3\, e^{-3x}\left\{\dfrac{1}{x+1} - 3\log(x+1)\right\}$

46. $\dfrac{1}{\sqrt{\cos x}}\left\{2x + \left(\dfrac{x^2+2}{2}\right)\tan x\right\}$

47. $2x(1-x^2)^2 \sec 2x\,\{1-4x^2+x(1-x^2)\tan 2x\}$

48. $-\sec x$

49. $e^{ax} \sec x\,\{a \tan 2x + \tan x \tan 2x + 2\sec^2 2x\}$

50. $-2x \tan x^2$

51. $\dfrac{-2\log x \sin(\log x)^2}{x}$

52. $\dfrac{1}{x^2-1}$

53. $\operatorname{cosec} x$

54. $\sin 2x + 2x\cos 2x + 5^x \log 5 + 6\tan^5 x \sec^2 x$

55. $\dfrac{3}{3x+2} - \dfrac{2x^2}{2x-1} - 2x\log(2x-1)$

56. $2x + \dfrac{2x^3}{\sqrt{x^4-1}}$

57. $\dfrac{1}{\sqrt{x^2+4x+1}}$

63. $\frac{2}{3}$ 64. $\frac{2}{\pi}$ 77. $-12\cos^2(\sec^2 2t)\sin(\sec^2 2t)\sec^2 2t\tan 2t$

10.5 DIFFERENTIATION BY USING TRIGONOMETRICAL SUBSTITUTIONS

Sometimes, it becomes very easy to differentiate a function by using trigonometrical transformations. Usually this is done in case of inverse trigonometrical functions. Some important results on trigonometrical and inverse trigonometrical functions are given below for ready reference.

(i) $\sin 2x = 2\sin x\cos x$ (ii) $1+\cos 2x = 2\cos^2 x$ or, $\cos 2x = 2\cos^2 x - 1$

(iii) $1-\cos 2x = 2\sin^2 x$ or, $\cos 2x = 1-2\sin^2 x$

(iv) $\sin 2x = \dfrac{2\tan x}{1+\tan^2 x}$ (v) $\cos 2x = \dfrac{1-\tan^2 x}{1+\tan^2 x}$

(vi) $\tan 2x = \dfrac{2\tan x}{1-\tan^2 x}$ (vii) $\sin 3x = 3\sin x - 4\sin^3 x$

(viii) $\cos 3x = 4\cos^3 x - 3\cos x$ (ix) $\tan 3x = \dfrac{3\tan x - \tan^3 x}{1-3\tan^2 x}$

(x) $\sin^{-1}\left\{x\sqrt{1-y^2}+y\sqrt{1-x^2}\right\}$

$$=\begin{cases}\sin^{-1}x+\sin^{-1}y & \text{, if } -1\le x, y<1 \text{ and } x^2+y^2\le 1 \text{ or, if } xy<0 \text{ and } x^2+y^2>1\\ \pi-(\sin^{-1}x+\sin^{-1}y) & \text{, if } 0<x, y\le 1 \text{ and } x^2+y^2>1\\ -\pi-(\sin^{-1}x+\sin^{-1}y) & \text{, if } -1\le x, y<0 \text{ and } x^2+y^2>1\end{cases}$$

$\sin^{-1}\left\{x\sqrt{1-y^2}-y\sqrt{1-x^2}\right\}$

$$=\begin{cases}\sin^{-1}x-\sin^{-1}y & \text{, if } -1\le x, y\le 1 \text{ and } x^2+y^2\le 1 \text{ or, if } xy>0\ \&\ x^2+y^2>1\\ \pi-(\sin^{-1}x-\sin^{-1}y) & \text{, if } 0<x\le 1, -1\le y\le 0 \text{ and } x^2+y^2>1\\ -\pi-(\sin^{-1}x-\sin^{-1}y) & \text{, if } -1\le x<0, 0<y\le 1 \text{ and } x^2+y^2\ge 1\end{cases}$$

(xi) $$\cos^{-1}\left\{xy-\sqrt{1-x^2}\sqrt{1-y^2}\right\}=\begin{cases}\cos^{-1}x+\cos^{-1}y, & \text{if } -1\le x, y\le 1 \text{ and } x+y\ge 0\\ 2\pi-(\cos^{-1}x+\cos^{-1}y), & \text{if } -1\le x, y\le 1 \text{ and } x+y\le 0\end{cases}$$

$$\cos^{-1}\left\{xy+\sqrt{1-x^2}\sqrt{1-y^2}\right\}=\begin{cases}\cos^{-1}x-\cos^{-1}y, & \text{if } -1\le x, y\le 1 \text{ and } x\le y\\ -(\cos^{-1}x-\cos^{-1}y), & \text{if } -1\le y\le 0, 0<x\le 1 \text{ and } x\ge y\end{cases}$$

(xii) $$\tan^{-1}\left(\frac{x+y}{1-xy}\right)=\begin{cases}\tan^{-1}x+\tan^{-1}y, & \text{if } xy<1\\ \pi-(\tan^{-1}x+\tan^{-1}y), & \text{if } x>0, y>0 \text{ and } xy>1\\ \pi+(\tan^{-1}x+\tan^{-1}y), & \text{if } x<0, y<0 \text{ and } xy>1\end{cases}$$

(xiii) $\tan^{-1}\left(\frac{x-y}{1+xy}\right) = \begin{cases} \tan^{-1}x - \tan^{-1}y, & \text{if } xy > -1 \\ \pi - (\tan^{-1}x - \tan^{-1}y), & \text{if } x > 0, y < 0 \text{ and } xy < -1 \\ -\pi - (\tan^{-1}x - \tan^{-1}y), & \text{if } x < 0, y > 0 \text{ and } xy < -1 \end{cases}$

(xiv) $\sin^{-1}x + \cos^{-1}x = \frac{\pi}{2}$, if $-1 \leq x \leq 1$

(xv) $\tan^{-1}x + \cot^{-1}x = \frac{\pi}{2}$ for all $x \in R$

(xvi) $\sec^{-1}x + \text{cosec}^{-1}x = \frac{\pi}{2}$, if $x \in (-\infty, -1] \cup [1, \infty)$

(xvii) $\cos^{-1}(-x) = \pi - \cos^{-1}x$ for $x \in [-1, 1]$

(xviii) $\tan^{-1}(-x) = -\tan^{-1}x$ for $x \in R$

(xix) $\sin^{-1}(-x) = -\sin^{-1}x$ for $x \in [-1,1]$

(xx) $\sin^{-1}x = \text{cosec}^{-1}\left(\frac{1}{x}\right)$, if $x \in (-\infty, -1] \cup [1, \infty)$

(xxi) $\cos^{-1}x = \sec^{-1}\frac{1}{x}$, if $x \in (-\infty, -1] \cup [1, \infty)$

(xxii) $\tan^{-1}x = \begin{cases} \cot^{-1}\left(\frac{1}{x}\right), & \text{if } x > 0 \\ -\pi + \cot^{-1}\left(\frac{1}{x}\right), & \text{if } x < 0 \end{cases}$ or, $\tan^{-1}\left(\frac{1}{x}\right) = \begin{cases} \cot^{-1}x, & x > 0 \\ -\pi + \cot^{-1}x, & x < 0 \end{cases}$

(xxiii) $\sin^{-1}(\sin\theta) = \theta$, if $-\frac{\pi}{2} \leq \theta \leq \frac{\pi}{2}$; $\cos^{-1}(\cos\theta) = \theta$, if $0 \leq \theta \leq \pi$

$\tan^{-1}(\tan\theta) = \theta$, if $-\frac{\pi}{2} < \theta < \frac{\pi}{2}$; $\text{cosec}^{-1}(\text{cosec}\,\theta) = \theta$, if $-\frac{\pi}{2} < \theta < \frac{\pi}{2}, \theta \neq 0$

$\sec^{-1}(\sec\theta) = \theta$, if $0 < \theta < \pi, \theta \neq \frac{\pi}{2}$; $\cot^{-1}(\cot\theta) = \theta$, if $0 < \theta < \pi$

Following are some substitutions useful in finding derivatives:

Expression	*Substitution*	*Expression*	*Substitution*
(i) $a^2 + x^2$	$x = a\tan\theta$ or, $a\cot\theta$	(iv) $\sqrt{\frac{a-x}{a+x}}$ or, $\sqrt{\frac{a+x}{a-x}}$	$x = a\cos 2\theta$
(ii) $a^2 - x^2$	$x = a\sin\theta$ or, $a\cos\theta$	(v) $\sqrt{\frac{a^2-x^2}{a^2+x^2}}$ or, $\sqrt{\frac{a^2+x^2}{a^2-x^2}}$	$x^2 = a^2\cos 2\theta$
(iii) $x^2 - a^2$	$x = a\sec\theta$ or, $a\,\text{cosec}\,\theta$		

ILLUSTRATIVE EXAMPLES

BASED ON BASIC CONCEPTS (BASIC)

EXAMPLE 1 *Differentiate the following functions with respect to x:*

(i) $\sin^{-1}(\sin x), x \in [0, 2\pi]$

(ii) $\cos^{-1}(\cos x), x \in [0, 2\pi]$

(iii) $\tan^{-1}(\tan x), x \in [0, \pi] - \left\{\frac{\pi}{2}\right\}$

SOLUTION (i) Let $y = \sin^{-1}(\sin x)$. Then,

$$y = \sin^{-1}(\sin x) = \begin{cases} x \ , & \text{if } x \in \left[0, \dfrac{\pi}{2}\right] \\ \pi - x \ , & \text{if } x \in \left[\dfrac{\pi}{2}, \dfrac{3\pi}{2}\right] \\ -2\pi + x \ , & \text{if } x \in \left[\dfrac{3\pi}{2}, 2\pi\right] \end{cases}$$

We observe that

$$\left(\text{LHD of } y \text{ at } x = \frac{\pi}{2}\right) = 1 \text{ and, } \left(\text{RHD of } y \text{ at } x = \frac{\pi}{2}\right) = -1$$

$$\left(\text{LHD of } y \text{ at } x = \frac{3\pi}{2}\right) = -1 \text{ and, } \left(\text{RHD of } y \text{ at } x = \frac{3\pi}{2}\right) = 1$$

So, $y = \sin^{-1}(\sin x)$ is not differentiable at $x = \dfrac{\pi}{2}, \dfrac{3\pi}{2}$.

$$\therefore \quad \frac{dy}{dx} = \begin{cases} 1 \ , & \text{if } x \in \left[0, \dfrac{\pi}{2}\right) \\ -1 \ , & \text{if } x \in \left(\dfrac{\pi}{2}, \dfrac{3\pi}{2}\right) \\ 1 \ , & \text{if } x \in \left(\dfrac{3\pi}{2}, 2\pi\right] \end{cases}$$

(ii) Let $y = \cos^{-1}(\cos x)$. Then,

$$y = \cos^{-1}(\cos x) = \begin{cases} -x \ , & \text{if } x \in [-\pi, 0] \\ x \ , & \text{if } x \in [0, \pi] \\ 2\pi - x \ , & \text{if } x \in [\pi, 2\pi] \\ -2\pi + x \ , & \text{if } x \in [2\pi, 3\pi] \text{ and so on.} \end{cases}$$

Clearly,

(LHD at $x = 0$) $= -1$ and (RHD at $x = 0$) $= 1$; (LHD at $x = \pi$) $= 1$ and (RHD at $x = \pi$) $= -1$

(LHD at $x = 2\pi$) $= -1$ and (RHD at $x = 2\pi$) $= 1$

So, $y = \cos^{-1}(\cos x)$ is not differentiable at $x = 0, \pi, 2\pi$. Hence, $\dfrac{dy}{dx} = \begin{cases} 1 \ , & \text{if } x \in (0, \pi) \\ -1 \ , & \text{if } x \in (\pi, 2\pi) \end{cases}$

(iii) Let $y = \tan^{-1}(\tan x)$. Then,

$$y = \tan^{-1}(\tan x) = \begin{cases} x \ , & \text{if } x \in \left[0, \dfrac{\pi}{2}\right) \\ x - \pi \ , & \text{if } x \in \left(\dfrac{\pi}{2}, \dfrac{3\pi}{2}\right) \\ x - 2\pi \ , & \text{if } x \in \left(\dfrac{3\pi}{2}, \dfrac{5\pi}{2}\right) \end{cases} \quad \text{and so on}$$

$\therefore \quad \frac{dy}{dx} = 1, \text{ if } x \in \left[0, \frac{\pi}{2}\right) \cup \left(\frac{\pi}{2}, \pi\right]$

EXAMPLE 2 *Differentiate* $\sin^{-1}\left(2x\sqrt{1-x^2}\right)$ *with respect to x, if*

(i) $-\frac{1}{\sqrt{2}} < x < \frac{1}{\sqrt{2}}$ (ii) $\frac{1}{\sqrt{2}} < x < 1$ (iii) $-1 < x < -\frac{1}{\sqrt{2}}$

SOLUTION Let $y = \sin^{-1}\left(2x\sqrt{1-x^2}\right)$. Putting $x = \sin\theta$, we get

$$y = \sin^{-1}(2\sin\theta\cos\theta) = \sin^{-1}(\sin 2\theta)$$

(i) If $-\frac{1}{\sqrt{2}} < x < \frac{1}{\sqrt{2}}$, then

$$x = \sin\theta \Rightarrow -\frac{1}{\sqrt{2}} < \sin\theta < \frac{1}{\sqrt{2}} \Rightarrow -\frac{\pi}{4} < \theta < \frac{\pi}{4} \Rightarrow -\frac{\pi}{2} < 2\theta < \frac{\pi}{2}$$

$\therefore \quad y = \sin^{-1}(\sin 2\theta) = 2\theta \qquad \left[\because -\frac{\pi}{2} < 2\theta < \frac{\pi}{2}\right]$

$\Rightarrow \quad y = 2\sin^{-1}x \qquad [\because \sin\theta = x \Rightarrow \theta = \sin^{-1}x]$

$\Rightarrow \quad \frac{dy}{dx} = \frac{2}{\sqrt{1-x^2}}$

(ii) If $\frac{1}{\sqrt{2}} < x < 1$, then

$$x = \sin\theta \Rightarrow \frac{1}{\sqrt{2}} < \sin\theta < 1 \Rightarrow \frac{\pi}{4} < \theta < \frac{\pi}{2} \Rightarrow \frac{\pi}{2} < 2\theta < \pi$$

$\therefore \quad y = \sin^{-1}(\sin 2\theta)$

$\Rightarrow \quad y = \sin^{-1}(\sin(\pi - 2\theta)) = \pi - 2\theta \qquad \left[\because \frac{\pi}{2} < 2\theta < \pi \Rightarrow 0 < \pi - 2\theta < \frac{\pi}{2}\right]$

$\Rightarrow \quad y = \pi - 2\sin^{-1}x \Rightarrow \frac{dy}{dx} = 0 - \frac{2}{\sqrt{1-x^2}} = -\frac{2}{\sqrt{1-x^2}}$

(iii) If $-1 < x < -\frac{1}{\sqrt{2}}$, then

$$x = \sin\theta \Rightarrow -1 < \sin\theta < -\frac{1}{\sqrt{2}} \Rightarrow -\frac{\pi}{2} < \theta < -\frac{\pi}{4} \Rightarrow -\pi < 2\theta < -\frac{\pi}{2}$$

$\therefore \quad y = \sin^{-1}(\sin 2\theta)$

$\Rightarrow \quad y = \sin^{-1}(-\sin(\pi + 2\theta))$

$\Rightarrow \quad y = \sin^{-1}(\sin(-\pi - 2\theta)) = -\pi - 2\theta \qquad \left[\because -\pi < 2\theta < -\frac{\pi}{2} \Rightarrow -\frac{\pi}{2} < \pi + 2\theta < 0\right]$

$\Rightarrow \quad y = -\pi - 2\sin^{-1}x \Rightarrow \frac{dy}{dx} = -0 - \frac{2}{\sqrt{1-x^2}} = -\frac{2}{\sqrt{1-x^2}}.$

EXAMPLE 3 *Differentiate* $\sin^{-1}(3x-4x^3)$ *with respect to x, if*

(i) $-\frac{1}{2}<x<\frac{1}{2}$ (ii) $\frac{1}{2}<x<1$ (iii) $-1<x<-\frac{1}{2}$

SOLUTION Let $y=\sin^{-1}(3x-4x^3)$. Putting $x=\sin\theta$, we get

$$y = \sin^{-1}(3\sin\theta-4\sin^3\theta) = \sin^{-1}(\sin 3\theta)$$

(i) If $-\frac{1}{2}<x<\frac{1}{2}$, then

$$x = \sin\theta \Rightarrow -\frac{1}{2} < \sin\theta < \frac{1}{2} \Rightarrow -\frac{\pi}{6} < \theta < \frac{\pi}{6} \Rightarrow -\frac{\pi}{2} < 3\theta < \frac{\pi}{2}$$

$\therefore$ $y = \sin^{-1}(\sin 3\theta) = 3\theta$ $\left[\because -\frac{\pi}{2} < 3\theta < \frac{\pi}{2}\right]$

$\Rightarrow$ $y = 3\sin^{-1}x \Rightarrow \frac{dy}{dx} = \frac{3}{\sqrt{1-x^2}}$

(ii) If $\frac{1}{2}<x<1$, then

$$x = \sin\theta \Rightarrow \frac{1}{2} < \sin\theta < 1 \Rightarrow \frac{\pi}{6} < \theta < \frac{\pi}{2} \Rightarrow \frac{\pi}{2} < 3\theta < \frac{3\pi}{2}$$

$\therefore$ $y = \sin^{-1}(\sin 3\theta)$

$\Rightarrow$ $y = \sin^{-1}\{\sin(\pi-3\theta)\} = \pi-3\theta$ $\left[\because \frac{\pi}{2} < 3\theta < \frac{3\pi}{2} \Rightarrow -\frac{\pi}{2} < \pi-3\theta < \frac{\pi}{2}\right]$

$\Rightarrow$ $y = \pi - 3\sin^{-1}x$ $[\because x = \sin\theta \Rightarrow \theta = \sin^{-1}x]$

$\Rightarrow$ $\frac{dy}{dx} = 0 - \frac{3}{\sqrt{1-x^2}} = -\frac{3}{\sqrt{1-x^2}}$

(iii) If $-1<x<-\frac{1}{2}$, then

$$x = \sin\theta \Rightarrow -1 < \sin\theta < -\frac{1}{2} \Rightarrow -\frac{\pi}{2} < \theta < -\frac{\pi}{6} \Rightarrow -\frac{3\pi}{2} < 3\theta < -\frac{\pi}{2}$$

$\therefore$ $y = \sin^{-1}(\sin 3\theta)$

$\Rightarrow$ $y = \sin^{-1}\{\sin(-\pi-3\theta)\} = -\pi-3\theta$ $\left[\because -\frac{3\pi}{2} < 3\theta < -\frac{\pi}{2} \Rightarrow -\frac{\pi}{2} < -\pi-3\theta < \frac{\pi}{2}\right]$

$\Rightarrow$ $y = -\pi - 3\sin^{-1}x \Rightarrow \frac{dy}{dx} = -0 - \frac{3}{\sqrt{1-x^2}} = -\frac{3}{\sqrt{1-x^2}}$

EXAMPLE 4 *Differentiate* $\cos^{-1}(2x^2-1)$ *with respect to x, if* (i) $0<x<1$ (ii) $-1<x<0$

SOLUTION Let $y=\cos^{-1}(2x^2-1)$. Putting $x=\cos\theta$, we get

$$y = \cos^{-1}(2\cos^2\theta-1) = \cos^{-1}(\cos 2\theta)$$

(i) If $0<x<1$, then

$$x = \cos\theta \Rightarrow 0 < \cos\theta < 1 \Rightarrow 0 < \theta < \frac{\pi}{2} \Rightarrow 0 < 2\theta < \pi$$

$\therefore$ $y = \cos^{-1}(\cos 2\theta) = 2\theta$ $[\because 0 < 2\theta < \pi$

$\Rightarrow$ $y = 2\cos^{-1}x$ $[\because x = \cos\theta \Rightarrow \theta = \cos^{-1}x]$

$\Rightarrow \quad \dfrac{dy}{dx} = -\dfrac{2}{\sqrt{1-x^2}}$

(ii) If $-1 < x < 0$, then

$x = \cos\theta \Rightarrow -1 < \cos\theta < 0 \Rightarrow \dfrac{\pi}{2} < \theta < \pi \Rightarrow \pi < 2\theta < 2\pi$

$\therefore \quad y = \cos^{-1}(\cos 2\theta)$

$\Rightarrow \quad y = \cos^{-1}\{\cos(2\pi - 2\theta)\} = 2\pi - 2\theta \qquad [\because \pi < 2\theta < 2\pi \Rightarrow 0 < 2\pi - 2\theta < \pi]$

$\Rightarrow \quad y = 2\pi - 2\cos^{-1}x \Rightarrow \dfrac{dy}{dx} = 0 + \dfrac{2}{\sqrt{1-x^2}} = \dfrac{2}{\sqrt{1-x^2}}$

EXAMPLE 5 *Differentiate* $\cos^{-1}(1-2x^2)$ *with respect to x, if*

(i) $0 < x < 1$ (ii) $-1 < x < 0$

SOLUTION Let $y = \cos^{-1}(1-2x^2)$. Putting $x = \sin\theta$, we get

$y = \cos^{-1}(1 - 2\sin^2\theta) = \cos^{-1}(\cos 2\theta)$

(i) If $0 < x < 1$, then

$x = \sin\theta \Rightarrow 0 < \sin\theta < 1 \Rightarrow 0 < \theta < \dfrac{\pi}{2} \Rightarrow 0 < 2\theta < \pi$

$\therefore \quad y = \cos^{-1}(\cos 2\theta) = 2\theta = 2\sin^{-1}x \qquad [\because x = \sin\theta \Rightarrow \theta = \sin^{-1}x]$

$\Rightarrow \quad \dfrac{dy}{dx} = \dfrac{2}{\sqrt{1-x^2}}$

(ii) If $-1 < x < 0$, then

$x = \sin\theta \Rightarrow -1 < \sin\theta < 0 \Rightarrow -\dfrac{\pi}{2} < \theta < 0 \Rightarrow -\pi < 2\theta < 0$

$\therefore \quad y = \cos^{-1}(\cos 2\theta)$

$\Rightarrow \quad y = \cos^{-1}(\cos(-2\theta)) = -2\theta = -2\sin^{-1}x \qquad [\because -\pi < 2\theta < 0 \Rightarrow 0 < -2\theta < \pi]$

$\Rightarrow \quad \dfrac{dy}{dx} = -\dfrac{2}{\sqrt{1-x^2}}$

EXAMPLE 6 *Differentiate* $\cos^{-1}(4x^3 - 3x)$ *with respect to x, if*

(i) $x \in \left(-\dfrac{1}{2}, \dfrac{1}{2}\right)$ (ii) $x \in \left(\dfrac{1}{2}, 1\right)$ (iii) $x \in \left(-1, -\dfrac{1}{2}\right)$

SOLUTION Let $y = \cos^{-1}(4x^3 - 3x)$. Putting $x = \cos\theta$, we get

$y = \cos^{-1}(4\cos^3\theta - 3\cos\theta) = \cos^{-1}(\cos 3\theta)$

(i) If $x \in \left(-\dfrac{1}{2}, \dfrac{1}{2}\right)$, then

$x = \cos\theta \Rightarrow -\dfrac{1}{2} < \cos\theta < \dfrac{1}{2} \Rightarrow \dfrac{\pi}{3} < \theta < \dfrac{2\pi}{3} \Rightarrow \pi < 3\theta < 2\pi$

$\therefore \quad y = \cos^{-1}(\cos 3\theta)$

$\Rightarrow \quad y = \cos^{-1}\{\cos(2\pi - 3\theta)\} = 2\pi - 3\theta \qquad [\because \pi < 3\theta < 2\pi \Rightarrow 0 < 2\pi - 3\theta < \pi]$

$\Rightarrow \quad y = 2\pi - 3\cos^{-1}x \qquad [\because x = \cos\theta \Rightarrow \theta = \cos^{-1}x]$

$\Rightarrow \quad \frac{dy}{dx} = 0 - 3 \times -\frac{1}{\sqrt{1-x^2}} = \frac{3}{\sqrt{1-x^2}}$

(ii) If $x \in \left(\frac{1}{2}, 1\right)$, then

$x = \cos\theta \Rightarrow \frac{1}{2} < \cos\theta < 1 \Rightarrow 0 < \theta < \frac{\pi}{3} \Rightarrow 0 < 3\theta < \pi$

$\therefore \quad y = \cos^{-1}(\cos 3\theta) = 3\theta \qquad [\because 0 < 3\theta < \pi]$

$\Rightarrow \quad y = 3\cos^{-1} x \qquad [\because x = \cos\theta \Rightarrow \theta = \cos^{-1} x]$

$\Rightarrow \quad \frac{dy}{dx} = -\frac{3}{\sqrt{1-x^2}}$

(iii) If $-1 < x < -\frac{1}{2}$, then

$x = \cos\theta \Rightarrow -1 < \cos\theta < -\frac{1}{2} \Rightarrow \frac{2\pi}{3} < \theta < \pi \Rightarrow 2\pi < 3\theta < 3\pi$

$\therefore \quad y = \cos^{-1}(\cos 3\theta)$

$\Rightarrow \quad y = \cos^{-1}\{\cos(2\pi - 3\theta)\}$

$\Rightarrow \quad y = \cos^{-1}\{\cos(3\theta - 2\pi)\} = 3\theta - 2\pi \qquad [\because 2\pi < 3\theta < 3\pi \Rightarrow 0 < 3\theta - 2\pi < \pi]$

$\Rightarrow \quad y = 3\cos^{-1} x - 2\pi \Rightarrow \frac{dy}{dx} = \frac{-3}{\sqrt{1-x^2}} - 0 = \frac{-3}{\sqrt{1-x^2}}$

EXAMPLE 7 *Differentiate* $\tan^{-1}\left(\frac{2x}{1-x^2}\right)$ *with respect to x, if*

(i) $x \in (-1, 1)$ (ii) $x \in (-\infty, -1)$ (iii) $x \in (1, \infty)$.

SOLUTION Let $y = \tan^{-1}\left(\frac{2x}{1-x^2}\right)$. Putting $x = \tan\theta$, we get : $y = \tan^{-1}(\tan 2\theta)$

(i) If $-1 < x < 1$, then

$x = \tan\theta \Rightarrow -1 < \tan\theta < 1 \Rightarrow -\frac{\pi}{4} < \theta < \frac{\pi}{4} \Rightarrow -\frac{\pi}{2} < 2\theta < \frac{\pi}{2}$

$\therefore \quad y = \tan^{-1}(\tan 2\theta) = 2\theta \qquad \left[\because -\frac{\pi}{2} < 2\theta < \frac{\pi}{2}\right]$

$\Rightarrow \quad y = 2\tan^{-1} x \qquad [\because x = \tan\theta \Rightarrow \theta = \tan^{-1} x]$

$\Rightarrow \quad \frac{dy}{dx} = \frac{2}{1+x^2}$

(ii) If $-\infty < x < -1$, then

$x = \tan\theta \Rightarrow -\infty < \tan\theta < -1 \Rightarrow -\frac{\pi}{2} < \theta < -\frac{\pi}{4} \Rightarrow -\pi < 2\theta < -\frac{\pi}{2}$

$\therefore \quad y = \tan^{-1}(\tan 2\theta)$

$\Rightarrow \quad y = \tan^{-1}\{\tan(\pi + 2\theta)\} = \pi + 2\theta \qquad \left[\because -\pi < 2\theta < -\frac{\pi}{2} \Rightarrow 0 < \pi + 2\theta < \frac{\pi}{2}\right]$

$\Rightarrow \quad y = \pi + 2\tan^{-1} x \Rightarrow \dfrac{dy}{dx} = 0 + \dfrac{2}{1+x^2} = \dfrac{2}{1+x^2}$

(iii) If $x \in (1, \infty)$, then

$x = \tan\theta \Rightarrow 1 < \tan\theta < \infty \Rightarrow \dfrac{\pi}{4} < \theta < \dfrac{\pi}{2} \Rightarrow \dfrac{\pi}{2} < 2\theta < \pi$

$\therefore \quad y = \tan^{-1}(\tan 2\theta) = \tan^{-1}\{-\tan(\pi - 2\theta)\} = \tan^{-1}\{\tan(2\theta - \pi)\}$

$\Rightarrow \quad y = 2\theta - \pi \qquad \left[\because \dfrac{\pi}{2} < 2\theta < \pi \Rightarrow -\dfrac{\pi}{2} < 2\theta - \pi < 0\right]$

$\Rightarrow \quad y = 2\tan^{-1} x - \pi \Rightarrow \dfrac{dy}{dx} = \dfrac{2}{1+x^2} - 0 = \dfrac{2}{1+x^2}$

EXAMPLE 8 *Differentiate* $\tan^{-1}\left(\dfrac{3x - x^3}{1 - 3x^2}\right)$, *if*

(i) $-\dfrac{1}{\sqrt{3}} < x < \dfrac{1}{\sqrt{3}}$ **[NCERT]** (ii) $x > \dfrac{1}{\sqrt{3}}$ (iii) $x < -\dfrac{1}{\sqrt{3}}$

SOLUTION Let $y = \tan^{-1}\left(\dfrac{3x - x^3}{1 - 3x^2}\right)$. Putting $x = \tan\theta$, we get

$$y = \tan^{-1}\left(\frac{3\tan\theta - \tan^3\theta}{1 - 3\tan^2\theta}\right) = \tan^{-1}(\tan 3\theta)$$

(i) If $-\dfrac{1}{\sqrt{3}} < x < \dfrac{1}{\sqrt{3}}$, then

$x = \tan\theta \Rightarrow -\dfrac{1}{\sqrt{3}} < \tan\theta < \dfrac{1}{\sqrt{3}} \Rightarrow -\dfrac{\pi}{6} < \theta < \dfrac{\pi}{6} \Rightarrow -\dfrac{\pi}{2} < 3\theta < \dfrac{\pi}{2}$

$\therefore \quad y = \tan^{-1}(\tan 3\theta) = 3\theta \qquad \left[\because -\dfrac{\pi}{2} < 3\theta < \dfrac{\pi}{2}\right]$

$\Rightarrow \quad y = 3\tan^{-1} x \qquad [\because x = \tan\theta \Rightarrow \theta = \tan^{-1} x]$

$\Rightarrow \quad \dfrac{dy}{dx} = \dfrac{3}{1+x^2}$

(ii) If $x > \dfrac{1}{\sqrt{3}}$, then

$x = \tan\theta \Rightarrow \tan\theta > \dfrac{1}{\sqrt{3}} \Rightarrow \dfrac{\pi}{6} < \theta < \dfrac{\pi}{2} \Rightarrow \dfrac{\pi}{2} < 3\theta < \dfrac{3\pi}{2}$

$\therefore \quad y = \tan^{-1}(\tan 3\theta) = \tan^{-1}\{-\tan(\pi - 3\theta)\} = \tan^{-1}\{\tan(3\theta - \pi)\}$

$\Rightarrow \quad y = 3\theta - \pi \qquad \left[\because \dfrac{\pi}{2} < 3\theta < \dfrac{3\pi}{2} \Rightarrow -\dfrac{\pi}{2} < 3\theta - \pi < \dfrac{\pi}{2}\right]$

$\Rightarrow \quad y = 3\tan^{-1} x - \pi \qquad [\because x = \tan\theta \Rightarrow \theta = \tan^{-1} x]$

$\Rightarrow \quad \dfrac{dy}{dx} = \dfrac{3}{1+x^2} - 0 = \dfrac{3}{1+x^2}$

(iii) If $x < -\dfrac{1}{\sqrt{3}}$, then

$$x = \tan\theta \Rightarrow -\infty < \tan\theta < -\frac{1}{\sqrt{3}} \Rightarrow -\frac{\pi}{2} < \theta < -\frac{\pi}{6} \Rightarrow -\frac{3\pi}{2} < 3\theta < -\frac{\pi}{2}$$

$\therefore \quad y = \tan^{-1}(\tan 3\theta) = \tan^{-1}\{\tan(\pi + 3\theta)\}$

$\Rightarrow \quad y = \pi + 3\theta = \pi + 3\tan^{-1} x \qquad \left[\because -\frac{3\pi}{2} < 3\theta < -\frac{\pi}{2} \Rightarrow -\frac{\pi}{2} < \pi + 3\theta < \frac{\pi}{2}\right]$

$\Rightarrow \quad \frac{dy}{dx} = 0 + \frac{3}{1+x^2} = \frac{3}{1+x^2}$

EXAMPLE 9 *Differentiate* $\sin^{-1}\left(\frac{2x}{1+x^2}\right)$ *with respect to x, when*

(i) $x \in (-1, 1)$ (ii) $x \in (1, \infty)$ (iii) $x \in (-\infty, -1)$

SOLUTION Let $y = \sin^{-1}\left(\frac{2x}{1+x^2}\right)$. Putting $x = \tan\theta$, we get

$$y = \sin^{-1}\left(\frac{2\tan\theta}{1+\tan^2\theta}\right) = \sin^{-1}(\sin 2\theta)$$

(i) If $x \in (-1, 1)$, then

$$x = \tan\theta \Rightarrow -1 < \tan\theta < 1 \Rightarrow -\frac{\pi}{4} < \theta < \frac{\pi}{4} \Rightarrow -\frac{\pi}{2} < 2\theta < \frac{\pi}{2}$$

$\therefore \quad y = \sin^{-1}(\sin 2\theta) = 2\theta \qquad \left[\because -\frac{\pi}{2} < 2\theta < \frac{\pi}{2}\right]$

$\Rightarrow \quad y = 2\tan^{-1} x \Rightarrow \frac{dy}{dx} = \frac{2}{1+x^2}$

(ii) If $x \in (1, \infty)$, then

$$x = \tan\theta \Rightarrow 1 < \tan\theta < \infty \Rightarrow \frac{\pi}{4} < \theta < \frac{\pi}{2} \Rightarrow \frac{\pi}{2} < 2\theta < \pi$$

$\therefore \quad y = \sin^{-1}(\sin 2\theta) = \sin^{-1}\{\sin(\pi - 2\theta)\} \qquad [\because \sin(\pi - 2\theta) = \sin 2\theta]$

$\Rightarrow \quad y = \pi - 2\theta \qquad \left[\because \frac{\pi}{2} < 2\theta < \pi \Rightarrow 0 < \pi - 2\theta < \frac{\pi}{2}\right]$

$\Rightarrow \quad y = \pi - 2\tan^{-1} x \qquad [\because x = \tan\theta \Rightarrow \theta = \tan^{-1} x]$

$\Rightarrow \quad \frac{dy}{dx} = 0 - \frac{2}{1+x^2} = -\frac{2}{1+x^2}$

(iii) If $x \in (-\infty, -1)$, then

$$x = \tan\theta \Rightarrow -\infty < \tan\theta < -1 \Rightarrow -\frac{\pi}{2} < \theta < -\frac{\pi}{4} \Rightarrow -\pi < 2\theta < -\frac{\pi}{2}$$

$\therefore \quad y = \sin^{-1}(\sin 2\theta) = \sin^{-1}\{-\sin(\pi + 2\theta)\} = \sin^{-1}\{\sin(-\pi - 2\theta)\}$

$\Rightarrow \quad y = -\pi - 2\theta \qquad \left[\because -\pi < 2\theta < -\frac{\pi}{2} \Rightarrow -\frac{\pi}{2} < -\pi - 2\theta < 0\right]$

$\Rightarrow \quad y = -\pi - 2\tan^{-1} x \qquad [\because x = \tan\theta \Rightarrow \theta = \tan^{-1} x]$

$\Rightarrow \quad \frac{dy}{dx} = 0 - \frac{2}{1+x^2} = -\frac{2}{1+x^2}$

EXAMPLE 10 *Differentiate* $\cos^{-1}\left(\dfrac{1-x^2}{1+x^2}\right)$ *with respect to x, when*

(i) $x \in (0, \infty)$ (ii) $x \in (-\infty, 0)$

SOLUTION Let $y = \cos^{-1}\left(\dfrac{1-x^2}{1+x^2}\right)$. Putting $x = \tan\theta$, we get

$$y = \cos^{-1}\left(\frac{1-\tan^2\theta}{1+\tan^2\theta}\right) = \cos^{-1}(\cos 2\theta)$$

(i) If $x \in (0, \infty)$, then

$$x = \tan\theta \Rightarrow 0 < \tan\theta < \infty \Rightarrow 0 < \theta < \frac{\pi}{2} \Rightarrow 0 < 2\theta < \pi$$

$\therefore \quad y = \cos^{-1}(\cos 2\theta) = 2\theta \qquad [\because 0 < 2\theta < \pi]$

$\Rightarrow \quad y = 2\tan^{-1} x \qquad [\because x = \tan\theta \Rightarrow \theta = \tan^{-1} x]$

$\Rightarrow \quad \dfrac{dy}{dx} = \dfrac{2}{1+x^2}$

(ii) If $x \in (-\infty, 0)$, then

$$x = \tan\theta \Rightarrow -\infty < \tan\theta < 0 \Rightarrow -\frac{\pi}{2} < \theta < 0 \Rightarrow -\pi < 2\theta < 0$$

$\therefore \quad y = \cos^{-1}(\cos 2\theta) = \cos^{-1}\{\cos(-2\theta)\} = -2\theta \qquad [\because -\pi < 2\theta < 0 \Rightarrow 0 < -2\theta < \pi]$

$\Rightarrow \quad y = -2\tan^{-1} x \Rightarrow \dfrac{dy}{dx} = -\dfrac{2}{1+x^2}$

EXAMPLE 11 *Differentiate each of the following functions with respect to x*

(i) $\cos^{-1}\left(\dfrac{1-x^2}{1+x^2}\right), 0 < x < 1$ [NCERT] (ii) $\sin^{-1}\left(\dfrac{1-x^2}{1+x^2}\right), 0 < x < 1$ [NCERT]

(iii) $\cos^{-1}\left(\dfrac{2x}{1+x^2}\right), -1 < x < 1$ [NCERT] (iv) $\sec^{-1}\left(\dfrac{1}{2x^2-1}\right), 0 < x < \dfrac{1}{\sqrt{2}}$ [NCERT]

SOLUTION (i) Let $y = \cos^{-1}\left(\dfrac{1-x^2}{1+x^2}\right)$, where $0 < x < 1$. Putting $x = \tan\theta$, we obtain

$$y = \cos^{-1}\left(\frac{1-\tan^2}{1+\tan^2\theta}\right) = \cos^{-1}(\cos 2\theta)$$

$\Rightarrow \quad y = 2\theta \qquad \left[\because 0 < x < 1 \Rightarrow 0 < \tan\theta < 1 \Rightarrow 0 < \theta < \dfrac{\pi}{4} \Rightarrow 0 < 2\theta < \dfrac{\pi}{2}\right]$

$\Rightarrow \quad y = 2\tan^{-1} x \qquad [\because x = \tan\theta \Rightarrow \theta = \tan^{-1} x]$

$\Rightarrow \quad \dfrac{dy}{dx} = \dfrac{2}{1+x^2}$

(ii) Let $y = \sin^{-1}\left(\frac{1-x^2}{1+x^2}\right)$, where $0 < x < 1$. Putting $x = \tan\theta$, we get

$$y = \sin^{-1}\left(\frac{1-\tan^2\theta}{1+\tan^2\theta}\right) = \sin^{-1}(\cos 2\theta) = \sin^{-1}\left\{\sin\left(\frac{\pi}{2} - 2\theta\right)\right\}$$

$\Rightarrow \quad y = \frac{\pi}{2} - 2\theta \quad \left[\because 0 < x < 1 \Rightarrow 0 < \tan\theta < 1 \Rightarrow 0 < \theta < \frac{\pi}{4} \Rightarrow 0 < 2\theta < \frac{\pi}{2} \Rightarrow 0 < \frac{\pi}{2} - 2\theta < \frac{\pi}{2}\right]$

$\Rightarrow \quad y = \frac{\pi}{2} - 2\tan^{-1}x \quad [\because x = \tan\theta \Rightarrow \theta = \tan^{-1}x]$

$\Rightarrow \quad \frac{dy}{dx} = 0 - \frac{2}{1+x^2} = -\frac{2}{1+x^2}$

(iii) Let $y = \cos^{-1}\left(\frac{2x}{1+x^2}\right)$, where $-1 < x < 1$. Putting $x = \tan\theta$, we get

$$y = \cos^{-1}\left(\frac{2\tan\theta}{1+\tan^2\theta}\right) = \cos^{-1}(\sin 2\theta) = \cos^{-1}\left\{\cos\left(\frac{\pi}{2} - 2\theta\right)\right\}$$

$\Rightarrow \quad y = \frac{\pi}{2} - 2\theta \left[\because -1 < x < 1 \Rightarrow -1 < \tan\theta < 1 \Rightarrow -\frac{\pi}{4} < \theta < \frac{\pi}{4} \Rightarrow -\frac{\pi}{2} < 2\theta < \frac{\pi}{2} \Rightarrow 0 < \frac{\pi}{2} - 2\theta < \pi\right]$

$\Rightarrow \quad y = \frac{\pi}{2} - 2\tan^{-1}x \Rightarrow \frac{dy}{dx} = \frac{-2}{1+x^2}$

(iv) Let $y = \sec^{-1}\left(\frac{1}{2x^2-1}\right)$, where $0 < x < \frac{1}{\sqrt{2}}$. Putting $x = \cos\theta$, we obtain

$$y = \sec^{-1}\left(\frac{1}{2\cos^2\theta - 1}\right) = \cos^{-1}(2\cos^2\theta - 1) \quad \left[\because \sec^{-1}\frac{1}{x} = \cos^{-1}x\right]$$

$\Rightarrow \quad y = \cos^{-1}(\cos 2\theta)$

$\Rightarrow \quad y = 2\theta \quad \left[\because 0 < x < \frac{1}{\sqrt{2}} \Rightarrow 0 < \cos\theta < \frac{1}{\sqrt{2}} \Rightarrow 0 < \theta < \frac{\pi}{4} \Rightarrow 0 < 2\theta < \frac{\pi}{2}\right]$

$\Rightarrow \quad y = 2\cos^{-1}x \quad [\because x = \cos\theta \Rightarrow \theta = \cos^{-1}x]$

$\Rightarrow \quad \frac{dy}{dx} = -\frac{2}{\sqrt{1-x^2}}$

EXAMPLE 12 *Differentiate each of the following functions with respect to x:*

(i) $\sin^{-1}\left(2x\sqrt{1-x^2}\right), -\frac{1}{\sqrt{2}} < x < \frac{1}{\sqrt{2}}$ (ii) $\cos^{-1}\left(2x\sqrt{1-x^2}\right), -\frac{1}{\sqrt{2}} < x < \frac{1}{\sqrt{2}}$

SOLUTION (i) Let $y = \sin^{-1}\left(2x\sqrt{1-x^2}\right)$, where $-\frac{1}{\sqrt{2}} < x < \frac{1}{\sqrt{2}}$. Putting $x = \sin\theta$, we get

$$y = \sin^{-1}(2\sin\theta\cos\theta) = \sin^{-1}(\sin 2\theta)$$

$\Rightarrow \quad y = 2\theta \quad \left[\because -\frac{1}{\sqrt{2}} < x < \frac{1}{\sqrt{2}} \Rightarrow -\frac{1}{\sqrt{2}} < \sin\theta < \frac{1}{\sqrt{2}} \Rightarrow -\frac{\pi}{4} < \theta < \frac{\pi}{4} \Rightarrow -\frac{\pi}{2} < 2\theta < \frac{\pi}{2}\right]$

$$\Rightarrow \quad y = 2\sin^{-1} x \qquad [\because x = \sin\theta \Rightarrow \theta = \sin^{-1} x]$$

$$\Rightarrow \quad \frac{dy}{dx} = \frac{2}{\sqrt{1-x^2}}$$

(ii) Let $y = \cos^{-1}\left(2x\sqrt{1-x^2}\right)$, where $-\frac{1}{\sqrt{2}} < x < \frac{1}{\sqrt{2}}$. Putting $x = \sin\theta$, we get

$$y = \cos^{-1}(2\sin\theta\cos\theta) = \cos^{-1}(\sin 2\theta) = \cos^{-1}\left\{\cos\left(\frac{\pi}{2} - 2\theta\right)\right\}$$

$$\Rightarrow \quad y = \frac{\pi}{2} - 2\theta \qquad \left[\begin{array}{l} \because -\frac{1}{\sqrt{2}} < x < \frac{1}{\sqrt{2}} \Rightarrow -\frac{1}{\sqrt{2}} < \sin\theta < \frac{1}{\sqrt{2}} \Rightarrow -\frac{\pi}{4} < \theta < \frac{\pi}{4} \\ \Rightarrow -\frac{\pi}{2} < 2\theta < \frac{\pi}{2} \Rightarrow 0 < \frac{\pi}{2} - 2\theta < \pi \end{array}\right]$$

$$\Rightarrow \quad y = \frac{\pi}{2} - 2\sin^{-1} x \qquad [\because x = \sin\theta \Rightarrow \theta = \sin^{-1} x]$$

$$\Rightarrow \quad \frac{dy}{dx} = 0 - \frac{2}{\sqrt{1-x^2}} \Rightarrow \frac{dy}{dx} = -\frac{2}{\sqrt{1-x^2}}$$

EXAMPLE 13 *Differentiate the following functions with respect to x:*

(i) $\tan^{-1}\left\{\frac{1-\cos x}{\sin x}\right\}, -\pi < x < \pi$ (ii) $\tan^{-1}\left\{\sqrt{\frac{1-\cos x}{1+\cos x}}\right\}, -\pi < x < \pi$

[NCERT EXEMPLAR]

(iii) $\tan^{-1}\left\{\sqrt{\frac{1+\cos x}{1-\cos x}}\right\}, 0 < x < \pi$ (iv) $\tan^{-1}\left\{\frac{\cos x}{1-\sin x}\right\}, -\frac{\pi}{2} < x < \frac{\pi}{2}$ [CBSE 2024]

(v) $\tan^{-1}\left\{\sqrt{\frac{1+\sin x}{1-\sin x}}\right\}, -\frac{\pi}{2} < x < \frac{\pi}{2}$ (vi) $\tan^{-1}(\sec x + \tan x), -\frac{\pi}{2} < x < \frac{\pi}{2}$

[NCERT EXEMPLAR]

SOLUTION (i) Let $y = \tan^{-1}\left\{\frac{1-\cos x}{\sin x}\right\}$. Then,

$$y = \tan^{-1}\left\{\frac{2\sin^2\frac{x}{2}}{2\sin\frac{x}{2}\cos\frac{x}{2}}\right\} = \tan^{-1}\left(\tan\frac{x}{2}\right) = \frac{x}{2} \qquad \left[\because -\pi < x < \pi \Rightarrow -\frac{\pi}{2} < \frac{x}{2} < \frac{\pi}{2}\right]$$

$$\therefore \quad \frac{dy}{dx} = \frac{1}{2}$$

(ii) Let $y = \tan^{-1}\left\{\sqrt{\frac{1-\cos x}{1+\cos x}}\right\}$. Then,

$$y = \tan^{-1}\left\{\sqrt{\frac{2\sin^2 x/2}{2\cos^2 x/2}}\right\} = \tan^{-1}\left|\tan\frac{x}{2}\right| = \begin{cases} \tan^{-1}\left(\tan\frac{x}{2}\right), & \text{if } \tan\frac{x}{2} \ge 0 \\ \tan^{-1}\left(-\tan\frac{x}{2}\right), & \text{if } \tan\frac{x}{2} < 0 \end{cases}$$

$$\Rightarrow \quad y = \begin{cases} \dfrac{x}{2}, & \text{if } 0 \le x < \pi \\ -\dfrac{x}{2}, & \text{if } -\pi < x < 0 \end{cases} \Rightarrow \frac{dy}{dx} = \begin{cases} \dfrac{1}{2}, & \text{if } 0 < x < \pi \\ -\dfrac{1}{2}, & \text{if } -\pi < x < 0 \end{cases}$$

(iii) Let $y = \tan^{-1}\left\{\sqrt{\dfrac{1+\cos x}{1-\cos x}}\right\}$. Then,

$$y = \tan^{-1}\left\{\sqrt{\frac{2\cos^2 x/2}{2\sin^2 x/2}}\right\} = \tan^{-1}\left|\cot\frac{x}{2}\right| = \tan^{-1}\left(\cot\frac{x}{2}\right)$$

$$\Rightarrow \quad y = \tan^{-1}\left\{\tan\left(\frac{\pi}{2}-\frac{x}{2}\right)\right\} = \frac{\pi}{2}-\frac{x}{2}$$

$$\therefore \quad \frac{dy}{dx} = 0 - \frac{1}{2} = -\frac{1}{2}.$$

(iv) Let $y = \tan^{-1}\left(\dfrac{\cos x}{1-\sin x}\right)$. Then,

$$y = \tan^{-1}\left\{\frac{\sin\left(\dfrac{\pi}{2}+x\right)}{1+\cos\left(\dfrac{\pi}{2}+x\right)}\right\} = \tan^{-1}\left\{\frac{2\sin\left(\dfrac{\pi}{4}+\dfrac{x}{2}\right)\cos\left(\dfrac{\pi}{4}+\dfrac{x}{2}\right)}{2\cos^2\left(\dfrac{\pi}{4}+\dfrac{x}{2}\right)}\right\}$$

$$\Rightarrow \quad y = \tan^{-1}\left\{\tan\left(\frac{\pi}{4}+\frac{x}{2}\right)\right\} = \frac{\pi}{4}+\frac{x}{2}$$

$$\therefore \quad \frac{dy}{dx} = 0 + \frac{1}{2} = \frac{1}{2}.$$

(v) Let $y = \tan^{-1}\left\{\sqrt{\dfrac{1+\sin x}{1-\sin x}}\right\}$. Then,

$$\Rightarrow \quad y = \tan^{-1}\left\{\sqrt{\frac{1-\cos(\pi/2+x)}{1+\cos(\pi/2+x)}}\right\} = \tan^{-1}\left\{\sqrt{\frac{2\sin^2(\pi/4+x/2)}{2\cos^2(\pi/4+x/2)}}\right\}$$

$$\Rightarrow \quad y = \tan^{-1}\left\{\tan\left(\frac{\pi}{4}+\frac{x}{2}\right)\right\} = \frac{\pi}{4}+\frac{x}{2} \qquad \left[\because -\frac{\pi}{2} < x < \frac{\pi}{2} \Rightarrow 0 < \frac{x}{4}+\frac{x}{2} < \frac{\pi}{2}\right]$$

$$\therefore \quad \frac{dy}{dx} = \frac{1}{2}$$

(vi) Let $y = \tan^{-1}(\sec x + \tan x)$. Then,

$$y = \tan^{-1}\left\{\frac{1}{\cos x}+\frac{\sin x}{\cos x}\right\} = \tan^{-1}\left\{\frac{1-\cos\left(\dfrac{\pi}{2}+x\right)}{\sin\left(\dfrac{\pi}{2}+x\right)}\right\}$$

$$\Rightarrow \quad y = \tan^{-1}\left\{\frac{2\sin^2\left(\frac{\pi}{4}+\frac{x}{2}\right)}{2\sin\left(\frac{\pi}{4}+\frac{x}{2}\right)\cos\left(\frac{\pi}{4}+\frac{x}{2}\right)}\right\} = \tan^{-1}\left\{\tan\left(\frac{\pi}{4}+\frac{x}{2}\right)\right\} = \frac{\pi}{4}+\frac{x}{2}$$

$$\therefore \quad \frac{dy}{dx} = \frac{1}{2}.$$

BASED ON HIGHER ORDER THINKING SKILLS (HOTS)

EXAMPLE 14 *Differentiate the following functions with respect to x:*

(i) $\tan^{-1}\left\{\sqrt{1+x^2}+x\right\},\ x \in R$ (ii) $\tan^{-1}\left\{\sqrt{1+x^2}-x\right\},\ x \in R$

(iii) $\tan^{-1}\left\{\frac{\sqrt{1+x^2}-1}{x}\right\},\ x \neq 0$ [CBSE 2004, 2012] (iv) $\tan^{-1}\left\{\frac{\sqrt{1+x^2}+1}{x}\right\},\ x \neq 0$

(v) $\cot^{-1}\left\{\sqrt{1+x^2}+x\right\}$ (vi) $\tan^{-1}\left\{\frac{\sqrt{1+\sin x}+\sqrt{1-\sin x}}{\sqrt{1+\sin x}-\sqrt{1-\sin x}}\right\},\ 0 < x < \pi.$

[CBSE 2004]

SOLUTION (i) Let $y = \tan^{-1}(\sqrt{1+x^2}+x)$. Putting $x = \cot\theta$, we get

$$y = \tan^{-1}(\text{cosec}\,\theta + \cot\theta) = \tan^{-1}\left(\frac{1}{\sin\theta}+\frac{\cos\theta}{\sin\theta}\right) = \tan^{-1}\left(\frac{1+\cos\theta}{\sin\theta}\right)$$

$$\Rightarrow \quad y = \tan^{-1}\left(\frac{2\cos^2\frac{\theta}{2}}{2\sin\frac{\theta}{2}\cos\frac{\theta}{2}}\right) = \tan^{-1}\left(\cot\frac{\theta}{2}\right) = \tan\left\{\tan\left(\frac{\pi}{2}-\frac{\theta}{2}\right)\right\} = \frac{\pi}{2}-\frac{1}{2}\theta$$

$$\Rightarrow \quad y = \frac{\pi}{2}-\frac{1}{2}\cot^{-1}x \qquad [\because x = \cot\theta \ \therefore\ \theta = \cot^{-1}x]$$

$$\therefore \quad \frac{dy}{dx} = 0 - \frac{1}{2}\left(-\frac{1}{1+x^2}\right) = \frac{1}{2(1+x^2)}$$

(ii) Let $y = \tan^{-1}(\sqrt{1+x^2}-x)$. Putting $x = \cot\theta$, we get

$$y = \tan^{-1}(\text{cosec}\,\theta - \cot\theta) = \tan^{-1}\left(\frac{1-\cos\theta}{\sin\theta}\right) = \tan^{-1}\left(\frac{2\sin^2\frac{\theta}{2}}{2\sin\frac{\theta}{2}\cos\frac{\theta}{2}}\right)$$

$$\Rightarrow \quad y = \tan^{-1}\left(\tan\frac{\theta}{2}\right) = \frac{1}{2}\theta = \frac{1}{2}\cot^{-1}x$$

$$\therefore \quad \frac{dy}{dx} = \frac{1}{2}\left(-\frac{1}{1+x^2}\right) = -\frac{1}{2(1+x^2)}$$

(iii) Let $y=\tan^{-1}\left(\frac{\sqrt{1+x^2}-1}{x}\right)$. Putting $x=\tan\theta$, we get

$$y=\tan^{-1}\left(\frac{\sec\theta-1}{\tan\theta}\right)=\tan^{-1}\left(\frac{1-\cos\theta}{\sin\theta}\right)=\tan^{-1}\left(\frac{2\sin^2\frac{\theta}{2}}{2\sin\frac{\theta}{2}\cos\frac{\theta}{2}}\right)=\tan^{-1}\left(\tan\frac{\theta}{2}\right)$$

$$\Rightarrow \quad y=\frac{1}{2}\theta=\frac{1}{2}\tan^{-1}x \Rightarrow \frac{dy}{dx}=\frac{1}{2}\left(\frac{1}{1+x^2}\right)$$

(iv) Let $y=\tan^{-1}\left(\frac{\sqrt{1+x^2}+1}{x}\right)$. Putting $x=\tan\theta$, we get

$$y=\tan^{-1}\left(\frac{\sec\theta+1}{\tan\theta}\right)=\tan^{-1}\left(\frac{1+\cos\theta}{\sin\theta}\right)=\tan^{-1}\left(\frac{2\cos^2\frac{\theta}{2}}{2\sin\frac{\theta}{2}\cos\frac{\theta}{2}}\right)$$

$$\Rightarrow \quad y=\tan^{-1}\left(\cot\frac{\theta}{2}\right)=\tan^{-1}\left\{\tan\left(\frac{\pi}{2}-\frac{\theta}{2}\right)\right\}=\frac{\pi}{2}-\frac{1}{2}\theta=\frac{\pi}{2}-\frac{1}{2}\tan^{-1}x$$

$$\therefore \quad \frac{dy}{dx}=0-\frac{1}{2}\times\frac{1}{1+x^2}=-\frac{1}{2(1+x^2)}$$

(v) Let $y=\cot^{-1}(\sqrt{1+x^2}+x)$. Putting $x=\cot\theta$, we get

$$y=\cot^{-1}(\operatorname{cosec}\theta+\cot\theta)=\cot^{-1}\left(\frac{1+\cos\theta}{\sin\theta}\right)=\cot^{-1}\left(\frac{2\cos^2\frac{\theta}{2}}{2\sin\frac{\theta}{2}\cos\frac{\theta}{2}}\right)=\cot^{-1}\left(\cot\frac{\theta}{2}\right)$$

$$\Rightarrow \quad y=\frac{1}{2}\theta=\frac{1}{2}\cot^{-1}x$$

$$\therefore \quad \frac{dy}{dx}=-\frac{1}{2(1+x^2)}$$

(vi) Let $y=\tan^{-1}\left\{\frac{\sqrt{1+\sin x}+\sqrt{1-\sin x}}{\sqrt{1+\sin x}-\sqrt{1-\sin x}}\right\}$. We know that:

$$\sqrt{1+\sin x}=\sqrt{\sin^2\frac{x}{2}+\cos^2\frac{x}{2}+2\sin\frac{x}{2}\cos\frac{x}{2}}=\sqrt{\left(\cos\frac{x}{2}+\sin\frac{x}{2}\right)^2}=\left|\cos\frac{x}{2}+\sin\frac{x}{2}\right|$$

$$\Rightarrow \quad \sqrt{1+\sin x}=\cos\frac{x}{2}+\sin\frac{x}{2}, \text{ for } 0<x<\pi.$$

and, $$\sqrt{1-\sin x}=\sqrt{\cos^2\frac{x}{2}+\sin^2\frac{x}{2}-2\sin\frac{x}{2}\cos\frac{x}{2}}=\sqrt{\left(\cos\frac{x}{2}-\sin\frac{x}{2}\right)^2}=\left|\cos\frac{x}{2}-\sin\frac{x}{2}\right|$$

$$\Rightarrow \quad \sqrt{1-\sin x} = \begin{cases} \cos\frac{x}{2} - \sin\frac{x}{2}, & \text{if } 0 < x < \frac{\pi}{2} \\ -\left(\cos\frac{x}{2} - \sin\frac{x}{2}\right), & \text{if } \frac{\pi}{2} < x < \pi \end{cases}$$

Thus, we have following cases:

Case I *When* $0 < x < \frac{\pi}{2}$: In this case, we obtain

$$y = \tan^{-1}\left\{\frac{\left(\cos\frac{x}{2} + \sin\frac{x}{2}\right) + \left(\cos\frac{x}{2} - \sin\frac{x}{2}\right)}{\left(\cos\frac{x}{2} + \sin\frac{x}{2}\right) - \left(\cos\frac{x}{2} - \sin\frac{x}{2}\right)}\right\} = \tan^{-1}\left(\cot\frac{x}{2}\right) = \tan^{-1}\left\{\tan\left(\frac{\pi}{2} - \frac{x}{2}\right)\right\}$$

$$\Rightarrow y = \frac{\pi}{2} - \frac{x}{2} \qquad \left[\because 0 < x < \frac{\pi}{2} \Rightarrow \frac{\pi}{4} < \frac{\pi}{2} - \frac{x}{2} < \frac{\pi}{2}\right]$$

$$\therefore \frac{dy}{dx} = 0 - \frac{1}{2} = -\frac{1}{2}$$

Case II *When* $\frac{\pi}{2} < x < \pi$: In this case, we obtain

$$y = \tan^{-1}\left\{\frac{\left(\cos\frac{x}{2} + \sin\frac{x}{2}\right) + \left(\sin\frac{x}{2} - \cos\frac{x}{2}\right)}{\left(\cos\frac{x}{2} + \sin\frac{x}{2}\right) - \left(\sin\frac{x}{2} - \cos\frac{x}{2}\right)}\right\} = \tan^{-1}\left(\tan\frac{x}{2}\right) = \frac{x}{2}$$

$$\therefore \quad \frac{dy}{dx} = \frac{1}{2}.$$

EXAMPLE 15 *Differentiate the following functions with respect to x:*

(i) $\tan^{-1}\left(\frac{a+x}{1-ax}\right)$ (ii) $\tan^{-1}\sqrt{\frac{a-x}{a+x}}, -a < x < a$

(iii) $\tan^{-1}\left(\frac{3a^2x - x^3}{a^3 - 3ax^2}\right), -\frac{1}{\sqrt{3}} < \frac{x}{a} < \frac{1}{\sqrt{3}}$ **[NCERT EXEMPLAR]**

(iv) $\tan^{-1}\left(\frac{a\cos x - b\sin x}{b\cos x + a\sin x}\right), -\frac{\pi}{2} < x < \frac{\pi}{2}$ *and* $\frac{a}{b}\tan x > -1$ **[NCERT EXEMPLAR]**

SOLUTION (i) $\frac{d}{dx}\left\{\tan^{-1}\left(\frac{a+x}{1-ax}\right)\right\} = \frac{d}{dx}\{\tan^{-1}a + \tan^{-1}x\} = \frac{d}{dx}(\tan^{-1}a) + \frac{d}{dx}(\tan^{-1}x)$

$$= 0 + \frac{1}{1+x^2} = \frac{1}{1+x^2}$$

(ii) Let $y = \tan^{-1}\left\{\sqrt{\frac{a-x}{a+x}}\right\}$, where $-a < x < a$. Substituting $x = a\cos\theta$, we get

$$y = \tan^{-1}\left\{\sqrt{\frac{a - a\cos\theta}{a + a\cos\theta}}\right\} = \tan^{-1}\left\{\sqrt{\frac{1-\cos\theta}{1+\cos\theta}}\right\} = \tan^{-1}\left\{\sqrt{\frac{2\sin^2\frac{\theta}{2}}{2\cos^2\frac{\theta}{2}}}\right\} = \tan^{-1}\left|\tan\frac{\theta}{2}\right|$$

Now,

$-a < x < a$ and $x = a\cos\theta \Rightarrow -a < a\cos\theta < a \Rightarrow -1 < \cos\theta < 1 \Rightarrow \theta \in (0, \pi) \Rightarrow \frac{\theta}{2} \in \left(0, \frac{\pi}{2}\right)$

$$\therefore \quad y = \tan^{-1}\left|\tan\frac{\theta}{2}\right| = \tan^{-1}\left(\tan\frac{\theta}{2}\right) = \frac{1}{2}\theta = \frac{1}{2}\cos^{-1}\left(\frac{x}{a}\right)$$

$$\Rightarrow \quad \frac{dy}{dx} = -\frac{1}{2} \times \frac{1}{\sqrt{1-\frac{x^2}{a^2}}} \times \frac{d}{dx}\left(\frac{x}{a}\right) = -\frac{1}{2\sqrt{a^2-x^2}}$$

(iii) Let $y = \tan^{-1}\left(\frac{3a^2x - x^3}{a^3 - 3ax^2}\right)$. Then,

$$y = \tan^{-1}\left(\frac{\frac{3x}{a} - \left(\frac{x}{a}\right)^3}{1 - 3\left(\frac{x}{a}\right)^2}\right) \qquad \text{[Dividing numerator and denominator by } a^3]$$

Putting $\frac{x}{a} = \tan\theta$, we get

$$y = \tan^{-1}\left(\frac{3\tan\theta - \tan^3\theta}{1 - 3\tan^2\theta}\right) = \tan^{-1}(\tan 3\theta)$$

$$\Rightarrow \quad y = 3\theta \qquad \left[\because -\frac{1}{\sqrt{3}} < \frac{x}{a} < \frac{1}{\sqrt{3}} \Rightarrow -\frac{\pi}{6} < \theta < \frac{\pi}{6} \Rightarrow -\frac{\pi}{2} < 3\theta < \frac{\pi}{2}\right]$$

$$\Rightarrow \quad y = 3\tan^{-1}\frac{x}{a}$$

$$\Rightarrow \quad \frac{dy}{dx} = \frac{3}{1+\frac{x^2}{a^2}} \times \frac{d}{dx}\left(\frac{x}{a}\right) = \frac{3a^2}{a^2+x^2} \times \frac{1}{a} = \frac{3a}{a^2+x^2}$$

(iv) Let $y = \tan^{-1}\left(\frac{a\cos x - b\sin x}{b\cos x + a\sin x}\right)$. Then,

$$y = \tan^{-1}\left(\frac{\frac{a}{b} - \tan x}{1 + \frac{a}{b}\tan x}\right) \qquad \text{[Dividing numerator and denominator by } b\cos x]$$

$$\Rightarrow \quad y = \tan^{-1}\left(\frac{a}{b}\right) - \tan^{-1}(\tan x) = \tan^{-1}\left(\frac{a}{b}\right) - x \qquad \left[\because -\frac{\pi}{2} < x < \frac{\pi}{2}\right]$$

$$\Rightarrow \quad \frac{dy}{dx} = 0 - 1 = -1$$

BASED ON HIGHER ORDER THINKING SKILLS (HOTS)

EXAMPLE 16 *If* $y = \sin^{-1}\left\{x\sqrt{1-x} - \sqrt{x}\sqrt{1-x^2}\right\}$ *and* $0 < x < 1$, *then find* $\frac{dy}{dx}$.

SOLUTION We have, [CBSE 2010]

$$y = \sin^{-1}\left\{x\sqrt{1-x} - \sqrt{x}\sqrt{1-x^2}\right\}, \text{ where } 0 < x < 1$$

$$\Rightarrow \quad y = \sin^{-1}\left\{x\sqrt{1-(\sqrt{x})^2} - \sqrt{x}\sqrt{1-x^2}\right\}$$

$$\Rightarrow \quad y = \sin^{-1} x - \sin^{-1}\sqrt{x} \quad \left[\text{Using} : \sin^{-1} x - \sin^{-1} y = \sin^{-1}\left\{x\sqrt{1-y^2} - y\sqrt{1-x^2}\right\}\right]$$

Differentiating with respect to x, we get

$$\frac{dy}{dx} = \frac{1}{\sqrt{1-x^2}} - \frac{1}{\sqrt{1-(\sqrt{x})^2}}\frac{d}{dx}(\sqrt{x}) = \frac{1}{\sqrt{1-x^2}} - \frac{1}{\sqrt{1-x}} \times \frac{1}{2\sqrt{x}}$$

EXAMPLE 17 *If* $y = \cos^{-1}\left\{x\sqrt{1-x} + \sqrt{x}\sqrt{1-x^2}\right\}$ *and* $0 < x < 1$, *find* $\frac{dy}{dx}$.

SOLUTION We have,

$$y = \cos^{-1}\left\{x\sqrt{1-x} + \sqrt{x}\sqrt{1-x^2}\right\} = \cos^{-1}\left\{x\sqrt{1-(\sqrt{x})^2} + \sqrt{x}\sqrt{1-x^2}\right\}$$

$$\Rightarrow \quad y = \frac{\pi}{2} - \sin^{-1}\left\{x\sqrt{1-(\sqrt{x})^2} + \sqrt{x}\sqrt{1-x^2}\right\} = \frac{\pi}{2} - \left\{\sin^{-1} x + \sin^{-1}\sqrt{x}\right\}$$

$$\Rightarrow \quad y = \left(\frac{\pi}{2} - \sin^{-1} x\right) - \sin^{-1}\sqrt{x} = \cos^{-1} x - \sin^{-1}\sqrt{x}$$

Differentiating with respect to x, we get

$$\frac{dy}{dx} = -\frac{1}{\sqrt{1-x^2}} - \frac{1}{\sqrt{1-(\sqrt{x})^2}}\frac{d}{dx}(\sqrt{x}) = -\frac{1}{\sqrt{1-x^2}} - \frac{1}{2\sqrt{x}\sqrt{1-x^2}}$$

EXAMPLE 18 *If* $y = \tan^{-1}\left\{\frac{\sqrt{1+x^2} + \sqrt{1-x^2}}{\sqrt{1+x^2} - \sqrt{1-x^2}}\right\}$, $-1 < x < 1, x \neq 0$ *find* $\frac{dy}{dx}$.

[CBSE 2015]

SOLUTION Putting $x^2 = \cos 2\theta$, we get

$$y = \tan^{-1}\left(\frac{\sqrt{1+\cos 2\theta} + \sqrt{1-\cos 2\theta}}{\sqrt{1+\cos 2\theta} - \sqrt{1-\cos 2\theta}}\right) = \tan^{-1}\left(\frac{\sqrt{2\cos^2\theta} + \sqrt{2\sin^2\theta}}{\sqrt{2\cos^2\theta} - \sqrt{2\sin^2\theta}}\right)$$

$$\Rightarrow \quad y = \tan^{-1}\left(\frac{\cos\theta + \sin\theta}{\cos\theta - \sin\theta}\right) = \tan^{-1}\left(\frac{1+\tan\theta}{1-\tan\theta}\right) = \tan^{-1}\left(\tan\left(\frac{\pi}{4} + \theta\right)\right)$$

$$\Rightarrow \quad y = \frac{\pi}{4} + \theta \quad \left[\because 0 < x^2 < 1 \Rightarrow 0 < \cos 2\theta < 1 \Rightarrow 0 < 2\theta < \frac{\pi}{2} \Rightarrow 0 < \theta < \frac{\pi}{4} \Rightarrow \frac{\pi}{4} < \frac{\pi}{4} + \theta < \frac{\pi}{2}\right]$$

$$\Rightarrow \quad y = \frac{\pi}{4} + \frac{1}{2}\cos^{-1} x^2 \quad \left[\because \cos 2\theta = x^2 \Rightarrow \theta = \frac{1}{2}\cos^{-1} x^2\right]$$

$$\therefore \quad \frac{dy}{dx} = \frac{d}{dx}\left(\frac{\pi}{4}\right) + \frac{1}{2}\frac{d}{dx}(\cos^{-1} x^2) = 0 + \frac{1}{2}\frac{(-1)}{\sqrt{1-x^4}}\frac{d}{dx}(x^2) = -\frac{1}{2} \times \frac{2x}{\sqrt{1-x^4}} = \frac{-x}{\sqrt{1-x^4}}$$

EXAMPLE 19 *Differentiate* $\sin^{-1}\left(\frac{2x}{1+x^2}\right)+\cos^{-1}\left(\frac{1-x^2}{1+x^2}\right)$. *with respect to x, if*

(i) $x \in (0, 1)$ (ii) $x \in (-1, 0)$ (iii) $x \in (1, \infty)$ (iv) $x \in (-\infty, -1)$

SOLUTION Let $y = \sin^{-1}\left(\frac{2x}{1+x^2}\right)+\cos^{-1}\left(\frac{1-x^2}{1+x^2}\right)$. Putting $x = \tan\theta$, we get

$$y = \sin^{-1}\left(\frac{2\tan\theta}{1+\tan^2\theta}\right)+\cos^{-1}\left(\frac{1-\tan^2\theta}{1+\tan^2\theta}\right) = \sin^{-1}(\sin 2\theta)+\cos^{-1}(\cos 2\theta)$$

(i) *When* $0 < x < 1$: We have,

$$x = \tan\theta \text{ and } 0 < x < 1 \Rightarrow 0 < \tan\theta < 1 \Rightarrow 0 < \theta < \frac{\pi}{4} \Rightarrow 0 < 2\theta < \frac{\pi}{2}$$

$$\therefore\ y = \sin^{-1}(\sin 2\theta)+\cos^{-1}(\cos 2\theta) = 2\theta+2\theta = 4\theta = 4\tan^{-1}x \quad [\because x = \tan\theta \Rightarrow \theta = \tan^{-1}x]$$

$$\Rightarrow \frac{dy}{dx} = \frac{4}{1+x^2}$$

(ii) *When* $-1 < x < 0$: We have,

$$x = \tan\theta \text{ and } -1 < x < 0 \Rightarrow -1 < \tan\theta < 0 \Rightarrow -\frac{\pi}{4} < \theta < 0 \Rightarrow -\frac{\pi}{2} < 2\theta < 0$$

$$\Rightarrow \sin^{-1}(\sin 2\theta) = 2\theta \text{ and } \cos^{-1}(\cos 2\theta) = \cos^{-1}\{\cos(-2\theta)\} = -2\theta.$$

$$\therefore\ y = \sin^{-1}(\sin 2\theta)+\cos^{-1}(\cos 2\theta) = 2\theta+(-2\theta) = 0$$

$$\Rightarrow \frac{dy}{dx} = 0.$$

(iii) *When* $x \in (1, \infty)$ We have,

$$x = \tan\theta \text{ and } 1 < x < \infty \Rightarrow 1 < \tan\theta < \infty \Rightarrow \frac{\pi}{4} < \theta < \frac{\pi}{2} \Rightarrow \frac{\pi}{2} < 2\theta < \pi$$

$$\Rightarrow \cos^{-1}(\cos 2\theta) = 2\theta \text{ and } \sin^{-1}(\sin 2\theta) = \sin^{-1}\{\sin(\pi-2\theta)\} = \pi-2\theta$$

$$\therefore\ y = \sin^{-1}(\sin 2\theta)+\cos^{-1}(\cos 2\theta) = \pi-2\theta+2\theta = \pi$$

$$\Rightarrow \frac{dy}{dx} = 0.$$

(iv) *When* $x \in (-\infty, -1)$: We have,

$$x = \tan\theta \text{ and } -\infty < x < -1 \Rightarrow -\infty < \tan\theta < -1 \Rightarrow -\frac{\pi}{2} < \theta < -\frac{\pi}{4} \Rightarrow -\pi < 2\theta < -\frac{\pi}{2}$$

$$\Rightarrow \sin^{-1}(\sin 2\theta) = \sin^{-1}\{-\sin(\pi+2\theta)\} = \sin^{-1}\{\sin(-\pi-2\theta)\} = -\pi-2\theta$$

$$\text{and, } \cos^{-1}(\cos 2\theta) = \cos^{-1}\{\cos(-2\theta)\} = -2\theta$$

$$\therefore\ y = \sin^{-1}(\sin 2\theta)+\cos^{-1}(\cos 2\theta) = -\pi-2\theta-2\theta = -\pi-4\tan^{-1}x$$

$$[\because x = \tan\theta \therefore \theta = \tan^{-1}x]$$

$$\Rightarrow \frac{dy}{dx} = 0-\frac{4}{1+x^2} = -\frac{4}{1+x^2}$$

EXAMPLE 20 *Differentiate* $\tan^{-1}\left(\frac{2x}{1-x^2}\right)+\cos^{-1}\left(\frac{1-x^2}{1+x^2}\right)$ *with respect to x, when*

(i) $x \in (0, 1)$ (ii) $x \in (1, \infty)$ (iii) $x \in (-1, 0)$ (iv) $x \in (-\infty, -1)$

SOLUTION Let $y = \tan^{-1}\left(\frac{2x}{1-x^2}\right) + \cos^{-1}\left(\frac{1-x^2}{1+x^2}\right)$. Putting $x = \tan\theta$, we get

$$y = \tan^{-1}\left(\frac{2\tan\theta}{1-\tan^2\theta}\right) + \cos^{-1}\left(\frac{1-\tan^2\theta}{1+\tan^2\theta}\right) = \tan^{-1}(\tan 2\theta) + \cos^{-1}(\cos 2\theta)$$

(i) *When* $x \in (0, 1)$: We have,

$$0 < x < 1 \text{ and } x = \tan\theta \Rightarrow 0 < \tan\theta < 1 \Rightarrow 0 < \theta < \frac{\pi}{4} \Rightarrow 0 < 2\theta < \frac{\pi}{2}$$

$\Rightarrow \tan^{-1}(\tan 2\theta) = 2\theta$ and $\cos^{-1}(\cos 2\theta) = 2\theta$

$\therefore\ y = \tan^{-1}(\tan 2\theta) + \cos^{-1}(\cos 2\theta) = 2\theta + 2\theta = 4\theta = 4\tan^{-1}x$ [$\because\ x = \tan\theta \Rightarrow \theta = \tan^{-1}x$]

$$\Rightarrow \frac{dy}{dx} = \frac{4}{1+x^2}$$

(ii) *When* $x \in (1, \infty)$: We have, $x > 1$ and $x = \tan\theta$

$$\Rightarrow \tan\theta > 1 \Rightarrow \frac{\pi}{4} < \theta < \frac{\pi}{2} \Rightarrow \frac{\pi}{2} < 2\theta < \pi \Rightarrow \frac{\pi}{2} < 2\theta < \pi \text{ and } -\frac{\pi}{2} < 2\theta - \pi < 0$$

$\therefore\ \cos^{-1}(\cos 2\theta) = 2\theta$

and, $\tan^{-1}(\tan 2\theta) = \tan^{-1}\left(-\tan(\pi - 2\theta)\right) = -\tan^{-1}\{\tan(\pi - 2\theta)\} = -(\pi - 2\theta) = 2\theta - \pi$.

$$\therefore\quad y = \tan^{-1}(\tan 2\theta) + \cos^{-1}(\cos 2\theta) = 2\theta - \pi + 2\theta = 4\theta - \pi = 4\tan^{-1}x - \pi$$

$$\Rightarrow\quad \frac{dy}{dx} = \frac{4}{1+x^2} - 0 = \frac{4}{1+x^2}$$

(iii) *When* $x \in (-1, 0)$: We have,

$$-1 < x < 0 \text{ and } x = \tan\theta \Rightarrow -1 < \tan\theta < 0 \Rightarrow -\frac{\pi}{4} < \theta < 0 \Rightarrow -\frac{\pi}{2} < 2\theta < 0$$

$$\Rightarrow\quad \tan^{-1}(\tan 2\theta) = 2\theta \text{ and } \cos^{-1}(\cos 2\theta) = \cos^{-1}\{\cos(-2\theta)\} = -2\theta$$

$$\therefore\quad y = \tan^{-1}(\tan 2\theta) + \cos^{-1}(\cos 2\theta) = 2\theta + (-2\theta) = 0$$

$$\Rightarrow\quad \frac{dy}{dx} = 0$$

(iv) *When* $x \in (-\infty, -1)$: We have, $-\infty < x < -1$ and $x = \tan\theta$

$$\Rightarrow\quad -\infty < \tan\theta < -1 \Rightarrow -\frac{\pi}{2} < \theta < -\frac{\pi}{4} \Rightarrow -\pi < 2\theta < -\frac{\pi}{2} \Rightarrow \frac{\pi}{2} < -2\theta < \pi \text{ and } 0 < \pi + 2\theta < \frac{\pi}{2}$$

$\Rightarrow \cos^{-1}(\cos 2\theta) = \cos^{-1}\{\cos(-2\theta)\} = -2\theta$

and, $\tan^{-1}(\tan 2\theta) = \tan^{-1}\{\tan(\pi + 2\theta)\} = \pi + 2\theta$

$$\therefore\quad y = \tan^{-1}(\tan 2\theta) + \cos^{-1}(\cos 2\theta) = \pi + 2\theta - 2\theta = \pi$$

$$\Rightarrow\quad \frac{dy}{dx} = 0.$$

EXAMPLE 21 *If* $y = \sin^{-1}x + \sin^{-1}\sqrt{1-x^2}$, *find* $\frac{dy}{dx}$ *in each of the following cases:*

(i) $x \in (0, 1)$ (ii) $x \in (-1, 0)$ **[NCERT]**

SOLUTION Putting $x = \sin\theta$, we obtain : $y = \sin^{-1}(\sin\theta) + \sin^{-1}(\cos\theta)$

(i) We have,

$$x \in (0, 1) \text{ and } x = \sin\theta \Rightarrow 0 < \sin\theta < 1 \Rightarrow 0 < \theta < \frac{\pi}{2} \Rightarrow 0 < \frac{\pi}{2} - \theta < \frac{\pi}{2}$$

$\therefore \quad y = \sin^{-1}(\sin\theta) + \sin^{-1}(\cos\theta) = \sin^{-1}(\sin\theta) + \sin\left\{\sin\left(\frac{\pi}{2}-\theta\right)\right\} = \theta + \frac{\pi}{2} - \theta = \frac{\pi}{2}$

$\therefore \quad \frac{dy}{dx} = 0$

(ii) We have, $x \in (-1, 0)$ and $x = \sin\theta \Rightarrow -1 < \sin\theta < 0 \Rightarrow -\frac{\pi}{2} < \theta < 0$

$\Rightarrow \quad \sin^{-1}(\sin\theta) = \theta$ and $\sin^{-1}(\cos\theta) = \sin^{-1}\left\{\sin\left(\frac{\pi}{2}+\theta\right)\right\} = \frac{\pi}{2} + \theta$

$\therefore \quad y = \sin^{-1}(\sin\theta) + \sin^{-1}(\cos\theta) = \theta + \frac{\pi}{2} + \theta = \frac{\pi}{2} + 2\sin^{-1}x$

$\Rightarrow \quad \frac{dy}{dx} = 0 + \frac{2}{\sqrt{1-x^2}} = \frac{2}{\sqrt{1-x^2}}$

EXERCISE 10.3

BASIC

Differentiate the following functions with respect to x:

1. $\cos^{-1}\left\{2x\sqrt{1-x^2}\right\}, \frac{1}{\sqrt{2}} < x < 1$

2. $\cos^{-1}\left\{\sqrt{\frac{1+x}{2}}\right\}, -1 < x < 1$

3. $\sin^{-1}\left\{\sqrt{\frac{1-x}{2}}\right\}, 0 < x < 1$

4. $\sin^{-1}\left\{\sqrt{1-x^2}\right\}, 0 < x < 1$

5. $\tan^{-1}\left\{\frac{x}{\sqrt{a^2-x^2}}\right\}, -a < x < a$

6. $\sin^{-1}\left\{\frac{x}{\sqrt{x^2+a^2}}\right\}$

7. $\sin^{-1}(2x^2-1), 0 < x < 1$

8. $\sin^{-1}(1-2x^2), 0 < x < 1$

9. $\cos^{-1}\left\{\frac{x}{\sqrt{x^2+a^2}}\right\}$

10. $\tan^{-1}\left(\frac{\sin x}{1+\cos x}\right), -\pi < x < \pi$ [NCERT]

11. $\sin^{-1}\left(\frac{1}{\sqrt{1+x^2}}\right)$

12. $\cos^{-1}\left(\frac{1-x^{2n}}{1+x^{2n}}\right), 0 < x < \infty$

13. $\sin^{-1}\left(\frac{1-x^2}{1+x^2}\right) + \sec^{-1}\left(\frac{1+x^2}{1-x^2}\right), x \in R$

14. $\tan^{-1}\left(\frac{a+x}{1-ax}\right)$

15. $\tan^{-1}\left(\frac{\sqrt{x}+\sqrt{a}}{1-\sqrt{xa}}\right)$

16. $\tan^{-1}\left(\frac{a+b\tan x}{b-a\tan x}\right)$

17. $\tan^{-1}\left(\frac{a+bx}{b-ax}\right)$

18. $\tan^{-1}\left(\frac{x-a}{x+a}\right)$

19. $\tan^{-1}\left(\frac{x}{1+6x^2}\right)$

20. $\tan^{-1}\left\{\frac{5x}{1-6x^2}\right\}, -\frac{1}{\sqrt{6}} < x < \frac{1}{\sqrt{6}}$

21. $\tan^{-1}\left\{\frac{\cos x+\sin x}{\cos x-\sin x}\right\}, -\frac{\pi}{4}<x<\frac{\pi}{4}$

22. $\tan^{-1}\left\{\frac{x^{1/3}+a^{1/3}}{1-(a\,x)^{1/3}}\right\}$

23. $\sin^{-1}\left(\frac{2^{x+1}}{1+4^x}\right)$ [CBSE 2013]

24. $\tan^{-1}\left\{\frac{4x}{1-4\,x^2}\right\}, -\frac{1}{2}<x<\frac{1}{2}$

25. $\tan^{-1}\left(\frac{2^{x+1}}{1-4^x}\right), -\infty<x<0$

26. $\tan^{-1}\left(\frac{2a^x}{1-a^{2x}}\right), a>1, -\infty<x<0$

27. $\tan^{-1}\left(\frac{1+\cos x}{\sin x}\right)$ [CBSE 2018]

BASED ON LOTS

28. $\sin^{-1}\left\{\frac{\sin x+\cos x}{\sqrt{2}}\right\}, -\frac{3\pi}{4}<x<\frac{\pi}{4}$

29. $\cos^{-1}\left\{\frac{\cos x+\sin x}{\sqrt{2}}\right\}, -\frac{\pi}{4}<x<\frac{\pi}{4}$ [NCERT EXEMPLAR]

30. $\tan^{-1}\left\{\frac{x}{1+\sqrt{1-x^2}}\right\}, -1<x<1$

31. $\tan^{-1}\left\{\frac{x}{a+\sqrt{a^2-x^2}}\right\}, -a<x<a$

32. $\sin^{-1}\left\{\frac{x+\sqrt{1-x^2}}{\sqrt{2}}\right\}, -\frac{1}{\sqrt{2}}<x<\frac{1}{\sqrt{2}}$

33. $\cos^{-1}\left\{\frac{x+\sqrt{1-x^2}}{\sqrt{2}}\right\}, -1<x<1$

34. $\sin^{-1}\left\{\frac{\sqrt{1+x}+\sqrt{1-x}}{2}\right\}, 0<x<1$

35. $\tan^{-1}\left\{\frac{\sqrt{1+a^2x^2}-1}{ax}\right\}, x\neq 0$

BASED ON HOTS

36. If $y=\sin^{-1}\left(\frac{2x}{1+x^2}\right)+\sec^{-1}\left(\frac{1+x^2}{1-x^2}\right), 0<x<1$, prove that $\frac{dy}{dx}=\frac{4}{1+x^2}$.

37. If $y=\sin^{-1}\left(\frac{x}{\sqrt{1+x^2}}\right)+\cos^{-1}\left(\frac{1}{\sqrt{1+x^2}}\right), 0<x<\infty$, prove that $\frac{dy}{dx}=\frac{2}{1+x^2}$.

38. Differentiate the following with respect to x:

(i) $\cos^{-1}(\sin x)$ (ii) $\cot^{-1}\left(\frac{1-x}{1+x}\right)$ [NCERT, CBSE 2004]

39. If $y=\cot^{-1}\left\{\frac{\sqrt{1+\sin x}+\sqrt{1-\sin x}}{\sqrt{1+\sin x}-\sqrt{1-\sin x}}\right\}$, show that $\frac{dy}{dx}$ is independent of x. [NCERT]

40. If $y=\tan^{-1}\left(\frac{2x}{1-x^2}\right)+\sec^{-1}\left(\frac{1+x^2}{1-x^2}\right), x>0$, prove that $\frac{dy}{dx}=\frac{4}{1+x^2}$.

41. If $y=\sec^{-1}\left(\frac{x+1}{x-1}\right)+\sin^{-1}\left(\frac{x-1}{x+1}\right), x>0$. Find $\frac{dy}{dx}$.

42. If $y = \sin\left[2\tan^{-1}\left\{\sqrt{\frac{1-x}{1+x}}\right\}\right]$, find $\frac{dy}{dx}$.

43. If $y = \cos^{-1}(2x) + 2\cos^{-1}\sqrt{1-4x^2}$, $0 < x < \frac{1}{2}$, find $\frac{dy}{dx}$.

44. If the derivative of $\tan^{-1}(a + bx)$ takes the value 1 at $x = 0$, prove that $1 + a^2 = b$.

45. If $y = \cos^{-1}(2x) + 2\cos^{-1}\sqrt{1-4x^2}$, $-\frac{1}{2} < x < 0$, find $\frac{dy}{dx}$.

46. If $y = \tan^{-1}\left\{\frac{\sqrt{1+x}-\sqrt{1-x}}{\sqrt{1+x}+\sqrt{1-x}}\right\}$, find $\frac{dy}{dx}$. [CBSE 2003, 2008]

47. If $y = \cos^{-1}\left\{\frac{2x-3\sqrt{1-x^2}}{\sqrt{13}}\right\}$, find $\frac{dy}{dx}$. [CBSE 2010]

48. Differentiate $\sin^{-1}\left\{\frac{2^{x+1}\cdot 3^x}{1+(36)^x}\right\}$ with respect to x. [CBSE 2013]

49. If $y = \sin^{-1}\left(6x\sqrt{1-9x^2}\right)$, $-\frac{1}{3\sqrt{2}} < x < \frac{1}{3\sqrt{2}}$, then find $\frac{dy}{dx}$. [CBSE 2017]

ANSWERS

1. $\frac{2}{\sqrt{1-x^2}}$
2. $-\frac{1}{2\sqrt{1-x^2}}$
3. $-\frac{1}{2\sqrt{1-x^2}}$
4. $-\frac{1}{\sqrt{1-x^2}}$
5. $\frac{1}{\sqrt{a^2-x^2}}$
6. $\frac{a}{a^2+x^2}$
7. $\frac{2}{\sqrt{1-x^2}}$
8. $\frac{-2}{\sqrt{1-x^2}}$
9. $-\frac{a}{a^2+x^2}$
10. $\frac{1}{2}$
11. $-\frac{1}{1+x^2}$
12. $\frac{2nx^{n-1}}{1+x^{2n}}$
13. 0
14. $\frac{1}{1+x^2}$
15. $\frac{1}{2\sqrt{x}(1+x)}$
16. 1
17. $\frac{1}{1+x^2}$
18. $\frac{a}{a^2+x^2}$
19. $\frac{3}{1+9x^2} - \frac{2}{1+4x^2}$
20. $\frac{3}{1+9x^2} + \frac{2}{1+4x^2}$
21. 1
22. $\frac{1}{3}\cdot\frac{x^{-2/3}}{1+x^{2/3}}$
23. $\frac{2^{x+1}}{1+4^x}\log 2$
24. $\frac{4}{1+4x^2}$
25. $\frac{2^{x+1}\log_e 2}{1+4^x}$
26. $\frac{2\cdot a^x\log a}{1+a^{2x}}$
27. $-\frac{1}{2}$
28. 1
29. -1
30. $\frac{1}{2\sqrt{1-x^2}}$
31. $\frac{1}{2\sqrt{a^2-x^2}}$
32. $\frac{1}{\sqrt{1-x^2}}$
33. $-\frac{1}{\sqrt{1-x^2}}$
34. $-\frac{1}{2\sqrt{1-x^2}}$
35. $\frac{1}{2}\left(\frac{a}{1+a^2x^2}\right)$
38. (i) -1 (ii) $\frac{1}{1+x^2}$
41. 0

42. $\frac{-x}{\sqrt{1-x^2}}$ 43. $\frac{2}{\sqrt{1-4x^2}}$ 45. $-\frac{6}{\sqrt{1-4x^2}}$ 46. $\frac{1}{2\sqrt{1-x^2}}$

47. $\frac{-1}{\sqrt{1-x^2}}$ 48. $\frac{2(\log 6)\,6^x}{1+36^x}$ 49. $\frac{6}{\sqrt{1-9x^2}}$

HINTS TO SELECTED PROBLEMS

15. Given function $= \tan^{-1}\sqrt{x} + \tan^{-1}\sqrt{a}$

16. Given function $= \tan^{-1}\left\{\frac{(a/b)+\tan x}{1-(a/b)\tan x}\right\} = \tan^{-1}(a/b) + \tan^{-1}(\tan x)$

17. Given function $I = \tan^{-1}\left\{\frac{(a/b)+x}{1-(a/b)x}\right\} = \tan^{-1}(a/b) + \tan^{-1} x$

18. Given function $= \tan^{-1}\left\{\frac{1-(a/x)}{1+(a/x)}\right\} = \tan^{-1}(1) - \tan^{-1}(a/x)$

19. Given function $= \tan^{-1}\left\{\frac{3x-2x}{1+(3x)(2x)}\right\} = \tan^{-1} 3x - \tan^{-1} 2x$

20. Given function $= \tan^{-1} 3x + \tan^{-1} 2x$

21. Given function $= \tan^{-1}\left(\frac{1+\tan x}{1-\tan x}\right) = \tan^{-1}(1) + \tan^{-1}(\tan x) = \frac{\pi}{4} + x$

22. Given function $= \tan^{-1} x^{1/3} + \tan^{-1} a^{1/3}$

36. Putting $x = \tan\theta$, we get $y = 2\tan^{-1} x + 2\tan^{-1} x = 4\tan^{-1} x$

39. We have,

$$y = \cot^{-1}\left\{\frac{\sqrt{1+\sin x}+\sqrt{1-\sin x}}{\sqrt{1+\sin x}-\sqrt{1-\sin x}}\right\}, 0 < x < \frac{\pi}{2}$$

$$\Rightarrow \quad y = \cot^{-1}\left\{\frac{\sqrt{\left(\cos\frac{x}{2}+\sin\frac{x}{2}\right)^2}+\sqrt{\left(\cos\frac{x}{2}+\sin\frac{x}{2}\right)^2}}{\sqrt{\left(\cos\frac{x}{2}+\sin\frac{x}{2}\right)^2}-\sqrt{\left(\cos\frac{x}{2}-\sin\frac{x}{2}\right)^2}}\right\}$$

$$\Rightarrow \quad y = \cot^{-1}\left\{\frac{\left|\cos\frac{x}{2}+\sin\frac{x}{2}\right|+\left|\cos\frac{x}{2}-\sin\frac{x}{2}\right|}{\left|\cos\frac{x}{2}+\sin\frac{x}{2}\right|-\left|\cos\frac{x}{2}-\sin\frac{x}{2}\right|}\right\}$$

$$\Rightarrow \quad y = \begin{cases} \cot^{-1}\left\{\dfrac{\left(\cos\dfrac{x}{2}+\sin\dfrac{x}{2}\right)+\left(\cos\dfrac{x}{2}-\sin\dfrac{x}{2}\right)}{\left(\cos\dfrac{x}{2}+\sin\dfrac{x}{2}\right)-\left(\cos\dfrac{x}{2}-\sin\dfrac{x}{2}\right)}\right\}, & 0 < x \leq \dfrac{\pi}{4} \\ \cot^{-1}\left\{\dfrac{\left(\cos\dfrac{x}{2}+\sin\dfrac{x}{2}\right)-\left(\cos\dfrac{x}{2}-\sin\dfrac{x}{2}\right)}{\left(\cos\dfrac{x}{2}+\sin\dfrac{x}{2}\right)+\left(\cos\dfrac{x}{2}-\sin\dfrac{x}{2}\right)}\right\}, & \dfrac{\pi}{4} < x < \dfrac{\pi}{2} \end{cases}$$

$$\Rightarrow \quad y = \begin{cases} \cot^{-1}\left(\cot\dfrac{x}{2}\right) & , 0 < x \; x \leq \dfrac{\pi}{4} \\ \cot^{-1}\left(\tan\dfrac{x}{2}\right) & , \dfrac{\pi}{4} < x < \dfrac{\pi}{2} \end{cases} \Rightarrow y = \begin{cases} \cot^{-1}\left(\cot\dfrac{x}{2}\right) & , 0 < x \leq \dfrac{\pi}{4} \\ \cot^{-1}\left\{\cot\left(\dfrac{\pi}{2}-\dfrac{x}{2}\right)\right\} & , \dfrac{\pi}{4} < x < \dfrac{\pi}{2} \end{cases}$$

$$\Rightarrow \quad y = \begin{cases} \dfrac{x}{2}, & 0 < x \leq \dfrac{\pi}{4} \\ \dfrac{\pi}{2}-\dfrac{x}{2}, & \dfrac{\pi}{4} < x < \dfrac{\pi}{2} \end{cases} \Rightarrow \quad \frac{dy}{dx} = \begin{cases} \dfrac{1}{2} & , 0 < x < \dfrac{\pi}{4} \\ -\dfrac{1}{2} & , \dfrac{\pi}{4} < x < \dfrac{\pi}{2} \end{cases}$$

Hence, $\dfrac{dy}{dx}$ is independent of x.

41. Use: $\sec^{-1}\left(\dfrac{x+1}{x-1}\right) = \cos^{-1}\dfrac{x-1}{x+1}$ and $\cos^{-1}\theta + \sin^{-1}\theta = \dfrac{\pi}{2}$

43. Putting $2x = \cos\theta$, we get

$$y = \theta + 2\cos^{-1}(\sin\theta) = \theta + 2\cos^{-1}\{\cos(\pi/2-\theta)\} = \theta + 2(\pi/2-\theta) = \pi - \theta = \pi - \cos^{-1}(2x)$$

10.6 RELATION BETWEEN $\frac{dy}{dx}$ AND $\frac{dx}{dy}$

Let x and y be two variables connected by a relation of the form $f(x, y) = 0$. Let Δx be a small change in x and let Δy be the corresponding change in y. Then,

$$\frac{dy}{dx} = \lim_{\Delta x \to 0} \frac{\Delta y}{\Delta x} \text{ and, } \frac{dx}{dy} = \lim_{\Delta x \to 0} \frac{\Delta x}{\Delta y}$$

Now, $\dfrac{\Delta y}{\Delta x} \times \dfrac{\Delta x}{\Delta y} = 1$

$$\Rightarrow \quad \lim_{\Delta x \to 0}\left(\frac{\Delta y}{\Delta x} \times \frac{\Delta x}{\Delta y}\right) = 1$$

$$\Rightarrow \quad \lim_{\Delta x \to 0}\frac{\Delta y}{\Delta x} \times \lim_{\Delta y \to 0}\frac{\Delta x}{\Delta y} = 1 \qquad [\because \Delta x \to 0 \Leftrightarrow \Delta y \to 0]$$

$$\Rightarrow \quad \frac{dy}{dx} \times \frac{dx}{dy} = 1 \Rightarrow \frac{dy}{dx} = \frac{1}{dx/dy}$$

10.7 DIFFERENTIATION OF IMPLICIT FUNCTIONS

Up till now we have discussed derivatives of functions of the form $y = f(x)$. If the variables x and y are connected by a relation of the form $f(x, y) = 0$ and it is not possible or convenient to express y as a function x in the form $y = \phi(x)$, then y is said to be an implicit function of x. To find $\frac{dy}{dx}$ in such a case, we differentiate both sides of the given relation with respect to x, keeping in mind that the derivative of $\phi(y)$ with respect to x is $\frac{d\phi}{dy} \cdot \frac{dy}{dx}$.

For example, $\frac{d}{dx}(\sin y) = \cos y \cdot \frac{dy}{dx}$, $\frac{d}{dx}(y^2) = 2y \frac{dy}{dx}$.

It should be noted that $\frac{d}{dy}(\sin y) = \cos y$ but $\frac{d}{dx}(\sin y) = \cos y \cdot \frac{dy}{dx}$.

Similarly, $\frac{d}{dy}(y^3) = 3y^2$ whereas $\frac{d}{dx}(y^3) = 3y^2 \frac{dy}{dx}$.

ILLUSTRATIVE EXAMPLES

BASED ON BASIC CONCEPTS (BASIC)

EXAMPLE 1 *If $ax^2 + 2hxy + by^2 + 2gx + 2fy + c = 0$, find $\frac{dy}{dx}$ and $\frac{dx}{dy}$. Also, show that $\frac{dy}{dx} \cdot \frac{dx}{dy} = 1$.*

SOLUTION We have, $ax^2 + 2hxy + by^2 + 2gx + 2fy + c = 0$ ...(i)

Differentiating both sides of this with respect to x, we get

$$\frac{d}{dx}(ax^2) + \frac{d}{dx}(2hxy) + \frac{d}{dx}(by^2) + \frac{d}{dx}(2gx) + \frac{d}{dx}(2fy) + \frac{d}{dx}(c) = \frac{d}{dx}(0)$$

$$\Rightarrow \quad a\frac{d}{dx}(x^2) + 2h\frac{d}{dx}(xy) + b\frac{d}{dx}(y^2) + 2g\frac{d}{dx}(x) + 2f\frac{d}{dx}(y) + 0 = 0$$

$$\Rightarrow \quad 2ax + 2h\left(x\frac{dy}{dx} + y\right) + b\,2y\frac{dy}{dx} + 2g \times 1 + 2f \times \frac{dy}{dx} = 0$$

$$\Rightarrow \quad \frac{dy}{dx}(2hx + 2by + 2f) + 2ax + 2hy + 2g = 0$$

$$\Rightarrow \quad \frac{dy}{dx} = -\frac{2(ax + hy + g)}{2(hx + by + f)} = -\left(\frac{ax + hy + g}{hx + by + f}\right) \qquad \text{...(ii)}$$

Differentiating both sides of (i) with respect to y, we obtain

$$\frac{d}{dy}(ax^2) + \frac{d}{dy}(2hxy) + \frac{d}{dy}(by^2) + \frac{d}{dy}(2gx) + \frac{d}{dy}(2fy) + \frac{d}{dy}(c) = \frac{d}{dy}(0)$$

$$\Rightarrow \quad a\frac{d}{dy}(x^2) + 2h\frac{d}{dy}(xy) + b\frac{d}{dy}(y^2) + 2g\frac{d}{dy}(x) + 2f\frac{d}{dy}(y) + \frac{d}{dy}(c) = 0$$

$$\Rightarrow \quad a\left(2x\frac{dx}{dy}\right) + 2h\left(y\frac{dx}{dy} + x\right) + b(2y) + 2g\frac{dx}{dy} + 2f \times 1 + 0 = 0$$

$$\Rightarrow \quad \frac{dx}{dy} = -\frac{2(hx + by + f)}{2(ax + hy + g)} = -\left(\frac{hx + by + f}{ax + hy + g}\right) \qquad \text{...(iii)}$$

From (ii) and (iii), we obtain

$$\frac{dy}{dx}\cdot\frac{dx}{dy}=-\left(\frac{ax+hy+g}{hx+by+f}\right)\times-\left(\frac{hx+by+f}{ax+hy+g}\right)=1$$

EXAMPLE 2 *If* $x^2+2xy+y^3=42$, *find* $\frac{dy}{dx}$

SOLUTION We have, $x^2+2xy+y^3=42$. Differentiating both sides of this with respect to x, we get

$$\frac{d}{dx}(x^2)+2\frac{d}{dx}(xy)+\frac{d}{dx}(y^3)=\frac{d}{dx}(42)$$

$$\Rightarrow \quad 2x+2\left(x\frac{dy}{dx}+y\right)+3y^2\frac{dy}{dx}=0$$

$$\Rightarrow \quad 2x+2y+\frac{dy}{dx}(2x+3y^2)=0 \Rightarrow \frac{dy}{dx}(2x+3y^2)=-2(x+y) \Rightarrow \frac{dy}{dx}=-\frac{2(x+y)}{(2x+3y^2)}.$$

EXAMPLE 3 *If* $x^3+y^3=3axy$, *find* $\frac{dy}{dx}$

SOLUTION Differentiating both sides of the given relation with respect to x, we get

$$\frac{d}{dx}(x^3)+\frac{d}{dx}(y^3)=3a\frac{d}{dx}(xy)$$

$$\Rightarrow \quad 3x^2+3y^2\frac{dy}{dx}=3a\left\{x\frac{dy}{dx}+y\right\}$$

$$\Rightarrow \quad (3y^2-3ax)\frac{dy}{dx}=3ay-3x^2 \Rightarrow 3(y^2-ax)\frac{dy}{dx}=3(ay-x^2) \Rightarrow \frac{dy}{dx}=\frac{ay-x^2}{y^2-ax}.$$

EXAMPLE 4 *If* $\log(x^2+y^2)=2\tan^{-1}\left(\frac{y}{x}\right)$, *show that* $\frac{dy}{dx}=\frac{x+y}{x-y}$.

SOLUTION Differentiating both sides of the given relation with respect to x, we get

$$\frac{d}{dx}\left\{\log(x^2+y^2)\right\}=2\frac{d}{dx}\left\{\tan^{-1}\left(\frac{y}{x}\right)\right\}$$

$$\Rightarrow \quad \frac{1}{x^2+y^2}\times\frac{d}{dx}(x^2+y^2)=2\times\frac{1}{1+(y/x)^2}\times\frac{d}{dx}\left(\frac{y}{x}\right)$$

$$\Rightarrow \quad \frac{1}{x^2+y^2}\left\{\frac{d}{dx}(x^2)+\frac{d}{dx}(y^2)\right\}=2\times\frac{x^2}{x^2+y^2}\left\{\frac{x\frac{dy}{dx}-y\times 1}{x^2}\right\}$$

$$\Rightarrow \quad \frac{1}{x^2+y^2}\left\{2x+2y\frac{dy}{dx}\right\}=\frac{2}{x^2+y^2}\left\{x\frac{dy}{dx}-y\right\}$$

$$\Rightarrow \quad 2\left\{x+y\frac{dy}{dx}\right\}=2\left\{x\frac{dy}{dx}-y\right\}$$

$$\Rightarrow \quad x+y\frac{dy}{dx}=x\frac{dy}{dx}-y \Rightarrow \frac{dy}{dx}(y-x)=-(x+y) \Rightarrow \frac{dy}{dx}=\frac{x+y}{x-y}$$

EXAMPLE 5 *If* $x\sqrt{1+y}+y\sqrt{1+x}=0$ *and* $x\neq y$, *prove that* $\frac{dy}{dx}=-\frac{1}{(x+1)^2}$. [CBSE 2012, NCERT]

SOLUTION We have,

$$x\sqrt{1+y} + y\sqrt{1+x} = 0$$

$$\Rightarrow \quad x\sqrt{1+y} = -y\sqrt{1+x}$$

$$\Rightarrow \quad x^2(1+y) = y^2(1+x) \qquad \text{[On squaring both sides]}$$

$$\Rightarrow \quad x^2 - y^2 = y^2 x - x^2 y$$

$$\Rightarrow \quad (x+y)(x-y) = -xy(x-y)$$

$$\Rightarrow \quad x + y = -xy \Rightarrow x = -y - xy \Rightarrow y(1+x) = -x \Rightarrow y = -\frac{x}{1+x} \qquad [\because x \neq y]$$

$$\Rightarrow \quad \frac{dy}{dx} = -\left\{\frac{(1+x)\times 1 - x(0+1)}{(1+x)^2}\right\} \Rightarrow \frac{dy}{dx} = -\frac{1}{(1+x)^2}$$

BASED ON LOWER ORDER THINKING SKILLS (LOTS)

EXAMPLE 6 *If* $\cos^{-1}\left(\frac{x^2-y^2}{x^2+y^2}\right) = \tan^{-1} a$, *prove that* $\frac{dy}{dx} = \frac{y}{x}$.

SOLUTION We have,

$$\cos^{-1}\left(\frac{x^2-y^2}{x^2+y^2}\right) = \tan^{-1} a \Rightarrow \frac{x^2-y^2}{x^2+y^2} = \cos(\tan^{-1} a) = \lambda, \text{ say}$$

$$\Rightarrow \quad \frac{2x^2}{-2y^2} = \frac{\lambda+1}{\lambda-1} \qquad \text{[Applying Componendo and dividendo]}$$

$$\Rightarrow \quad \frac{x^2}{y^2} = \frac{1+\lambda}{1-\lambda}$$

Differentiating both sides with respect to x, we get

$$\Rightarrow \quad \frac{y^2 \frac{d}{dx}(x^2) - x^2 \frac{d}{dx}(y^2)}{(y^2)^2} = 0 \Rightarrow \frac{y^2 \times 2x - x^2 \times 2y \frac{dy}{dx}}{y^4} = 0$$

$$\Rightarrow \quad 2xy^2 - 2x^2 y \frac{dy}{dx} = 0 \Rightarrow 2x^2 y \frac{dy}{dx} = 2xy^2 \Rightarrow \frac{dy}{dx} = \frac{2xy^2}{2x^2 y} \Rightarrow \frac{dy}{dx} = \frac{y}{x}$$

ALITER We have,

$$\cos^{-1}\left(\frac{x^2-y^2}{x^2+y^2}\right) = \tan^{-1} a \Rightarrow \cos^{-1}\left\{\frac{1-(y/x)^2}{1+(y/x)^2}\right\} = \tan^{-1} a$$

$$\Rightarrow \quad 2\tan^{-1}\left(\frac{y}{x}\right) = \tan^{-1} a \Rightarrow \tan^{-1}\left(\frac{y}{x}\right) = \frac{1}{2}\tan^{-1} a \Rightarrow \frac{y}{x} = \tan\left(\frac{1}{2}\tan^{-1} a\right)$$

$$\Rightarrow \quad \frac{d}{dx}\left(\frac{y}{x}\right) = 0 \Rightarrow \frac{x\frac{dy}{dx} - y \times 1}{x^2} = 0 \Rightarrow x\frac{dy}{dx} - y = 0 \Rightarrow \frac{dy}{dx} = \frac{y}{x}$$

EXAMPLE 7 *If* $\sin y = x \sin (a + y)$, *prove that* $\frac{dy}{dx} = \frac{\sin^2 (a + y)}{\sin a}$. **[CBSE 2009, 2011, 2012, 2024]**

SOLUTION Differentiating both sides of the given relation with respect to x, we get

$$\frac{d}{dx}(\sin y) = \frac{d}{dx}\left\{x \sin (a + y)\right\}$$

$$\Rightarrow \quad \cos y \frac{dy}{dx} = 1 \times \sin (a + y) + x \cos (a + y) \frac{d}{dx}(a + y)$$

$$\Rightarrow \quad \cos y \frac{dy}{dx} = \sin (a + y) + x \cos (a + y) \frac{dy}{dx}$$

$$\Rightarrow \quad \cos y \frac{dy}{dx} - x \cos (a + y) \frac{dy}{dx} = \sin (a + y)$$

$$\Rightarrow \quad \left\{\cos y - x \cos (a + y)\right\} \frac{dy}{dx} = \sin (a + y)$$

$$\Rightarrow \quad \left\{\cos y - \frac{\sin y}{\sin (a + y)} \cos (a + y)\right\} \frac{dy}{dx} = \sin (a + y) \qquad \left[\begin{array}{l} \because \sin y = x \sin (a + y) \\ \therefore x = \dfrac{\sin y}{\sin (a + y)} \end{array}\right]$$

$$\Rightarrow \quad \left\{\frac{\sin (a + y) \cos y - \sin y \cos (a + y)}{\sin (a + y)}\right\} \frac{dy}{dx} = \sin (a + y)$$

$$\Rightarrow \quad \frac{\sin (a + y - y)}{\sin (a + y)} \times \frac{dy}{dx} = \sin (a + y) \Rightarrow \frac{dy}{dx} = \frac{\sin^2 (a + y)}{\sin a}$$

ALITER 1 We have,

$$\sin y = x \sin (a + y) \Rightarrow x = \frac{\sin y}{\sin (a + y)}$$

Differentiating both sides with respect to y, we get

$$\frac{dx}{dy} = \frac{\sin (a + y) \cos y - \sin y \cos (a + y)}{\sin^2 (a + y)} = \frac{\sin (a + y - y)}{\sin^2 (a + y)}$$

$$\therefore \quad \frac{dy}{dx} = \frac{1}{dx/dy} = \frac{\sin^2 (a + y)}{\sin a}.$$

BASED ON HIGHER ORDER THINKING SKILLS (HOTS)

EXAMPLE 8 *If* $\sqrt{1 - x^6} + \sqrt{1 - y^6} = a (x^3 - y^3)$, *prove that* $\frac{dy}{dx} = \frac{x^2}{y^2} \sqrt{\frac{1 - y^6}{1 - x^6}}$, *where* $-1 \quad x < 1$ *and* $-1 < y < 1$.

SOLUTION Putting $x^3 = \sin A$ and $y^3 = \sin B$ in the given relation, we get

$$\sqrt{1 - \sin^2 A} + \sqrt{1 - \sin^2 B} = a (\sin A - \sin B)$$

$$\Rightarrow \quad \cos A + \cos B = a (\sin A - \sin B)$$

$$\Rightarrow \quad 2 \cos \left(\frac{A + B}{2}\right) \cos \left(\frac{A - B}{2}\right) = 2a \sin \left(\frac{A - B}{2}\right) \cos \left(\frac{A + B}{2}\right) \Rightarrow \cot \left(\frac{A - B}{2}\right) = a$$

$$\Rightarrow \quad \frac{A - B}{2} = \cot^{-1}(a) \Rightarrow A - B = 2 \cot^{-1}(a) \Rightarrow \sin^{-1} x^3 - \sin^{-1} y^3 = 2 \cot^{-1}(a).$$

Differentiating both sides with respect to x, we get

$$\frac{1}{\sqrt{1-x^6}} \times \frac{d}{dx}(x^3) - \frac{1}{\sqrt{1-y^6}} \times \frac{d}{dx}(y^3) = 0 \Rightarrow \frac{1}{\sqrt{1-x^6}} \times 3x^2 - \frac{1}{\sqrt{1-y^6}} \times 3y^2 \frac{dy}{dx} = 0$$

$$\Rightarrow \quad \frac{dy}{dx} = \frac{x^2}{y^2}\sqrt{\frac{1-y^6}{1-x^6}}$$

ALITER 1 We have, $\sqrt{1-x^6} + \sqrt{1-y^6} = a(x^3 - y^3)$ ...(i)

Differentiating both sides of the given relation with respect to x, we get

$$\frac{1}{2\sqrt{1-x^6}} \frac{d}{dx}(1-x^6) + \frac{1}{2\sqrt{1-y^6}} \frac{d}{dx}(1-y^6) = a\frac{d}{dx}(x^3 - y^3)$$

$$\Rightarrow \quad \frac{1}{2\sqrt{1-x^6}} \times -6x^5 + \frac{1}{2\sqrt{1-y^6}} \times -6y^5 \frac{dy}{dx} = a\left(3x^2 - 3y^2\frac{dy}{dx}\right)$$

$$\Rightarrow \quad \frac{-3x^5}{\sqrt{1-x^6}} - \frac{3y^5}{\sqrt{1-y^6}}\frac{dy}{dx} = 3ax^2 - 3ay^2\frac{dy}{dx} \Rightarrow \frac{dy}{dx}\left\{ay^2 - \frac{y^5}{\sqrt{1-y^6}}\right\} = ax^2 + \frac{x^5}{\sqrt{1-x^6}}$$

$$\Rightarrow \quad y^2\frac{dy}{dx}\frac{\left\{a\sqrt{1-y^6} - y^3\right\}}{\sqrt{1-y^6}} = x^2\frac{\left\{a\sqrt{1-x^6} + x^3\right\}}{\sqrt{1-x^6}} \Rightarrow \frac{dy}{dx} = \frac{x^2\sqrt{1-y^6}}{y^2\sqrt{1-x^6}}\left\{\frac{a\sqrt{1-x^6} + x^3}{a\sqrt{1-y^6} - y^3}\right\}$$

$$\Rightarrow \quad \frac{dy}{dx} = \frac{x^2\sqrt{1-y^6}}{y^2\sqrt{1-x^6}}\left\{\frac{\frac{\left\{\sqrt{1-x^6} + \sqrt{1-y^6}\right\}\sqrt{1-x^6}}{x^3 - y^3} + x^3}{\frac{\left\{\sqrt{1-x^6} + \sqrt{1-y^6}\right\}\sqrt{1-y^6}}{x^3 - y^3} - y^3}\right\}$$ [Using (i)]

$$\Rightarrow \quad \frac{dy}{dx} = \frac{x^2\sqrt{1-y^6}}{y^2\sqrt{1-x^6}}\left\{\frac{1 - x^6 + \sqrt{1-x^6}\sqrt{1-y^6} + x^6 - x^3y^3}{\sqrt{1-x^6}\sqrt{1-y^6} + 1 - y^6 - x^3y^3 + y^6}\right\}$$

$$\Rightarrow \quad \frac{dy}{dx} = \frac{x^2\sqrt{1-y^6}}{y^2\sqrt{1-x^6}}\left\{\frac{1 - x^3y^3 + \sqrt{1-x^6}\sqrt{1-y^6}}{1 - x^3y^3 + \sqrt{1-x^6}\sqrt{1-y^6}}\right\} \Rightarrow \frac{dy}{dx} = \frac{x^2}{y^2}\sqrt{\frac{1-y^6}{1-x^6}}$$

EXAMPLE 9 *If $x^2 + y^2 = t - \frac{1}{t}$ and $x^4 + y^4 = t^2 + \frac{1}{t^2}$, then prove that $\frac{dy}{dx} = \frac{1}{x^3 y}$.*

SOLUTION We have, $x^2 + y^2 = t - \frac{1}{t}$

$$\Rightarrow \quad (x^2 + y^2)^2 = \left(t - \frac{1}{t}\right)^2 \Rightarrow x^4 + y^4 + 2x^2y^2 = t^2 + \frac{1}{t^2} - 2$$

$$\Rightarrow \quad x^4 + y^4 + 2x^2y^2 = x^4 + y^4 - 2 \qquad \left[\because x^4 + y^4 = t^2 + \frac{1}{t^2}\right]$$

$$\Rightarrow \quad 2x^2y^2 = -2 \Rightarrow x^2y^2 = -1 \Rightarrow y^2 = -\frac{1}{x^2} \Rightarrow y^2 = -x^{-2}$$

Differentiating with respect to x, we get

$$2y\frac{dy}{dx} = -(-2)\,x^{-3} \Rightarrow y\frac{dy}{dx} = \frac{1}{x^3} \Rightarrow \frac{dy}{dx} = \frac{1}{x^3 y}$$

EXAMPLE 10 *If* $y = b\tan^{-1}\left(\frac{x}{a} + \tan^{-1}\frac{y}{x}\right)$, *find* $\frac{dy}{dx}$.

SOLUTION We have,

$$y = b\tan^{-1}\left(\frac{x}{a} + \tan^{-1}\frac{y}{x}\right) \Rightarrow \frac{y}{b} = \tan^{-1}\left(\frac{x}{a} + \tan^{-1}\frac{y}{x}\right) \Rightarrow \tan\frac{y}{b} = \frac{x}{a} + \tan^{-1}\frac{y}{x}$$

Differentiating both sides with respect to x, we get

$$\frac{1}{b}\sec^2\left(\frac{y}{b}\right)\frac{dy}{dx} = \frac{1}{a} + \frac{1}{1+\left(\frac{y}{x}\right)^2} \times \frac{x\frac{dy}{dx} - y}{x^2} \Rightarrow \frac{1}{b}\sec^2\left(\frac{y}{b}\right)\frac{dy}{dx} = \frac{1}{a} + \frac{x\frac{dy}{dx} - y}{x^2 + y^2}$$

$$\Rightarrow \quad \frac{dy}{dx}\left\{\frac{1}{b}\sec^2\left(\frac{y}{b}\right) - \frac{x}{x^2+y^2}\right\} = \frac{1}{a} - \frac{y}{x^2+y^2} \Rightarrow \frac{dy}{dx} = \frac{\frac{1}{a} - \frac{y}{x^2+y^2}}{\frac{1}{b}\sec^2\left(\frac{y}{b}\right) - \frac{x}{x^2+y^2}}$$

EXAMPLE 11 *If* $y = \cos^{-1}\sqrt{\frac{\cos 3x}{\cos^3 x}}$, *then show that* $\frac{dy}{dx} = \sqrt{\frac{3}{\cos x \cos 3x}}$.

SOLUTION We have, $y = \cos^{-1}\sqrt{\frac{\cos 3x}{\cos^3 x}}$

$$\Rightarrow \quad \cos y = \sqrt{\frac{\cos 3x}{\cos^3 x}} \qquad \ldots(\text{i})$$

$$\Rightarrow \quad \cos y = \sqrt{\frac{4\cos^3 x - 3\cos x}{\cos^3 x}} \Rightarrow \cos y = \sqrt{4 - 3\sec^2 x} \Rightarrow \cos^2 y = 4 - 3(1 + \tan^2 x)$$

$$\Rightarrow \quad 1 - \cos^2 y = 3\tan^2 x \Rightarrow \sin^2 y = 3\tan^2 x \Rightarrow \sin y = \sqrt{3}\tan x$$

Differentiating both sides with respect to x, we get

$$\cos y\frac{dy}{dx} = \sqrt{3}\sec^2 x$$

$$\Rightarrow \quad \frac{dy}{dx} = \frac{\sqrt{3}}{\cos y\cos^2 x} = \frac{\sqrt{3}}{\cos^2 x} \times \sqrt{\frac{\cos^3 x}{\cos 3x}} \qquad [\text{Using (i)}]$$

$$\Rightarrow \quad \frac{dy}{dx} = \sqrt{\frac{3}{\cos x \cos 3x}}$$

EXERCISE 10.4

BASIC

Find $\frac{dy}{dx}$ *in each of the following (1-11):*

1. $xy = c^2$
2. $y^3 - 3xy^2 = x^3 + 3x^2 y$
3. $x^{2/3} + y^{2/3} = a^{2/3}$

4. $4x + 3y = \log(4x - 3y)$ 5. $\frac{x^2}{a^2} + \frac{y^2}{b^2} = 1$ 6. $x^5 + y^5 = 5xy$

7. $(x + y)^2 = 2axy$ 8. $(x^2 + y^2)^2 = xy$ [CBSE 2009, 2018, 2023]

9. $\tan^{-1}(x^2 + y^2) = a$ 10. $e^{x-y} = \log\left(\frac{x}{y}\right)$ 11. $\sin xy + \cos(x + y) = 1$

12. If $xy = 1$, prove that $\frac{dy}{dx} + y^2 = 0$. 13. If $xy^2 = 1$, prove that $2\frac{dy}{dx} + y^3 = 0$.

BASED ON LOTS

14. If $\sqrt{1-x^2} + \sqrt{1-y^2} = a(x-y)$, prove that $\frac{dy}{dx} = \sqrt{\frac{1-y^2}{1-x^2}}$. [NCERT EXEMPLAR, CBSE 2024]

15. If $y\sqrt{1-x^2} + x\sqrt{1-y^2} = 1$, prove that $\frac{dy}{dx} = -\sqrt{\frac{1-y^2}{1-x^2}}$.

16. If $x\sqrt{1+y} + y\sqrt{1+x} = 0$, prove that $(1+x)^2\frac{dy}{dx} + 1 = 0$. [CBSE 2011]

17. If $\log\sqrt{x^2 + y^2} = \tan^{-1}\left(\frac{y}{x}\right)$, prove that $\frac{dy}{dx} = \frac{x+y}{x-y}$. [CBSE 2019, 2020]

18. If $\sec\left(\frac{x+y}{x-y}\right) = a$, prove that $\frac{dy}{dx} = \frac{y}{x}$.

19. If $\tan^{-1}\left(\frac{x^2 - y^2}{x^2 + y^2}\right) = a$, prove that $\frac{dy}{dx} = \frac{x}{y}\frac{(1 - \tan a)}{(1 + \tan a)}$.

20. If $xy\log(x + y) = 1$, prove that $\frac{dy}{dx} = -\frac{y(x^2y + x + y)}{x(xy^2 + x + y)}$.

21. If $y = x\sin(a + y)$, prove that $\frac{dy}{dx} = \frac{\sin^2(a + y)}{\sin(a + y) - y\cos(a + y)}$.

22. If $x\sin(a + y) + \sin a\cos(a + y) = 0$, prove that $\frac{dy}{dx} = \frac{\sin^2(a + y)}{\sin a}$. [NCERT EXEMPLAR]

23. If $y = x\sin y$, prove that $\frac{dy}{dx} = \frac{\sin y}{(1 - x\cos y)}$.

24. If $y\sqrt{x^2 + 1} = \log\left(\sqrt{x^2 + 1} - x\right)$, show that $(x^2 + 1)\frac{dy}{dx} + xy + 1 = 0$.

25. If $\sin(xy) + \frac{y}{x} = x^2 - y^2$, find $\frac{dy}{dx}$.

26. If $\tan(x + y) + \tan(x - y) = 1$, find $\frac{dy}{dx}$.

27. If $e^x + e^y = e^{x+y}$, prove that $\frac{dy}{dx} = -\frac{e^x(e^y - 1)}{e^y(e^x - 1)}$ or, $\frac{dy}{dx} + e^{y-x} = 0$ [CBSE 2014]

28. (i) If $\cos y = x\cos(a + y)$, with $\cos a \neq \pm 1$, prove that $\frac{dy}{dx} = \frac{\cos^2(a + y)}{\sin a}$. [NCERT]

(ii) If $x\cos(p+y)+\cos p\sin(p+y)=0$, prove that $\cos p\dfrac{dy}{dx}=-\cos^2(p+y)$. [CBSE 2024]

29. If $\sin^2 y+\cos xy=k$, find $\dfrac{dy}{dx}$ at $x=1,\ y=\dfrac{\pi}{4}$. [CBSE 2017]

BASED ON HOTS

30. If $y=\{\log_{\cos x}\sin x\}\{\log_{\sin x}\cos x\}^{-1}+\sin^{-1}\left(\dfrac{2x}{1+x^2}\right)$, find $\dfrac{dy}{dx}$ at $x=\dfrac{\pi}{4}$.

31. If $\sqrt{y+x}+\sqrt{y-x}=c$, show that $\dfrac{dy}{dx}=\dfrac{y}{x}-\sqrt{\dfrac{y^2}{x^2}-1}$.

ANSWERS

1. $-\dfrac{y}{x}$
2. $\dfrac{dy}{dx}=\dfrac{(x+y)^2}{y^2-2xy-x^2}$
3. $\left(-\dfrac{y}{x}\right)^{1/3}$
4. $\dfrac{4(1-4x+3y)}{3(4x-3y+1)}$
5. $-\dfrac{b^2x}{a^2y}$
6. $\dfrac{y-x^4}{y^4-x}$
7. $\dfrac{ay-x-y}{x+y-ax}$
8. $\dfrac{4x(x^2+y^2)-y}{x-4y(x^2+y^2)}$
9. $-\dfrac{x}{y}$
10. $\dfrac{y}{x}\cdot\dfrac{(xe^{x-y}-1)}{(ye^{x-y}-1)}$
11. $\dfrac{\sin(x+y)-y\cos(xy)}{x\cos(xy)-\sin(x+y)}$
25. $\dfrac{2x^3+y-x^2y\cos(xy)}{x\{x^2\cos xy+1+2xy\}}$
26. $\dfrac{\sec^2(x-y)+\sec^2(x+y)}{\sec^2(x-y)-\sec^2(x+y)}$
29. $\dfrac{\pi}{4}(\sqrt{2}+1)$
30. $8\left\{\dfrac{4}{\pi^2+16}-\dfrac{1}{\log 2}\right\}$

HINTS TO SELECTED PROBLEMS

12. We have,

$xy=1\Rightarrow y=\dfrac{1}{x}\Rightarrow\dfrac{dy}{dx}=-\dfrac{1}{x^2}$ Therefore, $\dfrac{dy}{dx}+y^2=-\dfrac{1}{x^2}+\dfrac{1}{x^2}=0$

13. We have,

$xy^2=1\Rightarrow x=\dfrac{1}{y^2}\Rightarrow\dfrac{dx}{dy}=-\dfrac{2}{y^3}\Rightarrow\dfrac{dy}{dx}=-\dfrac{y^3}{2}\Rightarrow 2\dfrac{dy}{dx}+y^3=0$

14. Put $x=\sin A,\ y=\sin B$ and proceed as in Ex. 8.

15. Put $x=\sin A$ and $y=\sin B$

28. We have,

$$\cos y=x\cos(a+y)$$
$$\Rightarrow x=\frac{\cos y}{\cos(a+y)}$$
$$\Rightarrow \frac{dx}{dy}=\frac{-\cos(a+y)\sin y-\cos y\times-\sin(a+y)}{\{\cos(a+y)\}^2}$$
$$\Rightarrow \frac{dx}{dy}=\frac{\sin(a+y)\cos y-\cos(a+y)\sin y}{\cos^2(a+y)}=\frac{\sin(a+y-y)}{\cos^2(a+y)}=\frac{\sin a}{\cos^2(a+y)}$$

$$\Rightarrow \quad \frac{dy}{dx} = \frac{\cos^2(a+y)}{\sin a}$$

10.8 LOGARITHMIC DIFFERENTIATION

We have learnt about the derivatives of the functions of the form $[f(x)]^n, n^{f(x)}$ and n^n, where $f(x)$ is a function of x and n is a constant. In this section, we will be mainly discussing derivatives of the functions of the form $[f(x)]^{g(x)}$ where $f(x)$ and $g(x)$ are functions of x. To find the derivative of this type of functions we proceed as follows:

Let $y = [f(x)]^{g(x)}$. Taking logarithm of both the sides, we get

$$\log y = g(x) \cdot \log \{f(x)\}$$

Differentiating with respect to x, we get

$$\frac{1}{y}\frac{dy}{dx} = g(x) \times \frac{1}{f(x)}\frac{d}{dx}\left(f(x)\right) + \log\{f(x)\} \cdot \frac{d}{dx}\left(g(x)\right)$$

$$\therefore \quad \frac{dy}{dx} = y\left\{\frac{g(x)}{f(x)} \cdot \frac{d}{dx}\left(f(x)\right) + \log\{f(x)\} \cdot \frac{d}{dx}\left(g(x)\right)\right\}$$

Alternatively, we may write

$$y = [f(x)]^{g(x)} = e^{g(x)\log\{f(x)\}}$$

Differentiating with respect to x, we get

$$\frac{dy}{dx} = e^{g(x)\log\{f(x)\}}\left\{g(x) \cdot \frac{1}{f(x)}\frac{d}{dx}\left(f(x)\right) + \log\{f(x)\} \cdot \frac{d}{dx}\left(g(x)\right)\right\}$$

$$\Rightarrow \quad \frac{dy}{dx} = [f(x)]^{g(x)}\left\{\frac{g(x)}{f(x)} \cdot \frac{d}{dx}\left(f(x)\right) + \log\{f(x)\} \cdot \frac{d}{dx}\left(g(x)\right)\right\}$$

ILLUSTRATIVE EXAMPLES

BASED ON BASIC CONCEPTS (BASIC)

EXAMPLE 1 *Differentiate the following functions with respect to x:*

(i) x^x (ii) $x^{\sin x}$ [NCERT] (iii) $(\sin x)^{\log x}$

SOLUTION (i) Let $y = x^x$. Then, $y = e^{x \cdot \log x}$ $\quad [\because a^b = e^{\log a^b} = e^{b \log a}]$

On differentiating both sides with respect to x, we get

$$\frac{dy}{dx} = e^{x\log x}\frac{d}{dx}(x\log x) = x^x\left\{\log x \times \frac{d}{dx}(x) + x \times \frac{d}{dx}(\log x)\right\} \quad [\because e^{x\log x} = x^x]$$

$$\Rightarrow \quad \frac{dy}{dx} = x^x\left(\log x + x \times \frac{1}{x}\right) = x^x\,(1+\log x)$$

(ii) Let $y = x^{\sin x}$. Then, $y = e^{\sin x \log x}$ $\quad [\because a^b = e^{\log a^b} = e^{b \log a}]$

On differentiating both sides with respect to x, we get

$$\frac{dy}{dx} = e^{\sin x \cdot \log x}\frac{d}{dx}(\sin x \cdot \log x)$$

$$\Rightarrow \quad \frac{dy}{dx} = x^{\sin x}\left\{\log x \frac{d}{dx}(\sin x) + \sin x \frac{d}{dx}(\log x)\right\} \qquad [\because e^{\sin x \log x} = x^{\sin x}]$$

$$\Rightarrow \quad \frac{dy}{dx} = x^{\sin x}\left\{\cos x \,.\, \log x + \frac{\sin x}{x}\right\}$$

(iii) Let $y = (\sin x)^{\log x}$. Then, $y = e^{\log x \,.\, \log \sin x}$ $[\because a^b = e^{b \log a}]$

On differentiating both sides with respect to x, we get

$$\frac{dy}{dx} = e^{\log x \,.\, \log \sin x} \frac{d}{dx}\{\log x \,.\, \log \sin x\}$$

$$\Rightarrow \quad \frac{dy}{dx} = (\sin x)^{\log x}\left\{\log \sin x \frac{d}{dx}(\log x) + \log x \frac{d}{dx}(\log \sin x)\right\}$$

$$\Rightarrow \quad \frac{dy}{dx} = (\sin x)^{\log x}\left\{\frac{\log \sin x}{x} + \log x \times \frac{1}{\sin x} \times \cos x\right\} = (\sin x)^{\log x}\left\{\frac{\log \sin x}{x} + \cot x \,.\, \log x\right\}$$

EXAMPLE 2 *Differentiate the following functions with respect to x:*

(i) $(\cos x)^x$ (ii) $x^{\sqrt{x}}$ (iii) $(\log x)^{\sin x}$ (iv) $(\sin x)^{\cos x}$

SOLUTION Let $y = (\cos x)^x$. Then, $y = e^{x \log \cos x}$

On differentiating both sides with respect to x, we get

$$\frac{dy}{dx} = e^{x \log \cos x} \frac{d}{dx}(x \log \cos x)$$

$$\Rightarrow \frac{dy}{dx} = (\cos x)^x \left\{\log \cos x \frac{d}{dx}(x) + x \frac{d}{dx}(\log \cos x)\right\} = (\cos x)^x \left\{\log \cos x + x \frac{1}{\cos x}(-\sin x)\right\}$$

$$\Rightarrow \frac{dy}{dx} = (\cos x)^x \,(\log \cos x - x \tan x)$$

(ii) Let $y = x^{\sqrt{x}}$. Then, $y = e^{\sqrt{x} \log x}$

On differentiating both sides with respect to x, we get

$$\frac{dy}{dx} = e^{\sqrt{x} \log x} \frac{d}{dx}(\sqrt{x} \log x)$$

$$\Rightarrow \quad \frac{dy}{dx} = x^{\sqrt{x}}\left\{\left(\log x\right)\frac{d}{dx}(\sqrt{x}) + \sqrt{x}\frac{d}{dx}(\log x)\right\}$$

$$\Rightarrow \quad \frac{dy}{dx} = x^{\sqrt{x}}\left\{\left(\log x\right)\frac{1}{2\sqrt{x}} + \sqrt{x} \times \frac{1}{x}\right\} = x^{\sqrt{x}}\left(\frac{\log x}{2\sqrt{x}} + \frac{1}{\sqrt{x}}\right)$$

(iii) Let $y = (\log x)^{\sin x}$. Then, $y = e^{\sin x \log(\log x)}$

On differentiating both sides with respect to x, we get

$$\frac{dy}{dx} = e^{\sin x \,.\, \log(\log x)} \frac{d}{dx}\{\sin x \,.\, \log(\log x)\}$$

$$\Rightarrow \quad \frac{dy}{dx} = (\log x)^{\sin x}\left\{\log(\log x)\frac{d}{dx}(\sin x) + \sin x \frac{d}{dx}(\log(\log x))\right\}$$

$$\Rightarrow \quad \frac{dy}{dx} = (\log x)^{\sin x}\left\{\log(\log x) \,.\, \cos x + \sin x \times \frac{1}{\log x} \times \frac{1}{x}\right\}$$

$$\Rightarrow \quad \frac{dy}{dx} = (\log x)^{\sin x} \left\{ \log(\log x) \cdot \cos x + \frac{\sin x}{x \log x} \right\}$$

(iv) Let $y = (\sin x)^{\cos x}$. Then, $y = e^{\cos x \cdot \log \sin x}$.

On differentiating both sides with respect to x, we get

$$\frac{dy}{dx} = e^{\cos x \cdot \log \sin x} \frac{d}{dx}(\cos x \cdot \log \sin x)$$

$$\Rightarrow \quad \frac{dy}{dx} = (\sin x)^{\cos x} \left\{ \log \sin x \frac{d}{dx}(\cos x) + \cos x \frac{d}{dx}(\log \sin x) \right\}$$

$$\Rightarrow \quad \frac{dy}{dx} = (\sin x)^{\cos x} \left\{ -\sin x \log \sin x + \cos x \times \frac{1}{\sin x} \times \cos x \right\}$$

$$\Rightarrow \quad \frac{dy}{dx} = (\sin x)^{\cos x} \left\{ -\sin x \log \sin x + \frac{\cos^2 x}{\sin x} \right\}$$

EXAMPLE 3 *Differentiate the following functions with respect to x :*

(i) $x^{\cos^{-1} x}$ (ii) $(\sin x)^{\cos^{-1} x}$

SOLUTION Let $y = x^{\cos^{-1} x}$. Then, $y = e^{\cos^{-1} x \cdot \log x}$

On differentiating both sides with respect to x, we get

$$\frac{dy}{dx} = e^{\cos^{-1} x \cdot \log x} \frac{d}{dx}(\cos^{-1} x \cdot \log x)$$

$$\Rightarrow \frac{dy}{dx} = x^{\cos^{-1} x} \left\{ \log x \frac{d}{dx}(\cos^{-1} x) + \cos^{-1} x \frac{d}{dx}(\log x) \right\} = x^{\cos^{-1} x} \left\{ \frac{-\log x}{\sqrt{1-x^2}} + \frac{\cos^{-1} x}{x} \right\}$$

(ii) Let $y = (\sin x)^{\cos^{-1} x}$. Then, $y = e^{\cos^{-1} x \cdot \log \sin x}$

On differentiating both sides with respect to x, we get

$$\frac{dy}{dx} = e^{\cos^{-1} x \cdot \log \sin x} \frac{d}{dx}(\cos^{-1} x \cdot \log \sin x)$$

$$\Rightarrow \quad \frac{dy}{dx} = (\sin x)^{\cos^{-1} x} \left\{ \cos^{-1} x \frac{d}{dx}(\log \sin x) + \log \sin x \frac{d}{dx}(\cos^{-1} x) \right\}$$

$$\Rightarrow \quad \frac{dy}{dx} = (\sin x)^{\cos^{-1} x} \left\{ \cos^{-1} x \times \frac{1}{\sin x} \times \cos x + (\log \sin x) \times \frac{-1}{\sqrt{1-x^2}} \right\}$$

$$\Rightarrow \quad \frac{dy}{dx} = (\sin x)^{\cos^{-1} x} \left\{ \cos^{-1} x \cot x - \frac{\log \sin x}{\sqrt{1-x^2}} \right\}.$$

BASED ON LOWER ORDER THINKING SKILLS (LOTS)

EXAMPLE 4 *Differentiate the following functions with respect to x:* (i) x^{x^x} (ii) $(x^x)^x$

SOLUTION (i) Let $y = x^{x^x}$. Then, $y = e^{x^x \cdot \log x}$

On differentiating both sides with respect to x, we get

$$\frac{dy}{dx} = e^{x^x \cdot \log x} \frac{d}{dx}(x^x \log x) = x^{x^x} \frac{d}{dx}(e^{x \log x} \log x)$$

$$\Rightarrow \quad \frac{dy}{dx} = x^{x^x} \left\{ \log x \frac{d}{dx}(e^{x \log x}) + e^{x \log x} \times \frac{d}{dx}(\log x) \right\}$$

$$\Rightarrow \quad \frac{dy}{dx} = x^{x^x} \left\{ \log x \cdot e^{x \log x} \frac{d}{dx}(x \log x) + e^{x \log x} \times \frac{1}{x} \right\}$$

$$\Rightarrow \quad \frac{dy}{dx} = x^{x^x} \left\{ (\log x)\, x^x \left(x \times \frac{1}{x} + \log x \right) + x^x \times \frac{1}{x} \right\}$$

$$\Rightarrow \quad \frac{dy}{dx} = x^{x^x} \left\{ x^x (1 + \log x) \log x + \frac{x^x}{x} \right\} = x^{x^x} x^x \left\{ (1 + \log x) \log x + \frac{1}{x} \right\}$$

(ii) Let $y = (x^x)^x$. Then, $y = x^{x \cdot x} = x^{x^2} \Rightarrow y = e^{x^2 \cdot \log x}$

On differentiating both sides with respect to x, we get

$$\frac{dy}{dx} = e^{x^2 \cdot \log x} \frac{d}{dx}(x^2 \log x) = e^{x^2 \cdot \log x} \left\{ \log x \frac{d}{dx}(x^2) + x^2 \right.$$

$$\Rightarrow \quad \frac{dy}{dx} = x^{x^2} \left\{ (\log x)\, 2x + x^2 \times \frac{1}{x} \right\}$$

$$\Rightarrow \quad \frac{dy}{dx} = x^{x^2}(2x \log x + x) = x\, x^{x^2}(2 \log x + 1).$$

EXAMPLE 5 *If* $y = (\sin x)^{\tan x} + (\cos x)^{\sec x}$, *find* $\frac{dy}{dx}$. [CBSE 2007]

SOLUTION We have, $y = (\sin x)^{\tan x} + (\cos x)^{\sec x} = e^{\tan x \cdot \log \sin x} \ldots$

On differentiating both sides with respect to x, we get

$$\frac{dy}{dx} = \frac{d}{dx}(e^{\tan x \log \sin x}) + \frac{d}{dx}(e^{\sec x \log \cos x})$$

$$\Rightarrow \quad \frac{dy}{dx} = e^{\tan x \log \sin x} \frac{d}{dx}(\tan x \log \sin x) + e^{\sec x \log \cos x} \ldots$$

$$\Rightarrow \quad \frac{dy}{dx} = (\sin x)^{\tan x} \left\{ \frac{d}{dx}(\tan x) \times \log \sin x + \tan x \times \frac{d}{dx}(\log \ldots \right.$$

$$+ (\cos x)^{\sec x} \left\{ \frac{d}{dx}(\sec x) \times \log \ldots \right.$$

$$\Rightarrow \quad \frac{dy}{dx} = (\sin x)^{\tan x} \left\{ \sec^2 x \log \sin x + \tan x \times \frac{1}{\sin x} \times \cos x \right\}$$

$$+ (\cos x)^{\sec x} \left\{ \sec x \tan x \log \cos \ldots \right.$$

$$\Rightarrow \quad \frac{dy}{dx} = (\sin x)^{\tan x} \left\{ \sec^2 x \log \sin x + 1 \right\} + (\cos x)^{\sec x} \{\sec x \tan \ldots$$

EXAMPLE 6 *Differentiate:* $(\log x)^x + x^{\log x}$ *with respect to* x. [CBSE 2020]

SOLUTION Let $y = (\log x)^x + x^{\log x}$. Then,

$$y = e^{\log (\log x)^x} + e^{\log (x^{\log x})} = e^{x \log (\log x)} + e^{\log x \cdot \log x}$$

On differentiating both sides with respect to x, we get

$$\frac{dy}{dx} = e^{x \log(\log x)} \times \frac{d}{dx}\{x \log(\log x)\} + e^{(\log x)^2} \times \frac{d}{dx}(\log x)^2$$

$$\Rightarrow \frac{dy}{dx} = (\log x)^x \left\{\log(\log x) \times \frac{d}{dx}(x) + x \times \frac{d}{dx}\{\log(\log x)\}\right\} + x^{\log x}\left\{2(\log x)\frac{d}{dx}(\log x)\right\}$$

$$\Rightarrow \frac{dy}{dx} = (\log x)^x \left\{\log(\log x) + x \times \frac{1}{\log x} \times \frac{1}{x}\right\} + x^{\log x}\left\{2(\log x)\frac{1}{x}\right\}$$

$$\Rightarrow \frac{dy}{dx} = (\log x)^x \left\{\log(\log x) + \frac{1}{\log x}\right\} + x^{\log x}\left\{\frac{2\log x}{x}\right\}$$

EXAMPLE 7 *Differentiate the following functions with respect to x :*

(i) $x^{\cot x} + \frac{2x^2 - 3}{x^2 + x + 2}$ [CBSE 2012] (ii) $\cos(x^x)$ (iii) $\log(x^x + \mathrm{cosec}^2 x)$ (iv) $x^x e^{2(x+3)}$

SOLUTION (i) Let $y = x^{\cot x} + \frac{2x^2 - 3}{x^2 + x + 2}$. Then,

$$y = e^{\cot x \log x} + \frac{2x^2 - 3}{x^2 + x + 2} \qquad \left[\because x^{\cot x} = e^{\log x^{\cot x}} = e^{\cot x \log x}\right]$$

On differentiating both sides with respect to x, we get

$$\Rightarrow \frac{dy}{dx} = \frac{d}{dx}(e^{\cot x \log x}) + \frac{d}{dx}\left(\frac{2x^2 - 3}{x^2 + x + 2}\right)$$

$$\Rightarrow \frac{dy}{dx} = e^{\cot x \log x}\frac{d}{dx}(\cot x \,.\, \log x) + \frac{(x^2 + x + 2)\frac{d}{dx}(2x^2 - 3) - (2x^2 - 3)\frac{d}{dx}(x^2 + x + 2)}{(x^2 + x + 2)^2}$$

$$\frac{dy}{dx} = x^{\cot x}\left\{(\log x)\frac{d}{dx}(\cot x) + (\cot x)\frac{d}{dx}(\log x)\right\} + \frac{(x^2 + x + 2)(4x) - (2x^2 - 3)(2x + 1)}{(x^2 + x + 2)^2}$$

$$\frac{dy}{dx} = x^{\cot x}\left\{-\mathrm{cosec}^2 x \,.\, \log x + \frac{\cot x}{x}\right\} + \frac{2x^2 + 14x + 3}{(x^2 + x + 2)^2}$$

(ii) Let $y = \cos(x^x)$. Then, $y = \cos(e^{x \log x})$ $\qquad [\because x^x = e^{x \log x}]$

On differentiating both sides with respect to x, we get

$$\frac{dy}{dx} = \frac{d}{dx}\left\{\cos(e^{x \log x})\right\} = -\sin(e^{x \log x})\frac{d}{dx}(e^{x \log x}) = -\sin(x^x)\, e^{x \log x}\frac{d}{dx}(x \log x)$$

$$\Rightarrow \frac{dy}{dx} = -\sin(x^x) \times x^x \left\{\frac{d}{dx}(x) \,.\, \log x + x\frac{d}{dx}(\log x)\right\}$$

$$\Rightarrow \frac{dy}{dx} = -x^x \sin(x^x)\left\{\log x + x \,.\, \frac{1}{x}\right\} = -x^x \sin(x^x)(\log x + 1)$$

(iii) Let $y = \log(x^x + \mathrm{cosec}^2 x)$. Then,

$$\frac{dy}{dx} = \frac{1}{x^x + \text{cosec}^2 x} \times \frac{d}{dx}(x^x + \text{cosec}^2 x) = \frac{1}{x^x + \text{cosec}^2 x}\left\{\frac{d}{dx}(x^x) + \frac{d}{dx}(\text{cosec}^2 x)\right\}$$

$$\Rightarrow \quad \frac{dy}{dx} = \frac{1}{x^x + \text{cosec}^2 x}\left\{\frac{d}{dx}(e^{x \log x}) + \frac{d}{dx}(\text{cosec}^2 x)\right\}$$

$$\Rightarrow \quad \frac{dy}{dx} = \frac{1}{x^x + \text{cosec}^2 x}\left\{e^{x \log x}\frac{d}{dx}(x \log x) + 2 \text{ cosec } x \frac{d}{dx}(\text{cosec } x)\right\}$$

$$\Rightarrow \quad \frac{dy}{dx} = \frac{1}{x^x + \text{cosec}^2 x}\left\{x^x(1 + \log x) - 2 \text{ cosec}^2 x \cot x\right\}$$

(iv) Let $y = x^x e^{2(x+3)}$. Then,

$$y = e^{x \log x} . e^{2(x+3)} \Rightarrow y = e^{x \log x + 2(x+3)} \qquad \left[\because x^x = e^{\log x^x} = e^{x \log x}\right]$$

On differentiating with respect to x, we get

$$\frac{dy}{dx} = e^{x \log x + 2(x+3)} \frac{d}{dx}\{x \log x + 2(x+3)\}$$

$$\Rightarrow \quad \frac{dy}{dx} = e^{x \log x} . e^{2(x+3)}\left\{\frac{d}{dx}(x \log x) + 2\frac{d}{dx}(x+3)\right\}$$

$$\Rightarrow \quad \frac{dy}{dx} = x^x e^{2(x+3)}(1 + \log x + 2) = x^x e^{2x+3}(3 + \log x)$$

EXAMPLE 8 *If $x^y = e^{x-y}$, prove that $\frac{dy}{dx} = \frac{\log x}{(1 + \log x)^2}$.*

[CBSE 2000 C, 2010 C, 2011, 2013, 2024, NCERT EXEMPLAR]

SOLUTION We have,

$$x^y = e^{x-y}$$

$$\Rightarrow \quad e^{y \log x} = e^{x-y} \qquad \left[\because x^y = e^{\log x^y} = e^{y \log x}\right]$$

$$\Rightarrow \quad y \log x = x - y \Rightarrow y \log x + y = x \Rightarrow y(1 + \log x) = x \Rightarrow y = \frac{x}{1 + \log x}$$

On differentiating both sides with respect to x, we get

$$\frac{dy}{dx} = \frac{(1 + \log x) \times 1 - x\left(0 + \frac{1}{x}\right)}{(1 + \log x)^2} = \frac{\log x}{(1 + \log x)^2}$$

EXAMPLE 9 *If $x^y + y^x = 2$, find $\frac{dy}{dx}$.* **[NCERT]**

SOLUTION We have,

$$x^y + y^x = 2 \Rightarrow e^{y \log x} + e^{x \log y} = 2$$

On differentiating both sides with respect to x, we get

$$\frac{d}{dx}\left(e^{y \log x}\right) + \frac{d}{dx}\left(e^{x \log y}\right) = \frac{d}{dx}(2)$$

$$\Rightarrow \quad e^{y \log x}\frac{d}{dx}(y \log x) + e^{x \log y}\frac{d}{dx}(x \log y) = 0$$

$$\Rightarrow \quad x^y \left\{\frac{dy}{dx} \times \log x + y \times \frac{1}{x}\right\} + y^x \left\{1 \times \log y + x \times \frac{1}{y}\frac{dy}{dx}\right\} = 0$$

$$\Rightarrow \quad \left\{x^y \log x + y^x \frac{x}{y}\right\} \frac{dy}{dx} + \left\{x^y \times \frac{y}{x} + y^x \times \log y\right\} = 0$$

$$\Rightarrow \quad \left\{x^y \log x + x\, y^{x-1}\right\} \frac{dy}{dx} + \left\{y\, x^{y-1} + y^x \log y\right\} = 0$$

$$\Rightarrow \quad \frac{dy}{dx} = -\left\{\frac{y\, x^{y-1} + y^x \log y}{x^y \log x + x\, y^{x-1}}\right\}$$

EXAMPLE 10 *If* $x^y = y^x$, *find* $\frac{dy}{dx}$. **[NCERT, CBSE 2024]**

SOLUTION We have, $x^y = y^x$. Taking log on both sides, we get

$$y \log x = x \log y$$

Differentiating both sides with respect to x, we get

$$y \frac{d}{dx}(\log x) + \log x \frac{d}{dx}(y) = x \frac{d}{dx}(\log y) + \log y \frac{d}{dx}(x)$$

$$\Rightarrow \quad y \times \frac{1}{x} + \log x \times \frac{dy}{dx} = x \times \frac{1}{y}\frac{dy}{dx} + (\log y)\, 1$$

$$\Rightarrow \quad \log x \frac{dy}{dx} - \frac{x}{y}\frac{dy}{dx} = \log y - \frac{y}{x}$$

$$\Rightarrow \quad \frac{dy}{dx}\left(\log x - \frac{x}{y}\right) = \log y - \frac{y}{x}$$

$$\Rightarrow \quad \frac{dy}{dx}\left(\frac{y \log x - x}{y}\right) = \frac{x \log y - y}{x} \Rightarrow \frac{dy}{dx} = \frac{y}{x}\left(\frac{x \log y - y}{y \log x - x}\right).$$

EXAMPLE 11 *If* $(\cos x)^y = (\sin y)^x$, *find* $\frac{dy}{dx}$. **[NCERT, CBSE 2009]**

SOLUTION We have, $(\cos x)^y = (\sin y)^x$. Taking log on both sides, we get

$$y \log \cos x = x \log \sin y$$

Differentiating both sides with respect to x, we get

$$y \frac{d}{dx}(\log \cos x) + \frac{dy}{dx}(\log \cos x) = x \frac{d}{dx}(\log \sin y) + (\log \sin y)\, 1$$

$$\Rightarrow \quad -\frac{y}{\cos x} \sin x + \frac{dy}{dx} \log \cos x = \frac{x}{\sin y} \cos y \frac{dy}{dx} + \log \sin y$$

$$\Rightarrow \quad \frac{dy}{dx}(\log \cos x - x \cot y) = \log \sin y + y \tan x \Rightarrow \frac{dy}{dx} = \frac{\log \sin y + y \tan x}{\log \cos x - x \cot y}.$$

EXAMPLE 12 *If* $y = a^x + e^x + x^x + x^a$, *find* $\frac{dy}{dx}$ at $x = a$. **[NCERT]**

SOLUTION We have,

$$y = a^x + e^x + x^x + x^a$$

$$\Rightarrow \quad y = a^x + e^x + e^{x \log x} + x^a$$

$$\Rightarrow \quad \frac{dy}{dx} = \frac{d}{dx}(a^x) + \frac{d}{dx}(e^x) + \frac{d}{dx}(e^{x\log x}) + \frac{d}{dx}(x^a)$$

$$\Rightarrow \quad \frac{dy}{dx} = a^x \log a + e^x + e^{x\log x}\frac{d}{dx}(x\log x) + a\,x^{a-1}$$

$$\Rightarrow \quad \frac{dy}{dx} = a^x \log a + e^x + x^x(1+\log x) + a\,x^{a-1}$$

$$\Rightarrow \quad \left(\frac{dy}{dx}\right)_{x=a} = a^a \log a + e^a + a^a(1+\log a) + a\,a^{a-1} = e^a + 2a^a(1+\log a)$$

REMARK *In order to find the derivative of a product of a number of functions or a quotient of a number of functions, we first take logarithm of both sides and then differentiate. The procedure is illustrated in the following examples.*

EXAMPLE 13 *If* $y = \dfrac{\sqrt{1-x^2}\,(2x-3)^{1/2}}{(x^2+2)^{2/3}}$, *find* $\dfrac{dy}{dx}$.

SOLUTION Taking log of both sides, we get

$$\log y = \frac{1}{2}\log(1-x^2) + \frac{1}{2}\log(2x-3) - \frac{2}{3}\log(x^2+2).$$

On differentiating both sides with respect to x, we get

$$\frac{1}{y}\frac{dy}{dx} = \frac{1}{2(1-x^2)}(-2x) + \frac{1}{2(2x-3)}\times 2 - \frac{2}{3}\times\frac{1}{x^2+2}\times 2x$$

$$\therefore \quad \frac{dy}{dx} = y\left\{-\frac{x}{1-x^2} + \frac{1}{2x-3} - \frac{4x}{3(x^2+2)}\right\} = \frac{\sqrt{1-x^2}\,(2x-3)^{1/2}}{(x^2+2)^{2/3}}\left\{-\frac{x}{1-x^2} + \frac{1}{2x-3} - \frac{4x}{3(x^2+2)}\right\}$$

EXAMPLE 14 *Find the derivative of* $\dfrac{\sqrt{x}\,(x+4)^{3/2}}{(4x-3)^{4/3}}$ *with respect to x.*

SOLUTION Let $y = \dfrac{\sqrt{x}\,(x+4)^{3/2}}{(4x-3)^{4/3}}$. Taking log of both sides, we get

$$\log y = \frac{1}{2}\log x + \frac{3}{2}\log(x+4) - \frac{4}{3}\log(4x-3)$$

On differentiating both sides with respect to x, we get

$$\frac{1}{y}\frac{dy}{dx} = \frac{1}{2x} + \frac{3}{2}\,\frac{1}{x+4}\,\frac{d}{dx}(x+4) - \frac{4}{3}\times\frac{1}{4x-3}\,\frac{d}{dx}(4x-3)$$

$$\Rightarrow \quad \frac{dy}{dx} = y\left\{\frac{1}{2x} + \frac{3}{2(x+4)} - \frac{4}{3(4x-3)}\times 4\right\} = \frac{\sqrt{x}\,(x+4)^{3/2}}{(4x-3)^{4/3}}\left\{\frac{1}{2x} + \frac{3}{2(x+4)} - \frac{16}{3(4x-3)}\right\}.$$

BASED ON HIGHER ORDER THINKING SKILLS (HOTS)

EXAMPLE 15 *If* $x^m y^n = (x+y)^{m+n}$, *prove that* $\dfrac{dy}{dx} = \dfrac{y}{x}$.

[CBSE 2000, 2014, 2017, NCERT EXAMPLAR]

SOLUTION We have, $x^m \cdot y^n = (x+y)^{m+n}$

Taking log on both sides, we get

$$m\log x + n\log y = (m+n)\log(x+y)$$

Differentiating both sides with respect to x, we get

$$m \times \frac{1}{x} + n \times \frac{1}{y}\frac{dy}{dx} = \frac{m+n}{x+y}\frac{d}{dx}(x+y)$$

$$\Rightarrow \quad \frac{m}{x} + \frac{n}{y} \times \frac{dy}{dx} = \frac{m+n}{x+y}\left(1 + \frac{dy}{dx}\right)$$

$$\Rightarrow \quad \left\{\frac{n}{y} - \frac{m+n}{x+y}\right\}\frac{dy}{dx} = \frac{m+n}{x+y} - \frac{m}{x}$$

$$\Rightarrow \quad \left\{\frac{nx+ny-my-ny}{y(x+y)}\right\}\frac{dy}{dx} = \left\{\frac{mx+nx-mx-my}{(x+y)x}\right\}$$

$$\Rightarrow \quad \frac{nx-my}{y(x+y)} \cdot \frac{dy}{dx} = \frac{nx-my}{(x+y)x} \Rightarrow \frac{dy}{dx} = \frac{y}{x}$$

EXAMPLE 16 *If* $y = \frac{ax^2}{(x-a)(x-b)(x-c)} + \frac{bx}{(x-b)(x-c)} + \frac{c}{x-c} + 1$, *prove that* $\frac{dy}{dx} = \frac{y}{x}\left\{\frac{a}{a-x} + \frac{b}{b-x} + \frac{c}{c-x}\right\}$.

SOLUTION We have,

$$y = \frac{ax^2}{(x-a)(x-b)(x-c)} + \frac{bx}{(x-b)(x-c)} + \frac{c}{x-c} + 1$$

$$\Rightarrow \quad y = \frac{ax^2}{(x-a)(x-b)(x-c)} + \frac{bx}{(x-b)(x-c)} + \left(\frac{c+x-c}{x-c}\right)$$

$$\Rightarrow \quad y = \frac{ax^2}{(x-a)(x-b)(x-c)} + \frac{bx}{(x-b)(x-c)} + \frac{x}{x-c}$$

$$\Rightarrow \quad y = \frac{ax^2}{(x-a)(x-b)(x-c)} + \frac{bx + x(x-b)}{(x-b)(x-c)}$$

$$\Rightarrow \quad y = \frac{ax^2}{(x-a)(x-b)(x-c)} + \frac{x^2}{(x-b)(x-c)}$$

$$\Rightarrow \quad y = \frac{ax^2 + x^2(x-a)}{(x-a)(x-b)(x-c)} \Rightarrow y = \frac{x^3}{(x-a)(x-b)(x-c)} \Rightarrow \log y = \log\left\{\frac{x^3}{(x-a)(x-b)(x-c)}\right\}$$

$$\Rightarrow \quad \log y = 3\log x - \left\{\log(x-a) + \log(x-b) + \log(x-c)\right\}$$

On differentiating with respect to x, we get

$$\frac{1}{y}\frac{dy}{dx} = \frac{3}{x} - \left\{\frac{1}{x-a} + \frac{1}{x-b} + \frac{1}{x-c}\right\}$$

$$\Rightarrow \quad \frac{dy}{dx} = y\left\{\left(\frac{1}{x} - \frac{1}{x-a}\right) + \left(\frac{1}{x} - \frac{1}{x-b}\right) + \left(\frac{1}{x} - \frac{1}{x-c}\right)\right\}$$

$$\Rightarrow \quad \frac{dy}{dx} = y\left\{-\frac{a}{x(x-a)} - \frac{b}{x(x-b)} - \frac{c}{x(x-c)}\right\} \Rightarrow \frac{dy}{dx} = \frac{y}{x}\left\{\frac{a}{a-x} + \frac{b}{b-x} + \frac{c}{c-x}\right\}$$

EXAMPLE 17 *Prove that the derivative of an even function is an odd function and that of an odd function is an even function.*

SOLUTION Let $f(x)$ be an even function. Then,

$$f(-x) = f(x) \Rightarrow \frac{d}{dx}\{f(-x)\} = \frac{d}{dx}\{f(x)\} \Rightarrow f'(-x) \cdot \frac{d}{dx}(-x) = f'(x)$$

$$\Rightarrow -f'(-x) = f'(x) \Rightarrow f'(-x) = -f'(x) \Rightarrow f'(x) \text{ is an odd function.}$$

Let $f(x)$ be an odd function. Then,

$$f(-x) = -f(x) \Rightarrow \frac{d}{dx}\{f(-x)\} = -\frac{d}{dx}\{f(x)\} \Rightarrow f'(-x)\frac{d}{dx}(-x) = -f'(x)$$

$$\Rightarrow -f'(-x) = -f'(x) \Rightarrow f'(-x) = f'(x) \Rightarrow f'(x) \text{ is an even function.}$$

EXAMPLE 18 *If* $y = f\left(\frac{2x-1}{x^2+1}\right)$ *and* $f'(x) = \sin x^2$, *find* $\frac{dy}{dx}$.

SOLUTION Let $z = \frac{2x-1}{x^2+1}$. Then,

$$y = f(z)$$

$$\Rightarrow \frac{dy}{dx} = \frac{d}{dx}\{f(z)\} = \frac{d}{dz}\{f(z)\} \cdot \frac{dz}{dx} = f'(z)\frac{d}{dx}\left(\frac{2x-1}{x^2+1}\right) = f'(z)\left\{\frac{2(x^2+1)-(2x-1)2x}{(x^2+1)^2}\right\}$$

$$\Rightarrow \frac{dy}{dx} = (\sin z^2)\frac{2(x^2+1)-(4x^2-2x)}{(x^2+1)^2} \qquad [\because f'(x) = \sin x^2 \therefore f'(z) = \sin z^2]$$

$$\Rightarrow \frac{dy}{dx} = 2\sin\left(\frac{2x-1}{x^2+1}\right)^2 \left\{\frac{1+x-x^2}{(x^2+1)^2}\right\}$$

EXAMPLE 19 *Given that* $\cos\frac{x}{2} \cdot \cos\frac{x}{4} \cdot \cos\frac{x}{8} \ldots = \frac{\sin x}{x}$, *prove that*

$$\frac{1}{2^2}\sec^2\frac{x}{2} + \frac{1}{2^4}\sec^2\frac{x}{4} + \ldots = \operatorname{cosec}^2 x - \frac{1}{x^2}$$

SOLUTION We have, $\cos\frac{x}{2} \cdot \cos\frac{x}{4} \cdot \cos\frac{x}{8} \ldots = \frac{\sin x}{x}$

Taking log on both sides, we get

$$\log\cos\frac{x}{2} + \log\cos\frac{x}{4} + \log\cos\frac{x}{8} \ldots = \log\sin x - \log x$$

Differentiating both sides with respect to x, we get

$$-\frac{1}{2}\frac{\sin\frac{x}{2}}{\cos\frac{x}{2}} - \frac{1}{4}\frac{\sin\frac{x}{4}}{\cos\frac{x}{4}} - \frac{1}{8}\frac{\sin\frac{x}{8}}{\cos\frac{x}{8}} \ldots = \frac{\cos x}{\sin x} - \frac{1}{x}$$

$$\Rightarrow -\frac{1}{2}\tan\frac{x}{2} - \frac{1}{4}\tan\frac{x}{4} - \frac{1}{8}\tan\frac{x}{8} \ldots = \cot x - \frac{1}{x}$$

Differentiating both sides with respect to x, we get

$$-\frac{1}{2^2}\sec^2\frac{x}{2} - \frac{1}{4^2}\sec^2\frac{x}{4} - \frac{1}{8^2}\sec^2\frac{x}{8} \ldots = -\operatorname{cosec}^2 x + \frac{1}{x^2}$$

$$\Rightarrow \quad \frac{1}{2^2}\sec^2\frac{x}{2}+\frac{1}{4^2}\sec^2\frac{x}{4}+\frac{1}{8^2}\sec^2\frac{x}{8}\ldots=\operatorname{cosec}^2 x-\frac{1}{x^2}$$

EXERCISE 10.5

BASIC

Differentiate the following functions with respect to x: (1-18)

1. $x^{1/x}$ [CBSE 2023] 2. $x^{\sin x}$ 3. $(1+\cos x)^x$ 4. $x^{\cos^{-1} x}$
5. $(\log x)^x$ 6. $(\log x)^{\cos x}$ 7. $(\sin x)^{\cos x}$ 8. $e^{x \log x}$
9. $(\sin x)^{\log x}$ 10. $10^{\log \sin x}$ 11. $(\log x)^{\log x}$ [NCERT] 12. $10^{(10^x)}$
13. $\sin(x^x)$ 14. $(\sin^{-1} x)^x$ 15. $x^{\sin^{-1} x}$ 16. $(\tan x)^{1/x}$
17. $x^{\tan^{-1} x}$ 18. (i) $(x^x)\sqrt{x}$ (ii) $x^{(\sin x-\cos x)}+\dfrac{x^2-1}{x^2+1}$

(iii) $x^{x\cos x}+\dfrac{x^2+1}{x^2-1}$ [NCERT, CBSE 2011] (iv) $(x\cos x)^x+(x\sin x)^{1/x}$ [NCERT]

(v) $\left(x+\dfrac{1}{x}\right)^x+x^{\left(1+\frac{1}{x}\right)}$ [NCERT] (vi) $e^{\sin x}+(\tan x)^x$ [CBSE 2003, 2024]

(vii) $(\cos x)^x+(\sin x)^{1/x}$ [CBSE 2010] (viii) $x^{x^2-3}+(x-3)^{x^2}$ [NCERT]

Find $\dfrac{dy}{dx}$, *(19-32) when:*

19. $y=e^x+10^x+x^x$
20. $y=x^n+n^x+x^x+n^n$
21. $y=\dfrac{(x^2-1)^3(2x-1)}{\sqrt{(x-3)(4x-1)}}$
22. $y=\dfrac{e^{ax}\sec x \log x}{\sqrt{1-2x}}$
23. $y=e^{3x}\sin 4x\cdot 2^x$
24. $y=\sin x\sin 2x\sin 3x\sin 4x$
25. $y=x^{\sin x}+(\sin x)^x$ [NCERT]
26. $y=(\sin x)^{\cos x}+(\cos x)^{\sin x}$
27. $y=(\tan x)^{\cot x}+(\cot x)^{\tan x}$
28. (i) $y=(\sin x)^x+\sin^{-1}\sqrt{x}$ [NCERT, CBSE 2009, 13, 17]
    (ii) $y=x^{\sin x}+\sin^{-1}\sqrt{x}$ [CBSE 20 20]
    (iii) $y=(\sin x)^x x^{\sin x}+a^x$ [CBSE 2024] (iv) $y=(\cos x)^x+\cos^{-1}\sqrt{x}$ [CBSE 2024]
29. (i) $y=x^{\cos x}+(\sin x)^{\tan x}$ [CBSE 2009] (ii) $y=x^x+(\sin x)^x$ [CBSE 2008]
30. $y=(\tan x)^{\log x}+\cos^2\left(\dfrac{\pi}{4}\right)$
31. $y=x^x+x^{1/x}$
32. $y=x^{\log x}+(\log x)^x$ [NCERT, CBSE 2013, 2019]

BASED ON LOTS

33. If $x^y-y^x=a^b$, find $\dfrac{dy}{dx}$. [CBSE 2019]
34. If $x^{16}y^9=(x^2+y)^{17}$, prove that $x\dfrac{dy}{dx}=2y$

35. If $y = \sin(x^x)$, prove that $\frac{dy}{dx} = \cos(x^x) \cdot x^x (1 + \log x)$

36. If $x^x + y^x = 1$, prove that $\frac{dy}{dx} = -\left\{ \frac{x^x (1 + \log x) + y^x \cdot \log y}{x \cdot y^{(x-1)}} \right\}$

37. If $x^y \cdot y^x = 1$, prove that $\frac{dy}{dx} = -\frac{y(y + x \log y)}{x(y \log x + x)}$

38. If $x^y + y^x = (x + y)^{x + y}$, find $\frac{dy}{dx}$

39. If $x^m y^n = 1$, prove that $\frac{dy}{dx} = -\frac{my}{nx}$

40. If $y^x = e^{y - x}$, prove that $\frac{dy}{dx} = \frac{(1 + \log y)^2}{\log y}$ [NCERT EXEMPLAR]

41. If $(\sin x)^y = (\cos y)^x$, prove that $\frac{dy}{dx} = \frac{\log \cos y - y \cot x}{\log \sin x + x \tan y}$

42. If $(\cos x)^y = (\tan y)^x$, prove that $\frac{dy}{dx} = \frac{\log \tan y + y \tan x}{\log \cos x - x \sec y \operatorname{cosec} y}$

43. If $e^x + e^y = e^{x + y}$, prove that $\frac{dy}{dx} + e^{y - x} = 0$ [CBSE 2014]

44. If $e^y = y^x$, prove that $\frac{dy}{dx} = \frac{(\log y)^2}{\log y - 1}$

45. If $e^{x + y} - x = 0$, prove that $\frac{dy}{dx} = \frac{1 - x}{x}$

46. If $y = x \sin(a + y)$, prove that $\frac{dy}{dx} = \frac{\sin^2(a + y)}{\sin(a + y) - y \cos(a + y)}$

47. If $x \sin(a + y) + \sin a \cos(a + y) = 0$, prove that $\frac{dy}{dx} = \frac{\sin^2(a + y)}{\sin a}$ [CBSE 2013]

48. If $(\sin x)^y = x + y$, prove that $\frac{dy}{dx} = \frac{1 - (x + y) y \cot x}{(x + y) \log \sin x - 1}$

49. If $xy \log(x + y) = 1$, prove that $\frac{dy}{dx} = -\frac{y(x^2 y + x + y)}{x(xy^2 + x + y)}$

50. If $y = x \sin y$, prove that $\frac{dy}{dx} = \frac{y}{x(1 - x \cos y)}$

51. Find the derivative of the function $f(x)$ given by $f(x) = (1 + x)(1 + x^2)(1 + x^4)(1 + x^8)$ and hence find $f'(1)$

52. If $y = \log \frac{x^2 + x + 1}{x^2 - x + 1} + \frac{2}{\sqrt{3}} \tan^{-1}\left(\frac{\sqrt{3}\, x}{1 - x^2}\right)$, find $\frac{dy}{dx}$.

53. If $y = (\sin x - \cos x)^{\sin x - \cos x}$, $\frac{\pi}{4} < x < \frac{3\pi}{4}$, find $\frac{dy}{dx}$. [CBSE 2010]

54. If $xy = e^{x - y}$, find $\frac{dy}{dx}$. [NCERT, CBSE 2023]

55. If $y^x + x^y + x^x = a^b$, find $\frac{dy}{dx}$. [NCERT]

56. If $(\cos x)^y = (\cos y)^x$ find $\frac{dy}{dx}$. [CBSE 2012, 2024]

57. If $\cos y = x \cos (a+y)$, where $\cos a \neq \pm 1$, prove that $\frac{dy}{dx} = \frac{\cos^2(a+y)}{\sin a}$. [CBSE 2014]

BASED ON HOTS

58. If $(x-y)\, e^{\frac{x}{x-y}} = a$, prove that $y\frac{dy}{dx} + x = 2y$. [CBSE 2014]

59. If $x = e^{x/y}$, prove that $\frac{dy}{dx} = \frac{\log x - 1}{(\log x)^2}$ [CBSE 2024, NCERT EXEMPLAR]

60. If $y = x^{\tan x} + \sqrt{\frac{x^2+1}{2}}$, find $\frac{dy}{dx}$ [NCERT EXEMPLAR]

61. If $y = 1 + \frac{\alpha}{\left(\frac{1}{x}-\alpha\right)} + \frac{\beta/x}{\left(\frac{1}{x}-\alpha\right)\left(\frac{1}{x}-\beta\right)} + \frac{\gamma/x^2}{\left(\frac{1}{x}-\alpha\right)\left(\frac{1}{x}-\beta\right)\left(\frac{1}{x}-\gamma\right)}$, find $\frac{dy}{dx}$.

ANSWERS

1. $x^{1/x}\left(\frac{1-\log x}{x^2}\right)$

2. $x^{\sin x}\left\{\frac{\sin x}{x} + (\cos x)\log x\right\}$

3. $(1+\cos x)^x\left\{\log(1+\cos x) - \frac{x\sin x}{1+\cos x}\right\}$

4. $x^{\cos^{-1} x}\left\{\frac{\cos^{-1} x}{x} - \frac{\log x}{\sqrt{1-x^2}}\right\}$

5. $(\log x)^x\left\{\log(\log x) + \frac{1}{\log x}\right\}$

6. $(\log x)^{\cos x}\left\{-\sin x \cdot \log(\log x) + \frac{\cos x}{x\log x}\right\}$

7. $(\sin x)^{\cos x}\{-\sin x \log \sin x + \cos x \cot x\}$

8. $x^x(1+\log x)$

9. $(\sin x)^{\log x}\left\{\frac{1}{x}\log \sin x + \log x \cdot \cot x\right\}$

10. $10^{\log \sin x} \cdot \log 10 \cdot \cot x$

11. $(\log x)^{\log x}\left\{\frac{1+\log(\log x)}{x}\right\}$

12. $10^{10^x}10^x(\log_e 10)^2$

13. $x^x(1+\log x)\cos(x^x)$

14. $(\sin^{-1} x)^x\left\{\log \sin^{-1} x + \frac{x}{\sin^{-1} x}\cdot\frac{1}{\sqrt{1-x^2}}\right\}$

15. $x^{\sin^{-1} x}\left\{\frac{\sin^{-1} x}{x} + \frac{\log x}{\sqrt{1-x^2}}\right\}$

16. $(\tan x)^{1/x}\left\{-\frac{1}{x^2}\log \tan x + \frac{1}{x}\frac{\sec^2 x}{\tan x}\right\}$

17. $x^{\tan^{-1} x}\left\{\frac{\tan^{-1} x}{x} + \frac{\log x}{1+x^2}\right\}$

18. (i) $x^{x+1/2}\left\{\left(\frac{2x+1}{2x}\right) + \log x\right\}$

(ii) $x^{(\sin x - \cos x)}\left\{\dfrac{\sin x - \cos x}{x} + (\cos x + \sin x)\log x\right\} + \dfrac{4x}{(x^2+1)^2}$

(iii) $x^{x\cos x}\{(1+\log x)\cos x - x\log x\sin x\} - \dfrac{4x}{(x^2-1)^2}$

(iv) $(x\cos x)^x\{1 - x\tan x + \log(x\cos x)\} + (x\sin x)^{1x}\dfrac{\{1 + x\cot x - \log(x\sin x)\}}{x^2}$

(v) $\left(x+\dfrac{1}{x}\right)^x\left\{\dfrac{x^2-1}{x^2+1} + \log\left(x+\dfrac{1}{x}\right)\right\} + x^{1+\frac{1}{x}}\left\{\dfrac{x+1}{x^2} - \dfrac{\log x}{x^2}\right\}$

(vi) $e^{\sin x}\cos x + (\tan x)^x\{\log\tan x + x\sec x\operatorname{cosec} x\}$

(vii) $(\cos x)^x(\log\cos x - x\tan x) + (\sin x)^{1/x}\left(-\dfrac{1}{x^2}\log\sin x + \dfrac{\cot x}{x}\right)$

(viii) $x^{x^2-3}\left\{\dfrac{x^2-3}{x} + 2x\log x\right\} + (x-3)^{x^2}\left\{\dfrac{x^2}{x-3} + 2x\log(x-3)\right\}$

19. $e^x + 10^x\log 10 + x^x\log(ex)$

20. $nx^{n-1} + n^x\log n + x^x\log(ex)$

21. $\dfrac{(x^2-1)^3(2x-1)}{\sqrt{(x-3)(4x-1)}}\left\{\dfrac{6x}{x^2-1} + \dfrac{2}{2x-1} - \dfrac{1}{2(x-3)} - \dfrac{2}{4x-1}\right\}$

22. $\dfrac{e^{ax}\sec x\log x}{\sqrt{1-2x}}\left\{a + \tan x + \dfrac{1}{x\log x} + \dfrac{1}{1-2x}\right\}$

23. $e^{3x}\sin 4x\,2^x(3 + 4\cot 4x + \log 2)$

24. $\sin x\sin 2x\sin 3x\sin 4x(\cot x + 2\cot 2x + 3\cot 3x + 4\cot 4x)$

25. $x^{\sin x}\left\{\cos x\log x + \dfrac{\sin x}{x}\right\} + (\sin x)^x\{\log\sin x + x\cot x\}$

26. $(\sin x)^{\cos x}\{-\sin x\log\sin x + \cos x\cot x\} + (\cos x)^{\sin x}\{\cos x\log\cos x - \sin x\tan x\}$

27. $(\tan x)^{\cot x}\operatorname{cosec}^2 x(1 - \log\tan x) + (\cot x)^{\tan x}\sec^2 x\{\log\cot x - 1\}$

28. (i) $(\sin x)^x(x\cot x + \log\sin x) + \dfrac{1}{2\sqrt{x-x^2}}$ (ii) $x^{\sin x}\left(\dfrac{\sin x}{x} + \cos x.\log x\right) + \dfrac{1}{2\sqrt{x-x^2}}$

(iii) $(\sin x)^x x^{\sin x}\left\{x\cot x + \log\sin x + \cos x\log x + \dfrac{\sin x}{x}\right\} + a^x\log_e a$

(iv) $(\cos x)^x\{\log\cos x - x\tan x\} - \dfrac{1}{2\sqrt{x-x^2}}$

29. (i) $x^{\cos x}\left\{\dfrac{\cos x}{x} - \sin x\log x\right\} + (\sin x)^{\tan x}\left\{1 + \sec^2 x\log\sin x\right\}$

(ii) $x^x(1+\log x) + (\sin x)^x(x\cot x + \log\sin x)$

30. $(\tan x)^{\log x}\left\{\log x \frac{\sec^2 x}{\tan x}+\frac{\log \tan x}{x}\right\}$

31. $x^x(1+\log x)+x^{1/x}\left\{\frac{1-\log x}{x^2}\right\}$

32. $x^{\log x}\left\{\frac{2\log x}{x}\right\}+(\log x)^x\left\{\log(\log x)+\frac{1}{\log x}\right\}$

33. $\frac{y^x \log y - yx^{y-1}}{x^y \log x - xy^{x-1}}$

38. $\frac{(x+y)^{(x+y)}\{1+\log(x+y)\}-yx^{y-1}-y^x\log y}{x^y\log x+xy^{x-1}-(x+y)^{x+y}\{1+\log(x+y)\}}$

51. $1+2x+3x^2+\ldots+15x^{14}, f'(1)=120$

52. $\frac{4}{x^4+x^2+1}$

53. $(\sin x-\cos x)^{\sin x-\cos x}\{(\sin x+\cos x)\log(\sin x-\cos x)+(\cos x+\sin x)\}$

54. $\frac{y(x-1)}{x(y+1)}$

55. $-\frac{y^x\log y+yx^{y-1}+x^x(1+\log x)}{xy^{x-1}+x^y\log x}$

56. $\frac{\log\cos y+y\tan x}{\log\cos x+x\tan y}$

60. $x^{\tan x}\left\{\sec^2 x\log x+\frac{\tan x}{x}\right\}+\frac{x}{\sqrt{2x^2+2}}$

61. $\frac{y}{x}\left\{\frac{\alpha}{\frac{1}{x}-\alpha}+\frac{\beta}{\frac{1}{x}-\beta}+\frac{\gamma}{\frac{1}{x}-\gamma}\right\}$

HINTS TO SELECTED PROBLEMS

11. Let $y=(\log x)^{\log x}$. Then, $y=e^{\log\left\{(\log x)^{\log x}\right\}} \Rightarrow y=e^{(\log x)\log(\log x)}$

$$\Rightarrow \frac{dy}{dx}=e^{(\log x)\log(\log x)}\frac{d}{dx}\left\{(\log x)\ \log(\log x)\right\}$$

$$=(\log x)^{\log x}\left\{\frac{d}{dx}(\log x)\cdot\log(\log x)+\log x\frac{d}{dx}\log(\log x)\right\}$$

$$=(\log x)^{\log x}\left\{\frac{\log(\log x)}{x}+\log x\times\frac{1}{\log x}\times\frac{1}{x}\right\}$$

$$=(\log x)^{\log x}\left\{\frac{\log(\log x)}{x}+\frac{1}{x}\right\}=(\log x)^{\log x}\left\{\frac{1+\log(\log x)}{x}\right\}$$

18. (iii) Let $y=x^{x\cos x}+\frac{x^2+1}{x^2-1}$. Then, $y=e^{x\cos x\log x}+\frac{x^2+1}{x^2-1}$

$$\therefore \frac{dy}{dx}=\frac{d}{dx}\left\{e^{x\cos x\log x}\right\}+\frac{d}{dx}\left(\frac{x^2+1}{x^2-1}\right)=e^{x\cos x\log x}\frac{d}{dx}(x\cos x\log x)+\frac{d}{dx}\left(\frac{x^2+1}{x^2-1}\right)$$

$$=x^{x\cos x}\{\cos x\log x-x\sin x\log x+\cos x\}+\frac{(x^2-1)\,2x-(x^2+1)\,2x}{(x^2-1)^2}$$

$$=x^{x\cos x}\{\cos x\log x-x\sin\log x+\cos x\}-\frac{4x}{(x^2-1)^2}$$

18. (iv) Let $y=(x\cos x)^x+(x\sin x)^{1/x}$. Then,

$$y = e^{\log(x\cos x)^x} + e^{\log(x\sin x)^{1/x}}$$

$$\Rightarrow \quad y = e^{x\log(x\cos x)} + e^{1/x\log(x\sin x)}$$

$$\Rightarrow \quad \frac{dy}{dx} = \frac{d}{dx}\left\{e^{x\log(x\cos x)}\right\} + \frac{d}{dx}\left\{e^{1/x\ \log(x\sin x)}\right\}$$

$$\Rightarrow \quad \frac{dy}{dx} = e^{x\log(x\cos x)}\frac{d}{dx}\{x\log(x\cos x)\} + e^{1/x\log(x\sin x)}\frac{d}{dx}\left\{\frac{1}{x}\log(x\sin x)\right\}$$

$$\Rightarrow \quad \frac{dy}{dx} = (x\cos x)^x\frac{d}{dx}\{x(\log x + \log\cos x)\} + (x\sin x)^{1/x}\frac{d}{dx}\left\{\frac{1}{x}(\log x + \log\sin x)\right\}$$

$$\Rightarrow \quad \frac{dy}{dx} = (x\cos x)^x\left\{(\log x + \log\cos x) + x\left(\frac{1}{x} - \tan x\right)\right\}$$

$$+ (x\sin x)^{1/x}\left\{\frac{1}{x}\left(\frac{1}{x} + \cot x\right) - \frac{1}{x^2}(\log x + \log\sin x)\right\}$$

$$= (x\cos x)^x\{\log(x\cos x) + (1 - x\tan x)\} + (x\sin x)^{1/x}\left\{\frac{1}{x^2} + \frac{\cot x}{x} - \frac{\log x}{x^2} - \frac{\log\sin x}{x^2}\right\}$$

$$= (x\cos x)^x\{\log(x\cos x) + 1 - x\tan x\} + (x\sin x)^{1/x}\left\{\frac{1 + x\cot x - \log(x\sin x)}{x^2}\right\}$$

18. (v) Let $y = \left(x + \frac{1}{x}\right)^x + x^{1+1/x}$. Then,

$$y = e^{x\log(x+1/x)} + e^{(1+1/x)\log x}$$

$$\Rightarrow \quad \frac{dy}{dx} = e^{x\log(x+1/x)}\frac{d}{dx}\left\{x\log\left(x + \frac{1}{x}\right)\right\} + e^{(1+1/x)\log x}\frac{d}{dx}\left\{\left(1 + \frac{1}{x}\right)\log x\right\}$$

$$\Rightarrow \quad \frac{dy}{dx} = \left(x + \frac{1}{x}\right)^x\left\{\log\left(x + \frac{1}{x}\right) + \frac{x}{x + \frac{1}{x}}\frac{d}{dx}\left(x + \frac{1}{x}\right)\right\} + x^{1+1/x}\left\{-\frac{1}{x^2}\log x + \left(1 + \frac{1}{x}\right)\frac{1}{x}\right\}$$

$$\Rightarrow \quad \frac{dy}{dx} = \left(x + \frac{1}{x}\right)^x\left\{\log\left(x + \frac{1}{x}\right) + \frac{x^2}{x^2+1}\left(1 - \frac{1}{x^2}\right)\right\} + x^{1+1/x}\left\{\frac{1 + x - \log x}{x^2}\right\}$$

$$\Rightarrow \quad \frac{dy}{dx} = \left(x + \frac{1}{x}\right)^x\left\{\log\left(x + \frac{1}{x}\right) + \frac{x^2 - 1}{x^2 + 1}\right\} + x^{1/x - 1}\{1 + x - \log x\}$$

18. (viii) Let $y = x^{x^2 - 3} + (x - 3)^{x^2}$. Then,

$$y = e^{\log x^{(x^2-3)}} + e^{\log(x-3)^{x^2}}$$

$$\Rightarrow \quad y = e^{(x^2-3)\log x} + e^{x^2\log(x-3)}$$

$$\Rightarrow \quad \frac{dy}{dx} = \frac{d}{dx}\left\{e^{(x^2-3)\log x}\right\} + \frac{d}{dx}\left\{e^{x^2\log(x-3)}\right\}$$

$$\Rightarrow \quad \frac{dy}{dx} = e^{(x^2-3)\log x} \frac{d}{dx}\left\{(x^2-3)\log x\right\} + e^{x^2 \log(x-3)} \frac{d}{dx}\left\{x^2 \log(x-3)\right\}$$

$$\Rightarrow \quad \frac{dy}{dx} = x^{x^2-3}\left\{2x\log x + \frac{x^2-3}{x}\right\} + (x-3)^{x^2}\left\{2x\log(x-3) + \frac{x^2}{x-3}\right\}$$

25. We have, $y = x^{\sin x} + (\sin x)^x$

$$\Rightarrow \quad y = e^{\log x^{\sin x}} + e^{\log(\sin x)^x} \Rightarrow y = e^{\sin x \log x} + e^{x \log \sin x}$$

$$\therefore \quad \frac{dy}{dx} = \frac{d}{dx}(e^{\sin x \log x}) + \frac{d}{dx}(e^{x \log \sin x})$$

$$\Rightarrow \quad \frac{dy}{dx} = e^{\sin x \log x}\frac{d}{dx}(\sin x \log x) + e^{x \log \sin x}\frac{d}{dx}(x \log \sin x)$$

$$\Rightarrow \quad \frac{dy}{dx} = x^{\sin x}\left\{\cos x \log x + \frac{\sin x}{x}\right\} + (\sin x)^x \{\log \sin x + x \cot x\}$$

28. Let $y = (\sin x)^x + \sin^{-1}\sqrt{x}$. Then, $y = e^{x \log \sin x} + \sin^{-1}\sqrt{x}$

$$\therefore \quad \frac{dy}{dx} = \frac{d}{dx}(e^{x \log \sin x}) + \frac{d}{dx}(\sin^{-1}\sqrt{x})$$

$$\Rightarrow \quad \frac{dy}{dx} = e^{x \log \sin x}\frac{d}{dx}(x \log \sin x) + \frac{d}{dx}(\sin^{-1}\sqrt{x})$$

$$\Rightarrow \quad \frac{dy}{dx} = (\sin x)^x\{\log \sin x + x \cot x\} + \frac{1}{\sqrt{1-x}} \times \frac{1}{2\sqrt{x}}$$

$$\Rightarrow \quad \frac{dy}{dx} = (\sin x)^x\{\log \sin x + x \cot x\} + \frac{1}{2\sqrt{x-x^2}}$$

32. We have, $y = x^{\log x} + (\log x)^x$

$$y = e^{\log(x^{\log x})} + e^{\log(\log x)^x} = e^{\log x \log x} + e^{x \log(\log x)} = e^{(\log x)^2} + e^{x \log(\log x)}$$

$$\therefore \quad \frac{dy}{dx} = e^{(\log x)^2}\frac{d}{dx}(\log x)^2 + e^{x \log(\log x)}\frac{d}{dx}\{x \log(\log x)\}$$

$$\Rightarrow \quad \frac{dy}{dx} = x^{\log x}\left(2\log x \times \frac{1}{x}\right) + (\log x)^x\left\{\log(\log x) + \frac{x}{\log x} \times \frac{1}{x}\right\}$$

$$\Rightarrow \quad \frac{dy}{dx} = \frac{2x^{\log x}}{x}\log x + (\log x)^x\left\{\log(\log x) + \frac{1}{\log x}\right\}$$

54. We have,

$$xy = e^{x-y} \Rightarrow \log(xy) = \log(e^{x-y}) \Rightarrow \log x + \log y = x - y$$

Differentiating with respect to x, we get

$$\frac{1}{x} + \frac{1}{y}\frac{dy}{dx} = 1 - \frac{dy}{dx} \Rightarrow \frac{dy}{dx}\left(\frac{1}{y}+1\right) = 1 - \frac{1}{x} \Rightarrow \frac{dy}{dx} = \frac{y(x-1)}{x(y+1)}$$

55. We have,

$$y^x + x^y + x^x = a^b$$

$$\Rightarrow \quad e^{\log y^x} + e^{\log x^y} + e^{\log x^x} = a^b \Rightarrow e^{x \log y} + e^{y \log x} + e^{x \log x} = a^b$$

Differentiating both sides with respect to x, we get

$$\frac{d}{dx}(e^{x \log y}) + \frac{d}{dx}(e^{y \log x}) + \frac{d}{dx}(e^{x \log x}) = \frac{d}{dx}(a^b)$$

$$\Rightarrow \quad e^{x \log y}\frac{d}{dx}(x \log y) + e^{y \log x}\frac{d}{dx}(y \log x) + e^{x \log x}\frac{d}{dx}(x \log x) = 0$$

$$\Rightarrow \quad y^x\left(\log y + \frac{x}{y}\frac{dy}{dx}\right) + x^y\left(\frac{dy}{dx}\log x + \frac{y}{x}\right) + x^x(1 + \log x) = 0$$

$$\Rightarrow \quad \frac{dy}{dx}(xy^{x-1} + x^y \log x) = -\{y^x \log y + y\, x^{y-1} + x^x(1 + \log x)\}$$

$$\Rightarrow \quad \frac{dy}{dx} = -\frac{\{y^x \log y + y\, x^{y-1} + x^x(1 + \log x)\}}{xy^{x-1} + x^y \log x}$$

10.9 DIFFERENTIATION OF INFINITE SERIES

Sometimes the value of y is given as an infinite series and we are asked to find $\frac{dy}{dx}$. In such cases we use the fact that if a term is deleted from an infinite series, it remains unaffected. The method of finding $\frac{dy}{dx}$ is explained in the following examples.

ILLUSTRATIVE EXAMPLES

BASED ON BASIC CONCEPTS (BASIC)

EXAMPLE 1 *If* $y = x^{x^{x^{\cdot^{\cdot^{\infty}}}}}$, *find* $\frac{dy}{dx}$.

SOLUTION Since by deleting a single term from an infinite series, it remains same. Therefore, the given function may be written as

$$y = x^y$$

$$\Rightarrow \quad \log y = y \log x \qquad \text{[On taking log of both sides]}$$

$$\Rightarrow \quad \frac{1}{y}\frac{dy}{dx} = \frac{dy}{dx}\log x + y\frac{d}{dx}(\log x) \qquad \text{[Differentiating both sides with respect to } x\text{]}$$

$$\Rightarrow \quad \frac{1}{y}\frac{dy}{dx} = \frac{dy}{dx}\log x + \frac{y}{x}$$

$$\Rightarrow \quad \frac{dy}{dx}\left\{\frac{1}{y} - \log x\right\} = \frac{y}{x} \Rightarrow \frac{dy}{dx}\frac{(1 - y \log x)}{y} = \frac{y}{x} \Rightarrow \frac{dy}{dx} = \frac{y^2}{x(1 - y \log x)}$$

EXAMPLE 2 *If* $y = \sqrt{\sin x + \sqrt{\sin x + \sqrt{\sin x + \ldots \text{to } \infty}}}$, *prove that* $\frac{dy}{dx} = \frac{\cos x}{2y - 1}$.

SOLUTION The given series may be written as

$$y = \sqrt{\sin x + y}$$

$$\Rightarrow \quad y^2 = \sin x + y \qquad \text{[Squaring both sides]}$$

$$\Rightarrow \quad 2y\frac{dy}{dx} = \cos x + \frac{dy}{dx} \qquad \text{[Differentiating both sides with respect to } x\text{]}$$

$$\Rightarrow \quad \frac{dy}{dx}(2y - 1) = \cos x \Rightarrow \frac{dy}{dx} = \frac{\cos x}{2y - 1}.$$

EXAMPLE 3 *If* $y = a^{x^{a^{x^{\cdot^{\cdot^{\infty}}}}}}$, *prove that* $\frac{dy}{dx} = \frac{y^2 \log y}{x(1 - y \log x \cdot \log y)}$.

SOLUTION The given series may be written as

$$y = a^{(x^y)}$$

$\Rightarrow \quad \log y = x^y \log a$ [Taking log of both sides]

$\Rightarrow \quad \log(\log y) = y \log x + \log(\log a)$ [Taking log of both sides]

$\Rightarrow \quad \frac{1}{\log y} \frac{d}{dx}(\log y) = \frac{dy}{dx} \log x + y \frac{d}{dx}(\log x) + 0$ [Differentiating both sides w.r.t. x]

$\Rightarrow \quad \frac{1}{\log y} \frac{1}{y} \frac{dy}{dx} = \frac{dy}{dx} \log x + y \times \frac{1}{x}$

$\Rightarrow \quad \frac{dy}{dx}\left\{\frac{1}{y \log y} - \log x\right\} = \frac{y}{x} \Rightarrow \frac{dy}{dx}\left\{\frac{1 - y \log y \log x}{y \log y}\right\} = \frac{y}{x} \Rightarrow \frac{dy}{dx} = \frac{y^2 \log y}{x\{1 - y \log y \log x\}}.$

EXAMPLE 4 *If* $y = e^{x + e^{x + e^{x + \dots \text{ to } \infty}}}$, *show that* $\frac{dy}{dx} = \frac{y}{1 - y}$.

SOLUTION The given function may be written as

$$y = e^{x + y}$$

$\Rightarrow \quad \log y = (x + y) \log e$ [Taking log of both sides]

$\Rightarrow \quad \log y = x + y$ [$\because \log e = 1$]

$\Rightarrow \quad \frac{1}{y} \frac{dy}{dx} = 1 + \frac{dy}{dx}$ [Differentiating with respect to x]

$\Rightarrow \quad \frac{dy}{dx}\left(\frac{1}{y} - 1\right) = 1 \Rightarrow \frac{dy}{dx} = \frac{y}{1 - y}$

EXAMPLE 5 *If* $y = (\sqrt{x})^{(\sqrt{x})^{(\sqrt{x})^{\dots \infty}}}$, *show that* $\frac{dy}{dx} = \frac{y^2}{x(2 - y \log x)}$.

SOLUTION The given function can be written as

$$y = (\sqrt{x})^y$$

$\Rightarrow \quad y = x^{y/2}$

$\Rightarrow \quad \log y = \frac{y}{2} \log x$ [On taking log of both sides]

$\Rightarrow \quad \frac{1}{y} \frac{dy}{dx} = \frac{y}{2} \times \frac{1}{x} + \frac{1}{2} \log x \frac{dy}{dx}$ [Differentiating both sides with respect to x]

$\Rightarrow \quad \frac{dy}{dx}\left\{\frac{1}{y} - \frac{1}{2} \log x\right\} = \frac{y}{2x} \Rightarrow \frac{dy}{dx}\left\{\frac{2 - y \log x}{2y}\right\} = \frac{y}{2x} \Rightarrow \frac{dy}{dx} = \frac{y^2}{x(2 - y \log x)}.$

BASED ON LOWER ORDER THINKING SKILLS (LOTS)

EXAMPLE 6 *If* $y = x + \cfrac{1}{x + \cfrac{1}{x + \cfrac{1}{x + \dots}}}$, *prove that* $\frac{dy}{dx} = \frac{y}{2y - x}$.

SOLUTION We have,

$$y = x + \cfrac{1}{x + \cfrac{1}{x + \cfrac{1}{x + \dots}}} \Rightarrow y = x + \frac{1}{y} \Rightarrow y^2 = xy + 1$$

Differentiating both sides with respect to x, we obtain

$$2y\frac{dy}{dx} = y + x\frac{dy}{dx} + 0 \Rightarrow \frac{dy}{dx}(2y - x) = y \Rightarrow \frac{dy}{dx} = \frac{y}{2y - x}.$$

EXAMPLE 7 *If* $y = \cfrac{\sin x}{1 + \cfrac{\cos x}{1 + \cfrac{\sin x}{1 + \cfrac{\cos x}{1 + \dots \text{ to } \infty}}}}$, *prove that* $\frac{dy}{dx} = \frac{(1 + y)\cos x + y \sin x}{1 + 2y + \cos x - \sin x}$.

SOLUTION We have,

$$y = \cfrac{\sin x}{1 + \cfrac{\cos x}{1 + y}} \Rightarrow y = \frac{(1 + y)\sin x}{1 + y + \cos x} \Rightarrow y + y^2 + y\cos x = (1 + y)\sin x$$

Differentiating both sides with respect to x, we get

$$\frac{dy}{dx} + 2y\frac{dy}{dx} + \frac{dy}{dx}\cos x - y\sin x = \frac{dy}{dx}\sin x + (1 + y)\cos x$$

$$\Rightarrow \quad \frac{dy}{dx}\{1 + 2y + \cos x - \sin x\} = (1 + y)\cos x + y\sin x$$

$$\Rightarrow \quad \frac{dy}{dx} = \frac{(1 + y)\cos x + y\sin x}{1 + 2y + \cos x - \sin x}.$$

EXERCISE 10.6

BASIC

1. If $y = \sqrt{x + \sqrt{x + \sqrt{x + \dots \text{ to } \infty}}}$, prove that $\frac{dy}{dx} = \frac{1}{2y - 1}$.
2. If $y = \sqrt{\cos x + \sqrt{\cos x + \sqrt{\cos x + \dots \text{ to } \infty}}}$, prove that $\frac{dy}{dx} = \frac{\sin x}{1 - 2y}$.
3. If $y = \sqrt{\log x + \sqrt{\log x + \sqrt{\log x + \dots \text{ to } \infty}}}$, prove that $(2y - 1)\frac{dy}{dx} = \frac{1}{x}$.
4. If $y = \sqrt{\tan x + \sqrt{\tan x + \sqrt{\tan x + \dots \text{ to } \infty}}}$, prove that $\frac{dy}{dx} = \frac{\sec^2 x}{2y - 1}$.
5. If $y = (\sin x)^{(\sin x)^{(\sin x)^{\dots \infty}}}$, prove that $\frac{dy}{dx} = \frac{y^2 \cot x}{(1 - y \log \sin x)}$.
6. If $y = (\tan x)^{(\tan x)^{(\tan x)^{\dots \infty}}}$, prove that $\frac{dy}{dx} = 2$ at $x = \frac{\pi}{4}$.

BASED ON LOTS

7. If $y = (\cos x)^{(\cos x)^{(\cos x)\dots \infty}}$, prove that $\frac{dy}{dx} = -\frac{y^2 \tan x}{(1 - y \log \cos x)}$. [NCERT EXEMPLAR]

BASED ON HOTS

8. If $y = e^{x^{e^x}} + x^{e^{e^x}} + e^{x^{x^e}}$, prove that

$$\frac{dy}{dx} = e^{x^{e^x}} \cdot x^{e^x}\left\{\frac{e^x}{x} + e^x \cdot \log x\right\} + x^{e^{e^x}} \cdot e^{e^x}\left\{\frac{1}{x} + e^x \cdot \log x\right\} + e^{x^{x^e}} x^{x^e} \cdot x^{e-1}\{1 + e \log x\}$$

10.10 DIFFERENTIATION OF PARAMETRIC FUNCTIONS

Sometimes x and y are given as functions of a single variable e.g. $x = \phi(t)$, $y = \psi(t)$ are two functions of a single variable. In such a case x and y are called parametric functions or parametric equations and t is called the parameter. To find $\frac{dy}{dx}$ in case of parametric functions, we first obtain the relationship between x and y by eliminating the parameter t and then we differentiate it with respect to x. But, it is not always convenient to eliminate the parameter. Therefore, $\frac{dy}{dx}$ can also be obtained by the following formula

$$\frac{dy}{dx} = \frac{dy/dt}{dx/dt}$$

In order to prove this, let Δx and Δy be the changes in x and y respectively corresponding to a small change Δt in t. Then,

$$\frac{\Delta y}{\Delta x} = \frac{\Delta y/\Delta t}{\Delta x/\Delta t} \Rightarrow \frac{dy}{dx} = \lim_{\Delta x \to 0} \frac{\Delta y}{\Delta x} = \frac{\lim\limits_{\Delta t \to 0} \frac{\Delta y}{\Delta t}}{\lim\limits_{\Delta t \to 0} \frac{\Delta x}{\Delta t}} = \frac{\frac{dy}{dt}}{\frac{dx}{dt}}$$

ILLUSTRATIVE EXAMPLES

BASED ON BASIC CONCEPTS (BASIC)

EXAMPLE 1 *Find $\frac{dy}{dx}$ in each of the following:*

(i) $x = a\left\{\cos t + \frac{1}{2}\log \tan^2 \frac{t}{2}\right\}$ and $y = a \sin t$. [CBSE 2011, 2019 NCERT]

(ii) $x = a(\theta - \sin\theta)$ and $y = a(1 - \cos\theta)$. [NCERT]

SOLUTION (i) $x = a\left\{\cos t + \frac{1}{2}\log \tan^2 \frac{t}{2}\right\}$ and $y = a \sin t$

$$\Rightarrow \quad x = a\left\{\cos t + \frac{1}{2} \times 2 \log \tan \frac{t}{2}\right\} \quad \text{and } y = a \sin t$$

$$\Rightarrow \quad x = a\left\{\cos t + \log \tan \frac{t}{2}\right\} \quad \text{and } y = a \sin t.$$

Differentiating with respect to t, we get

$$\frac{dx}{dt} = a\left\{-\sin t + \frac{1}{\tan t/2}\left(\sec^2 \frac{t}{2}\right) \times \frac{1}{2}\right\} \text{ and } \frac{dy}{dt} = a \cos t$$

$$\Rightarrow \quad \frac{dx}{dt} = a\left\{-\sin t + \frac{1}{2\sin(t/2)\cos(t/2)}\right\} \text{ and } \frac{dy}{dt} = a \cos t$$

$$\Rightarrow \quad \frac{dx}{dt} = a\left\{-\sin t + \frac{1}{\sin t}\right\} \text{ and } \frac{dy}{dt} = a\cos t$$

$$\Rightarrow \quad \frac{dx}{dt} = a\left\{\frac{-\sin^2 t + 1}{\sin t}\right\} \text{ and } \frac{dy}{dt} = a\cos t$$

$$\Rightarrow \quad \frac{dx}{dt} = \frac{a\cos^2 t}{\sin t} \text{ and } \frac{dy}{dt} = a\cos t \Rightarrow \frac{dy}{dx} = \frac{dy/dt}{dx/dt} = \frac{a\cos t}{\frac{a\cos^2 t}{\sin t}} = \tan t$$

(ii) We have, $x = a(\theta - \sin\theta)$ and $y = a(1 - \cos\theta)$

Differentiating with respect to θ, we get

$$\frac{dx}{d\theta} = a(1 - \cos\theta) \text{ and } \frac{dy}{d\theta} = a\sin\theta$$

$$\therefore \quad \frac{dy}{dx} = \frac{dy/d\theta}{dx/d\theta} = \frac{a\sin\theta}{a(1-\cos\theta)} = \frac{2\sin(\theta/2)\cos(\theta/2)}{2\sin^2(\theta/2)} = \cot\frac{\theta}{2}.$$

EXAMPLE 2 *If* $x = a\sec^3\theta$ and $y = a\tan^3\theta$, *find* $\frac{dy}{dx}$ at $\theta = \frac{\pi}{3}$. [NCERT EXEMPLAR]

SOLUTION We have, $x = a\sec^3\theta$ and $y = a\tan^3\theta$

Differentiating with respect to θ, we get

$$\frac{dx}{d\theta} = 3a\sec^2\theta\frac{d}{d\theta}(\sec\theta) \text{ and } \frac{dy}{d\theta} = 3a\tan^2\theta\frac{d}{d\theta}(\tan\theta)$$

$$\Rightarrow \quad \frac{dx}{d\theta} = 3a\sec^3\theta\tan\theta \text{ and } \frac{dy}{d\theta} = 3a\tan^2\theta\sec^2\theta$$

$$\therefore \quad \frac{dy}{dx} = \frac{dy/d\theta}{dx/d\theta} = \frac{3a\tan^2\theta\sec^2\theta}{3a\sec^3\theta\tan\theta} = \frac{\tan\theta}{\sec\theta} = \sin\theta \Rightarrow \left(\frac{dy}{dx}\right)_{\theta=\pi/3} = \sin\frac{\pi}{3} = \frac{\sqrt{3}}{2}$$

EXAMPLE 3 *Find* $\frac{dy}{dx}$, *when* $x = a\cos^3 t$ *and* $y = a\sin^3 t$.

SOLUTION We have, $x = a\cos^3 t$ and $y = a\sin^3 t$

$$\therefore \quad \frac{dx}{dt} = 3a\cos^2 t\frac{d}{dt}\cos(t) = -3a\cos^2 t\sin t \text{ and, } \frac{dy}{dt} = 3a\sin^2 t\frac{d}{dt}(\sin t) = 3a\sin^2 t\cos t$$

$$\therefore \quad \frac{dy}{dx} = \frac{dy/dt}{dx/dt} = \frac{3a\sin^2 t\cos t}{-3a\cos^2 t\sin t} = -\tan t$$

BASED ON LOWER ORDER THINKING SKILLS (LOTS)

EXAMPLE 4 *If* $x = \sqrt{a^{\sin^{-1} t}}$, $y = \sqrt{a^{\cos^{-1} t}}$, $a > 0$ *and* $-1 < t < 1$, *show that* $\frac{dy}{dx} = -\frac{y}{x}$. [CBSE 2012, NCERT]

SOLUTION We have,

$$x = \sqrt{a^{\sin^{-1} t}} \text{ and } y = \sqrt{a^{\cos^{-1} t}}$$

$$\Rightarrow \quad \frac{dx}{dt} = \frac{1}{2}\left(a^{\sin^{-1} t}\right)^{-1/2}\frac{d}{dt}\left(a^{\sin^{-1} t}\right) \text{ and } \frac{dy}{dt} = \frac{1}{2}\left(a^{\cos^{-1} t}\right)^{-1/2}\frac{d}{dt}\left(a^{\cos^{-1} t}\right)$$

$$\Rightarrow \quad \frac{dx}{dt} = \frac{1}{2}\left(a^{\sin^{-1} t}\right)^{-1/2} \left(a^{\sin^{-1} t} \log_e a\right) \frac{d}{dt}(\sin^{-1} t)$$

and,

$$\frac{dy}{dt} = \frac{1}{2}\left(a^{\cos^{-1} t}\right)^{-1/2} \left(a^{\cos^{-1} t} \log_e a\right) \frac{d}{dt}(\cos^{-1} t)$$

$$\Rightarrow \quad \frac{dx}{dt} = \frac{1}{2}\left(a^{\sin^{-1} t}\right)^{1/2} (\log_e a) \times \frac{1}{\sqrt{1-t^2}} = \frac{x \log_e a}{2\sqrt{1-t^2}}$$

and, $$\frac{dy}{dt} = \frac{1}{2}\left(a^{\cos^{-1} t}\right)^{1/2} (\log_e a) \times \frac{-1}{\sqrt{1-t^2}} = \frac{-y \log_e a}{2\sqrt{1-t^2}}$$

$$\therefore \quad \frac{dy}{dx} = \frac{\frac{dy}{dt}}{\frac{dx}{dt}} = \frac{-y \log_e a}{2\sqrt{1-t^2}} \times \frac{2\sqrt{1-t^2}}{x \log_e a} = \frac{-y}{x}.$$

ALITER Clearly, $x^2 y^2 = a^{\sin^{-1} t + \cos^{-1} t} \Rightarrow x^2 y^2 = a^{\pi/2}$ $\left[\because \sin^{-1} t + \cos^{-1} t = \frac{\pi}{2}\right]$

Differentiating with respect to x, we get

$$2xy^2 + 2x^2 y \frac{dy}{dx} = 0 \Rightarrow \frac{dy}{dx} = -\frac{y}{x}$$

BASED ON HIGHER ORDER THINKING SKILLS (HOTS)

EXAMPLE 5 *If* $x = \sin^{-1}\left(\frac{2t}{1+t^2}\right)$ *and* $y = \tan^{-1}\left(\frac{2t}{1-t^2}\right)$, $t > 1$. *Prove that* $\frac{dy}{dx} = -1$.

SOLUTION Let $t = \tan\theta$. Then,

$$t > 1 \Rightarrow \tan\theta > 1 \Rightarrow \frac{\pi}{4} < \theta < \frac{\pi}{2} \Rightarrow \frac{\pi}{2} < 2\theta < \pi$$

$$\therefore \quad x = \sin^{-1}\left\{\frac{2t}{1+t^2}\right\} = \sin^{-1}\left\{\frac{2\tan\theta}{1+\tan^2\theta}\right\}$$

$$\Rightarrow \quad x = \sin^{-1}(\sin 2\theta) = \sin^{-1}\{\sin(\pi - 2\theta)\} = \pi - 2\theta = \pi - 2\tan^{-1} t$$

$$\Rightarrow \quad \frac{dx}{dt} = 0 - \frac{2}{1+t^2} = \frac{-2}{1+t^2}$$

and, $$y = \tan^{-1}\left\{\frac{2t}{1-t^2}\right\}$$

$$\Rightarrow \quad y = \tan^{-1}\left\{\frac{2\tan\theta}{1-\tan^2\theta}\right\} = \tan^{-1}(\tan 2\theta) = \tan^{-1}\{-\tan(\pi - 2\theta)\}$$

$$\Rightarrow \quad y = -\tan^{-1}\{\tan(\pi - 2\theta)\} = -(\pi - 2\theta) = -\pi + 2\tan^{-1} t$$

$$\Rightarrow \quad \frac{dy}{dt} = 0 + \frac{2}{1+t^2} = \frac{2}{1+t^2}$$

$$\therefore \quad \frac{dy}{dx} = \frac{\frac{dy}{dt}}{\frac{dx}{dt}} = \frac{\frac{2}{1+t^2}}{-\frac{2}{1+t^2}} = -1.$$

EXAMPLE 6 *If $u = \sin(m \cos^{-1} x)$, $v = \cos(m \sin^{-1} x)$, prove that $\frac{du}{dv} = \frac{\sqrt{1-u^2}}{1-v^2}$.*

SOLUTION We have,

$$u = \sin(m \cos^{-1} x) \text{ and } v = \cos(m \sin^{-1} x)$$

$$\Rightarrow \quad \sin^{-1} u = m \cos^{-1} x \text{ and } \cos^{-1} v = m \sin^{-1} x$$

$$\Rightarrow \quad \sin^{-1} u + \cos^{-1} v = m(\cos^{-1} x + \sin^{-1} x) \Rightarrow \sin^{-1} u + \cos^{-1} v = \frac{m\pi}{2} \quad \left[\because \sin^{-1} x + \cos^{-1} x = \frac{\pi}{2}\right]$$

Differentiating both sides with respect to v, we obtain

$$\frac{1}{\sqrt{1-u^2}} \frac{du}{dv} - \frac{1}{\sqrt{1-v^2}} = 0 \Rightarrow \frac{du}{dv} = \sqrt{\frac{1-u^2}{1-v^2}}$$

EXAMPLE 7 *If $x = \sec\theta - \cos\theta$ and $y = \sec^n \theta - \cos^n \theta$, prove that $(x^2+4)\left(\frac{dy}{dx}\right)^2 = n^2(y^2+4)$*

SOLUTION We have,

$$x = \sec\theta - \cos\theta \text{ and } y = \sec^n \theta - \cos^n \theta$$

$$\therefore \quad \frac{dx}{d\theta} = \sec\theta \tan\theta + \sin\theta \text{ and, } \frac{dy}{d\theta} = n \sec^n \theta \tan\theta + n \cos^{n-1} \theta \sin\theta$$

$$\Rightarrow \quad \frac{dx}{d\theta} = \tan\theta(\sec\theta + \cos\theta) \text{ and, } \frac{dy}{d\theta} = n \tan\theta(\sec^n \theta + \cos^n \theta)$$

$$\therefore \quad \frac{dy}{dx} = \frac{dy/d\theta}{dx/d\theta} = \frac{n \tan\theta(\sec^n \theta + \cos^n \theta)}{\tan\theta(\sec\theta + \cos\theta)} = n \frac{\sec^n \theta + \cos^n \theta}{\sec\theta + \cos\theta}$$

$$\Rightarrow \quad \left(\frac{dy}{dx}\right)^2 = n^2 \frac{(\sec^n \theta + \cos^n \theta)^2}{(\sec\theta + \cos\theta)^2}$$

$$\Rightarrow \quad \left(\frac{dy}{dx}\right)^2 = n^2 \left\{\frac{(\sec^n \theta - \cos^n \theta)^2 + 4\sec^n \theta \cos^n \theta}{(\sec\theta - \cos\theta)^2 + 4\sec\theta\cos\theta}\right\} \quad [\because (a+b)^2 = (a-b)^2 + 4ab]$$

$$\Rightarrow \quad \left(\frac{dy}{dx}\right)^2 = n^2 \left(\frac{y^2+4}{x^2+4}\right) \Rightarrow (x^2+4)\left(\frac{dy}{dx}\right)^2 = n^2(y^2+4)$$

EXERCISE 10.7

BASIC

Find $\frac{dy}{dx}$, when

1. $x = at^2$ and $y = 2at$ [NCERT]
2. $x = a(\theta + \sin\theta)$ and $y = a(1 - \cos\theta)$ [NCERT]
3. $x = a\cos\theta$ and $y = b\sin\theta$
4. $x = ae^{\theta}(\sin\theta - \cos\theta)$, $y = ae^{\theta}(\sin\theta + \cos\theta)$ [CBSE 2014]
5. $x = b\sin^2\theta$ and $y = a\cos^2\theta$

6. $x = a(1 - \cos\theta)$ and $y = a(\theta + \sin\theta)$ at $\theta = \frac{\pi}{2}$ [NCERT]

7. $x = \frac{e^t + e^{-t}}{2}$ and $y = \frac{e^t - e^{-t}}{2}$

8. $x = \frac{3at}{1+t^2}$ and $y = \frac{3at^2}{1+t^2}$

9. $x = a(\cos\theta + \theta\sin\theta)$ and $y = a(\sin\theta - \theta\cos\theta)$ [NCERT]

10. $x = e^{\theta}\left(\theta + \frac{1}{\theta}\right)$ and $y = e^{-\theta}\left(\theta - \frac{1}{\theta}\right)$. [NCERT EXEMPLAR]

11. $x = \frac{2t}{1+t^2}$ and $y = \frac{1-t^2}{1+t^2}$.

12. $x = \cos^{-1}\frac{1}{\sqrt{1+t^2}}$ and $y = \sin^{-1}\frac{t}{\sqrt{1+t^2}}, t \in R$

13. $x = \frac{1-t^2}{1+t^2}$ and $y = \frac{2t}{1+t^2}$

14. If $x = 10(t - \sin t)$, $y = 12(1 - \cos t)$, find $\frac{dy}{dx}$. [NCERT]

15. If $x = a(\theta - \sin\theta)$ and, $y = a(1 + \cos\theta)$, find $\frac{dy}{dx}$ at $\theta = \frac{\pi}{3}$. [CBSE 2011]

16. If $x = \frac{1+\log t}{t^2}$, $y = \frac{3 + 2\log t}{t}$, find $\frac{dy}{dx}$. [NCERT EXEMPLAR]

17. If $x = 3\sin t - \sin 3t$, $y = 3\cos t - \cos 3t$, find $\frac{dy}{dx}$ at $t = \frac{\pi}{3}$. [NCERT EXEMPLAR]

18. If $\sin x = \frac{2t}{1+t^2}$, $\tan y = \frac{2t}{1-t^2}$, find $\frac{dy}{dx}$. [NCERT EXEMPLAR]

19. If $x = a(2\theta - \sin 2\theta)$ and $y = a(1 - \cos 2\theta)$, find $\frac{dy}{dx}$ when $\theta = \frac{\pi}{3}$. [CBSE 2018]

20. If $x = \sin^{-1}\left(\frac{2t}{1+t^2}\right)$ and $y = \tan^{-1}\left(\frac{2t}{1-t^2}\right)$, $-1 < t < 1$, prove that $\frac{dy}{dx} = 1$

BASED ON LOTS

21. If $x = 2\cos\theta - \cos 2\theta$ and $y = 2\sin\theta - \sin 2\theta$, prove that $\frac{dy}{dx} = \tan\left(\frac{3\theta}{2}\right)$. [CBSE 2013]

22. If $x = e^{\cos 2t}$ and $y = e^{\sin 2t}$, prove that $\frac{dy}{dx} = -\frac{y\log x}{x\log y}$ [CBSE 2024, NCERT EXEMPLAR]

23. If $x = a\left(t + \frac{1}{t}\right)$ and $y = a\left(t - \frac{1}{t}\right)$, prove that $\frac{dy}{dx} = \frac{x}{y}$.

24. If $x = \frac{\sin^3 t}{\sqrt{\cos 2t}}$, $y = \frac{\cos^3 t}{\sqrt{\cos 2t}}$, find $\frac{dy}{dx}$ [NCERT]

25. If $x = \left(t + \frac{1}{t}\right)^a$, $y = a^{t + \frac{1}{t}}$, find $\frac{dy}{dx}$

26. If $x = a\left(\frac{1+t^2}{1-t^2}\right)$ and $y = \frac{2t}{1-t^2}$, find $\frac{dy}{dx}$ [CBSE 2005]

27. If $x = a\sin 2t\,(1+\cos 2t)$ and $y = b\cos 2t\,(1-\cos 2t)$, show that at $t = \frac{\pi}{4}$, $\frac{dy}{dx} = \frac{b}{a}$.

[CBSE 2014, 2016, NCERT EXEMPLAR]

28. If $x = \cos t\,(3-2\cos^2 t)$ and $y = \sin t\,(3-2\sin^2 t)$ find the value of $\frac{dy}{dx}$ at $t = \frac{\pi}{4}$.

[CBSE 2014, NCERT EXEMPLAR]

ANSWERS

1. $\frac{1}{t}$	2. $\tan\frac{\theta}{2}$	3. $-\frac{b}{a}\cot\theta$	4. $\cot\theta$
5. $-\frac{a}{b}$	6. 1	7. $\frac{x}{y}$	8. $\frac{2t}{1-t^2}$
9. $\tan\theta$	10. $e^{-2\theta}\frac{(\theta^2-\theta^3+\theta+1)}{(\theta^3+\theta^2+\theta-1)}$	11. $-\frac{x}{y}$	12. 1
13. $\frac{t^2-1}{2t}$	14. $\frac{6}{5}\cot\left(\frac{t}{2}\right)$	15. $-\sqrt{3}$	16. t
17. $-\frac{1}{\sqrt{3}}$	18. 1	19. $\frac{1}{\sqrt{3}}$	24. $-\cot 3t$
25. $\frac{a^{t+\frac{1}{t}}\log a}{a\left(t+\frac{1}{t}\right)^{a-1}}$	26. $\frac{1+t^2}{2at}$	28. 1	

HINTS TO SELECTED PROBLEMS

22. We have, $x = e^{\cos 2t}$, $y = e^{\sin 2t}$

$$\Rightarrow \frac{dx}{dt} = e^{\cos 2t}(-2\sin 2t),\ \frac{dy}{dt} = e^{\sin 2t}(2\cos 2t)$$

$$\Rightarrow \frac{dx}{dt} = -2x\sin 2t,\ \frac{dy}{dt} = 2y\cos 2t$$

$$\Rightarrow \frac{dx}{dt} = -2x\log y,\ \frac{dy}{dt} = 2y\log x \qquad \left[\because x = e^{\cos 2t},\ y = e^{\sin 2t} \Rightarrow \log x = \cos 2t,\ \log y = \sin 2t\right]$$

$$\therefore \frac{dy}{dx} = \frac{dy/dt}{dx/dt} = \frac{2y\log x}{-2x\log y} = -\left(\frac{y\log x}{x\log y}\right)$$

ALITER We have,

$$x = e^{\cos 2t} \text{ and, } y = e^{\sin 2t}$$

$$\Rightarrow \log x = \cos 2t \text{ and, } \log y = \sin 2t \Rightarrow (\log x)^2 + (\log y)^2 = \cos^2 2t + \sin^2 2t$$

$$\Rightarrow (\log x)^2 + (\log y)^2 = 1$$

Differentiating both sides with respect to x, we get

$$2(\log x)\frac{1}{x}+2(\log y)\frac{1}{y}\frac{dy}{dx}=0 \Rightarrow \frac{dy}{dx}=-\frac{y\log x}{x\log y}$$

24. We have,

$$x = \frac{\sin^3 t}{\sqrt{\cos 2t}}, y = \frac{\cos^3 t}{\sqrt{\cos 2t}}$$

$$\Rightarrow \quad x = \sin^3 t\ (\cos 2t)^{-1/2},\ y = \cos^3 t\ (\cos 2t)^{-1/2}$$

$$\Rightarrow \quad \frac{dx}{dt} = \frac{3\sin^2 t\cos t}{\sqrt{\cos 2t}} + \sin^3 t \times -\frac{1}{2}(\cos 2t)^{-3/2}\frac{d}{dt}(\cos 2t)$$

$$\text{and, } \frac{dy}{dt} = \frac{-3\cos^2 t\sin t}{\sqrt{\cos 2t}} + \cos^3 t \times -\frac{1}{2}(\cos 2t)^{-3/2}\frac{d}{dt}(\cos 2t)$$

$$\Rightarrow \quad \frac{dx}{dt} = \frac{3\sin^2 t\cos t}{\sqrt{\cos 2t}} + \frac{\sin^3 t\sin 2t}{(\cos 2t)^{3/2}},\ \frac{dy}{dt} = \frac{-3\cos^2 t\sin t}{\sqrt{\cos 2t}} + \frac{\cos^3 t\sin 2t}{(\cos 2t)^{3/2}}$$

$$\Rightarrow \quad \frac{dx}{dt} = \frac{3\sin^2 t\cos t\cos 2t + \sin^3 t\sin 2t}{(\cos 2t)^{3/2}},\ \frac{dy}{dt} = \frac{-3\cos^2 t\sin t\cos 2t + \cos^3 t\sin 2t}{(\cos 2t)^{3/2}}$$

$$\Rightarrow \quad \frac{dx}{dt} = \frac{3\sin^2 t\cos t(1-2\sin^2 t) + 2\sin^4 t\cos t}{(\cos 2t)^{3/2}},$$

$$\frac{dy}{dt} = \frac{-3\cos^2 t\sin t(2\cos^2 t - 1) + 2\cos^4 t\sin t}{(\cos 2t)^{3/2}}$$

$$\Rightarrow \quad \frac{dx}{dt} = \frac{3\sin^2 t\cos t - 4\sin^4 t\cos t}{(\cos 2t)^{3/2}},\ \frac{dy}{dt} = \frac{-4\cos^4 t\sin t + 3\cos^2 t\sin t}{(\cos 2t)^{3/2}}$$

$$\Rightarrow \quad \frac{dx}{dt} = \frac{\sin t\cos t(3\sin t - 4\sin^3 t)}{(\cos 2t)^{3/2}},\ \frac{dy}{dt} = \frac{-\sin t\cos t(4\cos^3 t - 3\cos t)}{(\cos 2t)^{3/2}}$$

$$\Rightarrow \quad \frac{dx}{dt} = \frac{\sin 2t\sin 3t}{2(\cos 2t)^{3/2}},\ \frac{dy}{dt} = \frac{-\sin 2t\cos 3t}{(\cos 2t)^{3/2}}$$

$$\therefore \quad \frac{dy}{dx} = \frac{dy/dt}{dx/dt} = \frac{-\sin 2t\cos 3t}{\sin 2t\sin 3t} = -\cot 3t$$

10.11 DIFFERENTIATION OF A FUNCTION WITH RESPECT TO ANOTHER FUNCTION

So far we have discussed derivative of one variable, say, y with respect to other variable, say, x. In this section, we will discuss derivative of a function with respect to another function.

Let $u = f(x)$ and $v = g(x)$ be two functions of x. Then, to find the derivative of $f(x)$ with respect to $g(x)$ i.e., to find $\frac{du}{dv}$ we use the following formula

$$\frac{du}{dv} = \frac{du/dx}{dv/dx}$$

Thus, to find the derivative of $f(x)$ with respect to $g(x)$, we first differentiate both with respect to x and then divide the derivative of $f(x)$ with respect to x by the derivative of $g(x)$ with respect to x.

Following examples will illustrate the procedure.

ILLUSTRATIVE EXAMPLES

BASED ON BASIC CONCEPTS (BASIC)

EXAMPLE 1 *Differentiate* $\log \sin x$ *with respect to* $\sqrt{\cos x}$.

SOLUTION Let $u = \log \sin x$ and $v = \sqrt{\cos x}$. Then,

$$\frac{du}{dx} = \cot x \text{ and } \frac{dv}{dx} = -\frac{\sin x}{2\sqrt{\cos x}}$$

$$\therefore \quad \frac{du}{dv} = \frac{du/dx}{dv/dx} = -\frac{\cot x}{\frac{\sin x}{2\sqrt{\cos x}}} = -2\sqrt{\cos x}\cot x \operatorname{cosec} x$$

EXAMPLE 2 *Differentiate* $\tan^{-1}\left(\frac{1+2x}{1-2x}\right)$ *with respect to* $\sqrt{1+4x^2}$.

SOLUTION Let $u = \tan^{-1}\left(\frac{1+2x}{1-2x}\right)$ and $v = \sqrt{1+4x^2}$. Then,

$$u = \tan^{-1} 1 + \tan^{-1} 2x \text{ and } v = \sqrt{1+4x^2} \Rightarrow \frac{du}{dx} = \frac{2}{1+4x^2} \text{ and } \frac{dv}{dx} = \frac{1}{2\sqrt{1+4x^2}} \times 8x = \frac{4x}{\sqrt{1+4x^2}}$$

$$\therefore \quad \frac{du}{dv} = \frac{\frac{du}{dx}}{\frac{dv}{dx}} = \frac{\frac{2}{1+4x^2}}{\frac{4x}{\sqrt{1+4x^2}}} = \frac{1}{2x\sqrt{1+4x^2}}$$

EXAMPLE 3 *Differentiate* $\tan^{-1}\left(\frac{\sqrt{1+x^2}-1}{x}\right)$ *with respect to* $\tan^{-1} x$, $x \neq 0$.

SOLUTION Let $u = \tan^{-1}\left(\frac{\sqrt{1+x^2}-1}{x}\right)$ and $v = \tan^{-1} x$. Putting $x = \tan\theta$, we get

$$u = \tan^{-1}\left(\frac{\sqrt{1+x^2}-1}{x}\right) = \tan^{-1}\left(\frac{\sec\theta - 1}{\tan\theta}\right) = \tan^{-1}\left(\frac{1-\cos\theta}{\sin\theta}\right)$$

$$\Rightarrow \quad u = \tan^{-1}\left\{\frac{2\sin^2(\theta/2)}{2\sin(\theta/2)\cos(\theta/2)}\right\} = \tan^{-1}\left(\tan\frac{\theta}{2}\right) = \frac{1}{2}\theta = \frac{1}{2}\tan^{-1} x$$

Thus, we obtain

$$u = \frac{1}{2}\tan^{-1} x \text{ and } v = \tan^{-1} x \Rightarrow \frac{du}{dx} = \frac{1}{2} \times \frac{1}{1+x^2} \text{ and } \frac{dv}{dx} = \frac{1}{1+x^2}.$$

$$\therefore \quad \frac{du}{dv} = \frac{du/dx}{dv/dx} = \frac{1}{2(1+x^2)} \times (1+x^2) = \frac{1}{2}.$$

EXAMPLE 4 *Differentiate* $\sin^{-1}\left(\frac{2x}{1+x^2}\right)$ *with respect to* $\tan^{-1} x$, $-1 < x < 1$.

SOLUTION Let $u = \sin^{-1}\left(\frac{2x}{1+x^2}\right)$ and $v = \tan^{-1} x$. Putting $x = \tan\theta$, we get

$$u = \sin^{-1}\left(\frac{2\tan\theta}{1+\tan^2\theta}\right) = \sin^{-1}(\sin 2\theta)$$

$$\Rightarrow \quad u = 2\theta = 2\tan^{-1} x \qquad \left[\because -1 < x < 1 \Rightarrow -\frac{\pi}{4} < \theta < \frac{\pi}{4} \Rightarrow -\frac{\pi}{2} < 2\theta < \frac{\pi}{2}\right]$$

Thus, we obtain

$$u = 2\tan^{-1} x \text{ and } v = \tan^{-1} x \Rightarrow \frac{du}{dx} = \frac{2}{1+x^2} \text{ and } \frac{dv}{dx} = \frac{1}{1+x^2}$$

$$\therefore \quad \frac{du}{dv} = \frac{du/dx}{dv/dx} = \frac{2/1+x^2}{1/1+x^2} = 2$$

EXAMPLE 5 *Differentiate x^x with respect to $x \log x$.*

SOLUTION Let $u = x^x$ and $v = x \log x$. Then,

$$u = x^x = e^{\log x^x} = e^{x\log x} \text{ and } v = x\log x$$

$$\Rightarrow \quad \frac{du}{dx} = e^{x\log x} \times \frac{d}{dx}(x\log x) \text{ and } \frac{dv}{dx} = x \times \frac{1}{x} + 1 \times \log x$$

$$\Rightarrow \quad \frac{du}{dx} = x^x(1+\log x) \text{ and } \frac{dv}{dx} = 1 + \log x \Rightarrow \frac{du}{dv} = \frac{du/dx}{dv/dx} = \frac{x^x(1+\log x)}{(1+\log x)} = x^x$$

ALITER We have, $u = x^x \Rightarrow \log u = x\log x = v \Rightarrow u = e^v$

$$\therefore \quad \frac{du}{dv} = \frac{d}{dv}(e^v) = e^v = u \Rightarrow \frac{du}{dv} = x^x.$$

BASED ON LOWER ORDER THINKING SKILLS (LOTS)

EXAMPLE 6 *Differentiate $\tan^{-1}\left\{\frac{\sqrt{1+x^2}-\sqrt{1-x^2}}{\sqrt{1+x^2}+\sqrt{1-x^2}}\right\}$ with respect to $\cos^{-1} x^2$.* [CBSE 2019]

SOLUTION Let $\tan^{-1}\left\{\frac{\sqrt{1+x^2}-\sqrt{1-x^2}}{\sqrt{1+x^2}+\sqrt{1-x^2}}\right\}$ and $v = \cos^{-1} x^2$. Putting $x^2 = \cos\theta$, we get

$$u = \tan^{-1}\left\{\frac{\sqrt{1+\cos\theta}-\sqrt{1-\cos\theta}}{\sqrt{1+\cos\theta}+\sqrt{1-\cos\theta}}\right\} = \tan^{-1}\left\{\frac{\sqrt{2\cos^2\theta/2}-\sqrt{2\sin^2\theta/2}}{\sqrt{2\cos^2\theta/2}+\sqrt{2\sin^2\theta/2}}\right\}$$

$$\Rightarrow \quad u = \tan^{-1}\left\{\frac{\cos\theta/2 - \sin\theta/2}{\cos\theta/2 + \sin\theta/2}\right\}$$

$$\Rightarrow \quad u = \tan^{-1}\left\{\frac{1-\tan\theta/2}{1+\tan\theta/2}\right\} \qquad \left[\text{Dividing numerator and denominator by } \cos\frac{\theta}{2}\right]$$

$$\Rightarrow \quad u = \tan^{-1}\left\{\tan\left(\frac{\pi}{4}-\frac{\theta}{2}\right)\right\} = \frac{\pi}{4}-\frac{1}{2}\theta = \frac{\pi}{4}-\frac{1}{2}\cos^{-1}x^2 \quad [\because x^2=\cos\theta \therefore \theta=\cos^{-1}x^2]$$

$$\Rightarrow \quad \frac{du}{dx} = -\frac{1}{2}\times\frac{-2x}{\sqrt{1-x^4}} = \frac{x}{\sqrt{1-x^4}}$$

Now, $v=\cos^{-1}x^2 \Rightarrow \dfrac{dv}{dx} = \dfrac{-2x}{\sqrt{1-x^4}}$

$$\therefore \quad \frac{du}{dv} = \frac{du/dx}{dv/dx} = -\frac{1}{2}$$

EXAMPLE 7 *Differentiate* $x^{\sin^{-1}x}$ *with respect to* $\sin^{-1}x$.

SOLUTION Let $u=x^{\sin^{-1}x}$ and $v=\sin^{-1}x$. Then,

$$u = x^{\sin^{-1}x}$$

$$\Rightarrow \quad u = e^{\sin^{-1}x\,.\log x}$$

$$\Rightarrow \quad \frac{du}{dx} = e^{\sin^{-1}x\,.\log x}\cdot\frac{d}{dx}\{\sin^{-1}x\,.\log x\} = x^{\sin^{-1}x}\left\{\frac{\sin^{-1}x}{x}+\frac{\log x}{\sqrt{1-x^2}}\right\}$$

and, $v=\sin^{-1}x \Rightarrow \dfrac{dv}{dx} = \dfrac{1}{\sqrt{1-x^2}}$

$$\therefore \quad \frac{du}{dv} = \frac{\frac{du}{dx}}{\frac{dv}{dx}} = \frac{x^{\sin^{-1}x}\left\{\frac{\sin^{-1}x}{x}+\frac{\log x}{\sqrt{1-x^2}}\right\}}{\frac{1}{\sqrt{1-x^2}}} = x^{\sin^{-1}x}\left\{\log x+\frac{\sqrt{1-x^2}}{x}\sin^{-1}x\right\}$$

EXAMPLE 8 *If* $x\in\left(\frac{1}{\sqrt{2}},1\right)$, *differentiate* $\tan^{-1}\left(\frac{\sqrt{1-x^2}}{x}\right)$ *with respect to* $\cos^{-1}\left(2x\sqrt{1-x^2}\right)$.

[CBSE 2014, NCERT EXEMPLAR]

SOLUTION Let $u=\tan^{-1}\left(\frac{\sqrt{1-x^2}}{x}\right)$ and $v=\cos^{-1}\left(2x\sqrt{1-x^2}\right)$. Let $x=\sin\theta$. Then,

$$x\in\left(\frac{1}{\sqrt{2}},1\right) \Rightarrow \frac{1}{\sqrt{2}}<\sin\theta<1 \Rightarrow \frac{\pi}{4}<\theta<\frac{\pi}{2}$$

Now,

$$u = \tan^{-1}\left(\frac{\sqrt{1-x^2}}{x}\right) = \tan^{-1}\left(\frac{\sqrt{1-\sin^2\theta}}{\sin\theta}\right) = \tan^{-1}(\cot\theta) = \tan^{-1}\left\{\tan\left(\frac{\pi}{2}-\theta\right)\right\}$$

$\Rightarrow \quad u = \frac{\pi}{2} - \theta = \frac{\pi}{2} - \sin^{-1} x \qquad \left[\because \frac{\pi}{4} < \theta < \frac{\pi}{2} \Rightarrow 0 < \frac{\pi}{2} - \theta < \frac{\pi}{4}\right]$

$\Rightarrow \quad \frac{du}{dx} = 0 - \frac{1}{\sqrt{1-x^2}} = -\frac{1}{\sqrt{1-x^2}}$

$v = \cos^{-1}\left(2x\sqrt{1-x^2}\right)$

$\Rightarrow \quad v = \frac{\pi}{2} - \sin^{-1}\left(2x\sqrt{1-x^2}\right) = \frac{\pi}{2} - \sin^{-1}(\sin 2\theta) \qquad [\because x = \sin\theta]$

$\Rightarrow \quad v = \frac{\pi}{2} - \sin^{-1}\{\sin(\pi - 2\theta)\} = \frac{\pi}{2} - (\pi - 2\theta) \qquad \left[\because \frac{\pi}{4} < \theta < \frac{\pi}{2} \Rightarrow 0 < \pi - 2\theta < \frac{\pi}{2}\right]$

$\Rightarrow \quad v = -\frac{\pi}{2} + 2\theta = -\frac{\pi}{2} + 2\sin^{-1} x \Rightarrow \frac{dv}{dx} = \frac{2}{\sqrt{1-x^2}}$

$\therefore \quad \frac{du}{dv} = \frac{\frac{du}{dx}}{\frac{dv}{dx}} = \frac{\frac{-1}{\sqrt{1-x^2}}}{\frac{2}{\sqrt{1-x^2}}} = -\frac{1}{2}$

EXAMPLE 9 *Differentiate* $\tan^{-1}\left(\frac{2x}{1-x^2}\right)$ *with respect to* $\sin^{-1}\left(\frac{2x}{1+x^2}\right)$, *if*

(i) $x \in (-1, 1)$ (ii) $x \in (1, \infty)$ (iii) $x \in (-\infty, -1)$

SOLUTION Let $u = \tan^{-1}\left(\frac{2x}{1-x^2}\right)$ and $v = \sin^{-1}\left(\frac{2x}{1+x^2}\right)$. Putting $x = \tan\theta$, we get

$u = \tan^{-1}\left(\frac{2\tan\theta}{1-\tan^2\theta}\right) = \tan^{-1}(\tan 2\theta)$ and $v = \sin^{-1}\left(\frac{2\tan\theta}{1+\tan^2\theta}\right) = \sin^{-1}(\sin 2\theta)$

(i) *When* $x \in (-1, 1)$: We have,

$x \in (-1, 1)$ and $x = \tan\theta \Rightarrow -1 < \tan\theta < 1 \Rightarrow -\frac{\pi}{4} < \theta < \frac{\pi}{4} \Rightarrow -\frac{\pi}{2} < 2\theta < \frac{\pi}{2}$

$\therefore \quad u = \tan^{-1}(\tan 2\theta) = 2\theta$ and $v = \sin^{-1}(\sin 2\theta) = 2\theta$

$\Rightarrow \quad u = 2\tan^{-1} x$ and $v = 2\tan^{-1} x \qquad [\because x = \tan\theta \Rightarrow \theta = \tan^{-1} x]$

$\Rightarrow \quad \frac{du}{dx} = \frac{2}{1+x^2}$ and $\frac{dv}{dx} = \frac{2}{1+x^2}$

$\therefore \quad \frac{du}{dv} = \frac{\frac{du}{dx}}{\frac{dv}{dx}} = \frac{\frac{2}{1+x^2}}{\frac{2}{1+x^2}} = 1$

(ii) *When* $x \in (1, \infty)$: We have,

$x \in (1, \infty)$ and $x = \tan\theta \Rightarrow 1 < \tan\theta < \infty \Rightarrow \frac{\pi}{4} < \theta < \frac{\pi}{2} \Rightarrow \frac{\pi}{2} < 2\theta < \pi$

$\therefore \quad u = \tan^{-1}(\tan 2\theta) = \tan^{-1}\{-\tan(\pi - 2\theta)\} = \tan^{-1}\{\tan(2\theta - \pi)\} = 2\theta - \pi$

$\Rightarrow \quad u = 2\tan^{-1} x - \pi \qquad [\because \theta = \tan^{-1} x]$

$$\Rightarrow \quad \frac{du}{dx} = \frac{2}{1+x^2} - 0 = \frac{2}{1+x^2}$$

and, $\quad v = \sin^{-1}(\sin 2\theta) = \sin^{-1}\{\sin(\pi - 2\theta)\} = \pi - 2\theta = \pi - 2\tan^{-1} x$

$$\Rightarrow \quad \frac{dv}{dx} = 0 - \frac{2}{1+x^2} = \frac{-2}{1+x^2}$$

$$\therefore \quad \frac{du}{dv} = \frac{\frac{du}{dx}}{\frac{dv}{dx}} = \frac{\frac{2}{1+x^2}}{\frac{-2}{1+x^2}} = -1$$

(iii) *When* $x \in (-\infty, -1)$: We have,

$x = \tan\theta$ and $x \in (-\infty, -1) \Rightarrow -\infty < \tan\theta < -1 \Rightarrow -\frac{\pi}{2} < \theta < -\frac{\pi}{4} \Rightarrow -\pi < 2\theta < -\frac{\pi}{2}$

$$\therefore \quad u = \tan^{-1}(\tan 2\theta) = \tan^{-1}\{\tan(\pi + 2\theta)\} = \pi + 2\theta = \pi + 2\tan^{-1} x$$

$$\Rightarrow \quad \frac{du}{dx} = 0 + \frac{2}{1+x^2} = \frac{2}{1+x^2}$$

and, $v = \sin^{-1}(\sin 2\theta) = \sin^{-1}\{-\sin(\pi + 2\theta)\} = \sin^{-1}(\sin(-\pi - 2\theta)) = -\pi - 2\theta = -\pi - 2\tan^{-1} x$

$$\Rightarrow \quad \frac{dv}{dx} = -\frac{2}{1+x^2}$$

$$\therefore \quad \frac{du}{dv} = \frac{\frac{du}{dx}}{\frac{dv}{dx}} = \frac{\frac{2}{1+x^2}}{-\frac{2}{1+x^2}} = -1$$

EXAMPLE 10 *If* $-\frac{1}{\sqrt{3}} < x < \frac{1}{\sqrt{3}}$, *differentiate* $\tan^{-1}\left(\frac{3x - x^3}{1 - 3x^2}\right)$ *with respect to* $\tan^{-1}\left(\frac{2x}{1 - x^2}\right)$.

SOLUTION Let $u = \tan^{-1}\left(\frac{3x - x^3}{1 - 3x^2}\right)$ and $v = \tan^{-1}\left(\frac{2x}{1 - x^2}\right)$. Putting $x = \tan\theta$, we obtain

$$u = \tan^{-1}(\tan 3\theta) \text{ and } v = \tan^{-1}(\tan 2\theta)$$

$$\Rightarrow \quad u = 3\theta \text{ and } v = 2\theta \quad \left[\begin{array}{l} \because -\frac{1}{\sqrt{3}} < x < \frac{1}{\sqrt{3}} \Rightarrow -\frac{1}{\sqrt{3}} < \tan\theta < \frac{1}{\sqrt{3}} \Rightarrow -\frac{\pi}{6} < \theta < \frac{\pi}{6} \\ \Rightarrow -\frac{\pi}{2} < 3\theta < \frac{\pi}{2} \text{ and } -\frac{\pi}{3} < 2\theta < \frac{\pi}{3} \end{array}\right]$$

$$\Rightarrow \quad u = 3\tan^{-1} x \text{ and } v = 2\tan^{-1} x \Rightarrow \frac{du}{dx} = \frac{3}{1+x^2} \text{ and } \frac{dv}{dx} = \frac{2}{1+x^2}$$

$$\therefore \quad \frac{du}{dv} = \frac{\frac{du}{dx}}{\frac{dv}{dx}} = \frac{\frac{3}{1+x^2}}{\frac{2}{1+x^2}} = \frac{3}{2}.$$

EXERCISE 10.8

BASIC

1. Differentiate $\sec^2(x^2)$ with respect to x^2. [CBSE 2020]
2. Differentiate $\log(1 + x^2)$ with respect to $\tan^{-1} x$.

3. Differentiate $(\log x)^x$ with respect to $\log x$.

4. Differentiate $(\cos x)^{\sin x}$ with respect to $(\sin x)^{\cos x}$.

5. Differentiate $\tan^{-1}\left(\frac{1+ax}{1-ax}\right)$ with respect to $\sqrt{1+a^2x^2}$.

6. Differentiate $\sin^2 x$ with respect to $e^{\cos x}$. [CBSE 2020]

7. Differentiate $\tan^{-1}\left(\frac{\cos x}{1+\sin x}\right)$ with respect to $\sec^{-1} x$.

BASED ON LOTS

8. Differentiate $\sin^{-1}\sqrt{1-x^2}$ with respect to $\cos^{-1} x$, if (i) $x \in (0, 1)$ (ii) $x \in (-1, 0)$.

9. Differentiate $\sin^{-1}(4x\sqrt{1-4x^2})$ with respect to $\sqrt{1-4x^2}$, if

(i) $x \in \left(-\frac{1}{2\sqrt{2}}, \frac{1}{2\sqrt{2}}\right)$ (ii) $x \in \left(\frac{1}{2\sqrt{2}}, \frac{1}{2}\right)$ (iii) $x \in \left(-\frac{1}{2}, -\frac{1}{2\sqrt{2}}\right)$

10. Differentiate $\tan^{-1}\left(\frac{\sqrt{1+x^2}-1}{x}\right)$ with respect to $\sin^{-1}\left(\frac{2x}{1+x^2}\right)$, if $-1 < x < 1, x \neq 0$.

[CBSE 2014, 2016]

11. Differentiate $\sin^{-1}(2x\sqrt{1-x^2})$ with respect to $\sec^{-1}\left(\frac{1}{\sqrt{1-x^2}}\right)$, if:

(i) $x \in (0, 1/\sqrt{2})$ (ii) $x \in (1/\sqrt{2}, 1)$ [CBSE 2023]

12. Differentiate $\sin^{-1}\left(\frac{2x}{1+x^2}\right)$ with respect to $\cos^{-1}\left(\frac{1-x^2}{1+x^2}\right)$, if $0 < x < 1$.

13. Differentiate $\sin^{-1}\left(2x\sqrt{1-x^2}\right)$ with respect to $\tan^{-1}\left(\frac{x}{\sqrt{1-x^2}}\right)$, if $-\frac{1}{\sqrt{2}} < x < \frac{1}{\sqrt{2}}$.

14. Differentiate $\tan^{-1}\left(\frac{2x}{1-x^2}\right)$ with respect to $\cos^{-1}\left(\frac{1-x^2}{1+x^2}\right)$, if $0 < x < 1$.

15. Differentiate $\tan^{-1}\left(\frac{x-1}{x+1}\right)$ with respect to $\sin^{-1}(3x-4x^3)$, if $-\frac{1}{2} < x < \frac{1}{2}$.

16. Differentiate $\sin^{-1}\left(\frac{2x}{1+x^2}\right)$ with respect to $\tan^{-1}\left(\frac{2x}{1-x^2}\right)$, if $-1 < x < 1$.

17. Differentiate $\cos^{-1}(4x^3-3x)$ with respect to $\tan^{-1}\left(\frac{\sqrt{1-x^2}}{x}\right)$, if $\frac{1}{2} < x < 1$.

18. Differentiate $\tan^{-1}\left(\frac{x}{\sqrt{1-x^2}}\right)$ with respect to $\sin^{-1}\left(2x\sqrt{1-x^2}\right)$, if $-\frac{1}{\sqrt{2}} < x < \frac{1}{\sqrt{2}}$. [CBSE 2014]

19. Differentiate $\sin^{-1}\sqrt{1-x^2}$ with respect to $\cot^{-1}\left(\frac{x}{\sqrt{1-x^2}}\right)$, if $0 < x < 1$.

20. Differentiate $\sin^{-1}\left(2ax\sqrt{1-a^2x^2}\right)$ with respect to $\sqrt{1-a^2x^2}$, if $-\frac{1}{\sqrt{2}} < ax < \frac{1}{\sqrt{2}}$.

21. Differentiate $\tan^{-1}\left(\frac{1-x}{1+x}\right)$ with respect to $\sqrt{1-x^2}$, if $-1 < x < 1$.

ANSWERS

1. $2\sec^2(x^2)\tan(x^2)$ 2. $2x$ 3. $x(\log x)^{x-1}\{1+\log x \cdot \log(\log x)\}$

4. $\frac{(\cos x)^{\sin x}\{\cos x \cdot \log \cos x - \sin x \cdot \tan x\}}{(\sin x)^{\cos x}\{-\sin x \log \sin x + \cos x \cdot \cot x\}}$ 5. $\frac{1}{ax\sqrt{1+a^2x^2}}$

6. $-2e^{-\cos x}\cos x$ 7. $\frac{-x\sqrt{x^2-1}}{2}$ 8. (i) 1 (ii) -1 9. (i) $-\frac{1}{x}$ (ii) $\frac{1}{x}$ (iii) $\frac{1}{x}$

10. $\frac{1}{4}$ 11. (i) 2 (ii) -2 12. 1 13. 2 14. 1 15. $\frac{\sqrt{1-x^2}}{3(1+x^2)}$

16. 1 17. 3 18. $\frac{1}{2}$ 19. 1 20. $-\frac{2}{ax}$ 21. $\frac{\sqrt{1-x^2}}{x(1+x^2)}$

10.12 DIFFERENTIATION OF DETERMINANTS

In the previous sections, we have studied differentiation in detail. In this section, we shall discuss the differentiation of determinants.

To differentiate a determinant, we differentiate one row (or column) at a time, keeping others unchanged.

For example, if

$$\Delta(x) = \begin{vmatrix} f(x) & g(x) \\ u(x) & v(x) \end{vmatrix}, \text{ then}$$

$$\frac{d}{dx}\{\Delta(x)\} = \begin{vmatrix} f'(x) & g'(x) \\ u(x) & v(x) \end{vmatrix} + \begin{vmatrix} f(x) & g(x) \\ u'(x) & v'(x) \end{vmatrix}. \text{ Also, } \frac{d}{dx}\{\Delta(x)\} = \begin{vmatrix} f'(x) & g(x) \\ u'(x) & v(x) \end{vmatrix} + \begin{vmatrix} f(x) & g'(x) \\ u(x) & v'(x) \end{vmatrix}$$

Similar results hold for the differentiation of determinants of higher order. Following examples will illustrate the same.

ILLUSTRATIVE EXAMPLES

BASED ON LOWER ORDER THINKING SKILLS (LOTS)

EXAMPLE 1 *If* $f(x) = \begin{vmatrix} x+a^2 & ab & ac \\ ab & x+b^2 & bc \\ ac & bc & x+c^2 \end{vmatrix}$, *find* $f'(x)$.

SOLUTION We have,

$$f(x) = \begin{vmatrix} x+a^2 & ab & ac \\ ab & x+b^2 & bc \\ ac & bc & x+c^2 \end{vmatrix}$$

$$\Rightarrow \quad f'(x) = \begin{vmatrix} 1 & 0 & 0 \\ ab & x+b^2 & bc \\ ac & bc & x+c^2 \end{vmatrix} + \begin{vmatrix} x+a^2 & ab & ac \\ 0 & 1 & 0 \\ ac & bc & x+c^2 \end{vmatrix} + \begin{vmatrix} x+a^2 & ab & ac \\ ab & x+b^2 & bc \\ 0 & 0 & 1 \end{vmatrix}$$

$$\Rightarrow \quad f'(x) = \begin{vmatrix} x+b^2 & bc \\ bc & x+c^2 \end{vmatrix} + \begin{vmatrix} x+a^2 & ac \\ ac & x+c^2 \end{vmatrix} + \begin{vmatrix} x+a^2 & ab \\ ab & x+b^2 \end{vmatrix}$$

$$\Rightarrow \quad f'(x) = \left\{(x+b^2)(x+c^2) - b^2c^2\right\} + \left\{(x+a^2)(x+c^2) - a^2c^2\right\} + \left\{(x+a)^2(x+b^2) - a^2b^2\right\}$$

$$\Rightarrow \quad f'(x) = x^2 + x(b^2+c^2) + x^2 + x(a^2+c^2) + x^2 + x(a^2+b^2) = 3x^2 + 2x(a^2+b^2+c^2).$$

EXAMPLE 2 *If $f_r(x)$, $g_r(x)$ and $h_r(x)$; $r = 1, 2, 3$ are polynomials in x such that $f_r(a) = g_r(a) = h_r(a)$; $r = 1, 2, 3$ and*

$$F(x) = \begin{vmatrix} f_1(x) & f_2(x) & f_3(x) \\ g_1(x) & g_2(x) & g_3(x) \\ h_1(x) & h_2(x) & h_3(x) \end{vmatrix}, \text{ find } F'(x) \text{ at } x = a.$$

SOLUTION We have,

$$F(x) = \begin{vmatrix} f_1(x) & f_2(x) & f_3(x) \\ g_1(x) & g_2(x) & g_3(x) \\ h_1(x) & h_2(x) & h_3(x) \end{vmatrix}$$

$$\therefore \quad F'(x) = \begin{vmatrix} f_1'(x) & f_2'(x) & f_3'(x) \\ g_1(x) & g_2(x) & g_3(x) \\ h_1(x) & h_2(x) & h_3(x) \end{vmatrix} + \begin{vmatrix} f_1(x) & f_2(x) & f_3(x) \\ g_1'(x) & g_2'(x) & g_3'(x) \\ h_1(x) & h_2(x) & h_3(x) \end{vmatrix} + \begin{vmatrix} f_1(x) & f_2(x) & f_3(x) \\ g_1(x) & g_2(x) & g_3(x) \\ h_1'(x) & h_2'(x) & h_3'(x) \end{vmatrix}$$

$$\Rightarrow \quad F'(a) = \begin{vmatrix} f_1'(a) & f_2'(a) & f_3'(a) \\ g_1(a) & g_2(a) & g_3(a) \\ h_1(a) & h_2(a) & h_3(a) \end{vmatrix} + \begin{vmatrix} f_1(a) & f_2(a) & f_3(a) \\ g_1'(a) & g_2'(a) & g_3'(a) \\ h_1(a) & h_2(a) & h_3(a) \end{vmatrix} + \begin{vmatrix} f_1(a) & f_2(a) & f_3(a) \\ g_1(a) & g_2(a) & g_3(a) \\ h_1'(a) & h_2'(a) & h_3'(a) \end{vmatrix}$$

$$\Rightarrow \quad F'(a) = \begin{vmatrix} f'_1(a) & f'_2(a) & f'_3(a) \\ g_1(a) & g_2(a) & g_3(a) \\ g_1(a) & g_2(a) & g_3(a) \end{vmatrix} + \begin{vmatrix} f_1(a) & f_2(a) & f_3(a) \\ g'_1(a) & g'_2(a) & g'_3(a) \\ f_1(a) & f_2(a) & f_3(a) \end{vmatrix} + \begin{vmatrix} f_1(a) & f_2(a) & f_3(x) \\ f_1(a) & f_2(a) & f_3(a) \\ g_1'(a) & g_2'(a) & g_3'(a) \end{vmatrix}$$

[Using: $f_r(a) = g_r(a) = h_r(a)$; $r = 1, 2, 3$]

$\Rightarrow \quad F'(a) = 0 + 0 + 0 = 0$ [$\because$ Two rows are identical in each of the determinants]

EXAMPLE 3 *If $f(x)$, $g(x)$ and $h(x)$ are three polynomials of degree 2, then prove that*

$$\phi(x) = \begin{vmatrix} f(x) & g(x) & h(x) \\ f'(x) & g'(x) & h'(x) \\ f''(x) & g''(x) & h''(x) \end{vmatrix} \text{ is a constant polynomial.}$$

SOLUTION Let $f(x) = a_1 x^2 + a_2 x + a_3$, $g(x) = b_1 x^2 + b_2 x + b_3$ and $h(x) = c_1 x^2 + c_2 x + c_3$.

Then, $f'(x) = 2a_1 x + a_2$, $g'(x) = 2b_1 x + b_2$ and $h'(x) = 2c_1 x + c_2$

$f''(x) = 2a_1$, $g'' = 2b_1$, $h''(x) = 2c_1$ and, $f'''(x) = g'''(x) = h'''(x) = 0$ ...(i)

In order to prove that $\phi(x)$ is a constant polynomial, it is sufficient to show that $\phi''(x) = 0$ for all x.

Now,

$$\phi(x) = \begin{vmatrix} f(x) & g(x) & h(x) \\ f'(x) & g'(x) & h'(x) \\ f''(x) & g''(x) & h''(x) \end{vmatrix}$$

$$\Rightarrow \quad \phi'(x) = \begin{vmatrix} f'(x) & g'(x) & h'(x) \\ f'(x) & g'(x) & h'(x) \\ f''(x) & g''(x) & h''(x) \end{vmatrix} + \begin{vmatrix} f(x) & g(x) & h(x) \\ f''(x) & g''(x) & h''(x) \\ f''(x) & g''(x) & h''(x) \end{vmatrix} + \begin{vmatrix} f(x) & g(x) & h(x) \\ f'(x) & g'(x) & h'(x) \\ f'''(x) & g'''(x) & h'''(x) \end{vmatrix}$$

$$\Rightarrow \quad \phi'(x) = 0 + 0 + \begin{vmatrix} f(x) & g(x) & h(x) \\ f'(x) & g'(x) & h'(x) \\ 0 & 0 & 0 \end{vmatrix} \quad \text{[Using (i)]}$$

$\Rightarrow \quad \phi'(x) = 0 + 0 + 0 = 0$ for all $x \Rightarrow \phi(x) =$ Constant for all x.

Hence, $\phi(x)$ is a constant polynomial.

EXAMPLE 4 *If f, g, h are differentiable functions of x and* $\Delta = \begin{vmatrix} f & g & h \\ (xf)' & (xg)' & (xh)' \\ (x^2 f)'' & (x^2 g)'' & (x^2 h)'' \end{vmatrix}$,

prove that $\Delta' = \begin{vmatrix} f & g & h \\ f' & g' & h' \\ (x^3 f'')' & (x^3 g'')' & (x^3 h'')' \end{vmatrix}$.

SOLUTION We have,

$$(xf)' = xf' + f, (xg)' = xg' + g, (xh)' = xh' + h$$

$$(x^2 f)' = x^2 f' + 2xf, (x^2 g)' = x^2 g' + 2xg, (x^2 h)' = x^2 h' + 2xh$$

$$(x^2 f)'' = x^2 f'' + 4xf' + 2f, (x^2 g)'' = x^2 g'' + 4xg' + 2g \text{ and, } (x^2 h)'' = x^2 h'' + 4xh' + 2h$$

$$\therefore \quad \Delta = \begin{vmatrix} f & g & h \\ xf' + f & xg' + g & xh' + h \\ x^2 f'' + 4xf' + 2f & x^2 g'' + 4xg' + 2g & x^2 h'' + 4xh' + 2h \end{vmatrix}$$

$$\Rightarrow \quad \Delta = \begin{vmatrix} f & g & h \\ xf' & xg' & xh' \\ x^2 f'' + 4xf' & x^2 g'' + 4xg' & x^2 h'' + 4xh' \end{vmatrix} \quad \text{Applying } R_2 \to R_2 - R_1, \text{ and } R_3 \to R_3 - 2R_1$$

$$\Rightarrow \quad \Delta = \begin{vmatrix} f & g & h \\ xf' & xg' & xh' \\ x^2 f'' & x^2 g'' & x^2 h'' \end{vmatrix} \qquad \text{Applying } R_3 \to R_3 - 4R_2$$

$$\Rightarrow \quad \Delta = x \begin{vmatrix} f & g & h \\ f' & g' & h' \\ x^2 f'' & x^2 g'' & x^2 h'' \end{vmatrix} \qquad [\because \text{ Taking } x \text{ common from } R_2]$$

$$\Rightarrow \quad \Delta = \begin{vmatrix} f & g & h \\ f' & g' & h' \\ x^3 f'' & x^3 g'' & x^3 h'' \end{vmatrix} \qquad [\text{Multiplying } R_3 \text{ by } x]$$

$$\therefore \quad \Delta' = \begin{vmatrix} f' & g' & h' \\ f' & g' & h' \\ x^3 f'' & x^3 g'' & x^3 h'' \end{vmatrix} + \begin{vmatrix} f & g & h \\ f'' & g'' & h'' \\ x^3 f'' & x^3 g'' & x^3 h'' \end{vmatrix} + \begin{vmatrix} f & g & h \\ f' & g' & h' \\ (x^3 f'')' & (x^3 g'')' & (x^3 h'')' \end{vmatrix}$$

$$\Rightarrow \quad \Delta' = 0 + 0 + \begin{vmatrix} f & g & h \\ f' & g' & h' \\ (x^3 f'')' & (x^3 g'')' & (x^3 h'')' \end{vmatrix} = \begin{vmatrix} f & g & h \\ f' & g' & h' \\ (x^3 f'')' & (x^3 g'')' & (x^3 h'')' \end{vmatrix}$$

EXAMPLE 5 *If* $y = \begin{vmatrix} f(x) & g(x) & h(x) \\ l & m & n \\ a & b & c \end{vmatrix}$, *prove that* $\frac{dy}{dx} = \begin{vmatrix} f'(x) & g'(x) & h'(x) \\ l & m & n \\ a & b & c \end{vmatrix}$. **[NCERT]**

SOLUTION We have, $y = \begin{vmatrix} f(x) & g(x) & h(x) \\ l & m & n \\ a & b & c \end{vmatrix}$

$$\therefore \quad \frac{dy}{dx} = \begin{vmatrix} \frac{d}{dx}(f(x)) & \frac{d}{dx}(g(x)) & \frac{d}{dx}(h(x)) \\ l & m & n \\ a & b & c \end{vmatrix} + \begin{vmatrix} f(x) & g(x) & h(x) \\ 0 & 0 & 0 \\ a & b & c \end{vmatrix} + \begin{vmatrix} f(x) & g(x) & h(x) \\ l & m & n \\ 0 & 0 & 0 \end{vmatrix}$$

$$\Rightarrow \quad \frac{dy}{dx} = \begin{vmatrix} f'(x) & g'(x) & h'(x) \\ l & m & n \\ a & b & c \end{vmatrix}$$

FILL IN THE BLANKS TYPE QUESTIONS (VBQs)

1. If $y = x|x|$, then $\left(\frac{dy}{dx}\right)_{x=-1}$ = ...

2. If $y = 2x + |x|$, then $\left(\frac{dy}{dx}\right)_{x=-1}$ = ... and $\left(\frac{dy}{dx}\right)_{x=1}$ =................................ .

3. If $f(x) = |x^2 - x|$, then $f'(2)$ = ...

4. If $y = \sin x°$ and $\frac{dy}{dx} = k \cos x°$, then k = ...

5. If $f(x) = e^x g(x)$, $g(0) = 2$, $g'(0) = 1$, then $f'(0)$ = ...

6. If $f(x) = 3|x + 2|$, then $f'(-3)$ = ...

7. If $f(1) = 3$, $f'(2) = 1$, then $\frac{d}{dx}\left\{\ln f(e^x + 2x)\right\}$ = ...

8. If $f(x) = x|x|$, then $f'(x)$ = ...

9. If $f(x) = |x - 1| + |x - 3|$, then $f'(2)$ = ...

10. If $f(x) = |\cos x - \sin x|$, then $f'\left(\frac{\pi}{3}\right)$ = ...

11. If $f(x) = |\cos x|$, then $f'\left(\frac{\pi}{4}\right)$ = ...

12. The derivative of x^2 with respect to x^3 is ....

13. For the curve $\sqrt{x} + \sqrt{y} = 1$, $\frac{dy}{dx}$ at $\left(\frac{1}{4}, \frac{1}{4}\right)$ is ....

14. If $f(x) = |\sin x|$, then $f'\left(-\frac{\pi}{4}\right)$ = ...

15. If $f(x) = |\sin x - \cos x|$, then $f'\left(\frac{\pi}{6}\right)$ = ...

16. If $y = \tan x°$, then $\left(\frac{dy}{dx}\right)_{x=45°}$ = ...

17. If $y = \sin^{-1}(e^x) + \cos^{-1}(e^x)$, then $\frac{dy}{dx}$ = ...

18. If $y = \sin^{-1}(3x - 4x^3)$, $\frac{1}{2} < x < 1$, then $\frac{dy}{dx}$ = ...

19. If $y = \sec^{-1}\left(\frac{\sqrt{x}+1}{\sqrt{x}-1}\right) + \sin^{-1}\left(\frac{\sqrt{x}-1}{\sqrt{x}+1}\right)$, then $\frac{dy}{dx}$ is equal to ....

20. The derivative of $\cos x$ with respect to $\sin x$ is ....

21. The derivative of $\log_{10} x$ with respect to x is ....

22. If $\frac{d}{dx}(f(x)) = \frac{1}{1+x^2}$, then $\frac{d}{dx}\left\{f(x^3)\right\}$ = ...

23. If $y = \cos(\sin x^2)$, then $\frac{dy}{dx}$ at $x = \sqrt{\frac{\pi}{2}}$ is equal to ....

24. If $y = \log|x|$, $x \neq 0$, then $\frac{dy}{dx}$ = ...

25. If $f(x) = ax^2 + bx + c$, then $f'(1) + f'(4) - f'(5)$ is equal to ....

26. If $f'(1) = 2$ and $g'(\sqrt{2}) = 4$, then the derivative of $f(\tan x)$ with respect to $g(\sec x)$ at $x = \frac{\pi}{4}$ is equal to ....

ANSWERS

1. 2 2. 1, 3 3. 3 4. $\frac{\pi}{180}$ 5. 3 6. -3 7. 2 8. $2|x|, x \neq 0$

9. 0 10. $\frac{\sqrt{3}+1}{2}$ 11. $-\frac{1}{\sqrt{2}}$ 12. $\frac{3x}{2}$ 13. -1 14. $-\frac{1}{\sqrt{2}}$ 15. $-\left(\frac{\sqrt{3}+1}{2}\right)$

16. $\frac{\pi}{90}$ 17. 0 18. $\frac{-3}{\sqrt{1-x^2}}$ 19. 0 20. $-\tan x$ 21. $\frac{1}{x}\log_{10} e$

22. $\frac{3x^2}{1+x^6}$ 23. 0 24. $\frac{1}{x}$ 25. b 26. $\frac{1}{\sqrt{2}}$

VERY SHORT ANSWER QUESTIONS (VSAQs)

Answer each of the following questions in one word or one sentence or as per exact requirement of the question:

1. If $f(x) = \log_e(\log_e x)$, then write the value of $f'(e)$.
2. If $f(x) = x + 1$, then write the value of $\frac{d}{dx}(fof)(x)$. [CBSE 2019]
3. If $f'(1) = 2$ and $y = f(\log_e x)$, find $\frac{dy}{dx}$ at $x = e$.
4. If $f(1) = 4$, $f'(1) = 2$, find the value of the derivative of $\log(f(e^x))$ with respect to x at the point $x = 0$.
5. If $f'(x) = \sqrt{2x^2 - 1}$ and $y = f(x^2)$, then find $\frac{dy}{dx}$ at $x = 1$.
6. Let $g(x)$ be the inverse of an invertible function $f(x)$ which is derivable at $x = 3$. If $f(3) = 9$ and $f'(3) = 9$, write the value of $g'(9)$.
7. If $y = \sin^{-1}(\sin x)$, $-\frac{\pi}{2} \leq x \leq \frac{\pi}{2}$. Then, write the value of $\frac{dy}{dx}$ for $x \in \left(-\frac{\pi}{2}, \frac{\pi}{2}\right)$.
8. If $\frac{\pi}{2} \leq x \leq \frac{3\pi}{2}$ and $y = \sin^{-1}(\sin x)$, find $\frac{dy}{dx}$.
9. If $\pi \leq x \leq 2\pi$ and $y = \cos^{-1}(\cos x)$, find $\frac{dy}{dx}$.
10. If $y = \sin^{-1}\left(\frac{2x}{1+x^2}\right)$, write the value of $\frac{dy}{dx}$ for $x > 1$.
11. If $f(0) = f(1) = 0$, $f'(1) = 2$ and $y = f(e^x)\, e^{f(x)}$, write the value of $\frac{dy}{dx}$ at $x = 0$.
12. If $y = x|x|$, find $\frac{dy}{dx}$ for $x < 0$.
13. If $y = \sin^{-1} x + \cos^{-1} x$, find $\frac{dy}{dx}$.

14. If $x = a(\theta + \sin\theta)$, $y = a(1 + \cos\theta)$, find $\frac{dy}{dx}$.

15. If $-\frac{\pi}{2} < x < 0$ and $y = \tan^{-1}\sqrt{\frac{1-\cos 2x}{1+\cos 2x}}$, find $\frac{dy}{dx}$.

16. If $y = x^x$, find $\frac{dy}{dx}$ at $x = e$.

17. If $y = \tan^{-1}\left(\frac{1-x}{1+x}\right)$, find $\frac{dy}{dx}$.

18. If $y = \log_a x$, find $\frac{dy}{dx}$.

19. If $y = \log\sqrt{\tan x}$, write $\frac{dy}{dx}$.

20. If $y = \sin^{-1}\left(\frac{1-x^2}{1+x^2}\right) + \cos^{-1}\left(\frac{1-x^2}{1+x^2}\right)$, find $\frac{dy}{dx}$.

21. If $y = \sec^{-1}\left(\frac{x+1}{x-1}\right) + \sin^{-1}\left(\frac{x-1}{x+1}\right)$, then write the value of $\frac{dy}{dx}$.

22. If $|x| < 1$ and $y = 1 + x + x^2 + \ldots$ to ∞, then find the value of $\frac{dy}{dx}$.

23. If $u = \sin^{-1}\left(\frac{2x}{1+x^2}\right)$ and $v = \tan^{-1}\left(\frac{2x}{1-x^2}\right)$, where $-1 < x < 1$, then write the value of $\frac{du}{dv}$.

24. If $f(x) = \log\left\{\frac{u(x)}{v(x)}\right\}$, $u(1) = v(1)$ and $u'(1) = v'(1) = 2$, then find the value of $f'(1)$.

25. If $y = \log|3x|$, $x \neq 0$, find $\frac{dy}{dx}$.

26. If $f(x)$ is an even function, then write whether $f'(x)$ is even or odd.

27. If $f(x)$ is an odd function, then write whether $f'(x)$ is even or odd.

28. Write the derivative of $\sin x$ with respect to $\cos x$. [CBSE 2014]

29. If $y = \log(\cos e^x)$, then find $\frac{dy}{dx}$. [CBSE 2019]

30. If $f(x) = x + 7$ and $g(x) = x - 7$, $x \in R$, then find $\frac{d}{dx}(fog)(x)$. [CBSE 2019]

31. If $y = x^{1/x}$, then find $\frac{dy}{dx}$ at $x = 1$. [CBSE 2023]

32. If $x = a\sin 2t$, $y = a(\cos 2t + \log\tan t)$, find $\frac{dy}{dx}$. [CBSE 2023]

33. If $x^{1/3} + y^{1/3} = 1$, find $\frac{dy}{dx}$ at the point $\left(\frac{1}{8}, \frac{1}{8}\right)$. [CBSE 2024]

34. If $y = \sqrt{\cos x + y}$, prove that $\frac{dy}{dx} = \frac{\sin x}{1-2y}$. [CBSE 2024]

35. If $y = (\sin^{-1} x)^2$, then find $(1-x^2)\frac{d^2y}{dx^2} - x\frac{dy}{dx}$. [CBSE 2024]

ANSWERS

1. 1	2. 1	3. $\frac{2}{e}$	4. $\frac{1}{2}$	5. 2
6. $\frac{1}{9}$	7. 1	8. –1	9. –1	10. $\frac{-2}{1+x^2}$
11. 2	12. $-2x$	13. 0	14. $-\tan\frac{\theta}{2}$	15. –1
16. $2e^e$	17. $-\frac{1}{1+x^2}$	18. $\frac{1}{x \log_e a}$	19. cosec $2x$	20. 0
21. 0	22. $\frac{1}{(1-x)^2}$	23. 1	24. 0	25. $\frac{1}{x}$
26. odd	27. even	28. $-\cot x$	29. $-\tan(e^x) \cdot e^x$	30. 2
31. 1	32. $\cot 2t$	33. –1	35. 2	

CHAPTER 11

HIGHER ORDER DERIVATIVES

11.1 DEFINITION AND NOTATIONS

If $y = f(x)$, then $\frac{dy}{dx}$, the derivative of y with respect to x, is itself, in general, a function of x and can be differentiated again. To fix up the idea, we shall call $\frac{dy}{dx}$ as the first order derivative of y with respect to x and the derivative of $\frac{dy}{dx}$ with respect to x as the second order derivative of y with respect to x and will be denoted by $\frac{d^2y}{dx^2}$. Similarly the derivative of $\frac{d^2y}{dx^2}$ with respect to x will be termed as the third order derivative of y with respect to x and will be denoted by $\frac{d^3y}{dx^3}$ and so on. The nth order derivative of y with respect to x will be denoted by $\frac{d^n y}{dx^n}$.

If $y = f(x)$, then the other alternative notations for

$$\frac{dy}{dx}, \quad \frac{d^2y}{dx^2}, \quad \frac{d^3y}{dx^3}, \quad \dots, \quad \frac{d^ny}{dx^n} \text{ are}$$

$$\begin{array}{lllll} y_1, & y_2, & y_3, & \dots, & y_n \\ y', & y'', & y''', & \dots, & y^{(n)} \\ Dy, & D^2 y, & D^3 y, & \dots, & D^n y \\ f'(x), & f''(x), & f'''(x), & \dots, & f^n(x) \end{array}$$

The values of these derivatives at $x = a$ are denoted by $y_n(a)$, $y^n(a)$, $D^n y(a)$, $f^n(a)$ or, $\left(\frac{d^ny}{dx^n}\right)_{x=a}$.

ILLUSTRATIVE EXAMPLES

BASED ON BASIC CONCEPTS (BASIC)

Type I ON PROVING RELATIONS INVOLVING VARIOUS ORDER DERIVATIVES OF CARTESIAN FUNCTIONS

EXAMPLE 1 *If* $y = \sin^{-1} x$, *show that* $\frac{d^2 y}{dx^2} = \frac{x}{(1 - x^2)^{3/2}}$.

SOLUTION We have, $y = \sin^{-1} x$. On differentiating with respect to x, we get

$$\frac{dy}{dx} = \frac{1}{\sqrt{1 - x^2}}$$

On differentiating again with respect to x, we get

$$\frac{d^2y}{dx^2} = \frac{d}{dx}\left(\frac{1}{\sqrt{1-x^2}}\right) = \frac{d}{dx}\{(1-x^2)^{-1/2}\} = -\frac{1}{2}(1-x^2)^{-3/2} \times \frac{d}{dx}(1-x^2)$$

$$\Rightarrow \quad \frac{d^2y}{dx^2} = -\frac{1}{2(1-x^2)^{3/2}}(-2x) = \frac{x}{(1-x^2)^{3/2}}.$$

EXAMPLE 2 *If $y = \tan x + \sec x$, prove that* $\dfrac{d^2y}{dx^2} = \dfrac{\cos x}{(1-\sin x)^2}$.

[NCERT EXEMPLAR, CBSE 2023]

SOLUTION We have, $y = \tan x + \sec x$

$$\therefore \quad \frac{dy}{dx} = \sec^2 x + \sec x \tan x = \frac{1}{\cos^2 x} + \frac{\sin x}{\cos^2 x} = \frac{1+\sin x}{\cos^2 x}$$

$$\Rightarrow \quad \frac{dy}{dx} = \frac{1+\sin x}{1-\sin^2 x} = \frac{1}{1-\sin x}$$

$$\Rightarrow \quad \frac{d^2y}{dx^2} = \frac{d}{dx}\left\{\frac{1}{1-\sin x}\right\} = \frac{d}{dx}\{(1-\sin x)^{-1}\}$$

$$\Rightarrow \quad \frac{d^2y}{dx^2} = (-1)(1-\sin x)^{-2}\frac{d}{dx}(1-\sin x) = \frac{-1}{(1-\sin x)^2}(-\cos x) = \frac{\cos x}{(1-\sin x)^2}.$$

EXAMPLE 3 *If $y = \tan x$, prove that $y_2 = 2yy_1$.*

SOLUTION We have, $y = \tan x$

$$\therefore \quad \frac{dy}{dx} = \sec^2 x \quad \text{or,} \quad y_1 = \sec^2 x \qquad \left[\because y_1 = \frac{dy}{dx}\right]$$

$$\Rightarrow \quad \frac{d}{dx}(y_1) = \frac{d}{dx}(\sec^2 x)$$

$$\Rightarrow \quad y_2 = 2\sec x \frac{d}{dx}(\sec x) = 2\sec x \sec x \tan x = 2\tan x \sec^2 x$$

$$\Rightarrow \quad y_2 = 2yy_1 \qquad [\because y = \tan x \text{ and } y_1 = \sec^2 x]$$

EXAMPLE 4 *If $y = x^x$, find* $\dfrac{d^2y}{dx^2}$.

SOLUTION We have, $y = x^x$

$$\therefore \quad \log y = x \log x$$

Differentiating with respect to x, we get

$$\frac{1}{y}\frac{dy}{dx} = 1 \times \log x + x \times \frac{1}{x} \Rightarrow \frac{dy}{dx} = y(1+\log x) \qquad \text{...(i)}$$

Differentiating both sides of (i) with respect to x, we get

$$\frac{d^2y}{dx^2} = \frac{dy}{dx}(1+\log x) + y\frac{d}{dx}(1+\log x)$$

$$\Rightarrow \quad \frac{d^2y}{dx^2} = \frac{dy}{dx}(1+\log x) + y \times \frac{1}{x} = y(1+\log x)^2 + \frac{y}{x} \qquad \text{[Using (i)]}$$

$$\Rightarrow \quad \frac{d^2y}{dx^2} = x^x\left\{(1+\log x)^2 + \frac{1}{x}\right\}$$

EXAMPLE 5 *If* $y=\sqrt{ax+b}$, *prove that* $y\frac{d^2y}{dx^2}+\left(\frac{dy}{dx}\right)^2=0.$ [CBSE 2023]

SOLUTION We have, $y=\sqrt{ax+b} \Rightarrow y^2=ax+b$

Differentiating both sides with respect to x, we obtain

$$2y\frac{dy}{dx}=a$$

Differentiating both sides with respect to x, we obtain

$$2y\frac{d^2y}{dx^2}+2\left(\frac{dy}{dx}\right)^2=0 \Rightarrow y\frac{d^2y}{dx^2}+\left(\frac{dy}{dx}\right)^2=0.$$

BASED ON LOWER ORDER THINKING SKILLS (LOTS)

EXAMPLE 6 *If* $y=A\cos nx+B\sin nx$, *show that* $\frac{d^2y}{dx^2}+n^2y=0.$ [CBSE 2001C]

SOLUTION We have, $y=A\cos nx+B\sin nx$

On differentiating with respect to x, we get

$$\frac{dy}{dx} = -An\sin nx+Bn\cos nx$$

On differentiating again with respect to x, we get

$$\frac{d^2y}{dx^2} = -An^2\cos nx-Bn^2\sin nx = -n^2(A\cos nx+B\sin nx) = -n^2y$$

$$\therefore \quad \frac{d^2y}{dx^2}+n^2y = 0.$$

EXAMPLE 7 *If* $y=Ae^{mx}+Be^{nx}$, *show that* $\frac{d^2y}{dx^2}-(m+n)\frac{dy}{dx}+mny=0.$

[NCERT, CBSE 2007, 2014]

SOLUTION We have, $y = Ae^{mx}+Be^{nx}$

$$\therefore \quad \frac{dy}{dx} = Ame^{mx}+Bne^{nx} \qquad \text{[Differentiating with respect to } x\text{]}$$

$$\Rightarrow \quad \frac{d^2y}{dx^2} = Am^2e^{mx}+Bn^2e^{nx}$$

$$\therefore \quad \frac{d^2y}{dx^2}-(m+n)\frac{dy}{dx}+mny=(Am^2e^{mx}+Bn^2e^{nx})-(m+n)(Ame^{mx}+Bne^{nx})+mn(Ae^{mx}+Be^{nx})=0.$$

EXAMPLE 8 *If* $y=A\cos(\log x)+B\sin(\log x)$, *prove that* $x^2\frac{d^2y}{dx^2}+x\frac{dy}{dx}+y=0.$

[CBSE 2007, 2009]

SOLUTION We have, $y=A\cos(\log x)+B\sin(\log x)$.

On differentiating with respect to x, we get

$$\frac{dy}{dx}=-\frac{1}{x}A\sin(\log x)+\frac{B}{x}\cos(\log x) \Rightarrow x\frac{dy}{dx}=-A\sin(\log x)+B\cos(\log x)$$

On differentiating again with respect to x, we get

$$x\frac{d^2y}{dx^2}+\frac{dy}{dx} = -A\frac{\cos(\log x)}{x}-B\frac{\sin(\log x)}{x}$$

$$\Rightarrow \quad x^2 \frac{d^2y}{dx^2} + x\frac{dy}{dx} = -\{A\cos(\log x) + B\sin(\log x)\}$$

$$\Rightarrow \quad x^2 \frac{d^2y}{dx^2} + x\frac{dy}{dx} = -y \Rightarrow x^2\frac{d^2y}{dx^2} + x\frac{dy}{dx} + y = 0$$

EXAMPLE 9 *If* $y = \log\left\{x + \sqrt{x^2+a^2}\right\}$, *prove that:* $(x^2+a^2)\frac{d^2y}{dx^2} + x\frac{dy}{dx} = 0.$ [CBSE 2013]

SOLUTION We have, $y = \log\left\{x+\sqrt{x^2+a^2}\right\}$

On differentiating with respect to x, we get

$$\frac{dy}{dx} = \frac{1}{x+\sqrt{x^2+a^2}} \times \frac{d}{dx}\left\{x+\sqrt{x^2+a^2}\right\} = \frac{1}{x+\sqrt{x^2+a^2}}\left\{1+\frac{2x}{2\sqrt{x^2+a^2}}\right\}$$

$$\Rightarrow \quad \frac{dy}{dx} = \frac{1}{x+\sqrt{x^2+a^2}} \times \left\{\frac{\sqrt{x^2+a^2}+x}{\sqrt{x^2+a^2}}\right\}$$

$$\Rightarrow \quad y_1 = \frac{1}{\sqrt{x^2+a^2}}, \text{ where } y_1 = \frac{dy}{dx} \Rightarrow y_1^2\,(x^2+a^2) = 1$$

Differentiating with respect to x, we get

$$y_1^2\frac{d}{dx}(x^2+a^2) + (x^2+a^2)\frac{d}{dx}(y_1^2) = 0$$

$$\Rightarrow y_1^2(2x) + (x^2+a^2)\times 2y_1y_2 = 0 \qquad \left[\because \frac{d}{dx}(y_1^2) = 2(y_1)^{2-1}\frac{d}{dx}(y_1) = 2y_1\frac{d}{dx}\left(\frac{dy}{dx}\right) = 2y_1y_2\right]$$

$$\Rightarrow 2y_1\left\{y_2(x^2+a^2) + xy_1\right\} = 0 \Rightarrow y_2(x^2+a^2) + xy_1 = 0 \qquad [\because y_1 \neq 0]$$

EXAMPLE 10 *If* $y = \sin^{-1}x$, *then show that* $(1-x^2)\frac{d^2y}{dx^2} - x\frac{dy}{dx} = 0.$ [CBSE 2012, NCERT]

SOLUTION We have, $y = \sin^{-1}x$

Differentiating with respect to x, we obtain

$$\frac{dy}{dx} = \frac{1}{\sqrt{1-x^2}} \Rightarrow \sqrt{1-x^2}\frac{dy}{dx} = 1$$

Differentiating both sides with respect to x, we get

$$\sqrt{1-x^2}\frac{d^2y}{dx^2} - \frac{x}{\sqrt{1-x^2}}\frac{dy}{dx} = 0$$

$$\Rightarrow \quad (1-x^2)\frac{d^2y}{dx^2} - x\frac{dy}{dx} = 0 \qquad \left[\text{Multiplying both sides by } \sqrt{1-x^2}\right]$$

ALITER We have, $y = \sin^{-1}x \Rightarrow \frac{dy}{dx} = \frac{1}{\sqrt{1-x^2}} \Rightarrow (1-x^2)\left(\frac{dy}{dx}\right)^2 = 1$

Differentiating both sides with respect to x, we get

$$(1-x^2)\left\{2\frac{dy}{dx}\times\frac{d}{dx}\left(\frac{dy}{dx}\right)\right\} - 2x\left(\frac{dy}{dx}\right)^2 = 0$$

$$\Rightarrow \quad 2(1-x^2)\frac{dy}{dx}\frac{d^2y}{dx^2} - 2x\left(\frac{dy}{dx}\right)^2 = 0 \Rightarrow (1-x^2)\frac{d^2y}{dx^2} - x\frac{dy}{dx} = 0.$$

EXAMPLE 11 *If* $y = e^{m\sin^{-1}x}$, *prove that* $(1-x^2)\frac{d^2y}{dx^2} - x\frac{dy}{dx} - m^2y = 0.$ [CBSE 2015]

SOLUTION We have, $y = e^{m\sin^{-1}x}$.

Differentiating with respect to x, we obtain

$$\frac{dy}{dx} = e^{m\sin^{-1}x} \times \frac{m}{\sqrt{1-x^2}}$$

$$\Rightarrow \quad \frac{dy}{dx} = \frac{my}{\sqrt{1-x^2}} \qquad [\because e^{m\sin^{-1}x} = y]$$

$$\Rightarrow \quad \left(\frac{dy}{dx}\right)^2 = \frac{m^2y^2}{1-x^2} \Rightarrow (1-x^2)\left(\frac{dy}{dx}\right)^2 = m^2y^2 \Rightarrow (1-x^2)\ {y_1}^2 = m^2y^2, \text{ where } y_1 = \frac{dy}{dx}$$

Differentiating with respect to x, we obtain

$$(1-x^2)\frac{d}{dx}({y_1}^2) + ({y_1}^2)\frac{d}{dx}(1-x^2) = m^2\frac{d}{dx}(y^2)$$

$$\Rightarrow \quad (1-x^2)\,2y_1y_2 + {y_1}^2(-2x) = m^2(2yy_1) \qquad \left[\because \frac{d}{dx}({y_1}^2) = 2y_1y_2 \text{ and } \frac{d}{dx}(y^2) = 2yy_1\right]$$

$$\Rightarrow \quad 2y_1\left\{(1-x^2)\,y_2 - xy_1 - m^2y\right\} = 0 \Rightarrow (1-x^2)\,y_2 - xy_1 - m^2y = 0 \qquad [\because y_1 \neq 0]$$

EXAMPLE 12 *If* $y = \left\{x + \sqrt{x^2+1}\right\}^m$, *show that* $(x^2+1)\,y_2 + xy_1 - m^2y = 0.$ [CBSE 2013, 2015]

SOLUTION We have, $y = \left\{x + \sqrt{x^2+1}\right\}^m$. Differentiating with respect to x, we get

$$\frac{dy}{dx} = m\left\{x + \sqrt{x^2+1}\right\}^{m-1} \times \frac{d}{dx}\left\{x + \sqrt{x^2+1}\right\}$$

$$\Rightarrow \quad \frac{dy}{dx} = m\left\{[x + \sqrt{x^2+1}\right\}^{m-1} \times \left\{1 + \frac{2x}{2\sqrt{x^2+1}}\right\} = \frac{m\left\{\sqrt{x^2+1}+x\right\}^m}{\sqrt{x^2+1}}$$

$$\Rightarrow \quad \frac{dy}{dx} = \frac{my}{\sqrt{x^2+1}} \Rightarrow y_1 = \frac{my}{\sqrt{x^2+1}} \Rightarrow y_1\sqrt{x^2+1} = my$$

$$\Rightarrow \quad {y_1}^2(x^2+1) = m^2y^2 \qquad \text{[Squaring both sides]}$$

Differentiating with respect to x, we get

$$2y_1\,y_2\,(1+x^2) + {y_1}^2(2x) = 2m^2\,yy_1 \quad \Rightarrow y_2\,(1+x^2) + xy_1 - m^2\,y = 0$$

EXAMPLE 13 *If* $y = \frac{\sin^{-1}x}{\sqrt{1-x^2}}$, *show that* $(1-x^2)\frac{d^2y}{dx^2} - 3x\frac{dy}{dx} - y = 0.$ [CBSE 2013]

SOLUTION We have, $y = \frac{\sin^{-1}x}{\sqrt{1-x^2}} \Rightarrow y\sqrt{1-x^2} = \sin^{-1}x$

Differentiating both sides with respect to x, we get

$$\frac{dy}{dx}\sqrt{1-x^2}-\frac{x}{\sqrt{1-x^2}}y=\frac{1}{\sqrt{1-x^2}}\Rightarrow\frac{dy}{dx}(1-x^2)-xy=1$$

Differentiating both sides with respect to x, we get

$$\frac{d^2y}{dx^2}(1-x^2)-2x\frac{dy}{dx}-x\frac{dy}{dx}-y=0\Rightarrow(1-x^2)\frac{d^2y}{dx^2}-3x\frac{dy}{dx}-y=0$$

EXAMPLE 14 *If* $x=\tan\left(\frac{1}{a}\log y\right)$, *show that* $(1+x^2)\frac{d^2y}{dx^2}+(2x-a)\frac{dy}{dx}=0.$ [CBSE 2011, 2013]

SOLUTION We have,

$$x=\tan\left(\frac{1}{a}\log y\right)\Rightarrow\tan^{-1}x=\frac{1}{a}\log y\Rightarrow a\tan^{-1}x=\log y$$

Differentiating with respect to x, we get:

$$\frac{a}{1+x^2}=\frac{1}{y}\frac{dy}{dx}\Rightarrow(1+x^2)\frac{dy}{dx}=ay$$

Differentiating with respect to x

$$(1+x^2)\frac{d^2y}{dx^2}+2x\frac{dy}{dx}=a\frac{dy}{dx}\Rightarrow(1+x^2)\frac{d^2y}{dx^2}+(2x-a)\frac{dy}{dx}=0$$

Type II **ON FINDING SECOND ORDER DERIVATIVES OF PARAMETRIC FUNCTIONS**

EXAMPLE 15 *Find* $\frac{d^2y}{dx^2}$, *if* $x=at^2$, $y=2at$.

SOLUTION We have, $x=at^2$ and $y=2at$

$$\Rightarrow\quad\frac{dx}{dt}=2at\text{ and }\frac{dy}{dt}=2a\qquad\text{...(i)}$$

$$\therefore\quad\frac{dy}{dx}=\frac{dy/dt}{dx/dt}=\frac{2a}{2at}=\frac{1}{t}$$

Differentiating both sides with respect to x, we get

$$\frac{d^2y}{dx^2}=\frac{d}{dx}\left(\frac{1}{t}\right)=-\frac{1}{t^2}\frac{dt}{dx}=-\frac{1}{t^2}\times\frac{1}{2at}=-\frac{1}{2at^3}\qquad\left[\text{From (i)},\frac{dx}{dt}=2at\therefore\frac{dt}{dx}=\frac{1}{2at}\right]$$

EXAMPLE 16 *If* $x=a\cos^3\theta$, $y=a\sin^3\theta$, *find* $\frac{d^2y}{dx^2}$. *Also, find its value at* $\theta=\frac{\pi}{6}$.

SOLUTION We have, $x=a\cos^3\theta$ and $y=a\sin^3\theta$ [CBSE 2013, 2024]

$$\therefore\quad\frac{dx}{d\theta}=-3a\cos^2\theta\sin\theta\text{ and }\frac{dy}{d\theta}=3a\sin^2\theta\cos\theta$$

So, $$\frac{dy}{dx}=\frac{dy/d\theta}{dx/d\theta}=\frac{3a\sin^2\theta\cos\theta}{-3a\cos^2\theta\sin\theta}=-\tan\theta$$

Differentiating both sides with respect to x, we obtain,

$$\frac{d^2y}{dx^2}=\frac{d}{dx}(-\tan\theta)=-\sec^2\theta\frac{d\theta}{dx}=-\sec^2\theta\times\frac{1}{-3a\cos^2\theta\sin\theta}=\frac{1}{3a}\sec^4\theta\operatorname{cosec}\theta$$

$$\therefore\quad\left(\frac{d^2y}{dx^2}\right)_{\theta=\frac{\pi}{6}}=\frac{1}{3a}\sec^4\frac{\pi}{6}\operatorname{cosec}\frac{\pi}{6}=\frac{1}{3a}\times\left(\frac{2}{\sqrt{3}}\right)^4\times2=\frac{32}{27a}$$

EXAMPLE 17 *If* $x=a\sin t$ *and* $y=a\left(\cos t+\log\tan\frac{t}{2}\right)$, *find* $\frac{d^2y}{dx^2}$. [CBSE 2013]

SOLUTION We have,

$$x = a \sin t \text{ and } y = a\left(\cos t + \log \tan \frac{t}{2}\right)$$

$$\Rightarrow \quad \frac{dx}{dt} = a\cos t \text{ and } \frac{dy}{dt} = a\left(-\sin t + \frac{1}{\tan \frac{t}{2}} \times \sec^2 \frac{t}{2} \times \frac{1}{2}\right)$$

$$\Rightarrow \quad \frac{dx}{dt} = a\cos t \text{ and } \frac{dy}{dt} = a\left(-\sin t + \frac{1}{\sin t}\right)$$

$$\Rightarrow \quad \frac{dx}{dt} = a\cos t \text{ and } \frac{dy}{dt} = \frac{a(1-\sin^2 t)}{\sin t} \Rightarrow \frac{dx}{dt} = a\cos t \text{ and } \frac{dy}{dt} = \frac{a\cos^2 t}{\sin t}$$

$$\therefore \quad \frac{dy}{dx} = \frac{\frac{dy}{dt}}{\frac{dx}{dt}} = \frac{\frac{a\cos^2 t}{\sin t}}{a\cos t} = \frac{\cos t}{\sin t} = \cot t$$

$$\Rightarrow \quad \frac{d^2y}{dx^2} = \frac{d}{dx}\left(\frac{dy}{dx}\right) = \frac{d}{dx}(\cot t) = -\text{cosec}^2\, t\, \frac{dt}{dx} = -\text{cosec}^2\, t \times \frac{1}{a\cos t} = -\frac{1}{a\sin^2 t \cos t}$$

BASED ON HIGHER ORDER THINKING SKILLS (HOTS)

EXAMPLE 18 *If $y = \tan^{-1} x$, find $\frac{d^2y}{dx^2}$ in terms of y alone.* **[NCERT EXEMPLAR]**

SOLUTION We have,

$$y = \tan^{-1} x \Rightarrow x = \tan y$$

Differentiating with respect to y, we obtain

$$\frac{dx}{dy} = \sec^2 y \Rightarrow \frac{dy}{dx} = \frac{1}{\sec^2 y} = \cos^2 y \qquad \left[\because \frac{dy}{dx} = \frac{1}{dx/dy}\right]$$

Differentiating both sides with respect to x, we obtain

$$\frac{d^2y}{dx^2} = \frac{d}{dx}(\cos^2 y) = -2\cos y \sin y \frac{dy}{dx} = -2\cos y \sin y \times \cos^2 y \qquad \left[\because \frac{dy}{dx} = \cos^2 y\right]$$

$$\Rightarrow \quad \frac{d^2y}{dx^2} = -2\sin y \cos^3 y$$

EXAMPLE 19 *If $x^m y^n = (x+y)^{m+n}$, prove that $\frac{d^2y}{dx^2} = 0$.* **[NCERT EXEMPLAR]**

SOLUTION We have,

$$x^m y^n = (x+y)^{m+n} \Rightarrow \frac{dy}{dx} = \frac{y}{x}$$ [See Example 15 on page 11.75]

Differentiating both sides with respect to x, we obtain

$$\frac{d}{dx}\left(\frac{dy}{dx}\right) = \frac{d}{dx}\left(\frac{y}{x}\right) = \frac{x\frac{dy}{dx} - y \times 1}{x^2} = \frac{x\left(\frac{y}{x}\right) - y}{x^2} = 0 \qquad \left[\text{Using: } \frac{dy}{dx} = \frac{y}{x}\right]$$

EXAMPLE 20 *If $y^3 - y = 2x$, prove that $\frac{d^2y}{dx^2} = -\frac{24y}{(3y^2-1)^3}$.*

SOLUTION We have, $y^3 - y = 2x$

Differentiating both sides with respect to y, we obtain

$$(3y^2-1) = 2\frac{dx}{dy} \Rightarrow \frac{dy}{dx} = \frac{2}{(3y^2-1)}$$

Differentiating both sides with respect to x, we obtain

$$\frac{d^2y}{dx^2} = -\frac{2}{(3y^2-1)^2}\frac{d}{dx}(3y^2-1) = -\frac{2}{(3y^2-1)^2} \times 6y\frac{dy}{dx}$$

$$\Rightarrow \quad \frac{d^2y}{dx^2} = -\frac{12y}{(3y^2-1)^2} \times \frac{2}{(3y^2-1)} = -\frac{24y}{(3y^2-1)^3} \qquad \left[\because \frac{dy}{dx} = \frac{2}{3y^2-1}\right]$$

EXAMPLE 21 *If* $e^y(x+1) = 1$, *show that* $\frac{d^2y}{dx^2} = \left(\frac{dy}{dx}\right)^2$. **[NCERT]**

SOLUTION We have,

$$e^y(x+1) = 1 \Rightarrow e^y = \frac{1}{x+1} \Rightarrow \log e^y = \log\left(\frac{1}{x+1}\right) \Rightarrow y = -\log(x+1)$$

$$\Rightarrow \quad \frac{dy}{dx} = -\frac{1}{x+1} \text{ and } \frac{d^2y}{dx^2} = \frac{1}{(x+1)^2} \Rightarrow \frac{d^2y}{dx^2} = \left(\frac{dy}{dx}\right)^2$$

EXAMPLE 22 *If* $(a+bx)\,e^{y/x} = x$ *or,* $y = x\log\left(\frac{x}{a+bx}\right)$, *prove that* $x^3\frac{d^2y}{dx^2} = \left(x\frac{dy}{dx} - y\right)^2$.

[CBSE 2005, 2013, 2015]

SOLUTION We have, $(a+bx)\,e^{y/x} = x$

$$\Rightarrow \quad e^{y/x} = \frac{x}{a+bx} \Rightarrow \frac{y}{x} = \log\left(\frac{x}{a+bx}\right) \Rightarrow y = x\log\left(\frac{x}{a+bx}\right)$$

$$\Rightarrow \quad y = x\{\log x - \log(a+bx)\} \Rightarrow \frac{y}{x} = \log x - \log(a+bx)$$

On differentiating with respect to x, we get

$$\frac{x\frac{dy}{dx} - y}{x^2} = \frac{1}{x} - \frac{1}{a+bx}\frac{d}{dx}(a+bx) = \frac{1}{x} - \frac{b}{a+bx}$$

$$\Rightarrow \quad x\frac{dy}{dx} - y = x^2\left\{\frac{1}{x} - \frac{b}{a+bx}\right\} \Rightarrow x\frac{dy}{dx} - y = \frac{ax}{a+bx} \qquad \text{...(i)}$$

Differentiating both sides of (i) with respect to x, we get

$$x\frac{d^2y}{dx^2} + \frac{dy}{dx} - \frac{dy}{dx} = \frac{(a+bx)\,a - ax\,(0+b)}{(a+bx)^2}$$

$$\Rightarrow \quad x\frac{d^2y}{dx^2} = \frac{a^2}{(a+bx)^2}$$

$$\Rightarrow \quad x^3\frac{d^2y}{dx^2} = \frac{a^2x^2}{(a+bx)^2} \qquad \text{[Multiplying both sides by } x^2\text{]}$$

$$\Rightarrow \quad x^3\frac{d^2y}{dx^2} = \left(\frac{ax}{a+bx}\right)^2 \qquad \text{...(ii)}$$

From (i) and (ii), we obtain : $x^3 \frac{d^2y}{dx^2} = \left(x\frac{dy}{dx} - y\right)^2$.

EXAMPLE 23 *$y = x^x$, prove that* $\frac{d^2y}{dx^2} - \frac{1}{y}\left(\frac{dy}{dx}\right)^2 - \frac{y}{x} = 0.$ **[CBSE 2014, 2016]**

SOLUTION We have, $y = x^x$ or, $y = e^{\log x^x} = e^{x \log x}$

Differentiating with respect to x, we get

$$\frac{dy}{dx} = e^{x\log x}\frac{d}{dx}(x \log x) \Rightarrow \frac{dy}{dx} = x^x(1 + \log x) \Rightarrow \frac{dy}{dx} = y(1 + \log x) \quad ...(i)$$

Differentiating with respect to x, we get

$$\frac{d^2y}{dx^2} = y \times \frac{d}{dx}(1 + \log x) + \frac{dy}{dx} \times (1 + \log x)$$

$$\Rightarrow \quad \frac{d^2y}{dx^2} = y \times \frac{1}{x} + \frac{dy}{dx} \times (1 + \log x)$$

$$\Rightarrow \quad \frac{d^2y}{dx^2} = \frac{y}{x} + \frac{dy}{dx}\left(\frac{1}{y}\frac{dy}{dx}\right) \quad \left[\text{From (i)}, 1 + \log x = \frac{1}{y}\frac{dy}{dx}\right]$$

$$\Rightarrow \quad \frac{d^2y}{dx^2} = \frac{y}{x} + \frac{1}{y}\left(\frac{dy}{dx}\right)^2 \Rightarrow \frac{d^2y}{dx^2} - \frac{1}{y}\left(\frac{dy}{dx}\right)^2 - \frac{y}{x} = 0.$$

Type III ON PROVING RELATIONS INVOLVING VARIOUS ORDER DERIVATIVES OF PARAMETRIC FUNCTIONS

EXAMPLE 24 *If $x = a \cos\theta + b \sin\theta$ and $y = a \sin\theta - b\cos\theta$, prove that* $y^2\frac{d^2y}{dx^2} - x\frac{dy}{dx} + y = 0.$

[CBSE 2013, 2014, 2015]

SOLUTION We have, $x = a\cos\theta + b\sin\theta$ and $y = a\sin\theta - b\cos\theta$

$$\therefore \quad x^2 + y^2 = (a\cos\theta + b\sin\theta)^2 + (a\sin\theta - b\cos\theta)^2$$

$$\Rightarrow \quad x^2 + y^2 = a^2(\cos^2\theta + \sin^2\theta) + b^2(\sin^2\theta + \cos^2\theta) \Rightarrow x^2 + y^2 = a^2 + b^2$$

Differentiating with respect to x, we get

$$2x + 2y\frac{dy}{dx} = 0 \Rightarrow \frac{dy}{dx} = -\frac{x}{y} \quad ...(i)$$

Differentiating with respect to x, we get

$$\frac{d^2y}{dx^2} = -\left\{\frac{y \times 1 - x\frac{dy}{dx}}{y^2}\right\} = -\left\{\frac{y - x\left(-\frac{x}{y}\right)}{y^2}\right\} \quad \text{[Using (i)]}$$

$$\Rightarrow \quad \frac{d^2y}{dx^2} = -\frac{(x^2 + y^2)}{y^3} \quad ...(ii)$$

$$\therefore \quad y^2\frac{d^2y}{dx^2} - x\frac{dy}{dx} + y = -y^2\left(\frac{x^2 + y^2}{y^3}\right) - x\left(-\frac{x}{y}\right) + y = 0 \quad \text{[Using (i) and (ii)]}$$

EXAMPLE 25 *If $x=\sin t$ and $y=\sin pt$, prove that* $(1-x^2)\dfrac{d^2y}{dx^2}-x\dfrac{dy}{dx}+p^2y=0.$

[NCERT EXEMPLAR, CBSE 2016, 2019]

SOLUTION We have,

$$x=\sin t,\ y=\sin pt \Rightarrow \frac{dx}{dt}=\cos t \text{ and, } \frac{dy}{dt}=p\cos pt$$

$$\therefore \quad \frac{dy}{dx}=\frac{dy/dt}{dx/dt}=\frac{p\cos pt}{\cos t}=\frac{p\sqrt{1-\sin^2 pt}}{\sqrt{1-\sin^2 t}}=\frac{p\sqrt{1-y^2}}{\sqrt{1-x^2}}$$

$$\Rightarrow \quad \left(\frac{dy}{dx}\right)^2=\frac{p^2(1-y^2)}{1-x^2} \Rightarrow \left(\frac{dy}{dx}\right)^2(1-x^2)=p^2(1-y^2)$$

Differentiating with respect to x, we obtain

$$(1-x^2)\frac{d}{dx}\left(\frac{dy}{dx}\right)^2+\left(\frac{dy}{dx}\right)^2\frac{d}{dx}(1-x^2)=p^2\left(0-2y\frac{dy}{dx}\right)$$

$$\Rightarrow \quad (1-x^2)\,2\frac{dy}{dx}\frac{d^2y}{dx^2}+\left(\frac{dy}{dx}\right)^2(-2x)=-2p^2y\frac{dy}{dx}$$

$$\Rightarrow \quad 2\frac{dy}{dx}\left\{(1-x^2)\frac{d^2y}{dx^2}-x\frac{dy}{dx}+p^2y\right\}=0 \Rightarrow (1-x^2)\frac{d^2y}{dx^2}-x\frac{dy}{dx}+p^2y=0 \qquad \left[\because 2\frac{dy}{dx}\neq 0\right]$$

EXAMPLE 26 *If $x=\sin\theta$, $y=\cos p\theta$, prove that* $(1-x^2)\,y_2-xy_1+p^2\,y=0$, *where* $y_2=\dfrac{d^2y}{dx^2}$ *and* $y_1=\dfrac{dy}{dx}$.

SOLUTION We have, $x=\sin\theta$ and $y=\cos p\theta$.

$$\therefore \quad \frac{dy}{dx}=\frac{\dfrac{dy}{d\theta}}{\dfrac{dx}{d\theta}}=\frac{-p\sin p\theta}{\cos\theta}=\frac{-p\sqrt{1-\cos^2 p\theta}}{\sqrt{1-\sin^2\theta}}=\frac{-p\sqrt{1-y^2}}{\sqrt{1-x^2}}$$

$$\Rightarrow \quad \left(\frac{dy}{dx}\right)^2=\frac{p^2(1-y^2)}{(1-x^2)} \Rightarrow (1-x^2)\left(\frac{dy}{dx}\right)^2=p^2(1-y^2)$$

Differentiating both sides with respect to x, we get

$$(1-x^2)\,2\frac{dy}{dx}\times\frac{d^2y}{dx^2}-2x\left(\frac{dy}{dx}\right)^2=p^2\left(0-2y\frac{dy}{dx}\right) \Rightarrow (1-x^2)\frac{d^2y}{dx^2}-x\frac{dy}{dx}+p^2y=0$$

Type IV ON PROVING RELATIONS INVOLVING VARIOUS ORDER DERIVATIVES

EXAMPLE 27 *If $(x-a)^2+(y-b)^2=c^2$, prove that* $\dfrac{\left\{1+\left(\dfrac{dy}{dx}\right)^2\right\}^{3/2}}{\dfrac{d^2y}{dx^2}}$ *is a constant independent of a and b.*

[NCERT]

SOLUTION We have,

$$(x-a)^2+(y-b)^2=c^2 \qquad \text{...(i)}$$

Differentiating with respect to x, we get

$$2(x-a)+2(y-b)\frac{dy}{dx} = 0 \Rightarrow (x-a)+(y-b)\frac{dy}{dx} = 0 \quad ...(ii)$$

Differentiating with respect to x, we get

$$1+(y-b)\frac{d^2y}{dx^2}+\left(\frac{dy}{dx}\right)^2 = 0$$

$$\Rightarrow \quad (y-b)\frac{d^2y}{dx^2} = -\left\{1+\left(\frac{dy}{dx}\right)^2\right\} \Rightarrow \frac{d^2y}{dx^2} = -\frac{\left\{1+\left(\frac{dy}{dx}\right)^2\right\}}{y-b} \quad ...(iii)$$

From (ii), we obtain: $\dfrac{dy}{dx} = -\left(\dfrac{x-a}{y-b}\right)$

$$\therefore \quad 1+\left(\frac{dy}{dx}\right)^2 = 1+\frac{(x-a)^2}{(y-b)^2} = \frac{(x-a)^2+(y-b)^2}{(y-b)^2} = \frac{c^2}{(y-b)^2} \quad \text{[Using (i)]} \quad ...(iv)$$

$$\Rightarrow \quad \left\{1+\left(\frac{dy}{dx}\right)^2\right\}^{3/2} = \left\{\frac{c^2}{(y-b)^2}\right\}^{3/2} = \frac{c^3}{(y-b)^3} \quad ...(v)$$

From (iii) and (iv), we obtain

$$\frac{d^2y}{dx^2} = -\frac{\left\{1+\left(\frac{dy}{dx}\right)^2\right\}}{y-b} = -\frac{c^2/(y-b)^2}{(y-b)} = \frac{-c^2}{(y-b)^3} \quad ...(vi)$$

From (v) and (vi), we obtain

$$\frac{\left\{1+\left(\frac{dy}{dx}\right)^2\right\}^{3/2}}{\frac{d^2y}{dx^2}} = \frac{\frac{c^3}{(y-b)^3}}{\frac{-c^2}{(y-b)^3}} = -c, \text{ which is independent of } a \text{ and } b.$$

EXAMPLE 28 *If $y^2 = a^2\cos^2 x + b^2\sin^2 x$, then prove that $\dfrac{d^2y}{dx^2}+y = \dfrac{a^2b^2}{y^3}$.*

SOLUTION We have,

$$y^2 = a^2\cos^2 x + b^2\sin^2 x$$

$$\Rightarrow \quad 2y^2 = a^2(2\cos^2 x)+b^2(2\sin^2 x) = a^2(1+\cos 2x)+b^2(1-\cos 2x)$$

$$\Rightarrow \quad 2y^2 = (a^2+b^2)+(a^2-b^2)\cos 2x \quad ...(i)$$

Differentiating with respect to x, we get

$$4y\frac{dy}{dx} = -2(a^2-b^2)\sin 2x \Rightarrow 2y\frac{dy}{dx} = -(a^2-b^2)\sin 2x \quad ...(ii)$$

From (i), we obtain

$$2y^2-(a^2+b^2) = (a^2-b^2)\cos 2x \quad ...(iii)$$

Squaring (ii) and (iii) and adding, we get

$$4y^2\left(\frac{dy}{dx}\right)^2+\left\{2y^2-(a^2+b^2)\right\}^2 = (a^2-b^2)^2\{\sin^2 2x+\cos^2 2x\}$$

$$\Rightarrow \quad 4y^2\left(\frac{dy}{dx}\right)^2 + 4y^4 - 4y^2(a^2+b^2) + (a^2+b^2)^2 = (a^2-b^2)^2$$

$$\Rightarrow \quad 4y^2\left\{\left(\frac{dy}{dx}\right)^2 + y^2 - (a^2+b^2)\right\} = (a^2-b^2)^2 - (a^2+b^2)^2$$

$$\Rightarrow \quad 4y^2\left\{\left(\frac{dy}{dx}\right)^2 + y^2 - (a^2+b^2)\right\} = -4a^2b^2 \Rightarrow \left(\frac{dy}{dx}\right)^2 + y^2 - (a^2+b^2) = -\frac{a^2b^2}{y^2}$$

Differentiating both sides with respect to x, we get

$$2\left(\frac{dy}{dx}\right)\frac{d^2y}{dx^2} + 2y\frac{dy}{dx} = \frac{2a^2b^2}{y^3}\frac{dy}{dx} \Rightarrow \frac{d^2y}{dx^2} + y = \frac{a^2b^2}{y^3} \quad \left[\text{Dividing both sides by } 2\frac{dy}{dx}\right]$$

EXAMPLE 29 *If $f(x) = |x|^3$, show that $f''(x)$ exists for all real x and find it.*

SOLUTION We have, **[NCERT]**

$$f(x) = |x|^3 = \begin{cases} x^3, & \text{if } x \geq 0 \\ (-x)^3 = -x^3, & \text{if } x < 0 \end{cases}$$

Now,

$$(\text{LHD of } f(x) \text{ at } x=0) = \lim_{x \to 0^-} \frac{f(x)-f(0)}{x-0} = \lim_{x \to 0^-} \frac{-x^3-0}{x} = \lim_{x \to 0^-} -x^2 = 0$$

$$(\text{RHD of } f(x) \text{ at } x=0) = \lim_{x \to 0^+} \frac{f(x)-f(0)}{x-0} = \lim_{x \to 0^+} \frac{x^3-0}{x} = \lim_{x \to 0} x^2 = 0$$

$\therefore \quad (\text{LHD of } f(x) \text{ at } x=0) = (\text{RHD of } f(x) \text{ at } x=0)$

So, $f(x)$ is differentiable at $x=0$ and the derivative of $f(x)$ is given by

$$f'(x) = \begin{cases} 3x^2, & \text{if } x \geq 0 \\ -3x^2, & \text{if } x < 0 \end{cases}$$

Now,

$$(\text{LHD of } f'(x) \text{ at } x=0) = \lim_{x \to 0^-} \frac{f'(x)-f'(0)}{x-0} = \lim_{x \to 0^-} \frac{-3x^2-0}{x} = \lim_{x \to 0^-} -3x = 0$$

$$(\text{RHD of } f'(x) \text{ at } x=0) = \lim_{x \to 0^+} \frac{f'(x)-f'(0)}{x-0} = \lim_{x \to 0^+} \frac{3x^2-0}{x-0} = \lim_{x \to 0^+} 3x = 0$$

$\therefore \quad (\text{LHD of } f'(x) \text{ at } x=0) = (\text{RHD of } f'(x) \text{ at } x=0)$

So, $f'(x)$ is differentiable at $x=0$.

Hence, $f''(x) = \begin{cases} 6x, & \text{if } x \geq 0 \\ -6x, & \text{if } x < 0 \end{cases}$.

Type V MISCELLANEOUS PROBLEMS

EXAMPLE 30 *In $\frac{dy}{dx}$, x is independent variable and y is the dependent variable. If independent and dependent variables are interchanged $\frac{dy}{dx}$ becomes $\frac{dx}{dy}$ and these two are connected by the relation $\frac{dy}{dx}\cdot\frac{dx}{dy} = 1$. Find a relation between $\frac{d^2y}{dx^2}$ and $\frac{d^2x}{dy^2}$.*

SOLUTION We know that

$$\frac{d^2y}{dx^2} = \frac{d}{dx}\left(\frac{dy}{dx}\right)$$

$$\Rightarrow \quad \frac{d^2y}{dx^2} = \frac{d}{dx}\left(\frac{1}{dx/dy}\right) = \frac{d}{dx}\left\{\left(\frac{dx}{dy}\right)^{-1}\right\}$$

$$\Rightarrow \quad \frac{d^2y}{dx^2} = \frac{d}{dy}\left\{\left(\frac{dx}{dy}\right)^{-1}\right\}\frac{dy}{dx} = \left\{-\left(\frac{dx}{dy}\right)^{-2}\frac{d}{dy}\left(\frac{dx}{dy}\right)\right\} \times \frac{1}{dx/dy}$$

$$\Rightarrow \quad \frac{d^2y}{dx^2} = \left\{-\left(\frac{dx}{dy}\right)^{-2}\frac{d^2x}{dy^2}\right\} \times \left(\frac{dx}{dy}\right)^{-1} = -\left(\frac{dx}{dy}\right)^{-3}\frac{d^2x}{dy^2}$$

Hence, $\frac{d^2y}{dx^2} = -\left(\frac{dx}{dy}\right)^{-3}\frac{d^2x}{dy^2}$ or, $\left(\frac{dy}{dx}\right)^3\frac{d^2y}{dx^2} = -\frac{d^2x}{dy^2}$

EXAMPLE 31 *Find the equation to which the equation* $x\frac{d^2y}{dx^2} + \left(\frac{dy}{dx}\right)^2 - y\frac{dy}{dx} = 0$ *is transformed by interchanging the independent and dependent variables.*

SOLUTION We know that

$$\frac{dy}{dx} = \frac{1}{dx/dy} \text{ and } \frac{d^2y}{dx^2} = -\frac{1}{(dx/dy)^3}\frac{d^2x}{dy^2} \qquad \text{[See Example 29]}$$

Substituting these values in the equation $x\frac{d^2y}{dx^2} + \left(\frac{dy}{dx}\right)^2 - \left(\frac{dy}{dx}\right) = 0$, we get

$$-\frac{x}{\left(\frac{dx}{dy}\right)^3}\frac{d^2x}{dy^2} + \left(\frac{1}{\frac{dx}{dy}}\right)^2 - \frac{y}{\left(\frac{dx}{dy}\right)} = 0$$

$$\Rightarrow \quad -x\frac{d^2x}{dy^2} + \frac{dx}{dy} - y\left(\frac{dx}{dy}\right)^2 = 0 \qquad \left[\text{Multiplying both sides by } \left(\frac{dx}{dy}\right)^3\right]$$

$$\Rightarrow \quad x\frac{d^2x}{dy^2} + y\left(\frac{dx}{dy}\right)^2 - \frac{dx}{dy} = 0$$

EXERCISE 11.1

BASIC

1. Find the second order derivatives of each of the following functions:
   (i) $x^3 + \tan x$ (ii) $\sin(\log x)$ [NCERT] (iii) $\log(\sin x)$ [NCERT]
   (iv) $e^x \sin 5x$ [NCERT] (v) $e^{6x}\cos 3x$ [NCERT] (vi) $x^3 \log x$ [NCERT]
   (vii) $\tan^{-1} x$ [NCERT] (viii) $x\cos x$ [NCERT] (ix) $\log(\log x)$ [NCERT]
2. If $y = e^{-x}\cos x$, show that $\frac{d^2y}{dx^2} = 2e^{-x}\sin x$.
3. If $y = x + \tan x$, show that $\cos^2 x\frac{d^2y}{dx^2} - 2y + 2x = 0$. [CBSE 2007]

4. If $y = x^3 \log x$, prove that $\dfrac{d^4y}{dx^4} = \dfrac{6}{x}$.

5. If $y = \log(\sin x)$, prove that $\dfrac{d^3y}{dx^3} = 2\cos x \operatorname{cosec}^3 x$.

6. If $y = 2\sin x + 3\cos x$, show that $\dfrac{d^2y}{dx^2} + y = 0$.

7. If $y = \dfrac{\log x}{x}$, show that $\dfrac{d^2y}{dx^2} = \dfrac{2\log x - 3}{x^3}$.

8. If $x = a\sec\theta$, $y = b\tan\theta$, prove that $\dfrac{d^2y}{dx^2} = -\dfrac{b^4}{a^2 y^3}$.

9. If $x = a(\cos\theta + \theta\sin\theta)$, $y = a(\sin\theta - \theta\cos\theta)$, prove that
$\dfrac{d^2x}{d\theta^2} = a(\cos\theta - \theta\sin\theta)$, $\dfrac{d^2y}{d\theta^2} = a(\sin\theta + \theta\cos\theta)$ and $\dfrac{d^2y}{dx^2} = \dfrac{\sec^3\theta}{a\theta}$.

[NCERT, CBSE 2012, 2017]

10. If $y = e^x \cos x$, prove that $\dfrac{d^2y}{dx^2} = 2e^x \cos\left(x + \dfrac{\pi}{2}\right)$. [CBSE 2012]

11. If $x = a\cos\theta, y = b\sin\theta$, show that $\dfrac{d^2y}{dx^2} = -\dfrac{b^4}{a^2 y^3}$. [CBSE 2020]

12. If $x = a(1 - \cos^3\theta)$, $y = a\sin^3\theta$, prove that $\dfrac{d^2y}{dx^2} = \dfrac{32}{27a}$ at $\theta = \dfrac{\pi}{6}$.

13. If $x = a(\theta + \sin\theta)$, $y = a(1 + \cos\theta)$, prove that $\dfrac{d^2y}{dx^2} = -\dfrac{a}{y^2}$.

14. If $x = a(\theta - \sin\theta)$, $y = a(1 + \cos\theta)$ find $\dfrac{d^2y}{dx^2}$. [CBSE 2011]

15. If $x = a(1 - \cos\theta)$, $y = a(\theta + \sin\theta)$, prove that $\dfrac{d^2y}{dx^2} = -\dfrac{1}{a}$ at $\theta = \dfrac{\pi}{2}$.

16. If $x = a(1 + \cos\theta)$, $y = a(\theta + \sin\theta)$, prove that $\dfrac{d^2y}{dx^2} = \dfrac{-1}{a}$ at $\theta = \dfrac{\pi}{2}$.

BASED ON LOTS

17. If $x = \cos\theta, y = \sin^3\theta$, prove that $y\dfrac{d^2y}{dx^2} + \left(\dfrac{dy}{dx}\right)^2 = 3\sin^2\theta\,(5\cos^2\theta - 1)$. [CBSE 2013]

18. If $y = \sin(\sin x)$, prove that $\dfrac{d^2y}{dx^2} + \tan x\dfrac{dy}{dx} + y\cos^2 x = 0$. [CBSE 2018]

19. If $x = \sin t$, $y = \sin pt$, prove that $(1 - x^2)\dfrac{d^2y}{dx^2} - x\dfrac{dy}{dx} + p^2 y = 0$.

20. If $y = (\sin^{-1} x)^2$, prove that $(1 - x^2)y_2 - xy_1 - 2 = 0$. [CBSE 2019]

21. If $y = e^{\tan^{-1} x}$, prove that $(1 + x^2)y_2 + (2x - 1)y_1 = 0$.

22. If $y = 3\cos(\log x) + 4\sin(\log x)$, prove that $x^2y_2 + xy_1 + y = 0$.

[NCERT, CBSE 2009, 2012, 2016]

23. If $y = e^{2x}(ax + b)$, show that $y_2 - 4y_1 + 4y = 0$.

24. If $x = \sin\left(\frac{1}{a}\log y\right)$, show that $(1 - x^2)\, y_2 - x\, y_1 - a^2\, y = 0$. [CBSE 2010]

25. If $\log y = \tan^{-1} x$, show that $(1 + x^2)\, y_2 + (2x - 1)\, y_1 = 0$.

26. If $y = \tan^{-1} x$, show that $(1 + x^2)\frac{d^2y}{dx^2} + 2x\frac{dy}{dx} = 0$.

27. If $y = \left\{\log\left(x + \sqrt{x^2 + 1}\right)\right\}^2$, show that $(1 + x^2)\frac{d^2y}{dx^2} + x\frac{dy}{dx} = 2$. [CBSE 2008]

28. If $y = (\tan^{-1} x)^2$, then prove that $(1 + x^2)^2\, y_2 + 2x\,(1 + x^2)\, y_1 = 2$.
[CBSE 2012, 2024, [NCERT]

29. If $y = \cot x$ show that $\frac{d^2y}{dx^2} + 2y\frac{dy}{dx} = 0$.

30. Find $\frac{d^2y}{dx^2}$, where $y = \log\left(\frac{x^2}{e^2}\right)$. [CBSE 2000]

31. If $y = ae^{2x} + be^{-x}$, show that, $\frac{d^2y}{dx^2} - \frac{dy}{dx} - 2y = 0$. [CBSE 2000C]

32. If $y = e^x(\sin x + \cos x)$ prove that $\frac{d^2y}{dx^2} - 2\frac{dy}{dx} + 2y = 0$. [CBSE 2002, 2009]

33. If $y = \cos^{-1} x$, find $\frac{d^2y}{dx^2}$ in terms of y alone. [NCERT]

34. If $y = e^{a\cos^{-1} x}$, prove that $(1 - x^2)\frac{d^2y}{dx^2} - x\frac{dy}{dx} - a^2\, y = 0$. [NCERT, CBSE 2012, 2020]

35. If $y = 500\, e^{7x} + 600\, e^{-7x}$, show that $\frac{d^2y}{dx^2} = 49\, y$. [NCERT]

36. If $x = 2\cos t - \cos 2t$, $y = 2\sin t - \sin 2t$, find $\frac{d^2y}{dx^2}$ at $t = \frac{\pi}{2}$.

37. If $x = 4z^2 + 5$, $y = 6z^2 + 7z + 3$, find $\frac{d^2y}{dx^2}$.

38. If $y = \log(1 + \cos x)$, prove that $\frac{d^3y}{dx^3} + \frac{d^2y}{dx^2}\cdot\frac{dy}{dx} = 0$. [CBSE 2005]

39. If $y = \sin(\log x)$, prove that $x^2\frac{d^2y}{dx^2} + x\frac{dy}{dx} + y = 0$. [CBSE 2007]

40. If $y = 3\,e^{2x} + 2\,e^{3x}$, prove that $\frac{d^2y}{dx^2} - 5\frac{dy}{dx} + 6y = 0$. [NCERT, CBSE 2007, 2009]

41. If $y = (\cot^{-1} x)^2$, prove that $y_2\,(x^2 + 1)^2 + 2x\,(x^2 + 1)\, y_1 = 2$.

42. If $y = \operatorname{cosec}^{-1} x$, $x > 1$, then show that $x(x^2 - 1)\frac{d^2y}{dx^2} + (2x^2 - 1)\frac{dy}{dx} = 0$. [CBSE 2010]

43. If $x = \cos t + \log\tan\frac{t}{2}$, $y = \sin t$, then find the value of $\frac{d^2y}{dt^2}$ and $\frac{d^2y}{dx^2}$ at $t = \frac{\pi}{4}$. [CBSE 2012]

44. If $x = a\sin t$ and $y = a\left(\cos t + \log\tan\frac{t}{2}\right)$, find $\frac{d^2y}{dx^2}$. [CBSE 2013]

45. If $x = a(\cos t + t\sin t)$ and $y = a(\sin t - t\cos t)$, then find the value of $\frac{d^2y}{dx^2}$ at $t = \frac{\pi}{4}$. [CBSE 2014]

46. If $x = a\left(\cos t + \log\tan\frac{t}{2}\right)$, $y = a\sin t$, evaluate $\frac{d^2y}{dx^2}$ at $t = \frac{\pi}{3}$. [CBSE 2014]

47. If $x = a(\cos 2t + 2t\sin 2t)$ and $y = a(\sin 2t - 2t\cos 2t)$, then find $\frac{d^2y}{dx^2}$. [CBSE 2015]

48. If $x = 3\cos t - 2\cos^3 t$, $y = 3\sin t - 2\sin^3 t$, find $\frac{d^2y}{dx^2}$. [CBSE 2017]

BASED ON HOTS

49. If $x = a\sin t - b\cos t$, $y = a\cos t + b\sin t$, prove that $\frac{d^2y}{dx^2} = -\frac{x^2+y^2}{y^3}$.

50. Find A and B so that $y = A\sin 3x + B\cos 3x$ satisfies the equation

$$\frac{d^2y}{dx^2} + 4\frac{dy}{dx} + 3y = 10\cos 3x.$$

51. If $y = Ae^{-kt}\cos(pt + c)$, prove that $\frac{d^2y}{dt^2} + 2k\frac{dy}{dt} + n^2y = 0$, where $n^2 = p^2 + k^2$.

52. If $y = x^n\{a\cos(\log x) + b\sin(\log x)\}$, prove that $x^2\frac{d^2y}{dx^2} + (1-2n)x\frac{dy}{dx} + (1+n^2)y = 0$.

53. If $y = a\left\{x + \sqrt{x^2+1}\right\}^n + b\left\{x - \sqrt{x^2+1}\right\}^n$, prove that $(x^2+1)\frac{d^2y}{dx^2} + x\frac{dy}{dx} - n^2y = 0$.

ANSWERS

1. (i) $6x + 2\sec^2 x\tan x$ (ii) $\frac{-[\sin(\log x) + \cos(\log x)]}{x^2}$ (iii) $-\text{cosec}^2 x$

(iv) $2e^x(5\cos 5x - 12\sin 5x)$ (v) $9e^{6x}(3\cos 3x - 4\sin 3x)$ (vi) $x(5 + 6\log x)$

(vii) $\frac{-2x}{(1+x^2)^2}$ (viii) $-x\cos x - 2\sin x$ (ix) $-\frac{(1+\log x)}{(x\log x)^2}$

14. (ii) $\frac{1}{4a}\text{cosec}^4\frac{\theta}{2}$ 30. $-\frac{2}{x^2}$ 33. $-\cot y\,\text{cosec}^2 y$

36. $-\frac{3}{2}$ 37. $-\frac{7}{64z^3}$ 43. $\left(\frac{d^2y}{dt^2}\right)_{t=\frac{\pi}{4}} = -\frac{1}{\sqrt{2}}$, $\left(\frac{d^2y}{dx^2}\right)_{t=\frac{\pi}{4}} = 2\sqrt{2}$

44. $-\frac{1}{a\sin^2 t\cos t}$ 45. $\frac{8\sqrt{2}}{\pi a}$ 46. $\frac{8\sqrt{3}}{a}$ 47. $\frac{1}{2at}\sec^3 2t$

48. $-\frac{1}{3\sin^3 t\cos 2t}$ 50. $A = \frac{2}{3}, B = -\frac{1}{3}$

HINTS TO SELECTED PROBLEMS

1. (ii) Let $y = \sin(\log x)$. Then,

$$\frac{dy}{dx} = \frac{\cos(\log x)}{x} \Rightarrow \frac{d^2y}{dx^2} = \frac{d}{dx}\left(\frac{1}{x}\right)\cos(\log x) + \frac{1}{x}\frac{d}{dx}\{\cos(\log x)\}$$

$$\Rightarrow \frac{d^2y}{dx^2} = -\frac{\cos(\log x)}{x^2} - \frac{\sin(\log x)}{x^2} = -\frac{1}{x^2}\left\{\cos(\log x) + \sin(\log x)\right\}$$

(iii) Let $y = \log(\sin x)$. Then, $\frac{dy}{dx} = \cot x \Rightarrow \frac{d^2y}{dx^2} = -\text{cosec}^2 x$

(iv) Let $y = e^x \sin 5x$. Then,

$$\frac{dy}{dx} = e^x \sin 5x + e^x (5 \cos 5x) = e^x (\sin 5x + 5 \cos 5x)$$

$$\Rightarrow \frac{d^2y}{dx^2} = \frac{d}{dx}(e^x) \cdot (\sin 5x + 5 \cos 5x) + e^x \frac{d}{dx}(\sin 5x + 5 \cos 5x)$$

$$\Rightarrow \frac{d^2y}{dx^2} = e^x (\sin 5x + 5 \cos 5x) + e^x (5 \cos 5x - 25 \sin 5x) = e^x (-24 \sin 5x + 10 \cos 5x)$$

(v) Let $y = e^{6x} \cos 3x$. Then,

$$\frac{dy}{dx} = \frac{d}{dx}(e^{6x}) \cos 3x + e^{6x} \frac{d}{dx}(\cos 3x)$$

$$\Rightarrow \frac{dy}{dx} = 6 e^{6x} \cos 3x - 3 e^{6x} \sin 3x \Rightarrow \frac{dy}{dx} = 3 e^{6x} (2 \cos 3x - \sin 3x)$$

$$\Rightarrow \frac{d^2y}{dx^2} = 3 \frac{d}{dx}(e^{6x}) (2 \cos 3x - \sin 3x) + 3 e^{6x} \frac{d}{dx}(2 \cos 3x - \sin 3x)$$

$$\Rightarrow \frac{d^2y}{dx^2} = 18 e^{6x} (2 \cos 3x - \sin 3x) + 3e^{6x} (-6 \sin 3x - 3 \cos 3x)$$

$$\Rightarrow \frac{d^2y}{dx^2} = 9 e^{6x} \{4 \cos 3x - 2 \sin 3x - 2 \sin 3x - \cos 3x\} = 9 e^{6x} (3 \cos 3x - 4 \sin 3x)$$

(vi) Let $y = x^3 \log x$. Then,

$$\frac{dy}{dx} = \log x \frac{d}{dx}(x^3) + x^3 \frac{d}{dx}(\log x)$$

$$\Rightarrow \frac{dy}{dx} = 3x^2 \log x + x^3 \times \frac{1}{x} \Rightarrow \frac{dy}{dx} = x^2 (3 \log x + 1)$$

$$\Rightarrow \frac{d^2y}{dx^2} = (3 \log x + 1) \frac{d}{dx}(x^2) + x^2 \frac{d}{dx}(3 \log x + 1)$$

$$\Rightarrow \frac{d^2y}{dx^2} = 2x (3 \log x + 1) + x^2 \times \frac{3}{x} = x (6 \log x + 5)$$

(vii) Let $y = \tan^{-1} x$. Then,

$$\frac{dy}{dx} = \frac{1}{1 + x^2} = (1 + x^2)^{-1} \Rightarrow \frac{d^2y}{dx^2} = -(1 + x^2)^{-2} \frac{d}{dx}(1 + x^2) = -\frac{2x}{(1 + x^2)^2}$$

(viii) Let $y = x \cos x$. Then,

$$\frac{dy}{dx} = \cos x - x \sin x \Rightarrow \frac{d^2y}{dx^2} = -\sin x - (\sin x + x \cos x) = -2 \sin x - x \cos x$$

(ix) Let $y = \log(\log x)$. Then,

$$\frac{dy}{dx} = \frac{1}{\log x} \frac{d}{dx}(\log x) = \frac{1}{x \log x} = (x \log x)^{-1}$$

$$\Rightarrow \frac{d^2y}{dx^2} = \frac{d}{dx}\{(x \log x)^{-1}\}$$

$$\Rightarrow \frac{d^2y}{dx^2} = -(x \log x)^{-2} \frac{d}{dx}(x \log x) = -\frac{1}{(x \log x)^2}(1 + \log x) = \frac{-(1 + \log x)}{(x \log x)^2}$$

22. We have,

$$y = 3\cos(\log x) + 4\sin(\log x)$$

$$\Rightarrow \frac{dy}{dx} = -\frac{3}{x}\sin(\log x) + \frac{4}{x}\cos(\log x) \Rightarrow x\frac{dy}{dx} = -3\sin(\log x) + 4\cos(\log x)$$

Differentiating both sides with respect to x, we get

$$x\frac{d^2y}{dx^2} + \frac{dy}{dx} = \frac{-3}{x}\cos(\log x) - \frac{4}{x}\sin(\log x)$$

$$\Rightarrow x^2\frac{d^2y}{dx^2} + x\frac{dy}{dx} = -\{3\cos(\log x) + 4\sin(\log x)\}$$

$$\Rightarrow x^2\frac{d^2y}{dx^2} + x\frac{dy}{dx} = -y \Rightarrow x^2\frac{d^2y}{dx^2} + x\frac{dy}{dx} + y = 0$$

28. We have,

$$y = (\tan^{-1} x)^2$$

$$\Rightarrow \frac{dy}{dx} = 2(\tan^{-1} x)^{2-1}\frac{d}{dx}(\tan^{-1} x)$$

$$\Rightarrow \frac{dy}{dx} = \frac{2}{1+x^2}\tan^{-1} x \Rightarrow (1+x^2)\frac{dy}{dx} = 2\tan^{-1} x$$

$$\Rightarrow (1+x^2)^2\left(\frac{dy}{dx}\right)^2 = 4(\tan^{-1} x)^2 \qquad \text{[Squaring both sides]}$$

$$\Rightarrow (1+x^2)^2\left(\frac{dy}{dx}\right)^2 = 4y$$

Differentiating both sides with respect to x, we get

$$2(1+x^2)\times 2x\left(\frac{dy}{dx}\right)^2 + 2(1+x^2)^2\frac{dy}{dx}\frac{d^2y}{dx^2} = 4\frac{dy}{dx}$$

$$\Rightarrow 2x(1+x^2)\frac{dy}{dx} + (1+x^2)^2\frac{d^2y}{dx^2} = 2 \Rightarrow (1+x^2)^2 y_2 + 2x(1+x^2)y_1 = 2$$

33. We have,

$$y = \cos^{-1} x$$

$$\frac{dy}{dx} = -\frac{1}{\sqrt{1-x^2}} = -(1-x^2)^{-1/2}$$

$$\Rightarrow \frac{d^2y}{dx^2} = \frac{1}{2}(1-x^2)^{-3/2}\frac{d}{dx}(1-x^2) \Rightarrow \frac{d^2y}{dx^2} = \frac{-x}{(1-x^2)^{3/2}}$$

$$\Rightarrow \frac{d^2y}{dx^2} = \frac{-\cos y}{(1-\cos^2 y)^{3/2}} \qquad [\because y = \cos^{-1} x \Rightarrow x = \cos y]$$

$$\Rightarrow \frac{d^2y}{dx^2} = -\cot y \operatorname{cosec}^2 y$$

34. We have,

$$y = e^{a\cos^{-1} x}$$

$$\Rightarrow \frac{dy}{dx} = e^{a\cos^{-1} x}\frac{d}{dx}(a\cos^{-1} x) \Rightarrow \frac{dy}{dx} = e^{a\cos^{-1} x}\times -\frac{a}{\sqrt{1-x^2}} \Rightarrow \frac{dy}{dx} = \frac{-ay}{\sqrt{1-x^2}}$$

$\Rightarrow \quad \sqrt{1-x^2}\, \frac{dy}{dx} = -ay \Rightarrow (1-x^2)\left(\frac{dy}{dx}\right)^2 = a^2 y^2$ [On squaring both sides]

Differentiating with respect to x, we get

$$-2x\left(\frac{dy}{dx}\right)^2 + (1-x^2)\, 2\, \frac{dy}{dx}\frac{d^2y}{dx^2} = 2a^2 y \frac{dy}{dx}$$

$$\Rightarrow \quad -x\frac{dy}{dx} + (1-x^2)\frac{d^2y}{dx^2} = a^2 y \Rightarrow (1-x^2)\frac{d^2y}{dx^2} - x\frac{dy}{dx} - a^2 y = 0$$

35. We have,

$$y = 500\, e^{7x} + 600\, e^{-7x}$$

$$\Rightarrow \quad \frac{dy}{dx} = 3500\, e^{7x} - 4200\, e^{-7x}$$

$$\Rightarrow \quad \frac{d^2y}{dx^2} = 3500 \times 7\, e^{7x} + 4200 \times 7\, e^{-7x} \Rightarrow \frac{d^2y}{dx^2} = 49\,(500e^{7x} + 600e^{-7x}) \Rightarrow \frac{d^2y}{dx^2} = 49y$$

40. We have,

$$y = 3\, e^{2x} + 2\, e^{3x} \Rightarrow \frac{dy}{dx} = 6\, e^{2x} + 6\, e^{3x} \text{ and } \frac{d^2y}{dx^2} = 12\, e^{2x} + 18\, e^{3x}$$

$$\therefore \quad \frac{d^2y}{dx^2} - 5\frac{dy}{dx} + 6y = (12\, e^{2x} + 18\, e^{3x}) - 5\,(6\, e^{2x} + 6\, e^{3x}) + 6\,(3\, e^{2x} + 2\, e^{3x}) = 0$$

FILL IN THE BLANKS TYPE QUESTIONS (FBQs)

1. If $y = t^{10} + 1$ and $x = t^8 + 1$, then $\frac{d^2y}{dx^2} =$ ....
2. If $x = a\sin\theta$ and $y = b\cos\theta$, then $\frac{d^2y}{dx^2} =$ ....
3. If $y = x + e^x$, then $\frac{d^2y}{dx^2} =$ ....
4. If $y = 1 - x + \frac{x^2}{2!} - \frac{x^3}{3!} + \frac{x^4}{4!}$ ...., then $\frac{d^2y}{dx^2} =$ ....
5. If $y = x + e^x$, then $\frac{d^2x}{dy^2} =$ ....
6. If $y = \log_e x$, then $\frac{d^2y}{dx^2} =$ .... [CBSE 2020]

ANSWERS

1. $\frac{5}{16t^6}$ 2. $\frac{-b}{a^2}\sec^3\theta$ 3. e^x 4. e^{-x} 5. $-\frac{e^x}{(1+e^x)^3}$ 6. $-\frac{1}{x^2}$

VERY SHORT ANSWER QUESTIONS (VSAQs)

Answer each of the following questions in one word or one sentence or as per exact requirement of the question:

1. If $y = a\, x^{n+1} + bx^{-n}$ and $x^2 \frac{d^2y}{dx^2} = \lambda y$, then write the value of λ.
2. If $x = a\cos nt - b\sin nt$ and $\frac{d^2x}{dt^2} = \lambda x$, then find the value of λ.

3. If $x = t^2$ and $y = t^3$, find $\frac{d^2y}{dx^2}$.

4. If $x = 2at$, $y = at^2$, where a is a constant, then find $\frac{d^2y}{dx^2}$ at $x = \frac{1}{2}$.

5. If $x = f(t)$ and $y = g(t)$, then write the value of $\frac{d^2y}{dx^2}$.

6. If $y = 1 - x + \frac{x^2}{2!} - \frac{x^3}{3!} + \frac{x^4}{4!}$ ..... to ∞, then write $\frac{d^2y}{dx^2}$ in terms of y.

7. If $y = x + e^x$, find $\frac{d^2x}{dy^2}$.

8. If $y = |x - x^2|$, then find $\frac{d^2y}{dx^2}$.

9. If $y = |\log_e x|$, find $\frac{d^2y}{dx^2}$.

10. If $x = a\cos t$ and $y = b\sin t$, then find $\frac{d^2y}{dx^2}$. [CBSE 2023]

ANSWERS

1. $n(n+1)$
2. n^2
3. $\frac{3}{4t}$
4. $\frac{1}{2a}$
5. $\frac{f'g'' - g'f''}{f'^3}$
6. y
7. $\frac{-e^x}{(1+e^x)^3}$
8. $\frac{d^2y}{dx^2} = \begin{cases} -2, & 0 < x < 1 \\ 2, & x > 1, x < 0 \end{cases}$
9. $\frac{d^2y}{dx^2} = \begin{cases} \frac{1}{x^2}, & 0 < x < 1 \\ -\frac{1}{x^2}, & x > 1 \end{cases}$
10. $-\frac{b}{a^2}\operatorname{cosec}^3 t$

CHAPTER 12

DERIVATIVE AS A RATE MEASURER

12.1 DERIVATIVE AS A RATE MEASURER

Let $y = f(x)$ be a function of x. Let Δy be the change in y corresponding to a small change Δx in x. Then, $\frac{\Delta y}{\Delta x}$ represents the change in y due to a unit change in x. In other words, $\frac{\Delta y}{\Delta x}$ represents the average rate of change of y with respect to x as x changes from x to $x + \Delta x$.

As $\Delta x \to 0$, the limiting value of this average rate of change of y with respect to x in the interval $[x, x + \Delta x]$ becomes the instantaneous rate of change of y with respect to x.

Thus,

$$\lim_{\Delta x \to 0} \frac{\Delta y}{\Delta x} = \text{Instantaneous rate of change of } y \text{ with respect to } x$$

$$\Rightarrow \quad \frac{dy}{dx} = \text{Rate of change of } y \text{ with respect to } x \qquad \left[\because \lim_{\Delta x \to 0} \frac{\Delta y}{\Delta x} = \frac{dy}{dx}\right]$$

The word "instantaneous" is often dropped.

Hence, $\frac{dy}{dx}$ represents the rate of change of y with respect to x for a definite value of x.

REMARK 1 *The value of $\frac{dy}{dx}$ at $x = x_0$ i.e. $\left(\frac{dy}{dx}\right)_{x = x_0}$ represents the rate of change of y with respect to x at $x = x_0$.*

REMARK 2 *If $x = \phi(t)$ and $y = \psi(t)$, then $\frac{dy}{dx} = \frac{\frac{dy}{dt}}{\frac{dx}{dt}}$, provided that $\frac{dx}{dt} \neq 0$.*

Thus, the rate of change of y with respect to x can be calculated by using the rate of change of y and that of x each with respect to t.

REMARK 3 *Throughout this chapter, the term "rate of change" will mean the instantaneous rate of change unless stated otherwise.*

ILLUSTRATIVE EXAMPLES

BASED ON BASIC CONCEPTS (BASIC)

EXAMPLE 1 *A balloon, which always remains spherical, has a variable radius. Find the rate at which its volume is increasing with respect to its radius when the radius is 7 cm.*

SOLUTION Let x be the radius and y be the volume of the balloon. Then,

$$y = \frac{4}{3}\pi x^3 \Rightarrow \frac{dy}{dx} = 4\pi x^2 \Rightarrow \left(\frac{dy}{dx}\right)_{x=7} = 4\pi (7)^2 = 196\pi \text{ cm}^2$$

Hence, the volume is increasing with respect to its radius at the rate of $196\,\pi \text{ cm}^2$, when the radius is 7 cm.

EXAMPLE 2 *Find the rate of change of the area of a circle with respect to its radius. How fast is the area changing with respect to the radius when the radius is 3 cm?* **[NCERT]**

SOLUTION Let A be the area of the circle. Then,

$$A = \pi r^2 \Rightarrow \frac{dA}{dr} = 2\pi r$$

Thus, the rate of change of the area of the circle with respect to its radius r is $2\pi r$.
When $r = 3$ cm, we obtain

$$\frac{dA}{dr} = (2\pi \times 3) \text{ cm} = 6\pi \text{ cm}.$$

EXAMPLE 3 *A balloon, which always remains spherical, has a variable diameter $\frac{3}{2}(2x+3)$. Determine the rate of change of volume with respect to x.*

SOLUTION Let V be the volume of the balloon. Then,

$$V = \frac{4\pi}{3}\left\{\frac{3}{4}(2x+3)\right\}^3 = \frac{9\pi}{16}(2x+3)^3$$

$$\Rightarrow \quad \frac{dV}{dx} = \frac{9\pi}{16} \times 3(2x+3)^2 \frac{d}{dx}(2x+3) = \frac{27\pi}{8}(2x+3)^2$$

EXAMPLE 4 *The total cost C (x) associated with the production of x units of an item is given by*

$$C(x) = 0.005x^3 - 0.02x^2 + 30x + 5000$$

Find the marginal cost when 3 units are produced, where by marginal cost we mean the instantaneous rate of change of total cost at any level of output. **[CBSE 2018, NCERT]**

SOLUTION Since the marginal cost is the rate of change of total cost with respect to the output.

$$\therefore \quad \text{Marginal cost (MC)} = \frac{d}{dx}(C(x)) = \frac{d}{dx}(0.005x^3 - 0.02x^2 + 30x + 5000)$$

$$= 0.005(3x^2) - 0.02(2x) + 30$$

When $x = 3$, we get

$$\text{Marginal cost (MC)} = 0.005 \times 3 \times 3^2 - 0.02 \times 2 \times 3 + 30 = 0.135 - 0.12 + 30 = 30.015$$

Hence, the required marginal cost is ₹ 30.02 (nearly).

EXAMPLE 5 *The total revenue received from the sale of x units of a product is given by $R(x) = 3x^2 + 36x + 5$. Find the marginal revenue when $x = 5$, where by marginal revenue we mean the rate of change of total revenue with respect to the number of items sold at an instant.* **[NCERT]**

SOLUTION Since the marginal revenue is the rate of change of total revenue with respect to the number of units sold.

$$\therefore \quad \text{Marginal revenue (MR)} = \frac{dR}{dx} = \frac{d}{dx}(3x^2 + 36x + 5) = 6x + 36$$

When $x = 5$, we obtain

$$\text{Marginal revenue} = 6 \times 5 + 36 = 66$$

Hence, the required marginal revenue is ₹ 66.

EXAMPLE 6 *A car starts from a point P at time $t = 0$ second and stops at point Q. The distance x, in metres, covered by it, in t seconds is given by $x = t^2\left(2 - \frac{t}{3}\right)$. Find the time taken by it to reach at Q and also find distance between P and Q.* **[NCERT]**

SOLUTION We have,

$x = t^2\left(2 - \frac{t}{3}\right) \Rightarrow x = 2t^2 - \frac{t^3}{3} \Rightarrow \frac{dx}{dt} = 4t - t^2$. This gives velocity of the car at any time t.

Suppose the car stops at Q after t_1 second. Then, at $t = t_1$

$$\frac{dx}{dt} = 0$$

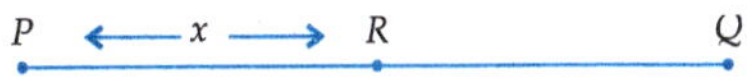

Fig. 12.1

or, $\left(\frac{dx}{dt}\right)_{t=t_1} = 0$

$\Rightarrow \quad 4t_1 - t_1^2 = 0 \Rightarrow t_1(4 - t_1) = 0 \Rightarrow t_1 = 4$ $\quad [\because t_1 = 0$ is for point $P]$

Thus, the car takes 4 seconds to reach at Q.

The distance between P and Q is the value of x at $t = t_1$ i.e. at $t = 4$.

$\therefore \quad PQ = (\text{Value of } x \text{ at } t = 4) = 2 \times 4^2 - \frac{4^3}{3} = 32 - \frac{64}{3} = \frac{32}{3}$ m

BASED ON LOWER ORDER THINKING SKILLS (LOTS)

EXAMPLE 7 *Find the rate of change of volume of a sphere with respect to its surface area when the radius is 2 cm.*

SOLUTION Let r be the radius, V the volume and S be the surface area of the sphere. Then,

$$V = \frac{4}{3}\pi r^3 \text{ and } S = 4\pi r^2$$

We have, to find $\frac{dV}{dS}$ when $r = 2$.

Now, $V = \frac{4}{3}\pi r^3$ and $S = 4\pi r^2 \Rightarrow \frac{dV}{dr} = 4\pi r^2$ and $\frac{dS}{dr} = 8\pi r$

$$\therefore \quad \frac{dV}{dS} = \frac{\frac{dV}{dr}}{\frac{dS}{dr}} = \frac{4\pi r^2}{8\pi r} = \frac{r}{2} \Rightarrow \left(\frac{dV}{dS}\right)_{r=2} = \frac{2}{2} = 1.$$

EXAMPLE 8 *If x and y are the sides of two squares such that $y = x - x^2$. Find the change of the area of second square with respect to the area of the first square.* **[NCERT EXEMPLAR]**

SOLUTION Let A_1 and A_2 denote the areas of squares of sides x and y respectively. Then,

$$A_1 = x^2 \text{ and } A_2 = y^2$$

$$\Rightarrow \quad A_1 = x^2 \text{ and } A_2 = (x - x^2)^2 \qquad [\because y = x - x^2 \text{ (given)}]$$

$$\Rightarrow \quad \frac{dA_1}{dx} = 2x \text{ and } \frac{dA_2}{dx} = 2(x - x^2)(1 - 2x)$$

$$\therefore \quad \frac{dA_2}{dA_1} = \frac{dA_2/dx}{dA_1/dx} = \frac{2(x - x^2)(1 - 2x)}{2x} = (1 - x)(1 - 2x) = 1 - 3x + 2x^2.$$

EXAMPLE 9 *A swimming pool is to be drained for cleaning. If L represents the number of litres of water in the pool t seconds after the pool has been plugged off to drain and $L = 200(10 - t)^2$. How fast is the water running out at the end of 5 seconds? What is the average rate at which the water flows out during the first 5 seconds?* **[NCERT EXEMPALR]**

SOLUTION We have to find $\frac{dL}{dt}$ at $t = 5$.

Now, $L = 200(10 - t)^2 \Rightarrow \frac{dL}{dt} = -400(10 - t) \Rightarrow \left(\frac{dL}{dt}\right)_{t=5} = -400(10 - 5) = -2000$

Thus, the water is running out at the rate of 2000 litres per second at the end of 5 seconds.

The average rate at which the water flows out during the first 5 seconds is given by

$$\frac{L(0)-L(5)}{5}=\frac{200\,(10-0)^2-200\,(10-5)^2}{5}=\frac{20000-5000}{5}=3000 \text{ litres/sec.}$$

EXERCISE 12.1

BASIC

1. Find the rate of change of the total surface area of a cylinder of radius r and height h, when the radius varies.
2. Find the rate of change of the volume of a sphere with respect to its diameter.
3. Find the rate of change of the volume of a cone with respect to the radius of its base.
4. Find the rate of change of the area of a circle with respect to its radius r when $r=5$ cm.
5. Find the rate of change of the volume of a ball with respect to its radius r. How fast is the volume changing with respect to the radius when the radius is 2 cm?
6. The total cost $C(x)$ associated with the production of x units of an item is given by $C(x)=0.007x^3-0.003x^2+15x+4000$. Find the marginal cost when 17 units are produced. [NCERT]
7. The total revenue received from the sale of x units of a product is given by $R(x)=13x^2+26x+15$. Find the marginal revenue when $x=7$. [NCERT]

BASED ON LOTS

8. Find the rate of change of the volume of a sphere with respect to its surface area when the radius is 2 cm.
9. Find the rate of change of the area of a circular disc with respect to its circumference when the radius is 3 cm.
10. The money to be spent for the welfare of the employees of a firm is proportional to the rate of change of its total revenue (Marginal revenue). If the total revenue (in rupees) received from the sale of x units of a product is given by $R(x)=3x^2+36x+5$, find the marginal revenue, when $x=5$, and write which value does the question indicate. [CBSE 2013]

ANSWERS

1. $4\pi r+2\pi h$ 2. $\frac{\pi r^2}{2}$, r is the diameter 3. $\frac{2}{3}\pi r h$ 4. $10\,\pi$ cm^2/cm
5. $4\pi r^2$, 16π m^3/m 6. ₹ 20.967 7. ₹ 208 8. 1 cm 9. 3 cm
10. MR = ₹ 66. It indicates the extra money spent when number of employees increase from 5 to 6.

HINTS TO SELECTED PROBLEMS

6. We have, $C(x)=0.007x^3-0.003x^2+15x+4000 \Rightarrow \frac{d}{dx}(C(x))=0.021x^2-0.006x+15$

$$\therefore \left(\frac{d}{dx}C(x)\right)_{x=17}=0.021\times 17^2-0.006\times 17+15.$$ Hence, marginal cost = ₹ 20.967

7. We have, $R(x)=13x^2+26x+15$

$$\therefore \frac{d}{dx}(R(x))=26x+26 \Rightarrow \left(\frac{d}{dx}(R(x))\right)_{x=7}=26\times 7+26=208$$

8. We have,

$$V=\frac{4}{3}\pi r^3 \text{ and, } S=4\pi r^2 \Rightarrow \frac{dV}{dr}=4\pi r^2 \text{ and, } \frac{dS}{dr}=8\pi r$$

$$\therefore \frac{dV}{dS}=\frac{dV/dr}{dS/dr}=\frac{4\pi r^2}{8\pi r}=\frac{r}{2} \Rightarrow \left(\frac{dV}{dS}\right)_{r=2}=\frac{2}{2}=1 \text{ cm}$$

9. We have, $A = \pi r^2$ and, $C = 2\pi r \Rightarrow \frac{dA}{dr} = 2\pi r$ and, $\frac{dC}{dr} = 2\pi$

$$\therefore \quad \frac{dA}{dC} = \frac{dA/dr}{dC/dr} = r \Rightarrow \left(\frac{dA}{dC}\right)_{r=3} = 3 \text{ cm}$$

12.2 RELATED RATES

Generally we come across with the problems in which the rate of change of one of the quantities involved is required corresponding to the given rate of change of another quantity. For example, suppose the rate of change of volume of a spherical balloon is required when the rate of change of its radius is given. In such type of problems, we must find a relation connecting such quantities and differentiate this relation w.r. to time. The procedure is illustrated in the following examples.

ILLUSTRATIVE EXAMPLES

BASED ON BASIC CONCEPTS (BASIC)

EXAMPLE 1 *An edge of a variable cube is increasing at the rate of 10 cm/sec. How fast the volume of the cube is increasing when the edge is 5 cm long?*

SOLUTION Let x be the length of the edge of the cube and V be its volume at any time t. Then,

$$V = x^3 \text{ and } \frac{dx}{dt} = 10 \text{ cm/sec} \qquad \text{[Given]}$$

Now, $V = x^3$

$$\Rightarrow \quad \frac{dV}{dt} = 3x^2 \frac{dx}{dt} = (3x^2)(10) = 30x^2 \qquad \left[\because \frac{dx}{dt} = 10\right]$$

$$\Rightarrow \quad \left(\frac{dV}{dt}\right)_{x=5} = 30(5)^2 = 750 \text{ cm}^3\text{sec.}$$

Thus, the volume of the cube is increasing at the rate of 750 cm^3/sec when the edge is 5 cm long.

EXAMPLE 2 *The radius of a circle is increasing uniformly at the rate of 4 cm/sec. Find the rate at which the area of the circle is increasing when the radius is 8 cm.*

SOLUTION Let r be the radius and A be the area of a circle at any time t. Then,

$$A = \pi r^2 \text{ and } \frac{dr}{dt} = 4 \text{ cm/sec} \qquad \text{[Given]}$$

Now, $A = \pi r^2 \Rightarrow \frac{dA}{dt} = 2\pi r \frac{dr}{dt} \Rightarrow \left(\frac{dA}{dt}\right)_{r=8} = 2\pi \times 8 \times 4 \text{ cm}^2/\text{sec} = 64\pi \text{ cm}^2/\text{sec.}$

EXAMPLE 3 *Find an angle θ, $0 < \theta < \frac{\pi}{2}$, which increases twice as fast as it sine.*

[NCERT EXEMPLAR]

SOLUTION It is given that

$$\frac{d\theta}{dt} = 2\frac{d}{dt}(\sin\theta) \Rightarrow \frac{d\theta}{dt} = 2\cos\theta\frac{d\theta}{dt} \Rightarrow 2\cos\theta = 1 \Rightarrow \cos\theta = \frac{1}{2} \Rightarrow \theta = 60° \left[\because \frac{d\theta}{dt} \neq 0\right]$$

Hence, the measure of angle is 60°.

EXAMPLE 4 *The median of an equilateral triangle is increasing at the rate of $2\sqrt{3}$ cm/sec. Find the rate at which its side is increasing.* **[CBSE 2023]**

SOLUTION Let l be the length of the median of an equilateral triangle whose each side is x cm. Then,

$$l = \frac{\sqrt{3}}{2}x$$

Differentiating both sides with respect to t, we obtain

$$\frac{dl}{dt} = \frac{\sqrt{3}}{2}\frac{dx}{dt} \Rightarrow 2\sqrt{3} = \frac{\sqrt{3}}{2}\frac{dx}{dt} \Rightarrow \frac{dx}{dt} = 4 \text{ cm/sec.} \qquad \left[\because \frac{dl}{dt} = 2\sqrt{3} \text{ cm/sec (given)}\right]$$

Hence, its sides are increasing at 4 cm/sec.

EXAMPLE 5 *The side of an equilateral triangle is increasing at the rate of 2 cm/sec. At what rate is its area increasing when the side of the triangle is 20 cm?* **[CBSE 2015]**

SOLUTION At any time t, let x cm be the length of a side of an equilateral triangle and A be its area. Then,

$$A = \frac{\sqrt{3}}{4}x^2 \Rightarrow \frac{dA}{dt} = \frac{\sqrt{3}}{4} \times 2x\frac{dx}{dt} = \frac{\sqrt{3}}{2}x\frac{dx}{dt}$$

$$\Rightarrow \left(\frac{dA}{dt}\right)_{x=20} = \frac{\sqrt{3}}{2} \times 20 \times 2 = 20\sqrt{3} \text{ cm}^2\text{/sec} \qquad \left[\because \frac{dx}{dt} = 2 \text{ cm/sec (given)}\right]$$

Hence, the area is increasing at the rate of $20\sqrt{3}$ cm^2/sec.

EXAMPLE 6 *The radius of a balloon is increasing at the rate of 10 cm/sec. At what rate is the surface area of the balloon increasing when the radius is 15 cm?*

SOLUTION Let r be the radius and S be the surface area of the balloon at any time t. Then,

$$S = 4\pi r^2 \text{ and } \frac{dr}{dt} = 10 \text{ cm/sec}$$

Now, $S = 4\pi r^2$

$$\Rightarrow \frac{dS}{dt} = 8\pi r\frac{dr}{dt} = 80\pi r \qquad \left[\because \frac{dr}{dt} = 10 \text{ cm/sec.}\right]$$

$$\Rightarrow \left(\frac{dS}{dt}\right)_{r=15} = 80\pi(15) = 1200\pi \text{ cm}^2\text{/sec.}$$

EXAMPLE 7 *A stone is dropped into a quiet lake and waves move in a circle at a speed of 3.5 cm/sec. At the instant when the radius of the circular wave is 7.5 cm, how fast is the enclosed area increasing?* **[NCERT]**

SOLUTION Let r be the radius and A be the area of the circular wave at any time t. Then,

$$A = \pi r^2 \text{ and } \frac{dr}{dt} = 3\cdot5 \text{ cm/sec.} \qquad \text{[Given]}$$

Now, $A = \pi r^2$

$$\Rightarrow \frac{dA}{dt} = \pi\left(2r\frac{dr}{dt}\right) = 2\pi r\frac{dr}{dt} = 2\pi r(3\cdot5) = 7\pi r \qquad \left[\because \frac{dr}{dt} = 3.5 \text{ cm/sec}\right]$$

$$\Rightarrow \left(\frac{dA}{dt}\right)_{r=7\cdot5} = 7\pi(7\cdot5) = 52\cdot5\pi \text{ cm}^2\text{/sec.}$$

EXAMPLE 8 *For the curve $y = 5x - 2x^3$, if x increases at the rate of 2 units/sec, then how fast is the slope of the curve changing when x = 3?* **[NCERT EXEMPLAR]**

SOLUTION Let m be the slope of the curve at an arbitrary point (x, y) on it. Then,

$$m = \frac{dy}{dx} \Rightarrow m = 5 - 6x^2 \qquad \left[\because\ y = 5x - 2x^3\ \therefore \frac{dy}{dx} = 5 - 6x^2\right]$$

It is given that $\frac{dx}{dt} = 2$ units/sec and we have to find $\frac{dm}{dt}$ when $x = 3$.

Now,

$$m = 5 - 6x^2 \Rightarrow \frac{dm}{dt} = -12\,x\,\frac{dx}{dt} \Rightarrow \left(\frac{dm}{dt}\right)_{x=3} = -12 \times 3 \times 2 = -72 \text{ units/sec} \left[\because x = 3 \text{ and } \frac{dx}{dt} = 2\right]$$

Thus, the slope of the curve is decreasing at the rate of 72 units/sec when x is increasing at the rate of 2 units/sec.

EXAMPLE 9 *The volume of a cube is increasing at a rate of 7 cm^3/ sec. How fast is the surface area increasing when the length of an edge is 12 cm?* **[CBSE 2024]**

SOLUTION Let x be the length of an edge of the cube, V be the volume and S be the surface area at any time t. Then, $V = x^3$ and $S = 6x^2$. It is given that

$$\frac{dV}{dt} = 7\text{cm}^3/\text{sec} \Rightarrow \frac{d}{dt}(x^3) = 7 \Rightarrow 3x^2\frac{dx}{dt} = 7 \Rightarrow \frac{dx}{dt} = \frac{7}{3x^2}$$

Now, $S = 6x^2$

$$\Rightarrow \frac{dS}{dt} = 12x\frac{dx}{dt} = 12x \times \frac{7}{3x^2} = \frac{28}{x} \qquad \left[\because \frac{dx}{dt} = \frac{7}{3x^2}\right]$$

$$\Rightarrow \left(\frac{dS}{dt}\right)_{x=12} = \frac{28}{12}\text{ cm}^2/\text{sec} = \frac{7}{3}\text{ cm}^2/\text{sec}$$

EXAMPLE 10 *Iqbal, a data analyst in a social media platform is tracking the number of active users on their site between 5 pm and 6 pm on a particular day. The user growth function is modelled by $N(t) = 1000\,e^{0.1t}$, where N(t) represents the number of active users at time t minutes during that period. Find how fast the number of active users are increasing or decreasing at 10 minutes past 5 pm.*

SOLUTION Given: $N(t) = 1000\,e^{0.1t}$

$$\therefore \quad \frac{d}{dt}N(t) = 1000 \times 0.1 \times e^{0.1t} \Rightarrow \frac{d}{dt}N(t) = 100\,e^{0.1t} \qquad \text{...(i)}$$

This is the rate of increase of active users at any time t.

As 10 minutes past 5, we have $t = 10$. Putting $t = 10$ in (i), we obtain

$$\left(\frac{d}{dt}N(t)\right)_{t=10} = 100\,e^{0.1\times 10} = 100e$$

Hence, the number of active users is increasing at the rate of $100e$ people per minute at 5 : 10 p.m on that day.

BASED ON LOWER ORDER THINKING SKILLS (LOTS)

EXAMPLE 11 *If the area of circle increases at a uniform rate, then prove that the perimeter varies inversely as the radius.* [NCERT EXEMPLAR]

SOLUTION Let r be the radius P be the perimeter and A be the area of the circle at any time t. Then, $A = \pi r^2$ and $P = 2\pi r$. It is given that $\frac{dA}{dt}$ = constant (k), where $k > 0$.

Now,

$$A = \pi r^2 \text{ and } P = 2\pi r$$

$$\Rightarrow \quad A = \pi\left(\frac{P}{2\pi}\right)^2 \qquad \left[\because P = 2\pi r \Rightarrow r = \frac{P}{2\pi}\right]$$

$$\Rightarrow \quad A = \frac{1}{4\pi}P^2$$

$$\Rightarrow \quad \frac{dA}{dt} = \frac{1}{4\pi} \times 2P\frac{dP}{dt} \Rightarrow k = \frac{1}{2\pi}P\frac{dP}{dt} \Rightarrow k = \frac{1}{2\pi}(2\pi r)\frac{dP}{dt} \qquad [\because P = 2\pi r]$$

$$\Rightarrow \quad \frac{dP}{dt} = \frac{k}{r} \Rightarrow P \text{ varies inversely as the radius } r.$$

ALITER We have,

$$A = \pi r^2 \text{ and } P = 2\pi r$$

$$\Rightarrow \quad \frac{dA}{dt} = 2\pi r\frac{dr}{dt} \text{ and } \frac{dP}{dt} = 2\pi\frac{dr}{dt} \Rightarrow k = 2\pi r\frac{dr}{dt} \text{ and } \frac{dP}{dt} = 2\pi\frac{dr}{dt} \qquad \left[\because \frac{dA}{dt} = k\right]$$

$$\Rightarrow \quad \frac{dP}{dt} = 2\pi\left(\frac{k}{2\pi r}\right) \qquad \left[\text{On eliminating } \frac{dr}{dt}\right]$$

$$\Rightarrow \quad \frac{dP}{dt} = \frac{k}{r} \Rightarrow P \text{ varies inversely as the radius } r.$$

EXAMPLE 12 *A spherical ball of salt is dissolving in water in such a manner that the rate of decrease of volume at any instant is proportional to the surface. Prove that the radius is decreasing at a constant rate.* [NCERT EXEMPLAR]

SOLUTION Let V, S and r denote respectively the volume, surface area and radius of the salt ball at any instant t. Then,

$$V = \frac{4}{3}\pi r^3 \text{ and } S = 4\pi r^2$$

It is given that the rate of decrease of the volume V is proportional to the surface area S.

i.e. $$\frac{dV}{dt} \propto S$$

$$\Rightarrow \quad \frac{dV}{dt} = -kS, \text{ where } k > 0 \text{ is the constant of proportionality}$$

It is given that V is decreasing with time, so that is why negative sign is taken.

Now,

$$\frac{dV}{dt} = -kS \Rightarrow \frac{d}{dt}\left(\frac{4}{3}\pi r^3\right) = -k\,(4\pi r^2) \Rightarrow 4\pi r^2\frac{dr}{dt} = -4\pi k r^2 \Rightarrow \frac{dr}{dt} = -k$$

$\therefore$ r decrease with a constant rate

Hence, the radius is decreasing at a constant rate.

EXAMPLE 13 *A particle moves along the curve $6y = x^3 + 2$. Find the points on the curve at which the y-coordinate is changing 8 times as fast as the x-coordinate.* [NCERT]

SOLUTION Let the required point be $P(x, y)$. It is given that

Rate of change of y coordinate = 8 (Rate of change of x-coordinate) i.e. $\frac{dy}{dt} = 8\frac{dx}{dt}$ ...(i)

Now, $6y = x^3 + 2$

$\Rightarrow \quad 6\frac{dy}{dt} = 3x^2\frac{dx}{dt}$ [Differentiating both sides with respect to t]

$\Rightarrow \quad 6\left(8\frac{dx}{dt}\right) = 3x^2\frac{dx}{dt}$ [Using (i)]

$\Rightarrow \quad 3x^2 = 48 \Rightarrow x^2 = 16 \Rightarrow x = \pm 4$

Now, $x = 4 \Rightarrow 6y = 4^3 + 2 = 66 \Rightarrow y = 11$ and, $x = -4 \Rightarrow 6y = (-4)^3 + 2 = -62 \; y = -\frac{31}{3}$

So, the required points are $(-4, -31/3)$ and $(4, 11)$.

EXAMPLE 14 *A particle moves along the curve $3y = ax^3 + 1$ such that at a point with x-coordinate 1, y-coordinate is changing twice as fast as x-coordinate. Find the value of a.* [CBSE 2023]

SOLUTION We have, $3y = ax^3 + 1$

Differentiating with respect to t, we obtain

$$3\frac{dy}{dt} = 3ax^2\frac{dx}{dt} \quad ...(i)$$

When $x = 1$, it is given that $\frac{dy}{dt} = 2\frac{dx}{dt}$. Substituting these values in (i), we obtain

$$\frac{dx}{dt} = 3a \times (1)^2 \times \frac{dx}{dt} \Rightarrow 6 = 3a \Rightarrow a = 2.$$

EXAMPLE 15 *The volume of a cube is increasing at a constant rate. Prove that the increase in surface area varies inversely as the length of the edge of the cube.* [NCERT EXEMPLAR]

SOLUTION Let x be the length of each edge of the cube, S be its surface area and V be its volume at any time t. Then, $S = 6x^2$ and $V = x^3$. It is given that $\frac{dV}{dt} = k$ (constant).

Now, $V = x^3 \Rightarrow \frac{dV}{dt} = 3x^2\frac{dx}{dt} \Rightarrow k = 3x^2\frac{dx}{dt} \Rightarrow \frac{dx}{dt} = \frac{k}{3x^2}$ ...(i)

and, $S = 6x^2$

$\Rightarrow \quad \frac{dS}{dt} = 12x\frac{dx}{dt} = 12x\left(\frac{k}{3x^2}\right) = \frac{4k}{x}$ [Using (i)]

$\Rightarrow \quad \frac{dS}{dt} \propto \frac{1}{x}.$

Hence, the rate of increase in surface area varies inversely as the length of the edge of the cube.

EXAMPLE 16 *Two men M_1 and M_2 start with velocities v at the same time from the junction of two roads inclined at 45° to each other. If they travel by different roads, find the rate at which they are separated.* [NCERT EXEMPLAR]

SOLUTION Let O be the junction and OA and OB be two roads inclined at an angle of 45°. Let men M_1 and M_2 travel by roads OA and OB respectively and let at any time P and Q be their positions such that $OP = OQ = x$ (both men travel with same speed v). Then,

$$\frac{dx}{dt} = v$$

Let $PQ = y$. We have to find $\frac{dy}{dt}$.

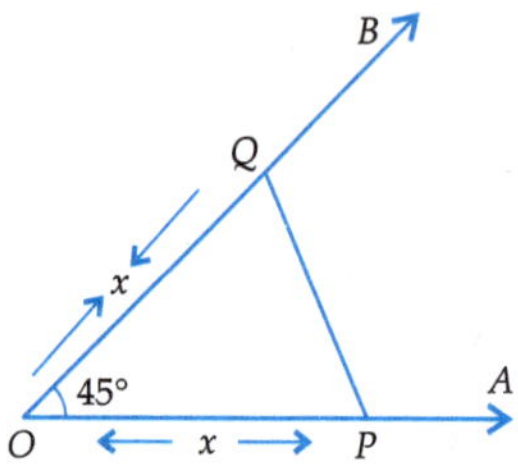

Fig. 12.2

Using cosine formula in ΔOPQ, we obtain

$$PQ^2 = OP^2 + OQ^2 - 2\, OP \cdot OQ \cos 45°$$

$$\Rightarrow \quad y^2 = x^2 + x^2 - 2x^2 \times \frac{1}{\sqrt{2}}$$

$$\Rightarrow \quad y = \sqrt{2-\sqrt{2}}\, x$$

$$\Rightarrow \quad \frac{dy}{dt} = \sqrt{2-\sqrt{2}}\, \frac{dx}{dt} = \sqrt{2-\sqrt{2}}\, v \qquad \left[\because \frac{dx}{dt} = v\right]$$

Hence, two men M_1 and M_2 are separated at the rate $\left(\sqrt{2-\sqrt{2}}\right) v$.

EXAMPLE 17 *The length x of a rectangle is decreasing at the rate of 2 cm/sec and the width y is increasing at the rate of 2 cm/sec. When x = 12 cm and y = 5 cm, find the rate of change of (i) the perimeter and (ii) the area of the rectangle.* **[NCERT]**

SOLUTION Let P be the perimeter and A be the area of the rectangle at any time t. Then,

$$P = 2(x+y) \text{ and } A = xy$$

It is given that $\frac{dx}{dt} = -2$ cm/sec and $\frac{dy}{dt} = 2$ cm/sec.

(i) We have, $P = 2(x+y)$

$$\Rightarrow \quad \frac{dP}{dt} = 2\left(\frac{dx}{dt} + \frac{dy}{dt}\right) = 2(-2+2) = 0 \text{ cm/sec i.e. the perimeter remains constant.}$$

(ii) We have, $A = xy$

$$\Rightarrow \quad \frac{dA}{dt} = \left(\frac{dx}{dt}\right) y + x\left(\frac{dy}{dt}\right) = -2\times 5 + 12\times 2 = 14 \text{ cm}^2/\text{sec.} \qquad [\because x = 12 \text{ cm and } y = 5 \text{ cm (given)}]$$

EXAMPLE 18 *A man 2 metres high, walks at a uniform speed of 6 metres per minute away from a lamp post, 5 metres high. Find the rate at which the length of his shadow increases.* **[NCERT]**

SOLUTION Let AB be the lamp-post. Let at any time t, the man CD be at a distance x metres from the lamp-post and y metres be the length of his shadow CE. Then,

$$\frac{dx}{dt} = 6 \text{ metres/minute} \qquad \text{[Given]} \quad ...(i)$$

Clearly, triangles ABE and CDE are similar.

$$\therefore \quad \frac{AB}{CD} = \frac{AE}{CE}$$

$$\Rightarrow \quad \frac{5}{2} = \frac{x+y}{y}$$

$$\Rightarrow \quad 3y = 2x \Rightarrow 3\frac{dy}{dt} = 2\frac{dx}{dt} \Rightarrow 3\frac{dy}{dt} = 2(6) \qquad \text{[Using (i)]}$$

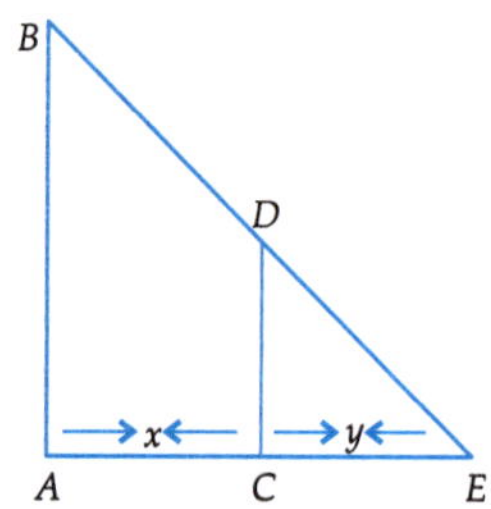

Fig. 12.3

$$\Rightarrow \quad \frac{dy}{dt} = 4$$

Thus, the shadow increases at the rate of 4 metres/minute.

EXAMPLE 19 *A man is walking at the rate of 6.5 km/hr towards the foot of a tower 120 m high. At what rate is he approaching the top of the tower when he is 50 m away from the tower?*

SOLUTION Let at any time t, the man be at distances of x and y metres from the foot and top of the tower respectively. Then,

$$y^2 = x^2 + (120)^2 \quad ...(i)$$

$$\Rightarrow \quad 2y\frac{dy}{dt} = 2x\frac{dx}{dt} \Rightarrow \frac{dy}{dt} = \frac{x}{y}\frac{dx}{dt}$$

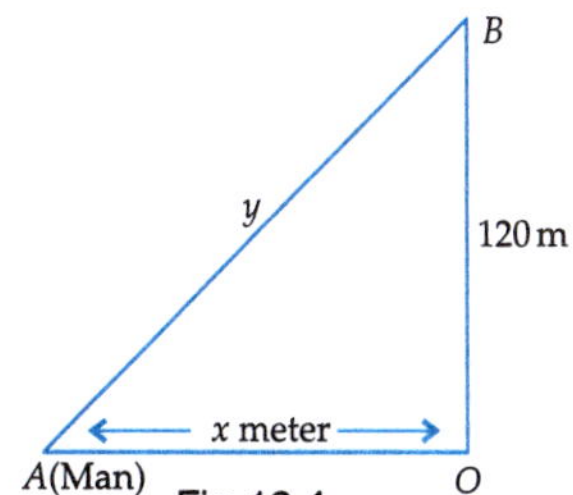

Fig. 12.4

We are given that $\frac{dx}{dt} = -6\cdot5$ km/hr (negative sign due to decreasing x). Therefore,

$$\frac{dy}{dt} = -\frac{6\cdot5x}{y} \quad ...(ii)$$

Putting $x = 50$ in (i), we get: $y = \sqrt{50^2 + 120^2} = 130$.

Putting $x = 50$, $y = 130$ in (ii), we get : $\frac{dy}{dt} = -\frac{6\cdot5 \times 50}{130} = -2\cdot5$.

Thus, the man is approaching the top of the tower at the rate of $2\cdot5$ km/hr.

EXAMPLE 20 *A man 2 m tall, walks at the rate of* $1\frac{2}{3}$ *m/sec towards a street light which is* $5\frac{1}{3}$ *m above the ground. At what rate is tip of his shadow moving? At what rate is the length of the shadow changing when he is* $3\frac{1}{3}$ *m from the base of the light?* **[NCERT EXEMPLAR]**

SOLUTION Let OA be the street light of height $5\frac{1}{3}$ m. At any time t, let PQ be the position of the man and let PR be the length of his shadow such that $PR = x$ and $OP = y$.

It is given that the man is walking at the rate of $\frac{5}{3}$ m/sec towards the street light.

$$\therefore \quad \frac{dy}{dt} = -\frac{5}{3} \text{ m/sec} \quad ...(i)$$

We have to find the rate at which the tip of the shadow is moving i.e. we have to find $\frac{d}{dt}(x+y)$.

For this we require the value of $\frac{dx}{dt}$. So, let us first find $\frac{dx}{dt}$.

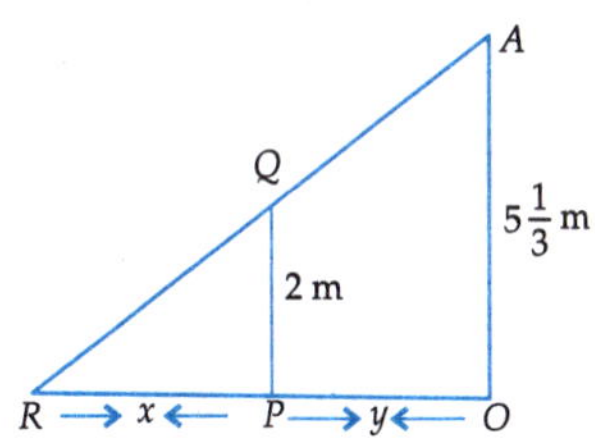

Fig. 12.5

Δ's AOR and QPR are similar triangles.

$$\therefore \quad \frac{AO}{PQ} = \frac{OR}{PR} \Rightarrow \frac{16/3}{2} = \frac{x+y}{x} \Rightarrow 8x = 3x + 3y \Rightarrow 5x = 3y$$

Differentiating with respect to t, we obtain

$$5\frac{dx}{dt} = 3\frac{dy}{dt} \Rightarrow 5\frac{dx}{dt} = 3 \times -\frac{5}{3} \Rightarrow \frac{dx}{dt} = -1 \text{ m/sec} \quad ...(ii)$$

$$\therefore \quad \frac{d}{dt}(OR) = \frac{d}{dt}(x+y) = \frac{dx}{dt} + \frac{dy}{dt} = -1 - \frac{5}{3} = -\frac{8}{3}$$

[Using (i) and (ii)]

Thus, the tip R of the shadow PR is moving towards the base of the street light at the rate of $8/3$ m/sec.

From (ii), we obtain : $\frac{dx}{dt} = -1$ for all x, y.

Thus, the length of the shadow is reducing at the rate of 1 m/sec when the man is $3\frac{1}{3}$ m from the base of light.

EXAMPLE 21 *A ladder 5 m long is leaning against a wall. The bottom of the ladder is pulled along the ground away from the wall at the rate of 2 m/sec. How fast its height on the wall decreasing when the foot of the ladder is 4 m away from the wall?* [CBSE 2012, NCERT, CBSE 2019]

SOLUTION Let AB be the position of the ladder at any time t such that $OA = x$ and $OB = y$. Then,

$$OA^2 + OB^2 = AB^2 \Rightarrow x^2 + y^2 = 5^2 \qquad ...(i)$$

It is given that the bottom of the ladder is pulled along the ground away from the wall at the rate of 2 m/sec.

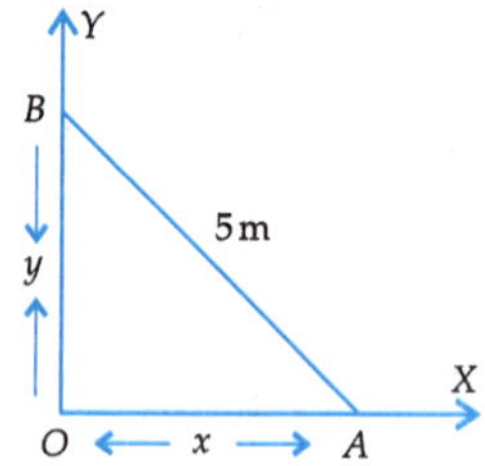

Fig. 12.6

$$\therefore \quad \frac{dx}{dt} = 2 \text{ m/sec.}$$

Now, $x^2 + y^2 = 5^2$

$$\Rightarrow \quad 2x\frac{dx}{dt} + 2y\frac{dy}{dt} = 0$$

$$\Rightarrow \quad 2x(2) + 2y\frac{dy}{dt} = 0 \qquad \left[\because \frac{dx}{dt} = 2\right]$$

$$\Rightarrow \quad \frac{dy}{dt} = -\frac{2x}{y} \qquad ...(ii)$$

Putting $x = 4$ in (i), we get: $y = \sqrt{25-16} = 3$. Putting $x = 4$ and $y = 3$ in (ii), we get:

$$\frac{dy}{dt} = -\frac{8}{3} \text{ m/sec.}$$

Hence, the rate of decrease in the height of the ladder on the wall is $\frac{8}{3}$ m/sec.

EXAMPLE 22 *The two equal sides of an isosceles triangle with fixed base b are decreasing at the rate of 3 cm/sec. How fast is the area decreasing when the two equal sides are equal to the base?* [NCERT]

SOLUTION Let at any time t, the length of each equal side be x cm and area of the triangle be A. Then,

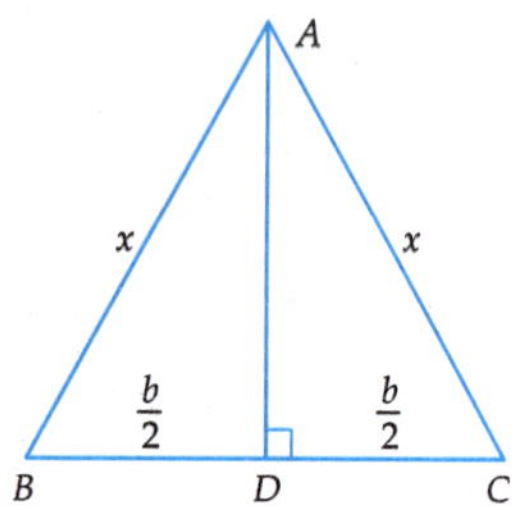

Fig. 12.7

$$A = \frac{1}{2}(BC \times AD)$$

$$\Rightarrow \quad A = \frac{1}{2} \times b \times \sqrt{x^2 - \frac{b^2}{4}}$$

$$\Rightarrow \quad A = \frac{b}{4}\sqrt{4x^2 - b^2}$$

$$\Rightarrow \quad \frac{dA}{dt} = \frac{b}{4} \times \frac{1}{2\sqrt{4x^2-b^2}} \frac{d}{dt}(4x^2 - b^2)$$

$$\Rightarrow \quad \frac{dA}{dt} = \frac{b}{8\sqrt{4x^2-b^2}} \times 8x\frac{dx}{dt}$$

$$\Rightarrow \quad \frac{dA}{dt} = \frac{bx}{\sqrt{4x^2-b^2}}\frac{dx}{dt} = \frac{3bx}{\sqrt{4x^2-b^2}} \qquad \left[\because \frac{dx}{dt} = 3 \text{ cm/sec (given)}\right]$$

$$\Rightarrow \quad \left(\frac{dA}{dt}\right)_{x=b} = \frac{3b^2}{\sqrt{4b^2-b^2}} = \sqrt{3}\, b \text{ cm}^2\text{/sec.}$$

BASED ON HIGHER ORDER THINKING SKILLS (HOTS)

EXAMPLE 23 *An airforce plane is ascending vertically at the rate of 100 km/h. If the radius of the earth is r km, how fast is the area of the earth, visible from the plane, increasing at 3 minutes after it started ascending? Given that the visible area A at height h is given by* $A = 2\pi r^2 \frac{h}{r+h}$.

SOLUTION It is given that the plane is ascending vertically at the constant rate of 100 km/h.

$$\therefore \quad \frac{dh}{dt} = 100 \text{ km/h} \qquad \text{...(i)}$$

$$\Rightarrow \quad \text{Height of the plane after 3 minutes} = 100 \times \frac{3}{60} = 5 \text{ km.} \qquad [\text{Using } h = vt]$$

Now, $A = 2\pi r^2 \frac{h}{r+h}$

$$\Rightarrow \quad \frac{dA}{dt} = 2\pi r^2 \frac{d}{dt}\left(\frac{h}{r+h}\right) = 2\pi r^2 \left\{\frac{(r+h)\frac{dh}{dt} - h\frac{d}{dt}(r+h)}{(r+h)^2}\right\} = 2\pi r^2 \left\{\frac{(r+h)\frac{dh}{dt} - h\frac{dh}{dt}}{(r+h)^2}\right\}$$

$$\Rightarrow \quad \frac{dA}{dt} = \frac{2\pi r^3}{(r+h)^2}\frac{dh}{dt} \Rightarrow \frac{dA}{dt} = \frac{2\pi r^3}{(r+h)^2} \times 100 = \frac{200\pi r^3}{(r+h)^2} \qquad \left[\because \frac{dh}{dt} = 100 \text{ km/h}\right]$$

We have to find $\frac{dA}{dt}$ when $t = 3$ minutes and at $t = 3$, we have $h = 5$ km.

$$\therefore \quad \left(\frac{dA}{dt}\right)_{t=3} = \frac{200\pi r^3}{(r+5)^2}.$$

EXAMPLE 24 *Water is dripping out from a conical funnel of semi-vertical angle* $\frac{\pi}{4}$ *at the uniform rate of* $2 \text{ cm}^2/\text{sec}$ *in its surface area through a tiny hole at the vertex in the bottom. When the slant height of the water is 4 cm, find the rate of decrease of the slant height of the water.* **[NCERT EXEMPLAR]**

SOLUTION Let VAB be a conical funnel of semi-vertical angle $\frac{\pi}{4}$. At any time t the water in the cone also forms a cone. Let r be its radius, l be the slant height and S be the surface area. Then,

$$VA' = l, \; O'A' = r \text{ and } \angle A'VO' = \frac{\pi}{4}.$$

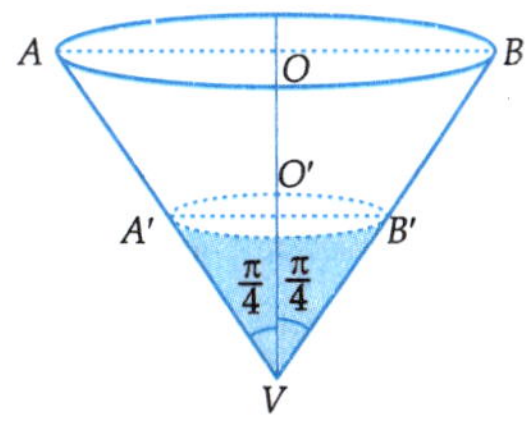

Fig. 12.8

In $\Delta VO'A'$, we obtain

$$\cos\frac{\pi}{4} = \frac{VO'}{VA'} = \frac{VO'}{l} \text{ and, } \sin\frac{\pi}{4} = \frac{O'A'}{VA'} = \frac{O'A'}{l}.$$

$$\Rightarrow \quad VO' = l\cos\frac{\pi}{4} \text{ and, } O'A' = l\sin\frac{\pi}{4}.$$

The surface area S of the conical funnel is given by

$$S = \pi(O'A')(VA') \qquad [\text{Using: } S = \pi r l]$$

$$\Rightarrow \quad S = \pi\left(l\sin\frac{\pi}{4}\right) l = \pi l^2 \sin\frac{\pi}{4} = \frac{\pi l^2}{\sqrt{2}}$$

$$\Rightarrow \quad \frac{dS}{dt} = \frac{2\pi l}{\sqrt{2}}\frac{dl}{dt}$$

$$\Rightarrow \quad -2 = \frac{2\pi l}{\sqrt{2}} \frac{dl}{dt} \qquad \left[\because \frac{dS}{dt} = -2 \text{ cm}^2/\text{sec}\right]$$

$$\Rightarrow \quad \frac{dl}{dt} = -\frac{\sqrt{2}}{\pi l} \Rightarrow \left(\frac{dl}{dt}\right)_{l=4} = -\frac{\sqrt{2}}{4\pi} \text{ cm/sec.}$$

Thus, the rate of decrease of the slant height is $\frac{\sqrt{2}}{4\pi}$ cm/sec.

EXAMPLE 25 *Sand is pouring from a pipe at the rate of 12 cm³/sec. The falling sand forms a cone on the ground in such a way that the height of the cone is always one-sixth of the radius of the base. How fast is the height of the sand-cone increasing when the height is 4 cm?* **[NCERT, CBSE 2011, 2024]**

SOLUTION Let r be the radius, h be the height and V be the volume of the sand-cone at any time t. Then,

$$V = \frac{1}{3}\pi r^2 h$$

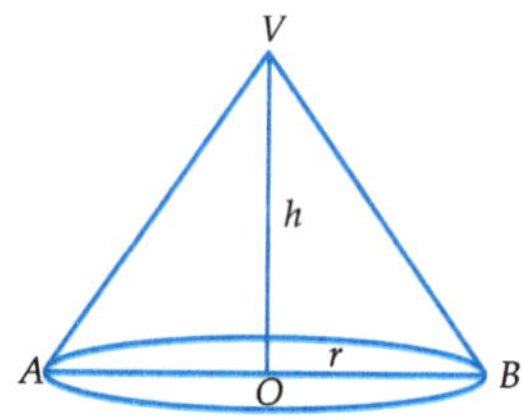

Fig. 12.9

$$\Rightarrow \quad V = \frac{1}{3}\pi(36h^2)h = 12\pi h^3 \qquad [\because r = 6h]$$

$$\Rightarrow \quad \frac{dV}{dt} = 36\pi h^2 \frac{dh}{dt} \qquad \text{...(i)}$$

$$\Rightarrow \quad \frac{dh}{dt} = \frac{1}{3\pi h^2} \qquad \left[\because \frac{dV}{dt} = 12 \text{ (Given)}\right]$$

$$\Rightarrow \quad \left(\frac{dh}{dt}\right)_{h=4} = \frac{1}{3\pi(4)^2} = \frac{1}{48\pi}$$

Thus, the height of the sand-cone is increasing at the rate of $\frac{1}{48\pi}$ cm/sec.

EXAMPLE 26 *An inverted cone has a depth of 10 cm and a base of radius 5 cm. Water is poured into it at the rate of 3/2 c.c. per minute. Find the rate at which the level of water in the cone is rising when the depth is 4 cm.*

SOLUTION Let α be the semi-vertical angle of the cone VAB whose height VO is 10 cm and radius $OB = 5$ cm. Then,

$$\tan\alpha = \frac{5}{10} = \frac{1}{2}$$

Let V be the volume of the water in the cone i.e. the volume of the cone $VA'B'$ after time t minutes and h be the height of water. Then,

$$V = \frac{1}{3}\pi(OB')^2(VO')$$

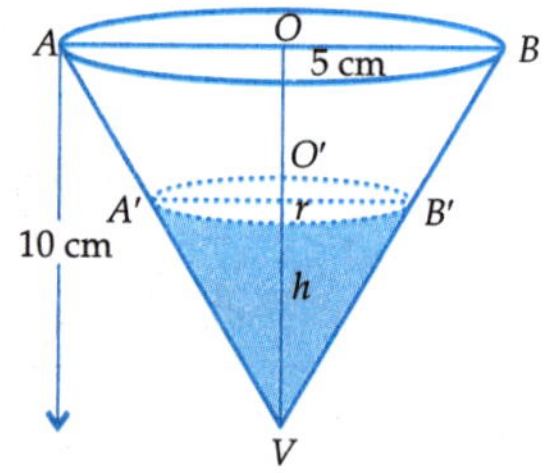

Fig. 12.10

$$\Rightarrow V = \frac{1}{3}\pi h^3 \tan^2\alpha \left[\because \tan\alpha = \frac{O'B'}{VO'} = \frac{O'B'}{h} \Rightarrow O'B' = h\tan\alpha\right]$$

$$\Rightarrow V = \frac{\pi}{12}h^3 \qquad \left[\because \tan\alpha = \frac{1}{2}\right]$$

$$\Rightarrow \frac{dV}{dt} = \frac{\pi}{12}3h^2\frac{dh}{dt} = \frac{\pi}{4}h^2\frac{dh}{dt}$$

$$\Rightarrow \quad \frac{3}{2} = \frac{\pi h^2}{4} \frac{dh}{dt} \qquad \left[\because \frac{dV}{dt} = \frac{3}{2} \text{ cm}^3/\text{minute (given)}\right]$$

$$\Rightarrow \quad \frac{dh}{dt} = \frac{6}{\pi h^2} \Rightarrow \left(\frac{dh}{dt}\right)_{h=4} = \frac{6}{\pi (4)^2} = \frac{3}{8\pi} \text{ cm/min.}$$

EXAMPLE 27 *Water is dripping out from a conical funnel at a uniform rate of 4 cm³/sec through a tiny hole at the vertex in the bottom. When the slant height of the water is 3 cm, find* the rate *of decrease of the slant height of the water-cone. Given that the vertical angle of the funnel is* 120°. **[NCERT EXEMPLAR]**

SOLUTION Let at any time t, V be the volume of the water in the cone i.e., the volume of the water-cone $VA'B'$, and let l be the slant height. Then,

$$O'A' = l \sin 60° = \frac{\sqrt{3}\, l}{2} \text{ and } VO' = l \cos 60° = \frac{l}{2}.$$

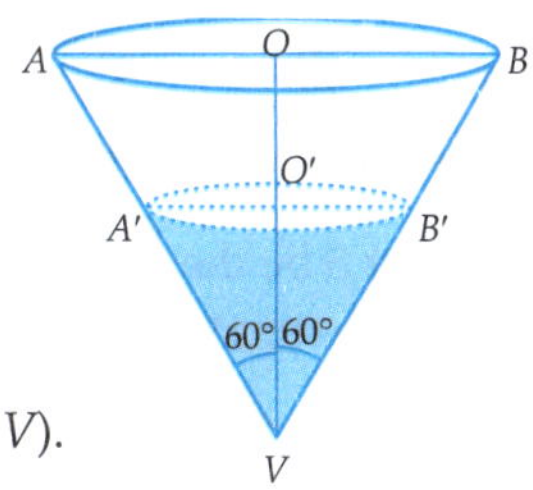

Fig. 12.11

$$\therefore \quad V = \frac{1}{3}\pi\left(\frac{\sqrt{3}\, l}{2}\right)^2\left(\frac{l}{2}\right) = \frac{\pi l^3}{8} \Rightarrow \frac{dV}{dt} = \frac{3\pi l^2}{8}\frac{dl}{dt} \qquad \text{...(i)}$$

We are given that $\frac{dV}{dt} = -4$ cm³/sec (negative sign due to decreasing V).

$$\therefore \quad -4 = \frac{3\pi}{8} l^2 \frac{dl}{dt} \qquad \left[\text{Putting } \frac{dV}{dt} = -4 \text{ in (i)}\right]$$

$$\Rightarrow \quad \frac{dl}{dt} = -\frac{32}{3\pi l^2} \Rightarrow \left(\frac{dl}{dt}\right)_{l=3} = -\frac{32}{3\pi (3)^2} = -\frac{32}{27\pi} \text{ cm/sec}$$

Thus, the slant height of the water-cone is decreasing at the rate of $\frac{32}{27}$ cm/sec.

EXAMPLE 28 *Water is running into a conical vessel, 15 cm deep and 5 cm in radius, at the rate of 0.1 cm³/sec. When the water is 6 cm deep, find at what rate is*

(i) *the water level rising?*

(ii) *the water-surface area increasing?*

(iii) *the wetted surface of the vessel increasing?*

SOLUTION Let V be the volume of the water in the cone i.e. the volume of the water-cone $VA'B'$ at any time t. Let $VO' = h$, $O'A' = r$ and $VA' = l$. Let α be the semi-vertical angle of the cone. Then,

$$\tan \alpha = \frac{OA}{VO} = \frac{5}{15} = \frac{1}{3}. \text{ Also, } \tan \alpha = \frac{O'A'}{VO'} = \frac{r}{h}$$

$$\therefore \quad \frac{1}{3} = \frac{r}{h} \Rightarrow 3r = h$$

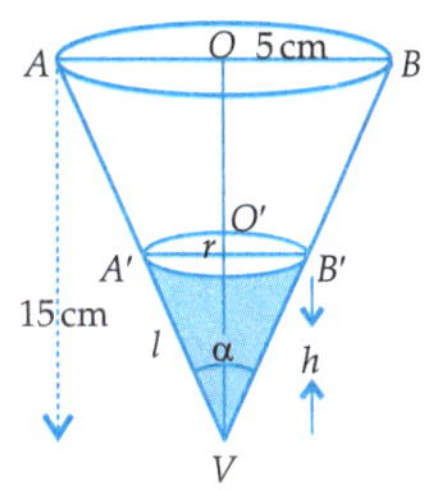

Fig. 12.12

(i) We have,

$$V = \frac{1}{3}\pi r^2 h = \frac{1}{3}\pi\left(\frac{h}{3}\right)^2 h = \frac{\pi}{27} h^3 \qquad [\because 3r = h]$$

$$\Rightarrow \quad \frac{dV}{dt} = \frac{3\pi}{27} h^2 \frac{dh}{dt}$$

$$\Rightarrow \quad 0.1 = \frac{3\pi}{27} h^2 \frac{dh}{dt} \qquad \left[\because \frac{dV}{dt} = 0.1 \text{ cm}^3/\text{sec (Given)}\right]$$

$$\Rightarrow \quad \frac{dh}{dt} = \frac{2.7}{3\pi h^2} \Rightarrow \left(\frac{dh}{dt}\right)_{h=6} = \frac{2.7}{3\pi (36)} = \frac{1}{40\pi}$$

Thus, the water level is rising at the rate of $\frac{1}{40\pi}$ cm/sec.

(ii) Let A be the water surface area at any time t. Then,

$$A = \pi r^2$$

$$\Rightarrow \quad A = \pi \frac{h^2}{9} \qquad [\because\ 3r = h]$$

$$\Rightarrow \quad \frac{dA}{dt} = \frac{2\pi h}{9} \frac{dh}{dt}$$

When $h = 6$, $\frac{dh}{dt} = \frac{1}{40\pi}$, we obtain:

$$\frac{dA}{dt} = \frac{2\pi \times 6}{9} \times \frac{1}{40\pi} = \frac{1}{30} \text{ cm}^2/\text{sec}$$

Thus, the water-surface area is increasing at the rate of $\frac{1}{30}$ cm^2/sec

(iii) Let S be the wetted surface area of the vessel at any time t. Then, $S = \pi rl$.

From Fig. 12.12, we obtain

$$l^2 = VA'^2 = VO'^2 + O'A'^2$$

$$\Rightarrow \quad l^2 = h^2 + r^2$$

$$\Rightarrow \quad l^2 = h^2 + \frac{h^2}{9} \qquad [\because\ 3r = h]$$

$$\Rightarrow \quad l = \frac{\sqrt{10}\, h}{3}$$

$$\therefore \quad S = \pi rl \Rightarrow S = \pi\left(\frac{h}{3}\right)\left(\frac{\sqrt{10}\, h}{3}\right) \Rightarrow S = \frac{\pi}{9}\sqrt{10}\, h^2 \Rightarrow \frac{dS}{dt} = \frac{2\pi\sqrt{10}\, h}{9}\frac{dh}{dt}$$

Since $h = 6$ and, $\frac{dh}{dt} = \frac{1}{40\pi}$. Therefore, $\frac{dS}{dt} = \frac{2\pi\sqrt{10}}{9} \times 6 \times \frac{1}{40\pi} = \frac{\sqrt{10}}{30}$ cm^2/sec.

Thus, the wetted surface area of the vessel is increasing at the rate of $\frac{\sqrt{10}}{30}$ cm^2/sec.

EXAMPLE 29 *A water tank has the slope of an inverted right circular cone with its axis vertical and vertex lower most. Its semi-vertical angle is* $\tan^{-1}(0.5)$. *Water is poured into it at a constant rate of 5 cubic metre per hour. Find the rate at which the level of the water is rising at the instant when the depth of water in the tank is 4 m.* **[NCERT]**

SOLUTION Let α be the semi-vertical angle of the water tank in the form of cone. Then,

$$\tan\alpha = 0.5 = \frac{1}{2} \Rightarrow \frac{r}{h} = \frac{1}{2} \Rightarrow r = \frac{h}{2}$$

Let $V\ A'\ B'$ be the water cone of volume V. Then,

$$\frac{dV}{dt} = 5 \text{ m}^3/\text{hr} \qquad \text{[Given]}$$

We have to find $\frac{dh}{dt}$ when $h = 4$ m.

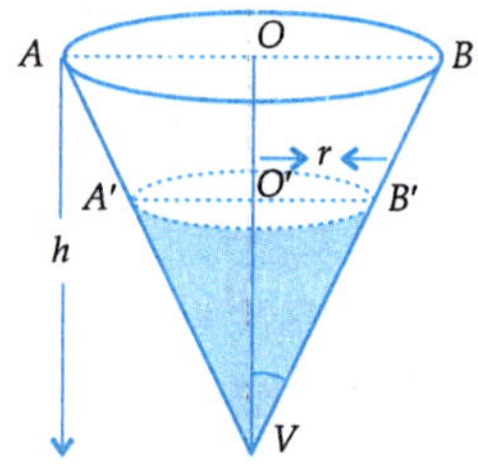

Fig. 12.13

Now,

$$V = \frac{1}{3} r^2 h$$

$$\Rightarrow \quad V = \frac{1}{3}\pi\left(\frac{h}{2}\right)^2 h = \frac{\pi}{12} h^3$$

$$\Rightarrow \quad \frac{dV}{dt} = \frac{\pi}{4}h^2\frac{dh}{dt} \Rightarrow 5 = \frac{\pi}{4}\times 4^2 \times \frac{dh}{dt} \Rightarrow \frac{dh}{dt} = \frac{5}{4\pi} = \frac{5}{4}\times\frac{7}{22}\text{ m/h} = \frac{35}{88}\text{ m/h}$$

Thus, the rate of change of water level is $\frac{35}{88}$ m/h.

EXAMPLE 30 *A man is moving away from a tower 41.6 m high at the rate of 2 m/sec. Find the rate at which the angle of elevation of the top of tower is changing, when he is at a distance of 30 m from the foot of the tower. Assume that the eye level of the man is 1.6 m from the ground.*

SOLUTION Let AB be the tower. Let at any time t, the man be at a distance of x metres from the tower AB and let θ be the angle of elevation at that time. Then,

$$\tan\theta = \frac{BC}{PC} \Rightarrow \tan\theta = \frac{40}{x} \Rightarrow x = 40\cot\theta \quad \text{...(i)}$$

$$\therefore \quad \frac{dx}{dt} = -40\,\text{cosec}^2\theta\,\frac{d\theta}{dt}$$

We are given that $\frac{dx}{dt} = 2$ m/sec.

$$\therefore \quad 2 = -40\,\text{cosec}^2\theta\,\frac{d\theta}{dt} \Rightarrow \frac{d\theta}{dt} = -\frac{1}{20\,\text{cosec}^2\theta} \quad \text{...(ii)}$$

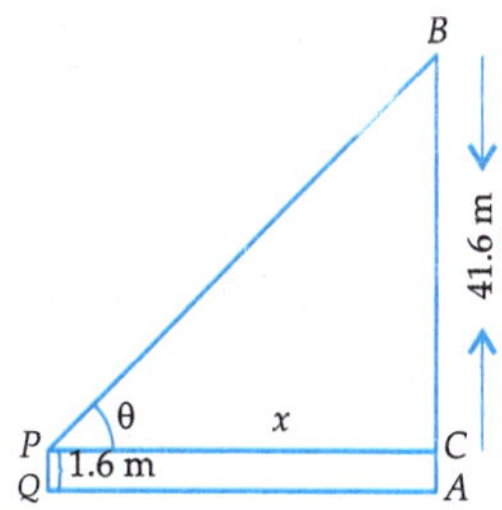

Fig.12.14

When $x = 30$, we get

$$\cot\theta = \frac{30}{40} = \frac{3}{4} \quad [\text{Putting } x = 30 \text{ in (i)}]$$

$$\therefore \quad \text{cosec}^2\theta = 1 + \cot^2\theta = 1 + \frac{9}{16} = \frac{25}{16}$$

Substituting $\text{cosec}^2\theta = \frac{25}{16}$ in (ii), we get: $\frac{d\theta}{dt} = -\frac{1}{20\times\frac{25}{16}} = -\frac{4}{125}$ radians/sec

Thus, the angle of elevation of the top of tower is decreasing at the rate of 4/125 radians/sec.

EXAMPLE 31 *A kite is moving horizontally at the height of 151.5 meters. If the speed of kite is 10 m/sec, how fast is the string being let out; when the kite is 250 m away from the boy who is flying the kite? The height of the boy is 1.5 m.* **[NCERT EXEMPLAR]**

SOLUTION Let OA be the boy of height 1.5 m and kite be flying at a height $OB = 151.5$ m from the horizon OX. Therefore, $AB = OB - OA = (151.5 - 1.5)$ m $= 150$m.

Let at any time t, kite be at P such that $BP = x$ and $AP = y$. It is given that the kite is moving horizontally at the speed of 10 m/sec.

$$\therefore \quad \frac{dx}{dt} = 10 \text{ m/sec}$$

We have to find the rate at which the string is being let out i.e. $\frac{dy}{dt}$ when $y = 250$ m.

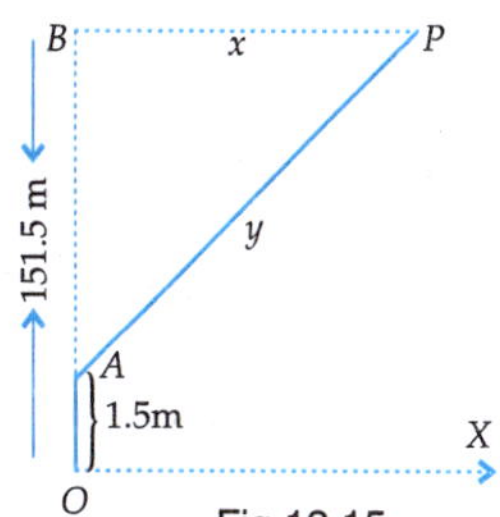

Fig.12.15

Applying Pythagoras theorem in ΔABP, we obtain

$$AP^2 = AB^2 + BP^2 \Rightarrow y^2 = 150^2 + x^2 \quad \text{...(i)}$$

Differentiating (i) with respect to t, we obtain

$$2y\frac{dy}{dt} = 2x\frac{dx}{dt} \Rightarrow \frac{dy}{dt} = \frac{x}{y}\times 10 \Rightarrow \frac{dy}{dt} = \frac{10x}{y} \quad \text{...(ii)}$$

Putting $y = 250$ in (i), we obtain

$$250^2 = 150^2 + x^2 \Rightarrow x^2 = 40000 \Rightarrow x = 200$$

Putting $x = 200$ and $y = 250$ in (ii), we obtain: $\frac{dy}{dt} = 10 \times \frac{200}{250} = 8.$

Hence, the string is being let out at the rate of 8 m/sec.

EXERCISE 12.2

BASIC

1. The side of a square sheet is increasing at the rate of 4 cm per minute. At what rate is the area increasing when the side is 8 cm long?
2. An edge of a variable cube is increasing at the rate of 3 cm per second. How fast is the volume of the cube increasing when the edge is 10 cm long?
3. The side of a square is increasing at the rate of 0.2 cm/sec. Find the rate of increase of the perimeter of the square.
4. The radius of a circle is increasing at the rate of 0.7 cm/sec. What is the rate of increase of its circumference? [NCERT]
5. The radius of a spherical soap bubble is increasing at the rate of 0.2 cm/sec. Find the rate of increase of its surface area, when the radius is 7 cm.
6. A balloon which always remains spherical, is being inflated by pumping in 900 cubic centimetres of gas per second. Find the rate at which the radius of the balloon is increasing when the radius is 15 cm. [NCERT]
7. The radius of an air bubble is increasing at the rate of 0.5 cm/sec. At what rate is the volume of the bubble increasing when the radius is 1 cm?
8. A stone is dropped into a quiet lake and waves move in circles at a speed of 4 cm/sec. At the instant when the radius of the circular wave is 10 cm, how fast is the enclosed area increasing? [NCERT]
9. A particle moves along the curve $y = x^3$. Find the points on the curve at which the y-coordinate changes three times more rapidly than the x-coordinate.
10. Find an angle θ
    (i) which increases twice as fast as its cosine.
    (ii) whose rate of increase is twice the rate of decrease of its consine.

BASED ON LOTS

11. A man 2 metres high walks at a uniform speed of 5 km/hr away from a lamp-post 6 metres high. Find the rate at which the length of his shadow increases.
12. A ladder 13 m long leans against a wall. The foot of the ladder is pulled along the ground away from the wall, at the rate of 1.5 m/sec. How fast is the angle θ between the ladder and the ground is changing when the foot of the ladder is 12 m away from the wall.
13. A particle moves along the curve $y = x^2 + 2x$. At what point(s) on the curve are the x and y coordinates of the particle changing at the same rate?
14. If $y = 7x - x^3$ and x increases at the rate of 4 units per second, how fast is the slope of the curve changing when $x = 2$?
15. The top of a ladder 6 metres long is resting against a vertical wall on a level pavement, when the ladder begins to slide outwards. At the moment when the foot of the ladder is 4 metres from the wall, it is sliding away from the wall at the rate of 0.5 m/sec. How fast is the top-sliding downwards at this instance?
    How far is the foot from the wall when it and the top are moving at the same rate?

16. A balloon in the form of a right circular cone surmounted by a hemisphere, having a diametre equal to the height of the cone, is being inflated. How fast is its volume changing with respect to its total height h, when $h = 9$ cm.
17. Water is running into an inverted cone at the rate of π cubic metres per minute. The height of the cone is 10 metres, and the radius of its base is 5 m. How fast the water level is rising when the water stands 7.5 m below the base.
18. The surface area of a spherical bubble is increasing at the rate of 2 cm²/s. When the radius of the bubble is 6 cm, at what rate is the volume of the bubble increasing? [CBSE 2005]
19. The radius of a cylinder is increasing at the rate 2 cm/sec. and its altitude is decreasing at the rate of 3 cm/sec. Find the rate of change of volume when radius is 3 cm and altitude 5 cm. [CBSE 2017]
20. The volume of metal in a hollow sphere is constant. If the inner radius is increasing at the rate of 1 cm/sec, find the rate of increase of the outer radius when the radii are 4 cm and 8 cm respectively.
21. A particle moves along the curve $y = \left(\frac{2}{3}\right)x^3 + 1$. Find the points on the curve at which the y-coordinate is changing twice as fast as the x-coordinate.
22. Find the point on the curve $y^2 = 8x$ for which the abscissa and ordinate change at the same rate. [CBSE 2002C]
23. (i) The volume of a cube is increasing at the rate of $9 \text{ cm}^3/\text{sec}$. How fast is the surface area increasing when the length of an edge is 10 cm?

    (ii) The surface area of a cube increases at the rate of $72 \text{ cm}^2/\text{sec}$. Find the rate of change of its volume when the edge of the cube measures 3 cm. [CBSE 2024]
24. The volume of a spherical balloon is increasing at the rate of $25 \text{ cm}^3/\text{sec}$. Find the rate of change of its surface area at the instant when radius is 5 cm. [CBSE 2004, 2017]
25. The length x of a rectangle is decreasing at the rate of 5 cm/minute and the width y is increasing at the rate of 4 cm/minute. When $x = 8$ cm and $y = 6$ cm, find the rates of change of (i) the perimeter (ii) the area of the rectangle. [CBSE 2009]
26. A circular disc of radius 3 cm is being heated. Due to expansion, its radius increases at the rate of 0.05 cm/sec. Find the rate at which its area is increasing when radius is 3.2 cm. [NCERT]

BASED ON HOTS

27. Sand is being poured onto a conical pile at the constant rate of 50 cm³/minute such that the height of the cone is always one half of the radius of its base. How fast is the height of the pile increasing when the sand is 5 cm deep.
28. A kite is 120 m high and 130 m of string is out. If the kite is moving away horizontally at the rate of 52 m/sec, find the rate at which the string is being paid out.

ANSWERS

1. 64 cm²/minute	2. 900 cm³/sec	3. 0.8 cm/sec	4. 1.4 π cm/sec
5. 11.2π cm²/sec	6. $1/\pi$ cm/sec	7. 2π cm³/sec	8. 80π cm²/sec
9. (1, 1), (–1, –1)	10. (i) $7\pi/6$ (ii) $\pi/6$	11. 5/2 km/h	12. 0.3 radian/sec
13. (–1/2, – 3/4)	14. 48	15. $\frac{1}{\sqrt{5}}$ m/sec, $3\sqrt{2}$m	16. 12π cm³/sec
17. 0.64 metre/minute	18. 6 cm³/sec	19. 33π cm³/sec	20. 1/4 cm/sec
21. (1, 5/3) and (–1, 1/3)		22. (2, 4)	23. (i) 3.6 cm²/sec
(ii) 54 cm³/sec	24. 10 cm²/sec	25. (i) – 2 cm/minute	(ii) 2 cm/minute
26. 0.320 π cm²/sec	27. $1/2\pi$ cm/minute	28. 20 m/sec.	

HINTS TO SELECTED PROBLEMS

10. (i) We have,

$$\frac{d\theta}{dt} = 2\frac{d}{dt}(\cos\theta) \Rightarrow \frac{d\theta}{dt} = -2\sin\theta\frac{d\theta}{dt} \Rightarrow \sin\theta = -\frac{1}{2} \Rightarrow \theta = \frac{7\pi}{6}$$

(ii) It is given that

$$\frac{d\theta}{dt} = -2\frac{d}{d\theta}(\cos\theta) \Rightarrow \frac{d\theta}{dt} = 2\sin\theta\frac{d\theta}{dt} \Rightarrow \sin\theta = \frac{1}{2} \Rightarrow \theta = \frac{\pi}{6}$$

12. Let the bottom of the ladder be at a distance x m from the wall and the top be at a height y from the ground. Then,

$$x^2 + y^2 = 13^2 \text{ and } \tan\theta = \frac{y}{x}$$

$$\therefore \quad 2x\frac{dx}{dt} + 2y\frac{dy}{dt} = 0 \text{ and } \sec^2\theta\frac{d\theta}{dt} = \frac{x\frac{dy}{dt} - y\frac{dx}{dt}}{x^2}$$

$$\Rightarrow \quad 3x + 2y\frac{dy}{dt} = 0 \text{ and } \sec^2\theta\frac{d\theta}{dt} = \frac{x\frac{dy}{dt} - \frac{3y}{2}}{x^2} \qquad \left[\because \frac{dx}{dt} = 15\right]$$

$$\Rightarrow \quad \frac{dy}{dt} = -\frac{3x}{2y} \text{ and } \sec^2\theta\frac{d\theta}{dt} = \frac{x \times -\frac{3x}{2y} - \frac{3y}{2}}{x^2}$$

$$\Rightarrow \quad \frac{d\theta}{dt} = -\frac{3}{2}\frac{(x^2+y^2)}{x^2 y\sec^2\theta} = -\frac{3}{2}\frac{(x^2+y^2)}{x^2 y(1+\tan^2\theta)} = -\frac{3}{2}\frac{(x^2+y^2)}{x^2 y\left(1+\frac{y^2}{x^2}\right)} = -\frac{3}{2y}$$

When $x = 12$, $x^2 + y^2 = 13^2 \Rightarrow y = 5$. $\therefore \frac{d\theta}{dt} = -\frac{3}{10}$

13. We have, $y = x^2 + 2x \Rightarrow \frac{dy}{dt} = (2x+2)\frac{dx}{dt} \Rightarrow 1 = 2x + 2 \Rightarrow x = -\frac{1}{2}$

14. We have, m = Slope of the curve $= \frac{dy}{dx} = 7 - 3x^2$.

Now, $m = 7 - 3x^2$

$$\Rightarrow \quad \frac{dm}{dt} = -6x\frac{dx}{dt} = -6x(4) = -24x \qquad \left[\because \frac{dx}{dt} = 4 \text{ (given)}\right]$$

$$\Rightarrow \quad \left(\frac{dm}{dt}\right)_{x=2} = -48$$

18. We have, $S = 4\pi r^2 \Rightarrow \frac{dS}{dt} = 8\pi r\frac{dr}{dt} \Rightarrow \frac{dr}{dt} = \frac{2}{8\pi r}$

Now,

$$V = \frac{4}{3}\pi r^3 \Rightarrow \frac{dV}{dt} = 4\pi r^2\frac{dr}{dt} \Rightarrow \frac{dV}{dt} = 4\pi r^2 \times \frac{2}{8\pi r} = r \qquad \text{[Using (i)]}$$

Hence, $\frac{dV}{dt} = 6$ when $r = 6$.

19. We have, $V = \pi r^2 h$, $\frac{dr}{dt} = 2$ and $\frac{dh}{dt} = -3$

$\therefore \quad V = \pi r^2 h \Rightarrow \frac{dV}{dt} = \pi \left\{ 2rh\frac{dr}{dt} + r^2\frac{dh}{dt} \right\} \Rightarrow \frac{dV}{dt} = \pi(4rh - 3r^2)$

When $r = 3, h = 5$, we obtain: $\frac{dV}{dt} = \pi(60 - 27) = 33\pi$

26. Let r be the radius and A be the area of the disc at any time t. Then, $A = \pi r^2$. It is given that $\frac{dr}{dt} = 0.05$ cm/sec.

Now, $A = \pi r^2$

$\Rightarrow \frac{dA}{dt} = 2\pi r\frac{dr}{dt} \Rightarrow \left(\frac{dA}{dt}\right)_{r=3.2} = 2\pi \times 3.2 \times 0.05 = 0.320\pi \text{ cm}^2\text{/sec.}$

28. We have, $y^2 = x^2 + (120)^2$

$\Rightarrow 2y\frac{dy}{dt} = 2x\frac{dx}{dt} \Rightarrow \frac{dy}{dt} = \frac{x}{y}\frac{dx}{dt} \Rightarrow \frac{dy}{dt} = 52\frac{x}{y} \quad \left[\because \frac{dx}{dt} = 52\right]$

Putting $y = 130$ in $y^2 = x^2 + (120)^2$, we get $x = 50$.

$\therefore \quad \frac{dy}{dt} = \frac{52 \times 50}{130} = 20.$

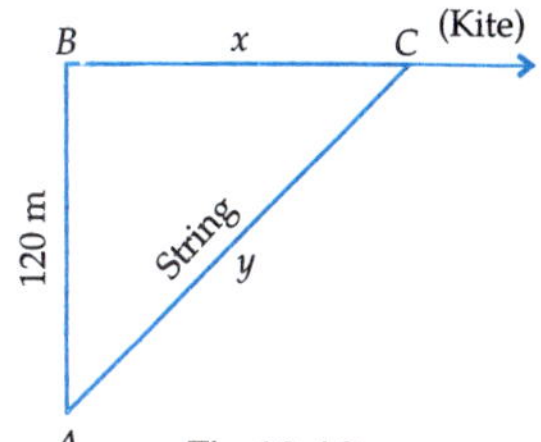

Fig.12.16

FILL IN THE BLANKS TYPE QUESTIONS (FBQs)

1. The rate of change of $\sqrt{x^2 + 16}$ with respect to $\frac{x}{x-1}$ at $x = 3$ is ....
2. The rate of change of the surface are of a sphere of radius r when the radius is increasing at the rate of 2 cm/sec is................................ .
3. The diagonal of a square is changing at the rate of $\frac{1}{2}$ cm/sec. Then the rate of change of area, when the area is 400 cm^2, is equal to ....
4. The rate of change of volume of a sphere with respect to its surface area, when the radius is 2 cm, is ....
5. The angle θ, $0 < \theta < \frac{\pi}{2}$, which increases twice as fast as its sine, is ....
6. The sides of an equilateral triangle are increasing at the rate of 2 cm/sec. The rate at which the area increases, when the side is 10 cm, is ....
7. Gas is being pumped into a spherical balloon at the rate of 30 cm^3/min. The rate at which the radius increases when it reaches the value 15 cm, is ....
8. The distance s described by a particle in t seconds is given by $s = ae^t + \frac{b}{e^t}$. Then the acceleration of the particle at time t is equal to ....
9. The volume V and depth x of water in a vessel are connected by the relation $V = 5x - \frac{x^2}{6}$ and the volume of water is increasing the rate of 5 cm^3/sec, when $x = 2$ cm. The rate of which the depth of water is increasing is equal to ....

10. Water is flowing into a vertical cylindrical tank of radius 2 ft at the rate of 8 cubic/minute. The rate at which the water level is rising, is ....

11. If the radius of a circle is increasing at the rate of 0.5 cm/sec, then the rate of increase of its circumference is .... [CBSE 2020]

12. The radius of a circle is increasing at the uniform rate of 3 cm/sec. At the instant when the radius of the circle is 2 cm, its area increases at the rate of .... cm^2/sec. [CBSE 2020]

ANSWERS

1. $\frac{-12}{5}$ 2. $16\pi r$ 3. $10\sqrt{2}$ cm^2/sec 4. 1 5. $\frac{\pi}{6}$ 6. $10\sqrt{3}$ sq.unit/sec
7. $\frac{1}{30\pi}$ cm/min 8. s 9. $\frac{15}{13}$ cm/sec 10. $\frac{2}{\pi}$ ft/minute 11. π cm/sec 12. 12π

VERY SHORT ANSWER QUESTIONS (VSAQs)

Answer each of the following questions in one word or one sentence or as per exact requirement of the question:

1. If a particle moves in a straight line such that the distance travelled in time t is given by $s = t^3 - 6t^2 + 9t + 8$. Find the initial velocity of the particle.
2. The volume of a sphere is increasing at 3 cubic centimeter per second. Find the rate of increase of the radius, when the radius is 2 cms.
3. The sides of an equilateral triangle are increasing at the rate of 2 cm/sec. How far is the area increasing when the side is 10 cms? [NCERT EXEMPLAR]
4. The side of a square is increasing at the rate of 0.1 cm/sec. Find the rate of increase of its perimeter.
5. The radius of a circle is increasing at the rate of 0.5 cm/sec. Find the rate of increase of its circumference.
6. The side of an equilateral triangle is increasing at the rate of $\frac{1}{3}$ cm/sec. Find the rate of increase of its perimeter.
7. Find the surface area of a sphere when its volume is changing at the same rate as its radius.
8. If the rate of change of volume of a sphere is equal to the rate of change of its radius, find the radius of the sphere.
9. The amount of pollution content added in air in a city due to x diesel vehicles is given by $P(x) = 0.005x^3 + 0.02x^2 + 30x$. Find the marginal increase in pollution content when 3 diesel vehicles are added and write which value is indicated in the above questions. [CBSE 2013]
10. A ladder, 5 meter long, standing on a horizontal floor, leans against a vertical wall. If the top of the ladder slides down wards at the rate of 10 cm/sec, then find the rate at which the angle between the floor and ladder is decreasing when lower end of ladder is 2 metres from the wall. [NCERT EXEMPLAR]
11. The area of a circle is increasing at a uniform rate of 2 cm^2/sec. How fast is the circumference of the circle increasing when the radius $r = 5$ cm? [CBSE 2024]

ANSWERS

1. 9 units/unit time
2. $3/16\pi$ cm/sec
3. $10\sqrt{3}$ cm^2/sec
4. 0.4 cm/sec
5. π cm/sec
6. 1 cm/sec
7. 1 square unit
8. $1/2\sqrt{\pi}$ units
9. 30.255 units, Pollution level due to x diesel vehicles.
10. 1/20 radian/second
11. 2/5 cm/sec

CHAPTER 13

INCREASING AND DECREASING FUNCTIONS

13.1 INTRODUCTION

In this chapter, we shall study monotonicity of functions. A function $f(x)$ is said to be a monotonically increasing function on $[a, b]$, if the values of $f(x)$ increase or decrease with the increase or decrease in x. If the values of $f(x)$ decrease with the increase in the values of x, then $f(x)$ is said to be a monotonically decreasing function. The monotonicity of functions in $[a, b]$ is strongly connected to the sign of its derivative in $[a, b]$. The relation between the two will be discused in section 13.4. In determining the intervals of monotonicity of a function in its domain, we shall be solving the inequations $f'(x) > 0$ and $f'(x) < 0$. So, we shall first discuss the procedure of solving inequations in the following section.

13.2 SOLUTION OF RATIONAL ALGEBRAIC INEQUATIONS

The following results are very useful in solving rational algebraic inequations:

(i) $ab > 0 \Rightarrow (a > 0 \text{ and } b > 0)$ or $(a < 0 \text{ and } b < 0)$

(ii) $ab < 0 \Rightarrow (a > 0 \text{ and } b < 0)$ or $(a < 0 \text{ and } b > 0)$

(iii) $ab > 0$ and $a > 0 \Rightarrow b > 0$

(iv) $ab < 0$ and $a < 0 \Rightarrow b > 0$

If $P(x)$ and $Q(x)$ are polynomials, then the inequations $\frac{P(x)}{Q(x)} > 0$, $\frac{P(x)}{Q(x)} < 0$, $\frac{P(x)}{Q(x)} \geq 0$ and $\frac{P(x)}{Q(x)} \leq 0$ are known as rational algebraic inequations. These inequations can be solved by using the following algorithm.

ALGORITHM

Step I *Factorize $P(x)$ and $Q(x)$ into linear factors.*

Step II *Make coefficient of x positive in all factors.*

Step III *Equate all the factors to zero and find the corresponding values of x. These values are generally known as critical points.*

Step IV *Plot the critical points on the number line. Note that n critical points will divide the number line in $(n+1)$ regions.*

Step V *In the right most region, the expression will be positive and in other regions it will be alternatively negative and positive. So, mark positive sign in the right most region and than mark alternatively negative and positive signs in the remaining regions.*

Step VI *Obtain the solution set of the given inequation by selecting the appropriate regions in step V.*

Following illustrations will illustrate the above algorithm.

ILLUSTRATION 1 *Solve:* $4x^3 - 24x^2 + 44x - 24 > 0$.

SOLUTION We have,

$$4x^3 - 24x^2 + 44x - 24 > 0 \Rightarrow 4(x^3 - 6x^2 + 11x - 6) > 0$$

$$\Rightarrow \quad x^3 - 6x^2 + 11x - 6 > 0 \qquad [\because 4 > 0 \text{ and } ab > 0, a > 0 \Rightarrow b > 0]$$

$$\Rightarrow \quad (x-1)(x^2 - 5x + 6) > 0 \Rightarrow (x-1)(x-2)(x-3) > 0 \qquad \ldots(i)$$

On equating all factors, on LHS of the inequation, to zero, we obtain $x = 1, 2, 3$ as critical points. Let us plot these critical points on the number line as shown in Fig. 13.1. These points divide the number line into four regions. In the right most region the expression on LHS of (i) bears positive sign and then alternatively negative and positive signs as marked in Fig. 13.1. Since the expression in (i) is positive. Therefore, solution set of inequation (i) is the union of the regions marked with + signs. Hence from Fig. 13.1, we obtain $(1, 2) \cup (3, \infty)$ as the solution set.

i.e. $\quad x^3 - 6x^2 + 11x - 6 > 0 \Rightarrow (x-1)(x-2)(x-3) > 0 \Rightarrow x \in (1, 2) \cup (3, \infty)$.

Hence, the solution set of the given inequality is $(1, 2) \cup (3, \infty)$.

Fig. 13.1 Signs of $(x-1)(x-2)(x-3)$ for different values of x

ILLUSTRATION 2 *Solve* : $\dfrac{1}{x+1} - \dfrac{4}{(2+x)^2} > 0,\ x \neq -1, -2.$

SOLUTION We have,

$$\frac{1}{x+1} - \frac{4}{(2+x)^2} = \frac{(2+x)^2 - 4(x+1)}{(2+x)^2(x+1)} = \frac{x^2}{(2+x)^2(x+1)}$$

$$\therefore \quad \frac{1}{x+1} - \frac{4}{(2+x)^2} > 0$$

$$\Rightarrow \quad \frac{x^2}{(2+x)^2(x+1)} > 0$$

$$\Rightarrow \quad \left(\frac{x}{2+x}\right)^2 \left(\frac{1}{x+1}\right) > 0$$

$$\Rightarrow \quad \frac{1}{x+1} > 0 \text{ and } x \neq 0 \qquad \left[\because \left(\frac{x}{2+x}\right)^2 > 0 \text{ and if } a > 0, \text{ then } ab > 0 \Rightarrow b > 0\right]$$

$$\Rightarrow \quad x + 1 > 0 \text{ and } x \neq 0 \qquad \left[\because \frac{a}{b} > 0 \text{ and } a > 0, \Rightarrow b > 0\right]$$

$$\Rightarrow \quad x > -1 \text{ and } x \neq 0 \Rightarrow x \in (-1, 0) \cup (0, \infty)$$

Hence, the solution set of the given inequality is $(-1, 0) \cup (0, \infty)$.

ILLUSTRATION 3 *Solve:* $\dfrac{1-x^2}{5x-6-x^2} < 0$

SOLUTION We have,

$$\frac{1-x^2}{5x-6-x^2} < 0 \Leftrightarrow \frac{-(x^2-1)}{-(x^2-5x+6)} < 0 \Leftrightarrow \frac{x^2-1}{x^2-5x+6} < 0 \Leftrightarrow \frac{(x-1)(x+1)}{(x-2)(x-3)} < 0 \qquad \text{...(i)}$$

Equating all the factors to zero, we obtain $x = 1, -1, 2, 3$ as the critical points.

Now, we plot these points on the number line as show in Fig. 13.2. These points divide the number line into 5 regions. In the right most region the expression in (i) bears '+' sign and in the other regions the expression bears alternate negative and positive signs as shown in Fig. 13.2.

Since the expression in (i) is negative, so solution set of the given inequation is the union of regions containing negative signs. Hence, from Fig. 13.2, we get $x \in (-1, 1) \cup (2, 3)$

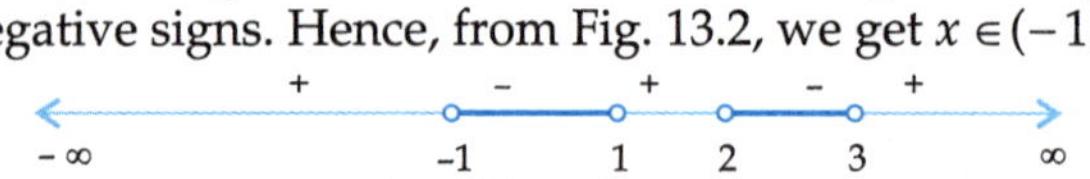

Fig. 13.2 Signs of $\dfrac{(x-1)(x+1)}{(x-2)(x-3)}$ for different values of x

i.e. $\quad \dfrac{1-x^2}{5x-6-x^2}<0 \Rightarrow x\in(-1,1)\cup(2,3)$

ILLUSTRATION 4 *Solve:* $\dfrac{8x^2+16x-51}{2x^2+5x-12}>3.$

SOLUTION We have,

$$\frac{8x^2+16x-51}{2x^2+5x-12}>3 \Leftrightarrow \frac{8x^2+16x-51}{2x^2+5x-12}-3>0 \Leftrightarrow \frac{8x^2+16x-51-6x^2-15x+36}{2x^2+5x-12}>0$$

$$\Leftrightarrow \frac{2x^2+x-15}{2x^2+5x-12}>0 \Leftrightarrow \frac{2x^2+6x-5x-15}{2x^2+8x-3x-12}>0 \Leftrightarrow \frac{(x+3)\ (2x-5)}{(x+4)\ (2x-3)}>0 \qquad \text{...(i)}$$

Equating all factors to zero, we obtain $x=-4,-3,3/2,5/2$. Now, we plot these points on the number line as shown in Fig. 13.3. These points divide the number line into five regions. In the right most region the expression in (i) bears positive sign and in all other regions it bears alternate negative and positive signs as shown in Fig. 13.3.

Fig. 13.3 Signs of $\dfrac{(x+3)(2x-5)}{(x+4)(2x-3)}$ for different values of x

Since the expression in (i) is positive, so the solution set of the given inequation is the union of regions containing '+' signs. Hence, from Fig 13.3, we get $x\in(-\infty,-4)\cup(-3,3/2)\cup(5/2,\infty)$.

i.e. $\quad \dfrac{8x^2+16x-51}{2x^2+5x-12}>3 \Rightarrow x\in(-\infty,-4)\cup(-3,3/2)\cup(5/2,\infty).$

ILLUSTRATION 5 *Solve:* $\dfrac{x^2-2x+5}{3x^2-2x-5}>\dfrac{1}{2}.$

SOLUTION We have,

$$\frac{x^2-2x+5}{3x^2-2x-5}>\frac{1}{2} \Leftrightarrow \frac{x^2-2x+5}{3x^2-2x-5}-\frac{1}{2}>0 \Leftrightarrow \frac{2(x^2-2x+5)-(3x^2-2x-5)}{2(3x^2-2x-5)}>0$$

$$\Leftrightarrow \frac{-x^2-2x+15}{2(3x^2-2x-5)}>0 \Leftrightarrow \frac{-(x^2+2x-15)}{2(3x^2-2x-5)}>0 \Leftrightarrow \frac{x^2+2x-15}{2(3x^2-2x-5)}<0 \Leftrightarrow \frac{x^2+2x-15}{3x^2-2x-5}>0$$

$$\Leftrightarrow \frac{(x+5)(x-3)}{(x+1)(3x-5)}<0 \qquad \text{...(i)}$$

On equating all factors to zero, we get $x=-5,-1,5/3,3$. Plotting these points on number line and marking alternatively '+' and '–' signs, we obtain as shown in Fig. 13.4.

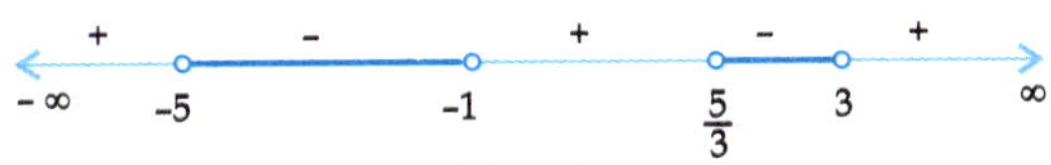

Fig. 13.4 Signs of $\dfrac{(x+5)(x-3)}{(x+1)(3x-5)}$ for different values of x

Since the expression in (i) is negative, so the solution set of the given inequation is the union of regions marked with '–' signs. Hence, from Fig. 13.4, we get $x\in(-5,-1)\cup(5/3,3)$.

i.e. $\quad \dfrac{x^2-2x+5}{3x^2-2x-5}>\dfrac{1}{2} \Rightarrow x\in(-5,-1)\cup(5/3,3).$

ILLUSTRATION 6 *Solve:* $\dfrac{x^2-2x+24}{x^2-3x+4}\le 4.$

SOLUTION We have,

$$\frac{x^2-2x+24}{x^2-3x+4} \le 4 \Leftrightarrow \frac{x^2-2x+24}{x^2-3x+4} - 4 \le 0 \Leftrightarrow \frac{(x^2-2x+24)-4(x^2-3x+4)}{x^2-3x+4} \le 0$$

$$\Leftrightarrow \quad \frac{-3x^2+10x+8}{x^2-3x+4} \le 0 \Leftrightarrow \frac{3x^2-10x-8}{x^2-3x+4} \ge 0 \Leftrightarrow \frac{(3x+2)(x-4)}{(x^2-3x+4)} \ge 0$$

$$\Leftrightarrow \quad (3x+2)(x-4) \ge 0 \qquad \left[\begin{array}{r} \because \text{Disc. of } x^2-3x+4 \text{ is } - \text{ve and coeff. of } x^2 \text{ is } + \text{ve} \\ \therefore x^2-3x+4>0 \text{ for all } x \end{array}\right]$$

$$\Leftrightarrow \quad x \le -\frac{2}{3} \text{ or } x \ge 4 \Leftrightarrow x \in (-\infty, -2/3] \cup [4, \infty) \qquad \text{[See Fig. 13.5]}$$

Thus, $\dfrac{x^2-2x+24}{x^2-3x+4} \le 4 \Rightarrow x \in (-\infty, -2/3 \cup [4, \infty)$.

Fig. 13.5 Signs of $(3x+2)(x-4)$ for different values of x.

ILLUSTRATION 7 *Solve:* $\dfrac{x^2-4x+7}{x^2-7x+12} \le \dfrac{2}{3}$.

SOLUTION We have,

$$\frac{x^2-4x+7}{x^2-7x+12} \le \frac{2}{3} \Leftrightarrow \frac{x^2-4x+7}{x^2-7x+12} - \frac{2}{3} \le 0$$

$$\Leftrightarrow \quad \frac{3(x^2-4x+7)-2(x^2-7x+12)}{x^2-7x+12} \le 0 \Leftrightarrow \frac{x^2+2x-3}{x^2-7x+12} \le 0 \Leftrightarrow \frac{(x+3)(x-1)}{(x-3)(x-4)} \le 0 \qquad ...(i)$$

On equating all factors in (i) to zero, we get $x = -3, 1, 3, 4$ as critical points. Plotting these points on the number line and marking alternatively '+' and '–' signs from the right most side, we obtain that the inequation in (i) has the signs as shown in Fig. 13.6. Since the expression in (i) is negative, so the solution set of the given in, equation is the union of the regions marked with '–' signs. Hence, from Fig 13.6, we get $x \in [-3, 1] \cup (3, 4)$.

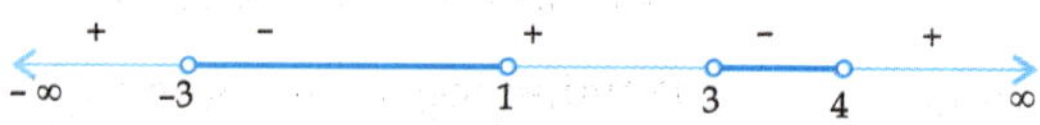

Fig. 13.6 Signs of $\dfrac{(x+3)(x-1)}{(x-3)(x-4)}$ for different values of x

i.e. $\dfrac{x^2-4x+7}{x^2-7x+12} \le \dfrac{2}{3} \Rightarrow x \in [-3, 1] \in (3, 4)$.

It should be noted that 3 and 4 are not included, because denominator becomes zero at $x = 3$ and $x = 4$.

13.3 SOME DEFINITIONS

STRICTLY INCREASING FUNCTION *A function $f(x)$ is said to be a strictly increasing function on (a, b), if*

$$x_1 < x_2 \Rightarrow f(x_1) < f(x_2) \text{ for all } x_1, x_2 \in (a, b)$$

Thus, $f(x)$ is strictly increasing on (a, b) if the values of $f(x)$ increase with the increase in the values of x.

Graphically, $f(x)$ is increasing on (a, b) if the graph $y = f(x)$ moves up as x moves to the right. The graph in Fig. 13.7 is the graph of a strictly increasing function on (a, b).

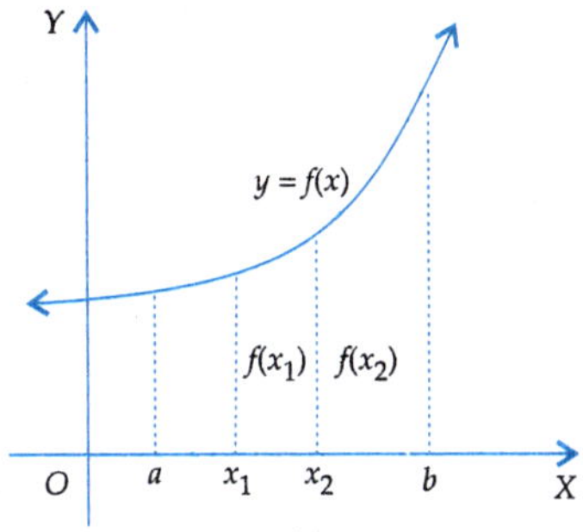

Fig. 13.7 Graph of an increasing function

ILLUSTRATION 1 *Show that the function $f(x) = 2x + 3$ is strictly increasing function on R.*

SOLUTION Let $x_1, x_2 \in R$ and let $x_1 < x_2$. Then,

$$x_1 < x_2 \Rightarrow 2x_1 < 2x_2 \Rightarrow 2x_1 + 3 < 2x_2 + 3 \Rightarrow f(x_1) < f(x_2)$$

Thus, $x_1 < x_2 \Rightarrow f(x_1) < f(x_2)$ for all $x_1, x_2 \in R$. So, $f(x)$ is strictly increasing function on R. This result is also evident from the graph of the function shown in Fig. 13.8.

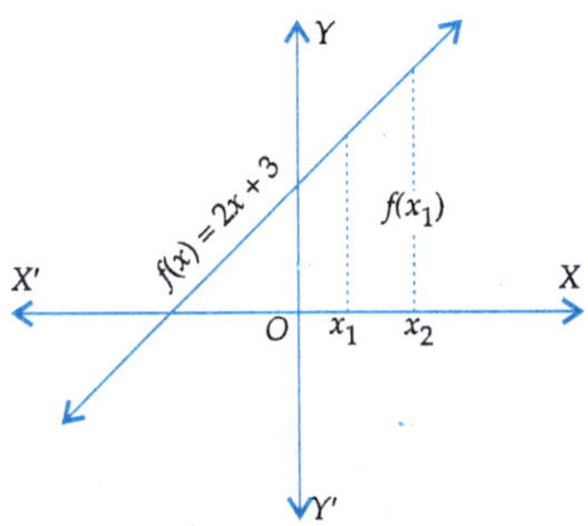

Fig. 13.8 Graph of $f(x) = 2x + 3$

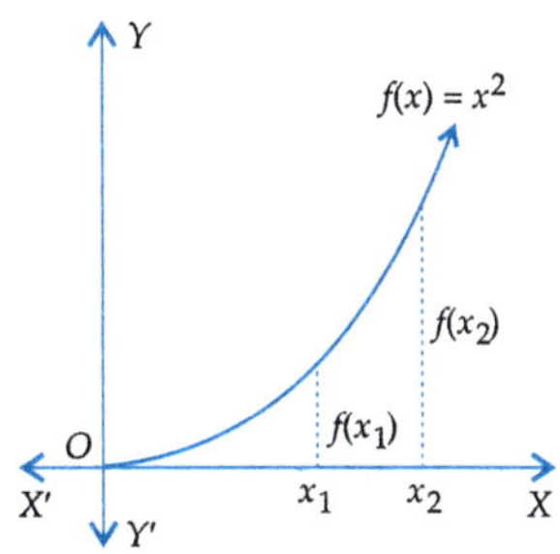

Fig. 13.9 Graph of $f(x) = x^2, x \geq 0$

ILLUSTRATION 2 *Show that the function $f(x) = x^2$ is strictly increasing function on $[0, \infty)$.*

SOLUTION Let $x_1, x_2 \in [0, \infty)$ such that $x_1 < x_2$. Then,

$$x_1 < x_2 \Rightarrow x_1^2 < x_1 x_2 \quad \text{[Multiplying both sides by } x_1] \quad ...(i)$$

again, $$x_1 < x_2 \Rightarrow x_1 x_2 < x_2^2 \quad \text{[Multiplying both sides by } x_2] \quad ...(ii)$$

From (i) and (ii), we get

$$x_1 < x_2 \Rightarrow x_1^2 < x_2^2 \Rightarrow f(x_1) < f(x_2)$$

Thus, $x_1 < x_2 \Rightarrow f(x_1) < f(x_2)$ for all $x_1, x_2 \in [0, \infty)$.

Hence, $f(x)$ is strictly increasing function on $[0, \infty)$ which is evident from the graph shown in Fig. 13.9.

ILLUSTRATION 3 *Show that the function $f(x) = a^x$, $a > 1$ is strictly increasing on R.*

SOLUTION Let $x_1, x_2 \in R$ such that $x_1 < x_2$. Then,

$$x_1 < x_2$$

$$\Rightarrow a^{x_1} < a^{x_2} \quad [\because a > 1 \therefore x_1 < x_2 \Rightarrow a^{x_1} < a^{x_2}]$$

$$\Rightarrow f(x_1) < f(x_2)$$

Thus, $x_1 < x_2 \Rightarrow f(x_1) < f(x_2)$ for all $x_1, x_2 \in R$.

Hence, $f(x)$ is strictly increasing function on R. This fact is also exhibited in the graph of this function as shown in Fig. 13.10.

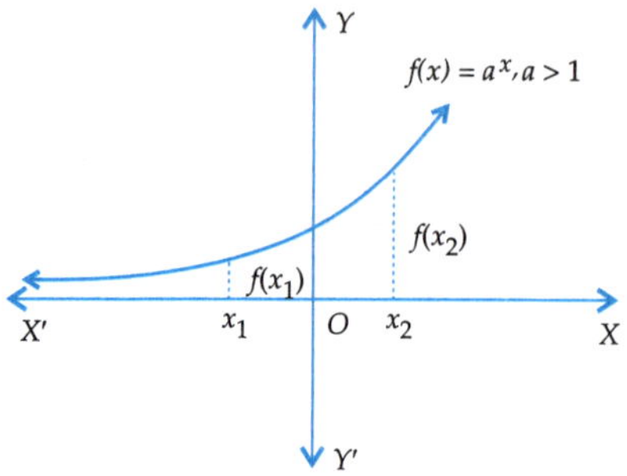

Fig. 13.10 Graph of $f(x) = a^x, a > 1$

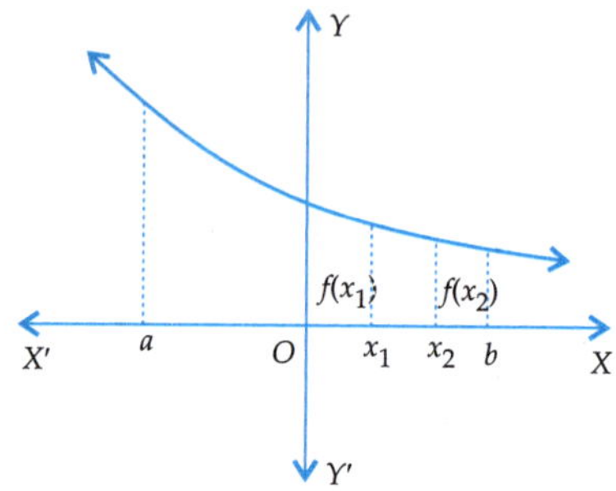

Fig. 13.11 Graph of decreasing function

REMARK *In the above example if we replace a by e (≈ 2.71), then we find that $f(x) = e^x$ is also increasing on R.*

STRICTLY DECREASING FUNCTION *A function $f(x)$ is said to be a strictly decreasing function on (a, b), if*

$$x_1 < x_2 \Rightarrow f(x_1) > f(x_2) \quad \text{for all } x_1, x_2 \in (a, b)$$

Thus, $f(x)$ is strictly decreasing on (a, b) if the values of $f(x)$ decrease with the increase in the values of x.

Graphically it means that $f(x)$ is a decreasing function on (a, b) if its graph moves down as x moves to the right. The graph in Fig. 13.11 is the graph of a strictly decreasing function.

ILLUSTRATION 4 *Show that the function $f(x) = -3x + 12$ is strictly decreasing function on R.*

SOLUTION Let $x_1, x_2 \in R$ be such that $x_1 < x_2$. Then,

$$x_1 < x_2 \Rightarrow -3x_1 > -3x_2 \Rightarrow -3x_1 + 12 > -3x_2 + 12 \Rightarrow f(x_1) > f(x_2)$$

Thus, $x_1 < x_2 \Rightarrow f(x_1) > f(x_2)$ for all $x_1, x_2 \in R$.

So, $f(x)$ is strictly decreasing function on R.

This fact can also be observed from the graph of the function as shown in Fig. 13.12

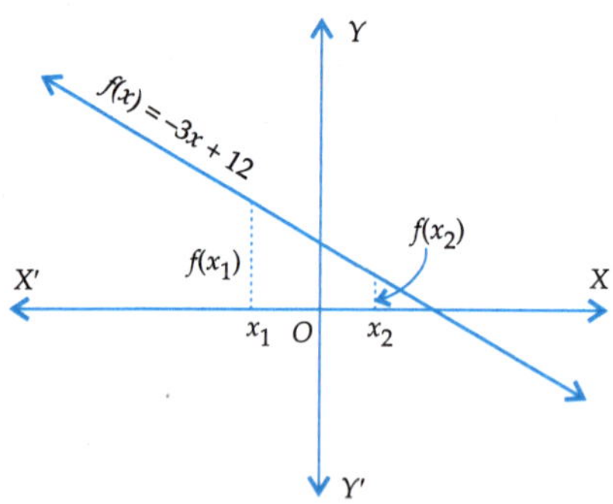

Fig. 13.12 Graph of $f(x) = -3x + 12$

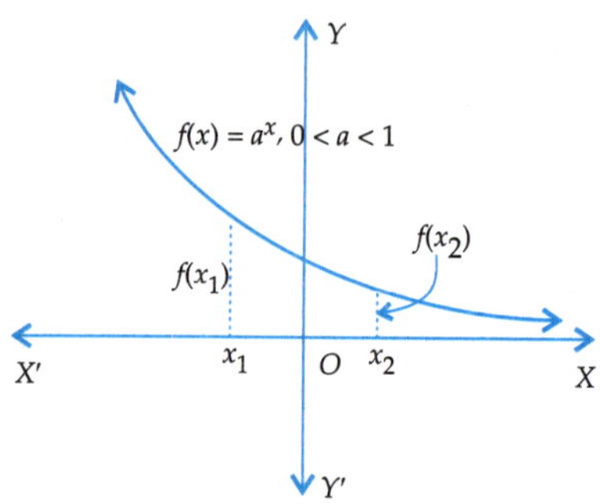

Fig. 13.13 Graph of $f(x) = a^x, 0 < a < 1$

ILLUSTRATION 5 *Show that the function $f(x) = a^x$, $0 < a < 1$ is strictly decreasing on R.*

SOLUTION Let $x_1, x_2 \in R$ such that $x_1 < x_2$. Then,

$$x_1 < x_2$$

$$\Rightarrow \quad a^{x_1} > a^{x_2} \qquad [\because 0 < a < 1 \therefore x_1 < x_2 \Rightarrow a^{x_1} > a^{x_2}]$$

$$\Rightarrow \quad f(x_1) > f(x_2)$$

Thus, $x_1 < x_2 \Rightarrow f(x_1) > f(x_2)$ for all $x_1, x_2, \in R$.

Hence, $f(x)$ is strictly decreasing function on R. This is also evident from the graph of $f(x)$ as shown in Fig. 13.13.

REMARK *Since* $0 < e^{-1} = \frac{1}{e} < 1$, *therefore* $f(x) = (e^{-1})^x = e^{-x}$ *is also a strictly decreasing function on R.*

ILLUSTRATION 6 *Show that the function* $f(x) = x^2$ *is a strictly decreasing function on* $(-\infty, 0]$.

SOLUTION Let $x_1, x_2 \in (-\infty, 0]$ be such that $x_1 < x_2$. Then,

$$x_1 < x_2 \Rightarrow x_1^2 > x_1 x_2 \quad ...(i) \quad \text{and,} \quad x_1 < x_2 \Rightarrow x_1 x_2 > x_2^2 \quad ...(ii)$$

From (i) and (ii), we obtain

$$x_1 < x_2 \Rightarrow x_1^2 > x_2^2 \Rightarrow f(x_1) > f(x_2)$$

Thus, $x_1 < x_2 \Rightarrow f(x_1) > f(x_2)$ for all $x_1, x_2 \in (-\infty, 0]$.

Hence, $f(x)$ is strictly decreasing on $(-\infty, 0]$. See also Fig. 13.14.

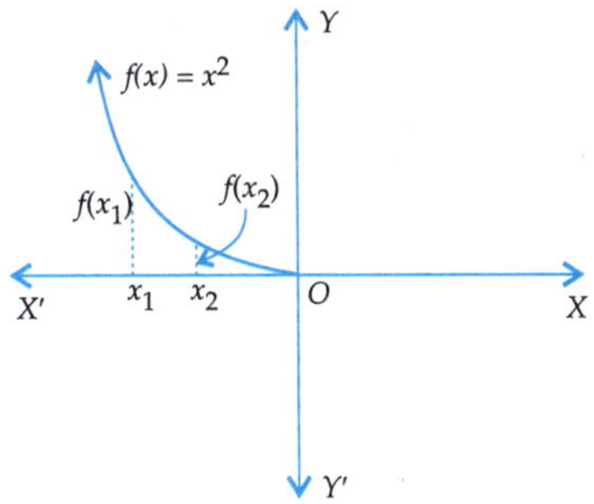

Fig. 13.14 Graph of $f(x) = x^2, x \le 0$

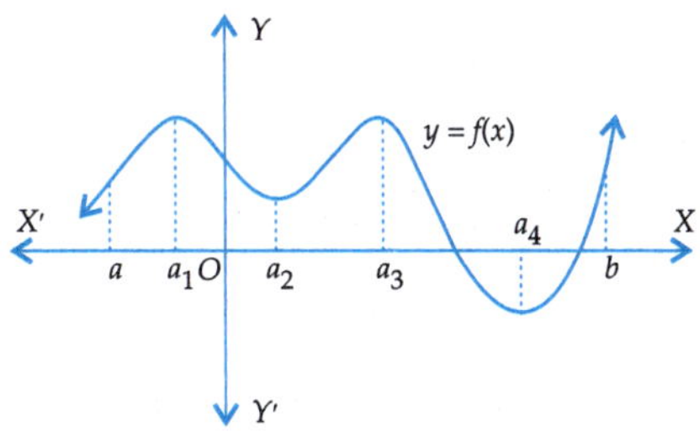

Fig. 13.15

Uptill now, we have been discussing about a strictly increasing or strictly decreasing functions. But, it is possible that a function may neither be strictly increasing nor strictly decreasing on a given interval. For example, $f(x)$ in Fig. 13.15 is neither strictly increasing nor strictly decreasing on (a, b). However, it is increasing on the sub-intervals (a, a_1), (a_2, a_3) and (a_4, b) and decreasing on the intervals (a_1, a_2) and (a_3, a_4).

ILLUSTRATION 7 *Show that the function* $f(x) = x^2$ *is neither strictly increasing nor strictly decreasing on R.*

SOLUTION In illustrations 3 and 6 we have seen that $f(x) = x^2$ is strictly increasing on $[0, \infty)$ and strictly decreasing on $(-\infty, 0]$. Hence, it is neither strictly increasing nor strictly decreasing on R i.e. $(-\infty, \infty)$.

Uptill now we were talking about strictly increasing and strictly decreasing functions. But, there can be functions which are increasing (decreasing) but not strictly increasing (decreasing). For example, consider the function whose graph is shown in Fig. 13.16. Clearly, $f(x)$ is increasing on (a, b) but it is strictly increasing only in the intervals (a, a_1) and (a_2, b). Such functions are called monotonically increasing function. In this chapter, we shall be studying only strictly increasing and strictly decreasing function.

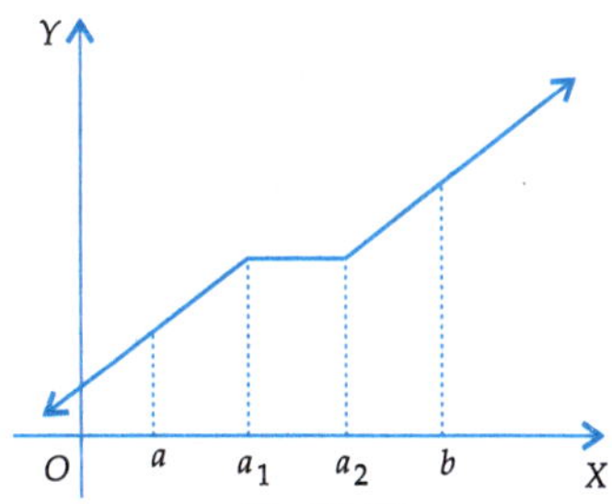

Fig. 13.16

NOTE *From now onwards, by an increasing or a decreasing function we shall mean a strictly increasing or a strictly decreasing function.*

MONOTONIC FUNCTION (i) *A function* $f(x)$ *is said to be monotonically on an interval* (a, b),

$$x_1 x_2 \Rightarrow f(x_1) \le f(x_2) \text{ for all } x_1, x_2 \in (a, b)$$

(ii) *A function* $f(x)$ *is said to be monotonically decreasing on an interval* (a, b), *if*

$$x_1 < x_2 \Rightarrow f(x_1) \ge f(x_2) \text{ for all } x_1, x_2 \in (a, b).$$

DEFINITION *A function $f(x)$ is said to be increasing (decreasing) at a point x_0 if there is an interval $(x_0 - h, x_0 + h)$ containing x_0 such that $f(x)$ is increasing (decreasing) on $(x_0 - h, x_0 + h)$.*

DEFINITION *A function $f(x)$ is said to be increasing on [a, b] if it is increasing (decreasing) on (a, b) and it is also increasing (decreasing) at $x = a$ and $x = b$.*

EXERCISE 13.1

BASIC

1. Prove that the function $f(x) = \log_e x$ is increasing on $(0, \infty)$.
2. Prove that the function $f(x) = \log_a x$ is increasing on $(0, \infty)$ if $a > 1$ and decreasing on $(0, \infty)$, if $0 < a < 1$.
3. Prove that $f(x) = ax + b$, where a, b are constants and $a > 0$ is an increasing function on R.
4. Prove that $f(x) = ax + b$, where a, b are constants and $a < 0$ is a decreasing function on R.
5. Show that $f(x) = \frac{1}{x}$ is a decreasing function on $(0, \infty)$.
6. Show that $f(x) = \frac{1}{1+x^2}$ decreases in the interval $[0, \infty)$ and increases in the interval $(-\infty, 0]$.
7. Show that $f(x) = \frac{1}{1+x^2}$ is neither increasing nor decreasing on R.
8. Without using the derivative, show that the function $f(x) = |x|$ is
   (a) strictly increasing in $(0, \infty)$ (b) strictly decreasing in $(-\infty, 0)$.
9. Without using the derivative show that the function $f(x) = 7x - 3$ is strictly increasing function on R.

HINTS TO SELECTED PROBLEMS

1. For any $x_1, x_2 \in (0, \infty)$, we have
   $x_1 < x_2 \Rightarrow \log_e x_1 < \log_e x_2 \Rightarrow f(x_1) < f(x_2) \Rightarrow f(x)$ is increasing on $(0, \infty)$.
2. Case I When $a > 1$: For any $x_1, x_2 \in (0, \infty)$
   $x_1 > x_2 \Rightarrow \log_a x_1 > \log_a x_2 \Rightarrow f(x_1) > f(x_2) \Rightarrow f(x)$ is increasing on $(0, \infty)$.
   Case II When $a < 1$: For any $x_1, x_2 \in (0, \infty)$
   $x_1 > x_2 \Rightarrow \log_a x_1 < \log_a x_2 \Rightarrow f(x_1) < f(x_2) \Rightarrow f(x)$ is decreasing on $(0, \infty)$

13.4 NECESSARY AND SUFFICIENT CONDITIONS FOR MONOTONICITY

In this section, we intend to see how we can use derivative of a function to determine where it is increasing and where it is decreasing.

THEOREM 1 *(Necessary Condition) Let $f(x)$ be continuous on $[a, b]$ and differentiable on (a, b).*

(i) If $f(x)$ is strictly increasing on (a, b), then $f'(x) > 0$ for all $x \in (a, b)$.

(ii) If $f(x)$ is strictly decreasing on (a, b), then $f'(x) < 0$ for all $x \in (a, b)$.

PROOF Let x be an arbitrary point in (a, b). Since $f(x)$ is differentiable on (a, b). So, it is differentiable at x.

$$\therefore \quad f'(x) = \lim_{h \to 0} \frac{f(x+h) - f(x)}{h}, h > 0 \text{ exists.}$$

(i) If $f(x)$ is strictly increasing on (a, b), then

$$f(x+h) > f(x) \text{ for all } h > 0$$

$$\Rightarrow \quad \frac{f(x+h)-f(x)}{h} > 0 \text{ for all } h > 0 \Rightarrow \lim_{h \to 0} \frac{f(x+h)-f(x)}{h} > 0 \Rightarrow f'(x) > 0.$$

Since x is an arbitrary point of (a, b). Therefore, $f'(x) > 0$ for all $x \in (a, b)$.

(ii) If $f(x)$ is strictly decreasing on (a, b), then

$$f(x+h) < f(x) \text{ for all } h > 0$$

$$\Rightarrow \quad \frac{f(x+h)-f(x)}{h} < 0 \text{ for all } h > 0 \Rightarrow \lim_{h \to 0} \frac{f(x+h)-f(x)}{h} < 0 \Rightarrow f'(x) < 0$$

Since x is an arbitrary point of (a, b). Therefore, $f'(x) < 0$ for all $x \in (a, b)$.

Q.E.D.

REMARK *If $f(x)$ is an increasing function on (a, b), then as shown in Fig. 13.17, the tangent at every point on the curve $y = f(x)$ makes an acute angle θ with the positive direction of x-axis.*

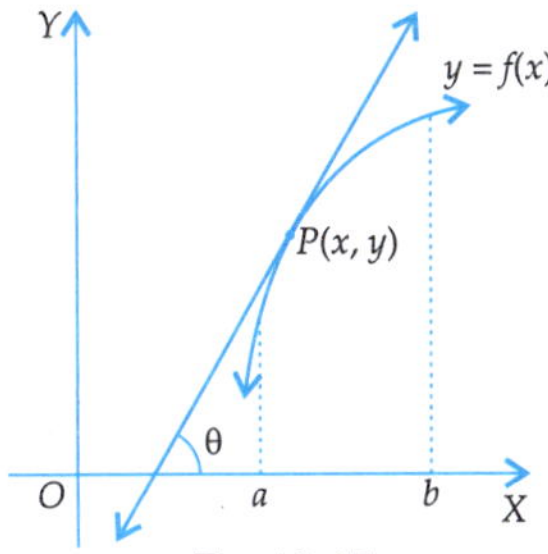

Fig. 13.17

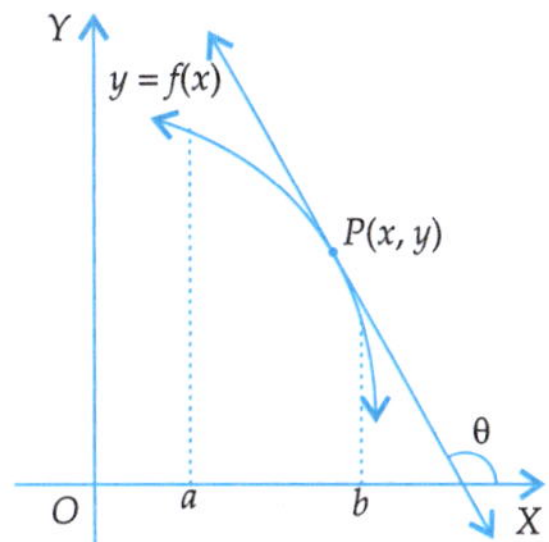

Fig. 13.18

$$\therefore \quad \tan\theta > 0 \Rightarrow \frac{dy}{dx} > 0 \text{ or, } f'(x) > 0 \textit{ for all } x \in (a, b)$$

If $f(x)$ is a decreasing function on (a, b), then as shown in Fig. 13.18, the tangent at every point on the curve $y = f(x)$ makes an obtuse angle θ with x-axis.

$$\therefore \quad \tan\theta < 0 \Rightarrow \frac{dy}{dx} < 0 \text{ or, } f'(x) < 0 \textit{ for all } x \in (a, b).$$

THEOREM 2 *(Sufficient Condition) Let f be a differentiable real function defined on an open interval (a, b).*

(i) If $f'(x) > 0$ for all $x \in (a, b)$, then $f(x)$ is increasing on (a, b).

(ii) If $f'(x) < 0$ for all $x \in (a, b)$, then $f(x)$ is decreasing on (a, b).

PROOF Let $x_1, x_2 \in (a, b)$ such that $x_1 < x_2$. Consider the sub-interval $[x_1, x_2]$. Since $f(x)$ is differentiable on (a, b) and $[x_1, x_2] \subset (a, b)$. Therefore, $f(x)$ is continuous on $[x_1, x_2]$ and differentiable on (x_1, x_2). By the Lagrange's mean value theorem, there exists $c \in (x_1, x_2)$ such that

$$f'(c) = \frac{f(x_2) - f(x_1)}{x_2 - x_1} \quad \text{...(i)}$$

(i) Since $f'(x) > 0$ for all $x \in (a, b)$, so in particular, $f'(c) > 0$.

Now, $f'(c) > 0$

$$\Rightarrow \quad \frac{f(x_2) - f(x_1)}{x_2 - x_1} > 0 \quad \text{[Using (i)]}$$

$$\Rightarrow \quad f(x_2) - f(x_1) > 0 \quad [\because x_2 - x_1 > 0 \text{ when } x_1 < x_2]$$

$\Rightarrow \quad f(x_2) > f(x_1)$ or, $f(x_1) < f(x_2)$

Since x_1, x_2 are arbitrary points in (a, b). Therefore, $x_1 < x_2 \Rightarrow f(x_1) < f(x_2)$ for all $x_1, x_2 \in (a, b)$.

Hence, $f(x)$ is increasing on (a, b).

(ii) Since $f'(x) < 0$ for all $x \in (a, b)$, so in particular, $f'(c) < 0$.

Now, $f'(c) < 0$

$$\Rightarrow \quad \frac{f(x_2) - f(x_1)}{x_2 - x_1} < 0 \qquad \text{[Using (i)]}$$

$$\Rightarrow \quad f(x_2) - f(x_1) < 0 \qquad [\because x_2 - x_1 > 0 \text{ when } x_1 < x_2]$$

$$\Rightarrow \quad f(x_2) < f(x_1) \Rightarrow f(x_1) > f(x_2)$$

Since x_1, x_2 are arbitrary points in (a, b). Therefore, $x_1 < x_2 \Rightarrow f(x_1) > f(x_2)$ for all $x_1, x_2 \in (a, b)$.

Hence, $f(x)$ is decreasing on (a, b).

COROLLARY *Let $f(x)$ be a function defined on (a, b).*

(i) *If $f'(x) > 0$ for all $x \in (a, b)$ except for a finite number of points, where $f'(x) = 0$, then $f(x)$ is increasing on $((a, b)$.*

(ii) *If $f'(x) < 0$ for all $x \in (a, b)$ except for a finite number of points, where $f'(x) = 0$, then $f(x)$ is decreasing on (a, b).*

In order to find the interval in which a given function is increasing or decreasing, we may use the following algorithm.

ALGORITHM

Step I *Obtain the function and put it equal to $f(x)$.*

Step II *Find $f'(x)$.*

Step III *Put $f'(x) > 0$ and solve this inequation.*

For the values of x obtained in step III $f(x)$ is increasing and for the remaining points in its domain it is decreasing.

ILLUSTRATIVE EXAMPLES

BASED ON BASIC CONCEPTS (BASIC)

Type I ON FINDING THE INTERVALS IN WHICH A FUNCTION IS INCREASING OR DECREASING

EXAMPLE 1 *Find the intervals in which $f(x) = -x^2 - 2x + 15$ is increasing or decreasing.*

SOLUTION We have,

$$f(x) = -x^2 - 2x + 15 \Rightarrow f'(x) = -2x - 2 = -2(x + 1)$$

For $f(x)$ to be increasing, we must have

$$f'(x) > 0$$

$$\Rightarrow \quad -2(x + 1) > 0$$

$$\Rightarrow \quad x + 1 < 0 \qquad [\because -2 < 0 \text{ and } ab > 0, a < 0 \Rightarrow b < 0]$$

$$\Rightarrow \quad x < -1 \Rightarrow x \in (-\infty, -1)$$

Thus, $f(x)$ is increasing on the interval $(-\infty, -1)$.

For $f(x)$ to be decreasing, we must have

$f'(x) < 0$

$\Rightarrow \quad -2(x+1) < 0$

$\Rightarrow \quad x+1 > 0$ $\quad [\because -2 < 0 \text{ and } ab < 0, a < 0 \Rightarrow b > 0]$

$\Rightarrow \quad x > -1 \Rightarrow x \in (-1, \infty)$

So, $f(x)$ is decreasing on $(-1, \infty)$.

EXAMPLE 2 *Find the intervals in which the function* $f(x) = 2x^3 - 9x^2 + 12x + 15$ *is (i) increasing, (ii) decreasing:* **[CBSE 2010, 2011]**

SOLUTION We have,

$$f(x) = 2x^3 - 9x^2 + 12x + 15 \Rightarrow f'(x) = 6x^2 - 18x + 12 = 6(x^2 - 3x + 2)$$

(i) For $f(x)$ to be increasing, we must have

$f'(x) > 0$

$\Rightarrow \quad 6(x^2 - 3x + 2) > 0$

$\Rightarrow \quad x^2 - 3x + 2 > 0$ $\quad [\because 6 > 0 \therefore 6(x^2 - 3x + 2) > 0 \Rightarrow x^2 - 3x + 2 > 0]$

$\Rightarrow \quad (x-1)(x-2) > 0$

$\Rightarrow \quad x < 1 \text{ or } x > 2 \Rightarrow x \in (-\infty, 1) \cup (2, \infty).$ [See Fig. 13.19]

So, $f(x)$ is increasing on $(-\infty, 1) \cup (2, \infty)$.

Fig. 13.19 Signs of $f'(x)$ for different values of x

(ii) For $f(x)$ to be decreasing , we must have

$f'(x) < 0$

$\Rightarrow \quad 6(x^2 - 3x + 2) < 0$

$\Rightarrow \quad x^2 - 3x + 2 < 0$ $\quad [\because 6 > 0 \therefore 6(x^2 - 3x + 2) < 0 \Rightarrow x^2 - 3x + 2 < 0]$

$\Rightarrow \quad (x-1)(x-2) < 0 \Rightarrow 1 < x < 2 \Rightarrow x \in (1, 2)$ [See Fig. 13.20]

So, $f(x)$ is decreasing on (1, 2).

Fig. 13.20 Signs of $f'(x)$ for different values of x

EXAMPLE 3 *Find the intervals in which the function* $f(x) = 2x^3 + 9x^2 + 12x + 20$ *is (i) increasing; (ii) decreasing:*

SOLUTION We have,

$$f(x) = 2x^3 + 9x^2 + 12x + 20 \Rightarrow f'(x) = 6x^2 + 18x + 12 = 6(x^2 + 3x + 2)$$

(i) For $f(x)$ to be increasing, we must have

$f'(x) > 0$

$\Rightarrow \quad 6(x^2 + 3x + 2) > 0$

$\Rightarrow \quad (x^2 + 3x + 2) > 0$ $\quad [\because 6 > 0 \text{ and } 6(x^2 + 3x + 2) > 0 \therefore x^2 + 3x + 2 > 0]$

$\Rightarrow \quad (x+1)(x+2) > 0$ [See Fig. 13.21]

$\Rightarrow \quad x < -2 \text{ or } x > -1$

$\Rightarrow \quad x \in (-\infty, -2) \cup (-1, \infty)$

So, $f(x)$ is increasing on $(-\infty, -2) \cup (-1, \infty)$

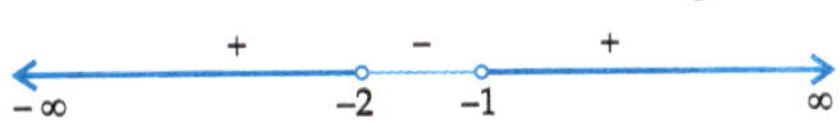

Fig. 13.21 Signs of $f'(x)$ for different values of x

(ii) For $f(x)$ to be decreasing, we must have

$f'(x) < 0$

$\Rightarrow \quad 6(x^2 + 3x + 2) < 0$

$\Rightarrow \quad x^2 + 3x + 2 < 0$ $\quad [\because 6 > 0 \text{ and } 6(x^2 + 3x + 2) < 0 \therefore x^2 + 3x + 2 < 0]$

$\Rightarrow \quad (x + 1)(x + 2) < 0$ $\quad$ [See Fig. 13.22]

$\Rightarrow \quad -2 < x < -1$

So, $f(x)$ is decreasing on $(-2, -1)$.

Fig. 13.22 Signs of $f'(x)$ for different values of x

EXAMPLE 4 *Find the intervals in which $f(x) = (x+1)^3 (x-3)^3$ is increasing or decreasing.* [NCERT, CBSE 2001C, 2011]

SOLUTION We have,

$$f(x) = (x+1)^3 (x-3)^3$$

$$\Rightarrow \quad f'(x) = \left\{3(x+1)^2 \frac{d}{dx}(x+1)\right\}(x-3)^3 + (x+1)^3 \left\{3(x-3)^2 \frac{d}{dx}(x-3)\right\}$$

$$\Rightarrow \quad f'(x) = 3(x+1)^2 (x-3)^3 + 3(x+1)^3 (x-3)^2 = 3(x+1)^2 (x-3)^2 (x+1+x-3)$$

$$\Rightarrow \quad f'(x) = 6(x+1)^2 (x-3)^2 (x-1)$$

For $f(x)$ to be increasing, we must have

$$f'(x) > 0$$

$$\Rightarrow \quad 6(x+1)^2 (x-3)^2 (x-1) > 0$$

$\Rightarrow \quad x - 1 > 0 \text{ and } x \neq -1, 3$ $\quad [\because 6(x+1)^2 (x-3)^2 > 0 \text{ for all } x \neq -1, 3]$

$\Rightarrow \quad x > 1 \text{ and } x \neq -1, 3 \Rightarrow x \in (1, 3) \cup (3, \infty)$

So, $f(x)$ is increasing on $(1, 3) \cup (3, \infty)$.

For $f(x)$ to be decreasing, we must have

$$f'(x) < 0$$

$$\Rightarrow \quad 6(x+1)^2 (x-3)^2 (x-1) < 0$$

$\Rightarrow \quad x - 1 < 0 \text{ and } x \neq -1, 3$ $\quad [\because 6(x+1)^2 (x-3)^2 > 0 \text{ for all } x \neq -1, 3]$

$\Rightarrow \quad x < 1 \text{ and } x \neq -1, 3 \Rightarrow x \in (-\infty, -1) \cup (-1, 1)$

So, $f(x)$ is decreasing on $(-\infty, -1) \cup (-1, 1)$.

EXAMPLE 5 *Find the intervals in which $f(x) = (x-1)^3 (x-2)^2$ is increasing or decreasing.*

SOLUTION We have,

$$f(x) = (x-1)^3 (x-2)^2$$

$$\Rightarrow \quad f'(x) = 3(x-1)^2 \left\{\frac{d}{dx}(x-1)\right\}(x-2)^2 + (x-1)^3 \, 2 \times (x-2) \frac{d}{dx}(x-2)$$

$$\Rightarrow \quad f'(x) = 3(x-1)^2 (x-2)^2 + 2(x-1)^3 (x-2) = (x-1)^2 (x-2)(3x-6+2x-2)$$

$$\Rightarrow \quad f'(x) = (x-1)^2 (x-2)(5x-8)$$

For $f(x)$ to be increasing, we must have

$$f'(x) > 0$$

$$\Rightarrow \quad (x-1)^2 (x-2)(5x-8) > 0$$

$\Rightarrow \quad (x-2)(5x-8) > 0 \text{ and } x \neq 1$ $\quad [\because (x-1)^2 > 0 \text{ for all } x \neq 1]$

$\Rightarrow \quad 5(x - 8/5)(x-2) > 0 \text{ and } x \neq 1$

$\Rightarrow \quad (x - 8/5)(x-2) > 0 \text{ and } x \neq 1$ $\quad [\because 5 > 0]$

$\Rightarrow \quad x < 8/5 \text{ or } x > 2 \text{ and } x \neq 1 \Rightarrow x \in (-\infty, 1) \cup (1, 8/5) \cup (2, \infty)$ $\quad$ [See Fig. 13.23]

So, $f(x)$ is increasing on $(-\infty, 1) \cup (1, 8/5) \cup (2, \infty)$.

For $f(x)$ to be decreasing, we must have

$$f'(x) < 0$$

$$\Rightarrow \quad (x-1)^2 (x-2)(5x-8) < 0$$

Fig. 13.23 Signs of $f'(x)$ for different values of x

$\Rightarrow \quad (x-2)(5x-8) < 0$ and $x \neq 1$ $\quad [\because (x-1)^2 > 0$ for all $x \neq 1]$

$\Rightarrow \quad 5(x-2)(x-8/5) < 0$ and $x \neq 1$

$\Rightarrow \quad (x-8/5)(x-2) < 0$ and $x \neq 1$ $\quad [\because 5 > 0]$

$\Rightarrow \quad x \in (8/5, 2)$ and $x \neq 1 \Rightarrow x \in (8/5, 2)$ $\quad$ [See Fig. 13.24]

So, $f(x)$ is decreasing on $(8/5, 2)$.

Fig. 13.24 Signs of $f'(x)$ for different values of x

EXAMPLE 6 *Find the intervals in which the function* $f(x) = x^4 - \frac{x^3}{3}$ *is increasing or decreasing.* [NCERT EXEMPLAR]

SOLUTION We have,

$$f(x) = x^4 - \frac{x^3}{3} \Rightarrow f'(x) = 4x^3 - x^2 = x^2(4x-1)$$

For $f(x)$ to be increasing, we must have

$$f'(x) > 0 \Rightarrow x^2(4x-1) > 0 \Rightarrow 4x - 1 > 0 \text{ and } x \neq 0 \qquad [\because x^2 > 0]$$

$$\Rightarrow \quad 4x > 1 \text{ and } x \neq 0 \Rightarrow x > \frac{1}{4} \Rightarrow x \in (1/4, \infty)$$

So, $f(x)$ is increasing on $(1/4, \infty)$.

For $f(x)$ to be decreasing, we must have

$$f'(x) < 0 \Rightarrow x^2(4x-1) > 0 \Rightarrow 4x - 1 < 0 \text{ and } x \neq 0 \qquad [\because x^2 > 0 \text{ for all } x \neq 0]$$

$$\Rightarrow \quad 4x < 1 \text{ and } x \neq 0 \Rightarrow x < 1/4 \text{ and } x \neq 0 \Rightarrow x \in (-\infty, 0) \cup (0, 1/4)$$

So, $f(x)$ is decreasing on $(-\infty, 0) \cup (0, 1/4)$.

EXAMPLE 7 *Find the intervals in which the function* $f(x) = \ln(1+x) - \frac{2x}{2+x}$ *is increasing or decreasing.* [CBSE 2012, NCERT]

SOLUTION We have, $f(x) = \ln(1+x) - \frac{2x}{2+x}$. Clearly, $f(x)$ is defined for all x satisfying $x + 1 > 0$ i.e. $x > -1$. So, domain $(f) = (-1, \infty)$.

Now,

$$f(x) = \ln(1+x) - \frac{2x}{2+x}$$

$$\Rightarrow \quad f'(x) = \frac{1}{1+x}\frac{d}{dx}(x+1) - \frac{(2+x)\times 2 - 2x(0+1)}{(2+x)^2} = \frac{1}{1+x} - \frac{4}{(2+x)^2}$$

$$\Rightarrow \quad f'(x) = \frac{(2+x)^2 - 4(1+x)}{(2+x)^2(1+x)} = \frac{x^2}{(2+x)^2(1+x)} = \left(\frac{x}{2+x}\right)^2 \frac{1}{x+1}$$

For $f(x)$ to be increasing, we must have

$$f'(x) > 0$$

$$\Rightarrow \quad \left(\frac{x}{2+x}\right)^2 \frac{1}{x+1} > 0$$

$$\Rightarrow \quad \frac{1}{x+1} > 0 \text{ and } x \neq 0 \qquad \left[\because \left(\frac{x}{2+x}\right)^2 > 0 \text{ for all } x \neq 0\right]$$

$$\Rightarrow \quad x + 1 > 0 \text{ and } x \neq 0 \Rightarrow x > -1 \text{ and } x \neq 0 \Rightarrow x \in (-1, 0) \cup (0, \infty)$$

So, $f(x)$ is increasing on $(-1, 0) \cup (0, \infty)$.

EXAMPLE 8 *Find the intervals in which* $f(x) = \dfrac{4x^2+1}{x}$ *is increasing or decreasing.* **[CBSE 2004]**

SOLUTION We have, $f(x) = \dfrac{4x^2+1}{x} = 4x + \dfrac{1}{x} \Rightarrow f'(x) = 4 - \dfrac{1}{x^2} = \dfrac{4x^2-1}{x^2}$.

For $f(x)$ to be increasing, we must have

$$f'(x) > 0$$

$$\Rightarrow \frac{4x^2-1}{x^2} > 0$$

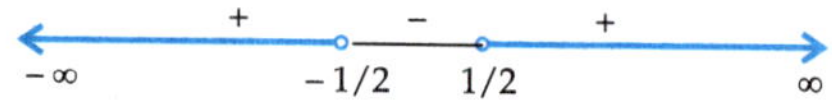

Fig. 13.25 Signs of $f'(x)$ for different values of x

$$\Rightarrow 4x^2 - 1 > 0$$

$$\Rightarrow (2x-1)(2x+1) > 0$$

$\Rightarrow (x - 1/2)(x + 1/2) > 0 \Rightarrow x < -1/2$ or, $x > 1/2 \Rightarrow x \in (-\infty, -1/2) \cup (1/2, \infty)$ [See Fig. 13.25]

So, $f(x)$ is increasing on $(-\infty, -1/2) \cup (1/2, \infty)$.

For $f(x)$ to be decreasing, we must have

$$f'(x) < 0$$

$$\Rightarrow \frac{4x^2-1}{x^2} < 0$$

$\Rightarrow 4x^2 - 1 < 0$ $[\because x^2 > 0]$

$\Rightarrow (2x-1)(2x+1) > 0 \Rightarrow -\dfrac{1}{2} < x < \dfrac{1}{2} \Rightarrow x \in (-1/2, 1/2)$ [See Fig. 13.26]

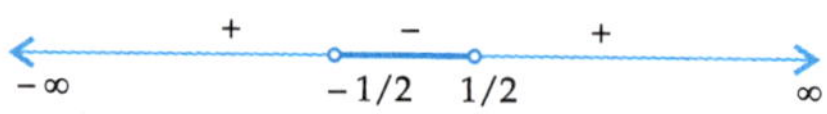

Fig. 13.26 Signs of $f'(x)$ for different values of x

But, domain $(f) = R - \{0\}$. So, $f(x)$ is decreasing on $(-1/2, 0) \cup (0, 1/2)$.

EXAMPLE 9 *Determine the intervals in which the function* $f(x) = x^4 - 8x^3 + 22x^2 - 24x + 21$ *is decreasing or increasing.*

SOLUTION We have,

$$f(x) = x^4 - 8x^3 + 22x^2 - 24x + 21$$

$$\Rightarrow f'(x) = 4x^3 - 24x^2 + 44x - 24 = 4(x^3 - 6x^2 + 11x - 6) = 4(x-1)(x^2 - 5x + 6)$$

For $f(x)$ to be increasing, we must have

$$f'(x) > 0$$

$$\Rightarrow 4(x-1)(x^2 - 5x + 6) > 0$$

Fig. 13.27 Signs of $f'(x)$ for different values of x

$\Rightarrow (x-1)(x^2 - 5x + 6) > 0$ $[\because 4 > 0]$

$\Rightarrow (x-1)(x-2)(x-3) > 0 \Rightarrow 1 < x < 2$ or, $3 < x < \infty \Rightarrow x \in (1, 2) \cup (3, \infty)$ [See Fig. 13.27]

So, $f(x)$ is increasing on $(1, 2) \cup (3, \infty)$.

For $f(x)$ to be decreasing, we must have

$$f'(x) < 0$$

$$\Rightarrow 4(x-1)(x^2 - 5x + 6) < 0$$

$\Rightarrow (x-1)(x^2 - 5x + 6) < 0$ $[\because 4 > 0]$

$\Rightarrow (x-1)(x-2)(x-3) < 0 \Rightarrow 2 < x < 3$ or, $x < 1 \Rightarrow x \in (2, 3) \cup (-\infty, 1)$ [See Fig. 13.28]

So, $f(x)$ is decreasing on $(2, 3) \cup (-\infty, 1)$.

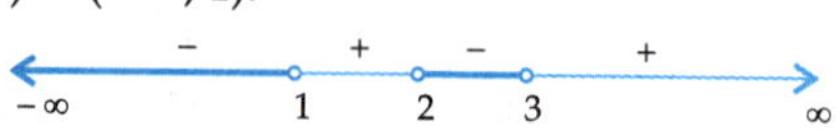

Fig. 13.28 Signs of $f'(x)$ for different values of x

EXAMPLE 10 *Find the intervals for which $f(x) = x^4 - 2x^2$ is increasing or decreasing.*

SOLUTION We have, $f(x) = x^4 - 2x^2 \Rightarrow f'(x) = 4x^3 - 4x = 4x(x^2 - 1)$

For $f(x)$ to be increasing, we must have

$$f'(x) > 0$$

$$\Rightarrow \quad 4x(x^2 - 1) > 0$$

$$\Rightarrow \quad x(x^2 - 1) > 0 \quad [\because 4 > 0]$$

Fig. 13.29 Signs of $f'(x)$ for different values of x

$$\Rightarrow \quad x(x-1)(x+1) > 0 \Rightarrow -1 < x < 0 \text{ or, } x > 1 \Rightarrow x \in (-1, 0) \cup (1, \infty) \quad \text{[See Fig. 13.29]}$$

So, $f(x)$ is increasing on $(-1, 0) \cup (1, \infty)$.

For $f(x)$ to be decreasing, we must have

$$f'(x) < 0$$

$$\Rightarrow \quad 4x(x^2 - 1) < 0$$

$$\Rightarrow \quad x(x^2 - 1) < 0 \quad [\because 4 > 0]$$

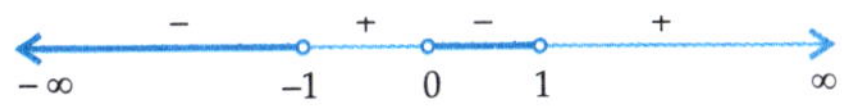

Fig. 13.30 Signs of $f'(x)$ for different values of x

$$\Rightarrow \quad x(x-1)(x+1) < 0 \Rightarrow x < -1 \text{ or, } 0 < x < 1 \Rightarrow x \in (-\infty, -1) \cup (0, 1) \quad \text{[See Fig. 13.30]}$$

So, $f(x)$ is decreasing on $(-\infty, -1) \cup (0, 1)$.

EXAMPLE 11 *Determine the values of x for which $f(x) = \frac{x-2}{x+1}$, $x \neq -1$ is increasing or decreasing.*

SOLUTION We have, $f(x) = \frac{x-2}{x+1}$, $x \neq -1$.

$$\Rightarrow \quad f'(x) = \frac{(x+1) \times 1 - (x-2) \times 1}{(x+1)^2} = \frac{3}{(x+1)^2}, \; x \neq -1.$$

Clearly, $f'(x) = \frac{3}{(x+1)^2} > 0$ for all $x \in R - \{-1\}$. So, $f(x)$ is increasing on $R - \{-1\}$.

EXAMPLE 12 *Find the intervals in which $f(x) = \frac{x}{2} + \frac{2}{x}$, $x \neq 0$ is increasing or decreasing.*

SOLUTION We have,

$$f(x) = \frac{x}{2} + \frac{2}{x} \Rightarrow f'(x) = \frac{1}{2} - \frac{2}{x^2} = \frac{x^2 - 4}{2x^2}$$

For $f(x)$ to be increasing, we must have

$$f'(x) > 0$$

$$\Rightarrow \quad \frac{x^2 - 4}{2x^2} > 0$$

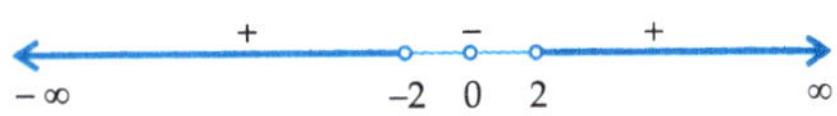

Fig. 13.31 Signs of $f'(x)$ for different values of x

$$\Rightarrow \quad x^2 - 4 > 0 \Rightarrow (x-2)(x+2) > 0 \Rightarrow x < -2 \text{ or, } x > 2 \Rightarrow x \in (-\infty, -2) \cup (2, \infty)$$

So, $f(x)$ is increasing on $(-\infty, -2) \cup (2, \infty)$. [See Fig. 13.31]

For $f(x)$ to be decreasing, we must have

$$f'(x) < 0$$

$$\Rightarrow \quad \frac{x^2 - 4}{2x^2} < 0$$

Fig. 13.32 Signs of $f'(x)$ for different values of x

$$\Rightarrow \quad x^2 - 4 < 0 \Rightarrow (x-2)(x+2) < 0 \Rightarrow x \in (-2, 2) \quad \text{[See Fig. 13.32]}$$

But, domain $(f) = R - \{0\}$. So, $f(x)$ is decreasing on $(-2, 0) \cup (0, 2)$.

EXAMPLE 13 *Find the intervals in which the function f given by $f(x) = x^3 + \frac{1}{x^3}$, $x \neq 0$ is*

(i) *increasing* (ii) *decreasing* **[NCERT, CBSE 2009]**

SOLUTION Clearly, domain $(f) = R - \{0\}$.

Now, $f(x) = x^3 + \dfrac{1}{x^3}$

$\Rightarrow \quad f'(x) = 3x^2 - \dfrac{3}{x^4} = \dfrac{3}{x^4}(x^6 - 1) = \dfrac{3}{x^4}(x^2-1)(x^4+x^2+1) = 3\left(\dfrac{x^4+x^2+1}{x^4}\right)(x^2-1)$

(i) For $f(x)$ to be increasing, we must have

$f'(x) > 0$

$\Rightarrow \quad 3\left(\dfrac{x^4+x^2+1}{x^4}\right)(x^2-1) > 0$

Fig. 13.33 Signs of $f'(x)$ for different values of x

$\Rightarrow \quad (x^2 - 1) > 0 \qquad \left[\because\ 3\left(\dfrac{x^4+x^2+1}{x^4}\right) > 0,\ x \neq 0\right]$

$\Rightarrow \quad (x-1)(x+1) > 0 \Rightarrow x \in (-\infty, -1) \cup (1, \infty)$ [See Fig. 13.33]

So, $f(x)$ is increasing on $(-\infty, -1) \cup (1, \infty)$

(ii) For $f(x)$ to be decreasing, we must have

$f'(x) < 0$

$\Rightarrow \quad 3\left(\dfrac{x^4+x^2+1}{x^4}\right)(x^2-1) < 0$

Fig. 13.34 Signs of $f'(x)$ for different values of x

$\Rightarrow \quad x^2 - 1 < 0 \qquad \left[\because\ 3\left(\dfrac{x^4+x^2+1}{x^4}\right) < 0\right]$

$\Rightarrow \quad (x-1)(x+1) < 0 \Rightarrow x \in (-1, 0) \cup (0, 1)$ [See Fig. 13.34] $[\because\ x \neq 0]$

Hence, $f(x)$ is decreasing an $(-1, 0) \cup (0, 1)$.

EXAMPLE 14 *For which values of x, the function* $f(x) = \dfrac{x}{x^2+1}$ *is increasing and for which values of x, it is decreasing.*

SOLUTION We have, $f(x) = \dfrac{x}{x^2+1} \Rightarrow f'(x) = \dfrac{(x^2+1)\times 1 - x(2x+0)}{(x^2+1)^2} = \dfrac{1-x^2}{(x^2+1)^2}$.

For $f(x)$ to be increasing, we must have

$f'(x) > 0$

$\Rightarrow \quad \dfrac{1-x^2}{(x^2+1)^2} > 0$

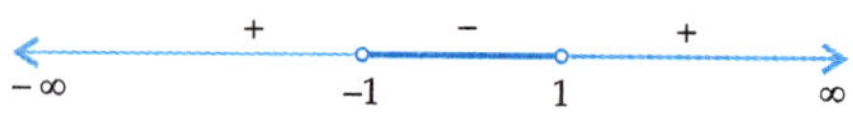

Fig. 13.35 Signs of $f'(x)$ for different values of x

$\Rightarrow \quad 1 - x^2 > 0 \qquad [\because\ (x^2+1)^2 > 0]$

$\Rightarrow \quad -(x^2-1) > 0 \Rightarrow x^2 - 1 < 0 \Rightarrow (x-1)(x+1) < 0 \Rightarrow -1 < x < 1$ [See Fig. 13.35]

$\Rightarrow \quad x \in (-1, 1)$

So, $f(x)$ is increasing on $(-1, 1)$.

For $f(x)$ to be decreasing, we must have

$f'(x) < 0$

$\Rightarrow \quad \dfrac{1-x^2}{(x^2+1)^2} < 0$

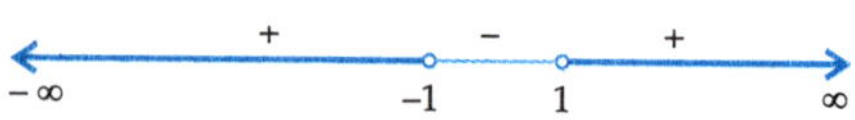

Fig. 13.36 Signs of $f'(x)$ for different values of x

$\Rightarrow \quad 1 - x^2 < 0 \qquad [\because (x^2+1)^2 > 0]$

$\Rightarrow \quad -(x^2-1) < 0 \Rightarrow x^2 - 1 > 0 \Rightarrow (x-1)(x+1) > 0 \Rightarrow x < -1$ or $x > 1$ [See Fig. 13.36]

So, $f(x)$ is decreasing on $(-\infty, -1) \cup (1, \infty)$.

EXAMPLE 15 *Find the intervals in which* $f(x) = 2 \ln (x-2) - x^2 + 4x + 1$ *is increasing or decreasing.*

SOLUTION Clearly, $f(x)$ is defined for all $x > 2$.

Now, $f(x) = 2 \ln (x-2) - x^2 + 4x + 1$

$$\Rightarrow \quad f'(x) = \frac{2}{x-2} - 2x + 4 = \frac{2 - 2x(x-2) + 4(x-2)}{x-2} = \frac{-2x^2 + 8x - 6}{x-2}$$

$$\Rightarrow \quad f'(x) = \frac{-2(x^2 + 4x - 3)}{x-2} = \frac{-2(x-1)(x-3)}{x-2}$$

For $f(x)$ to be increasing, we must have

$$f'(x) > 0 \Rightarrow \frac{-2(x-1)(x-3)}{x-2} > 0 \Rightarrow \frac{(x-1)(x-3)}{x-2} < 0$$

$\Rightarrow \quad x - 3 < 0 \qquad [\because x \in \text{Domain}(f) \Rightarrow x > 2 \Rightarrow x - 1 > 0 \text{ and } x - 2 > 0]$

$\Rightarrow \quad x < 3 \Rightarrow x \in (2, 3) \qquad [\because x > 2]$

So, $f(x)$ is increasing on $(2, 3)$.

For $f(x)$ to be decreasing, we must have

$$f'(x) < 0 \Rightarrow \frac{-2(x-1)(x-3)}{x-2} < 0 \Rightarrow \frac{(x-1)(x-3)}{x-2} > 0$$

$\Rightarrow \quad x - 3 > 0 \qquad [\because \text{For } x > 2, x - 2 > 0 \text{ and } x - 1 > 0]$

$\Rightarrow \quad x > 3 \Rightarrow x \in (3, \infty)$

So, $f(x)$ is decreasing on $(3, \infty)$.

EXAMPLE 16 *Separate* $[0, \pi/2]$ *into subintervals in which* $f(x) = \sin 3x$ *is increasing or decreasing.* **[NCERT]**

SOLUTION We have, $f(x) = \sin 3x$. Therefore, $f'(x) = 3 \cos 3x$.

Now, $x \in D(f) \Rightarrow 0 < x < \pi/2 \Rightarrow 0 < 3x < 3\pi/2$.

Since cosine function is positive in first quadrant and negative in the second and third quadrants. Therefore, we consider the following cases.

Case I *When* $0 < 3x < \pi/2$ i.e. $0 < x < \pi/6$: In this case, we have

$$0 < 3x < \pi/2 \Rightarrow \cos 3x > 0 \Rightarrow 3 \cos 3x > 0 \Rightarrow f'(x) > 0$$

Thus, $f'(x) > 0$ for $0 < 3x < \pi/2$ i.e. $0 < x < \pi/6$. So, $f(x)$ is increasing on $(0, \pi/6)$.

Case II *When* $\pi/2 < 3x < 3\pi/2$ i.e. $\pi/6 < x < \pi/2$: In this case, we have

$$\pi/2 < 3x < 3\pi/2 \Rightarrow \cos 3x < 0 \Rightarrow 3 \cos 3x < 0 \Rightarrow f'(x) < 0$$

Thus, $f'(x) < 0$ for $\pi/2 < 3x < 3\pi/2$ i.e. $\pi/6 < x < \pi/2$. So, $f(x)$ is decreasing on $(\pi/6, \pi/2)$.

Hence, $f(x)$ is increasing on $(0, \pi/6)$ and decreasing on $(\pi/6, \pi/2)$.

EXAMPLE 17 *Find the intervals in which the function f given by*

$$f(x) = \frac{4 \sin x - 2x - x \cos x}{2 + \cos x}, \; 0 \le x \le 2\pi$$ **[NCERT]**

is (i) increasing (ii) decreasing

SOLUTION We have,

$$f(x) = \frac{4 \sin x - 2x - x \cos x}{2 + \cos x}$$

$$\Rightarrow \quad f'(x) = \frac{(2+\cos x)(4\cos x - 2 - \cos x + x\sin x) + (4\sin x - 2x - x\cos x)\sin x}{(2+\cos x)^2}$$

$$\Rightarrow \quad f'(x) = \frac{\cos x\,(4-\cos x)}{(2+\cos x)^2}$$

(i) For $f(x)$ to be increasing, we must have

$$f'(x) > 0 \Rightarrow \frac{\cos x\,(4-\cos x)}{(2+\cos x)^2} > 0 \Rightarrow \cos x > 0 \qquad \left[\because \frac{4-\cos x}{(2+\cos x)^2} > 0\right]$$

$$\Rightarrow \quad x \in (0, \pi/2) \cup (3\pi/2, 2\pi)$$

Hence, $f(x)$ is increasing on $(0, \pi/2) \cup (3\pi/2, 2\pi)$.

(ii) For $f(x)$ to be decreasing, we must have

$$f'(x) < 0 \Rightarrow \frac{\cos x\,(4-\cos x)}{(2+\cos x)^2} < 0 \Rightarrow \cos x < 0 \Rightarrow x \in (\pi/2, 3\pi/2)$$

Hence, $f(x)$ is decreasing on $(\pi/2, 3\pi/2)$.

EXAMPLE 18 *Separate the interval* $[0, \pi/2]$ *into sub-intervals in which* $f(x) = \sin^4 x + \cos^4 x$ *is increasing or decreasing.* **[CBSE 2000 C]**

SOLUTION We have, $f(x) = \sin^4 x + \cos^4 x$

$$\Rightarrow \quad f'(x) = 4\sin^3 x\cos x - 4\cos^3 x\sin x = -4\sin x\cos x\,(\cos^2 x - \sin^2 x)$$

$$\Rightarrow \quad f'(x) = -2(2\sin x\cos x)(\cos 2x) = -2\sin 2x\cos 2x = -\sin 4x$$

We have, $0 < x < \pi/2 \Rightarrow 0 < 4x < 2\pi$.

Since sine function is positive in the first and second quadrants and negative in the third and fourth quadrants. So, we consider the following cases:

Case I *When* $0 < 4x < \pi$ i.e. $0 < x < \pi/4$: In this case, we have

$$\sin 4x > 0 \Rightarrow -\sin 4x < 0 \Rightarrow f'(x) < 0$$

$\therefore$ $f'(x) < 0$ for $0 < 4x < \pi$ i.e. $0 < x < \pi/4$. So, $f(x)$ is decreasing on $[0, \pi/4]$.

Case II *When*, $\pi < 4x < 2\pi$ i.e. $\pi/4 < x < \pi/2$: In this case, we have

$$\sin 4x < 0 \Rightarrow -\sin 4x > 0 \Rightarrow f'(x) > 0$$

$\therefore$ $f'(x) > 0$ for $\pi < 4x < 2\pi$ i.e. $\pi/4 < x < \pi/2$. So, $f(x)$ is increasing on $[\pi/4, \pi/2]$.

EXAMPLE 19 *Find the intervals in which the function f given by* $f(x) = \sin x + \cos x$, $0 \le x \le 2\pi$ *is increasing or decreasing.* **[NCERT, CBSE 2009, 2017, 2020]**

SOLUTION We have,

$$f(x) = \sin x + \cos x$$

$$\Rightarrow \quad f'(x) = \cos x - \sin x = \sqrt{2}\left(\cos x\sin\frac{\pi}{4} - \sin x\cos\frac{\pi}{4}\right) = \sqrt{2}\sin\left(\frac{\pi}{4} - x\right) = -\sqrt{2}\sin\left(x - \frac{\pi}{4}\right)$$

Now, $0 \le x \le 2\pi \Rightarrow 0 - \frac{\pi}{4} < x - \frac{\pi}{4} < 2\pi - \frac{\pi}{4} \Rightarrow -\frac{\pi}{4} < x - \frac{\pi}{4} < \frac{7\pi}{4}$

For $f(x)$ to be increasing, we must have

$$f'(x) > 0$$

$$\Rightarrow \quad -\sqrt{2}\sin\left(x - \frac{\pi}{4}\right) > 0$$

$$\Rightarrow \quad \sin\left(x-\frac{\pi}{4}\right)<0$$

$$\Rightarrow \quad -\frac{\pi}{4}<x-\frac{\pi}{4}<0 \text{ or, } \pi<x-\frac{\pi}{4}<\frac{7\pi}{4}$$

$$\Rightarrow \quad 0<x<\frac{\pi}{4} \text{ or, } \frac{5\pi}{4}<x<2\pi \Rightarrow x\in\left(0,\frac{\pi}{4}\right) \text{ or, } x\in\left(\frac{5\pi}{4},2\pi\right) \Rightarrow x\in(0,\pi/4)\cup(5\pi/4,2\pi)$$

Hence, $f(x)$ is increasing on $(0,\pi/4)\cup(5\pi/4,2\pi)$.

For $f(x)$ to be decreasing, we must have

$$f'(x)<0$$

$$\Rightarrow -\sqrt{2}\sin\left(x-\frac{\pi}{4}\right)<0 \Rightarrow \sin\left(x-\frac{\pi}{4}\right)>0 \Rightarrow 0<x-\frac{\pi}{4}<\pi \Rightarrow \frac{\pi}{4}<x<\frac{5\pi}{4} \Rightarrow x\in\left(\frac{\pi}{4},\frac{5\pi}{4}\right).$$

Hence, $f(x)$ is decreasing on $(\pi/4, 5\pi/4)$.

EXAMPLE 20 *Find the intervals in which $f(x)=\sin 3x-\cos 3x$, $0<x<\pi$, is strictly increasing or decreasing.* **[CBSE 2016]**

SOLUTION We have,

$$f(x) = \sin 3x-\cos 3x$$

$$\Rightarrow f'(x)=3(\cos 3x+\sin 3x)$$

$$\Rightarrow f'(x)=3\sqrt{2}\left(\frac{1}{\sqrt{2}}\cos 3x+\frac{1}{\sqrt{2}}\sin 3x\right)=3\sqrt{2}\left(\sin\frac{\pi}{4}\cos 3x+\cos\frac{\pi}{4}\sin 3x\right)=3\sqrt{2}\sin\left(3x+\frac{\pi}{4}\right)$$

It is given that

$$0<x<\pi \Rightarrow 0<3x<3\pi \Rightarrow \frac{\pi}{4}<3x+\frac{\pi}{4}<3\pi+\frac{\pi}{4} \Rightarrow \frac{\pi}{4}<3x+\frac{\pi}{4}<\frac{13\pi}{4}$$

(i) For $f(x)$ to be strictly increasing, we must have

$$f'(x)>0$$

$$\Rightarrow 3\sqrt{2}\sin\left(3x+\frac{\pi}{4}\right)>0$$

$$\Rightarrow \sin\left(3x+\frac{\pi}{4}\right)>0$$

$$\Rightarrow \frac{\pi}{4}<3x+\frac{\pi}{4}<\pi \text{ or, } 2\pi<3x+\frac{\pi}{4}<3\pi$$

$$\Rightarrow 0<3x<\frac{3\pi}{4} \text{ or, } \frac{7\pi}{4}<3\pi<\frac{11\pi}{4} \Rightarrow 0<x<\frac{\pi}{4} \text{ or, } \frac{7\pi}{12}<x<\frac{11\pi}{12} \Rightarrow x\in\left(0,\frac{\pi}{4}\right)\cup\left(\frac{7\pi}{12},\frac{11\pi}{12}\right)$$

So, $f(x)$ is strictly increasing on $\left(0,\frac{\pi}{4}\right)\cup\left(\frac{7\pi}{12},\frac{11\pi}{12}\right)$.

(ii) For $f(x)$ to be strictly decreasing we must have

$$f'(x)<0$$

$$\Rightarrow 3\sqrt{2}\sin\left(3x+\frac{\pi}{4}\right)<0$$

$$\Rightarrow \sin\left(3x+\frac{\pi}{4}\right)<0$$

$$\Rightarrow \pi<3x+\frac{\pi}{4}<2\pi \text{ or, } 3\pi<3x+\frac{\pi}{4}<\frac{13\pi}{4}$$

$$\Rightarrow \frac{3\pi}{4}<3x<\frac{7\pi}{4} \text{ or, } \frac{11\pi}{4}<3x<3\pi \Rightarrow \frac{\pi}{4}<x<\frac{7\pi}{12} \text{ or, } \frac{11\pi}{12}<x<\pi \Rightarrow x\in\left(\frac{\pi}{4},\frac{7\pi}{12}\right)\cup\left(\frac{11\pi}{12},\pi\right)$$

So, $f(x)$ is strictly decreasing on $\left(\frac{\pi}{4}, \frac{7\pi}{12}\right) \cup \left(\frac{11\pi}{12}, \pi\right)$.

Type II ON PROVING THE MONOTONICITY OF A FUNCTION ON A GIVEN INTERVAL

EXAMPLE 21 *Prove that the function $f(x) = x^3 - 3x^2 + 3x - 100$ is increasing on R.* [NCERT]

SOLUTION We have,

$$f(x) = x^3 - 3x^2 + 3x - 100 \Rightarrow f'(x) = 3x^2 - 6x + 3 = 3(x-1)^2$$

Now, $x \in R \Rightarrow (x-1)^2 \geq 0 \Rightarrow f'(x) \geq 0$.

Thus, $f'(x) \geq 0$ for all $x \in R$. Hence, $f(x)$ is increasing on R.

EXAMPLE 22 *Let I be an interval disjointed from $[-1, 1]$. Prove that the function $f(x) = x + \frac{1}{x}$ is increasing on I.* [NCERT]

SOLUTION We have,

$$f(x) = x + \frac{1}{x} \Rightarrow f'(x) = 1 - \frac{1}{x^2} = \frac{x^2 - 1}{x^2}$$

Now, $x \in I \Rightarrow x \notin [-1, 1] \Rightarrow x < -1$ or $x > 1 \Rightarrow x^2 > 1 \Rightarrow x^2 - 1 > 0 \Rightarrow \frac{x^2 - 1}{x^2} > 0 \Rightarrow f'(x) > 0$

Thus, $f'(x) > 0$ for all $x \in I$. Hence, $f(x)$ increasing on I.

EXAMPLE 23 *Show that the function $f(x) = \frac{3}{x} + 7$ is decreasing for $x \in R - \{0\}$.*

SOLUTION We have, $f(x) = \frac{3}{x} + 7 \Rightarrow f'(x) = -\frac{3}{x^2}$

Now, $x \in R, x \neq 0 \Rightarrow \frac{1}{x^2} > 0 \Rightarrow -\frac{3}{x^2} < 0 \Rightarrow f'(x) < 0$.

Hence, $f(x)$ is decreasing for $x \in R, x \neq 0$.

EXAMPLE 24 *Show that the function $x + 1/x$ is increasing for $x > 1$.*

SOLUTION Let $f(x) = x + \frac{1}{x}$. Then, $f'(x) = 1 - \frac{1}{x^2} = \frac{x^2 - 1}{x^2}$

Now, $x > 1 \Rightarrow x^2 > 1 \Rightarrow \frac{x^2 - 1}{x^2} > 0 \Rightarrow f'(x) > 0$. Hence, $f(x)$ is increasing for $x > 1$.

EXAMPLE 25 *The population P(t) of rabbits in a forest is modelled by the function given by:*

$P(t) = \frac{2000}{1 + e^{-0.5t}}$, *where P represent the population of rabbits in t years*

Determine whether the rabbit population is increasing or not, and justify your answer.

SOLUTION The population $P(t)$ of rabbits in t years is given by

$$P(t) = \frac{2000}{1 + e^{-0.5t}}$$

$$\Rightarrow \quad \frac{dP(t)}{dt} = 2000 \times -\frac{1}{(1 + e^{-0.5t})^2} \times \frac{d}{dt}(1 + e^{-0.5t})$$

$$\Rightarrow \quad \frac{dP(t)}{dt} = -\frac{2000}{(1 + e^{-0.5t})^2} \times -0.5 e^{-0.5t} = \frac{1000\, e^{-0.5t}}{(1 + e^{-0.5t})^2} > 0 \text{ for all } t.$$

Hence, $P(t)$ i.e. the rabbit population is increasing.

EXAMPLE 26 *Show that* $f(x) = \tan^{-1}(\sin x + \cos x)$ *is an increasing function on the interval* $(0, \pi/4)$.

[NCERT EXEMPLAR]

SOLUTION We have, $f(x) = \tan^{-1}(\sin x + \cos x)$

$$\Rightarrow \quad f'(x) = \frac{1}{1+(\sin x + \cos x)^2} \times \frac{d}{dx}(\sin x + \cos x) = \frac{1}{1+(\sin + \cos x)^2} \times (\cos x - \sin x)$$

$$\Rightarrow \quad f'(x) = \frac{\cos x(1-\tan x)}{1+(\sin x + \cos x)^2}$$

Now, $0 < x < \pi/4$

$$\Rightarrow \quad \cos x > 0, \frac{1}{1+(\sin x + \cos x)^2} \text{ and } 1 - \tan x > 0 \qquad [\because 0 < \tan x < 1 \text{ for } 0 < x < \pi/4]$$

$$\Rightarrow \quad \frac{\cos x(1-\tan x)}{1+(\sin x + \cos x)^2} > 0 \Rightarrow f'(x) > 0$$

Thus, $f'(x) > 0$ for all $x \in (0, \pi/4)$. Hence, $f(x)$ is increasing on $(0, \pi/4)$.

EXAMPLE 27 *Prove that* $f(\theta) = \frac{4\sin\theta}{2+\cos\theta} - \theta$ *is an increasing function of* θ *in* $\left[0, \frac{\pi}{2}\right]$.

[NCERT, CBSE 2011, 2024]

SOLUTION We have,

$$f(\theta) = \frac{4\sin\theta}{2+\cos\theta} - \theta$$

$$\Rightarrow f'(\theta) = \frac{(2+\cos\theta)(4\cos\theta) + 4\sin^2\theta}{(2+\cos\theta)^2} - 1 = \frac{8\cos\theta + 4}{(2+\cos\theta)^2} - 1 = \frac{4\cos\theta - \cos^2\theta}{(2+\cos\theta)^2}$$

$$\Rightarrow f'(\theta) = \frac{\cos\theta(4-\cos\theta)}{(2+\cos\theta)^2} > 0 \text{ for all } \theta \in \left(0, \frac{\pi}{2}\right). \quad [\because \cos\theta > 0, 4 - \cos\theta > 0 \text{ and } 2 + \cos\theta > 0]$$

Hence, $f(\theta)$ is increasing on $[0, \pi/2]$.

EXAMPLE 28 *Prove that the function* $f(x) = \tan x - 4x$ *is strictly decreasing on* $(-\pi/3, \pi/3)$.

[NCERT EXEMPLAR]

SOLUTION We have, $f(x) = \tan x - 4x$

$$\Rightarrow \quad f'(x) = \sec^2 x - 4 = \frac{1-4\cos^2 x}{\cos^2 x} = \frac{4}{\cos^2 x}\left(\frac{1}{4} - \cos^2 x\right) = \frac{4}{\cos^2 x}\left(\frac{1}{2} + \cos x\right)\left(\frac{1}{2} - \cos x\right)$$

Now,

$$x \in (-\pi/3, \pi/3) \Rightarrow -\frac{\pi}{3} < x < \frac{\pi}{3} \Rightarrow \frac{1}{2} < \cos x < 1 \Rightarrow \frac{1}{2} < \cos x \text{ and } \frac{1}{2} + \frac{1}{2} < \frac{1}{2} + \cos x < \frac{1}{2} + 1$$

$$\Rightarrow \quad \frac{1}{2} - \cos x < 0 \text{ and } 1 < \frac{1}{2} + \cos x < \frac{3}{2} \Rightarrow \frac{1}{2} - \cos x < 0 \text{ and } \frac{1}{2} + \cos x > 0$$

$$\Rightarrow \quad \left(\frac{1}{2} - \cos x\right)\left(\frac{1}{2} + \cos x\right) < 0 \Rightarrow \frac{4}{\cos^2 x}\left(\frac{1}{2} - \cos x\right)\left(\frac{1}{2} + \cos x\right) < 0 \Rightarrow f'(x) < 0$$

Hence, f is strictly decreasing on $(-\pi/3, \pi/3)$.

EXAMPLE 29 *Show that* $f(x) = 2x + \cot^{-1} x + \ln\left(\sqrt{1+x^2} - x\right)$ *is increasing on R.*

[NCERT EXEMPLAR]

SOLUTION We have,

$$f(x) = 2x + \cot^{-1} x + \ln\left(\sqrt{1+x^2} - x\right)$$

$$\Rightarrow \quad f'(x) = 2 - \frac{1}{1+x^2} + \frac{1}{\sqrt{1+x^2}-x}\left(\frac{x}{\sqrt{1+x^2}} - 1\right)$$

$$\Rightarrow \quad f'(x) = 2 - \frac{1}{1+x^2} + \frac{1}{\sqrt{1+x^2}-x}\left(\frac{x-\sqrt{1+x^2}}{\sqrt{1+x^2}}\right) = 2 - \frac{1}{1+x^2} - \frac{1}{\sqrt{1+x^2}}$$

$$\Rightarrow \quad f'(x) = \left(1 - \frac{1}{1+x^2}\right) + \left(1 - \frac{1}{\sqrt{1+x^2}}\right) > 0 \text{ for all } x \in R \Rightarrow f'(x) > 0 \text{ for all } x \in R,\ x \neq 0.$$

Hence, $f(x)$ is increasing on R.

EXAMPLE 30 *Test whether the function* $f(x) = x^3 - 8$ *is increasing on* $[1, 2]$.

SOLUTION We have,

$$f(x) = x^3 - 8 \Rightarrow f'(x) = 3x^2 \Rightarrow f'(x) > 0 \text{ for all } x \in [1, 2]$$

So, $f(x)$ is increasing on $[1, 2]$.

EXAMPLE 31 *Which of the following functions are decreasing on* $(0, \pi/2)$?

(i) $\cos x$ (ii) $\cos 2x$ (iii) $\tan x$ (iv) $\cos 3x$ **[NCERT]**

SOLUTION (i) We have, $f(x) = \cos x \Rightarrow f'(x) = -\sin x$

Now, $x \in (0, \pi/2) \Rightarrow \sin x > 0 \Rightarrow -\sin x < 0 \Rightarrow f'(x) < 0$

So, $f(x)$ is decreasing on $(0, \pi/2)$.

(ii) Let $f(x) = \cos 2x$. Then, $f'(x) = -2 \sin 2x$.

Now, $x \in (0, \pi/2) \Rightarrow 0 < x < \pi/2 \Rightarrow 0 < 2x < \pi \Rightarrow \sin 2x > 0 \Rightarrow -2 \sin 2x < 0 \Rightarrow f'(x) < 0$

So, $f(x)$ is decreasing on $(0, \pi/2)$.

(iii) Let $f(x) = \tan x$. Then, $f'(x) = \sec^2 x$.

Now, $x \in (0, \pi/2) \Rightarrow \sec^2 x > 0 \Rightarrow f'(x) > 0$. So, $f(x)$ is increasing on $(0, \pi/2)$.

(iv) Let $f(x) = \cos 3x$. Then, $f'(x) = -3 \sin 3x$

Now, $x \in (0, \pi/2) \Rightarrow 0 < x < \pi/2 \Rightarrow 0 < 3x < 3\pi/2 \Rightarrow \sin 3x$ can be positive as well as negative

$\Rightarrow f'(x) = -3 \sin 3x$ can be positive as well as negative

So, $f(x)$ is neither increasing nor decreasing on $(0, \pi/2)$.

EXAMPLE 32 *Prove that the function* $f(x) = x^2 - x + 1$ *is neither increasing nor decreasing on* $(-1, 1)$.

[CBSE 2014, NCERT]

SOLUTION We have, $f(x) = x^2 - x + 1 \Rightarrow f'(x) = 2x - 1 = 2(x - 1/2)$.

Now, $-1 < x < 1/2 \Rightarrow (x - 1/2) < 0 \Rightarrow 2(x - 1/2) < 0 \Rightarrow f'(x) < 0$

and, $1/2 < x < 1 \Rightarrow x - 1/2 > 0 \Rightarrow 2(x - 1/2) > 0 \Rightarrow f'(x) > 0$.

Thus, $f'(x)$ does not have the same sign throughout the interval $(-1, 1)$. Hence, $f(x)$ is neither increasing or decreasing on $(-1, 1)$.

EXAMPLE 33 *On which of the following intervals is the function* $f(x) = x^{100} + \sin x - 1$ *increasing?*

(i) $(0, \pi/2)$ (ii) $(\pi/2, \pi)$ (iii) $(0, 1)$ (iv) $(-1, 1)$. **[NCERT]**

SOLUTION We have, $f(x) = x^{100} + \sin x - 1 \Rightarrow f'(x) = 100x^{99} + \cos x$

(i) $x \in \left(0, \frac{\pi}{2}\right) \Rightarrow 0 < x < \frac{\pi}{2} \Rightarrow x^{99} > 0$ and $\cos x > 0 \Rightarrow 100x^{99} + \cos x > 0 \Rightarrow f'(x) > 0$.

Thus, $f(x)$ is increasing on $(0, \pi/2)$.

(ii) $x \in \left(\frac{\pi}{2}, \pi\right) \Rightarrow \frac{\pi}{2} < x < \pi \Rightarrow x^{99} > 1$ $\left[\because \frac{\pi}{2} < x < \pi \Rightarrow \frac{22}{14} < x < \frac{22}{7}\right]$

$\Rightarrow$ $100x^{99} > 100$ ...(i)

Again, $x \in (\pi/2, \pi) \Rightarrow -1 < \cos x < 0 \Rightarrow 0 > \cos x > -1$ ...(ii)

From (i) and (ii), we find that for $x \in (\pi/2, \pi)$

$100\, x^{99} > 100$ and $\cos x > -1$

$\Rightarrow$ $100x^{99} + \cos x > 100 - 1 \Rightarrow 100x^{99} + \cos x > 0 \Rightarrow f'(x) > 0$

Thus, $f(x)$ is increasing on $(\pi/2, \pi)$.

(iii) $x \in (0, 1) \Rightarrow x^{99} > 0 \Rightarrow 100x^{99} > 0$

Again, $x \in (0, 1)$

$\Rightarrow$ x lies between 0 and 1 radian

$\Rightarrow$ x lies between $0°$ and $57°$ $[\because 1° \simeq 57°]$

$\Rightarrow$ x lies in first quadrant $\Rightarrow \cos x > 0$

$\therefore$ $x \in (0, 1) \Rightarrow 100\, x^{99} > 0$ and $\cos x > 0 \Rightarrow 100x^{99} + \cos x > 0 \Rightarrow f'(x) > 0$

Thus, $f(x)$ is increasing on (0, 1).

(iv) We have seen in (iii) that $f'(x) > 0$ for $0 < x < 1$. But, $f'(x)$ can be positive as well as negative when $-1 < x < 0$. So, $f'(x)$ can be positive as well as negative for $x \in (-1, 1)$. Hence, $f(x)$ is neither increasing nor decreasing on (– 1, 1).

BASED ON LOWER ORDER THINKING SKILLS (LOTS)

Type I ON FINDING THE INTERVAL IN WHICH A FUNCTION IS INCREASING OR DECREASING

EXAMPLE 34 *Determine the values of x for which $f(x) = x^x$, $x > 0$ is increasing or decreasing.*

SOLUTION Clearly, $f(x) = x^x$ is defined for $x > 0$. So, domain $f = (0, \infty)$.

Now, $f(x) = x^x = e^{x \log x}$

$\Rightarrow$ $f'(x) = e^{x \log x} \frac{d}{dx}(x \log_e x) \Rightarrow f'(x) = x^x (1 + \log_e x)$

For $f(x)$ to be increasing, we must have

$f'(x) > 0$

$\Rightarrow$ $x^x (1 + \log_e x) > 0$

$\Rightarrow$ $1 + \log_e x > 0$ $[\because x^x > 0 \text{ for } x > 0]$

$\Rightarrow$ $\log_e x > -1$

$\Rightarrow$ $x > e^{-1}$ $[\because \log_a x > N \Rightarrow x > a^N$ for $a > 1$. Here, $e > 1$. So, $\log_e x > -1 \Rightarrow x > e^{-1}]$

$\Rightarrow$ $x \in (1/e, \infty)$

Thus, $f(x)$ is increasing on $(1/e, \infty)$.

For $f(x)$ to be decreasing, we must have

$f'(x) < 0$

$\Rightarrow$ $x^x (1 + \log_e x) < 0$

$\Rightarrow$ $1 + \log_e x < 0$ $[\because x^x > 0 \text{ for } x > 0]$

$\Rightarrow \quad \log_e x < -1 \Rightarrow x < e^{-1} \Rightarrow x \in (0, 1/e)$

Thus, $f(x)$ is decreasing on $(0, 1/e)$.

Hence, $f(x)$ is increasing on $(1/e, \infty)$ and decreasing on $(0, 1/e)$.

EXAMPLE 35 *Find the intervals in which* $f(x) = \dfrac{x}{\log x}$ *is increasing or decreasing.* **[CBSE 2024]**

SOLUTION Note that the domain of $f(x)$ is the set of all positive real numbers other than unity i.e. $(0, 1) \cup (1, \infty)$.

Now, $f(x) = \dfrac{x}{\log x} \Rightarrow f'(x) = \dfrac{\log x - 1}{(\log x)^2}$

For $f(x)$ to be increasing, we must have

$$f'(x) > 0$$

$$\Rightarrow \frac{\log x - 1}{(\log x)^2} > 0$$

$$\Rightarrow \log x - 1 > 0 \quad [\because (\log x)^2 > 0 \text{ for } x > 0, x \neq 1]$$

$$\Rightarrow \log x > 1$$

$$\Rightarrow x > e^1 \quad [\because \log_a x > N \Rightarrow x > a^N \text{ for } a > 1. \text{ Here, } e > 1 \therefore \log_e x > 1 \Rightarrow x > e^1]$$

$$\Rightarrow x \in (e, \infty).$$

So, $f(x)$ is increasing on (e, ∞).

For $f(x)$ to be decreasing, we must have

$$f'(x) < 0$$

$$\Rightarrow \frac{\log x - 1}{(\log x)^2} < 0$$

$$\Rightarrow \log x - 1 < 0 \quad [\because (\log x)^2 > 0 \text{ for } x > 0, x \neq 1]$$

$$\Rightarrow \log x < 1 \Rightarrow x < e^1 \Rightarrow x \in (0, e) - \{1\} \quad [\because f(x) \text{ is defined for } x > 0, x \neq 1]$$

So, $f(x)$ is decreasing on $(0, e) - \{1\}$.

BASED ON HIGHER ORDER THINKING SKILLS (HOTS)

EXAMPLE 36 *If* a, b, c *are real numbers, then find the intervals in which* $f(x) = \begin{vmatrix} x+a^2 & ab & ac \\ ab & x+b^2 & bc \\ ac & bc & x+c^2 \end{vmatrix}$ *is increasing or decreasing.*

SOLUTION We have,

$$f(x) = \begin{vmatrix} x+a^2 & ab & ac \\ ab & x+b^2 & bc \\ ac & bc & x+c^2 \end{vmatrix}$$

$$\Rightarrow f'(x) = \begin{vmatrix} 1 & 0 & 0 \\ ab & x+b^2 & bc \\ ac & bc & x+c^2 \end{vmatrix} + \begin{vmatrix} x+a^2 & ab & ac \\ 0 & 1 & 0 \\ ac & bc & x+c^2 \end{vmatrix} + \begin{vmatrix} x+a^2 & ab & ac \\ ab & x+b^2 & bc \\ 0 & 0 & 1 \end{vmatrix}$$

$$\Rightarrow f'(x) = (x+b^2)(x+c^2) - b^2c^2 + (x+a^2)(x+c^2) - a^2c^2 + (x+a)^2(x+b)^2 - a^2b^2$$

$\Rightarrow \quad f'(x) = 3x^2 + 2x(a^2 + b^2 + c^2).$

For $f(x)$ to be increasing, we must have

$$f'(x) > 0$$

$$\Rightarrow \quad 3x^2 + 2x(a^2 + b^2 + c^2) > 0$$

$$\Rightarrow \quad x\left\{3x + 2(a^2 + b^2 + c^2)\right\} > 0$$

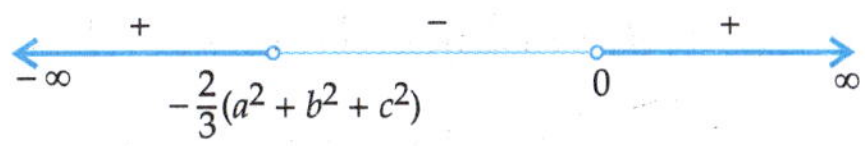

Fig. 13.37 Signs of $f'(x)$ for different values of x

$$\Rightarrow \quad x < -\frac{2}{3}(a^2 + b^2 + c^2) \text{ or, } x > 0 \qquad \text{[See Fig. 13.37]}$$

$$\Rightarrow \quad x \in \left(-\infty, -\frac{2}{3}(a^2 + b^2 + c^2)\right) \cup (0, \infty).$$

So, $f(x)$ is increasing on $\left(-\infty, -\frac{2}{3}(a^2 + b^2 + c^2)\right) \cup (0, \infty)$

For $f(x)$ to be decreasing, we must have

$$f'(x) < 0$$

$$\Rightarrow \quad 3x^2 + 2x(a^2 + b^2 + c^2) < 0$$

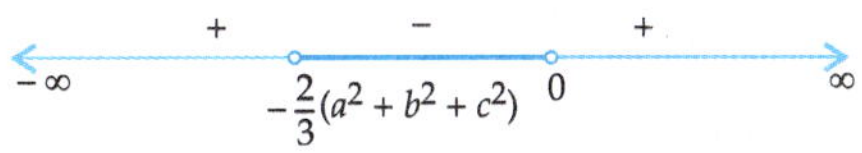

Fig. 13.38 Signs of $f'(x)$ for different values of x

$$\Rightarrow \quad x\left\{3x + 2(a^2 + b^2 + c^2)\right\} < 0$$

$$\Rightarrow \quad -\frac{2}{3}(a^2 + b^2 + c^2) < x < 0 \qquad \text{[See Fig. 13.38]}$$

$$\Rightarrow \quad x \in \left(-\frac{2}{3}(a^2 + b^2 + c^2), 0\right)$$

So, $f(x)$ is decreasing on $\left(-\frac{2}{3}(a^2 + b^2 + c^2), 0\right)$.

Hence, $f(x)$ is increasing on $\left(-\infty, -\frac{2}{3}(a^2 + b^2 + c^2)\right) \cup (0, \infty)$ and decreasing on $\left(-\frac{2}{3}(a^2 + b^2 + c^2), 0\right)$.

Type II ON PROVING MONOTONICITY OF A FUNCTION ON A GIVEN INTERVAL

EXAMPLE 37 *Show that for $a \geq 1$, $f(x) = \sqrt{3}\sin x - \cos x - 2ax + b$ is decreasing on R.*

SOLUTION We have,

$$f(x) = \sqrt{3}\sin x - \cos x - 2ax + b$$

$$\Rightarrow \quad f'(x) = \sqrt{3}\cos x + \sin x - 2a$$

$$\Rightarrow \quad f'(x) = 2\left(\frac{\sqrt{3}}{2}\cos x + \frac{1}{2}\sin x\right) - 2a$$

$$\Rightarrow \quad f'(x) = 2\left(\sin\frac{\pi}{3}\cos x + \cos\frac{\pi}{3}\sin x\right) - 2a = 2\sin\left(x + \frac{\pi}{3}\right) - 2a = 2\left\{\sin\left(x + \frac{\pi}{3}\right) - a\right\}$$

$$\Rightarrow \quad f'(x) < 0 \text{ for all } x \in R \qquad \left[\because \sin\left(x + \frac{\pi}{3}\right) \leq 1 \text{ and } a \geq 1 \text{ for all } x \in R\right]$$

Hence, $f(x)$ is decreasing on R.

EXAMPLE 38 *Show that $f(x) = \cos(2x + \pi/4)$ is an increasing function on $(3\pi/8, 7\pi/8)$.*

SOLUTION We have, $f(x) = \cos(2x + \pi/4) \Rightarrow f'(x) = -2\sin(2x + \pi/4)$

Now,

$$x \in (3\pi/8, 7\pi/8) \Rightarrow 3\pi/8 < x < 7\pi/8 \Rightarrow 3\pi/4 < 2x < 7\pi/4$$

$\Rightarrow$ $\pi/4 + 3\pi/4 < 2x + \pi/4 < 7\pi/4 + \pi/4 \Rightarrow \pi < 2x + \pi/4 < 2\pi$

$\Rightarrow$ $\sin(2x + \pi/4) < 0$ [$\because$ sine function is negative in third and fourth quadrants]

$\Rightarrow$ $-2\sin(2x + \pi/4) > 0 \Rightarrow f'(x) > 0$

Hence, $f(x)$ is increasing on $(3\pi/8, 7\pi/8)$.

EXAMPLE 39 *Find the least value of 'a' such that the function $f(x) = x^2 + ax + 1$ is increasing on $[1, 2]$. Also, find the greatest value of 'a' for which $f(x)$ is decreasing on $[1, 2]$.* [NCERT]

SOLUTION We have, $f(x) = x^2 + ax + 1$

$\therefore$ $f'(x) = 2x + a$ and $f''(x) = 2$ for all x.

Now, $f''(x) = 2$ for all $x \in (1, 2)$

$\Rightarrow$ $f''(x) > 0$ for all $x \in [1, 2]$

$\Rightarrow$ $f'(x)$ is an increasing function on $[1, 2]$

$\Rightarrow$ $f'(1)$ and $f'(2)$ are the least and the greatest values of $f'(x)$ on $[1, 2]$.

As $f(x)$ is increasing on $[1, 2]$. Therefore, $f'(x) > 0$ for all $x \in [1, 2]$. This is possible when least value of $f'(x)$ i.e. $f'(1) > 0$.

Now, $f'(1) > 0 \Rightarrow 2 + a > 0 \Rightarrow a > -2$

Thus, the least value of a is –2.

If $f(x)$ is decreasing on $[1, 2]$, then

$f'(x) < 0$ for all $x \in [1, 2]$

$\Rightarrow$ Greatest value of $f'(x) < 0$ for $x \in [1, 2]$

$\Rightarrow$ $f'(2) < 0$ [$\because$ $f'(x)$ is increasing on $[1, 2]$ $\therefore$ $f'(2)$ is the greatest value of $f(x)$]

$\Rightarrow$ $4 + a < 0 \Rightarrow a < -4$.

So, the greatest value of a is -4.

NOTE (i) *$ax^2 + bx + c > 0$ for all $x \Rightarrow a > 0$ and $b^2 - 4ac < 0$*

(ii) *$ax^2 + bx + c < 0$ for all $x \Rightarrow a < 0$ and $b^2 - 4ac < 0$*

(iii) *If the least value of $f(x)$ defined on $[a, b]$ is positive, then $f(x) > 0$ for all $x \in [a, b]$.*

(iv) *If the greatest value of $f(x)$ defined on $[a, b]$ is negative, then $f(x) < 0$ for all $x \in [a, b]$.*

EXAMPLE 40 *Find the values 'a' for which the function $f(x) = (a + 2)x^3 - 3ax^2 + 9ax - 1$ decreases for all real values of x.*

SOLUTION We have,

$$f(x) = (a + 2)x^3 - 3ax^2 + 9ax - 1 \Rightarrow f'(x) = 3(a + 2)x^2 - 6ax + 9a$$

Since $f(x)$ is decreasing for all real values of x. Therefore,

$f'(x) < 0$ for all $x \in R$

$\Rightarrow$ $3(a + 2)x^2 - 6ax + 9a < 0$ for all $x \in R$

$\Rightarrow$ $(a + 2)x^2 - 2ax + 3a < 0$ for all $x \in R$

$\Rightarrow$ $a + 2 < 0$ and $4a^2 - 4 \times (a + 2) \times 3a < 0$ [$\because$ $ax^2 + bx + c < 0$ for all $x \in R \Rightarrow a < 0$ and Disc < 0]

$\Rightarrow$ $a < -2$ and $a^2 - 3a^2 - 6a < 0$

$\Rightarrow$ $a < -2$ and $-2a^2 - 6a < 0$

$\Rightarrow$ $a < -2$ and $-2a(a + 3) < 0$

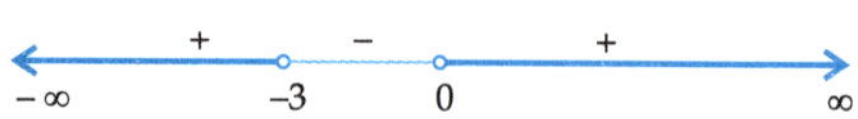

Fig. 13.39 Signs of $a(a + 3)$ for different values of x

Now,

$$-2a(a+3) < 0$$

$\Rightarrow \quad a(a+3) > 0$

$\Rightarrow \quad a < -3$ or, $a > 0$ [See Fig. 13.39]

$\Rightarrow \quad a \in (-\infty, -3) \cup (0, \infty)$

$\therefore \quad a < -2$ and $-2a(a+3) < 0 \Rightarrow a < -2$ and $a \in (-\infty, -3) \cup (0, \infty) \Rightarrow a \in (-\infty, -3)$.

Hence, $f(x)$ decreases for all $x \in R$, if $a \in (-\infty, -3)$.

EXAMPLE 41 *Find the values of k for which $f(x) = kx^3 - 9kx^2 + 9x + 3$ is increasing on R.*

SOLUTION It is given that $f(x)$ is increasing on R. Therefore,

$f'(x) > 0$ for all $x \in R$

$\Rightarrow \quad 3kx^2 - 18kx + 9 > 0$ for all $x \in R$

$\Rightarrow \quad kx^2 - 6kx + 3 > 0$ for all $x \in R$

$\Rightarrow \quad k > 0$ and $36k^2 - 12k < 0$ $[\because ax^2 + bx + c > 0$ for all $x \in R \Rightarrow a > 0$ and Disc $< 0]$

$\Rightarrow \quad k > 0$ and $12k(3k-1) < 0$

$\Rightarrow \quad k > 0$ and $k(3k-1) < 0$

$\Rightarrow \quad 3k - 1 < 0$ $[\because k > 0]$

$\Rightarrow \quad k < \frac{1}{3} \Rightarrow k \in (0, 1/3)$.

Hence, $f(x)$ is increasing on R, if $k \in (0, 1/3)$.

EXERCISE 13.2

BASIC

1. Find the intervals in which the following functions are increasing or decreasing.

(i) $f(x) = 10 - 6x - 2x^2$ [NCERT]

(ii) $f(x) = x^2 + 2x - 5$ [NCERT]

(iii) $f(x) = 6 - 9x - x^2$ [NCERT]

(iv) $f(x) = 2x^3 - 12x^2 + 18x + 15$

(v) $f(x) = 5 + 36x + 3x^2 - 2x^3$

(vi) $f(x) = 8 + 36x + 3x^2 - 2x^3$

(vii) $f(x) = 5x^3 - 15x^2 - 120x + 3$

(viii) $f(x) = x^3 - 6x^2 - 36x + 2$

(ix) $f(x) = 2x^3 - 15x^2 + 36x + 1$ [CBSE 2005, 2010]

(x) $f(x) = 2x^3 + 9x^2 + 12x + 20$ [CBSE 2011]

(xi) $f(x) = 2x^3 - 9x^2 + 12x - 5$

(xii) $f(x) = 6 + 12x + 3x^2 - 2x^3$

(xiii) $f(x) = 2x^3 - 24x + 107$

(xiv) $f(x) = -2x^3 - 9x^2 - 12x + 1$ [NCERT]

(xv) $f(x) = (x-1)(x-2)^2$

(xvi) $f(x) = x^3 - 12x^2 + 36x + 17$ [CBSE 2001]

(xvii) $f(x) = 2x^3 - 24x + 7$

(xviii) $f(x) = \frac{3}{10}x^4 - \frac{4}{5}x^3 - 3x^2 + \frac{36}{5}x + 11$ [NCERT]

(xix) $f(x) = x^4 - 4x$

(xx) $f(x) = \frac{x^4}{4} + \frac{2}{3}x^3 - \frac{5}{2}x^2 - 6x + 7$

(xxi) $f(x) = x^4 - 4x^3 + 4x^2 + 15$

(xxii) $f(x) = 5x^{3/2} - 3x^{5/2}, x > 0$

(xxiii) $f(x) = x^8 + 6x^2$

(xxiv) $f(x) = x^3 - 6x^2 + 9x + 15$ [CBSE 2000, 04]

(xxv) $f(x) = \{x(x-2)\}^2$ [NCERT, CBSE 2010, 14]

(xxvi) $f(x) = 3x^4 - 4x^3 - 12x^2 + 5$ [CBSE 2014]

(xxvii) $f(x) = \frac{3}{2}x^4 - 4x^3 - 45x^2 + 51$ [CBSE 2014]

(xxviii) $f(x) = \log(2+x) - \frac{2x}{2+x}, x \in R$ [CBSE 2014]

(xxix) $f(x) = \frac{x^4}{4} - x^3 - 5x^2 + 24x + 12$ [CBSE 2018]

(xxx) $f(x) = x^4 - 4x^3 + 10$ [CBSE 2024]

2. Determine the values of x for which the function $f(x) = x^2 - 6x + 9$ is increasing or decreasing. Also, find the coordinates of the point on the curve $y = x^2 - 6x + 9$ where the normal is parallel to the line $y = x + 5$.
3. Find the intervals in which $f(x) = \sin x - \cos x$, where $0 < x < 2\pi$ is increasing or decreasing.
4. Show that $f(x) = e^{2x}$ is increasing on R. [CBSE 2000, 2010]
5. Show that $f(x) = e^{1/x}, x \neq 0$ is a decreasing function for all $x \neq 0$.
6. Show that $f(x) = \ln_a x, 0 < a < 1$ is a decreasing function for all $x > 0$.
7. Show that $f(x) = \sin x$ is increasing on $(0, \pi/2)$ and decreasing on $(\pi/2, \pi)$ and neither increasing nor decreasing in $(0, \pi)$. [NCERT]
8. Show that $f(x) = \ln \sin x$ is increasing on $(0, \pi/2)$ and decreasing on $(\pi/2, \pi)$. [NCERT]
9. Show that $f(x) = x - \sin x$ is increasing for all $x \in R$.
10. Show that $f(x) = x^3 - 15x^2 + 75x - 50$ is an increasing function for all $x \in R$.
11. Show that $f(x) = \cos^2 x$ is a decreasing function on $(0, \pi/2)$.
12. Show that $f(x) = \sin x$ is an increasing function on $(-\pi/2, \pi/2)$.
13. Show that $f(x) = \cos x$ is a decreasing function on $(0, \pi)$, increasing in $(-\pi, 0)$ and neither increasing nor decreasing in $(-\pi, \pi)$.
14. Show that $f(x) = \tan x$ is an increasing function on $(-\pi/2, \pi/2)$.
15. Show that $f(x) = (x-1)e^x + 1$ is an increasing function for all $x > 0$.
16. Prove that the function $f(x) = x^3 - 6x^2 + 12x - 18$ is increasing on R. [CBSE 2002C]
17. State when a function $f(x)$ is said to be increasing on an interval $[a, b]$. Test whether the function $f(x) = x^2 - 6x + 3$ is increasing on the interval [4, 6].
18. Show that $f(x) = \sin x - \cos x$ is an increasing function on $(-\pi/4, \pi/4)$.
19. Show that $f(x) = \tan^{-1} x - x$ is a decreasing function on R.
20. Determine whether $f(x) = -\frac{x}{2} + \sin x$ is increasing or decreasing on $\left(-\frac{\pi}{3}, \frac{\pi}{3}\right)$.
21. Find the intervals in which $f(x) = \ln(1+x) - \frac{x}{1+x}$ is increasing or decreasing.

    [CBSE 2000 C]
22. Find the intervals in which $f(x) = (x+2)e^{-x}$ is increasing or decreasing.

    [CBSE 2000 C]
23. Show that the function f given by $f(x) = 10^x$ is increasing for all x.

24. Prove that the function f given by $f(x) = x - [x]$ is increasing in $(0, 1)$.

25. Prove that the following functions are increasing on R:

(i) $f(x) = 3x^5 + 40x^3 + 240x$ (ii) $f(x) = 4x^3 - 18x^2 + 27x - 27$ [CBSE 2017]

26. Prove that the function f given by $f(x) = \ln \cos x$ is strictly increasing on $(-\pi/2, 0)$ and strictly decreasing on $(0, \pi/2)$. [NCERT]

27. Prove that the function f given by $f(x) = x^3 - 3x^2 + 4x$ is strictly increasing on R. [NCERT]

28. Prove that the function $f(x) = \cos x$ is:

(i) strictly decreasing in $(0, \pi)$ (ii) strictly increasing in $(\pi, 2\pi)$

(iii) neither increasing nor decreasing in $(0, 2\pi)$ [NCERT]

BASED ON LOTS

29. Show that $f(x) = \tan^{-1}(\sin x + \cos x)$ is a decreasing function on the interval $(\pi/4, \pi/2)$.

30. Show that the function $f(x) = \sin(2x + \pi/4)$ is decreasing on $(3\pi/8, 5\pi/8)$.

31. Show that the function $f(x) = \cot^{-1}(\sin x + \cos x)$ is decreasing on $(0, \pi/4)$ and increasing on $(\pi/4, \pi/2)$.

32. Show that the function $x^2 - x + 1$ is neither increasing nor decreasing on $(0, 1)$.

33. Show that $f(x) = x^9 + 4x^7 + 11$ is an increasing function for all $x \in R$.

34. Show that the function $f(x) = \dfrac{16 \sin x}{4 + \cos x} - x$ is strictly decreasing in $\left(\dfrac{\pi}{2}, \pi\right)$. [CBSE 2023]

35. Show that the function $f(x) = e^x - e^{-x} + x - \tan^{-1} x$ is strictly increasing on its domain. [CBSE 2024]

36. Show that the function f given by $f(x) = \sin x + \cos x$ is strictly decreasing on the interval $\left(\dfrac{\pi}{4}, \dfrac{5\pi}{4}\right)$. [CBSE 2024]

BASED ON HOTS

37. Show that $f(x) = x^2 - x \sin x$ is an increasing function on $(0, \pi/2)$.

38. Find the value(s) of a for which $f(x) = x^3 - ax$ is an increasing function on R.

39. Find the values of b for which the function $f(x) = \sin x - bx + c$ is a decreasing function on R.

40. Show that $f(x) = x + \cos x - a$ is an increasing function on R for all values of a.

41. Let f defined on $[0, 1]$ be twice differentiable such that $|f''(x)| \le 1$ for all $x \in [0, 1]$. If $f(0) = f(1)$, then show that $|f'(x)| < 1$ for all $x \in [0, 1]$. [NCERT]

42. Find the intervals in which $f(x)$ is increasing or decreasing: [CBSE 2014]

(i) $f(x) = x|x|, x \in R$ (ii) $f(x) = \sin x + |\sin x|, 0 < x \le 2\pi$

(iii) $f(x) = \sin x(1 + \cos x), 0 < x < \dfrac{\pi}{2}$

ANSWERS

1.

	Increasing	Decreasing		Increasing	Decreasing
(i)	$(-\infty, -3/2)$	$(-3/2, \infty)$	(ii)	$(-1, \infty)$	$(-\infty, -1)$
(iii)	$(-\infty, -9/2)$	$(-9/2, \infty)$	(iv)	$(-\infty, 1) \cup (3, \infty)$	$(1, 3)$
(v)	$(-2, 3)$	$(-\infty, -2) \cup (3, \infty)$	(vi)	$(-2, 3)$	$(-\infty, -2) \cup (3, \infty)$

(vii) $(-\infty,-2)\cup(4,\infty)$ $(-2,4)$ (viii) $(-\infty,-2)\cup(6,\infty)$ $(-2,6)$

(ix) $(-\infty,2)\cup(3,\infty)$ $(2,3)$ (x) $(-\infty,-2)\cup(-1,\infty)$ $(-2,-1)$

(xi) $(-\infty,1)\cup(2,\infty)$ $(1,2)$ (xii) $(-1,2)$ $(-\infty,-1)\cup(2,\infty)$

(xiii) $(-\infty,-2)\cup(2,\infty)$ $(-2,2)$ (xiv) $(-2,-1)$ $(-\infty,-2)\cup(-1,\infty)$

(xv) $(-\infty,4/3)\cup(2,\infty)$ $(4/3,2)$ (xvi) $(-\infty,2)\cup(6,\infty)$ $(2,6)$

(xvii) $(-\infty,-2)\cup(2,\infty)$ $(-2,2)$ (xviii) $(-2,1)\cup(3,\infty)$ $(-\infty,-2)\cup(1,3)$

(xix) $(1,\infty)$ $(-\infty,1)$ (xx) $(-3,-1)\cup(2,\infty)$ $(-\infty,-3)\cup(-1,2)$

(xxi) $(0,1)\cup(2,\infty)$ $(-\infty,0)\cup(1,2)$ (xxii) $(0,1)$ $(1,\infty)$

(xxiii) $(0,\infty)$ $(-\infty,0)$ (xxiv) $(-\infty,-1)\cup(3,\infty)$ $(1,3)$

(xxv) $(0,1)\cup(2,\infty)$ $(-\infty,0)\cup(1,2)$ (xxvi) $(-1,0)\cup(2,\infty)$ $(-\infty,-1)\cup(0,2)$

(xxvii) $(-3,0)\cup(5,\infty)$ $(-\infty,-3)\cup(0,5)$ (xxviii) $(2,\infty)$ $(-2,2)$

(xxix) $(-3,2)\cup(4,\infty)$ $(-\infty,-3)\cup(2,4)$ (xxx) $(3,\infty)$ $(-\infty,3)$

2. Increasing on $(3,\infty)$ and decreasing on $(-\infty,3)$; $(5/2, 1/4)$

3. Increasing on $(0, 3\pi/4)\cup(7\pi/4, 2\pi)$; decreasing on $(3\pi/4, 7\pi/4)$

17. Increasing 20. Increasing 21. Increasing on $(0,\infty)$; decreasing on $(-1,0)$

22. Increasing on $(-\infty,-1)$; decreasing on $(-1,\infty)$

26. Increasing on $(-\infty,-1)$; decreasing on $(-1,\infty)$ 38. $a\le 0$ 39. $b\ge 1$

42. (i) Increasing for all $x\in R$

(ii) Increasing on $(0,\pi/2)$, decreasing on $(\pi/2,\pi)$, neither increasing nor decreasing on $(\pi, 2\pi)$

(iii) Increasing on $(0,\pi/3)$, decreasing on $(\pi/3,\pi/2)$

FILL IN THE BLANKS TYPE QUESTIONS (FBQs)

1. The values of 'a' for which the function $f(x)=\sin x - ax + b$ increases on R are ....

2. The function $f(x)=\dfrac{2x^2-1}{x^4}$, $x>0$, decreases in the interval ....

3. The function $g(x)=x+\dfrac{1}{x}$, $x\ne 0$ decreases in the closed interval ....

4. The largest open interval in which the function $f(x)=\dfrac{1}{1+x^2}$ decreases is ....

5. The set of values of x for which $f(x)=\tan x - x$ is increasing is ....

6. The set of values of 'a' for which the function $f(x)=\sin x-\cos x-ax+b$ decreases for all real values of x, is .... [NCERT EXEMPLAR]

7. The set of values of 'a' for which the $f(x)=ax+b$ is strictly increasing for all real x, is ....

8. If $k\pi$ is the length of the largest interval in which the function $f(x)=3\sin x-4\sin^3 x$ is increasing, then $k=$ ....

9. The set of values of λ for which the function $f(x)=\dfrac{\lambda\sin x+6\cos x}{2\sin x+3\cos x}$ is strictly increasing, is........................ .

10. The largest interval in which $f(x)=x^{1/x}$ is strictly increasing is ....

ANSWERS

1. $(-\infty, -1)$ 2. $(1, \infty)$ 3. $[-1, 1]$ 4. $(0, \infty)$
5. $R = \left\{(2n-1)\frac{\pi}{2}, n \in Z\right\}$ 6. $(\sqrt{2}, \infty)$ 7. $(0, \infty)$
8. $\frac{1}{3}$ 9. $(4, \infty)$ 10. $(1, e)$

VERY SHORT ANSWER QUESTIONS (VSAQs)

Answer each of the following questions in one word or one sentence or as per exact requirement of the question:

1. What are the values of 'a' for which $f(x) = a^x$ is increasing on R?
2. What are the values of 'a' for which $f(x) = a^x$ is decreasing on R?
3. Write the set of values of 'a' for which $f(x) = \log_a x$ is increasing in its domain.
4. Write the set of values of 'a' for which $f(x) = \log_a x$ is decreasing in its domain.
5. Find 'a' for which $f(x) = a(x + \sin x) + a$ is increasing on R.
6. Find the values of 'a' for which the function $f(x) = \sin x - ax + 4$ is increasing function on R.
7. Find the set of values of 'b' for which $f(x) = b(x + \cos x) + 4$ is decreasing on R.
8. Find the set of values of 'a' for which $f(x) = x + \cos x + ax + b$ is increasing on R.
9. Write the set of values of k for which $f(x) = kx - \sin x$ is increasing on R.
10. If $g(x)$ is a decreasing function on R and $f(x) = \tan^{-1}\{g(x)\}$. State whether $f(x)$ is increasing or decreasing on R.
11. Write the set of values of a for which the function $f(x) = ax + b$ is decreasing for all $x \in R$.
12. Write the interval in which $f(x) = \sin x + \cos x$, $x \in [0, \pi/2]$ is increasing.
13. State whether $f(x) = \tan x - x$ is increasing or decreasing its domain.
14. Write the set of values of a for which $f(x) = \cos x + a^2 x + b$ is strictly increasing on R.
15. If $f(x) = a(\tan x - \cot x)$, where $a > 0$, then find whether $f(x)$ is increasing or decreasing function in its domain. **[CBSE 2023]**

ANSWERS

1. $a > 1$ 2. $0 < a < 1$ 3. $a > 1$ 4. $0 < a < 1$
5. $a \in (0, \infty)$ 6. $a \in (-\infty, -1)$ 7. $b \in (-\infty, 0)$ 8. $a \in (0, \infty)$
9. $k \in (1, \infty)$ 10. Decreasing 11. $a \in (-\infty, 0)$ 12. $[0, \pi/4]$
13. Increasing 14. $a \in (-\infty, -1] \cup [1, \infty)$ 15. Increasing

CHAPTER 14

MAXIMA AND MINIMA

14.1 INTRODUCTION

In the previous chapters, we have learnt about various applications of differentiation. In this chapter, we will use differentiation to find the maximum and minimum values of differentiable functions in their domains. In the end of the chapter, we will discuss applications of maxima and minima in solving some applied problems.

14.2 MAXIMUM AND MINIMUM VALUES OF A FUNCTION IN ITS DOMAIN

MAXIMUM *Let $f(x)$ be a real function defined on an interval $[a, b]$. Then, $f(x)$ is said to have the maximum value in $[a, b]$, if there exists a point c in $[a, b]$ such that $f(x) \le f(c)$ for all $x \in [a, b]$.*

In such a case, the number $f(c)$ is called the maximum value of $f(x)$ in the interval $[a, b]$ and the point c is called a point of maximum value of f in the interval $[a, b]$.

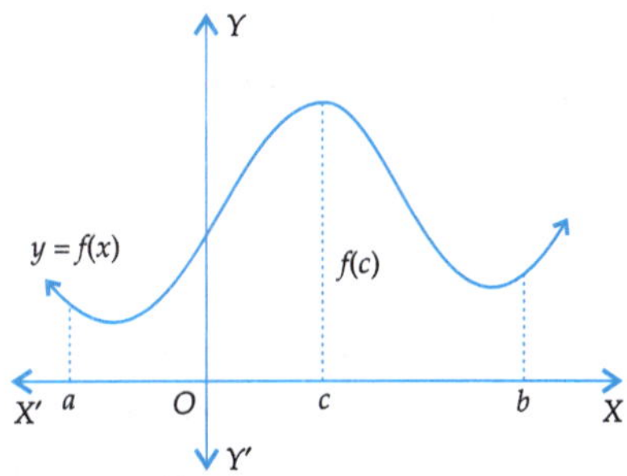

Fig. 14.1 Maximum value of $f(x)$ at $x = c$

Consider the function f given by $f(x) = -(x-1)^2 + 10$.

Clearly, domain $(f) = R = (-\infty, \infty)$.

We observe that

$$-(x-1)^2 \le 0 \text{ for all } x \in R$$

$$\Rightarrow \quad -(x-1)^2 + 10 \le 10 \text{ for all } x \in R$$

$$\Rightarrow \quad f(x) \le 10 \quad \text{for all } x \in R$$

$$\Rightarrow \quad f(x) \le f(1) \text{ for all } x \in R \qquad [\because f(1) = -(1-1)^2 + 10 = 10]$$

It follows from this expression that $f(1) = 10$ is the maximum value of function f and the point of maximum value of f is $x = 1$. This fact is also evident from the graph of function f as shown in Fig. 14.2.

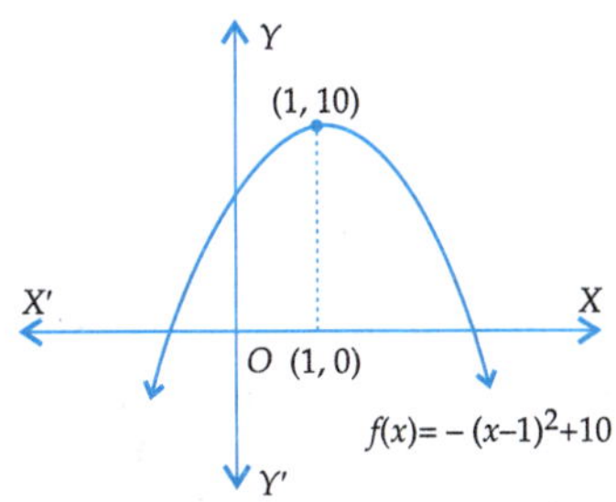

Fig. 14.2 Graph of $f(x) = -(x-1)^2 + 10$

MINIMUM *Let $f(x)$ be a real function defined on an interval $[a, b]$. Then $f(x)$ is said to have the minimum value in interval $[a, b]$, if there exists a point $c \in [a, b]$ such that $f(x) \ge f(c)$ for all $x \in [a, b]$.*

In such a case, the number $f(c)$ is called the minimum value of $f(x)$ in the interval $[a, b]$ and the point c is called a point of minimum value of f in the interval $[a, b]$.

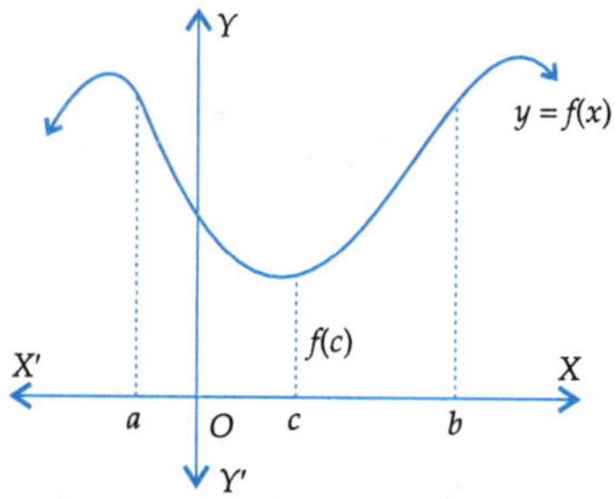

Fig. 14.3 Minimum value of $f(x)$ at $x = c$

Consider the function f given by $f(x) = x^2 + 5$. Clearly, domain $(f) = R = (-\infty, \infty)$.

Now,

$x^2 \geq 0$ for all $x \in R \Rightarrow x^2 + 5 \geq 5$ for all $x \in R \Rightarrow f(x) \geq 5$ for all $x \in R \Rightarrow f(x) \geq f(0)$ for all $x \in R$

It follows from this expression and the above definition that the minimum value of function $f(x) = x^2 + 5$ defined on R is 5 and the point of minimum value of f is $x = 0$. This observation is also evident from the graph of $f(x) = x^2 + 5$ as shown in Fig. 14.4.

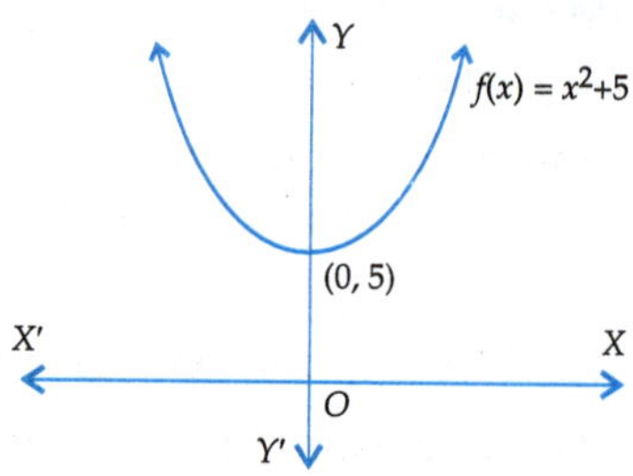

Fig. 14.4 Graph of $f(x) = x^2 + 5$

In the above discussion, we have seen that the function $f(x) = -(x-1)^2 + 10$, $x \in R$ has the maximum value but it does not attain the minimum value, because $-(x-1)^2 + 10$ can be made as small as we please, which is also evident from the graph (Fig. 14.2). The function $f(x) = x^2 + 5$ attains the minimum value 5 at $x = 0$, but it does not attain the maximum value at any point in its domain. In fact, $f(x)$ can be made as large as we please. From the graph of $f(x)$ (Fig. 14.4), we find that the values of $f(x)$ are increasing rapidly. That is why it does not attain the maximum value.

Let us now consider the function $f(x) = \sin x$ defined on the interval $[0, 2\pi]$.

Clearly, $-1 \leq \sin x \leq 1$ for all $x \in [0, 2\pi]$. So, $-1 \leq f(x) \leq 1$ for all $x \in [0, 2\pi]$.

Also, $f\left(\frac{\pi}{2}\right) = 1$ and $f\left(\frac{3\pi}{2}\right) = -1$.

$\therefore \quad f\left(\frac{3\pi}{2}\right) \leq f(x) \leq f\left(\frac{\pi}{2}\right)$ for all $x \in [0, 2\pi]$

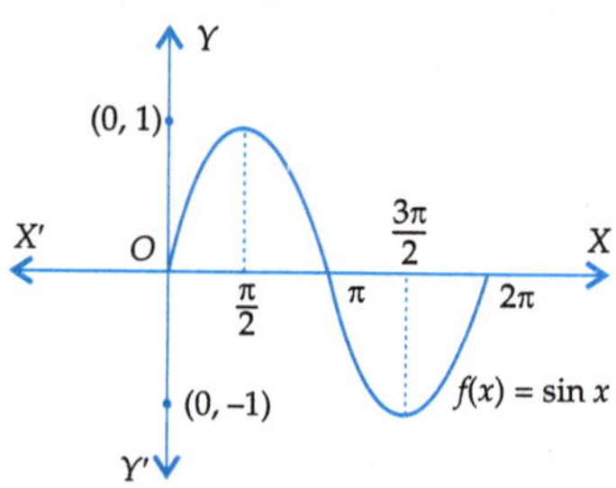

Fig. 14.5 Graph of $f(x) = \sin x, 0 \leq x \leq 2\pi$

Thus, $f(x)$ attains both the maximum value 1 and the minimum value -1 in the interval $[0, 2\pi]$. Points $x = \pi/2$ and $x = 3\pi/2$ are respectively the points of maximum and minimum values of f in the interval $[0, 2\pi]$. This is also evident from the graph of $f(x)$ as shown in Fig. 14.5.

Now, consider the function f given by $f(x) = x^3$ defined on $(-2, 2)$. Clearly, it is an increasing function in the given interval. So, it should have the minimum value at a point closest to -2 on its right and the maximum value at a point closest to 2 on the left. In fact, it is not possible to locate such points as shown in Fig. 14.6. Therefore, $f(x) = x^3$ has neither the maximum value nor the minimum value in the interval $(-2, 2)$.

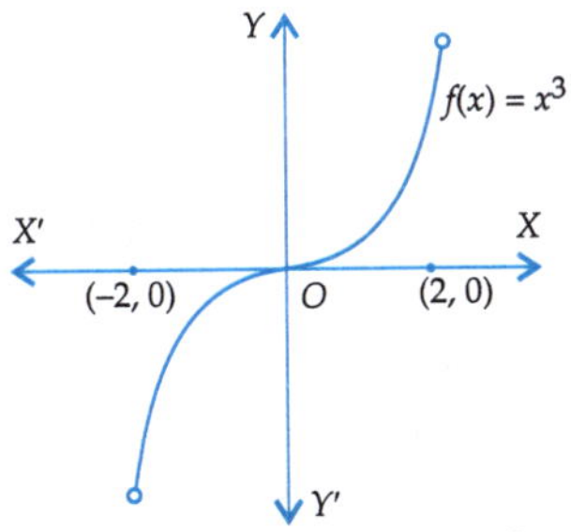

Fig. 14.6 Graph of $f(x) = x^3$

It follows from the above discussion that a function f defined on an interval I.

(i) may attain the maximum value at a point in I but not the minimum value at any point in I.

(ii) may attain the minimum at a point in I but not the maximum value at any point in I.

(iii) may attain both the maximum and minimum values at some points in I.

(iv) may not attain both the maximum and minimum values at any point in I.

Let us now discuss more examples on the maximum and minimum values of functions in their domains.

ILLUSTRATIVE EXAMPLES

BASED ON BASIC CONCEPTS (BASIC)

EXAMPLE 1 *Find the maximum and the minimum values, if any, of the following functions*

(i) $f(x) = 3x^2 + 6x + 8, x \in R$ (ii) $f(x) = -|x-1| + 5$ *for all* $x \in R$

(iii) $f(x) = \sin 3x + 4, x \in (-\pi/2, \pi/2)$ (iv) $f(x) = x^3 + 1$ *for all* $x \in R$ [NCERT]

(v) $f(x) = \sin(\sin x)$ *for all* $x \in R$ (vi) $f(x) = |x+3|$ *for all* $x \in R$.

SOLUTION (i) We have, $f(x) = 3x^2 + 6x + 8 = 3(x^2 + 2x + 1) + 5 = 3(x+1)^2 + 5$.

Clearly, $3(x+1)^2 \geq 0$ for all $x \in R$

$\Rightarrow \quad 3(x+1)^2 + 5 \geq 5$ for all $x \in R \Rightarrow f(x) \geq f(-1)$ for all $x \in R$. $[\because f(-1) = 5]$

Thus, 5 is the minimum value of $f(x)$ which it attains at $x = -1$.

Since $f(x)$ can be made as large as we please. Therefore, the maximum value does not exist which can be observed from Fig. 14.7.

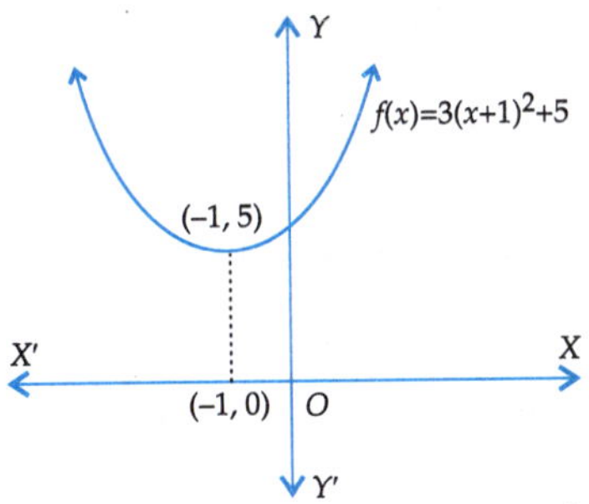

Fig. 14.7 Graph of $f(x) = 3(x+1)^2 + 5$

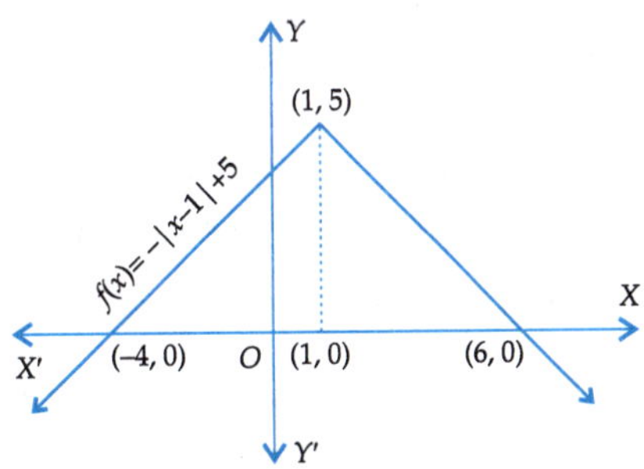

Fig. 14.8 Graph of $f(x) = -|x-1| + 5$

(ii) We have, $f(x) = -|x-1| + 5$ for all $x \in R$.

Clearly, $|x-1| \geq 0$ for all $x \in R$

$\Rightarrow \quad -|x-1| \leq 0$ for all $x \in R \Rightarrow -|x-1| + 5 \leq 5$ for all $x \in R \Rightarrow f(x) \leq 5$ for all $x \in R$.

So, 5 is the maximum value of $f(x)$.

Now, $f(x)=5 \Rightarrow -|x-1|+5=5 \Rightarrow |x-1|=0 \Rightarrow x=1.$

Thus, $f(x)$ attains the maximum value 5 at $x = 1$. Since $f(x)$ can be made as small as we please. Therefore the minimum value of $f(x)$ does not exist (see Fig. 14.8).

(iii) We have, $f(x) = \sin 3x + 4$ for all $x \in R$

Clearly, $-1 \le \sin 3x \le 1$ for all $x \in R$

$\Rightarrow \quad -1+4 \le \sin 3x + 4 \le 1+4$ for all $x \in R$

$\Rightarrow \quad 3 \le \sin 3x + 4 \le 5$ for all $x \in R \Rightarrow 3 \le f(x) \le 5$ for all $x \in R$.

Thus, the maximum value of $f(x)$ is 5 and the minimum value is 3.

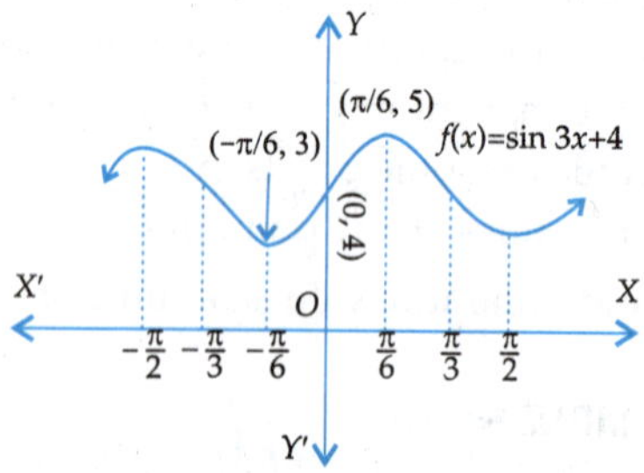

Fig. 14.9 Graph of $f(x) = \sin 3x + 4$

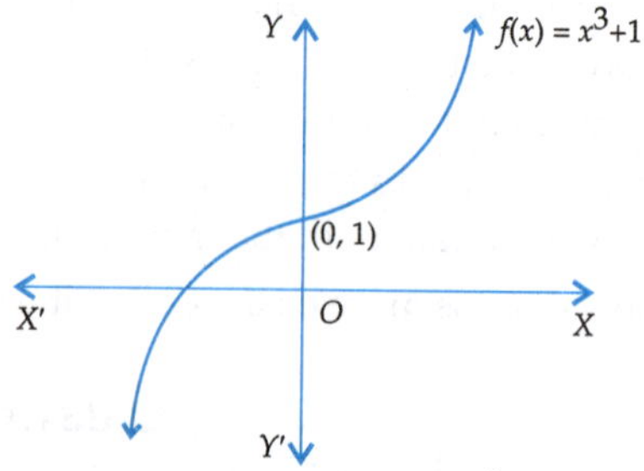

Fig. 14.10 Graph of $f(x) = x^3 + 1$

Now, $f(x) = 5 \Rightarrow \sin 3x + 4 = 5 \Rightarrow \sin 3x = 1 \Rightarrow 3x = \frac{\pi}{2} \Rightarrow x = \frac{\pi}{6}.$

So, $f(x)$ attains its maximum value 5 at $x = \frac{\pi}{6}$. (see Fig. 14.9).

Also, $f(x) = 3 \Rightarrow \sin 3x + 4 = 3 \Rightarrow \sin 3x = -1 \Rightarrow 3x = -\frac{\pi}{2} \Rightarrow x = -\frac{\pi}{6}.$

So, $f(x)$ attains the minimum value 3 at $x = -\frac{\pi}{6}$.

(iv) We have, $f(x) = x^3 + 1, x \in R$. Here, we observe that the values of $f(x)$ increase when the values of x are increased and $f(x)$ can be made as large as we please by giving large values to x. So, $f(x)$ does not have the maximum value. Similarly, $f(x)$ can be made as small as we please by giving smaller values to x. So $f(x)$ does not have the minimum value also. (See Fig. 14.10).

(v) We have, $f(x) = \sin(\sin x),\ x \in R$. Clearly,

$-1 \le \sin x \le 1$ for all $x \in R$

$\Rightarrow \quad \sin(-1) \le \sin(\sin x) \le \sin 1$ for all $x \in R$ [$\because \sin x$ is an increasing function on $[-1, 1]$]

$\Rightarrow \quad -\sin 1 \le f(x) \le \sin 1$ for all $x \in R$

This shows that the maximum value of $f(x)$ is $\sin 1$ and the minimum value is $-\sin 1$.

(vi) We have, $f(x) = |x+3|$ for all $x \in R$

Clearly, $|x+3| \ge 0$ for all $x \in R \Rightarrow f(x) \ge 0$ for all $x \in R$.

So, the minimum value of $f(x)$ is 0, which it attains at $x = -3$. Clearly, $f(x) = |x+3|$ does not have the maximum value. (See Fig. 14.11).

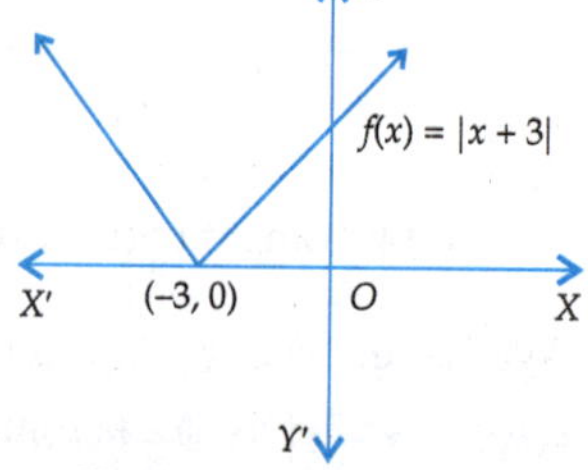

Fig. 14.11 Graph of $f(x) = |x+3|$

EXERCISE 14.1

BASIC

Find the maximum and the minimum values, if any, without using derivatives of the following functions:

1. $f(x) = 4x^2 - 4x + 4$ on R
2. $f(x) = -(x-1)^2 + 2$ on R [NCERT]
3. $f(x) = |x+2|$ on R
4. $f(x) = \sin 2x + 5$ on R [NCERT]
5. $f(x) = |\sin 4x + 3|$ on R [NCERT]
6. $f(x) = 2x^3 + 5$ on R [CBSE 2023]
7. $f(x) = -|x+1| + 3$ on R [NCERT]
8. $f(x) = 16x^2 - 16x + 28$ on R
9. $f(x) = x^3 - 1$ on R

ANSWERS

1. Min. = 3, Max. dose not exist.
2. Max. = 2, Min. does not exist.
3. Min. = 0, Max. does not exist.
4. Max. = 6, Min. = 4.
5. Max. = 4, Min. = 2.
6. Max and Min. both do not exist.
7. Max. = 3, Min. does not exist.
8. Min. = 24, Max. does not exist
9. Max. and Min. both do not exist.

HINTS TO SELECTED PROBLEMS

2. We have, $f(x) = -(x-1)^2$ for all $x \in R$

   Clearly, $-(x-1)^2 \le 0$ for all $x \in R \Rightarrow -(x-1)^2 + 2 \le 2$ for all $x \in R \Rightarrow f(x) \le 2$ for all $x \in R$.

   So, $f(x)$ attains maximum value 2 at $x = 1$ and the minimum value does not exist as $f(x)$ can be made as small as we please.

4. We have, $f(x) = \sin 2x + 5,\ x \in R$.

   Clearly, $-1 \le \sin 2x \le 1$ for all $x \in R$

   $\Rightarrow\ 5 - 1 \le \sin 2x + 5 \le 1 + 5$ for all $x \in R \Rightarrow 4 \le f(x) \le 6$ for all $x \in R$.

   So, the minimum and the maximum values of $f(x)$ are 4 and 6 respectively.

5. We have, $f(x) = |\sin 4x + 3|,\ x \in R$. We know that

   $-1 \le \sin 4x \le 1$ for all $x \in R$.

   $\Rightarrow\ 3 - 1 \le \sin 4x + 3 \le 1 + 3$ for all $x \in R$

   $\Rightarrow\ 2 \le \sin 4x + 3 \le 4$ for all $x \in R$

   $\Rightarrow\ 2 \le |\sin 4x + 3| \le 4$ for all $x \in R \Rightarrow 2 \le f(x) \le 4$ for all $x \in R$

   So, the minimum and the maximum values of $f(x)$ are 2 and 4 respectively.

7. We have, $f(x) = -|x+1| + 3,\ x \in R$. We know that

   $-|x+1| \le 0$ for all $x \in R \Rightarrow -|x+1| + 3 \le 3$ for all $x \in R \Rightarrow f(x) \le 3$ for all $x \in R$.

So, the maximum value of $f(x)$ is 3. As $f(x)$ can be made as small as we please. So, the minimum value of $f(x)$ does not exist.

14.3 LOCAL MAXIMA AND LOCAL MINIMA

In the previous section, we have discussed about the greatest (maximum) and the least (minimum) values of a function in its domain. But, there may be points in the domain of a function where the function does not attain the greatest (or the least) value but the values at these points are greater than or less than the values of the function at the neighbouring points. Such points are known as the points of local minimum or local maximum and we will be mainly discussing about the local maximum and local minimum values of a function.

LOCAL MAXIMUM *A function $f(x)$ is said to attain a local maximum at $x = a$ if there exists a neighbourhood $(a - \delta, a + \delta)$ of a such that*

$$f(x) < f(a) \text{ for all } x \in (a - \delta, a + \delta),\ x \ne a.$$

or, $\quad f(x) - f(a) < 0$ *for all* $x \in (a - \delta, a + \delta),\ x \neq a.$

In such a case, $f(a)$ is called the local maximum value of $f(x)$ at $x = a$.

LOCAL MINIMUM *A function $f(x)$ is said to attain a local minimum at $x = a$ if there exists a neighbourhood $(a - \delta, a + \delta)$ of a such that*

$$f(x) > f(a) \text{ for all } x \in (a - \delta, a + \delta), x \neq a$$

or, $\quad f(x) - f(a) > 0$ *for all* $x \in (a - \delta, a + \delta), x \neq a.$

The value of the function at $x = a$ i.e. $f(a)$ is called the local minimum value of $f(x)$ at $x = a$.

The points at which a function attains either the local maximum values or local minimum values are known as the extreme points or turning points and both local maximum and local minimum values are called the extreme values of $f(x)$. Thus, a function attains an extreme value at $x = a$ if $f(a)$ is either a local maximum value or a local minimum value. Consequently, at an extreme point 'a', $f(x) - f(a)$ keeps the same sign for all values of x in a deleted neighbourhood of a.

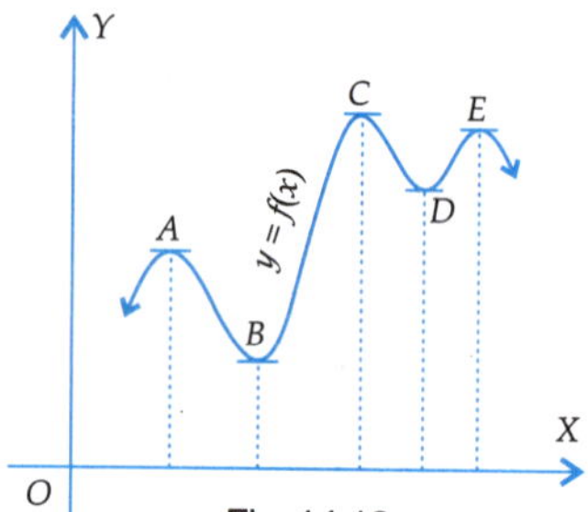

Fig. 14.12

In Fig. 14.12 we observe that the x-coordinates of the points A, C and E are points of local maximum and the values at these points i.e. their y-coordinates are the local maximum values of $f(x)$. The x-coordinates of points B and D are points of local minimum and their y-coordinates are the local minimum values of $f(x)$.

NOTE *By a local maximum (or local minimum) value of a function at a point $x = a$, we mean the greatest (or the least) value in the neighbourhood of point $x = a$ and not the maximum (or the minimum) in the domain of the function. In fact a function may have any number of points of local maximum (or local minimum) and even a local minimum value may be greater than a local maximum value. In Fig. 14.12 the minimum value at D is greater than the maximum value at A. Thus, a local maximum value may not be the greatest value and a local minimum value may not be the least value of the function in its domain.*

It follows from the above definition that if a is a point of local maximum of a function f, then in the neighbourhood of a the graph of f should be as shown in Fig. 14.13. Clearly, $f(x)$ is increasing in the left neighbourhood $(a - \delta, a)$ of point a and decreasing in the right neighbourhood of $x = a$.

$\therefore \quad f'(x) > 0$ for $x \in (a - \delta, a)$ and, $f'(x) < 0$ for $x \in (a, a + \delta)$

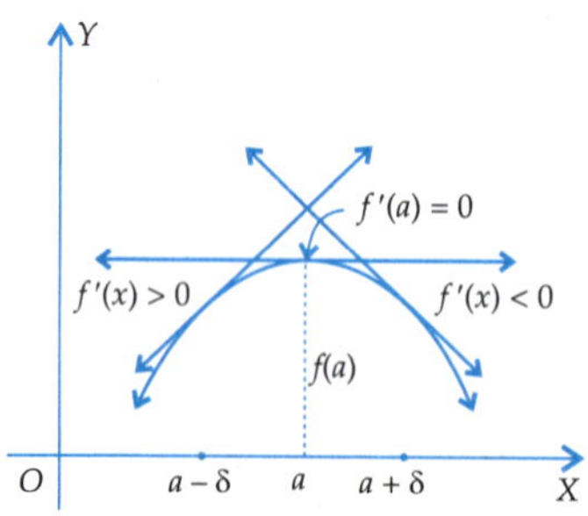

Fig. 14.13 Point of local maximum

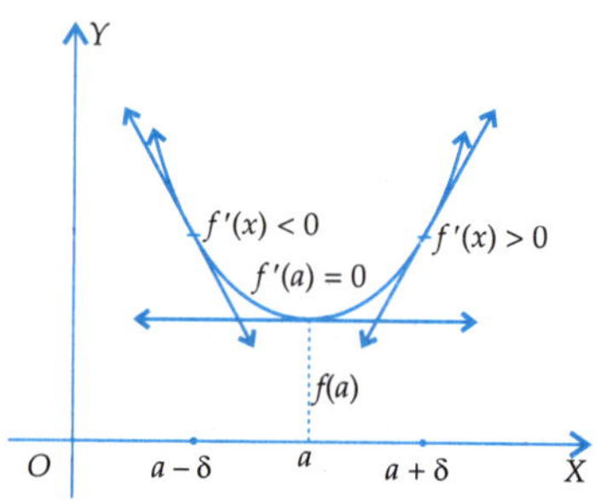

Fig. 14.14 Point of local minimum

This suggests that $f'(a)$ must be zero.

Similarly, if a is a point of local minimum of a function f, then in the neighbourhood of a the graph of f should be as shown in Fig. 14.14. Here, we observe that $f(x)$ is decreasing in the left neighbourhood $(a - \delta, a)$ of a and increasing in the right neighbourhood $(a, a + \delta)$ of a.

$\therefore \qquad f'(x) < 0$ for $x \in (a - \delta, a)$ and, $f'(x) > 0$ for $x \in (a, a + \delta)$.

This also suggests that $f'(a)$ must be zero.

In view of the above discussion we state the following theorem (without proof) which is known as the necessary condition for points of local maximum or minimum.

THEOREM *A necessary condition for f(a) to be an extreme value of a function f(x) is that $f'(a) = 0$, in case it exists.*

REMARK 1 *This result states that if the derivative exists, it must be zero at the extreme points. A function may however attain an extreme value at a point without being derivable thereat. For example, the function $f(x) = |x|$ attains the minimum value at the origin even though it is not derivable at $x = 0$.*

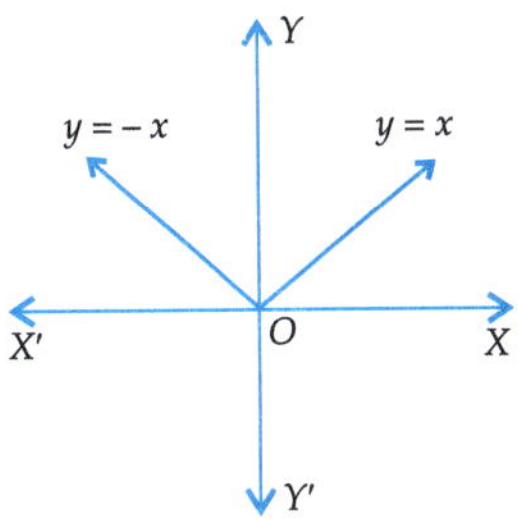

Fig. 14.15 Graph of $f(x) = |x|$

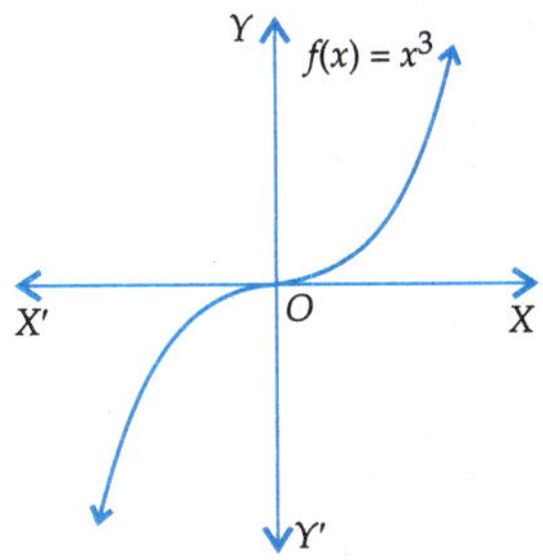

Fig. 14.16 Graph of $f(x) = x^3$

REMARK 2 *This condition is only a necessary condition for the point $x = a$ to be an extreme point. It is not sufficient i.e., $f'(a) = 0$ does not necessarily imply that $x = a$ is an extreme point. There are functions for which the derivatives vanish at a point but do not have an extreme value thereat. For example, for the function $f(x) = x^3$, we have $f'(0) = 0$ but at $x = 0$ the function does not attain an extreme value (See Fig. 14.16). In fact on the left of point $x = 0$, the curve is concave down and on its right the curve is concave up. That is, the concavity of $f(x)$ changes x as increases through O. Such points are called points of inflection. If $x = c$ is a point of inflection of a function $f(x)$, then $f''(c) = 0$ and $f''(x)$ change its sign as x increases through 'c'.*

REMARK 3 *Geometrically the above condition means that the tangent to the curve $y = f(x)$ at a point where the ordinate is maximum or minimum is parallel to the x-axis.*

REMARK 4 *As discussed in Remark 2 that all x, for which $f'(x) = 0$, do not give us the extreme values. The values of x for which $f'(x) = 0$ are called stationary points or turning points and the corresponding values of f(x) are called stationary or turning values of f(x).*

REMARK 5 *The values of x for which $f'(x) = 0$ or, $f'(x)$ does not exist are known as critical points.*

14.4 FIRST DERIVATIVE TEST FOR LOCAL MAXIMA AND MINIMA

In the previous section, we have seen that an extreme point (point of local maximum or minimum) the derivative of the function either does not exist or in case it exists, it must be zero. We have also seen that if a is a point of local maximum value of a function f, then there exists a neighbourhood $(a - \delta, a + \delta)$ of a such that

$f'(x) > 0 \quad$ for all $x \in (a - \delta, a)$ [See Fig. 14.13]

and, $\quad f'(x) < 0 \quad$ for all $x \in (a, a + \delta)$.

In case, a is a point of local minimum value of function f, then there exists a neighbourhood $(a - \delta, a + \delta)$ of a such that

$f'(x) < 0 \quad$ for all $x \in (a - \delta, a)$

and, $\quad f'(x) > 0 \quad$ for all $x \in (a, a + \delta)$ [See Fig. 14.14]

In the light of these observations, we state the following theorem (without proof) for finding the points of local maxima or local minima.

THEOREM 1 *(First derivative test) Let f be a differentiable function defined on an interval I and let $a \in I$. Then,*

(a) *$x = a$ is a point of local maximum value of f, if*

(i) $f'(a) = 0$

and, (ii) *$f'(x)$ changes sign from positive to negative as x increases through a*

i.e. $f'(x) > 0$ at every point sufficiently close to and to the left of a, and $f'(x) < 0$ at every point sufficiently close to and to the right of a.

(b) *$x = a$ is a point of local minimum value of f, if*

(i) $f'(a) = 0$

and, (ii) *$f'(x)$ changes sign from negative to positive as x increases through a*

i.e. $f'(x) < 0$ at every point sufficiently close to and to the left of a, and $f'(x) > 0$ at every point sufficiently close to and to the right of a.

(c) *If $f'(a) = 0$ and $f'(x)$ does not change sign as increases through a, that is, $f'(x)$ has the same sign in the complete neighbourhood of a, then a is neither a point of local maximum value nor a point of local minimum value. In fact, such a point is called a point of inflexion.*

The above theorem suggests the following algorithm to find the points to local maxima or local minima of differentiable functions.

ALGORITHM

Step I *Put $y = f(x)$*

Step II *Find $\frac{dy}{dx}$.*

Step III *Put $\frac{dy}{dx} = 0$ and solve this equation for x. Let $c_1, c_2, c_3, \ldots, c_n$ be the roots of this equation. Points $c_1, c_2, c_3, \ldots, c_n$ are critical points (stationary values of x) and these are the possible points where the function can attain a local maximum or a local minimum. So, we test the function at each one of these points.*

Step IV *Consider $x = c_1$.*

If $\frac{dy}{dx}$ changes its sign from positive to negative as x increases through c_1, then the function attains a local maximum at $x = c_1$.

If $\frac{dy}{dx}$ changes its sign from negative to positive as x increases through c_1, then the function attains a local minimum at $x = c_1$.

If $\frac{dy}{dx}$ does not change sign as x increases through c_1, then $x = c_1$ is neither a point of local maximum nor a point of local minimum. In this case $x = c_1$ is a point of inflexion.

Similarly, we may deal with other values of x.

Following examples will illustrate the above algorithm.

ILLUSTRATIVE EXAMPLES

BASED ON BASIC CONCEPTS (BASIC)

EXAMPLE 1 *Find all the points of local maxima and minima of the function* $f(x) = x^3 - 6x^2 + 9x - 8$. **[NCERT]**

SOLUTION Let $y = f(x) = x^3 - 6x^2 + 9x - 8$. Then, $\frac{dy}{dx} = f'(x) = 3x^2 - 12x + 9 = 3(x^2 - 4x + 3)$.

The critical points of $f(x)$ are given by $f'(x) = 0$ or, $\frac{dy}{dx} = 0$.

Now, $\frac{dy}{dx} = 0 \Rightarrow 3(x^2 - 4x + 3) = 0 \Rightarrow x = 1, 3.$

We have to examine whether these points are points of local maxima or local minima or neither of them.

Fig. 14.17 Signs of $\frac{dy}{dx}$ for different values of x.

We have, $\frac{dy}{dx} = 3(x-1)(x-3)$

The changes in signs of $\frac{dy}{dx}$ for different values of x are shown in Fig. 14.17. Clearly, $\frac{dy}{dx}$ changes sign from positive to negative as increases through 1. So, $x = 1$ is a point of local maximum. Also, $\frac{dy}{dx}$ changes sign from negative to positive as x increases through 3. So $x = 3$ is a point of local minimum.

EXAMPLE 2 *Find all the points of local maxima and local minima as well as the corresponding local maximum and local minimum values for the function* $f(x) = (x-1)^3 (x+1)^2$.

SOLUTION Let $y = f(x) = (x-1)^3 (x+1)^2$. Then,

$$\frac{dy}{dx} = 3(x-1)^2 (x+1)^2 + 2(x+1)(x-1)^3 = (x-1)^2 (x+1) \{3(x+1) + 2(x-1)\}$$

$$\Rightarrow \quad \frac{dy}{dx} = (x-1)^2 (x+1)(5x+1).$$

At points of local maxima or local minima, we must have

$$\frac{dy}{dx} = 0 \Rightarrow (x-1)^2 (x+1)(5x+1) = 0 \Rightarrow x = 1 \text{ or, } x = -1 \text{ or, } x = -\frac{1}{5}$$

Now, we have to examine whether these points are points of local maximum or local minimum or neither of them.

Since $(x-1)^2$ is always positive, therefore the sign of $\frac{dy}{dx}$ is same as that the $(x+1)(5x+1)$. The changes in signs of $\frac{dy}{dx}$ for different values of x are shown in Fig. 14.18.

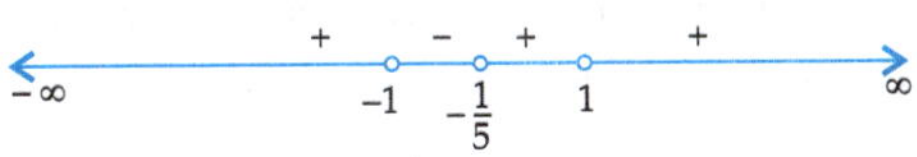

Fig. 14.18 Signs of $\frac{dy}{dx}$ for different values of x.

Clearly, $\frac{dy}{dx}$ does not change its sign as x passes through 1. So $x = 1$ is neither a point of local maximum nor a point of local minimum. In fact, $x = 1$ is a point of inflexion.

Clearly, $\frac{dy}{dx}$ changes sign from positive to negative as x passes through –1. So, $x = -1$ is a point of local maximum.

The local maximum value of $f(x)$ at $x=-1$ is $f(-1)=(-2)^3(-1+1)^2 = 0.$

It is evident from Fig. 14.18 that $\frac{dy}{dx}$ changes sign from negative to positive as x passes through $-1/5$. So, $x=-1/5$ is a point of local minimum.

The local minimum value of $f(x)$ at $x=-\frac{1}{5}$ is $f\left(-\frac{1}{5}\right)=\left(-\frac{1}{5}-1\right)^3\left(-\frac{1}{5}+1\right)^2=-\frac{3456}{3125}.$

EXAMPLE 3 *Find all the points of local maxima and local minima of the function* $f(x)=x^3-6x^2+12x-8.$

SOLUTION Let $y=f(x)=x^3-6x^2+12x-8$. Then, $\frac{dy}{dx}=3x^2-12x+12=3(x-2)^2.$

The critical points of $y=f(x)$ are given by $\frac{dy}{dx}=0.$

Fig. 14.19 Signs of $\frac{dy}{dx}$ for different values of x.

Now, $\frac{dy}{dx}=0 \Rightarrow 3(x-2)^2=0 \Rightarrow x=2.$

We observe that $\frac{dy}{dx}=3(x-2)^2>0$ for all $x\neq 2$. Thus, $\frac{dy}{dx}$ does not change sign as x increases through $x=2$.

Hence, $x=2$ is neither a point of local maximum nor a point of local minimum. In fact, it is a point of inflection.

EXAMPLE 4 *Show that the function* $f(x)=4x^3-18x^2+27x-7$ *has neither maxima nor minima.* **[NCERT EXEMPLAR, CBSE 2024]**

SOLUTION We have,

$$y=f(x)=4x^3-18x^2+27x-7 \Rightarrow \frac{dy}{dx}=12x^2-36x+27=3(4x^2-12x+9)=3(2x-3)^2$$

The critical points of $y=f(x)$ are given by $\frac{dy}{dx}=0.$

Now, $\frac{dy}{dx}=0 \Rightarrow 3(2x-3)^2=0 \Rightarrow 2x-3=0 \Rightarrow x=\frac{3}{2}$. Clearly, $\frac{dy}{dx}=3(2x-3)^2>0$ for all $x\neq\frac{3}{2}$

Thus, $\frac{dy}{dx}$ does not change its sign as x increases through $x=3/2$ as shown in Fig. 14.20. Hence, $x=3/2$ is neither a point of local maximum nor a point of local minimum. In fact, it is a point of inflection.

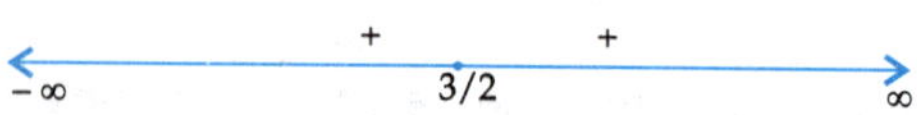

Fig. 14.20 Signs of $\frac{dy}{dx}$ for different values of x.

EXAMPLE 5 *Find the points of local maxima, local minima and the points of inflection of the function* $f(x)=x^5-5x^4+5x^3-1$. *Also, find the corresponding local maximum and local minimum values* **[NCERT EXEMPLAR]**

SOLUTION Let $y=f(x)=x^5-5x^4+5x^3-1$. Then,

$$\frac{dy}{dx}=5x^4-20x^3+15x^2=5x^2(x^2-4x+3)=5x^2(x-1)(x-3)$$

The critical points of $y=f(x)$ are given by $\frac{dy}{dx}=0.$

Now, $\frac{dy}{dx}=0 \Rightarrow 5x^2(x-1)(x-3)=0 \Rightarrow x=0, x=1, x=3.$

Clearly, $\frac{dy}{dx}$ does not change its sign as x increases through 0. So, $x = 0$ is a point of inflection.

It is evident from Fig. 14.21 that $\frac{dy}{dx}$ changes its sign from positive to negative as x increases through 1. So, $x = 1$ is a point of local maximum. The local maximum value of $f(x)$ is $f(1) = 1 - 5 + 5 - 1 = 0$.

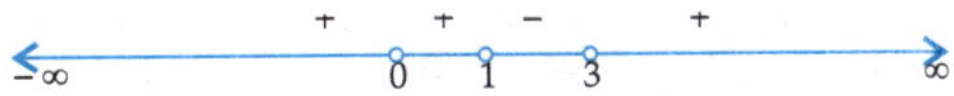

Fig. 14.21 Signs of $\frac{dy}{dx}$ for different values of x.

We observe, from Fig. 14.21, that $\frac{dy}{dx}$ changes its sign from negative to positive as x increases through 3. So, $x = 3$ is a point of local minimum. The local minimum value of $f(x)$ is

$$f(3) = 3^5 - 5 \times 3^4 + 5 \times 3^3 - 1 = -28.$$

EXAMPLE 6 *Find the local maxima or local minima, if any, of the function* $f(x) = \sin x + \cos x$, $0 < x < \frac{\pi}{2}$ *using the first derivative test.* [NCERT]

SOLUTION We have, $y = f(x) = \sin x + \cos x \Rightarrow \frac{dy}{dx} = \cos x - \sin x$

The critical points of $y = f(x)$ are given by $\frac{dy}{dx} = 0$.

Now, $\frac{dy}{dx} = 0 \Rightarrow \cos x - \sin x = 0 \Rightarrow \tan x = 1 \Rightarrow x = \frac{\pi}{4}$ $\left[\because 0 < x < \frac{\pi}{2}\right]$

Now, we will see whether $x = \frac{\pi}{4}$ is a point of local maximum or a point of local minimum or none of these.

In the left neighbourhood $x = \frac{\pi}{4}$, we have

$$x < \frac{\pi}{4} \Rightarrow \cos x > \sin x \Rightarrow \cos x - \sin x > 0 \Rightarrow \frac{dy}{dx} > 0$$

In the right neighbourhood of $x = \frac{\pi}{4}$, we have

$$x > \frac{\pi}{4} \Rightarrow \cos x < \sin x \Rightarrow \cos x - \sin x < 0 \Rightarrow \frac{dy}{dx} < 0$$

Thus, $\frac{dy}{dx}$ changes its sign from positive to negative as x increases through $\frac{\pi}{4}$. So, $f(x)$ attains a local maximum at $x = \frac{\pi}{4}$.

EXAMPLE 7 *Find the local maximum or local minimum, if any, of the function* $f(x) = \sin^4 x + \cos^4 x$, $0 < x < \frac{\pi}{2}$ *using the first derivative test.*

SOLUTION We have,

$$y = f(x) = \sin^4 x + \cos^4 x$$

$$\Rightarrow \frac{dy}{dx} = 4 \sin^3 x \cos x - 4 \cos^3 x \sin x = -4 \cos x \sin x (\cos^2 x - \sin^2 x)$$

$$\Rightarrow \frac{dy}{dx} = -2 \sin 2x \cos 2x = -\sin 4x$$

The critical points of $y = f(x)$ are given by $\frac{dy}{dx} = 0$.

Now, $\frac{dy}{dx} = 0 \Rightarrow -\sin 4x = 0 \Rightarrow \sin 4x = 0 \Rightarrow 4x = \pi \Rightarrow x = \frac{\pi}{4}$ $\left[\because 0 < x < \frac{\pi}{2} \therefore 0 < 4x < 2\pi\right]$

In the left neighbourhood of $x = \frac{\pi}{4}$, we have

$$x < \frac{\pi}{4} \Rightarrow 4x < \pi \Rightarrow \sin 4x > 0 \Rightarrow -\sin 4x < 0 \Rightarrow \frac{dy}{dx} < 0$$

In the right neighbourhood of $x = \frac{\pi}{4}$, we have

$$x > \frac{\pi}{4} \Rightarrow 4x > \pi \Rightarrow \sin 4x < 0 \Rightarrow -4\sin 4x > 0 \Rightarrow \frac{dy}{dx} > 0$$

Thus, $\frac{dy}{dx}$ changes sign from negative to positive as x increases through $\frac{\pi}{4}$. So, $x = \frac{\pi}{4}$ is a point of local minimum. The local minimum value of $f(x)$ at $x = \frac{\pi}{4}$ is

$$f\left(\frac{\pi}{4}\right) = \left(\sin\frac{\pi}{4}\right)^4 + \left(\cos\frac{\pi}{4}\right)^4 = \frac{1}{2}.$$

EXAMPLE 8 *Find the points at which the function f given by* $f(x) = (x-2)^4 (x+1)^3$ has

(i) *local maxima* (ii) *local minima* (iii) *points of inflexion* [NCERT]

SOLUTION We have,

$$f(x) = (x-2)^4 (x+1)^3$$

$$\Rightarrow \quad f'(x) = 4(x-2)^3 (x+1)^3 + 3(x-2)^4 (x+1)^2 = (x-2)^3 (x+1)^2 (7x-2)$$

$$\Rightarrow \quad f'(x) = (x-2)^2 (x+1)^2 (x-2)(7x-2)$$

The critical points of $f(x)$ are given by $f'(x) = 0$.

Now, $f'(x) = 0 \Rightarrow x = 2, -1, \frac{2}{7}$

Since $(x-2)^2 (x+1)^2$ is always positive. So, sign of $f'(x)$ depends upon the sign of $(x-2)(7x-2)$.

The changes in signs of $f'(x)$ as x increases through $\frac{2}{7}$ and 2 are shown in Fig. 14.22.

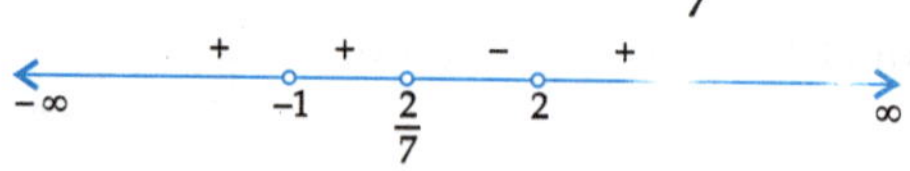

Fig. 14.22 Signs of $f'(x)$ for different values of x.

Clearly, $f'(x)$ changes its sign from positive to negative as increases through $\frac{2}{7}$. So, $x = \frac{2}{7}$ is a point of local maximum.

We observe that $f'(x)$ changes its sign from negative to positive as x increases through 2. So, $x = 2$ is a point of local minimum.

There is no change in the sign of $f'(x)$ as increases through -1. So, $x = -1$ is a point of inflexion.

EXERCISE 14.2

BASIC

Find the points of local maxima or local minima, if any, of the following functions, using the first derivative test. Also, find the local maximum or local minimum values, as the case may be:

1. $f(x) = (x-5)^4$
2. $f(x) = x^3 - 3x$ [NCERT]
3. $f(x) = x^3 (x-1)^2$
4. $f(x) = (x-1)(x+2)^2$

5. $f(x) = \frac{1}{x^2+2}$ [NCERT]
6. $f(x) = x^3 - 6x^2 + 9x + 15$
7. $f(x) = \sin 2x,\ 0 < x < \pi$
8. $f(x) = \sin x - \cos x,\ 0 < x < 2\pi$ [NCERT]
9. $f(x) = \cos x,\ 0 < x < \pi$
10. $f(x) = \sin 2x - x,\ -\frac{\pi}{2} \le x \le \frac{\pi}{2}$
11. $f(x) = 2\sin x - x,\ -\frac{\pi}{2} \le x \le \frac{\pi}{2}$
12. $f(x) = x\sqrt{1-x},\ 0 < x < 1$ [NCERT]
13. $f(x) = x^3(2x-1)^3$
14. $f(x) = \frac{x}{2} + \frac{2}{x},\ x > 0$

ANSWERS

1. $x = 5$ is a point of local minimum, local minimum value = 0.
2. $x = -1$ is a point of local maximum, local maximum value = 2
   $x = 1$ is a point of local minimum, local minimum value = – 2.
3. $x = 1$ is a point of local minimum, local minimum value = 0
   $x = \frac{3}{5}$ is a point of local maximum, local maximum value = $\frac{108}{3125}$.
4. $x = 0$ is a point of local minimum, local minimum value = – 4
   $x = -2$ is a point of local maximum, local maximum value = 0.
5. Local maximum at $x = 0$, Local maximum value $= \frac{1}{2}$
6. $x = 1$ is a point of local maximum, local maximum value = 19
   $x = 3$ is a point of local minimum, local minimum value = 15.
7. $x = \frac{\pi}{4}$ is a point of local maximum local maximum value = 1
   $x = \frac{3\pi}{4}$ is a point of local minimum local minimum value = – 1.
8. $x = \frac{3\pi}{4}$ is a point of local maximum, local maximum value = $\sqrt{2}$
   $x = \frac{7\pi}{4}$ is a point of local minimum, local minimum value = $-\sqrt{2}$.
9. None in the interval $(0, \pi)$
10. $x = \frac{\pi}{6}$ is a point of local maximum, local maximum value = $\frac{\sqrt{3}}{2} - \frac{\pi}{6}$
    $x = -\frac{\pi}{6}$ is a point of local minimum, local minimum value = $-\frac{\sqrt{3}}{2} + \frac{\pi}{6}$.
11. $x = \frac{\pi}{3}$ is a point of local maximum, local maximum value = $\sqrt{3} - \frac{\pi}{3}$
    $x = \frac{-\pi}{3}$ is a point of local minimum, local minimum value $= -\sqrt{3} + \frac{\pi}{3}$.
12. Local maximum at $x = \frac{2}{3}$, Local Maximum value $= \frac{2\sqrt{3}}{9}$
13. Minimum at $x = \frac{1}{4}$, Local Minimum value = $-\frac{1}{512}$
14. Minimum at $x = 2$, Local Minimum value = 2

HINTS TO SELECTED PROBLEMS

2. We have, $f(x) = x^3 - 3x \Rightarrow f'(x) = 3x^2 - 3 = 3(x-1)(x+1)$

The critical points of $f(x)$ are given by $f'(x) = 0$.

Now, $f'(x) = 0 \Rightarrow 3(x-1)\ (x+1) = 0 \Rightarrow x = 1, -1.$

The changes in signs of $f'(x)$ for different value of x are as shown in Fig. 14.23.

Fig. 14.23 Signs of $f'(x)$ for different values of x.

Clearly, $f'(x)$ changes its sign from positive to negative as x increases through -1. So, $x = -1$ is a point of local maximum with the local maximum value given by $f(-1) = (-1)^3 - 3(-1) = 2$.

As $f'(x)$ changes its sign from negative to positive as x increases through 1. So, $x = 1$ is a point of local minimum with the local minimum value $f(1) = 1 - 3 = -2$.

5. We have, $f(x) = \dfrac{1}{x^2+2} \Rightarrow f'(x) = \dfrac{-2x}{(x^2+2)^2}$

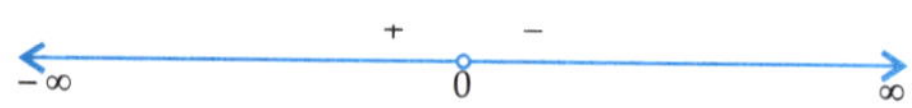

Fig. 14.24 Signs of $f'(x)$ for different values of x.

The critical points of $f(x)$ are given by $f'(x) = 0$.

Now, $f'(x) = 0 \Rightarrow \dfrac{-2x}{(x^2+2)^2} = 0 \Rightarrow x = 0$

The signs of $f'(x)$ for different values of x are shown in Fig. 14.24. Clearly, $f'(x)$ changes its sign from positive to negative as increases through 0. So, $x = 0$ is a point of local maximum with the local maximum value $f(0) = 1/2$.

8. We have, $f(x) = \sin x - \cos x,\ 0 < x < 2\pi \Rightarrow f'(x) = \cos x + \sin x$

For a local maximum or minimum, we must have

$$f'(x) = 0 \Rightarrow \cos x + \sin x = 0 \Rightarrow \tan x = -1 \Rightarrow x = \frac{3\pi}{4}, \frac{7\pi}{4}$$

Now, $f'(x) = \cos x + \sin x = \sqrt{2}\left(\dfrac{1}{\sqrt{2}}\cos x + \dfrac{1}{\sqrt{2}}\sin x\right) = \sqrt{2}\sin\left(x + \dfrac{\pi}{4}\right)$

In the left neighbourhood of $x = 3\pi/4$, we have

$$x < \frac{3\pi}{4} \Rightarrow x + \frac{\pi}{4} < \pi \Rightarrow \sqrt{2}\sin\left(x + \frac{\pi}{4}\right) > 0 \Rightarrow f'(x) > 0$$

In the right neighbourhood of $x = \dfrac{3\pi}{4}$, we have

$$x > \frac{3\pi}{4} \Rightarrow x + \frac{\pi}{4} > \pi \Rightarrow \sqrt{2}\sin\left(x + \frac{\pi}{4}\right) < 0 \Rightarrow f'(x) < 0$$

Thus, $f'(x)$ changes its sign from positive to negative as x increases through $\dfrac{3\pi}{4}$. So, $x = \dfrac{3\pi}{4}$ is a point of local maximum with the local maximum value given by

$$f\left(\frac{3\pi}{4}\right) = \sin\frac{3\pi}{4} - \cos\frac{3\pi}{4} = \sqrt{2}$$

In the left neighbourhood of $x = \dfrac{7\pi}{4}$, we have

$$x < \frac{7\pi}{4} \Rightarrow x + \frac{\pi}{4} < 2\pi \Rightarrow \sqrt{2}\sin\left(x + \frac{\pi}{4}\right) < 0 \Rightarrow f'(x) < 0$$

In the right neighbourhood of $x = \frac{7\pi}{4}$, we have

$$x > \frac{7\pi}{4} \Rightarrow x + \frac{\pi}{4} > 2\pi \Rightarrow \sqrt{2}\sin\left(x + \frac{\pi}{4}\right) > 0 \Rightarrow f'(x) > 0$$

Thus, $f'(x)$ changes its sign from negative to positive as x increases through $\frac{7\pi}{4}$.

So, $x = \frac{7\pi}{4}$ is a point of local minimum with local minimum value given by

$$f\left(\frac{7\pi}{4}\right) = \sin\frac{7\pi}{4} - \cos\frac{7\pi}{4} = -\sqrt{2}.$$

12. We have

$$f(x) = x\sqrt{1-x},\, x > 0 \Rightarrow f'(x) = \sqrt{1-x} - \frac{x}{2\sqrt{1-x}} = \frac{2-3x}{2\sqrt{1-x}}$$

At critical points of $f(x)$, we must have $f'(x) = 0 \Rightarrow \frac{2-3x}{2\sqrt{1-x}} = 0 \Rightarrow x = \frac{2}{3}$

Now, $f'(x) = \frac{2-3x}{2\sqrt{1-x}} = -3\left(\frac{x - \frac{2}{3}}{2\sqrt{1-x}}\right)$

Fig. 14.25 Signs of $f'(x)$ for different values of x.

The changes in signs of $f'(x)$ as x increases through $2/3$ are shown below:

Clearly, $f'(x)$ changes its sign from positive to negative as x increases through $2/3$. So, $x = 2/3$ is a point of local maximum with the local maximum value $f\left(\frac{2}{3}\right) = \frac{2}{3\sqrt{3}}$

14.5 HIGHER ORDER DERIVATIVE TEST

As we have seen in the previous section that finding the local maximum or local minimum by first derivative test is very time consuming and of course tedious for beginners because it is slightly difficult to determine the change in the sign of $f'(x)$ as x increases through the points given by $f'(x) = 0$. We have another test known as the Higher order derivative test which enables us to find the points of local maxima or local minima more easily and more quickly.

THEOREM *(Higher Order Derivative Test) Let f be a differentiable function defined on an interval I and let c be an interior point of I such that*

(i) $f'(c) = f''(c) = f'''(c) = \ldots = f^{n-1}(c) = 0$ *and, (ii)* $f^n(c)$ *exists and is non-zero.*

Then,

if n is even and $f^n(c) < 0 \Rightarrow x = c$ *is a point of local maximum*

if n is even and $f^n(c) > 0 \Rightarrow x = c$ *is a point of local minimum*

if n is odd, $x = c$ *is neither a point of local maximum nor a point of local minimum.*

This theorem suggests the following algorithm to find the points of local maximum and local minimum.

ALGORITHM

Step I *Find* $f'(x)$

Step II *Put* $f'(x) = 0$ *and solve this equation for x. Let* $c_1, c_2, \ldots, c_n$ *be the roots of this equation. Points* $c_1, c_2, \ldots, c_n$ *are stationary values or critical points of* $f(x)$ *and these are the possible points where the function can attain a local maximum or a local minimum. So, we test the function at each one of these points.*

Step III *Find $f''(x)$. Consider $x = c_1$.*

If $f''(c_1) < 0$, then $x = c_1$ is a point of local maximum.

If $f''(c_1) > 0$, then $x = c_1$ is a point of local minimum.

If $f''(c_1) = 0$, we must find $f'''(x)$ and substitute in it c_1 for x.

If $f'''(c_1) \neq 0$, then $x = c_1$ is neither a point of local maximum nor a point of local minimum and is called the point of inflection.

If $f'''(c_1) = 0$, we must find $f^{IV}(x)$ and substitute in it c_1 for x.

If $f^{IV}(c_1) < 0$, then $x = c_1$ is a point of local maximum and if $f^{IV}(c_1) > 0$, then $x = c_1$ is a point of local minimum.

If $f^{IV}(c_1) = 0$, we must find $f^{V}(x)$, and so on. Similarly, the points $c_2, c_3, \ldots$, may be tested.

POINT OF INFLECTION *An arc of a curve $y = f(x)$ is called concave upward if, at each of its points, the arc lies above the tangent at the point (see Fig. 14.26).*

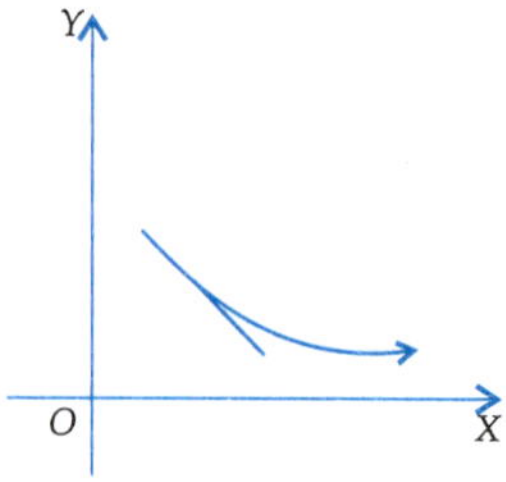

Fig. 14.26 Concave upward curve

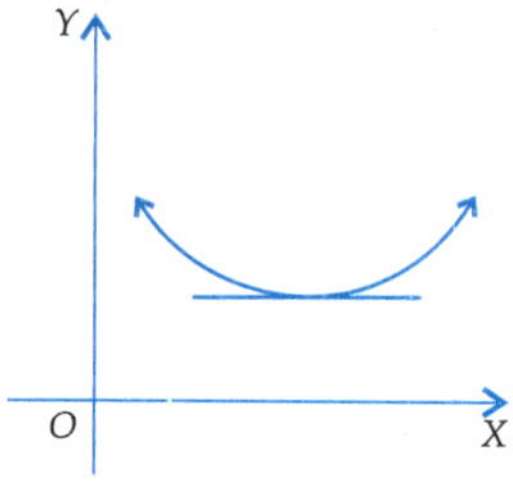

Fig. 14.27 Concave upward curve

If $y = f(x)$ is a concave upward curve, then as x increases, $f'(x)$ either is of the same sign and increasing (see Fig. 14.26) or changes sign from negative to positive (see Fig. 14.27). In either case $f'(x)$ is increasing and so $f''(x) > 0$. Thus, for a concave upward curve $f''(x) > 0$.

An arc of a curve $y = f(x)$ is called *concave downward* if, at each of its points, the arc lies below the tangent at the point.

If an arc of a curve $y = f(x)$ is *concave downward*, then as x increases, $f'(x)$ either is of the same sign and decreasing (see Fig. 14.28) or changes sign from positive to negative (see Fig. 14.29). In either case $f'(x)$ is decreasing and so $f''(x) < 0$. Thus, for a concave downward curve $f''(x) < 0$.

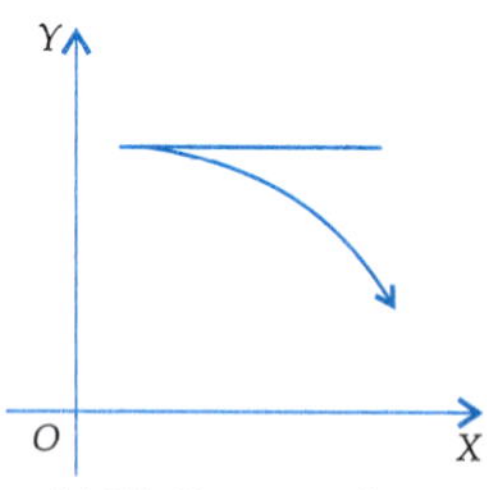

Fig. 14.28 Concave downward curve

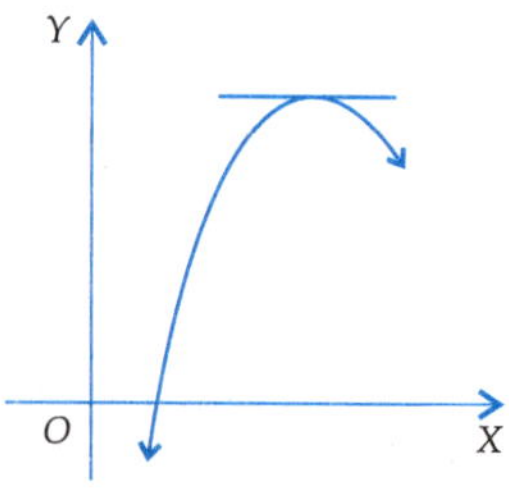

Fig. 14.29 Concave downward curve

POINT OF INFLEXION *A point of inflection is a point at which a curve is changing concave upward to concave downward, or vice-versa.*

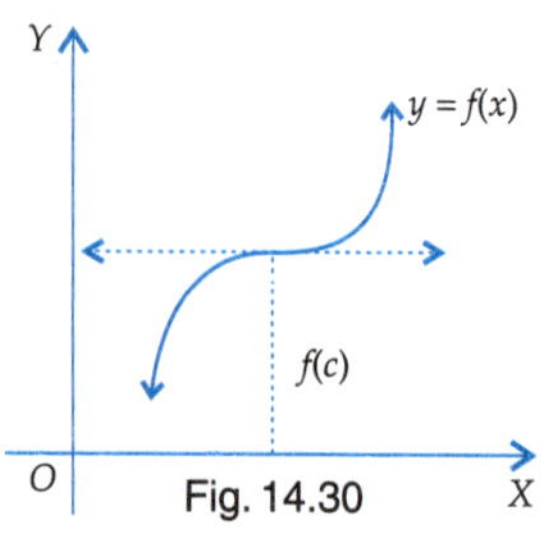

Fig. 14.30

A curve $y = f(x)$ has one of its points $x = c$ as an inflection point, if

(i) $f''(c) = 0$ or is not defined and

(ii) $f''(x)$ changes sign as x increases through $x = c$.

The later condition may be replaced by $f'''(c) \neq 0$ when $f'''(c)$ exists.

Thus, $x = c$ is a point of inflection if $f''(c) = 0$ and $f'''(c) \neq 0$.

PROPERTIES OF MAXIMA AND MINIMA

(i) If $f(x)$ is continuous function in its domain, then at least one maximum or one minimum must lie between two equal values of $f(x)$.

(ii) Maxima and Minima occur alternately, that is, between two maxima there is one minimum and vice-versa.

(iii) If $f(x) \to \infty$ as $x \to a$ or b and $f'(x) = 0$ only for one value of x (say c) between a and b, then $f(c)$ is necessarily the minimum and the least value.

If $f(x) \to -\infty$ as $x \to a$ or b, then $f(c)$ is necessarily the maximum and the greatest value.

ILLUSTRATIVE EXAMPLES

BASED ON BASIC CONCEPTS (BASIC)

EXAMPLE 1 *Find all the points of local maxima and minima and the corresponding maximum and minimum values of the function* $f(x) = -\frac{3}{4}x^4 - 8x^3 - \frac{45}{2}x^2 + 105$.

SOLUTION We have, **[NCERT EXEMPLAR]**

$$f(x) = -\frac{3}{4}x^4 - 8x^3 - \frac{45}{2}x^2 + 105 \Rightarrow f'(x) = -3x^3 - 24x^2 - 45x = -3x(x^2 + 8x + 15)$$

The critical points of $f(x)$ are given by $f'(x) = 0$.

Now, $f'(x) = 0 \Rightarrow -3x(x^2 + 8x + 15) = 0 \Rightarrow -3x(x + 3)(x + 5) = 0 \Rightarrow x = 0, -3, -5$

Thus, $x = 0$, $x = -3$ and $x = -5$ are the possible points of local maxima or minima.

Let us now test the function at each of these points. We have,

$$f'(x) = -3x^3 - 24x^2 - 45x \Rightarrow f''(x) = -9x^2 - 48x - 45$$

At $x = 0$: We have, $f''(0) = -45 < 0$.

So, $x = 0$ is a point of local maximum. The local maximum value of $f(x)$ at $x = 0$ is $f(0) = 105$.

At $x = -3$: We have, $f''(-3) = -9(-3)^2 - 48(-3) - 45 = 18 > 0$

So, $x = -3$ is a point of local minimum. The local minimum value of $f(x)$ at $x = -3$ is

$$f(-3) = -\frac{3}{4}(-3)^4 - 8(-3)^3 - \frac{45}{2}(-3)^2 + 105 = \frac{231}{4}$$

At $x = -5$: We have, $f''(-5) = -9(-5)^2 - 48(-5) - 45 = -30 < 0$

So, $x = -5$ is a point of local maximum. The local maximum value of $f(x)$ at $x = -5$ is

$$f(-5) = -\frac{3}{4}(-5)^4 - 8(-5)^3 - \frac{45}{2}(-5)^2 + 105 = \frac{295}{4}$$

EXAMPLE 2 *Find all the points of local maxima and minima and the corresponding maximum and minimum values of the function* $f(x) = 2x^3 - 21x^2 + 36x - 20$.

SOLUTION We have, $f(x) = 2x^3 - 21x^2 + 36x - 20 \Rightarrow f'(x) = 6x^2 - 42x + 36$

The critical points of $f(x)$ are given by $f'(x) = 0$.

Now, $f'(x) = 0 \Rightarrow 6x^2 - 42x + 36 = 0 \Rightarrow (x - 1)(x - 6) = 0 \Rightarrow x = 1, 6$.

Thus, $x = 1$ and $x = 6$ are the possible points of local maxima or minima.

Now, we test the function at each of these points.

We have, $f''(x) = 12x - 42$.

At $x = 1$: We have, $f''(1) = 12 - 42 = -30 < 0$.

So, $x = 1$ is a point of local maximum. The local maximum value is $f(1) = 2 - 21 + 36 - 20 = -3$.

At $x = 6$: We have, $f''(6) = 12(6) - 42 = 30 > 0$

So $x = 6$ is a point of local minimum. The local minimum value is

$$f(6) = 2(6)^3 - 21(6)^2 + 36 \times 6 - 20 = -128.$$

EXAMPLE 3 *If M and m denote local maximum and local minimum values of the function $f(x) = x + \frac{1}{x}$ $(x \neq 0)$ respectively, find the value of $(M - m)$.* **[CBSE 2024]**

SOLUTION We have, $f(x) = x + \frac{1}{x}, x \neq 0$

$$\therefore \quad f'(x) = 1 - \frac{1}{x^2} \text{ and } f''(x) = \frac{2}{x^3}$$

At points of local maximum or minimum, we must have

$$f'(x) = 0 \Rightarrow 1 - \frac{1}{x^2} = 0 \Rightarrow x^2 = 1 \Rightarrow x = \pm 1$$

We find that $f''(1) = 2 > 0$. So, $f(x)$ attains a local minimum m (say) at $x = 1$.

$$\therefore \quad m = f(1) = 1 + 1 = 2$$

Clearly, $f''(-1) = -2 < 0$. So, $f(x)$ attains a local maximum M (say) at $x = -1$.

$$\therefore \quad M = f(-1) = -1 - 1 = -2$$

Hence, $M - m = -2 - 2 = -4$.

EXAMPLE 4 *Find the points of local maxima and local minima, if any, of each of the following functions. Find also the local maximum and local minimum values, as the case may be:*

(i) $f(x) = \sin 2x - x$, *where* $-\frac{\pi}{2} < x < \frac{\pi}{2}$ (ii) $f(x) = \sin x + \frac{1}{2}\cos 2x$, *where* $0 < x < \frac{\pi}{2}$

(iii) $f(x) = \sin^4 x + \cos^4 x, \ 0 < x < \frac{\pi}{2}$

SOLUTION (i) We have, $f(x) = \sin 2x - x \Rightarrow f'(x) = 2\cos 2x - 1$

The critical points of $f(x)$ are given by $f'(x) = 0$.

$$\therefore \ f'(x) = 0 \Rightarrow 2\cos 2x - 1 = 0 \Rightarrow \cos 2x = \frac{1}{2} \Rightarrow 2x = -\frac{\pi}{3} \text{ or, } 2x = \frac{\pi}{3} \quad \left[\because -\frac{\pi}{2} < x < \frac{\pi}{2} \therefore -\pi < 2x < \pi\right]$$

$$\Rightarrow x = -\frac{\pi}{6} \text{ or, } x = \frac{\pi}{6}$$

Thus, $x = -\frac{\pi}{6}$ and $x = \frac{\pi}{6}$ are possible points of local maxima or minima.

Now, we test the function at each of these points.

Clearly, $f''(x) = -4\sin 2x$.

At $x = -\pi/6$: We have, $f''\left(-\frac{\pi}{6}\right) = -4\sin\left(-\frac{\pi}{3}\right) = -4 \times \frac{-\sqrt{3}}{2} = 2\sqrt{3} > 0$. So, $x = -\frac{\pi}{6}$ is a point of local minimum. The local minimum value is $f\left(-\frac{\pi}{6}\right) = \sin\left(-\frac{\pi}{3}\right) + \frac{\pi}{6} = -\frac{\sqrt{3}}{2} + \frac{\pi}{6}$.

At $x = \pi/6$: We have, $f''\left(\frac{\pi}{6}\right) = -4 \sin \frac{\pi}{3} = -4\left(\frac{\sqrt{3}}{2}\right) = -2\sqrt{3} < 0.$

So, $x = \frac{\pi}{6}$ is a point of local maximum. The local maximum value is $f\left(\frac{\pi}{6}\right) = \sin \frac{\pi}{3} - \frac{\pi}{6} = \frac{\sqrt{3}}{2} - \frac{\pi}{6}.$

(ii) We have, $f(x) = \sin x + \frac{1}{2} \cos 2x$, where $0 < x < \frac{\pi}{2} \Rightarrow f'(x) = \cos x - \sin 2x.$

The critical points of $f(x)$ are given by $f'(x) = 0$.

$\therefore\ f'(x) = 0 \Rightarrow \cos x - \sin 2x = 0 \Rightarrow \cos x - 2 \sin x \cos x = 0 \Rightarrow \cos x (1 - 2 \sin x) = 0$

$\Rightarrow \cos x = 0$ or, $1 - 2 \sin x = 0 \Rightarrow \cos x = 0$ or, $\sin x = \frac{1}{2} \Rightarrow x = \frac{\pi}{2}$ or $x = \frac{\pi}{6}$ $\left[\because 0 < x < \frac{\pi}{2}\right]$

Thus, $x = \frac{\pi}{6}$ is a point of local maximum or local minimum. Let us now test the function at this point.

Clearly, $f''(x) = -\sin x - 2 \cos 2x \Rightarrow f''\left(\frac{\pi}{6}\right) = -\sin \frac{\pi}{6} - 2 \cos \frac{\pi}{3} = -\frac{1}{2} - 2 \times \frac{1}{2} = -\frac{3}{2} < 0$

So, $x = \frac{\pi}{6}$ is the point of local maximum.

The local maximum value is $f\left(\frac{\pi}{6}\right) = \sin \frac{\pi}{6} + \frac{1}{2} \cos \frac{\pi}{3} = \frac{1}{2} + \frac{1}{2}\left(\frac{1}{2}\right) = \frac{3}{4}$

(iii) We have, $f(x) = \sin^4 x + \cos^4 x$, where $0 < x < \frac{\pi}{2}$.

$\therefore\ f'(x) = 4 \sin^3 x \cos x - 4 \cos^3 x \sin x = -4 \cos x \sin x (\cos^2 x - \sin^2 x) = -2 \sin 2x \cos 2x$

$\Rightarrow f'(x) = -\sin 4x.$

At points of local maximum and minimum, we must have

$$f'(x) = 0 \Rightarrow -\sin 4x = 0 \Rightarrow 4x = \pi \Rightarrow x = \frac{\pi}{4} \qquad \left[\because 0 < x < \frac{\pi}{2} \therefore 0 < 4x < 2\pi\right]$$

Now, $f''(x) = -4 \cos 4x \Rightarrow f''\left(\frac{\pi}{4}\right) = -4 \cos \pi = (-4)(-1) = 4 > 0$

So, $x = \frac{\pi}{4}$ is a point of local minimum and the local minimum value is

$$f\left(\frac{\pi}{4}\right) = \sin^4 \frac{\pi}{4} + \cos^4 \frac{\pi}{4} = \left(\frac{1}{\sqrt{2}}\right)^4 + \left(\frac{1}{\sqrt{2}}\right)^4 = \frac{1}{4} + \frac{1}{4} = \frac{1}{2}.$$

EXAMPLE 5 *Find the points of local maxima or local minima, if any, of the following functions. Find also the local maximum or local minimum values, as the case may be:*

(i) $f(x) = \sin x + \cos x$, *where* $0 < x < \frac{\pi}{2}$ (ii) $f(x) = \sin x - \cos x$, *where* $0 < x < 2\pi$

[CBSE 2015]

(iii) $f(x) = \sin 2x$, *where* $0 < x < \pi$ (iv) $f(x) = 2 \cos x + x$, *where* $0 < x < \pi$

(v) $f(x) = 2 \sin x - x$, $-\frac{\pi}{2} < x < \frac{\pi}{2}$.

SOLUTION (i) We have, $f(x) = \sin x + \cos x$, where $0 < x < \frac{\pi}{2}$.

$\therefore\ f'(x) = \cos x - \sin x.$

The critical points of $f(x)$ are given $f'(x) = 0$.

$\therefore \quad f'(x) = 0 \Rightarrow \cos x - \sin x = 0 \Rightarrow \cos x = \sin x \Rightarrow \tan x = 1 \Rightarrow x = \frac{\pi}{4} \quad \left[\because 0 < x < \frac{\pi}{2}\right]$

Thus, $x = \frac{\pi}{4}$ is a point of local maximum or minimum.

Now, $f''(x) = -\sin x - \cos x \Rightarrow f''\left(\frac{\pi}{4}\right) = -\sin\frac{\pi}{4} - \cos\frac{\pi}{4} = -\sqrt{2} < 0.$

So, $x = \frac{\pi}{4}$ is a point of local maximum.

The local maximum value is $f\left(\frac{\pi}{4}\right) = \sin\frac{\pi}{4} + \cos\frac{\pi}{4} = \frac{1}{\sqrt{2}} + \frac{1}{\sqrt{2}} = \frac{2}{\sqrt{2}} = \sqrt{2}.$

(ii) We have,

$f(x) = \sin x - \cos x$, where $0 < x < 2\pi \Rightarrow f'(x) = \cos x + \sin x$

At points of local maximum and local minimum, we must have

$f'(x) = 0$

$\Rightarrow \quad \cos x + \sin x = 0 \Rightarrow \sin x = -\cos x \Rightarrow \tan x = -1 \Rightarrow x = \frac{3\pi}{4}$ or, $x = \frac{7\pi}{4} \quad [\because 0 < x < 2\pi]$

Thus, $x = \frac{3\pi}{4}$ and $x = \frac{7\pi}{4}$ are possible points of local maximum or minimum. Let us now test the function at each of these points. Clearly, $f''(x) = -\sin x + \cos x$.

At $x = 3\pi/4$: We have,

$f''\left(\frac{3\pi}{4}\right) = -\sin\frac{3\pi}{4} + \cos\frac{3\pi}{4} = -\frac{1}{\sqrt{2}} - \frac{1}{\sqrt{2}} = -\frac{2}{\sqrt{2}} < 0.$ So, $x = \frac{3\pi}{4}$ is the point of local maximum.

The local maximum value is $f\left(\frac{3\pi}{4}\right) = \sin\frac{3\pi}{4} - \cos\frac{3\pi}{4} = \frac{1}{\sqrt{2}} + \frac{1}{\sqrt{2}} = \frac{2}{\sqrt{2}} = \sqrt{2}.$

At $x = \frac{7\pi}{4}$: We have, $f''\left(\frac{7\pi}{4}\right) = -\sin\frac{7\pi}{4} + \cos\frac{7\pi}{4} = \frac{1}{\sqrt{2}} + \frac{1}{\sqrt{2}} = \frac{2}{\sqrt{2}} > 0.$

So, the function attains a local minimum at $x = \frac{7\pi}{4}$.

The local minimum value is $f\left(\frac{7\pi}{4}\right) = \sin\frac{7\pi}{4} - \cos\frac{7\pi}{4} = -\frac{1}{\sqrt{2}} - \frac{1}{\sqrt{2}} = -\sqrt{2}.$

(iii) We have,

$f(x) = \sin 2x$, where $0 < x < \pi \Rightarrow f'(x) = 2\cos 2x.$

At points of local maximum or local minimum, we must have

$$f'(x) = 0 \Rightarrow 2\cos 2x = 0 \Rightarrow \cos 2x = 0 \Rightarrow 2x = \frac{\pi}{2}, \frac{3\pi}{2} \Rightarrow x = \frac{\pi}{4}, \frac{3\pi}{4} \quad [\because 0 < x < \pi \therefore 0 < 2x < 2\pi]$$

Thus, $x = \frac{\pi}{4}$ and $x = \frac{3\pi}{4}$ are possible points of local maximum or local minimum. Let us now test the function at these points. Clearly, $f''(x) = -4\sin 2x$.

At $x = \frac{\pi}{4}$: We have, $f''\left(\frac{\pi}{4}\right) = -4\sin\frac{\pi}{2} = -4 < 0.$ So, $x = \frac{\pi}{4}$ is a point of local maximum.

The local maximum value of $f(x)$ is $f\left(\frac{\pi}{4}\right) = \sin\frac{\pi}{2} = 1.$

At $x=\frac{3\pi}{4}$: We have, $f''\left(\frac{3\pi}{4}\right)=-4\sin\frac{3\pi}{2}=4>0$. So, $x=\frac{3\pi}{4}$, is a point of local minimum.

The local minimum value of $f(x)$ is $f\left(\frac{3\pi}{4}\right)=\sin\frac{3\pi}{2}=-1$.

(iv) We have, $f(x)=2\cos x+x$, where $0<x<\pi \Rightarrow f'(x)=-2\sin x+1$

At points of local maximum and minimum, we must have

$$f'(x)=0 \Rightarrow -2\sin x+1=0 \Rightarrow \sin x=\frac{1}{2} \Rightarrow x=\frac{\pi}{6},\frac{5\pi}{6} \qquad [\because 0<x<\pi]$$

Thus, $x=\frac{\pi}{6}$ and $x=\frac{5\pi}{6}$ are possible points of local maximum or minimum. Let us now test the function at these points.

Clearly, $f''(x)=-2\cos x$

At $x=\frac{\pi}{6}$: We have, $f''\left(\frac{\pi}{6}\right)=-2\cos\frac{\pi}{6}=-\sqrt{3}<0$. So, $x=\frac{\pi}{6}$ is a point of local maximum.

The local maximum value of $f(x)$ is $f\left(\frac{\pi}{6}\right)=2\cos\frac{\pi}{6}+\frac{\pi}{6}=\sqrt{3}+\frac{\pi}{6}$

At $x=\frac{5\pi}{6}$: We have, $f''\left(\frac{5\pi}{6}\right)=-2\cos\frac{5\pi}{6}=\sqrt{3}>0$. So, $x=\frac{5\pi}{6}$ is a point of local minimum.

The local minimum value of $f(x)$ is $f\left(\frac{5\pi}{6}\right)=2\cos\frac{5\pi}{6}+\frac{5\pi}{6}=-\sqrt{3}+\frac{5\pi}{6}$.

(v) We have, $f(x)=2\sin x-x$, where $-\pi/2<x<\pi/2 \Rightarrow f'(x)=2\cos x-1$

The critical points of $f(x)$ are given by $f'(x)=0$.

$$\therefore \quad f'(x)=0 \Rightarrow 2\cos x-1=0 \Rightarrow \cos x=1/2 \Rightarrow x=\pm\pi/3 \qquad [\because -\pi/2<x<\pi/2]$$

Thus, $x=\pm\pi/3$ are points of local maximum or minimum. Clearly, $f''(x)=-2\sin x$.

At $x=-\pi/3$: We have,

$$f''(-\pi/3)=-2\sin(-\pi/3)=2\sin\pi/3=2\sqrt{3}/2=\sqrt{3}>0.$$

So, $x=-\pi/3$ is a point of local minimum.

The local minimum value is $f(-\pi/3)=2\sin(-\pi/3)-(-\pi/3)=-\sqrt{3}+\pi/3$.

At $x=\pi/3$: We have, $f''(\pi/3)=-2\sin\pi/3=-\sqrt{3}<0$. So, $x=\pi/3$ is a point of local maximum.

The local maximum value is $f(\pi/3)=2\sin\pi/3-\pi/3=\sqrt{3}-\pi/3$.

EXAMPLE 6 *Find the local maximum and local minimum values of*

$$f(x)=\sec x+\log\cos^2 x,\ 0<x<2\pi. \qquad \textbf{[NCERT EXEMPLAR]}$$

SOLUTION We have,

$$f(x)=\sec x+2\log\cos x \Rightarrow f'(x)=\sec x\tan x-2\tan x=\tan x(\sec x-2)$$

The critical points of $f(x)$ are given by $f'(x)=0$.

$$\therefore \quad f'(x)=0 \Rightarrow \tan x(\sec x-2)=0 \Rightarrow \tan x=0 \text{ or } \sec x=2 \Rightarrow \tan x=0 \text{ or } \cos x=\frac{1}{2}$$

$$\Rightarrow \quad x=\pi,\ x=\frac{\pi}{3},\frac{5\pi}{3} \qquad [\because 0<x<2\pi]$$

Thus, $x=\pi$, $x=\frac{\pi}{3},\frac{5\pi}{3}$ are possible points of local maximum and local minimum.

Now, $f'(x)=\tan x(\sec x-2)$

$\Rightarrow \quad f''(x) = \sec^2 x(\sec x - 2) + \tan^2 x \sec x = \sec^2 x(\sec x - 2) + \sec x(\sec^2 x - 1)$

$\Rightarrow \quad f''(x) = 2\sec^3 x - 2\sec^2 x - \sec x$

Let us now investigate critical points for points of local maximum and local minimum.

At $x = \frac{\pi}{3}$: We obtain, $f''\left(\frac{\pi}{3}\right) = 2\sec^3\frac{\pi}{3} - 2\sec^2\frac{\pi}{3} - \sec\frac{\pi}{3} = 2\times 8 - 2\times 4 - 2 = 6 > 0$

Thus, $x = \frac{\pi}{3}$ is a point of local minimum. The local minimum value of $f(x)$ is given by

$$f\left(\frac{\pi}{3}\right) = \sec\frac{\pi}{3} + \log\cos^2\frac{\pi}{3} = 2 + \log\frac{1}{4} = 2 - 2\log 2$$

At $x = \pi$: We obtain, $f''(\pi) = 2\sec^3\pi - 2\sec^2\pi - \sec\pi = -2 - 2 + 1 = -3 < 0$

Thus, $x = \pi$ is a point of local maximum. The local maximum value of $f(x)$ is given by

$$f(\pi) = \sec\pi + \log\cos^2\pi = -1 + \log 1 = -1.$$

At $x = \frac{5\pi}{3}$: We obtain, $f''\left(\frac{5\pi}{3}\right) = 2\sec^3\frac{5\pi}{3} - 2\sec^2\frac{5\pi}{3} - \sec\frac{5\pi}{3} = 2(2)^3 - 2(2)^2 + 2 = 10 > 0$

Thus, $x = \frac{5\pi}{3}$ is a point of local minimum.

The local minimum value is given by $f\left(\frac{5\pi}{3}\right) = \sec\frac{5\pi}{3} + \log\cos^2\frac{5\pi}{3} = 2 + \log\frac{1}{4} = 2 - 2\log 2.$

EXAMPLE 7 *Show that none of the following functions has a local maximum or a local minimum:*

(i) $x^3 + x^2 + x + 1$ (ii) e^x (iii) $\log x$ (iv) $\cos x,\ 0 < x < \pi$ **[NCERT]**

SOLUTION (i) Let $f(x) = x^3 + x^2 + x + 1$. Then, $f'(x) = 3x^2 + 2x + 1$.

At points of local maximum or minimum, we have

$$f'(x) = 0 \Rightarrow 3x^2 + 2x + 1 = 0$$

But, this equation gives imaginary values of x. So, $f'(x) \neq 0$ for any real value of x. Hence, $f(x)$ does not have a maximum or minimum.

(ii) Let $f(x) = e^x$. Then, $f'(x) = e^x$. Clearly, $f'(x) \neq 0$ for any value of x. So, $f(x) = e^x$ does not have a maximum or a minimum.

(iii) Let $f(x) = \log x$. Then, $f'(x) = \frac{1}{x}$. Clearly, $f'(x) \neq 0$ for any value of $x \in$ Domain (f).

So, $f(x) = \log x$ does not have a maximum or a minimum.

(iv) Let $f(x) = \cos x$. Then, $f'(x) = -\sin x$. Clearly, $f'(x) \neq 0$ for any $x \in (0, \pi)$.

So, $f(x) = \cos x$ does not have a maximum or minimum on $(0, \pi)$.

EXAMPLE 8 *Find the maximum profit that a company can make, if the profit function is given* $P(x) = 41 + 24x - 18x^2$. **[NCERT]**

SOLUTION We have,

$$P(x) = 41 + 24x - 18x^2 \Rightarrow \frac{d}{dx}\left(P(x)\right) = 24 - 36x \text{ and } \frac{d^2}{dx^2}\left(P(x)\right) = -36$$

For maximum or minimum, we must have

$$\frac{d}{dx}\left(P(x)\right) = 0 \Rightarrow 24 - 36x = 0 \Rightarrow x = \frac{2}{3}$$

Also, $\left\{\frac{d^2}{dx^2}\left(P\ (x)\right)\right\}_{x=2/3} = -36 < 0$. So, profit is maximum when $x = \frac{2}{3}$.

Maximum profit = (Value of $P(x)$ at $x = 2/3$) $= 41 + 24 \times (2/3) - 18\,(2/3)^2 = 49$

EXAMPLE 9 *At what points, the slope of the curve $y = -x^3 + 3x^2 + 9x - 27$ is maximum? Also, find the maximum slope.* **[NCERT EXEMPLAR]**

SOLUTION The slope m of the curve $y = -x^3 + 3x^2 + 9x - 27$ at point (x, y) is given by

$$m = \frac{dy}{dx} = -3x^2 + 6x + 9 \qquad \ldots\text{(i)}$$

$$\therefore \quad \frac{dm}{dx} = -6x + 6 \text{ and } \frac{d^2m}{dx^2} = -6$$

For maximum or minimum values of m, we must have

$$\frac{dm}{dx} = 0 \Rightarrow -6x + 6 = 0 \Rightarrow x = 1$$

Clearly, $\frac{d^2m}{dx^2} = -6 < 0$ for all x. So, m is maximum at $x = 1$. Putting $x = 1$ in (i), we obtain $m = 12$.

Putting $x = 1$ in the equation $y = -x^3 + 3x^2 + 9x - 27$, we obtain $y = -16$. Hence, the slope of the given curve is maximum at the point $(1, -16)$ and the maximum value of the slope is 12.

EXAMPLE 10 *If $f(x) = a \log|x| + bx^2 + x$ has extreme values at $x = -1$ and at $x = 2$, then find a and b.*

SOLUTION We observe that $f(x)$ is defined for all $x \neq 0$.

Now, $f(x) = a \log|x| + bx^2 + x \Rightarrow f'(x) = \frac{a}{x} + 2bx + 1$

It is given that $f(x)$ has extreme values at $x = -1$ and $x = 2$.

$$\therefore \quad f'(-1) = 0 \text{ and } f'(2) = 0$$

$$\Rightarrow \quad -a - 2b + 1 = 0 \text{ and } \frac{a}{2} + 4b + 1 = 0 \Rightarrow a + 2b = 1 \text{ and } a + 8b = -2$$

Solving these equations, we get: $a = 2$ and $b = -1/2$.

EXAMPLE 11 *It is given that at $x = 1$, the function $x^4 - 62x^2 + ax + 9$ attains its maximum value. Find the value of 'a' and hence obtain all other points where the given function obtains local maximum or local minimum values.* **[CBSE 2024, NCERT]**

SOLUTION Let $f(x) = x^4 - 62x^2 + ax + 9$. Then, $f'(x) = 4x^3 - 124x + a$.

It is given that $f(x)$ attains its maximum at $x = 1$.

$$\therefore \quad f'(1) = 0 \Rightarrow 4 - 124 + a = 0 \Rightarrow a = 120$$

Now, $f(x) = x^4 - 62x^2 + 120x + 9$

$$\Rightarrow \quad f'(x) = 4x^3 - 124x + 120 \text{ and } f''(x) = 12x^2 - 124$$

For maximum or minimum values of x, we must have

$$f'(x) = 0$$

$$\Rightarrow \quad 4(x^3 - 31x + 30) = 0 \Rightarrow 4(x-1)(x-5)(x+6) = 0 \Rightarrow x = 1, 5, -6$$

Now, $f''(x) = 4(3x^2 - 31)$

$\Rightarrow \quad f''(1) = 4 \times -28 < 0, f''(5) = 4 \times 44 > 0$ and $f''(-6) = 4 \times 77 > 0$

Therefore, $f(x)$ attains local minimum values at $x = 5$ and $x = -6$.

BASED ON LOWER ORDER THINKING SKILLS (LOTS)

EXAMPLE 12 *If $y = \frac{ax - b}{(x-1)(x-4)}$ has a turning point $P(2, -1)$, find the values of a and b and show that y is maximum at P.*

SOLUTION We have,

$$y = \frac{ax-b}{(x-1)(x-4)} = \frac{ax-b}{x^2 - 5x + 4} \quad \text{...(i)}$$

$$\Rightarrow \frac{dy}{dx} = \frac{(x^2-5x+4)a - (ax-b)(2x-5)}{(x^2-5x+4)^2} \quad \text{...(ii)}$$

$$\Rightarrow \left(\frac{dy}{dx}\right)_P = \frac{(4-10+4)a - (2a-b)(4-5)}{(4-10+4)^2} = -\frac{b}{4}$$

Since P is a turning point of the curve (i). Therefore,

$$\left(\frac{dy}{dx}\right)_P = 0 \Rightarrow -\frac{b}{4} = 0 \Rightarrow b = 0 \quad \text{...(iii)}$$

Since $P(2, -1)$ lies on $y = \frac{ax-b}{(x-1)(x-4)}$. Therefore,

$$-1 = \frac{2a-b}{(2-1)(2-4)} \Rightarrow -1 = \frac{2a-b}{-2} \Rightarrow 2a - b = 2 \quad \text{...(iv)}$$

From (iii) and (iv), we get $a = 1, b = 0$. Substituting the values of a and b in (ii), we get

$$\frac{dy}{dx} = \frac{(x^2-5x+4) - x(2x-5)}{(x^2-5x+4)^2} = \frac{-x^2+4}{(x^2-5x+4)^2}$$

$$\Rightarrow \frac{d^2y}{dx^2} = \frac{(x^2-5x+4)^2(-2x) - (-x^2+4)\,2(x^2-5x+4)(2x-5)}{(x^2-5x+4)^4}$$

$$\Rightarrow \frac{d^2y}{dx^2} = \frac{-2x(x^2-5x+4) + 2(x^2-4)(2x-5)}{(x^2-5x+4)^3}$$

Now, $\left(\frac{dy}{dx}\right)_{(2,-1)} = 0$ and, $\left(\frac{d^2y}{dx^2}\right)_{(2,-1)} = \frac{(-2)(-4)}{(-2)^3} = -1 < 0$

So, y is maximum at P when $a = 1$ and $b = 0$.

BASED ON HIGHER ORDER THINKING SKILLS (HOTS)

EXAMPLE 13 *Show that the maximum value of $\left(\frac{1}{x}\right)^x$ is $e^{1/e}$.*

SOLUTION Let $y = \left(\frac{1}{x}\right)^x = x^{-x} = e^{-x \ln x}$. Differentiating with respect to x, we obtain

$$\frac{dy}{dx} = e^{-x \ln x} \frac{d}{dx}(-x \ln x)$$

$$\Rightarrow \quad \frac{dy}{dx} = -e^{-x\log x}(1+\ln x) = -y\,(1+\ln x)$$

$$\Rightarrow \quad \frac{d^2y}{dx^2} = -\frac{dy}{dx}(1+\ln x) - \frac{y}{x} \qquad \text{[Differentiating with respect to } x\text{]}$$

$$\Rightarrow \quad \frac{d^2y}{dx^2} = x^{-x}(1+\ln x)^2 - \frac{x^{-x}}{x} = x^{-x}(1+\ln x)^2 - x^{-x-1}$$

At points of local maximum and local minimum, we must have

$$\frac{dy}{dx} = 0 \Rightarrow -y\,(1+\ln x) = 0 \Rightarrow 1+\ln x = 0 \Rightarrow \ln x = -1 \Rightarrow x = e^{-1} = \frac{1}{e}$$

Now,

$$\left(\frac{d^2y}{dx^2}\right)_{x=1/e} = \left(\frac{1}{e}\right)^{-1/e}\left(1+\ln\frac{1}{e}\right)^2 - \left(\frac{1}{e}\right)^{-1/e-1} = -\left(\frac{1}{e}\right)^{-1/e} \times 0 - e^{e^{-1}+1} = -e^{e^{-1}+1} < 0$$

So, $x = 1/e$ is a point of local maximum. The local maximum value of y is obtained by putting $x = 1/e$ in y and is equal to $e^{1/e}$.

EXAMPLE 14 *Show that* $\sin^p\theta\cos^q\theta$ *attains a maximum, when* $\theta = \tan^{-1}\sqrt{\frac{p}{q}}$.

SOLUTION Let $y = \sin^p\theta\cos^q\theta$. Then,

$$\frac{dy}{d\theta} = p\sin^{p-1}\theta\cos\theta\cos^q\theta + \sin^p\theta\, q\cos^{q-1}\theta\,(-\sin\theta)$$

$$\Rightarrow \quad \frac{dy}{d\theta} = p\sin^{p-1}\theta\cos^{q+1}\theta - q\sin^{p+1}\theta\cos^{q-1}\theta = \sin^{p-1}\theta\cos^{q-1}\theta\,(p\cos^2\theta - q\sin^2\theta)$$

$$\Rightarrow \quad \frac{dy}{d\theta} = \sin^p\theta\cos^q\theta\left(\frac{p\cos^2\theta - q\sin^2\theta}{\sin\theta\cos\theta}\right) = \sin^p\theta\cos^q\theta\,(p\cot\theta - q\tan\theta)$$

For maximum or minimum, we must have

$$\frac{dy}{d\theta} = 0$$

$$\Rightarrow \quad \sin^p\theta\cos^q\theta\,(p\cot\theta - q\tan\theta) = 0$$

$$\Rightarrow \quad \sin^p\theta = 0 \text{ or, } \cos^q\theta = 0 \text{ or, } p\cot\theta - q\tan\theta = 0$$

$$\Rightarrow \quad \sin^p\theta = 0 \text{ or, } \cos^q\theta = 0 \text{ or, } \tan\theta = \sqrt{\frac{p}{q}} \Rightarrow \theta = 0 \text{ or, } \theta = \frac{\pi}{2} \text{ or, } \theta = \tan^{-1}\sqrt{\frac{p}{q}} = \alpha \text{ (say)}$$

Now, $\frac{dy}{d\theta} = \sin^p\theta\cos^q\theta\,(p\cot\theta - q\tan\theta) \Rightarrow \frac{dy}{d\theta} = y\,(p\cot\theta - q\tan\theta)$

$$\therefore \quad \frac{d^2y}{d\theta^2} = \frac{dy}{d\theta}(p\cot\theta - q\tan\theta) + y\,(-p\,\mathrm{cosec}^2\theta - q\sec^2\theta)$$

$$\Rightarrow \quad \left(\frac{d^2y}{d\theta^2}\right)_{\theta=\alpha} = \left(\frac{dy}{d\theta}\right)_{\theta=\alpha}\left(p\sqrt{\frac{q}{p}} - q\sqrt{\frac{p}{q}}\right) + \sin^p\theta\cos^q\theta\left(-p\,\mathrm{cosec}^2\theta - q\sec^2\theta\right)$$

$$\Rightarrow \quad \left(\frac{d^2y}{d\theta^2}\right)_{\theta=\alpha} = 0 - \sin^p\theta\cos^q\theta\,(p\,\mathrm{cosec}^2\theta + q\sec^2\theta) < 0$$

Hence, y is maximum when $\theta = \alpha = \tan^{-1}\sqrt{\frac{p}{q}}$.

EXERCISE 14.3

BASIC

1. Find the points of local maxima or local minima and corresponding local maximum and local minimum values of each of the following functions. Also, find the points of inflection, if any:

(i) $f(x) = x^4 - 62x^2 + 120x + 9$ (ii) $f(x) = x^3 - 6x^2 + 9x + 15$

(iii) $f(x) = (x-1)(x+2)^2$ (iv) $f(x) = 2/x - 2/x^2, x > 0$

(v) $f(x) = x\,e^x$ (vi) $f(x) = x/2 + 2/x, x > 0$

(vii) $f(x) = (x+1)(x+2)^{1/3}, x \geq -2$ (viii) $f(x) = x\sqrt{32 - x^2}, -5 \leq x \leq 5$

(ix) $f(x) = x^3 - 2ax^2 + a^2 x, a > 0, x \in R$ (x) $f(x) = x + \frac{a^2}{x}, \; a > 0, \; x \neq 0$

(xi) $f(x) = x\sqrt{2 - x^2} \; -\sqrt{2} \leq x \leq \sqrt{2}$ (xii) $f(x) = x + \sqrt{1 - x}, x \leq 1$

2. Find the local extremum values of the following functions :

(i) $f(x) = (x-1)(x-2)^2$ (ii) $f(x) = x\sqrt{1-x}, x \leq 1$ (iii) $f(x) = -(x-1)^3 (x+1)^2$

BASED ON LOTS

3. The function $y = a \log x + bx^2 + x$ has extreme values at $x = 1$ and $x = 2$. Find a and b.

4. Show that $\frac{\log x}{x}$ has a maximum value at $x = e$. [NCERT, CBSE 2024]

5. Find the maximum and minimum values of the function $f(x) = \frac{4}{x+2} + x$.

6. Find the maximum and minimum values of $f(x) = \tan x - 2x$.

7. If $f(x) = x^3 + ax^2 + bx + c$ has a maximum at $x = -1$ and minimum at $x = 3$. Determine a, b and c.

8. Prove that $f(x) = \sin x + \sqrt{3} \cos x$ has maximum value at $x = \frac{\pi}{6}$. [NCERT EXEMPLAR]

9. Find local maximum value and local minimum value (which ever exists) for the function $f(x) = 4x^2 + \frac{1}{x}, \; x \neq 0$. [CBSE 2024]

ANSWERS

1. (i) Local Max. at $x = 1$, Local Max. value = 68
Local Min. at $x = 5, -6$; Local Min. values are -316 and -1647.
(ii) Local Max. at $x = 1$, Local Max. value = 19, Local Min. at $x = 3$, Local Min. value = 15
(iii) Local Max. at $x = -2$, Local Max. value = 0, Local Min at $x = 0$, Local Min value = -4
(iv) Local Max. at $x = 2$, Local Max. value = $1/2$
(v) Local Min. at $x = -1$, Local Min. value = $-1/e$
(vi) Local Min. at $x = 2$, Local Min. value = 2
(vii) Local Min. at $x = -7/4$, Local Min. value $= -\frac{3}{4^{4/3}}$
(viii) Local Max. at $x = 4$; Local Max. value = 16, Local Min. at $x = -4$; Local Min. value = -16
(ix) Local Max. at $x = a/3$, Local Max. value $= \frac{4a^3}{27}$, Local Min. at $x = a$, Local Min. value = 0

(x) Local Max. at $x = -a$, Local Max value $= -2a$, Local Min. at $x = a$, Local Min. value $= 2a$

(xi) Local Max. at $x = 1$, Local Max. value $= 1$, Local Min. at $x = -1$, Local Min. value $= -1$

(xii) Local Max. at $x = 3/4$, Local Max. value $= 5/4$

2. (i) Local Max. value $= 4/27$ at $x = 4/3$, Local Min. value $= 0$ at $x = 2$

(ii) Local Max. value $= \dfrac{2}{3\sqrt{3}}$ at $x = 2/3$

(iii) Local Max. value $3456/3125$ at $x = -1/5$; Local Min. value $= 0$ at $x = -1$

3. $a = -2/3, b = -1/6$ 5. Local Max. value $= -6$ at $x = -4$; Local Min. value $= 2$ at $x = 0$.

6. Local Max. value $= -1 - 3\pi/2$ at $x = 3\pi/4$; Local Min. value $= 1 - \pi/2$ at $x = \pi/4$.

7. $a = -3, b = -9, c \in R$ 9. Local min. value $= 3$ at $x = \dfrac{1}{2}$.

14.6 MAXIMUM AND MINIMUM VALUES IN A CLOSED INTERVAL

Let $y = f(x)$ be a function defined on $[a, b]$. By a local maximum (or local minimum) value of a function at a point $c \in [a, b]$ we mean the greatest (or the least) value in the immediate neighbourhood of $x = c$. It does not mean the greatest or the maximum (or the least or the minimum) of $f(x)$ in the interval $[a, b]$. A function may have a number of local maxima or local minima in a given interval and even a local minimum may be greater than a local maximum.

Thus, a local maximum value may not be the greatest (the maximum) value and a local minimum value may not be the least (the minimum) value of the function in any given interval as shown in Fig. 14.31.

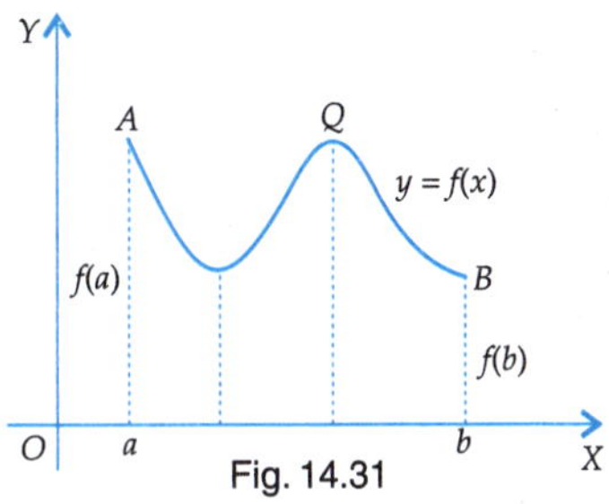

Fig. 14.31

However, if a function $f(x)$ is differentiable and consequently continuous on a closed interval $[a, b]$, then it attains the absolute maximum (absolute minimum) at stationary points (points where $f'(x) = 0$) or at the end points of the interval $[a, b]$. Thus, to find the absolute maximum (absolute minimum) value of the function, we choose the largest and the smallest amongst the numbers $f(a), f(c_1), f(c_2), \dots, f(c_n), f(b)$ where $x = c_1, c_2, \dots, c_n$ are the stationary points.

We may use the following algorithm for finding the maximum (absolute maximum) and the minimum (absolute minimum) of a function f defined on a closed interval $[a, b]$.

ALGORITHM

Step I *Find $f'(x)$*

Step II *Put $f'(x) = 0$ and find values of x. Let $c_1, c_2, \dots, c_n$ be the values of x.*

Step III *Take the maximum and minimum values out of the values $f(a), f(c_1), f(c_2), \dots, f(c_n), f(b)$.*

The maximum and minimum values obtained in step III are respectively the largest (or absolute maximum) and the smallest (or absolute minimum) values of the function.

ILLUSTRATIVE EXAMPLES

BASED ON BASIC CONCEPTS (BASIC)

EXAMPLE 1 *Find the maximum and minimum values of $f(x) = 2x^3 - 24x + 107$ in the interval* $[1, 3]$. [NCERT]

SOLUTION We have,

$$f(x) = 2x^3 - 24x + 107 \Rightarrow f'(x) = 6x^2 - 24$$

Now, $f'(x) = 0 \Rightarrow 6x^2 - 24 = 0 \Rightarrow x = \pm 2$

But, $x = -2 \notin [1, 3]$. So $x = 2$ is the only stationary point. Let us now compute the values of $f(x)$ at $x = 1, 2, 3$. We find that

$$f(1) = 2 - 24 + 107 = 85, \; f(2) = 2(2)^3 - 24(2) + 107 = 75$$

and, $f(3) = 2(3)^3 - 24 \times 3 + 107 = 89$

Clearly, largest of these values is 89 and the least is 75. Hence, the maximum value of $f(x)$ is 89 which it attains at $x = 3$ and the minimum value is 75 which is attained at $x = 2$.

EXAMPLE 2 *Find the maximum and minimum values of* $f(x) = \sin x$ *in the interval* $[\pi, 2\pi]$.

SOLUTION We have, $f(x) = \sin x$. Therefore, $f'(x) = \cos x$.

At stationary points, we must have

$$f'(x) = 0 \Rightarrow \cos x = 0 \Rightarrow x = \frac{3\pi}{2} \qquad [\because x \in [\pi, 2\pi]]$$

Let us now compute the values of $f(x)$ at $x = \pi, \frac{3\pi}{2}, 2\pi$. We find that

$$f(\pi) = \sin \pi = 0, f\left(\frac{3\pi}{2}\right) = \sin\frac{3\pi}{2} = -1 \text{ and } f(2\pi) = \sin 2\pi = 0.$$

The greatest and the least of these values are 0 and –1 respectively. Hence, the maximum value of $f(x)$ is 0 which it attains at $x = \pi$ and 2π, and the minimum value is – 1 which it attains at $x = 3\pi/2$.

EXAMPLE 3 *Find the absolute maximum value and the absolute minimum value of the following functions in the given intervals:*

(i) $f(x) = \left(\frac{1}{2} - x\right)^2 + x^3$ in $[-2, 2.5]$ (ii) $f(x) = \sin x + \cos x$ in $[0, \pi]$ **[NCERT]**

SOLUTION (i) We have,

$$f(x) = \left(\frac{1}{2} - x\right)^2 + x^3, \text{ where } x \in [-2, 2.5] \Rightarrow f'(x) = -2(1/2 - x) + 3x^2 = -1 + 2x + 3x^2$$

At the points of local maximum and local maximum, we must have

$$f'(x) = 0 \Rightarrow 3x^2 + 2x - 1 = 0 \Rightarrow (3x - 1)(x + 1) = 0 \Rightarrow x = 1/3, -1$$

The values of $f(x)$ at these points and also at the end-points of the interval are computed as given below.

$$f(-2) = \left(\frac{1}{2} + 2\right)^2 + (-2)^3 = \frac{25}{4} - 8 = -\frac{7}{4}, \; f\left(\frac{1}{3}\right) = \left(\frac{1}{2} - \frac{1}{3}\right)^2 + \left(\frac{1}{3}\right)^3 = \frac{1}{36} + \frac{1}{27} = \frac{7}{108},$$

$$f(-1) = \left(\frac{1}{2} + 1\right)^2 + (-1)^3 = \frac{5}{4} \text{ and, } f(2.5) = \left(\frac{1}{2} - 2.5\right)^2 + (2.5)^3 = \frac{157}{8}$$

Of these values, the maximum value of $f(x)$ is $\frac{157}{8}$ and the minimum value is $-\frac{7}{4}$.

Thus, the absolute maximum $= \frac{157}{8}$ and, the absolute minimum $= -\frac{7}{4}$.

(ii) We have,

$$f(x) = \sin x + \cos x, \text{ where } x \in [0, \pi] \Rightarrow f'(x) = \cos x - \sin x$$

The critical points of $f(x)$ are given by

$$f'(x) = 0 \Rightarrow \cos x - \sin x = 0 \Rightarrow \cos x = \sin x \Rightarrow \tan x = 1 \Rightarrow x = \pi/4$$

Let us now calculate the values of $f(x)$ at the critical points and the end-points of the interval.

$$f(0) = \sin 0 + \cos 0 = 1, \; f(\pi/4) = \sin \pi/4 + \cos \pi/4 = \sqrt{2} \text{ and, } f(\pi) = \sin \pi + \cos \pi = -1.$$

Of these values, the maximum and minimum values of $f(x)$ are $\sqrt{2}$ and -1 respectively.

So, absolute maximum = $\sqrt{2}$ and, absolute minimum = – 1.

EXAMPLE 4 *Find both the maximum and the minimum value of* $3x^4 - 8x^3 + 12x^2 - 48x + 1$ *on the interval* [1, 4].

SOLUTION Let $f(x) = 3x^4 - 8x^3 + 12x^2 - 48x + 1$. Then, $f'(x) = 12x^3 - 24x^2 + 24x - 48$.

The critical points of $f(x)$ are given by $f'(x) = 0$.

Now, $f'(x) = 0$

$\Rightarrow 12x^3 - 24x^2 + 24x - 48 = 0$

$\Rightarrow x^3 - 2x^2 + 2x - 4 = 0 \Rightarrow x^2(x-2) + 2(x-2) = 0 \Rightarrow (x-2)(x^2+2) = 0 \Rightarrow x = 2 \quad [\because x^2 + 2 \neq 0]$

The values of $f(x)$ at critical points and at the end-points of the interval are computed as follows:

$$f(2) = -59, \quad f(1) = -40 \text{ and } f(4) = 257.$$

Of these values the largest and the smallest values are $f(4) = 257$ and $f(2) = -59$.

So, the minimum and maximum values of $f(x)$ on [1, 4] are – 59 and 257 respectively.

EXAMPLE 5 *Find the absolute maximum and absolute minimum values of the function f given by* $f(x) = \frac{x}{2} + \frac{2}{x}$, *on the interval* [1, 2]. **[CBSE 2024]**

SOLUTION We have, $f(x) = \frac{x}{2} + \frac{2}{x}$, $x \in [1, 2]$

$$\therefore \quad f'(x) = \frac{1}{2} - \frac{2}{x^2} \Rightarrow f'(x) = \frac{x^2 - 4}{2x^2}$$

$$\therefore \quad f'(x) = 0 \Rightarrow \frac{x^2 - 4}{2x^2} = 0 \Rightarrow x^2 - 4 = 0 \Rightarrow x = 2 \qquad [\because -2 \notin [1, 2]]$$

Thus, we obtain the following points: 1, 2. Let us not compute the values of $f(x)$ at $x = 1, 2$. We find that

$$f(1) = \frac{1}{2} + \frac{2}{1} = \frac{5}{2} \text{ and, } f(2) = 1 + 1 = 2$$

$$\therefore \quad \text{Absolute maximum value} = \frac{5}{2}, \text{ Absolute minimum value} = 2.$$

BASED ON LOWER ORDER THINKING SKILLS (LOTS)

EXAMPLE 6 *Find the maximum and minimum values of* $f(x) = \sin x + \frac{1}{2} \cos 2x$ *in* $[0, \pi/2]$.

SOLUTION We have, $f(x) = \sin x + \frac{1}{2} \cos 2x$. Therefore, $f'(x) = \cos x - \sin 2x$.

At stationary points, we have

$$f'(x) = 0 \Rightarrow \cos x - 2 \sin x \cos x = 0 \Rightarrow \cos x = 0 \text{ or, } \sin x = \frac{1}{2} \Rightarrow x = \frac{\pi}{2} \text{ and } x = \frac{\pi}{6} \quad \left[\because 0 \leq x \leq \frac{\pi}{2}\right]$$

Let us now calculate the values of $f(x)$ at these points and at the end-points of the interval. We find that

$$f(0) = \sin 0 + \frac{1}{2} \cos 0 = \frac{1}{2}, \ f\left(\frac{\pi}{6}\right) = \sin \frac{\pi}{6} + \frac{1}{2} \cos \frac{\pi}{3} = \frac{3}{4} \text{ and, } f\left(\frac{\pi}{2}\right) = \sin \frac{\pi}{2} + \frac{1}{2} \cos \pi = \frac{1}{2}$$

Of these values, the leagest value is $\frac{3}{4}$ and the smallest value is $\frac{1}{2}$. Thus, the maximum and minimum values of $f(x)$ are $\frac{3}{4}$ and $\frac{1}{2}$ respectively which it attains at $x = \frac{\pi}{6}$ and $x = 0$, $x = \frac{\pi}{2}$ respectively.

EXAMPLE 7 *Find the maximum and minimum values of* $f(x) = x^{50} - x^{20}$ *in the interval* $[0, 1]$.

SOLUTION Let $f(x) = x^{50} - x^{20}$. Then, $f'(x) = 50x^{49} - 20x^{19}$.

At stationary points, we must have

$$f'(x) = 0 \Rightarrow 50x^{49} - 20x^{19} = 0 \Rightarrow x^{19}(50x^{30} - 20) = 0$$

$$\Rightarrow \quad x = 0 \text{ or, } 50x^{30} = 20 \Rightarrow x = 0 \text{ or, } x = \left(\frac{2}{5}\right)^{1/30}.$$

The values of $f(x)$ at these points and at the end-points of the interval $[0, 1]$ are as given below.

Now, $f(0) = 0, f\left(\frac{2}{5}\right)^{1/30} = \left(\frac{2}{5}\right)^{50/30} - \left(\frac{2}{5}\right)^{20/30} = \left(\frac{2}{5}\right)^{2/3}\left(\frac{2}{5} - 1\right) = -\frac{3}{5}\left(\frac{2}{5}\right)^{2/3}$ and, $f(1) = 1 - 1 = 0$.

Of these values, the maximum value is 0 and the minimum value is $-\frac{3}{5}\left(\frac{2}{5}\right)^{1/3}$.

Thus, the maximum value of $f(x)$ in $[0, 1]$ is 0 and the minimum value of $f(x)$ in $[0, 1]$ is $-\frac{3}{5}\left(\frac{2}{5}\right)^{2/3}$.

EXAMPLE 8 *Find the maximum and minimum values of* $f(x) = x + \sin 2x$ *in the interval* $[0, 2\pi]$. **[NCERT]**

SOLUTION We have, $f(x) = x + \sin 2x$. Therefore, $f'(x) = 1 + 2\cos 2x$.

At stationary points, we have

$$f'(x) = 0 \Rightarrow 1 + 2\cos 2x = 0 \Rightarrow \cos 2x = -\frac{1}{2}$$

$$\Rightarrow \quad 2x = \frac{2\pi}{3} \text{ or, } 2x = \frac{4\pi}{3} \Rightarrow x = \frac{\pi}{3} \text{ or, } x = \frac{2\pi}{3} \qquad [\because\ 0 \le x \le 2\pi \ \therefore\ 0 \le 2x \le 4\pi]$$

Let us now compute the values of $f(x)$ at these stationary points and at the end-points of the interval $[0, 2\pi]$.

Now, $f(0) = 0 + \sin 0 = 0$, $f\left(\frac{\pi}{3}\right) = \frac{\pi}{3} + \sin\frac{2\pi}{3} = \frac{\pi}{3} + \frac{\sqrt{3}}{2}$, $f\left(\frac{2\pi}{3}\right) = \frac{2\pi}{3} + \sin\frac{4\pi}{3} = \frac{2\pi}{3} - \frac{\sqrt{3}}{2}$

and, $f(2\pi) = 2\pi + \sin 4\pi = 2\pi + 0 = 2\pi$.

Of these values, the maximum value is 2π and the minimum value is 0. Thus, the maximum value of $f(x)$ is 2π and the minimum value is 0.

EXAMPLE 9 *Find the difference between the greatest and least values of the function* $f(x) = \sin 2x - x$ *on* $[-\pi/2, \pi/2]$. **[NCERT EXEMPLAR]**

SOLUTION We have, $f(x) = \sin 2x - x$. Therefore, $f'(x) = 2\cos 2x - 1$.

At stationary points, we must have

$$f'(x) = 0 \Rightarrow 2\cos 2x - 1 = 0 \Rightarrow \cos 2x = \frac{1}{2} \Rightarrow 2x = -\frac{\pi}{3}, \frac{\pi}{3} \Rightarrow x = -\frac{\pi}{6}, \frac{\pi}{6}$$

Let us now compute the values of $f(x)$ at these stationary points and also at the end-points of the interval $[-\pi/2, \pi/2]$.

Now, $f(x) = \sin 2x - x$

$$\Rightarrow \quad f\left(-\frac{\pi}{2}\right) = \sin(-\pi) + \frac{\pi}{2} = \frac{\pi}{2}, \quad f\left(-\frac{\pi}{6}\right) = \sin\left(-\frac{\pi}{3}\right) + \frac{\pi}{6} = -\frac{\sqrt{3}}{2} + \frac{\pi}{6}$$

$$f\left(\frac{\pi}{6}\right) = \sin\frac{\pi}{3} - \frac{\pi}{6} = \frac{\sqrt{3}}{2} - \frac{\pi}{6} \text{ and, } f\left(\frac{\pi}{2}\right) = \sin\pi - \frac{\pi}{2} = -\frac{\pi}{2}$$

Of these values, the largest is $\frac{\pi}{2}$ and the least is $-\frac{\pi}{2}$. So, the greatest and the least values of $f(x)$ on $[-\pi/2, \pi/2]$ are $\pi/2$ and $-\pi/2$ respectively. Hence, required difference $= \frac{\pi}{2} - \left(-\frac{\pi}{2}\right) = \pi$.

EXAMPLE 10 *Show that* $f(x) = \sin x(1 + \cos x)$ *is maximum at* $x = \frac{\pi}{3}$ *in the interval* $[0, \pi]$.

SOLUTION We have,

$$f(x) = \sin x(1 + \cos x).$$

$$\Rightarrow \quad f'(x) = \cos x(1 + \cos x) - \sin^2 x = \cos x + \cos^2 x - (1 - \cos^2 x)$$

$$\Rightarrow \quad f'(x) = 2\cos^2 x + \cos x - 1 = (2\cos x - 1)(\cos x + 1).$$

At stationary points, we have

$$f'(x) = 0 \Rightarrow (2\cos x - 1)(\cos x + 1) = 0 \Rightarrow \cos x = \frac{1}{2} \text{ or, } \cos x = -1 \Rightarrow x = \frac{\pi}{3} \text{ or, } x = \pi.$$

Let us now compute the values of x at these stationary points and at the end-points of the interval. We find that

$$f(0) = 0, f\left(\frac{\pi}{3}\right) = \sin\frac{\pi}{3}\left(1 + \cos\frac{\pi}{3}\right) = \frac{3\sqrt{3}}{4} \text{ and } f(\pi) = 0.$$

Of these values, the maximum value is $\frac{3\sqrt{3}}{4}$. Hence, $f(x)$ attains the maximum value $\frac{3\sqrt{3}}{4}$ at $x = \pi/3$.

EXERCISE 14.4

BASIC

1. Find the absolute maximum and the absolute minimum values of the following functions in the given intervals:
   (i) $f(x) = 4x - \frac{x^2}{2}$ in $[-2, 4.5]$ **[NCERT]** (ii) $f(x) = (x-1)^2 + 3$ in $[-3, 1]$ **[NCERT]**
   (iii) $f(x) = 3x^4 - 8x^3 + 12x^2 - 48x + 25$ in $[0, 3]$ **[NCERT]**
   (iv) $f(x) = (x-2)\sqrt{x-1}$ in $[1, 9]$
2. Find the maximum value of $2x^3 - 24x + 107$ in the interval $[1, 3]$. Find the maximum value of the same function in $[-3, -1]$. **[NCERT]**
3. Find absolute maximum and minimum values of a function f given by $f(x) = 12x^{4/3} - 6x^{1/3}, x \in [-1, 1]$. **[NCERT]**
4. Find the absolute maximum and minimum values of a function f given by $f(x) = 2x^3 - 15x^2 + 36x + 1$ on the interval $[1, 5]$. **[NCERT]**

BASED ON LOTS

5. Find the absolute maximum and minimum values of the function f given by $f(x) = \cos^2 x + \sin x, x \in [0, \pi]$. **[NCERT]**

ANSWERS

1. (i) Absolute Maximum = 8 at $x = 4$, Absolute Minimum = – 10 at $x = -2$
   (ii) Absolute Maximum = 19 at $x = -3$, Absolute Minimum = 3 at $x = 1$
   (iii) Absolute Maximum = 25 at $x = 0$, Absolute Minimum = – 39 at $x = 2$
   (iv) Absolute Maximum = $14\sqrt{2}$ at $x = 9$, Absolute Minimum $= -\frac{2}{3\sqrt{3}}$ at $x = \frac{4}{3}$
2. Maximum value = 89 at $x = 3$ in [1, 3], Maximum value = 139 at $x = -2$ in [– 3, – 1]
3. Absolute Maximum = 5/4, Absolute Minimum = 1
4. Absolute Minimum. value $= -\frac{9}{4}$ at $x = \frac{1}{8}$, Absolute Maximum value = 18 at $x = -1$
5. Absolute Maximum value = 56 at $x = 5$, Absolute Minimum value = 24 at $x = 1$

14.7 APPLIED PROBLEMS ON MAXIMA AND MINIMA

In this section, we will discuss some applied problems on maxima and minima for which following results will be very useful.

(i) For a square of side x: Area $= x^2$, Perimeter $= 4x$.

(ii) For a rectangle of sides x *and* y: Area $= xy$, Perimeter $= 2(x + y)$.

(iii) For a trapezium: Area $= \frac{1}{2}$ (Sum of parallel sides) × (Distance between them).

(iv) For a circle of radius r: Area $= \pi r^2$, Circumference $= 2\pi r$.

(v) For a sphere of radius r: Volume $= \frac{4}{3}\pi r^3$, Surface Area $= 4\pi r^2$.

(vi) For a right circular cylinder of base radius r and height h:
Volume $= \pi r^2 h$, Surface $= 2\pi rh + 2\pi r^2$, Curved surface $= 2\pi rh$.

(vii) For a right circular cone of height h, slant height l and radius of the base r:
Volume $= \left(\frac{1}{3}\right)\pi r^2 h$, Curved surface $= \pi rl$, Total surface $= \pi r^2 + \pi rl$.

(viii) For a cuboid of edges of lengths x, y *and* z: Volume $= xyz$, Surface $= 2(xy + yz + zx)$.

(ix) For a cube of edge length x: Volume $= x^3$, Surface Area $= 6x^2$.

(x) Area of an equilateral triangle $= \frac{\sqrt{3}}{4}(Side)^2$.

REMARK *If k is a positive constant, then a function of the form* $k\,f(x)$, $k + f(x)$, $\{f(x)\}^k$, $\{f(x)\}^{1/k}$, $\log f(x)$ *will be maximum or minimum according as* $f(x)$ *is maximum or minimum provided that* $f(x) > 0$.

ILLUSTRATIVE EXAMPLES

BASED ON BASIC CONCEPTS (BASIC)

EXAMPLE 1 *Find two numbers whose sum is 24 and whose product is as large as possible.* [NCERT]

SOLUTION Let the numbers be x and y. Then,

$$x + y = 24 \text{ (given)} \quad \text{...(i)}$$

Let P be the product of these numbers. Then,

$$P = xy = x(24 - x) \quad \text{[Using (i)]}$$

$$\Rightarrow \qquad P = 24x - x^2 \Rightarrow \frac{dP}{dx} = 24 - 2x \text{ and } \frac{d^2P}{dx^2} = -2$$

The critical points of P are given by $\frac{dP}{dx} = 0$.

$$\therefore \qquad \frac{dP}{dx} = 0 \Rightarrow 24 - 2x = 0 \Rightarrow x = 12$$

Also, $\left(\frac{d^2P}{dx^2}\right)_{x=12} = -2 < 0$. So, P is maximum when $x = 12$.

Putting $x = 12$ in (i), we obtain $y = 12$. Hence, the required numbers are both equal to 12.

EXAMPLE 2 *Find two positive numbers x and y such that $x + y = 60$ and xy^3 is maximum.* **[NCERT]**

SOLUTION Let $P = xy^3$. It is given that $x + y = 60$. Therefore, $x = 60 - y$.

Now, $P = xy^3$

$$\Rightarrow \qquad P = (60 - y)\, y^3 = 60y^3 - y^4 \Rightarrow \frac{dP}{dy} = 180y^2 - 4y^3 \text{ and } \frac{d^2P}{dy^2} = 360y - 12y^2$$

The critical points of P are given by $\frac{dP}{dy} = 0$.

$$\therefore \qquad \frac{dP}{dy} = 0.$$

$$\Rightarrow \qquad 180y^2 - 4y^3 = 0 \Rightarrow 4y^2(45 - y) = 0 \Rightarrow y = 0, y = 45 \Rightarrow y = 45 \quad [\because y = 0 \text{ is not possible}]$$

Now, $\left(\frac{d^2P}{dy^2}\right)_{y=45} = 360 \times 45 - 12(45)^2 = 12 \times 45\,(30 - 45) = -8100 < 0$

So, P is maximum when $y = 45$. Putting $y = 45$ in $x + y = 60$, we obtain $x = 15$.
Hence, xy^3 is maximum when $x = 15$ and $y = 45$.

EXAMPLE 3 *Find two positive numbers x and y such that their sum is 35 and the product $x^2 y^5$ is maximum.* **[NCERT]**

SOLUTION Let $P = x^2 y^5$. It is given that $x + y = 35 \Rightarrow x = 35 - y$ ...(i)

Putting $x = 35 - y$ in $P = x^2 y^5$, we get

$$P = (35 - y)^2 y^5$$

$$\Rightarrow \qquad \frac{dP}{dy} = -2(35 - y)\, y^5 + 5(35 - y)^2 y^4 = (35 - y)\, y^4 \{-2y + 5(35 - y)\} = y^4 (35 - y)(175 - 7y)$$

$$\Rightarrow \qquad \frac{dP}{dy} = 7y^4 (35 - y)(25 - y)$$

The critical points of P are given by $\frac{dP}{dy} = 0$.

$$\therefore \qquad \frac{dP}{dy} = 0 \Rightarrow 7y^4 (35 - y)(25 - y) = 0 \Rightarrow y = 0, 25, 35$$

But, $y = 0$ and $y = 35$ are not possible. So, $y = 25$.

Now, $\frac{d^2P}{dy^2} = 28y^3 (35 - y)(25 - y) - 7y^4 (25 - y) - 7y^4 (35 - y)$

$$\therefore \quad \left(\frac{d^2P}{dy^2}\right)_{y=25} = -7\,(25)^4\,(35-20) = -7\,(25)^4\,(10) < 0$$

Thus, P has maximum when $y = 25$. Putting $y = 25$ in (i), we obtain $x = 10$. Hence, x^2y^5 is maximum when $x = 10$, and $y = 25$.

EXAMPLE 4 *Amongst all pairs of positive numbers with product 256, find those whose sum is the least.*

SOLUTION Let the required numbers be x and y. Then, $xy = 256$ (given) ...(i)

Let $S = x + y$. Then,

$$S = x + \frac{256}{x} \qquad \text{[Using (i)]}$$

$$\Rightarrow \quad \frac{dS}{dx} = 1 - \frac{256}{x^2} \text{ and, } \frac{d^2S}{dx^2} = \frac{512}{x^3}$$

The critical points of S are given by $\frac{dS}{dx} = 0$.

$$\therefore \quad \frac{dS}{dx} = 0 \Rightarrow 1 - \frac{256}{x^2} = 0 \Rightarrow x^2 = 256 \Rightarrow x = 16$$

Now, $\left(\frac{d^2S}{dx^2}\right)_{x=16} = \frac{512}{(16)^3} = \frac{1}{8} > 0$. Thus, S is minimum when $x = 16$.

Putting $x = 16$ in (i) we get $y = 16$. Hence, the required numbers are both equal to 16.

EXAMPLE 5 *Find two positive numbers whose sum is 14 and the sum of whose squares is minimum.*

SOLUTION Let the numbers be x and y. Then,

$$x + y = 14 \qquad \text{...(i)}$$

Let S be the sum of the squares of x and y. Then,

$$S = x^2 + y^2$$

$$\Rightarrow \quad S = x^2 + (14 - x)^2 \qquad \text{[Using (i)]}$$

$$\Rightarrow \quad S = 2x^2 - 28x + 196 \Rightarrow \frac{dS}{dx} = 4x - 28 \text{ and } \frac{d^2S}{dx^2} = 4$$

The critical points of S are given by $\frac{dS}{dx} = 0$.

$$\therefore \quad \frac{dS}{dx} = 0 \Rightarrow 4x - 28 = 0 \Rightarrow x = 7$$

Clearly, $\frac{d^2S}{dx^2} = 4 > 0$. Thus, S is minimum when $x = 7$.

Putting $x = 7$ in (i), we obtain $y = 7$. Hence, the required numbers are both equal to 7.

EXAMPLE 6 *The combined resistance R of two resistors R_1 and R_2 $(R_1, R_2 > 0)$ is given by $\frac{1}{R} = \frac{1}{R_1} + \frac{1}{R_2}$.*

If $R_1 + R_2 = C$ (a constant), show that the maximum resistance R is obtained by choosing $R_1 = R_2$.

SOLUTION We have,

$$\frac{1}{R} = \frac{1}{R_1} + \frac{1}{R_2} \text{ and } R_1 + R_2 = C$$

$$\Rightarrow \quad \frac{1}{R} = \frac{R_1 + R_2}{R_1 R_2} = \frac{C}{R_1 R_2} = \frac{C}{R_1(C - R_1)} \qquad [\because R_2 = C - R_1]$$

$\Rightarrow \quad R = \dfrac{R_1 C - R_1^{\ 2}}{C} = R_1 - \dfrac{R_1^{\ 2}}{C} \Rightarrow \dfrac{dR}{dR_1} = 1 - \dfrac{2R_1}{C}$ and $\dfrac{d^2R}{dR_1^{\ 2}} = -\dfrac{2}{C}$

The critical numbers of R are given by $\dfrac{dR}{dR_1} = 0.$

$\therefore \quad \dfrac{dR}{dR_1} = 0 \Rightarrow 1 - \dfrac{2R_1}{C} = 0 \Rightarrow R_1 = \dfrac{C}{2}$

Clearly, $\dfrac{d^2R}{dR_1^2} = -\dfrac{2}{C} < 0$ for all values of R_1. Thus, R is maximum when $R_1 = \dfrac{C}{2}$.

Putting $R_1 = \dfrac{C}{2}$ in $R_1 + R_2 = C$, we get: $R_2 = C - \dfrac{C}{2} = \dfrac{C}{2}$. Hence, R is maximum when $R_1 = R_2 = C/2$.

EXAMPLE 7 *A beam of length l is supported at two ends and is uniformly loaded. If W is the uniform load per unit length, the bending moment M at a distance x from one end is given by $M = \dfrac{W}{2} lx - \dfrac{1}{2} Wx^2$. Find the point on the beam at which the bending moment has the maximum value.*

SOLUTION We have,

$$M = \frac{Wlx}{2} - \frac{Wx^2}{2} \Rightarrow \frac{dM}{dx} = \frac{Wl}{2} - Wx \text{ and } \frac{d^2M}{dx^2} = -W$$

The critical numbers of M are given by $\dfrac{dM}{dx} = 0.$

Now, $\dfrac{dM}{dx} = 0 \Rightarrow \dfrac{Wl}{2} - Wx = 0 \Rightarrow x = \dfrac{l}{2}$

Clearly, $\dfrac{d^2M}{dx^2} = -W < 0$ for all values of x. Thus, M is maximum when $x = l/2$.

Hence, the required point is at a distance of $l/2$ from the supporting end.

EXAMPLE 8 *Find the minimum value of $ax + by$, where $xy = c^2$ and a, b, c are positive.*

[CBSE 2015, 2020]

SOLUTION Let $z = ax + by$, where $xy = c^2$. Then,

$$z = ax + \frac{bc^2}{x} \qquad \left[\because\ xy = c^2 \Rightarrow y = \frac{c^2}{x}\right] \qquad \ldots\text{(i)}$$

$$\Rightarrow \quad \frac{dz}{dx} = a - \frac{bc^2}{x^2} \text{ and } \frac{d^2z}{dx^2} = \frac{2bc^2}{x^3}$$

The critical points of z are given by $\dfrac{dz}{dx} = 0.$

$$\therefore \quad \frac{dz}{dx} = 0 \Rightarrow a - \frac{bc^2}{x^2} = 0 \Rightarrow x^2 = \frac{bc^2}{a} \Rightarrow x = \pm\sqrt{\frac{b}{a}}\, c$$

At $x = \sqrt{\dfrac{b}{a}}\, c$: We find that $\dfrac{d^2z}{dx^2} = 2bc^2\left(\sqrt{\dfrac{a}{b}} \times \dfrac{1}{c}\right)^3 = 2\,\dfrac{a}{c}\sqrt{\dfrac{a}{b}} > 0$. So, z is minimum at $x = c\sqrt{\dfrac{b}{a}}$.

The minimum value of z is given by $z = a\sqrt{\dfrac{b}{a}}\, c + \dfrac{bc^2}{c}\sqrt{\dfrac{a}{b}} = 2\sqrt{ab}\, c \qquad \left[\text{Putting } x = \sqrt{\dfrac{b}{a}}\, c \text{ in (i)}\right]$

At $x=-\sqrt{\frac{b}{a}}c$: We find that $\frac{d^2z}{dx^2}=2bc^2\left(-\frac{a}{bc^3}\sqrt{\frac{a}{b}}\right)=-2\frac{a}{c}\sqrt{\frac{a}{b}}<0$. So, z is maximum at $x=-\sqrt{\frac{b}{a}}c$.

EXAMPLE 9 *Show that all the rectangles with a given perimeter, the square has the largest area.*

SOLUTION Let x and y be the lengths of two sides of the rectangle of fixed parameter P and let A be its area. Then,

$$P=2(x+y) \quad ...(i) \qquad \text{and,} \qquad A=xy \quad ...(ii)$$

Now, $P=2(x+y) \Rightarrow y=\frac{P}{2}-x$

$\therefore \quad A=xy=x\left(\frac{P}{2}-x\right)=\frac{Px}{2}-x^2 \Rightarrow \frac{dA}{dx}=\frac{P}{2}-2x$ and $\frac{d^2A}{dx^2}=-2$

The critical points of A are given by $\frac{dA}{dx}=0$.

$\therefore \quad \frac{dA}{dx}=0 \Rightarrow \frac{P}{2}-2x=0 \Rightarrow P=4x \Rightarrow 2x+2y=4x \Rightarrow 2x=2y \Rightarrow x=y$

Clearly, $\left(\frac{d^2A}{dx^2}\right)_{x=y}=-2<0$. Hence, A is maximum when $x=y$ i.e. the rectangle is a square.

EXAMPLE 10 *Show that of all the rectangles of given area, the square has the smallest perimeter.*

[CBSE 2011]

SOLUTION Let x and y be the lengths of two sides of a rectangle of given area A, and let P be the perimeter. Then,

$$A=xy \quad ...(i) \qquad \text{and,} \qquad P=2(x+y) \quad ...(ii)$$

Now, $A=xy \Rightarrow y=\frac{A}{x}$

$\therefore \quad P=2(x+y)=2\left(x+\frac{A}{x}\right) \Rightarrow \frac{dP}{dx}=2\left(1-\frac{A}{x^2}\right)$ and $\frac{d^2P}{dx^2}=\frac{4A}{x^3}$

The critical points of P are given by $\frac{dP}{dx}=0$.

$\therefore \quad \frac{dP}{dx}=0 \Rightarrow 2\left(1-\frac{A}{x^2}\right)=0 \Rightarrow 1-\frac{A}{x^2}=0 \Rightarrow x^2=A \Rightarrow x^2=xy \Rightarrow x=y.$

Clearly, $\frac{d^2P}{dx^2}=\frac{4A}{x^3}>0$ for all positive values of x. Hence, P is minimum when $x=y$ i.e the rectangle is a square.

EXAMPLE 11 *Show that of all the rectangles inscribed in a given circle, the square has the maximum area.*

[NCERT, CBSE 2002, 2006, 2008, 2011, 2013]

SOLUTION Let $ABCD$ be a rectangle inscribed in a given circle with centre at O and radius a. Let $AB=2x$ and $BC=2y$. Applying Pythagoras theorem in right triangle OAM, we obtain

$$OA^2=AM^2+OM^2 \Rightarrow a^2=x^2+y^2 \Rightarrow y=\sqrt{a^2-x^2} \quad ...(i)$$

Let A be the area of the rectangle $ABCD$. Then,

$$A = 4xy = 4x\sqrt{a^2 - x^2} \quad \text{[Using (i)]}$$

$$\Rightarrow \quad \frac{dA}{dx} = 4\left\{\sqrt{a^2 - x^2} - \frac{x^2}{\sqrt{a^2 - x^2}}\right\} = 4\left\{\frac{a^2 - 2x^2}{\sqrt{a^2 - x^2}}\right\}$$

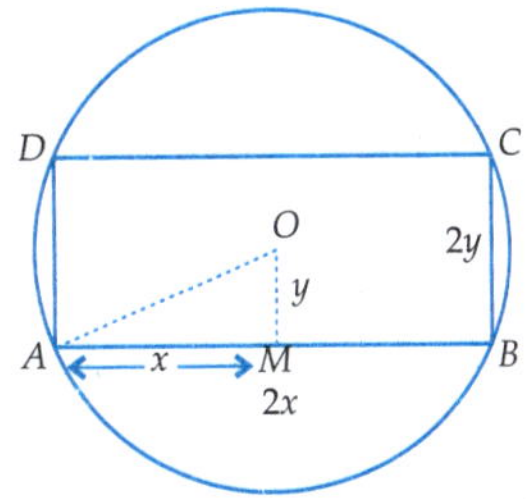

Fig. 14.32

The critical points of A are given by $\frac{dA}{dx} = 0$.

$$\therefore \quad \frac{dA}{dx} = 0$$

$$\Rightarrow \quad 4\left\{\frac{a^2 - 2x^2}{\sqrt{a^2 - x^2}}\right\} = 0 \Rightarrow a^2 - 2x^2 = 0 \Rightarrow x = \frac{a}{\sqrt{2}}$$

Now, $\frac{dA}{dx} = 4\left\{\frac{a^2 - 2x^2}{\sqrt{a^2 - x^2}}\right\}$

$$\Rightarrow \quad \frac{d^2A}{dx^2} = 4\frac{d}{dx}\left\{(a^2 - 2x^2)(a^2 - x^2)^{-1/2}\right\}$$

$$\Rightarrow \quad \frac{d^2A}{dx^2} = 4\left\{-4x(a^2 - x^2)^{-1/2} + (a^2 - 2x^2)(-1/2)(a^2 - x^2)^{-3/2}(-2x)\right\}$$

$$\Rightarrow \quad \frac{d^2A}{dx^2} = 4\left\{\frac{-4x}{\sqrt{a^2 - x^2}} + \frac{x(a^2 - 2x^2)}{(a^2 - x^2)^{3/2}}\right\}$$

Clearly, $\left(\frac{d^2A}{dx^2}\right)_{x = a/\sqrt{2}} = -16 < 0$. Thus, A is maximum when $x = \frac{a}{\sqrt{2}}$. Putting $x = \frac{a}{\sqrt{2}}$ in (i), we get $y = \frac{a}{\sqrt{2}}$.

Now, $x = y = a/\sqrt{2} \Rightarrow 2x = 2y = \sqrt{2}a \Rightarrow AB = BC \Rightarrow ABCD$ is a square.

Hence, area A is maximum when the rectangle is a square.

EXAMPLE 12 *Show that the rectangle of maximum perimeter which can be inscribed in a circle of radius a is a square of side $\sqrt{2}a$.* **[CBSE 2002]**

SOLUTION Let $ABCD$ be a rectangle in a given circle of radius a with centre at O. Let $AB = 2x$ and $AD = 2y$ be the sides of the rectangle. Applying Pythagoras theorem in ΔOAM, we get

$$AM^2 + OM^2 = OA^2 \Rightarrow x^2 + y^2 = a^2 \Rightarrow y = \sqrt{a^2 - x^2} \quad \text{...(i)}$$

Let P be the perimeter of the rectangle $ABCD$. Then,

$$P = 4x + 4y$$

$$\Rightarrow \quad P = 4x + 4\sqrt{a^2 - x^2} \quad \text{[Using (i)]}$$

$$\Rightarrow \quad \frac{dP}{dx} = 4 - \frac{4x}{\sqrt{a^2 - x^2}}$$

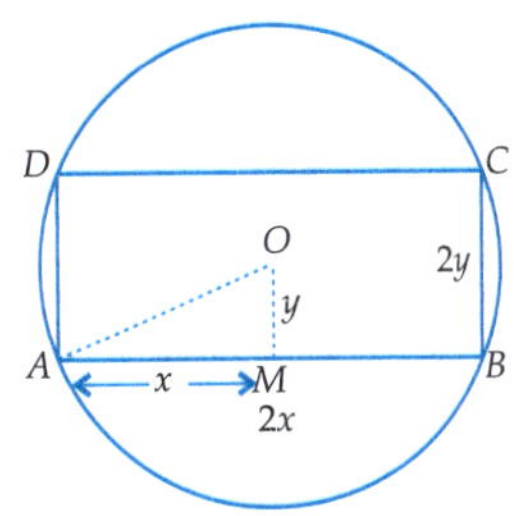

Fig. 14.33

The critical points of P are given by $\frac{dP}{dx} = 0$.

$$\therefore \quad \frac{dP}{dx} = 0$$

$$\Rightarrow \quad 4 - \frac{4x}{\sqrt{a^2 - x^2}} = 0$$

$$\Rightarrow \quad 4 = \frac{4x}{\sqrt{a^2 - x^2}} \Rightarrow \sqrt{a^2 - x^2} = x \Rightarrow a^2 - x^2 = x^2 \Rightarrow 2x^2 = a^2 \Rightarrow x = \frac{a}{\sqrt{2}}$$

Now, $\frac{dP}{dx} = 4 - \frac{4x}{\sqrt{a^2 - x^2}}$

$$\Rightarrow \quad \frac{d^2P}{dx^2} = \frac{-4\left\{\sqrt{a^2 - x^2} - \frac{x(-x)}{\sqrt{a^2 - x^2}}\right\}}{\left\{\sqrt{a^2 - x^2}\right\}^2} = \frac{-4a^2}{(a^2 - x^2)^{3/2}}$$

$\therefore \quad \left(\frac{d^2P}{dx^2}\right)_{x = a/\sqrt{2}} = \frac{-4a^2}{\left(a^2 - \frac{a^2}{2}\right)^{3/2}} = \frac{-8\sqrt{2}}{a} < 0$. Thus, P is maximum when $x = \frac{a}{\sqrt{2}}$.

Putting $x = \frac{a}{\sqrt{2}}$ in (i), we obtain $y = \frac{a}{\sqrt{2}}$.

Now, $x = y = a\sqrt{2} \Rightarrow 2x = 2y \Rightarrow AB = BC \Rightarrow ABCD$ is a square.

Hence, P is maximum when the rectangle is square of side $2x = \frac{2a}{\sqrt{2}} = \sqrt{2}\,a$.

EXAMPLE 13 *AB is a diameter of a circle and C is any point on the circle. Show that the area of ΔABC is maximum, when it is isosceles.* **[NCERT EXEMPLAR]**

SOLUTION Let $AB = 2a$, $AC = x$ and $CB = y$. Since AB is a diameter of the circle having centre O and C is a point on the semi-circle ACB. Therefore, $\angle ACB = \frac{\pi}{2}$.

Applying Pythagoras theorem in ΔACB, we obtain

$$AB^2 = AC^2 + CB^2 \Rightarrow (2a)^2 = x^2 + y^2 \Rightarrow y = \sqrt{4a^2 - x^2} \quad \ldots(i)$$

Let A be the area of ΔACB. Then,

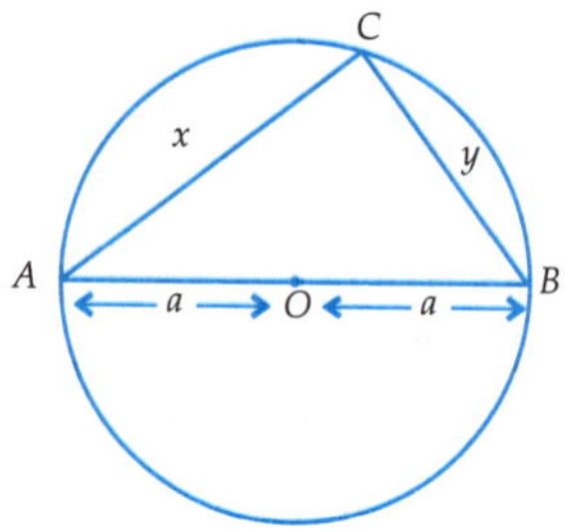

Fig. 14.34

$$A = \frac{1}{2} AC \times CB = \frac{1}{2} xy$$

$$\Rightarrow \quad A = \frac{1}{2} x \sqrt{4a^2 - x^2} \quad \text{[Using (i)]}$$

$$\Rightarrow \quad \frac{dA}{dx} = \frac{1}{2}\left\{\sqrt{4a^2 - x^2} - \frac{x^2}{\sqrt{4a^2 - x^2}}\right\} = \frac{2a^2 - x^2}{\sqrt{4a^2 - x^2}}$$

The stationary values of A are given by $\frac{dA}{dx} = 0$.

$$\therefore \quad \frac{dA}{dx} = 0 \Rightarrow \frac{2a^2 - x^2}{\sqrt{4a^2 - x^2}} = 0 \Rightarrow 2a^2 = x^2 \Rightarrow x = \sqrt{2}a$$

Now, $\frac{dA}{dx} = \frac{2a^2 - x^2}{\sqrt{4a^2 - x^2}} \Rightarrow \frac{d^2A}{dx^2} - \frac{\sqrt{4a^2 - x^2} \times -2x - (2a^2 - x^2) \times \frac{-x}{\sqrt{4a^2 - x^2}}}{\left(\sqrt{4a^2 - x^2}\right)^2} = -\frac{x(6a^2 - x^2)}{(4a^2 - x^2)^{3/2}}$

Clearly, $\left(\frac{d^2A}{dx^2}\right)_{x = \sqrt{2}a} = -2 < 0$. Thus, A is maximum when $x = \sqrt{2}a$ and $y = \sqrt{2}a$.

Hence, the area of ΔABC is maximum when it is isosceles.

EXAMPLE 14 *Tangent to the circle $x^2+y^2=a^2$ at any point on it in the first quadrant makes intercepts OA and OB on x and y axes respectively, O being the centre of the circle. Find the minimum value of OA + OB.* **[CBSE 2015]**

SOLUTION Let $P(a\cos\theta, a\sin\theta)$ be an arbitrary point on the circle $x^2+y^2=a^2$. If P lies in the first quadrant, then $0 \le \theta \le \pi/2$. The equation of tangent to $x^2+y^2=a^2$ at $P(a\cos\theta, a\sin\theta)$ is

$$x\cos\theta + y\sin\theta = a \qquad \left[\begin{array}{l}\text{The tangent to } x^2+y^2=a^2\\ \text{at } (x_1, y_1) \text{ is } xx_1+yy_1=a^2\end{array}\right]$$

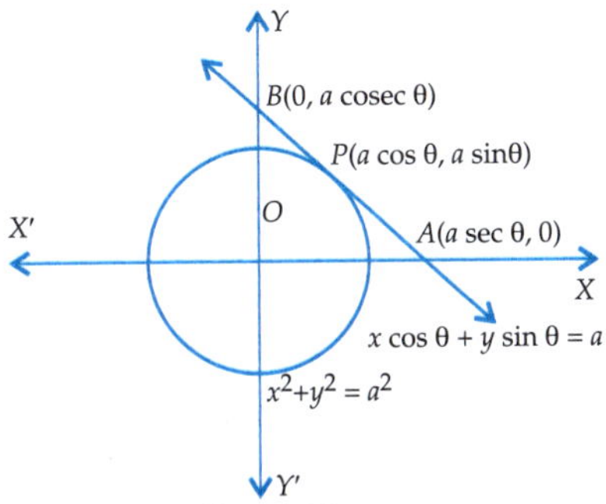

Fig. 14.35

This cuts x and y-axis at $A(a\sec\theta, 0)$ and $B(0, a\operatorname{cosec}\theta)$ respectively.

$\therefore \qquad OA = a\sec\theta$ and $OB = a\operatorname{cosec}\theta$

Let $S = OA + OB$. Then, $S = a(\sec\theta + \operatorname{cosec}\theta)$.

$$\therefore \qquad \frac{dS}{d\theta} = a(\sec\theta\tan\theta - \operatorname{cosec}\theta\cot\theta)$$

and,

$$\frac{d^2S}{d\theta^2} = a(\sec^3\theta + \sec\theta\tan^2\theta + \operatorname{cosec}^3\theta + \operatorname{cosec}\theta\cot^2\theta)$$

For maximum or minimum values of S, we must have

$$\frac{dS}{d\theta} = 0 \Rightarrow a(\sec\theta\tan\theta - \operatorname{cosec}\theta\cot\theta) = 0 \Rightarrow \tan^3\theta = 1 \Rightarrow \tan\theta = 1 \Rightarrow \theta = \frac{\pi}{4}$$

At $\theta = \frac{\pi}{4}$, we obtain : $\frac{d^2S}{d\theta^2} = a(2\sqrt{2}+\sqrt{2}+2\sqrt{2}+\sqrt{2}) = 6\sqrt{2}a > 0$

Hence, S is minimum at $\theta = \frac{\pi}{4}$ and the minimum value of S is given by

$$S = a\left(\sec\frac{\pi}{4} + \operatorname{cosec}\frac{\pi}{4}\right) = 2\sqrt{2}\,a$$

EXAMPLE 15 *If the sum of the lengths of the hypotenues and a side of a right angled triangle is given, show that the area of the triangle is maximum when the angle between them is $\pi/3$.*

[CBSE 2009, 2014, 2016, 2017]

SOLUTION Let ABC be a right angled triangle with base $BC = x$ and hypotenues $AC = y$ such that $x + y = k$, where k is a constant. Let θ be the angle between the base and hypotenues. Let A be the area of the triangle. Then,

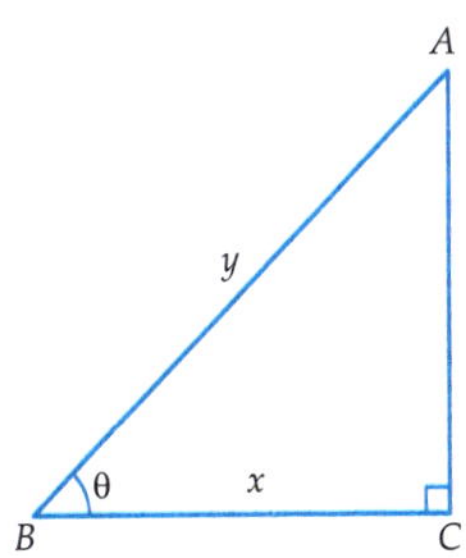

Fig. 14.36

$$A = \frac{1}{2}BC \times AC = \frac{1}{2}x\sqrt{y^2-x^2}$$

$$\Rightarrow \qquad A^2 = \frac{x^2}{4}(y^2-x^2)$$

$$\Rightarrow \qquad A^2 = \frac{x^2}{4}\{(k-x)^2-x^2\} \qquad [\because x+y=k]$$

$$\Rightarrow \qquad A^2 = \frac{k^2x^2-2kx^3}{4} \qquad \text{...(i)}$$

Differentiating with respect to x, we get

$$2A\frac{dA}{dx} = \frac{2k^2x-6kx^2}{4} \qquad \text{...(ii)}$$

$$\Rightarrow \quad \frac{dA}{dx} = \frac{k^2x - 3kx^2}{4A}$$

The critical numbers of A are given by $\frac{dA}{dx} = 0$.

Now, $\frac{dA}{dx} = 0 \Rightarrow \frac{k^2 x - 3kx^2}{4A} = 0 \Rightarrow x = \frac{k}{3}$.

Differentiating (ii) with respect to x, we get

$$2\left(\frac{dA}{dx}\right)^2 + 2A\frac{d^2A}{dx^2} = \frac{2k^2 - 12kx}{4} \qquad ...(iii)$$

When $x = \frac{k}{3}, \frac{dA}{dx} = 0$. Putting $\frac{dA}{dx} = 0$ and $x = \frac{k}{3}$ in (iii), we get: $\frac{d^2A}{dx^2} = \frac{-k^2}{4A} < 0$.

Thus, A is maximum when $x = \frac{k}{3}$. Putting $x = \frac{k}{3}$ in $x + y = k$, we obtain $y = \frac{2k}{3}$.

In ΔACB, $\cos\theta = \frac{BC}{AB} \Rightarrow \cos\theta = \frac{x}{y} \Rightarrow \cos\theta = \frac{k/3}{2k/3} = \frac{1}{2} \Rightarrow \theta = \frac{\pi}{3}$.

Thus, area of triangle ABC is maximum, when angle θ between base BC and hypotenuse AB is $\pi/3$.

EXAMPLE 16 *Prove that the area of right-angled triangle of given hypotenues is maximum when the triangle is isosceles.*

SOLUTION Let h be the hypotenues of the right-angled triangle, and let x be its altitude. Then, Base of the triangle $= \sqrt{h^2 - x^2}$. Let A be the area of the triangle. Then, ...(i)

$$A = \frac{1}{2}x\sqrt{h^2 - x^2}$$

$$\Rightarrow \quad \frac{dA}{dx} = \frac{1}{2}\left\{\sqrt{h^2 - x^2} + x\frac{1}{2}(h^2 - x^2)^{-1/2}\frac{d}{dx}(h^2 - x^2)\right\}$$

$$\Rightarrow \quad \frac{dA}{dx} = \frac{1}{2}\left\{\sqrt{h^2 - x^2} - \frac{x^2}{\sqrt{h^2 - x^2}}\right\} = \frac{1}{2}\left\{\frac{h^2 - 2x^2}{\sqrt{h^2 - x^2}}\right\}$$

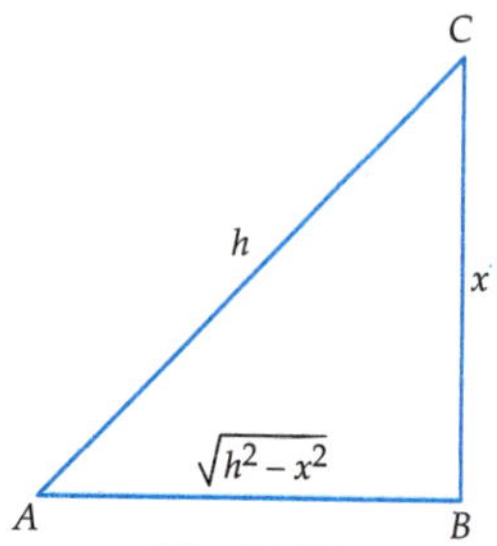

Fig. 14.37

The critical numbers of x are given by $\frac{dA}{dx} = 0$.

$$\therefore \quad \frac{dA}{dx} = 0 \Rightarrow \frac{1}{2}\left\{\frac{h^2 - 2x^2}{\sqrt{h^2 - x^2}}\right\} = 0 \Rightarrow h^2 = 2x^2 \Rightarrow x = \frac{h}{\sqrt{2}}$$

Now, $\frac{dA}{dx} = \frac{1}{2}\left\{\frac{h^2 - 2x^2}{\sqrt{h^2 - x^2}}\right\}$

$$\Rightarrow \quad \frac{d^2A}{dx^2} = \frac{1}{2}\left\{(-4x)\frac{1}{\sqrt{h^2 - x^2}} + (h^2 - 2x^2)\left(-\frac{1}{2}\right)(h^2 - x^2)^{-3/2}\frac{d}{dx}(h^2 - x^2)\right\}$$

$$\Rightarrow \quad \frac{d^2A}{dx^2} = \frac{1}{2}\left\{\frac{-4x}{\sqrt{h^2 - x^2}} + \frac{x(h^2 - 2x^2)}{(h^2 - x^2)^{3/2}}\right\} \Rightarrow \left(\frac{d^2A}{dx^2}\right)_{x = \frac{h}{\sqrt{2}}} = -2 < 0.$$

Thus, A is maximum when $x = \frac{h}{\sqrt{2}}$. Putting $x = \frac{h}{\sqrt{2}}$ in (i), we get: Base $= \sqrt{h^2 - \left(\frac{h^2}{2}\right)} = \frac{h}{\sqrt{2}}$.

Therefore, $AB = BC = \frac{h}{\sqrt{2}}$. Hence, A is maximum when the triangle is isosceles.

EXAMPLE 17 *Show that the surface area of a closed cuboid with square base and given volume is minimum, when it is a cube.*

SOLUTION Let V be the fixed volume of a closed cuboid with length x, breadth x and height y. Let S be the surface area of the cuboid. Then,

$$V = x^2 y \quad ...(i)$$

and, $$S = 2(x^2 + xy + xy) = 2x^2 + 4xy \quad ...(ii)$$

Now, $$S = 2x^2 + 4xy$$

$$\Rightarrow S = 2x^2 + 4x\left(\frac{V}{x^2}\right) \quad \left[\because V = x^2 y \therefore y = \frac{V}{x^2}\right]$$

$$\Rightarrow S = 2x^2 + \frac{4V}{x} \Rightarrow \frac{dS}{dx} = 4x - \frac{4V}{x^2} \quad ...(iii)$$

The critical numbers of S are given by $\frac{dS}{dx} = 0$.

$$\therefore \frac{dS}{dx} = 0 \Rightarrow 4x - \frac{4V}{x^2} = 0 \Rightarrow V = x^3 \Rightarrow x^2 y = x^3 \Rightarrow x = y. \quad [\because V = x^2 y]$$

Differentiating (iii) with respect to x, we get

$$\frac{d^2S}{dx^2} = 4 + \frac{8V}{x^3} = 4 + \frac{8x^2 y}{x^3} = 4 + \frac{8y}{x} \Rightarrow \left(\frac{d^2S}{dx^2}\right)_{y=x} = 12 > 0.$$

Hence, S is minimum when length $= x$, breadth $= x$ and height $= x$ i.e., when it is a cube.

EXAMPLE 18 *An open tank with a square base and vertical sides is to be constructed from a metal sheet so as to hold a given quantity of water. Show that the cost of the material will be least when depth of the tank is half of its width.* **[CBSE 2007, 2010, 2018]**

SOLUTION Let the length, width and height of the open tank be x, x and y units respectively. Then, its volume is $x^2 y$ and the total surface area is $x^2 + 4xy$. It is given that the tank can hold a given quantity of water. This means that its volume is constant. Let it be V. Then,

$$V = x^2 y \quad ...(i)$$

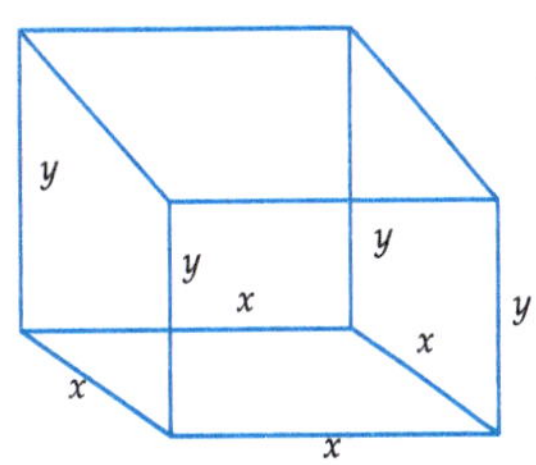

Fig. 14.38

The cost of the material will be least if the total surface area is least. Let S denote the total surface area. Then,

$$S = x^2 + 4xy \quad ...(ii)$$

We have to minimize S subject to the condition that the volume V is constant.

Now,

$$S = x^2 + 4xy$$

$$\Rightarrow S = x^2 + \frac{4V}{x} \quad \text{[Using (i)]}$$

$$\Rightarrow \quad \frac{dS}{dx} = 2x - \frac{4V}{x^2} \text{ and } \frac{d^2S}{dx^2} = 2 + \frac{8V}{x^3}$$

The critical numbers of S are given by $\frac{dS}{dx} = 0$.

Now, $\frac{dS}{dx} = 0 \Rightarrow 2x - \frac{4V}{x^2} = 0 \Rightarrow 2x^3 = 4V \Rightarrow 2x^3 = 4x^2 y \Rightarrow x = 2y \quad [\because V = x^2 y]$

Clearly, $\frac{d^2 S}{dx^2} = 2 + \frac{8V}{x^3} > 0$ for all x. Hence, S is minimum when $x = 2y$ i.e. the depth (height) of the tank is half of its width.

EXAMPLE 19 *A metal box with a square base and vertical sides is to contain 1024 cm^3 of water. the material for the top and bottom costs ₹ 5 per cm^2 and the material for the sides costs ₹ 2.50 per cm^2. Find the least cost of the box.* **[NCERT EXEMPALR]**

SOLUTION Let the length, breadth and height of the metal box be x cm, x cm and y cm respectively. It is given that the box can contain 1024 cm^3 of water.

$$\therefore \quad 1024 = x^2 y \Rightarrow y = \frac{1024}{x^2} \quad \ldots(i)$$

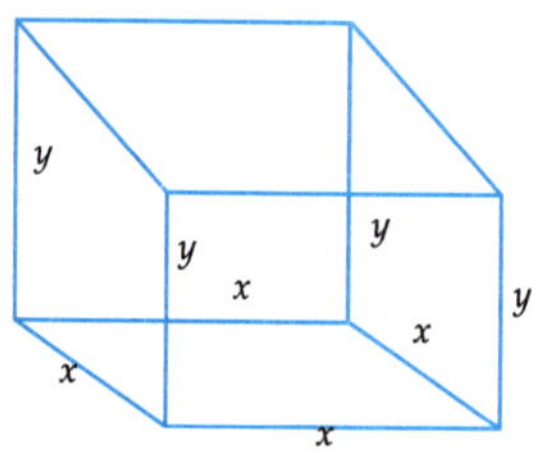

Fig. 14.39

Let C be the total cost in ₹ of material used to construct the box. Then,

$$C = 5x^2 + 5x^2 + \frac{5}{2} \times 4xy \Rightarrow C = 10x^2 + 10xy$$

We have to find the least value of C.

Now,

$$C = 10x^2 + 10xy$$

$$\Rightarrow \quad C = 10x^2 + 10x \times \frac{1024}{x^2} \qquad \text{[Using (i)]}$$

$$\Rightarrow \quad C = 10x^2 + \frac{10240}{x} \Rightarrow \frac{dC}{dx} = 20x - \frac{10240}{x^2} \text{ and } \frac{d^2C}{dx^2} = 20 + \frac{20480}{x^3}$$

The critical numbers for C are given by $\frac{dC}{dx} = 0$.

Now, $\frac{dC}{dx} = 0 \Rightarrow 20x - \frac{10240}{x^2} = 0 \Rightarrow x^3 = 512 \Rightarrow x^3 = 8^3 \Rightarrow x = 8$

Clearly, $\left(\frac{d^2C}{dx^2}\right)_{x=8} = 20 + \frac{20480}{8^3} > 0$. Thus, the cost of the box is least when $x = 8$. Putting $x = 8$ in (i), we obtain $y = 16$. So, the dimensions of the box are $8 \times 8 \times 16$.

Putting $x = 8$ and $y = 16$ in $C = 10x^2 + 10xy$, we obtain $C = 1920$.

Hence, the least cost of the box is ₹1920.

EXAMPLE 20 *An open box with a square base is to be made out of a given quantity of card board of area c^2 square units. Show that the maximum volume of the box is $\frac{c^3}{6\sqrt{3}}$ cubic units.*

[CBSE 2001C, 05, 2012, NCERT EXEMPLAR]

SOLUTION Let the length, breadth and height of the box x, x and y units respectively. It is given that the area of the card board is c^2 sq. units.

$$\therefore \quad x^2 + 4xy = c^2 \quad \text{...(i)}$$

Let V be the volume of the box. Then,

$$V = x^2 y \quad \text{...(ii)}$$

$$\Rightarrow \quad V = x^2\left(\frac{c^2 - x^2}{4x}\right) \quad \text{[Using (i)]}$$

$$\Rightarrow \quad V = \frac{c^2}{4}x - \frac{x^3}{4} \Rightarrow \frac{dV}{dx} = \frac{c^2}{4} - \frac{3x^2}{4} \text{ and } \frac{d^2V}{dx^2} = -\frac{3x}{2}$$

The critical points of V are given by $\frac{dV}{dx} = 0$.

Now, $\frac{dV}{dx} = 0 \Rightarrow \frac{c^2}{4} - \frac{3x^2}{4} = 0 \Rightarrow x = \frac{c}{\sqrt{3}}$

Clearly, $\left(\frac{d^2V}{dx^2}\right)_{x = c/\sqrt{3}} = \frac{-3c}{2\sqrt{3}} < 0$. Thus, V is maximum when $x = \frac{c}{\sqrt{3}}$.

Putting $x = \frac{c}{\sqrt{3}}$ in (i), we obtain $y = \frac{c}{2\sqrt{3}}$ Putting $x = \frac{c}{\sqrt{3}}$ and $y = \frac{c}{2\sqrt{3}}$ in (ii) the maximum volume of the box is given by $V = \frac{c^2}{3} \times \frac{c}{2\sqrt{3}} = \frac{c^3}{6\sqrt{3}}$ cubic units

EXAMPLE 21 *The sum of the surface areas of a rectangular parallelopiped with sides x, 2x and $\frac{x}{3}$ and a sphere is given to be constant. Prove that the sum of the volumes is minimum, if x is equal to three times the radius of the sphere. Also, find the minimum value of the sum of their volumes.*

[NCERT EXEMPLAR, CBSE 2016]

SOLUTION Let y be the radius of the sphere and let S be the constant value of the sum of the surface areas of the parallelopiped and the sphere. Then,

$$S = 2\left(x \times 2x + 2x \times \frac{x}{3} + \frac{x}{3} \times x\right) + 4\pi y^2 \Rightarrow S = 6x^2 + 4\pi y^2 \quad \text{...(i)}$$

Let V be the sum of the volumes of the sphere and the parallelepiped. Then,

$$V = \frac{4}{3}\pi y^3 + x \times 2x \times \frac{x}{3}$$

$$\Rightarrow \quad V = \frac{4}{3}\pi y^3 + \frac{2}{3}x^3 = \frac{4}{3}\pi\left(\frac{S - 6x^2}{4\pi}\right)^{3/2} + \frac{2}{3}x^3 \quad \left[\because S = 6x^2 + 4\pi y^2 \Rightarrow y^2 = \frac{S - 6x^2}{4\pi}\right]$$

$$\Rightarrow \quad V = \frac{1}{6\sqrt{\pi}}(S - 6x^2)^{3/2} + \frac{2}{3}x^3$$

$$\Rightarrow \quad \frac{dV}{dx} = \frac{1}{6\sqrt{\pi}} \times \frac{3}{2}(S - 6x^2)^{1/2}(-12x) + \frac{2}{3} \times 3x^2 \Rightarrow \frac{dV}{dx} = -\frac{3}{\sqrt{\pi}}(S - 6x^2)^{1/2}x + 2x^2 \quad \text{...(ii)}$$

The critical numbers of V are given by $\frac{dV}{dx} = 0$.

Now,

$$\frac{dV}{dx}=0 \Rightarrow -\frac{3}{\sqrt{\pi}}(S-6x^2)^{1/2}x+2x^2=0 \Rightarrow \frac{3x}{\sqrt{\pi}}(S-6x^2)^{1/2}=2x^2$$

$\Rightarrow \quad \frac{3}{\sqrt{\pi}}(S-6x^2)^{1/2}=2x \Rightarrow 9(S-6x^2)=4\pi x^2$ [Squaring both sides]

$\Rightarrow \quad 9(4\pi y^2)=4\pi x^2 \Rightarrow 9y^2=x^2 \Rightarrow x=3y$ [Using (i)]

Putting $x=3y$ or, $y=\frac{x}{3}$ in (i), we obtain $S=6x^2+\frac{4\pi x^2}{9}$.

Differentiating (ii), we obtain: $\frac{d^2V}{dx^2}=-\frac{3}{\sqrt{\pi}}(S-6x^2)^{1/2}+\frac{18x^2}{\sqrt{\pi}\sqrt{S-6x^2}}+4x$

When $x=3y$ or, $y=\frac{x}{3}$, we obtain

$$\frac{d^2V}{dx^2}=\frac{-3}{\sqrt{\pi}}\left(\frac{4\pi x^2}{9}\right)^{1/2}+\frac{18x^2}{\sqrt{\pi}\left(\frac{2}{3}\sqrt{\pi}x\right)}+4x=-2x+\frac{27x}{\pi}+4x=\frac{27x}{\pi}+2x>0$$

So, V is minimum when $x=3y$. Putting $x=3y$ or, $y=\frac{x}{3}$ in $V=\frac{4}{3}\pi y^3+\frac{2}{3}x^3$, we obtain

$$V=\frac{4}{3}\pi\left(\frac{x}{3}\right)^3+\frac{2}{3}x^3=\frac{2}{3}x^3\left(1+\frac{2\pi}{27}\right)$$

Hence, the sum of the volume is minimum when $x=3y$ i.e. x is equal to three times the radius of the sphere and the maximum value of the sum of the volumes is $V=\frac{2}{3}x^3\left(1+\frac{2\pi}{27}\right)$.

EXAMPLE 22 *Show that the triangle of maximum area that can be inscribed in a given circle is an equilateral triangle.*

SOLUTION Let ABC be a triangle inscribed in a given circle with centre O and radius r. The area of the triangle will be maximum if its vertex A opposite to the base BC is at a maximum distance from the base BC. This is possible only when A lies on the diameter perpendicular to BC. Thus, $AD \perp BC$. So, triangle ABC must be an isosceles triangle. Let $OD=x$.

Applying Pythagoras theorem in right triangle ODB, we get

$$OB^2=OD^2+BD^2 \Rightarrow r^2=x^2+BD^2 \Rightarrow BD=\sqrt{r^2-x^2}$$

$\therefore \quad BC=2BD=2\sqrt{r^2-x^2}$

Also, $AD=AO+OD=r+x$. Let A denote the area of ΔABC. Then,

$$A=\frac{1}{2}(BC\times AD)$$

$\Rightarrow \quad A=\frac{1}{2}\times 2\sqrt{r^2-x^2}\times(r+x)$

$\Rightarrow \quad A=(r+x)\sqrt{r^2-x^2}$

$\Rightarrow \quad \frac{dA}{dx}=\sqrt{r^2-x^2}-\frac{x(r+x)}{\sqrt{r^2-x^2}}$ [Differentiating with respect to x]

$\Rightarrow \quad \frac{dA}{dx}=\frac{r^2-rx-2x^2}{\sqrt{r^2-x^2}}$

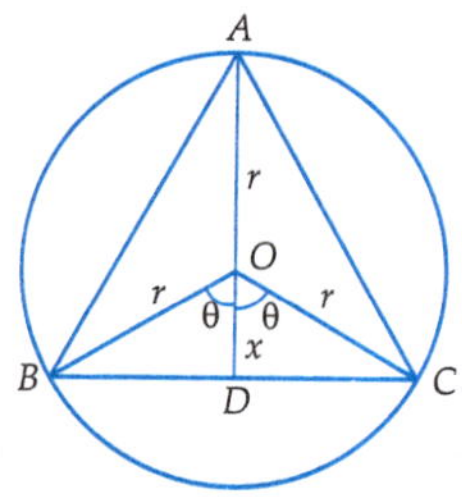

Fig. 14.40

The critical numbers of A are given by $\frac{dA}{dx}=0$.

$\therefore \quad \frac{dA}{dx} = 0 \Rightarrow \frac{r^2 - rx - 2x^2}{\sqrt{r^2 - x^2}} = 0 \Rightarrow (r - 2x)(r + x) = 0 \Rightarrow r - 2x = 0 \Rightarrow x = \frac{r}{2} \quad [\because r + x \neq 0]$

Now, $\frac{dA}{dx} = \frac{r^2 - rx - 2x^2}{\sqrt{r^2 - x^2}}$

$\Rightarrow \quad \frac{d^2 A}{dx^2} = \frac{(-r - 4x)}{\sqrt{r^2 - x^2}} + \frac{(r^2 - rx - 2x^2)\, x}{(r^2 - x^2)^{3/2}}$ [Differentiating both sides with respect to x]

$\Rightarrow \quad \left(\frac{d^2 A}{dx^2}\right)_{x = r/2} = -2\sqrt{3} < 0$

Thus, A is maximum when $x = \frac{r}{2}$. Therefore, $BD = \sqrt{r^2 - x^2} \Rightarrow BD = \frac{\sqrt{3}r}{2}$.

In $\Delta\, ODB$, we obtain

$$\tan\theta = \frac{BD}{OD} \Rightarrow \tan\theta = \frac{\sqrt{3}r/2}{r/2} = \sqrt{3} \Rightarrow \theta = 60° \Rightarrow \angle BAC = \theta = 60°$$

But, $AB = AC$. Therefore, $\angle B = \angle C = 60°$. Thus, we obtain $\angle A = \angle B = \angle C = 60°$.

Hence, A is maximum when $\Delta\, ABC$ is equilateral.

EXAMPLE 23 *A wire of length 36 m is to be cut into two pieces. One of the pieces is to be made into a square and the other into a circle. What should be the lengths of the two pieces, so that the combined area of the square and the circle is minimum?*

SOLUTION Let the length of a side of the square be x metres and the radius of the circle be y metres. It is given that the length of the wire is 36 m.

$\therefore \quad 4x + 2\pi y = 36 \Rightarrow 2x + \pi y = 18$ ...(i)

Let A be the combined area of the square and the circle. Then,

$A = x^2 + \pi y^2$ ...(ii)

$\Rightarrow \quad A = x^2 + \pi\left(\frac{18 - 2x}{\pi}\right)^2$ [Using (i)]

$\Rightarrow \quad A = x^2 + \frac{1}{\pi}(18 - 2x)^2$

$\Rightarrow \quad \frac{dA}{dx} = 2x + \frac{2}{\pi}(18 - 2x)(-2) = 2x - \frac{4}{\pi}(18 - 2x)$ and, $\frac{d^2A}{dx^2} = 2 - \frac{4}{\pi}(-2) = 2 + \frac{8}{\pi}$

The critical numbers of A are given by $\frac{dA}{dx} = 0$.

$\therefore \quad \frac{dA}{dx} = 0 \Rightarrow 2x - \frac{4}{\pi}(18 - 2x) = 0 \Rightarrow x = \frac{36}{\pi + 4}$

Clearly, $\left(\frac{d^2A}{dx^2}\right)_{x = 36/\pi + 4} = 2 + \frac{8}{\pi} > 0$. Thus, A is minimum when $x = \frac{36}{\pi + 4}$.

Putting $x = \frac{36}{\pi + 4}$ in (i), we obtain $y = \frac{18}{\pi + 4}$. So, lengths of the two pieces of wire are

$$4x = 4 \times \frac{36}{\pi + 4} = \frac{144}{\pi + 4} \text{ m and } 2\pi y = 2\pi \times \frac{18}{\pi + 4} = \frac{36\pi}{\pi + 4} \text{ m}$$

Hence, the combined area of the square and the circle is minimum when the lengths of two pieces are $\frac{144}{\pi+4}$ metres and $\frac{36\pi}{\pi+4}$ metres.

EXAMPLE 24 *A figure consists of a semi-circle with a rectangle on its diameter. Given the perimeter of the figure, find its dimensions in order that the area may be maximum.* **[CBSE 2002]**

SOLUTION Let $ABCD$ be a rectangle and let the semi-circle be described on side AB as diameter. Let $AB = 2x$ and $AD = 2y$. Let P be the perimeter and A be the area of the figure. Then,

$$P = 2x + 4y + \pi x \qquad \text{...(i)} \qquad \text{and,} \quad A = (2x)(2y) + \frac{\pi x^2}{2} \qquad \text{...(ii)}$$

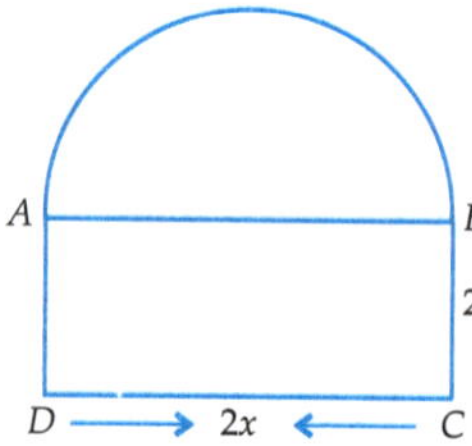

Fig. 14.41

Now $\quad A = 4xy + \frac{\pi x^2}{2}$

$\Rightarrow \quad A = x(P - 2x - \pi x) + \frac{\pi x^2}{2}$ [Using (i)]

$\Rightarrow \quad A = Px - 2x^2 - \pi x^2 + \frac{\pi x^2}{2}$

$\Rightarrow \quad A = Px - 2x^2 - \frac{\pi x^2}{2} \Rightarrow \frac{dA}{dx} = P - 4x - \pi x$ and $\frac{d^2A}{dx^2} = -4 - \pi$

The critical numbers of A are given by $\frac{dA}{dx} = 0$.

$\therefore \quad \frac{dA}{dx} = 0 \Rightarrow P - 4x - \pi x = 0 \Rightarrow x = \frac{P}{\pi + 4}$

Clearly, $\frac{d^2A}{dx^2} = -4 - \pi < 0$ for all values of x. Thus, A is maximum when $x = \frac{P}{\pi+4}$.

Putting $x = \frac{P}{\pi+4}$ in (i) we get $y = \frac{P}{2(\pi+4)}$. So, area of the figure is maximum when dimensions of the figure are: Length $= 2x = \frac{2P}{\pi+4}$ and Breadth $= 2y = \frac{P}{\pi+4}$.

EXAMPLE 25 *A square piece of tin of side 24 cm is to be made into a box without top by cutting a square from each corner and folding up the flaps to form a box. What should be the side of the square to be cut off so that the volume of the box is maximum? Also, find this maximum volume.*

SOLUTION Let x cm be the length of a side of the square which is cut-off from each corner of the plate. Then, dimensions of the box as shown in Fig. 14.42 are Length $= 24 - 2x$, Breadth $= 24 - 2x$ and height $= x$.

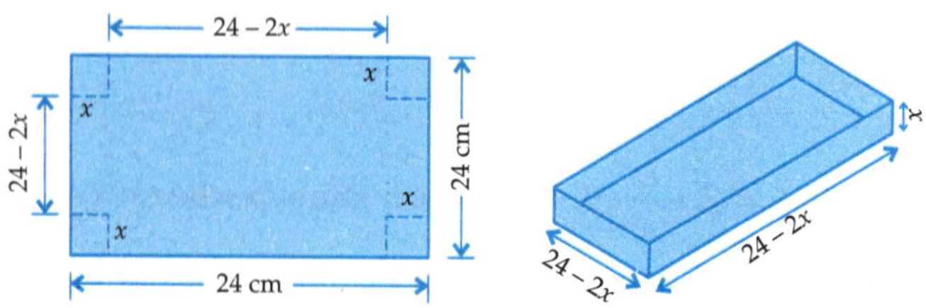

Fig. 14.42

Let V be the volume of the box. Then,

$$V = (24 - 2x)^2 x = 4x^3 - 96x^2 + 576x \Rightarrow \frac{dV}{dx} = 12x^2 - 192x + 576 \text{ and } \frac{d^2V}{dx^2} = 24x - 192$$

The critical numbers of V are given by $\frac{dV}{dx} = 0$.

$\therefore \quad \frac{dV}{dx} = 0 \Rightarrow 12x^2 - 192x + 576 = 0$

$\Rightarrow \quad x^2 - 16x + 48 = 0 \Rightarrow (x-12)(x-4) = 0 \Rightarrow x = 12, 4$

But, $x = 12$ is not possible. Therefore, $x = 4$.

Clearly, $\left(\frac{d^2V}{dx^2}\right)_{x=4} = 24 \times 4 - 192 < 0$. Thus, V is maximum when $x = 4$.

Hence, the volume of the box is maximum when the side of the square is 4 cm.

Putting $x = 4$ in $V = (24-2x)^2 x$, we obtain that the maximum volume of the box is given by $V = (24-8)^2 \times 4 = 1024 \text{ cm}^3$.

EXAMPLE 26 *A rectangular sheet of fix perimeter with sides having their lengths in the ratio 8 : 15 is converted into an open rectangular box by folding after removing squares of equal area from all four corners. If the total area of removed square is 100 square units, the resulting box has maximum volume. Find the length of the sides of the rectangular sheet.*

SOLUTION Let the sides of rectangular sheet be $8a$ and $15a$ units respectively. Let the length of each side of the squares of same size removed from each corner of the sheet be x units. Then, the dimensions of the open box, formed by folding up the flaps, are:

Length $= 15a - 2x$, breadth $= 8a - 2x$, height $= x$

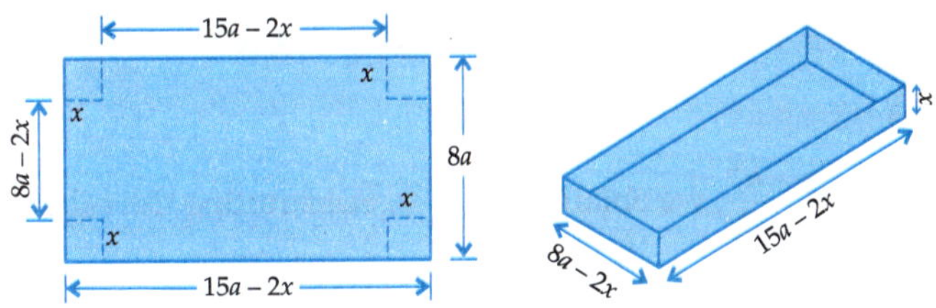

Fig. 14.43

Let V be the volume of the box formed. Then,

$$V = (15a - 2x)(8a - 2x)x$$

$\Rightarrow \quad V = 120a^2 x - 46ax^2 + 4x^3, \ \frac{dV}{dx} = 120a^2 - 92ax + 12x^2$ and $\frac{d^2V}{dx^2} = -92a + 24x$

The critical numbers of V are given by $\frac{dV}{dx} = 0$.

$\therefore \quad \frac{dV}{dx} = 0 \Rightarrow 120a^2 - 92ax + 12x^2 = 0$

$\Rightarrow \quad 30a^2 - 23ax + 3x^2 = 0 \Rightarrow (5a - 3x)(6a - x) = 0 \Rightarrow x = 6a, x = \frac{5a}{3}$

But, $x = 6a$ is not possible as for $x = 6a$ breadth $= 8a - 12a = -4a$, which is not possible.

So, $x = \frac{5a}{3}$. When $x = \frac{5a}{3}, \frac{d^2V}{dx^2} = -92a + 40a = -52a < 0$. Thus, V is maximum when $x = \frac{5a}{3}$.

It is given that total area of four squares removed from each corner of the sheet is 100 sq. units.

$\therefore \ 4x^2 = 100 \Rightarrow x^2 = 25 \Rightarrow \frac{25a^2}{9} = 25 \Rightarrow a^2 = 9 \Rightarrow a = 3$

Hence, the dimensions of the sheet are $15a = 45$ and $8a = 24$.

BASED ON LOTS

EXAMPLE 27 *Find the volume of the largest cylinder that can be inscribed in a sphere of radius r cm.* **[CBSE 2009, 2012]**

SOLUTION Let h be the height and R be the radius of the base of the inscribed cylinder. Let V be the volume of the cylinder. Then,

$$V = \pi R^2 h \qquad ...(i)$$

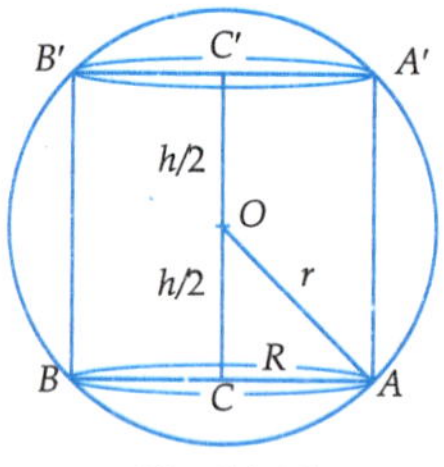

Fig. 14.44

Applying Pythagoras Theorem in ΔOCA, we get

$$\therefore \quad OA^2 = OC^2 + CA^2 \Rightarrow r^2 = \left(\frac{h}{2}\right)^2 + R^2 \Rightarrow R^2 = r^2 - \frac{h^2}{4}$$

Substituting the value of R^2 in (i), we get

$$V = \pi\left(r^2 - \frac{h^2}{4}\right)h$$

$$\Rightarrow \quad V = \pi r^2 h - \frac{\pi}{4}h^3, \ \frac{dV}{dh} = \pi r^2 - \frac{3\pi h^2}{4} \text{ and } \frac{d^2V}{dh^2} = -\frac{3\pi h}{2}$$

The critical numbers of V are given by $\frac{dV}{dh} = 0$.

$$\therefore \quad \frac{dV}{dh} = 0 \Rightarrow \pi r^2 - \frac{3\pi h^2}{4} = 0 \Rightarrow h^2 = \frac{4r^2}{3} \Rightarrow h = \frac{2}{\sqrt{3}}r$$

Clearly, $\left(\frac{d^2V}{dh^2}\right)_{h = \frac{2r}{\sqrt{3}}} = -\sqrt{3}\pi r < 0$. Thus, V is maximum when $h = \frac{2r}{\sqrt{3}}$.

Putting $h = \frac{2r}{\sqrt{3}}$ in $R^2 = r^2 - \frac{h^2}{4}$, we obtain $R = \sqrt{\frac{2}{3}}\,r$. Substituting the values of R^2 and h in (i), we find that the maximum volume of the cylinder is given by

$$V = \pi R^2 h = \pi\left(\frac{2}{3}r^2\right)\left(\frac{2r}{\sqrt{3}}\right) = \frac{4\pi r^3}{3\sqrt{3}}$$

EXAMPLE 28 *Show that a cylinder of a given volume which is open at the top, has minimum total surface area, provided its height is equal to the radius of its base.* **[CBSE 2011, 2014]**

SOLUTION Let r be the radius and h be the height of a cylinder of given volume V. Then,

$$V = \pi r^2 h \Rightarrow h = \frac{V}{\pi r^2} \qquad ...(i)$$

Let S be the total surface area of the cylinder which is open at the top. Then,

$$S = 2\pi rh + \pi r^2$$

$$\Rightarrow \quad S = 2\pi r \times \frac{V}{\pi r^2} + \pi r^2 \qquad \text{[Using (i)]}$$

$$\Rightarrow \quad S = \frac{2V}{r} + \pi r^2, \ \frac{dS}{dr} = -\frac{2V}{r^2} + 2\pi r \text{ and } \frac{d^2s}{dr^2} = \frac{4V}{r^3} + 2\pi$$

The critical numbers of S are given by $\frac{dS}{dr} = 0$.

$$\therefore \quad \frac{dS}{dr} = 0 \Rightarrow -\frac{2V}{r^2} + 2\pi r = 0 \Rightarrow V = \pi r^3 \Rightarrow \pi r^2 h = \pi r^3 \Rightarrow h = r \quad [\because V = \pi r^2 h]$$

Clearly, $\left(\frac{d^2S}{dr^2}\right)_{r=h} = \frac{4V}{h^3} + 2\pi > 0$. Hence, S is minimum when $h = r$ i.e., when the height of the cylinder is equal to the radius of the base.

EXAMPLE 29 *Show that the height of the closed cylinder of given surface and maximum volume, is equal to the diameter of its base.* **[NCERT, CBSE 2012]**

SOLUTION Let r be the radius of the base and h be the height of a closed cylinder of given surface area S. Then,

$$S = 2\pi r^2 + 2\pi rh \Rightarrow h = \frac{S - 2\pi r^2}{2\pi r} \quad \text{...(i)}$$

Let V be the volume of the cylinder. Then,

$$V = \pi r^2 h$$

$$\Rightarrow \quad V = \pi r^2 \left(\frac{S - 2\pi r^2}{2\pi r}\right) \quad \text{[Using (i)]}$$

$$\Rightarrow \quad V = \frac{rS - 2\pi r^3}{2} = \frac{rS}{2} - \pi r^3, \ \frac{dV}{dr} = \frac{S}{2} - 3\pi r^2 \text{ and } \frac{d^2V}{dr^2} = -6\pi r$$

The critical numbers of V are given by $\frac{dV}{dr} = 0$.

Now, $\frac{dV}{dr} = 0 \Rightarrow \frac{S}{2} - 3\pi r^2 = 0 \Rightarrow S = 6\pi r^2 \Rightarrow 2\pi r^2 + 2\pi rh = 6\pi r^2 \Rightarrow h = 2r$.

Clearly, $\frac{d^2V}{dr^2} = -6\pi r < 0$ for all r. Hence, V is maximum when $h = 2r$ i.e., when the height of the cylinder is equal to the diameter of the base.

EXAMPLE 30 *Show that the height of a cylinder, which is open at the top, having a given surface area and greatest volume, is equal to the radius of its base.* **[CBSE 2004, 2010]**

SOLUTION Let r be the radius and h be the height of a cylinder of given surface S. Then,

$$S = \pi r^2 + 2\pi rh \Rightarrow h = \frac{S - \pi r^2}{2\pi r} \quad \text{...(i)}$$

Let V be the volume of the cylinder. Then,

$$V = \pi r^2 h$$

$$\Rightarrow \quad V = \pi r^2 \left(\frac{S - \pi r^2}{2\pi r}\right) \quad \text{[Using (i)]}$$

$$\Rightarrow \quad V = \frac{Sr - \pi r^3}{2} = \frac{Sr}{2} - \frac{\pi r^3}{2} \Rightarrow \frac{dV}{dr} = \frac{S}{2} - \frac{3}{2}\pi r^2 \text{ and } \frac{d^2V}{dr^2} = -3\pi r$$

The critical numbers of V are given by $\frac{dV}{dr} = 0$.

$$\therefore \quad \frac{dV}{dr} = 0 \Rightarrow \frac{S}{2} - \frac{3}{2}\pi r^2 = 0 \Rightarrow S = 3\pi r^2 \Rightarrow \pi r^2 + 2\pi rh = 3\pi r^2 \Rightarrow r = h.$$

Clearly, $\frac{d^2V}{dr^2} = -3\pi r < 0$. Hence, V is maximum when $r = h$ i.e., when the height of the cylinder is equal to the radius of its base.

EXAMPLE 31 *Show that the height of the cylinder of maximum volume that can be inscribed in a sphere of radius a is $\frac{2a}{\sqrt{3}}$.* **[NCERT, CBSE 2001, 2012, 2013, 2014]**

SOLUTION Let r be the radius of the base and h be the height of the cylinder $ABCD$ which is inscribed in a sphere of radius a. It is obvious that for maximum volume the axis of the cylinder must be along the diameter of the sphere. Let O be the centre of the sphere such that $OL = x$. By symmetry, O is the mid-points of LM. Applying Pythagoras Theorem in ΔALO, we get

$$OA^2 = OL^2 + AL^2 \Rightarrow a^2 = x^2 + AL^2 \Rightarrow AL = \sqrt{a^2 - x^2}$$

Let V be the volume of the cylinder. Then,

$$V = \pi (AL)^2 \times LM$$

$$\Rightarrow \quad V = \pi (AL)^2 \times 2(OL) = \pi (a^2 - x^2) \times 2x = 2\pi (a^2 x - x^3)$$

$$\Rightarrow \quad \frac{dV}{dx} = 2\pi (a^2 - 3x^2) \text{ and } \frac{d^2 V}{dx^2} = -12\pi x$$

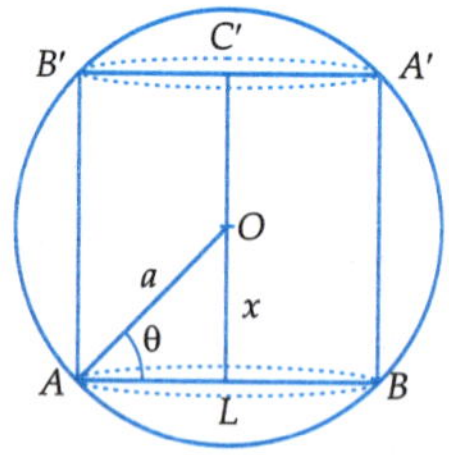

Fig. 14.45

The critical numbers of V are given by $\frac{dV}{dx} = 0$.

$$\therefore \quad \frac{dV}{dx} = 0 \Rightarrow 2\pi (a^2 - 3x^2) = 0 \Rightarrow x = \frac{a}{\sqrt{3}}$$

Clearly, $\left(\frac{d^2 V}{dx^2}\right)_{x = a/\sqrt{3}} = -12\pi \times \frac{a}{\sqrt{3}} < 0$. Hence, V is maximum when $x = \frac{a}{\sqrt{3}}$ and hence $LM = 2x = \frac{2a}{\sqrt{3}}$. In otherwords, the height of the cyclic of maximum volume is $2a/\sqrt{3}$.

EXAMPLE 32 *Show that the semi-vertical angle of a cone of maximum volume and given slant height is* $\tan^{-1}\sqrt{2}$ *or* $\cos^{-1}\frac{1}{\sqrt{3}}$. **[NCERT, CBSE 2011, 2014]**

SOLUTION Let α be the semi-vertical angle of a cone VAB of given slant height l.

In $\Delta\, AOV$,

$$\cos\alpha = \frac{VO}{VA} \text{ and } \sin\alpha = \frac{OA}{VA} \Rightarrow \cos\alpha = \frac{VO}{l} \text{ and } \sin\alpha = \frac{OA}{l} \Rightarrow VO = l\cos\alpha, OA = l\sin\alpha$$

Let V be the volume of the cone. Then,

$$V = \frac{1}{3}\pi (OA)^2 (VO)$$

$$\Rightarrow \quad V = \frac{1}{3}\pi (l \sin\alpha)^2 (l\cos\alpha)$$

$$\Rightarrow \quad V = \frac{1}{3}\pi l^3 \sin^2\alpha\cos\alpha \Rightarrow \frac{dV}{d\alpha} = \frac{\pi}{3} l^3 \left(-\sin^3\alpha + 2\sin\alpha\cos^2\alpha\right)$$

$$\Rightarrow \quad \frac{dV}{d\alpha} = \frac{\pi l^3}{3}\sin\alpha\left(-\sin^2\alpha + 2\cos^2\alpha\right) \quad \text{...(i)}$$

The critical points of V are given by $\frac{dV}{d\alpha} = 0$.

$$\therefore \quad \frac{dV}{d\alpha} = 0$$

$$\Rightarrow \quad \frac{\pi l^3}{3}\sin\alpha\left(-\sin^2\alpha + 2\cos^2\alpha\right) = 0$$

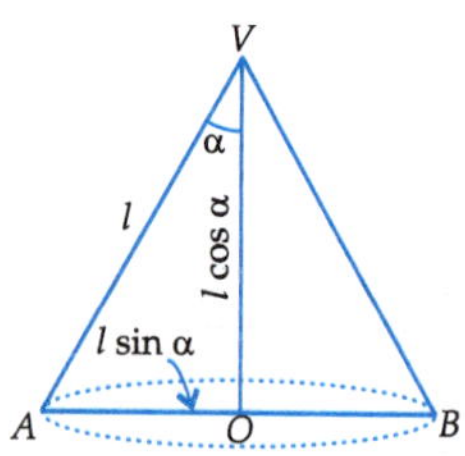

Fig. 14.46

$$\Rightarrow \quad 2\cos^2\alpha = \sin^2\alpha \Rightarrow \tan^2\alpha = 2 \Rightarrow \tan\alpha = \sqrt{2} \qquad [\because \alpha \text{ is acute} \therefore \sin\alpha \neq 0]$$

$$\therefore \quad \cos\alpha = \frac{1}{\sqrt{1+\tan^2\alpha}} = \frac{1}{\sqrt{3}} \qquad [\because \tan\alpha = \sqrt{2}]$$

Differentiating (i) with respect to α, we get

$$\frac{d^2V}{d\alpha^2} = \frac{\pi l^3}{3}(-3\sin^2\alpha\cos\alpha + 2\cos^3\alpha - 4\sin^2\alpha\cos\alpha) = \frac{\pi l^3}{3}\cos^3\alpha\,(2-7\tan^2\alpha)$$

$$\therefore \quad \left(\frac{d^2V}{d\alpha^2}\right)_{\tan\alpha=\sqrt{2}} = \frac{1}{3}\pi l^3\left(\frac{1}{\sqrt{3}}\right)^3(2-7\times 2) = \frac{-4\pi l^3}{3\sqrt{3}} < 0.$$

Thus, V is maximum, when $\tan\alpha = \sqrt{2}$ or, $\alpha = \tan^{-1}\sqrt{2}$ i.e. when the semi-vertical angle of the cone is $\tan^{-1}\sqrt{2}$.

EXAMPLE 33 *Show that the semi-vertical angle of a right circular cone of given surface area and maximum volume is* $\sin^{-1}\left(\frac{1}{3}\right)$. **[NCERT]**

SOLUTION Let r be radius, l be the slant height and h be the height of the cone VAB of given surface area S. Then,

$$S = \pi r^2 + \pi r l \Rightarrow l = \frac{S-\pi r^2}{\pi r} \qquad \text{...(i)}$$

Let V be the volume of the cone. Then,

$$V = \frac{1}{3}\pi r^2 h$$

$$\Rightarrow \quad V^2 = \frac{1}{9}\pi^2 r^4 h^2 = \frac{1}{9}\pi^2 r^4 (l^2 - r^2) \qquad [\because l^2 = r^2 + h^2]$$

$$\Rightarrow \quad V^2 = \frac{\pi^2}{9} r^4 \left\{\left(\frac{S-\pi r^2}{\pi r}\right)^2 - r^2\right\} \qquad \text{[Using (i)]}$$

$$\Rightarrow \quad V^2 = \frac{\pi^2 r^4}{9}\left\{\frac{(S-\pi r^2)^2 - \pi^2 r^4}{\pi^2 r^2}\right\} = \frac{1}{9}S(Sr^2 - 2\pi r^4)$$

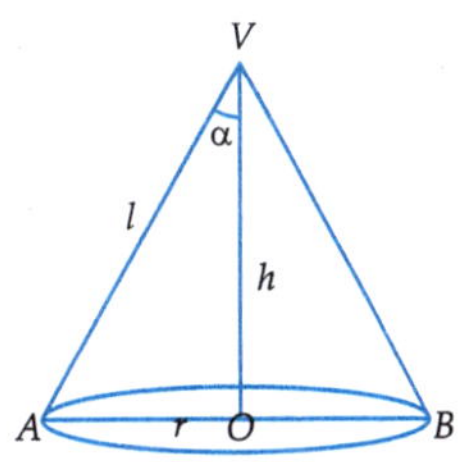

Fig. 14.47

Let $Z = V^2$. Then, V is maximum or minimum according as Z is maximum or minimum.

Now, $Z = \frac{1}{9}S(Sr^2 - 2\pi r^4) \Rightarrow \frac{dZ}{dr} = \frac{1}{9}S(2Sr - 8\pi r^3)$ and $\frac{d^2Z}{dr^2} = \frac{S}{9}(2S - 24\pi r^2)$

The critical numbers of Z are given by $\frac{dZ}{dr} = 0$.

$$\text{Now, } \frac{dZ}{dr} = 0 \Rightarrow 2Sr - 8\pi r^3 = 0 \Rightarrow S = 4\pi r^2 \Rightarrow r^2 = \frac{S}{4\pi} \qquad \text{...(iii)}$$

Clearly, $\left(\frac{d^2Z}{dr^2}\right)_{r^2=\frac{S}{4\pi}} = \frac{S}{9}\left(2S - 24\pi \times \frac{S}{4\pi}\right) = -\frac{4S^2}{9} < 0$. Thus, Z is maximum when $r^2 = \frac{S}{4\pi}$

i.e. $S = 4\pi r^2$. Hence, V is maximum when $S = 4\pi r^2$.

Now, $S = 4\pi r^2 \Rightarrow \pi rl + \pi r^2 = 4\pi r^2 \Rightarrow l = 3r.$

$\therefore \quad \sin\alpha = \frac{r}{l} = \frac{r}{3r} = \frac{1}{3}$. Hence, V is maximum when $\alpha = \sin^{-1}\left(\frac{1}{3}\right)$.

EXAMPLE 34 *Show that the volume of the largest cone that can be inscribed in a sphere of radius R is 8/27 of the volume of the sphere.* **[NCERT, CBSE 2008, 2010 C, 2012, 2013, 2014, 2016]**

SOLUTION Let VAB be a cone of greatest volume inscribed in a sphere of radius R. It is obvious that for maximum volume the axis of the cone must be along a diameter of the sphere. Let VC be the axis of the cone and O be the centre of the sphere such that $OC = x$. Then,

$$VC = VO + OC = R + x = \text{height of the cone.}$$

Applying Pythagoras Theorem in ΔACO, we get

$$OA^2 = AC^2 + OC^2 \Rightarrow AC^2 = OA^2 - OC^2 = R^2 - x^2$$

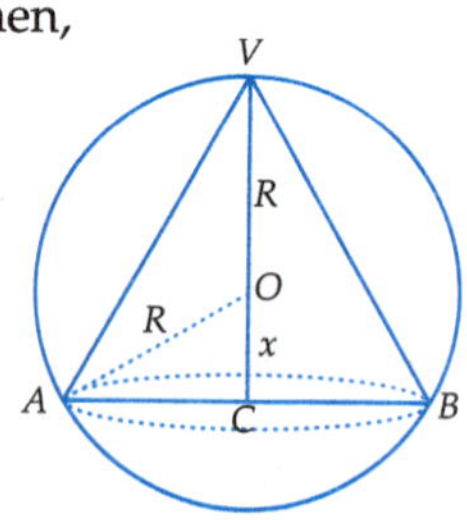

Fig. 14.48

Let V be the volume of the cone. Then,

$$V = \frac{1}{3}\pi (AC)^2 (VC)$$

$$\Rightarrow \quad V = \frac{1}{3}\pi (R^2 - x^2)(R + x) \quad \ldots(i)$$

$$\Rightarrow \quad \frac{dV}{dx} = \frac{1}{3}\pi \left\{R^2 - x^2 - 2x(R + x)\right\}$$

$$\Rightarrow \quad \frac{dV}{dx} = \frac{1}{3}\pi (R^2 - 2Rx - 3x^2) \text{ and } \frac{d^2V}{dx^2} = \frac{1}{3}\pi(-2R - 6x)$$

The critical numbers of V are given by $\frac{dV}{dx} = 0$.

$$\therefore \quad \frac{dV}{dx} = 0$$

$$\Rightarrow \quad R^2 - 2Rx - 3x^2 = 0 \Rightarrow (R - 3x)(R + x) = 0 \Rightarrow R - 3x = 0 \Rightarrow x = \frac{R}{3} \quad [\because R + x \neq 0]$$

Clearly, $\left(\frac{d^2V}{dx^2}\right)_{x = R/3} = -\frac{4}{3}R\pi < 0$. Thus, V is maximum when $x = \frac{R}{3}$.

Putting $x = \frac{R}{3}$ in (i), we obtain

$$V = \text{Maximum volume of the cone} = \frac{1}{3}\pi\left(R^2 - \frac{R^2}{9}\right)\left(R + \frac{R}{3}\right) = \frac{32\pi R^3}{81}$$

$$= \frac{8}{27}\left(\frac{4}{3}\pi R^3\right) = \frac{8}{27}\text{(Volume of the sphere)}.$$

EXAMPLE 35 *Prove that the radius of the right circular cylinder of greatest curved surface which can be inscribed in a given cone is half of that of the cone.* **[CBSE 2010 C, 2012, 2013, 2020]**

SOLUTION Let VAB be the cone of base radius $r = 0A$ and height $h = VO$. Let a cylinder of base radius $OC = x$ and height $= OO'$ be inscribed in the cone. Clearly, $\Delta VOB \sim \Delta B'DB$.

$$\therefore \quad \frac{VO}{B'D} = \frac{OB}{DB} \Rightarrow \frac{h}{B'D} = \frac{r}{r - x} \Rightarrow B'D = \frac{h(r - x)}{r}$$

Let S be the curved surface area of the cylinder. Then,

$$S = 2\pi (OC)(B'D)$$

$$\Rightarrow \quad S = 2\pi x \frac{h(r-x)}{r} = \frac{2\pi h}{r}(rx - x^2)$$

$$\Rightarrow \quad \frac{dS}{dx} = \frac{2\pi h}{r}(r-2x) \text{ and } \frac{d^2 S}{dx^2} = -\frac{4\pi h}{r}$$

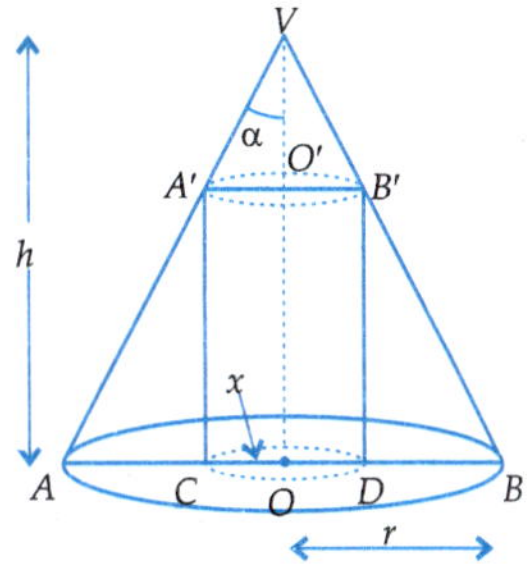

Fig. 14.49

The critical numbers of S are given by $\frac{dS}{dx} = 0$.

$$\therefore \quad \frac{dS}{dx} = 0 \Rightarrow \frac{2\pi h}{r}(r - 2x) = 0 \Rightarrow x = \frac{r}{2}$$

Clearly, $\frac{d^2 S}{dx^2} = \frac{-4\pi h}{r} < 0$ for all x. Hence, S is maximum when $x = \frac{r}{2}$ i.e. radius of the cylinder is half of the radius of the cone.

EXAMPLE 36 *Show that the volume of the greatest cylinder which can be inscribed in a cone of height h and semi-vertical angle α is $\frac{4}{27}\pi h^3 \tan^2 \alpha$. Also, show that height of the cylinder is $\frac{h}{3}$.*

[NCERT, CBSE 2001C, 2007, 2008, 2010, 2017, 2020]

SOLUTION Let VAB be a given cone of height h, semi-vertical angle α and let x be the radius of the base of the cylinder $A'B'DC$ which is inscribed in the cone VAB.

In $\Delta VO'A'$

$$\tan\alpha = \frac{O'A'}{VO'} = \frac{x}{VO'} \Rightarrow VO' = x\cot\alpha \Rightarrow OO' = VO - VO' = h - x\cot\alpha \qquad \text{...(i)}$$

Let V be the volume of the cylinder. Then,

$$V = \pi (O'B')^2 (OO')$$

$$\Rightarrow \quad V = \pi x^2 (h - x\cot\alpha) \qquad \text{...(ii)}$$

$$\Rightarrow \quad \frac{dV}{dx} = 2\pi xh - 3\pi x^2 \cot\alpha \text{ and } \frac{d^2V}{dx^2} = 2\pi h - 6\pi x\cot\alpha$$

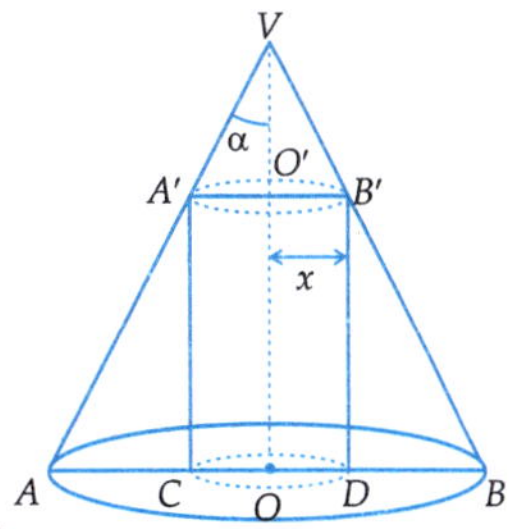

Fig. 14.50

The critical numbers of V are given by $\frac{dV}{dx} = 0$.

$$\therefore \quad \frac{dV}{dx} = 0 \Rightarrow 2\pi xh - 3\pi x^2 \cot\alpha = 0 \Rightarrow x = \frac{2h}{3}\tan\alpha \quad [\because x \neq 0]$$

Clearly, $\left(\frac{d^2V}{dx^2}\right)_{x=\frac{2h}{3}\tan\alpha} = \pi(2h - 4h) = -2\pi h < 0$. Hence, V is maximum when $x = \frac{2h}{3}\tan\alpha$.

Putting $x = \frac{2h}{3}\tan\alpha$ in (ii), the maximum volume of the cylinder is given by

$$V = \pi\left(\frac{2h}{3}\tan\alpha\right)^2\left(h - \frac{2h}{3}\right) = \frac{4}{27}\pi h^3 \tan^2\alpha.$$

Putting $x = \frac{2h}{3}\tan\alpha$ in (i), we get: $OO' = h - x\cot\alpha = h - \frac{2h}{3} = \frac{h}{3}$.

Hence, height of the cylinder $= OO' = \frac{h}{3}$.

BASED ON HIGHER ORDER THINKING SKILLS (HOTS)

EXAMPLE 37 *Let AP and BQ be two vertical poles at points A and B respectively. If $AP = 16$ m, $BQ = 22$ m and $AB = 20$ m, then find the distance of a point R on AB from the point A such that $RP^2 + RQ^2$ is minimum.* **[NCERT, CBSE 2010]**

SOLUTION Let R be a point on AB such that $AR = x$ m. Then, $RB = (20 - x)$ m.
Applying Pythagoras Theorem in Δ's RAP and RBQ, we get

$$PR^2 = x^2 + 16^2 \quad \text{...(i)}$$

and, $$RQ^2 = 22^2 + (20 - x)^2 \quad \text{...(ii)}$$

$\therefore$ $$PR^2 + RQ^2 = x^2 + 16^2 + 22^2 + (20 - x)^2 = 2x^2 - 40x + 1140$$

Let $Z = RP^2 + RQ^2$. Then,

$$Z = 2x^2 - 40x + 1140 \Rightarrow \frac{dZ}{dx} = 4x - 40 \text{ and } \frac{d^2Z}{dx^2} = 4$$

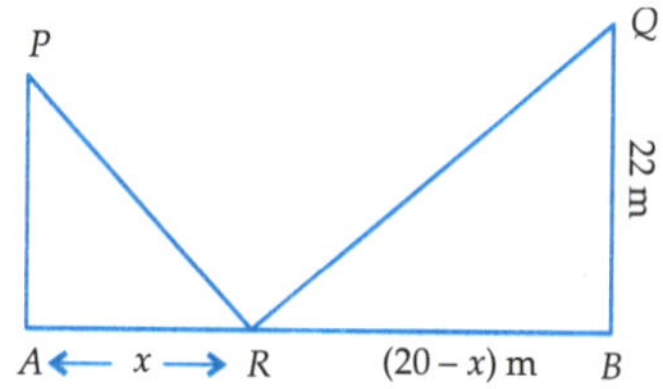

Fig. 14.51

The critical numbers of Z are given by $\frac{dZ}{dx} = 0$.

$$\therefore \quad \frac{dZ}{dx} = 0 \Rightarrow 4x - 40 = 0 \Rightarrow x = 10$$

Clearly, $\frac{d^2Z}{dx^2} = 4 > 0$ for all x. So, Z is minimum when $x = 10$. Thus, $RP^2 + RQ^2$ is minimum when, the distance of R from A is 10 m.

EXAMPLE 38 *If the length of three sides of a trapezium other than base are equal to 10 cm, then find the area of trapezium when it is maximum.* **[NCERT, CBSE 2010, 2013]**

SOLUTION Let $ABCD$ be the given trapezium such that $AD = DC = BC = 10$ cm. Draw DP and CQ perpendiculars from D and C respectively on AB. Clearly, $\Delta APD \cong \Delta BQC$. Let $AP = x$ cm. Then, $BQ = x$ cm.

Applying Pythagoras Theorem in ΔAPD and ΔBQC, we obtain: $DP = QC = \sqrt{100 - x^2}$.

Let A be the area of trapezium $ABCD$. Then,

$$A = \frac{1}{2}(AB + CD) \times DP$$

$$\Rightarrow \quad A = \frac{1}{2}(10 + 10 + 2x) \times \sqrt{100 - x^2}$$

$$\Rightarrow \quad A = (10 + x)\sqrt{100 - x^2} \quad \text{...(i)}$$

$$\Rightarrow \quad \frac{dA}{dx} = \sqrt{100 - x^2} - \frac{x(10 + x)}{\sqrt{100 - x^2}} = \frac{100 - 10x - 2x^2}{\sqrt{100 - x^2}}$$

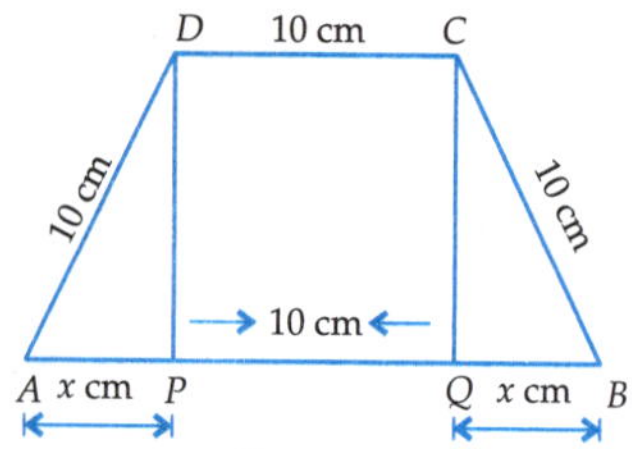

Fig. 14.52

The critical numbers of A are given by $\frac{dA}{dx} = 0$.

$$\therefore \quad \frac{dA}{dx} = 0 \Rightarrow \frac{100 - 10x - 2x^2}{\sqrt{100 - x^2}} = 0$$

$$\Rightarrow 100 - 10x - 2x^2 = 0 \Rightarrow x^2 + 5x - 50 = 0 \Rightarrow (x + 10)(x - 5) = 0 \Rightarrow x = 5 \quad [\because x > 0 \therefore x + 10 \neq 0]$$

Now, $\dfrac{dA}{dx} = \dfrac{100 - 10x - 2x^2}{\sqrt{100 - x^2}}$

$$\Rightarrow \quad \frac{d^2A}{dx^2} = \frac{\sqrt{100 - x^2}\,(-10 - 4x) + \dfrac{(100 - 10x - 2x^2)\,x}{\sqrt{100 - x^2}}}{100 - x^2} = \frac{2x^3 - 300x - 1000}{(100 - x^2)^{3/2}}$$

$$\Rightarrow \quad \left(\frac{d^2A}{dx^2}\right)_{x=5} = \frac{-30}{\sqrt{75}} < 0$$

Thus, the area of the trapezium is maximum when $x = 5$. Putting $x = 5$ in (i), the maximum area is given by

$$A = \frac{1}{2}\,(10 + 5)\,\sqrt{100 - 25} = \frac{75\sqrt{3}}{2}\ \text{cm}^2.$$

EXAMPLE 39 *A telephone company in a town has 500 subscribers on its list and collects fixed charges of ₹ 300 per subscriber. The company proposes to increase the annual subscription and it is believed that every increase of ₹ 1 one subscriber will discontinue the service. Find what increase will bring maximum revenue?* **[NCERT EXEMPLAR]**

SOLUTION Let the increase of ₹ x in annual subscription of ₹ 300 maximize the profit of the company. Due to this increase of ₹ x, x subscribers will discontinue the service. Therefore,

Number of subscriber using the service $= 500 - x$

Annual subscription of each subscriber $=$ ₹ $(300 + x)$

Let R be the total annual revenue of the company. Then,

$$R = (500 - x)\,(300 + x) \Rightarrow R = 150000 + 200x - x^2 \Rightarrow \frac{dR}{dx} = 200 - 2x \text{ and } \frac{d^2R}{dx^2} = -2$$

The stationary values of R are given by $\dfrac{dR}{dx} = 0$.

$$\therefore \quad \frac{dR}{dx} = 0 \Rightarrow 200 - 2x = 0 \Rightarrow x = 100$$

Clearly, $\dfrac{d^2R}{dx^2} = -2 < 0$ for all x. So, R is maximum when $x = 100$.

Thus, the total revenue received will be maximum if annual subscription is increased by ₹100.

EXAMPLE 40 *Find the point on the curve $y^2 = 4x$ which is nearest to the point* $(2, 1)$.

SOLUTION Let $P(x, y)$ be a point on $y^2 = 4x$ and $A(2, 1)$ be the given point. Then,

$$AP^2 = (x - 2)^2 + (y - 1)^2 \Rightarrow AP^2 = \left(\frac{y^2}{4} - 2\right)^2 + (y - 1)^2 \qquad \left[\because y^2 = 4x \ \therefore\ x = y^2/4\right]$$

Let $Z = AP^2$. Then, Z is maximum or minimum according as AP is maximum or minimum.

$$\text{Now,} \quad Z = \left(\frac{y^2}{4} - 2\right)^2 + (y - 1)^2 \Rightarrow \frac{dZ}{dy} = 2\left(\frac{y^2}{4} - 2\right)\left(\frac{2y}{4}\right) + 2\,(y - 1) = \frac{y^3}{4} - 2 \text{ and, } \frac{d^2Z}{dy^2} = \frac{3y^2}{4}$$

The critical numbers of Z are given by $\dfrac{dZ}{dy} = 0$.

$\therefore \quad \frac{dZ}{dy} = 0 \Rightarrow \frac{y^3}{4} - 2 = 0 \Rightarrow y^3 = 8 \Rightarrow y = 2$

Clearly, $\left(\frac{d^2Z}{dy^2}\right)_{y=2} = \frac{3(2)^2}{4} = 3 > 0$. Thus, Z is minimum when $y = 2$.

Putting $y = 2$ in $y^2 = 4x$, we obtain $x = 1$. So, the coordinates of P are (1, 2). Hence, the point (1, 2) on $y^2 = 4x$ is nearest to the point (2, 1).

EXAMPLE 41 *A jet of an enemy is flying along the curve $y = x^2 + 2$. A soldier is placed at the point (3, 2). What is the shortest distance between the soldier and the jet?*

SOLUTION Let $P(x, y)$ be the position of jet and the soldier is placed at A (3, 2). Then, the distance between the soldier and jet is given by

$$AP = \sqrt{(x-3)^2 + (y-2)^2} = \sqrt{(x-3)^2 + x^4} \qquad [\because y = x^2 + 2]$$

Let $\quad Z = AP^2$. Then, $Z = (x-3)^2 + x^4$

Clearly AP is maximum or minimum according as Z is maximum or minimum.

Now, $\quad Z = (x-3)^2 + x^4 \Rightarrow \frac{dZ}{dx} = 2(x-3) + 4x^3$ and $\frac{d^2Z}{dx^2} = 12x^2 + 2$

The critical numbers of Z are given by $\frac{dZ}{dx} = 0$.

$\therefore \quad \frac{dZ}{dx} = 0 \Rightarrow 2(x-3) + 4x^3 = 0 \Rightarrow 2x^3 + x - 3 = 0$

$\Rightarrow \quad (x-1)(2x^2 + 2x + 3) = 0 \Rightarrow x = 1 \qquad [\because 2x^2 + 2x + 3 = 0$ gives imaginary values of $x]$

Clearly, $\left(\frac{d^2Z}{dx^2}\right)_{x=1} = 12 + 2 = 14 > 0$. Thus, Z is minimum when $x = 1$. Putting $x = 1$ in $y = x^2 + 2$, we obtain $y = 3$. So, the coordinates of P are (1, 3). Hence, AP is minimum when jet is at the point (1, 3) on the curve.

Putting $x = 1$ and $y = 3$ in $AP = \sqrt{(x-3)^2 + (y-2)^2}$, we obtain: $AP = \sqrt{(1-3)^2 + 1^2} = \sqrt{5}$.

Hence, the shortest distance $= \sqrt{5}$.

EXAMPLE 42 *Find the shortest distance between the line $y - x = 1$ and the curve $x = y^2$.*

SOLUTION Let $P(t^2, t)$ be any point on the curve $x = y^2$. The distance S of P from the given line is

$$S = \left|\frac{t - t^2 - 1}{\sqrt{2}}\right| = \left|\frac{t^2 - t + 1}{\sqrt{2}}\right| = \frac{t^2 - t + 1}{\sqrt{2}} \qquad [\because t^2 - t + 1 > 0 \text{ for all } t \in R]$$

$\Rightarrow \quad \frac{dS}{dt} = \frac{2t - 1}{\sqrt{2}}$ and $\frac{d^2S}{dt^2} = \frac{2}{\sqrt{2}} = \sqrt{2}$

The critical numbers of S are given by $\frac{dS}{dt} = 0$.

$\therefore \quad \frac{dS}{dt} = 0 \Rightarrow 2t - 1 = 0 \Rightarrow t = \frac{1}{2}$

Clearly, $\frac{d^2S}{dt^2} = \sqrt{2} > 0$ for all t. So, S is minimum when $t = \frac{1}{2}$.

Putting $t = \frac{1}{2}$ in $S = \frac{t^2 - t + 1}{\sqrt{2}}$, the minimum value of S is $S = \frac{\left(\frac{1}{2}\right)^2 - \frac{1}{2} + 1}{\sqrt{2}} = \frac{3\sqrt{2}}{8}$.

EXAMPLE 43 *Find the shortest distance of the point* $(0, c)$ *from the parabola* $y = x^2$, *where* $0 \le c \le 5$. **[NCERT]**

SOLUTION Let $P(x, y)$ be any point on the parabola and $Q(0, c)$ be the given point. Then,

$$PQ^2 = x^2 + (y - c)^2 = x^2 + (x^2 - c)^2 \qquad [\because y = x^2]$$

$$\Rightarrow \quad PQ^2 = x^4 - x^2(2c - 1) + c^2$$

Clearly, PQ will be minimum when PQ^2 is minimum. Let $Z = PQ^2$. Then,

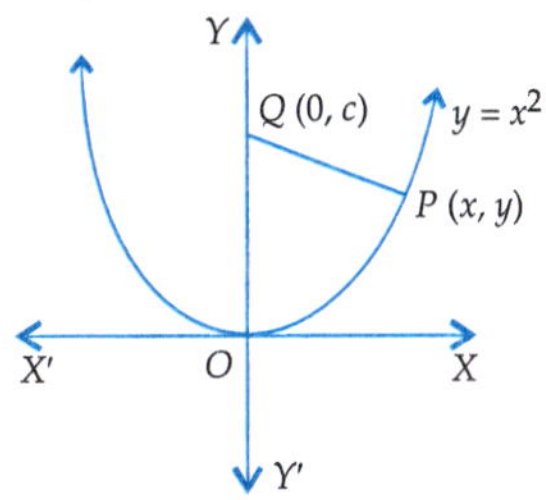

Fig. 14.53

$$Z = x^4 - x^2(2c - 1) + c^2$$

$$\Rightarrow \quad \frac{dZ}{dx} = 4x^3 - 2x(2c - 1) \text{ and } \frac{d^2Z}{dx^2} = 12x^2 - 2(2c - 1)$$

The critical numbers of Z are given by $\frac{dZ}{dx} = 0$.

$$\therefore \quad \frac{dZ}{dx} = 0$$

$$\Rightarrow \quad 4x^3 - 2x(2c - 1) = 0$$

$$\Rightarrow \quad 2x\{2x^2 - (2c - 1)\} = 0 \Rightarrow x = 0, x = \pm\sqrt{\frac{2c - 1}{2}} \Rightarrow x = 0, x = \pm\alpha, \text{ where } \alpha = \sqrt{\frac{2c - 1}{2}}$$

Clearly, $\left(\frac{d^2Z}{dx^2}\right)_{x = \pm\alpha} = 12\alpha^2 - 4\alpha^2 = 8\alpha^2 > 0$. So, Z is minimum at $x = \pm\alpha$.

Hence, PQ is minimum at $x = \pm\alpha$. Putting $x = \pm\alpha$ in $PQ^2 = x^2 + (x^2 - c)^2$, the minimum value of PQ is given by

$$PQ^2 = \alpha^2 + (\alpha^2 - c)^2 = \frac{2c - 1}{2} + \left(\frac{2c - 1}{2} - c\right)^2 = \frac{2c - 1}{2} + \frac{1}{4} = \frac{4c - 1}{4} \Rightarrow PQ = \frac{\sqrt{4c - 1}}{2}$$

Hence, the minimum distance is $\frac{\sqrt{4c - 1}}{2}$.

EXAMPLE 44 *Find the area of the greatest isosceles triangle that can be inscribed in a given ellipse having its vertex coincident with one end of the major axis.* **[NCERT, CBSE 2010]**

SOLUTION Let the equation of the ellipse be $\frac{x^2}{a^2} + \frac{y^2}{b^2} = 1$. Let APQ be an isosceles triangle having one vertex at $A(a, 0)$. Let the coordinates of P be $(a\cos\theta, b\sin\theta)$. Then the coordinates of Q are $(a\cos\theta, -b\sin\theta)$. Let A be the area of ΔAPQ. Then,

$$A = \frac{1}{2}(PQ)(AM) = \frac{1}{2}(2b\sin\theta)(a - a\cos\theta) = ab(\sin\theta - \sin\theta\cos\theta)$$

$$\Rightarrow \quad \frac{dA}{d\theta} = ab\,(\cos\theta - \cos^2\theta + \sin^2\theta)$$

$$\Rightarrow \quad \frac{dA}{d\theta} = ab\,(\cos\theta - \cos 2\theta)$$

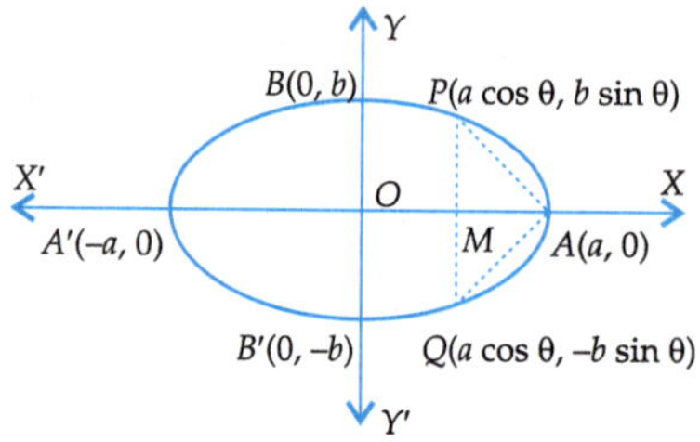

Fig. 14.54

The critical numbers of A are given by $\frac{dA}{d\theta} = 0$.

$$\therefore \quad \frac{dA}{d\theta} = 0$$

$$\Rightarrow \quad ab\,(\cos\theta - \cos 2\theta) = 0 \Rightarrow \cos\theta = \cos 2\theta \Rightarrow \theta = 2\pi - 2\theta \Rightarrow \theta = \frac{2\pi}{3}$$

Now, $\frac{dA}{d\theta} = ab\,(\cos\theta - \cos 2\theta) \Rightarrow \frac{d^2A}{d\theta^2} = ab\,(-\sin\theta + 2\sin 2\theta)$

For $\theta = \frac{2\pi}{3}$, we obtain: $\frac{d^2A}{d\theta^2} = ab\left(-\sin\frac{2\pi}{3} + 2\sin\frac{4\pi}{3}\right) = ab\left(-\frac{\sqrt{3}}{2} - 2\times\frac{\sqrt{3}}{2}\right) < 0$

Hence, A is maximum when $\theta = 2\pi/3$. The maximum area A is given by

$$A = ab\left(\sin\frac{2\pi}{3} - \sin\frac{2\pi}{3}\cos\frac{2\pi}{3}\right) = ab\left(\frac{\sqrt{3}}{2} + \frac{\sqrt{3}}{2}\times\frac{1}{2}\right) = \frac{3\sqrt{3}}{4}\,ab.$$

EXAMPLE 45 *Find the area of the greatest rectangle that can be inscribed in an ellipse* $\frac{x^2}{a^2} + \frac{y^2}{b^2} = 1.$

[CBSE 2013]

SOLUTION Let $PQRS$ be a rectangle inscribed in the ellipse $\frac{x^2}{a^2} + \frac{y^2}{b^2} = 1$. Let the coordinate of P be $(a\cos\theta, b\sin\theta)$. Then, the coordinates of Q, R and S are $(-a\cos\theta, b\sin\theta)$, $(-a\cos\theta, b\sin\theta)$ and $(a\cos\theta, -b\sin\theta)$ respectively. Let A be the area of rectangle $PQRS$. Then,

$$A = PQ \times PS = 2a\cos\theta \times 2b\sin\theta = 2ab\sin 2\theta \quad \text{...(i)}$$

$$\Rightarrow \frac{dA}{d\theta} = 4ab\cos 2\theta \text{ and } \frac{d^2A}{d\theta^2} = -8ab\sin 2\theta$$

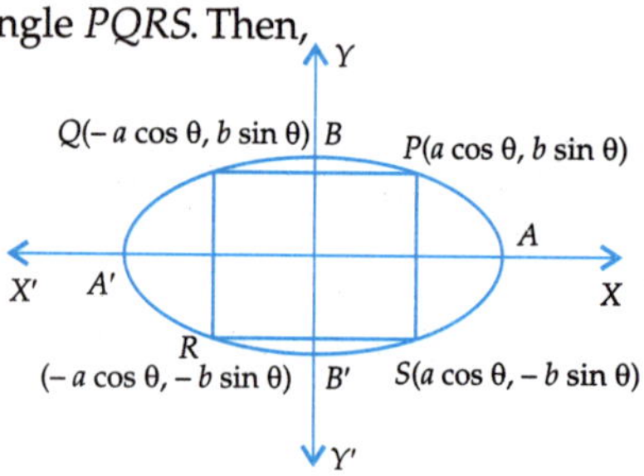

Fig. 14.55

The critical numbers of A are given by $\frac{dA}{d\theta} = 0$.

$$\therefore \frac{dA}{d\theta} = 0$$

$$\Rightarrow 4ab\cos 2\theta = 0 \Rightarrow \cos 2\theta = 0 \Rightarrow 2\theta = \frac{\pi}{2} \text{ or, } \frac{3\pi}{2} \Rightarrow \theta = \frac{\pi}{4} \text{ or, } \theta = \frac{3\pi}{4}$$

Clearly, $\left(\frac{d^2A}{d\theta^2}\right)_{\theta=\frac{\pi}{4}} = -8ab\sin\frac{\pi}{2} = -8ab < 0$. So, A is maximum when $\theta = \frac{\pi}{4}$. Putting $\theta = \frac{\pi}{4}$ in (i), the maximum value of A is given by $A = 2ab\sin\frac{\pi}{2} = 2ab$. Hence, the area of the greatest rectangle is $2ab$ sq. units.

EXAMPLE 46 *A point on the hypotenuse of a right triangle is at distances a and b from the sides of the triangle. Show that the minimum length of the hypotenuse is* $(a^{2/3} + b^{2/3})^{3/2}$.

[NCERT, CBSE 2008]

SOLUTION Let AOB be a right triangle with hypotenuse AB such that a point P on AB is at distances a and b from OA and OB respectively. i.e. $PL = a$ and $PM = b$.

Let $\angle OAB = \theta$. In Δ's ALP and PMB, we obtain

$$\sin\theta \frac{PL}{AP} \text{ and } \cos\theta = \frac{PM}{BP}$$

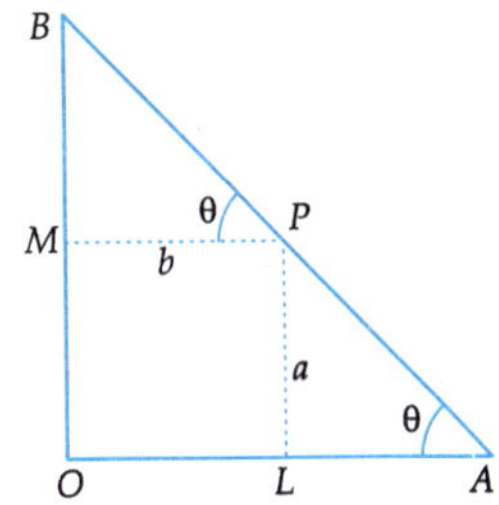

Fig. 14.56

$$\Rightarrow \quad \sin\theta = \frac{a}{AP} \text{ and } \cos\theta = \frac{b}{BP} \Rightarrow AP = a \operatorname{cosec}\theta \text{ and } BP = b\sec\theta$$

Let l be the length of the hypotenuse AB. Then,

$$l = AP + BP$$

$$\Rightarrow \quad l = a\operatorname{cosec}\theta + b\sec\theta$$

$$\Rightarrow \quad \frac{dl}{d\theta} = -a\operatorname{cosec}\theta\cot\theta + b\sec\theta\tan\theta$$

$$\text{and,} \quad \frac{d^2 l}{d\theta^2} = a\operatorname{cosec}^3\theta + a\operatorname{cosec}\theta\cot^2\theta + b\sec^3\theta + b\sec\theta\tan^2\theta$$

The critical numbers of l are given by $\frac{dl}{d\theta} = 0$.

$$\therefore \quad \frac{dl}{d\theta} = 0$$

$$\Rightarrow \quad -a\operatorname{cosec}\theta\cot\theta + b\sec\theta\tan\theta = 0 \Rightarrow -\frac{a\cos\theta}{\sin^2\theta} + \frac{b\sin\theta}{\cos^2\theta} = 0 \Rightarrow \tan^3\theta = \frac{a}{b}$$

$$\Rightarrow \quad \tan\theta = \left(\frac{a}{b}\right)^{1/3} \Rightarrow \sin\theta = \frac{a^{1/3}}{\sqrt{a^{2/3} + b^{2/3}}} \text{ and, } \cos\theta = \frac{b^{1/3}}{\sqrt{a^{2/3} + b^{2/3}}}$$

Clearly, $\frac{d^2 l}{d\theta^2} > 0$ for $\tan\theta = \left(\frac{a}{b}\right)^{1/3}$. Thus, l is minimum when $\tan\theta = \left(\frac{a}{b}\right)^{1/3}$.

The minimum value of l is given by

$$l = a\operatorname{cosec}\theta + b\sec\theta = a\sqrt{1 + \cot^2\theta} + b\sqrt{1 + \tan^2\theta} = a\sqrt{1 + \left(\frac{b}{a}\right)^{2/3}} + b\sqrt{1 + \left(\frac{a}{b}\right)^{2/3}}$$

$$\Rightarrow \quad l = (a^{2/3} + b^{2/3})^{3/2}.$$

EXERCISE 14.5

BASIC

1. Determine two positive numbers whose sum is 15 and the sum of whose squares is minimum.
2. Sum of two numbers is 5. If the sum of the cubes of these numbers is least, then find the sum of the squares of these numbers. [CBSE 2023]
3. How should we choose two numbers, each greater than or equal to -2, whose sum is $1/2$ so that the sum of the first and the cube of the second is minimum?
4. Divide 15 into two parts such that the square of one multiplied with the cube of the other is maximum.
5. (i) Of all the closed cylindrical cans (right circular), which enclose a given volume of 100 cm^3, which has the minimum surface area? [NCERT, CBSE 2014]

   (ii) Amongst all open (from the top) right circular cylindrical boxes of volume 125π cm^3, find the dimensions of the box which has the least surface area. [CBSE 2020]

6. A beam is supported at the two ends and is uniformly loaded. The bending moment M at a distance x from one end is given by

(i) $M = \frac{WL}{2} x - \frac{W}{2} x^2$ (ii) $M = \frac{Wx}{3} - \frac{W}{3} \frac{x^3}{L^2}$

Find the point at which M is maximum in each case.

7. A wire of length 28 m is to be cut into two pieces. One of the pieces is to be made into a square and the other into a circle. What should be the lengths of the two pieces so that the combined area of the circle and the square is minimum? **[NCERT, CBSE 2007, 2010]**

8. A wire of length 20 m is to be cut into two pieces. One of the pieces will be bent into shape of a square and the other into shape of an equilateral triangle. Where the wire should be cut so that the sum of the areas of the square and triangle is minimum? **[CBSE 2005]**

9. Given the sum of the perimeters of a square and a circle, show that the sum of their areas is least when one side of the square is equal to diameter of the circle. **[NCERT, CBSE 2005, 2011, 2014]**

10. Find the largest possible area of a right angled triangle whose hypotenuse is 5 cm long. **[CBSE 2000]**

11. Two sides of a triangle have lengths 'a' and 'b' and the angle between them is θ. What value of θ will maximize the area of the triangle? Find the maximum area of the triangle also. **[CBSE 2002 C]**

12. A square piece of tin of side 18 cm is to be made into a box without top by cutting a square from each corner and folding up the flaps to form a box. What should be the side of the square to be cut off so that the volume of the box is maximum? Also, find this maximum volume. **[NCERT]**

13. A rectangular sheet of tin 45 cm by 24 cm is to be made into a box without top, by cutting off squares from each corners and folding up the flaps. What should be the side of the square to be cut off so that the volume of the box is maximum possible? **[NCERT]**

14. A tank with rectangular base and rectangular sides, open at the top is to be constructed so that its depth is 2 m and volume is 8 m^3. If building of tank costs ₹ 70 per square metre for the base and ₹ 45 per square matre for sides, what is the cost of least expensive tank? **[NCERT, CBSE 2009, 2019]**

15. A window in the form of a rectangle is surmounted by a semi-circular opening. The total perimeter of the window is 10 m. Find the dimensions of the rectangular part of the window to admit maximum light through the whole opening. **[NCERT, CBSE 2000, 2002, 2011, 2014]**

16. A large window has the shape of a rectangle surmounted by an equilateral triangle. If the perimeter of the window is 12 metres find the dimensions of the rectangle that will produce the largest area of the window. **[CBSE 2011]**

17. Show that the height of the cylinder of maximum volume that can be inscribed in a sphere of radius R is $\frac{2R}{\sqrt{3}}$. **[NCERT]**

18. A rectangle is inscribed in a semi-circle of radius r with one of its sides on diameter of semi-circle. Find the dimensions of the rectangle so that its area is maximum. Find also the area.

BASED ON LOTS

19. Prove that a conical tent of given capacity will require the least amount of canvas when the height is $\sqrt{2}$ times the radius of the base. **[NCERT, CBSE 2007, 2011, 2013]**

20. Show that the cone of the greatest volume which can be inscribed in a given sphere has an altitude equal to $2/3$ of the diameter of the sphere.

21. Prove that the semi-vertical angle of the right circular cone of given volume and least curved surface is $\cot^{-1}(\sqrt{2})$. [CBSE 2014]
22. An isosceles triangle of vertical angle 2θ is inscribed in a circle of radius a. Show that the area of the triangle is maximum when $\theta = \frac{\pi}{6}$. [NCERT EXEMPLAR]
23. Prove that the least perimeter of an isosceles triangle in which a circle of radius r can be inscribed is $6\sqrt{3}r$. [CBSE 2016]
24. Find the dimensions of the rectangle of perimeter 36 cm which will sweep out a volume as large as possible when revolved about one of its sides. [NCERT EXEMPLAR]
25. Show that the height of the cone of maximum volume that can be inscribed in a sphere of radius 12 cm is 16 cm. [CBSE 2005]
26. A closed cylinder has volume 2156 cm^3. What will be the radius of its base so that its total surface area is minimum? [CBSE 2000C]
27. Show that the maximum volume of the cylinder which can be inscribed in a sphere of radius $5\sqrt{3}$ cm is 500 π cm^3. [CBSE 2004]
28. Show that among all positive numbers x and y with $x^2 + y^2 = r^2$, the sum $x + y$ is largest when $x = y = r/\sqrt{2}$.
29. Determine the points on the curve $x^2 = 4y$ which are nearest to the point (0, 5).
30. Find the point on the curve $y^2 = 4x$ which is nearest to the point (2,– 8).
31. Find the point on the curve $x^2 = 8y$ which is nearest to the point (2, 4). [CBSE 2007]
32. Find the point on the parabolas $x^2 = 2y$ which is closest to the point (0, 5).
33. Find the coordinates of a point on the parabola $y = x^2 + 7x + 2$ which is closest to the straight line $y = 3x - 3$. [CBSE 2015]
34. Find the point on the curve $y^2 = 2x$ which is at a minimum distance from the point (1, 4). [CBSE 2011]
35. Find the maximum slope of the curve $y = -x^3 + 3x^2 + 2x - 27$.
36. The total cost of producing x radio sets per day is ₹ $\left(\frac{x^2}{4} + 35x + 25\right)$ and the price per set at which they may be sold is ₹ $\left(50 - \frac{x}{2}\right)$. Find the daily output to maximize the total profit.
37. Manufacturer can sell x items at a price of ₹ $\left(5 - \frac{x}{100}\right)$ each. The cost price of x items is ₹$\left(\frac{x}{5} + 500\right)$. Find the number of items he should sell to earn maximum profit. [NCERT, CBSE 2009]
38. An open tank is to be constructed with a square base and vertical sides so as to contain a given quantity of water. Show that the expenses of lining with lead will be least, if depth is made half of width.
39. A box of constant volume c is to be twice as long as it is wide. The material on the top and four sides cost three times as much per square metre as that in the bottom. What are the most economic dimensions?
40. The sum of the surface areas of a sphere and a cube is given. Show that when the sum of their volumes is least, the diameter of the sphere is equal to the edge of the cube.

41. The perimeter of a rectangular metallic sheet is 300 cm. It is rolled along one of its sides to form a cylinder. Find the dimensions of the rectangular sheet so that the volume of cylinder so formed is maximum. **[CBSE 2024]**

BASED ON HOTS

42. A given quantity of metal is to be cast into a half cylinder with a rectangular base and semicircular ends. Show that in order that the total surface area may be minimum, the ratio of the length of the cylinder to the diameter of its semi-circular ends is $\pi:(\pi+2)$.

43. The strength of a beam varies as the product of its breadth and square of its depth. Find the dimensions of the strongest beam which can be cut from a circular log of radius a.

44. A straight line is drawn through a given point $P(1, 4)$. Determine the least value of the sum of the intercepts on the coordinate axes.

45. The total area of a page is 150 cm^2. The combined width of the margin at the top and bottom is 3 cm and the side 2 cm. What must be the dimensions of the page in order that the area of the printed matter may be maximum?

46. The space s described in time t by a particle moving in a straight line is given by $s=t^5-40t^3+30t^2+80t-250$. Find the minimum value of acceleration.

47. A particle is moving in a straight line such that its distance s at any time t is given by $s=\frac{t^4}{4}-2t^3+4t^2-7$. Find when its velocity is maximum and acceleration minimum.

ANSWERS

1. 15/2, 15/2 **2.** $\frac{25}{2}$ **3.** $\left(\frac{1}{2}-\frac{1}{\sqrt{3}}\right), \frac{1}{\sqrt{3}}$

4. 6, 9 **5.** (i) The cylinder with radius $\left(\frac{50}{\pi}\right)^{1/3}$ (ii) Radius = Height = 5 cm

6. (i) $x=\frac{L}{2}$ (ii) $x=\frac{L}{\sqrt{3}}$ **7.** $\frac{28\pi}{\pi+4}$ m, $\frac{112}{\pi+4}$ m **8.** $\frac{80\sqrt{3}}{9+4\sqrt{3}}, \frac{180}{9+4\sqrt{3}}$

10. $\frac{25}{4}$ cm^2 **11.** $\frac{\pi}{2}$, Area $=\frac{1}{2}ab$ **12.** 3 cm, 432 cm^3

13. 5 cm **14.** ₹ 1000 **15.** Length $=\frac{20}{\pi+4}$, Breadth $=\frac{10}{\pi+4}$

16. $\frac{12}{6-\sqrt{3}}, \frac{18-6\sqrt{3}}{6-\sqrt{3}}$ **18.** $\frac{r}{\sqrt{2}}, \sqrt{2}r$, Area $=r^2$ **24.** 12 cm, 6 cm

26. 7 cm **29.** $(\pm 2\sqrt{3}, 3)$ **30.** $(4, -4)$

31. (4, 2) **32.** $(\pm 2\sqrt{2}, 4)$ **33.** $(-2, -8)$

34. (2, 2) **35.** 5 at $(1, -23)$ **36.** 10 units **37.** 240

39. Length $=2\left(\frac{9c}{16}\right)^{1/3}$, Breadth $=\left(\frac{9c}{16}\right)^{1/3}$, Height $=\left(\frac{32c}{81}\right)^{1/3}$ **41.** 50 cm × 150 cm

43. Breadth $=\frac{2a}{\sqrt{3}}$, Depth $=2a\sqrt{\frac{2}{3}}$ **44.** 9

45. Length = 15 cm, Width = 10 cm **46.** $a=-260$ at $t=2$

47. Velocity is max. at $t=2-\frac{2}{\sqrt{3}}$, Acceleration is min. at $t=2$

HINTS TO SELECTED PROBLEMS

5. Let r be the radius and h be the height of the closed cylindrical cane of volume 100 cm^3. Then,

$$\pi r^2 h = 100 \Rightarrow h = \frac{100}{\pi r^2} \qquad ...(i)$$

Let S be the surface area of the can. Then,

$$S = 2\pi r h + 2\pi r^2 \Rightarrow S = \frac{200}{r} + 2\pi r^2 \qquad \text{[Using (i)}$$

$$\Rightarrow \frac{dS}{dr} = -\frac{200}{r^2} + 4\pi r \text{ and } \frac{d^2 S}{dr^2} = \frac{400}{r^3} + 4\pi$$

The critical numbers of S are given by $\frac{dS}{dr} = 0$.

$$\therefore \frac{dS}{dr} = 0 \Rightarrow -\frac{200}{r^2} + 4\pi r = 0 \Rightarrow 4\pi r^3 = 200 \Rightarrow r = \left(\frac{50}{\pi}\right)^{1/3}$$

Clearly, $\frac{d^2S}{dr^2} > 0$ for all r. Hence, S is minimum when $r = \left(\frac{50}{\pi}\right)^{1/3}$.

7. Let r be the radius of the circle and x meter be the length of each side of the square. Then,

$$2\pi r + 4x = 28 \Rightarrow \pi r + 2x = 14 \Rightarrow r = \frac{14 - 2x}{\pi} \qquad ...(i)$$

Let A be the combined area of the circle and the square. Then,

$$A = \pi r^2 + x^2 = \pi\left(\frac{14 - 2x}{\pi}\right)^2 + x^2 \qquad \text{[Using (i)]}$$

$$\Rightarrow A = \frac{1}{\pi}(14 - 2x)^2 + x^2 = \frac{4}{\pi}(7 - x)^2 + x^2 \Rightarrow \frac{dA}{dx} = -\frac{8}{\pi}(7 - x) + 2x \text{ and } \frac{d^2A}{dx^2} = \frac{8}{\pi}$$

The critical numbers of A are given by $\frac{dA}{dx} = 0$.

$$\therefore \frac{dA}{dx} = 0 \Rightarrow -\frac{8}{\pi}(7 - x) + 2x = 0 \Rightarrow x = \frac{28}{\pi + 4}$$

Clearly, $\frac{d^2A}{dx^2} = \frac{8}{\pi} > 0$ for all x. Hence, A is minimum when $x = \frac{28}{\pi + 4}$.

The lengths of two partions are $4x = \frac{112}{\pi + 4}$ meter and, $28 - \frac{112}{\pi + 4} = \frac{28\pi}{\pi + 4}$ m respectively.

9. Let x be the length of the each side of the square and y be the radius of the circle. Let S be the sum of their perimeters. Then,

$$S = 4x + 2\pi y \Rightarrow y = \frac{S - 4x}{2\pi} \qquad ...(i)$$

Let A be the sum of the areas of the square and the circle. Then,

$$A = x^2 + \pi y^2 = x^2 + \frac{1}{4\pi}(S - 4x)^2 \qquad \text{[Using (i)]}$$

$$\Rightarrow \frac{dA}{dx} = 2x - \frac{2}{\pi}(S - 4x) \text{ and } \frac{d^2A}{dx^2} = 2 + \frac{8}{\pi}$$

The critical numbers of A are given by $\frac{dA}{dx} = 0$.

$\therefore \quad \frac{dA}{dx} = 0 \Rightarrow 2x - \frac{2}{\pi}(S - 4x) = 0 \Rightarrow \pi x - S + 4x = 0 \Rightarrow x = \frac{S}{\pi + 4}$

Clearly, $\frac{d^2A}{dx^2} = 2 + \frac{8}{\pi} > 0$ for all x. So, A is minimum when $x = \frac{S}{\pi + 4}$ and for this value of x the value of y is given by $y = \frac{1}{2\pi}(S - 4x) = \frac{1}{2\pi}\left(S - \frac{4S}{\pi + 4}\right) = \frac{S}{2(\pi + 4)}$.

Clearly, $x = 2y$ i.e. side of the square is equal to the diameter of the circle.

Hence, A is minimum when side of the square is equal to the diameter of the circle.

12. Let the length of the each side of the square which is cut from each corner of the tin sheet be x cm. By folding up the flaps, a cuboidal box is formed whose length, breadth and height are $18 - 2x$, $18 - 2x$ and x respectively. Then, its volume V is given by

$$V = (18 - 2x)(18 - 2x)x = 324x - 72x^2 + 4x^3$$

$$\Rightarrow \frac{dV}{dx} = 324 - 144x + 12x^2 \text{ and } \frac{d^2V}{dx^2} = -144 + 24x$$

The critical numbers of V are given by

$$\frac{dV}{dx} = 0 \Rightarrow 324 - 144x + 12x^2 = 0 \Rightarrow x^2 - 12x + 27 = 0 \Rightarrow x = 3, 9.$$

But, $x = 9$ is not possible. Therefore, $x = 3$. Clearly, $\left(\frac{d^2V}{dx^2}\right)_{x=3} = -144 + 72 = -72 < 0.$

So, V is maximum when $x = 3$ i.e. the length of each side of the square to be cut is 3 cm.

13. Let the length of a side of the square be x cm and let V be the volume of the box. Then, $V = (45 - 2x)(24 - 2x)x$. Now, proceed as in Q. No. 10.

14. Let the length and breadth of the tank be x and y meters respectively. It is given that the volume of the tank is 8m^3 and height is 2m.

$$\therefore \quad 2xy = 8 \Rightarrow xy = 4 \Rightarrow y = \frac{4}{x} \qquad \text{...(i)}$$

Let C be the cost of the tank. Then,

$$C = 70xy + 45(2 \times 2y + 2 \times 2x) = 70xy + 180y + 180x$$

$$\Rightarrow C = 280 + \frac{720}{x} + 180x \qquad \text{[Using (i)]}$$

$$\Rightarrow \frac{dC}{dx} = -\frac{720}{x^2} + 180 \text{ and } \frac{d^2C}{dx^2} = \frac{1440}{x^3}$$

The critical numbers of C are given by $\frac{dC}{dx} = 0.$

$$\therefore \quad \frac{dC}{dx} = 0 \Rightarrow -\frac{720}{x^2} + 180 = 0 \Rightarrow x = 2$$

Clearly, $\left(\frac{d^2C}{dx^2}\right)_{x=2} = 180 > 0.$ So, C is minimum when $x = 2$.

Putting $x = 1$ in $C = 280 + \frac{720}{x} + 180x$, we get $C = 1000$. Hence, the cost of least expensive tank is ₹ 1000.

15. Let the width and height of window be $2x$ m and y m respectively. It is given that the perimeter of the window is 10 m.

$\therefore \quad 2x + 2y + \pi x = 10 \Rightarrow y = 5 - \frac{x}{2}(\pi + 2) \qquad \ldots(i)$

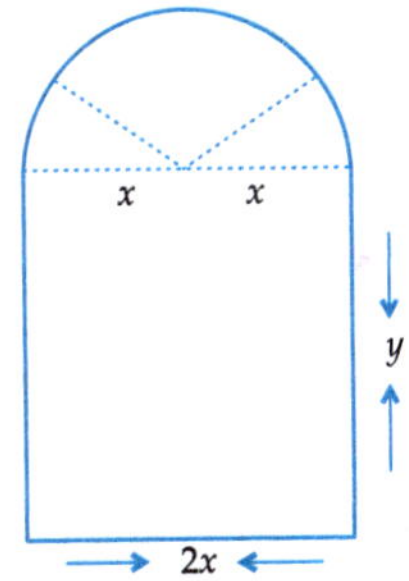

Fig. 14.57

Let A be the area of the window. Then

$$A = 2xy + \frac{\pi}{2}x^2$$

$$\Rightarrow A = 10x - (\pi + 2)x^2 + \frac{\pi}{2}x^2 \qquad \text{[Using (i)]}$$

$$\Rightarrow \frac{dA}{dx} = 10 - 2x(\pi + 2) + \pi x \text{ and, } \frac{d^2A}{dx^2} = -2(\pi + 2) + \pi = -\pi - 4$$

The critical numbers of A are given by $\frac{dA}{dx} = 0$.

$$\therefore \frac{dA}{dx} = 0 \Rightarrow 10 - 2x(\pi + 2) + \pi x = 0 \Rightarrow x = \frac{10}{\pi + 4}$$

Clearly, $\frac{d^2A}{dx^2} = -\pi - 4 < 0$ for all x. So, A is maximum when $x = \frac{10}{\pi + 4}$ and $y = 5 - \frac{5(\pi + 2)}{(\pi + 4)} = \frac{10}{\pi + 4}$. Hence, the dimensions of the window are $2x = \frac{20}{\pi + 4}$ and $y = \frac{10}{\pi + 4}$.

17. Let $OC = OG = x$. Then, $AC = \sqrt{R^2 - x^2}$.

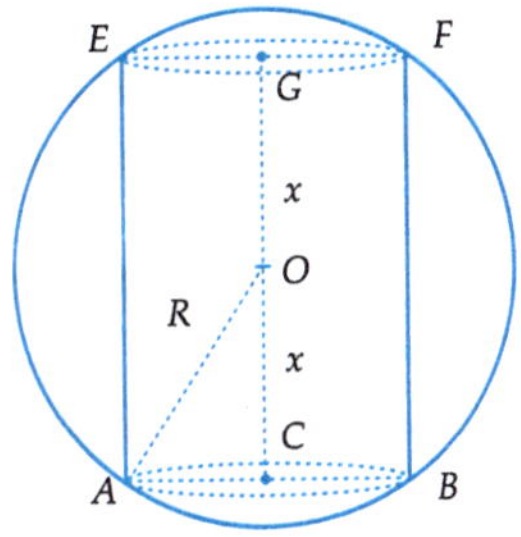

Fig. 14.58

Let V be the volume of the cylinder. Then.

$$V = \pi\left\{\sqrt{(R^2 - x^2)}\right\}^2 2x = 2\pi(R^2x - x^3)$$

$$\Rightarrow \frac{dV}{dx} = 2\pi(R^2 - 3x^2) \text{ and } \frac{d^2V}{dx^2} = -12\pi x$$

The critical numbers of V are given by $\frac{dV}{dx} = 0$.

Now, $\frac{dV}{dx} = 0 \Rightarrow R^2 - 3x^2 = 0 \Rightarrow x = \frac{R}{\sqrt{3}}$

Clearly, $\left(\frac{d^2V}{dx^2}\right)_{x = \frac{R}{\sqrt{3}}} = \frac{-12\pi R}{\sqrt{3}} < 0$. So, V is maximum when $x = \frac{R}{\sqrt{3}}$ and height of the cylinder $= 2x = \frac{2R}{\sqrt{3}}$.

19. Let r be the radius of the base h be the height and l be the slant height of the conical tent of volume V and surface area S. Then,

$$V = \frac{1}{3}\pi r^2 h \text{ and } S = \pi r l$$

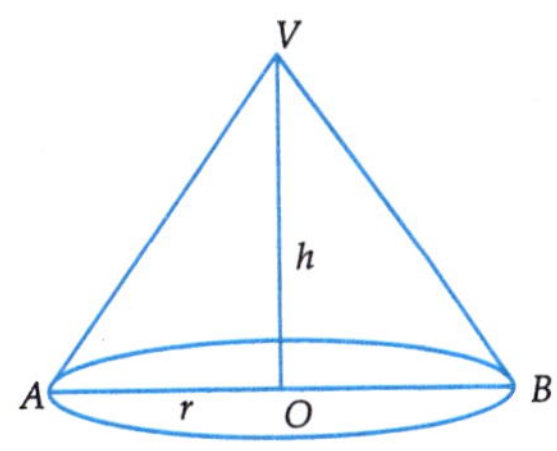

Fig. 14.59

Now, $S = \pi r l$

$$\Rightarrow S^2 = \pi^2 r^2 l^2 \Rightarrow Z = \pi^2 r^2(r^2 + h^2), \text{ where } Z = S^2$$

$$\Rightarrow Z = \pi^2 r^4 + \pi^2 r^2\left(\frac{9V^2}{\pi^2 r^4}\right) \qquad \left[\because V = \frac{1}{3}\pi r^2 h \Rightarrow h = \frac{3V}{\pi^2 r^4}\right]$$

$$\Rightarrow Z = \pi^2 r^4 + \frac{9V^2}{r^2} \Rightarrow \frac{dZ}{dr} = 4\pi^2 r^3 - \frac{18V^2}{r^3} \text{ and } \frac{d^2Z}{dr^2} = 12\pi^2 r^2 + \frac{54V^2}{r^4}$$

Clearly, Z is maximum or minimum according as S is maximum or minimum.

The critical numbers of Z are given by $\frac{dZ}{dr} = 0$.

$$\frac{dZ}{dr} = 0 \Rightarrow 4\pi^2 r^3 - \frac{18V^2}{r^3} = 0 \Rightarrow 4\pi^2 r^6 = 18V^2 \Rightarrow 2\pi^2 r^6 = \pi^2 r^4 h^2 \Rightarrow h = \sqrt{2}\, r$$

Clearly, $\frac{d^2Z}{dr^2} = 12\pi^2 r^2 + 54\frac{V^2}{r^4} > 0$ for all values of V and r.

So, Z and consequently S is minimum when $h = \sqrt{2}\, r$.

35. Slope m of the curve is given by $m = \frac{dy}{dx} = -3x^2 + 6x + 2$.

Now, $m = -3x^2 + 6x + 2 \Rightarrow \frac{dm}{dx} = -6x + 6$ and $\frac{d^2m}{dx^2} = -6$

The critical numbers of m are given by $\frac{dm}{dx} = 0$. Now, $\frac{dm}{dx} = 0 \Rightarrow -6x + 6 = 0 \Rightarrow x = 1$.

Clearly, $\frac{d^2m}{dx^2} = -6 < 0$ for all x. So, m is maximum when $x = 1$. Putting $x = 1$ in the equation of the curve, we get $y = -23$. Thus, slope is maximum at the point $(1, -23)$. The maximum value of slope is $m = 5$.

36. Profit P is given by

$$P = \text{Revenue} - \text{Cost} = ₹\left\{\left(50 - \frac{x}{2}\right)x - \left(\frac{x^2}{4} + 35x + 25\right)\right\} = ₹\left(-\frac{3}{4}x^2 + 15x - 25\right)$$

37. Suppose x items are sold to maximize the profit P. Then P = Revenue − Cost

$$\Rightarrow P = x\left(5 - \frac{x}{100}\right) - \left(\frac{x}{5} + 500\right) \Rightarrow P = \frac{24}{5}x - \frac{x^2}{100} - 500 \Rightarrow \frac{dP}{dx} = \frac{24}{5} - \frac{x}{50} \text{ and } \frac{d^2P}{dx^2} = -\frac{1}{50}$$

The critical numbers of P are given by $\frac{dP}{dx} = 0$.

$$\therefore \quad \frac{dP}{dx} = 0 \Rightarrow \frac{24}{5} - \frac{x}{50} = 0 \Rightarrow x = 240$$

Clearly, $\frac{d^2P}{dx^2} = -\frac{1}{50} < 0$ for all x. Hence, profit P is maximum when 240 items are sold.

44. The equation of a line passing through $P(1, 4)$ is $y - 4 = m(x - 1)$, where $m < 0$. Its intercepts on the axes are $\frac{m-4}{m}$ and $-(m-4)$ respectively.

Let S be the sum of the intercepts. Then,

$$S = \frac{m-4}{m} - (m-4) = -m + 5 - \frac{4}{m} \Rightarrow \frac{dS}{dm} = -1 + \frac{4}{m^2} \text{ and } \frac{d^2S}{dm^2} = -\frac{8}{m^3}$$

The critical numbers of S are given by $\frac{dS}{dm} = 0$.

Now, $\frac{dS}{dm} = 0 \Rightarrow -1 + \frac{4}{m^2} = 0 \Rightarrow m^2 = 4 \Rightarrow m = -2$ $\quad [\because m < 0]$

For $m = -2$, $\frac{d^2S}{dm^2} = 1 > 0$. So, S is minimum when $m = -2$.

For $m = -2$, The sum of the intercepts is given by $S = 2 + 5 + 2 = 9$.

FILL IN THE BLANKS TYPE QUESTIONS (FBQs)

1. If $f(x)=\dfrac{1}{4x^2+2x+1}$, then its maximum value is ....
2. The minimum value of $f(x)=\sin x$ in $\left[\dfrac{-\pi}{2},\dfrac{\pi}{2}\right]$ is ....
3. The maximum value of $f(x)=\sin x+\cos x$ is ....
4. If $f(x)$ has the second order derivative at $x=c$ such that $f'(c)=0$ and $f''(c)>0$, then c is a point of ....
5. If $f'(x)$ changes its sign from positive to negative as x increases through c in the interval $(c-h, c+h)$, then $x=c$ is a point of ....
6. If $f'(x)$ changes its sign from negative to positive as x increases through c in the interval $(c-h, c+h)$, then $x=c$ is a point of ....
7. The positive real number x when added to its reciprocal gives the minimum value of the sum when, $x=$ ....
8. The real number which must exceeds its cube is ....
9. The function $f(x)=ax+\dfrac{b}{x}$, $a, b, x>0$ takes on the least value at x equal to ....
10. If $y=a\log x+bx^2+x$ has its extreme values at $x=1$ and $x=2$, then $(a,b)=$ ....
11. If the function $f(x)=a\sin x+\dfrac{1}{3}\sin 3x$ has an extremum at $x=\dfrac{\pi}{3}$, then $a=$ ....
12. The maximum value of $f(x)=x\,e^{-x}$ is ....
13. If the function $f(x)=x^4-62x^2+ax+9$ attains a local maximum at $x=1$, then $a=$ ....
14. If the sum of two non-zero numbers is 4, then the minimum value of the sum of their reciprocals is ....
15. If x and y are two real numbers such that $x>0$ and $xy=1$. Then the minimum value of $x+y$ is ....
16. The number that exceeds its square by the greatest amount is ....
17. If m and M respectively denote the minimum and maximum values of $f(x)=(x-1)^2+3$ in the interval $[-3,1]$, then the ordered pair $(m, M)=$ ....
18. The minimum value of $f(x)=x^2+\dfrac{250}{x}$ is ....
19. The maximum slope of the curve $y=-x^3+3x^2+9x-27$ is ....
20. The function $f(x)=\dfrac{x}{2}+\dfrac{2}{x}$ has a local minimum at $x=$ ....
21. The least value of the function $f(x)=ax+\dfrac{b}{x}$ $(a>0, b>0, x>0)$ is ....

[CBSE 2020, NCERT EXEMPLAR]

ANSWERS

1. $\dfrac{4}{3}$ 2. -1 3. $\sqrt{2}$ 4. Local minimum 5. Local maximum

6. Local minimum 7. 1 8. $\dfrac{1}{\sqrt{3}}$ 9. $\sqrt{\dfrac{b}{a}}$ 10. $\left(-\dfrac{2}{3},-\dfrac{1}{6}\right)$ 11. 2

12. $\frac{1}{e}$ 13. 120 14. 1 15. 2 16. $\frac{1}{2}$ 17. (3, 19) 18. 75
19. 12 20. 2 21. $2\sqrt{ab}$

VERY SHORT ANSWER QUESTIONS (VSAQs)

Answer each of the following questions in one word or one sentence or as per exact requirement of the question:

1. Write necessary condition for a point $x = c$ to be an extreme point of the function $f(x)$.
2. Write sufficient conditions for a point $x = c$ to be a point of local maximum.
3. If $f(x)$ attains a local minimum at $x = c$, then write the values of $f'(c)$ and $f''(c)$.
4. Write the minimum value of $f(x) = x + \frac{1}{x}$, $x > 0$.
5. Write the maximum value of $f(x) = x + \frac{1}{x}$, $x < 0$.
6. Write the point where $f(x) = x \log_e x$ attains minimum value.
7. Find the least value of $f(x) = ax + \frac{b}{x}$, where $a > 0, b > 0$ and $x > 0$.
8. Write the minimum value of $f(x) = x^x$.
9. Write the maximum value of $f(x) = x^{1/x}$.
10. Write the maximum value of $f(x) = \frac{\log x}{x}$, if it exists.
11. Find the maximum and minimum values of the function given by $f(x) = 5 + \sin 2x$. [CBSE 2023]
12. Given that $f(x) = \frac{\log x}{x}$, find the point of local maximum of $f(x)$. [CBSE 2024]

ANSWERS

1. $f'(c) = 0$ 2. $f'(c) = 0$ and $f''(c) < 0$ 3. $f'(c) = 0$ and $f''(c) > 0$
4. 2 5. -2 6. $\left(\frac{1}{e}, -\frac{1}{e}\right)$ 7. $2\sqrt{ab}$
8. $e^{-1/e}$ 9. $e^{1/e}$ 10. $\frac{1}{e}$ 11. 6, 4 12. e

CHAPTER 15

INDEFINITE INTEGRALS

15.1 PRIMITIVE OR ANTIDERIVATIVE

DEFINITION *A function $\phi(x)$ is called a primitive (or an antiderivative or an integral) of a function $f(x)$, if $\phi'(x) = f(x)$.*

For example, $\frac{x^4}{4}$ is a primitive of x^3, because $\frac{d}{dx}\left(\frac{x^4}{4}\right) = x^3$.

Let $\phi(x)$ be a primitive of a function $f(x)$ and let C be any constant. Then,

$$\frac{d}{dx}\{\phi(x) + C\} = \phi'(x) = f(x) \qquad [\because \phi'(x) = f(x)]$$

$\therefore \quad \phi(x) + C$ is also a primitive of $f(x)$.

Thus, if a function $f(x)$ possesses a primitive, then it possesses infinitely many primitives which are contained in the expression $\phi(x) + C$, where C is a constant.

For example, $\frac{x^4}{4}, \frac{x^4}{4} + 2, \frac{x^4}{4} - 1$ etc. are primitives of x^3.

15.2 INDEFINITE INTEGRAL

DEFINITION *Let $f(x)$ be a function. Then the family of all its primitives (or antiderivatives) is called the indefinite integral of $f(x)$ and is denoted by $\int f(x)\, dx$.*

The symbol $\int f(x)\, dx$ is read as the indefinite integral of $f(x)$ with respect to x.

Thus, $$\frac{d}{dx}\left(\phi(x) + C\right) = f(x) \Leftrightarrow \int f(x)\, dx = \phi(x) + C \qquad \text{...(i)}$$

where $\phi(x)$ is primitive of $f(x)$ and C is an arbitrary constant known as the *constant of integration.*

Here, $\int$ is the integral sign, $f(x)$ is the integrand, x is the variable of integration and dx is the element of integration or differential of x.

DEFINITION *The process of finding an indefinite integral of a given function is called integration of the function.*

It follows from the above discussion that integrating a function $f(x)$ means finding a function $\phi(x)$ such that $\frac{d}{dx}\phi(x) = f(x)$.

15.3 FUNDAMENTAL INTEGRATION FORMULAS

We know that

$$\frac{d}{dx}\{\phi(x)\} = f(x) \Leftrightarrow \int f(x)\, dx = \phi(x) + C$$

Based upon this and various standard differentiation formulae, we obtain the following integration formulae:

(i) $\frac{d}{dx}\left(\frac{x^{n+1}}{n+1}\right) = x^n, n \neq -1 \qquad \Rightarrow \int x^n\, dx = \frac{x^{n+1}}{n+1} + C, n \neq -1$

(ii) $\frac{d}{dx}\left(\log_e x\right) = \frac{1}{x} \qquad \Rightarrow \int \frac{1}{x}\, dx = \log_e |x| + C$

(iii) $\frac{d}{dx}(e^x) = e^x \qquad \Rightarrow \int e^x\, dx = e^x + C$

(iv) $\frac{d}{dx}\left(\frac{a^x}{\log_e a}\right) = a^x, a > 0, a \neq 1 \qquad \Rightarrow \int a^x\, dx = \frac{a^x}{\log_e a} + C$

(v) $\frac{d}{dx}(-\cos x) = \sin x \qquad \Rightarrow \int \sin x\, dx = -\cos x + C$

(vi) $\frac{d}{dx}(\sin x) = \cos x \qquad \Rightarrow \int \cos x\, dx = \sin x + C$

(vii) $\frac{d}{dx}(\tan x) = \sec^2 x \qquad \Rightarrow \int \sec^2 x\, dx = \tan x + C$

(viii) $\frac{d}{dx}(-\cot x) = \text{cosec}^2 x \qquad \Rightarrow \int \text{cosec}^2 x\, dx = -\cot x + C$

(ix) $\frac{d}{dx}(\sec x) = \sec x \tan x \qquad \Rightarrow \int \sec x \tan x\, dx = \sec x + C$

(x) $\frac{d}{dx}(-\text{cosec}\, x) = \text{cosec}\, x \cot x \qquad \Rightarrow \int \text{cosec}\, x \cot x\, dx = -\text{cosec}\, x + C$

(xi) $\frac{d}{dx}(\log \sin x) = \cot x \qquad \Rightarrow \int \cot x\, dx = \log|\sin x| + C$

(xii) $\frac{d}{dx}(-\log \cos x) = \tan x \qquad \Rightarrow \int \tan x\, dx = -\log|\cos x| + C$

(xiii) $\frac{d}{dx}\{\log(\sec x + \tan x)\} = \sec x \qquad \Rightarrow \int \sec x\, dx = \log|\sec x + \tan x| + C$

(xiv) $\frac{d}{dx}\{\log(\text{cosec}\, x - \cot x)\} = \text{cosec}\, x \qquad \Rightarrow \int \text{cosec}\, x\, dx = \log|\text{cosec}\, x - \cot x| + C$

(xv) $\frac{d}{dx}\left(\sin^{-1}\frac{x}{a}\right) = \frac{1}{\sqrt{a^2 - x^2}} \qquad \Rightarrow \int \frac{1}{\sqrt{a^2 - x^2}}\, dx = \sin^{-1}\left(\frac{x}{a}\right) + C$

(xvi) $\frac{d}{dx}\left(\cos^{-1}\frac{x}{a}\right) = -\frac{1}{\sqrt{a^2 - x^2}} \qquad \Rightarrow \int -\frac{1}{\sqrt{a^2 - x^2}}\, dx = \cos^{-1}\left(\frac{x}{a}\right) + C$

(xvii) $\frac{d}{dx}\left(\frac{1}{a}\tan^{-1}\frac{x}{a}\right) = \frac{1}{a^2 + x^2} \qquad \Rightarrow \int \frac{1}{a^2 + x^2}\, dx = \frac{1}{a}\tan^{-1}\left(\frac{x}{a}\right) + C$

(xviii) $\frac{d}{dx}\left(\frac{1}{a}\cot^{-1}\frac{x}{a}\right) = -\frac{1}{a^2 + x^2} \qquad \Rightarrow \int -\frac{1}{a^2 + x^2}\, dx = \frac{1}{a}\cot^{-1}\left(\frac{x}{a}\right) + C$

(xix) $\frac{d}{dx}\left(\frac{1}{a}\sec^{-1}\frac{x}{a}\right) = \frac{1}{x\sqrt{x^2 - a^2}} \qquad \Rightarrow \int \frac{1}{x\sqrt{x^2 - a^2}}\, dx = \frac{1}{a}\sec^{-1}\left(\frac{x}{a}\right) + C$

(xx) $\frac{d}{dx}\left(\frac{1}{a}\text{cosec}^{-1}\frac{x}{a}\right) = -\frac{1}{x\sqrt{x^2 - a^2}} \qquad \Rightarrow \int -\frac{1}{x\sqrt{x^2 - a^2}}\, dx = \frac{1}{a}\text{cosec}^{-1}\left(\frac{x}{a}\right) + C$

Let us now discuss evaluation of some integrals based upon the above formulae.

ILLUSTRATIVE EXAMPLES

BASED ON BASIC CONCEPTS (BASIC)

EXAMPLE 1 *Evaluate the following integrals:*

(i) $\int x^4\,dx$ (ii) $\int \sqrt{x}\,dx$ (iii) $\int \frac{1}{\sqrt{x}}\,dx$ (iv) $\int \frac{1}{x^3}\,dx$ (v) $\int a^{3\log_a x}\,dx$

SOLUTION (i) $\int x^4\,dx = \frac{x^{4+1}}{4+1} + C = \frac{x^5}{5} + C$ [Using formula (i)]

(ii) $\int \sqrt{x}\,dx = \int x^{1/2}\,dx = \frac{x^{\frac{1}{2}+1}}{\frac{1}{2}+1} + C = \frac{2}{3}x^{3/2} + C$ [Using formula (i)]

(iii) $\int \frac{1}{\sqrt{x}}\,dx = \int x^{-1/2}\,dx = \frac{x^{-\frac{1}{2}+1}}{-\frac{1}{2}+1} + C = 2x^{1/2} + C$ [Using formula (i)]

(iv) $\int \frac{1}{x^3}\,dx = \int x^{-3}\,dx = \frac{x^{-3+1}}{-3+1} + C = -\frac{1}{2x^2} + C$ [Using formula (i)]

(v) $\int a^{3\log_a x}\,dx = \int a^{\log_a x^3}\,dx = \int x^3\,dx = \frac{x^{3+1}}{3+1} + C = \frac{x^4}{4} + C$ $[\because a^{\log_a x} = x]$

EXAMPLE 2 *Evaluate:* $\int \frac{e^{5\log_e x} - e^{4\log_e x}}{e^{3\log_e x} - e^{2\log_e x}}\,dx$

SOLUTION We know that $e^{a\log_e x} = x^a$

$$\therefore \quad \int \frac{e^{5\log_e x} - e^{4\log_e x}}{e^{3\log_e x} - e^{2\log_e x}} = \int \frac{x^5 - x^4}{x^3 - x^2}\,dx = \int \frac{x^4\,(x-1)}{x^2\,(x-1)}\,dx = \int x^2\,dx = \frac{x^3}{3} + C$$

EXAMPLE 3 *Evaluate:*

(i) $\int \frac{2}{1+\cos 2x}\,dx$ (ii) $\int \frac{2}{1-\cos 2x}\,dx$

SOLUTION We know that $1+\cos 2x = 2\cos^2 x$ and $1-\cos 2x = 2\sin^2 x$. Therefore,

(i) $\int \frac{2}{1+\cos 2x}\,dx = \int \frac{2}{2\cos^2 x}\,dx = \int \sec^2 x\,dx = \tan x + C$

(ii) $\int \frac{2}{1-\cos 2x}\,dx = \int \frac{2}{2\sin^2 x}\,dx = \int \text{cosec}^2 x\,dx = -\cot x + C$

EXAMPLE 4 *Evaluate:*

(i) $\int \frac{\cos 2x + 2\sin^2 x}{\cos^2 x}\,dx$ **[NCERT, CBSE 2018]** (ii) $\int \frac{2\cos^2 x - \cos 2x}{\sin^2 x}\,dx$

SOLUTION (i) We know that $1-\cos 2x = 2\sin^2 x$.

$$\therefore \quad \int \frac{\cos 2x + 2\sin^2 x}{\cos^2 x}\,dx$$

$$= \int \frac{1 - 2\sin^2 x + 2\sin^2 x}{\cos^2 x}\,dx = \int \frac{1}{\cos^2 x}\,dx = \int \sec^2 x\,dx = \tan x + C$$

(ii) We know that $\cos 2x = 2\cos^2 x - 1$.

$$\therefore \quad \int \frac{2\cos^2 x - \cos 2x}{\sin^2 x}\, dx = \int \frac{2\cos^2 x - (2\cos^2 x - 1)}{\sin^2 x}\, dx = \int \frac{1}{\sin^2 x}\, dx$$

$$= \int \text{cosec}^2 x\, dx = -\cot x + C$$

BASED ON LOWER ORDER THINKING SKILLS (LOTS)

EXAMPLE 5 *If $a > 0$ and $a \neq 1$ evaluate the following integrals:*

(i) $\int e^{x \log_e a}\, dx$ (ii) $\int e^{a \log_e x}\, dx$ (iii) $\int e^x a^x\, dx$ (iv) $\int 2^{\log_e x}\, dx$

SOLUTION (i) We know that $e^{\log_e k} = k$.

(i) $$\int e^{x \log_e a}\, dx = \int e^{\log_e a^x}\, dx = \int a^x\, dx = \frac{a^x}{\log_e a} + C$$

(ii) $$\int e^{a \log_e x}\, dx = \int e^{\log_e x^a}\, dx = \int x^a\, dx = \frac{x^{a+1}}{a+1} + C$$

(iii) $$\int e^x a^x\, dx = \int (ae)^x\, dx = \frac{(ae)^x}{\log(ae)} + C$$

(iv) We know that $x^{\log_a y} = y^{\log_a x}$

$$\therefore \quad \int 2^{\log_e x}\, dx = \int x^{\log_e 2}\, dx = \frac{x^{\log_e 2 + 1}}{\log_e 2 + 1} + C = \frac{x^{\log_e (2e)}}{\log_e (2e)} + C$$

EXERCISE 15.1

BASIC

1. *Evaluate each of the following integrals:*

(i) $\int x^4\, dx$ (ii) $\int x^{5/4}\, dx$ (iii) $\int \frac{1}{x^5}\, dx$ (iv) $\int \frac{1}{x^{3/2}}\, dx$

(v) $\int 3^x\, dx$ (vi) $\int \frac{1}{\sqrt[3]{x^2}}\, dx$ (vii) $\int 3^{2\log_3 x}\, dx$ (viii) $\int \log_x x\, dx$

2. *Evaluate each of the following integrals:*

(i) $\int \sqrt{\frac{1+\cos 2x}{2}}\, dx$ (ii) $\int \sqrt{\frac{1-\cos 2x}{2}}\, dx$

(iii) $\int \frac{\cos 2x + 2\sin^2 x}{\sin^2 x}\, dx$ (iv) $\int \frac{2\cos^2 x - \cos 2x}{\cos^2 x}\, dx$

(v) $\int \frac{e^{6\log_e x} - e^{5\log_e x}}{e^{4\log_e x} - e^{3\log_e x}}\, dx$ [NCERT] (vi) $\int \frac{1}{a^x b^x}\, dx$ (vii) $\int \frac{e^{\log\sqrt{x}}}{x}\, dx$

ANSWERS

1. (i) $\frac{x^5}{5} + C$ (ii) $\frac{4}{9} x^{9/4} + C$ (iii) $-\frac{1}{4x^4} + C$ (iv) $-\frac{2}{\sqrt{x}} + C$

(v) $\frac{3^x}{\log 3} + C$ (vi) $3x^{1/3} + C$ (vii) $\frac{x^3}{3} + C$ (viii) $x + C$

2. (i) $\sin x + C$ (ii) $-\cos x + C$ (iii) $-\cot x + C$ (iv) $\tan x + C$

(v) $\frac{x^3}{3}+C$ (vi) $\frac{a^{-x}b^{-x}}{-\log_e(ab)}+C$ (vii) $2\sqrt{x}+C$

HINTS TO SELECTED PROBLEMS

2.(v) $\int \frac{e^{6\log_e x}-e^{5\log_e x}}{e^{4\log_e x}-e^{3\log_e x}}\,dx=\int \frac{e^{\log_e x^6}-e^{\log_e x^5}}{e^{\log_e x^4}-e^{\log_e x^3}}\,dx=\int \frac{x^6-x^5}{x^4-x^3}\,dx=\int x^2 dx=\frac{x^3}{3}+C$

15.4 SOME STANDARD RESULTS ON INTEGRATION

THEOREM (i) $\frac{d}{dx}\left(\int f(x)\,dx\right)=f(x)$

i.e., the differentiation of an integral is the integrand itself or differentiation and integration are inverse operations.

(ii) $\int k\,f(x)\,dx=k\int f(x)\,dx$, *where k is a constant*

i.e., the integral of the product of a constant and a function = the constant × integral of the function.

(iii) $\int \{f(x)\pm g(x)\}\,dx=\int f(x)\,dx\pm\int g(x)\,dx$

i.e., the integral of the sum or difference of a finite number of functions is equal to the sum or difference of the integrals of the various functions.

PROOF (i) Let $\int f(x)\,dx=\phi(x)$. Then, by definition of an integral, we obtain

$$\frac{d}{dx}\left(\phi(x)\right)=f(x)\Rightarrow\frac{d}{dx}\left(\int f(x)\,dx\right)=f(x)$$

(ii) Let $\int f(x)\,dx=\phi(x)$. Then, by the definition of an integral, we obtain

$$\frac{d}{dx}\left(\phi(x)\right)=f(x) \quad \text{...(i)}$$

$\therefore\quad \frac{d}{dx}\{k\,\phi(x)\}=k\cdot\frac{d}{dx}(\phi(x))=k\,f(x)$ [Using (i)]

$\Rightarrow\quad \int k\,f(x)\,dx=k\,\phi(x)$ [By definition of an integral]

$\Rightarrow\quad \int k\,f(x)\,dx=k\int f(x)\,dx$ [$\because \int f(x)\,dx=\phi(x)$]

COROLLARY If $f(x)=1$, then $\int k\cdot dx=k\int 1\cdot dx=k\int x^0\,dx=kx+C$

Thus, integration of a constant k with respect to x is kx.

(iii) Let $\int f(x)\,dx=\phi(x)$ and $\int g(x)\,dx=\psi(x)$ ...(i)

Then, $\frac{d}{dx}(\phi(x))=f(x)$ and $\frac{d}{dx}(\psi(x))=g(x)$

$\Rightarrow\quad \frac{d}{dx}(\phi(x))\pm\frac{d}{dx}(\psi(x))=f(x)\pm g(x)$

$\Rightarrow\quad \frac{d}{dx}\{\phi(x)\pm\psi(x)\}=f(x)\pm g(x)$

$\Rightarrow\quad \int\{f(x)\pm g(x)\}\,dx=\phi(x)\pm\psi(x)$ [By definition of an integral]

$\Rightarrow\quad \int\{f(x)\pm g(x)\}\,dx=\int f(x)\,dx\pm\int g(x)\,dx$ [Using (i)]

GENERALIZATION *The above results can be generalized to the form*

$$\int \{k_1 f(x) \pm k_2 f_2(x) \pm \ldots \pm k_n f_n(x)\}\, dx = k_1 \int f_1(x)\, dx \pm k_2 \int f_2(x)\, dx \pm \ldots \pm k_n \int f_n(x)\, dx$$

i.e., the integration of the linear combination of a finite number of functions is equal to the linear combination of their integrals.

ILLUSTRATIVE EXAMPLES

BASED ON BASIC CONCEPTS (BASIC)

Type I **PROBLEMS BASED ON** $\int k f(x)\, dx = k \int f(x)\, dx$

EXAMPLE 1 *Evaluate:*

(i) $\int 4x^5\, dx$ (ii) $\int 2 \sin x\, dx$ (iii) $\int 3^{x+2}\, dx$ (iv) $\int \frac{1}{2} \sec^2 x\, dx$

SOLUTION Using $\int k f(x)\, dx = k \int f(x)\, dx$, we obtain

(i) $\int 4x^5\, dx = 4 \int x^5\, dx = 4\left(\frac{x^{5+1}}{5+1}\right) + C = \frac{4}{6} x^6 + C = \frac{2}{3} x^6 + C$

(ii) $\int 2 \sin x\, dx = 2 \int \sin x\, dx = -2 \cos x + C$

(iii) $\int 3^{x+2}\, dx = \int 3^x \cdot 3^2\, dx = 9 \int 3^x\, dx = 9\left(\frac{3^x}{\log 3}\right) + C$

(iv) $\int \frac{1}{2} \sec^2 x\, dx = \frac{1}{2} \int \sec^2 x\, dx = \frac{1}{2} \tan x + C$

Type II **EVALUATION OF INTEGRALS BY USING** $\int x^n\, dx = \frac{x^{n+1}}{n+1} + C$ **and** $\int \frac{1}{x}\, dx = \log_e x + C$

EXAMPLE 2 *Evaluate:*

(i) $\int x^3 + 5x^2 - 4 + \frac{7}{x} + \frac{2}{\sqrt{x}}\, dx$ (ii) $\int \frac{x^3 + 5x^2 + 4x + 1}{x^2}\, dx$ (iii) $\int (1 - x) \sqrt{x}\, dx$

(iv) $\int \left(\sqrt{x} + \frac{1}{\sqrt{x}}\right)^2 dx$ (v) $\int \left(x^2 + \frac{1}{x^2}\right)^3 dx$ (vi) $\int \frac{(1 + x)^2}{\sqrt{x}}\, dx$

(vii) $\int \frac{x^3 - x^2 + x - 1}{x - 1}\, dx$

SOLUTION (i) Let $I = \int x^3 + 5x^2 - 4 + \frac{7}{x} + \frac{2}{\sqrt{x}}\, dx$. Then,

$$I = \int x^3\, dx + \int 5x^2\, dx - \int 4 dx + \int \frac{7}{x}\, dx + \int \frac{2}{\sqrt{x}}\, dx$$

$$\Rightarrow \quad I = \int x^3\, dx + 5 \int x^2\, dx - 4 \int 1\, dx + 7 \int \frac{1}{x}\, dx + 2 \int x^{-1/2}\, dx$$

$$\Rightarrow \quad I = \frac{x^4}{4} + 5 \times \frac{x^3}{3} - 4x + 7 \log|x| + 2\left(\frac{x^{1/2}}{1/2}\right) + C = \frac{x^4}{4} + \frac{5}{3} x^3 - 4x + 7 \log|x| + 4\sqrt{x} + C$$

(ii) Let $I = \int \frac{x^3 + 5x^2 + 4x + 1}{x^2}\, dx$. Then,

$$I = \int \left(x + 5 + \frac{4}{x} + \frac{1}{x^2}\right) dx \qquad \text{[Dividing each term by } x^2\text{]}$$

$$\Rightarrow \quad I=\int x\,dx+\int 5dx+\int \frac{4}{x}\,dx+\int \frac{1}{x^2}\,dx$$

$$\Rightarrow \quad I=\int x\,dx+5\int 1dx+4\int \frac{1}{x}\,dx+\int x^{-2}\,dx$$

$$\Rightarrow \quad I=\frac{x^2}{2}+5x+4\log|x|+\left(\frac{x^{-1}}{-1}\right)+C=\frac{x^2}{2}+5x+4\log|x|-\frac{1}{x}+C$$

(iii) Let $I=\int (1-x)\sqrt{x}\,dx$. Then,

$$I=\int (\sqrt{x}-x\sqrt{x})\,dx=\int \sqrt{x}\,dx-\int x^{3/2}\,dx=\frac{x^{3/2}}{3/2}-\frac{x^{5/2}}{5/2}+C=\frac{2}{3}x^{3/2}-\frac{2}{5}x^{5/2}+C$$

(iv) Let $I=\int \left(\sqrt{x}+\frac{1}{\sqrt{x}}\right)^2 dx$. Then,

$$I=\int \left(x+\frac{1}{x}+2\right)dx=\int x\,dx+\int \frac{1}{x}\,dx+2\int 1\cdot dx=\frac{x^2}{2}+\log|x|+2x+C$$

(v) Let $I=\int \left(x^2+\frac{1}{x^2}\right)^3 dx$. Then,

$$I=\int \left(x^6+\frac{1}{x^6}+3x^2+\frac{3}{x^2}\right)dx=\int x^6\,dx+\int x^{-6}\,dx+3\int x^2\,dx+3\int x^{-2}\,dx$$

$$\Rightarrow \quad I=\frac{x^7}{7}+\left(\frac{x^{-5}}{-5}\right)+3\left(\frac{x^3}{3}\right)+3\left(\frac{x^{-1}}{-1}\right)+C=\frac{x^7}{7}-\frac{1}{5x^5}+x^3-\frac{3}{x}+C$$

(vi) Let $I=\int \frac{(1+x)^2}{\sqrt{x}}\,dx$. Then,

$$I=\int \frac{1+2x+x^2}{\sqrt{x}}\,dx$$

$$\Rightarrow \quad I=\int \frac{1}{\sqrt{x}}+2\sqrt{x}+x^{3/2}\,dx=\int x^{-1/2}\,dx+2\int x^{1/2}\,dx+\int x^{3/2}\,dx$$

$$\Rightarrow \quad I=\frac{x^{1/2}}{1/2}+2\times\frac{x^{3/2}}{3/2}+\frac{x^{5/2}}{5/2}+C=2x^{1/2}+\frac{4}{3}x^{3/2}+\frac{2}{5}x^{5/2}+C$$

(vii) Let $I=\int \frac{x^3-x^2+x-1}{x-1}\,dx$. Then,

$$I=\int \frac{x^2(x-1)+(x-1)}{x-1}\,dx=\int \frac{(x^2+1)(x-1)}{x-1}\,dx=\int x^2+1\,dx=\frac{x^3}{3}+x+C$$

EXAMPLE 3 *Evaluate:* $\int \frac{x^4+x^2+1}{x^2-x+1}\,dx$

SOLUTION Let $I=\int \frac{x^4+x^2+1}{x^2-x+1}\,dx$. Then,

$$I=\int \frac{(x^2+1)^2-x^2}{x^2-x+1}\,dx=\int \frac{(x^2+1+x)(x^2+1-x)}{(x^2-x+1)}\,dx=\int (x^2+x+1)\,dx=\frac{x^3}{3}+\frac{x^2}{2}+x+C$$

Type III INTEGRATION OF TRIGONOMETRIC FUNCTIONS

EXAMPLE 4 *Evaluate:*

(i) $\int (3\sin x - 2\cos x + 4\sec^2 x - 5\operatorname{cosec}^2 x)\, dx$ (ii) $\int \sqrt{1+\cos 2x}\, dx$

(iii) $\int \sqrt{1-\cos 2x}\, dx$ (iv) $\int \sqrt{1+\sin 2x}\, dx$

(v) $\int \sqrt{1-\sin 2x}\, dx, \frac{\pi}{4} < x < \frac{\pi}{2}$ [CBSE 2019] (vi) $\int \frac{\cos x - \cos 2x}{1-\cos x}\, dx$ [NCERT EXEMPLAR]

SOLUTION (i) Let $I = \int (3\sin x - 2\cos x + 4\sec^2 x - 5\operatorname{cosec}^2 x)\, dx$. Then,

$$I = 3\int \sin x\, dx - 2\int \cos x\, dx + 4\int \sec^2 x\, dx - 5\int \operatorname{cosec}^2 x\, dx$$

$$\Rightarrow \quad I = -3\cos x - 2\sin x + 4\tan x + 5\cot x + C$$

(ii) Let $I = \int \sqrt{1+\cos 2x}\, dx = \int \sqrt{2\cos^2 x}\, dx = \sqrt{2}\int \cos x\, dx = \sqrt{2}\sin x + C$

(iii) Let $I = \int \sqrt{1-\cos 2x}\, dx = \int \sqrt{2\sin^2 x}\, dx = \sqrt{2}\int \sin x\, dx = -\sqrt{2}\cos x + C$

(iv) Let $I = \int \sqrt{1+\sin 2x}\, dx = \int \sqrt{\sin^2 x + \cos^2 x + 2\sin x\cos x}\, dx$

$$\Rightarrow \quad I = \int (\sin x + \cos x)\, dx = \int \sin x\, dx + \int \cos x\, dx = -\cos x + \sin x + C$$

(v) Let $I = \int \sqrt{1-\sin 2x}\, dx = \int \sqrt{\sin^2 x + \cos^2 x - 2\sin x\cos x}\, dx$

$$\Rightarrow \quad I = \int \sqrt{\sin^2 x + \cos^2 x - 2\sin x\cos x}\, dx = \int \sqrt{(\sin x - \cos x)^2}\, dx = \int |\sin x - \cos x|\, dx$$

Now, following cases arise:

Case I *When* $\sin x > \cos x$: *In this case* $|\sin x - \cos x| = \sin x - \cos x$

$$\therefore \quad I = \int |\sin x - \cos x|\, dx = \int (\sin x - \cos x)\, dx = -\cos x + \sin x + C$$

Case II *When* $\sin x < \cos x$: *In this case* $|\sin x - \cos x| = -(\sin x - \cos x)$

$$\therefore \quad I = \int |\sin x - \cos x|\, dx = \int -(\sin x - \cos x)\, dx = -(-\cos x - \sin x) + C$$

(vi) Let $I = \int \frac{\cos x - \cos 2x}{1-\cos x}\, dx = \int \frac{\cos x - (2\cos^2 x - 1)}{1-\cos x}\, dx = \int \frac{-(2\cos^2 x - \cos x - 1)}{-(\cos x - 1)}\, dx$

$$\Rightarrow \quad I = \int \frac{(2\cos x + 1)(\cos x - 1)}{(\cos x - 1)}\, dx = \int (2\cos x + 1)\, dx = 2\sin x + x + C$$

EXAMPLE 5 *Evaluate:*

(i) $\int \tan^2 x\, dx$ (ii) $\int \cot^2 x\, dx$ (iii) $\int \frac{1}{\sin^2 x\cos^2 x}\, dx$

(iv) $\int \frac{\cos 2x}{\sin^2 x\cos^2 x}\, dx$ (v) $\int \frac{2+3\cos x}{\sin^2 x}\, dx$ (vi) $\int (2\tan x - 3\cot x)^2\, dx$

(vii) $\int \frac{\cos 2x - \cos 2\alpha}{\cos x - \cos\alpha}\, dx$ [NCERT, CBSE 2013]

SOLUTION (i) Let $I = \int \tan^2 x\, dx$. Then,

$$I = \int (\sec^2 x - 1)\, dx = \int \sec^2 x\, dx - \int 1\cdot dx = \tan x - x + C$$

(ii) Let $I = \int \cot^2 x\, dx$. Then,

$$I = \int (\operatorname{cosec}^2 x - 1)\, dx = \int \operatorname{cosec}^2 x\, dx - \int 1 \cdot dx = -\cot x - x + C$$

(iii) Let $I = \int \frac{1}{\sin^2 x \cos^2 x}\, dx$. Then,

$$\Rightarrow \quad I = \int \frac{\sin^2 x + \cos^2 x}{\sin^2 x \cos^2 x}\, dx$$

$$\Rightarrow \quad I = \int \frac{1}{\cos^2 x} + \frac{1}{\sin^2 x}\, dx = \int \sec^2 x\, dx + \int \operatorname{cosec}^2 x\, dx = \tan x - \cot x + C$$

(iv) Let $I = \int \frac{\cos 2x}{\sin^2 x \cos^2 x}\, dx$. Then,

$$I = \int \frac{\cos^2 x - \sin^2 x}{\sin^2 x \cos^2 x}\, dx$$

$$\Rightarrow \quad I = \int \left(\frac{1}{\sin^2 x} - \frac{1}{\cos^2 x} \right) dx = \int \operatorname{cosec}^2 x\, dx - \int \sec^2 x\, dx = -\cot x - \tan x + C$$

(v) Let $I = \int \frac{2 + 3\cos x}{\sin^2 x}\, dx$. Then,

$$I = \int \frac{2}{\sin^2 x} + \frac{3\cos x}{\sin^2 x}\, dx = \int (2\operatorname{cosec}^2 x + 3\cot x \operatorname{cosec} x)\, dx$$

$$\Rightarrow \quad I = 2\int \operatorname{cosec}^2 x\, dx + 3\int \operatorname{cosec} x \cot x\, dx = -2\cot x - 3\operatorname{cosec} x + C$$

(vi) Let $I = \int (2\tan x - 3\cot x)^2\, dx$. Then,

$$I = \int (4\tan^2 x + 9\cot^2 x - 12\tan x \cot x)\, dx = \int \{4(\sec^2 x - 1) + 9(\operatorname{cosec}^2 x - 1) - 12\}\, dx$$

$$\Rightarrow \quad I = \int (4\sec^2 x + 9\operatorname{cosec}^2 x - 25)\, dx = 4\tan x - 9\cot x - 25x + C$$

(vii) Let $I = \int \frac{\cos 2x - \cos 2\alpha}{\cos x - \cos \alpha}\, dx$. Then,

$$I = \int \frac{(2\cos^2 x - 1) - (2\cos^2 \alpha - 1)}{\cos x - \cos \alpha}\, dx = \int \frac{2(\cos^2 x - \cos^2 \alpha)}{\cos x - \cos \alpha}\, dx$$

$$\Rightarrow \quad I = 2\int (\cos x + \cos \alpha)\, dx = 2\int \cos x\, dx + 2\int \cos \alpha\, dx$$

$$\Rightarrow \quad I = 2\int \cos x\, dx + 2\cos \alpha \int 1 \cdot dx = 2\sin x + 2x\cos \alpha + C$$

EXAMPLE 6 *Evaluate:*

(i) $\int \frac{1}{1 + \sin x}\, dx$ (ii) $\int \frac{1}{1 + \cos x}\, dx$ (iii) $\int \frac{\sin x}{1 + \sin x}\, dx$ (iv) $\int \frac{\sec x}{\sec x + \tan x}\, dx$

SOLUTION (i) Let $I = \int \frac{1}{1 + \sin x}\, dx$. Then,

$$I = \int \frac{1}{1 + \sin x} \times \frac{1 - \sin x}{1 - \sin x}\, dx = \int \frac{1 - \sin x}{1 - \sin^2 x}\, dx = \int \frac{1 - \sin x}{\cos^2 x}\, dx$$

$$\Rightarrow \quad I = \int \frac{1}{\cos^2 x}\, dx - \int \frac{\sin x}{\cos^2 x}\, dx = \int \sec^2 x\, dx - \int \tan x \sec x\, dx = \tan x - \sec x + C$$

(ii) Let $I = \int \frac{1}{1+\cos x}\, dx$. Then,

$$I = \int \frac{1}{1+\cos x} \times \frac{1-\cos x}{1-\cos x}\, dx = \int \frac{1-\cos x}{1-\cos^2 x}\, dx$$

$$\Rightarrow \quad I = \int \frac{1-\cos x}{\sin^2 x}\, dx = \int \operatorname{cosec}^2 x\, dx - \int \cot x \operatorname{cosec} x\, dx = -\cot x + \operatorname{cosec} x + C$$

(iii) Let $I = \int \frac{\sin x}{1+\sin x}\, dx$. Then,

$$I = \int \frac{\sin x(1-\sin x)}{(1+\sin x)(1-\sin x)}\, dx = \int \frac{\sin x - \sin^2 x}{1-\sin^2 x}\, dx$$

$$\Rightarrow \quad I = \int \frac{\sin x - \sin^2 x}{\cos^2 x}\, dx = \int \frac{\sin x}{\cos^2 x} - \frac{\sin^2 x}{\cos^2 x}\, dx$$

$$\Rightarrow \quad I = \int \tan x \sec x\, dx - \int \tan^2 x\, dx = \int \tan x \sec x\, dx - \int (\sec^2 x - 1)\, dx$$

$$\Rightarrow \quad I = \int \sec x \tan x\, dx - \int \sec^2 x\, dx + \int 1 \cdot dx = \sec x - \tan x + x + C$$

(iv) Let $I = \int \frac{\sec x}{\sec x + \tan x}\, dx$. Then,

$$I = \int \frac{\sec x(\sec x - \tan x)}{(\sec x + \tan x)(\sec x - \tan x)}\, dx = \int \frac{\sec^2 x - \sec x \tan x}{\sec^2 x - \tan^2 x}\, dx$$

$$\Rightarrow \quad I = \int \sec^2 x - \sec x \tan x\, dx = \int \sec^2 x\, dx - \int \sec x \tan x\, dx = \tan x - \sec x + C$$

BASED ON LOWER ORDER THINKING SKILLS (LOTS)

EXAMPLE 7 *Evaluate:*

(i) $\int \frac{\sin^6 x + \cos^6 x}{\sin^2 x \cos^2 x}\, dx$ **[CBSE 2014]** (ii) $\int \frac{1+\cos 4x}{\cot x - \tan x}\, dx$

(iii) $\int \frac{1}{\tan x + \cot x + \sec x + \operatorname{cosec} x}\, dx$

SOLUTION (i) Let $I = \int \frac{\sin^6 x + \cos^6 x}{\sin^2 x \cos^2 x}\, dx$. Then,

$$I = \int \frac{(\sin^2 x + \cos^2 x)^3 - 3\sin^2 x \cos^2 x(\sin^2 x + \cos^2 x)}{\sin^2 x \cos^2 x}\, dx \quad \left[\begin{array}{l}\text{Using}: a^3 + b^3 \\ = (a+b)^3 - 3ab(a+b)\end{array}\right]$$

$$\Rightarrow \quad I = \int \frac{1 - 3\sin^2 x \cos^2 x}{\sin^2 x \cos^2 x}\, dx = \int \left\{ \frac{1}{\sin^2 x \cos^2 x} - 3 \right\} dx$$

$$\Rightarrow \quad I = \int \left\{ \frac{\sin^2 x + \cos^2 x}{\sin^2 x \cos^2 x} - 3 \right\} dx = \int (\sec^2 x + \operatorname{cosec}^2 x - 3)\, dx = \tan x - \cot x - 3x + C$$

(ii) Let $I = \int \frac{1+\cos 4x}{\cot x - \tan x}\, dx$. Then,

$$I = \int \frac{2\cos^2 2x \cos x \sin x}{\cos^2 x - \sin^2 x}\, dx = \int \cos 2x \sin 2x \, dx = \frac{1}{2}\int \sin 4x \, dx = -\frac{1}{8}\cos 4x + C$$

(iii) Let $I = \int \frac{1}{\tan x + \cot x + \sec x + \operatorname{cosec} x} dx$. Then,

$$I = \int \frac{1}{\frac{\sin x}{\cos x} + \frac{\cos x}{\sin x} + \frac{1}{\cos x} + \frac{1}{\sin x}} dx = \int \frac{\sin x \cos x}{\sin^2 x + \cos^2 x + \sin x + \cos x} dx$$

$$\Rightarrow \quad I = \frac{1}{2}\int \frac{2\sin x \cos x}{1 + \sin x + \cos x} dx = \frac{1}{2}\int \frac{(1 + 2\sin x \cos x) - 1}{1 + \sin x + \cos x} dx$$

$$\Rightarrow \quad I = \frac{1}{2}\int \frac{(\sin^2 x + \cos^2 x + 2\sin x \cos x) - 1}{1 + \sin x + \cos x} dx = \frac{1}{2}\int \frac{(\sin x + \cos x)^2 - 1^2}{\sin x + \cos x + 1} dx$$

$$\Rightarrow \quad I = \frac{1}{2}\int \frac{(\sin x + \cos x) + 1)(\sin x + \cos x - 1)}{\sin x + \cos x + 1} dx = \frac{1}{2}\int (\sin x + \cos x - 1)\, dx$$

$$\Rightarrow \quad I = \frac{1}{2}(-\cos x + \sin x - x) + C$$

EXAMPLE 8 *Evaluate*:

(i) $\int \sin^{-1}(\cos x)\, dx,\ 0 \le x \le \pi$ **[NCERT]** (ii) $\int \tan^{-1}\left\{\sqrt{\left(\frac{1 - \cos 2x}{1 + \cos 2x}\right)}\right\} dx,\ 0 < x < \pi/2$

(iii) $\int \tan^{-1}(\sec x + \tan x)\, dx, -\pi/2 < x < \pi/2$ **[CBSE 2003]**

SOLUTION (i) Let $I = \int \sin^{-1}(\cos x)\, dx$. Then,

$$I = \int \sin^{-1}\left\{\sin\left(\frac{\pi}{2} - x\right)\right\} dx = \int \left(\frac{\pi}{2} - x\right) dx = \frac{\pi}{2}\int 1 \cdot dx - \int x\, dx = \frac{\pi}{2}x - \frac{x^2}{2} + C$$

(ii) Let $I = \int \tan^{-1}\left\{\sqrt{\frac{1 - \cos 2x}{1 + \cos 2x}}\right\} dx$. Then,

$$I = \int \tan^{-1}\left\{\sqrt{\frac{2\sin^2 x}{2\cos^2 x}}\right\} dx = \int \tan^{-1}(\tan x)\, dx = \int x\, dx = \frac{x^2}{2} + C$$

(iii) Let $I = \int \tan^{-1}(\sec x + \tan x)\, dx$. Then,

$$I = \int \tan^{-1}\left(\frac{1 + \sin x}{\cos x}\right) dx$$

$$\Rightarrow \quad I = \int \tan^{-1}\left\{\frac{1 - \cos\left(\frac{\pi}{2} + x\right)}{\sin\left(\frac{\pi}{2} + x\right)}\right\} dx = \int \tan^{-1}\left\{\frac{2\sin^2\left(\frac{\pi}{4} + \frac{x}{2}\right)}{2\sin\left(\frac{\pi}{4} + \frac{x}{2}\right)\cos\left(\frac{\pi}{4} + \frac{x}{2}\right)}\right\} dx$$

$$\Rightarrow \quad I = \int \tan^{-1}\left\{\tan\left(\frac{\pi}{4} + \frac{x}{2}\right)\right\} dx = \int \frac{\pi}{4} + \frac{x}{2}\, dx = \frac{\pi}{4}\int 1 \cdot dx + \frac{1}{2}\int x\, dx = \frac{\pi}{4}x + \frac{x^2}{4} + C$$

EXAMPLE 9 *Evaluate:* $\int \tan^{-1}\left\{\sqrt{\frac{1-\sin x}{1+\sin x}}\right\} dx, -\pi/2 < x < \pi/2$ [CBSE 2003, 2006]

SOLUTION Let $I = \int \tan^{-1}\left\{\sqrt{\frac{1-\sin x}{1+\sin x}}\right\} dx$. Then,

$$I = \int \tan^{-1}\left\{\sqrt{\frac{1-\cos\left(\frac{\pi}{2}-x\right)}{1+\cos\left(\frac{\pi}{2}-x\right)}}\right\} dx = \int \tan^{-1}\left\{\sqrt{\frac{2\sin^2\left(\frac{\pi}{4}-\frac{x}{2}\right)}{2\cos^2\left(\frac{\pi}{4}-\frac{x}{2}\right)}}\right\} dx$$

$$\Rightarrow \quad I = \int \tan^{-1}\left\{\tan\left(\frac{\pi}{4}-\frac{x}{2}\right)\right\} = \int \left(\frac{\pi}{4}-\frac{x}{2}\right) dx = \frac{\pi}{4}x - \frac{x^2}{4} + C$$

Type IV INTEGRATION OF EXPONENTIAL FUNCTIONS

EXAMPLE 10 *Evaluate:*

(i) $\int e^{x\log a} + e^{a\log x} + e^{a\log a}\ dx$ (ii) $\int \left(\frac{x}{m}+\frac{m}{x}+x^m+m^x\right) dx$

SOLUTION (i) Let $I = \int e^{x\log a} + e^{a\log x} + e^{a\log a}\ dx$. Then,

$$I = \int e^{\log a^x} + e^{\log x^a} + e^{\log a^a}\ dx = \int (a^x + x^a + a^a)\ dx \qquad [\because e^{\log\lambda} = \lambda]$$

$$\Rightarrow \quad I = \int a^x\ dx + \int x^a\ dx + \int a^a\ dx = \frac{a^x}{\log a} + \frac{x^{a+1}}{a+1} + a^a\ x + C$$

(ii) Let $I = \int \left(\frac{x}{m}+\frac{m}{x}+x^m+m^x\right) dx$. Then,

$$I = \frac{1}{m}\int x\ dx + m\int \frac{1}{x}\ dx + \int x^m\ dx + \int m^x\ dx = \frac{x^2}{2m} + m\log|x| + \frac{x^{m+1}}{m+1} + \frac{m^x}{\log m} + C$$

EXAMPLE 11 *Evaluate:* (i) $\int \frac{2^x+3^x}{5^x} dx$ (ii) $\int \frac{(a^x+b^x)^2}{a^x b^x} dx$

SOLUTION (i) Let $I = \int \frac{2^x+3^x}{5^x} dx$. Then,

$$I = \int \left(\frac{2^x}{5^x}+\frac{3^x}{5^x}\right) dx = \int \left\{\left(\frac{2}{5}\right)^x + \left(\frac{3}{5}\right)^x\right\} dx = \frac{(2/5)^x}{\log_e(2/5)} + \frac{(3/5)^x}{\log_e(3/5)} + C$$

(ii) Let $I = \int \frac{(a^x+b^x)^2}{a^x b^x} dx$. Then,

$$I = \int \frac{a^{2x}+b^{2x}+2a^x b^x}{a^x b^x} dx$$

$$\Rightarrow \quad I = \int \frac{a^x}{b^x} + \frac{b^x}{a^x} + 2\ dx = \int \left\{\left(\frac{a}{b}\right)^x + \left(\frac{b}{a}\right)^x + 2\right\} dx = \frac{(a/b)^x}{\log_e(a/b)} + \frac{(b/a)^x}{\log_e(b/a)} + 2x + C$$

Type V MISCELLANEOUS PROBLEMS

EXAMPLE 12 *Evaluate:* (i) $\int (x^4 + x^2 + 1)\, d(x^2)$ (ii) $\int \sin(e^x)\, d(e^x)$

SOLUTION (i) Let $x^2 = t$. Then,

$$I = \int (x^4 + x^2 + 1)\, d(x^2) = \int (t^2 + t + 1)\, dt = \frac{t^3}{3} + \frac{t^2}{2} + t + C = \frac{x^6}{3} + \frac{x^4}{2} + x^2 + C \quad [\because t = x^2]$$

(ii) Let $e^x = t$. Then, $I = \int \sin(e^x)\, d(e^x) = \int \sin t\, dt = -\cos t + C = -\cos(e^x) + C$

EXAMPLE 13 *If* $f'(x) = 3x^2 - \frac{2}{x^3}$ *and* $f(1) = 0$, *find* $f(x)$.

SOLUTION We know that $f(x) = \int f'(x)\, dx$

$$\therefore \quad f(x) = \int \left(3x^2 - \frac{2}{x^3}\right) dx = 3\left(\frac{x^3}{3}\right) - 2\left(\frac{x^{-2}}{-2}\right) + C$$

$$\Rightarrow \quad f(x) = x^3 + \frac{1}{x^2} + C \qquad \text{...(i)}$$

$$\Rightarrow \quad f(1) = 1 + 1 + C \qquad [\text{Replacing } x \text{ by } 1]$$

$$\Rightarrow \quad 0 = C + 2 \Rightarrow C = -2 \qquad [\because f(1) = 0]$$

$$\therefore \quad f(x) = x^3 + \frac{1}{x^2} - 2 \qquad [\text{Putting } C = -2 \text{ in (i)}]$$

EXERCISE 15.2

BASIC

Evaluate the following integrals (1-44):

1. $\int (3x\sqrt{x} + 4\sqrt{x} + 5)\, dx$
2. $\int \left(2^x + \frac{5}{x} - \frac{1}{x^{1/3}}\right) dx$
3. $\int \left\{\sqrt{x}\,(ax^2 + bx + c)\right\} dx$
4. $\int (2 - 3x)(3 + 2x)(1 - 2x)\, dx$
5. $\int \left(\frac{m}{x} + \frac{x}{m} + m^x + x^m + mx\right) dx$
6. $\int \left(\sqrt{x} - \frac{1}{\sqrt{x}}\right)^2 dx$ [NCERT]
7. $\int \frac{(1 + x)^3}{\sqrt{x}}\, dx$
8. $\int \left\{x^2 + e^{\log x} + \left(\frac{e}{2}\right)^x\right\} dx$
9. $\int (x^e + e^x + e^e)\, dx$
10. $\int \sqrt{x}\left(x^3 - \frac{2}{x}\right) dx$
11. $\int \frac{1}{\sqrt{x}}\left(1 + \frac{1}{x}\right) dx$
12. $\int \frac{x^6 + 1}{x^2 + 1}\, dx$
13. $\int \frac{x^{-1/3} + \sqrt{x} + 2}{\sqrt[3]{x}}\, dx$
14. $\int \frac{(1 + \sqrt{x})^2}{\sqrt{x}}\, dx$
15. $\int \sqrt{x}\,(3 - 5x)\, dx$
16. $\int \frac{(x + 1)(x - 2)}{\sqrt{x}}\, dx$
17. $\int \frac{x^5 + x^{-2} + 2}{x^2}\, dx$
18. $\int (3x + 4)^2\, dx$
19. $\int \frac{2x^4 + 7x^3 + 6x^2}{x^2 + 2x}\, dx$
20. $\int \frac{5x^4 + 12x^3 + 7x^2}{x^2 + x}\, dx$
21. $\int \frac{\sin^2 x}{1 + \cos x}\, dx$
22. $\int (\sec^2 x + \operatorname{cosec}^2 x)\, dx$
23. $\int \frac{\sin^3 x - \cos^3 x}{\sin^2 x \cos^2 x}\, dx$ [NCERT]
24. $\int \frac{5\cos^3 x + 6\sin^3 x}{2\sin^2 x \cos^2 x}\, dx$
25. $\int \frac{1 - \cos 2x}{1 + \cos 2x}\, dx$

26. $\int \frac{1}{1-\cos x}\,dx$ 27. $\int \frac{1}{1-\sin x}\,dx$ 28. $\int \frac{1}{1+\cos 2x}\,dx$

29. $\int \frac{1}{1-\cos 2x}\,dx$ 30. $\int \frac{x^3-3x^2+5x-7+x^2 a^x}{2x^2}\,dx$

31. $\int \frac{1-\cos x}{1+\cos x}\,dx$ [NCERT] 32. $\int \left\{3\sin x - 4\cos x + \frac{5}{\cos^2 x} - \frac{6}{\sin^2 x} + \tan^2 x - \cot^2 x\right\} dx$

33. If $f'(x) = x - \frac{1}{x^2}$ and $f(1) = \frac{1}{2}$, find $f(x)$.

34. If $f'(x) = x + b$, $f(1) = 5$, $f(2) = 13$, find $f(x)$. 35. If $f'(x) = 8x^3 - 2x$, $f(2) = 8$, find $f(x)$.

36. If $f'(x) = a\sin x + b\cos x$ and $f'(0) = 4$, $f(0) = 3$, $f\left(\frac{\pi}{2}\right) = 5$, find $f(x)$.

37. Write the primitive or anti-derivative of $f(x) = \sqrt{x} + \frac{1}{\sqrt{x}}$.

BASED ON LOTS

38. $\int (\tan x + \cot x)^2\,dx$ 39. $\int \frac{\cos x}{1-\cos x}\,dx$ or $\int \frac{\cot x}{\operatorname{cosec} x - \cot x}\,dx$

40. $\int \frac{\cos^2 x - \sin^2 x}{\sqrt{1+\cos 4x}}\,dx$ 41. $\int \frac{\tan x}{\sec x + \tan x}\,dx$ 42. $\int \frac{\operatorname{cosec} x}{\operatorname{cosec} x - \cot x}\,dx$

43. $\int \tan^{-1}\left(\frac{\sin 2x}{1+\cos 2x}\right) dx$ 44. $\int \cos^{-1}(\sin x)\,dx$ 45. $\int \cot^{-1}\left(\frac{\sin 2x}{1-\cos 2x}\right) dx$

46. $\int \sin^{-1}\left(\frac{2\tan x}{1+\tan^2 x}\right) dx$ 47. $\int \frac{(x^3+8)(x-1)}{x^2-2x+4}\,dx$ 48. $\int (a\tan x + b\cot x)^2\,dx$

49. $\int \frac{\cos x}{1+\cos x}\,dx$ [NCERT]

ANSWERS

1. $\frac{6}{5}x^{5/2} + \frac{8}{3}x^{3/2} + 5x + C$

2. $\frac{2^x}{\log 2} + 5\log x - \frac{3}{2}x^{2/3} + C$

3. $\frac{2a}{7}x^{7/2} + \frac{2}{5}b\,x^{5/2} + \frac{2}{3}c\,x^{3/2} + C$

4. $3x^4 + \frac{4}{3}x^3 - \frac{17}{2}x^2 + 6x + C$

5. $m\log|x| + \frac{x^2}{2m} + \frac{m^x}{\log m} + \frac{x^{m+1}}{m+1} + \frac{mx^2}{2} + C$

6. $\frac{x^2}{2} - 2x + \log|x| + C$

7. $2\sqrt{x} + 2x^{3/2} + \frac{6}{5}x^{5/2} + \frac{2}{7}x^{7/2} + C$

8. $\frac{x^3}{3} + \frac{x^2}{2} + \frac{1}{\log\left(\frac{e}{2}\right)}\left(\frac{e}{2}\right)^x + C$

9. $\frac{x^{e+1}}{e+1} + e^x + e^e x + C$

10. $\frac{2}{9}x^{9/2} - 4\sqrt{x} + C$

11. $2\sqrt{x} - \frac{2}{\sqrt{x}} + C$

12. $\frac{x^5}{5} - \frac{x^3}{3} + x + C$

13. $3x^{1/3} + \frac{6}{7}x^{7/6} + 3x^{2/3} + C$

14. $2\sqrt{x} + 2x + \frac{2}{3}x^{3/2} + C$

15. $2x^{3/2} - 2x^{5/2} + C$

16. $\frac{2}{5}x^{5/2} - \frac{2}{3}x^{3/2} - 4\sqrt{x} + C$

17. $\frac{x^4}{4} - \frac{x^{-3}}{3} - \frac{2}{x} + C$

18. $\frac{1}{9}(3x+4)^3 + C$

19. $\frac{2}{3}x^3 + \frac{3}{2}x^2 + C$

20. $\frac{5}{3}x^3 + \frac{7}{2}x^2 + C$

21. $x - \sin x + C$

22. $\tan x - \cot x + C$

23. $\sec x + \operatorname{cosec} x + C$

24. $-\frac{5}{2}\operatorname{cosec} x + 3\sec x + C$

25. $\tan x - x + C$

26. $-\cot x - \operatorname{cosec} x + C$

27. $\tan x + \sec x + C$

28. $\frac{1}{2}\tan x + C$

29. $-\frac{1}{2}\cot x + C$

30. $\frac{1}{2}\left\{\frac{x^2}{2} - 3x + 5\log x + \frac{7}{x} + \frac{a^x}{\log a}\right\} + C$

31. $2(\operatorname{cosec} x - \cot x) - x + C$

32. $-3\cos x - 4\sin x + 6\tan x + 7\cot x + C$

33. $\frac{x^2}{2} + \frac{1}{x} - 1$

34. $\frac{x^2}{2} + \frac{13}{2}x - 2$

35. $2x^4 - x^2 - 20$

36. $f(x) = 2\cos x + 4\sin x + 1$

37. $\frac{2}{3}x^{3/2} + 2x^{1/2} + C$

38. $\tan x - \cot x + C$

39. $-\operatorname{cosec} x - \cot x - x + C$

40. $\frac{x}{\sqrt{2}} + C$

41. $\sec x - \tan x + x + C$

42. $-\cot x - \operatorname{cosec} x + C$

43. $\frac{x^2}{2} + C$

44. $\frac{\pi}{2}x - \frac{x^2}{2} + C$

45. $\frac{x^2}{2} + C$

46. $x^2 + C$

47. $\frac{x^3}{3} + \frac{x^2}{2} - 2x + C$

48. $a^2\tan x - b^2\cot x - (a^2 + b^2 - 2ab)x + C$

49. $-\operatorname{cosec} x + \cot x + x + C$

15.5 GEOMETRICAL INTERPRETATION OF INDEFINITE INTEGRAL

In order to understand the geometrical meaning of an indefinite integral, let us consider a function f given by $f(x) = -2x$.

Clearly,

$$\int f(x)\,dx = -x^2 + C, \text{ where C is the constant of integration.}$$

Let us now consider the family of curves given by $y = \int f(x)\,dx$ or, $y = -x^2 + C$.

Clearly, $y = -x^2 + C$ represents a family of parabolas having their common axis of symmetry along y-axis as shown in Fig. 15.1.

In other words, each integral of $f(x) = -2x$ represents a parabola with its axis of symmetry along y-axis.

Let us now consider the points of intersection of each of these parabolas with a line parallel to y-axis (a line orthogonal to the axis representing the variable of integration). Let $x = a$ be a line parallel to y-axis which cuts the parabolas $y = -x^2$, $y = -x^2 + 1$, $y = -x^2 + 2$, $y = -x^2 + 3$ etc. respectively at points P_1, P_2, P_3, P_4 etc. At each of these points, we have

$$\frac{dy}{dx} = -2a$$

That is the slopes of the tangents to the parabolas at P_1, P_2, P_3, P_4 etc. are same. Consequently, tangents at P_1, P_2, P_3, P_4 etc. are parallel.

Thus, the indefinite integral of a function may be interpreted geometrically as follows:

The indefinite integral of a function represents geometrically a family of curves having parallel tangents at their points of intersection with the lines orthogonal to the axis representing the variable of integration.

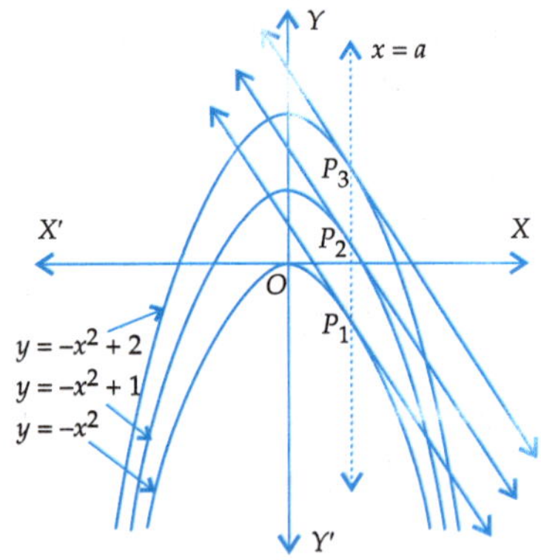

Fig. 15.1

15.6 COMPARISON BETWEEN DIFFERENTIATION AND INTEGRATION

Following points will help us to understand the difference between the differentiation and integration.

(i) The operations of differentiation and integration are defined on functions.

(ii) The derivative of a function, when it exists is a unique function whereas the integral of a function is not unique. In fact there are infinitely many integrals of a function such that any two integrals differ by a constant.

(iii) The derivative of a function at a point (if it exists) is meaningful but the integral of a function at a point does not have any sense.

(iv) Every function is not differentiable. Similarly, every function is not integrable.

(v) The derivative of a function at a point determines, the slope of the tangent to the corresponding curve at that point. The integral of a function represents a family of curves having parallel tangents at the points of intersection of the curves of the family with the lines orthogonal to the axis representing the variable of integration.

(vi) The processes of differentiation and integration are inverse of each other.

(vii) The operations of differentiation and integration are operations on functions.

(viii) Both the operations are linear.

i.e. $$\frac{d}{dx}(f(x) + g(x)) = \frac{d}{dx}(f(x)) + \frac{d}{dx}(g(x))$$

and, $$\int (f(x) + g(x))\,dx = \int f(x)\,dx + \int g(x)\,dx$$

(ix) The constant can be taken out side the differential as well as integral sign.

i.e. $\frac{d}{dx}(k\,f(x)) = k\frac{d}{dx}(f(x))$ and, $\int k\,f(x)\,dx = k\int f(x)\,dx$

(x) Differentiation and integration both are processes involving limits.

15.7 METHODS OF INTEGRATION

We have the following methods of integration:

(i) Integration by substitution (ii) Integration by parts

(iii) Integration of rational algebraic functions by using partial fractions.

We shall now discuss these methods in the sections to follow:

15.8 INTEGRATION BY SUBSTITUTION

In section 15.4, we have considered the problems on integration of functions in standard forms and the problems involving combinations of these functions. Integrals of certain functions cannot be obtained directly if they are not in one of the standard forms given in section 15.4, but they may be reduced to standard forms by proper substitution. The method of evaluating an integral by reducing it to standard form by a proper substitution is called *integration by substitution.*

If $\phi(x)$ is a continuously differentiable function, then to evaluate integrals of the form

$\int f(\phi(x))\ \phi'(x)\, dx$, we substitute $\phi(x) = t$ and $\phi'(x)\, dx = dt$.

This substitution reduces the above integral to $\int f(t)\, dt$. After evaluating this integral we substitute back the value of t.

15.8.1 INTEGRALS OF THE FORM $\int f(ax+b)\, dx$

THEOREM 1 *If* $\int f(x)\, dx = \phi(x)$, *then* $\int f(ax+b)\, dx = \frac{1}{a}\phi(ax+b)$

PROOF Let $I = \int f(ax+b)\, dx$ and let $ax+b = t$. Then, $d(ax+b) = dt \Rightarrow a\, dx = dt \Rightarrow dx = \frac{1}{a} dt$

Substituting $ax+b = t$ and $dx = \frac{1}{a} dt$, we get

$$I = \int f(ax+b)\, dx = \frac{1}{a}\int f(t)\, dt = \frac{1}{a}\phi(t) = \frac{1}{a}\phi(ax+b)$$

Q.E.D.

THEOREM 2 *Prove that* $\int (ax+b)^n\, dx = \frac{(ax+b)^{n+1}}{a(n+1)} + C,\ n \neq -1$

PROOF Let $ax+b = t$. Then, $d(ax+b) = dt \Rightarrow a\, dx = dt \Rightarrow dx = \frac{1}{a} dt$.

Putting $ax+b = t$ and $dx = \frac{1}{a} dt$, we get

$$\int (ax+b)^n\, dx = \frac{1}{a}\int t^n\, dt = \frac{1}{a}\times\frac{t^{n+1}}{n+1} + C = \frac{(ax+b)^{n+1}}{a(n+1)} + C$$

Q.E.D.

THEOREM 3 *Prove that* $\int \frac{1}{ax+b}\, dx = \frac{1}{a}\ln|ax+b| + C$

PROOF Let $ax+b = t$. Then, $d(ax+b) = dt \Rightarrow a\, dx = dt \Rightarrow dx = \frac{1}{a} dt$. Putting $ax+b = t$, and $dx = \frac{1}{a} dt$, we get

$$\int \frac{1}{ax+b}\, dx = \frac{1}{a}\int \frac{1}{t}\, dt = \frac{1}{a}\ln|t| + C = \frac{1}{a}\ln|ax+b| + C$$

Q.E.D.

THEOREM 4 *Prove that* $\int \sin(ax+b)\, dx = -\frac{1}{a}\cos(ax+b) + C$.

PROOF Let $ax+b = t$. Then, $d(ax+b) = dt \Rightarrow a\, dx = dt \Rightarrow dx = \frac{1}{a} dt$. Putting $ax+b = t$ and $dx = \frac{1}{a} dt$, we get

$$\int \sin(ax+b)\,dx = \frac{1}{a}\int \sin t\,dt = -\frac{1}{a}\cos t + C = -\frac{1}{a}\cos(ax+b) + C$$

Q.E.D.

On comparing these three results with

$$\int x^n\,dx = \frac{x^{n+1}}{n+1} + C,\ n \neq -1, \int \frac{1}{x}\,dx = \log|x| + C \text{ and, } \int \sin x\,dx = -\cos x + C$$

respectively we find that if x is replaced by $ax+b$, then the same formula is applicable but we must divide by the coefficient of x or derivative of $(ax+b)$ with respect to x i.e., a.

Thus, in any of the fundamental integration formulas given in section 15.3 if in place of x we have $ax+b$, then the same formula is applicable but we must divide by coefficient of x or derivative of $(ax+b)$ i.e. a.

We give below a list of some of them which are frequently used.

(i) $\int (ax+b)^n\,dx = \frac{(ax+b)^{n+1}}{a(n+1)} + C, n \neq -1$

(ii) $\int \frac{1}{ax+b}\,dx = \frac{1}{a}\ln|ax+b| + C$

(iii) $\int e^{ax+b}\,dx = \frac{1}{a}e^{ax+b} + C$

(iv) $\int a^{bx+c}\,dx = \frac{1}{b}\cdot\frac{a^{bx+c}}{\ln a} + C, a > 0$ and $a \neq 1$

(v) $\int \sin(ax+b)\,dx = -\frac{1}{a}\cos(ax+b) + C$

(vi) $\int \cos(ax+b)\,dx = \frac{1}{a}\sin(ax+b) + C$

(vii) $\int \sec^2(ax+b)\,dx = \frac{1}{a}\tan(ax+b) + C$

(viii) $\int \operatorname{cosec}^2(ax+b)\,dx = -\frac{1}{a}\cot(ax+b) + C$

(ix) $\int \sec(ax+b)\tan(ax+b)\,dx = \frac{1}{a}\sec(ax+b) + C$

(x) $\int \operatorname{cosec}(ax+b)\cot(ax+b)\,dx = -\frac{1}{a}\operatorname{cosec}(ax+b) + C$

(xi) $\int \tan(ax+b)\,dx = -\frac{1}{a}\ln|\cos(ax+b)| + C$

(xii) $\int \cot(ax+b)\,dx = \frac{1}{a}\ln|\sin(ax+b)| + C$

(xiii) $\int \sec(ax+b)\,dx = \frac{1}{a}\ln|\sec(ax+b) + \tan(ax+b)| + C$

(xiv) $\int \operatorname{cosec}(ax+b)\,dx = \frac{1}{a}\ln|\operatorname{cosec}(ax+b) - \cot(ax+b)| + C.$

Following examples illustrate the applications of these formulae to evaluate integrals.

ILLUSTRATIVE EXAMPLES

BASED ON BASIC CONCEPTS (BASIC)

Type I EVALUATION OF INTEGRALS DIRECTLY BASED UPON ABOVE GIVEN FORMULAE

EXAMPLE 1 *Evaluate:*

(i) $\int \left\{(2x-3)^5 + \frac{1}{(7x-5)^3} + \frac{1}{\sqrt{5x-4}} + \frac{1}{2-3x} + \sqrt{3x+2}\right\} dx$

(ii) $\int e^{2x-3}\,dx$ **[NCERT]**

(iii) $\int a^{3x+2}\,dx$

SOLUTION (i) Let $I = \int \left\{(2x-3)^5 + \frac{1}{(7x-5)^3} + \frac{1}{\sqrt{5x-4}} + \frac{1}{2-3x} + \sqrt{3x+2}\right\} dx$. Then,

$$I=\int (2x-3)^5\,dx+\int (7x-5)^{-3}\,dx+\int (5x-4)^{-1/2}\,dx+\int \frac{1}{2-3x}\,dx+\int \sqrt{3x+2}\,dx$$

$$\Rightarrow \quad I=\frac{(2x-3)^6}{2\times 6}+\frac{(7x-5)^{-2}}{7\times -2}+\frac{(5x-4)^{1/2}}{5\times \frac{1}{2}}+\left(\frac{1}{-3}\right)\log|2-3x|+\frac{(3x+2)^{3/2}}{3\times \frac{3}{2}}+C$$

$$\Rightarrow \quad I=\frac{1}{12}(2x-3)^6-\frac{1}{14}(7x-5)^{-2}+\frac{2}{5}\sqrt{5x-4}-\frac{1}{3}\log|2-3x|+\frac{2}{9}(3x+2)^{3/2}+C$$

(ii) $\int e^{2x-3}\,dx = \frac{1}{2}\times e^{2x-3}+C$

(iii) $\int a^{3x+2}\,dx=\frac{1}{3\log a}\times a^{3x+2}+C$

EXAMPLE 2 *Evaluate:*

(i) $\int \sec^2(7-4x)\,dx$ **[NCERT, CBSE 2009]** (ii) $\int \frac{1}{\sin^2 x\cos^2 x}\,dx$

(iii) $\int \operatorname{cosec}^2(3x+2)\,dx$ **[NCERT]** (iv) $\int \sin(ax+b)\cos(ax+b)\,dx$ **[NCERT]**

(v) $\int \frac{\sin 4x}{\sin 2x}\,dx$ (vi) $\int \frac{\sin 4x}{\cos 2x}\,dx$

SOLUTION (i) $\int \sec^2(7-4x)\,dx = -\frac{1}{4}\tan(7-4x)+C$

(ii) Let $I=\int \frac{1}{\sin^2 x\cos^2 x}\,dx$. Then,

$$I=\int \frac{4}{(2\sin x\cos x)^2}\,dx$$

$$\Rightarrow \quad I=4\int \frac{1}{\sin^2 2x}\,dx=4\int \operatorname{cosec}^2 2x\,dx=-\frac{4}{2}\cot 2x+C=-2\cot 2x+C$$

(iii) $\int \operatorname{cosec}^2(3x+2)\,dx=-\frac{1}{3}\cot(3x+2)+C$

(iv) Let $I=\int \sin(ax+b)\cos(ax+b)\,dx$. Then,

$$I=\frac{1}{2}\int 2\sin(ax+b)\cos(ax+b)\,dx=\frac{1}{2}\int \sin 2(ax+b)\,dx=-\frac{1}{4a}\cos(2ax+2b)+C$$

(v) Let $I=\int \frac{\sin 4x}{\sin 2x}\,dx$. Then,

$$I=\int \frac{2\sin 2x\cos 2x}{\sin 2x}\,dx=2\int \cos 2x\,dx=\frac{2}{2}\sin 2x+C=\sin 2x+C$$

(vi) Let $I=\int \frac{\sin 4x}{\cos 2x}\,dx$. Then,

$$I=\int \frac{2\sin 2x\cos 2x}{\cos 2x}\,dx=2\int \sin 2x\,dx=-\cos 2x+C$$

BASED ON LOWER ORDER THINKING SKILLS (LOTS)

EXAMPLE 3 *Evaluate:* $\int \frac{\sin^8 x-\cos^8 x}{1-2\sin^2 x\cos^2 x}\,dx$ **[NCERT]**

SOLUTION Let $I=\int \frac{\sin^8 x-\cos^8 x}{1-2\sin^2 x\cos^2 x}\,dx$. Then,

$$I = \int \frac{(\sin^4 x + \cos^4 x)(\sin^4 x - \cos^4 x)}{(\sin^2 x + \cos^2 x)^2 - 2\sin^2 x\cos^2 x}\,dx$$

$$\Rightarrow I = \int \frac{(\sin^4 x + \cos^4 x)(\sin^2 x + \cos^2 x)(\sin^2 x - \cos^2 x)}{\sin^4 x + \cos^4 x}\,dx = -\int \cos 2x\,dx = -\frac{1}{2}\sin 2x + C$$

EXAMPLE 4 *Evaluate:* $\int \sqrt{1 \mp \sin x}\,dx,\ 0 < x < \pi/2$

SOLUTION Let $I = \int \sqrt{1 \mp \sin x}\,dx$. Then,

$$I = \int \sqrt{\sin^2 \frac{x}{2} + \cos^2 \frac{x}{2} \mp 2\sin\frac{x}{2}\cos\frac{x}{2}}\,dx$$

$$\Rightarrow \quad I = \int \sqrt{\left(\cos\frac{x}{2} \mp \sin\frac{x}{2}\right)^2}\,dx = \int \left(\cos\frac{x}{2} \mp \sin\frac{x}{2}\right)dx = \int \cos\frac{x}{2}\,dx \mp \int \sin\frac{x}{2}\,dx$$

$$\Rightarrow \quad I = 2\sin\frac{x}{2} \pm 2\cos\frac{x}{2} + C = 2\left(\sin\frac{x}{2} \pm \cos\frac{x}{2}\right) + C$$

EXAMPLE 5 *Evaluate:*

(i) $\int \frac{1}{\sqrt{3x+4} - \sqrt{3x+1}}\,dx$ (ii) $\int \frac{1}{\sqrt{1-2x} + \sqrt{3-2x}}\,dx$

SOLUTION (i) Let $I = \int \frac{1}{\sqrt{3x+4} - \sqrt{3x+1}}\,dx$. Then,

$$I = \int \frac{\sqrt{3x+4} + \sqrt{3x+1}}{\left(\sqrt{3x+4} + \sqrt{3x+1}\right)\left(\sqrt{3x+4} - \sqrt{3x+1}\right)}\,dx = \int \frac{\sqrt{3x+4} + \sqrt{3x+1}}{(3x+4) - (3x+1)}\,dx$$

$$\Rightarrow \quad I = \frac{1}{3}\int \{\sqrt{3x+4} + \sqrt{3x+1}\}\,dx = \frac{1}{3}\int \sqrt{3x+4}\,dx + \frac{1}{3}\int \sqrt{3x+1}\,dx$$

$$\Rightarrow \quad I = \frac{1}{3}\left\{\frac{(3x+4)^{3/2}}{3 \times \frac{3}{2}}\right\} + \frac{1}{3}\left\{\frac{(3x+1)^{3/2}}{3 \times \frac{3}{2}}\right\} + C = \frac{2}{27}\{(3x+4)^{3/2} + (3x+1)^{3/2}\} + C$$

(ii) Let $I = \int \frac{1}{\sqrt{1-2x} + \sqrt{3-2x}}\,dx$. Then,

$$I = \int \frac{\sqrt{1-2x} - \sqrt{3-2x}}{(\sqrt{1-2x} + \sqrt{3-2x})(\sqrt{1-2x} - \sqrt{3-2x})}\,dx = \int \frac{\sqrt{1-2x} - \sqrt{3-2x}}{(1-2x) - (3-2x)}\,dx$$

$$\Rightarrow \quad I = -\frac{1}{2}\int \sqrt{1-2x}\,dx + \frac{1}{2}\int \sqrt{3-2x}\,dx$$

$$\Rightarrow \quad I = -\frac{1}{2}\left\{\frac{(1-2x)^{3/2}}{-2 \times \frac{3}{2}}\right\} + \frac{1}{2}\left\{\frac{(3-2x)^{3/2}}{-2 \times \frac{3}{2}}\right\} + C = \frac{1}{6}(1-2x)^{3/2} - \frac{1}{6}(3-2x)^{3/2} + C$$

EXAMPLE 6 *Evaluate:* $\int \frac{8^{1+x} + 4^{1-x}}{2^x}\,dx$

SOLUTION Let $I = \int \frac{8^{1+x} + 4^{1-x}}{2^x}\,dx$. Then,

$$I = \int \frac{2^{3x+3} + 2^{2-2x}}{2^x} \, dx$$

$$\Rightarrow \quad I = \int 2^{2x+3} + 2^{2-3x} \, dx = \frac{2^{2x+3}}{2 \ln 2} + \frac{2^{2-3x}}{(-3) \ln 2} + C = \frac{2^{2x+2}}{\ln 2} - \frac{2^{2-3x}}{3 \ln 2} + C$$

EXERCISE 15.3

BASIC

1. $\int (2x-3)^5 + \sqrt{3x+2} \, dx$
2. $\int \frac{1}{(7x-5)^3} + \frac{1}{\sqrt{5x-4}} \, dx$
3. $\int \frac{1}{2-3x} + \frac{1}{\sqrt{3x-2}} \, dx$
4. $\int \sin x \sqrt{1 + \cos 2x} \, dx$
5. $\int \frac{1 + \cos x}{1 - \cos x} \, dx$ [CBSE 2000]
6. $\int \frac{1 - \cos x}{1 + \cos x} \, dx$
7. $\int \frac{1}{1 + \cos 3x} \, dx$
8. $\int \tan^2 (2x-3) \, dx$ [NCERT]

BASED ON LOTS

9. $\int \frac{x+3}{(x+1)^4} \, dx$
10. $\int \frac{1}{\sqrt{x+1} + \sqrt{x}} \, dx$
11. $\int \frac{1}{\sqrt{2x+3} + \sqrt{2x-3}} \, dx$
12. $\int \frac{2x}{(2x+1)^2} \, dx$
13. $\int \frac{1}{\sqrt{x+a} + \sqrt{x+b}} \, dx$
14. $\int \frac{1}{1 - \sin \frac{x}{2}} \, dx$
15. $\int (e^x + 1)^2 e^x \, dx$
16. $\int \left(e^x + \frac{1}{e^x} \right)^2 dx$
17. $\int \frac{1 + \cos 4x}{\cot x - \tan x} \, dx$
18. $\int \frac{1}{\sqrt{x+3} - \sqrt{x+2}} \, dx$ [CBSE 2002]
19. $\int \frac{1}{\cos^2 x (1 - \tan x)^2} \, dx$ [NCERT]

ANSWERS

1. $\frac{(2x-3)^6}{12} + \frac{2}{9}(3x+2)^{3/2} + C$
2. $-\frac{1}{14}(7x-5)^{-2} + \frac{2}{5}\sqrt{5x-4} + C$
3. $-\frac{1}{3} \log |2-3x| + \frac{2}{3}\sqrt{3x-2} + C$
4. $-\frac{1}{2\sqrt{2}} \cos 2x + C$
5. $-2 \cot \left(\frac{x}{2} \right) - x + C$
6. $2 \tan \left(\frac{x}{2} \right) - x + C$
7. $\frac{1 - \cos 3x}{3 \sin 3x} + C$
8. $\frac{1}{2} \tan (2x-3) - x + C$
9. $-\frac{1}{2(x+1)^2} - \frac{2}{3(x+1)^3} + C$
10. $\frac{2}{3}\left\{ (x+1)^{3/2} - x^{3/2} \right\} + C$
11. $\frac{1}{18}\left\{ (2x+3)^{3/2} - (2x-3)^{3/2} \right\} + C$
12. $\frac{1}{2} \log |2x+1| + \frac{1}{2(2x+1)} + C$

13. $\frac{2}{3(a-b)}\left\{(x+a)^{3/2}-(x+b)^{3/2}\right\}+C$

14. $2\left(\tan\frac{x}{2}+\sec\frac{x}{2}\right)+C$

15. $\frac{1}{3}(e^x+1)^3+C$

16. $\frac{1}{2}e^{2x}+2x-\frac{1}{2}e^{-2x}+C$

17. $-\frac{1}{8}\cos 4x+C$

18. $\frac{2}{3}\left\{(x+3)^{3/2}+(x+2)^{3/2}\right\}+C$

19. $\frac{1}{2}\tan\left(\frac{\pi}{4}+x\right)+C$

15.8.2 EVALUATION OF INTEGRALS OF THE FORM $\frac{P(x)}{(ax+b)^n}$, $n \in N$, WHERE $p(x)$ IS A POLYNOMIAL

In order to evaluate this type of Integrals, we may follow the following algorithm.

Step I *Check whether degree of* $P(x) \geq$ *or* $< n$.

Step II *If degree of* $P(x) < n$, *express* $P(x)$ *in the form*

$$A_0 + A_1(ax+b) + A_2(ax+b)^2 + \ldots + A_{n-1}(ax+b)^{n-1}$$

Step III *Write* $\frac{P(x)}{(ax+b)^n}$ *as* $\frac{A_0}{(ax+b)^n}+\frac{A_1}{(ax+b)^{n-1}}+\frac{A_2}{(ax+b)^{n-2}}+\ldots+\frac{A_{n-1}}{ax+b}$

Step IV *Evaluate*

$$\int \frac{P(x)}{(ax+b)^n}dx = A_0\int\frac{1}{(ax+b)^n}dx + A_1\int\frac{1}{(ax+b)^{n-1}}dx+\ldots+A_{n-1}\int\frac{1}{ax+b}dx$$

Step V *If degree of* $P(x) \geq n$, *then divide* $P(x)$ *by* $(ax+b)^n$ *and express* $\frac{P(x)}{(ax+b)^n}$ *as*

$Q(x)+\frac{R(x)}{(ax+b)^n}$, *where degree of* $R(x)$ *is less than n.*

Step VI *Use step II and III to evaluate* $\int \frac{R(x)}{(ax+b)^n}dx$

Following examples will illustrate the above procedure.

ILLUSTRATIVE EXAMPLES

BASED ON HIGHER ORDER THINKING SKILLS (HOTS)

EXAMPLE 1 *Evaluate:*

(i) $\int \frac{x^3}{(x+2)^4}dx$ (ii) $\int \left(\frac{x-1}{x+1}\right)^4 dx$

SOLUTION (i) Let $I = \int \frac{x^3}{(x+2)^4}dx$. Then,

$$I=\int\frac{\{(x+2)-2\}^3}{(x+2)^4}dx=\int\frac{(x+2)^3-6(x+2)^2+12(x+2)-8}{(x+2)^4}dx$$

$$\Rightarrow I=\int\left\{\frac{1}{x+2}-\frac{6}{(x+2)^2}+\frac{12}{(x+2)^3}-\frac{8}{(x+2)^4}\right\}dx=\log|x+2|+\frac{6}{x+2}-\frac{6}{(x+2)^2}+\frac{8}{3(x+2)^3}+C$$

(ii) Let $I = \int \left(\frac{x-1}{x+1}\right)^4 dx$. Then,

$$I = \int \frac{\{(x+1)-2\}^4}{(x+1)^4} dx$$

$$\Rightarrow \quad I = \int \frac{(x+1)^4 - {}^4C_1 (x+1)^3 \times 2 + {}^4C_2 (x+1)^2 \times 2^2 - {}^4C_3 (x+1) \times 2^3 + {}^4C_4 (2)^4}{(x+1)^4} dx$$

$$\Rightarrow \quad I = \int \frac{(x+1)^4 - 8(x+1)^3 + 24(x+1)^2 - 32(x+1) + 16}{(x+1)^4} dx$$

$$\Rightarrow \quad I = \int \left\{1 - \frac{8}{x+1} + \frac{24}{(x+1)^2} - \frac{32}{(x+1)^3} + \frac{16}{(x+1)^4}\right\} dx$$

$$\Rightarrow \quad I = x - 8\log|x+1| - \frac{24}{x+1} + \frac{16}{(x+1)^2} - \frac{16}{3(x+1)^3} + C$$

EXAMPLE 2 *Evaluate:*

(i) $\int \frac{ax+b}{(cx+d)^2} dx$ (ii) $\int \frac{x+2}{(x+1)^2} dx$ (iii) $\int \frac{2+x+x^2}{x^2(2+x)} + \frac{2x-1}{(x+1)^2} dx$

SOLUTION (i) Let $I = \int \frac{ax+b}{(cx+d)^2} dx$

Let $ax+b = \lambda(cx+d) + \mu$. On equating coefficients of like powers of x, we get

$$a = \lambda c \text{ and } b = \lambda d + \mu \Rightarrow \lambda = \frac{a}{c} \text{ and } \mu = \frac{bc-ad}{c}$$

$$\therefore \quad I = \int \frac{ax+b}{(cd+d)^2} dx = \int \frac{\lambda(cx+d)+\mu}{(cx+d)^2} dx = \lambda \int \frac{1}{cx+d} dx + \mu \int \frac{1}{(cx+d)^2} dx$$

$$\Rightarrow \quad I = \frac{\lambda}{c} \log|cx+d| - \frac{\mu}{c(cx+d)} + C = \frac{a}{c^2} \log|cx+d| - \frac{(bc-ad)}{c^2} \times \frac{1}{cx+d} + C$$

ALITER Let

$$I = \int \frac{ax+b}{(cx+d)^2} dx. \text{ Then,}$$

$$I = a \int \frac{x + \frac{b}{a}}{(cx+d)^2} dx \quad \text{[Making coefficient of } x \text{ unity in the numerator]}$$

$$\Rightarrow \quad I = \frac{a}{c} \int \frac{cx + \frac{bc}{a}}{(cx+d)^2} dx \quad \text{[Making } c \text{ as the coefficient of } x \text{ in the numerator]}$$

$$\Rightarrow \quad I = \frac{a}{c} \int \frac{(cx+d) + \frac{bc}{a} - d}{(cx+d)^2} dx \quad \text{[Adding and subtracting } d \text{ in the numerator]}$$

$$\Rightarrow \quad I = \frac{a}{c} \int \frac{1}{(cx+d)} dx + \frac{(bc-ad)}{c} \int \frac{1}{(cx+d)^2} dx \quad \text{[Separating the integrals]}$$

$$\Rightarrow \quad I = \frac{a}{c^2} \log|cx+d| - \frac{(bc-ad)}{c^2} \times \frac{1}{(cx+d)} + C$$

(ii) Let $x+2 = \lambda(x+1) + \mu$. On equating the coefficients of like powers of x on both sides, we get

$\lambda = 1$ and $2 = \lambda + \mu \Rightarrow \lambda = 1, \mu = 1$

$\therefore \quad I = \int \frac{x+2}{(x+1)^2}\, dx = \int \frac{\lambda(x+1)+\mu}{(x+1)^2}\, dx = \int \left\{\frac{\lambda}{x+1} + \frac{\mu}{(x+1)^2}\right\} dx$

$\Rightarrow \quad I = \lambda \int \frac{1}{x+1}\, dx + \mu \int \frac{1}{(x+1)^2}\, dx = \lambda \ln|x+1| - \frac{\mu}{x+1} + C = \ln|x+1| - \frac{1}{x+1} + C$

ALITER $I = \int \frac{x+2}{(x+1)^2}\, dx = \int \frac{(x+1)+1}{(x+1)^2}\, dx = \int \left\{\frac{1}{x+1} + \frac{1}{(x+1)^2}\right\} dx = \ln|x+1| - \frac{1}{x+1} + C$

(iii) Let $I = \int \left\{\frac{2+x+x^2}{x^2(2+x)} + \frac{2x-1}{(x+1)^2}\right\} dx$. Then,

$I = \int \left\{\frac{(2+x)+x^2}{x^2(2+x)} + \frac{2(x+1)-3}{(x+1)^2}\right\} dx = \int \left\{\frac{1}{x^2} + \frac{1}{2+x} + \frac{2}{x+1} - \frac{3}{(x+1)^2}\right\} dx$

$\Rightarrow \quad I = -\frac{1}{x} + \ln|2+x| + 2\ln|x+1| + \frac{3}{x+1} + C$

EXAMPLE 3 *Evaluate:*

(i) $\int \frac{x^3}{(x+1)^2}\, dx$ (ii) $\int \frac{x^2}{(a+bx)^2}\, dx$ (iii) $\int \frac{x^2+1}{(x+1)^2}\, dx$ [CBSE 2006]

SOLUTION (i) Let $I = \int \frac{x^3}{(x+1)^2}\, dx$. Using long division method, we obtain

$$\frac{x^3}{(x+1)^2} = x - 2 + \frac{3x+2}{(x+1)^2} = x - 2 + \frac{3(x+1)-3+2}{(x+1)^2} = x - 2 + \frac{3}{x+1} - \frac{1}{(x+1)^2}$$

$\therefore \quad I = \int \frac{x^3}{(x+1)^2}\, dx = \int \left\{x - 2 + \frac{3}{x+1} - \frac{1}{(x+1)^2}\right\} dx = \frac{x^2}{2} - 2x + 3\ln|x+1| + \frac{1}{x+1} + C$

(ii) Let $I = \int \frac{x^2}{(a+bx)^2}\, dx$. Using Long division method, we get

$$\frac{x^2}{(a+bx)^2} = \frac{1}{b^2} + \frac{-\frac{2a}{b}x - \frac{a^2}{b^2}}{(bx+a)^2} = \frac{1}{b^2} - \frac{a}{b^2}\,\frac{(2bx+a)}{(bx+a)^2}$$

$\Rightarrow \quad \frac{x^2}{(a+bx)^2} = \frac{1}{b^2} - \frac{a}{b^2}\left\{\frac{2(bx+a)-a}{(bx+a)^2}\right\} = \frac{1}{b^2} - \frac{2a}{b^2} \times \frac{1}{bx+a} + \frac{a^2}{b^2} \times \frac{1}{(bx+a)^2}$

$\therefore \quad I = \int \frac{x^2}{(a+bx)^2}\, dx = \int \left\{\frac{1}{b^2} - \frac{2a}{b^2} \times \frac{1}{bx+a} + \frac{a^2}{b^2} \times \frac{1}{(bx+a)^2}\right\} dx$

$\Rightarrow \quad I = \frac{1}{b^2}\int 1 \cdot dx - \frac{2a}{b^2}\int \frac{1}{bx+a}\, dx + \frac{a^2}{b^2}\int \frac{1}{(bx+a)^2}\, dx$

$\Rightarrow \quad I = \frac{x}{b^2} - \frac{2a}{b^3}\ln|bx+a| - \frac{a^2}{b^3} \times \frac{1}{bx+a} + C = \frac{1}{b^3}\left\{bx - 2a\ln|bx+a| - \frac{a^2}{bx+a}\right\} + C$

ALITER We have,

$$I = \int \frac{x^2}{(a+bx)^2}\,dx = \frac{1}{b^2}\int \frac{b^2 x^2}{(a+bx)^2}\,dx = \frac{1}{b^2}\int \frac{(b^2x^2 + 2abx + a^2) - (2abx + a^2)}{(bx+a)^2}\,dx$$

$$\Rightarrow \quad I = \frac{1}{b^2}\int \frac{(bx+a)^2 - \{2a(bx+a) - 2a^2 + a^2\}}{(bx+a)^2}\,dx = \frac{1}{b^2}\int \frac{(bx+a)^2 - 2a(bx+a) + a^2}{(bx+a)^2}\,dx$$

$$\Rightarrow \quad I = \frac{1}{b^2}\int \left\{1 - \frac{2a}{bx+a} + \frac{a^2}{(bx+a)^2}\right\} dx = \frac{1}{b^2}\left\{x - \frac{2a}{b}\ln|bx+a| - \frac{a^2}{b(bx+a)}\right\} + C$$

$$\Rightarrow \quad I = \frac{1}{b^3}\left\{bx - 2a\ln|bx+a| - \frac{a^2}{bx+a}\right\} + C$$

(iii) Let $I = \int \frac{x^2+1}{(x+1)^2}\,dx$. Then,

$$I = \int \frac{x^2+1+2x-2x}{(x+1)^2}\,dx = \int \frac{(x+1)^2 - 2x}{(x+1)^2}\,dx = \int 1 - \frac{2x}{(x+1)^2}\,dx$$

$$\Rightarrow \quad I = \int 1\cdot dx - 2\int \frac{x}{(x+1)^2}\,dx = \int 1\cdot dx - 2\int \frac{(x+1)-1}{(x+1)^2}\,dx$$

$$\Rightarrow \quad I = \int 1\cdot dx - 2\int \left\{\frac{1}{x+1} - \frac{1}{(x+1)^2}\right\} dx$$

$$\Rightarrow \quad I = \int 1\cdot dx - 2\int \frac{1}{x+1}\,dx + 2\int \frac{1}{(x+1)^2}\,dx = x - 2\ln|x+1| - \frac{2}{x+1} + C$$

EXAMPLE 4 *Evaluate:*

(i) $\int \frac{x^3}{x+2}\,dx$ (ii) $\int \frac{x^7}{x+1}\,dx$ (iii) $\int \frac{x^6}{x-1}\,dx$

SOLUTION (i) Using long division method, we obtain

$$\frac{x^3}{x+2} = x^2 - 2x + 4 - \frac{8}{x+2}$$

$$\Rightarrow \quad \int \frac{x^3}{x+2}\,dx = \int \left\{x^2 - 2x + 4 - \frac{8}{x+2}\right\} dx = \frac{x^3}{3} - x^2 + 4x - 8\ln|x+2| + C$$

ALITER Let $I = \int \frac{x^3}{x+2}\,dx$. Then,

$$I = \int \frac{(x^3 + 2^3) - 2^3}{x+2}\,dx = \int \left\{\frac{(x+2)(x^2 - 2x + 4)}{x+2} - \frac{8}{x+2}\right\} dx$$

$$\Rightarrow \quad I = \int \left\{x^2 - 2x + 4 - \frac{8}{x+2}\right\} dx = \frac{x^3}{3} - x^2 + 4x - 8\ln|x+2| + C$$

(ii) Using long division method, we have

$$\frac{x^7}{x+1} = x^6 - x^5 + x^4 - x^3 + x^2 - x + 1 - \frac{1}{x+1}$$

$$\therefore \quad \int \frac{x^7}{x+1}\, dx = \int \left\{ x^6 - x^5 + x^4 - x^3 + x^2 - x + 1 - \frac{1}{x+1} \right\} dx$$

$$\Rightarrow \quad \int \frac{x^7}{x+1}\, dx = \frac{x^7}{7} - \frac{x^6}{6} + \frac{x^5}{5} - \frac{x^4}{4} + \frac{x^3}{3} - \frac{x^2}{2} + x - \log|x+1| + C$$

ALITER Let $I = \int \frac{x^7}{x+1}\, dx$. Then,

$$I = \int \frac{(x^7+1)-1}{x+1}\, dx = \int \frac{x^7+1}{x+1}\, dx - \int \frac{1}{x+1}\, dx = \int \frac{x^7-(-1)^7}{x-(-1)}\, dx - \int \frac{1}{x+1}\, dx$$

$$\Rightarrow \quad I = \int (x^6 - x^5 + x^4 - x^3 + x^2 - x + 1)\, dx - \int \frac{1}{x+1}\, dx \quad \left[\because \frac{x^n - a^n}{x-a} = x^{n-1} + x^{n-2}a + x^{n-3}a^2 + \ldots + x\,a^{n-2} + a^{n-1} \right]$$

$$\Rightarrow \quad I = \frac{x^7}{7} - \frac{x^6}{6} + \frac{x^5}{5} - \frac{x^4}{4} + \frac{x^3}{3} - \frac{x^2}{2} + x - \log|x+1| + C$$

(iii) Let $I = \int \frac{x^6}{x-1}\, dx = \int \frac{x^6 - 1^6 + 1^6}{x-1}\, dx = \int \frac{x^6 - 1^6}{x-1} + \frac{1}{x-1}\, dx$

$$\Rightarrow \quad I = \int \left\{ x^5 + x^4 + x^3 + x^2 + x + 1 + \frac{1}{x-1} \right\} dx \quad \left[\because \frac{x^n - a^n}{x-a} = x^{n-1} + x^{n-2}a + x^{n-3}a^2 + \ldots + x\,a^{n-2} + a^{n-1} \right]$$

$$\Rightarrow \quad I = \frac{x^6}{6} + \frac{x^5}{5} + \frac{x^4}{4} + \frac{x^3}{3} + \frac{x^2}{2} + x + \log|x-1| + C$$

EXERCISE 15.4

BASED ON HOTS

1. $\int \frac{x^2+5x+2}{x+2}\, dx$
2. $\int \frac{x^3}{x-2}\, dx$
3. $\int \frac{x^2+x+5}{3x+2}\, dx$
4. $\int \frac{2x+3}{(x-1)^2}\, dx$
5. $\int \frac{x^2+3x-1}{(x+1)^2}\, dx$
6. $\int \frac{2x-1}{(x-1)^2}\, dx$

ANSWERS

1. $\frac{x^2}{2} + 3x - 4\log|x+2| + C$
2. $\frac{x^3}{3} + x^2 + 4x + 8\log|x-2| + C$
3. $\frac{x^2}{6} + \frac{1}{9}x + \frac{43}{27}\log|3x+2| + C$
4. $2\log|x-1| - \frac{5}{x-1} + C$
5. $x + \log|x+1| + \frac{3}{x+1} + C$
6. $-\frac{1}{x-1} + 2\log|x-1| + C$

15.8.3 EVALUATION OF INTEGRALS OF THE FORM $\int (ax+b)\sqrt{cx+d}\, dx$ AND $\int \frac{ax+b}{\sqrt{cx+d}}\, dx$

In order to evaluate this type of integrals, we may use the following algorithm:

ALGORITHM

Step I *Write* $(ax+b)$ *in terms of* $(cx+d)$ *as follows:* $(ax+b) = \lambda(cx+d)+\mu$

Step II *Find* λ *and* μ *by equating coefficients of like powers of* x *on both sides.*

Step III *Replace* $ax+b$ *by* $\lambda(cx+d)+\mu$ *in the given integral to obtain*

$$\int (ax+b)\sqrt{cx+d}\ dx = \int \left\{\lambda(cx+d)+\mu\right\}\sqrt{cx+d}\ dx$$

$$= \lambda\int (cx+d)^{3/2}\, dx + \mu\int \sqrt{cx+d}\ dx$$

$$= \frac{2\lambda}{5c}(cx+d)^{5/2} + \frac{2\mu}{3c}(cx+d)^{3/2} + C$$

$$\int \frac{ax+b}{\sqrt{cx+d}}\, dx = \int \frac{\lambda(cx+d)+\mu}{\sqrt{cx+d}}\, dx = \lambda\int\sqrt{cx+d}\ dx + \mu\int\frac{1}{\sqrt{cx+d}}\, dx$$

$$= \frac{2\lambda}{3c}(cx+d)^{3/2} + \frac{2\mu}{c}(cx+d)^{1/2} + C$$

Following examples will illustrate the above procedure:

ILLUSTRATIVE EXAMPLES

BASED ON LOWER ORDER THINKING SKILLS (LOTS)

EXAMPLE 1 *Evaluate:* (i) $\int x\sqrt{x+2}\ dx$ (ii) $\int (7x-2)\sqrt{3x+2}\ dx$

SOLUTION (i) Let $I = \int x\sqrt{x+2}\ dx$. Then,

$$I = \int \{(x+2)-2\}\sqrt{x+2}\ dx \qquad [\because x = (x+2)-2]$$

$$\Rightarrow \quad I = \int \{(x+2)^{3/2} - 2(x+2)^{1/2}\}\, dx = \frac{2}{5}(x+2)^{5/2} - \frac{4}{3}(x+2)^{3/2} + C$$

(ii) Let $I = \int (7x-2)\sqrt{3x+2}\ dx$. Let $7x-2 = \lambda(3x+2)+\mu$

On equating the coefficients of like powers of x on both sides, we get

$$3\lambda = 7 \text{ and } -2 = 2\lambda+\mu \Rightarrow \lambda = \frac{7}{3} \text{ and } \mu = -\frac{20}{3}$$

$$\therefore \quad I = \int \{\lambda(3x+2)+\mu\}\sqrt{3x+2}\ dx = \int \{\lambda(3x+2)^{3/2} + \mu(3x+2)^{1/2}\}\, dx$$

$$\Rightarrow \quad I = \lambda\left\{\frac{(3x+2)^{5/2}}{\frac{5}{2}\times 3}\right\} + \mu\left\{\frac{(3x+2)^{3/2}}{3\times\frac{3}{2}}\right\} + C = \frac{14}{45}(3x+2)^{5/2} - \frac{40}{27}(3x+2)^{3/2} + C$$

ALITER Let $I = \int (7x-2)\sqrt{3x+2}\ dx$. Then,

$$I = \int 7\left(x-\frac{2}{7}\right)\sqrt{3x+2}\, dx = \int \frac{7}{3}\left(3x-\frac{6}{7}\right)\sqrt{3x+2}\, dx = \frac{7}{3}\int\left(3x+2-2-\frac{6}{7}\right)\sqrt{3x+2}\, dx$$

$$\Rightarrow I = \frac{7}{3}\int\left\{(3x+2)-\frac{20}{7}\right\}\sqrt{3x+2}\ dx = \frac{7}{3}\int\left\{(3x+2)^{3/2} - \frac{20}{7}\sqrt{3x+2}\right\} dx$$

$$\Rightarrow I = \frac{7}{3}\left\{\frac{(3x+2)^{5/2}}{3\times\frac{5}{2}} - \frac{20}{7}\times\frac{(3x+2)^{3/2}}{\frac{3}{2}\times 3}\right\} + C = \frac{14}{45}(3x+2)^{5/2} - \frac{40}{27}(3x+2)^{3/2} + C$$

EXAMPLE 2 *Evaluate:* (i) $\int \frac{x}{\sqrt{x+2}}\,dx$ (ii) $\int \frac{x+1}{\sqrt{2x-1}}\,dx$

SOLUTION (i) Let $I = \int \frac{x}{\sqrt{x+2}}\,dx$. Then,

$$I = \int \frac{(x+2)-2}{\sqrt{x+2}}\,dx = \int \left\{\sqrt{x+2} - \frac{2}{\sqrt{x+2}}\right\} dx$$

$$\Rightarrow \quad I = \left\{\frac{(x+2)^{3/2}}{\frac{3}{2}}\right\} - 2\left\{\frac{(x+2)^{1/2}}{\frac{1}{2}}\right\} + C = \frac{2}{3}(x+2)^{3/2} - 4(x+2)^{1/2} + C$$

(ii) Let $I = \int \frac{x+1}{\sqrt{2x-1}}\,dx$. Then,

$$I = \frac{1}{2}\int \frac{2x+2}{\sqrt{2x-1}}\,dx = \frac{1}{2}\int \frac{(2x-1)+3}{\sqrt{2x-1}}\,dx = \frac{1}{2}\int \left\{\sqrt{2x-1} + \frac{3}{\sqrt{2x-1}}\right\} dx$$

$$\Rightarrow \quad I = \frac{1}{2}\int \sqrt{2x-1}\,dx + \frac{3}{2}\,\frac{1}{\sqrt{2x-1}}\,dx$$

$$\Rightarrow \quad I = \frac{1}{2}\left\{\frac{(2x-1)^{3/2}}{2\times\frac{3}{2}}\right\} + \frac{3}{2}\left\{\frac{(2x-1)^{1/2}}{2\times\frac{1}{2}}\right\} + C = \frac{1}{6}(2x-1)^{3/2} + \frac{3}{2}(2x-1)^{1/2} + C$$

BASED ON HIGHER ORDER THINKING SKILLS (HOTS)

EXAMPLE 3 *Evaluate:* $\int \frac{8x+13}{\sqrt{4x+7}}\,dx$

SOLUTION Let $I = \int \frac{8x+13}{\sqrt{4x+7}}\,dx$. Let $8x+13 = \lambda(4x+7)+\mu$

On equating the coefficients of like powers of x on both sides, we get

$$8 = 4\lambda,\ 13 = 7\lambda + \mu \Rightarrow \lambda = 2 \text{ and } \mu = -1$$

Replacing $8x+13$ by $\lambda(4x+7)+\mu$ in the given integral, we obtain

$$I = \int \frac{\lambda(4x+7)+\mu}{\sqrt{4x+7}}\,dx = \int \left\{\lambda\sqrt{4x+7} + \frac{\mu}{\sqrt{4x+7}}\right\} dx$$

$$\Rightarrow \quad I = \lambda\int \sqrt{4x+7}\,dx + \mu\int \frac{1}{\sqrt{4x+7}}\,dx$$

$$\Rightarrow \quad I = \lambda\left\{\frac{(4x+7)^{3/2}}{4\times\frac{3}{2}}\right\} + \mu\left\{\frac{(4x+7)^{1/2}}{4\times\frac{1}{2}}\right\} + C = \frac{1}{3}(4x+7)^{3/2} - \frac{1}{2}(4x+7)^{1/2} + C$$

ALITER Let $I = \int \frac{8x+13}{\sqrt{4x+7}}\,dx$. Then,

$$I = 8 \int \frac{x + \frac{13}{8}}{\sqrt{4x+7}}\, dx$$

$$\Rightarrow \quad I = \frac{8}{4} \int \frac{4x + \frac{13}{2}}{\sqrt{4x+7}}\, dx = 2 \int \frac{(4x+7) + \left(\frac{13}{2} - 7\right)}{\sqrt{4x+7}}\, dx = 2 \int \frac{(4x+7) - \frac{1}{2}}{\sqrt{4x+7}}\, dx$$

$$\Rightarrow \quad I = 2 \int \left\{ \sqrt{4x+7} - \frac{1}{2} \times \frac{1}{\sqrt{4x+7}} \right\} dx$$

$$\Rightarrow \quad I = 2 \left\{ \frac{(4x+7)^{3/2}}{4 \times \frac{3}{2}} \right\} - \frac{1}{2} \left\{ \frac{(4x+7)^{1/2}}{4 \times \frac{1}{2}} \right\} + C = \frac{1}{3}\,(4x+7)^{3/2} - \frac{1}{2}\,(4x+7)^{1/2} + C$$

EXAMPLE 4 *Evaluate:* $\int \frac{x}{\sqrt{x+a} + \sqrt{x+b}}\, dx.$

SOLUTION Let $I = \int \frac{x}{\sqrt{x+a} + \sqrt{x+b}}\, dx$. Then,

$$I = \int \frac{x\left\{\sqrt{x+a} - \sqrt{x+b}\right\}}{\left\{\sqrt{x+a} + \sqrt{x+b}\right\}\left\{\sqrt{x+a} - \sqrt{x+b}\right\}}\, dx = \int \frac{x\left\{\sqrt{x+a} - \sqrt{x+b}\right\}}{a-b}\, dx$$

$$\Rightarrow \quad I = \frac{1}{a-b} \int \left\{ x\sqrt{x+a} - x\sqrt{x+b} \right\} dx$$

$$\Rightarrow \quad I = \frac{1}{a-b} \int \left\{ (x+a-a)\sqrt{x+a} - (x+b-b)\sqrt{x+b} \right\} dx$$

$$\Rightarrow \quad I = \frac{1}{a-b} \int \left\{ (x+a)^{3/2} - a\sqrt{x+a} - (x+b)^{3/2} + b\sqrt{x+b} \right\} dx$$

$$\Rightarrow \quad I = \frac{1}{a-b} \left\{ \frac{2}{5}\,(x+a)^{5/2} - \frac{2a}{3}\,(x+a)^{3/2} - \frac{2}{5}(x+b)^{5/2} + \frac{2b}{3}(x+b)^{3/2} \right\} + C$$

EXERCISE 15.5

BASED ON LOTS

1. $\int x\sqrt{1+2x}\, dx$ [CBSE 2024]
2. $\int \frac{x-1}{\sqrt{x+4}}\, dx$
3. $\int \frac{x}{\sqrt{x+4}}\, dx$
4. $\int \frac{x+1}{\sqrt{2x+3}}\, dx$

BASED ON HOTS

5. $\int (x+2)\sqrt{3x+5}\, dx$
6. $\int \frac{2x+1}{\sqrt{3x+2}}\, dx$
7. $\int \frac{3x+5}{\sqrt{7x+9}}\, dx$
8. $\int \frac{2-3x}{\sqrt{1+3x}}\, dx$
9. $\int (5x+3)\sqrt{2x-1}\, dx$
10. $\int \frac{x}{\sqrt{x+a} - \sqrt{x+b}}\, dx$

ANSWERS

1. $\frac{1}{10}(1+2x)^{5/2} - \frac{1}{6}(1+2x)^{3/2} + C$
2. $\frac{2}{3}(x+4)^{3/2} - 10\,(x+4)^{1/2} + C$

3. $\frac{2}{3}(x-8)\sqrt{x+4}+C$

4. $\frac{1}{6}(2x+3)^{3/2}-\frac{1}{2}(2x+3)^{1/2}+C$

5. $\frac{2}{135}(9x+20)(3x+5)^{3/2}+C$

6. $\frac{2}{27}(6x+1)\sqrt{3x+2}+C$

7. $\frac{2}{49}\sqrt{7x+9}\,(7x+17)+C$

8. $\frac{2}{9}(8-3x)\sqrt{1+3x}+C$

9. $\frac{1}{3}(3x+4)(2x-1)^{3/2}+C$

10. $\frac{1}{a-b}\left\{\frac{2}{5}(x+a)^{5/2}-\frac{2a}{3}(x+a)^{3/2}+\frac{2}{5}(x+b)^{5/2}-\frac{2b}{3}(x+b)^{3/2}\right\}+C$

15.8.4 EVALUATION OF INTEGRALS OF THE FORM $\int \sin^m x\,dx$, $\int \cos^m x\,dx$, WHERE $m \le 4$, $m \in N$

To evaluate integrals of the form $\int \sin^m x\,dx$, $\int \cos^m x\,dx$ where $m \le 4$, we express $\sin^m x$ and $\cos^m x$ in terms of sines and cosines of multiples of x by using the following trigonometrical identities:

(i) $\sin^2 x = \frac{1-\cos 2x}{2}$ (ii) $\cos^2 x = \frac{1+\cos 2x}{2}$

(iii) $\sin 3x = 3\sin x - 4\sin^3 x$ (v) $\cos 3x = 4\cos^3 x - 3\cos x$.

Following examples will illustrate the procedure.

ILLUSTRATIVE EXAMPLES

BASED ON BASIC CONCEPTS (BASIC)

EXAMPLE 1 *Evaluate:*

(i) $\int \sin^2 x\,dx$ (ii) $\int \cos^2 x\,dx$ [NCERT] (iii) $\int \sin^2 x \cos^2 x\,dx$

SOLUTION (i) Let $I = \int \sin^2 x\,dx$. Then,

$$I = \int \frac{1-\cos 2x}{2}\,dx = \frac{1}{2}\int (1-\cos 2x)\,dx = \frac{1}{2}\left\{x-\frac{\sin 2x}{2}\right\}+C$$

(ii) Let $I = \int \cos^2 x\,dx$. Then,

$$I = \int \frac{1+\cos 2x}{2}\,dx = \frac{1}{2}\int (1+\cos 2x)\,dx = \frac{1}{2}\left\{x+\frac{\sin 2x}{2}\right\}+C$$

(iii) Let $I = \int \sin^2 x \cos^2 x\,dx$. Then,

$$I = \frac{1}{4}\int (2\sin x\cos x)^2\,dx$$

$$\Rightarrow \quad I = \frac{1}{4}\int \sin^2 2x\,dx = \frac{1}{4}\int \frac{1-\cos 4x}{2}\,dx = \frac{1}{8}\int (1-\cos 4x)\,dx = \frac{1}{8}\left\{x-\frac{\sin 4x}{4}\right\}+C$$

EXAMPLE 2 *Evaluate:*

(i) $\int \sin^3 x\,dx$ [NCERT] (ii) $\int \cos^3 x\,dx$ (iii) $\int \sin^3 x \cos^3 x\,dx$ [NCERT]

SOLUTION (i) Let $I = \int \sin^3 x\,dx$. Then,

$$I = \int \frac{3\sin x - \sin 3x}{4}\,dx = \frac{1}{4}\int (3\sin x - \sin 3x)\,dx = \frac{1}{4}\left\{-3\cos x + \frac{\cos 3x}{3}\right\}+C$$

(ii) Let $I = \int \cos^3 x\, dx$. Then,

$$I = \int \frac{\cos 3x + 3\cos x}{4} dx = \frac{1}{4}\int \cos 3x + 3\cos x\, dx = \frac{1}{4}\left\{\frac{\sin 3x}{3} + 3\sin x\right\} + C$$

(iii) Let $I = \int \sin^3 x \cos^3 x\, dx$. Then,

$$I = \frac{1}{8}\int (2\sin x\cos x)^3\, dx = \frac{1}{8}\int \sin^3 2x\, dx = \frac{1}{8}\int \frac{3\sin 2x - \sin 6x}{4} dx$$

$$\Rightarrow \quad I = \frac{1}{32}\int (3\sin 2x - \sin 6x)\, dx = \frac{1}{32}\left\{-\frac{3}{2}\cos 2x + \frac{1}{6}\cos 6x\right\} + C$$

BASED ON LOWER ORDER THINKING SKILLS (LOTS)

EXAMPLE 3 *Evaluate:*

(i) $\int \sin^4 x\, dx$ [NCERT, CBSE 2000, 2004] (ii) $\int \cos^4 x\, dx$ [CBSE 2000, 2003]

(iii) $\int \sin^4 x \cos^4 x\, dx$

SOLUTION (i) Let $I = \int \sin^4 x\, dx$. Then,

$$I = \int \left(\frac{1 - \cos 2x}{2}\right)^2 dx \qquad \left[\because \sin^2\theta = \frac{1 - \cos 2\theta}{2}\right]$$

$$\Rightarrow \quad I = \frac{1}{4}\int 1 - 2\cos 2x + \cos^2 2x\, dx$$

$$\Rightarrow \quad I = \frac{1}{4}\int 1 - 2\cos 2x + \frac{1 + \cos 4x}{2} dx = \frac{1}{8}\int 2 - 4\cos 2x + 1 + \cos 4x\, dx$$

$$\Rightarrow \quad I = \frac{1}{8}\int 3 - 4\cos 2x + \cos 4x\, dx = \frac{1}{8}\left\{3x - 2\sin 2x + \frac{\sin 4x}{4}\right\} + C$$

(ii) Let $I = \int \cos^4 x\, dx$. Then,

$$I = \int \left(\frac{1 + \cos 2x}{2}\right)^2 dx \qquad \left[\because \cos^2\theta = \frac{1 + \cos 2\theta}{2}\right]$$

$$\Rightarrow \quad I = \frac{1}{4}\int 1 + 2\cos 2x + \cos^2 2x\, dx = \frac{1}{4}\int 1 + 2\cos 2x + \frac{1 + \cos 4x}{2} dx$$

$$\Rightarrow \quad I = \frac{1}{8}\int 3 + 4\cos 2x + \cos 4x\, dx = \frac{1}{8}\left\{3x + 2\sin 2x + \frac{\sin 4x}{4}\right\} + C$$

(iii) Let $I = \int \sin^4 x \cos^4 x\, dx$. Then,

$$I = \frac{1}{16}\int (2\sin x\cos x)^4\, dx = \frac{1}{16}\int (\sin 2x)^4\, dx = \frac{1}{16}\int (\sin^2 2x)^2\, dx$$

$$\Rightarrow \quad I = \frac{1}{16}\int \left(\frac{1 - \cos 4x}{2}\right)^2 dx$$

$$\Rightarrow \quad I = \frac{1}{64}\int (1 - 2\cos 4x + \cos^2 4x)\, dx = \frac{1}{64}\int \left\{1 - 2\cos 4x + \frac{1 + \cos 8x}{2}\right\} dx$$

$$\Rightarrow \quad I = \frac{1}{128}\int \left(3 - 4\cos 4x + \cos 8x\right) dx = \frac{1}{128}\left\{3x - \sin 4x + \frac{1}{8}\sin 8x\right\} + C$$

EXERCISE 15.6

BASIC

1. $\int \sin^2 (2x + 5)\, dx$ [NCERT]
2. $\int \sin^3 (2x + 1)\, dx$ [NCERT]

3. $\int \sin^2 bx\, dx$ 4. $\int \sin^2 \frac{x}{2}\, dx$ 5. $\int \cos^2 \frac{x}{2}\, dx$

6. $\int \cos^2 nx\, dx$ 7. $\int \sin x\sqrt{1-\cos 2x}\, dx$

BASED ON LOTS

8. $\int \cos^4 2x\, dx$ [NCERT] 9. $\int \frac{\sin 3x}{\sin x}\, dx$ [CBSE 2022] 10. $\int \frac{\cos 3x}{\cos x}\, dx$

ANSWERS

1. $\frac{x}{2}-\frac{1}{8}\sin(4x+10)+C$ 2. $-\frac{3}{8}\cos(2x+1)+\frac{1}{24}\cos(6x+3)+C$ 3. $\frac{x}{2}-\frac{\sin 2bx}{4b}+C$

4. $\frac{1}{2}(x-\sin x)+C$ 5. $\frac{1}{2}(x+\sin x)+C$ 6. $\frac{x}{2}+\frac{1}{4n}\sin 2nx+C$ 7. $\frac{1}{\sqrt{2}}x-\frac{\sin 2x}{2\sqrt{2}}+C$

8. $\frac{3x}{8}+\frac{\sin 4x}{8}+\frac{\sin 8x}{64}+C$ 9. $x+\sin 2x+C$ 10. $\sin 2x-x+C$

HINTS TO SELECTED PROBLEMS

1. $\int \sin^2(2x+5)\, dx = \frac{1}{2}\int\left\{1-\cos(4x+10)\right\}dx = \frac{1}{2}\left\{x-\frac{1}{4}\sin(4x+10)\right\}+C$

2. $I=\int \sin^3(2x+1)\, dx = \frac{1}{4}\int\left\{3\sin(2x+1)-\sin 3(2x+1)\right\}dx$

$\Rightarrow\quad I = \frac{1}{4}\int\left\{3\sin(2x+1)-\sin(6x+3\right\}dx = -\frac{3}{8}\cos(2x+1)+\frac{1}{24}\cos(6x+3)+C$

8. $I=\int \cos^4 2x\, dx = \int (\cos^2 2x)^2\, dx = \int\left(\frac{1+\cos 4x}{2}\right)^2 dx$

$= \frac{1}{4}\int(1+2\cos 4x+\cos^2 4x)\, dx = \frac{1}{4}\int 1+2\cos 4x+\frac{1+\cos 8x}{2}\, dx$

$\Rightarrow\quad I = \frac{1}{8}\int(3+4\cos 4x+\cos 8x)\, dx = \frac{1}{8}\left(3x+\sin 4x+\frac{1}{8}\sin 8x\right)+C$

15.8.5 EVALAUTION OF INTEGRALS OF THE FORM $\int \sin mx\cos nx\, dx$, $\int \sin mx\sin nx\, dx$, $\int \cos mx\cos nx\, dx$

To evaluate this type of integrals we use the following trigonometrical identities to express the products into sums.

$2\sin A\cos B=\sin(A+B)+\sin(A-B)$; $2\cos A\sin B=\sin(A+B)-\sin(A-B)$

$2\cos A\cos B=\cos(A+B)+\cos(A-B)$; $2\sin A\sin B=\cos(A-B)-\cos(A+B)$

Following examples will illustrate the procedure.

ILLUSTRATIVE EXAMPLES

BASED ON BASIC CONCEPTS (BASIC)

EXAMPLE 1 *Evaluate:*

(i) $\int \sin 4x\cos 3x\, dx$ (ii) $\int \sin 3x\sin 2x\, dx$ [CBSE 2022]

(iii) $\int \sin 3x\cos 4x\, dx$ [NCERT] (iv) $\int \cos 2x\cos 4x\, dx$ [CBSE 2007]

SOLUTION (i) Let $I = \int \sin 4x\cos 3x\, dx$. Then,

$I = \frac{1}{2}\int 2\sin 4x\cos 3x\, dx = \frac{1}{2}\int(\sin 7x+\sin x)\, dx = \frac{1}{2}\left\{-\frac{\cos 7x}{7}-\cos x\right\}+C$

(ii) Let $I = \int \sin 3x \sin 2x\, dx$. Then,

$$I = \frac{1}{2}\int 2\sin 3x \sin 2x\, dx = \frac{1}{2}\int (\cos x - \cos 5x)\, dx = \frac{1}{2}\left\{\sin x - \frac{\sin 5x}{5}\right\} + C$$

(iii) Let $I = \int \sin 3x \cos 4x\, dx$. Then,

$$I = \frac{1}{2}\int 2\sin 3x \cos 4x\, dx$$

$$\Rightarrow \quad I = \frac{1}{2}\int \left\{\sin 7x + \sin(-x)\right\} dx = \frac{1}{2}\int (\sin 7x - \sin x)\, dx = \frac{1}{2}\left\{-\frac{\cos 7x}{7} + \cos x\right\} + C$$

(iv) Let $I = \int \cos 2x \cos 4x\, dx$. Then,

$$I = \frac{1}{2}\int 2\cos 4x \cos 2x\, dx = \frac{1}{2}\int (\cos 6x + \cos 2x)\, dx = \frac{1}{2}\left\{\frac{\sin 6x}{6} + \frac{\sin 2x}{2}\right\} + C$$

BASED ON LOWER ORDER THINKING SKILLS (LOTS)

EXAMPLE 2 *Evaluate:*

(i) $\int \cos 2x \cos 4x \cos 6x\, dx$ [NCERT] (ii) $\int \sin x \sin 2x \sin 3x\, dx$ [CBSE 2012, NCERT]

SOLUTION (i) Let $I = \int \cos 2x \cos 4x \cos 6x\, dx$. Then,

$$I = \frac{1}{2}\int (2\cos 4x \cos 2x) \cos 6x\, dx$$

$$\Rightarrow \quad I = \frac{1}{2}\int (\cos 6x + \cos 2x)\cos 6x\, dx = \frac{1}{4}\int (2\cos^2 6x + 2\cos 6x \cos 2x)\, dx$$

$$\Rightarrow \quad I = \frac{1}{4}\int 1 + \cos 12x + \cos 8x + \cos 4x = \frac{1}{4}\left\{x + \frac{\sin 12x}{12} + \frac{\sin 8x}{8} + \frac{\sin 4x}{4}\right\} + C$$

(ii) Let $I = \int \sin x \sin 2x \sin 3x\, dx$. Then,

$$I = \frac{1}{2}\int (2\sin 2x \sin x) \sin 3x\, dx$$

$$\Rightarrow \quad I = \frac{1}{2}\int (\cos x - \cos 3x)\sin 3x\, dx = \frac{1}{4}\int (2\sin 3x \cos x - 2\sin 3x \cos 3x)\, dx$$

$$\Rightarrow \quad I = \frac{1}{4}\int (\sin 4x + \sin 2x - \sin 6x)\, dx = \frac{1}{4}\left\{-\frac{\cos 4x}{4} - \frac{\cos 2x}{2} + \frac{\cos 6x}{6}\right\} + C$$

EXAMPLE 3 *Evaluate:* $\int \frac{\sin 4x}{\sin x}\, dx$

SOLUTION Let $I = \int \frac{\sin 4x}{\sin x}\, dx$. Then,

$$I = \int \frac{2\sin 2x \cos 2x}{\sin x}\, dx = \int \frac{4\sin x \cos x \cos 2x}{\sin x}\, dx$$

$$\Rightarrow \quad I = 2\int 2\cos 2x \cos x\, dx = 2\int (\cos 3x + \cos x)\, dx = 2\left\{\frac{\sin 3x}{3} + \sin x\right\} + C$$

BASED ON HIGHER ORDER THINKING SKILLS (HOTS)

EXAMPLE 4 *Evaluate :* $\int \frac{\cos 5x + \cos 4x}{1 - 2\cos 3x}\, dx$ [NCERT EXEMPLAR]

SOLUTION Let $I = \int \frac{\cos 5x + \cos 4x}{1 - 2\cos 3x}\, dx$. Then,

$$\Rightarrow \quad I = \int \frac{\sin 3x (\cos 5x + \cos 4x)}{\sin 3x - 2 \sin 3x \cos 3x}\, dx$$

$$\Rightarrow \quad I = \int \frac{\left(2 \sin \frac{3x}{2} \cos \frac{3x}{2}\right)\left(2 \cos \frac{9x}{2} \cos \frac{x}{2}\right)}{\sin 3x - \sin 6x}\, dx = 4 \int \frac{\sin \frac{3x}{2} \cos \frac{3x}{2} \cos \frac{9x}{2} \cos \frac{x}{2}}{-2 \cos \frac{9x}{2} \sin \frac{3x}{2}}\, dx$$

$$\Rightarrow \quad I = -\int 2 \cos \frac{3x}{2} \cos \frac{x}{2}\, dx = -\int (\cos 2x + \cos x)\, dx = -\left(\frac{\sin 2x}{2} + \sin x\right) + C$$

EXERCISE 15.7

BASIC

Integrate the following integrals:

1. $\int \sin 4x \cos 7x\, dx$ [CBSE 2007]
2. $\int \cos 3x \cos 4x\, dx$
3. $\int \cos mx \cos nx\, dx, m \neq n$
4. $\int \sin mx \cos nx\, dx, \ m \neq n$

BASED ON LOTS

5. $\int \sin 2x \sin 4x \sin 6x\ dx$
6. $\int \sin x \cos 2x \sin 3x\, dx$

ANSWERS

1. $-\frac{1}{22} \cos 11\, x + \frac{1}{6} \cos 3x + C$
2. $\frac{1}{14} \sin 7x + \frac{1}{2} \sin x + C$
3. $\frac{1}{2}\left\{\frac{\sin (m+n)\, x}{m+n} + \frac{\sin (m-n)\, x}{m-n}\right\} + C$
4. $\frac{1}{2}\left\{-\frac{\cos (m+n)\, x}{m+n} - \frac{\cos (m-n)\, x}{m-n}\right\} + C$
5. $-\frac{1}{32} \cos 8x + \frac{1}{48} \cos 12x - \frac{1}{16} \cos 4x + C$
6. $\frac{x}{4} + \frac{1}{16} \sin 4x - \frac{1}{24} \sin 6x - \frac{1}{8} \sin 2x + C$

15.8.6 INTEGRALS OF THE FORM $\int \frac{f'(x)}{f(x)}\, dx$

THEOREM 1 $\int \frac{f'(x)}{f(x)}\, dx = \log \{f(x)\} + C$

PROOF Let $I = \int \frac{f'(x)}{f(x)}\, dx$. Putting $f(x) = t$ and $f'(x)\, dx = dt$, we get

$$I = \int \frac{1}{t}\, dt = \ln t + C = \ln |f(x)| + C$$

Q.E.D.

REMARK *It follows from the above theorem that if the numerator in integrand is exact differential of the denominator then its integral is logarithm of the denominator.*

SOME STANDARD RESULTS

THEOREM 2 *Prove that:* $\int \tan x\, dx = -\log |\cos x| + C$ or, $\int \tan x\, dx = \log |\sec x| + C$

PROOF Let $I = \int \tan x\, dx$. Then, $I = \int \frac{\sin x}{\cos x}\, dx$

Let $\cos x = t$. Then, $d(\cos x) = dt \Rightarrow -\sin x\, dx = dt \Rightarrow dx = -\frac{dt}{\sin x}$

Putting $\cos x = t$, and $dx = -dt/\sin x$, we get

$$I = \int \frac{\sin x}{\cos x} \times -\frac{dt}{\sin x} = -\int \frac{1}{t}\, dt = -\ln|t| + C = -\ln|\cos x| + C$$

Hence, $\int \tan x\, dx = -\ln|\cos x| + C$ or, $\int \tan x\, dx = \ln|\sec x| + C$

Q.E.D.

THEOREM 3 *Prove that:* $\int \cot x\, dx = \ln|\sin x| + C.$

PROOF Let $I = \int \cot x\, dx$. Then, $I = \int \frac{\cos x}{\sin x}\, dx.$

Let $\sin x = t$. Then, $d(\sin x) = dt \Rightarrow \cos x\, dx = dt \Rightarrow dx = \frac{dt}{\cos x}$

Putting $\sin x = t$, and $dx = dt/\cos x$, we get

$$I = \int \frac{\cos x}{t} \cdot \frac{dt}{\cos x} = \int \frac{1}{t}\, dt = \ln|t| + C = \ln|\sin x| + C$$

Hence, $\int \cot x\, dx = \ln|\sin x| + C.$ Q.E.D.

THEOREM 4 *Prove that:* $\int \sec x\, dx = \ln|\sec x + \tan x| + C.$

PROOF Let $I = \int \sec x\, dx$. Then, $I = \int \frac{\sec x(\sec x + \tan x)}{(\sec x + \tan x)}\, dx$

Let $\sec x + \tan x = t$. Then,

$$d(\sec x + \tan x) = dt \Rightarrow (\sec x \tan x + \sec^2 x)\, dx = dt \Rightarrow dx = \frac{dt}{\sec x(\sec x + \tan x)}$$

Putting $\sec x + \tan x = t$ and $dx = \frac{dt}{\sec x(\sec x + \tan x)}$, we get

$$I = \int \frac{\sec x(\sec x + \tan x)}{t} \times \frac{dt}{\sec x(\sec x + \tan x)} = \int \frac{1}{t}\, dt = \ln|t| + C = \ln|\sec x + \tan x| + C$$

Hence, $\int \sec x\, dx = |\sec x + \tan x| + C.$ Q.E.D.

THEOREM 5 *Prove that:* $\int \operatorname{cosec} x\, dx = \ln|\operatorname{cosec} x - \cot x| + C.$

PROOF Let $I = \int \operatorname{cosec} x\, dx$. Then, $I = \int \frac{\operatorname{cosec} x(\operatorname{cosec} x - \cot x)}{\operatorname{cosec} x - \cot x}\, dx$

Let $\operatorname{cosec} x - \cot x = t$. Then,

$$d(\operatorname{cosec} x - \cot x) = dt \Rightarrow (-\operatorname{cosec} x \cot x + \operatorname{cosec}^2 x)\, dx = dt \Rightarrow dx = \frac{dt}{\operatorname{cosec} x(\operatorname{cosec} x - \cot x)}$$

Putting $\operatorname{cosec} x - \cot x = t$ and, $dx = \frac{dt}{\operatorname{cosec} x(\operatorname{cosec} x - \cot x)}$, we get

$$I = \int \frac{\operatorname{cosec} x(\operatorname{cosec} x - \cot x)}{\operatorname{cosec} x - \cot x} \times \frac{dt}{(\operatorname{cosec} x - \cot x)\operatorname{cosec} x}$$

$$\Rightarrow \quad I = \int \frac{1}{t}\, dt = \ln|t| + C = \ln|\operatorname{cosec} x - \cot x| + C$$

Hence, $\int \operatorname{cosec} x\, dx = \ln|\operatorname{cosec} x - \cot x| + C$ Q.E.D.

ALTERATIVE FORMULAE FOR $\int \operatorname{cosec} x\, dx$ AND $\int \sec x\, dx$

Let $I = \int \operatorname{cosec} x\, dx = \int \frac{1}{\sin x} dx = \int \frac{1}{2 \sin x/2 \cos x/2} dx$. Then,

$$I = \int \frac{\sec^2 x/2}{2 \tan x/2} dx \qquad \left[\text{Divide both numerator and denumerator by } \cos^2 \frac{x}{2}\right]$$

Let $\tan \frac{x}{2} = t$. Then, $d\left(\tan \frac{x}{2}\right) = dt \Rightarrow \frac{1}{2} \sec^2 \frac{x}{2} dx = dt \Rightarrow dx = \frac{2\, dt}{\sec^2 \frac{x}{2}}$

Putting $\tan \frac{x}{2} = t$ and $dx = \frac{2dt}{\sec^2 \frac{x}{2}}$, we get

$$I = \int \frac{1}{t} dt = \ln |t| + C = \ln \left| \tan \frac{x}{2} \right| + C$$

Hence, $\int \operatorname{cosec} x\, dx = \ln \left| \tan \frac{x}{2} \right| + C$ ...(i)

$$\int \sec x\, dx = \int \operatorname{cosec}\left(\frac{\pi}{2} + x\right) dx = \log \left| \tan \left(\frac{\pi}{4} + \frac{x}{2}\right) \right| + C \qquad \text{[Using (i)]}$$

Hence, $\int \sec x\, dx = \ln \left| \tan \left(\frac{\pi}{4} + \frac{x}{2}\right) \right| + C$

ILLUSTRATIVE EXAMPLES

BASED ON BASIC CONCEPTS (BASIC)

Type I **PROBLEMS BASED ON** $\int \tan x\, dx, \int \cot x\, dx, \int \sec x\, dx, \int \operatorname{cosec} x\, dx$

EXAMPLE 1 *Evaluate:*

(i) $\int \frac{1}{\sqrt{1 + \cos 2x}} dx$ (ii) $\int \frac{1}{\sqrt{1 - \cos x}} dx$ (iii) $\int \sqrt{\frac{1 - \cos 2x}{1 + \cos 2x}}$ (iv) $\int \sqrt{\frac{1 + \cos x}{1 - \cos x}} dx$

SOLUTION (i) We have,

$$\int \frac{1}{\sqrt{1 + \cos 2x}} dx = \int \frac{1}{\sqrt{2 \cos^2 x}} dx = \frac{1}{\sqrt{2}} \int \sec x\, dx = \frac{1}{\sqrt{2}} \ln |\sec x + \tan x| + C$$

(ii) $$\int \frac{1}{\sqrt{1 - \cos x}} dx = \int \frac{1}{\sqrt{2 \sin^2 \frac{x}{2}}} dx = \frac{1}{\sqrt{2}} \int \operatorname{cosec} \frac{x}{2} dx = \sqrt{2} \ln \left| \operatorname{cosec} \frac{x}{2} - \cot \frac{x}{2} \right| + C$$

(iii) $$\int \sqrt{\frac{1 - \cos 2x}{1 + \cos 2x}} dx = \int \sqrt{\frac{2 \sin^2 x}{2 \cos^2 x}} dx = \int \tan x\, dx = \ln |\sec x| + C$$

(iv) $$\int \sqrt{\frac{1 + \cos x}{1 - \cos x}} dx = \int \sqrt{\frac{2 \cos^2 \frac{x}{2}}{2 \sin^2 \frac{x}{2}}} dx = \int \cot \frac{x}{2} dx = 2 \ln \left| \sin \frac{x}{2} \right| + C$$

BASED ON LOWER ORDER THINKING SKILLS (LOTS)

EXAMPLE 2 *Evaluate:*

(i) $\int \frac{1}{\sqrt{1+\sin 2x}}\,dx$ (ii) $\int \frac{1}{\sqrt{1-\sin x}}\,dx$

SOLUTION (i) Let $I = \int \frac{1}{\sqrt{1+\sin 2x}}\,dx$. Then,

$$I = \int \frac{1}{\sqrt{1-\cos\left(\frac{\pi}{2}+2x\right)}}\,dx = \int \frac{1}{\sqrt{2\sin^2\left(\frac{\pi}{4}+x\right)}}\,dx$$

$$\Rightarrow \quad I = \frac{1}{\sqrt{2}}\int \operatorname{cosec}\left(\frac{\pi}{4}+x\right)dx = \frac{1}{\sqrt{2}}\ln\left|\tan\left(\frac{\pi}{8}+\frac{x}{2}\right)\right| + C$$

(ii) Let $I = \int \frac{1}{\sqrt{1-\sin x}}\,dx$. Then,

$$I = \int \frac{1}{\sqrt{1+\cos\left(\frac{\pi}{2}+x\right)}}\,dx = \int \frac{1}{\sqrt{2\cos^2\left(\frac{\pi}{4}+\frac{x}{2}\right)}}\,dx = \frac{1}{\sqrt{2}}\int \sec\left(\frac{\pi}{4}+\frac{x}{2}\right)dx$$

$$\Rightarrow \quad I = \frac{2}{\sqrt{2}}\ln\left|\tan\left(\frac{\pi}{4}+\frac{\pi}{8}+\frac{x}{4}\right)\right| + C = \sqrt{2}\ln\left|\tan\left(\frac{3\pi}{8}+\frac{x}{4}\right)\right| + C$$

BASED ON HIGHER ORDER THINKING SKILLS (HOTS)

EXAMPLE 3 *Evaluate:*

(i) $\int \frac{\sin(x-a)}{\sin x}\,dx$ (ii) $\int \frac{\sin x}{\sin(x-a)}\,dx$ [NCERT, CBSE 2004]

(iii) $\int \frac{1}{\sin(x-a)\sin(x-b)}\,dx$

SOLUTION (i) Let $I = \int \frac{\sin(x-a)}{\sin x}\,dx$. Then,

$$I = \int \frac{\sin x\cos a - \cos x\sin a}{\sin x}\,dx = \int \cos a\,dx - \int \sin a\cot x\,dx$$

$$\Rightarrow \quad I = \cos a\int 1\cdot dx - \sin a\int \cot x\,dx = x\cos a - \sin a\ln|\sin x| + C$$

(ii) Let $I = \int \frac{\sin x}{\sin(x-a)}\,dx$. Then,

$$I = \int \frac{\sin\{(x-a)+a\}}{\sin(x-a)}\,dx$$

$$\Rightarrow \quad I = \int \frac{\sin(x-a)\cos a + \cos(x-a)\sin a}{\sin(x-a)}\,dx = \int \{\cos a + \cot(x-a)\sin a\}\,dx$$

$$\Rightarrow \quad I = \cos a\int 1\cdot dx + \sin a\int \cot(x-a)\,dx = x\cos a + \sin a\ln|\sin(x-a)| + C$$

(iii) Let $I = \int \frac{1}{\sin(x-a)\sin(x-b)}\,dx$. Then,

$$I = \frac{1}{\sin(a-b)}\int \frac{\sin\{(x-b)-(x-a)\}}{\sin(x-a)\sin(x-b)}\,dx$$

$$\Rightarrow \quad I = \frac{1}{\sin(a-b)}\int \frac{\sin(x-b)\cos(x-a) - \cos(x-b)\sin(x-a)}{\sin(x-a)\sin(x-b)}\,dx$$

$$\Rightarrow \quad I = \frac{1}{\sin(a-b)} \int \{\cot(x-a) - \cot(x-b)\}\, dx$$

$$\Rightarrow \quad I = \frac{1}{\sin(a-b)} \Big\{ \ln|\sin(x-a)| - \ln|\sin(x-b)| \Big\} + C$$

$$\Rightarrow \quad I = \operatorname{cosec}(a-b) \ln\left|\frac{\sin(x-a)}{\sin(x-b)}\right| + C$$

EXAMPLE 4 *Evaluate:*

(i) $\displaystyle\int \frac{1}{\sin(x-a)\cos(x-b)}\, dx$ (ii) $\displaystyle\int \frac{1}{\cos(x-a)\cos(x-b)}\, dx$ **[NCERT, CBSE 2023]**

SOLUTION (i) Let $I = \displaystyle\int \frac{1}{\sin(x-a)\cos(x-b)}\, dx$. Then,

$$I = \frac{1}{\cos(a-b)} \int \frac{\cos(a-b)}{\sin(x-a)\cos(x-b)}\, dx = \frac{1}{\cos(a-b)} \int \frac{\cos\{(x-b)-(x-a)\}}{\sin(x-a)\cos(x-b)}\, dx$$

$$\Rightarrow \quad I = \frac{1}{\cos(a-b)} \int \frac{\cos(x-a)\cos(x-b) + \sin(x-a)\sin(x-b)}{\sin(x-a)\cos(x-b)}\, dx$$

$$\Rightarrow \quad I = \frac{1}{\cos(a-b)} \int \Big\{ \cot(x-a) + \tan(x-b) \Big\}\, dx$$

$$\Rightarrow \quad I = \frac{1}{\cos(a-b)} \Big\{ \log_e|\sin(x-a)| - \log_e|\cos(x-b)| \Big\} + C$$

$$\Rightarrow \quad I = \frac{1}{\cos(a-b)} \log_e\left|\frac{\sin(x-a)}{\cos(x-b)}\right| + C$$

(ii) Let $I = \displaystyle\int \frac{1}{\cos(x-a)\cos(x-b)}\, dx$. Then,

$$I = \frac{1}{\sin(a-b)} \int \frac{\sin(a-b)}{\cos(x-a)\cos(x-b)}\, dx = \frac{1}{\sin(a-b)} \int \frac{\sin\{(x-b)-(x-a)\}}{\cos(x-a)\cos(x-b)}\, dx$$

$$\Rightarrow \quad I = \frac{1}{\sin(a-b)} \int \frac{\sin(x-b)\cos(x-a) - \cos(x-b)\sin(x-a)}{\cos(x-a)\cos(x-b)}\, dx$$

$$\Rightarrow \quad I = \frac{1}{\sin(a-b)} \int \Big\{ \tan(x-b) - \tan(x-a) \Big\}\, dx$$

$$\Rightarrow \quad I = \frac{1}{\sin(a-b)} \{-\log_e|\cos(x-b)| + \log_e|\cos(x-a)|\} + C$$

$$\Rightarrow \quad I = \frac{1}{\sin(a-b)} \log_e\left|\frac{\cos(x-a)}{\cos(x-b)}\right| + C$$

EXAMPLE 5 *Evaluate:* $\displaystyle\int \frac{\sin(x+a)}{\sin(x+b)}\, dx$

SOLUTION Let $I = \displaystyle\int \frac{\sin(x+a)}{\sin(x+b)}\, dx$. Then,

$$I = \int \frac{\sin(x+b+a-b)}{\sin(x+b)}\, dx = \int \frac{\sin\{(x+b)+(a-b)\}}{\sin(x+b)}\, dx$$

$$\Rightarrow I = \int \frac{\sin(x+b)\cos(a-b) + \cos(x+b)\sin(a-b)}{\sin(x+b)}$$

$$\Rightarrow I = \int \{\cos(a-b) + \cot(x+b)\sin(a-b)\}\, dx = \cos(a-b)\int 1\cdot dx + \sin(a-b)\int \cot(x+b)\, dx$$

$$\Rightarrow I = x\cos(a-b) + \sin(a-b)\log_e|\sin(x+b)| + C$$

Type II EVALUATION OF INTEGRALS BASED UPON $\int \frac{f'(x)}{f(x)}\, dx = \log_e|f(x)| + C$

In order to evaluate this type of integrals, we may use the following algorithm:

ALGORITHM

Step I *Obtain the integral, let it be* $I = \int \frac{f'(x)}{f(x)}\, dx$

Step II *Put* $f(x) = t$ *and replace* $f'(x)\, dx$ *by* dt *to obtain* $I = \int \frac{1}{t}\, dt$

Step III *Evaluate integral obtained in step II to obtain* $I = \log_e|t| + C$

Step IV *Replace t by* $f(x)$ *in step III to get* $I = \log_e|f(x)| + C$

Following examples will illustrate the above procedure.

BASED ON BASIC CONCEPTS (BASIC)

EXAMPLE 6 *Evaluate:*

(i) $\int \frac{2x+5}{x^2+5x-7}\, dx$ (ii) $\int \frac{1-\tan x}{1+\tan x}\, dx$ (iii) $\int \frac{\sec^2 x}{3+\tan x}\, dx$

(iv) $\int \frac{e^x - e^{-x}}{e^x + e^{-x}}\, dx$ [NCERT] (v) $\int e^{3\log x}(x^4+1)^{-1}\, dx$ [NCERT]

SOLUTION (i) Let $I = \int \frac{2x+5}{x^2+5x-7}\, dx$

Let $x^2+5x-7 = t$. Then, $d(x^2+5x-7) = dt \Rightarrow (2x+5)\, dx = dt \Rightarrow dx = \frac{dt}{2x+5}$

Putting $x^2+5x-7 = t$ and $dx = \frac{dt}{2x+5}$, we get

$$\therefore \quad I = \int \frac{2x+5}{x^2+5x-7}\, dx = \int \frac{1}{t}\, dt = \log_e|t| + C = \log_e|x^2+5x-7| + C$$

(ii) We have, $I = \int \frac{1-\tan x}{1+\tan x}\, dx = \int \frac{\cos x - \sin x}{\cos x + \sin x}\, dx$. Let $\cos x + \sin x = t$. Then,

$$d(\cos x + \sin x) = dt \Rightarrow (-\sin x + \cos x)\, dx = dt \Rightarrow dx = \frac{dt}{\cos x - \sin x}$$

Putting $\cos x + \sin x = t$ and $dx = \frac{dt}{\cos x - \sin x}$, we get

$$I = \int \frac{1-\tan x}{1+\tan x}\, dx = \int \frac{1}{t}\, dt = \log_e|t| + C = \log_e|\cos x + \sin x| + C$$

(iii) Let $I = \int \frac{\sec^2 x}{3+\tan x}\, dx$. Let $3+\tan x = t$. Then,

$d(3+\tan x) = dt \Rightarrow \sec^2 x\, dx = dt \Rightarrow dx = \frac{dt}{\sec^2 x}$. Putting $\tan x = t$ and $dx = \frac{dt}{\sec^2 x}$, we get

$$I = \int \frac{\sec^2 x}{3+t} \times \frac{dt}{\sec^2 x} = \int \frac{1}{3+t}\, dt = \ln|3+t| + C = \ln|3+\tan x| + C$$

(iv) Let $I = \int \frac{e^x - e^{-x}}{e^x + e^{-x}}\, dx.$

Let $e^x + e^{-x} = t$. Then, $d(e^x + e^{-x}) = dt \Rightarrow (e^x - e^{-x})\, dx = dt \Rightarrow dx = \frac{dt}{e^x - e^{-x}}$

Putting $e^x + e^{-x} = t$ and $dx = \frac{dt}{e^x - e^{-x}}$, we get

$$I = \int \frac{e^x - e^{-x}}{e^x + e^{-x}}\, dx = \int \frac{dt}{t} = \ln|t| + C = \ln|e^x + e^{-x}| + C$$

(v) Let $I = \int e^{3\log x} (x^4+1)^{-1}\, dx = \int \frac{e^{\log x^3}}{x^4+1}\, dx = \int \frac{x^3}{x^4+1}\, dx$

Let $x^4 + 1 = t$. Then, $d(x^4+1) = dt \Rightarrow 4x^3\, dx = dt \Rightarrow dx = \frac{dt}{4x^3}$. Putting $x^4 + 1 = t$ and $dx = \frac{dt}{4x^3}$, we get

$$I = \frac{1}{4}\int \frac{1}{t}\, dt = \frac{1}{4} \ln|t| + C = \frac{1}{4} \ln(x^4+1) + C$$

BASED ON LOWER ORDER THINKING SKILLS (LOTS)

EXAMPLE 7 *Evaluate:*

(i) $\int \frac{1}{1+e^{-x}}\, dx$ (ii) $\int \frac{\sin 2x}{a^2 \sin^2 x + b^2 \cos^2 x}\, dx$ [CBSE 2005]

(iii) $\int \frac{\tan x}{a + b\tan^2 x}\, dx$ (iv) $\int \frac{\sin x - x\cos x}{x(x+\sin x)}\, dx$ [CBSE 2015]

SOLUTION (i) Let $I = \int \frac{1}{1+e^{-x}}\, dx = \int \frac{1}{1+\frac{1}{e^x}}\, dx = \int \frac{e^x}{e^x+1}\, dx$

Let $e^x + 1 = t$. Then, $d(e^x+1) = dt \Rightarrow e^x dx = dt \Rightarrow dx = \frac{dt}{e^x}$. Putting $1 + e^x = t$ and $dx = \frac{dt}{e^x}$, we get

$$I = \int \frac{e^x}{e^x+1}\, dx = \int \frac{e^x}{t}\frac{dt}{e^x} = \int \frac{1}{t}\, dt = \ln|t| + C = \ln|1+e^x| + C$$

(ii) Let $I = \int \frac{\sin 2x}{a^2\sin^2 x + b^2\cos^2 x}\, dx$. Let $a^2 \sin^2 x + b^2 \cos^2 x = t$. Then,

$$d(a^2 \sin^2 x + b^2 \cos^2 x) = dt \Rightarrow (a^2 - b^2) \sin 2x \, dx = dt \Rightarrow dx = \frac{dt}{(a^2 - b^2) \sin 2x}$$

Putting $a^2 \sin^2 x + b^2 \cos^2 x = t$ and $dx = \dfrac{dt}{(a^2 - b^2) \sin 2x}$, we get

$$I = \int \frac{\sin 2x}{t} \times \frac{dt}{2 \sin x \cos x (a^2 - b^2)}$$

$$\Rightarrow \quad I = \frac{1}{(a^2 - b^2)} \int \frac{1}{t} \, dt = \frac{1}{(a^2 - b^2)} \ln |t| + C = \frac{1}{(a^2 - b^2)} \ln |a^2 \sin^2 x + b^2 \cos^2 x| + C$$

(iii) Let $I = \displaystyle\int \frac{\tan x}{a + b \tan^2 x}$. Then,

$$I = \int \frac{\sin x \cos x}{a + b \dfrac{\sin^2 x}{\cos^2 x}} \, dx = \int \frac{\sin x \cos x}{a \cos^2 x + b \sin^2 x} \, dx = \frac{1}{2} \int \frac{\sin 2x}{a \cos^2 x + b \sin^2 x} \, dx$$

$$\Rightarrow \quad I = \frac{1}{2(b-a)} \ln |a \cos^2 x + b \sin^2 x| + C \qquad \text{[See (ii)]}$$

(iv) Let $I = \displaystyle\int \frac{\sin x - x \cos x}{x(x + \sin x)} \, dx$. Then,

$$I = \int \frac{(x + \sin x) - x - x \cos x}{x(x + \sin x)} \, dx = \int \frac{(x + \sin x) - x(1 + \cos x)}{x(x + \sin x)} \, dx = \int \left\{ \frac{1}{x} - \frac{1 + \cos x}{x + \sin x} \right\} dx$$

$$\Rightarrow \quad I = \ln |x| - \ln (x + \sin x) + C = \ln \left| \frac{x}{x + \sin x} \right| + C$$

BASED ON HIGHER ORDER THINKING SKILLS (HOTS)

EXAMPLE 8 *Evaluate:*

(i) $\displaystyle\int \tan x \tan 2x \tan 3x \, dx$ (ii) $\displaystyle\int \tan (x - \theta) \tan (x + \theta) \tan 2x \, dx$

SOLUTION (i) We know that

$$\tan 3x = \tan (2x + x) = \frac{\tan 2x + \tan x}{1 - \tan 2x \tan x} \Rightarrow \tan 3x (1 - \tan 2x \tan x) = \tan 2x + \tan x$$

$$\Rightarrow \tan 3x - \tan 3x \tan 2x \tan x = \tan 2x + \tan x \Rightarrow \tan 3x \tan 2x \tan x = \tan 3x - \tan 2x - \tan x$$

$$\therefore \quad I = \int \tan x \tan 2x \tan 3x \, dx$$

$$\Rightarrow I = \int (\tan 3x - \tan 2x - \tan x) \, dx = -\frac{1}{3} \log_e |\cos 3x| + \frac{1}{2} \log_e |\cos 2x| + \log_e |\cos x| + C$$

(ii) We know that $2x = (x - \theta) + (x + \theta)$

$$\therefore \quad \tan 2x = \tan \{(x - \theta) + (x + \theta)\}$$

$$\Rightarrow \quad \tan 2x = \frac{\tan (x - \theta) + (x + \theta)}{1 - \tan (x - \theta) \tan (x + \theta)}$$

$$\Rightarrow \quad \tan 2x - \tan (x - \theta) \tan (x + \theta) \tan 2x = \tan (x - \theta) + \tan (x + \theta)$$

$$\Rightarrow \quad \tan (x - \theta) \tan (x + \theta) \tan 2x = \tan 2x - \tan (x - \theta) - \tan (x + \theta)$$

$$\therefore \quad I = \int \tan (x - \theta) \tan (x + \theta) \tan 2x \, dx = \int \{\tan 2x - \tan (x - \theta) - \tan (x + \theta)\} \, dx$$

$$\Rightarrow \quad I = -\frac{1}{2} \ln |\cos 2x| + \ln |\cos (x - \theta)| + \ln |\cos (x + \theta)| + C$$

EXAMPLE 9 *Evaluate:* $\int \left\{1 + 2\tan x(\tan x + \sec x)\right\}^{1/2} dx$

SOLUTION Let $I = \int \left\{1 + 2\tan x(\tan x + \sec x)\right\}^{1/2} dx$. Then,

$$I = \int \left\{1 + 2\tan^2 x + 2\tan x \sec x\right\}^{1/2} dx = \int \left\{1 + \tan^2 x + \tan^2 x + 2\tan x \sec x\right\}^{1/2} dx$$

$$\Rightarrow I = \int \left\{\sec^2 x + \tan^2 x + 2\tan x \sec x\right\}^{1/2} dx = \int \left\{(\sec x + \tan x)^2\right\}^{1/2} dx$$

$$\Rightarrow I = \int (\sec x + \tan x)\, dx = \ln|\sec x + \tan x| + \ln|\sec x| + C$$

EXAMPLE 10 *Evaluate:* $\int \frac{\sin 2x}{\sin\left(x - \frac{\pi}{3}\right)\sin\left(x + \frac{\pi}{3}\right)} dx$

SOLUTION Let $I = \int \frac{\sin 2x}{\sin\left(x - \frac{\pi}{3}\right)\sin\left(x + \frac{\pi}{3}\right)} dx$. Then,

$$I = \int \frac{\sin\left\{\left(x - \frac{\pi}{3}\right) + \left(x + \frac{\pi}{3}\right)\right\}}{\sin\left(x - \frac{\pi}{3}\right)\sin\left(x + \frac{\pi}{3}\right)} dx$$

$$\Rightarrow \quad I = \int \frac{\sin\left(x - \frac{\pi}{3}\right)\cos\left(x + \frac{\pi}{3}\right) + \cos\left(x - \frac{\pi}{3}\right)\sin\left(x + \frac{\pi}{3}\right)}{\sin\left(x - \frac{\pi}{3}\right)\sin\left(x + \frac{\pi}{3}\right)}$$

$$\Rightarrow \quad I = \int \left\{\cot\left(x + \frac{\pi}{3}\right) + \cot\left(x - \frac{\pi}{3}\right)\right\} dx = \ln\left|\sin\left(x + \frac{\pi}{3}\right)\right| + \ln\left|\sin\left(x - \frac{\pi}{3}\right)\right| + C$$

EXERCISE 15.8

BASIC

Evaluate the following integrals:

1. $\int \frac{1}{\sqrt{1 - \cos 2x}} dx$
2. $\int \frac{1}{\sqrt{1 + \cos x}} dx$
3. $\int \sqrt{\frac{1 + \cos 2x}{1 - \cos 2x}} dx$
4. $\int \sqrt{\frac{1 - \cos x}{1 + \cos x}} dx$
5. $\int \frac{e^{3x}}{e^{3x} + 1} dx$
6. $\int \frac{\sec x \tan x}{3\sec x + 5} dx$
7. $\int \frac{1}{x(3 + \log x)} dx$
8. $\int \frac{e^x + 1}{e^x + x} dx$
9. $\int \frac{1}{x \log x} dx$
10. $\int \frac{\cos x}{2 + 3\sin x} dx$
11. $\int \frac{1 - \sin x}{x + \cos x} dx$
12. $\int \frac{e^{4x} - 1}{e^{4x} + 1} dx$ [CBSE 2024]
13. $\int \frac{2\cos x - 3\sin x}{6\cos x + 4\sin x} dx$ [NCERT]
14. $\int \frac{\cos 2x + x + 1}{x^2 + \sin 2x + 2x} dx$

15. $\int \frac{-\sin x + 2\cos x}{2\sin x + \cos x}\,dx$

16. $\int \frac{\cos 4x - \cos 2x}{\sin 4x - \sin 2x}\,dx$

17. $\int \frac{\sec x}{\log(\sec x + \tan x)}\,dx$

18. $\int \frac{\operatorname{cosec} x}{\log \tan \frac{x}{2}}\,dx$

19. $\int \frac{\operatorname{cosec}^2 x}{1 + \cot x}\,dx$

20. $\int \frac{1 - \sin 2x}{x + \cos^2 x}\,dx$ [CBSE 2000]

21. $\int \frac{1 + \tan x}{x + \log \sec x}\,dx$ [CBSE 2000]

22. $\int \frac{\sin 2x}{a^2 + b^2 \sin^2 x}\,dx$

23. $\int \frac{x + 1}{x(x + \log x)}\,dx$

24. $\int \frac{1}{\sqrt{1 - x^2}\,(2 + 3\sin^{-1} x)}\,dx$

25. $\int \frac{\sec^2 x}{\tan x + 2}\,dx$

26. $\int \frac{2\cos 2x + \sec^2 x}{\sin 2x + \tan x - 5}\,dx$

BASED ON LOTS

27. $\int \frac{\sec x}{\sec 2x}\,dx$

28. $\int \frac{\cos 2x}{(\cos x + \sin x)^2}\,dx$ [NCERT]

29. $\int \frac{\sin(x - a)}{\sin(x - b)}\,dx$

30. $\int \frac{\sin(x - \alpha)}{\sin(x + \alpha)}\,dx$ [CBSE 2006, 2013, 2015]

31. $\int \frac{1 + \tan x}{1 - \tan x}\,dx$

32. $\int \frac{\cos x}{\cos(x - a)}\,dx$

33. $\int \sqrt{\frac{1 - \sin 2x}{1 + \sin 2x}}\,dx$

34. $\int \frac{1 - \cot x}{1 + \cot x}\,dx$

35. $\int \frac{\sec x \operatorname{cosec} x}{\log(\tan x)}\,dx$

36. $\int \frac{\sin 2x}{a\cos^2 x + b\sin^2 x}\,dx$

37. $\int \frac{a}{b + ce^x}\,dx$

38. $\int \frac{1}{e^x + 1}\,dx$ [CBSE 2003]

39. $\int \frac{\cot x}{\log \sin x}\,dx$

BASED ON HOTS

40. $\int \frac{1}{\cos(x + a)\cos(x + b)}\,dx$ [NCERT]

41. $\int \frac{1}{x \log x \log(\log x)}\,dx$

42. $\int \frac{10x^9 + 10^x \log_e 10}{10^x + x^{10}}\,dx$

43. $\int \frac{\sin 2x}{\sin 5x \sin 3x}\,dx$

44. $\int \frac{1 + \cot x}{x + \log \sin x}\,dx$ [CBSE 2000]

45. $\int \frac{\cos(x + a)}{\sin(x + b)}\,dx$ [CBSE 2019]

46. $\int \frac{1}{\sqrt{x}(\sqrt{x} + 1)}\,dx$

47. $\int \tan 2x \tan 3x \tan 5x\,dx$

48. $\int \{1 + \tan x \tan(x + \theta)\}\,dx$

49. $\int \frac{\sin 2x}{\sin\left(x - \frac{\pi}{6}\right)\sin\left(x + \frac{\pi}{6}\right)}\,dx$

50. $\int \frac{e^{x-1} + x^{e-1}}{e^x + x^e}\,dx$

51. $\int \frac{1}{\sin x \cos^2 x}\,dx$

52. $\int \frac{1}{\cos 3x - \cos x}\,dx$

ANSWERS

1. $\frac{1}{\sqrt{2}} \log\left|\tan \frac{x}{2}\right| + C$

2. $\sqrt{2} \log\left|\tan\left(\frac{\pi}{4} + \frac{x}{4}\right)\right| + C$

3. $\log|\sin x| + C$

4. $-2\log\left|\cos\frac{x}{2}\right|+C$
5. $\frac{1}{3}\log|e^{3x}+1|+C$
6. $\frac{1}{3}\log|3\sec x+5|+C$
7. $\log|3+\log x|+C$
8. $\log|e^{x}+x|+C$
9. $\log|\log x|+C$
10. $\frac{1}{3}\log|2+3\sin x|+C$
11. $\log|x+\cos x|+C$
12. $\frac{1}{2}\log|e^{2x}+e^{-2x}|+C$
13. $\frac{1}{2}\log|2\sin x+3\cos x|+C$
14. $\frac{1}{2}\log|x^2+\sin 2x+2x|+C$
15. $\log|\cos x+2\sin x|+C$
16. $\frac{1}{3}\log|\cos 3x|+C$
17. $\log|\log(\sec x+\tan x)|+C$
18. $\log\left|\log\tan\frac{x}{2}\right|+C$
19. $-\log|1+\cot x|+C$
20. $\log|x+\cos^2 x|+C$
21. $\log|x+\log\sec x|+C$
22. $\frac{1}{b^2}\log(a^2+b^2\sin^2 x)+C$
23. $\log|x+\log x|+C$
24. $\frac{1}{3}\log|2+3\sin^{-1}x|+C$
25. $\log|\tan x+2|+C$
26. $\log|\sin 2x+\tan x-5|+C$
27. $2\sin x-\log|\sec x+\tan x|+C$
28. $\log|\sin x+\cos x|+C$
29. $x\cos(b-a)+\sin(b-a)\log|\sin(x-b)|+C$
30. $x\cos 2\alpha-\sin 2\alpha\log|\sin(x+\alpha)|+C$
31. $-\log|\cos x-\sin x|+C$
32. $(x-a)\cos a-\sin a\log|\sec(x-a)|+C$
33. $\log\left|\cos\left(\frac{\pi}{4}-x\right)\right|+C$
34. $-\log|\cos x+\sin x|+C$
35. $\log(\log\tan x)+C$
36. $\frac{1}{b-a}\log|a\cos^2 x+b\sin^2 x|+C$
37. $-\frac{a}{b}\log|be^{-x}+c|+C$
38. $-\log|1+e^{-x}|+C$
39. $\log|\log\sin x|+C$
40. $\frac{1}{\sin(a-b)}\log\left|\frac{\cos(x+b)}{\cos(x+a)}\right|+C$
41. $\log\{\log(\log x)\}+C$
42. $\log|10^{x}+x^{10}|+C$
43. $\frac{1}{3}\log|\sin 3x|-\frac{1}{5}\log|\sin 5x|+C$
44. $\log|x+\log\sin x|+C$
45. $\cos(a-b)\log\sin(x+b)-x\sin(a-b)+C$
46. $2\log|\sqrt{x}+1|+C$
47. $\frac{1}{5}\log|\sec 5x|-\frac{1}{2}\log|\sec 2x|-\frac{1}{3}\log|\sec 3x|+C$
48. $\cot\theta\log\left|\frac{\cos x}{\cos(x+\theta)}\right|+C$
49. $\log\left|\sin^2 x-\frac{1}{4}\right|+C$
50. $\frac{1}{e}\log|e^{x}+x^{e}|+C$
51. $\sec x+\log\left|\tan\frac{x}{2}\right|+C$
52. $\frac{1}{4}\left\{\operatorname{cosec} x-\log|\sec x+\tan x|\right\}+C$

HINTS TO SELECTED PROBLEMS

27. $\int \frac{\sec x}{\sec 2x}\, dx = \int \frac{\cos 2x}{\cos x}\, dx = \int \frac{2\cos^2 x - 1}{\cos x}\, dx = \int 2\cos x - \sec x\, dx$

$$= 2\sin x - \ln \tan\left(\frac{\pi}{4} + \frac{x}{2}\right) + C$$

28. Let $I = \int \frac{\cos 2x}{(\cos x + \sin x)^2}\, dx$. Then, $I = \int \frac{\cos 2x}{1 + \sin 2x}\, dx$

Let $1 + \sin 2x = t$. Then, $d(1 + \sin 2x) = dt$ or, $2\cos 2x\, dx = dt$

$\therefore \quad I = \frac{1}{2}\int \frac{1}{t}\, dt = \frac{1}{2}\ln|t| + C = \frac{1}{2}\ln|1 + \sin 2x| + C$

ALITER $I = \int \frac{\cos 2x}{(\cos x + \sin x)^2}\, dx = \int \frac{\cos^2 x - \sin^2 x}{(\cos x + \sin x)^2}\, dx = \int \frac{\cos x - \sin x}{\cos x + \sin x}\, dx$

$\Rightarrow \quad I = \ln\left|\cos x + \sin x\right| + C$

40. Let $I = \int \frac{1}{\cos(x+a)\cos(x+b)}\, dx$. Then,

$$I = \frac{1}{\sin(b-a)} \int \frac{\sin\{(x+b)-(x+a)\}}{\cos(x+a)\cos(x+b)}\, dx$$

$$\Rightarrow \quad I = \frac{1}{\sin(b-a)} \int \frac{\sin(x+b)\cos(x+a) - \cos(x+b)\sin(x+a)}{\cos(x+a)\cos(x+b)}\, dx$$

$$\Rightarrow \quad I = \frac{1}{\sin(b-a)} \int \left\{\tan(x+b) - \tan(x+a)\right\} dx$$

$$\Rightarrow \quad I = \frac{1}{\sin(b-a)} \left\{-\ln\cos(x+b) + \ln\cos(x+a)\right\} + C = \frac{1}{\sin(a-b)} \ln\frac{\cos(x+b)}{\cos(x+a)} + C$$

50. $I = \int \frac{1}{\sin x \cos^2 x}\, dx = \int \frac{\sin^2 x + \cos^2 x}{\sin x \cos^2 x}\, dx = \int (\sec x \tan x + \operatorname{cosec} x)\, dx$

$$= \sec x + \ln\left|\tan\frac{x}{2}\right| + C$$

51. $\int \frac{1}{\cos 3x - \cos x}\, dx = \int \frac{\sin^2 x + \cos^2 x}{-2\sin 2x \sin x}\, dx = \int \frac{\sin^2 x + \cos^2 x}{-4\sin^2 x \cos x}\, dx$

$$= -\frac{1}{4}\int \left(\sec x + \operatorname{cosec} x \cot x\right) dx = -\frac{1}{4}\left\{\log(\sec x + \tan x) - \operatorname{cosec} x\right\} + C$$

15.8.7 INTEGRALS OF THE FORM $\int \{f(x)\}^n f'(x)\, dx$

THEOREM $\int \{f(x)\}^n f'(x)\, dx = \frac{\{f(x)\}^{n+1}}{n+1}, n \neq -1$

PROOF Let $I = \int \{f(x)\}^n f'(x)\, dx$. Putting $f(x) = t$ and $f'(x)\, dx = dt$, we get

$$I = \int \{f(x)\}^n f'(x)\, dx = \int t^n\, dt = \frac{t^{n+1}}{n+1} + C = \frac{\{f(x)\}^{n+1}}{n+1} + C, n \neq -1.$$

Q.E.D.

ILLUSTRATIVE EXAMPLES

BASED ON BASIC CONCEPTS (BASIC)

EXAMPLE 1 *Evaluate:*

(i) $\int \frac{3x+1}{(3x^2+2x+1)^3}\,dx$ (ii) $\int \sin^3 x \cos x\,dx$ (iii) $\int \tan^3 x \sec^2 x\,dx$ (iv) $\int \frac{(\log x)^3}{x}\,dx$

SOLUTION (i) Let $I = \int \frac{3x+1}{(3x^2+2x+1)^3}\,dx$. Let $3x^2+2x+1 = t$. Then,

$$d(3x^2+2x+1) = dt \Rightarrow (6x+2)\,dx = dt \Rightarrow dx = \frac{dt}{2(3x+1)}$$

Putting $3x^2+2x+1 = t$ and $dx = \frac{dt}{6x+2}$, we get

$$I = \int \frac{3x+1}{t^3} \times \frac{dt}{2(3x+1)} = \frac{1}{2}\int t^{-3}\,dt = \frac{1}{2}\left(\frac{t^{-2}}{-2}\right) + C = -\frac{1}{4t^2} + C = -\frac{1}{4(3x^2+2x+1)^2} + C$$

(ii) Let $I = \int \sin^3 x \cos x\,dx$. Let $\sin x = t$. Then, $d(\sin x) = dt \Rightarrow \cos x\,dx = dt \Rightarrow dx = \frac{dt}{\cos x}$.

Putting $\sin x = t$ and $dx = \frac{dt}{\cos x}$, we get

$$I = \int \sin^3 x \cos x\,dx = \int t^3 \cos x \times \frac{dt}{\cos x} = \int t^3\,dt = \frac{t^4}{4} + C = \frac{\sin^4 x}{4} + C$$

(iii) Let $I = \int \tan^3 x \sec^2 x\,dx$. Let $\tan x = t$. Then, $d(\tan x) = dt \Rightarrow \sec^2 x\,dx = dt \Rightarrow dx = \frac{dt}{\sec^2 x}$.

Putting $\tan x = t$ and $dx = dt \sec^2 x$, we get

$$I = \int \tan^3 x \sec^2 x\,dx = \int t^3 \sec^2 x \times \frac{dt}{\sec^2 x} = \int t^3\,dt = \frac{t^4}{4} + C = \frac{\tan^4 x}{4} + C$$

(iv) Let $I = \int \frac{(\log x)^3}{x}\,dx$. Let $\log x = t$. Then, $d(\log x) = dt \Rightarrow \frac{1}{x}\,dx = dt \Rightarrow dx = x\,dt$.

Putting $\log x = t$ and $dx = x\,dt$, we get

$$I = \int \frac{t^3}{x}\,x\,dt = \int t^3\,dt = \int \frac{t^4}{4} + C = \frac{(\log x)^4}{4} + C$$

EXAMPLE 2 *Evaluate:*

(i) $\int \frac{4(\sin^{-1} x)^3}{\sqrt{1-x^2}}\,dx$ (ii) $\int \frac{\log\left(\tan\frac{x}{2}\right)}{\sin x}\,dx$ (iii) $\int \frac{\sin x}{\sqrt{3+2\cos x}}\,dx$

SOLUTION (i) Let $I = \int \frac{4(\sin^{-1} x)^3}{\sqrt{1-x^2}}\,dx$. Let $\sin^{-1} x = t$. Then, $d(\sin^{-1} x) = dt$

$\Rightarrow \frac{1}{\sqrt{1-x^2}}\,dx = dt \Rightarrow dx = \sqrt{1-x^2}\,dt$. Putting $\sin^{-1} x = t$ and $dx = \sqrt{1-x^2}\,dt$, we get

$$I = \int \frac{4t^3}{\sqrt{1-x^2}} \sqrt{1-x^2}\; dt = 4\int t^3\, dt = t^4 + C = (\sin^{-1} x)^4 + C$$

(ii) Let $I = \int \frac{\log\left(\tan \frac{x}{2}\right)}{\sin x} dx$. Let $\log \tan \frac{x}{2} = t$. Then,

$$d\left(\log \tan \frac{x}{2}\right) = dt \Rightarrow \frac{1}{\tan \frac{x}{2}} \sec^2 \frac{x}{2} \times \frac{1}{2} dx = dt \Rightarrow dx = \sin x\, dt$$

Putting $\log \tan \frac{x}{2} = t$ and $dx = \sin x\, dt$, we get

$$I = \int \frac{t}{\sin x} \sin x\, dt = \int t\, dt = \frac{t^2}{2} + C = \frac{1}{2}\left(\log \tan \frac{x}{2}\right)^2 + C$$

(iii) Let $I = \int \frac{\sin x}{\sqrt{3 + 2\cos x}} dx$. Let $3 + 2\cos x = t$. Then,

$$d(3 + 2\cos x) = dt \Rightarrow -2\sin x\, dx = dt \Rightarrow dx = -\frac{dt}{2\sin x}.$$

Putting $3 + 2\cos x = t$ and $dx = -\frac{dt}{2\sin x}$, we get

$$I = \int \frac{\sin x}{\sqrt{t}} \times -\frac{dt}{2\sin x} = -\frac{1}{2}\int t^{-1/2}\, dt = -\frac{1}{2} \times \frac{t^{1/2}}{1/2} + C = -\sqrt{t} + C = -\sqrt{3 + 2\cos x} + C$$

EXAMPLE 3 *Evaluate:*

(i) $\int \frac{(1 + \log x)^2}{x} dx$ [NCERT, CBSE 2009] (ii) $\int \frac{\sec^2 (2\tan^{-1} x)}{1 + x^2} dx$

(iii) $\int \frac{\tan x \sec^2 x}{(a + b\tan^2 x)^2} dx$ (iv) $\int \sec^3 x \tan x\, dx$

SOLUTION (i) Let $\int \frac{(1 + \log x)^2}{x} dx$. Let $1 + \log x = t$. Then,

$d(1 + \log x) = dt \Rightarrow \frac{1}{x} dx = dt \Rightarrow dx = x\, dt$. Putting $1 + \log x = t$ and $dx = = x\, dt$, we get

$$\therefore \quad I = \int \frac{t^2}{x} \times x\, dt = \int t^2\, dt = \frac{t^3}{3} + C = \frac{(1 + \log x)^3}{3} + C$$

(ii) Let $I = \int \frac{\sec^2 (2\tan^{-1} x)}{1 + x^2} dx$. Let $2\tan^{-1} x = t$. Then,

$$d(2\tan^{-1} x) = dt \Rightarrow \frac{2}{1 + x^2} dx = dt \Rightarrow dx = \frac{1 + x^2}{2} dt.$$

Putting $2\tan^{-1} x = t$ and $dx = \frac{1 + x^2}{2} dt$, we get

$$I = \int \frac{\sec^2 t}{1 + x^2} \times \frac{1 + x^2}{2} dt = \frac{1}{2}\int \sec^2 t\, dt = \frac{1}{2}\tan t + C = \frac{1}{2}\tan(2\tan^{-1} x) + C$$

(iii) Let $I = \int \frac{\tan x \sec^2 x}{(a + b \tan^2 x)^2} dx$. Let $a + b \tan^2 x = t$. Then,

$$d(a + b \tan^2 x)\ dt \Rightarrow 2b \tan x \sec^2 x\, dx = dt \Rightarrow dx = \frac{dt}{2b \tan x \sec^2 x}$$

Putting $a + b \tan^2 x = t$, and $dx = \frac{dt}{2b \tan x \sec^2 x}$, we get

$$I = \int \frac{\tan x \sec^2 x}{t^2} \times \frac{dt}{2b \tan x \sec^2 x} = \frac{1}{2b} \int \frac{1}{t^2} dt = \frac{1}{2b} \int t^{-2} dt = -\frac{1}{2bt} + C$$

$$\Rightarrow \quad I = -\frac{1}{2b(a + b \tan^2 x)} + C$$

(iv) Let $I = \int \sec^3 x \tan x\, dx = \int \sec^2 x\ (\sec x \tan x)\, dx$

Let $\sec x = t$. Then, $d(\sec x) = dt \Rightarrow \sec x \tan x\, dx = dt \Rightarrow dx = \frac{dt}{\sec x \tan x}$

Putting $\sec x = t$ and $dx = \frac{dt}{\sec x \tan x}$, we get

$$I = \int t^2\, dt = \frac{t^3}{3} + C = \frac{1}{3} \sec^3 x + C$$

EXAMPLE 4 *Evaluate:*

(i) $\int x^3 \sin x^4\, dx$ (ii) $\int e^{-x} \operatorname{cosec}^2 (2e^{-x} + 5)\, dx$ (iii) $\int x^2 \frac{\tan^{-1} x^3}{1 + x^6} dx$

SOLUTION (i) Let $I = \int x^3 \sin x^4\, dx$.

Let $x^4 = t$. Then, $d(x^4) = dt \Rightarrow 4x^3\, dx = dt \Rightarrow dx = \frac{1}{4x^3} dt$

$$\therefore \quad I = \int x^3 \sin t \times \frac{dt}{4x^3} = \frac{1}{4} \int \sin t\, dt = -\frac{1}{4} \cos t + C = -\frac{1}{4} \cos x^4 + C$$

(ii) Let $I = \int e^{-x} \operatorname{cosec}^2 (2e^{-x} + 5)\, dx$.

Let $2e^{-x} + 5 = t$ Then, $d(2e^{-x} + 5) = dt \Rightarrow -2e^{-x}\, dx = dt \Rightarrow dx = -\frac{dt}{2e^{-x}}$

$$\therefore \quad I = \int e^{-x} \operatorname{cosec}^2 t \left(-\frac{dt}{2e^{-x}} \right) = -\frac{1}{2} \int \operatorname{cosec}^2 t\, dt = \frac{1}{2} \cot t + C = \frac{1}{2} \cot (2e^{-x} + 5) + C$$

(iii) Let $I = \int x^2 \frac{\tan^{-1} x^3}{1 + x^6} dx$.

Let $\tan^{-1} x^3 = t$. Then, $d(\tan^{-1} x^3) = dt \Rightarrow \frac{1}{1 + x^6} 3x^2\, dx = dt \Rightarrow dx = \frac{(1 + x^6)}{3x^2} dt$

$$\therefore \quad I = \int x^2 \times \frac{t}{1 + x^6} \times \frac{1 + x^6}{3x^2} dt = \frac{1}{3} \int t\, dt = \frac{1}{6} t^2 + C = \frac{1}{6} \{\tan^{-1} x^3\}^2 + C$$

EXAMPLE 5 *Evaluate:*

(i) $\int \sqrt{\tan x}\,(1+\tan^2 x)\,dx$ (ii) $\int \{f(ax+b)\}^n f'(ax+b)\,dx,\ n \neq -1$ [NCERT]

SOLUTION (i) Let $I = \int \sqrt{\tan x}\,(1+\tan^2 x)\,dx = \int \sqrt{\tan x}\,\sec^2 x\,dx$

Putting $\tan x = t$ and $\sec^2 x\,dx = dt$, we get

$$I = \int \sqrt{t}\,dt = \frac{t^{3/2}}{3/2} + C = \frac{2}{3}(\tan x)^{3/2} + C$$

(ii) Let $I = \int \{f(ax+b)\}^n f'(ax+b)\,dx$. Putting $f(ax+b) = t$ and $f'(ax+b).a\,dx = dt$, we get

$$I = \frac{1}{a}\int t^n\,dt = \frac{1}{a}\left(\frac{t^{n+1}}{n+1}\right) + C = \frac{\{f(ax+b)\}^{n+1}}{a(n+1)} + C,\ n \neq -1$$

BASED ON HIGHER ORDER THINKING SKILLS (HOTS)

EXAMPLE 6 *Evaluate:*

(i) $\int \frac{\sin 2x}{(a+b\cos x)^2}\,dx$ (ii) $\int 2^{2^{2^x}}\, 2^{2^x}\, 2^x\,dx$

(iii) $\int \frac{1}{\sqrt{\sin^3 x \sin(x+\alpha)}}\,dx,\ \alpha \neq n\pi,\ n \in Z$ [NCERT] (iv) $\int \frac{(x^4-x)^{1/4}}{x^5}\,dx$

SOLUTION (i) Let $I = \int \frac{\sin 2x}{(a+b\cos x)^2}\,dx = \int \frac{2\sin x\cos x}{(a+b\cos x)^2}\,dx$

Putting $a + b\cos x = t$ and $-b\sin x\,dx = dt$ or, $dx = -dt/b\sin x$, we get

$$I = \int \frac{2\sin x\cos x}{t^2} \times -\frac{dt}{b\sin x} = -\frac{2}{b}\int \frac{1}{t^2}\cdot\cos x\,dt$$

$$\Rightarrow \quad I = -\frac{2}{b}\int \frac{1}{t^2}\left(\frac{t-a}{b}\right)dt = -\frac{2}{b^2}\int\left(\frac{1}{t} - \frac{a}{t^2}\right)dt \quad \left[\because\ a+b\cos x = t \ \therefore\ \cos x = \frac{t-a}{b}\right]$$

$$\Rightarrow \quad I = -\frac{2}{b^2}\left\{\log|t| + \frac{a}{t}\right\} + C = -\frac{2}{b^2}\left\{\log|a+b\cos x| + \frac{a}{a+b\cos x}\right\} + C$$

(ii) Let $I = \int 2^{2^{2^x}}\, 2^{2^x}\, 2^x\,dx$. Let $2^{2^{2^x}} = t$. Then,

$$d\left(2^{2^{2^x}}\right) = dt \Rightarrow 2^{2^{2^x}}\, 2^{2^x}\, 2^x (\log 2)^3\,dx = dt.$$

Putting $2^{2^{2^x}} = t$ and $2^{2^{2^x}}\, 2^{2^x}\, 2^x (\log 2)^3\,dx = dt$, we get

$$I = \int \frac{1}{(\log 2)^3}\,dt = \frac{1}{(\log 2)^3}\,t + C = \frac{1}{(\log 2)^3}\, 2^{2^{2^x}} + C$$

(iii) We find that

$$\sin^3 x \sin(x+\alpha) = \sin^3 x(\sin x\cos\alpha + \cos x\sin\alpha) = \sin^4 x(\cos\alpha + \cot x\sin\alpha)$$

$\therefore \quad I = \int \frac{1}{\sqrt{\sin^3 x \sin(x+\alpha)}}\, dx$

$\Rightarrow \quad I = \int \frac{1}{\sin^2 x \sqrt{\cos\alpha + \cot x \sin\alpha}}\, dx = \int \frac{\operatorname{cosec}^2 x}{\sqrt{\cos\alpha + \cot x \sin\alpha}}\, dx$

Putting $\cos\alpha + \cot x \sin\alpha = t$ and, $-\operatorname{cosec}^2 x \sin\alpha\, dx = dt$, we get

$$I = \int -\frac{1}{\sin\alpha\sqrt{t}}\, dt = -\frac{1}{\sin\alpha}\int t^{-1/2}\, dt = -\frac{1}{\sin\alpha}\left(\frac{t^{1/2}}{1/2}\right) + C$$

$\Rightarrow \quad I = -2(\operatorname{cosec}\alpha)\sqrt{t} + C = -2\operatorname{cosec}\alpha(\cos\alpha + \cot x \sin\alpha)^{1/2} + C$

(iv) Let $I = \int \frac{(x^4 - x)^{1/4}}{x^5} = \int \frac{x\left(1 - \frac{1}{x^3}\right)^{1/4}}{x^5}\, dx = \int \frac{1}{x^4}\left(1 - \frac{1}{x^3}\right)^{1/4} dx$

Let $1 - \frac{1}{x^3} = t$. Then, $d\left(1 - \frac{1}{x^3}\right) = dt \Rightarrow \frac{3}{x^4}\, dx = dt \Rightarrow dx = \frac{x^4}{3}\, dt$

Putting $\left(1 - \frac{1}{x^3}\right) = t$ and, $dx = \frac{x^4}{3}\, dt$, we get

$$I = \frac{1}{3}\int \frac{1}{x^4} \times t^{1/4} \times x^4\, dt = \frac{1}{3}\int t^{1/4}\, dt = \frac{4}{15}t^{5/4} + C = \frac{4}{15}\left(1 - \frac{1}{x^3}\right)^{5/4} + C$$

EXAMPLE 7 *Evaluate:* (i) $\int \frac{\sec^4 x}{\sqrt{\tan x}}\, dx$ (ii) $\int \frac{\cos^9 x}{\sin x}\, dx$

SOLUTION (i) Let $I = \int \frac{\sec^4 x}{\sqrt{\tan x}}\, dx$. Putting $\tan x = t$ and $\sec^2 x\, dx = dt$, we get

$$I = \int \frac{\sec^4 x}{\sqrt{t}} \times \frac{dt}{\sec^2 x} = \int \frac{\sec^2 x}{\sqrt{t}}\, dt = \int \frac{1 + \tan^2 x}{\sqrt{t}}\, dt = \int \frac{1 + t^2}{\sqrt{t}}\, dt$$

$\Rightarrow \quad I = \int (t^{-1/2} + t^{3/2})\, dt = 2t^{1/2} + \frac{2}{5}t^{5/2} + C = 2\sqrt{\tan x} + \frac{2}{5}\tan^{5/2} x + C$

(ii) Let $I = \int \frac{\cos^9 x}{\sin x}\, dx$. Putting $\sin x = t$ and $\cos x\, dx = dt$, we get

$$I = \int \frac{\cos^9 x}{t} \times \frac{dt}{\cos x} = \int \frac{\cos^8 x}{t}\, dt = \int \frac{(1 - \sin^2 x)^4}{t}\, dt = \int \frac{(1 - t^2)^4}{t}\, dt$$

$\Rightarrow \quad I = \int \frac{1 - 4t^2 + 6t^4 - 4t^6 + t^8}{t}\, dt = \int \frac{1}{t} - 4t + 6t^3 - 4t^5 + t^7\, dt$

$\Rightarrow \quad I = \log|t| - 2t^2 + \frac{3}{2}t^4 - \frac{2}{3}t^6 + \frac{1}{8}t^8 + C$

$\Rightarrow \quad I = \log|\sin x| - 2\sin^2 x + \frac{3}{2}\sin^4 x - \frac{2}{3}\sin^6 x + \frac{1}{8}\sin^8 x + C$

EXAMPLE 8 *Evaluate:* $\int \frac{1}{\sqrt[4]{(x-1)^3 (x+2)^5}}\, dx$

SOLUTION Let $\int \frac{1}{\sqrt[4]{(x-1)^3 (x+2)^5}}\, dx$. Then,

$$I = \int \frac{1}{\sqrt[4]{\left(\frac{x-1}{x+2}\right)^3 (x+2)^8}}\, dx = \int \frac{1}{(x+2)^2 \left(\frac{x-1}{x+2}\right)^{3/4}}\, dx = \int \left(\frac{x-1}{x+2}\right)^{-3/4} \times \frac{1}{(x+2)^2}\, dx$$

Let $\frac{x-1}{x+2} = t$ or, $1 - \frac{3}{x+2} = t$. Then, $d\left(1 - \frac{3}{x+2}\right) = dt \Rightarrow \frac{3}{(x+2)^2}\, dx = dt \Rightarrow \frac{1}{(x+2)^2}\, dx = \frac{1}{3} dt.$

Putting $\frac{x-1}{x+2} = t$ and $\frac{1}{(x+2)^2} dx = \frac{1}{3} dt$, we obtain

$$I = \frac{1}{3} \int t^{-3/4}\, dt = \frac{4}{3} t^{1/4} + C = \frac{4}{3} \left(\frac{x-1}{x+2}\right)^{1/4} + C$$

EXAMPLE 9 *Evaluate:* (i) $\int x^x (1 + \log x)\, dx$ (ii) $\int x^{2x} (1 + \log x)\, dx$

SOLUTION (i) Let $x^x = t$. Then,

$$d(x^x) = dt \Rightarrow d(e^{x \log x}) = dt \Rightarrow e^{x \log x} (\log x + 1)\, dx = dt \Rightarrow x^x (1 + \log x)\, dx = dt$$

$$\therefore \quad I = \int x^x (1 + \log)\, dx = \int dt = t + C = x^x + C$$

(ii) Let $I = \int x^{2x} (1 + \log x)\, dx$. Putting $x^x = t$ and $x^x (1 + \log x)\, dx = dt$, we obtain

$$I = \int x^x\, x^x (1 + \log x)\, dx = \int t\, dt = \frac{1}{2} t^2 + C = \frac{1}{2} (x^x)^2 + C = \frac{1}{2} x^{2x} + C$$

EXAMPLE 10 *Evaluate:* $\int \frac{x}{x - \sqrt{x^2 - 1}}\, dx$

SOLUTION Let $I = \int \frac{x}{x - \sqrt{x^2 - 1}}\, dx$. Then,

$$I = \int \frac{x}{x - \sqrt{x^2 - 1}} \times \frac{x + \sqrt{x^2 - 1}}{x + \sqrt{x^2 - 1}}\, dx = \int \frac{x (x + \sqrt{x^2 - 1})}{x^2 - (x^2 - 1)}\, dx = \int x^2 + x \sqrt{x^2 - 1}\, dx$$

$$\Rightarrow \quad I = \int x^2 dx + \int \sqrt{x^2 - 1}\, x\, dx = \frac{x^3}{3} + \frac{1}{2} \int \sqrt{t}\, dt, \text{ where } t = x^2 - 1$$

$$\Rightarrow \quad I = \frac{x^3}{3} + \frac{1}{3} t^{3/2} + C = \frac{x^3}{3} + \frac{1}{3} (x^2 - 1)^{3/2} + C$$

EXAMPLE 11 *Evaluate:* $\int \frac{\cos^3 x}{\sin^2 x + \sin x}\, dx$

SOLUTION Let $I = \int \frac{\cos^3 x}{\sin^2 x + \sin x}\, dx$. Then,

$$I=\int \frac{\cos^2 x}{\sin x\,(\sin x+1)}\cos x\,dx=\int \frac{(1-\sin^2 x)}{\sin x\,(1+\sin x)}\cos x\,dx$$

Let $\sin x = t$. Then, $d(\sin x)=dt$ or, $\cos x\,dx = dt$, we obtain

$\therefore$ $$I=\int \frac{1-t^2}{t\,(1+t)}dt=\int \frac{1-t}{t}\,dt=\int\left(\frac{1}{t}-1\right)dt=\log|t|-t+C = \log|\sin x|-\sin x+C$$

EXERCISE 15.9

Evaluate the following integrals:

1. $\int \frac{\log x}{x}\,dx$
2. $\int \sqrt{1+e^x}\,e^x\,dx$
3. $\int \sqrt[3]{\cos^2 x}\,\sin x\,dx$
4. $\int \frac{e^x}{(1+e^x)^2}\,dx$
5. $\int \cot^3 x\,\text{cosec}^2\,x\,dx$
6. $\int \frac{\{e^{\sin^{-1} x}\}^2}{\sqrt{1-x^2}}\,dx$
7. $\int \frac{1+\sin x}{\sqrt{x-\cos x}}\,dx$
8. $\int \frac{1}{\sqrt{1-x^2}\,(\sin^{-1} x)^2}\,dx$
9. $\int \frac{1}{\sqrt{\tan^{-1} x\,(1+x^2)}}\,dx$
10. $\int \frac{1}{x}(\log x)^2\,dx$
11. $\int \cos^3 x\,e^{\log \sin x}dx$ [CBSE 2024]
12. $\int \tan^{3/2} x\,\sec^2 x\,dx$
13. $\int \frac{1+\cos x}{(x+\sin x)^3}\,dx$
14. $\int \frac{\cos x-\sin x}{1+\sin 2x}\,dx$ [NCERT]
15. $\int \frac{\sin 2x}{(a+b\cos 2x)^2}\,dx$
16. $\int \frac{\log x^2}{x}\,dx$
17. $\int \frac{\sin x}{(1+\cos x)^2}\,dx$
18. $\int x^3\cos x^4\,dx$
19. $\int \frac{x\sin^{-1} x^2}{\sqrt{1-x^4}}\,dx$
20. $\int x^3\sin(x^4+1)\,dx$
21. $\int x^2\,e^{x^3}\cos(e^{x^3})\,dx$
22. $\int 2x\sec^3(x^2+3)\tan(x^2+3)\,dx$
23. $\int \left(\frac{x+1}{x}\right)(x+\log x)^2\,dx$ [NCERT, CBSE 2002C]
24. $\int \frac{1}{x^2}\cos^2\left(\frac{1}{x}\right)dx$
25. $\int \frac{e^{\sqrt{x}}\cos(e^{\sqrt{x}})}{\sqrt{x}}\,dx$
26. $\int \frac{\sin\sqrt{x}}{\sqrt{x}}\,dx$ [NCERT, CBSE 2009]
27. $\int \frac{e^{m\sin^{-1} x}}{\sqrt{1-x^2}}\,dx$
28. $\int \frac{\cos\sqrt{x}}{\sqrt{x}}\,dx$ [NCERT, CBSE 2009]
29. $\int \frac{\sin(\log x)}{x}\,dx$
30. $\int \frac{e^{m\tan^{-1} x}}{1+x^2}\,dx$ [NCERT]
31. $\int \frac{(\sin^{-1} x)^3}{\sqrt{1-x^2}}\,dx$
32. $\int \frac{\sin(2+3\log x)}{x}\,dx$
33. $\int x\,e^{x^2}\,dx$
34. $\int \frac{\sec^2\sqrt{x}}{\sqrt{x}}dx$ [CBSE 2000]
35. $\int \frac{(1+\sqrt{x})^2}{\sqrt{x}}dx$

BASED ON LOTS

36. $\int \frac{\log\left(1+\frac{1}{x}\right)}{x(1+x)} dx$

37. $\int \frac{\cot x}{\sqrt{\sin x}} dx$

38. $\int \frac{\tan x}{\sqrt{\cos x}} dx$

39. $\int \frac{\cos^3 x}{\sqrt{\sin x}} dx$

40. $\int \frac{\sin^3 x}{\sqrt{\cos x}} dx$

41. (i) $\int \frac{\sqrt{\tan x}}{\sin x \cos x} dx$ [NCERT]

(ii) $\int \frac{\sqrt{\cot x}}{\sin x \cos x} dx$ [CBSE 2022]

42. $\int \frac{x^3}{(x^2+1)^3} dx$

43. $\int (4x+2)\sqrt{x^2+x+1}\, dx$ [NCERT]

44. $\int \frac{4x+3}{\sqrt{2x^2+3x+1}} dx$

45. $\int e^{\cos^2 x} \sin 2x\, dx$

46. $\int \cot x \log \sin x\, dx$ [NCERT]

47. $\int \sec x \ln(\sec x + \tan x)\, dx$ [NCERT]

48. $\int \operatorname{cosec} x \log(\operatorname{cosec} x - \cot x)\, dx$

49. $\int \frac{2x}{\sqrt[3]{x^2-1}} dx$ [CBSE 2020]

50. $\int \frac{(x+1)e^x}{\cos^2(xe^x)} dx$

51. $\int \frac{(x+1)e^x}{\sin^2(xe^x)} dx$

52. $\int \frac{x\tan^{-1}x^2}{1+x^4} dx$

53. $\int \frac{1}{1+\sqrt{x}} dx$

54. $\int \tan x \sec^2 x \sqrt{1-\tan^2 x}\, dx$

55. $\int \log x \frac{\sin\{1+(\log x)^2\}}{x} dx$

56. $\int \sec^4 x \tan x\, dx$

57. $\int \frac{\cos^5 x}{\sin x} dx$ [CBSE 2005]

58. $\int 5^{x+\tan^{-1}x}\left(\frac{x^2+2}{x^2+1}\right) dx$

59. $\int \frac{\sin(\tan^{-1}x)}{1+x^2} dx$ [CBSE 2002]

60. $\int \frac{x}{\sqrt{x^2+a^2}+\sqrt{x^2-a^2}} dx$

61. $\int \frac{e^{2x}}{1+e^x} dx$

62. $\int \tan^3 2x \sec 2x\, dx$ [NCERT]

63. $\int \frac{x+\sqrt{x+1}}{x+2} dx$

64. $\int 5^{5^{5^x}} 5^{5^x} 5^x\, dx$

65. $\int \frac{1}{x\sqrt{x^4-1}} dx$ [NCERT EXEMPLAR]

66. $\int \sqrt{e^x-1}\, dx$

67. $\int \frac{1}{(x+1)(x^2+2x+2)} dx$

68. $\int \frac{x^5}{\sqrt{1+x^3}} dx$

69. $\int 4x^3\sqrt{5-x^2}\, dx$

70. $\int \frac{1}{\sqrt{x}+x} dx$

71. $\int \frac{1}{x^2(x^4+1)^{3/4}} dx$ [NCERT]

72. $\int \frac{\sin^5 x}{\cos^4 x} dx$

73. $\int \frac{1}{\sqrt{\sin^3 x \cos(x-\alpha)}} dx$ [CBSE 2023]

ANSWERS

1. $\frac{(\log x)^2}{2}+C$

2. $\frac{2}{3}(1+e^x)^{3/2}+C$

3. $-\frac{3}{5}\cos^{5/3}x+C$

4. $-\dfrac{1}{(1+e^x)}+C$ 5. $-\dfrac{1}{4}\cot^4 x+C$ 6. $\dfrac{1}{2}\{e^{\sin^{-1}x}\}^2+C$

7. $2\sqrt{x-\cos x}+C$ 8. $-\dfrac{1}{\sin^{-1}x}+C$ 9. $2\sqrt{\tan^{-1}x}+C$

10. $\dfrac{1}{3}(\log x)^3+C$ 11. $-\dfrac{1}{4}\cos^4 x+C$ 12. $\dfrac{2}{5}\tan^{5/2}x+C$

13. $\dfrac{-1}{2(x+\sin x)^2}+C$ 14. $-\dfrac{1}{(\sin x+\cos x)}+C$ 15. $\dfrac{1}{2b(a+b\cos 2x)}+C$

16. $(\log x)^2+C$ 17. $\dfrac{1}{1+\cos x}+C$ 18. $\dfrac{1}{4}\sin x^4+C$

19. $\dfrac{1}{4}(\sin^{-1}x^2)^2+C$ 20. $-\dfrac{1}{4}\cos(x^4+1)+C$ 21. $\dfrac{1}{3}\sin(e^{x^3})+C$

22. $\dfrac{1}{3}\sec^3(x^2+3)+C$ 23. $\dfrac{1}{3}(x+\log x)^3+C$ 24. $-\dfrac{1}{2}\left(\dfrac{1}{x}\right)-\dfrac{1}{4}\sin\left(\dfrac{2}{x}\right)+C$

25. $2\sin(e^{\sqrt{x}})+C$ 26. $-2\cos\sqrt{x}+C$ 27. $\dfrac{1}{m}e^{m\sin^{-1}x}+C$

28. $2\sin\sqrt{x}+C$ 29. $-\cos(\log x)+C$ 30. $\dfrac{1}{m}e^{m\tan^{-1}x}+C$

31. $\dfrac{1}{4}(\sin^{-1}x)^4+C$ 32. $-\dfrac{1}{3}\cos(2+3\ln x)+C$ 33. $\dfrac{1}{2}e^{x^2}+C$

34. $2\tan\sqrt{x}+C$ 35. $\dfrac{2}{3}(1+\sqrt{x})^3+C$ 36. $-\dfrac{1}{2}\left\{\ln\left(1+\dfrac{1}{x}\right)\right\}^2+C$

37. $-\dfrac{2}{\sqrt{\sin x}}+C$ 38. $\dfrac{2}{\sqrt{\cos x}}+C$ 39. $2\sqrt{\sin x}-\dfrac{2}{5}(\sin x)^{5/2}+C$

40. $-2\sqrt{\cos x}+\dfrac{2}{5}\cos^{5/2}x+C$ 41. (i) $2\sqrt{\tan x}+C$ (ii) $-2\sqrt{\cot x}+C$

42. $-\dfrac{(1+2x^2)}{4(x^2+1)^2}+C$ 43. $\dfrac{4}{3}(x^2+x+1)^{3/2}+C$ 44. $2\sqrt{2x^2+3x+1}+C$

45. $-e^{\cos^2 x}+C$ 46. $\dfrac{1}{2}\left\{\log|\sin x|\right\}^2+C$ 47. $\dfrac{1}{2}\left\{\log|\sec x+\tan x|\right\}^2+C$

48. $\dfrac{1}{2}\left\{\log|\operatorname{cosec} x-\cot x|\right\}^2+C$ 49. $\dfrac{3}{2}(x^2-1)^{2/3}+C$

50. $\tan(xe^x)+C$ 51. $-\cot(xe^x)+C$ 52. $\dfrac{1}{4}(\tan^{-1}x^2)^2+C$

53. $2\sqrt{x}-2\ln|1+\sqrt{x}|+C$ 54. $-\dfrac{1}{3}(1-\tan^2 x)^{3/2}+C$ 55. $-\dfrac{1}{2}\cos\{1+(\ln x)^2\}+C$

56. $\dfrac{1}{2}\tan^2 x+\dfrac{1}{4}\tan^4 x+C$ 57. $\dfrac{1}{4}\sin^4 x-\sin^2 x+\log|\sin x|+C$

58. $\dfrac{1}{\ln 5}(5^{x+\tan^{-1}x})+C$ 59. $-\cos(\tan^{-1}x)+C$

60. $\dfrac{1}{6a^2}\{(x^2+a^2)^{3/2}-(x^2-a^2)^{3/2}\}+C$ 61. $e^x-\log(1+e^x)+C$

62. $\frac{1}{6}\sec^3 2x - \frac{1}{2}\sec 2x + C$ 63. $(x+1) + 2\sqrt{x+1} - 2\log|x+2| - 2\tan^{-1}\sqrt{x+1} + C$

64. $\frac{5^{5^{5^x}}}{(\log_e 5)^3} + C$ 65. $\frac{1}{2}\sec^{-1}(x^2) + C$ 66. $2\sqrt{e^x - 1} - 2\tan^{-1}\sqrt{e^x - 1} + C$

67. $\log\left|\frac{x+1}{\sqrt{x^2+2x+2}}\right| + C$ 68. $\frac{2}{9}(1+x^3)^{3/2} - \frac{2}{3}(1+x^3)^{1/2} + C$

69. $\frac{4}{5}(5-x^2)^{5/2} - \frac{20}{3}(5-x^2)^{3/2} + C$ 70. $2\log|1+\sqrt{x}| + C$

71. $-\left(1+\frac{1}{x^4}\right)^{1/4} + C$ 72. $-\cos x - \frac{2}{\cos x} + \frac{1}{3\cos^3 x} + C$

73. $-2\sec\alpha\,(\cot x\cos\alpha + \sin\alpha)^{1/2} + C$

15.8.8 INTEGRALS OF THE FORM $\int (ax+b)^n P(x)\,dx$, $\int \frac{P(x)}{(ax+b)^n}\,dx$, WHERE $P(x)$ IS A POLYNOMIAL AND n IS A POSITIVE RATIONAL NUMBER

In order to evaluate this type of integrals, we may follow the following algorithm.

ALGORITHM

Step I *Substitute* $ax + b = t$ *or*, $x = \frac{t-b}{a}$ *and* $dx = \frac{1}{a}\,dt$

Step II *Simplify the integrand in terms of t and integrate with respect to t by using* $\int t^n dt = \frac{t^{n+1}}{n+1} + C.$

Step III *Replace t by* $ax + b$

Following examples will illustrate the above procedure.

ILLUSTRATIVE EXAMPLES

BASED ON BASIC CONCEPTS (BASIC)

EXAMPLE 1 *Evaluate:* $\int \frac{x^2}{\sqrt{x+2}}\,dx$

SOLUTION Let $I = \int \frac{x^2}{\sqrt{x+2}}\,dx$. Substituting $x + 2 = t$ and $dx = dt$, we get

$$I = \int \frac{(t-2)^2}{\sqrt{t}}\,dt = \int \frac{t^2 - 4t + 4}{\sqrt{t}}\,dt = \int (t^{3/2} - 4t^{1/2} + 4t^{-1/2})\,dt$$

$$\Rightarrow \quad I = \frac{2}{5}t^{5/2} - \frac{8}{3}t^{3/2} + 8t^{1/2} + C = \frac{2}{5}(x+2)^{5/2} - \frac{8}{3}(x+2)^{3/2} + 8\sqrt{x+2} + C$$

EXAMPLE 2 *Evaluate:* $\int x^2\sqrt{1+x}\,dx$

SOLUTION Let $I = \int x^2\sqrt{1+x}\,dx$. Substituting $1 + x = t$ and $dx = dt$, we get

$$I = \int (t-1)^2\sqrt{t}\,dt = \int (t^2 - 2t + 1)\sqrt{t}\,dt = \int (t^{5/2} - 2t^{3/2} + t^{1/2})\,dt$$

$$\Rightarrow \quad I = \frac{2}{7}t^{7/2} - \frac{4}{5}t^{5/2} + \frac{2}{3}t^{3/2} + C = \frac{2}{7}(1+x)^{7/2} - \frac{4}{5}(1+x)^{5/2} + \frac{2}{3}(1+x)^{3/2} + C$$

EXAMPLE 3 *Evaluate:* $\int x(1-x)^n \, dx$

SOLUTION Let $I = \int x(1-x)^n \, dx$. Substituting $1-x=t$ and $dx=-dt$, we get

$$I = -\int (1-t)\, t^n \, dt = -\int (t^n - t^{n+1})\, dt$$

$$\Rightarrow \quad I = -\frac{t^{n+1}}{n+1} + \frac{t^{n+2}}{n+2} + C = -\frac{1}{n+1}(1-x)^{n+1} + \frac{1}{n+2}(1-x)^{n+2} + C$$

BASED ON LOWER ORDER THINKING SKILLS (LOTS)

EXAMPLE 4 *Evaluate:* $\int \frac{x^5}{x+1}\, dx$

SOLUTION Let $I = \int \frac{x^5}{x+1}\, dx$. Substituting $x+1=t$ and $dx=dt$, we get

$$I = \int \frac{(t-1)^5}{t}\, dt = \int \frac{1}{t}\left({}^5C_0\, t^5 - {}^5C_1\, t^4 + {}^5C_2\, t^3 - {}^5C_3\, t^2 + {}^5C_4\, t - {}^5C_5)\, dt\right) dt$$

$$\Rightarrow \quad I = \int \frac{1}{t}(t^5 - 5t^4 + 10t^3 - 10t^2 + 5t - 1)\, dt$$

$$\Rightarrow \quad I = \int \left(t^4 - 5t^3 + 10t^2 - 10t + 5 - \frac{1}{t}\right) dt = \frac{t^5}{5} - \frac{5}{4}t^4 + \frac{10}{3}t^3 - 5t^2 + 5t - \log|t| + C$$

$$\Rightarrow \quad I = \frac{1}{5}(x+1)^5 - \frac{5}{4}(x+1)^4 + \frac{10}{3}(x+1)^3 - 5(x+1)^2 + 5(x+1) - \log|x+1| + C$$

EXAMPLE 5 *Evaluate:* $\int \frac{x^2}{(a+bx)^2}\, dx$

SOLUTION Let $I = \int \frac{x^2}{(a+bx)^2}\, dx$. Substituting $a+bx=t$ and $d(a+bx)=dt$ or, $b\,dx=dt$, we get

$$I = \int \frac{(t-a)^2}{b^2 t^2} \times \frac{1}{b}\, dt = \frac{1}{b^3}\int \frac{t^2 - 2at + a^2}{t^2}\, dt = \frac{1}{b^3}\int \left(1 - \frac{2a}{t} + \frac{a^2}{t^2}\right) dt$$

$$\Rightarrow \quad I = \frac{1}{b^3}\left\{t - 2a\log|t| - \frac{a^2}{t}\right\} + C = \frac{1}{b^3}\left\{(a+bx) - 2a\log|a+bx| - \frac{a^2}{a+bx}\right\} + C$$

BASED ON HIGHER ORDER THINKING SKILLS (HOTS)

EXAMPLE 6 *Evaluate:* $\int \frac{1}{x^{1/2} + x^{1/3}}\, dx$ [NCERT, CBSE 2022]

SOLUTION Here, the exponents of x are $\frac{1}{2}$ and $\frac{1}{3}$ and the LCM of their denominators is 6.

So, to remove fractional exponents, we substitute $x = t^6$ and $dx = 6t^5\, dt$.

$$\therefore \quad I = \int \frac{1}{x^{1/2} + x^{1/3}}\, dx = \int \frac{6t^5}{t^3 + t^2}\, dt = 6\int \frac{t^3}{t+1}\, dt = 6\int \frac{(t^3+1)-1}{t+1}\, dt$$

$$\Rightarrow \quad I = 6\int \left(t^2 - t + 1 - \frac{1}{t+1}\right) dt$$

$$\Rightarrow \quad I = 6\left\{\frac{t^3}{3} - \frac{t^2}{2} + t - \log|t+1|\right\} + C = 2\sqrt{x} - 3x^{1/3} + 6x^{1/6} - 6\log|x^{1/6}+1| + C$$

EXAMPLE 7 *Evaluate:* $\int \frac{x^{1/2}}{1+x^{3/4}}\,dx$

SOLUTION Here, the LCM of the denominators 2 and 4 of the exponents $\frac{1}{2}$ and $\frac{3}{4}$ is 4. So, to remove fractional exponents, we substitute $x = t^4$ and $dx = 4t^3 dt$.

$$\therefore \quad I = \int \frac{x^{1/2}}{1+x^{3/4}}\,dx = \int \frac{t^2}{1+t^3}\,4t^3 dt = 4\int \frac{t^5}{t^3+1}\,dt = 4\int \frac{t^3}{t^3+1}\,t^2\,dt$$

Let $t^3 + 1 = u$. Then $3t^2 dt = du$ or, $t^2 dt = \frac{1}{3}du$.

$$\therefore \quad I = 4\int \frac{u-1}{u} \times \frac{1}{3}\,du = \frac{4}{3}\int\left(1 - \frac{1}{u}\right)du = \frac{4}{3}(u - \ln u) + C = \frac{4}{3}\left\{(t^3+1) - \ln(t^3+1)\right\} + C$$

$$\Rightarrow \quad I = \frac{4}{3}\left\{\left(x^{3/4}+1\right) - \ln\left(x^{3/4}+1\right)\right\} + C$$

EXAMPLE 8 *Evaluate :* $\int \frac{\sqrt{x}}{\sqrt{x} - \sqrt[3]{x}}\,dx$

SOLUTION Let $I = \int \frac{x^{1/2}}{x^{1/2} - x^{1/3}}\,dx$. Clearly, the LCM of 2 and 3 is 6. So, by putting $x = t^6$ and $dx = 6t^5\,dt$, we get

$$I = \int \frac{t^3}{t^3 - t^2}\cdot 6t^5\,dt = 6\int \frac{t^6}{t-1}\,dt = 6\int \frac{t^6 - 1 + 1}{t-1}\,dt = 6\int \frac{t^6 - 1^6}{t-1} + \frac{1}{t-1}\,dt$$

$$\Rightarrow \quad I = 6\int t^5 + t^4 + t^2 + t + 1 + \frac{1}{t-1}\,dt = 6\left\{\frac{t^6}{6} + \frac{t^5}{5} + \frac{t^3}{3} + \frac{t^2}{2} + t + \log(t-1)\right\} + C$$

$$\Rightarrow \quad I = 6\left\{\frac{x}{6} + \frac{x^{5/6}}{5} + \frac{x^{1/2}}{3} + \frac{x^{1/3}}{2} + x^{1/6} + \log(x^{1/6} - 1)\right\} + C$$

EXAMPLE 9 *Evaluate :* $\int \frac{1}{\sqrt[3]{x+1} + \sqrt{x+1}}\,dx.$

SOLUTION Let $\int \frac{1}{\sqrt[3]{x+1} + \sqrt{x+1}}\,dx$. Here the exponents of $(1+x)$ are $\frac{1}{2}$ and $\frac{1}{3}$ and the LCM of their denominators is 6. So, we substitute $x + 1 = t^6$ and $dx = 6t^5 dt$.

$$\therefore \quad I = \int \frac{1}{t^2 + t^3}\,6t^5\,dt = 6\int \frac{t^3}{t+1}\,dt = 6\int \frac{t^3 + 1 - 1}{t+1}\,dt$$

$$\Rightarrow \quad I = 6\int \frac{t^3+1}{t+1}\,dt - 6\int \frac{1}{t+1}\,dt = 6\int (t^2 - t + 1)\,dt - 6\int \frac{1}{t+1}\,dt$$

$$\Rightarrow \quad I = 6\left(\frac{t^3}{3} - \frac{t^2}{2} + t\right) - 6\log|t+1| + C = 2t^3 - 3t^2 + 6t - 6\log|t+1| + C$$

$$\Rightarrow \quad I = 2(x+1)^{1/2} - 3(x+1)^{1/3} + 6(x+1)^{1/6} - 6\log|(x+1)^{16} + 1| + C$$

EXERCISE 15.10

BASIC

1. $\int x^2 \sqrt{x+2}\, dx$
2. $\int \frac{x^2}{\sqrt{x-1}}\, dx$
3. $\int \frac{x^2}{\sqrt{3x+4}}\, dx$

BASED ON LOTS

4. $\int \frac{2x-1}{(x-1)^2}\, dx$
5. $\int (2x^2+3)\sqrt{x+2}\, dx$
6. $\int \frac{x^2+3x+1}{(x+1)^2}\, dx$
7. $\int \frac{x^2}{\sqrt{1-x}}\, dx$
8. $\int x(1-x)^{23}\, dx$

BASED ON HOTS

9. $\int \frac{1}{\sqrt{x}+\sqrt[4]{x}}\, dx$
10. $\int \frac{1}{x^{1/3}(x^{1/3}-1)}\, dx$

ANSWERS

1. $\frac{2}{7}(x+2)^{7/2}-\frac{8}{5}(x+2)^{5/2}+\frac{8}{3}(x+2)^{3/2}+C$
2. $\frac{2}{15}(3x^2+4x+8)\sqrt{x-1}+C$
3. $\frac{2}{135}(3x+4)^{5/2}-\frac{16}{81}(3x+4)^{3/2}+\frac{32}{27}(3x+4)^{1/2}+C$
4. $-\frac{1}{x-1}+2\log|x-1|+C$
5. $\frac{4}{7}(x+2)^{7/2}-\frac{16}{5}(x+2)^{5/2}+\frac{22}{3}(x+2)^{3/2}+C$
6. $x+\frac{1}{x+1}+\log|x+1|+C$
7. $\frac{2}{15}(3x^2+4x+8)\sqrt{1-x}+C$
8. $-\frac{1}{600}(1-x)^{24}(1+24x)+C$
9. $2\sqrt{x}-4x^{1/4}+4\log|1+x^{1/4}|+C$
10. $3x^{1/3}+3\log(x^{1/3}-1)+C$

15.8.9 INTEGRALS OF THE FORM $\int \tan^m x \sec^{2n} x\, dx, \int \cot^m x \operatorname{cosec}^{2n} x\, dx;\ m, n \in N$

In order to evaluate this type of integrals. We may follow the following algorithm.

ALGORITHM

Step I *Write the given integral as* $I = \int \tan^m x (\sec^2 x)^{(n-1)} \sec^2 x\, dx$

Step II *Put* $\tan x = t$ *and* $\sec^2 x\, dx = dt$ *and write the integral as*

$$I = \int \tan^m x (\sec^2 x)^{n-1} \sec^2 x\, dx = \int \tan^m x (1+\tan^2 x)^{n-1} \sec^2 x\, dx = \int t^m (1+t^2)^{n-1} dt$$

Step III *Expand* $(1+t^2)^{n-1}$ *by binomial theorem in step II and integrate.*

Step IV *Replace* t *by* $\tan x$ *in step III.*

Following examples will illustrate the above procedure.

ILLUSTRATIVE EXAMPLES

BASED ON BASIC CONCEPTS (BASIC)

EXAMPLE 1 *Evaluate:*

(i) $\int \tan^n x \sec^2 x\, dx$ (ii) $\int \tan^2 x \sec^4 x\, dx$ (iii) $\int \sec^4 x\, dx$

SOLUTION (i) Let $I = \int \tan^n x \sec^2 x\, dx$. Substituting $\tan x = t$ and $\sec^2 x\, dx = dt$, we get

$$I = \int t^n\, dt = \frac{t^{n+1}}{n+1} + C = \frac{1}{n+1} \tan^{n+1} x + C$$

(ii) Let $I = \int \tan^2 x \sec^4 x \; dx$. Then,

$$I = \int \tan^2 x \sec^2 x \sec^2 x \, dx = \int \tan^2 x (1 + \tan^2 x) \sec^2 x \, dx$$

Substituting $\tan x = t$ and $\sec^2 x \, dx = dt$, we get

$$I = \int t^2 (1 + t^2) \, dt = \int (t^2 + t^4) \, dt = \frac{t^3}{3} + \frac{t^5}{5} + C = \frac{1}{3} \tan^3 x + \frac{1}{5} \tan^5 x + C$$

(iii) Let $I = \int \sec^4 x \; dx$. Then,

$$I = \int \sec^2 x \sec^2 x \; dx = \int (1 + \tan^2 x) \sec^2 x \, dx$$

Putting $\tan x = t$ and $\sec^2 x \, dx = dt$, we get

$$I = \int (1 + t^2) \; dt = t + \frac{t^3}{3} + C = \tan x + \frac{1}{3} \tan^3 x + C$$

EXAMPLE 2 *Evaluate:*

(i) $\int \cot^2 x \operatorname{cosec}^4 x \; dx$ (ii) $\int \operatorname{cosec}^4 x \; dx$

SOLUTION (i) Let $I = \int \cot^2 x \operatorname{cosec}^4 x \; dx$. Then,

$$I = \int \cot^2 x \operatorname{cosec}^2 x \operatorname{cosec}^2 x \; dx$$

$$\Rightarrow \quad I = \int \cot^2 x (\cot^2 x + 1) \operatorname{cosec}^2 x \, dx = \int (\cot^4 x + \cot^2 x) \operatorname{cosec}^2 x \; dx$$

Substituting $\cot x = t$ and $-\operatorname{cosec}^2 x \, dx = dt$, we get

$$I = - \int (t^4 + t^2) \; dt = -\frac{t^5}{5} - \frac{t^3}{3} + C = -\frac{1}{5} \cot^5 x - \frac{1}{3} \cot^3 x + C$$

(ii) Let $I = \int \operatorname{cosec}^4 x \; dx$. Then,

$$I = \int \operatorname{cosec}^2 x \operatorname{cosec}^2 x \, dx = \int (1 + \cot^2 x) \operatorname{cosec}^2 x \, dx$$

Substituting $\cot x = t$ and $-\operatorname{cosec}^2 x \, dx = dt$, we get

$$I = - \int (1 + t^2) \; dt = -t - \frac{t^3}{3} + C = -\cot x - \frac{1}{3} \cot^3 x + C$$

BASED ON LOWER ORDER THINKING SKILLS (LOTS)

EXAMPLE 3 *Evaluate:* $\int \tan^8 x \sec^4 x \, dx$ [NCERT EXEMPLAR]

SOLUTION Let $I = \int \tan^8 x \sec^4 x \; dx$. Then,

$$I = \int \tan^8 x \sec^2 x \sec^2 x \, dx = \int \tan^8 x (1 + \tan^2 x) \sec^2 x \, dx$$

Let $\tan x = t$. Then, $d(\tan x) = dt \Rightarrow \sec^2 x \, dx = dt$.

$$I = \int t^8 (1 + t^2) \, dt = \int t^8 + t^{10} \, dt = \frac{t^9}{9} + \frac{t^{11}}{11} + C = \frac{1}{9} \tan^9 x + \frac{1}{11} \tan^{11} x + C$$

15.8.10 INTEGRALS OF THE FORM $\int \tan^{2m+1} x \sec^{2n+1} x\, dx$, WHERE m, n ARE NON-NEGATIVE INTEGERS

In order to evaluate this type of integrals, we may follow the following algorithm.

ALGORITHM

Step I *Write the given integral as* $I = \int (\tan^2 x)^m (\sec x)^{2n} \sec x \tan x\, dx$

Step II *Substitute* $\sec x = t$ *and* $\sec x \tan x\, dx = dt$ *and write the integrals as*

$$I = \int (\sec^2 x - 1)^m (\sec x)^{2n} \sec x \tan x\, dx = \int (t^2 - 1)^m t^n\, dt$$

Step III *Expand* $(t^2 - 1)^m$ *by binomial theorem in step II and integrate.*

Step IV *Replace* t *by* $\sec x$ *in step III.*

Following examples will illustrate the above procedure.

ILLUSTRATIVE EXAMPLES

BASED ON BASIC CONCEPTS (BASIC)

EXAMPLE 1 *Evaluate:* $\int \tan^3 x \sec^3 x\, dx$ [CBSE 2020]

SOLUTION Let $I = \int \tan^3 x \sec^3 x\, dx$. Then,

$$I = \int \tan^2 x \sec^2 x (\sec x \tan x)\, dx = \int (\sec^2 x - 1) \sec^2 x (\sec x \tan x)\, dx$$

Substituting $\sec x = t$ and $\sec x \tan x\, dx = dt$, we get

$$I = \int (t^2 - 1) t^2\, dt = \int (t^4 - t^2)\, dt = \frac{t^5}{5} - \frac{t^3}{3} + C = \frac{1}{5} \sec^5 x - \frac{1}{3} \sec^3 x + C$$

EXAMPLE 2 *Evaluate:* $\int \sec^n x \tan x\, dx$

SOLUTION Let $I = \int \sec^n x \tan x\, dx$. Then,

$$I = \int \sec^{n-1} x (\sec x \tan x)\, dx$$

Substituting $\sec x = t$ and $\sec x \tan x\, dx = dt$, we get

$$I = \int t^{n-1}\, dt = \frac{t^n}{n} + C = \frac{1}{n} \sec^n x + C$$

ILLUSTRATIVE EXAMPLES

BASED ON LOWER ORDER THINKING SKILLS (LOTS)

15.8.11 INTEGRALS OF THE FORM $\int \tan^n x\, dx, \int \cot^n x\, dx$

EXAMPLE 1 *Evaluate:*

(i) $\int \tan^3 x\, dx$ (ii) $\int \tan^4 x\, dx$ [NCERT] (iii) $\int \cot^3 x\, dx$ (iv) $\int \cot^4 x\, dx$

SOLUTION (i) Let $I = \int \tan^3 x\, dx$. Then,

$$I = \int \tan^2 x \tan x\, dx = \int (\sec^2 x - 1) \tan x\, dx = \int \tan x \sec^2 x\, dx - \int \tan x\, dx$$

Putting $\tan x = t$ and $\sec^2 x\, dx = dt$ in first integral, we get

$$I = \int t\, dt - \int \tan x\, dx = \frac{t^2}{2} + \log|\cos x| + C = \frac{1}{2} \tan^2 x + \log|\cos x| + C$$

(ii) Let $I = \int \tan^4 x\, dx$. Then,

$$I = \int \tan^2 x \times \tan^2 x \; dx = \int \tan^2 x \; (\sec^2 x - 1) \; dx = \int (\tan^2 x \sec^2 x - \tan^2 x) \, dx$$

$$\Rightarrow \quad I = \int \tan^2 x \sec^2 x \; dx - \int \tan^2 x \; dx = \int \tan^2 x \sec^2 x \, dx - \int (\sec^2 x - 1) \; dx$$

Putting $\tan x = t$ and $\sec^2 dx = dt$ in first integral, we get

$$I = \int t^2 \, dt - \int (\sec^2 x - 1) \; dt = \frac{t^3}{3} - (\tan x - x) + C = \frac{\tan^3 x}{3} - \tan x + x + C$$

(iii) Let $I = \int \cot^3 x \; dx$. Then,

$$I = \int \cot^2 x \cot x \, dx = \int (\text{cosec}^2 x - 1) \cot x \; dx = \int (\cot x \, \text{cosec}^2 x - \cot x) \; dx$$

$$\Rightarrow \quad I = \int \cot x \, \text{cosec}^2 x \; dx - \int \cot x \; dx$$

Substituting $\cot x = t$ and $-\text{cosec}^2 x \, dx = dt$ in first integral, we get

$$I = -\int t \; dt - \int \cot x \, dx = -\frac{t^2}{2} - \log|\sin x| + C = -\frac{1}{2}\cot^2 x - \log|\sin x| + C$$

(iv) Let $I = \int \cot^4 x \; dx$. Then,

$$I = \int \cot^2 x \cot^2 x \; dx = \int (\text{cosec}^2 x - 1) \cot^2 x \, dx = \int (\cot^2 x \, \text{cosec}^2 x - \cot^2 x) \; dx$$

$$\Rightarrow \quad I = \int \cot^2 x \, \text{cosec}^2 x \, dx - \int \cot^2 x \; dx = \int \cot^2 x \, \text{cosec}^2 x \, dx - \int (\text{cosec}^2 x - 1) \, dx$$

Substituting $\cot x = t$ and $-\text{cosec}^2 x \, dx = dt$ in the first integral, we get

$$I = -\int t^2 \, dt - \int (\text{cosec}^2 x - 1) \, dx = -\frac{t^3}{3} - (-\cot x - x) + C = -\frac{1}{3}\cot^3 x + \cot x + x + C$$

BASED ON HIGHER ORDER THINKING SKILLS (HOTS)

EXAMPLE 2 *Prove that:* $\int \tan^n x \; dx = \frac{1}{n-1} \tan^{n-1} x - \int \tan^{n-2} x \; dx$

SOLUTION Let $I_n = \int \tan^n x \; dx$. Then,

$$I_n = \int \tan^{n-2} x \tan^2 x \; dx = \int \tan^{n-2} x \, (\sec^2 x - 1) \; dx$$

$$\Rightarrow \quad I_n = \int \tan^{n-2} x \sec^2 x \; dx - \int \tan^{n-2} x \; dx$$

Substituting $\tan x = t$, $\sec^2 x \, dx = dt$ in the first integral on the right hand side, we get

$$I_n = \int t^{n-2} \, dt - \int \tan^{n-2} x \, dx = \frac{t^{n-1}}{n-1} - \int \tan^{n-2} x \; dx$$

$$\Rightarrow \quad \int \tan^n x \, dx = \frac{1}{n-1} \tan^{n-1} x - \int \tan^{n-2} x \, dx$$

EXERCISE 15.11

BASED ON LOTS

Evaluate the following integrals (1-12):

1. $\int \tan^3 x \; \sec^2 x \; dx$
2. $\int \tan x \sec^4 x \; dx$
3. $\int \tan^5 x \sec^4 x \, dx$
4. $\int \sec^6 x \tan x \; dx$
5. $\int \tan^5 x \; dx$
6. $\int \sqrt{\tan x} \; \sec^4 x \; dx$
7. $\int \sec^4 2x \; dx$
8. $\int \text{cosec}^4 3x \; dx$
9. $\int \cot^n x \, \text{cosec}^2 x \; dx, n \neq -1$

10. $\int \cot^5 x \operatorname{cosec}^4 x \; dx$ 11. $\int \cot^5 x \; dx$ 12. $\int \cot^6 x \, dx$

13. If $\frac{d}{dx}(F(x)) = \frac{\sec^4 x}{\operatorname{cosec}^4 x}$ and $F\left(\frac{\pi}{4}\right) = \frac{\pi}{4}$, then find $F(x)$. [CBSE 2022]

ANSWERS

1. $\frac{1}{4} \tan^4 x + C$
2. $\frac{1}{2} \tan^2 x + \frac{1}{4} \tan^4 x + C$
3. $\frac{1}{6} \tan^6 x + \frac{1}{8} \tan^8 x + C$
4. $\frac{1}{6} \sec^6 x + C$
5. $\frac{1}{4} \tan^4 x - \frac{1}{2} \tan^2 x + \log|\sec x| + C$
6. $\frac{2}{3} \tan^{3/2} x + \frac{2}{7} \tan^{7/2} x + C$
7. $\frac{1}{2} \tan 2x + \frac{1}{6} \tan^3 2x + C$
8. $-\frac{1}{3} \cot 3x - \frac{1}{9} \cot^3 3x + C$
9. $-\frac{1}{n+1} \cot^{n+1} x + C$
10. $-\frac{1}{6} \cot^6 x - \frac{1}{8} \cot^8 x + C$
11. $-\frac{1}{4} \cot^4 x + \frac{1}{2} \cot^2 x + \log|\sin x| + C$
12. $-\frac{1}{5} \cot^5 x + \frac{1}{3} \cot^3 x - \cot x - x + C$
13. $F(x) = \frac{1}{3} \tan^3 x - \tan x + x + \frac{2}{3}$

15.8.12 INTEGRALS OF THE FORM $\int \sin^m x \cos^n x \, dx, m, n \in N$

In order to evaluate the integrals of the form $\int \sin^m x \cos^n x \, dx$, we may use the following algorithm.

ALGORITHM

Step I *Obtain the integral, say,* $\int \sin^m x \cos^n x \, dx$.

Step II *Check the exponents of* $\sin x$ *and* $\cos x$.

Step III *If the exponent of* $\sin x$ *is an odd positive integer put* $\cos x = t$.

If the exponent of $\cos x$ *is an odd positive integer put* $\sin x = t$.

If the exponents of $\sin x$ *and* $\cos x$ *both are odd positive integers put either* $\sin x = t$ *or,* $\cos x = t$.

If the exponents of $\sin x$ *and* $\cos x$ *both are even positive integers, then express* $\sin^m x \cos^n x$ *in terms of* sines *and* cosines *of multiples of* x *by using trigonometric results or De' Moivere's theorem.*

Step IV *Evaluate the integral obtained in step III.*

Following examples will illustrate the procedure.

ILLUSTRATIVE EXAMPLES

BASED ON LOWER ORDER THINKING SKILLS (LOTS)

EXAMPLE 1 *Evaluate:*

(i) $\int \sin^3 x \cos^4 x \, dx$ (ii) $\int \sin^2 x \cos^5 x \, dx$ (iii) $\int \sin^3 x \cos^5 x \, dx$

SOLUTION (i) Let $I = \int \sin^3 x \cos^4 x \, dx$. Here, power of $\sin x$ is odd, so we substitute

$$\cos x = t \Rightarrow -\sin x \, dx = dt \Rightarrow dx = -\frac{dt}{\sin x}$$

$$\therefore \quad I = \int \sin^3 x \, t^4 \left(-\frac{dt}{\sin x}\right) = -\int \sin^2 x \, t^4 \, dt = -\int (1-t^2) \, t^4 \, dt = -\int (t^4 - t^6) \, dt$$

$\Rightarrow \quad I = -\frac{t^5}{5} + \frac{t^7}{7} + C = -\frac{\cos^5 x}{5} + \frac{\cos^7 x}{7} + C$

(ii) Let $I = \int \sin^2 x \cos^5 x \, dx$. Here, power of $\cos x$ is odd, so we substitute

$$\sin x = t \Rightarrow \cos x \, dx = dt \Rightarrow dx = \frac{dt}{\cos x}$$

$\therefore \quad I = \int t^2 \cos^5 x \frac{dt}{\cos x} = \int t^2 (1 - \sin^2 x)^2 \, dt = \int t^2 (1 - t^2)^2 \, dt$

$\Rightarrow \quad I = \int (t^2 - 2t^4 + t^6) \, dt = \frac{t^3}{3} - \frac{2}{5} t^5 + \frac{t^7}{7} + C = \frac{\sin^3 x}{3} - \frac{2}{5} \sin^5 x + \frac{\sin^7 x}{7} + C$

(iii) Let $I = \int \sin^3 x \cos^5 x \, dx$. Here, powers of both $\sin x$ and $\cos x$ are odd. So we can substitute either $\sin x = t$ or, $\cos x = t$. Putting $\cos x = t$ and $-\sin x \, dx = dt$ or, $dx = -\frac{dt}{\sin x}$, we get

$$I = \int \sin^3 x \, t^5 \times -\frac{dt}{\sin x} = -\int t^5 \sin^2 x \, dt = -\int t^5 (1 - t^2) \, dt = -\int (t^5 - t^7) \, dt$$

$\Rightarrow \quad I = -\frac{t^6}{6} + \frac{t^8}{8} + C = -\frac{\cos^6 x}{6} + \frac{\cos^8 x}{8} + C$

EXAMPLE 2 *Evaluate:* $\int \cos^3 x \, e^{\log \sin x} \, dx$.

SOLUTION We have, $I = \int \cos^3 x \, e^{\log \sin x} \, dx = \int \cos^3 x \sin x \, dx$

Putting $\cos x = t$ and $-\sin x \, dx = dt$ or, $\sin x \, dx = -dt$, we get

$$I = -\int t^3 \, dt = -\frac{t^4}{4} + C = -\frac{\cos^4 x}{4} + C$$

15.8.13 TO EVALUATE INTEGRALS OF THE FORM $\int \sin^m x \cos^n x \, dx$, WHERE $m, n \in Q$ SUCH THAT $m + n$ IS A NEGATIVE EVEN INTEGER

ALGORITHM

Step I *Change the integrand in terms of* $\tan x$ and $\sec^2 x$ *by, dividing numerator and denominator by* $\cos^k x$, *where* $k = -(m + n)$.

Step II *Substitute* $\tan x = t$.

Following examples will illustrate the above procedure.

ILLUSTRATIVE EXAMPLES

BASED ON LOWER ORDER THINKING SKILLS (LOTS)

EXAMPLE 1 *Evaluate:* (i) $\int \frac{\sin^4 x}{\cos^8 x} \, dx$ (ii) $\int \frac{1}{\sqrt{\sin^3 x \cos^5 x}} \, dx$

SOLUTION (i) Let $I = \int \frac{\sin^4 x}{\cos^8 x} \, dx$. Here $k = -(m + n) = -(4 - 8) = 4$. Dividing numerator and denominator by $\cos^4 x$, we obtain

$$I = \int \frac{\dfrac{\sin^4 x}{\cos^4 x}}{\dfrac{\cos^8 x}{\cos^4 x}}\, dx = \int \tan^4 x \sec^4 x \; dx = \int \tan^4 x\,(1 + \tan^2 x) \sec^2 x \, dx$$

$$\Rightarrow \quad I = \int \tan^4 x\,(1 + \tan^2 x) \sec^2 x \, dx$$

Putting $\tan x = t$ and $\sec^2 x \, dx = dt$, we get

$$I = \int t^4 (1 + t^2)\, dt = \frac{t^5}{5} + \frac{t^7}{7} + C = \frac{\tan^5 x}{5} + \frac{\tan^7 x}{7} + C$$

(ii) Let $I = \displaystyle\int \frac{1}{\sqrt{\sin^3 x \cos^5 x}}\, dx$. Then, $I = \displaystyle\int \frac{1}{\sin^{3/2} x \cos^{5/2} x}\, dx = \int \sin^{-3/2} x \cos^{-5/2} x \, dx$

Here $k = -(m+n) = -\left(-\frac{3}{2} - \frac{5}{2}\right) = 4$. Dividing numerator and denominator by $\cos^4 x$, we obtain

$$I = \int \frac{\sec^4 x}{\tan^{3/2} x}\, dx = \int \frac{(1 + \tan^2 x)}{\tan^{3/2} x} \sec^2 x \; dx$$

Putting $\tan x = t$ and $\sec^2 x \, dx = dt$, we get

$$I = \int \frac{1 + t^2}{t^{3/2}}\, dt = \int (t^{-3/2} + t^{1/2})\, dt = \frac{-2}{\sqrt{t}} + \frac{t^{3/2}}{3/2} + C = -\frac{2}{\sqrt{\tan x}} + \frac{2}{3} (\tan x)^{3/2} + C$$

EXAMPLE 2 *Evaluate:* $\displaystyle\int \sec^{4/3} x \operatorname{cosec}^{8/3} x \, dx$

SOLUTION Let $I = \displaystyle\int \sec^{4/3} x \operatorname{cosec}^{8/3} x \, dx$ Then,

$$I = \int \frac{1}{\cos^{4/3} x \; \sin^{8/3} x}\, dx = \int \cos^{-4/3} x \; \sin^{-8/3} x \, dx$$

Here $k = -(m+n) = -\left(\frac{4}{3} - \frac{8}{3}\right) = 4$. So, we divide both numerator and denominator by $\cos^4 x$.

$\therefore \; I = \displaystyle\int \frac{\sec^4 x}{\tan^{8/3} x}\, dx = \int \frac{(1 + \tan^2 x)}{\tan^{8/3} x} \sec^2 x \, dx$. Putting $\tan x = t$ and $\sec^2 x \, dx = dt$, we get

$$I = \int \frac{1 + t^2}{t^{8/3}}\, dt = \int (t^{-8/3} + t^{-2/3})\, dt = -\frac{3}{5} t^{-5/3} + 3 t^{1/3} + C$$

$$\Rightarrow I = -\frac{3}{5} \tan^{-5/3} x + 3 \tan^{1/3} x + C$$

BASED ON HIGHER ORDER THINKING SKILLS (HOTS)

EXAMPLE 3 *Evaluate:* $\displaystyle\int \sqrt[3]{\frac{\sin^2 x}{\cos^{14} x}}\, dx$

SOLUTION Let $I = \displaystyle\int \sqrt[3]{\frac{\sin^2 x}{\cos^{14} x}}\, dx = \int \sin^{2/3} x \; \cos^{-14/3} x \, dx$

Here, the sum of the exponents of sin x and cos x in -4, which is a negative even integer. So, we divide and multiply by $\cos^4 x$ to get

$$I = \int \sin^{2/3} x \cos^{-14/3} x \cos^4 x \sec^4 x\, dx = \int \frac{\sin^{2/3} x}{\cos^{2/3} x} \sec^4 x\, dx$$

$$\Rightarrow \quad I = \int \tan^{2/3} x\,(1+\tan^2 x) \sec^2 x\, dx$$

Putting $\tan x = t$, and $\sec^2 x\, dx = dt$, we get

$$I = \int (t^{2/3} + t^{8/3})\, dt = \frac{3}{5} t^{5/3} + \frac{3}{11} t^{11/3} + C = \frac{3}{5} \tan^{5/3} x + \frac{3}{11} \tan^{11/3} x + C$$

EXERCISE 15.12

BASIC

Evaluate the following integrals:

1. $\int \sin^4 x \cos^3 x\, dx$
2. $\int \sin^5 x\, dx$
3. $\int \cos^5 x\, dx$
4. $\int \sin^5 x \cos x\, dx$
5. $\int \sin^3 x \cos^6 x\, dx$
6. $\int \sin^3 x \cos^5 x\, dx$

BASED ON LOTS

7. $\int \cos^7 x\, dx$
8. $\int x \cos^3 x^2 \sin x^2\, dx$
9. $\int \sin^7 x\, dx$

BASED ON HOTS

10. $\int \frac{1}{\sin^4 x \cos^2 x}\, dx$
11. $\int \frac{1}{\sin^3 x \cos^5 x}\, dx$
12. $\int \frac{1}{\sin^3 x \cos x}\, dx$
13. $\int \frac{1}{\sin x \cos^3 x}\, dx$ [NCERT]

ANSWERS

1. $\frac{1}{5} \sin^5 x - \frac{1}{7} \sin^7 x + C$
2. $-\left\{\cos x - \frac{2}{3} \cos^3 x + \frac{1}{5} \cos^5 x\right\} + C$
3. $\left\{\sin x - \frac{2}{3} \sin^3 x + \frac{1}{5} \sin^5 x\right\} + C$
4. $\frac{\sin^6 x}{6} + C$
5. $-\left\{\frac{\cos^7 x}{7} - \frac{\cos^9 x}{9}\right\} + C$
6. $-\frac{1}{6} \cos^6 x + \frac{1}{8} \cos^8 x + C$
7. $\sin x - \sin^3 x + \frac{3}{5} \sin^5 x - \frac{1}{7} \sin^7 x + C$
8. $-\frac{1}{8} \cos^4 x^2 + C$
9. $-\cos x + \cos^3 x - \frac{3}{5} \cos^5 x + \frac{1}{7} \cos^7 x + C$
10. $-\frac{1}{3} \cot^3 x - 2 \cot x + \tan x + C$
11. $-\frac{1}{2} (\tan x)^{-2} + 3 \log|\tan x| + \frac{3}{2} \tan^2 x + \frac{1}{4} \tan^4 x + C$
12. $\log|\tan x| - \frac{1}{2 \tan^2 x} + C$
13. $\frac{1}{2} \tan^2 x + \log|\tan x| + C$

HINTS TO SELECTED PROBLEMS

13. $I = \int \frac{1}{\sin x \cos^3 x} dx = \int \frac{\sec^4 x}{\tan x} dx$ [Diving numerator and denominator by $\cos^4 x$]

$$\Rightarrow \quad I = \int \frac{(1+\tan^2 x)}{\tan x} \sec^2 x \, dx = \int \left(\frac{1+t^2}{t}\right) dt, \text{ where } t = \tan x \text{ and } dt = \sec^2 x \, dx$$

$$\Rightarrow \quad I = \int \left(\frac{1}{t} + t\right) dt = \frac{t^2}{2} + \log t + C = \frac{1}{2}\tan^2 x + \log \tan x + C$$

15.9 EVALUATION OF INTEGRALS BY USING TRIGONOMETRIC SUBSTITUTIONS

In this section, we will discuss evaluation of integrals by using trigonometric substitutions. Following are some substitutions useful in evaluating integrals.

Expression	*Substitution*	*Expression*	*Substitution*
(i) $a^2 + x^2$	$x = a\tan\theta$ or $a\cot\theta$	(iv) $\sqrt{\frac{a-x}{a+x}}$ or, $\sqrt{\frac{a+x}{a-x}}$	$x = a\cos 2\theta$
(ii) $a^2 - x^2$	$x = a\sin\theta$ or $a\cos\theta$	(v) $\sqrt{\frac{x-\alpha}{\beta-x}}$ or, $\sqrt{(x-\alpha)(x-\beta)}$	$x = \alpha\cos^2\theta + \beta\sin^2\theta$.
(iii) $x^2 - a^2$	$x = a\sec\theta$ or $a\,\text{cosec}\,\theta$		

Let us discuss some problems on evaluation of integrals by making above substitutions.

ILLUSTRATIVE EXAMPLES

BASED ON HIGHER ORDER THINKING SKILLS (HOTS)

Type I EVALUATION OF INTEGRALS BY MAKING SUBSTITUTION $x = a\sin\theta$ or, $x = a\sin^2\theta$

EXAMPLE 1 *Evaluate:* $\int \frac{1}{(a^2 - x^2)^{3/2}} dx.$

SOLUTION Let $I = \int \frac{1}{(a^2-x^2)^{3/2}} dx$ and $x = a\sin\theta$. Then, $dx = d(a\sin\theta) \Rightarrow dx = a\cos\theta \, d\theta$.

$$\therefore \quad I = \int \frac{1}{(a^2 - a^2\sin^2\theta)^{3/2}} a\cos\theta \, d\theta = \int \frac{a\cos\theta}{a^3\cos^3\theta} d\theta = \frac{1}{a^2}\int \sec^2\theta \, d\theta$$

$$\Rightarrow \quad I = \frac{1}{a^2}\tan\theta + C = \frac{1}{a^2}\frac{\sin\theta}{\sqrt{1-\sin^2\theta}} + C = \frac{x}{a^3\sqrt{1-\frac{x^2}{a^2}}} + C = \frac{x}{a^2\sqrt{a^2-x^2}} + C$$

EXAMPLE 2 *Evaluate:* $\int \frac{x^2}{\sqrt{1-x^2}} dx.$

SOLUTION Let $I = \int \frac{x^2}{\sqrt{1-x^2}} dx$ and $x = \sin\theta$. Then, $dx = d(\sin\theta) = \cos\theta \, d\theta$.

$$I = \int \frac{\sin^2\theta}{\sqrt{1-\sin^2\theta}} \cos\theta \, d\theta = \int \sin^2\theta \, d\theta = \frac{1}{2}\int (1 - \cos 2\theta) \, d\theta$$

$$\Rightarrow \quad I = \frac{1}{2}\left(\theta - \frac{1}{2}\sin 2\theta\right) + C = \frac{1}{2}\theta - \frac{1}{2}\sin\theta\cos\theta + C = \frac{1}{2}\sin^{-1}x - \frac{1}{2}x\sqrt{1-x^2} + C$$

EXAMPLE 3 *Evaluate:* $\int \frac{x^2 - 3x + 1}{\sqrt{1-x^2}}\, dx.$ **[CBSE 2015]**

SOLUTION Let $I = \int \frac{x^2 - 3x + 1}{\sqrt{1-x^2}}\, dx$ and $x = \sin\theta$. Then, $dx = d(\sin\theta) = \cos\theta\, d\theta$.

$$\therefore \quad I = \int \frac{\sin^2\theta - 3\sin\theta + 1}{\sqrt{1-\sin^2\theta}} \cos\theta\, d\theta = \int (\sin^2\theta - 3\sin\theta + 1)\, d\theta$$

$$\Rightarrow \quad I = \int \left(\frac{1-\cos 2\theta}{2} - 3\sin\theta + 1\right) d\theta = \frac{1}{2}\int (3 - 6\sin\theta - \cos 2\theta)\, d\theta$$

$$\Rightarrow \quad I = \frac{1}{2}\left(3\theta + 6\cos\theta - \frac{1}{2}\sin 2\theta\right) + C = \frac{1}{2}\left\{3\theta + 6\sqrt{1-\sin^2\theta} - \sin\theta\sqrt{1-\sin^2\theta}\right\} + C$$

$$\Rightarrow \quad I = \frac{1}{2}\left\{3\sin^{-1}x + 6\sqrt{1-x^2} - x\sqrt{1-x^2}\right\} + C$$

EXAMPLE 4 *Evaluate:* $\int \frac{x^2}{\sqrt{1-x}}\, dx$

SOLUTION Let $I = \int \frac{x^2}{\sqrt{1-x}}\, dx = \int \frac{x^2}{\sqrt{1-(\sqrt{x})^2}}\, dx.$

Let $\sqrt{x} = \sin\theta$ or, $x = \sin^2\theta$. Then, $dx = d(\sin^2\theta) = 2\sin\theta\cos\theta\, d\theta$.

$$\therefore \quad I = \int \frac{(\sin^2\theta)^2}{\sqrt{1-\sin^2\theta}} 2\sin\theta\cos\theta\, d\theta = 2\int \sin^5\theta\, d\theta = 2\int (1-\cos^2\theta)^2 \sin\theta\, d\theta.$$

Let $\cos\theta = u$. Then, $d(\cos\theta) = du$ or, $-\sin\theta\, d\theta = du$.

$$I = -2\int (1-u^2)^2\, du = -2\int (1 - 2u^2 + u^4)\, du = -2\left(u - \frac{2}{3}u^3 + \frac{u^5}{5}\right) + C$$

$$\Rightarrow \quad I = -\frac{2}{15} u(15 - 10u^2 + 3u^4) + C = -\frac{2}{15}(15 - 10\cos^2\theta + 3\cos^4\theta)\cos\theta + C$$

$$\Rightarrow \quad I = -\frac{2}{15}\left\{15 - 10(1-\sin^2\theta) + 3(1-\sin^2\theta)^2\right\}\sqrt{1-\sin^2\theta} + C$$

$$\Rightarrow \quad I = -\frac{2}{15}\left\{8 + 4\sin^2\theta + 3\sin^4\theta\right\}\sqrt{1-\sin^2\theta} + C$$

$$\Rightarrow \quad I = -\frac{2}{15}\left\{8 + 4\sin^2\theta + 3\sin^4\theta\right\}\sqrt{1-\sin^2\theta} + C = -\frac{2}{15}(8 + 4x + 3x^2)\sqrt{1-x} + C$$

Type II INTEGRALS BASED UPON THE SUBSTITUTION $x = a\tan\theta$ OR, $x = a\tan^2\theta$

EXAMPLE 5 *Evaluate:* $\int \frac{1}{(a^2+x^2)^2}\, dx$

SOLUTION Let $I = \int \frac{1}{(a^2+x^2)^2}\, dx$ and $x = a\tan\theta$. Then, $dx = d(a\tan\theta) = a\sec^2\theta\, d\theta$.

$$\therefore \quad I = \int \frac{1}{(a^2 + a^2\tan^2\theta)^2} a\sec^2\theta\, d\theta = \frac{1}{a^3}\int \cos^2\theta\, d\theta = \frac{1}{2a^3}\int (1 + \cos 2\theta)\, d\theta$$

$$I = \frac{1}{2a^3}\left(\theta + \frac{1}{2}\sin 2\theta\right) + C = \frac{1}{2a^3}\left(\theta + \frac{\tan\theta}{1+\tan^2\theta}\right) + C = \frac{1}{2a^3}\left(\tan^{-1}\frac{x}{a} + \frac{ax}{a^2+x^2}\right) + C$$

EXAMPLE 6 *Evaluate* : $\int \frac{1}{x^4 + x^6}\, dx$

SOLUTION Let $I = \int \frac{1}{x^4 + x^6}\, dx$. Then, $I = \int \frac{1}{x^4 + x^6}\, dx = \int \frac{1}{x^4(1+x^2)}\, dx$

Let $x = \tan\theta$. Then, $dx = \sec^2\theta\, d\theta$.

$$\therefore \quad I = \int \frac{1}{x^4(1+x^2)}\, dx = \int \frac{1}{\tan^4\theta\,(1+\tan^2\theta)}\sec^2\theta\, d\theta = \int \cot^4\theta\, d\theta$$

$$\Rightarrow \quad I = \int \cot^2\theta\,(\text{cosec}^2\theta - 1)\, d\theta = \int \cot^2\theta\,\text{cosec}^2\theta\, d\theta - \int \cot^2\theta\, d\theta$$

$$\Rightarrow \quad I = \int \cot^2\theta\,\text{cosec}^2\theta\, d\theta - \int (\text{cosec}^2\theta - 1)\, d\theta$$

$$\Rightarrow \quad I = -\int t^2 dt - \int (\text{cosec}^2\theta - 1)\, d\theta, \text{ where } t = \cot\theta$$

$$\Rightarrow \quad I = -\frac{1}{3}t^3 - (-\cot\theta - \theta) + C = -\frac{1}{3}\cot^3\theta + \cot\theta + \theta + C = -\frac{1}{3x^3} + \frac{1}{x} + \tan^{-1}x + C$$

Type III EVALUATION OF INTEGRALS BY MAKING SUBSTITUTION $x = a\sec\theta$ OR, $x = a\sec^2\theta$

EXAMPLE 7 *Evaluate* : $\int \frac{1}{x^3\sqrt{x^2 - a^2}}\, dx$

SOLUTION Let $I = \int \frac{1}{x^3\sqrt{x^2 - a^2}}\, dx$ and $x = a\sec\theta$. Then, $dx = a\sec\theta\tan\theta\, d\theta$.

$$\therefore \quad I = \int \frac{1}{(a\sec\theta)^3\sqrt{a^2\sec^2\theta - a^2}}\, a\sec\theta\tan\theta\, d\theta = \frac{1}{a^3}\int \cos^2\theta\, d\theta = \frac{1}{2a^3}\int (1 + \cos 2\theta)\, d\theta$$

$$\Rightarrow \quad I = \frac{1}{2a^3}\left(\theta + \frac{1}{2}\sin 2\theta\right) + C = \frac{1}{2a^3}(\theta + \sin\theta\cos\theta) + C = \frac{1}{2a^3}\left(\sec^{-1}\frac{x}{a} + \frac{a}{x^2}\sqrt{x^2 - a^2}\right) + C$$

EXAMPLE 8 *Evaluate* : $\int \frac{1}{x\sqrt{x^4 - 1}}\, dx$

SOLUTION Let $\int \frac{1}{x\sqrt{x^4 - 1}}\, dx$. Then, $I = \int \frac{1}{x\sqrt{(x^2)^2 - 1}}\, dx = \int \frac{1}{x^2\sqrt{(x^2)^2 - 1}}\, x\, dx$

Let $x^2 = \sec\theta$. Then, $d(x^2) = d(\sec\theta)$ or, $2x\, dx = \sec\theta\tan\theta\, d\theta$ or, $dx = \frac{\sec\theta\tan\theta}{2x}d\theta$.

$$\therefore \quad I = \int \frac{1}{\sec\theta\sqrt{\sec^2\theta - 1}} \times \frac{1}{2}\sec\theta\tan\theta\, d\theta = \frac{1}{2}\int 1\cdot d\theta = \frac{1}{2}\theta + C = \frac{1}{2}\sec^{-1}x^2 + C$$

ALITER $I = \int \frac{1}{x\sqrt{(x^2)^2 - 1}}\, x\, dx = \frac{1}{2}\int \frac{1}{t\sqrt{t^2 - 1}}\, dt$, where $t = x^2$

$$\Rightarrow \quad I = \frac{1}{2}\sec^{-1}t + C = \frac{1}{2}\sec^{-1}x^2 + C$$

Type I INTEGRALS BASED ON THE SUBSTITUTION $x = a\sin^2\theta$ or $x = a\sin\theta$

EXAMPLE 9 *Evaluate:* $\int \frac{x}{(1 - x^4)^{3/2}}\, dx$.

SOLUTION Let $I = \int \frac{x}{(1 - x^4)^{3/2}}\, dx = \int \frac{x}{\left\{1 - (x^2)^2\right\}^{3/2}}\, dx$.

Let $x^2 = \sin\theta$. Then, $d(x^2) = d(\sin\theta) \Rightarrow 2x\,dx = \cos\theta\,d\theta \Rightarrow dx = \frac{\cos\theta}{2x}dx$

$$\therefore \quad I = \int \frac{x}{(1-\sin^2\theta)^{3/2}}\frac{\cos\theta}{2x}dx = \frac{1}{2}\int \sec^2\theta\,d\theta = \frac{1}{2}\tan\theta + C = \frac{1}{2}\frac{\sin\theta}{\sqrt{1-\sin^2\theta}} + C = \frac{1}{2}\frac{x^2}{\sqrt{1-x^4}} + C$$

EXAMPLE 10 *Evaluate:* $\int \frac{x^7}{(1-x^2)^5}dx.$

SOLUTION Let $x = \sin\theta$. Then, $dx = d(\sin\theta) = \cos\theta\,d\theta$.

$$\therefore \quad I = \int \frac{x^7}{(1-x^2)^5}dx = \int \frac{\sin^7\theta}{(1-\sin^2\theta)^5}\cos\theta\,d\theta = \int \tan^7\theta\sec^2\theta\,d\theta$$

Let $\tan\theta = u$. Then, $\sec^2\theta\,d\theta = du$ or, $d\theta = \frac{du}{\sec^2\theta}$

$$\therefore \quad I = \int u^7\,du = \frac{u^8}{8} + C = \frac{1}{8}\tan^8\theta + C = \frac{1}{8}\frac{\sin^8\theta}{(1-\sin^2\theta)^4} + C = \frac{1}{8}\frac{x^8}{(1-x^2)^4} + C$$

EXAMPLE 11 *Evaluate :* $\int \frac{1}{(1+\sqrt{x})\sqrt{x-x^2}}dx.$

SOLUTION Putting $x = \sin^2 t$ and $dx = 2\sin t\cos t\,dt$, we get

$$I = \int \frac{1}{(1+\sqrt{x})\sqrt{x-x^2}}dx = \int \frac{1}{(1+\sin t)\sqrt{\sin^2 t - \sin^4 t}}\,2\sin t\cos t\,dt$$

$$\Rightarrow \quad I = 2\int \frac{1}{1+\sin t}dt = 2\int \frac{1-\sin t}{\cos^2 t}dt = 2\int(\sec^2 t - \tan t\sec t)\,dt$$

$$\Rightarrow \quad I = 2(\tan t - \sec t) + C = 2\left(\frac{\sin t}{\sqrt{1-\sin^2 t}} - \frac{1}{\sqrt{1-\sin^2 t}}\right) + C = 2\sqrt{\frac{x}{1-x}} - \frac{2}{\sqrt{1-x}} + C$$

Type II INTEGRALS BASED ON THE SUBSTITUTION $x = a\tan\theta$ OR $x = a\tan^2\theta$

EXAMPLE 12 *Evaluate :* $\int \frac{1}{(x^2+2x+2)^2}dx$

SOLUTION Let $I = \int \frac{1}{(x^2+2x+2)^2}dx$. Then, $I = \int \frac{1}{\left\{(x+1)^2+1^2\right\}^2}dx$

Let $x+1 = \tan\theta$. Then, $d(x+1) = d(\tan\theta) \Rightarrow dx = \sec^2\theta\,d\theta$.

$$\therefore \quad I = \int \frac{1}{(\tan^2\theta+1)^2}\sec^2\theta\,d\theta = \int \cos^2\theta\,d\theta = \frac{1}{2}\int(1+\cos 2\theta)\,d\theta$$

$$\Rightarrow \quad I = \frac{1}{2}\left(\theta + \frac{1}{2}\sin 2\theta\right) + C = \frac{1}{2}\left(\theta + \frac{\tan\theta}{1+\tan^2\theta}\right) + C = \frac{1}{2}\left\{\tan^{-1}(x+1) + \frac{x+1}{x^2+2x+2}\right\} + C$$

EXAMPLE 13 *Evaluate :* $\int \frac{1+x^2}{(1-x^2)\sqrt{1+x^2+x^4}}dx$

SOLUTION Let $I = \int \frac{1+x^2}{(1-x^2)\sqrt{1+x^2+x^4}}dx$. Then,

$$I = \int \frac{\frac{1+x^2}{x^2}}{\left(\frac{1}{x}-x\right)\sqrt{\frac{1+x^2+x^4}{x^2}}}\,dx \qquad \text{[Dividing } N^r \text{ and } D^r \text{ by } x^2]$$

$$\Rightarrow \quad I = -\int \frac{1+\frac{1}{x^2}}{\left(x-\frac{1}{x}\right)\sqrt{x^2+\frac{1}{x^2}+1}}\,dx = -\int \frac{1}{\left(x-\frac{1}{x}\right)\sqrt{\left(x-\frac{1}{x}\right)^2+3}}\left(1+\frac{1}{x^2}\right)dx$$

Let $x-\frac{1}{x}=t$. Then, $d\left(x-\frac{1}{x}\right)=dt \Rightarrow \left(1+\frac{1}{x^2}\right)dx = dt.$

$$\therefore \quad I = -\int \frac{dt}{t\sqrt{t^2+3}} = -\int \frac{u\,du}{(u^2-3)\sqrt{u^2}}, \text{ where } t^2+3=u^2 \text{ and } 2t\,dt = 2u\,du$$

$$\Rightarrow \quad I = -\int \frac{1}{u^2-3}\,du = -\frac{1}{2\sqrt{3}}\log\left|\frac{u-\sqrt{3}}{u+\sqrt{3}}\right| + C$$

$$\Rightarrow \quad I = -\frac{1}{2\sqrt{3}}\log\left|\frac{\sqrt{t^2+3}-\sqrt{3}}{\sqrt{t^2+3}+\sqrt{3}}\right| + C = -\frac{1}{2\sqrt{3}}\log\left|\frac{\sqrt{x^2+\frac{1}{x^2}+1}-\sqrt{3}}{\sqrt{x^2+\frac{1}{x^2}+1}+\sqrt{3}}\right| + C$$

EXAMPLE 14 *Evaluate :* $\int \frac{x-1}{(x+1)\sqrt{x^3+x^2+x}}\,dx.$

SOLUTION Let $I = \int \frac{x-1}{(x+1)\sqrt{x^3+x^2+x}}\,dx.$

$$\Rightarrow \quad I = \int \frac{x^2-1}{(x+1)^2\sqrt{x^3+x^2+x}}\,dx \qquad \left[\text{Multiplying the } N^r \text{ and } D^r \text{ by } (x+1)\right]$$

$$\Rightarrow \quad I = \int \frac{(x^2-1)}{(x^2+2x+1)\sqrt{x^3+x^2+x}}\,dx$$

$$\Rightarrow \quad I = \int \frac{1-\frac{1}{x^2}}{\left(x+\frac{1}{x}+2\right)\sqrt{x+\frac{1}{x}+1}}\,dx \qquad \text{[Dividing } N^r \text{ and } D^r \text{ by } x^2]$$

Let $x+\frac{1}{x}+1=t^2$. Then, $d\left(x+\frac{1}{x}+1\right)=d(t^2) \Rightarrow \left(1-\frac{1}{x^2}\right)dx = 2t\,dt$

$$\Rightarrow \quad I = \int \frac{2t\,dt}{(t^2+1)\sqrt{t^2}} = 2\int \frac{1}{t^2+1}\,dt = 2\tan^{-1}(t) + C = 2\tan^{-1}\sqrt{x+\frac{1}{x}+1} + C$$

EXERCISE 15.13

BASED ON HOTS

Evaluate the following integrals:

1. $\int \frac{x^2}{(a^2 - x^2)^{3/2}} dx$
2. $\int \frac{x^7}{(a^2 - x^2)^5} dx$
3. $\int \cos\left\{2\cot^{-1}\sqrt{\frac{1+x}{1-x}}\right\} dx$
4. $\int \frac{\sqrt{1+x^2}}{x^4} dx$
5. $\int \frac{1}{(x^2 + 2x + 10)^2} dx$

ANSWERS

1. $\frac{x}{\sqrt{a^2 - x^2}} - \sin^{-1}\frac{x}{a} + C$
2. $\frac{1}{8a^2}\frac{x^8}{(a^2 - x^2)^4} + C$
3. $\frac{x^2}{2} + C$
4. $-\frac{1}{3}\frac{(x^2+1)^{3/2}}{x^3} + C$
5. $\frac{1}{54}\left\{\tan^{-1}\frac{x+1}{3} + \frac{3(x+1)}{x^2 + 2x + 10}\right\} + C$

15.10 SOME SPECIAL INTEGRALS

Let us discuss problems on evaluation of integrals by making above substitutions.

THEOREM *For any constant a, prove the following:*

(i) $\int \frac{1}{x^2 + a^2} dx = \frac{1}{a}\tan^{-1}\left(\frac{x}{a}\right) + C$

(ii) $\int \frac{1}{x^2 - a^2} dx = \frac{1}{2a}\log\left|\frac{x-a}{x+a}\right| + C$

(iii) $\int \frac{1}{a^2 - x^2} dx = \frac{1}{2a}\log\left|\frac{a+x}{a-x}\right| + C$

(iv) $\int \frac{1}{\sqrt{a^2 - x^2}} dx = \sin^{-1}\left(\frac{x}{a}\right) + C$

(v) $\int \frac{1}{\sqrt{a^2 + x^2}} dx = \log|x + \sqrt{a^2 + x^2}| + C$

(vi) $\int \frac{1}{\sqrt{x^2 - a^2}} dx = \log|x + \sqrt{x^2 - a^2}| + C$

PROOF (i) Let $I = \int \frac{1}{x^2 + a^2} dx$. Putting $x = a\tan\theta$ and $dx = a\sec^2\theta\, d\theta$, we get

$$I = \int \frac{a\sec^2\theta\, d\theta}{a^2 + a^2\tan^2\theta} = \frac{1}{a}\int 1 \cdot d\theta = \frac{1}{a}\theta + C = \frac{1}{a}\tan^{-1}\frac{x}{a} + C \quad \left[\because \tan\theta = \frac{x}{a} \Rightarrow \theta = \tan^{-1}\frac{x}{a}\right]$$

Similarly by making substitution $x = a\cot\theta$, we obtain: $\int -\frac{1}{a^2 + x^2} dx = \frac{1}{a}\cot^{-1}\left(\frac{x}{a}\right) + C$

(ii) We find that

$$\frac{1}{x^2 - a^2} = \frac{1}{(x-a)(x+a)} = \frac{1}{2a}\left\{\frac{1}{x-a} - \frac{1}{x+a}\right\}$$

$$\therefore \quad I = \int \frac{1}{x^2 - a^2} dx = \frac{1}{2a}\int\left\{\frac{1}{x-a} - \frac{1}{x+a}\right\} dx = \frac{1}{2a}\left\{\int \frac{1}{x-a} dx - \int \frac{1}{x+a} dx\right\}$$

$$\Rightarrow \quad I = \frac{1}{2a}\left\{\log|x-a| - \log|x+a|\right\} + C = \frac{1}{2a}\log\left|\frac{x-a}{x+a}\right| + C$$

(iii) Clearly, $\frac{1}{a^2-x^2} = \frac{1}{(a-x)(a+x)} = \frac{1}{2a}\left\{\frac{1}{a+x}+\frac{1}{a-x}\right\}$

$$\therefore \quad I = \int \frac{1}{a^2-x^2}\,dx = \frac{1}{2a}\left\{\int \frac{1}{a+x}\,dx + \int \frac{1}{a-x}\,dx\right\}$$

$$\Rightarrow \quad I = \frac{1}{2a}\left\{\log|a+x| - \log|a-x|\right\} + C = \frac{1}{2a}\log\left|\frac{a+x}{a-x}\right| + C$$

(iv) Let $I = \int \frac{1}{\sqrt{a^2-x^2}}\,dx$. Putting $x = a\sin\theta$ and $dx = a\cos\theta\,d\theta$, we get

$$I = \int \frac{a\cos\theta\,d\theta}{\sqrt{a^2-a^2\sin^2\theta}} = \int 1\cdot d\theta = \theta + C$$

$$\Rightarrow \quad I = \sin^{-1}\left(\frac{x}{a}\right) + C \qquad \left[\because x = a\sin\theta \Rightarrow \sin\theta = \frac{x}{a} \Rightarrow \theta = \sin^{-1}\frac{x}{a}\right]$$

Similarly, by making substitution $x = a\cos\theta$, we obtain

$$\int -\frac{1}{\sqrt{a^2-x^2}}\,dx = \cos^{-1}\left(\frac{x}{a}\right) + C$$

(v) Let $I = \int \frac{1}{\sqrt{a^2+x^2}}\,dx$. Putting $x = a\tan\theta$ and $dx = a\sec^2\theta\,d\theta$, we get

$$I = \int \frac{1}{\sqrt{a^2+a^2\tan^2\theta}}\,a\sec^2\theta\,d\theta = \int \sec\theta\,d\theta$$

$$\Rightarrow \quad I = \log|\sec\theta + \tan\theta| + C = \log\left|\tan\theta + \sqrt{1+\tan^2\theta}\right| + C$$

$$\Rightarrow \quad I = \log\left|\frac{x}{a} + \sqrt{1+\frac{x^2}{a^2}}\right| + C = \log\left|x + \sqrt{a^2+x^2}\right| - \log a + C \qquad \left[\because \tan\theta = \frac{x}{a}\right]$$

$$\Rightarrow \quad I = \log\left|x + \sqrt{a^2+x^2}\right| + C_1, \text{ where } C_1 = C - \log a$$

(vi) Let $I = \int \frac{1}{\sqrt{x^2-a^2}}\,dx$. Putting $x = a\sec\theta$ and $dx = a\sec\theta\tan\theta\,d\theta$, we get

$$I = \int \frac{1}{\sqrt{a^2\sec^2\theta - a^2}}\,a\sec\theta\tan\theta\,d\theta = \int \sec\theta\,d\theta = \log|\sec\theta + \tan\theta| + C$$

$$\Rightarrow \quad I = \log\left|\sec\theta + \sqrt{\sec^2\theta - 1}\right| + C = \log\left|\frac{x}{a} + \sqrt{\frac{x^2}{a^2} - 1}\right| + C \qquad \left[\because \sec\theta = \frac{x}{a}\right]$$

$$\Rightarrow \quad I = \log\left|x + \sqrt{x^2-a^2}\right| - \log a + C = \log\left|x + \sqrt{x^2-a^2}\right| + C_1, \text{ where } C_1 = C - \log a.$$

ILLUSTRATIVE EXAMPLES

BASED ON BASIC CONCEPTS (BASIC)

EXAMPLE 1 *Evaluate:*

(i) $\int \frac{1}{4+9x^2}\,dx$ (ii) $\int \frac{1}{9x^2-4}\,dx$ (iii) $\int \frac{1}{16-9x^2}\,dx$

SOLUTION (i) Let $I = \int \frac{1}{4+9x^2}\,dx$. Then,

$$I = \frac{1}{9}\int \frac{1}{\frac{4}{9}+x^2}\,dx = \frac{1}{9}\int \frac{1}{(2/3)^2+x^2}\,dx = \frac{1}{9}\times\frac{1}{(2/3)}\tan^{-1}\left(\frac{x}{2/3}\right)+C = \frac{1}{6}\tan^{-1}\left(\frac{3x}{2}\right)+C$$

(ii) Let $I = \int \frac{1}{9x^2-4}\,dx$. Then,

$$I = \frac{1}{9}\int \frac{1}{x^2-(2/3)^2}\,dx = \frac{1}{9}\times\frac{1}{2\times\frac{2}{3}}\log\left|\frac{x-\frac{2}{3}}{x+\frac{2}{3}}\right|+C = \frac{1}{12}\log\left|\frac{3x-2}{3x+2}\right|+C$$

(iii) Let $I = \int \frac{1}{16-9x^2}\,dx$. Then,

$$I = \frac{1}{9}\int \frac{1}{\frac{16}{9}-x^2}\,dx = \frac{1}{9}\int \frac{1}{\left(\frac{4}{3}\right)^2-x^2}\,dx = \frac{1}{9}\times\frac{1}{2\left(\frac{4}{3}\right)}\times\log\left|\frac{\frac{4}{3}+x}{\frac{4}{3}-x}\right|+C = \frac{1}{24}\log\left|\frac{4+3x}{4-3x}\right|+C$$

EXAMPLE 2 *Evaluate:*

(i) $\int \frac{1}{\sqrt{9-25x^2}}\,dx$ **[NCERT, CBSE 2020]** (ii) $\int \frac{1}{\sqrt{16x^2+25}}\,dx$ (iii) $\int \frac{1}{\sqrt{4x^2-9}}\,dx$

SOLUTION (i) Let $I = \int \frac{1}{\sqrt{9-25x^2}}\,dx$. Then,

$$I = \frac{1}{5}\int \frac{1}{\sqrt{\frac{9}{25}-x^2}}\,dx = \frac{1}{5}\int \frac{1}{\sqrt{\left(\frac{3}{5}\right)^2-x^2}}\,dx = \frac{1}{5}\sin^{-1}\left(\frac{x}{3/5}\right)+C = \frac{1}{5}\sin^{-1}\left(\frac{5x}{3}\right)+C$$

(ii) Let $I = \int \frac{1}{\sqrt{16x^2+25}}\,dx$. Then,

$$I = \frac{1}{4}\int \frac{1}{\sqrt{x^2+\left(\frac{5}{4}\right)^2}}\,dx = \frac{1}{4}\log\left|x+\sqrt{x^2+\left(\frac{5}{4}\right)^2}\right|+C = \frac{1}{4}\log\left|\frac{4x+\sqrt{16x^2+25}}{4}\right|+C$$

$$\Rightarrow \quad I = \frac{1}{4}\log\left|4x+\sqrt{16x^2+25}\right| - \frac{1}{4}\log 4 + C = \frac{1}{4}\log\left|4x+\sqrt{16x^2+25}\right| + C_1,$$

where $C_1 = -\frac{1}{4}\log 4 + C$

(iii) Let $I = \int \frac{1}{\sqrt{4x^2-9}}\,dx$. Then,

$$I = \frac{1}{2}\int \frac{1}{\sqrt{x^2-\frac{9}{4}}}\,dx = \frac{1}{2}\int \frac{1}{\sqrt{x^2-\left(\frac{3}{2}\right)^2}}\,dx$$

$$\Rightarrow I = \frac{1}{2}\log\left|x+\sqrt{x^2-\left(\frac{3}{2}\right)^2}\right|+C = \frac{1}{2}\log\left|x+\sqrt{x^2-\frac{9}{4}}\right|+C = \frac{1}{2}\log\left|\frac{2x+\sqrt{4x^2+9}}{2}\right|+C$$

$$\Rightarrow I = \frac{1}{2}\log\left|2x+\sqrt{4x^2-9}\right| - \frac{1}{2}\log 2 + C = \frac{1}{2}\log\left|2x+\sqrt{4x^2-9}\right|+C_1, \text{ where } C_1 = -\frac{1}{2}\log 2 + C$$

BASED ON LOWER ORDER THINKING SKILLS (LOTS)

EXAMPLE 3 *Evaluate:* $\int \frac{x^4}{x^2+1}\,dx$

SOLUTION Let $I = \int \frac{x^4}{x^2+1}\,dx$. Then,

$$I = \int \frac{x^4-1+1}{x^2+1}\,dx$$

$$\Rightarrow \quad I = \int \frac{x^4-1}{x^2+1} + \frac{1}{x^2+1}\,dx = \int (x^2-1)\,dx + \int \frac{1}{x^2+1}\,dx = \frac{x^3}{3} - x + \tan^{-1} x + C$$

EXERCISE 15.14

BASIC

Evaluate the following integrals:

1. $\int \frac{1}{a^2-b^2x^2}\,dx$
2. $\int \frac{1}{a^2x^2-b^2}\,dx$
3. $\int \frac{1}{a^2x^2+b^2}\,dx$
4. $\int \frac{x^2-1}{x^2+4}\,dx$
5. $\int \frac{1}{\sqrt{1+4x^2}}\,dx$ [NCERT]
6. $\int \frac{1}{\sqrt{a^2+b^2x^2}}\,dx$
7. $\int \frac{1}{\sqrt{a^2-b^2x^2}}\,dx$
8. $\int \frac{1}{\sqrt{(2-x)^2+1}}\,dx$
9. $\int \frac{1}{\sqrt{(2-x)^2-1}}\,dx$

BASED ON LOTS

10. $\int \frac{x^4+1}{x^2+1}\,dx$ [CBSE 2002 C]

ANSWERS

1. $\frac{1}{2ab}\log\left|\frac{a+bx}{a-bx}\right|+C$
2. $\frac{1}{2\,ab}\log\left|\frac{ax-b}{ax+b}\right|+C$
3. $\frac{1}{ab}\tan^{-1}\left(\frac{ax}{b}\right)+C$
4. $x-\frac{5}{2}\tan^{-1}\left(\frac{x}{2}\right)+C$
5. $\frac{1}{2}\log|2x+\sqrt{4x^2+1}|+C$
6. $\frac{1}{b}\log\left|bx+\sqrt{a^2+b^2x^2}\right|+C$
7. $\frac{1}{b}\sin^{-1}\left(\frac{bx}{a}\right)+C$
8. $-\log\left|(2-x)+\sqrt{(2-x)^2+1}\right|+C$
9. $-\log\left|2-x+\sqrt{(2-x)^2-1}\right|+C$
10. $\frac{x^3}{3}-x+2\tan^{-1}x+C$

HINTS TO SELECTED PROBLEMS

4. $\int \frac{x^2-1}{x^2+4} dx = \int 1 - \frac{5}{x^2+4} dx = \int 1 \cdot dx - 5 \int \frac{1}{x^2+2^2} dx = x - \frac{5}{2} \tan^{-1}\left(\frac{x}{2}\right) + C$

5. $\int \frac{1}{\sqrt{1+4x^2}} dx = \int \frac{1}{\sqrt{1+(2x)^2}} dx = \frac{1}{2} \log\left|2x + \sqrt{1+4x^2}\right| + C$

8. $\int \frac{1}{\sqrt{(2-x)^2+1}} dx = -\int \frac{1}{\sqrt{(2-x)^2+1^2}} d(2-x) = -\log\left|(2-x) + \sqrt{(2-x)^2+1}\right| + C$

9. $\int \frac{1}{\sqrt{(2-x)^2-1^2}} dx = -\int \frac{1}{\sqrt{(2-x)^2-1^2}} d(2-x) = -\log\left|2-x + \sqrt{(2-x)^2-1}\right| + C$

15.10.1 EVALUATION OF INTEGRALS OF THE TYPE $\int \frac{1}{ax^2+bx+c} dx$

To evaluate this type of integrals we express ax^2+bx+c as the sum or difference of two squares by using the following algorithm.

ALGORITHM

Step I *Make the coefficient of x^2 unity, if it is not, by multiplying and dividing by it.*

Step II *Add and subtract the square of the half of coefficient of x to express ax^2+bx+c in the form a*

$$\left\{\left(x+\frac{b}{2a}\right)^2 + \frac{4ac-b^2}{4a^2}\right\}$$

Step III *Use the suitable formula from the following formulas:*

$$\int \frac{1}{a^2+x^2} dx = \frac{1}{a} \tan^{-1}\left(\frac{x}{a}\right) + C, \quad \int \frac{1}{a^2-x^2} dx = \frac{1}{2a} \log\left|\frac{a+x}{a-x}\right| + C$$

$$\int \frac{1}{x^2-a^2} dx = \frac{1}{2a} \log\left|\frac{x-a}{x+a}\right| + C.$$

ILLUSTRATIVE EXAMPLES

BASED ON BASIC CONCEPTS (BASIC)

EXAMPLE 1 *Evaluate*

(i) $\int \frac{1}{x^2-x+1} dx$ (ii) $\int \frac{1}{2x^2+x-1} dx$ (iii) $\int \frac{1}{3+2x-x^2} dx$

SOLUTION (i) Let $I = \int \frac{1}{x^2-x+1} dx$. Then,

$$I = \int \frac{1}{x^2 - x + \frac{1}{4} - \frac{1}{4} + 1} dx = \int \frac{1}{(x-1/2)^2 + 3/4} dx$$

$$\Rightarrow \quad I = \int \frac{1}{(x-1/2)^2 + (\sqrt{3}/2)^2} dx = \frac{1}{\sqrt{3}/2} \tan^{-1}\left(\frac{x-12}{\sqrt{3}/2}\right) + C = \frac{2}{\sqrt{3}} \tan^{-1}\left(\frac{2x-1}{\sqrt{3}}\right) + C$$

(ii) Let $I = \int \frac{1}{2x^2+x-1} dx$. Then,

$$I = \frac{1}{2}\int \frac{1}{x^2 + \frac{x}{2} - \frac{1}{2}}\, dx$$

$$\Rightarrow \quad I = \frac{1}{2}\int \frac{1}{x^2 + x/2 + (1/4)^2 - (1/4)^2 - 1/2}\, dx = \frac{1}{2}\int \frac{1}{(x+1/4)^2 - (3/4)^2}\, dx$$

$$\Rightarrow \quad I = \frac{1}{2} \times \frac{1}{2\,(3/4)} \log\left|\frac{x + 1/4 - 3/4}{x + 1/4 + 3/4}\right| + C = \frac{1}{3}\log\left|\frac{x - 1/2}{x+1}\right| + C = \frac{1}{3}\log\left|\frac{2x-1}{2\,(x+1)}\right| + C$$

(iii) Let $I = \int \frac{1}{3 + 2x - x^2}\, dx$. Then,

$$I = \int \frac{1}{-(x^2 - 2x - 3)}\, dx = \int \frac{1}{-(x^2 - 2x + 1 - 1 - 3)}\, dx = \int \frac{1}{-\left\{(x-1)^2 - 2^2\right\}}\, dx$$

$$\Rightarrow \quad I = \int \frac{1}{2^2 - (x-1)^2}\, dx = \frac{1}{2\,(2)} \log\left|\frac{2 + (x-1)}{2 - (x-1)}\right| + C = \frac{1}{4}\log\left|\frac{x+1}{3-x}\right| + C$$

EXAMPLE 2 *Evaluate:*

(i) $\int \frac{1}{3x^2 + 13x - 10}\, dx$ **[NCERT]** (ii) $\int \frac{1}{4x^2 - 4x + 3}\, dx$

(iii) $\int \frac{1}{x^2 + 4x + 8}$ **[CBSE 2002, 2017]** (iv) $\int \frac{1}{9x^2 + 6x + 10}$

SOLUTION (i) Let $I = \int \frac{1}{3x^2 + 13x - 10}\, dx$. Then,

$$I = \frac{1}{3}\int \frac{1}{x^2 + \frac{13}{3}x - \frac{10}{3}}\, dx$$

$$\Rightarrow \quad I = \frac{1}{3}\int \frac{1}{x^2 + \frac{13}{3}x + \left(\frac{13}{6}\right)^2 - \left(\frac{13}{6}\right)^2 - \left(\frac{10}{3}\right)}\, dx = \frac{1}{3}\int \frac{1}{\left(x + \frac{13}{6}\right)^2 - \left(\frac{17}{6}\right)^2}\, dx$$

$$\Rightarrow \quad I = \frac{1}{3} \times \frac{1}{2\left(\frac{17}{6}\right)} \log\left|\frac{x + \frac{13}{6} - \frac{17}{6}}{x + \frac{13}{6} + \frac{17}{6}}\right| + C = \frac{1}{17}\log\left|\frac{x - 4/6}{x+5}\right| + C = \frac{1}{17}\log\left|\frac{3x-2}{3\,(x+5)}\right| + C$$

(ii) Let $I = \int \frac{1}{4x^2 - 4x + 3}\, dx$. Then,

$$I = \frac{1}{4}\int \frac{1}{x^2 - x + 3/4}\, dx = \frac{1}{4}\int \frac{1}{x^2 - x + \frac{1}{4} - \frac{1}{4} + \frac{3}{4}}\, dx = \frac{1}{4}\int \frac{1}{\left(x - \frac{1}{2}\right)^2 + \left(\frac{1}{\sqrt{2}}\right)^2}\, dx$$

$$\Rightarrow \quad I = \frac{1}{4} \times \frac{1}{(1/\sqrt{2})} \tan^{-1}\left(\frac{x - 1/2}{1/\sqrt{2}}\right) + C = \frac{1}{2\sqrt{2}} \tan^{-1}\left(\frac{2x-1}{\sqrt{2}}\right) + C$$

(iii) Let $I = \int \frac{1}{x^2 + 4x + 8}\, dx$. Then,

$$I = \int \frac{1}{x^2 + 4x + 4 + 4}\, dx = \int \frac{1}{(x+2)^2 + 2^2}\, dx = \frac{1}{2}\tan^{-1}\left(\frac{x+2}{2}\right) + C$$

(iv) Let $I = \int \frac{1}{9x^2+6x+10}\,dx$. Then,

$$I = \frac{1}{9}\int \frac{1}{x^2+\frac{2}{3}x+\frac{10}{9}}\,dx = \frac{1}{9}\int \frac{1}{x^2+\frac{2}{3}x+\frac{1}{9}-\frac{1}{9}+\frac{10}{9}}\,dx$$

$$\Rightarrow \quad I = \frac{1}{9}\int \frac{1}{\left(x+\frac{1}{3}\right)^2+1^2}\,dx = \frac{1}{9}\times\frac{1}{1}\tan^{-1}\left(\frac{x+\frac{1}{3}}{1}\right)+C = \frac{1}{9}\tan^{-1}\left(\frac{3x+1}{3}\right)+C$$

EXERCISE 15.15

Evaluate the following integrals:

1. $\int \frac{1}{4x^2+12x+5}\,dx$
2. $\int \frac{1}{5+4x-x^2}\,dx$ [CBSE 2024]
3. $\int \frac{1}{1+x-x^2}\,dx$
4. $\int \frac{1}{2x^2-x-1}\,dx$
5. $\int \frac{1}{x^2+6x+13}\,dx$ [NCERT]
6. $\int \frac{x+1}{(x+2)(x+3)}\,dx$ [CBSE 2020]

ANSWERS

1. $\frac{1}{8}\log\left|\frac{2x+1}{2x+5}\right|+C$
2. $\frac{1}{6}\log\left|\frac{x+1}{x-5}\right|+C$
3. $\frac{1}{\sqrt{5}}\log\left|\frac{\sqrt{5}-1+2x}{\sqrt{5}+1-2x}\right|+C$
4. $\frac{1}{3}\log\left|\frac{x-1}{2x+1}\right|+C$
5. $\frac{1}{2}\tan^{-1}\left(\frac{x+3}{2}\right)+C$
6. $\log\left|\frac{(x+3)^2}{x+2}\right|+C$

15.10.2 INTEGRALS REDUCIBLE TO THE FORM $\int \frac{1}{ax^2+bx+c}\,dx$

Following examples will illustrate the procedure of evaluating the above type of integrals.

ILLUSTRATIVE EXAMPLES

BASED ON BASIC CONCEPTS (BASIC)

EXAMPLE 1 *Evaluate:*

(i) $\int \frac{x}{x^4+x^2+1}\,dx$ (ii) $\int \frac{e^x}{e^{2x}+6e^x+5}\,dx$ (iii) $\int \frac{\sin x}{1+\cos^2 x}\,dx$ (iv) $\int \frac{2x^3}{4+x^8}\,dx$

SOLUTION (i) Let $I = \int \frac{x}{x^4+x^2+1}\,dx = \int \frac{x}{(x^2)^2+x^2+1}\,dx$

Let $x^2 = t$. Then, $d(x^2) = dt \Rightarrow 2x\,dx = dt \Rightarrow dx = \frac{dt}{2x}$

$$\therefore \quad I = \int \frac{x}{t^2+t+1}\times\frac{dt}{2x} = \frac{1}{2}\int \frac{1}{t^2+t+1}\,dt = \frac{1}{2}\int \frac{1}{\left(t+\frac{1}{2}\right)^2+\left(\frac{\sqrt{3}}{2}\right)^2}\,dt$$

$$\Rightarrow \quad I = \frac{1}{2}\times\frac{1}{\frac{\sqrt{3}}{2}}\tan^{-1}\left(\frac{t+\frac{1}{2}}{\frac{\sqrt{3}}{2}}\right)+C = \frac{1}{\sqrt{3}}\tan^{-1}\left(\frac{2t+1}{\sqrt{3}}\right)+C = \frac{1}{\sqrt{3}}\tan^{-1}\left(\frac{2x^2+1}{\sqrt{3}}\right)+C$$

(ii) Let $I = \int \frac{e^x}{e^{2x} + 6e^x + 5}\, dx = \int \frac{e^x}{(e^x)^2 + 6e^x + 5}\, dx$. Let $e^x = t$. Then, $d(e^x) = dt \Rightarrow e^x dx = dt$

$$\therefore \quad I = \int \frac{dt}{t^2 + 6t + 5} = \int \frac{1}{(t+3)^2 - 2^2}\, dt = \frac{1}{2 \times 2} \log\left|\frac{t+3-2}{t+3+2}\right| + C = \frac{1}{4}\log\left|\frac{e^x + 1}{e^x + 5}\right| + C$$

(iii) Let $I = \int \frac{\sin x}{1 + \cos^2 x}\, dx$. Let $\cos x = t$ Then, $d(\cos x) = dt \Rightarrow -\sin x\, dx = dt \Rightarrow dx = -dt \sin x$

$$\therefore \quad I = \int \frac{\sin x}{1 + t^2} \times -\frac{dt}{\sin x} = -\int \frac{1}{1+t^2}\, dt = -\tan^{-1}(t) + C = -\tan^{-1}(\cos x) + C$$

(iv) $I = \int \frac{2x^3}{4 + x^8}\, dx = \int \frac{2x^3}{2^2 + (x^4)^2}\, dx.$

Let $x^4 = t$. Then, $d(x^4) = dt \Rightarrow 4x^3\, dx = dt \Rightarrow dx = \frac{dt}{4x^3}$

$$\therefore \quad I = \int \frac{2x^3}{4 + t^2} \times \frac{dt}{4x^3} = \frac{1}{2}\int \frac{1}{2^2 + t^2}\, dt = \frac{1}{2} \times \frac{1}{2}\tan^{-1}\left(\frac{t}{2}\right) + C = \frac{1}{4}\tan^{-1}\left(\frac{x^4}{2}\right) + C$$

EXAMPLE 2 *Evaluate:* (i) $\int \frac{1}{x\{6(\log x)^2 + 7\log x + 2\}}\, dx$ (ii) $\int \frac{e^{-x}}{16 + 9e^{-2x}}\, dx$

SOLUTION (i) Let $I = \int \frac{1}{x\{6(\log x)^2 + 7\log x + 2\}}\, dx$

Let $\log x = t$. Then, $d(\log x) = dt \Rightarrow \frac{1}{x}\, dx = dt \Rightarrow dx = x\, dt$

$$\therefore \quad I = \int \frac{1}{6t^2 + 7t + 2}\, dt$$

$$I = \frac{1}{6}\int \frac{1}{t^2 + \frac{7}{6}t + \frac{1}{3}}\, dt = \frac{1}{6}\int \frac{1}{\left(t + \frac{7}{12}\right)^2 + \frac{1}{3} - \frac{49}{144}}\, dt = \frac{1}{6}\int \frac{1}{\left(t + \frac{7}{12}\right)^2 - \left(\frac{1}{12}\right)^2}\, dt$$

$$\Rightarrow \quad I = \frac{1}{6} \times \frac{1}{2\left(\frac{1}{12}\right)} \log\left|\frac{t + \frac{7}{12} - \frac{1}{12}}{t + \frac{7}{12} + \frac{1}{12}}\right| + C = \log\left|\frac{2t+1}{3t+2}\right| + C = \log\left|\frac{2\log x + 1}{3\log x + 2}\right| + C$$

(ii) Let $I = \int \frac{e^{-x}}{16 + 9e^{-2x}}\, dx = \int \frac{e^{-x}}{4^2 + (3e^{-x})^2}\, dx$. Let $3e^{-x} = t$. Then,

$d(3e^{-x}) = dt \Rightarrow -3e^{-x}dx = dt \Rightarrow dx = -\frac{dt}{3e^{-x}}$. Putting $3e^{-x} = t$ and $dx = -\frac{dt}{3e^{-x}}$, we get

$$\therefore \quad I = \int \frac{e^{-x}}{16 + t^2}\left(-\frac{dt}{3e^{-x}}\right) = -\frac{1}{3}\int \frac{dt}{16 + t^2} = -\frac{1}{3}\int \frac{1}{(4)^2 + t^2}\, dt$$

$$\Rightarrow I = -\frac{1}{3} \times \frac{1}{4}\tan^{-1}\left(\frac{t}{4}\right) + C = -\frac{1}{12}\tan^{-1}\left(\frac{3t}{4}\right) + C = -\frac{1}{12}\tan^{-1}\left(\frac{3e^{-x}}{4}\right) + C$$

EXAMPLE 3 *Evaluate:* (i) $\int \frac{1}{x(x^n+1)}\,dx$ **[CBSE 2000C]** (ii) $\int \frac{1}{x(x^5+1)}\,dx$

SOLUTION We have, $I = \int \frac{1}{x(x^n+1)}\,dx = \int \frac{x^{n-1}}{x^n(x^n+1)}\,dx$

Let $x^n+1 = t$. Then, $d(x^n+1) = dt \Rightarrow n\,x^{n-1}\,dx = dt \Rightarrow dx = \frac{dt}{n\,x^{n-1}}$

$$\therefore \quad I = \int \frac{1}{n\,x^n\,t}\,dt = \frac{1}{n}\int \frac{1}{(t-1)\,t}\,dt \qquad [\because x^n+1=t \;\therefore\; x^n=t-1]$$

$$\Rightarrow \quad I = \frac{1}{n}\int \frac{1}{t^2-t}\,dt = \frac{1}{n}\int \frac{dt}{t^2-t+1/4-1/4} = \frac{1}{n}\int \frac{1}{(t-1/2)^2-(1/2)^2}\,dt$$

$$\Rightarrow \quad I = \frac{1}{n}\times\frac{1}{2(1/2)}\log\left|\frac{t-1/2-1/2}{t-1/2+1/2}\right| + C = \frac{1}{n}\log\left|\frac{t-1}{t}\right| + C = \frac{1}{n}\log\left|\frac{x^n}{x^n+1}\right| + C$$

(ii) $I = \int \frac{1}{x(x^5+1)}\,dx = \int \frac{x^4}{x^5(x^5+1)}\,dx$

Let $x^5+1 = t$. Then, $d(x^5+1) = dt \Rightarrow 5x^4\,dx = dt \Rightarrow dx = \frac{dt}{5x^4}$

$$\therefore \quad I = \frac{1}{5}\int \frac{1}{tx^5}\,dt = \frac{1}{5}\int \frac{1}{t(t-1)}\,dt = \frac{1}{5}\int \frac{1}{t^2-t}\,dt$$

$$\Rightarrow \quad I = \frac{1}{5}\int \frac{1}{t^2-t+1/4-1/4}\,dt = \frac{1}{5}\int \frac{1}{(t-1/2)^2-(1/2)^2}$$

$$\Rightarrow \quad I = \frac{1}{5}\times\frac{1}{2(1/2)}\log\left|\frac{t-1/2-1/2}{t-1/2+1/2}\right| + C = \frac{1}{5}\log\left|\frac{t-1}{t}\right| + C = \frac{1}{5}\log\left|\frac{x^5}{x^5+1}\right| + C$$

BASED ON HIGHER ORDER THINKING SKILLS (HOTS)

EXAMPLE 4 *Evaluate :* $\int \frac{\sin x+\cos x}{9+16\sin 2x}\,dx$

SOLUTION We observe that $\sin x+\cos x$ occurs in the derivative of $-\cos x+\sin x$. So, we express $9+16\sin 2x$ in terms of $-\cos x+\sin x$ as follows.

$$\because \quad (-\cos x+\sin x)^2 = 1-\sin 2x \text{ or, } \sin 2x = 1-(-\cos x+\sin x)^2$$

$$\therefore \quad 9+16\sin 2x = 9+16\left\{1-(\cos x+\sin x)^2\right\} = 25-\left\{4(-\cos x+\sin x)\right\}^2$$

Thus, $I = \int \frac{\sin x+\cos x}{9+16\sin 2x}\,dx = \int \frac{\sin x+\cos x}{25-\left\{4(-\cos x+\sin x)\right\}^2}\,dx$

Let $4(-\cos x+\sin x) = t$. Then,

$$d\{4(-\cos x+\sin x)\} = dt \text{ or, } 4(\sin x+\cos x)\,dx = dt \text{ or, } dx = \frac{dt}{4(\sin x+\cos x)}$$

$$\therefore \quad I = \int \frac{\sin x+\cos x}{25-t^2}\times\frac{dt}{4(\sin x+\cos x)}$$

$$\Rightarrow \quad I = \frac{1}{4}\int \frac{1}{25-t^2}\,dt = \frac{1}{4}\times\frac{1}{10}\log\left|\frac{5+t}{5-t}\right| + C = \frac{1}{40}\log\left|\frac{5+4(-\cos x+\sin x)}{5-4(-\cos x+\sin x)}\right| + C$$

EXAMPLE 5 *Evaluate :* $\int \frac{1}{\sin x + \sec x} dx$

SOLUTION Let $I = \int \frac{1}{\sin x + \sec x} dx$. Then,

$$I = \int \frac{\cos x}{1 + \sin x \cos x} dx = \int \frac{2 \cos x}{2 + 2 \sin x \cos x} dx = \int \frac{(\cos x + \sin x) + (\cos x - \sin x)}{2 + 2 \sin x \cos x} dx$$

$$\Rightarrow \quad I = \int \frac{\cos x + \sin x}{2 + 2 \sin x \cos x} dx + \int \frac{\cos x - \sin x}{2 + 2 \sin x \cos x} dx$$

$$\Rightarrow \quad I = \int \frac{\cos x + \sin x}{3 - (1 - 2 \sin x \cos x)} dx + \int \frac{\cos x - \sin x}{1 + (1 + 2 \sin x \cos x)} dx$$

$$\Rightarrow \quad I = \int \frac{(\cos x + \sin x)}{3 - (\sin x - \cos x)^2} dx + \int \frac{\cos x - \sin x}{1 + (\sin x + \cos x)^2} dx$$

$$\Rightarrow \quad I = \int \frac{1}{(\sqrt{3})^2 - u^2} du + \int \frac{1}{1 + v^2} dv, \text{ where } u = \sin x - \cos x \text{ and } v = \sin x + \cos x$$

$$\Rightarrow \quad I = \frac{1}{2\sqrt{3}} \log \left| \frac{\sqrt{3} + u}{\sqrt{3} - u} \right| + \tan^{-1} v + C = \frac{1}{2\sqrt{3}} \log \left| \frac{\sqrt{3} + (\sin x - \cos x)}{\sqrt{3} - (\sin x - \cos x)} \right| + \tan^{-1} (\sin x + \cos x) + C$$

EXERCISE 15.16

BASIC

Evaluate the following integrals:

1. $\int \frac{\sec^2 x}{1 - \tan^2 x} dx$
2. $\int \frac{e^x}{1 + e^{2x}} dx$
3. $\int \frac{\cos x}{\sin^2 x + 4 \sin x + 5} dx$
4. $\int \frac{e^x}{e^{2x} + 5 e^x + 6} dx$
5. $\int \frac{e^{3x}}{4 e^{6x} - 9} dx$
6. $\int \frac{1}{e^x + e^{-x}} dx$
7. $\int \frac{x}{x^4 + 2x^2 + 3} dx$
8. $\int \frac{3x^5}{1 + x^{12}} dx$
9. $\int \frac{x^2}{x^6 - a^6} dx$
10. $\int \frac{x^2}{x^6 + a^6} dx$
11. $\int \frac{1}{x (x^6 + 1)} dx$
12. $\int \frac{x}{x^4 - x^2 + 1} dx$ [CBSE 2007]
13. $\int \frac{x}{3x^4 - 18x^2 + 11} dx$
14. $\int \frac{e^x}{(1 + e^x)(2 + e^x)} dx$ [CBSE 2022]
15. $\int \frac{\tan^2 x \sec^2 x}{1 - \tan^6 x} dx$ [CBSE 2019]
16. $\int \frac{1}{x \{(\log x)^2 - 3 \log x - 4\}} dx$ [CBSE 2024]

BASED ON LOTS

17. $\int \frac{1}{\cos x + \operatorname{cosec} x} dx$
18. $\int \frac{\sin x \cos x}{\sin 3x} dx$ [CBSE2023]
19. $\int \frac{\sin x \cos x}{\cos 3x} dx$
20. $\int \frac{1}{\sqrt{x}(\sqrt{x} + 1)(\sqrt{x} + 2)} dx$ [CBSE 2023]

ANSWERS

1. $\frac{1}{2} \log \left| \frac{1 + \tan x}{1 - \tan x} \right| + C$
2. $\tan^{-1} \left(\frac{e^x}{1} \right) + C$
3. $\tan^{-1} (\sin x + 2) + C$
4. $\log \left| \frac{e^x + 2}{e^x + 3} \right| + C$
5. $\frac{1}{36} \log \left| \frac{2e^{3x} - 3}{2e^{3x} + 3} \right| + C$
6. $\tan^{-1} (e^x) + C$

7. $\frac{1}{2\sqrt{2}}\tan^{-1}\left(\frac{x^2+1}{\sqrt{2}}\right)+C$ 8. $\frac{1}{2}\tan^{-1}(x^6)+C$ 9. $\frac{1}{6a^3}\log\left|\frac{x^3-a^3}{x^3+a^3}\right|+C$

10. $\frac{1}{3a^3}\tan^{-1}\left(\frac{x^3}{a^3}\right)+C$ 11. $\frac{1}{6}\log\left|\frac{x^6}{x^6+1}\right|+C$ 12. $\frac{1}{\sqrt{3}}\tan^{-1}\left(\frac{2x^2-1}{\sqrt{3}}\right)+C$

13. $\frac{\sqrt{3}}{48}\log\left|\frac{x^2-3-\frac{4}{\sqrt{3}}}{x^2-3+\frac{4}{\sqrt{3}}}\right|+C$ 14. $\log\left|\frac{1+e^x}{2+e^x}\right|+C$ 15. $\frac{1}{6}\log\left|\frac{1+\tan^3 x}{1-\tan^3 x}\right|+C$

16. $\frac{1}{5}\left|\frac{\log x-4}{\log x+1}\right|+C$ 17. $\frac{1}{2\sqrt{3}}\log\left|\frac{\sqrt{3}+\sin x-\cos x}{\sqrt{3}-\sin x+\cos x}\right|-\tan^{-1}(\sin x+\cos x)+C$

18. $\frac{1}{4\sqrt{3}}\log\left|\frac{\sqrt{3}+2\sin x}{\sqrt{3}-2\sin x}\right|+C$ 19. $-\frac{1}{4\sqrt{3}}\log\left|\frac{\sqrt{3}+2\cos x}{\sqrt{3}-2\cos x}\right|+C$ 20. $2\log\left(\frac{\sqrt{x}+1}{\sqrt{x}+2}\right)+C$

15.10.3 INTEGRALS OF THE TYPE $\int \frac{1}{\sqrt{ax^2+bx+c}}\,dx$

In order to evaluate this type of integrals, we may use the following algorithm.

ALGORITHM

Step I *Make the coefficient of x^2 unity, if it is not.*

Step II *Find half of the coefficient of x.*

Step III *Add and subtract $\left(\frac{1}{2}\text{ Coeff. of } x\right)^2$ inside the square root to express the quantity inside the square root in the form* $\left(x+\frac{b}{2a}\right)^2+\frac{4ac-b^2}{4a^2}$ or, $\frac{4ac-b^2}{4a^2}-\left(x+\frac{b}{2a}\right)^2$.

Step IV *Use the suitable formula from the following formulas:*

$$\int \frac{1}{\sqrt{a^2+x^2}}\,dx = \log\left|x+\sqrt{a^2+x^2}\right|+C,\quad \int \frac{1}{\sqrt{x^2-a^2}}\,dx=\log\left|x+\sqrt{x^2-a^2}\right|+C$$

$$\int \frac{1}{\sqrt{a^2-x^2}}\,dx = \sin^{-1}\left(\frac{x}{a}\right)+C$$

ILLUSTRATIVE EXAMPLES

BASED ON BASIC CONCEPTS (BASIC)

EXAMPLE 1 *Evaluate:*

(i) $\int \frac{1}{\sqrt{(x-1)(x-2)}}\,dx$ (ii) $\int \frac{1}{\sqrt{9+8x-x^2}}\,dx$ (iii) $\int \frac{1}{\sqrt{x(1-2x)}}\,dx$ (iv) $\int \frac{1}{\sqrt{2x^2+3x-2}}\,dx$

[NCERT]

SOLUTION (i) Let $I = \int \frac{1}{\sqrt{(x-1)(x-2)}}\,dx$. Then,

$$I = \int \frac{1}{\sqrt{x^2-3x+2}}\,dx = \int \frac{1}{\sqrt{x^2-3x+\frac{9}{4}-\frac{9}{4}+2}}\,dx = \int \frac{1}{\sqrt{\left(x-\frac{3}{2}\right)^2-\left(\frac{1}{2}\right)^2}}\,dx$$

$$\Rightarrow \quad I = \log\left|\left(x-\frac{3}{2}\right)+\sqrt{\left(x-\frac{3}{2}\right)^2-\left(\frac{1}{2}\right)^2}\right|+C = \log\left|\left(x-\frac{3}{2}\right)+\sqrt{x^2-3x+2}\right|+C$$

(ii) Let $I = \int \frac{1}{\sqrt{9+8x-x^2}}\,dx$. Then,

$$I = \int \frac{1}{\sqrt{-\left(x^2-8x-9\right)}}\,dx = \int \frac{1}{\sqrt{-\left(x^2-8x+16-25\right)}}\,dx$$

$$\Rightarrow \quad I = \int \frac{1}{\sqrt{-\{(x-4)^2-5^2\}}}\,dx = \int \frac{1}{\sqrt{5^2-(x-4)^2}}\,dx = \sin^{-1}\left(\frac{x-4}{5}\right)+C.$$

(iii) Let $I = \int \frac{1}{\sqrt{x(1-2x)}}\,dx$. Then,

$$I = \int \frac{1}{\sqrt{x-2x^2}}\,dx$$

$$\Rightarrow \quad I = \frac{1}{\sqrt{2}}\int \frac{1}{\sqrt{-\left\{x^2-\frac{x}{2}+\left(\frac{1}{4}\right)^2-\left(\frac{1}{4}\right)^2\right\}}}\,dx = \frac{1}{\sqrt{2}}\int \frac{1}{\sqrt{-\left\{\left(x-\frac{1}{4}\right)^2-\left(\frac{1}{4}\right)^2\right\}}}\,dx$$

$$\Rightarrow \quad I = \frac{1}{\sqrt{2}}\int \frac{1}{\sqrt{\left(\frac{1}{4}\right)^2-\left(x-\frac{1}{4}\right)^2}}\,dx = \frac{1}{\sqrt{2}}\sin^{-1}\left(\frac{x-1/4}{1/4}\right)+C = \frac{1}{\sqrt{2}}\sin^{-1}(4x-1)+C.$$

(iv) Let $I = \int \frac{1}{\sqrt{2x^2+3x-2}}\,dx$. Then,

$$I = \frac{1}{\sqrt{2}}\int \frac{1}{\sqrt{x^2+\frac{3}{2}x-1}}\,dx = \frac{1}{\sqrt{2}}\int \frac{1}{\sqrt{\left(x+\frac{3}{4}\right)^2-\frac{9}{16}-1}}\,dx$$

$$\Rightarrow \quad I = \frac{1}{\sqrt{2}}\int \frac{1}{\sqrt{\left(x+\frac{3}{4}\right)^2-\left(\frac{5}{4}\right)^2}}\,dx = \frac{1}{\sqrt{2}}\log\left|\left(x+\frac{3}{4}\right)+\sqrt{x^2+\frac{3}{2}x-1}\right|+C.$$

EXAMPLE 2 *Evaluate:* (i) $\int \frac{1}{\sqrt{(x-a)(x-b)}}\,dx$ **[CBSE 2001C]** (ii) $\int \frac{1}{\sqrt{x^2-4x+2}}\,dx$

SOLUTION (i) Let $I = \int \frac{1}{\sqrt{(x-a)(x-b)}}\,dx$. Then,

$$I = \int \frac{1}{\sqrt{x^2-x(a+b)+ab}}\,dx$$

$$\Rightarrow I = \int \frac{1}{\sqrt{x^2-x(a+b)+\left(\frac{a+b}{2}\right)^2-\left(\frac{a+b}{2}\right)^2+ab}}\,dx = \int \frac{1}{\sqrt{\left\{x-\left(\frac{a+b}{2}\right)\right\}^2-\left(\frac{a-b}{2}\right)^2}}\,dx$$

$$\Rightarrow I = \log\left|\left\{x-\left(\frac{a+b}{2}\right)\right\}+\sqrt{\left\{x-\left(\frac{a+b}{2}\right)\right\}^2-\left(\frac{a-b}{2}\right)^2}\right|+C$$

$$\Rightarrow I = \log\left|\left(\frac{2x-a-b}{2}\right)+\sqrt{(x-a)(x-b)}\right|+C=\log\left|\frac{(x-a)+(x-b)+2\sqrt{(x-a)(x-b)}}{2}\right|+C$$

$$\Rightarrow I = \log\left|\left(\sqrt{x-a}+\sqrt{x-b}\right)^2\right|-\log 2+C=2\log\left|\sqrt{x-a}+\sqrt{x-b}\right|+C, \text{ where } C_1=C-\log 2$$

(ii) Let $I = \int \frac{1}{\sqrt{x^2-4x+2}}\,dx$. Then,

$$I = \int \frac{1}{\sqrt{x^2-4x+4-4+2}}\,dx = \int \frac{1}{\sqrt{(x-2)^2-(\sqrt{2})^2}}\,dx$$

$$\Rightarrow I = \log\left|(x-2)+\sqrt{(x-2)^2-(\sqrt{2})^2}\right|+C = \log\left|x-2+\sqrt{x^2-4x+2}\right|+C$$

EXERCISE 15.17

BASIC

Evaluate the following integrals:

1. $\int \frac{1}{\sqrt{2x-x^2}}\,dx$
2. $\int \frac{1}{\sqrt{8+3x-x^2}}\,dx$ [NCERT]
3. $\int \frac{1}{\sqrt{5-4x-2x^2}}\,dx$ [CBSE 2009, 2019]
4. $\int \frac{1}{\sqrt{3x^2+5x+7}}\,dx$
5. $\int \frac{1}{\sqrt{(x-\alpha)(\beta-x)}}\,dx, (\beta>\alpha)$
6. $\int \frac{1}{\sqrt{7-3x-2x^2}}\,dx$
7. $\int \frac{1}{\sqrt{16-6x-x^2}}\,dx$
8. $\int \frac{1}{\sqrt{7-6x-x^2}}\,dx$ [NCERT, CBSE 2002]
9. $\int \frac{1}{\sqrt{5x^2-2x}}\,dx$ [NCERT]

ANSWERS

1. $\sin^{-1}(x-1)+C$
2. $\sin^{-1}\left(\frac{2x-3}{\sqrt{41}}\right)+C$
3. $\frac{1}{\sqrt{2}}\sin^{-1}\left\{\sqrt{\frac{2}{7}}(x+1)\right\}+C$
4. $\frac{1}{\sqrt{3}}\log\left|x+\frac{5}{6}+\sqrt{x^2+\frac{5}{3}x+\frac{7}{3}}\right|+C$
5. $2\sin^{-1}\left(\sqrt{\frac{x-\alpha}{\beta-\alpha}}\right)+C$
6. $\frac{1}{\sqrt{2}}\sin^{-1}\left(\frac{4x+3}{\sqrt{65}}\right)+C$
7. $\sin^{-1}\left(\frac{x+3}{5}\right)+C$
8. $\sin^{-1}\left(\frac{x+3}{4}\right)+C$
9. $\frac{1}{\sqrt{5}}\log\left|\frac{5x-1}{5}+\frac{\sqrt{5x^2-2x}}{\sqrt{5}}\right|+C$

15.10.4 INTEGRALS REDUCIBLE TO THE FORM $\int \frac{1}{\sqrt{ax^2+bx+c}}\,dx$

Following examples will illustrate the procedure of evaluating this type of integrals:

ILLUSTRATIVE EXAMPLES

BASED ON BASIC CONCEPTS (BASIC)

EXAMPLE 1 *Evaluate:*

(i) $\int \frac{e^x}{\sqrt{4-e^{2x}}}\,dx$ (ii) $\int \frac{x^2}{\sqrt{1-x^6}}\,dx$

(iii) $\int \frac{\sec^2 x}{\sqrt{16+\tan^2 x}}\,dx$ [NCERT] (iv) $\int \frac{1}{x\sqrt{(\log x)^2-5}}\,dx$

SOLUTION (i) Let $I = \int \frac{e^x}{\sqrt{4-e^{2x}}}\,dx = \int \frac{e^x}{\sqrt{2^2-(e^x)^2}}\,dx$

Let $e^x = t$. Then, $d(e^x) = dt \Rightarrow e^x\,dx = dt \Rightarrow dx = \frac{dt}{e^x}$

$$\therefore \quad I = \int \frac{dt}{\sqrt{4-t^2}} = \int \frac{dt}{\sqrt{2^2-t^2}} = \sin^{-1}\left(\frac{t}{2}\right)+C = \sin^{-1}\left(\frac{e^x}{2}\right)+C$$

(ii) Let $I = \int \frac{x^2}{\sqrt{1-x^6}}\,dx = \int \frac{x^2}{\sqrt{1^2-(x^3)^2}}\,dx$

Let $x^3 = t$. Then, $d(x^3) = dt \Rightarrow 3x^2\,dx = dt \Rightarrow dx = \frac{dt}{3x^2}$

$$\therefore \quad I = \frac{1}{3}\int \frac{dt}{\sqrt{1-t^2}} = \frac{1}{3}\sin^{-1}(t)+C = \frac{1}{3}\sin^{-1}(x^3)+C$$

(iii) Let, $I = \int \frac{\sec^2 x}{\sqrt{16+\tan^2 x}}\,dx = \int \frac{\sec^2 x}{\sqrt{4^2+\tan^2 x}}\,dx.$

Let $\tan x = t$. Then, $d(\tan x) = dt \Rightarrow \sec^2 x\,dx = dt \Rightarrow dx = \frac{dt}{\sec^2 x}$

$$\therefore \quad I = \int \frac{dt}{\sqrt{16+t^2}} = \int \frac{dt}{\sqrt{4^2+t^2}} = \log\left|t+\sqrt{4^2+t^2}\right|+C = \log\left|\tan x+\sqrt{16+\tan^2 x}\right|+C$$

(iv) Let $I = \int \frac{1}{x\sqrt{(\log x)^2-5}}\,dx$. Let $\log x = t$. Then, $d(\log x) = dt \Rightarrow \frac{1}{x}\,dx = dt \Rightarrow dx = x\,dt$

$$\therefore \quad I = \int \frac{1}{\sqrt{t^2-(\sqrt{5})^2}} = \log\left|t+\sqrt{t^2-5}\right|+C = \log\left|\log x+\sqrt{(\log x)^2-5}\right|+C$$

EXAMPLE 2 *Evaluate:*

(i) $\int \frac{a^x}{\sqrt{1-a^{2x}}}\,dx$ (ii) $\int \frac{2x}{\sqrt{1-x^2-x^4}}\,dx$ [CBSE 2005]

(iii) $\int \frac{e^x}{\sqrt{5-4e^x-e^{2x}}}\,dx$ [CBSE 2009, 2023] (iv) $\int \frac{\cos x}{\sqrt{\sin^2 x-2\sin x-3}}\,dx$

(v) $\int \sqrt{\frac{x}{a^3 - x^3}}\, dx$ [CBSE 2016] (vi) $\int \frac{\sin 2x \cos 2x}{\sqrt{9 - \cos^4 2x}}\, dx$

SOLUTION (i) Let $I = \int \frac{a^x}{\sqrt{1 - a^{2x}}}\, dx = \int \frac{a^x}{\sqrt{1^2 - (a^x)^2}}\, dx.$

Let $a^x = t$. Then, $d(a^x) = dt \Rightarrow a^x \log_e a\, dx = dt \Rightarrow dx = \frac{dt}{a^x \log_e a}$

$$\therefore \quad I = \int \frac{a^x}{\sqrt{1^2 - t^2}} \cdot \frac{dt}{a^x \log a} = \frac{1}{\log a} \int \frac{dt}{\sqrt{1^2 - t^2}} = \frac{1}{\log a} \times \sin^{-1}(t) + C = \frac{1}{\log a} \sin^{-1}(a^x) + C$$

(ii) Let $I = \int \frac{2x}{\sqrt{1 - x^2 - x^4}}\, dx = \int \frac{2x}{\sqrt{1 - x^2 - (x^2)^2}}\, dx.$

Let $x^2 = t$. Then, $d(x^2) = dt \Rightarrow 2x\, dx = dt \Rightarrow dx = \frac{dt}{2x}$

$$\therefore \quad I = \int \frac{1}{\sqrt{1 - t - t^2}}\, dt = \int \frac{1}{\sqrt{-(t^2 + t - 1)}}\, dt = \int \frac{1}{\sqrt{-\left\{t^2 + t + \frac{1}{4} - \frac{1}{4} - 1\right\}}}\, dt$$

$$\Rightarrow \quad I = \int \frac{1}{\sqrt{-\left\{\left(t + \frac{1}{2}\right)^2 - \frac{5}{4}\right\}}}\, dt = \int \frac{1}{\sqrt{\frac{5}{4} - \left(t + \frac{1}{2}\right)^2}}\, dt = \int \frac{1}{\sqrt{\left(\frac{\sqrt{5}}{2}\right)^2 - \left(t + \frac{1}{2}\right)^2}}\, dt$$

$$\Rightarrow \quad I = \sin^{-1}\left(\frac{t + 1/2}{\sqrt{5}/2}\right) + C = \sin^{-1}\left(\frac{2t + 1}{\sqrt{5}}\right) + C = \sin^{-1}\left(\frac{2x^2 + 1}{\sqrt{5}}\right) + C$$

(iii) Let $I = \int \frac{e^x}{\sqrt{5 - 4e^x - e^{2x}}}\, dx = \int \frac{e^x}{\sqrt{5 - 4e^x - (e^x)^2}}\, dx.$

Let $e^x = t$. Then, $d(e^x) = dt \Rightarrow e^x\, dx = dt \Rightarrow dx = \frac{dt}{e^x}$

$$\therefore \quad I = \int \frac{1}{\sqrt{5 - 4t - t^2}}\, dt = \int \frac{1}{\sqrt{-(t^2 + 4t - 5)}}\, dt = \int \frac{1}{\sqrt{-\{(t + 2)^2 - 3^2\}}}\, dt$$

$$\Rightarrow \quad I = \int \frac{1}{\sqrt{3^2 - (t + 2)^2}}\, dt = \sin^{-1}\left(\frac{t + 2}{3}\right) + C = \sin^{-1}\left(\frac{e^x + 2}{3}\right) + C$$

(iv) Let $I = \int \frac{\cos x}{\sqrt{\sin^2 x - 2\sin x - 3}}\, dx$. Let $\sin x = t$. Then,

$$d(\sin x) = dt \Rightarrow \cos x\, dx = dt \Rightarrow dx = \frac{dt}{\cos x}$$

$$\therefore \quad I = \int \frac{dt}{\sqrt{t^2 - 2t - 3}} = \int \frac{dt}{\sqrt{t^2 - 2t + 1 - 1 - 3}} = \int \frac{dt}{\sqrt{(t - 1)^2 - 2^2}}$$

$$\Rightarrow \quad I = \log\left|(t - 1) + \sqrt{(t - 1)^2 - 2^2}\right| + C$$

$$\Rightarrow \quad I = \log\left|t - 1 + \sqrt{t^2 - 2t - 3}\right| + C = \log\left|(\sin x - 1) + \sqrt{\sin^2 x - 2\sin x - 3}\right| + C$$

(v) Let $I = \int \sqrt{\frac{x}{a^3 - x^3}}\, dx = \int \frac{\sqrt{x}}{\sqrt{\left(a^{3/2}\right)^2 - \left(x^{3/2}\right)^2}}\, dx.$

Let $x^{3/2} = t$. Then, $d\left(x^{3/2}\right) = dt \Rightarrow \frac{3}{2} x^{1/2}\, dx = dt \Rightarrow dx = \frac{2}{3\sqrt{x}}\, dt$

$$\therefore \quad I = \frac{2}{3} \int \frac{1}{\sqrt{\left(a^{3/2}\right)^2 - t^2}}\, dt = \frac{2}{3} \sin^{-1}\left(\frac{t}{a^{3/2}}\right) + C = \frac{2}{3} \sin^{-1}\left(\frac{x^{3/2}}{a^{3/2}}\right) + C$$

(vi) Let $I = \int \frac{\sin 2x \cos 2x}{\sqrt{9 - \cos^4 2x}}\, dx$. Then, $I = \int \frac{\sin 2x \cos 2x}{\sqrt{3^2 - (\cos^2 2x)^2}}\, dx$

Putting $\cos^2 2x = t$ and $-4 \sin 2x \cos 2x\, dx = dt$, we get

$$I = -\frac{1}{4} \int \frac{1}{\sqrt{3^2 - t^2}}\, dt = -\frac{1}{4} \sin^{-1}\left(\frac{t}{3}\right) + C = -\frac{1}{4} \sin^{-1}\left(\frac{\cos^2 2x}{3}\right) + C$$

BASED ON LOWER ORDER THINKING SKILLS (LOTS)

EXAMPLE 3 *Evaluate:* (i) $\int \sqrt{\sec x - 1}\, dx$ (ii) $\int \frac{1}{\sqrt{1 - e^{2x}}}\, dx$

SOLUTION (i) Let $I = \int \sqrt{\sec x - 1}\, dx = \int \sqrt{\frac{1 - \cos x}{\cos x}}\, dx$. Then,

$$\Rightarrow \quad I = \int \sqrt{\frac{(1 - \cos x)}{\cos x} \times \frac{(1 + \cos x)}{(1 + \cos x)}}\, dx = \int \sqrt{\frac{1 - \cos^2 x}{\cos x + \cos^2 x}}\, dx = \int \frac{\sin x}{\sqrt{\cos^2 x + \cos x}}\, dx$$

Let $\cos x = t$. Then, $d(\cos x) = dt \Rightarrow -\sin x\, dx = dt \Rightarrow dx = -\frac{dt}{\sin x}$

$$\therefore \quad I = \int \frac{-dt}{\sqrt{t^2 + t}} = -\int \frac{dt}{\sqrt{\left(t + \frac{1}{2}\right)^2 - \left(\frac{1}{2}\right)^2}} = -\log\left|\left(t + \frac{1}{2}\right) + \sqrt{\left(t + \frac{1}{2}\right)^2 - \left(\frac{1}{2}\right)^2}\right| + C$$

$$\Rightarrow \quad I = -\log\left|\left(t + \frac{1}{2}\right) + \sqrt{t^2 + t}\right| + C = -\log\left|\left(\cos x + \frac{1}{2}\right) + \sqrt{\cos^2 x + \cos x}\right| + C$$

(ii) Let $I = \int \frac{1}{\sqrt{1 - e^{2x}}}\, dx = \int \frac{1}{\sqrt{1 - \frac{1}{e^{-2x}}}}\, dx = \int \frac{e^{-x}}{\sqrt{e^{-2x} - 1}}\, dx = \int \frac{e^{-x}}{\sqrt{(e^{-x})^2 - 1^2}}\, dx$

Let $e^{-x} = t$. Then, $d(e^{-x}) = dt \Rightarrow -e^{-x}\, dx = dt \Rightarrow dx = -\frac{dt}{e^{-x}}$

$$\therefore \quad I = -\int \frac{dt}{\sqrt{t^2 - 1^2}} = -\log\left|t + \sqrt{t^2 - 1}\right| + C = -\log\left|e^{-x} + \sqrt{e^{-2x} - 1}\right| + C$$

BASED ON HIGHER ORDER THINKING SKILLS (HOTS)

EXAMPLE 4 *Evaluate:* $\int \sqrt{\frac{\sin(x - \alpha)}{\sin(x + \alpha)}}\, dx$

SOLUTION Let $I = \int \sqrt{\frac{\sin(x-\alpha)}{\sin(x+\alpha)}}\, dx$

$$\Rightarrow I = \int \sqrt{\frac{\sin(x-\alpha)}{\sin(x+\alpha)} \times \frac{\sin(x-\alpha)}{\sin(x-\alpha)}}\, dx = \int \frac{\sin(x-\alpha)}{\sqrt{\sin^2 x - \sin^2 \alpha}}\, dx = \int \frac{\sin x \cos\alpha - \cos x \sin\alpha}{\sqrt{\sin^2 x - \sin^2\alpha}}\, dx$$

$$\Rightarrow I = \cos\alpha \int \frac{\sin x}{\sqrt{1-\cos^2 x - 1 + \cos^2\alpha}}\, dx - \sin\alpha \int \frac{\cos x}{\sqrt{\sin^2 x - \sin^2\alpha}}\, dx$$

$$\Rightarrow \quad I = \cos\alpha \int \frac{\sin x}{\sqrt{\cos^2\alpha - \cos^2 x}}\, dx - \sin\alpha \int \frac{\cos x}{\sqrt{\sin^2 x - \sin^2\alpha}}\, dx$$

In the first integral we put $\cos x = t$, so that $-\sin x\, dx = dt$ and in the second integral we put $\sin x = u$, so that $\cos x\, dx = du$.

$$\therefore \quad I = -\cos\alpha \int \frac{dt}{\sqrt{\cos^2\alpha - t^2}} - \sin\alpha \int \frac{du}{\sqrt{u^2 - \sin^2\alpha}}$$

$$\Rightarrow \quad I = -\cos\alpha \sin^{-1}\left(\frac{t}{\cos\alpha}\right) - \sin\alpha \log\left|u + \sqrt{u^2 - \sin^2\alpha}\right| + C$$

$$\Rightarrow \quad I = -\cos\alpha \sin^{-1}\left(\frac{\cos x}{\cos\alpha}\right) - \sin\alpha \log\left|\sin x + \sqrt{\sin^2 x - \sin^2\alpha}\right| + C$$

EXAMPLE 5 *Evaluate* : $\int \frac{\sin x + \cos x}{\sqrt{1+\sin 2x}}\, dx$ [NCERT EXAMPLAR]

SOLUTION Let $I = \int \frac{\sin x + \cos x}{\sqrt{1+\sin 2x}}\, dx$. Here, the integration of the numerator of the integrand is $-\cos x + \sin x$. That is the numerator of the integrand occurs in the derivative of $-\cos x + \sin x$. So, we express $1 + \sin 2x$ in terms of $-\cos x + \sin x$. We observe that $(-\cos x + \sin x)^2 = 1 - \sin 2x$. Therefore, we write $1 + \sin 2x = 2 - (1 - \sin 2x) = 2 - (\sin x - \cos x)^2$.

$$\therefore \quad I = \int \frac{\sin x + \cos x}{\sqrt{2 - (\sin x - \cos x)^2}}\, dx$$

Let $\sin x - \cos x = t$. Then, $d(\sin x - \cos x) = dt$ or, $(\cos x + \sin x)\, dx = dt$

$$\therefore \quad I = \int \frac{1}{\sqrt{2 - t^2}}\, dt = \int \frac{1}{\sqrt{(\sqrt{2})^2 - t^2}}\, dt = \sin^{-1}\left(\frac{t}{\sqrt{2}}\right) + C$$

$$\Rightarrow \quad I = \sin^{-1}\left\{\frac{1}{\sqrt{2}}(\sin x - \cos x)\right\} + C = \sin^{-1}\left\{\sin\left(x - \frac{\pi}{4}\right)\right\} + C$$

EXERCISE 15.18

BASIC

Evaluate the following integrals:

1. $\int \frac{x}{\sqrt{x^4 + a^4}}\, dx$

2. $\int \frac{\sec^2 x}{\sqrt{4 + \tan^2 x}}\, dx$ [NCERT, CBSE 2019]

3. $\int \frac{e^x}{\sqrt{16 - e^{2x}}}\, dx$

4. $\int \frac{\cos x}{\sqrt{4+\sin^2 x}}\,dx$ 5. $\int \frac{\sin x}{\sqrt{4\cos^2 x-1}}\,dx$ 6. $\int \frac{x}{\sqrt{4-x^4}}\,dx$

7. $\int \frac{1}{x\sqrt{4-9(\log x)^2}}\,dx$ 8. $\int \frac{\sin 8x}{\sqrt{9+\sin^4 4x}}\,dx$ 9. $\int \frac{\cos 2x}{\sqrt{\sin^2 2x+8}}\,dx$

10. $\int \frac{\sin 2x}{\sqrt{\sin^4 x+4\sin^2 x-2}}\,dx$ 11. $\int \frac{\sin 2x}{\sqrt{\cos^4 x-\sin^2 x+2}}\,dx$ 12. $\int \frac{\cos x}{\sqrt{4-\sin^2 x}}\,dx$

13. $\int \frac{1}{x^{2/3}\sqrt{x^{2/3}-4}}\,dx$ 14. $\int \frac{1}{\sqrt{(1-x^2)\{9+(\sin^{-1}x)^2\}}}\,dx$

BASED ON LOTS

15. $\int \frac{\cos x}{\sqrt{\sin^2 x-2\sin x-3}}\,dx$ 16. $\int \sqrt{\operatorname{cosec} x-1}\,dx$

17. $\int \frac{\sin x-\cos x}{\sqrt{\sin 2x}}\,dx$ [CBSE 2011] 18. $\int \frac{\cos x-\sin x}{\sqrt{8-\sin 2x}}\,dx$

ANSWERS

1. $\frac{1}{2}\log\left|x^2+\sqrt{x^4+a^4}\right|+C$ 2. $\log\left|\tan x+\sqrt{4+\tan^2 x}\right|+C$

3. $\sin^{-1}\left(\frac{e^x}{4}\right)+C$ 4. $\log\left|\sin x+\sqrt{4+\sin^2 x}\right|+C$

5. $-\frac{1}{2}\log\left|2\cos x+\sqrt{4\cos^2 x-1}\right|+C$ 6. $\frac{1}{2}\sin^{-1}\left(\frac{x^2}{2}\right)+C$

7. $\frac{1}{3}\sin^{-1}\left(\frac{3\log x}{2}\right)+C$ 8. $\frac{1}{4}\log\left|\sin^2 4x+\sqrt{9+\sin^4 4x}\right|+C$

9. $\frac{1}{2}\log\left|\sin 2x+\sqrt{\sin^2 2x+8}\right|+C$ 10. $\log\left|\sin^2 x+2+\sqrt{\sin^4 x+4\sin^2 x-2}\right|+C$

11. $-\log\left|\left(\cos^2 x+\frac{1}{2}\right)+\sqrt{\cos^4 x+\cos^2 x+1}\right|+C$

12. $\sin^{-1}\left(\frac{\sin x}{2}\right)+C$ 13. $3\log\left|x^{1/3}+\sqrt{x^{2/3}-4}\right|+C$

14. $\log\left|\sin^{-1}x+\sqrt{9+(\sin^{-1}x)^2}\right|+C$ 15. $\log\left|(\sin x-1)+\sqrt{\sin^2 x-2\sin x-3}\right|+C$

16. $\log\left|\left(\sin x+\frac{1}{2}\right)+\sqrt{\sin^2 x+\sin x}\right|+C$ 17. $-\log\left|(\sin x+\cos x)+\sqrt{\sin 2x}\right|+C$

18. $\sin^{-1}\left\{\frac{1}{3}(\sin x+\cos x)\right\}+C$

15.10.5 INTEGRALS OF THE FORM $\int \frac{px+q}{ax^2+bx+c}\,dx$

To evaluate this type of integrals, we use the following algorithm.

ALGORITHM

Step I *Write the numerator px + q in the following form:*

$$px+q = \lambda\left\{\frac{d}{dx}(ax^2+bx+c)\right\}+\mu \text{ i.e. } px+q = \lambda(2ax+b)+\mu$$

Step II *Obtain the values of λ and μ by equating the coefficients of like powers of x on both sides.*

Step III *Replace px + q by λ (2ax + b) + μ in the given integral to get*

$$\int \frac{px+q}{ax^2+bx+c}\,dx = \lambda\int\frac{2ax+b}{ax^2+bx+c}\,dx+\mu\int\frac{1}{ax^2+bx+c}\,dx$$

Step IV *Integrate RHS in step III and put the values of λ and μ obtained in step II.*

Following examples illustrate the above algorithm.

ILLUSTRATIVE EXAMPLES

BASED ON BASIC CONCEPTS (BASIC)

EXAMPLE 1 *Evaluate:*

(i) $\int \frac{x}{x^2+x+1}\,dx$ (ii) $\int\frac{4x+1}{x^2+3x+2}\,dx$ (iii) $\int\frac{2x-3}{x^2+3x-18}\,dx$

SOLUTION (i) Let $x=\lambda\frac{d}{dx}(x^2+x+1)+\mu$. Then, $x=\lambda(2x+1)+\mu$

Comparing the coefficients of like powers of x, we get

$$1 = 2\lambda \text{ and } \lambda+\mu = 0 \Rightarrow \lambda = \frac{1}{2} \text{ and } \mu = -\lambda = -\frac{1}{2}$$

$$\therefore \quad I = \int\frac{x}{x^2+x+1}\,dx = \int\frac{1/2\,(2x+1)-1/2}{x^2+x+1}\,dx = \frac{1}{2}\int\frac{2x+1}{x^2+x+1}\,dx - \frac{1}{2}\int\frac{1}{x^2+x+1}\,dx$$

$$\Rightarrow \quad I = \frac{1}{2}\int\frac{2x+1}{x^2+x+1}\,dx - \frac{1}{2}\int\frac{1}{\left(x^2+x+\frac{1}{4}\right)+\frac{3}{4}}\,dx$$

$$\Rightarrow \quad I = \frac{1}{2}\int\frac{2x+1}{x^2+x+1}\,dx - \frac{1}{2}\int\frac{1}{\left(x+\frac{1}{2}\right)^2+\left(\frac{\sqrt{3}}{2}\right)^2}\,dx$$

$$\Rightarrow \quad I = \frac{1}{2}\log|x^2+x+1| - \frac{1}{2}\times\frac{1}{(\sqrt{3/2})}\tan^{-1}\left(\frac{x+1/2}{\sqrt{3/2}}\right)+C$$

$$\Rightarrow \quad I = \frac{1}{2}\log|x^2+x+1| - \frac{1}{\sqrt{3}}\tan^{-1}\left(\frac{2x+1}{\sqrt{3}}\right)+C$$

(ii) Let $4x+1=\lambda\frac{d}{dx}(x^2+3x+2)+\mu$. Then, $4x+1=\lambda(2x+3)+\mu$.

Comparing coefficients of like powers of x, we get: $2\lambda=4$ and $3\lambda+\mu=1 \Rightarrow \lambda=2$ and $\mu=-5$

$\therefore \quad I = \int \frac{4x+1}{x^2+3x+2}\,dx = \int \frac{2(2x+3)-5}{x^2+3x+2}\,dx = 2\int \frac{2x+3}{x^2+3x+2}\,dx - 5\int \frac{1}{x^2+3x+2}\,dx$

$\Rightarrow \quad I = 2\log|x^2+3x+2| - 5\int \frac{1}{x^2+3x+(9/4)-(9/4)+2}\,dx$

$\Rightarrow \quad I = 2\log|x^2+3x+2| - 5\int \frac{1}{(x+3/2)^2-(1/2)^2}\,dx$

$\Rightarrow \quad I = 2\log|x^2+3x+2| - 5\times\frac{1}{2(1/2)}\log\left|\frac{x+\frac{3}{2}-\frac{1}{2}}{x+\frac{3}{2}+\frac{1}{2}}\right| + C$

$\Rightarrow \quad I = 2\log|x^2+3x+2| - 5\log\left|\frac{x+1}{x+2}\right| + C$

(iii) Let $2x-3 = \lambda\frac{d}{dx}(x^2+3x-18)+\mu$. Then, $2x-3=\lambda(2x+3)+\mu$.

Comparing coefficients of like powers of x, we get

$2\lambda = 2$ and $3\lambda+\mu = -3 \Rightarrow \lambda = 1$ and $\mu = -6$

$\therefore \quad I = \int \frac{2x-3}{x^2+3x-18}\,dx = \int \frac{2x+3-6}{x^2+3x-18}\,dx = \int \frac{2x+3}{x^2+3x-18}\,dx - 6\int \frac{1}{x^2+3x-18}\,dx$

$\Rightarrow \quad I = \log|x^2+3x-18| - 6\int \frac{1}{x^2+3x+\frac{9}{4}-\frac{9}{4}-18}\,dx$

$\Rightarrow \quad I = \log|x^2+3x-18| - 6\int \frac{1}{\left(x+\frac{3}{2}\right)^2-\left(\frac{9}{2}\right)^2}\,dx$

$\Rightarrow \quad I = \log|x^2+3x-18| - 6\times\frac{1}{2\left(\frac{9}{2}\right)}\log\left|\frac{x+\frac{3}{2}-\frac{9}{2}}{x+\frac{3}{2}+\frac{9}{2}}\right| + C$

$\Rightarrow \quad I = \log|x^2+3x-18| - \frac{2}{3}\log\left|\frac{x-3}{x+6}\right| + C$

EXAMPLE 2 *Evaluate:*

(i) $\int \frac{2\sin 2\phi - \cos\phi}{6-\cos^2\phi - 4\sin\phi}\,d\phi$ (ii) $\int \frac{x^3+x}{x^4-9}\,dx$ [CBSE 2022] (iii) $\int \frac{1}{2e^{2x}+3e^x+1}\,dx$

SOLUTION (i) Let $I = \int \frac{2\sin 2\phi-\cos\phi}{6-\cos^2\phi-4\sin\phi}\,d\phi$. Then,

$$I = \int \frac{(4\sin\phi-1)\cos\phi}{6-(1-\sin^2\phi)-4\sin\phi}\,d\phi = \int \frac{(4\sin\phi-1)\cos\phi}{\sin^2\phi-4\sin\phi+5}\,d\phi$$

Putting $\sin\phi = t$ and $\cos\phi\,d\phi = dt$, we get

$$I = \int \frac{4t-1}{t^2-4t+5}\,dt$$

Let $\quad (4t-1) = \lambda\frac{d}{dt}(t^2-4t+5)+\mu \Rightarrow (4t-1) = \lambda(2t-4)+\mu.$

Comparing coefficients of like powers of t, we get: $2\lambda = 4,\ -4\lambda+\mu = -1 \Rightarrow \lambda = 2,\ \mu = 7$

$\therefore \quad I = \int \frac{\lambda(2t-4)+\mu}{t^2-4t+5}\,dt = 2\int \frac{2t-4}{t^2-4t+5}\,dt + 7\int \frac{1}{t^2-4t+5}\,dt$

$\Rightarrow \quad I = 2\log|t^2-4t+5| + 7\int \frac{1}{(t-2)^2+1^2}\,dt = 2\log|t^2-4t+5| + 7\tan^{-1}(t-2) + C$

$\Rightarrow \quad I = 2\log|\sin^2\phi - 4\sin\phi + 5| + 7\tan^{-1}(\sin\phi - 2) + C$

(ii) Let $I = \int \frac{x^3+x}{x^4-9}\,dx$. Then,

$$I = \int \frac{x^3}{x^4-9}\,dx + \int \frac{x}{x^4-9}\,dx = I_1 + I_2 \text{ (say), where } I_1 = \int \frac{x^3}{x^4-9}\,dx \text{ and } I_2 = \int \frac{x}{x^4-9}\,dx.$$

Putting $x^4 - 9 = t$ and $4x^3\,dx = dt$, we get

$$I_1 = \int \frac{x^3}{t} \times \frac{dt}{4x^3} = \frac{1}{4}\int \frac{1}{t}\,dt = \frac{1}{4}\log|t| = \frac{1}{4}\log|x^4-9|$$

Putting $x^2 = t$ and $2xdx = dt$, we get

$$I_2 = \int \frac{x}{x^4-9}\,dx = \int \frac{x}{(x^2)^2-3^2}\,dx = \frac{1}{2}\int \frac{dt}{t^2-3^2} = \frac{1}{2}\times\frac{1}{2\times 3}\log\left|\frac{t-3}{t+3}\right| = \frac{1}{12}\log\left|\frac{x^2-3}{x^2+3}\right|$$

Hence, $I = I_1 + I_2 = \frac{1}{4}\log|x^4-9| + \frac{1}{12}\log\left|\frac{x^2-3}{x^2+3}\right| + C$

(iii) We have,

$$I = \int \frac{1}{2e^{2x}+3e^x+1}\,dx = \int \frac{1}{\frac{2}{e^{-2x}}+\frac{3}{e^{-x}}+1}\,dx = \int \frac{e^{-2x}}{2+3e^{-x}+e^{-2x}}\,dx$$

Let $e^{-x} = t$. Then, $d(e^{-x}) = dt \Rightarrow -e^{-x}\,dx = dt \Rightarrow dx = -\frac{dt}{e^{-x}}$

$$\therefore \quad I = \int \frac{-t\,dt}{2+3t+t^2} = -\int \frac{t}{t^2+3t+2}\,dt$$

Let $t = \lambda(2t+3)+\mu$. Comparing the coefficients of like powers of t, we get

$$2\lambda = 1,\ 3\lambda+\mu = 0 \Rightarrow \lambda = 1/2,\ \mu = -3/2$$

$$\therefore \quad I = -\int \frac{\lambda(2t+3)+\mu}{t^2+3t+2}\,dt = -\lambda\int \frac{2t+3}{t^2+3t+2}\,dt - \mu\int \frac{1}{t^2+3t+2}\,dt$$

$$\Rightarrow \quad I = -\frac{1}{2}\int \frac{2t+3}{t^2+3t+2}\,dt + \frac{3}{2}\int \frac{1}{(t+3/2)^2-(1/2)^2}\,dt$$

$$\Rightarrow \quad I = -\frac{1}{2}\log\left|t^2+3t+2\right| + \frac{3}{2}\times\frac{1}{2\left(\frac{1}{2}\right)}\log\left|\frac{t+\frac{3}{2}-\frac{1}{2}}{t+\frac{3}{2}+\frac{1}{2}}\right| + C$$

$$\Rightarrow \quad I = -\frac{1}{2}\log|e^{-2x}+3e^{-x}+2| + \frac{3}{2}\log\left|\frac{e^{-x}+1}{e^{-x}+2}\right| + C$$

BASED ON HIGHER ORDER THINKING SKILLS (HOTS)

EXAMPLE 3 *Evaluate:* $\int \frac{x^3}{x^4+3x^2+2}\,dx$ [NCERT EXEMPLAR]

SOLUTION (i) Let $I = \int \frac{x^3}{x^4+3x^2+2}\,dx$. Then, $I = \frac{1}{2}\int \frac{x^2}{(x^2)^2+3x^2+2}\,2x\,dx.$

Let $x^2 = t$. Then, $d(x^2) = dt$ or, $2x\,dx = dt$

$$\therefore \quad I = \frac{1}{2}\int \frac{t}{t^2+3t+2}\,dt = \frac{1}{4}\int \frac{(2t+3)-3}{t^2+3t+2}\,dt = \frac{1}{4}\int \frac{2t+3}{t^2+3t+2}\,dt - \frac{3}{4}\int \frac{1}{t^2+3+2}\,dt$$

$$\Rightarrow \quad I = \frac{1}{4}\int \frac{2t+3}{t^2+3t+2}\,dt - \frac{3}{4}\int \frac{1}{\left(t+\frac{3}{2}\right)^2-\left(\frac{1}{2}\right)^2}\,dt$$

$$\Rightarrow \quad I = \frac{1}{4}\log|t^2+3t+2| - \frac{3}{4}\log\left|\frac{t+\frac{3}{2}-\frac{1}{2}}{t+\frac{3}{2}+\frac{1}{2}}\right| + C = \frac{1}{4}\log|x^4+3x^2+2| - \frac{3}{4}\log\left|\frac{x^2+1}{x^2+2}\right| + C$$

EXERCISE 15.19

BASIC

Evaluate the following integrals:

1. $\int \frac{x}{x^2+3x+2}\,dx$ [CBSE 2022]
2. $\int \frac{x+1}{x^2+x+3}\,dx$
3. $\int \frac{x-3}{x^2+2x-4}\,dx$
4. $\int \frac{2x-3}{x^2+6x+13}\,dx$
5. $\int \frac{x-1}{3x^2-4x+3}\,dx$
6. $\int \frac{2x}{2+x-x^2}\,dx$
7. $\int \frac{1-3x}{3x^2+4x+2}\,dx$
8. $\int \frac{2x+5}{x^2-x-2}\,dx$
9. $\int \frac{ax^3+bx}{x^4+c^2}\,dx$
10. $\int \frac{(3\sin x-2)\cos x}{5-\cos^2 x-4\sin x}\,dx$ [CBSE 2013, 2016]
11. $\int \frac{x+2}{2x^2+6x+5}\,dx$ [CBSE 2007]
12. $\int \frac{5x-2}{1+2x+3x^2}\,dx$ [CBSE 2013, 2014]
13. $\int \frac{x+5}{3x^2+13x-10}\,dx$ [CBSE 2017]
14. $\int \frac{(3\sin x-2)\cos x}{13-\cos^2 x-7\sin x}\,dx$ [CBSE 2017]
15. $\int \frac{x+7}{3x^2+25x+28}\,dx$ [CBSE 2017]
16. $\int \frac{3x+5}{x^2+3x-18}\,dx$ [CBSE 2019]
17. $\int \frac{(3\cos x-2)\sin x}{5-\sin^2 x-4\cos x}\,dx$ [CBSE 2024]

BASED ON HOTS

18. $\int \frac{x^3}{x^4+x^2+1}\,dx$
19. $\int \frac{x^3-3x}{x^4+2x^2-4}\,dx$

ANSWERS

1. $\frac{1}{2}\log|x^2+3x+2| - \frac{3}{2}\log\left|\frac{x+1}{x+2}\right| + C$
2. $\frac{1}{2}\log|x^2+x+3| + \frac{1}{\sqrt{11}}\tan^{-1}\left(\frac{2x+1}{\sqrt{11}}\right) + C$
3. $\frac{1}{2}\log|x^2+2x-4| - \frac{2}{\sqrt{5}}\log\left|\frac{x+1-\sqrt{5}}{x+1+\sqrt{5}}\right| + C$
4. $\log|x^2+6x+13| - \frac{9}{2}\tan^{-1}\left(\frac{x+3}{2}\right) + C$

5. $\frac{1}{6}\log|3x^2-4x+3|-\frac{\sqrt{5}}{15}\tan^{-1}\left(\frac{3x-2}{\sqrt{5}}\right)+C$ 6. $-\log|2+x-x^2|+\frac{1}{3}\log\left|\frac{1+x}{2-x}\right|+C$

7. $-\frac{1}{2}\log|3x^2+4x+2|+\frac{3}{\sqrt{2}}\tan^{-1}\left(\frac{3x+2}{\sqrt{2}}\right)+C$ 8. $\log|x^2-x-2|+2\log\left|\frac{x-2}{x+1}\right|+C$

9. $\frac{a}{4}\log|x^4+c^2|+\frac{b}{2c}\tan^{-1}\left(\frac{x^2}{c}\right)+C$ 10. $3\log|2-\sin x|+\frac{4}{2-\sin x}+C$

11. $\frac{1}{4}\log(2x^2+6x+5)+\frac{1}{2}\tan^{-1}(2x+3)+C$

12. $\frac{5}{6}\log\left|3x^2+2x+1\right|-\frac{11}{3\sqrt{2}}\tan^{-1}\frac{3x+1}{\sqrt{2}}+C$ 13. $\frac{1}{6}\log|3x^2+13x-10|+\frac{1}{6}\log\left|\frac{3x-2}{3(x+5)}\right|+C$

14. $10\log(4-\sin x)-7\log(3-\sin x)+C$ 15. $\frac{1}{3}\log|3x+4|+C$

16. $\frac{3}{2}\log|x^2+3x-18|+\frac{1}{18}\log\left|\frac{x-3}{x+6}\right|+C$ 17. $-3\log(2-\cos x)+\frac{4}{\cos x-2}+C$

18. $\frac{1}{2}\log|x^4+x^2+1|-\frac{1}{\sqrt{3}}\tan^{-1}\left(\frac{2x^2+1}{\sqrt{3}}\right)+C$

19. $\frac{1}{2}\log|x^4+2x^2-4|-\frac{2}{\sqrt{5}}\log\left|\frac{x^2+1-\sqrt{5}}{x^2+1+\sqrt{5}}\right|+C$

15.10.6 INTEGRALS OF THE FORM $\int \frac{P(x)}{ax^2+bx+c}\,dx$, WHERE $P(x)$ IS A POLYNOMIAL OF DEGREE TWO OR MORE

To evaluate this type of integrals we divide the numerator by the denominator and express the integrand as

$$Q(x)+\frac{R(x)}{ax^2+bx+c},$$ where $R(x)$ is a linear function of x.

$$\therefore \quad \int \frac{P(x)}{ax^2+bx+c}\,dx = \int Q(x)\,dx + \int \frac{R(x)}{ax^2+bx+c}\,dx$$

Now to evaluate the second integral on RHS apply the method discussed earlier.

ILLUSTRATIVE EXAMPLES

BASED ON BASIC CONCEPTS (BASIC)

EXAMPLE 1 *Evaluate:* (i) $\int \frac{x^3+x+1}{x^2-1}\,dx$ (ii) $\int \frac{x^2+5x+3}{x^2+3x+2}\,dx$

SOLUTION (i) Let $I=\int \frac{x^3+x+1}{x^2-1}\,dx$. Then,

$$I=\int x+\frac{2x+1}{x^2-1}\,dx$$

$$\Rightarrow \quad I = \int x\,dx + \int \frac{2x}{x^2-1}\,dx + \int \frac{1}{x^2-1}\,dx = \frac{x^2}{2} + \log|x^2-1| + \frac{1}{2}\log\left|\frac{x-1}{x+1}\right| + C$$

(ii) Let $I = \int \frac{x^2+5x+3}{x^2+3x+2}\,dx$. Then,

$$I = \int \left(1 + \frac{2x+1}{x^2+3x+2}\right) dx = \int 1 \cdot dx + \int \frac{2x+3-2}{x^2+3x+2}\,dx$$

$$\Rightarrow \quad I = \int 1 \cdot dx + \int \frac{2x+3}{x^2+3x+2}\,dx - 2\int \frac{1}{x^2+3x+2}\,dx$$

$$\Rightarrow \quad I = x + \log|x^2+3x+2| - 2\int \frac{1}{\left(x+\frac{3}{2}\right)^2 - \left(\frac{1}{2}\right)^2}\,dx$$

$$\Rightarrow \quad I = x + \log|x^2+3x+2| - 2 \times \frac{1}{2\left(\frac{1}{2}\right)} \log\left|\frac{x+\frac{3}{2}-\frac{1}{2}}{x+\frac{3}{2}+\frac{1}{2}}\right| + C$$

$$\Rightarrow \quad I = x + \log|x^2+3x+2| - 2\log\left|\frac{x+1}{x+2}\right| + C$$

EXERCISE 15.20

BASIC

Evaluate the following integrals:

1. $\int \frac{x^2+x+1}{x^2-x}\,dx$
2. $\int \frac{x^2+x-1}{x^2+x-6}\,dx$
3. $\int \frac{(1-x^2)}{x(1-2x)}\,dx$ [CBSE 2010]
4. $\int \frac{x^2+1}{x^2-5x+6}\,dx$ [NCERT]
5. $\int \frac{x^2}{x^2+7x+10}\,dx$
6. $\int \frac{x^2+x+1}{x^2-x+1}\,dx$
7. $\int \frac{(x-1)^2}{x^2+2x+2}\,dx$
8. $\int \frac{x^3+x^2+2x+1}{x^2-x+1}\,dx$
9. $\int \frac{x^2(x^4+4)}{x^2+4}\,dx$
10. $\int \frac{x^2}{x^2+6x+12}\,dx$ [CBSE 2005]
11. $\int \frac{x^3+1}{x^3-x}\,dx$ [CBSE 2020]

ANSWERS

1. $x + \log|x^2-x| + 2\log\left|\frac{x-1}{x}\right| + C$
2. $x + \log\left|\frac{x-2}{x+3}\right| + C$
3. $\frac{1}{2}x + \log|x| - \frac{3}{4}\log|1-2x| + C$
4. $x - 5\log|x-2| + 10\log|x-3| + C$
5. $x - \frac{7}{2}\log|x^2+7x+10| + \frac{29}{6}\log\left|\frac{x+2}{x+5}\right| + C$
6. $x + \log|x^2-x+1| + \frac{2}{\sqrt{3}}\tan^{-1}\left(\frac{2x-1}{\sqrt{3}}\right) + C$
7. $x - 2\log|x^2+2x+2| + 3\tan^{-1}(x+1) + C$

8. $\frac{1}{2}x^2 + 2x + \frac{3}{2}\log|x^2 - x + 1| + \frac{1}{\sqrt{3}}\tan^{-1}\left(\frac{2x-1}{\sqrt{3}}\right) + C$

9. $\frac{1}{5}x^5 - \frac{4}{3}x^3 + 20x - 40\tan^{-1}\left(\frac{x}{2}\right) + C$

10. $x - 3\log|x^2 + 6x + 12| + 2\sqrt{3}\tan^{-1}\left(\frac{x+3}{\sqrt{3}}\right) + C$

11. $x + \log\left|\frac{x-1}{x}\right| + C$

15.10.7 INTEGRALS OF THE FORM $\int \frac{px+q}{\sqrt{ax^2+bx+c}}\,dx$

In order to evaluate this type of integrals, we use the following algorithm:

ALGORITHM

Step I *Write the numerator px + q in the following form:*

$$px + q = \lambda\left\{\frac{d}{dx}(ax^2+bx+c)\right\} + \mu \quad i.e. \quad px+q = \lambda(2ax+b)+\mu$$

Step II *Obtain the values of* λ and μ *by equating the coefficients of like powers of x on both sides.*

Step III *Replace* $px + q$ *by* $\lambda(2ax + b) + \mu$ *in the given integral to get*

$$\int \frac{px+q}{\sqrt{ax^2+bx+c}}\,dx = \lambda\int \frac{2ax+b}{\sqrt{ax^2+bx+c}}\,dx + \mu\int \frac{1}{\sqrt{ax^2+bx+c}}\,dx$$

Step IV *Integrate RHS in step III and put the values of* λ *and* μ *obtained in step II.*

Following examples will illustrate the above algorithm.

ILLUSTRATIVE EXAMPLES

BASED ON BASIC CONCEPTS (BASIC)

EXAMPLE 1 *Evaluate:*

(i) $\int \frac{2x+3}{\sqrt{x^2+4x+1}}\,dx$ (ii) $\int \frac{x+2}{\sqrt{x^2+5x+6}}\,dx$ [CBSE 2010] (iii) $\int \sqrt{\frac{1+x}{x}}\,dx$

SOLUTION (i) Let $2x + 3 = \lambda\frac{d}{dx}(x^2+4x+1) + \mu$. Then, $2x+3 = \lambda(2x+4)+\mu$.

Comparing the coefficients of like powers of x, we get: $2\lambda = 2$ and $4\lambda + \mu = 3 \Rightarrow \lambda = 1$ and $\mu = -1$

$$\therefore \quad I = \int \frac{2x+3}{\sqrt{x^2+4x+1}}\,dx = \int \frac{(2x+4)-1}{\sqrt{x^2+4x+1}}\,dx = \int \frac{2x+4}{\sqrt{x^2+4x+1}}\,dx - \int \frac{1}{\sqrt{x^2+4x+1}}\,dx$$

$$\Rightarrow \quad I = \int \frac{dt}{\sqrt{t}} - \int \frac{1}{\sqrt{(x+2)^2-(\sqrt{3})^2}}\,dx, \text{ where } t = x^2+4x+1$$

$$\Rightarrow \quad I = 2\sqrt{t} - \log\left|(x+2)+\sqrt{x^2+4x+1}\right| + C = 2\sqrt{x^2+4x+1} - \log|x+2+\sqrt{x^2+4x+1}| + C$$

(ii) Let $x + 2 = \lambda\frac{d}{dx}(x^2+5x+6)+\mu$. Then, $x+2 = \lambda(2x+5)+\mu$. Comparing the coefficients of like powers of x, we get: $1 = 2\lambda$ and $5\lambda + \mu = 2 \Rightarrow \lambda = \frac{1}{2}$ and $\mu = -\frac{1}{2}$

$$\therefore \ I = \int \frac{x+2}{\sqrt{x^2+5x+6}}\,dx = \int \frac{\frac{1}{2}(2x+5)-\frac{1}{2}}{\sqrt{x^2+5x+6}}\,dx = \frac{1}{2}\int \frac{2x+5}{\sqrt{x^2+5x+6}}\,dx - \frac{1}{2}\int \frac{1}{\sqrt{x^2+5x+6}}\,dx$$

$$\Rightarrow I = \frac{1}{2}\int \frac{dt}{\sqrt{t}} - \frac{1}{2}\int \frac{1}{\sqrt{\left(x+\frac{5}{2}\right)^2 - \left(\frac{1}{2}\right)^2}}\,dx, \text{ where } t = x^2+5x+6$$

$$\Rightarrow I = \sqrt{t} - \frac{1}{2}\log\left|\left(x+\frac{5}{2}\right)+\sqrt{x^2+5x+6}\right| + C = \sqrt{x^2+5x+6} - \frac{1}{2}\log\left|\left(x+\frac{5}{2}\right)+\sqrt{x^2+5x+6}\right| + C$$

(iii) Let $I = \int \sqrt{\frac{1+x}{x}}\,dx = \int \sqrt{\frac{1+x}{x}} \times \sqrt{\frac{1+x}{1+x}}\,dx = \int \frac{1+x}{\sqrt{x(1+x)}}\,dx = \int \frac{1+x}{\sqrt{x^2+x}}\,dx$

Let $x+1 = \lambda \frac{d}{dx}(x^2+x) + \mu$. Then, $x+1 = \lambda(2x+1)+\mu$.

Comparing the coefficients of like powers of x, we get: $1 = 2\lambda$ and $\lambda + \mu = 1 \Rightarrow \lambda = \frac{1}{2}, \mu = \frac{1}{2}$

$$\therefore I = \int \sqrt{\frac{1+x}{x}}\,dx = \int \frac{x+1}{\sqrt{x^2+x}}\,dx = \int \frac{\frac{1}{2}(2x+1)+\frac{1}{2}}{\sqrt{x^2+x}}\,dx = \frac{1}{2}\int \frac{2x+1}{\sqrt{x^2+x}}\,dx + \frac{1}{2}\int \frac{1}{\sqrt{x^2+x}}\,dx$$

$$\Rightarrow I = \frac{1}{2}\int \frac{1}{\sqrt{t}}\,dt + \frac{1}{2}\int \frac{1}{\sqrt{\left(x+\frac{1}{2}\right)^2 - \left(\frac{1}{2}\right)^2}}\,dx, \text{ where } t = x^2+x$$

$$\Rightarrow I = \sqrt{t} + \frac{1}{2}\log\left|\left(x+\frac{1}{2}\right)+\sqrt{x^2+x}\right| + C = \sqrt{x^2+x} + \frac{1}{2}\log\left|\left(x+\frac{1}{2}\right)+\sqrt{x^2+x}+C\right.$$

EXAMPLE 2 *Evaluate:*

(i) $\int \sqrt{\frac{a-x}{a+x}}\,dx$ (ii) $\int x\sqrt{\frac{a^2-x^2}{a^2+x^2}}\,dx$

SOLUTION (i) Let $I = \int \sqrt{\frac{a-x}{a+x}}\,dx = \int \sqrt{\frac{a-x}{a+x} \times \frac{a-x}{a-x}}\,dx = \int \frac{a-x}{\sqrt{a^2-x^2}}\,dx$. Then,

$$I = \int \frac{a}{\sqrt{a^2-x^2}}\,dx - \int \frac{x}{\sqrt{a^2-x^2}}\,dx$$

$$\Rightarrow \quad I = a\int \frac{1}{\sqrt{a^2-x^2}}\,dx + \frac{1}{2}\int \frac{-2x}{\sqrt{a^2-x^2}}\,dx = a\sin^{-1}\left(\frac{x}{a}\right) + \frac{1}{2}\int \frac{-2x}{\sqrt{a^2-x^2}}\,dx$$

Putting $a^2 - x^2 = t$ and $-2x\,dx = dt$, we get

$$I = a\sin^{-1}\left(\frac{x}{a}\right) + \frac{1}{2}\int \frac{dt}{\sqrt{t}} = a\sin^{-1}\left(\frac{x}{a}\right) + \frac{1}{2}\left(\frac{t^{1/2}}{1/2}\right) + C$$

$$\Rightarrow \quad I = a\sin^{-1}\left(\frac{x}{a}\right) + \sqrt{t} + C = a\sin^{-1}\left(\frac{x}{a}\right) + \sqrt{a^2-x^2} + C$$

(ii) Let $I = \int x\sqrt{\frac{a^2-x^2}{a^2+x^2}}\,dx$. Putting $x^2 = t$, and $2x\,dx = dt$ or, $dx = \frac{dt}{2x}$, we get

$$I = \int x\sqrt{\frac{a^2-t}{a^2+t}}\,\frac{dt}{2x} = \frac{1}{2}\int \sqrt{\frac{a^2-t}{a^2+t}}\,dt = \frac{1}{2}\int \sqrt{\frac{a^2-t}{a^2+t} \times \frac{a^2-t}{a^2-t}}\,dt$$

$$\Rightarrow \quad I = \frac{1}{2}\int \frac{a^2 - t}{\sqrt{a^4 - t^2}}\, dt = \frac{1}{2}\int \frac{a^2}{\sqrt{a^4 - t^2}}\, dt - \frac{1}{2}\int \frac{t\, dt}{\sqrt{a^4 - t^2}}$$

$$\Rightarrow \quad I = \frac{1}{2}a^2 \int \frac{1}{\sqrt{(a^2)^2 - t^2}}\, dt + \frac{1}{4}\int \frac{-2t}{\sqrt{a^4 - t^2}}\, dt$$

$$\Rightarrow \quad I = \frac{1}{2}a^2 \sin^{-1}\left(\frac{t}{a^2}\right) + \frac{1}{4}\int \frac{du}{\sqrt{u}}, \text{ where } a^4 - t^2 = u$$

$$\Rightarrow \quad I = \frac{1}{2}a^2 \sin^{-1}\left(\frac{t}{a^2}\right) + \frac{1}{4}\left(\frac{u^{1/2}}{1/2}\right) + C$$

$$\Rightarrow \quad I = \frac{1}{2}a^2 \sin^{-1}\left(\frac{t}{a^2}\right) + \frac{1}{2}\sqrt{a^4 - t^2} + C = \frac{1}{2}a^2 \sin^{-1}\left(\frac{x^2}{a^2}\right) + \frac{1}{2}\sqrt{a^4 - x^4} + C$$

EXERCISE 15.21

BASIC

Evaluate the following integrals:

1. $\int \frac{x}{\sqrt{x^2 + 6x + 10}}\, dx$
2. $\int \frac{2x + 1}{\sqrt{x^2 + 2x - 1}}\, dx$
3. $\int \frac{x + 1}{\sqrt{4 + 5x - x^2}}\, dx$
4. $\int \frac{6x - 5}{\sqrt{3x^2 - 5x + 1}}\, dx$
5. $\int \frac{3x + 1}{\sqrt{5 - 2x - x^2}}\, dx$
6. $\int \frac{x}{\sqrt{8 + x - x^2}}\, dx$
7. $\int \frac{x + 2}{\sqrt{x^2 + 2x - 1}}\, dx$
8. $\int \frac{x + 2}{\sqrt{x^2 - 1}}\, dx$ [NCERT]
9. $\int \frac{x - 1}{\sqrt{x^2 + 1}}\, dx$ [NCERT]
10. $\int \frac{x}{\sqrt{x^2 + x + 1}}\, dx$
11. $\int \frac{x + 1}{\sqrt{x^2 + 1}}\, dx$
12. $\int \frac{3x + 5}{\sqrt{x^2 + 2x + 4}}\, dx$ [CBSE 2024]
13. $\int \frac{3x + 1}{\sqrt{5 - 2x - x^2}}\, dx$
14. $\int \sqrt{\frac{1 - x}{1 + x}}\, dx$
15. $\int \frac{2x + 1}{\sqrt{x^2 + 4x + 3}}\, dx$ [CBSE2000]
16. $\int \frac{2x + 3}{\sqrt{x^2 + 4x + 5}}\, dx$ [CBSE 2001]
17. $\int \frac{5x + 3}{\sqrt{x^2 + 4x + 10}}\, dx$ [CBSE 2011, 12]
18. $\int \frac{x + 2}{\sqrt{x^2 + 2x + 3}}$ [CBSE 2013]
19. $\int \frac{5x - 3}{\sqrt{1 + 4x - 2x^2}}\, dx$ [CBSE 2024]

ANSWERS

1. $\sqrt{x^2 + 6x + 10} - 3 \log |(x + 3) + \sqrt{x^2 + 6x + 10}| + C$
2. $2\sqrt{x^2 + 2x - 1} - \log |x + 1 + \sqrt{x^2 + 2x - 1}| + C$
3. $-\sqrt{4 + 5x - x^2} + \frac{7}{2}\sin^{-1}\left(\frac{2x - 5}{\sqrt{41}}\right) + C$
4. $2\sqrt{3x^2 - 5x + 1} + C$
5. $-3\sqrt{5 - 2x - x^2} - 2\sin^{-1}\left(\frac{x + 1}{\sqrt{6}}\right) + C$
6. $-\sqrt{8 + x - x^2} + \frac{1}{2}\sin^{-1}\left(\frac{2x - 1}{\sqrt{33}}\right) + C$
7. $\sqrt{x^2 + 2x - 1} + \log |(x + 1) + \sqrt{x^2 + 2x - 1}| + C$
8. $\sqrt{x^2 - 1} + 2\log |x + \sqrt{x^2 - 1}| + C$

9. $\sqrt{x^2+1} - \log|x+\sqrt{x^2+1}| + C$

10. $\sqrt{x^2+x+1} - \frac{1}{2}\left\{\log\left|\frac{2x+1}{2} + \sqrt{x^2+x+1}\right|\right\} + C$

11. $\sqrt{x^2+1} + \log|x+\sqrt{x^2+1}| + C$

12. $3\sqrt{x^2+2x+4} - \frac{1}{2}\log|x+1+\sqrt{x^2+2x+4}| + C$

13. $-3\sqrt{5-2x-x^2} - 2\sin^{-1}\left(\frac{x+1}{\sqrt{6}}\right) + C$

14. $\sin^{-1}x + \sqrt{1-x^2} + C$

15. $2\sqrt{x^2+4x+3} - 3\log|x+2+\sqrt{x^2+4x+3}| + C$

16. $2\sqrt{x^2+4x+5} - \log\left|x+2+\sqrt{x^2+4x+5}\right| + C$

17. $5\sqrt{x^2+4x+10} - 7\log\left|x+2+\sqrt{x^2+4x+10}\right| + C$

18. $\sqrt{x^2+2x+3} + \log\left|(x+1)+\sqrt{x^2+2x+3}\right| + C$

19. $-\frac{5}{2}\sqrt{1+4x-2x^2} + \sqrt{2}\sin^{-1}\left\{\frac{2}{3}(x-1)\right\} + C$

15.10.8 INTEGRALS OF THE FORM $\int \frac{1}{a\sin^2 x + b\cos^2 x}dx, \int \frac{1}{a + b\sin^2 x}dx,$ $\int \frac{1}{a+b\cos^2 x}dx, \int \frac{1}{(a\sin x + b\cos x)^2}dx, \int \frac{1}{a+b\sin^2 x + c\cos^2 x}dx$

To evaluate this type of integrals we use the following algorithm.

ALGORITHM

Step I *Divide numerator and denominator both by* $\cos^2 x$.

Step II *Replace* $\sec^2 x$, *if any, in denominator by* $1+\tan^2 x$.

Step III *Put* $\tan x = t$ *so that* $\sec^2 x\, dx = dt$. *This substitution reduces the integral in the form* $\int \frac{1}{at^2+bt+c}dt$.

Step IV *Evaluate the integral obtained in step III by using the methods discussed earlier.*

Following examples will illustrate the procedure.

ILLUSTRATIVE EXAMPLES

BASED ON BASIC CONCEPTS (BASIC)

EXAMPLE 1 *Evaluate:*

(i) $\int \frac{1}{a^2\sin^2 x + b^2\cos^2 x}dx$ (ii) $\int \frac{1}{1+3\sin^2 x + 8\cos^2 x}dx$

(iii) $\int \frac{\sin x}{\sin 3x}dx$ (iv) $\int \frac{1}{(2\sin x + 3\cos x)^2}dx$

SOLUTION (i) Dividing the numerator and denominator of the given integrand by $\cos^2 x$, we get

$$I = \int \frac{1}{a^2\sin^2 x + b^2\cos^2 x}dx = \int \frac{\sec^2 x}{a^2\tan^2 x + b^2}dx$$

Putting $\tan x = t$ and $\sec^2 x\, dx = dt$, we get

$$I = \int \frac{dt}{a^2 t^2 + b^2} = \frac{1}{a^2}\int \frac{dt}{t^2 + (b/a)^2} = \frac{1}{a^2} \times \frac{1}{b/a} \tan^{-1}\left(\frac{t}{b/a}\right) + C$$

$$\Rightarrow \quad I = \frac{1}{ab}\tan^{-1}\left(\frac{at}{b}\right) + C = \frac{1}{ab}\tan^{-1}\left(\frac{a \tan x}{b}\right) + C$$

(ii) Dividing the numerator and denominator of the given integrand by $\cos^2 x$, we get

$$I = \int \frac{1}{1 + 3\sin^2 x + 8\cos^2 x}\, dx$$

$$\Rightarrow \quad I = \int \frac{\sec^2 x}{\sec^2 x + 3\tan^2 x + 8}\, dx = \int \frac{\sec^2 x}{1 + \tan^2 x + 3\tan^2 x + 8}\, dx = \int \frac{\sec^2 x\, dx}{4\tan^2 x + 9}$$

Putting $\tan x = t$ and $\sec^2 x\, dx = dt$, we get

$$\Rightarrow \quad I = \int \frac{dt}{4t^2 + 9} = \frac{1}{4}\int \frac{dt}{t^2 + (3/2)^2} = \frac{1}{4} \times \frac{1}{3/2}\tan^{-1}\left(\frac{t}{3/2}\right) + C$$

$$\Rightarrow \quad I = \frac{1}{6}\tan^{-1}\left(\frac{2t}{3}\right) + C = \frac{1}{6}\tan^{-1}\left(\frac{2\tan x}{3}\right) + C$$

(iii) Let $I = \int \frac{\sin x}{\sin 3x}\, dx = \int \frac{\sin x}{3\sin x - 4\sin^3 x}\, dx = \int \frac{1}{3 - 4\sin^2 x}\, dx$

$$\Rightarrow \quad I = \int \frac{\sec^2 x}{3\sec^2 x - 4\tan^2 x}\, dx \qquad \text{[Dividing numerator and denominator by } \cos^2 x\text{]}$$

Putting $\tan x = t$ and $\sec^2 x\, dx = dt$, we get

$$I = \int \frac{dt}{3(1 + t^2) - 4t^2} = \int \frac{dt}{3 - t^2} = \int \frac{1}{(\sqrt{3})^2 - t^2}\, dt$$

$$\Rightarrow \quad I = \frac{1}{2\sqrt{3}}\log\left|\frac{\sqrt{3} + t}{\sqrt{3} - t}\right| + C = \frac{1}{2\sqrt{3}}\log\left|\frac{\sqrt{3} + \tan x}{\sqrt{3} - \tan x}\right| + C$$

(iv) Dividing the numerator and denominator by $\cos^2 x$, we get

$$I = \int \frac{1}{(2\sin x + 3\cos x)^2}\, dx = \int \frac{\sec^2 x}{(2\tan x + 3)^2}\, dx$$

Putting $\tan x = t$ and $\sec^2 x\, dx = dt$, we get

$$\therefore \quad I = \int \frac{dt}{(2t + 3)^2} = -\frac{1}{2(2t + 3)} + C = -\frac{1}{2(2\tan x + 3)} + C$$

EXAMPLE 2 *Evaluate:* (i) $\int \frac{1}{3 + \sin 2x}\, dx$ (ii) $\int \frac{1}{2 - 3\cos 2x}\, dx$

SOLUTION (i) Let

$$I = \int \frac{1}{3 + \sin 2x}\, dx = \int \frac{1}{3(\sin^2 x + \cos^2 x) + 2\sin x \cos x}\, dx$$

$$\Rightarrow \quad I = \int \frac{\sec^2 x}{3\tan^2 x + 2\tan x + 3}\, dx \qquad \text{[Dividing numerator and denominator by } \cos^2 x\text{]}$$

Putting $\tan x = t$ and $\sec^2 x\, dx = dt$, we get

$$\therefore\ I = \int \frac{dt}{3t^2+2t+3} = \frac{1}{3}\int \frac{dt}{t^2+\frac{2}{3}t+1} = \frac{1}{3}\int \frac{dt}{\left(t+\frac{1}{3}\right)^2+\left(\frac{2\sqrt{2}}{3}\right)^2}$$

$$\Rightarrow I = \frac{1}{3}\times\frac{1}{\left(\frac{2\sqrt{2}}{3}\right)}\tan^{-1}\left(\frac{t+\frac{1}{3}}{\frac{2\sqrt{2}}{3}}\right)+C = \frac{1}{2\sqrt{2}}\tan^{-1}\left(\frac{3t+1}{2\sqrt{2}}\right)+C = \frac{1}{2\sqrt{2}}\tan^{-1}\left(\frac{3\tan x+1}{2\sqrt{2}}\right)+C$$

(ii) Let $I = \int \frac{1}{2-3\cos 2x}\,dx$. Then,

$$\Rightarrow\quad I = \int \frac{1}{2-3(\cos^2 x-\sin^2 x)}\,dx$$

$$\Rightarrow\quad I = \int \frac{\sec^2 x}{2\sec^2 x-3+3\tan^2 x}\,dx \quad \text{[Dividing numerator and denominator by } \cos^2 x]$$

$$\Rightarrow\quad I = \int \frac{\sec^2 x}{2(1+\tan^2 x)-3+3\tan^2 x}\,dx = \int \frac{\sec^2 x}{5\tan^2 x-1}\,dx$$

Putting $\tan x = t$ and $\sec^2 x\,dx = dt$, we get

$$\therefore\quad I = \int \frac{dt}{5t^2-1} = \frac{1}{5}\int \frac{dt}{t^2-\left(\frac{1}{\sqrt{5}}\right)^2} = \frac{1}{5}\times\frac{1}{2\left(\frac{1}{\sqrt{5}}\right)}\log\left|\frac{t-\frac{1}{\sqrt{5}}}{t+\frac{1}{\sqrt{5}}}\right|+C$$

$$\Rightarrow\quad I = \frac{1}{2\sqrt{5}}\log\left|\frac{\sqrt{5}t-1}{\sqrt{5}t+1}\right|+C = \frac{1}{2\sqrt{5}}\log\left|\frac{\sqrt{5}\tan x-1}{\sqrt{5}\tan x+1}\right|+C$$

EXERCISE 15.22

BASIC

Evaluate the following integrals:

1. $\int \frac{1}{4\cos^2 x+9\sin^2 x}\,dx$
2. $\int \frac{1}{4\sin^2 x+5\cos^2 x}\,dx$
3. $\int \frac{2}{2+\sin 2x}\,dx$
4. $\int \frac{\cos x}{\cos 3x}\,dx$
5. $\int \frac{1}{1+3\sin^2 x}\,dx$
6. $\int \frac{1}{3+2\cos^2 x}\,dx$
7. $\int \frac{1}{\cos 2x+3\sin^2 x}\,dx$
8. $\int \frac{\sin 2x}{\sin^4 x+\cos^4 x}\,dx$
9. $\int \frac{1}{\cos x(\sin x+2\cos x)}\,dx$
10. $\int \frac{1}{\sin^2 x+\sin 2x}\,dx$
11. $\int \frac{1}{(\sin x-2\cos x)(2\sin x+\cos x)}\,dx$

ANSWERS

1. $\frac{1}{6}\tan^{-1}\left(\frac{3\tan x}{2}\right)+C$
2. $\frac{1}{2\sqrt{5}}\tan^{-1}\left(\frac{2\tan x}{\sqrt{5}}\right)+C$
3. $\frac{2}{\sqrt{3}}\tan^{-1}\left(\frac{2\tan x+1}{\sqrt{3}}\right)+C$
4. $\frac{1}{2\sqrt{3}}\log\left|\frac{1+\sqrt{3}\tan x}{1-\sqrt{3}\tan x}\right|+C$
5. $\frac{1}{2}\tan^{-1}(2\tan x)+C$
6. $\frac{1}{\sqrt{15}}\tan^{-1}\left(\frac{\sqrt{3}\tan x}{\sqrt{5}}\right)+C$

7. $\frac{1}{\sqrt{2}}\tan^{-1}(\sqrt{2}\tan x)+C$ 8. $\tan^{-1}(\tan^2 x)+C$ 9. $\log|\tan x+2|+C$

10. $\frac{1}{2}\log\left|\frac{\tan x}{\tan x+2}\right|+C$ 11. $\frac{1}{5}\log\left|\frac{\tan x-2}{2\tan x+1}\right|+C$

15.10.9 INTEGRALS OF THE FORM $\int \frac{1}{a\sin x+b\cos x}dx$, $\int \frac{1}{a+b\sin x}dx$, $\int \frac{1}{a+b\cos x}dx$, $\int \frac{1}{a\sin x+b\cos x+c}dx$

To evaluate this type of integrals we use the following algorithm.

ALGORITHM

Step I *Put* $\sin x=\frac{2\tan x/2}{1+\tan^2 x/2}$ *and,* $\cos x=\frac{1-\tan^2 x/2}{1+\tan^2 x/2}$ *and simplify.*

Step II *Replace* $1+\tan^2\frac{x}{2}$ *in the numerator by* $\sec^2\frac{x}{2}$.

Step III *Put* $\tan\frac{x}{2}=t$ *so that* $\frac{1}{2}\sec^2\frac{x}{2}dx=dt$. *This substitution reduces the integral in the form* $\int\frac{1}{at^2+bt+c}dt$.

Step IV *Evaluate the integral obtained in step III by using methods discussed earlier.*

Following examples will illustrate the above procedure.

ILLUSTRATIVE EXAMPLES

BASED ON BASIC CONCEPTS (BASIC)

EXAMPLE 1 *Evaluate:*

(i) $\int\frac{1}{1+\sin x+\cos x}dx$ (ii) $\int\frac{1}{2+\cos x}dx$ (iii) $\int\frac{1+\sin x}{\sin x(1+\cos x)}dx$ (iv) $\int\frac{1}{1-2\sin x}dx$

SOLUTION (i) Putting $\sin x=\frac{2\tan x/2}{1+\tan^2 x/2}$ and $\cos x=\frac{1-\tan^2 x/2}{1+\tan^2 x/2}$, we get

$$I=\int\frac{1}{1+\sin x+\cos x}dx=\int\frac{1}{1+\frac{2\tan x/2}{1+\tan^2 x/2}+\frac{1-\tan^2 x/2}{1+\tan^2 x/2}}dx$$

$$\Rightarrow\quad I=\int\frac{1+\tan^2 x/2}{1+\tan^2 x/2+2\tan x/2+1-\tan^2 x/2}dx=\int\frac{\sec^2 x/2}{2+2\tan x/2}dx$$

Putting $\tan\frac{x}{2}=t$ and $\frac{1}{2}\sec^2\frac{x}{2}dx=dt$ or, $\sec^2\frac{x}{2}dx=2dt$, we get

$$I=\int\frac{2dt}{2+2t}=\int\frac{1}{t+1}dt=\log|t+1|+C=\log\left|\tan\frac{x}{2}+1\right|+C$$

(ii) Let $I=\int\frac{1}{2+\cos x}dx=\int\frac{1}{2+\frac{1-\tan^2 x/2}{1+\tan^2 x/2}}dx$ $\left[\because \cos x=\frac{1-\tan^2 x/2}{1+\tan^2 x/2}\right]$

$$\Rightarrow \quad I = \int \frac{1 + \tan^2 x/2}{2(1 + \tan^2 x/2) + 1 - \tan^2 x/2} dx = \int \frac{\sec^2 x/2}{\tan^2 x/2 + 3} dx$$

Putting $\tan x/2 = t$ and $(1/2 \sec^2 (x/2) = dt$ or, $\sec^2 (x/2)\, dx = 2dt$, we get

$$I = \int \frac{2dt}{t^2 + 3} = 2\int \frac{dt}{t^2 + (\sqrt{3})^2} = \frac{2}{\sqrt{3}} \tan^{-1}\left(\frac{t}{\sqrt{3}}\right) + C = \frac{2}{\sqrt{3}} \tan^{-1}\left(\frac{\tan x/2}{\sqrt{3}}\right) + C$$

(iii) Let $I = \int \frac{1 + \sin x}{\sin x (1 + \cos x)} dx$. Putting $\sin x = \frac{2\tan x/2}{1 + \tan^2 x/2}$ and $\cos x = \frac{1 - \tan^2 x/2}{1 + \tan^2 x/2}$, we get

$$I = \int \frac{1 + \frac{2 \tan x/2}{1 + \tan^2 x/2}}{\frac{2 \tan x/2}{1 + \tan^2 x/2}\left(1 + \frac{1 - \tan^2 x}{1 + \tan^2 x/2}\right)} dx$$

$$\Rightarrow \quad I = \int \frac{(1 + \tan^2 x/2 + 2 \tan x/2)(1 + \tan^2 x/2)}{2 \tan x/2 (1 + \tan^2 x/2 + 1 - \tan^2 x/2)} dx = \int \frac{(1 + \tan x/2)^2 \sec^2 x/2}{4 \tan x/2} dx$$

Putting $\tan x/2 = t$ and $(1/2) \sec^2 (x/2)\, dx = dt$ *or*, $\sec^2 (x/2)\, dx = 2\, dt$, we get

$$I = \int \frac{(1 + t)^2}{4t} 2\, dt = \frac{1}{2}\int \frac{1 + t^2 + 2t}{t} dt = \frac{1}{2}\int \left(\frac{1}{t} + t + 2\right) dt$$

$$\Rightarrow \quad I = \frac{1}{2}\left\{\log|t| + \frac{t^2}{2} + 2t\right\} + C = \frac{1}{2}\left\{\log|\tan x/2| + \frac{\tan^2 x/2}{2} + 2 \tan x/2\right\} + C$$

(iv) Let $I = \int \frac{1}{1 - 2\sin x} dx$. Putting $\sin x = \frac{2 \tan x/2}{1 + \tan^2 x/2}$, we get

$$I = \int \frac{1}{1 - \frac{4 \tan x/2}{1 + \tan^2 x/2}} dx = \int \frac{1 + \tan^2 x/2}{1 + \tan^2 x/2 - 4 \tan x/2} dx = \int \frac{\sec^2 x/2}{1 + \tan^2 x/2 - 4 \tan x/2} dx$$

Putting $\tan x/2 = t$ and $\frac{1}{2} \sec^2 (x/2)\, dx = dt$ or, $\sec^2 (x/2)\, dx = 2dt$, we get

$$I = \int \frac{2}{1 + t^2 - 4t} dt = 2\int \frac{1}{t^2 - 4t + 4 - 4 + 1} dt = 2\int \frac{1}{(t - 2)^2 - (\sqrt{3})^2} dt$$

$$\Rightarrow \quad I = 2 \times \frac{1}{2\sqrt{3}} \log\left|\frac{t - 2 - \sqrt{3}}{t - 2 + \sqrt{3}}\right| + C = \frac{1}{\sqrt{3}} \log\left|\frac{\tan x/2 - 2 - \sqrt{3}}{\tan x/2 - 2 + \sqrt{3}}\right| + C$$

EXERCISE 15.23

BASIC

Evaluate the following integrals:

1. $\int \frac{1}{5 + 4 \cos x} dx$ [CBSE 2003] 2. $\int \frac{1}{5 - 4 \sin x} dx$ 3. $\int \frac{1}{1 - 2 \sin x} dx$

4. $\int \frac{1}{4\cos x - 1}\,dx$ 5. $\int \frac{1}{1-\sin x+\cos x}\,dx$ 6. $\int \frac{1}{3+2\sin x+\cos x}\,dx$ [CBSE 2004]

7. $\int \frac{1}{13+3\cos x+4\sin x}\,dx$ 8. $\int \frac{1}{\cos x-\sin x}\,dx$ 9. $\int \frac{1}{\sin x+\cos x}\,dx$

10. $\int \frac{1}{5-4\cos x}\,dx$ 11. $\int \frac{1}{2+\sin x+\cos x}\,dx$ 12. $\int \frac{1}{\sin x+\sqrt{3}\cos x}\,dx$

13. $\int \frac{1}{\sqrt{3}\sin x+\cos x}\,dx$ 14. $\int \frac{1}{\sin x-\sqrt{3}\cos x}\,dx$ 15. $\int \frac{1}{5+7\cos x+\sin x}\,dx$

ANSWERS

1. $\frac{2}{3}\tan^{-1}\left(\frac{\tan x/2}{3}\right)+C$

2. $\frac{2}{3}\tan^{-1}\left(\frac{5\tan x/2-4}{3}\right)+C$

3. $\frac{1}{\sqrt{3}}\log\left|\frac{\tan\frac{x}{2}-2-\sqrt{3}}{\tan\frac{x}{2}-2+\sqrt{3}}\right|+C$

4. $\frac{1}{\sqrt{15}}\log\left|\frac{\sqrt{3}+\sqrt{5}\tan x/2}{\sqrt{3}-\sqrt{5}\tan x/2}\right|+C$

5. $-\log\left|1-\tan\frac{x}{2}\right|+C$

6. $\tan^{-1}\left(1+\tan\frac{x}{2}\right)+C$

7. $\frac{1}{6}\tan^{-1}\left(\frac{5\tan x/2+2}{6}\right)+C$

8. $\frac{1}{\sqrt{2}}\log\left|\frac{\sqrt{2}+\tan x/2+1}{\sqrt{2}-\tan x/2-1}\right|+C$

9. $\frac{1}{\sqrt{2}}\log\left|\frac{\sqrt{2}+\tan x/2-1}{\sqrt{2}-\tan x/2+1}\right|+C$

10. $\frac{2}{3}\tan^{-1}\left(3\tan\frac{x}{2}\right)+C$

11. $\sqrt{2}\tan^{-1}\left(\frac{\tan(x/2)+1}{\sqrt{2}}\right)+C$

12. $\frac{1}{2}\log\left|\frac{1+\sqrt{3}\tan x/2}{3-\sqrt{3}\tan x/2}\right|+C$

13. $\frac{1}{2}\log\left|\tan\left(\frac{x}{2}+\frac{\pi}{12}\right)\right|+C$

14. $\frac{1}{2}\log\left|\tan\left(\frac{x}{2}-\frac{\pi}{6}\right)\right|+C$

15. $\frac{1}{5}\log_e\left|\frac{\tan x/2+2}{\tan x/2-3}\right|+C$

15.10.10 ALTERNATIVE METHOD TO EVALUATE INTEGRALS OF THE FORM $\int \frac{1}{a\sin x+b\cos x}\,dx$

To evaluate this type of integrals, we substitute

$$a=r\cos\theta, b=r\sin\theta \text{ so that } r=\sqrt{a^2+b^2} \text{ and, } \theta=\tan^{-1}\left(\frac{b}{a}\right)$$

$\therefore$ $a\sin x+b\cos x = r\cos\theta\sin x+r\sin\theta\cos x = r\sin(x+\theta)$

So, $I = \int \frac{1}{a\sin x+b\cos x}\,dx = \frac{1}{r}\int \frac{1}{\sin(x+\theta)}\,dx = \frac{1}{r}\int \text{cosec}\,(x+\theta)\,dx$

$\Rightarrow$ $I = \frac{1}{r}\log\left|\tan\left(\frac{x}{2}+\frac{\theta}{2}\right)\right|+C = \frac{1}{\sqrt{a^2+b^2}}\log\left|\tan\left(\frac{x}{2}+\frac{1}{2}\tan^{-1}\frac{b}{a}\right)\right|+C$

Following examples will illustrate the above algorithm.

ILLUSTRATIVE EXAMPLES

BASED ON BASIC CONCEPTS (BASIC)

EXAMPLE 1 *Evaluate:* (i) $\int \frac{1}{\sqrt{3}\sin x+\cos x}\,dx$ (ii) $\int \frac{1}{\sin x+\sqrt{3}\cos x}\,dx$

SOLUTION (i) Let $\sqrt{3}=r\sin\theta$ and $1=r\cos\theta$. Then

$$r=\sqrt{(\sqrt{3})^2+1^2} \text{ and } \tan\theta=\frac{\sqrt{3}}{1}\Rightarrow r=2 \text{ and } \theta=\frac{\pi}{3}$$

$$\therefore \quad I=\int \frac{1}{\sqrt{3}\sin x+\cos x}\,dx=\int \frac{1}{r\sin\theta\sin x+r\cos\theta\cos x}\,dx$$

$$\Rightarrow \quad I=\frac{1}{r}\int \frac{1}{\cos(x-\theta)}\,dx=\frac{1}{r}\int \sec(x-\theta)\,dx=\frac{1}{r}\log\left|\tan\left(\frac{\pi}{4}+\frac{x}{2}-\frac{\theta}{2}\right)\right|+C$$

$$\Rightarrow \quad I=\frac{1}{2}\log\left|\tan\left(\frac{\pi}{4}+\frac{x}{2}-\frac{\pi}{6}\right)\right|+C=\frac{1}{2}\log\left|\tan\left(\frac{x}{2}+\frac{\pi}{12}\right)\right|+C$$

(ii) Let $1=r\cos\theta$ and $\sqrt{3}=r\sin\theta$. Then, $r=\sqrt{1^2+(\sqrt{3})^2}$ and $\tan\theta=\frac{\sqrt{3}}{1}\Rightarrow r=2$ and $\theta=\frac{\pi}{3}$

$$\therefore \quad I=\int \frac{1}{\sin x+\sqrt{3}\cos x}\,dx=\frac{1}{r}\int \frac{1}{\sin x\cos\theta+\cos x\sin\theta}\,dx=\frac{1}{r}\int \frac{1}{\sin(x+\theta)}\,dx$$

$$\Rightarrow \quad I=\frac{1}{r}\int \operatorname{cosec}(x+\theta)\,dx=\frac{1}{r}\log\left|\tan\left(\frac{x}{2}+\frac{\theta}{2}\right)\right|+C=\frac{1}{2}\log\left|\tan\left(\frac{x}{2}+\frac{\pi}{6}\right)\right|+C$$

15.10.11 INTEGRALS OF THE FORM $\int \frac{a\sin x+b\cos x}{c\sin x+d\cos x}\,dx$

To evaluate this type of integrals, we use the following algorithm.

ALGORITHM

Step I *Write, Numerator* $=\lambda$ *(Diff. of denominator)* $+\mu$ *(Denominator)*

i.e. $a\sin x+b\cos x=\lambda(c\cos x-d\sin x)+\mu(c\sin x+d\cos x)$

Step II *Obtain the values of* λ *and* μ *by equating the coefficients of* $\sin x$ *and* $\cos x$ *on both the sides.*

Step III *Replace numerator in the integrand by* $\lambda(c\cos x-d\sin x)+\mu(c\sin x+d\cos x)$ *to obtain*

$$\int \frac{a\sin x+b\cos x}{c\sin x+d\cos x}\,dx=\lambda\int \frac{c\cos x-d\sin x}{c\sin x+d\cos x}\,dx+\mu\int \frac{c\sin x+d\cos x}{c\sin x+d\cos x\,dx}$$

$$=\lambda\log|c\sin x+d\cos x|+\mu x+C$$

Following examples will illustrate the above procedure.

ILLUSTRATIVE EXAMPLES

BASED ON BASIC CONCEPTS (BASIC)

EXAMPLE 1 *Evaluate:* (i) $\int \frac{3\sin x+2\cos x}{3\cos x+2\sin x}\,dx$ (ii) $\int \frac{1}{1+\tan x}\,dx$

SOLUTION (i) Let $I=\int \frac{3\sin x+2\cos x}{3\cos x+2\sin x}\,dx$

Let $3\sin x+2\cos x=\lambda\frac{d}{dx}(3\cos x+2\sin x)+\mu(3\cos x+2\sin x)$

i.e. $3\sin x + 2\cos x = \lambda(-3\sin x + 2\cos x) + \mu(3\cos x + 2\sin x)$

Comparing the coefficients of sin x and cos x on both sides, we get

$$-3\lambda + 2\mu = 3 \text{ and } 2\lambda + 3\mu = 2 \Rightarrow \mu = \frac{12}{13} \text{ and } \lambda = -\frac{5}{13}$$

$$\therefore \quad I = \int \frac{\lambda(-3\sin x + 2\cos x) + \mu(3\cos x + 2\sin x)}{3\cos x + 2\sin x}\, dx$$

$$\Rightarrow \quad I = \mu\int 1\cdot dx + \lambda\int \frac{-3\sin x + 2\cos x}{3\cos x + 2\sin x}\, dx = \mu x + \lambda\int \frac{dt}{t}, \text{ where } t = 3\cos x + 2\sin x$$

$$\Rightarrow \quad I = \mu x + \lambda \log|t| + C = \frac{12}{13}x - \frac{5}{13}\log|3\cos x + 2\sin x| + C$$

(ii) $$I = \int \frac{1}{1+\tan x}\, dx = \int \frac{\cos x}{\cos x + \sin x}\, dx$$

Let $\cos x = \lambda \frac{d}{dx}(\cos x + \sin x) + \mu(\cos x + \sin x)$. Then,

$$\cos x = \lambda(-\sin x + \cos x) + \mu(\sin x + \cos x)$$

Comparing the coefficients of sin x and cos x on both sides, we get :

$$-\lambda + \mu = 0 \text{ and } \lambda + \mu = 1 \Rightarrow \lambda = \mu = \frac{1}{2}$$

$$\therefore \quad I = \int \frac{\cos x}{\cos x + \sin x}\, dx = \int \frac{1/2(-\sin x + \cos x) + 1/2(\cos x + \sin x)}{\cos x + \sin x}\, dx$$

$$\Rightarrow \quad I = \frac{1}{2}\int \frac{-\sin x + \cos x}{\cos x + \sin x}\, dx + \frac{1}{2}\int \frac{\cos x + \sin x}{\cos x + \sin x}\, dx$$

$$\Rightarrow \quad I = \frac{1}{2}\int \frac{dt}{t} + \frac{1}{2}\int 1\cdot dx, \text{ where } t = \cos x + \sin x$$

$$\Rightarrow \quad I = \frac{1}{2}\log|t| + \frac{1}{2}x + C = \frac{1}{2}x + \frac{1}{2}\log|\sin x + \cos x| + C$$

EXAMPLE 2 *Evaluate:* $\int \frac{1}{1+\cot x}\, dx$

SOLUTION Let $I = \int \frac{1}{1+\cot x}\, dx = \int \frac{1}{1+\frac{\cos x}{\sin x}}\, dx = \int \frac{\sin x}{\sin x + \cos x}\, dx$

Let $\sin x = \lambda \frac{d}{dx}(\sin x + \cos x) + \mu(\sin x + \cos x)$ i.e. $\sin x = \lambda(\cos x - \sin x) + \mu(\sin x + \cos x)$

Comparing the coefficients of sin x and cos x on both sides, we get

$$0 = \lambda + \mu \text{ and } 1 = -\lambda + \mu \Rightarrow \lambda = -1/2, \mu = 1/2$$

$$\therefore \quad I = \int \frac{\lambda(\cos x - \sin x) + \mu(\sin x + \cos x)}{\sin x + \cos x}\, dx = \lambda\int \frac{\cos x - \sin x}{\sin x + \cos x}\, dx + \mu\int \frac{\sin x + \cos x}{\sin x + \cos x}\, dx$$

$$\Rightarrow I = \lambda\int \frac{dt}{t} + \mu\int 1\cdot dx, \quad \text{where } t = \sin x + \cos x$$

$$\Rightarrow I = \lambda\log|t| + \mu x + C = -(1/2)\log|\sin x + \cos x| + (1/2)x + C$$

15.10.12 INTEGRALS OF THE FORM $\int \frac{a\sin x + b\cos x + c}{p\sin x + q\cos x + r}\, dx$

To evaluate this type of integrals, we use the following algorithm.

ALGORITHM

Step I *Write: Numerator* $= \lambda$ *(Diff. of denominator)* $+ \mu$ *(Denominator)* $+ \nu$

i.e. $a\sin x + b\cos x + c = \lambda(p\cos x - q\sin x) + \mu(p\sin x + q\cos x + r) + \nu$

Step II *Obtain the values of* λ and μ *by equating the coefficients of* $\sin x$ and $\cos x$ *and the constant terms on both the sides.*

Step III *Replace the numerator in the integrand by* $\lambda\,(p\cos x - q\sin x) + \mu\,(p\sin x + q\cos x + r) + \nu$ *to obtain*

$$I = \int \frac{a\sin x + b\cos x + c}{p\sin x + q\cos x + r}\,dx$$

$$\Rightarrow \quad I = \lambda\int \frac{p\cos x - q\sin x}{p\sin x + q\cos x + r}\,dx + \mu\int \frac{p\sin x + q\cos x + r}{p\sin x + q\cos x + r} + \nu\int \frac{1}{p\sin x + q\cos x + r}\,dx$$

$$\Rightarrow \quad I = \lambda\log|p\sin x + q\cos x + r| + \mu\,x + \nu\int \frac{1}{p\sin x + q\cos x + r}\,dx$$

Step IV *Evaluate the integral on RHS in step III by using the method discussed earlier.*

The following example will illustrates the procedure.

ILLUSTRATIVE EXAMPLES

BASED ON BASIC CONCEPTS (BASIC)

EXAMPLE *Evaluate:* $\displaystyle\int \frac{3\cos x + 2}{\sin x + 2\cos x + 3}\,dx$

SOLUTION Let $I = \displaystyle\int \frac{3\cos x + 2}{\sin x + 2\cos x + 3}\,dx$

Let $3\cos x + 2 = \lambda(\sin x + 2\cos x + 3) + \mu(\cos x - 2\sin x) + \nu$

Comparing the coefficients of $\sin x$, $\cos x$ and constant term on both sides, we get

$$\lambda - 2\mu = 0,\ 2\lambda + \mu = 3,\ 3\lambda + \nu = 2 \Rightarrow \lambda = \frac{6}{5},\ \mu = \frac{3}{5} \text{ and } \nu = -\frac{8}{5}$$

$$\therefore \quad I = \int \frac{\lambda(\sin x + 2\cos x + 3) + \mu(\cos x - 2\sin x) + \nu}{\sin x + 2\cos x + 3}\,dx$$

$$\Rightarrow \quad I = \lambda\int dx + \mu\int \frac{\cos x - 2\sin x}{\sin x + 2\cos x + 3}\,dx + \nu\int \frac{1}{\sin x + 2\cos x + 3}\,dx$$

$$\Rightarrow \quad I = \lambda x + \mu\log|\sin x + 2\cos x + 3| + \nu I_1, \text{ where } I_1 = \int \frac{1}{\sin x + 2\cos x + 3}\,dx$$

Putting $\sin x = \dfrac{2\tan x/2}{1 + \tan^2 x/2}$ and $\cos x = \dfrac{1 - \tan^2 x/2}{1 + \tan^2 x/2}$, we get

$$I_1 = \int \frac{1}{\dfrac{2\tan x/2}{1 + \tan^2 x/2} + \dfrac{2(1 - \tan^2 x/2)}{1 + \tan^2 x/2} + 3}\,dx$$

$$\Rightarrow I_1 = \int \frac{1 + \tan^2 x/2}{2\tan x/2 + 2 - 2\tan^2 x/2 + 3(1 + \tan^2 x/2)}\,dx = \int \frac{\sec^2 x/2}{\tan^2 x/2 + 2\tan x/2 + 5}\,dx$$

Putting $\tan\dfrac{x}{2} = t$ and $\dfrac{1}{2}\sec^2\dfrac{x}{2}\,dx = dt$ or, $\sec^2\dfrac{x}{2}\,dx = 2\,dt$, we get

$$I_1 = \int \frac{2dt}{t^2 + 2t + 5} = 2\int \frac{dt}{(t+1)^2 + 2^2} = \frac{2}{2}\tan^{-1}\left(\frac{t+1}{2}\right) = \tan^{-1}\left(\frac{\tan\frac{x}{2} + 1}{2}\right)$$

$\therefore \quad I = \lambda x + \mu \log|\sin x + 2\cos x + 3| + \nu \tan^{-1}\left(\frac{\tan\frac{x}{2}+1}{2}\right) + C$

$\Rightarrow \quad I = \frac{6}{5}x + \frac{3}{5}\log|\sin x + 2\cos x + 3| - \frac{8}{5}\tan^{-1}\left(\frac{\tan\frac{x}{2}+1}{2}\right) + C$

EXERCISE 15.24

BASIC

Evaluate the following integrals:

1. $\int \frac{1}{1-\cot x}\,dx$
2. $\int \frac{1}{1-\tan x}\,dx$
3. $\int \frac{3+2\cos x+4\sin x}{2\sin x+\cos x+3}\,dx$
4. $\int \frac{1}{p+q\tan x}\,dx$
5. $\int \frac{5\cos x+6}{2\cos x+\sin x+3}\,dx$
6. $\int \frac{2\sin x+3\cos x}{3\sin x+4\cos x}\,dx$
7. $\int \frac{1}{3+4\cot x}\,dx$
8. $\int \frac{2\tan x+3}{3\tan x+4}\,dx$
9. $\int \frac{1}{4+3\tan x}\,dx$
10. $\int \frac{8\cot x+1}{3\cot x+2}\,dx$
11. $\int \frac{4\sin x+5\cos x}{5\sin x+4\cos x}\,dx$

ANSWERS

1. $\frac{1}{2}x + \frac{1}{2}\log|\sin x - \cos x| + C$
2. $\frac{1}{2}x - \frac{1}{2}\log|\sin x - \cos x| + C$
3. $2x - 3\tan^{-1}\left(\tan\frac{x}{2}+1\right) + C$
4. $\frac{p}{p^2+q^2}x + \frac{q}{p^2+q^2}\log|p\cos x + q\sin x| + C$
5. $2x + \log|2\cos x + \sin x + 3| + C$
6. $\frac{18}{25}x + \frac{1}{25}\log|3\sin x + 4\cos x| + C$
7. $\frac{3}{25}x - \frac{4}{25}\log|3\sin x + 4\cos x| + C$
8. $\frac{18}{25}x + \frac{1}{25}\log|3\sin x + 4\cos x| + C$
9. $\frac{4}{25}x + \frac{3}{25}\log|4\cos x + 3\sin x| + C$
10. $2x + \log|2\sin x + 3\cos x| + C$
11. $\frac{40}{41}x + \frac{9}{41}\log|5\sin x + 4\cos x| + C$

15.11 INTEGRATION BY PARTS

THEOREM *If u and v are two functions of x, then*

$$\int uv\,dx = u\left(\int v\,dx\right) - \int\left\{\frac{du}{dx}\int v\,dx\right\}dx$$

i.e. *The integral of the product of two functions = (First function) × (Integral of second function) – Integral of {(Diff. of first function) × (integral of second function)}*

PROOF For any two functions $f(x)$ and $g(x)$, we know that

$$\frac{d}{dx}\{f(x)\cdot g(x)\} = f(x)\cdot\frac{d}{dx}\{g(x)\} + g(x)\cdot\frac{d}{dx}\{f(x)\}$$

$$\therefore \quad \int\left\{f(x)\cdot\frac{d}{dx}\{g(x)\} + g(x)\cdot\frac{d}{dx}\{f(x)\}\right\}dx = f(x)\,g(x)$$

$$\Rightarrow \quad \int \left\{ f(x) \cdot \frac{d}{dx}\{g(x)\} \right\} dx + \int \left\{ g(x) \cdot \frac{d}{dx}\{f(x)\} \right\} dx = f(x)\, g(x)$$

$$\Rightarrow \quad \int \left\{ f(x) \cdot \frac{d}{dx}\{g(x)\} \right\} dx = f(x) \cdot g(x) - \int \left\{ g(x) \cdot \frac{d}{dx}\{f(x)\} \right\} dx \qquad \text{...(i)}$$

Let $f(x) = u$ and $\frac{d}{dx}\{g(x)\} = v$ so that $g(x) = \int v\, dx$. Substituting these in (i), we get

$$\therefore \quad \int uv\, dx = u\left\{\int v\, dx\right\} - \int \left\{\frac{du}{dx} \cdot \int v\, dx\right\} dx$$

NOTE 1 *Proper choice of first and second function —*

Integration with the help of the above rule is called the integration by parts. In the above rule there are two terms on RHS and in both the terms the integral of the second function is involved. Therefore in the product of two functions if one of the two functions is not directly integrable (e.g., $\log x$, $\sin^{-1} x$, $\cos^{-1} x$, $\tan^{-1} x$ etc.), we take it as the first function and the remaining function is taken as the second function. If there is no other function, then unity is taken as the second function. If in the integral both the functions are easily integrable, then the first function is chosen in such a way that the derivative of the function is a simple function and the function thus obtained under the integral sign is easily integrable than the original function.

NOTE 2 *We can also choose the first function as the function which comes first in the word* **ILATE**, *where*

I – stands for the inverse trigonometric function ($\sin^{-1} x$, $\cos^{-1} x$, $\tan^{-1} x$ etc.)

L – stands for the logarithmic functions

A – stands for the algebraic functions

T – stands for the trigonometric functions

E – stands for the exponential functions

ILLUSTRATIVE EXAMPLES

BASED ON BASIC CONCEPTS (BASIC)

EXAMPLE 1 *Evaluate:*

(i) $\int x \sin 3x\, dx$ [NCERT] (ii) $\int x \sec^2 x\, dx$ [NCERT]

(iii) $\int x \log x\, dx$ [NCERT] (iv) $\int x \sin^2 x\, dx$

SOLUTION (i) Here both the functions viz. x and $\sin 3x$ are easily integrable and the derivative of x is one, a less complicated function. Therefore, we take x as the first function and $\sin 3x$ as the second function.

$$\therefore \quad I = \int \underset{\text{I}}{x} \underset{\text{II}}{\sin 3x}\, dx = x\left\{\int \sin 3x\, dx\right\} - \int \left\{\frac{d}{dx}(x) \times \int \sin 3x\, dx\right\} dx$$

$$\Rightarrow \quad I = x \times -\frac{1}{3}\cos 3x - \int \left\{-\frac{1}{3}\cos 3x\right\} dx$$

$$\Rightarrow \quad I = -\frac{1}{3} x \cos 3x + \frac{1}{3}\int \cos 3x\, dx = -\frac{1}{3} x \cos 3x + \frac{1}{9}\sin 3x + C.$$

(ii) Let $I = \int \underset{\text{I}}{x} \underset{\text{II}}{\sec^2 x}\, dx$. Then,

$$I = x\left\{\int \sec^2 x\, dx\right\} - \int \left\{\frac{d}{dx}(x) \times \int \sec^2 x\, dx\right\} dx$$

$$\Rightarrow \quad I = x \tan x - \int 1 \times \tan x \, dx = x \tan x + \log|\cos x| + C$$

(iii) Let $I = \int \underset{\text{II}}{x} \underset{\text{I}}{\log x} \, dx$. Then,

$$I = \log x \left\{ \int x \, dx \right\} - \int \left\{ \frac{d}{dx}(\log x) \times \int x \, dx \right\} dx = (\log x) \frac{x^2}{2} - \int \frac{1}{x} \times \frac{x^2}{2} \, dx$$

$$\Rightarrow \quad I = \frac{x^2}{2} \log x - \frac{1}{2} \int x \, dx = \frac{x^2}{2} \log x - \frac{1}{2}\left(\frac{x^2}{2}\right) + C = \frac{x^2}{2} \log x - \frac{1}{4} x^2 + C$$

(iv) Let $I = \int x \sin^2 x \, dx$. Then,

$$I = \int x \left\{ \frac{1 - \cos 2x}{2} \right\} dx = \frac{1}{2} \int x \, dx - \frac{1}{2} \int \underset{\text{I}}{x} \underset{\text{II}}{\cos 2x} \, dx$$

$$\Rightarrow \quad I = \frac{1}{2}\left(\frac{x^2}{2}\right) - \frac{1}{2}\left[x \left\{ \int \cos 2x \, dx \right\} - \int \left\{ \frac{d}{dx}(x) \times \int \cos 2x \, dx \right\} dx \right]$$

$$\Rightarrow \quad I = \frac{1}{4} x^2 - \frac{1}{2} \left\{ \frac{x}{2} \sin 2x - \int \frac{\sin 2x}{2} \, dx \right\} = \frac{x^2}{4} - \frac{1}{2} \left\{ \frac{x}{2} \sin 2x - \frac{1}{2} \int \sin 2x \, dx \right\}$$

$$\Rightarrow \quad I = \frac{x^2}{4} - \frac{1}{2} \left\{ \frac{x}{2} \sin 2x - \frac{1}{2}\left(-\frac{1}{2} \cos 2x \right) \right\} + C = \frac{1}{4} x^2 - \frac{x}{4} \sin 2x - \frac{1}{8} \cos 2x + C$$

EXAMPLE 2 *Evaluate:* (i) $\int x^2 \sin x \, dx$ (ii) $\int x^2 e^x \, dx$ **[NCERT]**

SOLUTION (i) Let $I = \int \underset{\text{I}}{x^2} \underset{\text{II}}{\sin x} \, dx$. Then,

$$I = x^2 \left\{ \int \sin x \, dx \right\} - \int \left\{ \frac{d}{dx}(x^2) \int \sin x \, dx \right\} dx$$

$$\Rightarrow \quad I = -x^2 \cos x - \int 2x(-\cos x) \, dx = -x^2 \cos x + 2 \int \underset{\text{I}}{x} \underset{\text{II}}{\cos x} \, dx$$

$$\Rightarrow \quad I = -x^2 \cos x + 2 \left[x \left\{ \int \cos x \, dx \right\} - \int \left\{ \frac{d}{dx}(x) \times \int \cos x \, dx \right\} dx \right]$$

$$\Rightarrow \quad I = -x^2 \cos x + 2 \left\{ x \sin x - \int \sin x \, dx \right\} = -x^2 \cos x + 2(x \sin x + \cos x) + C$$

(ii) Let $I = \int \underset{\text{I}}{x^2} \underset{\text{II}}{e^x} \, dx$. Then,

$$I = x^2 \left\{ \int e^x \, dx \right\} - \int \left\{ \frac{d}{dx}(x^2) \times \int e^x \, dx \right\} dx$$

$$\Rightarrow \quad I = x^2 e^x - \int 2x \, e^x \, dx = x^2 e^x - 2 \int \underset{\text{I}}{x} \underset{\text{II}}{e^x} \, dx$$

$$\Rightarrow \quad I = x^2 e^x - 2 \left[x \left\{ \int e^x \, dx \right\} - \int \left\{ \frac{d}{dx}(x) \times \int e^x \, dx \right\} dx \right]$$

$$\Rightarrow \quad I = x^2 e^x - 2 \left\{ x \, e^x - \int e^x \, dx \right\} = x^2 e^x - 2(x e^x - e^x) + C$$

EXAMPLE 3 *Evaluate:* (i) $\int \log x \, dx$ [NCERT] (ii) $\int (\log x)^2 \, dx$

SOLUTION (i) Let $I = \int \underset{\text{I}}{\log x} \cdot \underset{\text{II}}{1} \, dx = \log x \cdot \left\{\int 1 \cdot dx\right\} - \int \left\{\frac{d}{dx}(\log x) \cdot \int 1 \, dx\right\} dx$

$\Rightarrow \quad I = (\log x)\, x - \int \frac{1}{x} \cdot x \, dx = x(\log x) - \int 1 \cdot dx = x(\log x) - x + C$

(ii) Let $I = \int \underset{\text{I}}{(\log x)^2} \cdot \underset{\text{II}}{1} \, dx$. Then,

$$I = (\log x)^2 \left\{\int 1 \cdot dx\right\} - \int \left\{\frac{d}{dx}(\log x)^2 \cdot \int 1 \cdot dx\right\} dx$$

$\Rightarrow \quad I = (\log x)^2 \, x - \int 2 \log x \cdot \frac{1}{x} \cdot x \, dx = x(\log x)^2 - 2\int \underset{\text{I}}{\log x} \cdot \underset{\text{II}}{1} \, dx$

$\Rightarrow \quad I = x(\log x)^2 - 2\left[(\log x)\left\{\int 1 \cdot dx\right\} - \int \left\{\frac{d}{dx}(\log x) \int 1 \cdot dx\right\} dx\right]$

$\Rightarrow \quad I = x(\log x)^2 - 2\left\{(\log x)\, x - \int \frac{1}{x} \cdot x \, dx\right\} = x(\log x)^2 - 2(x \log x - x) + C$

EXAMPLE 4 *Evaluate:*

(i) $\int \sin^{-1} x \, dx$ [NCERT, CBSE 2022] (ii) $\int \tan^{-1} x \, dx$ [NCERT, CBSE 2022]

(iii) $\int \sec^{-1} x \, dx$ [NCERT]

SOLUTION (i) Let $\sin^{-1} x = t$. Then, $x = \sin t \Rightarrow dx = d(\sin t) = \cos t \, dt$

$\therefore \quad I = \int \sin^{-1} x \, dx$

$\Rightarrow \quad I = \int \underset{\text{I}}{t} \, \underset{\text{II}}{\cos t} \, dt = t \sin t - \int 1 \cdot (\sin t) \, dt = t \sin t - \int \sin t \, dt = t \sin t + \cos t + C$

$\Rightarrow \quad I = x \sin^{-1} x + \sqrt{1 - \sin^2 t} + C = x \sin^{-1} x + \sqrt{1 - x^2} + C$

(ii) Let $\tan^{-1} x = t$. Then, $x = \tan t$ and $dx = \sec^2 t \, dt$

$\therefore \quad I = \int \tan^{-1} x \, dx = \int \underset{\text{I}}{t} \, \underset{\text{II}}{\sec^2 t} \, dt = t(\tan t) - \int 1 \cdot \tan t \, dt = t \tan t + \log|\cos t| + C$

$\Rightarrow \quad I = x \tan^{-1} x + \log\left|\frac{1}{\sqrt{1 + x^2}}\right| + C \quad \left[\because \tan t = x \Rightarrow \cos t = \frac{1}{\sqrt{1 + \tan^2 t}} = \frac{1}{\sqrt{1 + x^2}}\right]$

$\Rightarrow \quad I = x \tan^{-1} x - \frac{1}{2} \log|1 + x^2| + C$

(iii) Let $\sec^{-1} x = t$ then, $x = \sec t \Rightarrow dx = \sec t \tan t \, dt$

$\therefore \; I = \int \sec^{-1} x \, dx = \int \underset{\text{I}}{t} \, \underset{\text{II}}{(\sec t \tan t)} \, dt = t(\sec t) - \int 1 \cdot \sec t \, dt = t \sec t - \log|(\sec t + \tan t)| + C$

$\Rightarrow I = t \sec t - \log|\sec t + \sqrt{\sec^2 t - 1}| + C = x(\sec^{-1} x) - \log|x + \sqrt{x^2 - 1}| + C$

EXAMPLE 5 *Evaluate:*

(i) $\int x \tan^{-1} x \, dx$ [NCERT, CBSE 2000C, 2019] (ii) $\int \frac{\log x}{x^2} \, dx$

(iii) $\int \frac{x - \sin x}{1 - \cos x} \, dx$ (iv) $\int \log(1 + x^2) \, dx$

SOLUTION (i) Let $I = \int \underset{\text{II}}{x} \underset{\text{I}}{\tan^{-1} x}\, dx$. Then,

$$I = (\tan^{-1} x)\frac{x^2}{2} - \int \frac{1}{1+x^2} \times \frac{x^2}{2}\, dx = \frac{x^2}{2}\tan^{-1} x - \frac{1}{2}\int \frac{x^2+1-1}{x^2+1}\, dx$$

$$\Rightarrow \quad I = \frac{x^2}{2}\tan^{-1} x - \frac{1}{2}\int 1 - \frac{1}{x^2+1}\, dx = \frac{x^2}{2}\tan^{-1} x - \frac{1}{2}\left(x - \tan^{-1} x\right) + C$$

(ii) Let $I = \int \frac{\log x}{x^2}\, dx = \int \underset{\text{II}}{\frac{1}{x^2}} \underset{\text{I}}{\log x}\, dx = (\log x)\left(-\frac{1}{x}\right) - \int \frac{1}{x}\left(-\frac{1}{x}\right) dx$

$$\Rightarrow \quad I = -\frac{1}{x}\log x + \int x^{-2}\, dx = -\frac{1}{x}\log x - \frac{1}{x} + C = -\frac{1}{x}(1 + \log x) + C$$

(iii) Let $I = \int \frac{x - \sin x}{1 - \cos x}\, dx$. Then,

$$I = \int \frac{x}{1-\cos x}\, dx - \int \frac{\sin x}{1 - \cos x}\, dx = \int \frac{x}{2}\operatorname{cosec}^2 \frac{x}{2}\, dx - \int \frac{2 \sin x/2 \cos x/2}{2 \sin^2 x/2}\, dx$$

$$\Rightarrow \quad I = \frac{1}{2}\int \underset{\text{I}}{x} \underset{\text{II}}{\operatorname{cosec}^2 \frac{x}{2}} - \int \cot \frac{x}{2}\, dx$$

$$\Rightarrow \quad I = \frac{1}{2}\left\{ x\left(-2\cot\frac{x}{2}\right) - \int 1 \cdot \left(-2\cot\frac{x}{2}\right) dx \right\} - \int \cot\frac{x}{2}\, dx + C$$

$$\Rightarrow \quad I = -x\cot\frac{x}{2} + \int \cot\frac{x}{2}\, dx - \int \cot\frac{x}{2}\, dx + C = -x\cot\frac{x}{2} + C$$

(iv) Let $I = \int \log(1+x^2)\, dx = \int \underset{\text{I}}{\log(1+x^2)} \cdot \underset{\text{II}}{1}\, dx = x\log(1+x^2) - \int \left(\frac{1}{1+x^2} \cdot 2x\right) x\, dx$

$$\Rightarrow \quad I = x\log(1+x^2) - 2\int \frac{x^2}{x^2+1}\, dx = x\log(x^2+1) - 2\int \frac{x^2+1-1}{x^2+1}\, dx$$

$$\Rightarrow \quad I = x\log(x^2+1) - 2\int 1 - \frac{1}{x^2+1}\, dx = x\log(x^2+1) - 2\left(x - \tan^{-1} x\right) + C$$

$$\Rightarrow \quad I = x\log(x^2+1) - 2x + 2\tan^{-1} x + C$$

EXAMPLE 6 *Evaluate:*

(i) $\int \sec^3 x\, dx$ **[CBSE 2024]** (ii) $\int \sin\sqrt{x}\, dx$

(iii) $\int \frac{\sin^{-1} x}{(1-x^2)^{3/2}}\, dx$ (iv) $\int (\sin^{-1} x)^2\, dx$ **[NCERT, CBSE 2004]**

SOLUTION (i) Let $I = \int \sec^3 x\, dx$

$$\Rightarrow \quad I = \int \underset{\text{I}}{\sec x} \cdot \underset{\text{II}}{\sec^2 x}\, dx = \sec x\left\{\int \sec^2 x\, dx\right\} - \int \left\{\left(\frac{d}{dx}(\sec x)\right)\left(\int \sec^2 x\, dx\right)\right\} dx$$

$$\Rightarrow \quad I = \sec x \tan x - \int \sec x \tan x \tan x\, dx = \sec x \tan x - \int \sec x \tan^2 x\, dx$$

$$\Rightarrow \quad I = \sec x \tan x - \int \sec x(\sec^2 x - 1)\, dx = \sec x \tan x - \int \sec^3 x\, dx + \int \sec x\, dx$$

$\Rightarrow \quad I = \sec x \tan x - I + \log|\sec x + \tan x| + C$

$\Rightarrow \quad 2I = \sec x \tan x + \log|\sec x + \tan x| + C = \frac{1}{2} \sec\tan x + \frac{1}{2} \log|\sec x + \tan x| + C$

(ii) Let $I = \int \sin\sqrt{x}\, dx$. Let $\sqrt{x} = t$. Then, $d(\sqrt{x}) = dt \Rightarrow \frac{1}{2\sqrt{x}} dx = dt \Rightarrow dx = 2\sqrt{x}\, dt$

$\therefore \quad I = \int \sin\sqrt{x}\, dx = \int (\sin t)\, 2t\, dt = 2\int \underset{\text{I}}{t} \underset{\text{II}}{\sin t}\, dt$

$\Rightarrow \quad I = 2\left\{t(-\cos t) - \int 1\,(-\cos t)\, dt\right\} = 2\left\{-t\cos t + \int \cos t\, dt\right\}$

$\Rightarrow \quad I = 2(-t\cos t + \sin t) + C = 2(-\sqrt{x}\cos\sqrt{x} + \sin\sqrt{x}) + C$

(iii) Let $x = \sin t$ Then, $dx = \cos t\, dt$

$\therefore \quad I = \int \frac{\sin^{-1} x}{(1-x^2)^{3/2}} dx = \int \frac{t}{(1-\sin^2 t)^{3/2}} \cos t\, dt = \int \underset{\text{I}}{t} \underset{\text{II}}{\sec^2 t}\, dt$

$\Rightarrow \quad I = t\tan t - \int 1 \times \tan t\, dt = t\tan t + \log|\cos t| + C$

$\Rightarrow \quad I = \frac{t\sin t}{\sqrt{1-\sin^2 t}} + \log|\sqrt{1-\sin^2 t}| + C$

$\Rightarrow \quad I = (\sin^{-1} x)\frac{x}{\sqrt{1-x^2}} + \log|\sqrt{1-x^2}| + C = \frac{x\sin^{-1} x}{\sqrt{1-x^2}} + \frac{1}{2}\log|1-x^2| + C$

(iv) Let $\sin^{-1} x = t$ Then, $x = \sin t \Rightarrow dx = \cos t\, dt$

$\therefore \quad I = \int (\sin^{-1} x)^2\, dx$

$\Rightarrow \quad I = \int \underset{\text{I}}{t^2} \underset{\text{II}}{\cos t}\, dt = t^2(\sin t) - \int 2t\sin t\, dt = t^2\sin t - 2\int \underset{\text{I}}{t} \underset{\text{II}}{\sin t}\, dt$

$\Rightarrow \quad I = t^2\sin t - 2\left\{t(-\cos t) - \int 1 \times (-\cos t)\, dt\right\}$

$\Rightarrow \quad I = t^2\sin t - 2\left\{-t\cos t + \int \cos t\, dt\right\}$

$\Rightarrow \quad I = t^2\sin t - 2\left(-t\cos t + \sin t\right) + C = t^2\sin t - 2\left\{-t\sqrt{1-\sin^2 t} + \sin t\right\} + C$

$\Rightarrow \quad I = x(\sin^{-1} x)^2 - 2\left\{-\sqrt{1-x^2}\sin^{-1} x + x\right\} + C$

EXAMPLE 7 *Evaluate:*

(i) $\int x\log(1+x)\, dx$ (ii) $\int x\cot^{-1} x\, dx$

(iii) $\int x\sin^{-1} x\, dx$ **[NCERT, CBSE 2000, 2009]** (iv) $\int x^2\tan^{-1} x\, dx$

(v) $\int x^3\log 2x\, dx$ (vi) $\int x^3 e^x\, dx$

SOLUTION (i) Let $I = \int \underset{\text{II}}{x} \underset{\text{I}}{\log(x+1)}\, dx$. Then,

$I = \log(x+1)\frac{x^2}{2} - \int \frac{1}{x+1} \times \frac{x^2}{2} dx$

$$\Rightarrow \quad I = \frac{x^2}{2}\log(x+1) - \frac{1}{2}\int \frac{x^2}{x+1}\,dx = \frac{x^2}{2}\log(x+1) - \frac{1}{2}\int \frac{x^2-1+1}{x+1}\,dx$$

$$\Rightarrow \quad I = \frac{x^2}{2}\log(x+1) - \frac{1}{2}\int \frac{x^2-1}{x+1} + \frac{1}{x+1}\,dx = \frac{x^2}{2}\log(x+1) - \frac{1}{2}\left\{\int \left((x-1) + \frac{1}{x+1}\right)dx\right\}$$

$$\Rightarrow \quad I = \frac{x^2}{2}\log(x+1) - \frac{1}{2}\left\{\frac{x^2}{2} - x + \log|x+1|\right\} + C$$

(ii) Let $I = \int \underset{\text{II}}{x}\ \underset{\text{I}}{\cot^{-1} x}\,dx$. Then,

$$I = (\cot^{-1} x)\left(\frac{x^2}{2}\right) - \int \frac{-1}{1+x^2} \times \frac{x^2}{2}\,dx$$

$$\Rightarrow \quad I = \frac{x^2}{2}\cot^{-1} x + \frac{1}{2}\int \frac{x^2}{x^2+1}\,dx = \frac{x^2}{2}\cot^{-1} x + \frac{1}{2}\int \frac{x^2+1-1}{x^2+1}\,dx$$

$$\Rightarrow \quad I = \frac{x^2}{2}\cot^{-1} x + \frac{1}{2}\int \left(1 - \frac{1}{x^2+1}\right)dx = \frac{x^2}{2}\cot^{-1} x + \frac{1}{2}\left(x - \tan^{-1} x\right) + C$$

(iii) Let $I = \int \underset{\text{II}}{x}\ \underset{\text{I}}{\sin^{-1} x}\,dx$. Then,

$$I = (\sin^{-1} x)\,\frac{x^2}{2} - \int \frac{1}{\sqrt{1-x^2}} \times \frac{x^2}{2}\,dx = \frac{x^2}{2}\sin^{-1} x + \frac{1}{2}\int \frac{-x^2}{\sqrt{1-x^2}}\,dx$$

$$\Rightarrow \quad I = \frac{x^2}{2}\sin^{-1} x + \frac{1}{2}\int \frac{1-x^2-1}{\sqrt{1-x^2}}\,dx = \frac{x^2}{2}\sin^{-1} x + \frac{1}{2}\left\{\int \frac{1-x^2}{\sqrt{1-x^2}}\,dx - \int \frac{1}{\sqrt{1-x^2}}\,dx\right\}$$

$$\Rightarrow \quad I = \frac{x^2}{2}\sin^{-1} x + \frac{1}{2}\left\{\int \sqrt{1-x^2}\,dx - \int \frac{1}{\sqrt{1-x^2}}\,dx\right\}$$

$$\Rightarrow \quad I = \frac{x^2}{2}\sin^{-1} x + \frac{1}{2}\left[\left\{\frac{1}{2}x\sqrt{1-x^2} + \frac{1}{2}\sin^{-1} x\right\} - \sin^{-1} x\right] + C$$

$$\Rightarrow \quad I = \frac{1}{2}x^2\sin^{-1} x + \frac{1}{4}x\sqrt{1-x^2} - \frac{1}{4}\sin^{-1} x + C$$

(iv) Let $I = \int \underset{\text{II}}{x^2}\ \underset{\text{I}}{\tan^{-1} x}\,dx$. Then,

$$I = (\tan^{-1} x)\,\frac{x^3}{3} - \int \frac{1}{1+x^2} \times \frac{x^3}{3}\,dx = \frac{x^3}{3}\tan^{-1} x - \frac{1}{3}\int \frac{x^3}{x^2+1}\,dx$$

$$\Rightarrow \quad I = \frac{x^3}{3}\tan^{-1} x - \frac{1}{3}\int \left(x - \frac{x}{x^2+1}\right)dx = \frac{x^3}{3}\tan^{-1} x - \frac{1}{3}\left\{\int x\,dx - \int \frac{x}{x^2+1}\,dx\right\}$$

$$\Rightarrow \quad I = \frac{x^3}{3}\tan^{-1} x - \frac{1}{3}\int x\,dx + \frac{1}{3}\int \frac{x}{x^2+1}\,dx$$

$\Rightarrow \quad I = \frac{x^3}{3} \tan^{-1} x - \frac{1}{3}\left(\frac{x^2}{2}\right) + \frac{1}{3}\int \frac{1}{2t}\, dt$, where $x^2 + 1 = t$

$\Rightarrow \quad I = \frac{x^3}{3} \tan^{-1} x - \frac{1}{6} x^2 + \frac{1}{6} \log|t| + C = \frac{x^3}{3} \tan^{-1} x - \frac{1}{6} x^2 + \frac{1}{6} \log|x^2 + 1| + C$

(v) Let $I = \int \underset{\text{II}}{x^3} \underset{\text{I}}{\log 2x}\, dx$. Then,

$$I = (\log 2x)\, \frac{x^4}{4} - \int \frac{1}{2x} \times 2 \times \frac{x^4}{4}\, dx = \frac{x^4}{4} \log 2x - \frac{1}{4}\int x^3\, dx = \frac{x^4}{4} \log 2x - \frac{x^4}{16} + C$$

(vi) Let $I = \int \underset{\text{I}}{x^3} \underset{\text{II}}{e^x}\, dx$. Then,

$$I = x^3 e^x - \int 3x^2 e^x\, dx = x^3 e^x - 3\int \underset{\text{I}}{x^2} \underset{\text{II}}{e^x}\, dx$$

$\Rightarrow \quad I = x^3 e^x - 3\left\{x^2 e^x - \int 2x\, e^x\, dx\right\} = x^3 e^x - 3\left\{x^2 e^x - 2\int \underset{\text{I}}{x} \underset{\text{II}}{e^x}\, dx\right\}$

$\Rightarrow \quad I = x^3 e^x - 3\left[x^2 e^x - 2\left\{x\, e^x - \int 1 \cdot e^x\, dx\right\}\right]$

$\Rightarrow \quad I = x^3 e^x - 3\left\{x^2 e^x - 2\left(x\, e^x - e^x\right)\right\} + C$

$\Rightarrow \quad I = x^3 e^x - 3x^2 e^x + 6x\, e^x - 6e^x + C = (x^3 - 3x^2 + 6x - 6)\, e^x + C$

BASED ON LOWER ORDER THINKING SKILLS (LOTS)

EXAMPLE 8 *Evaluate* : $\int \sin 2x \tan^{-1}(\sin x)\, dx$

SOLUTION Let $I = \int \sin 2x \tan^{-1}(\sin x)\, dx$. Putting $\sin x = t$ and $\cos x\, dx = dt$, we get

$$I = \int \sin 2x \tan^{-1}(\sin x)\, dx = 2\int \underset{\text{II}}{t} \underset{\text{I}}{\tan^{-1} t}\, dt = 2\left\{(\tan^{-1} t)\frac{t^2}{2} - \int \frac{1}{1+t^2} \times \frac{t^2}{2}\, dt\right\}$$

$\Rightarrow \quad I = t^2 (\tan^{-1} t) - \int \frac{(t^2+1) - 1}{1+t^2}\, dt = t^2 \tan^{-1} t - \int \left(1 - \frac{1}{1+t^2}\right) dt$

$\Rightarrow \quad I = t^2 \tan^{-1} t - t + \tan^{-1} t + C$

$\Rightarrow \quad I = \sin^2 x \tan^{-1}(\sin x) - \sin x + \tan^{-1}(\sin x) + C$

EXAMPLE 9 *Evaluate* : $\int \cot^{-1}(1 - x + x^2)\, dx$

SOLUTION Let $I = \int \cot^{-1}(1 - x + x^2)\, dx$. Then,

$$I = \int \cot^{-1}\left\{1 - x(1-x)\right\} dx = \int \tan^{-1}\left\{\frac{1}{1 - x(1-x)}\right\} dx$$

$\Rightarrow \quad I = \int \tan^{-1}\left\{\frac{x + (1-x)}{1 - x(1-x)}\right\} dx = \int \left\{\tan^{-1} x + \tan^{-1}(1-x)\right\} dx$

$\Rightarrow \quad I = \int \tan^{-1} x\, dx + \int \tan^{-1}(1-x)\, dx = I_1 + I_2 \quad \text{...(i)}$

where $I_1 = \int \tan^{-1} x\, dx$ and $I_2 = \int \tan^{-1}(1-x)\, dx$.

Now,

$$I_1 = \int \tan^{-1} x \, dx = \int \underset{\text{I}}{\tan^{-1} x} \; \underset{\text{II}}{1} \, dx = x \tan^{-1} x - \int \frac{x}{1+x^2} dx$$

$$\Rightarrow \quad I_1 = x \tan^{-1} x - \frac{1}{2} \int \frac{1}{1+x^2} 2x \, dx = x \tan^{-1} x - \frac{1}{2} \log(1+x^2) \quad \text{...(ii)}$$

and,

$$I_2 = \int \tan^{-1}(1-x)\, dx = -\int \tan^{-1} t \, dt, \text{ where } t = 1-x.$$

$$\Rightarrow \quad I_2 = -\left\{ t \tan^{-1} t - \frac{1}{2} \log(1+t^2) \right\} \quad \text{[Using (ii)]}$$

$$\Rightarrow \quad I_2 = -\left[(1-x) \tan^{-1}(1-x) - \frac{1}{2} \log\left\{ 1 + (1-x)^2 \right\} \right]$$

Substituting the values of I_1 and I_2 in (i), we get

$$\int \cot^{-1}(1-x+x^2)\, dx = x \tan^{-1} x - \frac{1}{2} \log(1+x^2) - (1-x) \tan^{-1}(1-x) + \frac{1}{2} \log\left\{1+(1-x)^2\right\} + C$$

BASED ON HIGHER ORDER THINKING SKILLS (HOTS)

EXAMPLE 10 *Evaluate* : $\int \left(3x^2 \tan \frac{1}{x} - x \sec^2 \frac{1}{x} \right) dx$

SOLUTION Let $I = \int \left\{ 3x^2 \tan \frac{1}{x} - x \sec^2 \frac{1}{x} \right\} dx$

$$\Rightarrow \quad I = \int \underset{\text{II}}{3x^2} \; \underset{\text{I}}{\tan \frac{1}{x}} \, dx - \int x \sec^2 \frac{1}{x} \, dx$$

$$\Rightarrow \quad I = x^3 \tan\left(\frac{1}{x}\right) - \int \left(\sec^2 \frac{1}{x} \right) \times -\frac{1}{x^2} \times x^3 \, dx - \int x \sec^2 \frac{1}{x} \, dx$$

$$\Rightarrow \quad I = x^3 \tan \frac{1}{x} + \int x \sec^2 \frac{1}{x} \, dx - \int x \sec^2 \frac{1}{x} \, dx + C = x^3 \tan\left(\frac{1}{x}\right) + C$$

EXAMPLE 11 *Evaluate* : $\int \frac{\log(1+x^2)}{x^3} dx$

SOLUTION Let $I = \int \frac{\log(1+x^2)}{x^3} dx$. Then,

$$I = \int \underset{\text{I}}{\log(1+x^2)} \; \underset{\text{II}}{x^{-3}} \, dx = -\frac{1}{2x^2} \log(1+x^2) + \int \frac{x \, dx}{x^2(1+x^2)}$$

$$\Rightarrow \quad I = -\frac{1}{2x^2} \log(1+x^2) + \frac{1}{2} \int \frac{dt}{t(1+t)}, \quad \text{where } t = x^2$$

$$\Rightarrow \quad I = -\frac{1}{2x^2} \log(1+x^2) + \frac{1}{2} \int \left(\frac{1}{t} - \frac{1}{t+1} \right) dt = -\frac{1}{2x^2} \log(1+x^2) + \frac{1}{2} \left\{ \log t - \log(t+1) \right\} + C$$

$$\Rightarrow \quad I = -\frac{1}{2x^2} \log(1+x^2) + \frac{1}{2} \log \left| \frac{x^2}{x^2+1} \right| + C$$

EXAMPLE 12 *Evaluate:* $\int \frac{\sin^{-1}\sqrt{x}-\cos^{-1}\sqrt{x}}{\sin^{-1}\sqrt{x}+\cos^{-1}\sqrt{x}}\,dx$ **[NCERT]**

SOLUTION We know that $\sin^{-1}x+\cos^{-1}x=\frac{\pi}{2}$

$$\therefore \quad I = \int \frac{\sin^{-1}\sqrt{x}-\cos^{-1}\sqrt{x}}{\sin^{-1}\sqrt{x}+\cos^{-1}\sqrt{x}}\,dx = \int \frac{\sin^{-1}\sqrt{x}-\left(\frac{\pi}{2}-\sin^{-1}\sqrt{x}\right)}{\frac{\pi}{2}}\,dx$$

$$\Rightarrow \quad I = \frac{2}{\pi}\int \left(2\sin^{-1}\sqrt{x}-\frac{\pi}{2}\right)dx = \frac{4}{\pi}\int \sin^{-1}\sqrt{x}\,dx - \int 1\cdot dx$$

$$\Rightarrow \quad I = \frac{4}{\pi}\int \sin^{-1}\sqrt{x}\,dx - x + C = \frac{4}{\pi}I_1 - x + C, \text{ where } I_1 = \int \sin^{-1}\sqrt{x}\,dx \qquad \text{...(i)}$$

Putting $x=\sin^2\theta$ and $dx = 2\sin\theta\cos\theta\,d\theta = \sin 2\theta\,d\theta$, we get

$$I_1 = \int \underset{\text{I}}{\theta}\ \underset{\text{II}}{\sin 2\theta}\,d\theta = -\theta\frac{\cos 2\theta}{2} + \int \frac{1}{2}\cos 2\theta\,d\theta = -\frac{\theta}{2}\cos 2\theta + \frac{1}{4}\sin 2\theta$$

$$\Rightarrow \quad I_1 = -\frac{1}{2}\theta(1-2\sin^2\theta) + \frac{1}{2}\sin\theta\sqrt{1-\sin^2\theta}$$

$$\Rightarrow \quad I_1 = -\frac{1}{2}(1-2x)\sin^{-1}\sqrt{x} + \frac{1}{2}\sqrt{x}\sqrt{1-x} \qquad \text{...(ii)}$$

From (i) and (ii), we get

$$I = \frac{4}{\pi}\left\{-\frac{1}{2}(1-2x)\sin^{-1}\sqrt{x} + \frac{1}{2}\sqrt{x-x^2}\right\} - x + C$$

$$\Rightarrow \quad I = \frac{2}{\pi}\left\{\sqrt{x-x^2} - (1-2x)\sin^{-1}\sqrt{x}\right\} - x + C$$

EXAMPLE 13 *Evaluate:* $\int \frac{\sqrt{x^2+1}\left\{\log(x^2+1)-2\log x\right\}}{x^4}\,dx$ **[CBSE 2012, NCERT]**

SOLUTION Let

$$I = \int \frac{\sqrt{x^2+1}\left\{\log(x^2+1)-2\log x\right\}}{x^4}\,dx$$

$$\Rightarrow \quad I = \int \frac{\sqrt{x^2+1}}{x^4}\left\{\log(x^2+1)-\log x^2\right\}dx = \int \sqrt{1+\frac{1}{x^2}}\,\log\left(1+\frac{1}{x^2}\right)\frac{1}{x^3}\,dx$$

Let $1+\frac{1}{x^2}=t$. Then, $d\left(1+\frac{1}{x^2}\right) = dt \Rightarrow -\frac{2}{x^3}dx = dt \Rightarrow \frac{1}{x^3}dx = -\frac{1}{2}dt$

$$\therefore \quad I = -\frac{1}{2}\int \underset{\text{II}}{\sqrt{t}}\ \underset{\text{I}}{\log t}\,dt$$

$$\Rightarrow \quad I = -\frac{1}{2}\left\{\frac{2}{3}(\log t)\,t^{3/2} - \frac{2}{3}\int \frac{1}{t}\times t^{3/2}\,dt\right\} = -\frac{1}{2}\left\{\frac{2}{3}(\log t)\,t^{3/2} - \frac{4}{9}t^{3/2}\right\} + C$$

$$\Rightarrow \quad I = -\frac{1}{3}t^{3/2}\left\{\log t - \frac{2}{3}\right\} + C = -\frac{1}{3}\left(1+\frac{1}{x^2}\right)^{3/2}\left\{\log\left(1+\frac{1}{x^2}\right) - \frac{2}{3}\right\} + C.$$

EXAMPLE 14 *Evaluate:* $\int \frac{x^2}{(x \sin x + \cos x)^2} dx$

SOLUTION Let $I = \int \frac{x^2}{(x \sin x + \cos x)^2} dx$. Then, $I = \int \underset{\text{I}}{(x \sec x)} \times \underset{\text{II}}{\frac{x \cos x}{(x \sin x + \cos x)^2}} dx$

Let $t = x \sin x + \cos x$. Then,

$$\int \frac{x \cos x}{(x \sin x + \cos x)^2} dx = \int \frac{1}{t^2} dt = -\frac{1}{t} = -\frac{1}{x \sin x + \cos x}$$

Using this as a result and integrating by parts, we obtain

$$I = (x \sec x) \times \frac{-1}{x \sin x + \cos x} - \int (\sec x + x \sec x \tan x) \times \frac{-1}{x \sin x + \cos x} dx$$

$$\Rightarrow \quad I = -\frac{x \sec x}{x \sin x + \cos x} + \int \sec^2 x \, dx$$

$$\Rightarrow \quad I = \frac{-x}{\cos x (x \sin x + \cos x)} + \tan x + C = \frac{(\sin x - x \cos x)}{x \sin x + \cos x} + C$$

EXAMPLE 15 *Find an anti-derivative of the function* $f(x) g''(x) - f''(x) g(x)$

SOLUTION Required anti-derivative of $f(x) g''(x) - f''(x) g(x)$ is given by

$$\int \{f(x) g''(x) - f''(x) g(x)\} dx$$

$$= \int \underset{\text{I}}{f(x)} \underset{\text{II}}{g''(x)} dx - \int \underset{\text{II}}{f''(x)} \underset{\text{I}}{g(x)} dx$$

$$= \left\{f(x) g'(x) - \int f'(x) g'(x) dx\right\} - \left\{g(x) f'(x) - \int f'(x) g'(x) dx\right\} + C$$

$$= f(x) g'(x) - g(x) f'(x) + C$$

EXAMPLE 16 *Evaluate :* $\int \sin^{-1} \left\{\frac{2x+2}{\sqrt{4x^2 + 8x + 13}}\right\} dx$

SOLUTION Let

$$I = \int \sin^{-1} \left\{\frac{2x+2}{\sqrt{4x^2 + 8x + 13}}\right\} dx = \sin^{-1} \left\{\frac{2x+2}{\sqrt{(2x+2)^2 + 3^2}}\right\} dx$$

Substituting $2x + 2 = 3 \tan \theta$ and $dx = \frac{3}{2} \sec^2 \theta \, d\theta$, we get

$$I = \int \sin^{-1} \left(\frac{3 \tan \theta}{3 \sec \theta}\right) \times \frac{3}{2} \sec^2 \theta \, d\theta = \frac{3}{2} \int \underset{\text{I}}{\theta} \underset{\text{II}}{\sec^2 \theta} \, d\theta$$

$$\Rightarrow \quad I = \frac{3}{2} \left\{\theta \tan \theta - \int \tan \theta \, d\theta\right\} = \frac{3}{2} \left\{\theta \tan \theta - \log |\sec \theta|\right\}$$

$$\Rightarrow \quad I = \frac{3}{2} \left\{\left(\frac{2x+2}{3}\right) \tan^{-1} \left(\frac{2x+2}{3}\right) - \log \sqrt{1 + \left(\frac{2x+2}{3}\right)^2}\right\} + C$$

$$\Rightarrow \quad I = \frac{3}{2} \left\{\left(\frac{2x+2}{3}\right) \tan^{-1} \left(\frac{2x+2}{3}\right) - \log \sqrt{4x^2 + 8x + 13}\right\} + C$$

$$\Rightarrow \quad I = (x+1) \tan^{-1} \left(\frac{2x+2}{3}\right) - \frac{3}{4} \log (4x^2 + 8x + 13) + C$$

EXERCISE 15.25

BASIC

Evaluate the following integrals:

1. $\int x \cos x \, dx$
2. $\int \log (x+1) \, dx$
3. $\int x^3 \log x \, dx$
4. $\int x e^x \, dx$ [NCERT]
5. $\int x e^{2x} \, dx$
6. $\int x^2 e^{-x} \, dx$
7. $\int x^2 \cos x \, dx$
8. $\int x^2 \cos 2x \, dx$
9. $\int x \sin 2x \, dx$
10. $\int \frac{\log (\log x)}{x} \, dx$
11. $\int \cos x \tan^{-1} (\sin x) \, dx$ [CBSE 2022]
12. $\int x \operatorname{cosec}^2 x \, dx$
13. $\int x^n \log x \, dx$ [CBSE 2020]
14. $\int \frac{\log x}{x^n} \, dx$
15. $\int x \sin x \cos x \, dx$
16. $\int (\log x)^2 \, x \, dx$
17. $\int \frac{\log (x+2)}{(x+2)^2} \, dx$
18. $\int \log_{10} x \, dx$
19. $\int \frac{\log x}{(x+1)^2} \, dx$ [CBSE 2015]
20. $\int x \tan^2 x \, dx$
21. $\int x \left(\frac{\sec 2x - 1}{\sec 2x + 1} \right) dx$
22. $\int (x+1) \log x \, dx$ [CBSE 2002C]
23. $\int (e^{\log x} + \sin x) \cos x \, dx$
24. $\int \sin^{-1} 2x \, dx$ [CBSE2019]
25. $\int x \cos^2 x \, dx$

BASED ON LOTS

26. $\int x^2 \sin^2 x \, dx$
27. $\int 2x^3 e^{x^2} \, dx$
28. $\int x^3 \cos x^2 \, dx$
29. $\int \sin x \log (\cos x) \, dx$ [CBSE 2019]
30. $\int e^{\sqrt{x}} \, dx$
31. $\int \frac{x + \sin x}{1 + \cos x} \, dx$
32. $\int \cos \sqrt{x} \, dx$
33. $\int \frac{x \cos^{-1} x}{\sqrt{1 - x^2}} \, dx$ [CBSE 2014]
34. $\int \operatorname{cosec}^3 x \, dx$
35. $\int \sec^{-1} \sqrt{x} \, dx$
36. $\int \sin^{-1} \sqrt{x} \, dx$
37. $\int (x+1) e^x \log (x e^x) \, dx$
38. $\int \sin^{-1} (3x - 4x^3) \, dx$
39. $\int \sin^{-1} \left(\frac{2x}{1 + x^2} \right) dx$ [NCERT]
40. $\int \tan^{-1} \left(\frac{3x - x^3}{1 - 3x^2} \right) dx$
41. $\int x^2 \sin^{-1} x \, dx$
42. $\int \frac{\sin^{-1} x}{x^2} \, dx$ [CBSE 2004]
43. $\int \frac{x^2 \tan^{-1} x}{1 + x^2} \, dx$
44. $\int \cos^{-1} (4x^3 - 3x) \, dx$
45. $\int \cos^{-1} \left(\frac{1 - x^2}{1 + x^2} \right) dx$
46. $\int \tan^{-1} \left(\frac{2x}{1 - x^2} \right) dx$
47. $\int x^2 \tan^{-1} x \, dx$ [CBSE 2012]
48. $\int \frac{(x \tan^{-1} x)}{(1 + x^2)^{3/2}} \, dx$
49. $\int \tan^{-1} (\sqrt{x}) \, dx$
50. $\int x \sin x \cos 2x \, dx$
51. $\int (\tan^{-1} x^2) \, x \, dx$
52. $\int \frac{x \sin^{-1} x}{\sqrt{1 - x^2}} \, dx$ [CBSE2012, 2016, NCERT]
53. $\int x^2 \log (x^2 + 1) \, dx$ [CBSE 2023]
54. $\int x^2 \sin^{-1} (x^{3/2}) \, dx$ [CBSE 2024]

BASED ON HOTS

55. $\int \sin^3 \sqrt{x}\, dx$

56. $\int x \sin^3 x\, dx$

57. $\int \cos^3 \sqrt{x}\, dx$

58. $\int x \cos^3 x\, dx$

59. $\int \tan^{-1} \sqrt{\frac{1-x}{1+x}}\, dx$ [NCERT]

60. $\int \sin^{-1} \sqrt{\frac{x}{a+x}}\, dx$

61. $\int \frac{x^3 \sin^{-1} x^2}{\sqrt{1-x^4}}\, dx$

62. $\int \frac{x^2 \sin^{-1} x}{(1-x^2)^{3/2}}\, dx$

ANSWERS

1. $x \sin x + \cos x + C$
2. $x \log(x+1) - x + \log(x+1) + C$
3. $\frac{x^4}{4} \log x - \frac{x^4}{16} + C$
4. $(x-1) e^x + C$
5. $\left(\frac{x}{2} - \frac{1}{4}\right) e^{2x} + C$
6. $-e^{-x}(x^2 + 2x + 2) + C$
7. $x^2 \sin x + 2x \cos x - 2 \sin x + C$
8. $\frac{x^2}{2} \sin 2x + \frac{x}{2} \cos 2x - \frac{\sin 2x}{4} + C$
9. $-\frac{x}{2} \cos 2x + \frac{1}{4} \sin 2x + C$
10. $\log x \{\log(\log x) - 1\} + C$
11. $\sin x (\tan^{-1} x) - \log(1 + \sin^2 x) + C$
12. $-x \cot x + \log|\sin x| + C$
13. $\frac{x^{n+1}}{n+1} \log x - \frac{x^{n+1}}{(n+1)^2} + C$
14. $\frac{x^{1-n}}{1-n} \log x - \frac{x^{1-n}}{(1-n)^2} + C$
15. $-\frac{1}{4} x \cos 2x + \frac{1}{8} \sin 2x + C$
16. $\frac{x^2}{2}\left\{(\log x)^2 - \log x + \frac{1}{2}\right\} + C$
17. $-\frac{1}{(x+2)} - \frac{\log(x+2)}{(x+2)} + C$
18. $\frac{1}{\log 10}\left\{x(\log x - 1)\right\} + C$
19. $-\frac{\log x}{x+1} + \log\left|\frac{x}{x+1}\right| + C$
20. $x \tan x - \log|\sec x| - \frac{x^2}{2} + C$
21. $x \tan x - \log|\sec x| - \frac{x^2}{2} + C$
22. $\left(x + \frac{x^2}{2}\right) \log x - \left(x + \frac{x^2}{4}\right) + C$
23. $x \sin x + \cos x + \frac{1}{2} \sin^2 x + C$
24. $x \sin^{-1} 2x + \frac{1}{2}\sqrt{1 - 4x^2} + C$
25. $\frac{x^2}{4} + \frac{x \sin 2x}{4} + \frac{\cos 2x}{8} + C$
26. $\frac{1}{6} x^3 - \frac{1}{4} x^2 \sin 2x - \frac{1}{4} x \cos 2x + \frac{1}{8} \sin 2x + C$
27. $e^{x^2}(x^2 - 1) + C$
28. $\frac{1}{2} x^2 \sin x^2 + \frac{1}{2} \cos x^2 + C$
29. $\cos x (1 - \log \cos x) + C$
30. $2 e^{\sqrt{x}} (\sqrt{x} - 1) + C$
31. $x \tan \frac{x}{2} + C$
32. $2\left\{\sqrt{x} \sin \sqrt{x} + \cos \sqrt{x}\right\} + C$
33. $-\left\{\sqrt{1 - x^2} \cos^{-1} x + x\right\} + C$
34. $-\frac{1}{2} \operatorname{cosec} x \cot x + \frac{1}{2} \log\left|\tan \frac{x}{2}\right| + C$
35. $x \sec^{-1} \sqrt{x} - \sqrt{x - 1} + C$
36. $\frac{1}{2}(2x - 1) \sin^{-1} \sqrt{x} + \frac{1}{2}\sqrt{x - x^2} + C$

37. $x e^x \left\{\log (x e^x) - 1\right\} + C$

38. $3x \sin^{-1} x + 3\sqrt{1-x^2} + C$

39. $2x \tan^{-1} x - \log|1+x^2| + C$

40. $3x \tan^{-1} x - \frac{3}{2}\log|x^2+1| + C$

41. $\frac{x^3}{3}\sin^{-1} x + \frac{1}{3}\sqrt{1-x^2} - \frac{1}{9}(1-x^2)^{3/2} + C$

42. $-\frac{\sin^{-1} x}{x} + \log\left|\frac{1+\sqrt{1+x^2}}{x}\right| + C$

43. $x \tan^{-1} x - \frac{1}{2}\log|1+x^2| - \frac{1}{2}(\tan^{-1} x)^2 + C$

44. $3x \cos^{-1} x - 3\sqrt{1-x^2} + C$

45. $2x \tan^{-1} x - \log|1+x^2| + C$

46. $2x \tan^{-1} x - \log|1+x^2| + C$

47. $\frac{x^3}{3}\tan^{-1} x - \frac{x^2}{6} + \frac{1}{6}\log|x^2+1| + C$

48. $-\frac{\tan^{-1} x}{\sqrt{1+x^2}} + \frac{x}{\sqrt{1+x^2}} + C$

49. $(x+1)\tan^{-1}\sqrt{x} - \sqrt{x} + C$

50. $\frac{1}{2}\left\{-\frac{x\cos 3x}{3} + \frac{\sin 3x}{9} + x\cos x - \sin x\right\} + C$

51. $\frac{1}{2}x^2 \tan^{-1} x^2 - \frac{1}{4}\log(1+x^4) + C$

52. $-\sqrt{1-x^2}\sin^{-1} x + x + C$

53. $\frac{x^3}{3}\log(x^2+1) - \frac{2}{9}x^3 + \frac{2}{3}x - \frac{2}{3}\tan^{-1} x + C$

54. $\frac{x^3}{3}\sin^{-1}(x^{3/2}) + \frac{x^{3/2}}{6}\sqrt{1-x^3} - \frac{1}{6}\sin^{-1}(x^{3/2}) + C$

55. $-\frac{3}{2}\sqrt{x}\cos\sqrt{x} + \frac{3}{2}\sin\sqrt{x} + \frac{1}{6}\sqrt{x}\cos 3\sqrt{x} - \frac{1}{18}\sin 3\sqrt{x} + C$

56. $-\frac{3x\cos x}{4} + \frac{3\sin x}{4} + \frac{x\cos 3x}{12} - \frac{\sin 3x}{36} + C$

57. $\frac{\sqrt{x}}{6}\sin 3\sqrt{x} + \frac{\cos 3\sqrt{x}}{18} + \frac{3}{2}\sqrt{x}\sin\sqrt{x} + \frac{3}{2}\cos\sqrt{x} + C$

58. $\frac{x\sin 3x}{12} + \frac{\cos 3x}{36} + \frac{3}{4}x\sin x + \frac{3}{4}\cos x + C$

59. $\frac{1}{2}x(\cos^{-1} x) - \frac{1}{2}\sqrt{1-x^2} + C$

60. $x\tan^{-1}\sqrt{\frac{x}{a}} - \sqrt{ax} + a\tan^{-1}\sqrt{\frac{x}{a}} + C$

61. $\frac{1}{2}\left\{x^2 - \sqrt{1-x^4}\sin^{-1} x^2\right\} + C$

62. $\frac{x\sin^{-1} x}{\sqrt{1-x^2}} - \frac{1}{2}(\sin^{-1} x)^2 + \frac{1}{2}\log(1-x^2) + C$

15.11.1 INTEGRALS OF THE FORM $\int e^x\left\{f(x) + f'(x)\right\}dx$

THEOREM *Prove that:* $\int e^x\left\{f(x) + f'(x)\right\}dx = e^x f(x) + C.$

PROOF We have,

$$\int e^x\{f(x) + f'(x)\}\,dx = \int \underset{\text{II}}{e^x}\,\underset{\text{I}}{f(x)}\,dx + \int e^x f'(x)\,dx$$

$$\Rightarrow \quad \int e^x\{f(x) + f'(x)\}\,dx = f(x)\cdot e^x - \int f'(x)\,e^x\,dx + \int e^x f'(x)\,dx + C$$

$$\Rightarrow \quad \int e^x\{f(x) + f'(x)\}\,dx = e^x f(x) + C$$

Q.E.D.

This theorem suggests the following algorithm to evaluate integrals of the form

$$\int e^x \left\{ f(x) + f'(x) \right\} dx.$$

ALGORITHM

Step I *Express the integral as the sum of two integrals, one consisting of $f(x)$ and other containing $f'(x)$.*

i.e. $\int e^x \left\{ f(x) + f'(x) \right\} dx = \int e^x f(x)\, dx + \int e^x f'(x)\, dx$

Step II *Evaluate the first integral on RHS using integration by parts by taking e^x as the second function. The second integral on RHS will cancel out from the second term obtained by evaluating the first integral.*

NOTE *The above theorem is also true if we have e^{kx} in place of e^x.*

i.e. $\int e^{kx} \left\{ k f(x) + f'(x) \right\} dx = e^{kx} f(x) + C$

ILLUSTRATIVE EXAMPLES

BASED ON BASIC CONCEPTS (BASIC)

EXAMPLE 1 *Evaluate:*

(i) $\int e^x \left(\frac{1}{x} - \frac{1}{x^2} \right) dx$ [NCERT] (ii) $\int e^x (\sin x + \cos x)\, dx$ [NCERT]

(iii) $\int \{\sin(\log x) + \cos(\log x)\}\, dx$

SOLUTION (i) Let $I = \int e^x \left(\frac{1}{x} - \frac{1}{x^2} \right) dx$. Then, $I = \int e^x \left(\underset{f}{\frac{1}{x}} + \underset{f'}{\frac{(-1)}{x^2}} \right) dx$

$\Rightarrow \quad I = \int \underset{\text{II}}{e^x} \underset{\text{I}}{\frac{1}{x}}\, dx - \int e^x \frac{1}{x^2}\, dx = \frac{1}{x} \cdot e^x - \int -\frac{1}{x^2} e^x\, dx - \int e^x \cdot \frac{1}{x^2}\, dx + C$

$\Rightarrow \quad I = \frac{1}{x} \cdot e^x + \int \frac{1}{x^2} \cdot e^x\, dx - \int \frac{1}{x^2} \cdot e^x\, dx + C = \frac{1}{x} e^x + C$

(ii) Let $I = \int e^x (\underset{f}{\sin x} + \underset{f'}{\cos x})\, dx = \int \underset{\text{II}}{e^x} \underset{\text{I}}{\sin x}\, dx + \int e^x \cos x\, dx$

$\Rightarrow \quad I = (\sin x) e^x - \int (\cos x) e^x\, dx + \int e^x \cos x\, dx + C = e^x \sin x + C$

(iii) Let $I = \int \{\sin(\log x) + \cos(\log x)\}\, dx$. Let $\log x = t$. Then, $x = e^t \Rightarrow dx = d(e^t) = e^t\, dt$

$\therefore \quad I = \int e^t (\underset{f}{\sin t} + \underset{f'}{\cos t})\, dt = \int \underset{\text{II}}{e^t} \underset{\text{I}}{\sin t}\, dt + \int e^t \cos t\, dt$

$\Rightarrow \quad I = \sin t \cdot e^t - \int \cos t \cdot e^t\, dt + \int \cos t \cdot e^t\, dt + C$

$\Rightarrow \quad I = e^t \cdot \sin t + C = e^{\log x} \sin(\log x) + C = x \sin(\log x) + C$

EXAMPLE 2 *Evaluate:*

(i) $\int e^x (\tan x + \log \sec x)\, dx$ (ii) $\int e^x \left(\frac{2 + \sin 2x}{1 + \cos 2x} \right) dx$ [NCERT, CBSE 2024]

(iii) $\int e^x \left(\frac{1 + \sin x \cos x}{\cos^2 x} \right) dx$ (iv) $\int e^x \left(\frac{1 - \sin x}{1 - \cos x} \right) dx$ [NCERT]

SOLUTION (i) Let $I = \int e^x (\tan x + \log \sec x)\, dx = \int e^x \left(\underset{f}{\log \sec x} + \underset{f'}{\tan x} \right) dx$

$\Rightarrow \quad I = \int \underset{\text{II}}{e^x} \underset{\text{I}}{\log \sec x}\, dx + \int e^x \tan x\, dx$

$\Rightarrow \quad I = (\log \sec x)\, e^x - \int \frac{1}{\sec x} \times \sec x \tan x\, e^x\, dx + \int e^x \tan x\, dx + C$

$\Rightarrow \quad I = e^x \log \sec x - \int e^x \tan x\, dx + \int e^x \tan x\, dx + C = e^x \cdot \log \sec x + C$

(ii) Let $I = \int e^x \left(\frac{2 + \sin 2x}{1 + \cos 2x} \right) dx$. Then,

$I = \int e^x \left(\frac{2 + 2 \sin x \cos x}{2 \cos^2 x} \right) dx$

$\Rightarrow \quad I = \int e^x (\underset{f'}{\sec^2 x} + \underset{f}{\tan x})\, dx = \int \underset{\text{II}}{e^x} \underset{\text{I}}{\tan x}\, dx + \int e^x \sec^2 x\, dx$

$\Rightarrow \quad I = (\tan x)\, e^x - \int \sec^2 x\, e^x\, dx + \int e^x \sec^2 x\, dx + C = e^x \tan x + C$

(iii) Let $I = \int e^x \left(\frac{1 + \sin x \cos x}{\cos^2 x} \right) dx = \int e^x \left(\frac{1}{\cos^2 x} + \frac{\sin x \cos x}{\cos^2 x} \right) dx$

$\Rightarrow \quad I = \int e^x (\underset{f'}{\sec^2 x} + \underset{f}{\tan x})\, dx = \int \underset{\text{II}}{e^x} \underset{\text{I}}{\tan x}\, dx + \int e^x \sec^2 x\, dx$

$\Rightarrow \quad I = (\tan x)\, e^x - \int \sec^2 x\, e^x\, dx + \int e^x \sec^2 x\, dx + C = e^x \tan x + C$

(iv) Let $I = \int e^x \left(\frac{1 - \sin x}{1 - \cos x} \right) dx$. Then,

$I = \int e^x \left(\frac{1 - 2 \sin \frac{x}{2} \cos \frac{x}{2}}{2 \sin^2 \frac{x}{2}} \right) dx = \int e^x \left(\frac{1}{2} \operatorname{cosec}^2 \frac{x}{2} - \cot \frac{x}{2} \right) dx$

$\Rightarrow \quad I = \int e^x \left\{ \underset{f}{\left(-\cot \frac{x}{2} \right)} + \underset{f'}{\frac{1}{2} \operatorname{cosec}^2 \frac{x}{2}} \right\} dx = -\int \underset{\text{II}}{e^x} \underset{\text{I}}{\cot \frac{x}{2}}\, dx + \frac{1}{2} \int e^x \operatorname{cosec}^2 \frac{x}{2}\, dx$

$\Rightarrow \quad I = -\left\{ \cot \frac{x}{2} \cdot e^x - \int -\operatorname{cosec}^2 \frac{x}{2} \cdot \frac{1}{2} e^x\, dx \right\} + \frac{1}{2} \int e^x \operatorname{cosec}^2 \frac{x}{2}\, dx$

$\Rightarrow \quad I = -e^x \cot \frac{x}{2} - \frac{1}{2} \int e^x \operatorname{cosec}^2 \frac{x}{2}\, dx + \frac{1}{2} \int e^x \operatorname{cosec}^2 \frac{x}{2}\, dx + C = -e^x \cot \frac{x}{2} + C$

BASED ON LOWER ORDER THINKING SKILLS (LOTS)

EXAMPLE 3 *Evaluate:*

(i) $\int e^x \frac{x}{(x+1)^2}\, dx$ [NCERT] (ii) $\int e^x \frac{x-3}{(x-1)^3}\, dx$ [NCERT] (iii) $\int \frac{\log x}{(1 + \log x)^2}\, dx$

SOLUTION (i) Let $I = \int e^x \cdot \frac{x}{(x+1)^2}\, dx$. Then,

$$I = \int e^x \frac{x+1-1}{(x+1)^2}\, dx = \int e^x \left\{ \underset{f}{\frac{1}{x+1}} + \underset{f'}{\frac{-1}{(x+1)^2}} \right\} dx = \int \underset{\text{II}}{e^x} \underset{\text{I}}{\frac{1}{x+1}}\, dx + \int e^x \frac{(-1)}{(x+1)^2}\, dx$$

$$\Rightarrow \quad I = \frac{1}{x+1} e^x - \int \frac{-1}{(x+1)^2} e^x\, dx + \int e^x \frac{(-1)}{(x+1)^2}\, dx + C = \frac{1}{x+1}\, e^x + C$$

(ii) Let $I = \int e^x \frac{x-3}{(x-1)^3}\, dx$. Then,

$$I = \int e^x \frac{(x-1)-2}{(x-1)^3}\, dx = \int e^x \left\{ \underset{f}{\frac{1}{(x-1)^2}} + \underset{f'}{\frac{(-2)}{(x-1)^3}} \right\} dx$$

$$\Rightarrow \quad I = \int \underset{\text{II}}{e^x} \times \underset{\text{I}}{\frac{1}{(x-1)^2}}\, dx + \int e^x \times \frac{-2}{(x-1)^3}\, dx$$

$$\Rightarrow \quad I = \frac{1}{(x-1)^2} e^x - \int \frac{-2}{(x-1)^3} \times e^x dx + \int e^x \times \frac{-2}{(x-1)^3}\, dx + C$$

$$\Rightarrow \quad I = \frac{e^x}{(x-1)^2} + 2\int \frac{e^x}{(x-1)^3}\, dx - 2\int \frac{e^x}{(x-1)^3}\, dx + C = \frac{e^x}{(x-1)^2} + C$$

(iii) $I = \int \frac{\log x}{(1+\log x)^2}\, dx$. Let $\log x = t$. Then, $x = e^t \Rightarrow dx = d(e^t) = e^t\, dt$

$$\therefore \quad I = \int \frac{t\, e^t}{(t+1)^2}\, dt = \int \frac{(t+1)-1}{(t+1)^2} e^t\, dt = \int \left\{ \underset{f}{\frac{1}{t+1}} + \underset{f'}{\frac{-1}{(t+1)^2}} \right\} e^t\, dt$$

$$\Rightarrow \quad I = \int \underset{\text{I}}{\frac{1}{t+1}} \underset{\text{II}}{e^t}\, dt + \int \frac{-1}{(t+1)^2} e^t dt = \frac{1}{t+1} e^t - \int \frac{-1}{(t+1)^2} e^t dt + \int \frac{-1}{(t+1)^2} e^t dt + C$$

$$\Rightarrow \quad I = \frac{e^t}{t+1} + C = \frac{x}{(\log x + 1)} + C$$

EXAMPLE 4 *Evaluate:*

(i) $\int \left\{ \frac{1}{\log x} - \frac{1}{(\log x)^2} \right\} dx$ (ii) $\int \left\{ \log(\log x) + \frac{1}{(\log x)^2} \right\} dx$ **[CBSE 2010]**

SOLUTION (i) Let $I = \int \left\{ \frac{1}{\log x} - \frac{1}{(\log x)^2} \right\} dx$. Putting $\log_e x = t$ or $x = e^t$ and $dx = e^t\, dt$, we obtain

$$I = \int \left(\underset{f}{\frac{1}{t}} + \underset{f'}{\frac{(-1)}{t^2}}\right) e^t\, dt = \int \underset{\text{II}}{e^t} \underset{\text{I}}{\frac{1}{t}}\, dt - \int e^t \frac{1}{t^2}\, dt$$

$$\Rightarrow \quad I = \frac{1}{t} e^t - \int -\frac{1}{t^2} \times e^t\, dt - \int e^t \times \frac{1}{t^2}\, dt + C = \frac{1}{t} e^t + C = \frac{x}{\log x} + C$$

(ii) Let $I = \int \left\{\log(\log x) + \frac{1}{(\log x)^2}\right\} dx$. Let $\log x = t$. Then, $x = e^t \Rightarrow dx = d(e^t) = e^t\, dt$.

$$\therefore \quad I = \int \left\{\log t + \frac{1}{t^2}\right\} e^t\, dt$$

$$\Rightarrow \quad I = \int \left\{\log t + \frac{1}{t} - \frac{1}{t} + \frac{1}{t^2}\right\} e^t\, dt = \int \left(\underset{f}{\log t} + \underset{f'}{\frac{1}{t}}\right) e^t\, dt + \int \left(\underset{f}{-\frac{1}{t}} + \underset{f'}{\frac{1}{t^2}}\right) e^t\, dt$$

$$\Rightarrow \quad I = \int \underset{\text{II}}{e^t} \underset{\text{I}}{\log t}\, dt + \int e^t \cdot \frac{1}{t}\, dt + \int \underset{\text{II}}{e^t} \underset{\text{I}}{(-1/t)}\, dt + \int e^t \frac{1}{t^2}\, dt$$

$$\Rightarrow \quad I = (\log t)\, e^t - \int \frac{1}{t} \cdot e^t\, dt + \int e^t \cdot \frac{1}{t}\, dt + \left(\frac{-1}{t}\right) e^t - \int \frac{1}{t^2} \cdot e^t\, dt + \int e^t \frac{1}{t^2}\, dt + C$$

$$\Rightarrow \quad I = e^t \cdot \log t - \frac{1}{t} e^t + C = x \log(\log x) - \frac{x}{\log x} + C$$

BASED ON HIGHER ORDER THINKING SKILLS (HOTS)

EXAMPLE 5 *Evaluate:* (i) $\int e^x \frac{x^2 + 1}{(x+1)^2}\, dx$ (ii) $\int e^x \frac{(1-x)^2}{(1+x^2)^2}\, dx$

SOLUTION (i) Let $I = \int e^x \frac{x^2 + 1}{(x+1)^2}\, dx = \int e^x \left\{1 - \frac{2x}{(x+1)^2}\right\} dx = \int e^x dx - 2\int e^x \frac{x}{(x+1)^2}\, dx$

$$\Rightarrow \quad I = e^x - 2\int e^x \cdot \frac{x+1-1}{(x+1)^2}\, dx = e^x - 2\int e^x \left\{\underset{f}{\frac{1}{x+1}} + \underset{f'}{\frac{-1}{(x+1)^2}}\right\} dx$$

$$\Rightarrow \quad I = e^x - 2\left\{\int \underset{\text{II}}{e^x} \cdot \underset{\text{I}}{\frac{1}{x+1}}\, dx - \int e^x \frac{1}{(x+1)^2}\, dx\right\}$$

$$\Rightarrow \quad I = e^x - 2\left\{\frac{1}{x+1} e^x - \int -\frac{1}{(x+1)^2} e^x\, dx - \int e^x \frac{1}{(x+1)^2}\, dx\right\}$$

$$\Rightarrow \quad I = e^x - 2\left\{\frac{1}{x+1} \cdot e^x + \int e^x \cdot \frac{1}{(x+1)^2}\, dx - \int e^x \cdot \frac{1}{(x+1)^2}\, dx\right\} + C$$

$$\Rightarrow \quad I = e^x - \frac{2e^x}{x+1} + C$$

(ii) Let $I = \int e^x \dfrac{(1-x)^2}{(1+x^2)^2}\, dx$. Then,

$$I = \int e^x \frac{1-2x+x^2}{(1+x^2)^2}\, dx = \int e^x \frac{(1+x^2)+(-2x)}{(1+x^2)^2}\, dx = \int e^x \Bigg\{ \underset{f}{\frac{1}{1+x^2}} + \underset{f'}{\frac{(-2x)}{(1+x^2)^2}} \Bigg\}\, dx$$

$$\Rightarrow \quad I = \int \underset{\text{II}}{e^x} \underset{\text{I}}{\frac{1}{(1+x^2)}}\, dx + \int e^x \frac{(-2x)}{(1+x^2)^2}\, dx$$

$$\Rightarrow \quad I = \frac{1}{1+x^2}\, e^x - \int \frac{(-2x)}{(1+x^2)^2}\, e^x dx + \int e^x \frac{(-2x)}{(1+x^2)^2}\, dx + C = \frac{e^x}{1+x^2} + C$$

EXAMPLE 6 *Evaluate:* $\int e^{2x} \left(\dfrac{1+\sin 2x}{1+\cos 2x} \right) dx$ [CBSE 2010]

SOLUTION Let $I = \int e^{2x} \left(\dfrac{1+\sin 2x}{1+\cos 2x} \right) dx = \int e^{2x} \left\{ \dfrac{1+2\sin x\cos x}{2\cos^2 x} \right\} dx$

$$\Rightarrow \quad I = \int e^{2x} \left\{ \frac{1}{2}\sec^2 x + \tan x \right\} dx = \int e^{2x} \Bigg\{ 2\Bigg(\underset{f}{\frac{1}{2}\tan x} \Bigg) + \underset{f'}{\frac{1}{2}\sec^2 x} \Bigg\}\, dx$$

$$\Rightarrow \quad I = \int \underset{\text{II}}{e^{2x}} \cdot \underset{\text{I}}{\tan x}\, dx + \frac{1}{2}\int e^{2x} \cdot \sec^2 x\, dx$$

$$\Rightarrow \quad I = (\tan x)\frac{e^{2x}}{2} - \int \sec^2 x \cdot \frac{e^{2x}}{2}\, dx + \frac{1}{2}\int e^{2x} \sec^2 x\, dx + C$$

$$\Rightarrow \quad I = \frac{1}{2}e^{2x}\tan x - \frac{1}{2}\int e^{2x}\sec^2 x\, dx + \frac{1}{2}\int e^{2x}\sec^2 x\, dx + C = \frac{1}{2}e^{2x}\tan x + C$$

EXERCISE 15.26

BASIC

Evaluate the following integrals:

1. $\int e^x (\cos x - \sin x)\, dx$
2. $\int e^x \left(\dfrac{1}{x^2} - \dfrac{2}{x^3} \right) dx$
3. $\int e^x \left(\dfrac{1+\sin x}{1+\cos x} \right) dx$ [NCERT]
4. $\int e^x (\cot x - \operatorname{cosec}^2 x)\, dx$
5. $\int e^x \left(\dfrac{x-1}{2x^2} \right) dx$
6. $\int e^x \sec x\,(1+\tan x)\, dx$
7. $\int e^x (\tan x - \log \cos x)\, dx$
8. $\int e^x [\sec x + \log(\sec x + \tan x)]\, dx$
9. $\int e^x (\cot x + \log \sin x)\, dx$
10. $\int e^x \left(\dfrac{\sin 4x - 4}{1-\cos 4x} \right) dx$ [CBSE 2010]
11. $\int e^x \left(\log x + \dfrac{1}{x} \right) dx$
12. $\int e^x \cdot \dfrac{\sqrt{1-x^2}\,\sin^{-1} x + 1}{\sqrt{1-x^2}}\, dx$

13. $\int e^x \left(\tan^{-1} x + \frac{1}{1+x^2}\right) dx$

14. $\int e^x \left(\frac{\sin x \cos x - 1}{\sin^2 x}\right) dx$

BASED ON LOTS

15. $\int e^x \frac{x-1}{(x+1)^3} dx$

16. $\int \frac{2-x}{(1-x)^2} e^x dx$

17. $\int e^x \frac{1+x}{(2+x)^2} dx$

18. $\int \frac{\sqrt{1-\sin x}}{1+\cos x} e^{-x/2} dx$ [CBSE 2013]

19. $\int e^x \left(\log x + \frac{1}{x^2}\right) dx$

20. $\int \frac{e^x}{x} \left\{x (\log x)^2 + 2 \log x\right\} dx$

21. $\int e^{2x} (-\sin x + 2 \cos x) dx$

22. $\int \{\tan (\log x) + \sec^2 (\log x)\} dx$

23. $\int e^{2x} \left(\frac{1-\sin 2x}{1-\cos 2x}\right) dx$ [CBSE 2013]

24. $\int \frac{\log x - 3}{(\log x)^4} dx$ [CBSE 2022]

25. $\int e^{x^2} (x^5 + 2x^3) dx$ [CBSE 2023]

26. $\int e^x \left\{\frac{1}{(1+x^2)^{3/2}} + \frac{x}{\sqrt{1+x^2}}\right\} dx$ [CBSE 2024]

BASED ON HOTS

27. $\int e^x \frac{(x-4)}{(x-2)^3} dx$ [CBSE 2009]

28. $\int e^{\cot^{-1} x} \left(\frac{1-x+x^2}{1+x^2}\right) dx$ [CBSE 2023]

ANSWERS

1. $e^x \cos x + C$
2. $\frac{e^x}{x^2} + C$
3. $e^x \tan \frac{x}{2} + C$
4. $e^x \cot x + C$
5. $\frac{e^x}{2x} + C$
6. $e^x \sec x + C$
7. $e^x \log \sec x + C$
8. $e^x \log (\sec x + \tan x) + C$
9. $e^x \log \sin x + C$
10. $e^x \cot 2x + C$
11. $e^x \log x + C$
12. $e^x \sin^{-1} x + C$
13. $e^x \tan^{-1} x + C$
14. $e^x \cot x + C$
15. $\frac{e^x}{(x+1)^2} + C$
16. $\frac{e^x}{1-x} + C$
17. $\frac{e^x}{x+2} + C$
18. $-e^{-x/2} \sec\left(\frac{x}{2}\right) + C$
19. $e^x\left(\log x - \frac{1}{x}\right) + C$
20. $e^x (\log x)^2 + C$
21. $e^{2x} \cos x + C$
22. $x \tan (\log x) + C$
23. $-\frac{1}{2} e^{2x} \cot x + C$
24. $\frac{x}{(\log x)^3} + C$
25. $\frac{x^4}{2} e^{x^2} + C$
26. $\frac{e^x x}{\sqrt{1+x^2}} + C$
27. $\frac{e^x}{(x-2)^2} + C$
28. $x e^{\cot^{-1} x} + C$

15.11.2 INTEGRALS OF THE FORM $\int e^{ax} \sin bx \, dx$ AND $\int e^{ax} \cos bx \, dx$

In this section, we will discuss problems based upon integrals of the form $\int e^{ax} \sin bx \, dx$ and $\int e^{ax} \cos bx \, dx$. In order to evaluate this type of integrals, we may use the following formulae:

THEOREM *Prove that:*

(i) $\int e^{ax} \sin bx \, dx = \frac{e^{ax}}{a^2 + b^2} (a \sin bx - b \cos bx) + C$ [CBSE 2002]

(ii) $\int e^{ax} \cos bx \, dx = \frac{e^{ax}}{a^2+b^2}(a \cos bx + b \sin bx) + C$

PROOF (i) Let $I = \int e^{ax} \sin bx \, dx$. Then,

$$I = \int \underset{\text{I}}{e^{ax}} \underset{\text{II}}{\sin bx} \, dx = -e^{ax} \frac{\cos bx}{b} - \int a e^{ax} \left(\frac{-\cos bx}{b} \right) dx$$

$$\Rightarrow \quad I = -\frac{1}{b} e^{ax} \cos bx + \frac{a}{b} \int \underset{\text{I}}{e^{ax}} \underset{\text{II}}{\cos bx} \, dx = -\frac{1}{b} e^{ax} \cos bx + \frac{a}{b} \left\{ e^{ax} \frac{\sin bx}{b} - \int a e^{ax} \frac{\sin bx}{b} dx \right\}$$

$$\Rightarrow \quad I = -\frac{1}{b} e^{ax} \cos bx + \frac{a}{b^2} e^{ax} \sin bx - \frac{a^2}{b^2} \int e^{ax} \sin bx \, dx$$

$$\Rightarrow \quad I = -\frac{1}{b} e^{ax} \cos bx + \frac{a}{b^2} e^{ax} \sin bx - \frac{a^2}{b^2} I$$

$$\Rightarrow \quad I + I \cdot \frac{a^2}{b^2} = \frac{e^{ax}}{b^2}(a \sin bx - b \cos bx) \Rightarrow I \left(\frac{a^2+b^2}{b^2} \right) = \frac{e^{ax}}{b^2}(a \sin bx - b \cos bx)$$

$$\Rightarrow \quad I = \frac{e^{ax}}{a^2+b^2}(a \sin bx - b \cos bx) + C$$

(ii) Similarly, we can prove that $\int e^{ax} \cos bx \, dx = \frac{e^{ax}}{a^2+b^2}(a \cos bx + b \sin bx) + C$ **Q.E.D.**

ILLUSTRATIVE EXAMPLES

BASED ON BASIC CONCEPTS (BASIC)

EXAMPLE 1 *Evaluate:*

(i) $\int e^{2x} \sin 3x \, dx$ (ii) $\int e^{-x} \cos x \, dx$

SOLUTION (i) Let $I = \int e^{2x} \sin 3x \, dx$. Then,

$$I = \int \underset{\text{I}}{e^{2x}} \underset{\text{II}}{\sin 3x} \, dx$$

$$\Rightarrow \quad I = e^{2x} \left(-\frac{\cos 3x}{3} \right) - \int 2e^{2x} \left(-\frac{\cos 3x}{3} \right) dx = -\frac{1}{3} e^{2x} \cos 3x + \frac{2}{3} \int \underset{\text{I}}{e^{2x}} \underset{\text{II}}{\cos 3x} \, dx$$

$$\Rightarrow \quad I = -\frac{1}{3} e^{2x} \cos 3x + \frac{2}{3} \left\{ e^{2x} \frac{\sin 3x}{3} - \int 2e^{2x} \frac{\sin 3x}{3} dx \right\}$$

$$\Rightarrow \quad I = -\frac{1}{3} e^{2x} \cos 3x + \frac{2}{9} e^{2x} \sin 3x - \frac{4}{9} \int e^{2x} \sin 3x \, dx$$

$$\Rightarrow \quad I = -\frac{1}{3} e^{2x} \cos 3x + \frac{2}{9} e^{2x} \sin 3x - \frac{4}{9} I$$

$$\Rightarrow \quad I + \frac{4}{9} I = \frac{e^{2x}}{9}(2 \sin 3x - 3 \cos 3x)$$

$$\Rightarrow \quad \frac{13}{9} I = \frac{e^{2x}}{9}(2 \sin 3x - 3 \cos 3x) \Rightarrow I = \frac{e^{2x}}{13}(2 \sin 3x - 3 \cos 3x) + C$$

(ii) Let $I = \int e^{-x} \cos x \, dx$. Then,

$$I = \int \underset{\text{I}}{e^{-x}} \underset{\text{II}}{\cos x}\, dx$$

$\Rightarrow \quad I = e^{-x} \sin x - \int -e^{-x} \sin x \, dx$

$\Rightarrow \quad I = e^{-x} \sin x + \int \underset{\text{I}}{e^{-x}} \underset{\text{II}}{\sin x}\, dx$

$\Rightarrow \quad I = e^{-x} \sin x + e^{-x}(-\cos x) - \int (-e^{-x})(-\cos x)\, dx$

$\Rightarrow \quad I = e^{-x} \sin x - e^{-x} \cos x - \int e^{-x} \cos x \, dx$

$\Rightarrow \quad I = e^{-x} \sin x - e^{-x} \cos x - I$

$\Rightarrow \quad 2I = e^{-x}(\sin x - \cos x) \Rightarrow I = \dfrac{e^{-x}}{2}(\sin x - \cos x) + C$

EXAMPLE 2 *Evaluate:*

(i) $\int e^{ax} \cos (bx + c)\, dx$ (ii) $\int \sin (\log x)\, dx$ (iii) $\int e^{x} \cos^2 x \, dx$

SOLUTION (i) Let $I = \int \underset{\text{I}}{e^{ax}} \underset{\text{II}}{\cos (bx + c)}\, dx$. Integrating by parts, we get

$$I = \frac{e^{ax}}{b} \sin (bx + c) - \int a e^{ax} \frac{\sin (bx + c)}{b}\, dx$$

$\Rightarrow \quad I = \dfrac{e^{ax}}{b} \sin (bx + c) - \dfrac{a}{b} \int \underset{\text{I}}{e^{ax}} \underset{\text{II}}{\sin (bx + c)}\, dx$

$\Rightarrow \quad I = \dfrac{e^{ax}}{b} \sin (bx + c) - \dfrac{a}{b}\left\{-e^{ax} \dfrac{\cos (bx + c)}{b} - \int a\, e^{ax} \dfrac{\cos (bx + c)}{b}\, dx\right\}$

$\Rightarrow \quad I = \dfrac{e^{ax}}{b} \sin (bx + c) - \dfrac{a}{b}\left\{-\dfrac{e^{ax}}{b} \cos (bx + c) + \dfrac{a}{b} \int e^{ax} \cos (bx + c)\, dx\right\}$

$\Rightarrow \quad I = \dfrac{e^{ax}}{b} \sin (bx + c) - \dfrac{a}{b}\left\{-\dfrac{e^{ax}}{b} \cos (bx + c) + \dfrac{a}{b} I\right\}$

$\Rightarrow \quad I = \dfrac{e^{ax}}{b} \sin (bx + c) + \dfrac{a}{b^2} e^{ax} \cos (bx + c) - \dfrac{a^2}{b^2} I$

$\Rightarrow \quad I + \dfrac{a^2}{b^2} I = \dfrac{b^{ax}}{b^2}\left\{b \sin (bx + c) + a \cos (bx + c)\right\}$

$\Rightarrow \quad I\left(\dfrac{a^2 + b^2}{b^2}\right) = \dfrac{e^{ax}}{b^2}\left\{a \cos (bx + c) + b \sin (bx + c)\right\}$

$\Rightarrow \quad I = \dfrac{e^{ax}}{a^2 + b^2}\left\{a \cos (bx + c) + b \sin (bx + c)\right\}$

Hence, $\int e^{ax} \cos (bx + c)\, dx = \dfrac{e^{ax}}{a^2 + b^2}\left\{a \cos (bx + c) + b \sin (bx + c)\right\} + C_1$

(ii) Let $I = \int \sin (\log x)\, dx$. Let $\log x = t$. Then, $x = e^t \Rightarrow dx = d(e^t) = e^t\, dt$

$\therefore \quad I = \int \underset{II}{\sin t}\, \underset{I}{e^t}\, dt = -e^t \cos t - \int e^t (-\cos t)\, dt$ [Integrating by parts]

$\Rightarrow \quad I = -e^t \cos t + \int \underset{I}{e^t}\, \underset{II}{\cos t}\, dt = -e^t \cos t + \left\{ e^t \sin t - \int e^t \sin t\, dt \right\}$

$\Rightarrow \quad I = -e^t \cos t + e^t \sin t - I \Rightarrow 2I = e^t (\sin t - \cos t) \Rightarrow I = \frac{e^t}{2} (\sin t - \cos t) + C$

Hence, $\int \sin (\log x)\, dx = \frac{x}{2} \{\sin (\log x) - \cos (\log x)\} + C.$

(iii) Let $I = \int e^x \cos^2 x\, dx$. Then,

$\Rightarrow \quad I = \int e^x \left(\frac{1 + \cos 2x}{2} \right) dx = \frac{1}{2} \int e^x (1 + \cos 2x)\, dx = \frac{1}{2} \int e^x\, dx + \frac{1}{2} \int e^x \cos 2x\, dx$

$\Rightarrow \quad I = \frac{1}{2} e^x + \frac{1}{2} I_1 + C$ ...(i)

where $I_1 = \int e^x \cos 2x\, dx.$

Now,

$I_1 = \int \underset{I}{e^x}\, \underset{II}{\cos 2x}\, dx = e^x \frac{\sin 2x}{2} - \int e^x \frac{\sin 2x}{2}\, dx$ [Integrating by parts]

$\Rightarrow \quad I_1 = \frac{1}{2} e^x \sin 2x - \frac{1}{2} \int \underset{I}{e^x}\, \underset{II}{\sin 2x}\, dx$

$\Rightarrow \quad I_1 = \frac{1}{2} e^x \sin 2x - \frac{1}{2} \left\{ -e^x \frac{\cos 2x}{2} - \int e^x \left(\frac{-\cos 2x}{2} \right) dx \right\}$

$\Rightarrow \quad I_1 = \frac{1}{2} e^x \sin 2x + \frac{1}{4} e^x \cos 2x - \frac{1}{4} \int e^x \cos 2x\, dx$

$\Rightarrow \quad I_1 = \frac{1}{2} e^x \sin 2x + \frac{1}{4} e^x \cos 2x - \frac{1}{4} I_1$

$\Rightarrow \quad I_1 + \frac{1}{4} I_1 = \frac{1}{4} e^x (\cos 2x + 2 \sin 2x) \Rightarrow \frac{5}{4} I_1 = \frac{1}{4} e^x (\cos 2x + 2 \sin 2x)$

$\Rightarrow \quad I_1 = \frac{e^x}{5} (\cos 2x + 2 \sin 2x)$ ...(ii)

$\therefore \quad I = \frac{1}{2} e^x + \frac{e^x}{10} (\cos 2x + 2 \sin 2x) + C$

BASED ON LOWER ORDER THINKING SKILLS (LOTS)

EXAMPLE 3 If $I_1 = \int e^{ax} \cos b\, x\, dx$ and $I_2 = \int e^{ax} \sin bx\, dx$, prove that

(i) $(a^2 + b^2)(I_1^{\,2} + I_2^{\,2}) = e^{2ax}$ (ii) $\tan^{-1} \left(\frac{I_2}{I_1} \right) + \tan^{-1} \frac{b}{a} = bx.$

SOLUTION (i) We have,

$I_1 = \int e^{ax} \cos bx\, dx = \frac{e^{ax}}{a^2 + b^2} (a \cos bx + b \sin bx)$

and, $I_2 = \int e^{ax} \sin bx\, dx = \frac{e^{ax}}{a^2 + b^2} (a \sin bx - b \cos bx)$

$\therefore \quad I_1^2 + I_2^2 = \frac{e^{2ax}}{(a^2+b^2)^2}\left\{(a\cos bx + b\sin bx)^2 + (a\sin bx - b\cos bx)^2\right\}$

$\Rightarrow \quad I_1^2 + I_2^2 = \frac{e^{2ax}}{(a^2+b^2)^2}(a^2+b^2) = \frac{e^{2ax}}{a^2+b^2}$

$\Rightarrow \quad (a^2+b^2)(I_1^2 + I_2^2) = e^{2ax}$

(ii) $\frac{I_2}{I_1} = \frac{a\sin bx - b\cos bx}{a\cos bx + b\sin bx} = \frac{\tan bx - \frac{b}{a}}{1 + \frac{b}{a}\tan bx}$ [Diving N^r and D^r by $\cos bx$]

$\Rightarrow \quad \frac{I_2}{I_1} = \frac{\tan bx - \tan\{\tan^{-1}(b/a)\}}{1 + \tan bx \,.\, \tan^{-1}(b/a)} = \tan\left\{bx - \tan^{-1}\left(\frac{b}{a}\right)\right\}$

$\Rightarrow \quad \tan^{-1}\left(\frac{I_2}{I_1}\right) = bx - \tan^{-1}\frac{b}{a} \Rightarrow \tan^{-1}\left(\frac{I_2}{I_1}\right) + \tan^{-1}\left(\frac{b}{a}\right) = bx.$

EXERCISE 15.27

BASIC

Evaluate the following integrals:

1. $\int e^{ax}\cos bx\, dx$ **[CBSE 2002]**

2. $\int e^{ax}\sin(bx+c)\, dx$

3. $\int \cos(\log x)\, dx$

4. $\int e^{2x}\cos(3x+4)\, dx$

5. $\int e^{2x}\sin x\cos x\, dx$

6. $\int e^{2x}\sin x\, dx$ **[NCERT]**

7. $\int e^{2x}\sin(3x+1)\, dx$ **[CBSE 2015]**

8. $\int e^{-2x}\sin x\, dx$

BASED ON LOTS

9. $\int \frac{1}{x^3}\sin(\log x)\, dx$

10. $\int e^{2x}\cos^2 x\, dx$

11. $\int e^x \sin^2 x\, dx$

12. $\int x^2 e^{x^3}\cos x^3\, dx$

ANSWERS

1. $\frac{e^{ax}}{a^2+b^2}(a\cos bx + b\sin bx) + C$

2. $\frac{e^{ax}}{a^2+b^2}\left\{a\sin(bx+c) - b\cos(bx+c)\right\} + C_1$

3. $\frac{x}{2}\left\{\cos(\log x) + \sin(\log x)\right\} + C$

4. $\frac{e^{2x}}{13}\left\{2\cos(3x+4) + 3\sin(3x+4)\right\} + C$

5. $\frac{e^{2x}}{8}(\sin 2x - \cos 2x) + C$

6. $\frac{e^{2x}}{5}(2\sin x - \cos x) + C$

7. $\frac{e^{2x}}{13}\left\{2\sin(3x+1) - 3\cos(3x+1)\right\} + C$

8. $\frac{e^{-2x}}{5}(-2\sin x - \cos x) + C$

9. $-\frac{1}{5x^2}\left\{\cos(\log x) + 2\sin(\log x)\right\} + C$

10. $\frac{e^{2x}}{4} + \frac{e^{2x}}{8}(\cos 2x + \sin 2x) + C$

11. $\frac{1}{2}e^x - \frac{e^x}{10}(\cos 2x + 2\sin 2x) + C$

12. $\frac{e^{x^3}}{6}(\sin x^3 + \cos x^3) + C$

15.12 SOME IMPORTANT INTEGRALS

In this section, we will prove three formulae which will be used in evaluating integrals of the form $\int \sqrt{ax^2+bx+c}\, dx$ and $\int (px+q)\sqrt{ax^2+bx+c}\, dx$.

THEOREM *Prove that:*

(i) $\int \sqrt{a^2-x^2}\, dx = \frac{1}{2} x \sqrt{a^2-x^2} + \frac{1}{2} a^2 \sin^{-1}\left(\frac{x}{a}\right) + C$

(ii) $\int \sqrt{a^2+x^2}\, dx = \frac{1}{2} x \sqrt{a^2+x^2} + \frac{1}{2} a^2 \log\left| x + \sqrt{a^2+x^2} \right| + C$

(iii) $\int \sqrt{x^2-a^2}\, dx = \frac{1}{2} x \sqrt{x^2-a^2} - \frac{1}{2} a^2 \log\left| x + \sqrt{x^2-a^2} \right| + C$

PROOF (i) Let $I = \int \sqrt{a^2-x^2}\, dx$. Then, $I = \int \underset{\text{I}}{\sqrt{a^2-x^2}}\ \underset{\text{II}}{1} \cdot dx$. Integrating by parts, we get

$$I = \sqrt{a^2-x^2}\, x - \int \frac{1}{2}(a^2-x^2)^{-1/2}(0-2x)\, x\, dx = x\sqrt{a^2-x^2} - \int \frac{-x^2}{\sqrt{a^2-x^2}}\, dx$$

$$\Rightarrow \quad I = x\sqrt{a^2-x^2} - \int \frac{(a^2-x^2)-a^2}{\sqrt{a^2-x^2}}\, dx = x\sqrt{a^2-x^2} - \int \sqrt{a^2-x^2}\, dx + a^2 \int \frac{1}{\sqrt{a^2-x^2}}\, dx$$

$$\Rightarrow \quad I = x\sqrt{a^2-x^2} - I + a^2 \sin^{-1}\left(\frac{x}{a}\right) + C$$

$$\Rightarrow \quad 2I = x\sqrt{a^2-x^2} + a^2 \sin^{-1}\left(\frac{x}{a}\right) + C = \frac{1}{2} x\sqrt{a^2-x^2} + \frac{1}{2} a^2 \sin^{-1}\left(\frac{x}{a}\right) + C$$

(ii) Let $I = \int \sqrt{a^2+x^2}\, dx$. Then, $I = \int \underset{\text{I}}{\sqrt{a^2+x^2}}\ \underset{\text{II}}{1} \cdot dx$. Integrating by parts, we obtain

$$I = \sqrt{a^2+x^2}\, x - \int \frac{1}{2}(a^2+x^2)^{-1/2}(0+2x)\, x\, dx = x\sqrt{a^2+x^2} - \int \frac{x^2}{\sqrt{a^2+x^2}}\, dx$$

$$\Rightarrow \quad I = x\sqrt{a^2+x^2} - \int \frac{(a^2+x^2)-a^2}{\sqrt{a^2+x^2}}\, dx = x\sqrt{a^2+x^2} - \int \sqrt{a^2+x^2}\, dx + a^2 \int \frac{1}{\sqrt{a^2+x^2}}\, dx$$

$$\Rightarrow \quad I = x\sqrt{a^2+x^2} - I + a^2 \log| x + \sqrt{a^2+x^2} |$$

$$\Rightarrow \quad 2I = x\sqrt{a^2+x^2} + a^2 \log| x + \sqrt{a^2+x^2} |$$

$$\Rightarrow \quad I = \frac{1}{2} x\sqrt{a^2+x^2} + \frac{1}{2} a^2 \log| x + \sqrt{a^2+x^2} | + C$$

(iii) Let $I = \sqrt{x^2-a^2}\, dx$. Then, $I = \int \underset{\text{I}}{\sqrt{x^2-a^2}}\ \underset{\text{II}}{1} \cdot dx$. Integrating by parts, we obtain

$$I = \sqrt{x^2-a^2} \cdot x - \int \frac{1}{2}(x^2-a^2)^{-1/2}(2x)\, x\, dx$$

$$\Rightarrow \quad I = x\sqrt{x^2-a^2} - \int \frac{x^2}{\sqrt{x^2-a^2}}\, dx = x\sqrt{x^2-a^2} - \int \frac{(x^2-a^2)+a^2}{\sqrt{x^2-a^2}}\, dx$$

$$\Rightarrow \quad I = x\sqrt{x^2-a^2} - \int \sqrt{x^2-a^2}\,dx - a^2 \int \frac{1}{\sqrt{x^2-a^2}}\,dx$$

$$\Rightarrow \quad I = x\sqrt{x^2-a^2} - I - a^2 \log|x+\sqrt{x^2-a^2}|$$

$$\Rightarrow \quad 2I = x\sqrt{x^2-a^2} - a^2 \log|x+\sqrt{x^2-a^2}| \Rightarrow I = \frac{1}{2}x\sqrt{x^2-a^2} - \frac{1}{2}a^2 \log|x+\sqrt{x^2-a^2}| + C$$

15.12.1 INTEGRALS OF THE FORM $\int \sqrt{ax^2+bx+c}\,dx$

In order to evaluate the above type of integrals, we use the following algorithm.

ALGORITHM

Step I *Make coefficient of x^2 as one by taking 'a' common to obtain $x^2 + \frac{b}{a}x + \frac{c}{a}$.*

Step II *Add and subtract $\left(\frac{b}{2a}\right)^2$ in $x^2 + \frac{b}{a}x + \frac{c}{a}$ to obtain $\left(x + \frac{b}{2a}\right)^2 + \frac{4ac-b^2}{4a^2}$.*

After applying these two steps the integral reduces to one of the following three forms:

$$\int \sqrt{a^2+x^2}\,dx, \int \sqrt{a^2-x^2}\,dx, \int \sqrt{x^2-a^2}\,dx.$$

Step III *Use the appropriate formula.*

ILLUSTRATIVE EXAMPLES

BASED ON BASIC CONCEPTS (BASIC)

EXAMPLE 1 *Evaluate:*

(i) $\int \sqrt{4x^2+9}\,dx$ (ii) $\int \sqrt{x^2+2x+5}\,dx$ [NCERT]

SOLUTION (i) Let $I = \int \sqrt{4x^2+9}\,dx$. Then,

$$I = 2\int \sqrt{x^2+\frac{9}{4}}\,dx = 2\int \sqrt{x^2+\left(\frac{3}{2}\right)^2}\,dx$$

$$\Rightarrow \quad I = 2\left\{\frac{1}{2}x\sqrt{x^2+\frac{9}{4}} + \frac{1}{2}\left(\frac{3}{2}\right)^2 \log\left|x+\sqrt{x^2+\frac{9}{4}}\right|\right\} + C$$

$$\Rightarrow \quad I = \frac{x}{2}\sqrt{4x^2+9} + \frac{9}{4}\log|2x+\sqrt{4x^2+9}| + C$$

(ii) $$I = \int \sqrt{x^2+2x+5}\,dx = \int \sqrt{x^2+2x+1+4}\,dx = \int \sqrt{(x+1)^2+2^2}\,dx$$

$$\Rightarrow \quad I = \frac{1}{2}(x+1)\sqrt{(x+1)^2+2^2} + \frac{1}{2}(2)^2 \log\left|(x+1)+\sqrt{(x+1)^2+2^2}\right| + C$$

$$\Rightarrow \quad I = \frac{1}{2}(x+1)\sqrt{x^2+2x+5} + 2\log\left|(x+1)+\sqrt{x^2+2x+5}\right| + C$$

EXAMPLE 2 *Evaluate:* (i) $\int \sqrt{7x-10-x^2}\,dx$ (ii) $\int \sqrt{(x-3)(5-x)}\,dx$

SOLUTION (i) Let $I = \int \sqrt{-(x^2-7x+10)}\,dx$. Then,

$$I = \int \sqrt{-\left(x^2-7x+\frac{49}{4}-\frac{49}{4}+10\right)}\,dx$$

$$\Rightarrow \quad I = \int \sqrt{-\left\{\left(x-\frac{7}{2}\right)^2 - \left(\frac{3}{2}\right)^2\right\}}\, dx = \int \sqrt{\left(\frac{3}{2}\right)^2 - \left(x-\frac{7}{2}\right)^2}\, dx$$

$$\Rightarrow \quad I = \frac{1}{2}\left(x-\frac{7}{2}\right)\sqrt{\left(\frac{3}{2}\right)^2 - \left(x-\frac{7}{2}\right)^2} + \frac{1}{2}\left(\frac{3}{2}\right)^2 \sin^{-1}\left(\frac{x-7/2}{3/2}\right) + C$$

$$\Rightarrow \quad I = \frac{1}{4}(2x-7)\sqrt{7x-10-x^2} + \frac{9}{8}\sin^{-1}\left(\frac{2x-7}{3}\right) + C.$$

(ii) Let $I = \int \sqrt{(x-3)(5-x)}\, dx$. Then,

$$I = \int \sqrt{-x^2+8x-15}\, dx = \int \sqrt{-\left\{x^2-8x+16-16+15\right\}}\, dx$$

$$\Rightarrow \quad I = \int \sqrt{-\left\{(x-4)^2 - 1^2\right\}}\, dx = \int \sqrt{1^2-(x-4)^2}\, dx$$

$$\Rightarrow \quad I = \frac{1}{2}(x-4)\sqrt{1^2-(x-4)^2} + \frac{1}{2}(1)^2 \sin^{-1}\left(\frac{x-4}{1}\right) + C$$

$$\Rightarrow \quad I = \frac{1}{2}(x-4)\sqrt{(x-3)(5-x)} + \frac{1}{2}\sin^{-1}(x-4) + C$$

BASED ON HIGHER ORDER THINKING SKILLS (HOTS)

EXAMPLE 3 *Evaluate :* $\int x\sqrt{\frac{1+x}{1-x}}\, dx$

SOLUTION Let $I = \int x\sqrt{\frac{1+x}{1-x}}\, dx$. Then,

$$I = \int \frac{x(1+x)}{\sqrt{1-x^2}}\, dx = \int \frac{x}{\sqrt{1-x^2}}\, dx + \int \frac{x^2}{\sqrt{1-x^2}}\, dx = -\frac{1}{2}\int \frac{-2x}{\sqrt{1-x^2}}\, dx - \int \frac{(1-x^2)-1}{\sqrt{1-x^2}}\, dx$$

$$\Rightarrow I = -\sqrt{1-x^2} - \int \sqrt{1-x^2}\, dx + \int \frac{1}{\sqrt{1-x^2}}\, dx = -\sqrt{1-x^2} - \frac{1}{2}x\sqrt{1-x^2} - \frac{1}{2}\sin^{-1}x + \sin^{-1}x + C$$

$$\Rightarrow I = -\sqrt{1-x^2} - \frac{1}{2}x\sqrt{1-x^2} + \frac{1}{2}\sin^{-1}x + C$$

EXAMPLE 4 *Evaluate:* $\int \sqrt{\frac{1-\sqrt{x}}{1+\sqrt{x}}}\, dx$ **[NCERT]**

SOLUTION Let $I = \int \sqrt{\frac{1-\sqrt{x}}{1+\sqrt{x}}}\, dx$. Putting $x = t^2$ and $dx = 2t\, dt$, we get

$$I = 2\int \sqrt{\frac{1-t}{1+t}}\,.\,t\, dt = 2\int \frac{t(1-t)}{\sqrt{1-t^2}}\, dt = \int \frac{2t}{\sqrt{1-t^2}}\, dt + 2\int \frac{-t^2}{\sqrt{1-t^2}}\, dt$$

$$\Rightarrow I = \int \frac{2t}{\sqrt{1-t^2}}\, dt + 2\int \frac{(1-t^2)-1}{\sqrt{1-t^2}}\, dt = -\int \frac{-2t}{\sqrt{1-t^2}}\, dt + 2\int \sqrt{1-t^2}\, dt - 2\int \frac{1}{\sqrt{1-t^2}}\, dt$$

$$\Rightarrow I = -2\sqrt{1-t^2} + 2\times\frac{1}{2}\left\{t\sqrt{1-t^2} + \sin^{-1}t\right\} - 2\sin^{-1}t + C$$

$$\Rightarrow I = -2\sqrt{1-t^2} + t\sqrt{1-t^2} - \sin^{-1} t + C = (1-x)(\sqrt{x}-2) - \sin^{-1}\sqrt{x} + C$$

EXAMPLE 5 *Evaluate :* $\int \frac{x^2}{\sqrt{1-2x-x^2}}\, dx$

SOLUTION Let $I = \int \frac{x^2}{\sqrt{1-2x-x^2}}\, dx$. Then,

$$I = -\int \frac{-x^2}{\sqrt{1-2x-x^2}}\, dx = -\int \frac{(1-2x-x^2)+(2x-1)}{\sqrt{1-2x-x^2}}\, dx$$

$$\Rightarrow I = -\int \sqrt{1-2x-x^2}\, dx - \int \frac{2x-1}{\sqrt{1-2x-x^2}}\, dx = -\int \sqrt{1-2x-x^2}\, dx + \int \frac{-2x-2+3}{\sqrt{1-2x-x^2}}\, dx$$

$$\Rightarrow I = -\int \sqrt{1-2x-x^2}\, dx + \int \frac{-2x-2}{\sqrt{1-2x-x^2}}\, dx + 3\int \frac{1}{\sqrt{1-2x-x^2}}\, dx$$

$$\Rightarrow I = -\int \sqrt{(\sqrt{2})^2-(x+1)^2}\, dx + \int \frac{1}{\sqrt{1-2x-x^2}}\, d(1-2x-x^2) + 3\int \frac{1}{\sqrt{(\sqrt{2})^2-(x+1)^2}}\, dx$$

$$\Rightarrow I = -\frac{1}{2}\left\{(x+1)\sqrt{1-2x-x^2} + 2\sin^{-1}\frac{x+1}{\sqrt{2}}\right\} + 2\sqrt{1-2x-x^2} + 3\sin^{-1}\left(\frac{x+1}{\sqrt{2}}\right) + C$$

EXERCISE 15.28

BASIC

Evaluate the following integrals:

1. $\int \sqrt{3+2x-x^2}\, dx$ [NCERT]
2. $\int \sqrt{x^2+x+1}\, dx$
3. $\int \sqrt{x-x^2}\, dx$
4. $\int \sqrt{1+x-2x^2}\, dx$
5. $\int \cos x\sqrt{4-\sin^2 x}\, dx$
6. $\int e^x\sqrt{e^{2x}+1}\, dx$
7. $\int \sqrt{9-x^2}\, dx$
8. $\int \sqrt{16x^2+25}\, dx$
9. $\int \sqrt{4x^2-5}\, dx$
10. $\int \sqrt{2x^2+3x+4}\, dx$
11. $\int \sqrt{3-2x-2x^2}\, dx$
12. $\int \sqrt{3-x^2}\, dx$
13. $\int \sqrt{x^2-2x}\, dx$ [CBSE 2017]
14. $\int \sqrt{2x-x^2}\, dx$ [CBSE 2017]

BASED ON LOTS

15. $\int x\sqrt{x^4+1}\, dx$
16. $\int x^2\sqrt{a^6-x^6}\, dx$
17. $\int \frac{\sqrt{16+(\log x)^2}}{x}\, dx$ [CBSE 2005]
18. $\int \sqrt{2ax-x^2}\, dx$

ANSWERS

1. $\frac{(x-1)}{2}\sqrt{3+2x-x^2} + 2\sin^{-1}\left(\frac{x-1}{2}\right) + C$
2. $\left(\frac{2x+1}{4}\right)\sqrt{x^2+x+1} + \frac{3}{8}\log\left|(2x+1)+\sqrt{x^2+x+1}\right| + C$

3. $\frac{1}{4}(2x-1)\sqrt{x-x^2}+\frac{1}{8}\sin^{-1}(2x-1)+C$

4. $\frac{1}{8}(4x-1)\sqrt{1+x-2x^2}+\frac{9\sqrt{2}}{32}\sin^{-1}\left(\frac{4x-1}{3}\right)+C$

5. $\frac{1}{2}\sin x\sqrt{4-\sin^2 x}+2\sin^{-1}\left(\frac{\sin x}{2}\right)+C$

6. $\frac{1}{2}e^x\sqrt{e^{2x}+1}+\frac{1}{2}\log\left|e^x+\sqrt{e^{2x}+1}\right|+C$

7. $\frac{1}{2}x\sqrt{9-x^2}+\frac{9}{2}\sin^{-1}\left(\frac{x}{3}\right)+C$

8. $2x\sqrt{x^2+\frac{25}{16}}+\frac{25}{8}\log\left|x+\sqrt{x^2+\frac{25}{16}}\right|+C$

9. $x\sqrt{x^2-\frac{5}{4}}-\frac{5}{4}\log\left|x+\sqrt{x^2-\frac{5}{4}}\right|+C$

10. $\left(\frac{4x+3}{8}\right)\sqrt{2x^2+3x+4}+\frac{23\sqrt{2}}{32}\log\left|\left(x+\frac{3}{4}\right)+\sqrt{x^2+\frac{3}{2}x+2}\right|+C$

11. $\frac{1}{4}(2x+1)\sqrt{3-2x-2x^2}+\frac{7}{4\sqrt{2}}\sin^{-1}\left(\frac{2x+1}{\sqrt{7}}\right)+C$

12. $\frac{1}{2}x\sqrt{3-x^2}+\frac{3}{2}\sin^{-1}\left(\frac{x}{\sqrt{3}}\right)+C$

13. $\frac{1}{2}(x-1)\sqrt{x^2-2x}-\frac{1}{2}\log\left|(x-1)+\sqrt{x^2-2x}\right|+C$

14. $\frac{1}{2}(x-1)\sqrt{2x-x^2}+\frac{1}{2}\sin^{-1}(x-1)+C$

15. $\frac{1}{4}x^2\sqrt{x^4+1}+\frac{1}{4}\log\left|x^2+\sqrt{x^4+1}\right|+C$

16. $\frac{1}{6}x^3\sqrt{a^6-x^6}+\frac{a^6}{6}\sin^{-1}\left(\frac{x^3}{a^3}\right)+C$

17. $\frac{1}{2}\log x\sqrt{(\log x)^2+16}+8\log|\log x+\sqrt{(\log x)^2+16}|+C$

18. $\frac{1}{2}(x-a)\sqrt{2ax-x^2}+\frac{a^2}{2}\sin^{-1}\left(\frac{x-a}{a}\right)+C$

15.12.2 INTEGRALS OF THE FORM $\int (px+q)\sqrt{ax^2+bx+c}\,dx$

In order to evaluate this type of integrals, we use the following algorithm.

ALGORITHM

Step I *Express $px+q$ as*

$$px+q = \lambda\frac{d}{dx}(ax^2+bx+c)+\mu \quad i.e.\quad px+q = \lambda(2ax+b)+\mu$$

Step II *Obtain the values of λ and μ by equating the coefficients of x and constant terms on both sides.*

Step III *Replace $px+q$ by $\lambda(2ax+b)+\mu$ in the integral to obtain*

$$\int(px+q)\sqrt{ax^2+bx+c}\,dx=\lambda\int(2ax+b)\sqrt{ax^2+bx+c}\,dx+\mu\int\sqrt{ax^2+bx+c}\,dx$$

Step IV *To evaluate first integral on RHS, use the formula $\int(f(x))^n f'(x)\,dx=\frac{\{f(x)\}^{n+1}}{n+1}$.*

Evaluate second integral on RHS by the method discussed in the previous section.

ILLUSTRATIVEEXAMPLES

BASED ON BASIC CONCEPTS (BASIC)

EXAMPLE 1 *Evaluate:*

(i) $\int (x-5)\sqrt{x^2+x}\,dx$ (ii) $\int (3x-2)\sqrt{x^2+x+1}\,dx$ **[CBSE 2014]**

SOLUTION Let $(x-5) = \lambda \frac{d}{dx}(x^2+x) + \mu$ i.e. $x-5 = \lambda(2x+1)+\mu$

Comparing coefficients of like powers of x, we get

$$1 = 2\lambda \text{ and } \lambda+\mu = -5 \Rightarrow \lambda = \frac{1}{2} \text{ and } \mu = -\frac{11}{2}$$

$$\therefore \quad I = \int (x-5)\sqrt{x^2+x}\,dx$$

$$\Rightarrow \quad I = \int \left(\frac{1}{2}(2x+1) - \frac{11}{2}\right)\sqrt{x^2+x}\,dx$$

$$\Rightarrow \quad I = \int \frac{1}{2}(2x+1)\sqrt{x^2+x}\,dx - \frac{11}{2}\int \sqrt{x^2+x}\,dx$$

$$\Rightarrow \quad I = \frac{1}{2}\int (2x+1)\sqrt{x^2+x}\,dx - \frac{11}{2}\int \sqrt{x^2+x}\,dx$$

$$\Rightarrow \quad I = \frac{1}{2}\int \sqrt{t}\,dt - \frac{11}{2}\int \sqrt{\left(x+\frac{1}{2}\right)^2 - \left(\frac{1}{2}\right)^2}\,dx, \quad \text{where } t = x^2+x$$

$$\Rightarrow \quad I = \frac{1}{2}\times\frac{t^{3/2}}{3/2} - \frac{11}{2}\left\{\frac{1}{2}\left(x+\frac{1}{2}\right)\sqrt{\left(x+\frac{1}{2}\right)^2 - \left(\frac{1}{2}\right)^2}\right.$$

$$\left. - \frac{1}{2}\left(\frac{1}{2}\right)^2 \log\left|\left(x+\frac{1}{2}\right) + \sqrt{\left(x+\frac{1}{2}\right)^2 - \left(\frac{1}{2}\right)^2}\right| + C\right.$$

$$\Rightarrow \quad I = \frac{1}{3}t^{3/2} - \frac{11}{2}\left\{\frac{2x+1}{4}\sqrt{x^2+x} - \frac{1}{8}\log\left|\left(x+\frac{1}{2}\right) + \sqrt{x^2+x}\right|\right\} + C$$

$$\Rightarrow \quad I = \frac{1}{3}(x^2+x)^{3/2} - \frac{11}{2}\left\{\frac{2x+1}{4}\sqrt{x^2+x} - \frac{1}{8}\log\left|\left(x+\frac{1}{2}\right)\sqrt{x^2+x}\right|\right\}$$

(ii) Let $3x-2 = \lambda \frac{d}{dx}(x^2+x+1) + \mu$ i.e. $3x-2 = \lambda(2x+1)+\mu$

Comparing the coefficients of like powers of x, we get

$$2\lambda = 3 \text{ and } \lambda+\mu = -2 \Rightarrow \lambda = \frac{3}{2} \text{ and } \mu = -\frac{7}{2}$$

$$\therefore \quad I = \int (3x-2)\sqrt{x^2+x+1}\,dx$$

$$\Rightarrow \quad I = \int \left\{\frac{3}{2}(2x+1) - \frac{7}{2}\right\}\sqrt{x^2+x+1}\,dx$$

$$\Rightarrow \quad I = \frac{3}{2}\int (2x+1)\sqrt{x^2+x+1}\,dx - \frac{7}{2}\int \sqrt{x^2+x+1}\,dx$$

$$\Rightarrow \quad I = \frac{3}{2}\int \sqrt{t}\,dt - \frac{7}{2}\int \sqrt{\left(x+\frac{1}{2}\right)^2 + \left(\frac{\sqrt{3}}{2}\right)^2}\,dx, \quad \text{where } t = x^2+x+1$$

$$\Rightarrow \quad I = t^{3/2} - \frac{7}{4}\left\{\left(x+\frac{1}{2}\right)\sqrt{x^2+x+1} + \left(\frac{\sqrt{3}}{2}\right)^2 \log\left|x+\frac{1}{2}+\sqrt{x^2+x+1}\right|\right\} + C$$

$$\Rightarrow \quad I = (x^2+x+1)^{3/2} - \frac{7}{2}\left\{\left(x+\frac{1}{2}\right)\sqrt{x^2+x+1} + \frac{3}{8}\log\left|x+\frac{1}{2}+\sqrt{x^2+x+1}\right|\right\} + C$$

EXAMPLE 2 *Evaluate:*

(i) $\int x\sqrt{1+x-x^2}\, dx$ (ii) $\int (x+1)\sqrt{1-x-x^2}\, dx$

SOLUTION Let $x = \lambda \frac{d}{dx}(1+x-x^2) + \mu$ i.e. $x = \lambda(1-2x) + \mu$

Comparing the coefficients of like powers of x, we get

$$1 = -2\lambda \text{ and } \lambda + \mu = 0 \Rightarrow \lambda = -\frac{1}{2} \text{ and } \mu = \frac{1}{2}$$

$$\therefore \quad I = \int x\sqrt{1+x-x^2}\, dx$$

$$\Rightarrow \quad I = \int \left\{-\frac{1}{2}(1-2x) + \frac{1}{2}\right\}\sqrt{1+x-x^2}\, dx$$

$$\Rightarrow \quad I = -\frac{1}{2}\int (1-2x)\sqrt{1+x-x^2}\, dx + \frac{1}{2}\int \sqrt{1+x-x^2}\, dx$$

$$\Rightarrow \quad I = -\frac{1}{2}\int \sqrt{t}\, dt + \frac{1}{2}\int \sqrt{-\left(x^2-x+\frac{1}{4}-\frac{1}{4}-1\right)}\, dx$$

$$\Rightarrow \quad I = -\frac{1}{2}\left(\frac{t^{3/2}}{3/2}\right) + \frac{1}{2}\int \sqrt{\left(\frac{\sqrt{5}}{2}\right)^2 - \left(x-\frac{1}{2}\right)^2}\, dx, \text{ where } t = 1+x-x^2$$

$$\Rightarrow \quad I = -\frac{1}{3}t^{3/2} + \frac{1}{2}\left\{\left(x-\frac{1}{2}\right)\sqrt{\left(\frac{\sqrt{5}}{2}\right)^2 - \left(x-\frac{1}{2}\right)^2} + \frac{1}{2}\left(\frac{\sqrt{5}}{2}\right)^2 \sin^{-1}\left(\frac{x-1/2}{\sqrt{5}/2}\right)\right\} + C$$

$$\Rightarrow \quad I = -\frac{1}{3}(1+x-x^2)^{3/2} + \frac{1}{2}\left\{\frac{1}{2}\left(x-\frac{1}{2}\right)\sqrt{1+x-x^2} + \frac{5}{8}\sin^{-1}\left(\frac{2x-1}{\sqrt{5}}\right)\right\} + C$$

(ii) Let $x+1 = \lambda \frac{d}{dx}(1-x-x^2) + \mu$ i.e. $x+1 = \lambda(-1-2x) + \mu$

Comparing the coefficients of like powers of x, we get

$$-2\lambda = 1 \text{ and } \mu - \lambda = 1 \Rightarrow \lambda = -\frac{1}{2} \text{ and } \mu = \frac{1}{2}$$

$$\therefore \quad I = \int (x+1)\sqrt{1-x-x^2}\, dx = \int \left\{-\frac{1}{2}(-1-2x) + \frac{1}{2}\right\}\sqrt{1-x-x^2}\, dx$$

$$\Rightarrow \quad I = -\frac{1}{2}\int (-1-2x)\sqrt{1-x-x^2}\, dx + \frac{1}{2}\int \sqrt{1-x-x^2}\, dx$$

$$\Rightarrow \quad I = \frac{1}{2}\int (-1-2x)\sqrt{1-x-x^2}\, dx + \frac{1}{2}\int \sqrt{\left\{1-\left(x^2+x+\frac{1}{4}-\frac{1}{4}\right)\right\}}\, dx$$

$$\Rightarrow \quad I = -\frac{1}{2}\int \sqrt{t}\, dt + \frac{1}{2}\int \sqrt{\left(\frac{\sqrt{5}}{2}\right)^2 - \left(x+\frac{1}{2}\right)^2}\, dx, \text{ where } t = 1-x-x^2$$

$$\Rightarrow \quad I = -\frac{1}{2}\left(\frac{t^{3/2}}{3/2}\right) + \frac{1}{2}\left\{\frac{1}{2}\left(x + \frac{1}{2}\right)\sqrt{1 - x - x^2} + \frac{1}{2} \times \frac{5}{4}\sin^{-1}\left(\frac{x + 1/2}{\sqrt{5}/2}\right)\right\} + C$$

$$\Rightarrow \quad I = -\frac{1}{3}(1 - x - x^2)^{3/2} + \frac{1}{8}(2x + 1)\sqrt{1 - x - x^2} + \frac{5}{16}\sin^{-1}\left(\frac{2x + 1}{\sqrt{5}}\right) + C$$

BASED ON HIGHER ORDER THINKING SKILLS (HOTS)

EXAMPLE 3 *Evaluate:* $\int \frac{x}{x - \sqrt{x^2 - 1}}\, dx$

SOLUTION Let

$$I = \int \frac{x}{x - \sqrt{x^2 - 1}}\, dx = \int x \frac{\left(x + \sqrt{x^2 - 1}\right)}{\left(x - \sqrt{x^2 - 1}\right)\left(x + \sqrt{x^2 - 1}\right)}\, dx$$

$$\Rightarrow \quad I = \int \frac{x\left(x + \sqrt{x^2 - 1}\right)}{x^2 - (x^2 - 1)}\, dx = \int \left(x^2 + x\sqrt{x^2 - 1}\right) dx = \int x^2\, dx + \int x\sqrt{x^2 - 1}\, dx$$

$$\Rightarrow \quad I = \int x^2\, dx + \frac{1}{2}\int \sqrt{t}\, dt, \text{ where } t = x^2 - 1$$

$$\Rightarrow \quad I = \frac{x^3}{3} + \frac{1}{3}t^{3/2} + C = \frac{x^3}{3} + \frac{1}{3}(x^2 - 1)^{3/2} + C$$

EXERCISE 15.29

BASIC

Evaluate the following integrals:

1. $\int (x + 1)\sqrt{x^2 - x + 1}\, dx$
2. $\int (x + 1)\sqrt{2x^2 + 3}\, dx$
3. $\int (2x - 5)\sqrt{2 + 3x - x^2}\, dx$
4. $\int (x + 2)\sqrt{x^2 + x + 1}\, dx$
5. $\int (4x + 1)\sqrt{x^2 - x - 2}\, dx$
6. $\int (x - 2)\sqrt{2x^2 - 6x + 5}\, dx$
7. $\int (x + 1)\sqrt{x^2 + x + 1}\, dx$
8. $\int (2x + 3)\sqrt{x^2 + 4x + 3}\, dx$
9. $\int (2x - 5)\sqrt{x^2 - 4x + 3}\, dx$
10. $\int x\sqrt{x^2 + x}\, dx$
11. $\int (x - 3)\sqrt{x^2 + 3x - 18}\, dx$ **[CBSE 2014]**
12. $\int (x + 3)\sqrt{3 - 4x - x^2}\, dx$ **[CBSE 14, 2015]**
13. $\int (3x + 1)\sqrt{4 - 3x - 2x^2}\, dx$ **[CBSE 2016]**
14. $\int (2x + 5)\sqrt{10 - 4x - 3x^2}\, dx$ **[CBSE 2016]**

ANSWERS

1. $\frac{(x^2 - x + 1)^{3/2}}{3} + \frac{3}{8}(2x - 1)\sqrt{x^2 - x + 1} + \frac{9}{16}\log\left|\left(x - \frac{1}{2}\right) + \sqrt{x^2 + x + 1}\right| + C$

2. $\frac{1}{6}(2x^2 + 3)^{3/2} + \frac{x}{2}\sqrt{2x^2 + 3} + \frac{3\sqrt{2}}{4}\log\left|\frac{\sqrt{2}\, x + \sqrt{2x^2 + 3}}{\sqrt{3}}\right| + C$

3. $-\frac{2}{3}(2+3x-x^2)^{3/2}-\left(\frac{2x-3}{2}\right)\sqrt{2+3x-x^2}-\frac{17}{4}\sin^{-1}\left(\frac{2x-3}{\sqrt{17}}\right)+C$

4. $\frac{1}{3}(x^2+x+1)^{3/2}+\frac{3(2x+1)}{8}\sqrt{x^2+x+1}+\frac{9}{16}\log\left|\left(x+\frac{1}{2}\right)+\sqrt{x^2+x+1}\right|+C$

5. $\frac{4}{3}(x^2-x-2)^{3/2}+\frac{3}{4}(2x-1)\sqrt{x^2-x-2}-\frac{27}{8}\log\left|\left(x-\frac{1}{2}\right)+\sqrt{x^2-x-2}\right|+C$

6. $\frac{1}{6}(2x^2-6x+5)^{3/2}-\frac{1}{\sqrt{2}}\left\{\frac{2x-3}{4}\sqrt{x^2-3x+\frac{5}{2}}+\frac{1}{8}\log\left|\frac{2x-3}{2}+\sqrt{x^2-3x+\frac{5}{2}}\right|\right\}+C$

7. $\frac{1}{3}(x^2+x+1)^{3/2}+\frac{1}{2}\left\{\frac{2x+1}{4}\sqrt{x^2+x+1}+\frac{3}{8}\log\left|\left(x+\frac{1}{2}\right)+\sqrt{x^2+x+1}\right|\right\}+C$

8. $\frac{2}{3}(x^2+4x+3)^{3/2}-\left\{\frac{1}{2}(x+2)\sqrt{x^2+4x+3}-\frac{1}{2}\log\left|(x+2)+\sqrt{x^2+4x+3}\right|\right\}+C$

9. $\frac{2}{3}(x^2-4x+3)^{3/2}-\left\{\frac{1}{2}(x-2)\sqrt{x^2-4x+3}-\frac{1}{2}\log\left|x-2+\sqrt{x^2-4x+3}\right|\right\}+C$

10. $\frac{1}{3}(x+x^2)^{3/2}-\frac{1}{8}(2x+1)\sqrt{x^2+x}+\frac{1}{16}\log\left|\left(x+\frac{1}{2}\right)+\sqrt{x^2+x}\right|+C$

11. $\frac{1}{3}(x^2+3x-18)^{3/2}-\frac{3}{4}(2x+3)\sqrt{x^2+3x-18}+\frac{243}{8}\log\left|\left(x+\frac{3}{2}\right)+\sqrt{x^2+3x-18}\right|+C$

12. $-\frac{1}{3}(3-4x-x^2)^{3/2}+\frac{1}{2}(x+2)\sqrt{3-4x-x^2}+\frac{7}{2}\sin^{-1}\left(\frac{x+2}{\sqrt{7}}\right)+C$

13. $-\frac{1}{2}(4-3x-2x^2)^{3/2}-\frac{5}{32}(4x+3)\sqrt{4-3x-2x^2}-\frac{205}{64\sqrt{2}}\sin^{-1}\frac{4x+3}{\sqrt{41}}+C$

14. $-\frac{2}{9}(10-4x-3x^2)^{3/2}+\frac{11}{18}(3x+2)\sqrt{10-4x-3x^2}+\frac{187}{9\sqrt{3}}\sin^{-1}\left(\frac{3x+2}{\sqrt{34}}\right)+C$

15.13 INTEGRATION OF RATIONAL ALGEBRAIC FUNCTIONS BY USING PARTIAL FRACTIONS

PARTIAL FRACTIONS *If $f(x)$ and $g(x)$ are two polynomials, then $\frac{f(x)}{g(x)}$ defines a rational algebraic function or a rational function of x.*

If degree of $f(x)<$ degree of $g(x)$, then $\frac{f(x)}{g(x)}$ is called a proper rational function.

If degree of $f(x)\geq$ degree of $g(x)$, then $\frac{f(x)}{g(x)}$ is called an improper rational function.

If $\frac{f(x)}{g(x)}$ is an improper rational function, we divide $f(x)$ by $g(x)$ so that the rational function $\frac{f(x)}{g(x)}$ is expressed in the form $\phi(x)+\frac{\psi(x)}{g(x)}$ where $\phi(x)$ and $\psi(x)$ are polynomials such that the degree of $\psi(x)$ is less than that of $g(x)$. Thus, $\frac{f(x)}{g(x)}$ is expressible as the sum of a polynomial and a proper rational function.

Any proper rational function $\frac{f(x)}{g(x)}$ can be expressed as the sum of rational functions, each having a simple factor of $g(x)$. Each such fraction is called a partial fraction and the process of obtaining them is called the resolution or decomposition of $\frac{f(x)}{g(x)}$ into partial fractions.

The resolution of $\frac{f(x)}{g(x)}$ into partial fractions depends mainly upon the nature of the factors of $g(x)$ as discussed below.

CASE I When denominator is expressible as the product of non-repeating linear factors.

Let $g(x) = (x - a_1)(x - a_2) \dots (x - a_n)$. Then, we assume that

$$\frac{f(x)}{g(x)} = \frac{A_1}{x - a_1} + \frac{A_2}{x - a_2} + \dots + \frac{A_n}{x - a_n}$$

where $A_1, A_2, .. A_n$ are constants and can be determined by equating the numerator on RHS to the numerator on LHS after taking LCM on RHS and then substituting $x = a_1, a_2, \dots, a_n$.

ILLUSTRATION 1 *Resolve* $\frac{3x+2}{x^3 - 6x^2 + 11x - 6}$ *into partial fractions.*

SOLUTION We have, $\frac{3x+2}{x^3 - 6x^2 + 11x - 6} = \frac{3x+2}{(x-1)(x-2)(x-3)}$

Let $\frac{3x+2}{(x-1)(x-2)(x-3)} = \frac{A}{x-1} + \frac{B}{x-2} + \frac{C}{x-3}$. Then,

$$\Rightarrow \quad \frac{3x+2}{(x-1)(x-2)(x-3)} = \frac{A(x-2)(x-3) + B(x-1)(x-3) + C(x-1)(x-2)}{(x-1)(x-2)(x-3)}$$

$$\Rightarrow \quad 3x + 2 = A(x-2)(x-3) + B(x-1)(x-3) + C(x-1)(x-2) \quad \text{...(i)}$$

Putting $x - 1 = 0$ or, $x = 1$ in (i), we get $5 = A(1-2)(1-3) \Rightarrow A = \frac{5}{2}$

Putting $x - 2 = 0$ or, $x = 2$ in (i), we obtain $8 = B(2-1)(2-3) \Rightarrow B = -8$

Putting $x - 3 = 0$ or, $x = 3$ in (i), we obtain $11 = C(3-1)(3-2) \Rightarrow C = \frac{11}{2}$

$$\therefore \quad \frac{3x+2}{x^3 - 6x^2 + 11x - 6} = \frac{3x+2}{(x-1)(x-2)(x-3)} = \frac{5}{2(x-1)} - \frac{8}{x-2} + \frac{11}{2(x-3)}$$

REMARK *In order to determine the values of constants in the numerator of the partial fraction corresponding to the non-repeated linear factor $px + q$ in the denominator of a rational expression, we may proceed as follows:*

Replace $x = -q/p$ (obtained by putting $px + q = 0$) everywhere in the given rational expression except in the factor $px + q$ itself. For example, in the above illustration the value of A is obtained by replacing x by 1 in all factors of $\frac{3x+2}{(x-1)(x-2)(x-3)}$ except $(x-1)$.

i.e. $$A = \frac{3 \times 1 + 2}{(1-2)(1-3)} = \frac{5}{2}$$

Similarly, B is obtained by putting $x = 2$ in all factors of $\frac{3x+2}{(x-1)(x-2)(x-2)}$ except $(x-2)$ in denominator.

$$B = \frac{3 \times 2 + 1}{(2-2)(2-3)} = -8$$

To find C, we put $x = 3$ in all factors of $\frac{3x+2}{(x-1)(x-2)(x-3)}$ except $(x-3)$ in denominator.

$$\therefore \quad C = \frac{3 \times 3 + 2}{(3-1)(3-2)} = \frac{11}{2}$$

ILLUSTRATION 2 *Resolve* $\frac{x^3 - 6x^2 + 10x - 2}{x^2 - 5x + 6}$ *into partial fractions.*

SOLUTION Here, the given function is an improper rational function. On dividing, we get

$$\frac{x^3 - 6x^2 + 10x - 2}{x^2 - 5x + 6} = x - 1 + \frac{(-x+4)}{x^2 - 5x + 6} \qquad \text{...(i)}$$

Now, $\frac{-x+4}{x^2 - 5x + 6} = \frac{-x+4}{(x-2)(x-3)}$

So, let $\frac{-x+4}{(x-2)(x-3)} = \frac{A}{x-2} + \frac{B}{x-3}$

$$\therefore \quad -x + 4 = A(x-3) + B(x-2) \qquad \text{...(ii)}$$

Putting $x - 3 = 0$ or, $x = 3$ in (ii), we get: $1 = B(1) \Rightarrow B = 1$.

Putting $x - 2 = 0$ or, $x = 2$ in (ii), we get: $2 = A(2-3) \Rightarrow A = -2$

$$\therefore \quad \frac{-x+4}{(x-2)(x-3)} = \frac{-2}{x-2} + \frac{1}{x-3}$$

Hence, $\frac{x^3 - 6x^2 + 10x - 2}{x^2 - 5x + 6} = x - 1 - \frac{2}{x-2} + \frac{1}{x-3}$

Case II *When the denominator $g(x)$ is expressible as the product of the linear factors such that some of them are repeating.*

Let $g(x) = (x-a)^k (x-a_1)(x-a_2)\dots(x-a_r)$. Then we assume that

$$\frac{f(x)}{g(x)} = \frac{A_1}{x-a} + \frac{A_2}{(x-a)^2} + \frac{A_3}{(x-a)^3} + \dots + \frac{A_k}{(x-a)^k} + \frac{B_1}{x-a} + \frac{B_2}{x-a_2} + \dots + \frac{B_r}{(x-a_r)}$$

i.e., corresponding to non-repeating factors we assume as in Case I and for each repeating factor $(x-a)^k$, we assume partial fractions

$$\frac{A_1}{x-a} + \frac{A_2}{(x-a)^2} + \frac{A_3}{(x-a)^3} + \dots + \frac{A_k}{(x-a)^k}, \text{ where } A_1, A_2, \dots, A_k \text{ are constants.}$$

Now, to determine constants we equate numerators on both sides. Some of the constants are determined by substitution as in case I and remaining are obtained by comparing coefficients of equal powers of x on both sides.

Following illustration illustrates the procedure.

ILLUSTRATION 3 *Resolve* $\frac{3x-2}{(x-1)^2(x+1)(x+2)}$ *into partial fractions.*

SOLUTION Let $\frac{3x-2}{(x-1)^2(x+1)(x+2)} = \frac{A_1}{x-1} + \frac{A_2}{(x-1)^2} + \frac{A_3}{x+1} + \frac{A_4}{x+2}$

$$\Rightarrow 3x - 2 = A_1(x-1)(x+1)(x+2) + A_2(x+1)(x+2) + A_3(x-1)^2(x+2) + A_4(x-1)^2(x+1) \qquad \text{...(i)}$$

Putting $x - 1 = 0$ or, $x = 1$ in (i), we get: $1 = A_2(1+1)(1+2) \Rightarrow A_2 = \frac{1}{6}$

Putting $x + 1 = 0$ or, $x = -1$ in (i), we get: $-5 = A_3(-2)^2(-1+2) \Rightarrow A_3 = -\frac{5}{4}$

Putting $x + 2 = 0$ or, $x = -2$ in (i), we get: $-8 = A_4(-3)^2(-1) \Rightarrow A_4 = \frac{8}{9}$

Now, equating coefficient of x^3 on both sides, we get

$$0 = A_1 + A_3 + A_4 \Rightarrow A_1 = -A_3 - A_4 = \frac{5}{4} - \frac{8}{9} = \frac{13}{36}$$

$$\therefore \quad \frac{3x-2}{(x-1)^2 (x+1)(x+2)} = \frac{13}{36(x-1)} + \frac{1}{6(x-1)^2} - \frac{5}{4(x+1)} + \frac{8}{9(x+2)}$$

Case III *When some of the factors of denominator $g(x)$ are quadratic but non-repeating.*

Corresponding to each quadratic factor $ax^2 + bx + c$, we assume partial fraction of the type $\frac{Ax + B}{ax^2 + bx + c}$, where A and B are constants to be determined by comparing coefficients of similar powers of x in the numerator of both sides. In practice it is advisable to assume partial fractions of the type $\frac{A(2ax+b)}{ax^2+bx+c} + \frac{B}{ax^2+bx+c}$.

Following illustration illustrates the procedure.

ILLUSTRATION 4 *Resolve* $\frac{2x-1}{(x+1)(x^2+2)}$ *into partial fractions.*

SOLUTION Let $\frac{2x-1}{(x+1)(x^2+2)} = \frac{A}{x+1} + \frac{Bx+C}{x^2+2}$. Then,

$$\frac{2x-1}{(x+1)(x^2+2)} = \frac{A(x^2+2) + (Bx+C)(x+1)}{(x+1)(x^2+2)} \Rightarrow 2x-1 = A(x^2+2) + (Bx+C)(x+1) \quad ...(i)$$

Putting $x + 1 = 0$ or, $x = -1$ in (i), we get: $-3 = A(3) \Rightarrow A = -1$.

Comparing coefficients of like powers of x on both sides of (i), we get

$$A + B = 0,\ C + 2A = -1 \text{ and } C + B = 2$$

$$\therefore \quad -1 + B = 0,\ C - 2 = -1 \Rightarrow B = 1,\ C = 1 \qquad [\text{Putting } A = -1]$$

$$\therefore \quad \frac{2x-1}{(x+1)(x^2+2)} = -\frac{1}{x+1} + \frac{x+1}{x^2+2}$$

Case IV *When some of the factors of the denominator $g(x)$ are quadratic and repeating.*

For every quadratic repeating factor of the type $(ax^2 + bx + c)^k$, we assume $2k$ partial fractions of the form

$$\left\{\frac{A_0(2ax+b)}{ax^2+bx+c} + \frac{A_1}{ax^2+bx+c}\right\} + \left\{\frac{A_1(2ax+b)}{(ax^2+bx+c)^2} + \frac{A_2}{(ax^2+bx+c)^2}\right\}$$
$$+ \ldots + \left\{\frac{A_{2k-1}(2ax+b)}{(ax^2+bx+c)^k} + \frac{A_{2k}}{(ax^2+bx+c)^k}\right\}$$

Following illustrations will illustrate the procedure.

ILLUSTRATION 5 *Resolve* $\frac{2x-3}{(x-1)(x^2+1)^2}$ *into partial fractions.*

SOLUTION Let $\frac{2x-3}{(x-1)(x^2+1)^2} = \frac{A}{x-1} + \frac{Bx+C}{x^2+1} + \frac{Dx+E}{(x^2+1)^2}$. Then,

$$2x - 3 = A(x^2+1)^2 + (Bx+C)(x-1)(x^2+1) + (Dx+E)(x-1) \quad ...(i)$$

Putting $x = 1$ in (i), we get: $-1 = A(1+1)^2 \Rightarrow A = -\frac{1}{4}$

Equating coefficients of like powers of x, we get

$$A + B = 0,\ C - B = 0,\ 2A + B - C + D = 0,\ C + E - B - D = 2 \text{ and } A - C - E = -3$$

Putting $A = -\frac{1}{4}$ and solving these equations, we get: $B = \frac{1}{4} = C,\ D = \frac{1}{2}$ and $E = \frac{5}{2}$.

$$\therefore \quad \frac{2x-3}{(x-1)(x^2+1)^2} = \frac{-1}{4(x-1)} + \frac{x+1}{4(x^2+1)} + \frac{x+5}{2(x^2+1)^2}$$

ILLUSTRATION 6 *Resolve* $\frac{2x}{x^3-1}$ *into partial fractions.*

SOLUTION We have, $\frac{2x}{x^3-1} = \frac{2x}{(x-1)(x^2+x+1)}$

So, let $\frac{2x}{(x-1)(x^2+x+1)} = \frac{A}{x-1} + \frac{Bx+C}{x^2+x+1}$. Then,

$$2x = A(x^2+x+1) + (Bx+C)(x-1) \quad \text{...(i)}$$

Putting $x-1=0$ or, $x=1$ in (i), we get : $2 = 3A \Rightarrow A = \frac{2}{3}$

Putting $x=0$ in (i), we get : $A - C = 0 \Rightarrow C = A = \frac{2}{3}$

Putting $x=-1$ in (i), we get : $-2 = A + 2B - 2C \Rightarrow -2 = \frac{2}{3} - 2B - \frac{4}{3} \Rightarrow B = \frac{2}{3}$

$$\therefore \quad \frac{2x}{x^3-1} = \frac{2}{3}\cdot\frac{1}{x-1} + \frac{2/3\,x + 2/3}{x^2+x+1} \text{ or, } \frac{2x}{x^3-1} = \frac{2}{3}\cdot\frac{1}{x-1} + \frac{2}{3}\cdot\frac{x+1}{x^2+x+1}$$

Let us now use partial fractions in evaluating integrals containing rational algebraic functions.

ILLUSTRATIVE EXAMPLES

BASED ON BASIC CONCEPTS (BASIC)

Type I WHEN THE DENOMINATOR IS EXPRESSIBLE AS A PRODUCT OF DISTINCT LINEAR FACTORS

EXAMPLE 1 *Evaluate:*

(i) $\int \frac{x-1}{(x+1)(x-2)}\,dx$ (ii) $\int \frac{2x-1}{(x-1)(x+2)(x-3)}\,dx$ [CBSE 2005] (iii) $\int \frac{x^3}{(x-1)(x-2)}\,dx$

SOLUTION (i) Let $\frac{x-1}{(x+1)(x-2)} = \frac{A}{x+1} + \frac{B}{x-2}$ ...(i)

$$\Rightarrow \quad x-1 = A(x-2) + B(x+1) \quad \text{...(ii)}$$

Putting $x-2=0$ or, $x=2$ in (ii), we get: $1 = 3B \Rightarrow B = 1/3$

Putting $x+1=0$ or, $x=-1$ in (ii), we get: $-2 = -3A \Rightarrow A = 2/3$

Substituting the values of A and B in (i), we get

$$\frac{x-1}{(x+1)(x-2)} = \frac{2}{3}\cdot\frac{1}{x+1} + \frac{1}{3}\cdot\frac{1}{x-2}$$

$$\therefore \quad I = \int \frac{x-1}{(x+1)(x-2)}\,dx = \frac{2}{3}\int\frac{1}{x+1}\,dx + \frac{1}{3}\int\frac{1}{x-2}\,dx = \frac{2}{3}\log|x+1| + \frac{1}{3}\log|x-2| + C$$

(ii) Let $\frac{2x-1}{(x-1)(x+2)(x-3)} = \frac{A}{x-1} + \frac{B}{x+2} + \frac{C}{x-3}$ ...(i)

$$\Rightarrow \quad 2x-1 = A(x+2)(x-3) + B(x-1)(x-3) + C(x-1)(x+2) \quad \text{...(ii)}$$

Putting $x+2=0$ or, $x=-2$ in (ii), we get: $-5 = B(-3)(-5) \Rightarrow B = -1/3$

Putting $x-3=0$ or, $x=3$ in (ii), we get: $5=C\,(2)\,(5) \Rightarrow C=1/2$

Putting $x-1=0$ or, $x=1$ in (ii), we get: $1=A\,(3)\,(-2) \Rightarrow A=-1/6$

Substituting the values of A, B and C in (i), we obtain

$$\frac{2x-1}{(x-1)(x+2)(x-3)} = -\frac{1}{6}\cdot\frac{1}{x-1} - \frac{1}{3}\cdot\frac{1}{x+2} + \frac{1}{2}\cdot\frac{1}{x-3}$$

$$\therefore \quad I = \int \frac{2x-1}{(x-1)(x+2)(x-3)}\,dx = -\frac{1}{6}\int\frac{1}{x-1}\,dx - \frac{1}{3}\int\frac{1}{x+2}\,dx + \frac{1}{2}\int\frac{1}{x-3}\,dx$$

$$\Rightarrow \quad I = -\frac{1}{6}\log|x-1| - \frac{1}{3}\log|x+2| + \frac{1}{2}\log|x-3| + C$$

(iii) Here, the degree of numerator is greater than that of denominator. So, we divide the numerator by denominator to obtain

$$\frac{x^3}{(x-1)(x-2)} = x+3+\frac{7x-6}{(x-1)(x-2)} \qquad \text{...(i)}$$

Now, let $\dfrac{7x-6}{(x-1)(x-2)} = \dfrac{A}{x-1} + \dfrac{B}{x-2}$ ...(ii)

$$\Rightarrow \quad 7x-6 = A(x-2) + B(x-1) \qquad \text{...(iii)}$$

Putting $x-2=0$ or, $x=2$ in (iii), we get: $B=8$. Putting $x-1=0$ or, $x=1$ in (iii), we get: $A=-1$

Substituting the values of A and B in (ii), we obtain

$$\frac{7x-6}{(x-1)(x-2)} = -\frac{1}{x-1} + \frac{8}{x-2}$$

$$\therefore \quad \frac{x^3}{(x-1)(x-2)} = x+3-\frac{1}{x-1}+\frac{8}{x-2} \qquad \text{[From (i)]}$$

$$\therefore \quad I = \int \frac{x^3}{(x-1)(x-2)}\,dx$$

$$\Rightarrow \quad I = \int\left(x+3-\frac{1}{x-1}+\frac{8}{x-2}\right)dx = \frac{x^2}{2} + 3x - \log|x-1| + 8\log|x-2| + C$$

EXAMPLE 2 *Evaluate:*

(i) $\displaystyle\int \frac{2x}{(x^2+1)(x^2+2)}\,dx$ **[NCERT]** (ii) $\displaystyle\int \frac{\cos\theta}{(2+\sin\theta)(3+4\sin\theta)}\,d\theta$ **[CBSE 2019]**

(iii) $\displaystyle\int \frac{1}{\sin x - \sin 2x}\,dx$ **[CBSE 2010]** (iv) $\displaystyle\int \frac{1-\cos x}{\cos x\,(1+\cos x)}\,dx$

SOLUTION (i) Let $I = \displaystyle\int \frac{2x}{(x^2+1)(x^2+2)}\,dx$. Putting $x^2=t$ and $2x\,dx = dt$, we get

$$I = \int \frac{dt}{(t+1)(t+2)}$$

Let $\dfrac{1}{(t+1)(t+2)} = \dfrac{A}{t+1} + \dfrac{B}{t+2}$ ...(i)

$$\Rightarrow \quad 1 = A(t+2) + B(t+1) \qquad \text{...(ii)}$$

Putting $t=-2$ in (ii), we obtain: $B=-1$. Putting $t=-1$ in (ii), we obtain: $A=1$.

Substituting the values of A and B in (i), we get

$$\frac{1}{(t+1)(t+2)} = \frac{1}{t+1} - \frac{1}{t+2}$$

$\therefore \quad I = \int \frac{1}{(t+1)(t+2)}\, dt = \int \left(\frac{1}{t+1} - \frac{1}{t+2} \right) dt$

$\Rightarrow \quad I = \log|t+1| - \log|t+2| + C = \log|x^2+1| - \log|x^2+2| + C$

(ii) Let $I = \int \frac{\cos\theta}{(2+\sin\theta)(3+4\sin\theta)}\, d\theta$. Putting $\sin\theta = t$, and $\cos\theta\, d\theta = dt$, we get

$$I = \int \frac{dt}{(2+t)(3+4t)}$$

Let $\frac{1}{(2+t)(3+4t)} = \frac{A}{2+t} + \frac{B}{3+4t}$ ...(i)

$\Rightarrow \quad 1 = A(3+4t) + B(2+t)$ ...(ii)

Putting $3+4t=0$ i.e. $t = -\frac{3}{4}$ in (ii), we get: $1 = B\left(2 - \frac{3}{4}\right) \Rightarrow B = \frac{4}{5}$

Putting $2+t=0$ i.e. $t=-2$ in (ii), we get: $1 = A(3-8) \Rightarrow A = -\frac{1}{5}$

Substituting the values of A and B in (i), we obtain

$$\frac{1}{(2+t)(3+4t)} = -\frac{1}{5}\cdot\frac{1}{2+t} + \frac{4}{5}\cdot\frac{1}{3+4t}$$

$\therefore \quad I = \int \frac{1}{(2+t)(3+4t)}\, dt = -\frac{1}{5}\int \frac{1}{2+t}\, dt + \frac{4}{5}\int \frac{1}{3+4t}\, dt$

$\Rightarrow \quad I = -\frac{1}{5}\log|2+t| + \frac{4}{5}\cdot\frac{1}{4}\log|3+4t| + C = -\frac{1}{5}\log|2+\sin\theta| + \frac{1}{5}\log|3+4\sin\theta| + C$

(iii) We have,

$$I = \int \frac{1}{\sin x - \sin 2x}\, dx$$

$\Rightarrow \quad I = \int \frac{1}{(\sin x - 2\sin x\cos x)}\, dx = \int \frac{1}{\sin x(1-2\cos x)}\, dx = \int \frac{\sin x}{\sin^2 x(1-2\cos x)}\, dx$

$\Rightarrow \quad I = \int \frac{\sin x}{(1-\cos^2 x)(1-2\cos x)}\, dx$

Putting $\cos x = t$, and $-\sin x\, dx = dt$ or, $\sin x\, dx = -dt$, we get

$$I = \int \frac{-dt}{(1-t^2)(1-2t)} = \int \frac{-1}{(1-t)(1+t)(1-2t)}\, dt$$

Let $\frac{-1}{(1-t)(1+t)(1-2t)} = \frac{A}{1-t} + \frac{B}{1+t} + \frac{C}{1-2t}$. Then,

$-1 = A(1+t)(1-2t) + B(1-t)(1-2t) + C(1-t)(1+t)$ ...(i)

Putting $t+1=0$ or, $t=-1$ in (i), we get: $-1 = 6B \Rightarrow B = -\frac{1}{6}$.

Putting $1-t=0$ or, $t=1$ in (i), we get: $-1 = -2A \Rightarrow A = \frac{1}{2}$.

Putting $1-2t=0$ or, $t=\frac{1}{2}$ in (i), we get: $-1 = C\left(\frac{1}{2}\right)\left(\frac{3}{2}\right) \Rightarrow C = -\frac{4}{3}$.

$\therefore \quad \frac{-1}{(1-t)(1+t)(1-2t)} = \frac{1}{2}\cdot\frac{1}{1-t} - \frac{1}{6}\cdot\frac{1}{1+t} - \frac{4}{3}\cdot\frac{1}{1-2t}$

$$\Rightarrow \quad I = \int \frac{-dt}{(1-t)(1+t)(1-2t)} = \frac{1}{2}\int \frac{1}{1-t}\,dt - \frac{1}{6}\int \frac{1}{1+t}\,dt - \frac{4}{3}\int \frac{1}{1-2t}\,dt$$

$$\Rightarrow \quad I = -\frac{1}{2}\log|1-t| - \frac{1}{6}\log|1+t| - \frac{4}{3} \times -\frac{1}{2}\log|1-2t| + C$$

$$\Rightarrow \quad I = -\frac{1}{2}\log|1-\cos x| - \frac{1}{6}\log|1+\cos x| + \frac{2}{3}\log|1-2\cos x| + C$$

(iv) Let $I = \int \frac{1-\cos x}{\cos x\,(1+\cos x)}\,dx$ and let $\cos x = y$. Then, $\frac{1-\cos x}{\cos x\,(1+\cos x)} = \frac{1-y}{y(1+y)}$

Let $\quad \frac{1-y}{y\,(1+y)} = \frac{A}{y} + \frac{B}{1+y}$ ...(i)

$\Rightarrow \quad 1-y = A\,(1+y) + By$ ...(ii)

Putting $y=0$ in (ii), we get $A=1$. Putting $y=-1$ in (ii), we get $B=-2$.

Substituting the values of A and B in (i), we obtain

$$\frac{1-y}{y\,(1+y)} = \frac{1}{y} - \frac{2}{1+y} \Rightarrow \frac{1-\cos x}{\cos x(1+\cos x)} = \frac{1}{\cos x} - \frac{2}{1+\cos x} \quad [\because y = \cos x]$$

$$\therefore \quad I = \int \frac{1-\cos x}{\cos x\,(1+\cos x)}\,dx = \int \frac{1}{\cos x}\,dx - \int \frac{2}{1+\cos x}\,dx$$

$$\Rightarrow \quad I = \int \sec x\,dx - \int \frac{2}{2\cos^2 x/2}\,dx = \int \sec x - \int \sec^2 x/2\;dx$$

$$\Rightarrow \quad I = \log|\sec x + \tan x| - 2\tan x/2 + C$$

EXAMPLE 3 *Evaluate:* $\int \frac{(x-1)(x-2)(x-3)}{(x-4)(x-5)(x-6)}\,dx.$

SOLUTION Let $\frac{(x-1)(x-2)(x-3)}{(x-4)(x-5)(x-6)} = 1 + \frac{A}{(x-4)} + \frac{B}{x-5} + \frac{C}{x-6}$ ...(i)

Then, $(x-1)(x-2)(x-3) = (x-4)(x-5)(x-6) + A(x-5)(x-6) + B(x-4)(x-6) + C(x-4)(x-5)$ ...(ii)

Putting $x = 4, 5$ and 6 successively in (ii), we obtain: $A=3$, $B=-24$ and $C=30$

Substituting values of A, B and C in (i), we obtain

$$\frac{(x-1)(x-2)(x-3)}{(x-4)(x-5)(x-6)} = 1 + \frac{3}{x-4} - \frac{24}{x-5} + \frac{30}{x-6}$$

$$\therefore \quad I = \int \frac{(x-1)(x-2)(x-3)}{(x-4)(x-5)(x-6)}\,dx = \int 1\cdot dx + 3\int \frac{1}{x-4}\,dx - 24\int \frac{1}{x-5}\,dx + 30\int \frac{1}{x-6}\,dx$$

$$\Rightarrow \quad I = x + 3\log|x-4| - 24\log|x-5| + 30\log|x-6| + C$$

Type II WHEN DENOMINATOR CONTAINS SOME REPEATING LINEAR FACTORS

EXAMPLE 4 *Evaluate:*

(i) $\int \frac{3x+1}{(x-2)^2(x+2)}\,dx$ [CBSE 2007] (ii) $\int \frac{x^2+1}{(x-1)^2(x+3)}\,dx$ [CBSE 2012]

SOLUTION (i) Let $\frac{3x+1}{(x-2)^2(x+2)} = \frac{A}{x-2} + \frac{B}{(x-2)^2} + \frac{C}{x+2}$ ...(i)

$\Rightarrow \quad 3x+1 = A\,(x-2)(x+2) + B\,(x+2) + C\,(x-2)^2$ ...(ii)

Putting $x - 2 = 0$ i.e. $x = 2$ in (ii), we get: $7 = 4B \Rightarrow B = \frac{7}{4}$

Putting $x + 2 = 0$ i.e. $x = -2$ in (ii), we get: $-5 = 16C \Rightarrow C = -\frac{5}{16}$

Comparing coefficients of x^2 on both sides of the identity (ii), we get

$$A + C = 0 \Rightarrow A = -C \Rightarrow A = \frac{5}{16}$$

Substituting the values of A, B and C in (i), we get

$$\frac{3x+1}{(x-2)^2(x+2)} = \frac{5}{16} \cdot \frac{1}{x-2} + \frac{7}{4} \frac{1}{(x-2)^2} - \frac{5}{16(x+2)}$$

$$\therefore \quad I = \int \frac{3x+1}{(x-2)^2(x+2)} dx = \frac{5}{16} \int \frac{1}{x-2} dx + \frac{7}{4} \int \frac{1}{(x-2)^2} dx - \frac{5}{16} \int \frac{1}{x+2} dx$$

$$\Rightarrow \quad I = \frac{5}{16} \log|x-2| - \frac{7}{4(x-2)} - \frac{5}{16} \log|x+2| + C$$

(ii) We have, $I = \int \frac{x^2+1}{(x-1)^2(x+3)} dx$

Let $$\frac{x^2+1}{(x-1)^2(x+3)} = \frac{A}{x-1} + \frac{B}{(x-1)^2} + \frac{C}{x+3} \quad \text{...(i)}$$

$$\Rightarrow \quad x^2 + 1 = A(x-1)(x+3) + B(x+3) + C(x-1)^2 \quad \text{...(ii)}$$

Putting $x - 1 = 0$ i.e. $x = 1$ in (ii), we get: $2 = 4B \Rightarrow B = \frac{1}{2}$

Putting $x + 3 = 0$ i.e. $x = -3$ in (ii), we get: $10 = 16C \Rightarrow C = \frac{5}{8}$

Equating the coefficients of x^2 on both sides of the identity (ii), we get

$$1 = A + C \Rightarrow A = 1 - C = 1 - \frac{5}{8} = \frac{3}{8}$$

Substituting the values of A, B and C in (i), we get

$$\frac{x^2+1}{(x-1)^2(x+3)} = \frac{3}{8} \cdot \frac{1}{x-1} + \frac{1}{2} \cdot \frac{1}{(x-1)^2} + \frac{5}{8}(x+3)$$

$$\Rightarrow \quad I = \int \frac{x^2+1}{(x-1)^2(x+3)} dx = \frac{3}{8} \int \frac{1}{x-1} dx + \frac{1}{2} \int \frac{1}{(x-1)^2} dx + \frac{5}{8} \int \frac{1}{x+3} dx$$

$$\Rightarrow \quad I = \frac{3}{8} \log|x-1| - \frac{1}{2(x-1)} + \frac{5}{8} \log|x+3| + C$$

EXAMPLE 5 *Evaluate:* $\int \frac{x^2+x+1}{(x-1)^3} dx.$

SOLUTION We have, $I = \int \frac{x^2+x+1}{(x-1)^3} dx$. Putting $x - 1 = t$ and $dx = dt$, we get

$$I = \int \frac{(t+1)^2 + (t+1) + 1}{t^3} dt = \int \frac{t^2 + 3t + 3}{t^3} dt = \int \left(\frac{1}{t} + \frac{3}{t^2} + \frac{3}{t^3} \right) dt$$

$\Rightarrow \quad I = \log|t| - \frac{3}{t} - \frac{3}{2t^2} + C = \log|x-1| - \frac{3}{x-1} - \frac{3}{2(x-1)^2} + C$

NOTE *This sum can also be done by using partial fractions. We write*

$$\frac{x^2+x+1}{(x-1)^3} = \frac{A}{x-1} + \frac{B}{(x-1)^2} + \frac{C}{(x-1)^3}$$

EXAMPLE 6 *Evaluate:* $\int \frac{x^2}{(x-1)^3(x+1)}\, dx$

SOLUTION We have, $I = \int \frac{x^2}{(x-1)^3(x+1)}\, dx$

Let $\frac{x^2}{(x-1)^3(x+1)} = \frac{A}{x-1} + \frac{B}{(x-1)^2} + \frac{C}{(x-1)^3} + \frac{D}{x+1}$ ...(i)

$\Rightarrow \quad x^2 = A(x-1)^2(x+1) + B(x-1)(x+1) + C(x+1) + D(x-1)^3$ ...(ii)

Putting $x-1=0$ i.e. $x=1$ in (ii), we get: $1 = 2C \Rightarrow C = \frac{1}{2}$

Putting $x+1=0$ i.e. $x=-1$ in (ii), we get: $1 = -8D \Rightarrow D = -\frac{1}{8}$

Putting $x=0$ in (iii), we get: $0 = A - B + C - D \Rightarrow A - B = -\frac{5}{8}$

Putting $x=2$ in (ii), we get: $4 = 3A + 3B + 3C + D \Rightarrow 4 = 3(A+B+C) + D \Rightarrow A + B = \frac{7}{8}$

Now, $A - B = -\frac{5}{8}$ and $A + B = \frac{7}{8} \Rightarrow A = \frac{1}{8}$ and $B = \frac{3}{4}$

Thus, we obtain $A = \frac{1}{8}, B = \frac{3}{4}, C = \frac{1}{2}, D = -\frac{1}{8}$

Substituting the values of A, B, C and D in (i), we get

$$\frac{x^2}{(x-1)^3(x+1)} = \frac{1}{8(x-1)} + \frac{3}{4(x-1)^2} + \frac{1}{2(x-1)^3} - \frac{1}{8(x+1)}$$

$\therefore \quad I = \int \frac{x^2}{(x-1)^3(x+1)}\, dx$

$\Rightarrow \quad I = \frac{1}{8}\int \frac{1}{x-1}\, dx + \frac{3}{4}\int \frac{1}{(x-1)^2}\, dx + \frac{1}{2}\int \frac{1}{(x-1)^3}\, dx - \frac{1}{8}\int \frac{1}{x+1}\, dx$

$\Rightarrow \quad I = \frac{1}{8}\log|x-1| - \frac{3}{4(x-1)} - \frac{1}{4(x-1)^2} - \frac{1}{8}\log|x+1| + C$

$\Rightarrow \quad I = \frac{1}{8}\log\left|\frac{x-1}{x+1}\right| - \frac{3}{4(x-1)} - \frac{1}{4(x-1)^2} + C$

Type III THE DENOMINATOR CONTAINS IRREDUCIBLE QUADRATIC FACTORS

EXAMPLE 7 *Evaluate:*

(i) $\int \frac{8}{(x+2)(x^2+4)}\, dx$ [CBSE 2013] (ii) $\int \frac{x}{(x-1)(x^2+4)}\, dx$

SOLUTION (i) Let $\frac{8}{(x+2)(x^2+4)} = \frac{A}{x+2} + \frac{Bx+C}{x^2+4}$ ...(i)

Then, $8 = A(x^2+4) + (Bx+C)(x+2)$ ...(ii)

Putting $x+2=0$ i.e. $x=-2$ in (ii), we get: $8 = 8A \Rightarrow A = 1$

Putting $x = 0$ and 1 respectively in (ii), we get: $8 = 4A + 2C$ and $8 = 5A + 3B + 3C$

Solving these equations, we obtain: $A = 1, C = 2$ and $B = -1$.

Substituting the values of A, B and C in (i), we obtain

$$\frac{8}{(x+2)(x^2+4)} = \frac{1}{x+2} + \frac{-x+2}{x^2+4}$$

$$\therefore \quad I = \int \frac{8}{(x+2)(x^2+4)}\,dx$$

$$\Rightarrow \quad I = \int \frac{1}{x+2}\,dx + \int \frac{-x+2}{x^2+4}\,dx = \int \frac{1}{x+2}\,dx - \int \frac{x}{x^2+4}\,dx + 2\int \frac{1}{x^2+4}\,dx$$

$$\Rightarrow \quad I = \log|x+2| - \frac{1}{2}\int \frac{1}{t}\,dt + 2 \times \frac{1}{2}\tan^{-1}\frac{x}{2} + C, \text{ where } t = x^2+4$$

$$\Rightarrow \quad I = \log|x+2| - \frac{1}{2}\log t + \tan^{-1}\frac{x}{2} + C = \log|x+2| - \frac{1}{2}\log(x^2+4) + \tan^{-1}\frac{x}{2} + C$$

(ii) Let $\frac{x}{(x-1)(x^2+4)} = \frac{A}{x-1} + \frac{Bx+C}{x^2+4}$ ...(i)

$\Rightarrow \quad x = A(x^2+4) + (Bx+C)(x-1)$ ...(ii)

Putting $x = 1$ in (ii), we get: $1 = 5A$. Putting $x = 0$ in (ii), we get: $0 = 4A - C$. Putting $x = -1$ in (ii), we get: $-1 = 5A + 2B - 2C$

Solving these equations, we obtain: $A = \frac{1}{5}, B = -\frac{1}{5}$ and $C = \frac{4}{5}$.

Substituting the values of A, B and C in (i), we obtain

$$\frac{x}{(x-1)(x^2+4)} = \frac{1}{5(x-1)} + \frac{-\frac{1}{5}x + \frac{4}{5}}{x^2+4}$$

$$\Rightarrow \quad \frac{x}{(x-1)(x^2+4)} = \frac{1}{5(x-1)} - \frac{1}{5}\frac{(x-4)}{(x^2+4)}$$

$$\therefore \quad I = \int \frac{x}{(x-1)(x^2+4)}\,dx = \int \left\{\frac{1}{5(x-1)} - \frac{1}{5}\cdot\frac{x-4}{x^2+4}\right\}dx = \frac{1}{5}\int \frac{1}{x-1}\,dx - \frac{1}{5}\int \frac{x-4}{x^2+4}\,dx$$

$$\Rightarrow \quad I = \frac{1}{5}\int \frac{1}{x-1}\,dx - \frac{1}{10}\int \frac{2x}{x^2+4}\,dx + \frac{4}{5}\int \frac{1}{x^2+4}\,dx$$

$$\Rightarrow \quad I = \frac{1}{5}\log|x-1| - \frac{1}{10}\log(x^2+4) + \frac{4}{5} \times \frac{1}{2}\tan^{-1}\frac{x}{2} + C$$

$$\Rightarrow \quad I = \frac{1}{5}\log|x-1| - \frac{1}{10}\log(x^2+4) + \frac{2}{5}\tan^{-1}\left(\frac{x}{2}\right) + C$$

EXAMPLE 8 *Evaluate:* $\int \frac{x^4}{(x-1)(x^2+1)}\, dx$ **[CBSE 2023]**

SOLUTION Let $I = \int \frac{x^4}{(x-1)(x^2+1)}\, dx$. Then,

$$I = \int \frac{(x^4-1)+1}{(x-1)(x^2+1)}\, dx = \int \left\{ \frac{(x^2-1)(x^2+1)}{(x-1)(x^2+1)} + \frac{1}{(x-1)(x^2+1)} \right\} dx$$

$$\Rightarrow \quad I = \int (x+1)\, dx + \int \frac{1}{(x-1)(x^2+1)}\, dx \quad \text{...(i)}$$

Let $\frac{1}{(x-1)(x^2+1)} = \frac{A}{x-1} + \frac{Bx+C}{x^2+1} \Rightarrow I = A(x^2+1) + (Bx+C)(x-1)$ ...(ii)

Putting $x = 1$ in (ii), we obtain: $1 = 2A \Rightarrow A = \frac{1}{2}$.

On equating the coefficients of x^2 and constant terms on both sides, we obtain

$$A + B = 0 \text{ and } A - C = 1 \Rightarrow B = -\frac{1}{2} \text{ and } C = -\frac{1}{2}$$

Substituting the values of A, B and C in (ii), we obtain

$$I = \int (x+1)\, dx + \frac{1}{2} \int \left(\frac{1}{x-1} - \frac{x+1}{x^2+1} \right) dx$$

$$\Rightarrow \quad I = \int (x+1)\, dx + \frac{1}{2} \int \frac{1}{x-1}\, dx - \frac{1}{2} \int \frac{x}{x^2+1}\, dx - \frac{1}{2} \int \frac{1}{x^2+1}\, dx$$

$$\Rightarrow \quad I = \frac{x^2}{2} + x + \frac{1}{2} \ln |x-1| - \frac{1}{4} \ln (x^2+1) - \frac{1}{2} \tan^{-1} x + C$$

IMPORTANT NOTE *If a rational function contains only even powers of x in both the numerator and denominator, then to resolve it into partial fractions, we proceed as follows:*

Step I *Put $x^2 = y$ in the given rational function.*

Step II *Resolve the rational function obtained in step I into partial fractions.*

Step III *Replace y by x^2.*

EXAMPLE 8 *Evaluate:*

(i) $\int \frac{x^2}{(x^2+1)(x^2+4)}\, dx$ **[CBSE 2013, 2014]** (ii) $\int \frac{x^2+1}{(x^2+2)(2x^2+1)}\, dx$

SOLUTION Let $x^2 = y$. Then,

$$\frac{x^2}{(x^2+1)(x^2+4)} = \frac{y}{(y+1)(y+4)}$$

Let $\frac{y}{(y+1)(y+4)} = \frac{A}{y+1} + \frac{B}{y+4}$ ...(i)

$$\Rightarrow \quad y = A(y+4) + B(y+1) \quad \text{...(ii)}$$

Putting $y = -1$ and $y = -4$ successively in (ii), we get: $A = -\frac{1}{3}$ and $B = \frac{4}{3}$.

Substituting the values of A and B in (i), we obtain

$$\frac{y}{(y+1)(y+4)} = -\frac{1}{3(y+1)} + \frac{4}{3(y+4)}$$

Replacing y by x^2, we obtain

$$\frac{x^2}{(x^2+1)(x^2+4)} = -\frac{1}{3(x^2+1)} + \frac{4}{3(x^2+4)}$$

$$\therefore \quad I = \int \frac{x^2}{(x^2+1)(x^2+4)}\,dx = \int \left\{-\frac{1}{3(x^2+1)} + \frac{4}{3(x^2+4)}\right\} dx = -\frac{1}{3}\int \frac{1}{x^2+1}\,dx + \frac{4}{3}\int \frac{1}{x^2+4}\,dx$$

$$\Rightarrow I = -\frac{1}{3}\tan^{-1} x + \frac{4}{3}\times\frac{1}{2}\tan^{-1}\left(\frac{x}{2}\right) + C = -\frac{1}{3}\tan^{-1} x + \frac{2}{3}\tan^{-1}\left(\frac{x}{2}\right) + C$$

(ii) Let $x^2 = y$. Then,

$$\frac{x^2+1}{(x^2+2)(2x^2+1)} = \frac{y+1}{(y+2)(2y+1)}$$

Let $\frac{y+1}{(y+2)(2y+1)} = \frac{A}{y+2} + \frac{B}{2y+1}$ ...(i)

$\Rightarrow y+1 = A(2y+1) + B(y+2)$ ...(ii)

Putting $y+2=0$ i.e. $y=-2$ in (ii), we get: $-1 = -3A \Rightarrow A = \frac{1}{3}$.

Putting $2y+1=0$ i.e. $y = -\frac{1}{2}$ in (ii), we get: $\frac{1}{2} = B\left(\frac{3}{2}\right) \Rightarrow B = \frac{1}{3}$.

Substituting the values of A and B in (i), we obtain

$$\frac{y+1}{(y+2)(2y+1)} = \frac{1}{3}\cdot\frac{1}{y+2} + \frac{1}{3}\frac{1}{(2y+1)}$$

Replacing y by x^2, we get

$$\frac{x^2+1}{(x^2+2)(2x^2+1)} = \frac{1}{3}\cdot\frac{1}{x^2+2} + \frac{1}{3(2x^2+1)}$$

$$\therefore \quad I = \int \frac{x^2+1}{(x^2+2)(2x^2+1)}\,dx = \frac{1}{3}\int \frac{1}{x^2+2}\,dx + \frac{1}{3}\int \frac{1}{(\sqrt{2}x)^2+1}\,dx$$

$$\Rightarrow \quad I = \frac{1}{3}\times\frac{1}{\sqrt{2}}\tan^{-1}\left(\frac{x}{\sqrt{2}}\right) + \frac{1}{3\sqrt{2}}\tan^{-1}(\sqrt{2}x) + C = \frac{1}{3\sqrt{2}}\left\{\tan^{-1}\frac{x}{\sqrt{2}} + \tan^{-1}\sqrt{2}\,x\right\} + C$$

BASED ON HIGHER ORDER THINKING SKILLS (HOTS)

EXAMPLE 9 *Evaluate* : $\int \frac{x+1}{x(1+x e^x)^2}\,dx$

SOLUTION Let $I = \int \frac{x+1}{x(1+x e^x)^2}\,dx = \int \frac{(x+1)e^x}{x e^x(1+x e^x)^2}\,dx$

Let $x e^x = t$. Then $d(x e^x) = dt$ or, $(x+1)e^x dx = dt$.

$\therefore \quad I = \int \frac{1}{t(1+t)^2}\, dt$, where $t = x e^x$.

Let $\quad \frac{1}{t(1+t)^2} = \frac{A}{t} + \frac{B}{1+t} + \frac{C}{(1+t)^2}$ ...(i)

$\Rightarrow \quad 1 = A(1+t)^2 + Bt(1+t) + Ct$ ...(ii)

Putting $t = 0$ and $t = -1$ respectively in (ii) we get: $A = 1, C = -1$

Now, putting $t = 1$ in (ii) we get: $1 = 4A + 2B + C \Rightarrow 1 = 4 + 2B - 1 \Rightarrow B = -1$

Substituting the values of A, B and C in (i), we get

$$\frac{1}{t(1+t)^2} = \frac{1}{t} - \frac{1}{1+t} - \frac{1}{(1+t)^2}$$

$$\therefore \quad I = \int \frac{1}{t(1+t)^2}\, dt = \int \left(\frac{1}{t} - \frac{1}{1+t} - \frac{1}{(1+t)^2} \right) dt$$

$$\Rightarrow \quad I = \log|t| - \log|1+t| + \frac{1}{1+t} + C = \log(xe^x) - \log(1 + xe^x) + \frac{1}{1+xe^x} + C$$

EXAMPLE 10 *Evaluate* : $\int \frac{1}{x + \sqrt{x^2 - x + 1}}\, dx$

SOLUTION Let $I = \int \frac{1}{x + \sqrt{x^2 - x + 1}}\, dx$. Let $x + \sqrt{x^2 - x + 1} = t$. Then,

$$\sqrt{x^2 - x + 1} = t - x \Rightarrow x^2 - x + 1 = (t - x)^2 \Rightarrow -2x + 1 = t^2 - 2tx \Rightarrow x = \frac{t^2 - 1}{2t - 1}$$

$$\therefore \quad dx = \frac{(2t-1)\,2t - 2(t^2 - 1)}{(2t-1)^2}\, dt = \frac{2t^2 - 2t + 2}{(2t-1)^2}\, dt$$

Substituting these values, we get

$$I = \int \frac{1}{t} \times \frac{2t^2 - 2t + 2}{(2t-1)^2}\, dt = 2 \int \frac{t^2 - t + 1}{t(2t-1)^2}\, dt$$

Let $\frac{t^2 - t + 1}{t(2t-1)^2} = \frac{A}{t} + \frac{B}{2t-1} + \frac{C}{(2t-1)^2}$ ...(i)

Using cover-up method, we obtain $A = 1$ and $C = \frac{3}{2}$.

From (i), we obtain: $t^2 - t + 1 = A(2t-1)^2 + B(2t-1)t + Ct$

On equating the coefficient of t^2 on both sides, we get: $1 = 4A + 2B \Rightarrow B = -\frac{3}{2}$

Substituting the values of A, B, C in (i), we get

$$\frac{t^2 - t + 1}{t(2t-1)^2} = \frac{1}{t} - \frac{3}{2(2t-1)} + \frac{3}{2} \frac{1}{(2t-1)^2}$$

$$\therefore \; I = 2\int \frac{1}{t}\, dt - 3\int \frac{1}{2t-1}\, dt + \frac{3}{2}\int \frac{1}{(2t-1)^2}\, dt = 2\log t - \frac{3}{2}\log(2t-1) - \frac{3}{4}\frac{1}{(2t-1)} + C$$

$$\Rightarrow I = 2\log\left(x+\sqrt{x^2-x+1}\right) - \frac{3}{2}\log\left\{(2x-1)+2\sqrt{x^2-x+1}\right\} - \frac{3}{4\left\{(2x-1)+2\sqrt{x^2-x+1}\right\}} + C$$

EXAMPLE 11 *Evaluate:* $\int \frac{\sin x}{\sin 4x}\, dx$

SOLUTION We have,

$$I = \int \frac{\sin x}{\sin 4x}\, dx = \int \frac{\sin x}{2\sin 2x \cos 2x}\, dx = \int \frac{\sin x}{4 \sin x \cos x \cos 2x}\, dx$$

$$\Rightarrow \quad I = \frac{1}{4}\int \frac{1}{\cos x \cos 2x}\, dx = \frac{1}{4}\int \frac{\cos x}{\cos^2 x \cos 2x}\, dx = \frac{1}{4}\int \frac{\cos x}{(1-\sin^2 x)(1-2\sin^2 x)}\, dx$$

Putting $\sin x = t$ and $\cos x\, dx = dt$, we get

$$I = \frac{1}{4}\int \frac{dt}{(1-t^2)(1-2t^2)}$$

Let $t^2 = y$. Then,

$$\frac{1}{(1-t^2)(1-2t^2)} = \frac{1}{(1-y)(1-2y)}$$

Let $\frac{1}{(1-y)(1-2y)} = \frac{A}{1-y} + \frac{B}{1-2y}$. Then, $1 = A(1-2y) + B(1-y)$ ...(i)

Putting $y = 1$ and $y = \frac{1}{2}$ respectively in (i), we get: $A = -1$ and $B = 2$.

$$\therefore \quad \frac{1}{(1-y)(1-2y)} = \frac{-1}{1-y} + \frac{2}{1-2y}$$

$$\Rightarrow \quad \frac{1}{(1-t^2)(1-2t^2)} = -\frac{1}{1-t^2} + \frac{2}{1-2t^2}$$

$$\Rightarrow \quad I = \frac{1}{4}\int \frac{dt}{(1-t^2)(1-2t^2)} = \frac{1}{4}\int -\frac{1}{1-t^2} + \frac{2}{1-2t^2}\, dt$$

$$\Rightarrow I = -\frac{1}{4}\int \frac{1}{1-t^2}\, dt + \frac{2}{4}\int \frac{1}{1-(\sqrt{2}\,t)^2}\, dt = -\frac{1}{4}\times\frac{1}{2}\log\left|\frac{1+t}{1-t}\right| + \frac{1}{2}\times\frac{1}{2\sqrt{2}}\log\left|\frac{1+\sqrt{2}\,t}{1-\sqrt{2}\,t}\right| + C$$

$$\Rightarrow I = -\frac{1}{8}\log\left|\frac{1+t}{1-t}\right| + \frac{1}{4\sqrt{2}}\log\left|\frac{1+\sqrt{2}t}{1-\sqrt{2}t}\right| + C = -\frac{1}{8}\log\left|\frac{1+\sin x}{1-\sin x}\right| + \frac{1}{4\sqrt{2}}\log\left|\frac{1+\sqrt{2}\sin x}{1-\sqrt{2}\sin x}\right| + C$$

EXAMPLE 12 *Evaluate:* $\int \frac{\tan\theta + \tan^3\theta}{1+\tan^3\theta}\, d\theta$

SOLUTION We have,

$$I = \int \frac{\tan\theta + \tan^3\theta}{1+\tan^3\theta}\, d\theta = \int \frac{\tan\theta\,(1+\tan^2\theta)}{1+\tan^3\theta}\, d\theta = \int \frac{\tan\theta \sec^2\theta}{(1+\tan^3\theta)}\, d\theta$$

Putting $\tan\theta = t$ and $\sec^2\theta\, d\theta = dt$, we get

$$I = \int \frac{t\, dt}{(1+t^3)} = \int \frac{t}{(1+t)(t^2-t+1)}\, dt$$

Let $\dfrac{t}{(1+t)(1-t+t^2)} = \dfrac{A}{1+t} + \dfrac{Bt+C}{1-t+t^2}$. Then, $t = A(1-t+t^2) + (Bt+C)(t+1)$ ...(i)

Putting $1+t=0$ or, $t=-1$ in (i), we get: $A = -\dfrac{1}{3}$.

Comparing the coefficients of t^2 on both sides of (i), we get: $A + B = 0 \Rightarrow B = -A = \dfrac{1}{3}$

Comparing, constant terms on both sides of (i), we get: $A + C = 0 \Rightarrow C = -A = \dfrac{1}{3}$

$$\therefore \quad \frac{t}{1+t^3} = -\frac{1}{3(1+t)} + \frac{\frac{1}{3}t + \frac{1}{3}}{1-t+t^2} = -\frac{1}{3(t+1)} + \frac{1}{3} \cdot \frac{t+1}{(1-t+t^2)}$$

$$\Rightarrow \quad I = -\frac{1}{3}\int \frac{1}{1+t}\,dt + \frac{1}{3}\int \frac{t+1}{t^2-t+1}\,dt = -\frac{1}{3}\int \frac{1}{1+t}\,dt + \frac{1}{6}\int \frac{2t-1+3}{t^2-t+1}\,dt$$

$$\Rightarrow \quad I = -\frac{1}{3}\int \frac{1}{1+t}\,dt + \frac{1}{6}\int \frac{2t-1}{t^2-t+1}\,dt + \frac{3}{6}\int \frac{1}{t^2-t+1}\,dt$$

$$\Rightarrow \quad I = -\frac{1}{3}\log|1+t| + \frac{1}{6}\log|t^2-t+1| + \frac{1}{2}\int \frac{1}{\left(t-\frac{1}{2}\right)^2 + \left(\frac{\sqrt{3}}{2}\right)^2}\,dt$$

$$\Rightarrow \quad I = -\frac{1}{3}\log|1+t| + \frac{1}{6}\log|t^2-t+1| + \frac{1}{2} \times \frac{1}{\frac{\sqrt{3}}{2}}\tan^{-1}\left(\frac{t-\frac{1}{2}}{\frac{\sqrt{3}}{2}}\right) + C$$

$$\Rightarrow \quad I = -\frac{1}{3}\log|1+t| + \frac{1}{6}\log|t^2-t+1| + \frac{1}{\sqrt{3}}\tan^{-1}\left(\frac{2t-1}{\sqrt{3}}\right) + C$$

$$\Rightarrow \quad I = -\frac{1}{3}\log|1+\tan\theta| + \frac{1}{6}\log|\tan^2\theta - \tan\theta + 1| + \frac{1}{\sqrt{3}}\tan^{-1}\left(\frac{2\tan\theta - 1}{\sqrt{3}}\right) + C$$

EXAMPLE 13 *Evaluate :* $\displaystyle\int \frac{1}{\sin x\,(2\cos^2 x - 1)}\,dx$

SOLUTION Putting $\cos x = t$ and $d(\cos x) = dt$ or, $-\sin x\,dx = dt$, we get

$$I = \int \frac{1}{\sin x\,(2\cos^2 x - 1)}\,dx = \int \frac{1}{\sin x\,(2t^2-1)} \times -\frac{dt}{\sin x}$$

$$\Rightarrow \quad I = -\int \frac{1}{(1-t^2)(2t^2-1)}\,dt$$

$$\therefore \quad I = -\int \left(\frac{1}{1-t^2} + \frac{2}{2t^2-1}\right)dt = -\int \frac{1}{1-t^2}\,dt - 2\int \frac{1}{2t^2-1}\,dt$$

$$\Rightarrow \quad I = -\int \frac{1}{1^2-t^2}\,dt - \int \frac{1}{t^2-(1/\sqrt{2})^2}\,dt$$

$$\Rightarrow \quad I = -\frac{1}{2}\log\left|\frac{1+t}{1-t}\right| - \frac{1}{\sqrt{2}}\log\left|\frac{\sqrt{2}t-1}{\sqrt{2}t+1}\right| + C = -\frac{1}{2}\log\left|\frac{1+\cos x}{1-\cos x}\right| - \frac{1}{\sqrt{2}}\left|\frac{\sqrt{2}\cos x - 1}{\sqrt{2}\cos x + 1}\right| + C$$

EXERCISE 15.30

BASIC

Evaluate the following integrals:

1. $\int \frac{2x+1}{(x+1)(x-2)} dx$

2. $\int \frac{1}{x(x-2)(x-4)} dx$

3. $\int \frac{x^2}{(x-1)(x-2)(x-3)} dx$

4. $\int \frac{5x}{(x+1)(x^2-4)} dx$ [NCERT]

5. $\int \frac{x^2+1}{x(x^2-1)} dx$

6. $\int \frac{2x-3}{(x^2-1)(2x+3)} dx$

7. $\int \frac{x^2+x+1}{(x^2+1)(x+2)} dx$ [CBSE 2015, 2023]

8. $\int \frac{ax^2+bx+c}{(x-a)(x-b)(x-c)} dx$, where a, b, c are distinct.

9. $\int \frac{x}{(x^2+1)(x-1)} dx$ [CBSE 2013]

10. $\int \frac{1}{(x-1)(x+1)(x+2)} dx$

11. $\int \frac{5x^2-1}{x(x-1)(x+1)} dx$

12. $\int \frac{x^2+6x-8}{x^3-4x} dx$

13. $\int \frac{x^2+1}{(2x+1)(x^2-1)} dx$

14. $\int \frac{3x-2}{(x+1)^2(x+3)} dx$ [CBSE 2013]

15. $\int \frac{2x+1}{(x+2)(x-3)^2} dx$

16. $\int \frac{x^2+1}{(x-2)^2(x+3)} dx$

17. $\int \frac{x}{(x-1)^2(x+2)} dx$ [NCERT, CBSE 2020]

18. $\int \frac{x^2}{(x-1)(x+1)^2} dx$

19. $\int \frac{x^2+x-1}{(x+1)^2(x+2)} dx$

20. $\int \frac{5x^2+20x+6}{x^3+2x^2+x} dx$

21. $\int \frac{18}{(x+2)(x^2+4)} dx$ [CBSE 2013]

22. $\int \frac{5}{(x^2+1)(x+2)} dx$

23. $\int \frac{x}{(x+1)(x^2+1)} dx$ [CBSE 2002, 05]

24. $\int \frac{1}{1+x+x^2+x^3} dx$

25. $\int \frac{1}{(x+1)^2(x^2+1)} dx$

26. $\int \frac{2x}{x^3-1} dx$

27. $\int \frac{3x+5}{x^3-x^2-x+1} dx$ [NCERT, CBSE 2013]

28. $\int \frac{x^3-1}{x^3+x} dx$

29. $\int \frac{x^2+x+1}{(x+1)^2(x+2)} dx$ [NCERT, CBSE 2014]

30. $\int \frac{3}{(1-x)(1+x^2)} dx$ [CBSE 2012]

31. $\int \frac{\cos x}{(1-\sin x)^3 (2+\sin x)} dx$

32. $\int \frac{\cos x}{(1-\sin x)(2-\sin x)} dx$ [CBSE 2007]

33. $\int \frac{2x+1}{(x-2)(x-3)} dx$ [CBSE 2007]

34. $\int \frac{2x}{(x^2+1)(x^2+2)^2} dx$ [CBSE 2017]

BASED ON LOTS

35. $\int \frac{x^2+x-1}{x^2+x-6} dx$

36. $\int \frac{3+4x-x^2}{(x+2)(x-1)} dx$

37. $\int \frac{x^2+1}{x^2-1} dx$

38. $\int \frac{x^3}{(x-1)(x-2)(x-3)} dx$

39. $\int \frac{\sin 2x}{(1+\sin x)(2+\sin x)} dx$ [CBSE 2004]

40. $\int \frac{2x}{(x^2+1)(x^2+3)} dx$ [CBSE 2004, 11]

41. $\int \frac{1}{x \log x (2+\log x)} dx$

42. $\int \frac{x^2}{(x^2+4)(x^2+9)} dx$ [CBSE 2013]

43. $\int \frac{1}{x\left\{6(\log x)^2+7\log x+2\right\}} dx$

44. $\int \frac{1}{x(x^n+1)} dx$ [NCERT]

45. $\int \frac{x}{(x^2-a^2)(x^2-b^2)} dx$

46. $\int \frac{x^2+1}{(x^2+4)(x^2+25)} dx$ [CBSE 2013]

47. $\int \frac{x^3+x+1}{x^2-1} dx$

48. $\int \frac{2x^2+7x-3}{x^2(2x+1)} dx$

49. $\int \frac{x^2}{(x^2+9)(x^2+4)} dx$ [CBSE 2024]

50. $\int \frac{x^2}{(x^2+1)(3x^2+4)} dx$

51. $\int \frac{1}{x(x^4+1)} dx$

52. $\int \frac{1}{x(x^3+8)} dx$ [CBSE 2013]

53. $\int \frac{2x^2+1}{x^2(x^2+4)} dx$ [CBSE 2013]

54. $\int \frac{1}{(x^2+1)(x^2+2)} dx$ [CBSE 2010]

55. $\int \frac{1}{x(x^4-1)} dx$ [NCERT]

56. $\int \frac{1}{x^4-1} dx$ [NCERT]

57. $\int \frac{x^2}{(x-1)(x^2+1)} dx$ [CBSE 2017]

58. $\int \frac{x^2+1}{(x^2+2)(x^2+4)} dx$ [CBSE 2024]

59. $\int \frac{\sqrt{x}}{(x+1)(x-1)} dx$ [CBSE 2024]

60. $\int \frac{1}{x(x^2-1)} dx$ [CBSE 2024]

61. $\int \frac{2x+3}{x^2(x+3)} dx$ [CBSE 2024]

62. $\int \frac{2x}{(x^2+1)(x^2-4)} dx$ [CBSE 2024]

BASED ON HOTS

63. $\int \frac{x^2}{(x^2+a^2)(x^2+b^2)} dx$

64. $\int \frac{1}{\cos x(5-4\sin x)} dx$

65. $\int \frac{1}{\sin x\ (3 + 2\cos x)}\, dx$

66. $\int \frac{1}{\sin x + \sin 2x}\, dx$ [CBSE 2015]

67. $\int \frac{x+1}{x(1 + x e^x)}\, dx$

68. $\int \frac{(x^2+1)(x^2+2)}{(x^2+3)(x^2+4)}\, dx$

69. $\int \frac{4x^4 + 3}{(x^2+2)(x^2+3)(x^2+4)}\, dx$

70. $\int \frac{x^4}{(x-1)(x^2+1)}\, dx$

71. $\int \frac{x^2}{x^4 - x^2 - 12}\, dx$

72. $\int \frac{x^2}{1 - x^4}\, dx$

73. $\int \frac{x^2}{x^4 + x^2 - 2}\, dx$ [NCERT, CBSE 2016]

74. $\int \frac{(x^2+1)(x^2+4)}{(x^2+3)(x^2-5)}\, dx$ [CBSE 2016]

75. $\int \frac{2\cos x}{(1-\sin x)(1+\sin^2 x)}\, dx$ [CBSE 2018]

ANSWERS

1. $\frac{1}{3}\log|x+1| + \frac{5}{3}\log|x-2| + C$

2. $\frac{1}{8}\log\left|\frac{x(x-4)}{(x-2)^2}\right| + C$

3. $\frac{1}{2}\log|x-1| - 4\log|x-2| + \frac{9}{2}\log|x-3| + C$

4. $\frac{5}{6}\log\left|\frac{(x+1)^2(x-2)}{(x+2)^3}\right| + C$

5. $\log\left|\frac{x^2-1}{x}\right| + C$

6. $\frac{5}{2}\log|x+1| - \frac{1}{10}\log|x-1| - \frac{12}{5}\log|2x+3| + C$

7. $\frac{3}{5}\log|x+2| + \frac{1}{5}\log(x^2+1) + \frac{1}{5}\tan^{-1}x + C$

8. $\frac{a^3 + ab + c}{(a-b)(a-c)}\log|x-a| + \frac{ab^2 + b^2 + c}{(b-a)(b-c)}\log|x-b| + \frac{ac^2 + bc + c}{(c-a)(c-b)}\log|x-c| + K$

9. $\frac{1}{2}\log|x-1| - \frac{1}{4}\log(x^2+1) + \frac{1}{2}\tan^{-1}x + C$

10. $\frac{1}{6}\log\left|\frac{(x-1)(x+2)^2}{(x+1)^3}\right| + C$

11. $\log|x(x^2-1)^2| + C$

12. $\log\left|\frac{x^2(x-2)}{(x+2)^2}\right| + C$

13. $-\frac{5}{6}\log|2x+1| + \frac{1}{3}\log|x-1| + \log|x+1| + C$

14. $\frac{11}{4}\log|x+1| + \frac{5}{2(x+1)} - \frac{11}{4}\log|x+3| + C$

15. $-\frac{3}{25}\log|x+2| + \frac{3}{25}\log|x-3| - \frac{7}{5(x-3)} + C$

16. $\frac{2}{5}\log|x+3| + \frac{3}{5}\log|x-2| - \frac{1}{x-2} + C$

17. $\frac{2}{9}\log\left|\frac{x-1}{x+2}\right| - \frac{1}{3(x-1)} + C$

18. $\frac{1}{4}\log|x-1| + \frac{3}{4}\log|x+1| + \frac{1}{2(x+1)} + C$

19. $\frac{1}{x+1} + \log|x+2| + C$

20. $6\log|x| - \log|x+1| - \frac{9}{(x+1)} + C$

21. $\frac{9}{4}\left\{\log|x+2| - \frac{1}{2}\log|x^2+4| + \tan^{-1}\left(\frac{x}{2}\right)\right\} + C$

22. $2\tan^{-1}x - \frac{1}{2}\log|x^2+1| + \log|x+2| + C$

23. $-\frac{1}{2}\log|x+1| + \frac{1}{4}\log|x^2+1| + \frac{1}{2}\tan^{-1}x + C$

24. $\frac{1}{2}\log|x+1| - \frac{1}{4}\log|1+x^2| + \frac{1}{2}\tan^{-1}x + C$

25. $\frac{1}{2}\log|x+1| - \frac{1}{2(x+1)} - \frac{1}{4}\log|x^2+1| + C$

26. $\frac{2}{3}\log|x-1| - \frac{1}{3}\log|x^2+x+1| + \frac{2}{\sqrt{3}}\tan^{-1}\left(\frac{2x+1}{\sqrt{3}}\right) + C$

27. $\frac{1}{2}\log\left|\frac{x+1}{x-1}\right| - \frac{4}{x-1} + C$

28. $x - \log|x| - \tan^{-1}x + \frac{1}{2}\log(x^2+1) + C$

29. $-2\log|x+1| - \frac{1}{x+1} + 3\log|x+2| + C$

30. $\frac{3}{4}\left\{\log\frac{x^2+1}{(1-x)^2} + 2\tan^{-1}x\right\} + C$

31. $-\frac{1}{27}\log|1-\sin x| + \frac{1}{9(1-\sin x)} + \frac{1}{6(1-\sin x)^2} + \frac{1}{27}\log|2+\sin x| + C$

32. $\log\left|\frac{2-\sin x}{1-\sin x}\right| + C$

33. $\log\left|\frac{(x-3)^7}{(x-2)^5}\right| + C$

34. $\log\left(\frac{x^2+1}{x^2+2}\right) + \frac{1}{x^2+2} + C$

35. $x - \log|x+3| + \log|x-2| + C$

36. $-x + 3\log|x+2| + 2\log|x-1| + C$

37. $x + \log\left|\frac{x-1}{x+1}\right| + C$

38. $x + \frac{1}{2}\log|x-1| - 8\log|x-2| + \frac{27}{2}\log|x-3| + C$

39. $\log\left|\frac{(2+\sin x)^4}{(1+\sin x)^2}\right| + C$

40. $\frac{1}{2}\log\left|\frac{x^2+1}{x^2+3}\right| + C$

41. $\frac{1}{2}\log\left|\frac{\log x}{2+\log x}\right| + C$

42. $-\frac{2}{5}\tan^{-1}\frac{x}{2} + \frac{3}{5}\tan^{-1}\frac{x}{3} + C$

43. $\log|2\log x + 1| - \log|3\log x + 2| + C$

44. $\frac{1}{n}\log\left|\frac{x^n}{x^n+1}\right| + C$

45. $\frac{1}{2(a^2-b^2)}\log\left|\frac{x^2-a^2}{x^2-b^2}\right| + C$

46. $-\frac{1}{14}\tan^{-1}\frac{x}{2} + \frac{8}{35}\tan^{-1}\frac{x}{5} + C$

47. $\frac{x^2}{2}+\log|x^2-1|+\frac{1}{2}\log\left|\frac{x-1}{x+1}\right|+C$

48. $\frac{3}{x}+13\log|x|-12\log|2x+1|+C$

49. $\frac{3}{5}\tan^{-1}\frac{x}{3}-\frac{2}{5}\tan^{-1}\left(\frac{x}{2}\right)+C$

50. $\frac{2}{\sqrt{3}}\tan^{-1}\left(\frac{\sqrt{3}x}{2}\right)-\tan^{-1}x+C$

51. $\frac{1}{4}\log\left(\frac{x^4}{x^4+1}\right)+C$

52. $\frac{1}{8}\log|x|-\frac{1}{24}\log\left|x^3+8\right|+C$

53. $-\frac{1}{4x}+\frac{7}{8}\tan^{-1}\left(\frac{x}{2}\right)+C$

54. $-\frac{1}{\sqrt{2}}\tan^{-1}\frac{x}{\sqrt{2}}+\tan^{-1}x+C$

55. $\frac{1}{4}\log\left|\frac{x^4-1}{x^4}\right|+C$

56. $\frac{1}{4}\log\left|\frac{x-1}{x+1}\right|-\frac{1}{2}\tan^{-1}x+C$

57. $\frac{1}{2}\log|x-1|+\frac{1}{4}\log(x^2+1)+\frac{1}{2}\tan^{-1}x+C$

58. $\frac{3}{4}\tan^{-1}\frac{x}{2}-\frac{1}{2\sqrt{2}}\tan^{-1}\frac{x}{\sqrt{2}}+C$

59. $\tan^{-1}\sqrt{x}+\frac{1}{2}\log\left|\frac{\sqrt{x}-1}{\sqrt{x}+1}\right|+C$

60. $\frac{1}{2}\ln\left(\frac{x^2-1}{x^2}\right)+C$

61. $\frac{1}{3}\ln\left|\frac{x}{x+3}\right|-\frac{1}{x}+C$

62. $\frac{1}{5}\ln\left|\frac{x^2-4}{x^2+1}\right|+C$

63. $\frac{a}{a^2-b^2}\tan^{-1}\frac{x}{a}-\frac{b}{a^2-b^2}\tan^{-1}\frac{x}{b}+C$

64. $\frac{1}{18}\log|1+\sin x|-\frac{1}{2}\log|1-\sin x|+\frac{4}{9}\log|5-4\sin x|+C$

65. $-\frac{1}{2}\log|1+\cos x|+\frac{1}{10}\log|1-\cos x|+\frac{2}{5}\log|3+2\cos x|+C$

66. $\frac{1}{6}\log|1-\cos x|+\frac{1}{2}\log|1+\cos x|-\frac{2}{3}\log|1+2\cos x|+C$

67. $\log\left|\frac{xe^x}{1+xe^x}\right|+C$

68. $x+\frac{2}{\sqrt{3}}\tan^{-1}\left(\frac{x}{\sqrt{3}}\right)-3\tan^{-1}\left(\frac{x}{2}\right)+C$

69. $\frac{19}{2\sqrt{2}}\tan^{-1}\left(\frac{x}{\sqrt{2}}\right)-\frac{39}{\sqrt{3}}\tan^{-1}\left(\frac{x}{\sqrt{3}}\right)+\frac{67}{4}\tan^{-1}\left(\frac{x}{2}\right)+C$

70. $\frac{x^2}{2}+x+\frac{1}{2}\log|x-1|-\frac{1}{4}\log(x^2+1)-\frac{1}{2}\tan^{-1}x+C$

71. $\frac{1}{7}\log\left|\frac{x-2}{x+2}\right|+\frac{\sqrt{3}}{7}\tan^{-1}\frac{x}{\sqrt{3}}+C$

72. $\frac{1}{4}\log\left|\frac{1-x}{1+x}\right|-\frac{1}{2}\tan^{-1}x+C$

73. $\frac{\sqrt{2}}{3}\tan^{-1}\frac{x}{\sqrt{2}}+\frac{1}{6}\log\left|\frac{x-1}{x+1}\right|+C$

74. $x+\frac{1}{4\sqrt{3}}\tan^{-1}\frac{x}{\sqrt{3}}+\frac{27}{8\sqrt{5}}\log\left|\frac{x-\sqrt{5}}{x+\sqrt{5}}\right|+C$

75. $-\log(1-\sin x)+\frac{1}{2}\log(1+\sin^2 x)+\tan^{-1}(\sin x)+C$

15.14 INTEGRALS OF THE FORM

$$\int\frac{x^2+1}{x^4+\lambda x^2+1}dx,\ \int\frac{x^2-1}{x^4+\lambda x^2+1}dx,\ \int\frac{1}{x^4+\lambda x^2+1}dx, \text{where } \lambda\in R$$

To evaluate this type of integrals, we use the following algorithm.

ALGORITHM

Step I *Divide numerator and denominator by* x^2.

Step II *Express the denominator of integrand in the form* $\left(x+\frac{1}{x}\right)^2 \pm k^2$.

Step III *Introduce* $d\left(x+\frac{1}{x}\right)$ *or,* $d\left(x-\frac{1}{x}\right)$ *or both in the numerator.*

Step IV *Substitute* $x+\frac{1}{x}=t$ *or,* $x-\frac{1}{x}=t$ *as the case may be.*

This substitution reduces the integral in one of the following forms $\int \frac{1}{x^2+a^2}\,dx$, $\int \frac{1}{x^2-a^2}\,dx$.

Step V *Use the appropriate formula.*

ILLUSTRATIVE EXAMPLES

BASED ON LOWER ORDER THINKING SKILLS (LOTS)

EXAMPLE 1 *Evaluate:*

(i) $\int \frac{x^2+1}{x^4+1}\,dx$ **[CBSE 2007, 11]** (ii) $\int \frac{x^2-1}{x^4+x^2+1}\,dx$ (iii) $\int \frac{x^2+4}{x^4+16}\,dx$ **[CBSE 2007]**

SOLUTION (i) Let $I=\int \frac{x^2+1}{x^4+1}\,dx$. Dividing the numerator and denominator by x^2, we obtain

$$I = \int \frac{1+\frac{1}{x^2}}{x^2+\frac{1}{x^2}}\,dx = \int \frac{1+\frac{1}{x^2}}{\left(x-\frac{1}{x}\right)^2+2}\,dx$$

Let $x-\frac{1}{x} = t \Rightarrow d\left(x-\frac{1}{x}\right) = dt \Rightarrow \left(1+\frac{1}{x^2}\right)dx = dt$.

$$\therefore\ I=\int \frac{dt}{t^2+(\sqrt{2})^2}=\frac{1}{\sqrt{2}}\tan^{-1}\left(\frac{t}{\sqrt{2}}\right)+C=\frac{1}{\sqrt{2}}\tan^{-1}\left(\frac{x-1/x}{\sqrt{2}}\right)+C=\frac{1}{\sqrt{2}}\tan^{-1}\left(\frac{x^2-1}{\sqrt{2}x}\right)+C$$

(ii) Let $I = \int \frac{x^2-1}{x^4+x^2+1}\,dx$. Dividing the numerator and denominator by x^2, we obtain

$$I = \int \frac{1-\frac{1}{x^2}}{x^2+1+\frac{1}{x^2}}\,dx = \int \frac{1-\frac{1}{x^2}}{\left(x+\frac{1}{x}\right)^2-1^2}\,dx$$

Let $x+\frac{1}{x} = u$. Then, $d\left(x+\frac{1}{x}\right) = du \Rightarrow \left(1-\frac{1}{x^2}\right)dx = du$

$$\therefore\ I = \int \frac{du}{u^2-1^2} = \frac{1}{2(1)}\log\left|\frac{u-1}{u+1}\right| + C = \frac{1}{2}\log\left|\frac{x+\frac{1}{x}-1}{x+\frac{1}{x}+1}\right| + C = \frac{1}{2}\log\left|\frac{x^2-x+1}{x^2+x+1}\right| + C$$

(iii) Let $I = \int \frac{x^2+4}{x^4+16}\,dx$. Dividing the numerator and denominator by x^2, we obtain

$$I = \int \frac{1+\frac{4}{x^2}}{x^2+\frac{16}{x^2}}\,dx = \int \frac{1+\frac{4}{x^2}}{x^2+\left(\frac{4}{x}\right)^2-8+8}\,dx = \int \frac{1+\frac{4}{x^2}}{\left(x-\frac{4}{x}\right)^2+8}\,dx.$$

Let $x-\frac{4}{x}=t$. Then, $d\left(x-\frac{4}{x}\right) = dt \Rightarrow \left(1+\frac{4}{x^2}\right)dx = dt$

$$\therefore \quad I = \int \frac{dt}{t^2+(2\sqrt{2})^2}$$

$$\Rightarrow \quad I = \frac{1}{2\sqrt{2}}\tan^{-1}\left(\frac{t}{2\sqrt{2}}\right)+C = \frac{1}{2\sqrt{2}}\tan^{-1}\left(\frac{x-\frac{4}{x}}{2\sqrt{2}}\right)+C = \frac{1}{2\sqrt{2}}\tan^{-1}\left(\frac{x^2-4}{2x\sqrt{2}}\right)+C$$

EXAMPLE 2 *Evaluate:*

(i) $\int \frac{1}{x^4+1}\,dx$ (ii) $\int \frac{x^2}{x^4+1}\,dx$ (iii) $\int \sqrt{\tan\theta}\,d\theta$

SOLUTION (i) Let $I = \int \frac{1}{x^4+1}\,dx$. Dividing numerator and denominator by x^2, we obtain

$$\Rightarrow \quad I = \int \frac{\frac{1}{x^2}}{x^2+\frac{1}{x^2}}\,dx = \frac{1}{2}\int \frac{\frac{2}{x^2}}{x^2+\frac{1}{x^2}}\,dx = \frac{1}{2}\int \frac{1+\frac{1}{x^2}}{x^2+\frac{1}{x^2}} - \frac{1-\frac{1}{x^2}}{x^2+\frac{1}{x^2}}\,dx$$

$$\Rightarrow \quad I = \frac{1}{2}\int \frac{1+\frac{1}{x^2}}{x^2+\frac{1}{x^2}}\,dx - \frac{1}{2}\int \frac{1-\frac{1}{x^2}}{x^2+\frac{1}{x^2}}\,dx = \frac{1}{2}\int \frac{1+\frac{1}{x^2}}{\left(x-\frac{1}{x}\right)^2+2}\,dx - \frac{1}{2}\int \frac{1-\frac{1}{x^2}}{\left(x+\frac{1}{x}\right)^2-2}\,dx$$

Substituting $x-\frac{1}{x}=u$ in first integral and $x+\frac{1}{x}=v$ in second integral, we obtain

$$I = \frac{1}{2}\int \frac{du}{u^2+(\sqrt{2})^2} - \frac{1}{2}\int \frac{dv}{v^2-(\sqrt{2})^2}$$

$$\Rightarrow \quad I = \frac{1}{2\sqrt{2}}\tan^{-1}\left(\frac{u}{\sqrt{2}}\right) - \frac{1}{2}\times\frac{1}{2\sqrt{2}}\log\left|\frac{v-\sqrt{2}}{v+\sqrt{2}}\right| + C$$

$$\Rightarrow \quad I = \frac{1}{2\sqrt{2}}\tan^{-1}\left(\frac{x-1/x}{\sqrt{2}\,x}\right) - \frac{1}{4\sqrt{2}}\log\left|\frac{x+1/x-\sqrt{2}}{x+1/x+\sqrt{2}}\right| + C$$

$$\Rightarrow \quad I = \frac{1}{2\sqrt{2}}\tan^{-1}\left(\frac{x^2-1}{\sqrt{2}\,x}\right) - \frac{1}{4\sqrt{2}}\log\left|\frac{x^2-\sqrt{2}\,x+1}{x^2+\sqrt{2}\,x+1}\right| + C$$

(ii) $I = \int \frac{x^2}{x^4+1}\,dx$. Dividing numerator and denominator by x^2, we obtain

$$\Rightarrow \quad I = \int \frac{1}{x^2 + 1/x^2}\, dx = \frac{1}{2} \int \frac{2}{x^2 + 1/x^2}\, dx = \int \frac{(1 + 1/x^2) + (1 - 1/x^2)}{x^2 + 1/x^2}\, dx$$

$$\Rightarrow \quad I = \frac{1}{2} \int = \frac{1}{2} \int \frac{1 + 1/x^2}{x^2 + 1/x^2}\, dx + \frac{1}{2} \int \frac{1 - 1/x^2}{x^2 + 1/x^2}\, dx$$

$$\Rightarrow \quad I = \frac{1}{2} \int \frac{1 + 1/x^2}{(x - 1/x)^2 + 2}\, dx + \frac{1}{2} \int \frac{1 - 1/x^2\, dx}{(x + 1/x)^2 - 2}$$

Putting $x - \frac{1}{x} = u$ in first integral and $x + \frac{1}{x} = v$ in second integral, we obtain

$$I = \frac{1}{2} \int \frac{du}{u^2 + (\sqrt{2})^2} + \frac{1}{2} \int \frac{dv}{v^2 - (\sqrt{2})^2}$$

$$\Rightarrow \quad I = \frac{1}{2} \times \frac{1}{\sqrt{2}} \tan^{-1}\left(\frac{u}{\sqrt{2}}\right) + \frac{1}{2} \times \frac{1}{2\sqrt{2}} \log\left|\frac{v - \sqrt{2}}{v + \sqrt{2}}\right| + C$$

$$\Rightarrow \quad I = \frac{1}{2\sqrt{2}} \tan^{-1}\left(\frac{x - 1/x}{\sqrt{2}}\right) + \frac{1}{4\sqrt{2}} \log\left|\frac{x + 1/x - \sqrt{2}}{x + 1/x + \sqrt{2}}\right| + C$$

$$\Rightarrow \quad I = \frac{1}{2\sqrt{2}} \tan^{-1}\left(\frac{x^2 - 1}{x\sqrt{2}}\right) + \frac{1}{4\sqrt{2}} \log\left|\frac{x^2 - x\sqrt{2} + 1}{x^2 + x\sqrt{2} + 1}\right| + C$$

(iii) Let $I = \int \sqrt{\tan\theta}\, d\theta$. Let $\tan\theta = x^2$. Then,

$$d(\tan\theta) = d(x^2) \Rightarrow \sec^2\theta\, d\theta = 2x\, dx \Rightarrow d\theta = \frac{2x\, dx}{\sec^2\theta} = \frac{2x\, dx}{1 + \tan^2\theta} = \frac{2x\, dx}{1 + x^4}$$

$$I = \int \sqrt{x^2} \cdot \frac{2x\, dx}{1 + x^4} = \int \frac{2x^2}{x^4 + 1}\, dx = \int \frac{2}{x^2 + 1/x^2}\, dx = \int \frac{1 + 1/x^2 + 1 - 1/x^2}{x^2 + 1/x^2}\, dx$$

$$\Rightarrow \quad I = \int \frac{1 + 1/x^2}{x^2 + 1/x^2}\, dx + \int \frac{1 - 1/x^2}{x^2 + 1/x^2}\, dx = \int \frac{1 + 1/x^2}{(x - 1/x)^2 + 2}\, dx + \int \frac{1 - 1/x^2\, dx}{(x + 1/x)^2 - 2}$$

Substituting $x - \frac{1}{x} = u$ in first integral and $x + \frac{1}{x} = v$ in second integral, we get

$$I = \int \frac{du}{u^2 + (\sqrt{2})^2} + \int \frac{dv}{v^2 - (\sqrt{2})^2} = \frac{1}{\sqrt{2}} \tan^{-1}\left(\frac{u}{\sqrt{2}}\right) + \frac{1}{2\sqrt{2}} \log\left|\frac{v - \sqrt{2}}{v + \sqrt{2}}\right| + C$$

$$\Rightarrow \quad I = \frac{1}{\sqrt{2}} \tan^{-1}\left(\frac{x - 1/x}{\sqrt{2}}\right) + \frac{1}{2\sqrt{2}} \log\left|\frac{x + 1/x - \sqrt{2}}{x + 1/x + \sqrt{2}}\right| + C$$

$$\Rightarrow \quad I = \frac{1}{\sqrt{2}} \tan^{-1}\left(\frac{x^2 - 1}{\sqrt{2}\, x}\right) + \frac{1}{2\sqrt{2}} \log\left|\frac{x^2 - \sqrt{2}\, x + 1}{x^2 + \sqrt{2}\, x + 1}\right| + C$$

$$\Rightarrow \quad I = \frac{1}{\sqrt{2}} \tan^{-1}\left(\frac{\tan\theta - 1}{\sqrt{2\tan\theta}}\right) + \frac{1}{2\sqrt{2}} \log\left|\frac{\tan\theta - \sqrt{2\tan\theta} + 1}{\tan\theta + \sqrt{2\tan\theta} + 1}\right| + C$$

EXAMPLE 3 *Evaluate:* $\int \left\{\sqrt{\tan\theta} + \sqrt{\cot\theta}\right\} d\theta$ **[CBSE 2010, 2013, 2014, 2020]**

SOLUTION Let $I = \int \left\{\sqrt{\tan\theta} + \sqrt{\cot\theta}\right\} d\theta$. Then,

$$I = \int \left\{\sqrt{\tan\theta} + \frac{1}{\sqrt{\tan\theta}}\right\} d\theta \Rightarrow I = \int \frac{\tan\theta + 1}{\sqrt{\tan\theta}}\, d\theta.$$

Let $\tan\theta = x^2$. Then,

$$d(\tan\theta) = d(x^2) \Rightarrow \sec^2\theta\, d\theta = 2x\, dx \Rightarrow d\theta = \frac{2x\, dx}{\sec^2\theta} = \frac{2x\, dx}{1+\tan^2\theta} = \frac{2x\, dx}{1+x^4}$$

$$\therefore \quad I = \int \frac{x^2+1}{\sqrt{x^2}} \times \frac{2x\, dx}{1+x^4} = 2\int \frac{x^2+1}{x^4+1} = 2\int \frac{1+1/x^2}{x^2+1/x^2}\, dx = 2\int \frac{1+1/x^2}{(x-1/x)^2+2}\, dx$$

$$\Rightarrow \quad I = 2\int \frac{1+1/x^2}{(x-1/x)^2+(\sqrt{2})^2}\, dx = 2\int \frac{du}{u^2+(\sqrt{2})^2} = \frac{2}{\sqrt{2}}\tan^{-1}\left(\frac{u}{\sqrt{2}}\right) + C, \text{ where } x - \frac{1}{x} = u$$

$$\Rightarrow \quad I = \sqrt{2}\tan^{-1}\left(\frac{x-1/x}{\sqrt{2}}\right) + C = \sqrt{2}\tan^{-1}\left(\frac{x^2-1}{\sqrt{2}\,x}\right) + C = \sqrt{2}\tan^{-1}\left\{\frac{\tan\theta - 1}{\sqrt{2\tan\theta}}\right\} + C$$

EXAMPLE 4 *Evaluate:* $\int \frac{1}{\sin^4 x + \cos^4 x}\, dx.$ **[CBSE 2014]**

SOLUTION Let $I = \int \frac{1}{\sin^4 x + \cos^4 x}\, dx$. Then,

$$\Rightarrow I = \int \frac{1/\cos^4 x}{\frac{\sin^4 x + \cos^4 x}{\cos^4 x}}\, dx = \int \frac{\sec^4 x}{\tan^4 x + 1}\, dx = \int \frac{\sec^2 x \cdot \sec^2 x}{\tan^4 x + 1}\, dx = \int \left\{\frac{1+\tan^2 x}{1+\tan^4 x}\right\} \sec^2 x\, dx$$

Putting $\tan x = t$ and $\sec^2 x\, dx = dt$, we get

$$I = \int \frac{1+t^2}{1+t^4}\, dt = \frac{1}{\sqrt{2}}\tan^{-1}\left(\frac{t^2-1}{\sqrt{2}t}\right) + C = \frac{1}{\sqrt{2}}\tan^{-1}\left(\frac{\tan^2 x - 1}{\sqrt{2}\tan x}\right) + C$$ [Proceed as in Example 3]

BASED ON HIGHER ORDER THINKING SKILLS (HOTS)

EXAMPLE 5 *Evaluate:* $\int \frac{1}{\cos^6 x + \sin^6 x}\, dx$

SOLUTION Let $I = \int \frac{1}{\cos^6 x + \sin^6 x}\, dx$. Then,

$$I = \int \frac{1}{(\cos^2 x + \sin^2 x)(\cos^4 x + \sin^4 x - \cos^2 x \sin^2 x)}\, dx$$

$$\Rightarrow \quad I = \int \frac{1}{(\cos^2 x + \sin^2 x)^2 - 3\sin^2 x \cos^2 x}\, dx$$

$$\Rightarrow \quad I = \int \frac{1}{1 - 3\sin^2 x \cos^2 x}\, dx = \int \frac{\sec^4 x}{\sec^4 x - 3\tan^2 x}\, dx$$ [Dividing N^r and D^r by $\cos^4 x$]

$$\Rightarrow \quad I = \int \frac{(1+\tan^2 x)\sec^2 x}{(1+\tan^2 x)^2 - 3\tan^2 x}\, dx = \int \frac{t^2+1}{t^4 - t^2 + 1}\, dt, \quad \text{where } t = \tan^2 x$$

$$\Rightarrow \quad I = \int \frac{1+\frac{1}{t^2}}{t^2 + \frac{1}{t^2} - 1}\, dt = \int \frac{1+\frac{1}{t^2}}{\left(t-\frac{1}{t}\right)^2 + 1} = \int \frac{du}{u^2+1}, \text{ where } u = t - \frac{1}{t}$$

$$\Rightarrow \quad I = \tan^{-1} u + C = \tan^{-1}(\tan x - \cot x) + C$$

EXAMPLE 6 *Evaluate* : $\int \frac{x^4+1}{x^6+1}\, dx$

SOLUTION Let $I = \int \frac{x^4+1}{x^6+1}\, dx$. Then,

$$I = \int \frac{(x^2+1)^2 - 2x^2}{(x^2+1)(x^4-x^2+1)}\, dx = \int \frac{x^2+1}{x^4-x^2+1}\, dx - 2\int \frac{x^2}{x^6+1}\, dx$$

$$\Rightarrow \quad I = \int \frac{1+\frac{1}{x^2}}{x^2 - 1 + \frac{1}{x^2}}\, dx - \frac{2}{3}\int \frac{3x^2\, dx}{(x^3)^2+1}\, dx = \int \frac{1+\frac{1}{x^2}}{\left(x-\frac{1}{x}\right)^2 + 1^2} - \frac{2}{3}\int \frac{1}{(x^3)^2+1^2}\, 3x^2\, dx$$

$$\Rightarrow \quad I = \int \frac{1}{u^2+1^2}\, du - \frac{2}{3}\int \frac{1}{v^2+1^2}\, dv, \text{ where } u = x - \frac{1}{x} \text{ and } v = x^3$$

$$\Rightarrow \quad I = \tan^{-1} u - \frac{2}{3}\tan^{-1} v + C = \tan^{-1}\left(x - \frac{1}{x}\right) - \frac{2}{3}\tan^{-1} x^3 + C$$

EXAMPLE 7 *Evaluate* : $\int \frac{x^3}{x^{16}+4}\, dx$

SOLUTION Let $I = \int \frac{x^3}{x^{16}+4}\, dx = \int \frac{x^3}{(x^4)^4+4}\, dx$. Putting $x^4 = t$ and $4x^3\, dx = dt$, we get

$$I = \frac{1}{4}\int \frac{1}{t^4+4}\, dt = \frac{1}{4}\int \frac{\frac{1}{t^2}}{t^2+\frac{4}{t^2}}\, dt \qquad [\text{Dividing N}^r \text{ and D}^r \text{ by } t^2]$$

$$\Rightarrow I = \frac{1}{16}\int \frac{\frac{4}{t^2}}{t^2+\frac{4}{t^2}}\, dt = \frac{1}{16}\int \frac{\left(1+\frac{2}{t^2}\right) - \left(1-\frac{2}{t^2}\right)}{t^2+\frac{4}{t^2}}\, dt$$

$$\Rightarrow I = \frac{1}{16}\int \frac{1+\frac{2}{t^2}}{t^2+\frac{4}{t^2}}\, dt - \frac{1}{16}\int \frac{1-\frac{2}{t^2}}{t^2+\frac{4}{t^2}}\, dt = \frac{1}{16}\int \frac{1+\frac{2}{t^2}}{\left(t-\frac{2}{t}\right)^2+4}\, dt - \frac{1}{16}\int \frac{1-\frac{2}{t^2}}{\left(t+\frac{2}{t}\right)^2-4}\, dt$$

$$\Rightarrow I = \frac{1}{16}\int \frac{du}{u^2+2^2} - \frac{1}{16}\int \frac{dv}{v^2-2^2}, \text{ where } u = t - \frac{2}{t} \text{ and } v = t + \frac{2}{t}$$

$$\Rightarrow I = \frac{1}{32}\tan^{-1}\left(\frac{u}{2}\right) - \frac{1}{16} \times \frac{1}{2 \times 2}\log\left|\frac{v-2}{v+2}\right| + C = \frac{1}{32}\tan^{-1}\left(\frac{t^2-2}{2t}\right) - \frac{1}{64}\log\left|\frac{t^2-2t+2}{t^2+2t+2}\right| + C$$

$$\Rightarrow I = \frac{1}{32}\tan^{-1}\left(\frac{x^8-2}{2x^4}\right) - \frac{1}{64}\log\left|\frac{x^8-2x^4+2}{x^8+2x^4+2}\right| + C$$

EXAMPLE 8 *Evaluate* : $\int \frac{x^2-1}{(x^2+1)\sqrt{x^4+1}}\,dx$

SOLUTION Let $I = \int \frac{x^2-1}{(x^2+1)\sqrt{x^4+1}}\,dx$. Then,

$$I = \int \frac{1-\frac{1}{x^2}}{\left(x+\frac{1}{x}\right)\sqrt{x^2+\frac{1}{x^2}}}\,dx = \int \frac{1-\frac{1}{x^2}}{\left(x+\frac{1}{x}\right)\sqrt{\left(x+\frac{1}{x}\right)^2-2}}\,dx \qquad \text{[Dividing } N^r \text{ and } D^r \text{ by } x^2]$$

Let $x+\frac{1}{x} = t$. Then, $d\left(x+\frac{1}{x}\right) = dt$ or, $\left(1-\frac{1}{x^2}\right)dx = dt$.

$$\therefore\ I = \int \frac{1}{t\sqrt{t^2-2}}\,dt = \int \frac{1}{t\sqrt{t^2-(\sqrt{2})^2}}\,dt = \frac{1}{\sqrt{2}}\sec^{-1}\left(\frac{t}{\sqrt{2}}\right) + C = \frac{1}{\sqrt{2}}\sec^{-1}\left(\frac{x-\frac{1}{x}}{\sqrt{2}}\right) + C$$

EXERCISE 15.31

BASED ON LOTS

Evaluate the following integrals:

1. $\int \frac{x^2+1}{x^4+x^2+1}\,dx$
2. $\int \sqrt{\cot\theta}\,d\theta$
3. $\int \frac{x^2+9}{x^4+81}\,dx$
4. $\int \frac{1}{x^4+x^2+1}\,dx$
5. $\int \frac{x^2-3x+1}{x^4+x^2+1}\,dx$
6. $\int \frac{x^2+1}{x^4-x^2+1}\,dx$
7. $\int \frac{x^2-1}{x^4+1}\,dx$ **[CBSE 2007]**
8. $\int \frac{x^2+1}{x^4+7x^2+1}\,dx$
9. $\int \frac{(x-1)^2}{x^4+x^2+1}\,dx$
10. $\int \frac{1}{x^4+3x^2+1}\,dx$
11. $\int \frac{1}{\sin^4 x+\sin^2 x\cos^2 x+\cos^4 x}\,dx$ **[CBSE 2014]**

ANSWERS

1. $\frac{1}{\sqrt{3}}\tan^{-1}\left(\frac{x^2-1}{\sqrt{3}x}\right) + C$
2. $-\frac{1}{\sqrt{2}}\tan^{-1}\left(\frac{\cot\theta-1}{\sqrt{2\cot\theta}}\right) - \frac{1}{2\sqrt{2}}\log\left|\frac{\cot\theta+1-\sqrt{2\cot\theta}}{\cot\theta+1+\sqrt{2\cot\theta}}\right| + C$

3. $\frac{1}{3\sqrt{2}}\tan^{-1}\left(\frac{x^2-9}{3\sqrt{2}\,x}\right)+C$

4. $\frac{1}{2\sqrt{3}}\tan^{-1}\left(\frac{x^2-1}{x\sqrt{3}}\right)-\frac{1}{4}\log\left|\frac{x^2-x+1}{x^2+x+1}\right|+C$

5. $\frac{1}{\sqrt{3}}\tan^{-1}\left(\frac{x^2-1}{\sqrt{3}x}\right)+\sqrt{3}\tan^{-1}\left(\frac{2x^2+1}{\sqrt{3}}\right)+C$

6. $\tan^{-1}\left(\frac{x^2-1}{x}\right)+C$

7. $\frac{1}{2\sqrt{2}}\log\left|\frac{x^2-\sqrt{2}\,x+1}{x^2+\sqrt{2}\,x+1}\right|+C$

8. $\frac{1}{3}\tan^{-1}\left(\frac{x^2-1}{3x}\right)+C$

9. $\frac{1}{\sqrt{3}}\tan^{-1}\left(\frac{x^2-1}{\sqrt{3}\,x}\right)-\frac{2}{\sqrt{3}}\tan^{-1}\left(\frac{2x^2+1}{\sqrt{3}}\right)+C$

10. $\frac{1}{2\sqrt{5}}\tan^{-1}\left(\frac{x^2-1}{\sqrt{5}x}\right)-\frac{1}{2}\tan^{-1}\left(\frac{x^2+1}{x}\right)+C$

11. $\frac{1}{\sqrt{3}}\tan^{-1}\left(\frac{\tan x-\cot x}{\sqrt{3}}\right)+C$

15.15 INTEGRATION OF SOME SPECIAL IRRATIONAL ALGEBRAIC FUNCTIONS

In this section, we shall discuss four integrals of the form $\int\frac{\phi(x)}{P\sqrt{Q}}\,dx$, where P and Q are polynomial functions of x.

15.15.1 INTEGRALS OF THE FORM $\int\frac{\phi(x)}{P\sqrt{Q}}\,dx$, WHERE P AND Q BOTH ARE LINEAR FUNCTIONS OF x

To evaluate this type of integrals we put $Q=t^2$ i.e., to evaluate integrals of the form $\int\frac{1}{(ax+b)\sqrt{cx+d}}\,dx$, put $cx+d=t^2$.

Following examples illustrate the procedure.

ILLUSTRATIVE EXAMPLES

BASED ON BASIC CONCEPTS (BASIC)

EXAMPLE 1 *Evaluate:* $\int\frac{1}{(x-3)\sqrt{x+1}}\,dx$

SOLUTION Let $I=\int\frac{1}{(x-3)\sqrt{x+1}}\,dx$

Here, P and Q both are linear, so we substitute $Q=t^2$ *i.e.* $x+1=t^2$ and $dx=2t\,dt$.

$$\therefore\quad I=\int\frac{1}{(t^2-1-3)}\frac{2t}{\sqrt{t^2}}\,dt=2\int\frac{dt}{t^2-2^2}=2\times\frac{1}{2(2)}\log\left|\frac{t-2}{t+2}\right|+C=\frac{1}{2}\log\left|\frac{\sqrt{x+1}-2}{\sqrt{x+1}+2}\right|+C.$$

EXAMPLE 2 *Evaluate* $\int\frac{\sqrt{x}}{x+1}\,dx.$

SOLUTION Let $I=\int\frac{\sqrt{x}}{x+1}\,dx=\int\frac{x}{\sqrt{x}\,(x+1)}\,dx$. Putting $x=t^2$ and $dx=2t\,dt$, we get

$$I = \int \frac{t^2}{\sqrt{t^2}} \frac{2t\,dt}{(t^2+1)} = 2\int \frac{t^2}{t^2+1}\,dt = 2\int \frac{t^2+1-1}{t^2+1}\,dt$$

$$\Rightarrow \quad I = 2\int 1 - \frac{1}{t^2+1}\,dt = 2\left(t - \tan^{-1} t\right) + C = 2\left(\sqrt{x} - \tan^{-1}\sqrt{x}\right) + C$$

15.15.2 INTEGRALS OF THE FORM $\int \frac{\phi(x)}{P\sqrt{Q}}\,dx$, WHERE P IS A QUADRATIC EXPRESSION AND Q IS A LINEAR EXPRESSION

To evaluate this type of integrals we put $Q = t^2$ i.e., to evaluate integrals of the form $\int \frac{1}{(ax^2+bx+c)\sqrt{px+q}}\,dx$, we put $px+q=t^2$.

Following examples will illustrate the procedure.

ILLUSTRATIVE EXAMPLES

BASED ON LOWER ORDER THINKING SKILLS (LOTS)

EXAMPLE 1 *Evaluate:* $\int \frac{1}{(x^2-4)\sqrt{x+1}}\,dx$

SOLUTION Let $I = \int \frac{1}{(x^2-4)\sqrt{x+1}}\,dx$. Putting $x+1=t^2$ and $dx = 2t\,dt$, we get

$$I = \int \frac{2t\,dt}{\left\{(t^2-1)^2-4\right\}\sqrt{t^2}} = 2\int \frac{dt}{(t^2-1-2)(t^2-1+2)} = 2\int \frac{dt}{(t^2-3)(t^2+1)}$$

Let $t^2 = y$. Then, $\frac{1}{(t^2-3)(t^2+1)} = \frac{1}{(y-3)(y+1)}$

$$\text{Let} \quad \frac{1}{(y-3)(y+1)} = \frac{A}{y-3} + \frac{B}{y+1} \qquad ...(i)$$

$$\Rightarrow \quad 1 = A(y+1) + B(y-3) \qquad ...(ii)$$

Putting $y=-1, 3$ respectively in (ii), we get: $B = -\frac{1}{4}$ and $A = \frac{1}{4}$.

Substituting the values of A and B in (i), we obtain

$$\frac{1}{(y-3)(y+1)} = \frac{1}{4(y-3)} - \frac{1}{4(y+1)} \Rightarrow \frac{1}{(t^2-3)(t^2+1)} = \frac{1}{4(t^2-3)} - \frac{1}{4(t^2+1)} \qquad [\because y = t^2]$$

$$\therefore \quad I = 2\int \left\{\frac{1}{4(t^2-3)} - \frac{1}{4(t^2+1)}\right\} dt = \frac{1}{2}\int \frac{1}{t^2-(\sqrt{3})^2}\,dt - \frac{1}{2}\int \frac{1}{t^2+1^2}\,dt$$

$$\Rightarrow I = \frac{1}{2} \times \frac{1}{2\sqrt{3}} \log\left|\frac{t-\sqrt{3}}{t+\sqrt{3}}\right| - \frac{1}{2}\tan^{-1}(t) + C = \frac{1}{4\sqrt{3}} \log\left|\frac{\sqrt{x+1}-\sqrt{3}}{\sqrt{x+1}+\sqrt{3}}\right| - \frac{1}{2}\tan^{-1}\left(\frac{\sqrt{x+1}}{1}\right) + C$$

BASED ON HIGHER ORDER THINKING SKILLS (HOTS)

EXAMPLE 2 *Evaluate:* $\int \frac{x+2}{(x^2+3x+3)\sqrt{x+1}}\,dx$

SOLUTION Let $I = \int \frac{x+2}{(x^2+3x+3)\sqrt{x+1}}\,dx$. Putting $x+1=t^2$, and $dx = 2t\,dt$, we get

$$I = \int \frac{(t^2+1)\,2t}{\left\{(t^2-1)^2 + 3(t^2-1) + 3\right\}\sqrt{t^2}}\,dt$$

$$\Rightarrow \quad I = 2\int \frac{(t^2+1)}{t^4+t^2+1}\,dt = 2\int \frac{1+\frac{1}{t^2}}{t^2+\frac{1}{t^2}+1}\,dt \qquad \text{[Dividing } N^r \text{ and } D^r \text{ by } t^2]$$

$$\Rightarrow \quad I = 2\int \frac{1+\frac{1}{t^2}}{\left(t-\frac{1}{t}\right)^2 + (\sqrt{3})^2}\,dt = 2\int \frac{du}{u^2+(\sqrt{3})^2}, \text{ where } t-\frac{1}{t}=u$$

$$\Rightarrow \quad I = \frac{2}{\sqrt{3}}\tan^{-1}\left(\frac{u}{\sqrt{3}}\right) + C = \frac{2}{\sqrt{3}}\tan^{-1}\left\{\frac{t-\frac{1}{t}}{\sqrt{3}}\right\} + C$$

$$\Rightarrow \quad I = \frac{2}{\sqrt{3}}\tan^{-1}\left(\frac{t^2-1}{\sqrt{3}\,t}\right) + C = \frac{2}{\sqrt{3}}\tan^{-1}\left\{\frac{x}{\sqrt{3(x+1)}}\right\} + C$$

15.15.3 INTEGRALS OF THE FORM $\int \frac{\phi(x)}{P\sqrt{Q}}\,dx$, WHERE P IS A LINEAR EXPRESSION AND Q IS A QUADRATIC EXPRESSION

To evaluate this type of integrals we put $P = 1/t$ i.e. to evaluate integrals of the form $\int \frac{1}{(ax+b)\sqrt{px^2+qx+r}}\,dx$, we put $ax+b=\frac{1}{t}$.

Following examples will illustrate the procedure.

ILLUSTRATIVE EXAMPLES

BASED ON LOWER ORDER THINKING SKILLS (LOTS)

EXAMPLE 1 *Evaluate* (i) $\int \frac{1}{(x+1)\sqrt{x^2-1}}\,dx$ (ii) $\int \frac{1}{(x-1)\sqrt{x^2+4}}\,dx$

SOLUTION (i) Let $I = \int \frac{1}{(x+1)\sqrt{x^2-1}}\,dx$. Putting $x+1=\frac{1}{t}$ and $dx = -\frac{1}{t^2}\,dt$, we get

$$\therefore \quad I = \int \frac{1}{\frac{1}{t}\sqrt{\left(\frac{1}{t}-1\right)^2-1}}\cdot\left(-\frac{1}{t^2}\right)dt = -\int \frac{dt}{\sqrt{1-2t}} = -\int (1-2t)^{-1/2}\,dt = -\frac{(1-2t)^{1/2}}{(-2)\left(\frac{1}{2}\right)} + C$$

$$\Rightarrow \quad I = \sqrt{1-2t} + C = \sqrt{1-\frac{2}{x+1}} + C = \sqrt{\frac{x-1}{x+1}} + C$$

(ii) Let $I = \int \frac{1}{(x-1)\sqrt{x^2+4}}\,dx$. Putting $x-1 = \frac{1}{t}$, and $dx = -\frac{1}{t^2}\,dt$, we get

$$\therefore \quad I = \int \frac{-\frac{1}{t^2}\,dt}{\frac{1}{t}\sqrt{\left(\frac{1}{t}+1\right)^2+4}} = -\int \frac{dt}{\sqrt{5t^2+2t+1}} = -\frac{1}{\sqrt{5}}\int \frac{dt}{\sqrt{t^2+\frac{2}{5}t+\frac{1}{5}}}$$

$$\Rightarrow \quad I = -\frac{1}{\sqrt{5}}\int \frac{dt}{\sqrt{\left(t^2+\frac{2}{5}t+\frac{1}{25}\right)+\frac{1}{5}-\frac{1}{25}}} = -\frac{1}{\sqrt{5}}\int \frac{1}{\sqrt{\left(t+\frac{1}{5}\right)^2+\left(\frac{2}{5}\right)^2}}\,dt$$

$$\Rightarrow \quad I = -\frac{1}{\sqrt{5}}\log\left|\left(t+\frac{1}{5}\right)+\sqrt{\left(t+\frac{1}{5}\right)^2+\left(\frac{2}{5}\right)^2}\right|+C = -\frac{1}{\sqrt{5}}\log\left|\left(t+\frac{1}{5}\right)+\sqrt{t^2+\frac{2}{5}t+\frac{1}{5}}\right|+C$$

$$\Rightarrow \quad I = -\frac{1}{\sqrt{5}}\log\left|\left(\frac{1}{x-1}+\frac{1}{5}\right)+\sqrt{\frac{1}{(x-1)^2}+\frac{2}{5(x-1)}+\frac{1}{5}}\right|+C$$

$$\Rightarrow \quad I = -\frac{1}{\sqrt{5}}\log\left|\frac{1}{x-1}+\frac{1}{5}+\sqrt{\frac{x^2+4}{5(x-1)^2}}\right|+C$$

15.15.4 INTEGRALS OF THE FORM $\int \frac{\phi(x)}{P\sqrt{Q}}\,dx$, WHERE P AND Q BOTH ARE PURE QUADRATIC EXPRESSION IN x i.e. $P = ax^2 + b$ AND $Q = cx^2 + d$

To evaluate this type of integrals we put $x = \frac{1}{t}$ *and then* $c + dt^2 = u^2$ *i.e., to evaluate integrals of the form* $\int \frac{1}{(ax^2+b)\sqrt{cx^2+d}}\,dx$, *we put* $x = \frac{1}{t}$ *to obtain* $\int \frac{-t\,dt}{(a+bt^2)\sqrt{c+dt^2}}$ *and then substitute* $c + dt^2 = u^2$.

Following examples will illustrate the procedure.

ILLUSTRATIVE EXAMPLES

BASED ON LOWER ORDER THINKING SKILLS (LOTS)

EXAMPLE 1 *Evaluate:* $\int \frac{1}{x^2\sqrt{1+x^2}}\,dx$

SOLUTION Let $I = \int \frac{1}{x^2\sqrt{1+x^2}}\,dx$. Putting $x = \frac{1}{t}$ and $-\frac{1}{x^2}\,dx = dt$ or, $dx = -x^2\,dt$, we get

$$I = \int \frac{-dt}{\sqrt{1+\frac{1}{t^2}}} = -\int \frac{t\,dt}{\sqrt{t^2+1}} = -\int \frac{u\,du}{\sqrt{u^2}}, \quad \text{where } t^2+1 = u^2$$

$$\Rightarrow \quad I = \int -1\cdot du = -u + C = -\sqrt{t^2+1}+C = -\sqrt{\frac{1}{x^2}+1}+C = -\frac{\sqrt{1+x^2}}{x}+C$$

BASED ON HIGHER ORDER THINKING SKILLS (HOTS)

EXAMPLE 2 *Evaluate:* $\int \frac{\sqrt{1+x^2}}{1-x^2}\,dx$

SOLUTION Let $I = \int \frac{\sqrt{1+x^2}}{1-x^2}\,dx = \int \frac{\sqrt{1+x^2}}{1-x^2} \times \sqrt{\frac{1+x^2}{1+x^2}}\,dx = \int \frac{1+x^2}{(1-x^2)\sqrt{1+x^2}}\,dx$

$$\Rightarrow \quad I = \int \frac{1}{(1-x^2)\sqrt{1+x^2}}\,dx + \int \frac{x^2}{(1-x^2)\sqrt{1+x^2}}\,dx$$

$$\Rightarrow \quad I = \int \frac{1}{(1-x^2)\sqrt{1+x^2}}\,dx - \int \frac{-x^2}{(1-x^2)\sqrt{1+x^2}}\,dx$$

$$\Rightarrow \quad I = \int \frac{1}{(1-x^2)\sqrt{1+x^2}}\,dx - \int \frac{(1-x^2)-1}{(1-x^2)\sqrt{1+x^2}}\,dx$$

$$\Rightarrow \quad I = \int \frac{1}{(1-x^2)\sqrt{1+x^2}}\,dx - \int \left\{\frac{1-x^2}{(1-x^2)\sqrt{1+x^2}} - \frac{1}{(1-x^2)\sqrt{1+x^2}}\right\}dx$$

$$\Rightarrow \quad I = \int \frac{1}{(1-x^2)\sqrt{1+x^2}}\,dx - \int \frac{1}{\sqrt{1+x^2}}\,dx + \int \frac{1}{(1-x^2)\sqrt{1+x^2}}\,dx$$

$$\Rightarrow \quad I = 2\int \frac{1}{(1-x^2)\sqrt{1+x^2}}\,dx - \int \frac{1}{\sqrt{1+x^2}}\,dx$$

$$\Rightarrow \quad I = 2I_1 - \log\left|x+\sqrt{1+x^2}\right| + C, \text{ where } I_1 = \int \frac{1}{(1-x^2)\sqrt{1+x^2}}\,dx$$

Putting $x = \frac{1}{t}$ and $dx = -\frac{1}{t^2}\,dt$ in I_1, we get

$$I_1 = \int \frac{\left(-\frac{1}{t^2}\right)dt}{\left(1-\frac{1}{t^2}\right)\sqrt{1+\frac{1}{t^2}}}$$

$$\Rightarrow \quad I_1 = -\int \frac{t\,dt}{(t^2-1)\sqrt{t^2+1}} = -\int \frac{u\,du}{(u^2-2)\sqrt{u^2}}, \text{ where } t^2+1 = u^2 \text{ and } t\,dt = u\,du$$

$$\Rightarrow \quad I_1 = -\int \frac{du}{u^2-(\sqrt{2})^2} = -\frac{1}{2\sqrt{2}}\log\left|\frac{u-\sqrt{2}}{u+\sqrt{2}}\right| = -\frac{1}{2\sqrt{2}}\log\left|\frac{\sqrt{t^2+1}-\sqrt{2}}{\sqrt{t^2+1}+\sqrt{2}}\right|$$

$$\Rightarrow \quad I_1 = -\frac{1}{2\sqrt{2}}\log\left|\frac{\sqrt{\frac{1}{x^2}+1}-\sqrt{2}}{\sqrt{\frac{1}{x^2}+1}+\sqrt{2}}\right| = -\frac{1}{2\sqrt{2}}\log\left|\frac{\sqrt{1+x^2}-\sqrt{2}\,x}{\sqrt{1+x^2}+\sqrt{2}\,x}\right|$$

$$\therefore \quad I = -\frac{1}{\sqrt{2}} \log \left| \frac{\sqrt{1+x^2} - \sqrt{2}\, x}{\sqrt{1+x^2} + \sqrt{2}\, x} \right| - \log \left| x + \sqrt{1+x^2} \right| + C$$

EXAMPLE 3 *Evaluate:* $\int \frac{1}{x\sqrt{ax - x^2}}\, dx$ **[NCERT]**

SOLUTION Let $I = \int \frac{1}{x\sqrt{ax-x^2}}\, dx$. Putting $x = \frac{1}{t}$ and $dx = -\frac{1}{t^2}\, dt$, we get

$$I = \int \frac{1}{\frac{1}{t}\sqrt{\frac{a}{t} - \frac{1}{t^2}}} \times -\frac{1}{t^2}\, dt = -\int \frac{1}{\sqrt{at-1}}\, dt = -\int (at-1)^{-1/2}\, dt = -\frac{(at-1)^{1/2}}{\frac{1}{2}a} + C$$

$$\Rightarrow \quad I = \frac{-2}{a}\sqrt{at-1} + C = \frac{-2}{a}\sqrt{\frac{a}{x} - 1} + C = \frac{-2}{a}\sqrt{\frac{a-x}{x}} + C$$

ALITER $I = \int \frac{1}{x\sqrt{ax-x^2}}\, dx = \int \frac{1}{x^2\sqrt{\frac{a}{x} - 1}}\, dx$

Let $\frac{a}{x} - 1 = t$. Then, $\frac{-a}{x^2}\, dx = dt$ or, $\frac{1}{x^2}\, dx = -\frac{1}{a}\, dt$

$$\therefore \quad I = -\frac{1}{a}\int \frac{1}{\sqrt{t}}\, dt = -\frac{2}{a}\sqrt{t} + C = -\frac{2}{a}\sqrt{\frac{a}{x} - 1} + C$$

EXAMPLE 4 *Evaluate:* $\int \frac{1}{\cos x \sqrt{\cos 2x}}\, dx$ **[CBSE 2024]**

SOLUTION Let $I = \int \frac{1}{\cos x\sqrt{\cos 2x}}\, dx$. Then,

$$I = \int \frac{\cos x}{\cos^2 x\sqrt{\cos 2x}}\, dx = \int \frac{\cos x}{(1 - \sin^2 x)\sqrt{1 - 2\sin^2 x}}\, dx$$

$$\Rightarrow \quad I = \int \frac{1}{(1-t^2)\sqrt{1-2t^2}}\, dt, \text{ where } t = \sin x$$

$$\Rightarrow \quad I = -\int \frac{u}{(u^2-1)\sqrt{u^2-2}}\, du, \text{ where } t = \frac{1}{u} \text{ and } dt = -\frac{1}{u^2}\, du$$

$$\Rightarrow \quad I = -\int \frac{1}{v^2+1}\, dv, \text{ where } u^2 - 2 = v^2$$

$$\Rightarrow \quad I = -\tan^{-1} v + C = -\tan^{-1}\sqrt{u^2-2} + C = -\tan^{-1}\frac{\sqrt{1-2t^2}}{t} + C$$

$$\Rightarrow \quad I = -\tan^{-1}\frac{\sqrt{1-2\sin^2 x}}{\sin x} + C = -\tan^{-1}\left(\frac{\sqrt{\cos 2x}}{\sin x}\right) + C$$

EXERCISE 15.32

BASED ON LOWER ORDER THINKING SKILLS (LOTS)

Evaluate the following integrals:

1. $\int \frac{1}{(x-1)\sqrt{x+2}}\, dx$
2. $\int \frac{1}{(x-1)\sqrt{2x+3}}\, dx$
3. $\int \frac{x+1}{(x-1)\sqrt{x+2}}\, dx$

4. $\int \frac{x^2}{(x-1)\sqrt{x+2}}\,dx$ 5. $\int \frac{x}{(x-3)\sqrt{x+1}}\,dx$ 6. $\int \frac{1}{(x^2+1)\sqrt{x}}\,dx$

7. $\int \frac{x}{(x^2+2x+2)\sqrt{x+1}}\,dx$ 8. $\int \frac{1}{(x-1)\sqrt{x^2+1}}\,dx$ 9. $\int \frac{1}{(x+1)\sqrt{x^2+x+1}}\,dx$

10. $\int \frac{1}{(x^2-1)\sqrt{x^2+1}}\,dx$ 11. $\int \frac{x}{(x^2+4)\sqrt{x^2+1}}\,dx$ 12. $\int \frac{1}{(1+x^2)\sqrt{1-x^2}}\,dx$

13. $\int \frac{1}{(2x^2+3)\sqrt{x^2-4}}\,dx$ 14. $\int \frac{x}{(x^2+4)\sqrt{x^2+9}}\,dx$

ANSWERS

1. $\frac{1}{\sqrt{3}}\log\left|\frac{\sqrt{x+2}-\sqrt{3}}{\sqrt{x+2}+\sqrt{3}}\right|+C$ 2. $\frac{1}{\sqrt{5}}\log\left|\frac{\sqrt{2x+3}-\sqrt{5}}{\sqrt{2x+3}+\sqrt{5}}\right|+C$

3. $2\sqrt{x+2}+\frac{2}{\sqrt{3}}\log\left|\frac{\sqrt{x+2}-\sqrt{3}}{\sqrt{x+2}+\sqrt{3}}\right|+C$

4. $\frac{2}{3}(x+2)^{3/2}-2\sqrt{x+2}+\frac{1}{\sqrt{3}}\log\left|\frac{\sqrt{x+2}-\sqrt{3}}{\sqrt{x+2}+\sqrt{3}}\right|+C$ 5. $2\sqrt{x+1}+\frac{3}{2}\log\left|\frac{\sqrt{x+1}-2}{\sqrt{x+1}+2}\right|+C$

6. $\frac{1}{\sqrt{2}}\tan^{-1}\left(\frac{x-1}{\sqrt{2x}}\right)-\frac{1}{2\sqrt{2}}\log\left|\frac{x-\sqrt{2x}+1}{x+\sqrt{2x}+1}\right|+C$ 7. $\frac{1}{\sqrt{2}}\log\left|\frac{(x+2)-\sqrt{2(x+1)}}{(x+2)+\sqrt{2(x+1)}}\right|+C$

8. $-\frac{1}{\sqrt{2}}\log\left|\left(t+\frac{1}{2}\right)+\sqrt{\left(t+\frac{1}{2}\right)^2+\frac{1}{4}}\right|+C$, where $t=\frac{1}{x-1}$

9. $-\log\left|\frac{1}{x+1}-\frac{1}{2}+\frac{\sqrt{x^2+x+1}}{x+1}\right|+C$ 10. $-\frac{1}{2\sqrt{2}}\log\left|\frac{\sqrt{2}\,x+\sqrt{x^2+1}}{\sqrt{2}\,x-\sqrt{x^2+1}}\right|+C$

11. $\frac{1}{\sqrt{3}}\tan^{-1}\left(\sqrt{\frac{x^2+1}{3}}\right)+C$ 12. $-\frac{1}{\sqrt{2}}\tan^{-1}\left(\sqrt{\frac{1-x^2}{2x^2}}\right)+C$

13. $\frac{1}{2\sqrt{33}}\log\left|\frac{\sqrt{11}\,x+\sqrt{3x^2-12}}{\sqrt{11}\,x-\sqrt{3x^2-12}}\right|+C$ 14. $\frac{1}{2\sqrt{5}}\log\left|\frac{\sqrt{x^2+9}-\sqrt{5}}{\sqrt{x^2+9}+\sqrt{5}}\right|+C$

REVISION EXERCISE

Evaluate the following integrals :

1. $\int \frac{1}{\sqrt{x}+\sqrt{x+1}}\,dx$ 2. $\int \frac{1-x^4}{1-x}\,dx$ 3. $\int \frac{x+2}{(x+1)^3}\,dx$

4. $\int \frac{8x+13}{\sqrt{4x+7}}\,dx$ 5. $\int \frac{1+x+x^2}{x^2(1+x)}\,dx$ 6. $\int \frac{(2^x+3^x)^2}{6^x}\,dx$

7. $\int \frac{\sin x}{1+\sin x}\,dx$ 8. $\int \frac{x^4+x^2-1}{x^2+1}\,dx$ 9. $\int \sec^2 x\cos^2 2x\,dx$

10. $\int \operatorname{cosec}^2 x \cos^2 2x \, dx$

11. $\int \sin^4 2x \, dx$

12. $\int \cos^3 3x \, dx$

13. $\int \frac{\sin 2x}{a^2 + b^2 \sin^2 x}$

14. $\int \frac{1}{(\sin^{-1} x)\sqrt{1-x^2}} \, dx$

15. $\int \frac{(\sin^{-1} x)^3}{\sqrt{1-x^2}} \, dx$

16. $\int \frac{1}{e^x + 1} \, dx$

17. $\int \frac{e^x - 1}{e^x + 1} \, dx$

18. $\int \frac{1}{e^x + e^{-x}} \, dx$

19. $\int \frac{\cos^7 x}{\sin x} \, dx$

20. $\int \sin x \sin 2x \sin 3x \, dx$

21. $\int \cos x \cos 2x \cos 3x \, dx$

22. $\int \frac{\sin x + \cos x}{\sqrt{\sin 2x}} \, dx$

23. $\int \frac{\sin x - \cos x}{\sqrt{\sin 2x}} \, dx$

24. $\int \frac{1}{\sin (x-a) \sin (x-b)} \, dx$

25. $\int \frac{1}{\cos (x-a) \cos (x-b)} \, dx$

26. $\int \frac{\sin x}{\sqrt{1 + \sin x}} \, dx$

27. $\int \frac{\sin x}{\cos 2x} \, dx$

28. $\int \tan^3 x \, dx$

29. $\int \tan^4 x \, dx$

30. $\int \tan^5 x \, dx$

31. $\int \cot^4 x \, dx$

32. $\int \cot^5 x \, dx$

33. $\int \frac{x^2}{(x-1)^3} \, dx$

34. $\int x \sqrt{2x + 3} \, dx$

35. $\int \frac{x^3}{(1 + x^2)^2} \, dx$

36. $\int x \sin^5 x^2 \cos x^2 \, dx$

37. $\int \sin^3 x \cos^4 x \, dx$

38. $\int \sin^5 x \, dx$

39. $\int \cos^5 x \, dx$

40. $\int \sqrt{\sin x} \cos^3 x \, dx$

41. $\int \frac{\sin 2x}{\sin^4 x + \cos^4 x} \, dx$

42. $\int \frac{1}{\sqrt{x^2 - a^2}} \, dx$

43. $\int \frac{1}{\sqrt{x^2 + a^2}} \, dx$

44. $\int \frac{1}{4x^2 + 4x + 5} \, dx$

45. $\int \frac{1}{x^2 + 4x - 5} \, dx$

46. $\int \frac{1}{1 - x - 4x^2} \, dx$

47. $\int \frac{1}{3x^2 + 13x - 10} \, dx$

48. $\int \frac{\sin x}{\sqrt{\cos^2 x - 2 \cos x - 3}} \, dx$

49. $\int \sqrt{\operatorname{cosec} x - 1} \, dx$

50. $\int \frac{1}{\sqrt{3 - 2x - x^2}} \, dx$

51. $\int \frac{x + 1}{x^2 + 4x + 5} \, dx$

52. $\int \frac{5x + 7}{\sqrt{(x-5)(x-4)}} \, dx$

53. $\int \sqrt{\frac{1 + x}{x}} \, dx$

54. $\int \sqrt{\frac{1 - x}{x}} \, dx$

55. $\int \frac{\sqrt{a} - \sqrt{x}}{1 - \sqrt{ax}} \, dx$

56. $\int \frac{1}{(\sin x - 2 \cos x)(2 \sin x + \cos x)} \, dx$

57. $\int \frac{1}{4 \sin^2 x + 4 \sin x \cos x + 5 \cos^2 x} \, dx$

58. $\int \frac{1}{a + b \tan x} \, dx$

59. $\int \frac{1}{\sin^2 x + \sin 2x} \, dx$

60. $\int \frac{\sin x + 2 \cos x}{2 \sin x + \cos x} \, dx$

61. $\int \frac{x^3}{\sqrt{x^8 + 4}} \, dx$

62. $\int \frac{1}{2 - 3 \cos 2x} \, dx$

63. $\int \frac{\cos x}{\frac{1}{4} - \cos^2 x} \, dx$

64. $\int \frac{1}{1+2\cos x}\,dx$ 65. $\int \frac{1}{1-2\sin x}\,dx$ 66. $\int \frac{1}{\sin x\,(2+3\cos x)}\,dx$

67. $\int \frac{1}{\sin x+\sin 2x}\,dx$ 68. $\int \frac{1}{\sin^4 x+\cos^4 x}\,dx$ 69. $\int \frac{1}{5-4\sin x}\,dx$

70. $\int \sec^4 x\,dx$ 71. $\int \operatorname{cosec}^4 2x\,dx$ 72. $\int \frac{1+\sin x}{\sin x\,(1+\cos x)}\,dx$

73. $\int \frac{1}{2+\cos x}\,dx$ 74. $\int \sqrt{\frac{a+x}{x}}\,dx$ 75. $\int \frac{6x+5}{\sqrt{6+x-2x^2}}\,dx$

76. $\int \frac{\sin^5 x}{\cos^4 x}\,dx$ 77. $\int \frac{\cos^5 x}{\sin x}\,dx$ 78. $\int \frac{\sin^6 x}{\cos x}\,dx$

79. $\int \frac{\sin^2 x}{\cos^6 x}\,dx$ 80. $\int \sec^6 x\,dx$ 81. $\int \tan^5 x\sec^3 x\,dx$

82. $\int \tan^3 x\sec^4 x\,dx$ 83. $\int \frac{1}{\sec x+\operatorname{cosec} x}\,dx$ 84. $\int \sqrt{a^2+x^2}\,dx$

85. $\int \sqrt{x^2-a^2}\,dx$ 86. $\int \sqrt{a^2-x^2}\,dx$ 87. $\int \sqrt{3x^2+4x+1}\,dx$

88. $\int \sqrt{1+2x-3x^2}\,dx$ 89. $\int x\sqrt{1+x-x^2}\,dx$ 90. $\int (2x+3)\sqrt{4x^2+5x+6}\,dx$

91. $\int (1+x^2)\cos 2x\,dx$ 92. $\int \log_{10} x\,dx$ 93. $\int \frac{\log(\log x)}{x}\,dx$

94. $\int x\sec^2 2x\,dx$ 95. $\int x\sin^3 x\,dx$ 96. $\int (x+1)^2 e^x\,dx$

97. $\int \log\left(x+\sqrt{x^2+a^2}\right)dx$ 98. $\int \frac{\log x}{x^3}\,dx$ 99. $\int \frac{\log(1-x)}{x^2}\,dx$

100. $\int x^3(\log x)^2\,dx$ 101. $\int \frac{1}{x\sqrt{1+x^n}}\,dx$ 102. $\int \frac{x^2}{\sqrt{1-x}}\,dx$

103. $\int \frac{x^5}{\sqrt{1+x^3}}\,dx$ 104. $\int \frac{1+x^2}{\sqrt{1-x^2}}\,dx$ 105. $\int x\sqrt{\frac{1-x}{1+x}}\,dx$

106. $\int \frac{1}{x\sqrt{1+x^3}}\,dx$ 107. $\int \frac{\sin x+\cos x}{\sin^4 x+\cos^4 x}\,dx$ 108. $\int x^2\tan^{-1} x\,dx$

109. $\int \tan^{-1}\sqrt{x}\,dx$ 110. $\int \sin^{-1}\sqrt{x}\,dx$ 111. $\int \sec^{-1}\sqrt{x}\,dx$

112. $\int \tan^{-1}\sqrt{\frac{1-x}{1+x}}\,dx$ 113. $\int \sin^{-1}\sqrt{\frac{x}{a+x}}\,dx$ 114. $\int \sin^{-1}(3x-4x^3)\,dx$

115. $\int (\sin^{-1} x)^3\,dx$ 116. $\int \cos^{-1}(1-2x^2)\,dx$ 117. $\int \frac{x\sin^{-1} x}{(1-x^2)^{3/2}}\,dx$

118. $\int e^{2x}\left(\frac{1+\sin 2x}{1+\cos 2x}\right)dx$ 119. $\int \frac{\sqrt{1-\sin x}}{1+\cos x}\,e^{-x/2}\,dx$ 120. $\int e^x\,\frac{(1-x)^2}{(1+x^2)^2}\,dx$

121. $\int \frac{e^{m\tan^{-1} x}}{(1+x^2)^{3/2}}\,dx$ 122. $\int \frac{x^2}{(x-1)^3(x+1)}\,dx$ 123. $\int \frac{x}{x^3-1}\,dx$

124. $\int \frac{1}{1+x+x^2+x^3}\,dx$ **125.** $\int \frac{1}{(x^2+2)(x^2+5)}\,dx$ **126.** $\int \frac{x^2-2}{x^5-x}\,dx$

127. $\int \sqrt{\frac{1-\sqrt{x}}{1+\sqrt{x}}}\,dx$ **128.** $\int \frac{x^2+x+1}{(x+1)^2(x+2)}\,dx$ **129.** $\int \frac{\sin 4x-2}{1-\cos 4x}e^{2x}\,dx$

130. $\int \frac{\{\cot x+\cot^3\}\,x}{1+\cot^3 x}\,dx$

ANSWERS

1. $\frac{2}{3}\left\{(x+1)^{3/2}-x^{3/2}\right\}+C$ **2.** $x+\frac{x^2}{2}+\frac{x^3}{3}+\frac{x^4}{4}+C$ **3.** $-\frac{1}{x+1}-\frac{1}{2(x+1)^2}+C$

4. $\frac{1}{3}(4x+7)^{3/2}-\frac{1}{2}\sqrt{4x+7}+C$ **5.** $-\frac{1}{x}+\log|x+1|+C$

6. $\left(\frac{2}{3}\right)^x\frac{1}{\log\left(\frac{2}{3}\right)}+\left(\frac{3}{2}\right)^x\frac{1}{\log\left(\frac{3}{2}\right)}+2x+C$ **7.** $x-\tan x+\sec x+C$

8. $\frac{x^3}{3}-\tan^{-1}x+C$ **9.** $\sin 2x+\tan x-2x+C$ **10.** $-\cot x-\sin 2x-2x+C$

11. $\frac{3}{8}x+\frac{\sin 8x}{64}-\frac{\sin 4x}{8}+C$ **12.** $\frac{\sin 3x}{3}-\frac{\sin^3 3x}{9}+C$ **13.** $\frac{1}{b^2}\log(a^2+b^2\sin^2 x)+C$

14. $\log|\sin^{-1}x|+C$ **15.** $\frac{1}{4}(\sin^{-1}x)^4+C$ **16.** $x-\log(e^x+1)+C$

17. $2\log(e^x+1)-x+C$ **18.** $\tan^{-1}(e^x)+C$

19. $\log|\sin x|-\frac{\sin^6 x}{6}-\frac{3\sin^2 x}{2}+\frac{3\sin^4 x}{4}+C$

20. $\frac{\cos 4x}{16}-\frac{\cos 2x}{8}+\frac{\cos 6x}{24}+C$ **21.** $\frac{x}{4}+\frac{\sin 6x}{24}+\frac{\sin 4x}{16}+\frac{\sin 2x}{8}+C$

22. $\sin^{-1}(\sin x-\cos x)+C$ **23.** $-\log|(\sin x+\cos x)+\sqrt{\sin 2x}|+C$

24. $\frac{1}{\sin(a-b)}\log\left|\frac{\sin(x-a)}{\sin(x-b)}\right|+C$ **25.** $\frac{1}{\sin(a-b)}\log\left|\frac{\cos(x-a)}{\cos(x-b)}\right|+C$

26. $2\left(\sin\frac{x}{2}-\cos\frac{x}{2}\right)-\sqrt{2}\log\left|\tan\left(\frac{x}{4}+\frac{\pi}{8}\right)\right|+C$ **27.** $\frac{1}{2\sqrt{2}}\log\left|\frac{1+\sqrt{2}\cos x}{1-\sqrt{2}\cos x}\right|+C$

28. $\frac{1}{2}\tan^2 x-\log|\sec x|+C$ **29.** $\frac{1}{3}\tan^3 x-\tan x+x+C$

30. $\frac{1}{4}\tan^4 x-\frac{1}{2}\tan^2 x+\log|\sec x|+C$ **31.** $-\frac{1}{3}\cot^3 x+\cot x+x+C$

32. $-\frac{1}{4}\cot^4 x+\frac{1}{2}\cot^2 x+\log|\sin x|+C$ **33.** $\log|x-1|-\frac{2}{x-1}-\frac{1}{2(x-1)^2}+C$

34. $\frac{1}{10}(2x+3)^{5/2}-\frac{1}{2}(2x+3)^{3/2}+C$ **35.** $\frac{1}{2}\left\{\log(1+x^2)+\frac{1}{1+x^2}\right\}+C$

36. $\frac{1}{12}\sin^6 x^2 + C$

37. $-\frac{\cos^5 x}{5} + \frac{\cos^7 x}{7} + C$

38. $-\cos x + \frac{2}{3}\cos^3 x - \frac{1}{5}\cos^5 x + C$

39. $\sin x + \frac{1}{5}\sin^5 x - \frac{2}{3}\sin^3 x + C$

40. $\frac{2}{3}\sin^{3/2} x - \frac{2}{7}\sin^{7/2} x + C$

41. $\tan^{-1}(\tan^2 x) + C$

42. $\log|x + \sqrt{x^2 - a^2}| + C$

43. $\log|x + \sqrt{x^2 + a^2}| + C$

44. $\frac{1}{4}\tan^{-1}\left(x + \frac{1}{2}\right) + C$

45. $\frac{1}{6}\log\left|\frac{x-1}{x+5}\right| + C$

46. $\frac{1}{2}\log\left|\left(x + \frac{1}{8}\right) + \frac{1}{2}\sqrt{1 - x - 4x^2}\right| + C$

47. $\frac{1}{17}\log\left|\frac{3x-2}{3x+15}\right| + C$

48. $-\log\left|(1 - \cos x) + \sqrt{\cos^2 x - 2\cos x - 3}\right| + C$

49. $\log\left|\left(\sin x + \frac{1}{2}\right) + \sqrt{\sin^2 x + \sin x}\right| + C$

50. $\sin^{-1}\left(\frac{x+1}{2}\right) + C$

51. $\frac{1}{2}\log|x^2 + 4x + 5| + \tan^{-1}(x+2) + C$

52. $6\sqrt{x^2 - 9x + 20} + 34\log\left|\left(x - \frac{9}{2}\right) + \sqrt{x^2 - 9x + 20}\right| + C$

53. $\sqrt{x^2 + x} + \frac{1}{2}\log\left|\left(x + \frac{1}{2}\right) + \sqrt{x^2 + x}\right| + C$

54. $\sqrt{x - x^2} + \frac{1}{2}\sin^{-1}(2x - 1) + C$

55. $-\frac{2}{a\sqrt{a}}\left\{(a-1)\log|1 - \sqrt{ax}| + (2-a)(1 - \sqrt{ax}) - \frac{1}{2}(1 - \sqrt{ax})^2\right\} + C$

56. $\frac{1}{5}\log\left|\frac{\tan x - 2}{2\tan x + 1}\right| + C$

57. $\frac{1}{4}\tan^{-1}\left(\tan x + \frac{1}{2}\right) + C$

58. $\frac{a}{a^2 + b^2}x + \frac{b}{a^2 + b^2}\log|a\cos x + b\sin x| + C$

59. $\frac{1}{2}\log\left|\frac{\tan x}{\tan x + 2}\right| + C$

60. $\frac{4}{5}x + \frac{3}{5}\log|2\sin x + \cos x| + C$

61. $\frac{1}{4}\log\left|x^8 + \sqrt{x^8 + 4}\right| + C$

62. $\frac{1}{2\sqrt{5}}\log\left|\frac{\sqrt{5}\tan x - 1}{\sqrt{5}\tan x + 1}\right| + C$

63. $\frac{1}{\sqrt{3}}\log\left|\frac{2\sin x - \sqrt{3}}{2\sin x + \sqrt{3}}\right| + C$

64. $\frac{1}{\sqrt{3}}\log\left|\frac{\sqrt{3} + \tan\frac{x}{2}}{\sqrt{3} - \tan\frac{x}{2}}\right| + C$

65. $\frac{1}{\sqrt{3}}\log\left|\frac{\tan\frac{x}{2} - 2 - \sqrt{3}}{\tan\frac{x}{2} - 2 + \sqrt{3}}\right| + C$

66. $\frac{1}{10}\log|\cos x - 1| + \frac{1}{2}\log|\cos x + 1| - \frac{3}{5}\log|3\cos x + 2| + C$

67. $\frac{1}{6}\log|\cos x - 1| + \frac{1}{2}\log|\cos x + 1| - \frac{2}{3}\log|2\cos x + 1| + C$

68. $\frac{1}{\sqrt{2}} \tan^{-1}\left(\frac{1}{\sqrt{2}} \tan 2x\right) + C$

69. $\frac{2}{3} \tan^{-1}\left\{\frac{5 \tan \frac{x}{2} - 4}{3}\right\} + C$

70. $\tan x + \frac{1}{3} \tan^3 x + C$

71. $-\frac{1}{2} \cot 2x - \frac{1}{6} \cot^3 2x + C$

72. $\frac{1}{4} \tan^2 \frac{x}{2} + \tan \frac{x}{2} + \frac{1}{2} \log\left|\tan \frac{x}{2}\right| + C$

73. $\frac{2}{\sqrt{3}} \tan^{-1}\left(\frac{1}{\sqrt{3}} \tan \frac{x}{2}\right) + C$

74. $\sqrt{x^2 + ax} + \frac{a}{2} \log\left|x + \frac{a}{2} + \sqrt{x^2 + ax}\right| + C$

75. $-3\sqrt{6 + x - 2x^2} + \frac{13}{2\sqrt{2}} \sin^{-1}\left(\frac{4x - 1}{7}\right) + C$

76. $-\cos x - \frac{2}{\cos x} + \frac{1}{3 \cos^3 x} + C$

77. $\frac{1}{4} \sin^4 x - \sin^2 x + \log|\sin x| + C$

78. $-\frac{1}{5} \sin^5 x - \frac{1}{3} \sin^3 x - \sin x + \frac{1}{2} \log\left|\frac{1 + \sin x}{1 - \sin x}\right| + C$

79. $\frac{1}{3} \tan^3 x + \frac{1}{5} \tan^5 x + C$

80. $\tan x + \frac{2}{3} \tan^3 x + \frac{1}{5} \tan^5 x + C$

81. $\frac{1}{7} \sec^7 x - \frac{2}{5} \sec^5 x + \frac{1}{3} \sec^3 x + C$

82. $\frac{1}{4} \tan^4 x + \frac{1}{6} \tan^6 x + C$

83. $-\frac{1}{2} \cos x + \frac{1}{2} \sin x - \frac{1}{2\sqrt{2}} \log\left|\tan\left(\frac{x}{2} + \frac{\pi}{8}\right)\right| + C$

84. $\frac{1}{2} x \sqrt{a^2 + x^2} + \frac{1}{2} a^2 \log|x + \sqrt{x^2 + a^2}| + C$

85. $\frac{1}{2} x \sqrt{x^2 - a^2} - \frac{1}{2} a^2 \log|x + \sqrt{x^2 - a^2}| + C$

86. $\frac{1}{2} x \sqrt{a^2 - x^2} + \frac{1}{2} a^2 \sin^{-1}\left(\frac{x}{a}\right) + C$

87. $\frac{1}{6}(3x + 2)\sqrt{3x^2 + 4x + 1} - \frac{\sqrt{3}}{18} \log\left|\left(x + \frac{2}{3}\right) + \sqrt{x^2 + \frac{4x}{3} + \frac{1}{3}}\right| + C$

88. $\left(\frac{3x - 1}{6}\right)\sqrt{1 + 2x - 3x^2} + \frac{2\sqrt{3}}{9} \sin^{-1}\left(\frac{3x - 1}{2}\right) + C$

89. $\frac{1}{24}(8x^2 - 2x - 11)\sqrt{1 + x - x^2} + \frac{5}{16} \sin^{-1}\left(\frac{2x - 1}{\sqrt{5}}\right) + C$

90. $\frac{1}{192}(128x^2 + 328x + 297)\sqrt{4x^2 + 5x + 6} + \frac{497}{256} \log\left|\left(x + \frac{5}{8}\right) + \sqrt{x^2 + \frac{5}{4}x + \frac{3}{2}}\right| + C$

91. $\frac{1}{2}(1 + x^2) \sin 2x + \frac{x}{2} \cos 2x - \frac{\sin 2x}{4} + C$

92. $x(\log x - 1) \cdot \log_{10} e + C$

93. $\log\{\log(\log x)\} - \log x + C$

94. $\frac{1}{2} x \tan 2x - \frac{1}{4} \log|\sec 2x| + C$

95. $\frac{1}{4}\left\{-3x \cos x + 3 \sin x + \frac{x}{3} \cos 3x - \frac{\sin 3x}{9}\right\} + C$

96. $e^x (x^2 + 1) + C$

97. $x \log|x + \sqrt{x^2 + a^2}| - \sqrt{x^2 + a^2} + C$

98. $-\frac{1}{4x^2}(2 \log x + 1) + C$

99. $\left(1-\frac{1}{x}\right)\log(1-x)-\log x+C$

100. $\frac{x^4}{4}(\log x)^2-\frac{1}{8}x^4\log x+\frac{1}{32}x^4+C$

101. $\frac{1}{n}\log\left|\frac{\sqrt{1+x^n}-1}{\sqrt{1+x^n}+1}\right|+C$

102. $-\frac{2}{15}\sqrt{1-x}\left(3x^2+4x+8\right)+C$

103. $\frac{2}{9}\sqrt{1+x^3}(x^3-2)+C$

104. $\frac{3}{2}\sin^{-1}x-\frac{x}{2}\sqrt{1-x^2}+C$

105. $\left(\frac{x}{2}-1\right)\sqrt{1-x^2}-\frac{1}{2}\sin^{-1}x+C$

106. $\frac{1}{3}\log\left|\frac{\sqrt{1+x^3}-1}{\sqrt{1+x^3}+1}\right|+C$

107. $\frac{1}{\sqrt{2}}\left[\frac{1}{2\sqrt{\sqrt{2}+1}}\log\left|\frac{\sqrt{\sqrt{2}+1}+t}{\sqrt{\sqrt{2}+1}-t}\right|+\frac{1}{\sqrt{\sqrt{2}-1}}\tan^{-1}\left(\frac{t}{\sqrt{\sqrt{2}-1}}\right)\right]$, where $t=\sin x-\cos x$

108. $\frac{x^3}{3}\tan^{-1}x-\frac{x^2}{6}+\frac{1}{6}\log|x^2+1|+C$

109. $(x+1)\tan^{-1}\sqrt{x}-\sqrt{x}+C$

110. $-\frac{1}{2}(1-2x)^2\sin^{-1}\sqrt{x}+\frac{1}{2}\sqrt{x-x^2}+C$

111. $x\sec^{-1}\sqrt{x}-\sqrt{x-1}+C$

112. $\frac{1}{2}\left\{x\cos^{-1}x-\sqrt{1-x^2}\right\}+C$

113. $(x+a)\tan^{-1}\sqrt{\frac{x}{a}}-\sqrt{ax}+C$

114. $3\left\{x\sin^{-1}x+\sqrt{1-x^2}\right\}+C$

115. $x\sin^{-1}x\left\{(\sin^{-1}x)^2-6\right\}+3\left\{(\sin^{-1}x)^2-2\right\}\sqrt{1-x^2}+C$

116. $2\left(x\sin^{-1}x+\sqrt{1-x^2}\right)+C$

117. $\frac{\sin^{-1}x}{\sqrt{1-x^2}}-\frac{1}{2}\log\left|\frac{1+x}{1-x}\right|+C$

118. $\frac{1}{2}e^{2x}\tan x+C$

119. $-e^{-x/2}\sec\left(\frac{x}{2}\right)+C$

120. $\frac{e^x}{1+x^2}+C$

121. $\frac{e^{m\tan^{-1}x}}{\sqrt{m^2+1}}\cos\left\{\tan^{-1}x-\cot^{-1}m\right\}+C$

122. $\frac{1}{8}\log\left|\frac{x-1}{x+1}\right|-\frac{3}{4(x-1)}-\frac{1}{4(x-1)^2}+C$

123. $\frac{1}{3}\log|x-1|-\frac{1}{6}\log|x^2+x+1|+\frac{1}{\sqrt{3}}\tan^{-1}\left(\frac{2x+1}{\sqrt{3}}\right)+C$

124. $\frac{1}{2}\log\left(\frac{|x+1|}{\sqrt{x^2+1}}\right)+\frac{1}{2}\tan^{-1}x+C$

125. $\frac{1}{3\sqrt{2}}\tan^{-1}\left(\frac{x}{\sqrt{2}}\right)-\frac{1}{3\sqrt{5}}\tan^{-1}\left(\frac{x}{\sqrt{5}}\right)+C$

126. $2\log|x|-\frac{1}{4}\log|x^2-1|-\frac{3}{4}\log|x^2+1|+C$

127. $-2\sqrt{1-x}+\cos^{-1}\sqrt{x}+\sqrt{x}\sqrt{1-x}+C$

128. $-2\log|1+x|-\frac{1}{x+1}+3\log|x+2|+C$

129. $\frac{1}{2}e^{2x}\cot 2x + C$

130. $-\frac{1}{6}\log|\cot^2 x - \cot x + 1| + \frac{1}{3}\log|\cot x + 1| - \frac{1}{\sqrt{3}}\tan^{-1}\left(\frac{2\cot x - 1}{\sqrt{3}}\right) + C$

FILL IN THE BLANKS TYPE QUESTIONS (FBQs)

1. If $0 < x < \frac{\pi}{4}$, then $\int \sqrt{1-\sin 2x}\, dx$ is equal to ....
2. If $\frac{\pi}{4} < x < \frac{\pi}{2}$, then $\int \sqrt{1-\sin 2x}\, dx$ is equal to ....
3. If $\int \frac{1}{\tan x + \cot x} dx = k\cos 2x + C$, then $k =$ ....
4. The value of the integral $\int e^{2\log x} + e^{x\log 2}\, dx$ is ....
5. If the value of integral $\int \frac{\sin^6 x}{\cos^8 x} dx$ is $k\tan^7 x + c$, then $k =$ ....
6. $\int \frac{x+3}{(x+4)^2} e^x dx =$ ....
7. $\int \cos x\, e^{2\sin x}\, dx =$ ....
8. $\int e^x \frac{x}{(x+1)^2} dx =$ ....
9. $\int \frac{\sin x}{3+4\cos^2 x} dx =$ ....
10. $\int \frac{x^2+1}{x^2-1} dx =$ ....
11. $\int \frac{e^{5\log_e x} - e^{4\log_e x}}{e^{3\log_e x} - e^{2\log_e x}} dx =$ ....
12. $\int \frac{x^4+x^2+1}{x^2-x+1} dx =$ ....
13. $\int \frac{\cos x - \sin x}{1+\sin 2x} dx =$ ....
14. $\int e^x \sin e^x\, dx =$ ....
15. $\int \frac{x}{e^{3x^2}} dx =$ ....
16. $\int x^x(1+\log x)\, dx =$ ....
17. $\int \frac{e^x}{e^x+1} dx =$ ....
18. $\int (x+3)(x^2+6x+10)^9\, dx =$ ....
19. $\int \frac{(\tan^{-1} x)^3}{1+x^2} dx =$ ....
20. $\int e^x(1-\cot x+\operatorname{cosec}^2 x)\, dx =$ ....

ANSWERS

1. $\sin x + \cos x + C$
2. $-\cos x - \sin x + C$
3. $-\frac{1}{4}$
4. $\frac{x^3}{3} + \frac{2^x}{\log 2} + C$
5. $\frac{1}{7}$
6. $\frac{e^x}{x+4} + C$
7. $\frac{1}{2}e^{2\sin x} + C$
8. $\frac{e^x}{x+1} + C$
9. $-\frac{1}{2\sqrt{3}}\tan^{-1}\left(\frac{2\cos x}{\sqrt{3}}\right) + C$
10. $x + \log\left|\frac{x-1}{x+1}\right| + C$
11. $\frac{x^3}{3} + C$
12. $\frac{1}{3}x^3 + \frac{1}{2}x^2 + x + C$
13. $-\frac{1}{\sin x + \cos x} + C$
14. $-\cos(e^x) + C$
15. $-\frac{1}{6}e^{-3x^2} + C$

16. $x^x + C$

17. $\log|e^x + 1| + C$

18. $\frac{1}{20}(x^2 + 6x + 10)^{10} + C$

19. $\frac{1}{4}(\tan^{-1} x)^4 + C$

20. $e^x (1 - \cot x) + C$

VERY SHORT ANSWER QUESTIONS (VSAQs)

Answer each of the following questions in one word or, one sentence or, as per exact requirement of the question:

1. Write a value of $\int \frac{1 + \cot x}{x + \log \sin x} dx$.
2. Write a value of $\int e^{3 \log x} x^4 dx$.
3. Write a value of $\int x^2 \sin x^3 dx$.
4. Write a value of $\int \tan^3 x \sec^2 x dx$.
5. Write a value of $\int e^x (\sin x + \cos x) dx$.
6. Write a value of $\int \tan^6 x \sec^2 x dx$.
7. Write a value of $\int \frac{\cos x}{3 + 2 \sin x} dx$.
8. Write a value of $\int e^x \sec x (1 + \tan x) dx$.
9. Write a value of $\int \frac{\log x^n}{x} dx$.
10. Write a value of $\int \frac{(\log x)^n}{x} dx$.
11. Write a value of $\int e^{\log \sin x} \cos x dx$.
12. Write a value of $\int \sin^3 x \cos x dx$.
13. Write a value of $\int \cos^4 x \sin x dx$.
14. Write a value of $\int \tan x \sec^3 x dx$.
15. Write a value of $\int \frac{1}{1 + e^x} dx$.
16. Write a value of $\int \frac{1}{1 + 2e^x} dx$.
17. Write a value of $\int \frac{(\tan^{-1} x)^3}{1 + x^2} dx$.
18. Write a value of $\int \frac{\sec^2 x}{(5 + \tan x)^4} dx$.
19. Write a value of $\int \frac{\sin x + \cos x}{\sqrt{1 + \sin 2x}} dx$.
20. Write a value of $\int \log_e x dx$.
21. Write a value of $\int a^x e^x dx$.
22. Write a value of $\int e^{2x^2 + \ln x} dx$.
23. Write a value of $\int (e^{x \log_e a} + e^{a \log_e x}) dx$.
24. Write a value of $\int \frac{\cos x}{\sin x \log \sin x} dx$.
25. Write a value of $\int \frac{\sin 2x}{a^2 \sin^2 x + b^2 \cos^2 x} dx$.
26. Write a value of $\int \frac{a^x}{3 + a^x} dx$.
27. Write a value of $\int \frac{1 + \log x}{3 + x \log x} dx$.
28. Write a value of $\int \frac{\sin x}{\cos^3 x} dx$.
29. Write a value of $\int \frac{\sin x - \cos x}{\sqrt{1 + \sin 2x}} dx$.
30. Write a value of $\int \frac{1}{x (\log x)^n} dx$.
31. Write a value of $\int e^{ax} \sin bx dx$.
32. Write a value of $\int e^{ax} \cos bx dx$.
33. Write a value of $\int e^x \left(\frac{1}{x} - \frac{1}{x^2}\right) dx$.
34. Write a value of $\int e^{ax} \{a f(x) + f'(x)\} dx$.
35. Write a value of $\int \sqrt{4 - x^2} dx$.
36. Write a value of $\int \sqrt{9 + x^2} dx$.
37. Write a value of $\int \sqrt{x^2 - 9} dx$.
38. Evaluate: $\int \frac{x^2}{1 + x^3} dx$ [CBSE 2008]
39. Evaluate: $\int \frac{x^2 + 4x}{x^3 + 6x^2 + 5} dx$ [CBSE 2008]
40. Evaluate: $\int \frac{\sec^2 \sqrt{x}}{\sqrt{x}} dx$ [CBSE 2009]

41. Evaluate: $\int \frac{\sin \sqrt{x}}{\sqrt{x}} dx$ [CBSE 2009]

42. Evaluate: $\int \frac{\cos \sqrt{x}}{\sqrt{x}} dx$ [CBSE 2009]

43. Evaluate: $\int \frac{(1+\log x)^2}{x} dx$ [CBSE 2009]

44. Evaluate: $\int \sec^2 (7-4x)\, dx$ [CBSE 2009]

45. Evaluate: $\int \frac{\log x}{x} dx$ [CBSE 2010]

46. Evaluate: $\int 2^x dx$ [CBSE 2010]

47. Evaluate: $\int \frac{1-\sin x}{\cos^2 x} dx$ [CBSE 2010]

48. Evaluate: $\int \frac{x^3-1}{x^2} dx$ [CBSE 2010]

49. Evaluate: $\int \frac{x^3-x^2+x-1}{x-1} dx$ [CBSE 2011]

50. Evaluate: $\int \frac{e^{\tan^{-1} x}}{1+x^2} dx$ [CBSE 2011]

51. Evaluate: $\int \frac{1}{\sqrt{1-x^2}} dx$ [CBSE 2011]

52. Evaluate: $\int \sec x (\sec x + \tan x)\, dx$ [CBSE 2011]

53. Evaluate: $\int \frac{1}{x^2+16} dx$ [CBSE 2011]

54. Evaluate: $\int (1-x)\sqrt{x}\, dx$ [CBSE 2012]

55. Evaluate: $\int \frac{x+\cos 6x}{3x^2+\sin 6x} dx$ [CBSE 2012]

56. If $\int \left(\frac{x-1}{x^2}\right) e^x\, dx = f(x)\, e^x + C$, then write the value of $f(x)$. [CBSE 2012]

57. If $\int e^x (\tan x + 1) \sec x\, dx = e^x f(x) + C$, then write the value $f(x)$. [CBSE 2012]

58. Evaluate: $\int \frac{2}{1-\cos 2x} dx$ [CBSE 2012]

59. Write the anti derivative of $\left(3\sqrt{x}+\frac{1}{\sqrt{x}}\right)$. [CBSE 2014]

60. Evaluate : $\int \cos^{-1}(\sin x)\, dx$ [CBSE 2014]

61. Evaluate $\int \frac{1}{\sin^2 x \cos^2 x} dx$ [CBSE 2014]

62. Evaluate : $\int \frac{1}{x(1+\log x)} dx$ [CBSE 2017]

63. $\int \frac{1}{x(x^2+4)} dx$ [CBSE 2022]

64. Given $\frac{d}{dx}F(x) = \frac{1}{\sqrt{2x-x^2}}$ and $F(1)=0$, find $F(x)$. [CBSE 2024]

65. Evaluate : $\int \frac{x^3-1}{x^3-x} dx$ [CBSE 2024]

ANSWERS

1. $\log|x + \log \sin x| + C$
2. $\frac{x^8}{8} + C$
3. $-\frac{1}{3}\cos x^3 + C$
4. $\frac{\tan^4 x}{4} + C$
5. $e^x \sin x + C$
6. $\frac{\tan^7 x}{7} + C$
7. $\frac{1}{2}\log|3+2\sin x| + C$
8. $e^x \sec x + C$
9. $\frac{n}{2}(\log x)^2 + C$
10. $\frac{(\log x)^{n+1}}{n+1} + C$
11. $\frac{\sin^2 x}{2} + C$
12. $\frac{\sin^4 x}{4} + C$

13. $-\dfrac{\cos^5 x}{5}+C$

14. $\dfrac{\sec^3 x}{3}+C$

15. $-\log(1+e^{-x})+C$

16. $-\log|2+e^{-x}|+C$

17. $\dfrac{(\tan^{-1} x)^4}{4}+C$

18. $\dfrac{1}{-3(5+\tan x)^3}+C$

19. $x+C$

20. $x(\log_e x-1)+C$

21. $\dfrac{(ae)^x}{\log(ae)}+C$

22. $\dfrac{1}{4}e^{2x^2}+C$

23. $\dfrac{a^x}{\log_e a}+\dfrac{x^{a+1}}{a+1}+C$

24. $\log(\log \sin x)+C$

25. $\dfrac{1}{a^2-b^2}\log(a^2\sin^2 x+b^2\cos^2 x)+C$

26. $\dfrac{1}{\log a}\log(3+a^x)+C$

27. $\log(3+x\log x)+C$

28. $\dfrac{1}{2}\sec^2 x+C$

29. $-\log|\sin x+\cos x|+C$

30. $\dfrac{(\log x)^{1-n}}{1-n}+C$

31. $\dfrac{e^{ax}}{a^2+b^2}(a\sin bx-b\cos bx)+C$

32. $\dfrac{e^{ax}}{a^2+b^2}(a\cos bx+b\sin bx)+C$

33. $\dfrac{e^x}{x}+C$

34. $e^{ax}f(x)+C$

35. $\dfrac{1}{2}x\sqrt{4-x^2}+2\sin^{-1}\dfrac{x}{2}+C$

36. $\dfrac{1}{2}x\sqrt{9+x^2}+\dfrac{9}{2}\log\left|x+\sqrt{9+x^2}\right|+C$

37. $\dfrac{1}{2}x\sqrt{x^2-9}-\dfrac{9}{2}\log\left|x+\sqrt{x^2-9}\right|+C$

38. $\dfrac{1}{3}\log|1+x^3|+C$

39. $\dfrac{1}{3}\log|x^3+6x^2+5|+C$

40. $2\tan\sqrt{x}+C$

41. $-2\cos\sqrt{x}+C$

42. $2\sin\sqrt{x}+C$

43. $\dfrac{(1+\log x)^3}{3}+C$

44. $-\dfrac{1}{4}\tan(7-4x)+C$

45. $\dfrac{1}{2}(\log x)^2+C$

46. $\dfrac{2^x}{\log_e 2}+C$

47. $\tan x-\sec x+C$

48. $\dfrac{x^2}{2}+\dfrac{1}{x}+C$

49. $\dfrac{x^3}{3}+x+C$

50. $e^{\tan^{-1}x}+C$

51. $\sin^{-1}x+C$

52. $\sec x+\tan x+C$

53. $\dfrac{1}{4}\tan^{-1}\left(\dfrac{x}{4}\right)+C$

54. $\dfrac{2}{3}x^{3/2}-\dfrac{2}{5}x^{5/2}+C$

55. $\dfrac{1}{6}\log|3x^2+\sin 6x|+C$

56. $\dfrac{1}{x}$

57. $\sec x$

58. $-\cot x+C$

59. $2(x^{3/2}+x^{1/2})+C$

60. $\dfrac{\pi}{2}x-\dfrac{x^2}{2}+C$

61. $-2\cot 2x+C$

62. $\log(1+\log x)+C$

63. $\dfrac{1}{8}\log\left(\dfrac{x^2}{x^2+4}\right)+C$

64. $\sin^{-1}(x-1)$

65. $x+\log\left|\dfrac{x}{x+1}\right|+C$